Communication Yearbook 2

Communication Yearbook 2

Edited by
Brent D. Ruben

An Annual Review
Published by the
International Communication Association

Transaction Books
New Brunswick, New Jersey

Library of Congress Catalog Number 76-45943
ISBN: 0-87855-282-0 (cloth)
Printed in the United States of America

CONTENTS

COMMUNICATION YEARBOOK 2

EDITOR

CONTRIBUTING EDITORS

THE INTERNATIONAL COMMUNICATION ASSOCIATION

Communication Yearbook is an annual review. The series is sponsored by the International Communication Association, one of the several major scholarly organizations in the communication field. It is composed of 2,500 communication scholars, teachers, and practitioners.

Throughout its 29-year history, the Association has been particularly important to those in the field of communication who have sought a forum where the behavioral science perspective was predominant. The International Communication Association has also been attractive to a number of individuals from a variety of disciplines who hold communication to be central to work within their primary fields of endeavor. The Association has been an important stimulant to the infusion of behavioral concepts in communication study and teaching, and has played a significant role in defining a broadened set of boundaries for the discipline as a whole.

The International Communication Association is composed of eight subdivisions: information systems, interpersonal communication, mass communication, organizational communication, intercultural communication, political communication, instructional communication, and health communication.

In addition to *Communication Yearbook*, the Association publishes *Human Communication Research*, the *ICA Newsletter*, *ICA Directory* and is affiliated with the *Journal of Communication*. Several divisions also publish newsletters and occasional papers.

PREFACE

With the completion of *Communication Yearbook 2*, the first phase of the *Yearbook* series and my own editorship come to an end. There are many persons who should be thanked individually for their commitment and interest in the series and for the help they provided me during the developmental stages of the project. To each of these persons let me simply say, again, thanks.

To the Contributing Editors for Volumes 1 and 2 who have given so generously of their support and their time, a very special thanks. Whatever status the series has thus far achieved is in no small sense a tribute to your involvement with the project.

I again want to express appreciation to those who contributed Review and Commentary articles for Volume 1, and to Contributing Editors Frank Dance and Gerry Miller, who prepared pieces for this year's volume. Sincere appreciation is also expressed to Edward Hall, Michael Burgoon, Lee Thayer, and Walter Weimer, who were also kind enough to provide Review and Commentary articles with no compensation beyond our thanks.

I am grateful for the assistance of the "Overview" authors for this volume: B. Aubrey Fisher, Dean Hewes, Joe Foley, Harry Dennis, Gerry Goldhaber, Mike Yates, Mike Prosser, Keith Sanders, Linda Lee Kaid, Velma Lashbrook, Bud Wheeless, and Don Cassata. A note of appreciation is also due contributors of Selected Studies for their cooperation in preparing their manuscripts for publication.

Special thanks to Marty Freedman, Jo Ann Zsilavetz, Dolores Palazzo, and Jayne Ghuzzi for their valuable editorial assistance in preparing this *Yearbook*.

Particular recognition is due Mike Cheney and Dave Davidson, both colleagues at Rutgers. Throughout the preparation of Volume 2, Mike has given unselfishly of his energies and expertise to oversee the various phases of manuscript preparation, as well as galley and page proof editing. He has assisted in a variety of other ways as well. Dave Davidson, as with Volume 1, has had sole responsibility for the preparation of the Index. Those who are familiar with this task recognize the amount of work involved, particularly given the fiscal and time constraints within which we are operating. Special thanks to you both.

Lastly, I want to thank my wife Jann and the children Robbi and Marc, who have again cheerfully put up with the time and energy commitment which seem to accompany the *Yearbook*. Take joy in the knowledge that next year, the manuscripts, revised manuscripts, revisions of revised manuscripts, references, and correspondence concerning missing references will accumulate in Dan Nimmo's home office rather than mine.

March 1978

Brent D. Ruben
Belle Mead, N.J.

OVERVIEW

OVERVIEW OF THE COMMUNICATION YEARBOOK SERIES

There are a number of publications devoted primarily, if not exclusively, to the publication of specialized studies in communication. There are few, if any, whose primary function is overview and synthesis. It is the pursuit of these generic goals which inspired the development of the *Communication Yearbook* series. The *Yearbook* series consists of: (1) disciplinary reviews and commentaries, (2) overviews of subdivisions within the field, (3) current research selected to represent the interest areas within the field, and (4) topic and author index.

Reviews and Commentaries

A primary means of fostering integration are the *Review and Commentary* papers, solicited on generic topics selected by the editor with input from contributing editors. The aim of these articles is to provide substantive input of generic relevance to scholars and researchers in all subdivisions of the field. In *Communication Yearbook 2*, *Reviews and Commentaries* focus on Human Communication Theory, Technology and Culture, Persuasion Research, Communication Philosophy, Communication and Psychological Models of Man.

A second means of facilitating synthesis are annual Overviews. Prepared by International Communication Association divisional chairpersons or their designates, Overviews examine trends in theory and research in various substantive domains within the field.

Communication Yearbook also provides a forum for the presentation of edited versions of outstanding current research, competitively selected for presentation at the annual conference of the International Communication Association. In *Communication Yearbook 2*, competitively selected studies are included which represent information systems, interpersonal communication, mass communication, organizational communication, political communication, intercultural communication, and health communication. Each work appearing in the volume has been indexed on *author, topic*, and *methodology* dimensions. The intent is to provide easy access to persons or ideas of interest that may be cited in *Reviews and Commentaries*, *Overviews*, or *Selected Studies* from various subdivisions within the field.

Organization of the Communication Yearbook

The volume is organized in the following manner: Section One consists of disciplinary-wide *Reviews and Commentaries*. For each of the following sections, the first piece included is the *Theory and Research Overview* followed by three *Selected Studies* which exemplify research in the area.

COMMUNICATION

Reviews and Commentaries

HUMAN COMMUNICATION THEORY: A HIGHLY SELECTIVE REVIEW AND TWO COMMENTARIES

FRANK E.X. DANCE
University of Denver

Where to begin? With the first human who reflected on the way spoken language worked? With Herodotus, Confucius, Plato, Pericles, Aristotle, Augustine, St. Thomas, Descartes, Hume, Hobbes, Kant, Locke, von Humboldt, Wittgenstein, Whitehead, Condillac, Pavlov? What to include? Contributions from philosophy, rhetoric, anthropology, the philosophy of science, psychology, history, literature, mathematics, physics, mass communication, sociology, speech communication, speech science? What not to include? Where to end?

The problem is that the study of human communication, and the resultant theorizing about human communication, has been central to the study of humans ever since humans began to turn their attention inward upon their own condition and outward upon how they affect the rest of the world in which they live.

Given the magnitude of the possible universe one could draw upon in a review of human communication theory, hopefully the reader will allow a somewhat arbitrary drawing of boundaries.

The year 1950 will serve as the first boundary. It was in 1950 that the National Society for the Study of Communication, the organization that eventuated into the International Communication Association, was formed (Weaver, 1977). By 1950 the seminal publications in statistical information theory (Shannon, 1948) and cybernetics (Wiener, 1948) had been made, and the level of human communication consciousness within the academic community was well on its way to being raised. It was in that time that scholars from various disciplines began to become more self-consciously aware of their own interest in something that could be labeled human communication theory, and schools and universities were starting to introduce courses in communication theory into their formal curricula. (This is not to say that some scholars were not earlier concerned with communication theory, or that some formal institutions had not earlier introduced courses touching upon human communication theory—it is just to suggest that around 1950 the number of such scholars and of such courses began to grow noticeably, and that as a result the interdisciplinary study of human communication entered upon a new stage.)

As a result of the important work of Wiener and of Shannon, the study of human communication theory in the early 1950s was often confused with the study of statistical information theory. Perhaps it was this initial confusion which led to the later, but still extant, confusion of the study of human communication theory with statistical technique and with the experimental method (Budd, 1977). It is apparent that to limit a content area, such as human communication theory, to a particular methodology, such as the experimental or quantitative method, is to limit the questions that can be appropriately asked and the answers that can possibly be derived. What is more, theory, of its nature, is a search for abstract principles that may be applied across many differing situations, while the experimental method often has as its appropriate goal the specification of variables in such a manner as to give highly specific results, verifiable within a highly specific set of controlled boundaries. Obviously, theory construction must take into account all appropriate methodologies, including the experimental. Just as obviously, it would be self-destructive for theory construction to rely solely on any given methodological technique.

A research area, by its intrinsic nature, affects the methodologies appropriate to its examination. Human communication is both an internal and an external phenomenon and thus hovers between the subjective and the objective. Human communication has profound personal effects as well as profound social effects and thus must be studied critically, historically, descriptively, empirically, and so forth. Rather than allowing a method to dictate the questions, (after the manner of Kaplan's famous duo "The Law of the Hammer" and the model of "The Drunkard's Search") the questions to which a human communication theorist directs his attention should direct us to the method most appropriate for finding possible answers. A human communication theorist might be engaged by such questions as:

> "What is the phylogenetic origin of human communication?"
> "Is human communication any different from the communication of other organisms?"
> "If so, in what way or ways?"
> "Does human communication have any peculiar effect on the manner in which humans come to be more humane?"
> "What is the effect of the use of human communication on the individual?"
> "What is the effect of human communication on society?"
> "What are the reciprocal effects of human communication and the mass media?"
> "What are the ethical dimensions of human communication?"

The purpose of the above list is not to suggest boundaries but to suggest that the various questions call for various methodologies, rather than one, in the search for possible answers.

A human communication theorist spends his or her time and cognitive efforts in consciously trying to answer the fundamental question (and the questions which flow from the fundamental question) of, "What is human about human communication and how does human communication help us in becoming ever more humane individually and socially?" Such an overall question lends focus and also carries with it innumerable subsidiary concerns guaranteed to keep numerous persons busy for a long time to come. For example, on the way to answering the fundamental question, we can concentrate on the human as the instrument of human communication, on the messages of human communication, on the means of reproducing the messages of human communication, on the means of technically extending the messages of human communication, on the best ways of communicating humanly, on the effects of different styles of human messages on individuals and society, on the effects of media on human communication, on the effects of human communication on emerging cultures, and on and on and on! Whatever questions the theorist deals with, the questions must involve the "human" element, and must be allowed to suggest a methodology rather than allowing a predetermined methodology to decide the appropriate questions.

The year 1950 has been set as one boundary for the review portion of this essay. A second boundary for the literature reviewed is the author's intent to make a contribution to human communication theory. The intent must be either stated or else be so manifest as to be clearly inferable.

The boundaries of year and intent are essentially outside the manner in which the author treats the subject of human communication theory. There are, however, two tensions which I believe do affect the treatment of the content, and these two tensions play an important part in lending a direction to the construction of human communication theory.

The first tension is that between *rationalism* and *empiricism*. The second tension is that between *interaction* and *conceptualization-mentation* as primary goals of human communication.

In *Zen and the Art of Motorcycle Maintenance*, Robert Pirsig (1974) discusses the problems created by Hume's extreme empiricism for the process of "knowing." Hume's position is that an individual is born a tabula rasa or clean slate, and that all that the individual ever comes to know is because of the experiences of that individual's senses across time. For Hume, experience writes upon the clean slate and that writing constitutes the totality of the individual's knowledge. Knowledge then would be totally experiential and, in a fashion, totally idiosyncratic. Kant, challenged by the solipsistic nature of Hume's proposal, countered, in his "Critique of Pure Reason," that "though all our knowledge begins with experience, it by no means follows that all rises out of experience" (1952, p. 14). Whereas Hume suggests that all knowledge, in reference to experience, is *a posteriori*, Kant says that some knowledge, rather than being *a posteriori*, exists *a priori* and that experience, rather than giving rise to *a priori* knowledge, simply serves to activate *a priori* knowledge in the individual. For example, the concepts of space and time are not deducible from discrete sensory stimuli, they are not arrived at *a posteriori*, but, according to Kant's position, are concepts which are outside of the specific sense experiences even though they are concepts which are triggered by the discrete experiences—they are *a priori* concepts.

The struggle between a rationalist interpretation of human nature and an empiricist interpretation of human nature has existed since the beginning of Western thought. Plato's suggestion of innate ideas is a rationalist suggestion; the word "education," in its origins, intimated that the process of education was one of drawing out of the individual certain ideas already present, rather than filling the individual with completely new ideas. In some ways, within the discipline of psychology today, Carl Rogers might be viewed as a believer in a rationalist position concerning human nature while B.F. Skinner would be much closer to the empiricism end of a rationalist-empiricist continuum. I am suggesting that, in the construction of human communication theory we can find this rationalist-empiricist struggle evidenced, and that understanding this tension may assist us in understanding the current state of human communication theory in the academy.

The second tension mentioned above was the tension between an interactionist perspective as the goal of human communication and a conceptualization-mentation perspective as the goal of human communication. Again, this is not a new distinction. Plato, Locke, and Swift, among others, tend to view the primary goal and purpose of human communication in terms of its fostering interaction among human beings. Descartes, von Humboldt and others espouse the position that the primary goal and purpose of human communication is to foster conceptualization. This historical division of thought regarding the main purpose of human communication is today mirrored in different treatments of human communication theory, and has practical impact on teaching and research in the field. Thus, the tensions between rationalism/empiricism, and interaction/mentation will also be taken into consideration in our selected literature review.

Even with the boundaries thus far set forth, there is still too large a body of literature open to review, so rather than pretending to any degree of exhaustiveness, writings will be chosen which are representative of some categories dealing with human communication theory.

The human communication theory literature, dating since 1950, is open to many different categorizations. For our purposes, the literature has been distributed into what seem to be five categories.

1. Literature dealing with applications of human communication. This would include essays and books giving advice and instruction in such areas as public speaking, advertising, managerial communication, conflict resolution, and so forth.
2. Literature dealing with the metatheoretical aspects of human communication theory. This would include writings setting forth metatheoretical prerequisites for building human communication theory, writings assessing the current state of theory-building qua theory-building in human communication, and writings suggesting metatheoretical strategies for building human communication theory.
3. Literature presenting collections, reviews, or synopses of materials dealing with human communication theory, although not trying to synthesize such materials.
4. Literature which not only presents a collection or synopsis of other materials, but which also makes an effort or an attempt to analyze or snythesize the material reviewed.
5. Literature which has as its stated or clearly inferable purpose the actual building of human communication theory.

A HIGHLY SELECTIVE REVIEW

Literature dealing with applications of human communication

Since those writings which would be found in the first category are generally not intended as contributions to human communication *theory*, this essay will not concern itself with that body of literature.

Literature dealing with metatheoretical aspects of human communication theory

For the most part, I suspect that productive theorists spend little time on metatheoretical concerns. Not that such concerns are either irrelevant or inconsequential to outcomes, but that, as in most creative enterprises (and theory building is a creative enterprise), those *doing* theory construction are not always conscious of, or much concerned with, the metatheoretical constraints and techniques actually underlying the construction of a specific disciplinary or content theory. Perhaps the rules of theory construction are best viewed as constitutive rules rather than as prescriptive rules. The result of such a view would be that successful attempts at theory construction usually mirror the metatheoretical rules, but that simply following the metatheoretical processes seldom if ever results in successful theory construction. I have the feeling that trying to teach human communication theory construction by immersing a student in the metatheoretical literature is similar to trying to teach creative writing by immersing the student in grammar and syntax. An epic poem or a sonnet can indeed be written by following rules, but without the necessary creative spark, the poem is likely to be absolutely correct in form and absolutely sterile in content.

On the other hand, there is still much to be learned from the reading and study of metatheoretical literature. Certainly such study better arms us for the tasks of analyzing and criticizing proposed theories of human communication. For the practicing theoretician, such concerns, when studied after the fact of theory construction, may highlight methodological shortcomings which may hinder conceptual breakthroughs. Certainly, recognizing the goals and attributes of theory construction may excite the would-be theorizer to seek for both power and precision in the nascent theory. The criteria of range and elegance may serve as tests and as goals for theories, but in truly creative theory construction they are usually viewed after the fact, rather than being held in consciousness throughout the creative theory-building process.

The metatheoretical literature in human communication theory is presently in a stage of proliferation. As recently as 1968, there was comparatively little metatheoretical literature, at least in the field of speech communication theory (Fischer, 1969). Prior to 1968, again in the field of speech communication, there was little evidence of metatheoretical sophistication. In the years since 1968 matters have changed rapidly. Scholars such as Lee Thayer, Leonard Hawes, Jesse Delia, W. Barnett Pearce, Gerald Miller and others have published increasingly penetrating and wise considerations of the metatheoretical bases and constraints for the building of human communication theory.

In 1963, Lee Thayer set forth his metatheoretical commentary by tying it directly to what he considers aspects of the human communicative reality—this is an example of how the subject matter itself dictates the possible methodological constraints. Thayer presented ten metatheoretical obstacles which he felt militated against successful theory building in human communication. Whereas some of Thayer's obstacles come from outside the human communicative act itself (such as those he refers to as "the myths of objectivity, rationality, and logicality"), other obstacles come from what he considers to be the nature of human communication (such as the problem presented to theory construction by the problems of meaning). In my opinion, Thayer illustrates a scholar who recognizes the two tensions affecting the building of theory, and constantly seems to be struggling to adjust those tensions in his own contributions.

Pragmatics of analoguing. Leonard Hawes (1975) set out to demonstrate that doing social science research is an exhilirating intellectual experience, and takes as his point of departure the observation that, at the heart of the social scientist's activity, we will always find the process of analogizing and developing analogies. Hawes's treatment of the roles of metaphor and analogy in language is indeed illuminating and helpful to theorists and critics of theory alike. What is more, Hawes puts his own metatheoretical convictions to the test by examining several well-known models of human communication in terms of the degree to which the models serve as examples of well-developed analogies. In addition, Hawes makes clear the distinction between partial theories and grand, or total, theories. With regard to Hawes' distinction, it certainly seems, at least at present, that the theories of human communication that now exist come closer to being partial rather than grand theories; and that many statements masquerading under the guise of theoretical statements come closer to being miniscule or particularistic observations based upon a single experimental study.

Both Thayer and Hawes go beyond the simple presentation of metatheoretical statements and, in Hawes's case, makes applications for the sake of example, or in Thayer's case, indicate how statements peculiar to the subject matter can themselves serve in a metatheoretical manner in terms of further theory construction (for example, his concern as to whether or not communication can even be studied apart from the totality of the human organism).

Other essays published in the field of human communication dealing with metatheory make certain metatheoretical observations but fail to make adequate disciplinary application of those observations. In the recent past, there have been a number of essays dealing with a rule-governed approach to human communication. These essays indicate what may be considered a possible metatheoretical approach, but never, at least to me, make the step into actual theory construction in human communication.

The growing interest and literature concerning the application of metatheoretical considerations to human communication theory is timely, valuable, and warranted. However, it should be understood that it is most often a body of literature about doing human communication theory, rather than literature which itself presents human communication theory either in the doing or done.

Literature presenting collections, reviews, or synopses of materials dealing with human communication theory, although not trying to synthesize such materials

Within this category falls the majority of those collections of readings with which we are all familiar. The major goal of such contributions seems to be to make available to the readership easily accessible collections of essays dealing with human communication theory. Given the fact that normally such essays are scattered in a variety of periodicals and are difficult to acquire, the goal seems a worthy one. This category includes only those collections consisting of previously published materials. Such collections sometimes include relatively brief editorial remarks prefatory to various groupings of the reprinted materials. It is often the case that the prefatory editorial remarks serve more as explanations of the editor's rationale for the inclusion of certain reprinted materials than as attempts at creative synthesis. Whereas such prefatory remarks may assist the reader in understanding the editorial point of view, seldom do the remarks approach making an original contribution to human communication theory itself.

Given the degree of growth in the area of our concern, such collections become rapidly dated, although they certainly serve a historical purpose in providing a record of content development. The selections themselves also point to emerging trends in the study of human communication, and the manner in which the various editors see fit to partition the field suggests how the academic conceptualization of the area might be emerging. Indeed, these collections also testify to the breadth of interdisciplinary interest in the phenomenon of human communication and often serve to alert the reader to areas of investigation with which he or she might not have been previously familiar.

From among a multitude of such contributions, examples are Mortensen (1972), Sereno and Mortensen (1970), and DeVito (1973).

As with Category Two, the writing within Category Three seldom actually constructs human communication theory, but rather presents windows which allow the reader to gaze upon samples of human communication theorizing that have been done elsewhere.

Literature presenting collections, reviews, or synopses of materials dealing with human communication theory and trying to synthesize such materials

Here we find a variety of styles of contribution:

1. collections of previously published materials, also including either editorial essays or essays

by other contributors, which try to creatively analyze and synthesize the previously published materials in terms of human communication theory;

2. compilations of original essays from various contributors, the original essays themselves being either new reviews of the literature from various fields, or efforts to suggest the domain of human communication theory within various disciplines, or how human communication might be viewed from differing disciplinary perspectives, or simply, essays dealing with some aspect of human communication theory;
3. efforts on the behalf of an author to creatively review the overall area of human communication theory for the purpose of presenting a fresh analysis and often suggest the path for future investigation and development.

Barker and Kibler (1971), and Barnlund (1968) may serve as paradigms of those collections of reprints which make a serious effort to draw from the reprinted materials so as to present at least partial syntheses of the first style. Barnlund's book has a specific subfocus within human communication theory, namely, interpersonal communication. However, Barnlund's definition of communication as an "effort after meaning," provides a prism through which he views the contributions of others. The book presents the results of an obviously exhaustive review of appropriate research literature and then goes on to present a series of insightful and clearly written review/syntheses which serve to introduce each of the book's divisions.

Among compilations of original essays, one could cite Dance (1967), Hanneman and McEwen (1975), Pool and Schramm (1973), and Budd and Ruben (1972). Of these four selections, three (Dance, Budd and Ruben, Pool and Schramm), while displaying editorial focus, seem not to have intended to make a synthesis of the original essays, but rather allow the essays to stand on their own with the implicit suggestion that the editorial selection and arrangement of the essays may serve as testimony to the editorial point of view. Hanneman, in Hanneman and McEwen, makes an effort to set forth a theoretical framework which might assist the reader in organizing the materials presented by other contributors to the collection. Oftentimes, these collections of original essays indeed serve to present some materials which themselves make contributions to human communication theory. However, it is the nature of the beast that more often the contributed essays serve to review prior contributions rather than to allow the author the luxury of original theoretical writing.

The third style of contribution within the fourth category includes serious efforts by a single author to review and synthesize the materials dealing with human communication theory, with the goal of presenting an overview and possible outline of future directions. Two such contributions would be those of Cherry (1961) and of Mortensen (1972). Cherry tries to present a view of the historical development of fields interested in human communication, and also tries to extract concepts or ideas which seem to be common to the diverse contributing disciplines and fields of interest. He also presents a glossary of terms and a fine listing of references. Cherry's engineering background is evident in his transactional approach to human communication. Mortensen does an exemplary job of gathering and weaving together into a coherent and persuasive narrative multitudinous contributions from many fields and disciplines. Mortensen states his own belief that communication, rather than being a unified discipline, is more likely an umbrella term for a host of general principles and orienting statements. Given such a belief, it is to be expected that Mortensen fails to present a unique or primitive contribution to human communication theory, even though his book serves as an admirable overview, as does Cherry's. However, due to the growth in the area, both Cherry and Mortensen are rapidly becoming dated.

A recent attempt within this subcategory is that of Littlejohn (1978). Littlejohn attempts to approach human communication theory from the point of view of various contributing disciplines. Within each of the disciplines he endeavors to analyze and synthesize the various developmental threads. Given the challenge of such a task, Littlejohn has done well.

All of the literature within Categories Three and Four is on the eclectic end of a continuum between primitive and eclectic (actually a third continuum affecting the content of human communication theory). Certainly such an eclectic bent seems to be the nature of the literature when one is considering collections of materials. On the other hand, there is no reason why books of the type by Cherry, Littlejohn, or Mortensen must, of necessity, take an eclectic approach to human communication theory. Is the pervading eclecticism the result of tradition, the reality of the phenomenon being examined, or an example of an assumption that might be disciplinarily entrenched and yet erroneous? Although the eclecticism militates against a very strong position for either an interactionist or a mentation perspective, the materials thus far certainly tend more towards the interactionist point of view. Given the emphasis on quantitative studies in most of the literature, I also consider that most of the contributions also lean towards an empiricist rather than a rationalist viewpoint.

Literature which has as its goal the formulation of human communication theory

Whereas none of the preceding bodies of literature seem to constitute human communication theory, as much as literature about human communication theory, this final grouping includes sustained contributions clearly discernible as having the intent of building a theory of human communication. The range of the theories reflected in this category include mostly partial or middle-range theories, although I am confident that some of the contributing scholars have a long-range goal of suggesting total or grand theories of human communication.

Given the lack of a single disciplinary focus in human communication theory up to this time, it is not surprising that contributions to theory should flow from many sources. Represented in the ranks of contributing theoreticians are anthropologists (Hewes, 1973; Sapir, 1921; Hymes, 1962; Birdwhistell, 1970); engineers (Shannon, 1948; Pierce, 1961); linguists (Chomsky, 1975; McNeil, 1970); psychiatrists (Ruesch, 1972; Shands, 1960); psychologists, including experimental, cognitive, comparative, humanistic and clinical (Watzlawick, 1976; Skinner, 1957; Fouts, 1975; Rumbaugh, 1974; Bever, 1974; Fodor, 1975; Werner & Kaplan, 1963); philosophers (Adler, 1967; Langer, 1967, 1972); sociologists (Mead, 1934; Duncan, 1962); political scientists (Deutsch, 1963; Pye, 1963; scholars in mass communication (Schramm, 1954; DeFleur & Ball-Rokeach, 1976); psycho-linguistics (Brown, 1973; Miller, 1956; Clark & Clark, 1977); persons from journalism (Stephenson, 1967); speech communication (Dance, 1975; Miller, 1966; Smith, 1970); and others who I find difficult to classify within a disciplinary boundary (Thayer, 1967, 1968, 1973; Berlo, 1960; Burke, 1970; Menyuk, 1971; Rosenstock-Huessy, 1970). Obviously, even such an approach at listing leaves out many whose names will occur to the reader of this essay.

Some of the contributions to human communication theory are purposeful—the individual has set out with the intent to so contribute [Thayer (1967, 1968, 1973), Stephenson (1967), Dance and Larson (1972), Dance (1976)]. Other human communication theory contributions, although clear, seem incidental to other pursuits of the scholars involved [Luria (1966), Ruesch (1972), Shands (1960), Rumbaugh (1974)]. The accidental or fortuitous contributions are those which in their conception did not design to specifically bear on the building of human communication theory, yet in their execution clearly do so.

Of those who are primarily interested in the building of human communication theory, their focus on such a goal seems to me to be obvious and sustained. For example, almost all of Chomsky's work (with the exception of his political writings) clearly bear on human communication theory. Others, such as Ruesch and Burke, have contributed both inside and outside of human communication theory, but a number of the works of each seems to have human communication theory-construction as a major goal. Authors such as Shands and Stephenson have probably written more outside than inside the focus of human communication theory, yet their contributions must be considered important ones. Berlo's (1960) book, although bordering on being a synthesizing review rather than an original contribution, must be included because of its impact on the entire field of interest, as well as because of Berlo's attempt to set forth a comprehensive model of an interactionist/empiricist perspective on human communication theory. Eco's work (1976), unfortunately not well known in the United States, centers upon human communication theory under the rubric of semiotics, and makes an effort to take into consideration both the interactionist and mentation perspective. Langer (1972), in her solitary and exemplary dedication, has centered almost completely on the philosophical entities underlying the entire spectrum of human communication phenomena. A review of the many essays of Critchley (1970), and Luria (1966), indicates a persevering interest in explicating the intricacies of human communication. Essays and research by Sander (1977), Freedle and Lewis (1977), Sigel and Cocking (1977), and Bates, Benigni, Bretherton, Camaroni and Volterra (1977), bear directly on the elemental concerns of human communication theory.

Obviously, any partial literature review such as this will be noted as much for what is left out as for what is included. However, it is intended to be a paradigmatic review rather than a comprehensive bibliography, and, thus, its touchstone must be the exemplars of the genre rather than all the contributions to the literature.

COMMENTARY

Having been commenting throughout the review section, above, I was somewhat confounded when I came to that part of this essay concerned with a commentary. So, in the best tradition, I consulted a number of dictionaries to find out exactly what might be expected of me. In essence, say those who purport to know, a commentary consists of some sort of explanatory treatise or systematic series of interpretations, often by someone who was involved in the activities about which the commentary is being made. To a certain extent, I have been involved in the activities surrounding human communication theory since close to 1950, and it has been my pleasure to meet and mingle with many of those scholars to whom I have already alluded. At least part of this commentary will thus meet definitional requirements. What I mean to do is to present both a review commentary (that is, a commentary dealing with the current situation as I see it) and a prospectus commentary (that is, a commentary setting forth the direction in which I would like to move in trying to contribute to the continuing process of building a grand theory of human communication).

A Review Commentary

Given everything which has been considered up to this point, as well as all of the prior knowledge of my readers, where are we vis-a-vis human communication theory in 1978? Where does this leave us?

It is clear, I believe, that there is currently no grand or total theory of human communication to which we can refer. As a matter of fact, it seems that almost no one has even set out to construct a grand theory in our field of interest.

It is also clear that we are certainly left with a few theories of the middle-range, or partial variety, for example Thayer, who attempts to account for the working of human communication within a restricted ambient, or Shands, who attempts to account for one or more aspects of human communication across a number of settings. Almost all, if not all, of the theories set forth by the scholars mentioned under Category Five of the literature review fall within the scope of partial theories.

In addition to a number of partial theories, we have available many partial, or particularistic, theoretical bits and pieces. Every piece of competent experimental research adds to our bank of theoretical tidbits. Unfortunately, all too often the research lacks a theoretical surrounding and thus it is difficult to exactly place the experimental results. There are times when experimental research seems to be following a hidden assumption that a multitude of unrelated but proven facts cannot possibly be wrong. Yet these contributions are important and call for organization and tailoring to a theoretical framework.

The situation is that we have no grand theories, a number of partial theories, and many particularistic, theoretical bits and pieces. Obviously, such a situation is less than satisfying to anyone concerned. The field, and many of those in it, exhibits fragmentation, pique, and frustration. The subject matter, and our efforts to deal with it thus far, seems to have left us truly bewitched, bothered, and bewildered.

How have we come to this state of affairs? Why

are we where we seem to be? First of all, I do not really think that our present situation is all that undesirable. The innate complexity and difficulty in the enterprise of constructing a theory of human communication, indeed of human communication itself, imbues all of our efforts with inherent problems. For example, Berlo has pointed out that human communication is processual. The process quality of human communication is not, I think, a primitive aspect of human communication, but is derived from the fact that human communication acts upon information. Process is manifestly part and parcel of information if one considers information to involve the reduction of uncertainty. One cannot reduce uncertainty without automatically involving an alteration of the status quo. Then, when human communication acts upon information, change will always be involved and change necessitates process. The processual or change aspect of human communication carries with it another attribute which make the search for theory difficult. As with all things involving human beings, unless one believes in strict reductionism, human communication theory must be probabilistic rather than absolutist. When dealing with humans we deal with probabilities. Thus, the effort to find an absolutist theory of human communication seems to be foreordained to failure. The probabilistic nature of human communication theory results in an uncertainty which some find distressing.

In addition to the processual and probabilistic aspect of human communication, it is omnipresent and ubiquitous. Human communication permeates the human condition. Human communication surrounds us and is an inbuilt aspect of everything human beings are and do. That makes any effort to explain, predict, and to some extent control human communication a pretty big order. How does one get a handle on the totality of human communication? Perhaps this may be an insurmountable difficulty which may doom our efforts to construct a grand theory and constrain us to the production of partial theories, at best.

Lastly, we are faced with the problem of using an instrument to examine the instrument itself. If, as many of us believe, human communication is closely related to conceptual processes and we are trying to examine human communication through mental activities, there is bound to be a blind spot. Maybe there is a point where mind and human communication are so fused that it is impossible for the human instrument, or any prosthetic extension of the human instrument, to discern, much less understand, that point of fusion. This may indeed be the ultimate human frailty which will confound our theory-building efforts.

In addition to the problems of process, probability, omnipresence, and the limitation of the instrument in examining itself, our current state is also traceable to the effects on scholars of those tensions which have been mentioned earlier.

The tension between rationalism and empiricism is apparent in the different approaches of Chomsky (rationalist) and Gerald Miller (empiricist). This is not to say that either gentleman espouses a total commitment to one or the other end of the continuum, but rather that their position on such a continuum is fairly obvious. The tension between rationalism and empiricism carries itself into entire schools of research and teaching. As with all such things, this particular tension also seems to cause some scholars to rigidify and condemn.

The tension between mentation and interaction is represented in the current state by the differing approaches of individuals such as Langer (mentation) and Cherry (interactionist). Indeed, almost all present professionals in the field of human communication seem to espouse an interactionist perspective. The majority of textbooks and courses serve interactionist goals and seldom treat the mentation perspective, save as mentation may be used to facilitate interaction. The almost disastrous emphasis on the clinical extremes of interpersonal communication courses in some schools is directly traceable to an exclusive interactionist commitment on the part of many practitioners.

Jerry Fodor (1975) has done a clean job of considering the problems of reductionism in considering some aspects of human communication. The tension between a holistic approach (Thayer) and a reductionist approach (Skinner) has served to introduce almost paralyzing confusion into theory-building efforts. It is against the negative results of undue tension on this dimension that Duncan (1968) wrote.

There is another tension at work in the field

which is almost invisible because it is so widely accepted. There is a prevailing belief that the study of human communication in its essence is totally eclectic. The tension then is one between the belief that human communication is a primitive area of study, and the opposite belief that human communication is almost epiphenomenal (that it arises out of human behavior and can only be considered when we consider every other aspect of human behavior). This tension between a primitive and an eclectic approach to the phenomenon is reflected in the contemporary fragmentation of research and theory.

Confounding the problems inherent to the phenomenon and the tensions surrounding the study of the phenomenon is the modern ritual of scholarship. The artificial compartmentalization of the academic superstructure results in a competitiveness and disciplinary isolationism culminating in jealousy and waste. Academic snobbery and one-upmanship inhibits rather than facilitates the common sharing and searching which should be hallmarks of the academy. An abusive amount of effort is wasted in looking over our shoulders to see who might be close behind us rather than standing together, in defiance of common ignorance, and in pursuit of common goals.

All of this explains, at least in part, why we are where we are. Unless things change radically it seems likely we'll continue doing more of the same. Tomorrow is always an extension of today. Unless a concerted effort is made by practitioners, researchers, teachers, and theoreticians, the future development of human communication theory will most likely be extended along the lines currently visible.

So much for Cassandra.

A Prospectus Commentary

Like Janus, a human communication theoretician should stand in the present with an eye towards both the past the the future. Eugen Rosenstock-Huessy (1970) states that speech situates the individual in the middle of a cross so that the individual at one and the same time, through speech, faces inward, outward, forward and backward. In the remainder of this essay I would like to look forward, and in a very personal vein set forth a perspective concerning where I, as a human communication theoretician, would like to go in trying to make a contribution to the eventual development of a grand theory of human communication.

All of those tensions we have been considering have to be adjusted. Note that I do not suggest that the tensions should be resolved. I am simply not for doing away with tensions. As a matter of fact, I believe that tensions are part and parcel of being human and that the proper adjustment of tensions is what helps set the appropriate tone for all of our human efforts. Just as with a violin, if the tension of a string is stretched too taut, the string breaks, tension totally disappears, and no tone is possible. On the other hand, if the string is allowed to be too loose, then tension also disappears, and no tone is possible. It is not a question of resolving or eliminating tensions, as much as a matter of seeking for the appropriate adjustment of tension so as to permit the development of the most resonant and satisfying tone. What must be done is to understand the tensions that are operating in human communication theory-construction and then to adjust those tensions for the individual theorist.

Here is how I have presently adjusted the tensions for myself.

Rationalism/empiricism. I believe that there is sufficient evidence to indicate that humans contain possibilities other than those induced by experience. On the other hand, without experience, human possibilities, whatever they may be, are doomed to lie fallow. If there is anything such as a "Language Acquisition Device" innate in human beings, that device needs to be activated by interfacing the neonate with a social environment. There certainly seems to be, in human beings, an innate or genetically determined thrust toward vocalization, but socialization and experience is demanded if this vocalization is ever to be joined with the cultural heritage imbedded in natural languages. There are effects of human communication upon the intrapersonal human condition, as well as upon interpersonal human settings, which do not seem to be amenable to empirical explanation. The work of phenomenological philosophers such as Husserl and Heidegger touch upon such matters and seem to me to call for an admission of rationalist possibilities. The ubiquitousness of human vocalization, *symboling*, and speech communication, when joined with reflections on the possibility of other linguistic universals, also suggest the fruitfulness of allowing for both a rationalist and an empiricist approach to theory construction. The possibility of universal functions of human communication again contributes to my belief that it will be most helpful for us theoretically to allow for rationalist or *a priori* human communication attributes, which, when elucidated, may then be related to experience and empirically tested and organized.

Mentation/interaction. At least within the traditions of speech communication and mass communication as disciplines, most of us have grown up immersed in the hegemony of *interaction* as the essence and the goal of human communication. Finally I have come to the point where, although I believe in interaction as a vital and essential component of human communication, I no longer believe interaction to be the primary goal of that which is peculiarly *human* in human communication. Nature, if I may be permitted some personification, is both prudent and tightfisted. When in the course of evolution, attributes or capacities are developed in a species which satisfactorily fulfill what seem to be the goals of the species in such a fashion as to allow the species to survive, indeed to grow and flourish, then nature seldom, if ever, provides additional attributes or capacities to the same species for duplicative purposes. In fact, much of evolution seems to consist of a constant move to diminish duplicative systems, for example, from four legs to two. I would like to suggest that the attributes and capacities which characterize much of nonhuman animal communication satisfactorily fulfill all the interactive goals necessary to the survival and continued growth of the animal kingdom. Response to the environment, food gathering, self-protection, rudimentary organizational needs, reproduction, all are adequately supported by the interaction aspect of most animal communication systems. If this is so, then why would evolution squander the valuable attribute of symbolicity to accomplish exactly the same goals which were already being accomplished by extant communicative attributes, capacities, and systems. There really is no adequate answer to this simple question. I think it quite apparent that the nature would do no such thing. However, humans *do* symbolize. In fact, for some, spoken symboling is more of an indicator of the species specificity of humans than is wisdom or rational thought—*homo symbolicum* rather than *homo sapiens*. If spoken symboling is indeed what is peculiarly or uniquely human about human communication, then what purpose does this additional attribute or capacity of spoken symboling serve. It must serve, unless nature has suddenly become both capricious and wasteful.

The answer is mentation. The raison d'etre of human communication is mentation, or the facilitation of conceptualization. Given the fact that humans are also members of the animal kingdom, humans have access to all of the communicative attributes and capacities distributed throughout the rest of the animal kingdom (often within different ranges of application), so humans, by virtue of their evolutionary birthright, have access to and make great use of the interactive aspect of animal communication.

The unique goal of human communication—mentation—is then superimposed on the previous animal communicative goal of interaction. The consequence is that uniquely human communication has as its primary purpose and goal, its raison d'etre, mentation, but that humans also communicate interactively as a result of access to other attributes and capacities with evolutionary primacy. This focus on mentation also suggests that, whereas the first goal of truly human communication is mentation, following close behind is the goal of sharing this mentation through interaction, the second goal of human communication and the first goal of animal communication.

It is also possible for human beings to seemingly suspend their uniquely human communicative capacity and behaviorally focus their communicative activities on the attributes and capacities of their animal heritage. Except for such anomalous human behavior, I do not believe that humans, when communicating, are ever successful in concentrating their communicative behaviors in either a totally mentative or a totally interactive manner. Human communication uses mentation to lend a uniquely human flavor to interaction. It is through the potentiating quality of mentation that interaction by humans is allowed to go beyond ordinary animal interaction and acquire characteristics which allow it to be called humane.

If this analysis is at all valid, then human communication theorists are given assistance in the discernment of appropriate avenues of investigation for the construction of a total theory of human communication. The research on animal communication assumes a contributing role within human communication theory, but researchers, theorists, and practitioners are all provided the needed guidance in terms of both priorities and range.

Let me state once again that I am not suggesting the abandonment of the study of communicative interaction, or the study of the role of human communication in interaction, I am instead stating that interaction is a secondary goal of what constitutes uniquely *human* communication, the primary goal of which was, is, and shall remain mentation.

Holism/reductionism. For many years I have been an admirer of the work of Ivan Petrovich Pavlov and his cognitive descendants. There is something very seductive about reductionism. Wouldn't it be simpler if everything was simple? Maybe so, but at least as far as can be seen everything is not simple, and often the whole is more than the sum of its parts. On this tension I have decided in favor of holism, with the understanding that the constant reductionist search is necessary for us to even approach a holistic understanding.

Primitive/eclectic. Eclecticism is simpler than primitivism. It is easier to decide that everything contributes to human communication rather than human communication, in some primitive manner, contributing to everything else. This tension is one which not only affects disciplinary identification, but more importantly affects conceptual identification. If human communication is an eclectic concept, then disciplinary organizations will be of necessity eclectic. This is what has actually happened. This is why, in Lee Thayer's words, we are always looking for a place to stand. This is why some of those disciplines concerned with human communication are always looking for a central core. Human communication is not only a tie that binds, but more importantly a primitive prism through which humans view everything else.

Hans Zetterberg (1965) provides some help in resolving this primitive/eclectic tension when he states that:

> It should be plain that a theory does not have any subject matter that can be called exclusively its own if all its primitive terms are borrowed terms from other sciences. If so, anything that it talks about can be exhaustively presented within the framework of theories from other sciences. On the other hand, if we have one or more terms that can properly be called minimum terms, we also have a unique subject matter. Any phenomenon, then, that has to be defined in these minimum terms is our exclusive subject matter. (p. 50-51)

Given Zetterberg's viewpoint, rather than ask the continuing question, "What, if any, is the proper subject matter for human communication theory?" we are able to ask, "What, if any, are the minimum terms of human communication theory?"

Zetterberg divides all terms into logical terms, such as "and," "or," "not," "imply," and "equal to" (similar to what Adler (1967) identifies as syncategorematic terms) and into extralogical terms, which constitute the content words of the subject under consideration (what Adler labels categorematic terms). In the search for primitive terms we restrict ourselves to a consideration of the extralogical terms.

Extralogical terms include: (1) *primitive terms*, a small group of extralogical words, which in different combinations with each other and with logical terms can define all other extralogical terms of the theory, and (2) *derived terms*, which are obtained by combinations of the primitive terms and the logical words. All derived terms may be explained or defined by arrangements of primitive terms.

Primitive terms include: (1) *minimum terms*, primitive terms unique to a given theory or academic discipline, and (2) *borrowed terms*, primitive terms shared with other theories or academic disciplines.

Note that in his quoted statement concerning

FIGURE 1
Tension Adjustment Profile

minimum (and therefore primitive) terms, Zetterberg states that a theory need have only "one or more" of what can be considered a minimum term in order to indicate the theory's exclusive subject matter.

As I see it, the resolution of this tension between eclecticism and primitivism has an importance beyond that of the sociology of knowledge. The resolution of this tension, like the resolution of the other tensions, may allow us to more fruitfully concentrate our efforts on the search for a total theory of human communication.

What we are left with is the question, "What, if any is the primitive minimum term(s) of human communication, and thus of human communication theory?" From a position I have been promoting in lectures and papers over the past two decades, I would like to suggest that one primitive minimum term of human communication is "spoken symbolism," "spoken language," or "speech communication." There may be other such terms. However, my own present resolution of the primitive/eclectic tension is adequately adjusted by the above-mentioned primitive minimum term. The search for other primitive terms, and the organization of all of the terms dealing with human communication, should also contribute to the ongoing construction of an adequate conceptual taxonomy for our pursuits. Another benefit of the isolation of one or more primitive terms may be the closer cooperation of scholars who share the same primitive terms (those in the borrowed subcategory) in their pursuits, rather than the same departmental affiliations.

I hope that it is apparent that taking a primitive position in human communication theory construction does not in any way restrict the theorists opportunity to draw upon research and thought from any appropriate source in the process of theorizing.

Earlier I suggested that the manner in which these tensions are adjusted will serve to set the tone which characterizes the activities and output of any theoretician. By plotting a tension adjustment profile, we may be able to make some helpful speculations as to what a given theorist's product is going to be like, in terms of its tone on at least these four dimensions. For myself I think it would look like that shown in Figure 1.

SOME PROPOSITIONS FOR A THEORY OF HUMAN COMMUNICATION

In bringing this essay to a close I would like to present some of the working hypotheses which direct my own efforts at human communication theory construction. The presentation of such bald statements is fraught with danger—the danger that I might feel committed to such statements even after they are disproven, the danger that the statements might be interpreted as if I meant them to be taken as laws, or facts, rather than as working hypotheses. Duncan (1968), when engaged in a similar pursuit, made clear the spirit in which the propositions are offered and in which it is trusted they shall be taken.

> Propositions often repel us because of their dogmatic sound. The following propositions are to be read not as dogma, but as points in conversation with others, or in the talk with inner selves we call thought. . . .
>
> These axioms should be read therefore, as a guide into discussion, not as a dogmatic report of discovered truths. (p. 43)

These are certainly not all the propositions I

might present, but they are more than a representative sample of the ones that often serve to direct my own efforts at theory-building. In many cases I have made statements elsewhere concerning the directions which might be set by following one or more of these propositions. Certainly, I shall not abuse your patience by repeating those observations here. Following most of the propositions, I will set down a very few lines suggesting some of the possible implications of the proposition.

The communicative repertoire of humans includes communicative attributes shared with other animal species through our evolutionary heritage, as well as uniquely human attributes. Although when communicating, humans have access to techniques evolutionarily shared with other species, humans have additional communication attributes unique to themselves. The study of animal communication thus bears directly upon the building of a grand theory of human communication, but the findings from research on animal communication must be interpreted with great caution and with regard for differences in range.

Human communication is a phenomenon in its own right. The use of the term "human" qualitatively rather than quantitatively modifies the term "communication." Human communication is not epiphenomenal or something which arises from the behavior of humans, but is itself a central organizing attribute from which that behavior which is considered uniquely human arises.

Human communication is unique in its capacity for the development and production of spoken symbols. The spoken modality has developmental dominance in the acquisition of normal human communication. Human communication, spoken language, and speech communication are all terms referring to the same concept (namely the jointure of genetically determined speech—vocalizations—of humans with culturally determined language).

Human communication results in an acoustic trigger to conceptualization. The fact that symbols, in their genesis and natural development, are spoken, is nontrivial. By nontrivial is meant that the fact that human symbols are spoken is essential to the realization of the primary goal of human communication, mentation. Mentation, although not identical with spoken symbolism, depends on spoken symbolism. Vocalization of infants in nurturing environments where the infant is in contact with responding others who themselves possess speech communication, leads to decentering, displacements, and the birth of the symbol.

The nature of the acoustic trigger has not been fully investigated; the trigger may be a one time event, or it may consist of a number of steps each of which builds upon the preceding step, but all of which taken together constitute a single routine.

There also seems to me to be the possibility that in the absence of a natural acoustic trigger (as with profoundly deaf infants) a different sensory modality may be substituted (such as pressure, or vision), but only with the assistance of intervening others, at the expense of great effort, and with results substantially lower than those produced by the natural trigger, the acoustic trigger to conceptualization.

The human infant, in order to develop speech communication, must be situated in an environment where responding others possess speech communication. In the process of speech communication acquisition, the infant moves from external speech communication to inner speech communication and thence to the production of external speech communication which is undergirded and informed by inner speech communication. In the initial exposure to responding others, the infant acquires models that assist in the development of early external speech communication on an interpersonal level. Thence the child moves to intrapersonal speech communication, to intrapersonal inner speech communication (intrapersonal level and inner speech communication are different concepts with different attributes), thence back to the interpersonal level of human communication and finally, in some instances, to speech communication on the third level of person to persons.

The fact that humans utter spoken symbols enjoins certain functional outcomes. The three presently discernible and supportable functions of human communication are: (1) *linking* (linking the individual with the human environment), (2) *mentation* (the development of higher mental processes), (3) *regulation* (the regulation of human behavior).

As a result of these functions of the spoken symbol, humans develop self-concepts. Speech communication plays a nurturing, integrative role throughout the individual lifespan. The functions, although present without intent, may be intentionally facilitated.

The functions of human communication are projected onto all human social organizations. Individuals compose social groupings. Social groupings, as a result of their being constituted by individuals, will exhibit role enactments of linking, mentation, and regulation.

Human communication functions underlie the many purposes to which human communication may be put. The intentional, purposive use of speech communication always rests on the underlying functions of human communication and are affected by those functions.

Human communication leads to the development of choice, intentionality, individual values, and social ethics. There is possibly a specific ethical value inherent in human communication which thus constitutes human communication as an end rather than as a means in the human enterprise.

Enough! The concern with human communication theory is a human concern, and I believe, a most important concern. All contributions are needed, all contributions are welcome, and perhaps from all contributions we will come ever closer to the eventual goal of a probabilistic, heuristic, grand theory of human communication.

REFERENCES

ADLER, M.J. *The difference of man and the difference it makes*. New York: Holt, Rinehart & Winston, 1967.

BARKER, L. & KIBLER, R.J. *Speech communication behavior: Perspectives and principles*. Englewood Cliffs, N.J.: Prentice-Hall, 1971.

BARNLUND, D.C. *Interpersonal communication: Survey and studies*. Boston: Houghton Mifflin, 1968.

BATES, E., BENIGNI, L., BRETHERTON, I., CAMAIONI, L., & VOLTERRA, V. From gesture to the first word: On cognitive and social prerequisites. In M. Lewis & L.A. Rosenblum (Eds.), *Interaction, conversation, and the development of language*. New York: Wiley, 1977, 247-307.

BERLO, D. *The process of communication*. New York: Holt, Rinehart & Winston, 1960.

BIRDWHISTELL, R.L. *Kinesics and context: Essays on body motion communication*. Philadelphia: University of Pennsylvania Press, 1970.

BROWN, R. *A first language: The early stages*. Cambridge, Mass.: Harvard University Press, 1973.

BUDD, R.W. Perspectives on a discipline: Review and commentary. In B.D. Ruben (Ed.), *Communication yearbook I*. New Brunswick, N.J.: Transaction-International Communication Association, 1977.

BUDD, R.W., & RUBEN, B.D. (Eds.). *Approaches to human communication*. New York: Spartan-Hayden, 1972.

BURKE, K. *The rhetoric of religion: Studies in logology*. Berkeley: University of California Press, 1970.

CHERRY, C. *On human communication* (2nd ed.). New York: Wiley, 1961.

CHOMSKY, N. *Reflections on language*. New York: Pantheon, 1975.

CLARK, H.H., & CLARK, E.V. *Psychology and language*. New York: Harcourt, Brace & Jovanovich, 1977.

CRITCHLEY, M. *Aphasiaology and other aspects of language*. London: Arnold, 1970.

DANCE, F.E.X. (Ed.). *Human communication theory: Original essays*. New York: Holt, Rinehart & Winston, 1967.

DANCE, F.E.X. Speech communication: The sign of mankind. In J. Van Doren (Ed.), *The great ideas today 1975*. Chicago: Encyclopedia Britannica Press, 1975, 40-57.

DANCE, F.E.X., & LARSON, C.E. *Speech communication: Concepts and behaviors*. New York: Holt, Rinehart & Winston, 1972.

DANCE, F.E.X. *The functions of human communication: A theoretical approach*. New York: Holt, Rinehart & Winston, 1976.

DE FLEUR, M.L., & BALL-ROKEACH, S. *The theories of mass communication* (3rd ed.). New York: McKay, 1976.

DELIA, J.G. Constructivism and the study of human communication. *Quarterly Journal of Speech*, 1977, 63, 66-83.

DE VITO, J.A. *Language: Concepts and processes*. Englewood Cliffs, N.J.: Prentice-Hall, 1973.

DEUTSCH, K.W. *The nerves of government*. New York: Free Press of Glencoe, 1963.

DUNCAN, H.D. *Communication and social order*. Totowa, N.J.: Bedminster Press, 1962.

DUNCAN, H.D. *Symbols in society*. New York: Oxford University Press, 1968, 43.

ECO, U. *A theory of semiotics*. Bloomington: Indiana University Press, 1976.

FISHER, M.J. A metatheoretical analysis of the literature on theory-construction in speech communication. Unpublished thesis, Department of Communication, University of Wisconsin-Milwaukee, 1969.

FODOR, J.A. *The language of thought*. New York: Crowell, 1975.

FODOR, J.A., BEVER, T.G., & GARRETT, M.F. *The psychology of language*. New York: McGraw-Hill, 1974.

FOUTS, R. The development of human linguistic behavior in chimpanzees. In J. Van Doren (Ed.), *The great ideas today 1975*. Chicago: Encyclopedia Britannica Press, 1975, 9-24.

FREEDLE, R., & LEWIS, M. Prelinguistic conversations. In M. Lewis & L.A. Rosenblum (Eds.), *Interaction, conversation, and the development of language*, New York: Wiley, 1977, 157-185.

HANNEMAN, G.J., & McEWEN, W.J. (Eds.). *Communication and behavior*. Reading, Mass.: Addison-Wesley, 1975.

HAWES, L. *Pragmatics of analoguing: Theory and model construction in communication*. Reading, Mass.: Addison-Wesley, 1975.

HAWES, L. Alternative theoretical bases: Toward a presuppositional critique. *Communication Quarterly*, 1977, 25, 63-68.

HEWES, G.W. Primate communication and the gestural origin of language. *Current Anthropology*, 1973, 14, 5-24.

HYMES, D. The ethnography of speaking. In T. Gladwin & W.C. Sturtevant (Eds.), *Anthropology and Human Behavior*. Washington, D.C.: Anthropological Society of Washington, 1962.

KANT, E. Critique of pure reason. In M. Adler (Ed.), *Great books of the western world* Vol. 42. Chicago: Encyclopedia Britannica Press, 1952, 14.

KAPLAN, A. *The conduct of inquiry*. San Francisco: Chandler, 1964.

LANGER, S. *Mind: An essay in human feeling* (2 vols.). Baltimore: Johns Hopkins Press, 1967, 1972.

LITTLEJOHN, S.W. *Theories of human communication*. Columbus, Ohio: Merrill, 1978.

LURIA, A.R. *Higher cortical functions in man*. New York: Basic, 1966.

McNEIL, D. *The acquisition of language: The study of developmental psycho-linguistics*. New York: Harper & Row, 1970.

MEAD, G.H. *Mind, self and society*. Chicago: University of Chicago Press, 1934.

MENYUK, P. *The acquisition and development of language*. Englewood Cliffs, N.J.: Prentice-Hall, 1971.

MILLER, G.A. The magical number seven plus or minus two: Some limits on our capacity for processing information. *Psychological Review*, 1956, 63, 81-96.

MILLER, G. *Speech communication: A behavioral approach*. Indianapolis: Bobbs-Merrill, 1966.

MILLER, G. Theory in quantitative speech research. *Western Speech*, 1964, 28, 15-22.

MORTENSEN, C.D. *Communication: The study of human interaction*. New York: McGraw-Hill, 1972.

MORTENSEN, C.D. *Basic readings in communication theory*. New York: Harper & Row, 1973.

PEARCE, W.B. Metatheoretical concerns in communication. *Communication Quarterly*, 1977, 25, 3-6.

PIERCE, J. *Symbols, signals and noise*. New York: Harper & Row, 1961.

PIRSIG, R.M. *Zen and the art of motorcycle maintenance*. New York: Morrow, 1974.

POOL, I. de Sola, & SCHRAMM, W. (Eds.). *Handbook of communication*. Chicago: Rand McNally, 1973.

PYE, L.W. (Ed.). *Communication and political development*. Princeton, N.J.: Princeton University Press, 1963.

ROSENSTOCK-HUSSEY, E. *Speech and reality*. Norwich Vt.: Argo, 1970.

RUESCH, J. *Semiotic approaches to human relations*. The Hague: Mouton, 1972.

RUMBAUGH, D.M. Lane (chimpanzee) learning language: A progress report. *Brain and language*, 1974, 1, 205-212.

SANDER, L.W. The regulation of exchange in the infant-caretaker system and some aspects of the context-content relationship. In M. Lewis & L.A. Rosenblum (Eds.), *Interaction, conversation, and the development of language*, New York: Wiley, 1977, 133-156.

SAPIR, E. *Language*. New York: Harcourt, Brace & World, 1921.

SCHRAMM, W. How communication works. In W. Schramm (Ed.), *Process and effects of mass communication*, Urbana: University of Illinois Press, 1954.

SERENO, K.K. & MORTENSEN, C.D. *Foundations of communication theory*. New York: Harper & Row, 1970.

SHANDS, H.C. *Thinking and psychotherapy*. Cambridge, Mass.: Harvard University Press, 1960.

SHANNON, C.E. The mathematical theory of communication. *Bell System Technical Journal*, 1948, July and Oct.

SIGEL, E.I. & COCKING, R.R. Cognition and communication: A dialectic paradigm for development. In M. Lewis & L.A. Rosenblum (Eds.), *Interaction, conversation, and the development of language*, New York: Wiley, 1977, 207-226.

SKINNER, B.F. *Verbal behavior*. New York: Appleton-Century-Crofts, 1957.

SMITH, R.G. *Speech communication theory and models*. New York: Harper & Row, 1970.

STEPHENSON, W. *The play theory of mass communication*. Chicago: University of Chicago Press, 1967.

THAYER, L. On theory-building in communication: Some conceptual problems. *Journal of Communication*, 1963, 13, 217-235.

THAYER, L. Communication and organizational theory. In F.E.X. Dance (Ed.), *Human communication theory: Original essays*, New York: Holt, Rinehart & Winston, 1967, 70-115.

THAYER, L. *Communication and communication systems*. Homewood, Ill.: Irwin, 1968.

THAYER, L. Toward an ethics of communication. In L. Thayer (Ed.), *Communication: ethical and moral issues*, New York: Gordon & Breach, 1973, 345-360.

WATZLAWICK, R. *How real is real?* New York: Vintage, 1976.

WEAVER, C. A history of the International Communication Association. In B.D. Ruben (Ed.), *Communication Yearbook I*, New Brunswick, N.J.: Transaction-International Communication Association, 1977.

WERNER, H. & KAPLAN, B. *Symbol formation*. New York: Wiley, 1963.

WIENER, N. *Cybernetics: Or control and communication in the animal and the machine*. New York: Wiley, 1948.

ZETTERBERG, H.L. *On theory and verification in sociology* (3rd ed.). Totowa, N.J.: Bedminster Press, 1965.

AUTONOMY AND DEPENDENCE IN TECHNOLOGICAL ENVIRONMENTS: REVIEW AND COMMENTARY

EDWARD T. HALL
Northwestern University

Culture is man's primary mode of coding information in a way that enables him to cope with an increasingly complex life. But one might also say that culture is a series of solutions to past problems and challenges and is therefore past-oriented. This means that culture is a deficient in its inventory of solutions to future problems.

Culture also provides ways of organizing and managing, in the sense that Drucker (1970) uses the term, the tremendous diversity of talents present in the human race. But in so doing, it takes on mass—incredible mass—which like the iceberg is only partially visible. To fully appreciate both its magnitude and complexity, one must look beneath the surface. It is this mass that makes cultures so slow to change on the deep levels. Superficial changes can be rapid but the basic fabric of culture—the mental processes—changes slowly, which can lead to adjustment problems, sometimes on a monumental scale.

This paper does not spring from any grand theory or plan and it does not take an elitist stand; in fact, just the opposite. My view has always been that one should start with the data, which in my case is human beings: how they behave and what they produce. I then try to discover where they are, what they are saying, how they are responding to the world at large, and what this means in the larger sense. I work with an open score rather than a closed score (Halprin, 1969). This enables me to keep my hand on the pulse of the people I am observing, but it also prevents me from taking any strong position on issues (in this case technology). As I see it, my function is to ascertain the issues and point up some of the options that are open to mankind.

Experience has taught me that human beings are not always completely aware of their own motives nor do they always see the collective impact that can result from combined individual acts. The human race is made up of individuals who are the battleground for many divergent and often conflicting drives and impulses. Similarly, on a larger stage, one can see many forces in society that do not always pull in the same direction either. This paper will deal with two of these contradictory trends that transcend some, if not all cultures, and bear directly on how technology affects mankind. My remarks should be considered in the context of my books (Hall, 1959, 1966, 1976), but particularly *The Silent Language* and *Beyond Culture* because the overall frame of culture as communication is the base on which my thinking rests. In this instance I am not concerned with the interface between cultures, but with what one can learn from the study of technology from the viewpoint of a *living systems* scientist.

It is unfortunate that in the beginning of this century Franz Boas and his followers dealt so harshly with Clark Whistler in his attempts to apply the linguistic models of the times to technological studies of the material culture of the American Indians. The result was that the study of *things*—man's material extensions (Hall, 1959), has never taken its proper place in the field of anthropology. On the other hand, this may be a good thing. At least the inherent richness and complexity of technological systems has not been further complicated by a mountain of theory of doubtful relevance.

MAN AND TECHNOLOGY

There are several factors to be considered in any discussion of man and technology:

1. For the past million years, the human species has set itself apart from other species by virtue of a strong and continuous drive to evolve its extensions. These extensions are rooted in two complementary processes (Hall, 1959): (a) those that

contain a strong *information* component, such as language; and (b) those that have a *material-technological* base in which the substances of the universe are organized and reorganized in such a way as to perform and enhance functions formerly performed by the body. A knife is an extension of the teeth; a hammer or club an extension of the fist; a pot or basket an extension of cupped hands to hold grain or berries. There is no break with the past between the highly evolved systems that we see today and the rudimentary tools and records dating back 136,000 years, when stone-age hunters first began to abstract usable data from the universe by recording the moon's movements, and the solstices and seasons on the dried ribs of bison (Marschak, 1972). While some extensions emphasize either information or technology, today's telephone, radio, and television combine both functions.

2. All human beings that I know about have two conflicting and powerful drives that exert a constant influence on how they relate to different technologies. These two drives can be summarized as *autonomy* and *dependency* (Hall, 1976a).

3. There is the media-message dichotomy made famous by our colleague Marshall McLuhan (1962).

4. It is also possible to identify systems in which the technology, by virtue of inherent characteristics, fuels its own development. Complexity grows exponentially as the system becomes larger. Telephone systems are an example—a two-station system needs no switchboard, but for any system beyond eight parties, a boundary is crossed requiring more complex switching arrangements. As the system grows, complexity increases with each new subscriber. The sheer mass of the network forces increased miniaturization and sophistication. Computers follow this same pattern.

5. When properly managed, some technological systems—and the emphasis is on *systems*—result in the development and enhancement of the social and economic matrix in which it is imbedded. The railroads in the days of the steam locomotive are a case in point. Because of frequent stops to take on fuel and water it cost nothing to load, produce, and freight at the same time. This factor alone played a prominent role in the overall uniform economic development of the central and western portions of the North American continent. Later, the invention of the Diesel locomotive reversed this trend and resulted in greater population concentration in large centers several hundred miles apart.

6. The size of a given system is crucial and probably has as much to do with its dynamics and growth as anything else. In the United States, the investment in the machinery that produces automobiles fostered, indeed virtually dictated, that automobile manufacturers manage their markets (Galbraith, 1967). This in turn set in motion forces by which the public became the captive servant of enterprise. Today the world is in an energy crunch, yet the sheer mass of the automobile industry's investment in capital, plant, and people is such that it is difficult to see how the United States is going to extricate itself from the automobile complex without major economic and social dislocations. Highways now cost several times as much per mile to build as railroads, while the ton-mile energy cost of moving freight by rail is considerably less than by truck. But in this case it is not just economic considerations such as "the bottom line" but many other factors that determine what happens. If railroads are expanded, what will become of the automobile industry, to say nothing of the highway construction industry? It is known from past experience that they won't take it lying down.

Since the time of the invention of movable type (McLuhan, 1962) and throughout the industrial revolution, Western culture has looked for linearly oriented, closed score (Hall, 1976b), technological solutions to virtually all problems. We have devoted most of our talents and resources to developing and improving technological solutions. Unfortunately, these efforts have been at the expense of knowledge about mankind. If the same kind of push, money, and interest had gone into the study of the human species as has gone into the development of technology, I would predict that more progress would have been made in solving the social and psychic ills that plague us today. The following come to mind as examples: Why has it been so difficult for human beings to understand that the economic growth on which we depend for prosperity cannot go on forever? Why do we seem to be unable to come up with an adequate steady-state model for modern economies? It is Garret Hardin's "Tragedy of the Commons" all over again (1976). The term homeostasis might as well not exist for all the good it does. Why in the United States do we continue to pave thousands of square miles of agricultural land to make way for streets, parking lots, and housing at a time in history when the world is facing food shortages, shortages that are going to get worse as time goes on because of the increase in world population. Again the population problem seems to have defeated us. We can send a man to the moon but are helpless in the face of a population explosion. People everywhere seem ignorant of the phenomenon I have termed *extension transference* (Hall, 1976), which is the confusion of the extension with the process extended. Perhaps if this process were better understood, the search for answers would shift from technology to studying man himself and concentrating on the interface between man and technology. Having spent considerable time studying and observing this interface (Hall, 1959, 1976b), I have found the process not only fascinating but very rich in data. Consider the matter of man's needs for autonomy and dependency which was mentioned earlier.

AUTONOMY AND DEPENDENCE

This contrasting pair—*autonomy* and *dependence* seems to be worldwide, transcultural and omnipresent among humans. In the United States there is great pride in individual autonomy, yet we permit our automobile manufacturers to swaddle us in the infantile comfort of a machine that does everything for us. This is not only counterproductive both physically and psychologically, but wasteful of materials and labor since such machines are expensive to build and maintain. There are also unforseen but important consequences of these machines because they are also dangerous to drive. Furthermore, my own research has identified a type of human being who depends very much on muscular feedback from his body in order to fix information in his brain. Such people are disoriented by the American car because it insulates them all too successfully from the surface of the road, and they have no way of relating the continuity of the surface of the earth with the continuity of their life stream as it is laid down in their central nervous system (Hall, 1976b). It is risky to take too much for granted when dealing with man's extensions because we often do not understand their impact on man.

Housing

This brings to mind our problems with housing, another system of extensions. My partner, Mildred Hall, and I were asked to consult on an internationally known public housing project—a world famous disaster known as Pruitt-Igoe homes in St. Louis. As is almost always the case, our advice was sought only after the damage had been done and what eventually proved to be an uncongenial environment had been constructed in concrete. To compound this error, the housing was totally cut off from the resources of the community and further handicapped by lack of public transportation, as well as poor maintenance from the city. The tenants were literally destroying that environment. The cost to the U.S. taxpayers was 28 million dollars. Clearly, there is little that experts can do in a case like this, but it does illustrate the necessity for including inputs on human needs at the programmatic phase of architectural planning.

In Latin America there are similar examples, instances in which the housing which was built by the people themselves out of scraps of wood and tin was actually preferred to the monstrosities constructed by public funds. Again, the people frequently destroyed what was built for them, because it was alien and did not fit their needs. They wanted *autonomy* and instead designs were imposed on them that were alien and ill-conceived. Even the great architect Corbusier made grievous errors in design at Chandigarh in India. He used a European model for South Asian people. While Corbusier himself was a genius and was well-intentioned, there was little that was humane in what he did. This is an example of why it is more important to meet man's cultural needs in housing than it is to meet the esthetic standards of architects (Hall, 1966). All over the industrialized world there have been a series of little-publicized and therefore little-known public and private housing disasters. Several years ago when Mildred Hall and I were interviewing town planners in Europe, many of them commented on the worldwide epidemic of vandalism. For example, English youths would smash and burn anything that could be destroyed in a project like Thames-Mead, even before it was completed. In the United States the recent past is replete with similar incidents in which youths, often from middle-class families, have gone on destructive sprees. Much of what happened in both Britain and the United States was a communication—a message directed at an unresponsive system. These examples only illustrate part of the point I am about to make which is that *when human beings rebel and destroy their habitat it is usually due to a failure to find a correct balance between their autonomy and dependence needs*. Hong Kong public housing is a move in the right direction. In the space and time available here I cannot properly reproduce the incredibly complex and subtle administrative structures, as well as the guiding principles that make Hong Kong public housing work. Indeed, I am not even sure that it really works as well as I think it does. I can only look at it from the viewpoint of my own experience. It certainly seems more effective than many public housing projects in the United States, in which highrise complexes were built with little regard for such basic human needs as the necessity to supervise children during play. In Hong Kong, instead of a complete finished apartment, people were given the architectural equivalent of the Model T Ford: four cement walls, some electrical outlets, pipes but no fixtures. To make the place habitable, the tenants had to provide their own amenities. This they could do without interference from a meddling bureaucracy. Those who proved to be responsible and industrious were later rewarded by an opportunity to move into even more desirable quarters. Nurseries and playrooms for small children were provided on every other floor so that mothers were not tied to apartments a hundred or more feet from ground-level play areas. It is important to note that the very strong Chinese family with its control over its members and great self-discipline is partially responsible for the success of the Hong Kong projects. In this case autonomy was given to the family to improve its environment and the individual could function under the family's umbrella.

As you can perceive, the model being suggested departs from the conventional one of words and political-economic acts and is based more on what people *do* as a consequence of their culture. I have chosen to focus on technology, because it is thought to be universally applicable regardless of culture, which it clearly is not. It is this image of the transferability of material things (including architecture) that is like a time bomb, because it can so radically alter the fabric of existence as to make it unrecognizable and in so doing destroy the continuity of life.

I make these statements as a result of over a half century of observation of other cultures as well as my own. While I was growing up in New Mexico, I observed the process of change in both the Spanish villagers and the Navaho Indians from a life with a minimum of gadgets to one that is almost totally mechanized. In my early lifetime, the whole material inventory for a great many people amounted to little more than horse gear, wagons, axes and saws, guns, shovels, cast iron stoves, leather boots, shoes, and machine woven clothes. This perspective on material culture systems as they evolved into their present form enables me to draw a few conclusions about how to handle and integrate material culture to avoid some of the pitfalls occasioned by technology—be it home grown or imported. It makes little difference.

Model T Fords

Early in the 1900s, Henry Ford visited one of Armour & Company's meat packing plants and watched a whole cow enter and later emerge as steaks, roasts, sausage, stew beef, tripe, dog food, glue and hides. Nothing was lost nor wasted. Ford asked himself, why not reverse the process starting with parts travelling along conveyers ending up with an entire automobile? This was the seed of the idea of the conveyer belt assembly line—a mixed blessing. While the assembly line helped provide inexpensive automobiles, it was just another step in the direction of a fragmented life for the worker. It has taken almost sixty years to begin to correct this mistake, and it still has not been accomplished. In Sweden and the United States, factories are now experimenting with plans to permit employees to complete whole manufacturing processes. This is done to somewhat reduce the boredom experienced by most assembly-line workers.

However, there was another side to Ford's thinking. His original desire was twofold: (1) to build a car his workers could afford, and (2) to pay them enough so they could buy it. He succeeded in both. But, the ultimate impact of his Model T Ford was of a different sort entirely. For those of you who may remember it, the Model T Ford was a particularly fortunate combination of simplicity and good basic design: almost anyone could fix it; it performed reasonably well in the flatlands for which it was designed, but required modification in other environments. In mountainous country the engine would neither properly lubricate itself nor stay cool enough to run. The adaptations that were available—a water pump and a tube to take oil from the flywheel magneto case to the front bearing of the camshaft—were inexpensive and could be bolted on. Shock absorbers were not provided but could be purchased as an accessory, as could high-compression heads and racing accessories. An entire industry grew up that thrived on improving the performance of Ford's basic model. What is even more remarkable, two generations of self-taught mechanics (not the kind that are employed by garages, but men who could fix things at home) were produced from the necessity of keeping these cantankerous, noisy, frequently temperamental machines running. The Model T Ford was designed to enhance man's needs for autonomy. The Model T's descendants have done just the opposite by catering to dependence with power windows, power brakes, power everything, including more than is safe for the average driver.

CONCLUSION

Each culture has developed over the years a unique inventory of talents, things that they do well and with ease. But, the peoples of the world have yet to learn how to tap the talents of other ethnic groups. This is hardly sensible, particularly when people of other cultures may live inside one's political boundaries. Not to be allowed to use one's talents is not only frustrating but it can drive people mad (Fromm-Reichman, 1950). I feel that what I have termed "The Model T - Hong Kong Housing Model" contains a message not only for developing nations, but particularly for those I would term the overdeveloped nations. There should always be a proper balance between meeting the autonomy and dependency needs of people, otherwise technology serves man poorly.

It is also important to identify the position of autonomy units in the social organization of the society. In the United States, for those ethnic groups of North European extraction, it is the individual who seeks autonomy. For those ethnic groups whose ancestors came from Southern Europe there is the strong pull of a large family unit—namely the extended family. Everything revolves around this one crucial contrast between individual and family. For example, Americans brought up in the North European Calvinist tradition feel it is good for both the individual and the state to "make it on his own" without help from family and friends. In fact, the use of influence of this sort is called nepotism. Americans of Mediterranean heritage place much more emphasis on binding ties to family friends and on human relations generally. For them, it is mandatory that one do what one can to help any family member by getting him a job. To the South European the North European looks harsh and unfeeling, whereas when the tables are turned the South European seems grasping and venal.

Mankind has had very little experience developing and using cultural insights as a way of building harmony in this world. He has spent much too much time and energy on the technological, political, and economic side of life: Man is now so preoccupied with evolving his extensions that he is not aware that he knows very little about himself. It is quite evident that culture has been oriented towards the past and has had, as one of its principal functions, the provision of models to enable members of a given culture to find clearcut ways of relating to each other. To my knowledge, no culture has developed special skills in relating to outsiders in any terms other than its own. Yet technology, transportation and communication, brings all of us closer and closer together.

Nowhere do we find well-developed techniques for dealing with the covert cultures of others. As a consequence, man's experience in the international field has been fraught with difficulties because people use different "silent languages" (Hall, 1959), most of which function outside conscious awareness.

One of the unforeseen consequences of technology has been the destruction of the balance between man's autonomy and his dependency needs as technology takes over. While it has not been all bad, neither has it been all good. In housing, in automobiles and machines in general, an important lesson for all is to structure things so that people have a voice and play an active part in what they use and produce. Clearly, technology will be with us for years to come. It should be used with wisdom and caution, however, because it has proved to be a mixed blessing. Mankind can do much better and can learn much more than we have in the past from each other.

REFERENCES

DRUCKER, P. *Technology, management and society*. New York: Harper & Row, 1970.

FROMM-REICHMANN, F. *Principles of intensive psychotherapy*. Chicago: University of Chicago Press, 1950.

GALBRAITH, J.K. *Economics and public purpose*. Boston: Houghton Mifflin, 1973.

GALBRAITH, J.K. *The new industrial state*. Boston: Houghton Mifflin, 1967.

HALL, E.T. *The silent language*. Garden City, N.Y.: Anchor/Doubleday, 1959.

HALL, E.T. *The hidden dimension*. Garden City, N.Y.: Anchor/Doubleday, 1966.

HALL, E.T. Cultural models in transcultural communication. In Condon & Saitol (Eds.), *Communicating across cultures for what*? Tokyo: Simul Press, 1976a.

HALL, E.T. *Beyond culture*. Garden City, N.Y.: Anchor/Doubleday, 1976b.

HALPRIN, I. *The RSVP cycles*. New York: Braziller, 1969.

HARDIN, G. *Exploring new ethics for survival: The voyage of the spaceship 'Beagle'*. New York: Viking, 1972.

MARSCHACK, A. *The roots of civilization*. New York: McGraw-Hill, 1972.

McLUHAN, M. *The Gutenberg galaxy*. Toronto: University of Toronto Press, 1962.

PERSUASION RESEARCH: REVIEW AND COMMENTARY

GERALD R. MILLER and MICHAEL BURGOON
Michigan State University

Can a persuasive case currently be made for persuasion research? Scarcely a decade ago, such a question would have seemed strange and puzzling. Casual perusal of the communication, psychology, and sociology journals of 1968 quickly reveals that the lion's share of the communication research action still lay in the pursuit of problems dealing with symbolic influence. For many students of communication, the classic volumes of the "Yale Group" (e.g., Hovland, Lumsdaine & Sheffield, 1949; Hovland, Janis & Kelley, 1953; Hovland, 1957; Hovland & Janis, 1959; Hovland & Rosenberg, 1960; Sherif & Hovland, 1961), which largely concerned the persuasion process, were accorded a seminal status comparable to that conferred on the Book of Genesis by devoted followers of the Judeo-Christian religious faith. William McGuire (1969) was about to publish a synthetic tour de force of the literature on attitudes and attitude change, a masterful essay spanning 132 pages of text and 42 pages of references. The unchallenged hegemony of cognitive consistency theories (e.g., Feldman, 1966; Abelson, Aronson, McGuire, Newcomb, Rosenberg & Tannenbaum, 1968), with their emphasis on the motivating properties of cognitively imbalanced attitudes and behaviors, stimulated investigators to pursue new persuasive paradigms such as role-playing (Elms & Janis, 1965; Miller & Burgoon, 1973) and counterattitudinal advocacy (Festinger & Carlsmith, 1959; Elms, 1969; Miller, 1972a, 1974). Publication of new books dealing with persuasion and attitude change was a seasonal commonplace. In short, few, if any, questioned the scientific vitality and centrality of persuasion research.

Ten years later, the picture has changed dramatically. While it would be hyperbolic to state that the guns are silent on the persuasive battleground, their roar has grown sporadic and muted. No longer are the pages of journals glutted with the results of persuasion studies. Attribution and equity theories have ended the reign of cognitive consistency in the social-psychological domain. Although excellent volumes of persuasive relevance continue to appear (e.g., Rokeach, 1973; Wyer, 1974; Fishbein & Ajzen, 1975; Cushman & McPhee, in press), they grace the advertising lists with considerably less frequency; indeed, a quick examination of the 1977 Program for the American Psychological Association Convention reveals but a single advertisement for a book centering on persuasion or attitude change (specifically, Zimbardo, Ebbesen & Maslach, 1977). As a result of these disciplinary trends, bedrock pessimists proclaim that persuasion research is a dying enterprise, while skeptics content themselves with the observation that it has become an area of limited, secondary import.

Are these pessimistic prognoses justified? This paper seeks to assess the current case for persuasion research. To provide a framework for this assessment, we will first suggest several reasons for the apparent decline of interest in persuasion research during the past decade. Drawing upon a somewhat expanded view of persuasive communication, we will next discuss two examples of areas where significant theoretical and research activities are presently taking place. Finally, to anticipate our argument, we will indicate that persuasion research is not in such dire straits as the pessimists and skeptics would have us believe; in fact, we will conclude that continued interest in this problem area is essential to our eventual understanding of human communication.

WHAT WENT WRONG? SOME REASONS FOR THE APPARENT DECLINE IN PERSUASION RESEARCH

To a large extent, traditional persuasion research has been swimming against both the ideological and scholarly currents of the past decade. The social and political upheaval of the late 1960s was accompanied by a widely professed revulsion against all things admittedly manipulative. Concepts such as *control* and *power* became devil words that provided a rallying point for the radical social ideology which infused numerous academic disciplines, including communication. As various strains of humanistic psychology delighted in reminding us, self-awareness was infinitely more important that other-compliance; sensitivity and encounter groups, not political conventions or advertising campaigns, were the staff of communicative life. Indeed, some of the more radical carried the argument to its anti-intellectual extreme, contending that any effort to impose analysis or understanding on the raw, experiential "stuff" of human communication was itself an ill-fated effort at manipulation and control: "vibes," rather than theories and hypotheses, were the best we could hope for.

As with all sweeping generalizations, the one we have just offered is not without paradox or exception. One ironic paradox lies in the persuasive zeal manifested by many adherents of the anti-persuasion school. Heartfelt expressions of contempt for manipulative activities were themselves manipulative activities—persuasive messages, if you will—calculated to engender certain attitudes and beliefs about the functions of human discourse. To disagree with these messages insured the wrath and censure of the anti-persuasionists, with the offending party or parties certain to fall heir to some currently popular acrimonious label—"fascist pig," "capitalist warmonger," "establishment tool," or the like. Viewed in isolation, this inconsistency seems little more than an amusing anomaly between thought and action; located within the broader context of this paper's major thrust, it illustrates a vexing problem: as with such staple commodities as sin, it is one thing to renounce verbally the use of persuasive communication and and quite another to cease its practice.

This difficulty is further underscored by one of the notable exceptions to the late 1960s and early 1970s disenchantment with persuasion research, the keen interest evidenced during that period in the rhetoric of social protest (e.g., Bachrach & Baratz, 1970; Burgess, 1972; Edelman, 1964, 1977; Raven & Kruglanski, 1970; Scott & Brockriede, 1969 Simons, 1970, 1972, 1974). Not only did most students of social protest movements assign a central role to the persuasion process, they adopted a decidedly tough-minded view of it. After emphasizing the limits of a concept such as "pure persuasion" and indicting the prevailing "drawing room controversy" approach to persuasive discourse, Simons (1974) captures the crux of this tough-minded position nicely:

> Contrary to the prevailing view of persuasion as clearly separable from constraints (i.e., coercive influence) and inducements (i.e., reward influence), I shall argue here that in conflict situations, *persuasion, broadly defined, is not so much an alternative to the power of constraints and inducements as it is an instrument of that power, an accompaniment to that power, or a consequence of that power*. (p. 177, italics in original)

In other words, persuasion, when woven into the fabric of social protest, becomes a power dependent communicative activity whose effectiveness depends largely on the capabilities of the would-be persuader(s) to carry a big stick and/or to blandish a juicy carrot. Moreover, as Simons notes (pp. 178-179), one of the most formidable tasks faced by the conflicting parties is to persuade "the other side" (to use a phrase whose currency has been assured by the rhetoric of the Vietnam conflict) of the wherewithal and willingness to employ constraints and inducements—in the argot of traditional persuasion research, to establish *credibility* with the intended audience.

If manipulation is, indeed, odious, how is a scholarly concern with this Pier Six brawl concept of persuasion to be justified? A conservative cynic might dismiss the whole matter as a case of schizophrenic ideological labeling; persuasion is "Machiavellian manipulation" when employed by social and political enemies and a manifestation of "righteous social indignation" when practiced by friendly forces. Though such a claim is not without merit for parties of *all* ideological bents, another explanation is more relevant to the concerns of this paper. It is a dubious tribute to the field's ability to generate myopic category systems, that the theory and research dealing with social protest are typically not treated as part of the domain of persuasion research. Instead, new labels have been invoked, so that topics such as "communication and conflict," though much in vogue both in the research laboratory and the classroom, seem somehow removed from our longstanding interest in persuasive communication. Thus, communication researchers can both have and consume their scholarly cake; while dismissing the utility of traditional persuasion research, they can sing the plaudits of inquiry concerning the role of communication in social conflict.

This latter fact suggests an important point about the apparent decline of persuasion research: *students of persuasion may have fallen captive to the limits imposed by their own operational definitions of the area*. Stated differently, "persuasion research" has typically been defined as the paradigms employed, the problems investigated, and the outcomes assessed by those who call themselves persuasion researchers. Although such a concern with matters ostensive has much to recommend it, sole reliance upon prevailing research practices as defining criteria for a problem area is virtually certain to produce conceptual sterility. Hence, persuasion research has suffered from its continued association with research paradigms and practices that are currently "out-of-synch" with its relevant scholarly community. Consideration of four such outmoded factors will serve to reinforce this point.

Persuasion as a Linear, Unidirectional Communicative Activity

Unquestionably, most researchers have approached persuasion from a linear, unidirectional vantage point: an active source (persuader) constructs messages with intent to influence the attitudes and/or behaviors of relatively passive receivers (persuadees). In other words, emphasis is placed on factors that facilitate or inhibit the ability of one party to exert influence over the other; or as Lin (1977, p. 56) puts it when speaking of the *directive* perspective toward communication research, "the major thrust clearly is to determine the best 'directive' mix for achieving the best result—to mold and change the receiving participants." Thus, a common way of focusing research questions or classroom discussion about persuasive communication has been to consider the effect of source characteristics *on* persuasive outcomes; the effect of message strategies *on* persuasive outcomes; the effect of channel alternatives *on* persuasive outcomes; the effect of receiver characteristics *on* persuasive outcomes; and, as research designs have grown more sophisticated, the conjunctive effects of two or more of these classes of variables *on* persuasive outcomes. Always, *cause* resides conceptually in these antecedent source, message, channel, and receiver variables, while *effect* is measured in terms of the extent of attitudinal and/or behavioral influence; the persuader *acts* and the persuadees are *acted upon* (Miller, 1974).

Although at one time most students of communication were comfortable with this conceptual perspective, it has recently run afoul of the increasingly prevailing commitment to a transactional, reciprocal view of communication. Berlo (1977) characterizes the paradigm shift that has occurred thusly:

> If we look on the "source" as intentional and initiatory and the "receiver" as passive and a receptive container—e.g., if the message is stimulus and the effect is response—the relationship is directional. On the other hand, if the relationship is one in which both users approach the engagement with expectations, plans, and anticipation, the uncertainty reduction attributable to the contact may better be understood in terms of how both parties use and approach a message-event than in terms of how one person uses the contact to direct the other. (p. 20)

In short, communicative transactions are typically interdependent, with the participating parties exerting reciprocal influence on each other. Moreover, satisfactory understanding of the communication process requires the researcher to adopt a transactional stance, a caveat as applicable to persuasive transactions as to other types of communicative exchanges.

Perhaps a hypothetical example, taken from the recent pages of American history, will effectively illustrate the difference between the two perspectives. During the hectic months of Watergate, the

Nixon administration employed a variety of persuasive tactics aimed at convincing the American public of the administration's innocence of political wrongdoing. A linear, unidirectional analysis of this situation places Nixon, or other key members of his administration, in the role of source/persuader, with the American public, or at least key segments of it, cast as receiver/persuadees. Given such an analysis, the questions that readily come to mind concern factors that might enhance or diminish the success of this tactical venture; e.g., questions concerning ways to structure messages so as to persuade the public of the merits of the administration's position. Note that this approach places the Nixon administration in the position of *acting*, and the American public in the position of being *acted upon*.

But as everyone who witnessed the dramatic unfolding of daily events is aware, the responses of the American public exerted a powerful reciprocal impact on the president and his cohorts. As the news media reacted skeptically to persuasive messages emanating from the White House and as the public opinion polls continued to reflect rising disenchantment with the "official versions" of political events, dramatic changes were wrought in the apparent attitudes and ongoing behaviors of administrative spokespersons. Although admittedly sketchy, accounts of these changes suggest that some members of the administration grew increasingly uncertain of the validity of its moral premises while others became even more dogmatic in their support of its political integrity. As for the paramount persuader, the president himself, his apparent lack of persuasive success seemed to exacerbate his bitterness and hostility, as well as reinforcing his belief that he was being unfairly deprived of his honored place in American history. Thus, an adequate explanation of the persuasive dynamics of the Watergate crisis cannot stop with an account of the effects of the administration on the American public, it must also include a description of the reciprocal effect of the public on the administration.

The preceding example was not chosen idly, for it can be used to underscore a second reason why the linear, unidirectional view of persuasive communication has fallen upon hard times. Critics argue that this conceptual perspective ensures a status quo, establishment flavor to most persuasion research. Stated bluntly, the argument goes as follows: usually it is the dominant institutions of a society who are most concerned with establishing areas of behavioral control and who have the resources to discover effective ways of attaining this objective. Consequently, funding for persuasion research is most likely to originate from these institutions, and the problems and studies receiving financial priority are almost certain to be those calculated to enhance the funding agency's control-exerting potential. Thus, whether intentionally or not, persuasion researchers become the handmaidens of government, business, and industry—the "haves" of society—and the results of their studies further strengthen the position of these privileged elites.

Certainly this argument is not without merit. Although it is easy to imagine a large corporation spending thousands of dollars to identify effective ways of persuading consumers to buy its products, it is difficult to conceive of the investigative shoe being on the other foot; that is, of individual consumers spending thousands to discover ways of resisting the persuasive wiles of the manufacturer. Furthermore, the problem is accentuated by the fact that what sells most easily often takes precedence over considerations of social responsibility. Thus, if it is simpler to persuade prospective car buyers of the virtues of tail fins or vinyl tops than of air bags or better gas mileage, the former persuasive appeals are likely to prevail. As a consequence, it is hardly surprising that numerous socially conscious individuals have expressed concern about some of the fruits of traditional persuasion research.

Persuasion as a One-to-Many Communicative Activity

A second, closely related characteristic of most persuasion research is its reliance on a one-to-many situational context. In the traditional persuasion study, a relatively large aggregate of receiver/persuadees—a classroom of students, the members of a PTA, and so forth—is exposed to a message attributed to a particular individual or institutional source. With few exceptions, the linear, unidirectional view of the "transaction" is reinforced by the fact that the message is not even presented live. Instead, the persuadees read it, or see and/or hear it on video or audiotape, a procedure that prevents any meaningful reciprocal influence by the audience. After message exposure, the persuadees respond to some measure of persuasive effect, usually a paper-and-pencil assessment of attitude change. Thus, the entire enterprise closely resembles a public speaking or mass media setting, though even here the fit is far from perfect, since there is little opportunity for the kinds of audience social facilitation effects one would expect in real-life communicative settings.

With the growing interest in interpersonal communication that has occurred over the past decade, students of communication have become increasingly aware of the potential limitations of this one-to-many situational context. Elsewhere, one of us has offered the following assessment of this approach:

> The prevailing tendency to use public-speaking situations for hypothesis testing stems largely from historical concerns of the discipline. But when one reflects on the communicative transactions of most persons, it becomes clear that only a small percentage of them consist of lengthy periods of uninterrupted discourse directed at sizable target audiences. In the give-and-take of dyadic dialogue, the communication flow of the small group . . . one finds most of the communication action. (Miller, 1972b, p. 397)

Applied specifically to persuasion, this assessment suggests that most social influence attempts take place in one-to-one or one-to-few situational contexts, not in the sort of communicator-audience setting that characterizes most persuasion research. Furthermore, the one-to-one and one-to-few contexts differ from the one-to-many situation in numerous ways which cast doubt on the generalizability of findings obtained in the latter setting. Consequently, while not devoid of scientific utility, the results of most traditional persuasion research are of limited import.

Consistent with our earlier remarks, this problem is accentuated by the widespread tendency to avoid terms like "persuasion" when dealing with certain areas of research. For instance, studies of negotiation and bargaining (e.g., Esser & Komroita, 1975; Turnbull, Strickland & Shaver, 1976; Donohue, 1976; Donohue & Cegala, 1977), many of which employ intimate, face-to-face communicative settings, are typically not thought of as persuasion studies, even though they obviously deal with variables which influence persuasive success. For that matter, much of the literature dealing with group pressure and its effects on conformity (e.g., Asch, 1951; Crutchfield, 1955; Milgram, 1963, 1965), could fruitfully be conceived of as persuasion research, but such a conceptual strategy is seldom encountered. Instead, persuasion and group pressure go their merry ways as separate topics of concern to most social psychologists and communication researchers, an unfortunate circumstance that will be mentioned again later in this paper.

Persuasion as an Action-Centered or Issue-Centered Activity

Actions and issues have consistently been the primary message ingredients used by persuasion researchers. Attempts to influence attitudes and/or behaviors have centered on such actions as proper toothbrushing, wearing automobile seat belts, getting tetanus shots, or quitting smoking—to mention but a few of the myriad actions that have been advocated. Similarly, issues such as student residence policies, civil rights legislation, nuclear weapons development, and capital punishment have been subjected to persuasive scrutiny. Indeed, persuasion seems to have been equated with selling actions, products, or policies.

On the surface, it may appear that this preoccupation with actions and issues constitutes a reasonably comprehensive approach to persuasive communication. A moment's thought, however, suggests that most people devote the preponderance of their persuasive energies to selling *themselves*, and to a lesser extent, other persons. In other words, people, rather than actions or policies, are the substantive mainstay of persuasion—unless, of course, the term "action" is defined broadly enough to embrace responding favorably to specific others. Stated in the vernacular of traditional persuasion research, the relevant attitudes are those concerning persuadees' cognitive, affective, and behavioral stances toward other persons, rather than their views about some action or policy.

To be sure, traditional persuasion research has evinced a concern for these person-oriented attitudes, as attested to by the voluminous literature dealing with communicator credibility (e.g., Hovland & Weiss, 1951; McCroskey, 1966; Berlo, Lemert & Mertz, 1970). With few exceptions, however, credibility has been treated as an antecedent, independent variable which influences subsequent persuasive outcomes, rather than a *persuasive outcome* worthy of study in its own right. As a result, some persuasion researchers seem to have deluded themselves with the belief that a good deal more is known about credibility than is actually the case. After all, it is neither earthshaking nor particularly helpful to discover that a communicator who is competent, trustworthy, dynamic, and sociable (in short, who conforms with all the glowing adjectives of the Scout Oath) is more persuasive than his or her incompetent, untrustworthy, phlegmatic, antisocial counterpart. Rather, what is needed are data bearing on the persuasive process of credibility formation (e.g., Miller & Hewgill, 1964; Baker, 1965; Sharp & McClung, 1966; Sereno & Hawkins, 1967), the verbal and nonverbal message strategies that can be used to engender more favorable personal perceptions on the part of others.

How has this lack of concern for person-oriented persuasive outcomes contributed to the apparent decline of persuasion research during the past decade? Quite simply, the problems associated with this area have been pursued by researchers who have adopted other conceptual handles to describe their work: person perception, interpersonal attraction, self-concept formation, and the like. Indeed, the list reads like a summary of the hottest contemporary research topics in social psychology. Granted, terms such as "interpersonal attraction" and "persuasion" are far from perfect synonyms; the former undoubtedly embraces phenomena that fall outside the domain of the latter. Nevertheless, unless common sense and writers such as Goffman (1959) are completely off-base, people spend considerable time trying to persuade others to perceive them as attractive, socially desirable individuals; that is, they deliberately employ certain verbal and nonverbal strategies to maximize the likelihood of creating favorable impressions. Such efforts not only could, but should be considered fair game for persuasion researchers.

Persuasion as an Attitude Change-Centered Activity

So pervasive has been the tendency of persuasion researchers to employ attitude change as their principal measure of persuasive effect that the terms "persuasion" and "attitude change" are virtually synonymous. Underlying the prevailing preoccupation with attitude change is the assumption that attitudes are motivational precursors of behavior; hence, messages which produce attitude change toward some action or issue should ultimately culminate in attitudinally consistent behaviors. Obviously, the argument goes, if people manifest more positive attitudes about wearing automobile seat belts, they are more likely to buckle up on their next trip to the grocery store or the summer cottage.

Unfortunately, what must have seemed like a perfectly reasonable methodological credo to the pioneers of persuasion research has consistently fallen upon empirical hard times. The voluminous literature concerning the attitude versus behavior problem (e.g., LaPiere, 1934; Campbell, 1963; DeFleur & Westie, 1963; Liska, 1975; Seibold, 1975; Ajzen & Fishbein, 1977) is familiar to most readers, and little is to be gained from yet another summary of it. Suffice it to say that any relationships which may exist between attitudes and behaviors—or, stated more accurately, between paper-and-pencil measures of attitude change and other classes of attitudinally consistent behavior (Miller, 1967)—are far from obvious. Indeed, until quite recently, only a handful of studies had attempted to demonstrate the existence of such a relationship, and as Festinger (1964) has noted, these attempts have met with limited success. The fact that people may change their markings on some scalar measure of attitudes following exposure to a persuasive message simply does not permit very confident inferences about the way they will behave vis-a-vis the attitude-object in other situations.

Failure to demonstrate convincingly a relatively consistent relationship between the measures of effect typically used in research settings and the measures of effect which usually concern persuasive practitioners in actual social situations has caused a number of communication scholars to question the scientific and social utility of traditional persuasion research. Although such indictments are leveled more frequently in casual office or barroom conversations than in the pages of professional journals, it is not unusual to hear colleagues speak of the sterility or the banality of most persuasion studies. Pointing to a hiatus in attitude change research which occurred from 1920 through 1945, McGuire (1969) has placed part of the blame on overly elaborate conceptual undertakings. We believe that the apparent decline in persuasion research during the years from 1968 through 1977 can be partially attributed to increasing disenchantment with an operational "law of the instrument"; that is, "give a small boy a hammer, and he will find that everything he encounters needs pounding" (Kaplan, 1964, p. 28). Despite all the "pounding" persuasion researchers have done with their Guttman, Likert, and semantic differential-type scales, an edifice of theoretically and socially significant research findings has been slow in rising.

Taken together, the four factors discussed above have contributed to an impoverished view of persuasion research, a perspective which does not jibe closely with the conceptual and research interests of most contemporary students of communication. One way to resolve this discrepancy, of course, would be to write off the area of persuasion research as a central empirical concern of communication. This solution strikes us as both conceptually and socially unwise, for few, if any, would seriously question the centrality of social influence to the communicative enterprise. A second, more defensible alternative is to adopt a somewhat expanded view of the persuasion process, to loosen the fetters imposed by defining persuasion largely in terms of the prior paradigms and practices of persuasion researchers. Such an approach not only yields greater conceptual robustness, it also permits identification of some areas where theoretical and research enterprises of relevance to persuasive communication are presently being pursued.

SOME ELEMENTS OF AN EXPANDED VIEW OF THE PERSUASION PROCESS

To a large extent, we have alluded to some important elements of an expanded view of persuasion in our previous discussion of several shortcomings of the traditional view of persuasion research. In its broadest sense, persuasion can be conceived of as any exercise, or attempted exercise of social influence. For the student of communication, however, only those attempts that rely primarily on symbolic transactions are of central concern. Thus, merely pulling a gun on another individual may be sufficient to cause the person to surrender his or her money, with no recourse to verbal messages needed. Although such a successful robbery can be broadly conceived of as an instance of *persuasion*, it does not qualify as an act of *persuasive communication*. On the other hand, the same gun-pulling behavior, accompanied by the command, "Hand over your money right now or you're dead!" does satisfy the defining criteria for persuasive communication. Indeed, even this relatively straightforward situation is more persuasively complex than it first appears. Not only does the robber seek to persuade the victim to part with his or her money, but in order to do so, the robber must also persuade the victim that the threat is credible. Harking back to the Woody Allen movie, *Take the Money and Run*, Simons reminds us of an amusing failure to persuasively establish the credibility of a threat. "By contrast to truly credible bank robbers, poor, inept Woody is holding a rain-damaged pistol made of soap. Moreover, when he nervously hands the bank teller a note demanding money, she calmly explains to him that he has not spelled 'm-o-n-e-y' correctly" (1974, p. 180). Though intended as parody, Woody's woes are sometimes paralleled in real life, for we occasionally read of a teller chasing a would-be bandit from the bank or verbally enticing him or her to abandon the robbery attempt.

Surely, robberies appear to be among the most linear, unidirectional persuasive transactions imaginable. But as the preceding example reveals, the opportunity for reciprocal influence exists even here: not only do robbers influence victims, victims also influence robbers. Hence, one indispensible element of an expanded view of persuasion is the notion of *reciprocity*, or interdependence. Persuasion is not a one-way street; rather, participants in a persuasive transaction usually exert mutual influence on each other. This is particularly true when different ends are sought, as in the case of negotiation and bargaining transactions. It is grossly oversimplified to speak of General Motors persuading the United Auto Workers or of the UAW persuading GM: an inevitable consequence of contract bargaining sessions is the modification and accomodation of both parties' positions. Furthermore, this same interdependence holds for personal relationships, an arena where much of the daily persuasive action unfolds. Even in what appear to be highly complementary interpersonal relationships (Watzlawick, Beavin & Jackson, 1967; Farace & Rogers, 1975), the potential for persuasive success is distributed between the participants. As Miller and Steinberg (1975, p. 236) suggest, "The person who says, 'I can't live without you,' is often more in control than the one to whom the plea is addressed."

Not only must an expanded view of persuasion allow for reciprocal influence, it must also recognize that persuasive transactions are an essential ingredient of all social situations. As we have indicated, traditional persuasion research has focused almost exclusively on one-to-many communicative settings, so that persuasion appears to be endemic to public speaking and mass media contexts. Although the findings of these studies have yielded useful information, persuasion researchers should also examine persuasive communication within small group and dyadic settings. To be sure, such studies are likely to be more costly and time-consuming. One of the probable reasons for the popularity of traditional persuasion research lies in the ease with which data can be collected: it does not seem overly pejorative to point out that many persuasion studies are, indeed, "quick and dirty." By contrast, observation of dyadic and small group interaction requires more time and effort by the researcher, particularly if message exchanges are themselves objects of scrutiny that are allowed to vary freely, rather than independent variables that are held constant, save for one or two relevant dimensions. Despite the added difficulties it poses, the former approach seems meritorious, for as Hawes (1977) has argued, a good deal of initial descriptive work is needed in order to identify the kinds of messages people use when attempting to exert social influence in face-to-face settings.

An expanded view of persuasion also suggests that researchers should devote greater attention to persuasive messages aimed at engendering more favorable attitudes toward the communicators themselves; that is, communications which seek to heighten interpersonal attractiveness or communicator credibility. As we have stated, communicative efforts to enhance attractiveness or credibility can be viewed as either legitimate persuasive ends in their own right (as when the communicators would simply like others to be more positively inclined toward them) or as essential means toward some other persuasive objective (as when influence is contingent upon establishing the credibility of threats and promises). In either case, the traditional approach of listing attributes which contribute to positive perceptions of credibility is clearly inadequate, since the key issue concerns the strategies that can be used to foster these positive perceptions. To resort to a whimsical example, one is reminded of the trauma faced by Charlie Brown in his desire to impress the attractive new girl at school. The best advice traditional persuasion research has to offer Charlie is to be competent, trustworthy, and dynamic, so that he will be able to plead his case persuasively with the girl. Charlie, of course, realizes that he is none of these, but rather an unknown interpersonal commodity. Consequently, he is occupied with *what* to say to the new girl and *how* to say it in order to make a favorable impression; that is, he is interested in beginning to establish his credibility with her.

A final element of an expanded view of persuasion involves increased concern for persuasive outcomes other than attitude change. There is no good reason why researchers should continue to limit their investigative horizons to this dependent variable, particularly in view of the continued skepticism concerning its scientific and social robustness. Much persuasive communication aims at influencing overt behavior, rather than affecting changes in some unobservable set of motivational dispositions called "attitudes." Indeed, the dispositional, attitude-oriented approach to persuasion has recently been questioned by several writers. Bem (1965, 1972), for instance, has challenged the commonly shared assumption that attitudes shape and direct behavior, suggesting instead that behavior may often shape and direct attitudes. Bem argues that our best evidence for how we feel about something (i.e., our attitudes) may often consist of examining the ways we behave in respect to it. Thus, to use a well-known example of Bem's, if someone is asked whether he or she likes brown bread, he or she may respond, "I must, because I'm always eating it." This approach to persuasion implies that if people can be induced to behave in certain ways, their attitudes will take care of themselves, a position which comports with both radical behavioristic (e.g., Skinner, 1974; Bem, 1965) and cognitive consistency (e.g., Festinger, 1957) conceptions of human action.

Larson and Sanders (1975) have also attacked the continued tendency to conceive of persuasion as a communicative activity that primarily seeks to alter people's motivational states. Rather, they contend, persuasion aims at aligning behaviors to conform with situational constraints and demands. Although the rationale for their *behavioral alignment hypothesis* draws heavily on a rule-governed perspective of human communication, the thrust of their position is akin to that of some early behaviorists, who advocated that paper-and-pencil, verbal measures of attitude should be treated as nothing more than one class of attitudinally-related responses. Indeed, so pervasive has been the reliance on these paper-and-pencil measures that many persuasion researchers have fallen prey to a reification fallacy: they have argued as if the responses to their attitude scales were, in some mysterious way, *the attitude*, while other responses such as contributing money, ringing doorbells, or going to jail were *the behaviors*. Actually, of course, responses to attitude scale items constitute verbal behavior; they are no more isomorphic with attitudes than are other classes of attitudinally consistent responses. Moreover, as we shall note later, attitudes can be grouped into more general dispositional constructs such as values, and if persuasion researchers wish to continue their love affair with dispositional states, these more general constructs may provide greater behavioral predictability.

One purpose for outlining some important elements of an expanded view of persuasion is to suggest priorities for future research activities. A second motive, however, is to lay the groundwork for a brief discussion of some examples of potentially significant research that is presently being conducted. As previously mentioned, we believe a great deal of important persuasion research has recently been carried out by investigators using other labels to describe their problem areas. As we examine two examples of this work, their relevance to our expanded conception of persuasion should become apparent.

TWO EXAMPLES OF RECENT PERSUASION RESEARCH

Research Dealing with Credibility Formation

Considerable attention has been given to identifying factors which influence people's initial perceptions of others, with most of this work falling under the rubric of *interpersonal attraction*. This research is highly relevant to our expanded view of persuasion on at least two counts: first, most of the studies have dealt with communicative contexts other than the one-to-many situation, with primary concern directed at dyadic encounters; second, and perhaps more important, the construct of *attraction* refers to a constellation of person-centered attitudes and is thus intimately related to the process of credibility formation. Notice, for example, how closely Huston's (1974) conceptualization of *attraction* corresponds with typical definitions of the construct *attitude*:

> There are two basic ways of examining attraction as a multifaceted attitude. First, attraction can be viewed as a constellation of sentiments which comprise the evaluative orientation of one person toward another. . . . Second, attraction-based attitudes can be seen as including the following three elements: (a) an *evaluative* component, which refers to the quality and strength of one's sentiments toward another person; (b) a *cognitive* component, which refers to the belief or beliefs one has about another person, as well as the cognitive processes by which these beliefs are developed; and (c) a *behavioral* component, which refers to one's tendency to approach or avoid another person, as well as to the manner in which these behavioral tendencies are manifested. The composite of feelings, beliefs, and behavioral dispositions provide a comprehensive description of the attitude toward that person. (p. 11)

In other words, judgments of attraction *are* manifestations of attitudes toward people. Granted, such judgments are constantly being formed, and sometimes occur apart from any conscious persuasive efforts to influence them on the part of the judged party or parties. For example, unobtrusive observation of a stranger at a social gathering may lead to tentative judgments of his or her attractiveness, even though the stranger is unaware that he or she is being observed. For that matter, behavioral accounts provided by third parties are often sufficient to establish initial perceptions of attractiveness, particularly if these accounts emanate from positively perceived persons. But these exceptions do not negate the fact that people often strive consciously to curry each other's approval: in the language of our expanded view of persuasion, they seek to influence others' judgments of their attractiveness or credibility.

Probably the largest body of literature dealing with this area concerns the variable of *attitude similarity* (Byrne, 1969, 1971; Huston, 1974). Both reinforcement and cognitive consistency theories imply that people should be more strongly attracted to individuals who see eye-to-eye with them: likes should attract more than opposites. Although many issues remain unresolved, results of numerous studies tend to support this proposition. Indeed, some investigators (e.g., Rokeach, 1960; Rokeach & Mezei, 1966) have contended that belief similarity is a more powerful determinant of initial attraction than a variable such as race, which has typically been viewed as a strong predictor of social preferences. Overall, it appears that the process of credibility formation can be furthered by communicating messages which suggest shared attitudes and beliefs.

This possibility has not been overlooked by the sycophant, the proverbial "yes-person" of our society. As typically practiced, ingratiation (Jones, 1964) is a persuasive strategy calculated to engender positive perceptions on the part of others. By expressing conformity with the beliefs and attitudes of significant others, the ingratiator seeks to maximize his or her favorable outcomes. Regardless of their moral evaluation of the ingratiation strategy, most people will begrudgingly grant its frequent persuasive effectiveness. "Jones is the only one who seems in touch with what's going on around here," thunders the boss, and this favorable personal evaluation signals the success of Jones's apple-polishing technique to other workers.

Obviously, however, issues concerning the role of attitude similarity in shaping initial perceptions of credibility transcend crass attempts at ingratiation. Suppose, for instance, that disagreement is inevitable: what communicative strategies can be used to dampen its effect on interpersonal judgments? Instructive in this regard is a study by Hodges and Byrne (1972), which revealed that disagreeing persons were more favorably evaluated when they expressed disagreement in open-minded, rather than dogmatic terms. Griffitt (1974) underscores the importance of the general question posed above, expressing the hope that future studies will reveal a variety of factors which are effective in reducing the impact of attitudinal disagreement on subsequent attractiveness judgments. To the extent that such studies focus on potentially available communicative strategies, they are central to our expanded, person-oriented view of persuasion.

Needless to say, initial perceptions of attractiveness are not solely influenced by the substance of the communicators' beliefs and attitudes. Rather, as the Hodges and Byrne study suggests, reactions to relative strangers may be as much or more determined by *how* they say things as by *what* they say. Stated more formally, *communicator style* undoubtedly exerts a strong impact on initial judgments of attractiveness or credibility. Although this relationship is intuitively obvious to almost everyone—as witnessed by the wide usage of such phrases as "comes on too strong," "rubs me the wrong way," and "spaced out"—persuasion researchers have devoted relatively little attention to teasing out the effects of various dimensions of communicator style on subsequent perceptions of attractiveness.

One reason for this paucity of research probably rests in the impoverished, action-oriented and issue-oriented view that has traditionally guided the concerns of persuasion researchers. An additional research deterrent lies in the difficulties that are sure to be encountered when researchers attempt to come to grips conceptually and operationally with the communicator style construct. Obviously, the construct embraces a host of stylistic and presentational variables, and it is hard to identify an overall scheme for attacking the problem, or for that matter, for assigning priorities to the variables which could conceivably be investigated. Norton (1977) puts the issue this way:

> What should be included in a communicator style construct? The problem is aggravated because there is no established domain of communicator style similar to such heavily validated constructs as attraction, credibility, or empathy. Fragments of assorted variables focusing on one's style of reacting, negotiating, and talking are found in the literature, but no researcher has pulled together variable sets to be identified and justified as "communicator style," a construct in its own right. (p. 1)

Furthermore, even after they are selected, the operational treatment of many of these variables is no easy task: the researcher may choose to observe actual communicative exchanges, which makes it almost impossible to sort out the many aspects of communicator style that are varying, or he or she may seek to manipulate a few variables while holding others constant, a procedure which is not only very time-consuming but which also introduces the issue of priority, or relative importance, mentioned above.

Given these problems, it is hardly surprising that research on communicator style conducted thus far has focused largely on identifying useful dimensions of the construct, with some interest also directed at determining which ones exert the greatest impact on perceptions of the communicator. For instance, Norton (1977) posits nine variables that pertain to communicator style: dominant, dramatic, animated, open, contentious, relaxed, friendly, attentive, and impression-leaving. As a result of two studies, he concludes that these variables do cluster to form meaningful dimensions of a multidimensional construct, and that certain components, particularly dominance and impression-leaving, are strongly related to perceptions of the communicator. It is important to note, however, that Norton relied entirely on self-report data, rather than asking other persons to evaluate communicators in terms of the style components. As Norton himself points out, self-report data may yield a preponderance of positive ratings of communicative effectiveness regardless of style; that is, people may report they are effective communicators across widely divergent styles. Thus, a necessary next step would be to obtain similar ratings from other persons, instead of the communicators themselves.

A study by Brandt, Kanaga, and Stoyanoff (1977) accomplished this step by requiring raters to evaluate a series of communicators who were recorded engaging in initial interactions with a stranger. To a large extent, their findings coincide with those of Norton: the pattern of relationships among style components was quite similar, and once again, impression-leaving and dominance were strongly related to effectiveness and attractiveness. Unlike the Norton studies, however, the animated style component was highly correlated with both communicative effectiveness and social attractiveness, a difference that, according to the authors, may stem from obtaining the style and effectiveness ratings from others, rather than from self-reports. Finally, these investigators suggest another refinement in the communicator style construct:

> It may be of some theoretical and practical utility to distinguish stylistic components which are primarily *expressionistic* in nature (i.e., those which reflect observable, expressive behaviors of communicators) from those which are primarily *impressionistic* in nature (i.e., those which reflect impressions formed by actors and/or observers of their actions). For example, attentive, animated, and precise seem to describe observable communication behaviors and would thus fall into the expressionistic category. On the other hand, friendly, relaxed, and impression leaving seem better suited to the impressionistic category. (1977, pp. 20-21)

It should be emphasized that the studies on communicator style have yet to specify the kinds of communicative behaviors which contribute to perceptions of particular styles. In this respect, they resemble much of the traditional persuasion research dealing with dimensions of credibility; that is, they permit ennumeration of some of the components of communicator style which engender favorable ratings of attractiveness, but they do not tell persons *how* to communicate so as to be perceived as possessing these stylistic compo-

FIGURE 1
An Accommodation Model of Speech Style

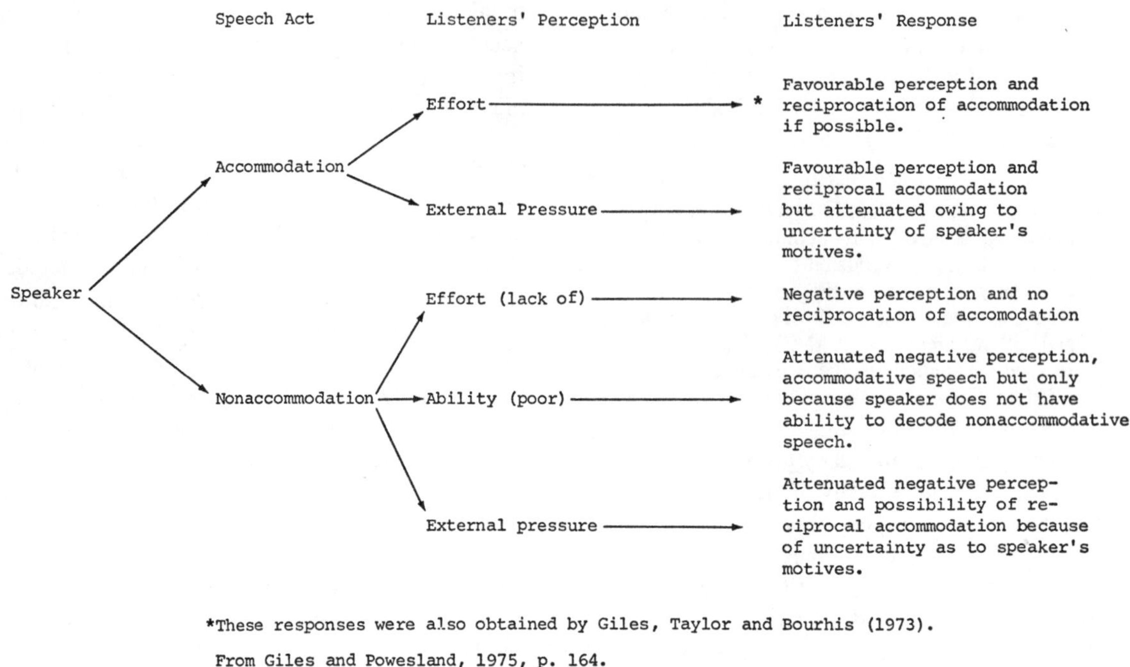

*These responses were also obtained by Giles, Taylor and Bourhis (1973).

From Giles and Powesland, 1975, p. 164.

nents. Thus, considering the present state of knowledge, it is easy to imagine this kind of exchange between a persuasion researcher and a communication practitioner:

> Practitioner: "What can I do to enhance my credibility with others?"
> Researcher: "You should employ a dominant communicator style."
> Practitioner: "How do I do that?"
> Researcher: "Try to come across as being more dominant."

Given the limited utility of this kind of advice, much work remains to be done on the relationship between specific verbal and nonverbal messages, and subsequent perceptions of both communicator style and communicator credibility.

Recently, Giles and Powesland (1975) have provided an excellent synthesis of prior research dealing with the influence of speech style (specifically, pronunciation, accent, dialect, and language) on social evaluation, as well as reporting the results of a number of their own studies. The final chapter of their volume illustrates the kinds of analyses that communication researchers, armed with an expanded view of persuasion, might well be contributing. Giles and Powesland posit the accomodation model of speech diversity found in Figure 1. The model rests on the assumption, taken from the attitude similarity research discussed earlier, that a person can ensure more favorable evaluations from another by reducing dissimilarities which exist between them. Thus, "accomodation through speech can be regarded as an attempt on the part of a speaker to modify or disguise his persona in order to make it more acceptable to the person addressed" (p. 158). In other words, accomodation constitutes a general persuasive strategy aimed at fostering initial credibility.

When applied specifically to speech style, the model identifies several variables that contribute to perceptions of accomodation or nonaccomodation, and ultimately, to reciprocated or nonreciprocated accomodation. For instance, if the listener perceives that the speaker is exerting considerable effort to accomodate his or her speech to the listener, then the latter will probably perceive the speaker favorably and reciprocate the accomodation. This response is particularly likely if the speaker is under no apparent external pressures to accomodate; that is, if he or she appears to be expending the effort solely from a desire to reduce dissimilarities, not because it is in his or her best interest to do so. Conversely, if the speaker appears to exert little effort to accomodate, especially when there are no apparent external pressures militating against accomodation, the listener will evaluate him or her unfavorably and will make no attempt at reciprocal accomodation. Examination of the model reveals other hypotheses concerning accomodation and nonaccomodation that are implied by it.

At first glance, the Giles and Powesland model may seem vulnerable to the linear, unidirectional charge leveled earlier against most traditional persuasion research. A moment's scrutiny reveals that the emphasis in the accomodation model is on *reciprocal* accomodation or nonaccomodation: although the terms "speaker" and "listener" are employed, the model deals with a situation where two communicators either do or do not achieve speech convergence through a series of communicative transactions. Thus, within the limits imposed by ordinary language, the accomodation model is concerned with reciprocal influence. Furthermore, it treats credibility as the persuasive outcome of interest, instead of relegating it to a secondary, instrumental status.

Without a doubt, numerous variables other than those discussed here influence initial judgments of attractiveness or communicator credibility. We have not sought to provide a complete inventory, but to identify an ongoing area of research that is central to persuasive communication. Hopefully, persuasion researchers will lay claim to some of the future research action in this area, rather than forfeiting it to investigators who hail from other disciplines and who are ostensibly interested in other problem areas.

Research Dealing with Persuasive Message Strategies

Several recent studies have sought to establish comprehensive typologies of persuasive message strategies, as well as to discover how strategy use may vary across types of situations and persons. Marwell and Schmitt (1967) provide the following justification for pursuing this problem:

> It is clear that people spend a great deal of time trying to get others to act in ways they desire. It is equally clear that people vary in the ways they go about attempting such interpersonal control. Yet students of social control have only recently begun to explore these variations. Most research has concentrated on why people comply rather than on how they go about gaining compliance. . . . What research findings there are on the selection of behaviors tend to concentrate on selected techniques in various situations. . . . None of this research . . . has systematically explored the range of compliance-gaining behaviors or elaborated the factors involved in their enactment. (pp. 350-351)

Since persuasion researchers have traditionally pursued message strategy research, it may be unclear why this area was selected as relevant to our expanded view of persuasion. First, as Marwell and Schmitt point out, prior work on message strategies has focused on the effectiveness of particular persuasive message strategies, not on developing a comprehensive set of strategies. For instance, there exists a voluminous literature dealing with the persuasive impact of fear-arousing message appeals (e.g., Janis, 1967; Higbee, 1969; Leventhal, 1970), yet relatively few studies have examined the effectiveness of reward-extending strategies—to mention only one possible alternative. Moreover, as Marwell and Schmitt's list of compliance-gaining strategies illustrates, several different strategies can be used to motivate fear-arousal. The influence agent may threaten to punish the persuadee if he or she does not comply, or the influence agent may try to link failure to comply with subsequent negative self-feelings on the persuadee's part (see the "threat" and "self-feeling, negative" strategies in Table 1). Both strategies rely on fear-arousal, but motivationally they function quite differently. Hence, the category "fear-arousing appeals" appears to be a catch-all label which embraces several strategy alternatives, rather than a descriptive title for a single strategy. In order to understand the substantive aspects of persuasive message exchanges, a more exhaustive set of strategies is necessary.

A second reason for including these message strategy studies lies in the fact that they investigate attempted influence in dyadic situations, not in the one-to-many context which typifies most prior persuasion research. Granted, the studies do not conform with ideal methodological circumstances, since they describe situations to respondents instead of actually observing the respondents in the situations. Consequently, questions regarding the extent of correspondence between *saying* and *doing* remain open. Some respondents may say they would use particular strategies in certain situations, but refrain from using these strategies when actually placed in the situations. Given this possible discrepancy, future researchers might well employ actual communicative situations, rather than descriptions of them. But even with this procedural shortcoming, the studies represent a needed break from the traditional one-to-many audience situation and an attempt to examine persuasion in a more interpersonal milieu. In this respect, they fit within our expanded view of persuasion.

Finally, the studies described here approach the issue of message strategies from a different perspective than most traditional persuasion research. Instead of being concerned with the persuasive impact of the various strategies, these studies center on the *message choices* made by the potential persuader. When people seek to communicate persuasively, they must choose from a set of symbolic alternatives at their disposal. Obviously, numerous personal and situational variables affect strategy preferences and selections. Despite the fact that our knowledge of the persuasion process remains incomplete without an understanding of how particular persuasive strategies are chosen, little attention has been devoted to this problem.

In their initial study, Marwell and Schmitt (1968) identified 16 compliance-gaining message strategies. These strategies are summarized in Table 1, using an example of a persuasive transaction in which a father attempts to persuade his son to study more conscientiously. To produce a dimensional structure for these 16 strategies, Marwell and Schmitt had respondents indicate how likely they would be to use each of the strategies in four differing dyadic situations: a job situation, a family situation, a sales situation, and a situation involving a roommate. Subsequent analysis produced five, first-order factors: *rewarding activity* (I), *punishing activity* (II), *expertise* (III), *activation of impersonal commitments* (IV), and *activation of personal commitments* (V). In addition, a further analysis was performed to generate second-order factors. The first, second-order factor, which was defined by first-order factors I, III, and IV, was labeled *socially acceptable techniques*, while the second, second-order factor, defined by first-order factors II and V, was named *socially unacceptable techniques*. Table 1 indicates the strategies contained in each of the factors.

Miller, Boster, Roloff, and Seibold (1977) extended the work of Marwell and Schmitt by subjecting the 16 strategies to cluster analysis and by examining the likelihood of their use in noninterpersonal and interpersonal relationships (Miller, 1975; Miller & Steinberg, 1975). Although one of their objectives was to generate a smaller, more abstract typology of compliance-gaining strategies than the one that Marwell and Schmitt reported, Miller et al. were unsuccessful in their attempt. Instead, the strategies were found to be highly situationally bound. In terms of strategy selection, some differences were observed between noninterpersonal and interpersonal situations. Even though the respondents tended to prefer socially acceptable, reward-oriented strategies in all situations, they indicated a higher likelihood of using the threat strategy in noninterpersonal relationships. Furthermore, strategy preferences were more varied in the noninterpersonal situations:

> When compared with interpersonal situations, noninterpersonal situations may be characterized as containing more strategies that have a high likelihood of use. . . . [Also] the cluster solutions in the noninterpersonal situations produce smaller structures. This is particularly true in the noninterpersonal, short-term consequences situation in which a one-cluster structure is the best solution. Considering both findings jointly, it is plausible to conclude that in the noninterpersonal situations persons are somewhat more uncertain as to what type of strategy to employ and, hence, tend to rate more strategies as highly likely to be used. This interpretation follows closely from Miller and Steinberg's argument that interpersonal relationships, which are based upon psychological data, facilitate one's ability to predict the other's behavior. This ability to predict, in turn, produces

TABLE 1
Sixteen Compliance-Gaining Techniques with Examples from Family Situations

Technique	Description and Example
1. Promise (I)†	(If you comply, I will reward you.) "You offer to increase Dick's allowance if he increases his studying."
2. Threat (II)	(If you do not comply, I will punish you.) "You threaten to forbid Dick the use of the car if he does not increase his studying."
3. Expertise (Positive) (III)	(If you comply, you will be rewarded because of "the nature of things.") "You point out to Dick that if he gets good grades he will be able to get into a good college and get a good job."
4. Expertise (Negative) (III)	(If you do not comply, you will be punished because of "the nature of things.") "You point out to Dick that if he does not get good grades he will not be able to get into a good college or get a good job."
5. Liking (I)	(Actor is friendly and helpful to get target in "good frame of mind" so that he will comply with request.) "You try to be as friendly and pleasant as possible to get Dick in the 'right frame of mind' before asking him to study."
6. Pre-Giving (I)	(Actor rewards target before requesting compliance.) "You raise Dick's allowance and tell him you now expect him to study."
7. Aversive Stimulation (II)	(Actor continuously punishes target making cessation contingent on compliance.) "You forbid Dick the use of the car and tell him he will not be allowed to drive until he studies more."
8. Debt (V)	(You owe me compliance because of past favors.) "You point out that you have sacrificed and saved to pay for Dick's education and that he owes it to you to get good enough grades to get into a good college."
9. Moral Appeal (IV)	(You are immoral if you do not comply.) "You tell Dick that it is morally wrong for anyone not to get as good grades as he can and that he should study more."
10. Self-Feeling (Positive) (IV)	(You will feel better about yourself if you comply.) "You tell Dick he will feel proud if he gets himself to study more."
11. Self-Feeling (Negative) (IV)	(You will feel worse about yourself if you do not comply.) "You tell Dick he will feel ashamed of himself if he gets bad grades."
12. Altercasting (Positive) (IV)	(A person with "good" qualities would comply.) "You tell Dick that since he is a mature and intelligent boy he naturally will want to study more and get good grades."
13. Altercasting (Negative) (IV)	(Only a person with "bad" qualities would not comply.) "You tell Dick that only someone very childish does not study as he should."
14. Altruism (V)	(I need your compliance very badly, so do it for me.) "You tell Dick that you really want very badly for him to get into a good college and that you wish he would study more as a personal favor to you."
15. Esteem (Positive) (IV)	(People you value will think better of you if you comply.) "You tell Dick that the whole family will be very proud of him if he gets good grades."
16. Esteem (Negative) (IV)	(People you value will think worse of you if you do not comply.) "You tell Dick that the whole family will be very disappointed in him if he gets poor grades."

*From Marwell and Schmitt, 357-358.

†Indicates first-order factors. As stated in text, the socially acceptable second-order factor consists of strategies in first-order factors I, III, and IV; while the socially unacceptable second-order factor consists of strategies in first-order factors II and V.

> the ability to control by choosing an appropriate persuasive strategy to produce the desired behavioral effect. But in noninterpersonal situations such data on others are lacking and, hence, prediction and control become somewhat more tenuous processes. In response to their uncertainty, persons may grab at any strategic straw which promises to produce some measure of control over an uncertain environment. (1977, p. 49)

It should be reemphasized that these findings deal with a relatively neglected aspect of the persuasion process, since they concern variables which influence the selection of persuasive strategies, rather than focusing on the persuasive efficacy of the various strategies.

Roloff (1976) has recently proposed a set of *prosocial* and *antisocial* communication strategies that may be used by relational participants. The former strategies "reflect people's attempts to obtain relational rewards by techniques that facilitate understanding of their attitudes and needs," while the latter "represent people's attempts to obtain relational rewards by imposing their position on another through force or deception" (p. 181). Roloff then presents six propositions that relate strategy selection to relational development and relational change. Although he adduces scattered evidence for the propositions from the findings of prior research, each of the propositions suggests testable hypotheses that should be of interest to persuasion researchers.

Obviously, the studies on persuasive message strategies described here have but scratched the surface of this problem area. Research currently underway at Michigan State University is seeking to isolate other situational factors which influence strategy selection. In addition, Roloff has commenced to investigate the effects of such personality characteristics as Machiavellianism (Christie & Geis, 1970) on strategy preferences and usage. Additional information about these matters cannot help but contribute to our understanding of the nature and substance of persuasive transactions, particularly in small, face-to-face settings.

The two areas discussed above exemplify the sorts of current research that are congruent with my expanded view of persuasion. Certainly, we have not exhausted the alternatives. As we previously stated, much of the recent research on social conflict falls within the purview of persuasion. Moreover, Rokeach's (1973) work on value change suggests a viable alternative to the traditional preoccupation with the persuasive outcome of attitude change. Speaking of the relationship between cognitive change and behavioral change, Rokeach argues for the superiority of values over attitudes, asserting that "as long as the values underlying a changed attitude remain intact, there is no compelling theoretical reason why a short-term attitude change should lead to a behavioral change" (1973, p. 232). On the other hand, he contends, value change should lead to behavioral change, suggesting that if persuasion researchers wish to continue measuring persuasive outcomes in terms of cognitive change, they would be better advised to concentrate on value change. Whether or not one agrees with Rokeach, his position underscores one of the major points of this paper: the traditional view of persuasion research has seriously handicapped researchers by imposing a narrow perspective on the problems to be investigated and the persuasive outcomes to be measured.

THE CASE FOR PERSUASION RESEARCH: SUMMING UP

If forced to condense the message of this paper to a single sentence, we would probably opt for that old communication adage, "Meanings are in people." We have argued that one's assessment of the current intellectual and scientific vigor of persuasion research depends upon the meaning he or she assigns to the term "persuasion research." If that meaning is restricted to the paradigms, practices, and outcomes that have traditionally been investigated by persuasion researchers, then there is probably serious cause for concern about the continued vitality of the area. Lest we are misunderstood, we hasten to stress that this pessimistic prognosis does not stem from a negative evaluation of previous persuasion research. Indeed, we believe that the methodological and substantive quality of most of this research is as good or better than research conducted in other problem areas—a not surprising assessment, considering the fact that we have been responsible for some of it. The problem lies not with the quality of individual studies, but rather with the impoverished conceptual foundation imposed by the traditional view of persuasion. Because of this conceptual inadequacy, persuasion researchers have been overly restrictive in defining issues and problems, with the result being that much of the important research action has been carried out by investigators ostensibly (though not necessarily actually) concerned with other problem areas.

On the other hand, if one's meaning of persuasion research embraces the kind of wider conceptual stance advocated in this paper, there is no compelling reason to be concerned about the health and vitality of persuasion research. Many of the most interesting, significant issues of the field are inextricably bound up in persuasive communication. The difficulty is not with persuasion research *per se*, but rather with the way persuasion research has traditionally been conceived and conducted. Hopefully, the expanded view of persuasion we have outlined clearly underscores this fact, as well as reestablishing the centrality of persuasion inquiry to our eventual understanding of human communication.

Finally, we must confess that our belief in the inexorable pervasiveness of the persuasion process has virtually dictated that we would arrive at a clean bill of intellectual and scientific health for persuasion research. No matter how fervently some well-meaning individuals try to deny or to wish the fact away, questions concerning control and influence will remain an integral aspect of humanity's daily communicative activities. Given the centrality of these questions, it seems both foolhardy and fruitless to assume that our understanding of human communication can go on advancing without continued research attention to the persuasion process. Thus, we conclude that the case for persuasion research is as strong today as it was a decade or a century ago.

REFERENCES

ABELSON, R.P., ARONSON, E., McGUIRE, W.J., NEWCOMB, T.M., ROSENBERG, M.J., & TANNENBAUM, P.H. (Eds.). *Theories of cognitive consistency: A sourcebook*. Chicago: Rand McNally, 1968.

AJZEN, I., & FISHBEIN, M. Attitude-behavior relations: A theoretical analysis and review of empirical research. *Psychological Bulletin*, 1977, 84, 888-918.

ASCH, S.E. Effects of group pressure upon the modification and distortion of judgments. In H. Guetzkow (Ed.), *Groups, leadership, and men*. Pittsburgh: Carnegie Press, 1951, 177-205.

BACHRACH, P., & BARATZ, M.S. *Power and poverty: Theory and practice*. New York: Oxford University Press, 1970.

BAKER, E.E. The immediate effects of perceived speaker disorganization on speaker credibility and audience attitude change in persuasive speaking. *Western Speech*, 1965, 29, 148-161.

BRANDT, D.R., KANAGA, K.R., & STOYANOFF, N.J. The relation between communicator style and observers' perceptions of communicative effectiveness and attractiveness. Paper presented at the annual meeting of the Central States Speech Association, Southfield, Michigan, April 1977.

BEM, D.J. An experimental analysis of self persuasion. *Journal of Experimental Social Psychology*, 1965, 1, 199-218.

BEM, D.J. Self-perception theory. In L. Berkowitz (Ed.), *Advances in experimental social psychology* Vol. 6. New York: Academic Press, 1972, 1-62.

BERLO, D.K. Communication as process: Review and commentary. In B.D. Ruben (Ed.), *Communication Yearbook I*. New Brunswick, N.J.: Transaction-International Communication Association, 1977, 11-27.

BERLO, D.K., LEMERT, J.B., & MERTZ, R.J. Dimensions for evaluating the acceptability of message source. *Public Opinion Quarterly*, 1970. 33, 563-576.

BURGESS, P. Crisis rhetoric: Coercion versus force. *Quarterly Journal of Speech*, 1972, 59, 61-73.

BYRNE, D. Attitudes and attraction. In L. Berkowitz (Ed.), *Advances in experimental social psychology* Vol. 4. New York: Academic Press, 1969, 35-89.

BYRNE, D. *The attraction paradigm*. New York: Academic Press, 1971.

CAMPBELL, D.T. Social attitudes and other acquired behavioral dispositions. In S. Koch (Ed.), *Psychology: A study of a science* Vol. 6. New York: McGraw-Hill, 1963, 94-172.

CHRISTIE, R., & GEIS, F.L. *Studies in Machiavellianism*. New York: Academic Press, 1970.

CRUTCHFIELD, R.S. Conformity and character. *American Psychologist*, 1955, 10, 191-198.

CUSHMAN, D.P., & McPHEE, R. (Eds.). *Theoretical issues in attitude and behavior change*. East Lansing: Michigan State University Press, in press.

DeFLEUR, M.L., & WESTIE, F.R. Attitude as a scientific concept. *Social Forces*, 1963, 42, 17-31.

DONOHUE, W.A. A reconceptualization of negotiation. Unpublished doctoral dissertation, Department of Communication, Ohio State University, Columbus, Ohio, 1976.

DONOHUE, W.A., & CEGALA, D.J. An examination of the implementation of social power in dyadic negotiations. Paper presented at the annual meeting of the International Communication Association, West Berlin, Germany, June 1977.

EDELMAN, M. *The symbolic uses of politics*. Urbana: University of Illinois Press, 1964.

EDELMAN, M. The language of participation and the language of resistance. *Human Communication Research*, 1977, 3, 159-170.

ELMS, A.C. (Ed.). *Role playing, reward, and attitude change*. New York: Van Nostrand Reinhold, 1969.

ELMS, A.C., & JANIS, I.L. Counter-norm attitudes induced by consonant versus dissonant conditions of role-playing. *Journal of Experimental Research in Personality*, 1965, 1, 50-60.

ESSER, J.K., & KOMROITA, S.S. Reciprocity and concession making in bargaining. *Journal of Personality and Social Psychology*, 1975, 31, 864-872.

FARACE, R.V., & ROGERS, L.E. Analysis of relational communication in dyads: New measurement procedures. *Human Communication Research*, 1975, 1, 222-239.

FELDMAN, S. (Ed.). *Cognitive consistency: Motivational antecedents and behavioral consequents*. New York: Academic Press, 1966.

FESTINGER, L. *A theory of cognitive dissonance*. Stanford, Cal.: Stanford University Press, 1957.

FESTINGER, L. Behavioral support for opinion change. *Public Opinion Quarterly*, 1964, 28, 404-417.

FESTINGER, L., & CARLSMITH, J.M. Cognitive consequences of forced compliance. *Journal of Abnormal and Social Psychology*, 1959, 58, 203-210.

FISHBEIN, M., & AJZEN, I. *Belief, attitude, intention and behavior*. Reading, Mass.: Addison-Wesley, 1975.

GILES, H., & POWESLAND, P.F. *Speech style and social evaluation*. New York: Academic Press, 1975.

GOFFMAN, E. *The presentation of self in everyday life*. Garden City, N.Y.: Doubleday, 1959.

GRIFFITT, W. Attitude similarity and attraction. In T.L. Huston (Ed.), *Foundations of interpersonal attraction*. New York: Academic Press, 1974, 285-308.

HAWES, L.C. Alternative theoretical bases: Toward a presuppositional critique. *Communication Quarterly*, 1977, 25, 63-68.

HIGBEE, K.L. Fifteen years of fear arousal. Research on threat appeals: 1953-1968. *Psychological Bulletin*, 1969, 72, 426-444.

HODGES, L.A., & BYRNE, D. Verbal dogmatism as a potentiator of intolerance. *Journal of Personality and Social Psychology*, 1972, 21, 312-317.

HOVLAND, C.I. (Ed.). *The order of presentation in persuasion*. New Haven, Conn.: Yale University Press, 1957.

HOVLAND, C.I., & JANIS, I.L. (Eds.). *Personality and persuasibility*. New Haven, Conn.: Yale University Press, 1959.

HOVLAND, C.I., JANIS, I.L., & KELLEY, H.H. *Communication and persuasion*. New Haven, Conn.: Yale University Press, 1953.

HOVLAND, C.I., LUMSDAINE, A.A., & SHEFFIELD, F.D. *Experiments on mass communication*. Princeton, N.J.: Princeton University Press, 1949.

HOVLAND, C.I., & ROSENBERG, M.J. (Eds.). *Attitude organization and change*. New Haven, Conn.: Yale University Press, 1960.

HOVLAND, C.I., & WEISS, W. The influence of source credibility on communication effectiveness. *Public Opinion Quarterly*, 1951, 15, 635-650.

HUSTON, T.L. A perspective on interpersonal attraction. In T.L Huston (Ed.), *Foundations of interpersonal attraction*. New York: Academic Press, 1974, 3-28.

JANIS, I.L. Effects of fear arousal on attitude change: Recent developments in theory and experimental research. In L. Berkowitz (Ed.), *Advances in experimental social psychology* Vol. 3. New York: Academic Press, 1967, 166-224.

JONES, E.E. *Ingratiation*. New York: Appleton-Century-Crofts, 1964.

KAPLAN, A. *The conduct of inquiry*. San Francisco: Chandler, 1964.

LaPIERE, R.T. Attitudes versus actions. *Social Forces*, 1934, 13, 230-237.

LARSON, C., & SANDERS, R. Faith, mystery, and data: An analysis of "scientific" studies of persuasion. *Quarterly Journal of Speech*, 1975, 61, 178-194.

LEVENTHAL, H. Findings and theory in the study of fear communications. In L. Berkowitz (Ed.), *Advances in experimental social psychology* Vol. 5. New York: Academic Press, 1970, 119-186.

LIN, N. Communication effects: Review and commentary. In B.D. Ruben (Ed.), *Communication Yearbook I*. New Brunswick, N.J.: Transaction-International Communication Association, 1977, 55-72.

LISKA, A.E. (Ed.). *The consistency controversy*. New York: Schenkman, 1975.

MARWELL, G., & SCHMITT, D.R. Dimensions of compliance-gaining behavior: An empirical analysis. *Sociometry*, 1967, 30, 350-364.

McCROSKEY, J.C. Scales for the measurement of ethos. *Speech Monographs*, 1966, 33, 65-72.

McGUIRE, W.J. The nature of attitudes and attitude change. In G. Lindzey and E. Aronson (Eds.), *Handbook of social psychology* Vol. 3 (2nd Ed.). Reading, Mass.: Addison-Wesley, 1969, 136-314.

MILGRAM, S. Behavioral study of obedience. *Journal of Abnormal and Social Psychology*, 1963, 67, 317-378.

MILGRAM, S. Some conditions of obedience and disobedience. *Human Relations*, 1965, 18, 57-76.

MILLER, G.R. A crucial problem in attitude research. *Quarterly Journal of Speech*, 1967, 53, 235-240.

MILLER, G.R. Counterattitudinal advocacy: A current appraisal. In C.D. Mortensen and K.K. Sereno (Eds.), *Advances in communication research*. New York: Harper & Row, 1972a, 105-152.

MILLER, G.R. Speech: An approach to human communication. In R.W. Budd and B.D. Ruben (Eds.), *Approaches to human communication*. Rochelle Park, N.J.: Spartan-Hayden, 1972b, 383-400.

MILLER, G.R. Toward a rhetoric of counterattitudinal advocacy. In W.R. Fisher (Ed.), *Rhetoric: A tradition in transition*. East Lansing: Michigan State University Press, 1974, 279-299.

MILLER, G.R. Interpersonal communication: A conceptual perspective. *Communication*, 1975, 2, 93-105.

MILLER, G.R., BOSTER, F., ROLOFF, M., & SEIBOLD, D. Compliance-gaining message strategies: A typology and some findings concerning effects of situational differences. *Communication Monographs*, 1977, 44, 37-50.

MILLER, G.R., & BURGOON, M. *New techniques of persuasion*. New York: Harper & Row, 1973.

MILLER, G.R., & HEWGILL, M.A. The effect of variations in nonfluency on audience ratings of source credibility. *Quarterly Journal of Speech*, 1964, 50, 36-44.

MILLER, G.R., & STEINBERG, M. *Between people: A new analysis of interpersonal communication*. Chicago: Science Research Associates, 1975.

NORTON, R.W. Foundation of a communicator style construct. Unpublished manuscript, Department of Communication, Purdue University, Lafayette, Indiana, 1977.

RAVEN, B.H., & KRUGLANSKI, A.W. Conflict and power.

In P. Swingle (Ed.), *The structure of conflict*. New York: Academic Press, 1970, 69-109.

ROKEACH, M. *The open and closed mind*. New York: Basic, 1960.

ROKEACH, M. *The nature of human values*. New York: Free Press, 1973.

ROKEACH, M., & MEZEI, L. Race and shared belief as factors in social choice. *Science*, 1966, 151, 167-172.

ROLOFF, M.E. Communication strategies, relationships, and relational change. In G.R. Miller (Ed.), *Perspectives on interpersonal communication*. Beverly Hills, Cal.: Sage, 1976, 173-195.

SCOTT, R.C., & BROCKRIEDE, W. *The rhetoric of black power*. New York: Harper & Row, 1969.

SEIBOLD, D.R. Communication research and the attitude-verbal report-behavior relationship: A critique and theoretic reformulation. *Human Communication Research*, 1975, 2, 3-32.

SERENO, K.K., & HAWKINS, G.J. The effects of variations in speakers' nonfluency upon audience ratings of attitude toward the speech topic and speakers' credibility. *Speech Monographs*, 1967, 34, 58-64.

SHARP, H., JR., & McCLUNG, T. Effects of organization on the speaker's ethos. *Speech Monographs*, 1966, 33, 182-183.

SHERIF, M., & HOVLAND, C.I. *Social judgment*. New Haven, Conn.: Yale University Press, 1961.

SIMONS, H.W. Requirements, problems, and strategies: A theory of persuasion for social movements. *Quarterly Journal of Speech*, 1970, 56, 1-11.

SIMONS, H.W. Persuasion in social conflicts: A critique of prevailing conceptions and a framework for future research. *Speech Monographs*, 1972, 39, 227-248.

SIMONS, H.W. The carrot and stick as handmaidens of persuasion in conflict situations. In G.R. Miller and H.W. Simons (Eds.), *Perspectives on communication in social conflict*. Englewood Cliffs, N.J.: Prentice-Hall, 1974, 172-205.

SKINNER, B.F. *About behaviorism*. New York: Knopf, 1974.

TURNBULL, A.A., STICKLAND, L., & SHAVER, K.G. Medium of communication, differential power, and phasing of concessions: Negotiating success and attributions to the opponent. *Human Communication Research*, 1976, 2, 262-270.

WATZLAWICK, P., BEAVIN, J.G., & JACKSON, D.D. *Pragmatics of human communication*. New York: Norton, 1967.

WYER, R.S., JR. *Cognitive organization and change: An information processing approach*. New York: Lawrence Erlbaum Associates, 1974.

ZIMBARDO, P.G., EBBESEN, E.E., & MASLACH, C. *Influencing attitudes and changing behavior* (2nd Ed.). Reading, Mass.: Addison-Wesley, 1977.

THE IDEA OF COMMUNICATION—LOOKING FOR A PLACE TO STAND: REVIEW AND COMMENTARY

LEE THAYER
University of Houston

If, as Alan Watts once remarked, "Trying to define yourself is like trying to bite your own teeth,"

Then what is to be said of *communication*?

I

Etymologically, there is a close relationship between "speak" and "sperm." They share root meanings like "to sprout," "to strew," "to sprinkle," "to scatter." So what's all the fuss about?

II

From the SUFI we have this observation:

For a long time now people have been claiming that what is wrong with society is that there is a failure of communication.

Many of these have had nothing to communicate other than the assertion that they cannot communicate.

They have communicated this effectively enough.

III

Why have we come to our concern with communication when we have, where we have, how we have? Is it possible that communication, like sex, for people of declining civilizations, may be a natural substitute for faculties we no longer quite have? (Fair, 1974, p. 196)

IV

Or is our curiosity a desperate attempt to regain something we once had?

A monk once asked the great Sekito: "What is it that makes up this Self?"

To this the master answered: "What do you want from me?"

The monk persisted: "If I do not ask you, where can I get the solution?"

"Did you ever lose it?" concluded the master (Suziki, 1951).

V

What is it we want to know? Max Weber (1949) said that "a person who attempted to govern his mode of walking continuously by anatomical knowledge would be in danger of stumbling" (p. 115). What of the person who attempted to govern his mode of talking . . . ?

Whitehead believed it to be profoundly erroneous to assume that we should cultivate the habit of thinking what we are doing. "The precise opposite is the case. Civilization advances by extending the number of important operations we can perform without thinking about them" (Hayek, 1948, p. 88).

"The great enemy of communication," Pierre Martineau once commented, "is the illustion of it."

VI

What would we know if we knew what we wanted to know?

That communication becomes problematical where individualism has been achieved?

If autonomous individuality is, as Hegel said, "the pivot and the centre of the difference between antiquity and modern times," is our interest in communication but a symptom of a much deeper split in our psyches, our civilization?

VII

". . . to be too conscious is an illness—a real

thoroughgoing illness'' (Dostoevsky, 1969).

The heroine of John Barth's *The End of the Road* says: "I think all our trouble comes from thinking too much and talking too much. We talk ourselves into all kinds of messes that would disappear if everybody just shut up about them.''

And communication?

VIII

. . . What is man that thou art mindful of him? (Psalm 8)

IX

"One who is aware does not talk.

One who talks is not aware.'' *Tao Tê Ching*, ch. 56.

X

Is our interest in words to multiply them or to stay them?

Walker Percy is a physician and a novelist. He recently made a great contribution to communication theory (1976) by discovering that his inability to grasp what it was about communication that fascinated him was precisely the fact that he could not grasp it.

He thereby becomes a Fellow of the Order of Ignored Savants. We want words, not wisdom.

XI

Words.

Another Fellow: "A civilization of words is a civilization distraught. . . . We . . . speak far too much, far too easily, making common what was private, arresting into the clichés of false certitude that which was provisional, personal, and therefore alive on the shadow-side of speech. We live in a culture which is, increasingly, a wind-tunnel of gossip; gossip that reaches from theology and politics to an unprecedented noising of private concerns . . .'' (Steiner, 1967, p. 73).

College catalog, under "Communication'': Gossip I, Gossip II, Advanced Gossip, Graduate Seminar in Advanced Gossipry. Lab: Discussion or encounter groups: If you are bored when alone, join others like yourself and share the richness of your inner being.

Words.

XII

And communication "theory?''

"It was no wonder that God had ceased to love him, for he had, from his own free will, exchanged the things of the Lord—the moon, the sea, friendship, fights—for the words that describe them'' (Dinesen, 1942, p. 11).

And when one exchanges the things of communication for the words that describe them, has one gained them?

Is a word about a word a word?

XIII

To talk, to talk, to catch a. . . .

"Generally it is true,'' wrote J.H. van den Berg (1975), "that the more people talk to each other, the worse their understanding is'' (p. 68).

Us and the American Telephone & Telegraph Company, whose advertisement read: "At least talk to each other. To communicate is the beginning of understanding.''

XIV

John B. Calhoun (1976) is a scientist at the National Institutes of Mental Health. He is interested in behavioral pathologies. He said, "Too many interactions among individuals produces the ultimate behavioral pathology. . . .''

Emily Dickinson is not a scientist at NIMH—perhaps she was not a scientist at all. She said:

> "Speech is one symptom of Affection
> And Silence one—
> The perfectest communication
> Is heard of none—.''

A theory of silence?

XV

Truth, then. And reality.

Steiner again, in one of yesterday's *Psychology*

Today's: "Language is not a description of reality, but an answer to it, an evasion from it."

Joseph Conrad, who was never interviewed in *Psychology Today*, was nonetheless of similar mind: "Words, as is well known, are the great foes of reality."

Theoretical question: If, as Bacon said, "All perceptions, as well of the sense as of the mind, accord to the measure of the individual, not to the measure of the universe," what then would a theory of communication be a measure of?

What is the reality of human communication, if words are an evasion from reality?

XVI

Expression? Communion? Ritual? Game? Function?

Suzanne Langer (1942) speculated that, with the first word, the first experience of "communication," ". . . the two creatures would look at one another with a light of understanding dawning . . . and would say some more words, and grin at some more objects. Perhaps they would join hands and chant words together" (p. 114).

Is our assumption that something has changed a part of the problem?

It is perhaps true that we don't grin as much as we once did. Or join hands.

Has anything else changed much?

XVII

We're "literate." We bear the weight of all that knowledge. We have to take life seriously. We have to make a theory about life. About communication. About talking.

"Life is far too important a thing ever to talk about," said Oscar Wilde.

If we exchange living for knowing, talking for loving, what shall we exchange for knowing about knowing, for knowing about knowing about talking?

> Vladimir: "To have lived is not enough for them."
> Estragon: "They have to talk about it" (Beckett, 1954).

XVIII

About what is a theory of communication?

"People," wrote William Hazlitt (1821-1822), "do not seem to talk for the sake of expressing their opinions, but to maintain an opinion for the sake of talking."

If a theory is for the sake of talking, what is it *about*?

For the sake of what is talking?

XIX

Nietzsche's Zarathustra: "Speaking is a beautiful folly: with that man dances over all things."

Is that a theory?

What would be a theory of that?

XX

"The true use of speech is not so much to express our wants as to conceal them" (Goldsmith, 1759).

What is it that a theory of communication is supposed to reveal?

How?

To speak of what one believes one knows about communication is to conceal . . . what?

XXI

If a clock tells time, what is it that people tell?

Much communication, like much money, is dope, a tranquillizer against the effects of not knowing what to do.

When in doubt, communicate.

"Man is a creature," said Robert Louis Stevenson, "who lives not upon bread alone, but principally by catchwords."

"People say what is said." At least that is what Ortega y Gasset said.

"What d'ya say?"

Say something. "Being confirmed by others frees me from being responsible for the absurdity of my belief" (Geiger, 1969, p. 218).

XXII

If speech, as Thomas Mann remarked, is civilization itself, what is speech itself?

XXIII

For Karl Kraus, language was not so much a means of communicating what he knew, but of finding out what he did not yet know.

Heidegger (1962): "Any interpretation which is to contribute understanding, must already have understood what is to be interpreted" (p. 194).

How was he able to understand *that*?

XXIV

And William James (1918): "The only things which we perceive are those we preperceive, and the only things which we preperceive are those which have been labelled for us and the labels stamped into our mind."

Is James talking about some*thing*? or some*one*?

Richard Faynman says that his father told him: "If you know the names of things you know a little something about people, but you don't necessarily know anything about those things."

What Peter tells me about Paul, Spinoza wrote, tells me more about Peter than it does about Paul.

So suppose I want to tell you something about Paul?

And if I wanted to tell you something about telling . . . ?

XXV

Another Fellow of the Order: "Understanding what some one says to you is thus attributing to him the idea which his words arouse in yourself . . ." (Collingwood, 1928, p. 250).

What, then, is a theory of communication a theory of?

XXVI

Why is it that the only people I listen to are the people I understand?

How is it that I can understand that I don't understand?

Sign: "Will someone please tell me who I am?"

Sign of what?

Would a theory of communication be a countersign?

XXVII

Let's be specific. Simplify.

For "Literalness is the devil's weapon" (Roethke, 1972, p. 170).

"The things that concern you most can't be put into prose. In prose the tendency is to avoid inner responsibility" (p. 171).

Is a theory prose? Or poetry?

XXVIII

There is understanding. And there is "inner responsibility."

Which is which?

There was once a person who didn't understand what communication was all about. I understood him.

Then there was another person who understood what communication was all about. I didn't understand him.

Then I got to wondering how it was I understood the difference.

XXIX

To communicate, then.

"It is idle to think that, by means of words, any real communication can ever pass from one man to another . . . from the moment that we have something to say to each other we are compelled to hold our peace" (Maeterlinck).

Or Steiner (1971): "The notion that we can express to our deaf selves, let alone communicate to any other human beings, blind, deaf, insensate as they are, a complete truth, fact, sensation—a fifth, tenth, millionth of such aforesaid truth, fact, or sensation—is arrogant folly" (p. 17).

The folly that makes all other follies possible?

XXX

"That's the flaw with words," the Yaqui sorcerer said, ". . . they always force us to feel enlightened, but then when we turn around to face the world they always fail us and we end up facing the world as we always have, without enlightenment" (Castaneda, 1974, p. 32).

Is that because "The nets for catching words are made of words . . ." because "language is a condition of man's existence . . ."? (Paz, 1973).

Is the question, "What is communication?"

Or is the question, "How shall we invent the notion of communication *so that* . . . ?"

XXXI

". . . as soon as one scratches the surface of the familiar and comes face to face with the nature of . . . [communication] . . . , one also finds himself face to face with the nature of man" (Percy, 1976, p. 150).

Is communication, is man, something separate from us, merely to be "discovered" by us?

If "The image of man affects the nature of man," then our idea of communication affects the nature of our communication.

If "What determines one's being human is the image one adopts . . . ," if "the truth of a theory about man is either creative or irrelevant, but never merely descriptive" (Herschel, 1965, p. 8), what of the truth of a theory of communication?

XXXII

"Life without structure is un-seen" (Cage, 1961).

What structure shall we give our lives in the saying of them?

XXXIII

Rilke: "Could anyone feel quite unconstrained in the face of forms that have a name?"

How shall we name the forms that will constrain us?

XXXIV

"Man is a being who has created himself in creating a language. By means of the word, man is a metaphor of himself" (Paz, 1973).

By means of what words shall we create ourselves?

XXXV

If, as Huizinga (1954) argues, "Without metaphor it is impossible to express a single thought" (p. 223), by what metaphors shall we express the idea of communication?

How shall we express human nature in expressing the nature of communication?

How shall we communicate ourselves that we may be?

As we communicate, so shall we be.

Knot: How shall we be? ". . . and we do not understand what we are, unless we know what we ought to be" (Eliot, 1935).

Knots: How shall we say how we say?

XXXVI

"People were looking for people, to talk to, for nothing really exists until we say it, a lesson the human animal either can't or doesn't want to learn" (Deal, 1942, p. 104).

And what shall we say of that which doesn't exist until we say it?

XXXVII

Neti, Neti.

"We have to *be* something before we can *know* anything. And when we have become something, the something we can know is less than the something we have become" (Wheelis, 1973).

What shall he who would know about communication become?

If what we can say of communication is a measure of the sayer, how shall we sayers measure up?

What are people for?

"The imperfect is our paradise.
Note that, in this bitterness, delight,
Since the imperfect is so hot in us,
Lies in flawed words and stubborn sounds" (Stevens, 1947, pp. 93-94).

Communication theory: a theory about how to enhance our imperfections.

A perfect theory, this. Imperfect!

XXXVIII

Martin Buber said that the source of all conflict

between men is that they do not say what they mean and they do not mean what they say.

Did he mean that?

And Max Stirner: "What I say I don't mean—and what I mean cannot be said."

What did he mean by that?

Empirical datum upon which any theory of communication would have to be based:

I cannot tell you what I mean.
I can only tell you what I say.
All the rest is up to you.

XXXIX

Thurber said: "A word to the wise is not sufficient if it doesn't make any sense."

And Collingwood (1939): ". . . a statement is not meaningful until the unstated question it answers is known, and the statement is misunderstood if the question is incorrectly inferred."

What was the question to which that is the answer?

A theory of communication would be the answer . . . to what question?

XL

If "The development and elaboration of heresy is the business of communication," (Seeley, 1962, p. 215)

Then what is the question?

If, as Blake said, anything capable of being believed is an image of truth,

What, then, is the truth of communication?

XLI

Mass communication?

What is it that we could know about "mass communication" that we don't, or can't, know about communication?

Is there anything significant about "mass communication" apart from what is said of it?—apart from what is believed of it?

An archaic method of scattering seeds is called "broadcasting."

Would a theory of "mass communication" be a theory of collecting or a theory of ingesting? Or of asseverating?

Or what is the *communication* part of it?

XLII

Kenneth Burke (1969) said that "Only those voices from without are effective which can speak in the language of the voice within" (p. 563).

And Baba Ram Dass: "Only that in you which is me can hear what I'm saying."

What is that in you which is me?

What is that in me which is you?

Is it the question?

Or the answer?

XLIII

And if "The language of experience is not the language of classification" (Ciardi, 1960, p. 666).

Then what shall be the language of a theory of communication?

XLIV

How shall we know?

How shall we know that what we know is what we need to know?

Nietzsche: "To know is merely to work with one's favorite metaphors."

And to know oneself?

And knowing what one knows?

And knowing that one knows what one knows?

To communicate: To tell what one knows?

And if I know what I believe another knows, will I thereby know what is worth knowing?

XLV

To understand: To be pleased with what one knows?

XLVI

What is it that I might know
Which, if I knew it,
I could no longer know
What I know?

What shall we be for?

For whom shall I be a metaphor? For whom shall my metaphors be?

What shall we be for?

A theory of communication is a metaphor . . . what?

XLVII

Cioran says that "civilization instructs us how to take hold of things, whereas it is the art of letting them go that it should teach us . . ." (Cioran, 1975, p. 95).

How are we to take hold (let go?) of that?

Can I let go that which I have not taken hold of?

Like the narrator in Henry Miller's *Tropic of Cancer*, ". . . I can't get it out of my mind what a discrepancy there is between ideas and living."

Is a theory of communication to be a theory of ideas or of living?

Or a theory of the difference?

Or is it the difference itself?

XLVIII

Of what is the idea of communication to be an idea?

Where shall we stand to look for it?

How shall we be to know it?

REFERENCES

BECKETT, S. *Waiting for Godot*. New York: Grove Press, 1954.

BURKE, K. *A Rhetoric of Motives*. Berkeley: University of California Press, 1969.

CAGE, J. Lecture on nothing. *Silence*, Cambridge, Mass: MIT Press, 1961.

CALHOUN, J.B. Scientific quest for a path to the future. *Populi*, 1976.

CASTANEDA, C. *Tales of power*. New York: Simon & Schuster, 1974.

CIARDI, J. *How does a poem mean*? Boston: Houghton & Mifflin, 1960.

CIORAN, E.M. Civilization: A portrait. In R. Boyers (Ed.), *Psychological man*. New York: Harper & Row, 1975.

COLLINGWOOD, R.G. *The principles of art*. Oxford: Clarendon Press, 1938.

COLLINGWOOD, R.G. *An autobiography*. Oxford: Oxford University Press, 1939.

DEAL, B.H. *The walls came tumbling down*. New York: Random House, 1942.

DICKINSON, E. *Poems*, c. 1862-1886.

DINESEN, I. *Winter's tales*. New York: Doubleday, 1942.

DOSTOEVSKY, F. *Notes from the underground*. New York: Crowell, 1969.

ELIOT, T.S. Religion and literature. 1935.

FAIR, C. *The new nonsense: The end of the rational consensus*. New York: Simon & Schuster, 1974.

GEIGER, T. *On social order and mass society*. Chicago: University of Chicago Press, 1969.

GOLDSMITH, O. *The bee*, October 20, 1779.

HAYEK, F.A. *Individualism and economic order*. Chicago: University of Chicago Press, 1948.

HAZLITT, W. On coffee house politicians. *Table Talk*, 1821-1822.

HEIDEGGER, M. In J. Mcquarrie & E. Robinson (Trans.) *Being and time*. London: SCM Press, 1962.

HERSCHEL, A.J. *Who is man*? Stanford, Cal.: Stanford University Press, 1965.

HUIZINGA, J. *The waning of the middle ages*. New York: Doubleday, 1954.

JAMES, W. *Principles of psychology*. New York: Holt, Rinehart & Winston, 1918.

LANGER, S. *Philosophy in a new key*. Cambridge, Mass.: Harvard University Press, 1942.

PAZ, O. *The bow and the lyre*. Austin: University of Texas Press, 1973.

PERCY, W. *The message in the bottle: How queer man is, how queer language is, and what one has to do with the other*. New York: Farrar, Straus & Giroux, 1976.

ROETHKE, T. *Straw for the fire: From the notebooks*. New York: Doubleday, 1972.

SEELEY, J.R. "Communication, communications and community." In J. Irving (Ed.), *Mass media in Canada*. Toronto: Ryerson Press, 1962.

SHILS, E. & FINCH, H. (Eds.) *The methodology of the social sciences*. New York: Free Press, 1949.

STEINER, G. *Language and silence: Essays 1958-66*. London: Farber & Farber, 1967.

STEINER, G. *Extraterritorial*. New York: Atheneum, 1971.

STEVENS, W. The poems of our climate. In *Poems*. New York: Vintage, 1947.

SUZUKI, D.T. Reason and intuition in Buddhist philosophy. In C.A. Moore (Ed.), *Essays in East-West philosophy*. Honolulu: University of Honolulu Press, 1951.

VAN DEN BERG, J.H. *The changing nature of man*. New York: Dell, 1975.

WHEELIS, A. *The moralist*. New York: Basic, 1973.

COMMUNICATION, SPEECH, AND PSYCHOLOGICAL MODELS OF MAN: REVIEW AND COMMENTARY

WALTER B. WEIMER
Pennsylvania State University

Two fields of crucial importance to communication are: the philosophy-methodology of science, which supplies a model of acceptable method and technique for research; and psychology, which supplies a model of man. The manner in which philosophy and psychology constrain developments in speech and communication is usually tacit, exercising a subtle influence upon the researcher's views of how communication studies ought to proceed. Because scientific status is sufficient to guarantee funding for research, graduate students, and course programs, communication has begun to sell itself (to both students and grant agencies) as a model of science. Communication researchers are influenced by dominant views in philosophy of science, and there seems to be considerable polarization between those who wish to ape the "hardheaded" sciences, and those who hold that the field does not fit the accepted picture of a hard "science." Psychological considerations constrain the field because at least an implicit (often explicit) model of man underlies studies of communication, the rhetorical process, and so forth. Thus, as with methodological considerations, communication researchers tend to split between those who endorse the view of man implicit in behaviorism and information processing psychologies, and researchers who protest that speech and communication cannot be modeled upon those psychological views.

These polarizations tend to dovetail: researchers who wish their field to enjoy the benefits and status of science adopt a behavioristic or computer model of psychological man because they perceive it to be scientific, and their opponents adopt a literary or humanistic position because they perceive a rigidity and mechanism in behaviorism and computerese which appears antithetical to the richness of human discourse and experience. The question arises as to whether this polarization, so much the product of other fields' effects, will ultimately tear communication apart, or whether there is some way to preserve the major points emphasized by these protagonists in a unified field.

This chapter argues that it is possible to preserve both the emphasis upon science and the scientific outlook that the "hardheaded" camp endorses, and also the cultural-humanistic-literary emphasis of the "softheaded" camp, but that doing so requires abandonment of the heretofore dominant models of both *methodology* and *man*. A conceptually adequate approach can result only if the positivistic conception of science found in logical empiricism and related philosophies of science is recognized to be inadequate and abandoned, and if the behavioristic-information processing model of man is recognized to be inadequate and replaced by an adequate cognitive psychology. Communication has been a self-inflicted victim of Procrustes's bed, cutting off or distorting various of its features due to an uncritical acceptance of previously dominant positions in philosophy and psychology. Further, instead of passive acceptance of philosophy and psychology, communication and speech should critically evaluate and actively shape significant aspects of those fields. By overviewing major features and themes in current cognitive research, this chapter attempts to show how that interaction can aid and be aided by cognitive psychology.

METHODOLOGICAL INTERLUDE: SCIENTISM IN THE STUDY OF HUMANITY

Before overviewing cognitive psychology, we must pause to note one particularly pernicious effect of uncritical acceptance of the positivistic conception of science that has damaged both psychology, speech, and communication: *scientism*. In *The Counter-Revolution of Science* (1952a), F.A. Hayek coined the term "scientism," to refer to: "an attitude which is decidedly unscientific in the true sense of the word, since it involves a mechanical and uncritical application of habits of thought to fields different from those in which they have been formed. The scientistic (as distinguished from the scientific) view is not an unprejudiced but a very prejudiced approach which, before it has considered its subject, claims to know what is the most appropriate way of investigating it'' (pp. 15-16). Scientism, in other words, is the requirement that a field conducts its inquiry (both theoretical and empirical) in a manner strictly analogous to a preconceived notion of what constitutes ''genuine science'' or ''true scientific method.''

Scientism is a major factor in the recent separation of communication from traditional areas such as speech,[1] and also in the adoption of a behavioristic and information-processing methodology in communication. Behaviorism, as it has developed in psychology and infiltrated into other human and cultural fields, is without doubt the most scientistic methodology in history. But behaviorism is both a methodology (which claims to be scientific because it endorses the logical positivist's and empiricist's strictures as to what constitutes ''scientific method'') and a substantive psychological position (which claims that behavior is the true subject of psychology and that it can be encompassed in the stimulus-organism-response-reinforcement schema). While a successful challenge to behaviorism must replace both aspects with more viable formulations, the task of this chapter is to attack and replace behavioristic and information processing psychology. (The philosophy of science issues are treated in detail elsewhere, both in other chapters of this and the previous *Yearbook*, and in the works of Kuhn, 1970a, 1970b; Popper, 1959, 1963, 1972; Lakatos, 1968, 1970; Feyerabend, 1965, 1970a, 1970b. A detailed analysis of major arguments, which incorporates both psychological and rhetorical material, is found in Weimer, 1978.) We must note that, although they are closely allied, the methodological and substantive aspects of behaviorism can be separated. Some theorists (e.g., G.R. Miller, 1976) have abandoned substantive behaviorism while clinging to the methodology (thus mummifying the discipline to preserve its ''scientific'' appearance at the expense of its vitality). Other theorists (e.g., Phillips, 1977) take the opposite tact, arguing against behavioristic (scientistic) methodology only to propose behaviorist substantive theories. This chapter attempts to provide a framework which will enable theorists in this latter camp to escape the last vestiges of behaviorism.

RECENT HISTORY IN PSYCHOLOGY

It is often said of psychologists that their philosophy of science is 20 years out of date (and limited to one hurried course in graduate school). It may likewise be said that the speech communication theorist's psychology is nearly 20 years out of date (e.g., enthusiastic embrace of ''neobehaviorism,'' information theoretic approaches to communication, scientistic statistical methodology [or better, methodolatry!], and increasing reliance upon the computer as a model of cognitive processes). Without realizing it, speech and communication theorists display a tendency to mimic psychological fashions that are (at least) a decade out of date. Many recent communication infatuations and ''discoveries'' are thus tragicomic. At the risk of seeming to patronize, it is worth noting the communalities and shared inadequacies of several psychological approaches now in vogue in speech communication. By seeing their problems we can begin to come to grips with what an adequate psychology might look like.

Psychology has had several paradigmatic successors (or candidates to be successor) to the behaviorism of the 1930s. Behaviorism had attempted to understand the psychological domain in terms of: (1) *physically specifiable* stimuli; (2) the organism (as a black box, with minimal internal wiring); (3) physically specifiable overt responses; and (4) reinforcement (which satisfied classical tissue needs or drives). First came neobehaviorism, which was forced (chiefly by so-called ''latent learning'' studies) to admit that reinforcement was both impossibly difficult to specify and that it was not necessary for learning (as had been assumed). Neobehaviorism also became mediational. It admitted that things went on *inside* the organism. Although it tried vainly to model those internal processes upon overt, physically specifiable stimuli and responses, the downfall of neobehaviorism for human psychology came with the serious study of the higher mental processes such as thinking, reasoning, problem solving, imagery, and so forth, but most especially language. Chomsky's revolution in linguistics, which replaced structural linguistics by transformational linguistics, made exbehaviorists out of most psychologists interested in cognition (see Jenkins, 1968, 1974, for a personal historical account).

It is worth noting that the last ditch defense of neobehaviorism was scientistic—its defenders (e.g., Osgood 1963, 1968, 1971) claimed to be scientific because they eschewed "mentalism" in favor of "physically" specifiable concepts. This position died (in the sense that it ceased to direct research in language and cognition) when it became obvious that its concepts were functionally specified rather than physically definable, and that the entire S-O-R framework simply made no sense when applied to cognition. It became clear to all but the most zealous that it was either vacuous or false to claim (as did Osgood, 1971) that we speak because talking reduces an internal drive state.

Thus, from the late 1950s to the early 1960s, it became increasingly clear that the theoretical vocabulary of behaviorism, regardless of how many neomodifications were effected, was bankrupt. It was no longer informative to say, for example, that the meaning of a word was a person's "internal response" to the word as a stimulus, or to think that anything theoretically useful was "measured" by techniques such as the semantic differential (Osgood, Suci, & Tannebaum, 1957). But where could one find a more useful theoretical framework? At first some theorists looked to motor skills learning, but it was obvious that its (then available) concepts were word for word substitutions for neobehavioristic formulations (e.g., what the subject receives is "knowledge of results" rather than "reinforcement"). Then the field rediscovered information theory, largely through rereading George A. Miller's (1951) book *Language and Communication*, which had made pioneering psychological applications of Shannon and Weaver's views, and incorporated Markov modeling of learning processes. Another landmark in this tradition was Colin Cherry's *On Human Communication* (1956).

Unfortunately, it soon became obvious that Chomsky's arguments against behavioristic formulations devastated the information theoretic-stochastic modeling views also, and the original proponents abandoned the position (see G.A. Miller, 1974). But the terminology is still current, largely because during this period the computer came into general use, and it seemed plausible to regard cognition as "information processing," and even to claim that the computer was an adequate model of human cognitive processes (e.g., Newell, Shaw, & Simon, 1958; Simon, 1969). But during this period, few theorists realized that the once precise concept of information was becoming an accordion, stretching this way and that to accommodate everything in sight, just as "association" or "habit" had been stretched by behaviorists. However, when confronted with a choice between an information processing approach to cognition, on one hand, and the only remaining behaviorist position, the radical behaviorism of Skinner, on the other, one can understand why sensory information processing became the dominant approach to cognitive psychology.

Is information-processing psychology any better than behaviorism? I think not, because it shares too much in common with its predecessor. A conceptually adequate psychology must make a sharper break with the past, and relearn many lessons that speech and communication theorists, especially rhetoricians, have known for a considerable time. One way to understand this is to examine the metatheoretical framework underlying both behaviorism and information processing approaches, which I have called the *sensory metatheory of mind* (Weimer, 1977). When we do so, it becomes clear that speech and communication (which must acknowledge the active, creative nature of man) cannot accept the sensory model provided by the information processors.

An introductory text by Mortensen (1972) typifies the problem facing the field. Mortensen wishes to defend the claim that: "incoming sensory data are not so much arranged and stamped into categories as they are amplified, selected, and transferred into patterns that fit the expectations of the individual. The notion of man as a detached bystander, an objective and dispassionate reader of the environment, is nothing more than a convenient artifact. Among living creatures man is the most spectacular example of an agent who amplifies his every activity" (pp. 17-18). The manner in which Mortensen defends this claim, however, is by marshalling a model of man based upon the sensory metatheory (largely in Chapter 3, entitled "Human Information Processing"). Let us first argue against the information processing approach by criticizing the sensory metatheory on which it is based and then outline a psychological model of man that can both defend Mortensen's claim, and unite psychology, speech, and communication.

THE SENSORY METATHEORY

A root metaphor of mind has evolved from looking at the world. Vision, conceived as the reception of information that both exists and possesses an intrinsic character independently of the organism, has been the paradigm of mental processes. Similarly, behavior or motor activity has been a consequence that follows from sensory (or mental) events. In great oversimplification, the sensory metatheory holds that the mental or cognitive domain involves the classical sensory component of the nervous system, and has nothing to do with the motor component. Cognition is thus "nothing but" sensory information processing. Consider this statement by Ulric Neisser in his famous textbook, *Cognitive Psychology* (1967):

> The term "cognition" refers to all the processes by which the sensory input is transformed, reduced, elaborated, stored, recovered, and used. It is concerned with these processes even when they operate in the absence of relevant stimulation, as in images and hallucinations. Such terms as *sensation*, *perception*, *imagery*, *retention*, *recall*, *problem solving*, and *thinking*, among many others, refer to hypothetical stages or aspects of cognition. . . . The organization of this book follows a sequence which is logically implied by the [above] definition. . . . It follows stimulus information "inward" from the organs of sense, through many transformations and reconstructions, through to eventual use in memory and thought. (pp. 4, vii)

Note that one never gets beyond sensory processing to behavior: Neisser has no discussion of behavior or skilled performance at all.[2]

This conception is so unquestioned by information processors that it is assumed to be uncontroversial matter-of-fact. Consider this book review comment:

> When stimulation is first presented to the mind, it is automatically acted upon by the system in a series of stages. At each stage features are abstracted and used for subsequent stages of abstraction. Thus, a word presented visually may be encoded in features first representing areas of dark and light, then lines, angles, shapes, and so on, then letters, then letter groups, then words coded linguistically and semantically, then synonyms and associates, then the overall context or situation in which the word appears. . . . The features that are abstracted are placed in the short-term memory store, where they may be used by the subject. . . . Eventually some portion of this information in short-term memory is transferred to, and stored in, long-term memory and the coding process is complete. (Shiffrin, 1973, p. 400)

Such views implicitly assume that cognition is to be understood "from the outside inward," that it is a matter of structuring and restructuring sensory information by sensory systems, and that only then is cognition somehow married to action (which is not assumed to be a cognitive phenomenon). And perhaps most important, these are constructive theorists who emphasize the active nature of the cognizing organism, in contrast to passive, empty organism stimulus-response models such as behaviorism. The communalities within the sensory metatheory far outweigh the differences, and even the change from behaviorism to information processing is minor when one looks at the essentially unchanged framework in which it occurred.

We can sketch the communalities in sensory approaches by outlining three problem areas that have been addressed by both behaviorists and sensory information processors: (1) perception and the nature of stimulus information; (2) concept formation and creativity; (3) memory and the utilization of stored "information." These three topics are enough to show that, despite their surface differences, both approaches represent the same metatheory.

Perception and Stimulus Information

Classic behaviorism presumed that stimuli were physically specifiable independently of the organism. The retreat from classic to neobehaviorism acknowledged the abstract nature of the stimulus, and the functional versus physical distinction arose. Thus, by 1966 Bourne (1966) defined the "stimulus" in concept learning as a relational concept. With such admissions, behaviorism became just as abstract as its "cognitive" successors. Where is any revolutionary difference between the information processor and behaviorist when both acknowledge that the informational basis of perception is abstract?

Concept Formation and Creativity

Behaviorism borrowed an ancient philosophical doctrine, the subtractive theory of abstraction, for its theory of concept formation and productivity (see Cassirer, 1953; Weimer, 1973). This position asserts that what is "learned" in concept formation are new combinations of old, already available elements. Thus, the behaviorist's account of creativity is that genuine creativity is nonexistent. All that can occur is relative creativity in new combinations of old (stimulus or response) "elements." But is the information processor's account fundamentally different? Recall the quotations from Neisser and Shiffrin and it will be obvious that, like the behaviorist, they assume a specifiable population of initial stimulus "elements" which are subsequently "processed." Thus, their account of creativity, even after the transformational revolution in linguistics, fails to address the problem, except in terms of the combination and recombination (although the terminology is now "transformation and retransformation") of sensory "information." The "constructive" information processor is no different from the behaviorist on this point.

Memory and The Utilization of "Stored" Information

Classic behaviorism proposed that what was learned and what was remembered were enduring entities that were "stored," in some specifiable sense, in the organism. The cognitive revolution has abandoned the storage of surface structure "elements" in favor of the storage of deep structural rules for the generation of elements (see Neisser, 1967, Chapter 11, where he defends the reconstructive "utilization hypothesis" against the earlier "reappearance hypothesis"). But such an approach lands Neisser with strange bedfellows: radical behaviorists such as Skinner. Here is a recent comment of Skinner's (1974) in this regard: "The metaphor of storage in memory . . . has caused a great deal of trouble. The computer is a bad model . . . (it is not the behaviorist incidentally, but the cognitive psychologist, with his computer-model of the mind, who represents man as a machine)" (p. 110). Skinner has even become a constructive theorist in his dotage. One can hardly imagine a more characteristic constructive slogan than "seeing does not imply something seen," yet Skinner (1969) is in complete agreement: "A man need not copy the stimulating environment in order to perceive it, and he need not make a copy in order to perceive it in the future. When an organism exposed to a set of contingencies of reinforcement is modified by them and as a result behaves in a different way in the future, we do not need to say that it stores the contingencies. What is 'stored' is a modified organism, not a record of the modifying variables" (p. 274).

These issues (and others) will recur throughout subsequent discussions, but for now they are illustrative of the point of this section: seemingly disparate theoretical formulations, especially when the theorists involved want to distantiate their positions from their opposition, may nonetheless be identical or quite similar on crucial points because they are variants of the same metatheory.

I have elaborated some aspects of sensory theories in psychology elsewhere (Weimer, 1977), and that account must substitute for our lack of discussion here. Below we will characterize the sensory approach obliquely, criticizing it in comparison to a more adequate metatheory. For the present, consider the position as underlying the remarks quoted from Mortensen, in light of the discussion above. It is not a strawman, but without a doubt the dominant position in speech and communication.

TOWARD AN ADEQUATE CONSTRUCTIVE PSYCHOLOGY: THE MOTOR METATHEORY[3]

Consider another conception of the functioning of the nervous system and the cognitive capacities that result from it. Consider the nervous system as fundamentally motoric in nature, such that both the traditional "motor" nervous system (which generates behavior through the muscles) and the "sensory" systems are generative, constructive systems which create both their own input and output. Startling as it may seem, this is what the voluminous neurophysiological data indicate (e.g., Eccles, 1970, 1973; Hayek, 1952b; Penfield, 1975; Pribram, 1971a, 1971b; Sperry, 1969). This conception requires us to abandon the program of analysis "from the outside in" of the sensory metatheory in favor of one which attempts to unravel how the "inside" generates both itself, our knowledge of the world, and action upon it. What was assumed to be relatively unproblematically given (sensory "information") is actually a motoric construction generated by the nervous system, and indeed everything we can know, experience, or do, results from the nervous system's ability to structure and restructure its own activity. The communality of otherwise diverse skills, such as acting, perceiving, communicating, and comprehending is simply that they are all skills of the functioning nervous system. Cognitive psychology is simply that discipline which studies how the nervous system manifests its skill in the (so-called) higher mental processes.

Cognition as Skilled Action

Consider the changes that result in our model of man when the motor metatheory is employed. We can see the flavor of the approach by examining various problem areas common to speech and psychology: (1) thinking, (2) concept formation, (3) memory, (4) comprehension, (5) knowledge, (6) perception, (7) the nature of experience, (8) tacit knowledge, and (9) meaning.

Thought as skilled behavior. Bartlett (1958) made the basic point well: "Thinking is an advanced form of skilled behavior. . . . that has grown out of earlier established forms of flexible adaptation to the environment" (p. 199). The immense power of thought resides in its creativity or productivity (as the linguist uses those terms: making infinite use of finite means), which frees the thinker who employs symbolic systems from the momentary environment. "The skills of the body are attached to the demands of the world of the moment, but thinking can meet those far away in any direction and even those which have no time or place. And because, now, body movement is supplemented by signs and symbols—all the varied media of its expression which thinking can employ—the thinker is in a position to attain a vast increase in the range and delicacy of his adaptability" (Bartlett, p. 200). Man *generates* his environment by thinking about it symbolically rather than merely responding to it (in behavioristic fashion) or elaborating its input (in information processing). The ability to conceptualize is a skill of the nervous system that far exceeds the mere amplification or selection of sensory data.

Concept formation and creativity. Concept formation emphasizes the problem of productivity. The number of experienced particulars (or sensory presentations) required to learn the simplest concepts is indefinitely large. To know a concept is to be able to apply it appropriately to totally novel instances. Each of us possesses the ability (both trivial and presently inexplicable) to exhaustively categorize everything in the universe as either a "face" or "nonface." But how do we come to know faces (or triangles, or behaviorists)? The problem is analogous to that of productivity in language, but the focus is upon comprehension rather than production.

We have no answer, in the form of an explanatorily adequate theory, for creativity in either production or comprehension. Both skills are instances of what Polanyi (1958, 1966) felicitously called tacit knowledge. No explicit knowledge suffices to account for concept formation (or its limiting case of thing-kind identification, such as "recognizing" Δ as a triangle) or our utilization of novel utterances. The best accounts we have are modeled upon transformational linguistics, where productivity can at least be addressed by grammars which range over fundamentally abstract (and therefore not physically specifiable) entities and allow indefinite recursion in the derivation of surface structures from deep conceptual structures. Concepts appear to be similar, in that they can be adequately characterized only by the abstract rules of determination which are their grammar. Thus, there are no perceptual (or sensory) concepts at all.

What is "learned" in concept formation is never purely perceptual nor particular; it is instead the rules of determination that constitute the invariant relations in a group (in the mathematical, or symmetry theoretic sense (see Shaw & McIntyre, 1974; Shaw, McIntyre, & Mace, 1974). Our "perceptual" knowledge is based upon deep conceptual rules of "seeing" that determine invariance in the ambient array. No sensory experience, no matter how elaborated or transformed, is alone identical with any concept. The concept is invariably both the underlying rules of determination and the surface structure that is "experienced." Consider triangularity. What it constitutes is "any three sided (plane) figure the sum of whose interior angles is 180 degrees." Such a definition is not perceptual at all—instead it constitutes a recipe for conceiving perceptual "input" as instantiating triangularity.

Concept formation is thus productive, fundamentally abstract, and nonperceptual. Attempting to understand it in behavioristic terms, as a matter of learning (and the identical elements theory of transfer) results in the insoluable paradoxes Plato first called attention to in the *Meno* (see Weimer, 1973). Relabeling it as information that is somehow repackaged by sensory systems ignores both its nonperceptual nature (which was quite clear to Cassirer [1953] long ago) and the abstractness of its rules of determination. The only framework that can even address these aspects of concept formation is the motor one.

Memory and the representation of information. The sensory approach proposes that memory is a matter of storage and retrieval of items previously learned or associated by some habit mechanism. For information processors, the terminology is very fancy but it amounts to the initial encoding of input, its storage (in frozen form in some deepfreeze in the brain), and subsequent retrieval (see Neisser, 1967; Melton & Martin, 1972). Unfortunately, the storage metaphor is not ecologically valid. Unless one is forced to rote memorize material à la Ebbinghaus it has no application. Our normal memory, for conversation, the affairs of everyday life, and so forth, is not storage at all, but the active subsumption of information to a context which renders it comprehensible. Memory is a matter of the active, ongoing modulation of information to provide a meaningful gestalt, rather than the retrieval of items (no matter how abstractly construed). No one has demonstrated this more effectively than Bransford and his associates (see Bransford & Franks, 1971; Bransford & Johnson, 1972; Branford & McCarrell, 1974; Bransford, McCarrell, Franks, & Nitsch, 1977). Bransford's research indicates that "input" (or information, etc.) will be remembered if it can be assimilated into a meaningful context but will be ignored otherwise. This makes memory a problem for comprehension rather than "stimulus encoding," and renders storage virtually nonexistent. Faced with an involved utterance pertaining to the imminent arrival of a magistrate, we do not store it—rather we understand it by abstracting the gist of it, and subsequently we will paraphrase it as "here come da judge," despite the fact that that is not what the "input" was. We don't store information at all (that is done by the environment, by libraries, signs, river beds, etc.); we assimilate it to our ongoing conceptual framework. That is, we *comprehend* information: "Our approach to comprehension focuses on the comprehender's ability to use his general knowledge to create situations that permit the relations specified in input sentences to be realized, or to postulate situations (e.g., instigating forces) that allow perceptual events to be understood. In short, the ability to create some level of semantic content sufficient to achieve a click of comprehension depends upon the comprehender's ability to think" (Bransford & McCarrell, 1974, p. 220).

Comprehension and the nature of knowledge. Comprehension indispensibly involves the assimilation of information to a conceptual context. That process utilizes and manifests *knowledge*, not memory in the sense of retrieved information. One does not remember his name, the place of his birth, or even "facts," such as that there are 12 inches in a foot: rather, one *knows* such things. But what is knowledge, and how is it acquired?

Perhaps the most cogent account we possess is due to Piaget's voluminous research and writings. Piaget's genetic epistemology is a motor theoretic approach: Piaget holds that the child comes to know the world and remember its objects in terms of actions upon that world, rather than in terms of passively noticing relations among objects. Knowing is adapting to the environment in a biological sense. To know is to do. What our knowledge consists of is skilled activities, such as being able to speak and comprehend, act upon our goals and desires, and so forth. Knowledge is not static, something stored in a computer or in a library—rather it is the ability to use information (and much more) in our commerce with the environment and other persons. To relate knowing to speech communication, all knowledge is a matter of making claims, that is, argument in favor of an assertion (a proposition to the philosopher). Knowing is intrinsically arguing: a suasory and inherently rhetorical occurrence. This is one area in which psychologists could learn much from the current school (as Arnold, 1972, dubbed it) which claims that rhetoric is a way of knowing. But it is not simply that rhetoric is one way of knowing. Rather, all knowledge is gained by rhetorical interaction. The history of science and methodology of research is replete with accounts that support that position, and it is informative to study Kuhn (1970a, 1970b), Hanson (1958, 1970), Feyerabend (1965, 1970a, 1970b), and other methodologists in that light. But to return to the main point, knowing as a generative process is a motoric activity. Because knowledge usually connotes static or fixed objects that are somehow stored in the organism, it is not surprising that Piaget speaks of the processes of adaptation and the exhibition of intelligence rather than knowledge: "With increasing adaptation in mental development the undifferentiated matrix of organism-in-environment becomes structured into organism-knows-environment. The structure that is thus built up is intelligence, considered as the general framework within which we know the world" (Furth, 1969, p. 181). This means that sensation or input alone cannot constitute knowledge. Indeed, there must be a structure (or schema) within the organism to which input can be assimilated (or accommodated) or it will not even lead to knowledge. Contrast this to the information processing assumptions of Neisser, Shiffrin, and Mortensen quoted earlier.

The nature of perception. Instead of involving the sensory encoding of independently specifiable stimulus input, perception is a motoric activity, in the sense that experience within a modality results from the involvement of the same neurophysiological apparatus that is involved in producing (as sender, rather than receiver) that information. One may begin to see what is involved by considering the theory of speech perception that has developed (largely at Haskins Laboratories) in the last three decades. What that theory has come to assume is that: "*Underlying the experience of language at the phonological level, in every form of language use, are processes which are basically identical to the motor coordination processes involved in speaking, with the motor commands being in someway inhibited in all cases but that of overt speech*" (Halwes & Wire, 1974, p. 386). Speech perception appears to utilize the same neural machinery that is involve in speaking. If we could not speak a language, we would not be able to experience speech.

This general form of account can explain how we perceive any skilled action that we can perform. Touch, taste, and the experienced aspects of locomotion through the environment presumably involve the motor command systems involved in touching, tasting, and locomoting. In such cases it is easy to construe the systems involved as production systems; however, the classic distance senses such as vision, which do not seem to be production systems, require more comment. With the exception of imagery and hallucination, we do not produce visual experience the way we do speech or locomotion. Is there any plausible account of visual experience as a motoric phenomenon?

Once again the answer is yes when we look at the neurophysiological data. The question to ask is "What determines visual perceptual experience when input is received?" A quarter of a century ago, Sperry (1952) provided the answer: "If there be any objectively demonstrable fact about perception . . . it is the following: insofar as an organism perceives a given object, it is prepared to respond with reference to it. This preparation-to-respond is absent in an organism that has failed to perceive . . . The presence or absence of adaptive reaction potentialities of this sort, ready to discharge into motor patterns, makes the difference between perceiving and not perceiving'' (p. 301). The point to note is that input (sensory information) to the visual system is one thing, and the conscious, or experiential, aspect of perception is another. In the absence of appropriate motor activity, what Sperry characterized as a preparation-to-respond, there will be no experience even though input to the retina is present. Festinger and his associates have experimented with contrasting the effects of motor expectation (called ''efferent readiness'' in the literature) with actual visual input, and found that perceptual experience follows expectation rather than input (Festinger, Burnham, Ono, & Bamber, 1967). Startling as it may seem, a line will be seen as either straight or curved depending upon the expectation (motor commands) established rather than the actual shape. It is not that perception is independent of all input, a matter of pure hallucination; it is the case that conscious experience depends crucially on the efferent command, the readiness to respond, rather than the retinal stimulation. This merely demonstrates, at the level of contour perception, what has been obvious to philosophers and dramatists for a long time: what we perceive in a situation is determined by our prior expectations. By the time one progresses from ''simple'' visual phenomena to person perception and social interaction it should not be surprising that the biases and expectations of one's audience are a more potent determiner of ''what is said and done'' than one's actual words and actions. Visual experience, like speech perception, is a matter of comprehension—when the click of understanding occurs in either, it is only because the perceiver has assimilated the input into a context that is meaningful and prepared for. If the perceiver cannot render input meaningful in terms of his conceptual framework (prior knowledge and present expectation), it will not be ''seen'' at all. Small wonder, then, that models of social interaction based upon ''objectively specified stimuli'' or stimulus ''information'' are so often contradictory or unreplicable: the variables the experimenter is manipulating are only of marginal importance to his subject's perceptions.

We have discussed vision primarily because it has been assumed to be the stronghold of the sensory approach. But it should be obvious that this is an expository strategy only. Wherever human experience is meaningful, one will find exactly the motor command preparation-to-respond that Sperry emphasized in the case of vision. Our experience is meaningful only because we are prepared for it, and one can as easily speak of ''tactile readiness'' or ''olfactory readiness.'' Philosophers have delighted in citing examples. ''Gratiolet relates that when two medical students were engaged in dissection, one playfully passed the handle of his scalpel across the fingers of his friend, who started, shrieked, and then, laughing at his error, confessed that he felt the pain of the blade cutting through to the bone'' (Lewes, 1879, p. 279). There is also the familiar phenomenon that a putrid, slightly nauseating smell suddenly becomes delectable when it is labeled ''limburger cheese.'' Such examples, which are common in all the perceptual modalities, are well catalogued in Chapter 19 of William James's (1890) classic *The Principles of Psychology*. Such illustrations point out that the rules which define meaningful experience are both context sensitive and define what *ought* to be rather than what *is* the case. To presage our discussion below, meaningful perception is a matter of contractual obligation, and both are motoric phenomena.

The sensory order. Since no sensory theory can even begin to address data such as Festinger's, or plausibly handle motor constructions such as imagery and hallucination, it would appear that the motor theory framework rules by default in the domain of perception. The motor metatheory also addresses one other area by default: the sensory order and the problem of the modality of our experiences. Why should sights be sights, or sounds be sounds, or within the visual mode, why should reds be red? These are the problems of the sensory order.

First, an epistemological disclaimer must be stated: The absolute quality of experience is not within the bounds of human inquiry; all we can intelligibly discuss is whether different sensory qualities differ in the same way for different individuals. As Hayek (1952b) put it in *The Sensory Order*: ''Nothing can become a problem about sensory qualities which cannot in principle also be described in words; and such description in words will always have to be description in terms of the relation of the quality in question to other sensory qualities'' (p. 31).

But how can the existence of sensory qualities be accounted for in terms of neural functioning? For some time, we have known that it is not due to the receptors (e.g., a blow on the head or electrical brain stimulation will cause visual sensation), nor to the central termination of the neural impulses (there is only minimal localization), nor to any properties unique to the various sensory pathways. If there is no anatomical localization unique to the sensory orders, there must be a functional one, or all experience would be qualitatively identical (which is to say, ambiguous). By abandoning anatomical localization, Hayek provided the only answer compatible with known neural functioning: the sensory orders result from the patterns of impulses and activity within the central nervous system. ''The sensory order (or other mental) qualities are not in some manner originally attached to, or an original attribute of, the individual physiological impulses, but . . . the whole of these qualities is determined by the system of connexions by which the impulses can be transmitted. It is thus the position of the individual impulse or group of impulses in the whole system of such connexions which gives it its distinctive quality'' (Hayek, 1952b, p. 53).

Experience versus knowledge. At this point it may be wise to make another philosophical excursus to point out that experience and knowledge, like experience and stimulus input, are two quite different things. Knowledge is conceptual; it is not, and can never be, experiential. We can have knowledge *of* experience, but that knowledge is itself not experiential. We can make the point by introducing Bertrand Russell's (1948) distinction between *acquaintance* and *description*. We ''know'' experience, what is given in the sensory orders, by being acquainted with it while we undergo it. Knowledge, of the sort disclosed by both science and enlightened common sense, is not acquaintance but description. We are never acquainted with the properties of scientific or theoretical entities—we know them entirely by propositions asserting their structural properties by description. Maxwell (1968, 1970) has put this by comparing science, as a search for structural relations known by description, to a detective story, in which an unknown culprit is identified solely by description but is not personally known to the other characters (until the denouement, when someone says ''I know him! That's John Smith, the butler!''). Proper names indicate that someone is acquainted with the person, rather than knowing him only in terms of descriptions (e.g., walks with a limp, is six feet tall, etc.). Science has no proper names. No scientific researcher ever concludes, ''And that's how I met Paula Proton.'' The information that science discloses about the *nonmental* realm is entirely structural and therefore divorced from phenomenal experience. We can know vastly more than we can experience only because knowledge is not linked to (or limited by) experience. We can conceive of and comprehend propositions such as ''light is the limiting velocity of stable objects in the universe,'' or ''protons are more massive than electrons,'' despite the fact that they can never be experienced perceptually. Indeed we never ''experience'' anything external to our own mental realm. What we take to be perceptible qualities of external objects are actually properties of our own mental life (see Russell, 1948; Maxwell, 1968, 1970, 1972; Weimer, 1973, 1975).

Thus, somewhat paradoxically, it is physical science and epistemology, rather than psychology, which guarantee that all experience is a construction in the mind of man. The ''input'' to a percipient being consists in structural properties of objects and events in the ambient array, but what one experiences is the ''raw feels'' of phenomenal acquaintance. To take vision as an example, the color of objects is due solely to the wavelength of reflected light that reaches our retinae. Even if the object itself, or the light rays themselves, were of a particular color, it would not matter—the hue we see is due to wavelength only. All the sights, sounds, feels, smells, tastes, and other sensations which we commonly attribute to external objects result from our nervous systems' responses to those objects rather than the objects themselves. In that sense, it is always a truism that our experience of the world is a construction of the nervous system of man.

On the other side of the coin, there definitely is

an informational basis for our perceptual experience. The information from the ambient array is, in itself, sufficient to specify our experience. Perception results when the senses, as perceptual systems in Gibson's (1966) sense, pick up the information (available at a station point) in an ambient array.

Gibson argues that the pickup of information that the perceptual systems perform is not a constructive activity that utilizes memorial or inferential processes. By contrast, the sensory information processor often argues that cognition performs a task that would literally be miraculous—constructing meaning from meaningless "snippets" of stimulus input. Consider Gregory's (1972) claim: "Perceptions are constructed, by complex brain processes, from fleeting fragmentary scraps of data signalled by the senses and drawn from the brain's memory banks—themselves constructions from snippets of the past" (p. 707). From the fact that experience is a construction in the nervous system, one cannot conclude that the information upon which perception is based consists of meaningless "snippets" (see Mace, 1974, 1977). Meaningful perception (which is to say, understanding) results when information from the perceptual systems is assimilated to the abstract pattern of neural activity which is our ongoing "knowledge of the world," and although that assimilation is a constructive process (in several senses), it is not a miraculous process. All this leads to an important point: despite the fact that all experience is a construction, the highly abstract, ecologically significant information which we perceive from our environment is picked up directly, without the mediation of symbolic or constructive activities such as images or inferences. Structural realism makes the first claim plausible, Gibson's "direct" realism makes the second equally plausible.

Tacit knowledge. All experience is both a construction and meaningful. A "meaningless experience" is a purely conceptual notion which, like "square circle," can never occur in the reality of human existence. Why must this be the case? The answer to that question poses an enormous problem for psychology: it is because of the pervasive presence of tacit knowledge that there can be no meaningless experience, and tacit knowledge labels a problem to be solved rather than providing any solution. Experience, as we have noted, is a construction of the nervous system that is dependent upon the patterning of activity relative to the background in the system. Only a tiny portion of that activity ever becomes conscious, or registers in our experience. What does finally reach conscious levels (Polanyi's explicit awareness) is totally dependent upon prior tacit processing. All meaning in experience is thus created by prior acts of classification and reclassification that must be tacit.

An experiment by Worthington (1964) shows that tacit meaning precedes any conscious awareness. Worthington had dark-adapted subjects seated in a black room view a designated area in which they were told a dim white light would appear. Ostensibly the experiment had to do with the time course of adaptation. All the subjects had to do was report when they first saw the light by pressing a button as soon as they saw anything in the designated area. Unknown to the subjects, the stimulus was a disc with a word printed on it in black, and the words employed were either obscene or geometrically similar neutral ones. Button pressing latency is considerably longer for those trials in which obscene words are on the disc. But the thing to note is that while the semantic status of the word determined latency, no subject ever reported seeing anything in the white disc.

Although the Worthington study is particularly tantalizing, there are numerous others that show the primacy of tacit over explicit knowing, awareness, and meaning. Michael Turvey (1974) put the problem they pose clearly: "The question we should ask of all these experiments is: How can 'higher-order' properties of stimulation, such as symmetry and familiarity and meaning, affect the identification of 'lower-order' properties from which the 'higher-order' properties are apparently derived?" (p. 175). The answer, of course, is that the apparent order is incorrect. It is the sensory theorist who proposes that meaning is "added" to the "lower-order" properties of stimulation (by an as yet undisclosed and miraculous process). Turvey's counter-proposal is an endorsement of Gibson's notion that tacit processing is relatively direct, a matter of the pickup of the affordance structure of events in the ambient array. While this is no doubt correct, it labels a problem to be tackled rather than states any solution. At present, the problems of tacit knowledge are an insurmountable stumbling block for all of psychology. While it is easy to see the absurdity of the sensory information processing approach in this domain, it is clear that available alternatives (such as Gibson's ecological approach to perception) are at best descriptions rather than explanations. And it should be noted that information, as Gibson uses the term, refers to something which is not *experienced* by the organism.

The point to be stressed, however, is that the motor theory framework at least enables one to address the problems of the tacit dimension in a noncontradictory manner. For the sensory theorist who must add meaning and understanding in a last processing step, studies such as Worthington's are all but unintelligible, and the only recourse available is to deny the data. But the data, which are literally everywhere, are undeniable, and that ostrich-like approach will not work for long. On the other hand, if knowledge and meaning are motoric processes, exhibitions of the skills of the nervous system in structuring and restructuring its own activity, then the data are no longer inconceivable, even though they remain presently inexplicable.

And what about meaning? At this point it would be delightful to pull the rabbit out of the hat by delivering the goods on "and this is what meaning is, and how it works." Unfortunately I am not about to do so—meaning is the most difficult problem that we have failed to face in the last several millennia. I can hardly improve upon these earlier caustic remarks:

> There is only one problem that has ever existed in psychology, and everything the field has investigated is merely a manifestation of that problem, a different aspect of the same elephant, an elephant that we have grasped at since the dawn of reflective thought without ever reaching at all. "This problem has many names. In the language of behaviorism, it is a matter of stimulus generalization or of stimulus equivalence. In the terminology of Gestalt psychology, it is the problem of contact between perceptual processes and memory trace: the so-called 'Höffding step.' Among philosophers, the question is usually formulated in terms of 'universals' and of 'abstraction from particulars.' For Bruner and his associates, it is the problem of categorization. In computer technology, it is called 'character recognition' when only letters and numbers are to be identified, or more generally 'pattern recognition' " (Neisser, 1967, p. 47). The problem, "When are stimuli equivalent?", *is* the problem of stimulus recognition, which *is* the problem of concept formation, *ad infinitum*, all of which together constitute the problems of meaning. Stimuli are equivalent, in the final analysis, only because they mean the same thing. No matter where one goes in psychology there comes a point at which one runs straight into an insurmountable wall that is, conceptually speaking, infinitely high and wide. All we can do is look up and see that written on that wall are all the problems of the manifestations of meaning. (Weimer, 1974, 427-429)

We can say little if anything about what meaning is. That issue, like the absolute nature of sensory qualities, is beyond the bounds of inquiry. But we can say a little about how it is manifested, and here again it is easy to criticize earlier accounts. Classic behaviorism, for example, thought of meaning as an internal response that could function as a stimulus for further responses (Osgood's semantic differential is based upon this idea). Other traditional accounts attempted to identify meaning with some other *thing*, and preferably a very concrete one, such as images, the favorite of associationist philosophers. The information processor often refers to meanings as constructions from sensory snippets, as in the Gregory quotation. This notion is quite parallel to the linguist's attempt to treat meaning in terms of abstract (and quite implausible) entities called features, which somehow "add up" to miraculously yield meanings. The problem for such static accounts is *context sensitivity*: the same "response" or "image" or "snippet" or "feature" can be meaningful or meaningless depending upon its context. Meaning and comprehension require a context-sensitive specification that just is not found in "sensory" psychology.

The problem that forces context sensitivity upon psychology is ambiguity. In order to understand, or know the meaning of objects or events (such as an utterance, a person's behavior, or a perceptual experience), we must be able to disambiguate the information with which we are presented. Linguists have often faced the problem, and the transformational grammarian's distinctions between lexical item, surface, and deep structural ambiguity are helpful. Some lexical items have multiple meanings, as "port" in, "The sailors love the port." Here we need a context, providing information about either a seaport or wine, to know to which the word refers. Surface structure ambiguities require a knowledge of how the utterance is to be parsed. Consider, "They are flying planes." This can mean either those persons are flying or those objects are in fact flying planes. Again, in context, there is no difficulty in comprehension. But there is also deep structural ambiguity, which was unknown (although it occurs all the time) prior to Chomsky's revolution in linguistics. Consider, "Flying planes can be dangerous." Here the ambiguity cannot be resolved by understanding a lexical item or parsing the constituents. One must know the derivational history of the utterance, from deep conceptual structures to surface items, in order to disambiguate it. This description of the problem (and that's all it is) shows that deep structural ambiguity is a conceptual problem. One thing or object is simultaneously two (or more) things at once. What has become obvious since the transformational revolution is that literally everything is deep structurally ambiguous, and the only reason why we are not overwhelmed by ambiguity is because we automatically supply a context which renders one interpretation so plausible that we never even conceive of alternatives.

The history of science is a case study in deep structural ambiguity. Literally every scientific revolution has overturned one conceptual perspective on a domain in favor of another. Consider Hanson's (1958) beautiful description of the difference between a Ptolemaic and a Galilean sunrise:

> If in the brilliant disc of which he is visually aware Tycho sees only the sun, then he cannot but see that it is a body which will behave in characteristically "Tychonic" ways. These serve as the foundation for Tycho's general geocentric-geostatic theories about the sun. . . . Tycho sees the sun beginning its journey from horizon to horizon. He sees that from some celestial vantage point the sun (carrying with it the moon and planets) could be watched circling our fixed earth. Watching the sun at dawn through Tychonic spectacles would be to see it in something like this way. Kepler's visual field, however, has a different conceptual organization. Yet a drawing of what he sees at dawn could be a drawing of exactly what Tycho saw, and could be recognized as such by Tycho. But Kepler will see the horizon dipping, or turning away, from our fixed local star (p. 23).

One can study Kuhn (1970b, 1974) and other methodologists for numerous examples in science in which the phenomena (at least their reference), are not in doubt but their interpretation (intension or sense) is. Scientific concept formation, like that in everyday life, is always an effort to grasp meaning.

Psychology texts are replete with examples from the perceptual domain also. One need only consider the Necker cube, or the Peter-Paul Goblet, to literally "see" one entity which can be interpreted as two different and incompatible phenomena. And it should be obvious by now that the motor metatheory is a conceptual alternative to traditional thought about the psychological domain that shows psychology is deep structurally ambiguous.

Applications of the Motor Metatheory: Meaning as Contractual Obligation

What sort of psychology can address the problems of context sensitivity and ambiguity? The recent research on comprehension by Bransford and his collaborators suggests one possibility. Comprehension, the ability to render incoming information meaningful, is basically the skill of resolving (or ignoring) ambiguity. To comprehend is to disambiguate, and much of Bransford's research consists in demonstration that if a subject is given an appropriate context he can understand virtually anything, remember it easily, and so forth. Conversely, even readily intelligible input is incomprehensible if one's expectations go against it when supplied the wrong context.

This leads to a new analogy or metaphor for meaning as a motoric process. Meaning (as a phenomenal experience) results from the activity of comprehending, and its exhibition is an indication of the craftsmanship or skill of the comprehender. *Craftsmanship* is the root metaphor of the cognitive processes in the motor theoretic framework. The motor theory asserts that the manifestation of meaning is a product of the skill of the nervous system, instanced in every act of either the reception of information or the production of behavior. Meaning thus becomes the underlying interrelationship of all the higher mental processes, manifested in each but not identifiable with any single one of them.

Context, however, is not the ultimate determiner of comprehension: there are higher order constraints that determine when a given context will or will not produce certain effects. Proffitt (1976) called such constraints *contracts*, and the determining factor in the effects of context *contractual obligation*. Contractual obligation is a matter of the perceiver coming to treat incoming information as bound up within a contract which specifies what contexts are appropriate for use in the assimilation of subsequent information. Contractual obligation is not just a larger context, but an obligatory framework: contracts define the way things are by specifying how they ought to be.

How should (note the modal term) one study contracts? One way has been available for a long time. Drama and the theater provide explicit examples of the contractual obligation set up between a playwright and his audience, and thus the dramatistic perspective can be informative. How one interprets, say, an art form such as a play, depends upon the manner in which one is led to treat the happenings upon a stage. We readily admit, for example, a poorly hung curtain is "really" a wall in the context of a play, but moments afterward it is nothing but a stage prop. One *participates* in a play in a very different way from what one does in just being in a theater or sitting in an audience. We are contractually obligated to accept certain contexts and ignore others, because that is what the playwright has specified *must be the case*.

Kenneth Burke's voluminous writings are equally good dramatic criticism, rhetoric, and psychology, and his lifelong study of symbolic form is largely a study of the manner in which contracts are manifested. It would be wise to study the aesthetic spectrum from his perspective, because "art is the dial on which fundamental psychological processes of *all* living are recorded" (Burke, 1959, p. 202). As one example of how Burke's dramatistic analysis relates to the current conception of meaning as determined by contractual obligation, consider this remark in *Counter Statement*, published nearly 50 years ago: "From a few speeches of Falstaff, for instance, we advance unconsciously to a synthesis of Falstaff; and thereafter, each time he appears on the stage, we know what to expect of him in essence, or quality, and we enjoy the poet's translation of this essence, or quality, into particulars, or quantity." (1968, p. 61) Analyses from the dramatistic and rhetorical perspective, even though they are "old hat" and "unscientific" to communication theorists who prefer to talk of the encoding and decoding of message units (with or without transactional analysis, interpersonal relations, etc.) are much more likely to be of lasting value to our understanding of meaning and its manifestations. At least those perspectives allow one to talk about skill, and the rhetorical and argumentative dimensions of comprehending, meaning, and communicating, which cannot be done in the scientistic perspectives of behaviorism and computerese.

From my perspective, the most obvious problem with the accounts of meaning in sensory approaches to communication centers around the all but universal assumption that meaning is an entity which is carried or conveyed from a sender to a receiver in some medium, such as language (speech). One receives the impression that man is particularly gifted at both transmitting meanings and constructing "richer" meanings from impoverished input (recall Mortenson and Gregory, quoted above). One should ask of this approach how language "carries" meaning, and how the perceiver "enriches" it. Once one steps outside the sensory framework, however, it becomes obvious that these questions are inappropriate, for *there is neither meaning nor knowledge in language*. Language does not carry meaning, it triggers or releases it in the perceiver. Unless a perceiver can generate a context which renders input (linguistic, visual, or other) comprehensible, that input has no meaning at all. Consider the parallel to the problem of finding meanings in a dictionary. Usually, we assume that the meanings of words are listed in a dictionary, but minimal reflection indicates that is not the case. If one were not already familiar with "what and how words mean" in human conceptualization, it would not be possible to use a dictionary: there are no meanings in dictionaries, only paraphrases. Meaning is in the comprehender, or thinker, who uses the dictionary, and it is not the sort of thing which is conveyed by language (or the dictionary) but rather is presupposed by it. We don't convey meaning, we trigger it in the conceptual framework of like-minded beings who attempt to comprehend what we have in mind. Communication could not carry meaning for the simple reason that all that can be "communicated" is inherently ambiguous. The pervasive presence of ambiguity guarantees that comprehension will be a triggering of meanings within the perceiver rather than the conveyance of packaged meanings to him. In this regard, man is a far more gifted constructive device than the mere information processor and elaborator envisaged by the sensory theorist.

What is the source of meaning in the perceiver? We don't know, and the answer can only emerge when the domain of pragmatics and intentionality, which is the framework for all human action (and hence communication) is explored. There is an obvious heirarchical structuring of domains relevant to the understanding of man that is informative in this regard (Morris, 1939). Morris distinguished *syntactic* study, *semantics*, and *pragmatics*. One can study syntactic structuring in relative isolation, so long as one is not concerned with the semantic content of the structures in question (thus Chomsky was correct to assert that syntax is "independent" of semantics, at least in this one sense). But studying semantic phenomena requires simultaneous syntactic study and presupposes pragmatics. Understanding of semantic fundamentals, however, requires understanding pragmatics. Psychology and the other human "sciences" will not advance very far without a thorough grounding in pragmatics, and until we are at that point it will be fruitless to speculate on how meaning is intrinsic to the human existential predicament. All we presently know is that it is so.

PSYCHOLOGY AND THE RHETORICAL NATURE OF MAN

Much of our discussion has been negative, emphasizing what we don't know and what is obviously wrong in popular approaches. We can end this chapter on a more promising, if still promissory, note by considering some obvious interrelationships of cognition and communication in the area of rhetoric. Consider contractual obligation and meaning as a rhetorical phenomenon. The participation in a contract is rhetorical and suasory: we present information to ourselves through contracts which define the way events and experiences ought to be. Thus, when one comprehends meaning in his experience, it involves advocating contractually specified relationships within what may be called the argumentative mode of behavior. To comprehend (meaning) is to argue for it: understanding is always advocacy.

One can see this clearly in cases of deception. Consider entering a room with a desk upon which are familiar appearing articles such as paper, pens, and so forth. If one were to hold up a yellow, cylindrical object and ask "What is this?" the reply would be "It's a pencil." Pressed for his reasoning in such an identification, a subject would no doubt say, "Well, it's shaped like a pencil, sharpened like one, says No. 2 pencil on the side, has an eraser, etc." If I were then to show him that it fails to write on paper, bends flexibly in my fingers, and so forth, or perhaps chewed it and then blew a bubble, the subject would, with some embarrassment, reply "You tricked me: it looks like a pencil but it's really bubble gum." Why the embarrassment? Because in even the "simple" act of identification, we are advocating a position: the attribution of meaning is an argumentative process. Having, on the basis of the context, decided that the the object must be a pencil, we are surprised and then chagrined when it does not behave according to our expectations for pencils, for it is then obvious that our identification was erroneous. The possibility of deception, of erroneous identification and interpretation of our experiences, is both the strongest possible support for the constructive nature of experience and the motor theoretic approach to cognition, on the one hand; and the argumentative and suasory, hence rhetorical, nature of cognition, on the other hand. Psychology, no less than rhetoric, requires adequate conceptions of argumentation, advocacy, and audience. Indeed, it will require a detailed understanding of the entire rhetorical-conceptual transaction. Both fields will be necessary to specify the primitive concepts of each discipline.

We can make these points in somewhat more detail by considering two cases in which meaning is both contractually specified and rhetorically grounded: the nature of scientific theorizing and the perceptual demonstrations of Adelbert A. Ames. Consider theoretical understanding first.

To explain a phenomenon is to conjecture a tentative theory which argues that that phenomenon must occur, given the theory's correctness in picturing reality. All explanation is argument within a pragmatic context. Theories are arguments, and hence rhetorical and suasory, because they are conceptual points of view that organize observations (data) into meaningful patterns. Thus, they argue for a particular pattern, or way of seeing reality, by imposing a contractual obligation upon their advocates that the world must be seen in that way. The quotation from Hanson above about Tycho and Kepler makes this point well.

Explanatory science is thus intrinsically argumentative. Theories are always modal statements. They argue that reality must *of necessity* be the way they specify it to be. To reject a theory as incorrect is to admit that it has deceived us in its representation of reality, but one does not thereby obviate its modal force. Indeed, one can only reject one theory by endorsing the perspective of another. Thus, explanatory science is never merely descriptive; even to describe requires an interpretive framework that specifies contractual obligation.

But how is scientific knowledge communicated? In both communication between initiates and in the instruction of apprentices, science requires injunction, literally commends, rather than amodal description. Both scientific articles and research training enjoin their audience to experience reality correctly. G. Spencer Brown (1972) put this clearly:

> Natural science appears to be more dependent upon injunction than we are prepared to admit. The professional initiation of the man of science consists not so much in reading the proper textbooks, as in obeying injunctions such as "look down that microscope." But it is not out of order for men of science, having looked down the microscope, now to describe to each other, and to discuss amongst themselves, what they have seen, and to write papers and textbooks describing it. Similarly, it is not out of order for mathematicians, each having obeyed a given set of injunctions, to describe to each other, and to discuss amongst themselves, what they have seen, and to write papers and textbooks describing it. But in each case, the description is dependent upon, and secondary to, the set of injunctions having been obeyed first. (p. 78)

Understanding in science, on this account, is a matter of illustrating to ourselves the commands of the paradigm. The scientific report institutes contracts for the creation of meanings in our acquaintance:

> When we attempt to realize a piece of music composed by another person, we do so by *illustrating*, to ourselves, with a musical instrument of some kind, the composer's commands. Similarly, if we are to realize a piece of mathematics, we must find a way of illustrating, to ourselves, the commands of the mathematician. . . . In this report it is comparable with practical art forms like cookery, in which the taste of a cake, although literally indescribable, can be conveyed to a reader in the form of a set of injunctions called a recipe. (Spencer Brown, pp. 77-78)

Thus, in science, the meaning of objects and events is defined by the contractual obligations which those objects and events ought to have, given the theory in which they are embedded. Their meanings cannot be defined independently of such contractual obligations. In that sense, it is a truism that scientific knowledge is relational, like a mathematical equation. An equation such as $F=MA$ specifies a comprehensive entity (in Polanyi's terms) which can never define its terms in isolation. The meaning of force can never be known in isolation from mass and acceleration, and the multiplicative relationship which unites all three terms. An explicit, noncircular definition of a theoretical entity is thus impossible to achieve. Theoretical science is explanatory only insofar as it is argumentative and suasory, enjoining us to see reality in the manner that it specifies.

A second way to make the point that contractual obligation and the manifestation of meaning is rhetorical is to consider psychological research such as that of Ames (see Ittleson, 1968). The Ames perceptual demonstrations, such as those in a deceptive enclosure known as the Ames room, primarily concern the problem of accounting for the inferential element in perceptual experience. Ames's account is clear that perception is contractual, a matter of what ought to be the case rather than what is (Proffitt, 1976). A typical experiment would construct a situation in which the observer would be deceived by following his habitual contracts for how things ought to be. Consider the "star point demonstration" which studies the perceptual constancy rule that "the brighter an object, the nearer it ought to be to the observer." When inflated balloons are illuminated in the otherwise dark Ames room, brighter balloons are indeed seen as nearer. But there is also a common perceptual rule which states that "the larger the object, the closer it ought to be." What happens in a conflict? Size is more potent that brightness—the observer will say that a larger balloon is nearer than a smaller, brigher one.

Thus, even though relative constancies exist in perception, they are contractually specified and their meaning as a constant is not inevitable or invariant.[4] This is clear also in the "bouncing balls demonstration." After seeing a steel ball drop, "rike a plate, and rebound several times, an observer was quite surprised when one which looked and weighed the same as the others did not bounce. A similar demonstration with malleable clay balls is surprising when they do bounce. In these cases, observers have certain contractual obligations (which they bring with them to a situation) concerning bouncing balls: steel balls *ought* to bounce, and spongy clay balls *ought not* to. When these contracts are violated, surprise results. Surprise is thus an indication of (the violation of) contractual obligation. If an organism never registers surprise, it is either because it is perfectly preattuned to its environment, or because its experience has no meaning. In either case it could never learn.

Consider now the problem of learning to cope with a "surprising" world. How should we view learning? The traditional answers are, for the behaviorist, that learning is the associational linkage of stimuli and responses, and, for the information processor, that it is either the differentiation (pace Gibson) or the enrichment (pace most constructive theorists) of stimulus information. While such pleonastic accounts have been accepted in the past, it is much more informative to view learning as contractual change.

Ames's "putting demonstration" makes this point well. Subjects were required to practice putting golf balls across a short distance into a small circle. With some practice, most subjects became quite proficient. If, however, the original balls were replaced by identical-appearing ones especially constructed to vary in resiliency, these balls would travel different distances when struck by the same force. Some of Ames's subjects gave up, in dismay or disgust, after varying numbers of trials. Others looked for slight differences in the appearance of the various balls and came to learn to improve their putting. The meaning of the original golf balls included the specification that they ought to be equal in physical properties such as resiliency. When that contract was broken with the new balls, their meaning changed, and the subjects had to learn a new set of relationships to play the game. Learning became a matter of contractual change, of expecting different obligatory relationships to obtain between the objects and events involved.

In order to learn the meanings of cultural entities, a child must discover the contractual obligations which such entities manifest to his peers and superiors. Thus, to know what a particular artificial entity such as a football is, the child must uncover the contractual obligations that have been "built in" to the object. "Natural" objects are defined in the same manner—by the contractual obligations which they ought to have relative to the observer's context. The child comes to give meaning to his experience by building up the vast and rich web of contractual obligations which define his culture in its particular social and historical (as well as geographical) milieu. The manner in which the child comes to do so, of course, is rhetorical in virtually every sense of the term in speech and communication.

Thus, psychology and rhetoric must be united and further developed if we are to understand how we perceive in a meaningful way. Wherever there is comprehension there is meaning, and, as Burke would emphasize, wherever there is meaning there is persuasion and thus rhetoric. Meaning can exist only in the pragmatic framework of intention and action, and it can be conveyed to an audience only by employing the argumentative mode of discourse and behavior. Meaning is our conceptual creation, very literally "what we make it," and in both comprehension and communication our "making it" is a matter of persuasion and argumentation. Even naming an object, or identifying an instance of a thing-kind classification, whether tacitly or explicitly, is a matter of rhetorical persuasion, of arguing for the appropriateness of that name or classification. The manifestation of meaning, even in its most primitive and tacit forms, requires a pragmatic context that is persuasive, and this units cognitive psychology and rhetoric. It is thus incumbent upon speech and communication to adopt a model of man that is capable of that unification. This chapter has pointed toward the only framework presently available that makes that unification possible.

SUMMARY

We have overviewed two alternative models of man in relation to psychology, communication, and speech. The sensory metatheory arose as an initially plausible attempt to make the mind and its cognitive processes a matter of sensory information processing, modeled upon the classic conception of vision as a distance sense. From it have arisen both behaviorism and information-processing psychologies.

Although it is prima facie plausible to regard cognition as a sensory phenomenon, the sensory framework falters on numerous problems. Those we have overviewed fall into three major categories. The first is the requirement that sensory input (stimulation) must be meaningfully specifiable independently of the cognizing organism. Behaviorism tried vainly to account for behavior in terms of the linkages of physically specifiable stimuli (and responses), but admitted defeat with the "functional specification" of its concepts, which licensed the linkage of anything to everything when accounting for the generation of behavior. Information processors, yielding to functional specification and transformations of input, became "constructive" theorists, but are still faced with the impossible task of constructing meaning from impoverished "snippets" of information. The sensory approach can deal with abstract entities and functional specification only by begging the questions of meaning and comprehension.

The second problem facing the sensory framework concerns the infinite variability of both cognition and action. Behaviorism tried to deny the data, often by insisting that it was a theory of (what the linguist called) performance rather than competence. The transformational revolution in linguistics and psycholinguistics has made that failure so well known as to require little comment. Less well-recognized is the failure of the information processing approach in this regard, but even the constructive information processor cannot address productivity except by postulating a "generative" cognitive apparatus. Even then the problem of meaning arises, for one simply cannot generate meaningful experience out of stimulus information unless it is already meaningful. When asked how it is already meaningful, the sensory theorist has no answer. Once again, the sensory approach can address productivity only by begging the questions of meaning and comprehension.

The problems of meaning lead to a third problem for the sensory metatheory: deep structural ambiguity. How the same stimulus information can be multiply meaningful is beyond the sensory framework. Not surprisingly, behaviorism denied or misrepresented the data. The information processor must assume that cognition can transform input in more than one manner, and provide an interpretation in each case. While this description may be correct, no theory of how this is accomplished has yet been proposed. Indeed, in the traditional information-processing literature, these problems are relegated to the "strategy" of problem solving, and most accounts of problem solving equate it with searching: problem solution is assumed to be successful search. How can a search be successful if the solution is ambiguous?

Once again, the sensory metatheory can deal with ambiguity only by presupposing meaning and comprehension. At its best, it provides a paraphrase of data to be explained; in no case does it succeed in explaining any of that data.

Any viable psychological theory must be capable of dealing with fundamental problems such as abstraction, productivity, and ambiguity, and eventually must propose explanatory models which account for man's skills in those areas. The motor metetheory can at least address these issues as they are manifested in traditional research areas such as perception, concept formation, memory, and thinking. It also addresses issues completely untouched by the sensory metatheory, such as tacit knowing, the sensory order and the nature of experience, comprehension, and manifestations of meaning, and the communality of action and cognition.

If it can avoid the scientism and methodolatry that have all too often characterized sensory-based theories in the past, there is considerable promise that explanatory theories within the motor metatheory can be developed for many, if not all, of the problem areas we have mentioned. Since that is the case, it would seem advisable for communication researchers to abandon the psychological model of man they have inherited from the sensory metatheory, and explore those models within the motor theory framework which seem most capable of uniting speech, communication, and psychology.

NOTES

1. One might note the progression from amorphous departments of speech, which included not only rhetoric and communication studies but sometimes even speech pathology and broadcasting, to the recent trend toward "speech communication" departments, and now the separation of communication as an independent program or department. This series of changes is entirely without *theoretical* motivation: no substantive theory has emerged in the area which dictates either the desirability or necessity of such separation. Instead, the changes appear to be dependent upon scientistic factors, such as the prestige and ease of obtaining funding for programs which can call themselves "scientific" (compare the vocational-technical schools whose radio ads offer training in the secretarial "sciences," and ROTC programs listed in college catalogues as departments of "military sciences"), and the claim of contemporary behaviorists (after the abject failure of behaviorism as a substantive psychological theory) that behaviorism alone provides "the true scientific method" in social and human studies. Consider the scientism in Gerald Miller's (1972) claim that anyone who does not employ a behavioristic "objective method" lives in "an intellectual never-never-land, where no 'real' answers to questions are ever unearthed" (p. 28). Scientism is rampant in communication and speech, and it is perhaps the strongest factor in favor of behavioristic and information-processing approaches.
2. The sensory information processors are thus modern descendents of the "cognitive behaviorism" of E.C. Tolman (1932, 1959), in that cognition is a matter of the linkages between stimuli (S-S learning) rather than stimuli and muscle-responses (S-R learning). They are thus subject to E.R. Guthrie's (1959) criticism of Tolman, that Tolman left the psychological subject (the rat, of course) "buried in thought" at a choice point, incapable of action. The motor metatheory which we shall overview below, because it conceives of cognition and action as the same sort of deep conceptual processes, is the first framework available to unite thinking and doing without facing conceptual stumbling blocks, such as leaving the subject computing away but incapable of acting, or participating in a shotgun wedding of cognition and action that is theoretically inexplicable. Theorists such as Neisser and Shiffrin are devastated by Guthrie's quit to Tolman, while others (e.g., Posner, 1973) have nothing but a shotgun to force cognition into action: "Many complex memory representations appear to have a dual character. On the one hand, they can be brought to consciousness and inspected like an image. On the other, they can produce a particular behavior" (Posner, p. 8).
3. Metatheories are abstract conceptual points of view which lie behind substantive theories in a domain. They serve to intellectually rationalize the particular characteristics and emphases of theories which are consonant with them, but metatheories do not have the detailed content of substantive theories. On that respect they are the vantage points from which things are viewed. Thus, many substantive theories, even though sometimes in conflict, may share the same metatheoretical point of view.
4. Gibson (1966, in press) has argued that the meaning of objects and events is directly specified in the affordance structure which they are said to have: the affordance structure of events specify their ecologically relevant meaning directly to the organism (see 1966, pp. 147, 285). Consider this description: "When the constant properties of constant objects are perceived (the shape, size, color, texture, composition, motion, animation, and position relative to other objects) the observer can go on to detect their *affordances*" (1966, p. 285). With this statement, Gibson puts himself in the same camp as Gregory and the information processors, requiring that we add meanings upon directly perceived constant properties. This position is, however, even more "miraculous" than the snippeting one, for it posits that we are directly aware of "constant properties." Unfortunately for Gibson's account, these properties are also contractually specified, as the myriad Ames demonstrations indicate. Perceptual "information" is detected only within a functional context determined by the observer's activity. Thus, even "constant" properties are detected to be constant only relative to the percipient's motives and actions. Constancy is an abstract entity which is contractually specified relative to observers and not independently of them, as Gibson's account must assume.

REFERENCES

ARNOLD, C.C. *Inventio* and *Pronuntiatio* in a "new rhetoric." Paper presented at the annual meeting of the Central States Speech Association, 1972.

BARTLETT, F.C. *Thinking*. New York: Basic, 1958.

BOURNE, L. *Human conceptual behavior*. Boston: Allyn & Bacon, 1966.

BRANSFORD, J.D., & FRANKS, J.J. The abstraction of linguistic ideas. *Cognitive Psychology*, 1971, 2, 331-350.

BRANSFORD, J.D., & JOHNSON, M.K. Contextual prerequisites for understanding: Some investigations of comprehension and recall. *Journal of Verbal Learning and Verbal Behavior*, 1972, 11, 717-726.

BRANSFORD, J.D., & McCARRELL, N.S. A sketch of a cognitive approach to comprehension: Some thoughts about understanding what it means to comprehend. In W.B. Weimer and D.S. Palmero (Eds.), *Cognition and the symbolic processes*. Hillsdale, N.J.: Lawrence Erlbaum Associates, 1974, 189-229.

BRANSFORD, J.D., McCARRELL, N.S., FRANKS, J.J., & NITSCH, K.E. Toward unexplaining memory. In R.E. Shaw and J.D. Bransford (Eds.), *Perceiving, acting, and knowing: Toward an ecological psychology*. Hillsdale, N.J.: Lawrence Erlbaum Associates, 1977, 431-466.

BURKE, K. *Attitudes toward history* (Rev. ed.). Boston: Beacon Press, 1959.

BURKE, K. *Counter statement* (Rev. ed.). Berkeley: University of California Press, 1968.

CASSIRER, E. *Substance and function and Einstein's theory of relativity*. New York: Dover, 1953, original 1923.

CHERRY, E.C. *On human communication*. New York: Wiley, 1956.

ECCLES, J.C. *Facing reality*. New York: Springer-Verlag, 1970.

ECCLES, J.C. *The understanding of the brain*. New York: McGraw-Hill, 1973.

FESTINGER, L., BURNHAM, C.A., ONO, H., & BAMBER, D. Efference and the conscious experience of perception. *Journal of Experimental Psychology*, 1967, 74, 1-36. (Monograph supplement)

FEYERABEND, P.K. Reply to criticism. In R.S. Cohen and M.W. Wartofsky (Eds.), *Boston studies in the philosophy of science*. Vol. 2. New York: Humanities Press, 1965, 223-261.

FEYERABEND, P.K. Against method. In M. Radner and S. Winokur (Eds.), *Minnesota studies in the philosophy of science*. Vol. 4. Minneapolis: University of Minnesota Press, 1970a, 17-130.

FEYERABEND, P.K. Problems of empiricism, part II. In R. Colodny (Ed.), *The nature and function of scientific theories*. Pittsburgh: University of Pittsburgh Press, 1970b, 275-353.

FURTH, H. *Piaget and knowledge*. Englewood Cliffs, N.J.: Prentice-Hall, 1969.

GIBSON, J.J. *The senses considered as perceptual systems*. Boston: Houghton-Mifflin, 1966.

GIBSON, J.J. *An ecological approach to visual perception*. Boston: Houghton-Mifflin, in press.

GREGORY, R.L. Seeing as thinking: An active theory of perception. *The Times Literary Supplement* (London), June 23, 1972, pp. 707-708.

GUTHRIE, E.R. Association by contiguity. In S. Koch (Ed.), *Psychology: A study of a science*. Vol. 3. New York: McGraw-Hill, 1959, 158-195.

HALWES, T., & WIRE, B. A possible solution to the pattern recognition problem in the speech modality. In W.B. Weimer and D.S. Palermo (Eds.), *Cognition and the symbolic processes*. Hillsdale, N.J.: Lawrence Erlbaum Associates, 1974, 385-388.

HANSON, N.R. *Patterns of discovery*. Cambridge: Cambridge University Press, 1958.

HANSON, N.R. A picture theory of theory meaning. In R. Colodny (Ed.), *The nature and function of scientific theories*. Pittsburgh: University of Pittsburgh Press. 1970, 233-274.

HAYEK, F.A. *The counter-revolution of science*. Glencoe, Ill.: The Free Press, 1952a.

HAYEK, F.A. *The sensory order*. Chicago: University of Chicago Press, 1952b.

ITTLESON, W.H. *The Ames demonstrations in perception*. New York: Hafner, 1968.

JAMES, W. *The principles of psychology*. New York: Holt, 1890.

JENKINS, J.J. The challenge to psychological theorists. In T.R. Dixon and D.L. Horton (Eds.), *Verbal behavior and general behavior theory*. Englewood Cliffs, N.J.: Prentice-Hall, 1968.

JENKINS, J.J. Remember that old theory of memory? Well, forget it! *American Psychologist*, 1974, 29, 785-795.

KUHN, T.S. Reflections on my critics. In I. Lakatos and A. Musgrave (Eds.), *Criticism and the growth of knowledge*. Cambridge: Cambridge University Press, 1970a, 237-278.

KUHN, T.S. *The structure of scientific revolutions* (Rev. ed.). Chicago: University of Chicago Press, 1970b.

KUHN, T.S. Second thoughts on paradigms. In F. Suppe (Ed.), *The structure of scientific theories*. Urbana: University of Illinois Press, 1974, 459-482.

LAKATOS, I. Changes in the problem of inductive logic. In I. Lakatos (Ed.), *The problem of inductive logic*. Amsterdam: North-Holland, 1968, 315-417.

LAKATOS, I. Falsification and the methodology of scientific research programmes. In I. Lakatos and A. Musgrave (Eds.), *Criticism and the growth of knowledge*. Cambridge: Cambridge University Press, 1970, 91-196.

LEWES, G.H. *Problems of life and mind* (2 vols.). Boston: Houghton, Osgood, 1879.

MACE, W.M. Ecologically stimulating cognitive psychology: Gibsonian perspectives. In W.B. Weimer and D.S. Palermo (Eds.), *Cognition and the symbolic processes*. Hillsdale, N.J.: Lawrence Erlbaum Associates, 1974, 37-64.

MACE, W.M. James J. Gibson's strategy for perceiving: Ask not what's inside your head, but what your head's inside of. In R.E. Shaw and J.D. Bransford (Eds.), *Perceiving, acting, and knowing: Toward an ecological psychology*.Hillsdale, N.J.: Lawrence Erlbaum Associates, 1977, 43-65.

MAXWELL, G. Scientific methodology and the causal theory of perception. In I. Lakatos and A. Musgrave (Eds.), *Problems in the philosophy of science*. Amsterdam: North-Holland, 1968, 148-160.

MAXWELL, G. Theories, perception, and structural realism. In R. Colodny (Ed.), *The nature and function of scientific theories*. Pittsburgh: University of Pittsburgh Press, 1970, 3-34.

MAXWELL, G. Russell on perception: A study in philosophical method. In D.F. Pears (Ed.), *Bertrand Russell: A collection of critical essays*. Garden City, N.Y.: Doubleday, 1972, 110-146.

MELTON, A.W., & MARTIN, E. (Eds.). *Coding processes in human memory*. Washington, D.C.: Winston, 1972.

MILLER, G.A. *Language and communication*. New York: McGraw-Hill, 1951.

MILLER, G.A. Toward a third metaphor for psycholinguistics. In W.B. Weimer and D.S. Palmero (Eds.), *Cognition and the symbolic processes*. Hillsdale, N.J.: Lawrence Erlbaum Associates, 1974, 397-413.

MILLER, G.R. *An introduction to speech communication* (Rev. ed.). Indianapolis: Bobbs-Merrill, 1972.

MILLER, G.R. The person as actor—cognitive psychology on the attack. *Quarterly Journal of Speech*, 1976, 62, 82-87.

MORRIS, C.W. Foundation of the theory of signs. In *International encyclopedia of unified science*. Chicago: University of Chicago Press, 1939.

MORTENSON, C.D. *Communication: The study of human interaction*. New York: McGraw-Hill, 1972.

NEISSER, U. *Cognitive psychology*. New York: Appleton-Century-Crofts, 1967.

NEWELL, A., SHAW, J.C., & SIMON, H.A. Elements of a theory of human problem solving. *Psychological Review*, 1958, 65, 151-166.

OSGOOD, C.E. On understanding and creating sentences. *American Psychologist*, 1963, 18, 735-751.

OSGOOD, C.E. Toward a wedding of insufficiencies. In T.R. Dixon and D.L. Horton (Eds.), *Verbal behavior and general behavior theory*, Englewood Cliffs, N.J.: Prentice-Hall, 1968, 495-519.

OSGOOD, C.E. Where do sentences come from? In D.D. Steinberg and L.A. Jakobovits (Eds.), *Semantics: An interdisciplinary reader*. Cambridge: Cambridge University Press, 1971, 497-529.

OSGOOD, C.E., SUCI, G.J., & TANNENBAUM, P.H. *The measurement of meaning*. Urbana: University of Illinois Press, 1957.

PENFIELD, W. *The mystery of the mind*. Princeton, N.J.: Princeton University Press, 1975.

PHILLIPS, G.M. Rhetoritherapy versus the medical model: Dealing with reticence. *Communication Education*, 1977, 26, 34-43.

POLANYI, M. *Personal knowledge*. New York: Harper, 1958.

POLANYI, M. *The tacit dimension*. Garden City, N.Y.: Doubleday, 1964.

POPPER, K.R. *The logic of scientific discovery*. New York: Harper, 1959.

POPPER, K.R. *Conjectures and refutations*. New York: Harper, 1963.

POPPER, K.R. *Objective knowledge*. Oxford: Oxford University Press, 1972.

POSNER, M. *Cognition: An introduction*. Glenview, Ill: Scott, Foresman, 1973.

PRIBRAM, K.H. *Languages of the brain*. Englewood Cliffs, N.J.: Prentice-Hall, 1971a.

PRIBRAM, K.H. *What makes man human*? New York: The American Museum of Natural History, 1971b.

PROFFITT, D.R. Demonstrations to investigate the meaning of every day experience. Unpublished doctoral dissertation, Pennsylvania State University, 1976.

RUSSELL, B.A. *Human knowledge: Its scope and limits*. New York: Simon & Schuster, 1948.

SHAW, R.E., & McINTYRE, M. Algoristic foundations for cognitive psychology. In W.B. Weimer and D.S. Palermo (Eds.), *Cognition and the symbolic processes*. Hillsdale, N.J.: Lawrence Erlbaum Associates, 1974, 305-362.

SHAW, R.E., McINTRYE, M., & MACE, W.M. The role of symmetry in event perception. In R.B. MacLeod and H. Pick (Eds.), *Perception: Essays in honor of James J. Gibson*. Ithaca, N.Y.: Cornell University Press, 1974.

SHIFFRIN, R.M. Information processing (review of *Coding processes in human memory*, A.W. Melton and E. Martin, [Eds.]). *Science*, 1973, 180, 400.

SIMON, H.A. *The sciences of the artificial*. Cambridge, Mass.: M.I.T. Press, 1969.

SKINNER, B.F. *Contingencies of reinforcement*. New York: Appleton-Century-Crofts, 1969.

SKINNER, B.F. *About behaviorism*. New York: Knopf, 1974.

SPENCER BROWN, G. *Laws of form*. New York: Julian Press, 1972.

SPERRY, R.W. Neurology and the mind-brain problem. *American Scientist*, 1952, 40, 291-312.

SPERRY, R.W. A modified concept of consciousness. *Psychological Review*, 1969, 76, 532-536.

TOLMAN, E.C. *Purposive behavior in animals and men*. New York: Appleton-Century-Crofts, 1932.

TOLMAN, E.C. Principles of purposive behavior. In S. Koch (Ed.), *Psychology: A study of a science*. New York: McGraw-Hill, 1959, 92-157.

WORTHINGTON, A.G. Differential rates of dark adaptation to "taboo" and "neutral" stimuli. *Canadian Journal of Psychology*, 1964, 18, 757-768.

WEIMER, W.B. Psycholinguistics and Plato's paradoxes of the *Meno*. *American Psychologist*, 1973, 28, 15-33.

WEIMER, W.B. Overview of a cognitive conspiracy: Reflections on the volume. In W.B. Weimer and D.S. Palermo (Eds.), *Cognition and the symbolic processes*. Hillsdale, N.J.: Lawrence Erlbaum Associates, 1974, 415-443.

WEIMER, W.B. The psychology of inference and expectation: Some preliminary remarks. In G. Maxwell and R.M. Anderson (Eds.), *Minnesota studies in the philosophy of science*. Vol. 6. Minneapolis: University of Minnesota, 1975, 430-486.

WEIMER, W.B. A conceptual framework for cognitive psychology: Motor theories of the mind. In R.E. Shaw and J.D. Bransford (Eds.), *Perceiving, acting, and knowing: Toward an ecological psychology*. Hillsdale, N.J.: Lawrence Erlbaum Associates, 1977, 267-311

WEIMER, W.B. *Notes on the methodology of scientific research*. Hillsdale, N.J.: Lawrence Erlbaum Associates, 1978.

INFORMATION SYSTEMS

Theory and Research: An Overview
Selected Studies

INFORMATION SYSTEMS THEORY AND RESEARCH: AN OVERVIEW

B. AUBREY FISHER
University of Utah

Each of the eight divisions of the International Communication Association is, for the most part, intuitively recognizable in terms of the unifying interests of the members. Four of the divisions are structured on the basis of levels in a sociological hierarchy—interpersonal communication, organizational communication, mass communication, and intercultural communication. Three other divisions are organized as to topical settings or purposes of the communication setting—political communication, instructional communication, and health communication. The lone division whose identity is not immediately apparent is division 1—information systems.

Reading the papers submitted to this division for presentation at the 1977 convention, I was struck with the extraordinary diversity of purposes, interests, and emphases of the divisional membership. To discover some unifying principle, recognizable as "information systems," among those papers was virtually impossible. Apparently, those interests fundamental to members of the information systems division is unclear to many members of our international organization.

Clearly the basic unifying principle of division 1 is or should be a theoretical perspective—specifically system theory. Consequently, one would expect that those communication scholars actively applying system principles to communication are capable of identifying the common elements which unite the members of the division. Paradoxically enough, that seems not to be the case. Several years ago, I attended a postdoctoral seminar on system theory and communication held at Purdue University. Systems enthusiasts all, we discussed and debated a variety of issues over the several days of the seminar. Agreement was minimal, at best. Some of us considered system theory, when applied to communication inquiry, to be a study of networks. To others, system theory seemed synonymous with cybernetics or a Parsonian-based brand of structural-functionalism. I even experienced an uneasy feeling that to some of us system theory provided only a vocabulary of new terms and concepts which could be used to label traditional variables. During two days of concentrated effort, we attempted valiantly, and ultimately futilely, to agree on recommendations for future systems research in communication. Moreover, we did not even agree on what constitutes systems approaches to communication inquiry.

Certainly the members in division 1 do not reflect a "scientific community" of scholars, at least in Diesing's (1971, pp. 319-320) sense of a body of scholars engaged in "regular, effective collaboration with other members." Nevertheless, the elements which unite the members of the Information Systems Division must inevitably be found in the tenets of system theory. And these elements should not be unfamiliar to our division. Numerous attempts to define systems approaches to communication research are abundant in the literature (see, e.g., Monge, 1973 & 1977; Ruben & Kim, 1975; Thayer, 1972; Fisher & Hawes, 1971) and include the overview article in *Communication Yearbook I*. Obviously, this article is but another in a long list. But rather than reiterate a do-it-again-until-we-get-it-right analysis, the present purpose seeks to provide some insight into the reasons for the evident confusion and apparent lack of unanimity among our membership.

The present essay does not attempt to distinguish between system and nonsystem approaches to communication theory and research. Krippendorff (1977, pp. 152-155) has amply demonstrated such a distinction. Rather, the present analysis employs the broadest definition of systems approaches to communication in order to include the present diversity of research which is recognizable, or claims to be recognizable as systems research in communication. One assumption underlying this analysis is that system theory constitutes one approach to communication theory and research—a viable and eminently useful perspective among many perspectives, each of which is viable and useful. The purpose is to gain an understanding of and appreciation for systems approaches to communication theory and research in order to render a realistic appraisal of their merits.

SOME COMMON MISCONCEPTIONS OF SYSTEMS

For every protagonist of systems approaches in communication inquiry, there seems to be an antagonist. Few contemporary communication scholars assume a neutral attitude toward system theory. Typically, they embrace the principles of information systems and actively espouse them, or else they denegrate them. Every theoretical perspective possesses strengths and weaknesses and one's choice of a perspective probably reflects rather egocentric reasons. That is, one chooses to use a theoretical perspective in a field as preparadigmatic (or multiparadigmatic) as communication, ultimately by responding to the question, "What does it do for me, conceptually and/or empirically?" The perspective which seems most useful to accomplishing one's purposes is thus the perspective embraced by the scholar.

The failure to advocate or utilize a systems approach (or any other approach, for that matter) is by no means a scholarly "error" in the sense that one has denied an obvious "truth." Principles of system theory do not represent "truths," any more than do the principles of any other theoretical perspective. Nor do the common misconceptions of system theory typically attempt to distort its principles. Rather, most misconceptions result from unfairly delimiting system approaches so that a rejection of system theory relies on reasons which are generally superficial. To repeat, there is nothing "wrong" in not choosing systems approaches to communication inquiry. But to do so for the wrong reasons is self-defeating.

Misconception: Systems are Mere Analogies without Explanatory Value

One of the most pervasive criticisms of system theory in communication focuses on the theory's emphasis on analogies. That is, the very existence of a system is metaphorical and is, theoretically at least, devoid of any essential empirical reality. The criticism goes something like this. "An analogy does not focus specifically on the phenomena of my interest. Therefore, it is a metaphor without particular usefulness." Such a criticism is, unfortunately, shortsighted.

Ackoff and Emery (1972, p. 14), discussing cybernetics, state, "Some psychologists and sociologists, however, realize that the phenomena they are concerned with are not captured in the cybernetician's definitions; hence, they look at his offerings simply as metaphors or analogies. Therefore, some behavioral scientists ignore work that could be at least very suggestive to them." To Ackoff and Emery, then, the greater danger is to engage in the scholarly exercise of throwing the theoretical baby out with the empirical bathwater. That is, the theoretical principles are discarded due to their metaphorical abstractness in guiding empirical inquiry.

More importantly, however, systems approaches to communication inquiry are not merely metaphors. Rather, they are attempts to establish a heuristic basis for the discovery of generalizable laws or rules which serve to explain the phenomena of human communication. Van Gigch (1974) emphasizes such a purpose in his description of "applied general systems theory" which he calls the "systems approach": "One of the objectives of the systems approach . . . is to search for similarities of structure and or properties, as well as for common phenomena which take place in systems of different disciplines. In doing so, it seeks to "raise the level of generality of the laws" which apply to narrow fields of endeavor. Generalizations ("isomorphisms," in the jargon of General Systems Theory) of the kind sought go beyond mere analogies" (p. 33). In this respect, the application of general system theory in any discipline, including communication, goes beyond merely analogical existence. Rather, system theory provides an heuristic framework which serves to focus inquiry and analysis of specific applications to phenomena within a given discipline. The application of system theory, therefore, becomes not a generalized metaphor but a suggestive framework notable for its heuristic potential. Berrien (1968, p. 191) thus describes his own purpose: "The present effort . . . has attempted to deal with the age old issues within a framework of generalized concepts and propositions in which the various levels of analysis represent not analogies but special cases" (author's emphasis deleted).

What, then, is the purpose of systems approaches to communication inquiry? Clearly, systems research relies on analogies, models, or metaphors developed from principles of much greater generality. Concepts such as structure, homestasis, equifinality, wholeness, etc., do not "belong to" communication. But in their application to the phenomena of communication, they go beyond their metaphorical existence and become principles which serve to explain and have a referent in the phenomena of human communication.

Systems principles without phenomenal existence are, of course, of limited usefulness. But in their existence as "special cases" (i.e., applied to communication), they can then be judged on their own merits. In this way, system theory in communication is not a single metaphor or unitary approach. To the contrary, it involves many different approaches utilizing diverse empirical referents or operationalizations of the more abstract concepts. In this way, the analogy itself does indeed have little explanatory value. The application, however, in the form of a specific heuristic framework composed of empirical referents, provides tremendous potential for scientific explanation.

Sutherland (1973, pp. 127-128) places system theory in its proper perspective: "Grand operational principles then, in the hands of the serious scientist, simply become systemic, encompassing heuristics whose utility lies not in their reification but in their perspectives—and here rests the general systems theorists's concerns with the analogy-building aspects of his approach."

Systems approaches to communication are indeed analogies. As analogies alone, they are of limited usefulness and provide little explanatory power. But as a framework for organizing empirical phenomena and generating research questions, they provide the basis for scientific explanation which can then be judged as to its utilitarian value.

Misconception: The Goal of System Theory is to Provide a General Theory for the Unification of all Science—Physical and Social

Science philosophers have for decades been enamored with the goal of uniting the disparate branches of science under one theoretical umbrella. The positivists sought to achieve this goal by generalizing the mathematical formalism of physics to all of science. That the unity of science is the goal of many systems philosophers is quite obvious. Certainly Bertalanffy (1968) and Laszlo (1972) perceive the unification of all science as a major, if not the primary, objective of *general* system theory. Whether such a goal is possible or even desirable is a matter for debate. But whether such a goal is paramount in systems approaches to communication inquiry is not.

Ruben and Kim (1975), in their editorial introduction to a volume in general system theory and communication, explicitly state the viewpoint of most protagonists of system theory within communication:

> Whether or not general systems is a way of thinking, a set of concepts, a theory, a metatheory, a philosophy, truly a new world view, or a combination, is a question with which we have wrestled since our earliest acquaintance with the area. And while we have yet to resolve this dilemma, we are convinced of the value of the thinking of scholars who have contributed to the writings on general systems theory. It is the belief that the student of human communication and the behavioral scientist will find the ideas of general systems as insightful, provocative and intellectually expansive as we have, which has prompted us to prepare this volume. (p. 3)

Will or can general system theory unify the physical and social sciences within its rubrics? The issue is a philosophical one and of little import in determining the value of systems approaches to communication. Clearly our concern is first with communication. System theory is thus only a perspective which may be used to gain insights into the phenomena of human communication. Whether system theory is or can be a general theory or metatheory for all sciences is clearly a superfluous issue and of minimal practical value.

Misconception: System Theory is a Rigid Logical Formalization which Imposes Its Structure on the Empirical World

Cushman (1977, p. 33) presents a rather damning criticism of system theory: "By treating lawful regularities as principles of logically conceivable systems and evaluating such regularities in terms of their usefulness rather than their truth value, the systems perspective provides a flexible and rigorous method of invention and judgment. Such an approach to theory construction emphasizes explanation and control at the expense of prediction." It is not difficult to conceive of the systems approach to communication as a logical and relatively rigid formal structure, i.e., a mathematical form (see, e.g., A. Kuhn, 1974). Those approaches emphasizing cybernetics and structural-functionalism (Monge, 1977, p. 23) clearly include a formalized logic intrinsic to the specific approach. But to define all systems approaches within specific logical structures is myopic and quite inaccurate.

For example, Cushman (1977, p. 33) also asserts, "While general systems analysts and systems scientists may disagree in regard to the ultimate goal of the systems perspective, they are in basic agreement on the methods to be employed and the types of theory to be constructed." A later discussion will illustrate that systems analysts and scientists in communication certainly cannot be characterized as being "in basic agreement" on either methods or theoretical structures. In fact, quite the opposite is true.

More importantly, to depict a formalization of logical structures as the sine qua non of any theoretical perspective is to ignore the potential fruitfulness or usefulness of that theory. The logical system is not the theory, regardless of the perspective. Bohm (1974, p. 389) states emphatically that our tendency to regard mathematical formalisms as some sort of truth is blatantly false. Mathematics provides only an extension of ordinary language in order to endow the expressed relationships among empirical phenomena with greater precision, thereby allowing the drawing of inferences. Logic is thus only a tool, no more and no less, and has no truth value in and of itself. Furthermore, Kaplan (1974) has argued convincingly for the employment of "logics-in-use" when a theory is adapted to a specific discipline. Monge (1973) has suggested developing such specialized logical forms specifically in employing systems approaches in communication inquiry.

Logical systems are historically and conceptually adapted to empirical purposes, not the other way around. Cushman is certainly correct that Meehan (1968) has argued for control as a prime criterion for research methodology. (The issue of control in systems approaches is a subject for a later discussion.) But applications of system theory do not, as Cushman implies, impose undue conceptual constraint upon inquiry. Meehan (1968, p. 83) is emphatic on this point when he writes, "The most important and most difficult part of explanation is the selection of concepts to load the system." Meehan goes on to indicate that we have no guidelines to assist us in conceptualizing. Rules and principles related to methods and techniques of formalizing explanations abound in virtually every field of scientific endeavor. But we are left on our own to develop our concepts.

Regardless of our theoretical perspective, the concepts we employ arise inevitably from our specific purposes and interests. Jantsch (1975, pp. 191-205) discusses this phenomenon as a "feedback loop" between our models and our myths. Systems approaches to communicative phenomena employ a great disparity of conceptualizations, research methods, observational techniques, and formal structures. A systems perspective is not nearly so rigidly structured as one might be led to believe.

Under any circumstances, the logical structure of any theoretical perspective should not be confused with the theory itself as it is applied in scientific inquiry. To do so is to engage in cart-before-the-horse reasoning. That is, any theory is capable of being formalized (see Suppe, 1974, p. 63), but the formalization of a theory inevitably comes *after* those theoretical principles have received widespread empirical support. (See Suppe, 1974, pp. 113-114 for a discussion of the distinction between axiomatization and formalization of theories, the latter being subject to semantic or empirical interpretation and not exclusively tautological.) The logical system is thus not a prior constraint on the empirical phenomena within a theoretical perspective but arises as an issue to be determined in the latter stages of theoretical development. Certainly communication theory is currently in a very early stage.

Misconception: Systems Approaches are Dependent upon the Purposes of Inquiry

Cushman (1977, p. 33) condemns a systems perspective of communication on the basis that it searches "for patterns of organization which are 'created' rather than discovered in 'phenomena'." Apparently, then, the observation of organizational patterns employed in systems inquiry are somehow less "real" because they are "created" rather than "discovered." On the other hand, one can argue that every epistemological perspective, systems included, is a creation rather than a discovery. That is, understanding is created and cannot be discovered in some sort of physicalistic or idealistic sense. Berlo (1960, p. 25) explains, ". . . the structure of physical reality cannot be *discovered* by man; it must be *created* by man. In 'constructing reality,' the theorist chooses to organize his perceptions one way or another. He may choose to say that we can call certain things 'elements' or 'ingredients.' In doing this, he realizes that he has not discovered anything, he has created a set of tools which may or may not be useful in describing the world."

Popper (1962, p. 73) provides much the same analysis: "Without waiting, passively, for repetitions to impress or impose regularities on us, we actively try to impose regularities upon the world." Any act of explanation, then, is not a discovery of something "real" which exists de facto in the world. Rather, it is an epistemological patterning imposed by the observer on the world in order to understand it more completely. This is the purpose and the benefit of the use of any theory in scientific inquiry.

This misconception is not so much a distortion of the systems approach but an assumption that the systems approach is somehow unique among the various epistemological perspectives because it imposes some explanatory framework upon empirical phenomena. But this structure is not to assume that the theoretical perspective necessarily imposes *a priori* truth upon empirical observation. Sutherland (1972, pp. 26-27) argues specifically against such a practice, which he considers nonsystemic. He concludes, "At the extreme, then, analogy-building can take on procrustean characteristics, just as the a priori denial of any structural isomorphisms or causal analogies leads us into the scientifically sterile world of the phenomenolgist. It is in the interval between the extremes, however, that the general systems theorist elects to work." (I do not necessarily subscribe to Sutherland's slap at phenomenology. In fact, the issue which Sutherland interprets as "scientific sterility" is probably the difference between epistemological and ontological concerns, a subject for later discussion.)

Of potentially greater danger here is an issue that goes beyond systems approaches to communication to the nature of theory itself. There is an implicit assumption in Cushman's argument that truth is "out there" to be discovered in reality. A "good" theory is one that facilitates its discovery. Such an assumption, whether intended or not, should be discarded. The choice between scientific theories is rarely, if ever, one that involves assessing the accuracy of a theory. Suppe (1974, p. 215) states a philosophical truism when he indicates that any choice between competing theories can be made only "on some basis other than their factual adequacy." Even though he represents a different philosophical position, Kaplan (1964, p. 312) nonetheless agrees: "Truth itself is plainly useless as a criterion for the acceptability of a theory."

Are systems approaches to communication a function of the purpose of inquiry? Of course they are. But virtually any epistemologically-based theory begins with a focus on the purposes of the investigation. The concepts used to load the system are a function of the investigator's purposes. Such an occurrence is perfectly normal. But such a constraint does not suggest that all systems approaches are similar or even that they include similar concepts. Nor are those of other approaches. In terms of a rules perspective, for example,

Cushman (1977) employs as his epistemological basis the self-concept. He later joins with Pearce (1977) in using von Wright's (1971) "practical syllogism" of goal-directed behavior, an epistemological basis advocated earlier by Pearce (1976). Another basis for employing a rules perspective in communication was based on regularity of interaction patterns (Fisher, 1976). Because systems approaches to communication emanate from the purposes of the inquiry does not imply that they employ a specific or limited method of performing inquiry. Like other perspectives, systems approaches reflect a methodological and conceptual disparity.

GENERAL CHARACTERISTICS OF SYSTEM THEORY

To reiterate those inherent characteristics of system theory is probably superfluous. Nevertheless, a brief discussion of those characteristics follows, not because I anticipate that the reader is unfamiliar with them, but because of the necessity to begin with a common conceptual basis of what we mean by system theory. Before discussing systems approaches to communication, then, a brief discussion of selected characteristics significant to system theory is included.

Holism and Nonsummativity

The principle of wholeness is such a prevalent characteristic of systems that it requires little explanation. Weiss (1969, pp. 11-12) defines the holistic principle: "Pragmatically defined, a system is a rather circumscribed complex of relatively bounded phenomena, which within those bounds, retains a relatively stationary pattern of structure in space or of sequential configuration in time in spite of a high degree of variability in the details of distribution and interrelations among its constituent units of lower order." Although the degree of structure and organization varies widely, the emphasis is upon holistic rather than reductionistic analysis. Simply speaking, the system as a whole is different from the sum of its component parts. Watzlawick, Beavin, and Jackson (1967, p. 125) indicate, "A system cannot be taken for the sum of its parts; indeed formal analysis of artificially isolated segments would destroy the very object of interest." Thus, reductionistic analysis is antisystemic in nature. The focus, instead, is on the organizing processes of the system rather than on analyzing the component parts.

Openness

Nearly every discussion of the principles of system theory includes, sooner or later, the inevitable discussion of open and closed systems. This discussion is no exception. System theorists have generally approached systemic openess by delineating the properties of open systems. The most common property is probably the free exchange of information with the environment (see, e.g., Rapoport, 1968, p. xviii). Other properties of open systems, interrelated with the permeable-boundaries property, include the following:

1. Open systems are characterized by equifinality, and thus the state of a system at any time is relatively independent of the initial arrangement of the component parts of the system (see, e.g., Bertalanffy, 1968, p. 132).
2. Open systems are not subject to the Second Law of Thermodynamics; hence, order and organization may increase in the system. The corollary is that entropy may decrease in an open system (see, e.g., Bertalanffy, 1968, p. 150; Pringle, 1968, p. 261).
3. Open systems are characterized by evolutionary processes leading to increased complexity (see, e.g., Pringle, 1968, pp. 262ff.).
4. Open systems are capable of self-regulation and thus are capable of adapting to internal and external change. Corollary—open systems include both positive and negative feedback processes of varying strengths. (See, e.g., Buckley, 1968; Maruyama, 1963.)

Unfortunately, students of systems tend to perceive systemic openness in dichotomous terms. That is, they perceive a system to be either open or closed. In reality, systems are always open to some degree. The totally open or totally closed system is an ideal type which could probably be maintained only under severely controlled laboratory conditions, if at all. Berrien (1968, p. 16) is explicit on this point: "We are compelled to view all real systems as open, recognizing that the degree of openness may vary among systems." Social systems clearly vary in their degree of openness although they are inevitably open to some extent. To close arbitrarily all social systems for the sake of empirical convenience seems utterly unrealistic.

Because open systems do not function consistently in accord with the principle of entropy (the Second Law of Thermodynamics), theorists are often at a loss to characterize the fluctuating maintenance and change of systemic order and structure. Homeostasis, as a "steady state" of equilibriated entropy/negentropy, seems a rationalization of the Second Law. Some prefer to coin the term "dynamic equilibrium" to denote the evolutionary change toward successively more complex "steady states." Pringle (1968, p. 261), for example, refers to a "steady-state equilibrium" maintained by replication "processes [which] are subject to variation." The conceptual insistence on preserving the Second Law within an equifinal, self-regulating system precipitates conceptual incongruity and ultimately confusion.

Laszlo (1972) provides direction out of this conceptual maze by suggesting the notion of "stationary or quasi-stationary, non-equilibrium states." He writes:

> The reasons are potent for discarding the concept of the equilibrium state in favor of that of a non-equilibrium steady state in *natural* systems: (i) equilibrium states do not have available usable energy whereas natural systems of the widest variety do; (ii) equilibrium states are "memoryless" whereas natural systems behave in large part in function of their past histories. . . . Thus, although a machine may go to equilibrium as its preferred state, natural systems go to increasingly organized *non*-equilibrium states. (pp. 42-43)

Laszlo provides several implications for systems analysis. First, open systems may develop an increasingly higher level of organization and, theoretically, may never reach equilibrium, in the sense of the final state of a closed system. Second, natural and social systems have available usable energy which can be utilized to maintain or achieve a functional steady state despite potential environmental disturbances. In the sense of information as the counterpart of "energy" in a social system (a topic of later discussion), social systems have the capacity not only to store information but to create it as well. Perhaps the most important implication is the clear importance of the time dimension and the functioning of the past on the present. Laszlo suggests that a complete investigation of an open system should include retrospective analysis of the system's history in a longitudinal view of system operation.

Hierarchical Organization

The organization of systems into a hierarchical succession is an axiomatic assumption of system theory. Every system is a suprasystem to the systems within it, and every system is a subsystem to the system which environs it. In other words, systems are always nested within other systems so that in every systems approach to empirical phenomena, subsystems and suprasystems exist below and above the system being observed. Choosing any specific hierarchical level for analysis is, of course, an essential preliminary task for the investigator and, largely, an arbitrary one.

Koestler (1969) uses the concept of "holon" to distinguish that systemic level of interest. He defines holon as "any stable sub-whole in an organismic, cognitive, or social hierarchy which displays rule-governed behavior and/or structural Gestalt constancy" (p. 97). The holon is thus a system existing within a hierarchy of systems. According to Koestler, "the holon is a system of relations which is represented on the next higher level as a unit." (p. 200, authors emphasis deleted.)

Recognizing that the system being observed exists within a hierarchy of systems, however, requires further conceptual consideration in order to maximize the benefits of empirical research and analysis. Ozbekhan (1971, p. 179) contributes a further implication concerning the significance of systemic hierarchy: "a part of the hierarchical structure is an organization of communications between levels, which forcus us to face the important problem of communication across system boundaries and levels. . . . Each level could be considered as a system unto itself, and that the *whole*—

the all-encompassing system represents a highly complex interdependent entity whose behavior cannot be causally derived from the summed up behaviors of its levels." Ozbekhan is emphatic in insisting that the investigator of systems consider the hierarchical structure and the relationships between hierarchical levels. That consideration must include some understanding of the information exchange across systemic boundaries and, thus, how one system is organized or functions in relation to its suprasystem.

Quoting Mesarovic and Macko, Ozbekhan (1971, p. 182) explains the advantages of such a research strategy. "Starting from any given stratum, understanding of a system increases by crossing (boundaries): moving down the hierarchy one obtains a deeper understanding of its significance [i.e., meaning]." Weick (1969, p. 45) expands on this same point in discussing social organizing: "If there are different levels of analysis (e.g., individual, group, organization, society), the only way we can learn much about any of these levels is if we know how they are tied together, that is, how one level interacts with another level. . . . 'Lower' levels constrain 'higher' levels and . . . 'higher' levels are distinct from 'lower' levels."

Laszlo (1972, p. 47) provides a final recommendation to the empiricist: "The processes of self-organization require that the strategic level of the next higher suprasystem be chosen for clear conceptual grasp. . . . Self-organization is better amenable to conceptualization from the viewpoint of a population of systems than it is from that of the self-organizing single system itself."

The implications for systems approaches to empirical inquiry, then, are clear. Considering the hierarchical organization of systems suggests inquiry into how systems are tied together, that is, the exchange of information across system boundaries. Such a consideration of the hierarchical organization of systems implies two foci of analysis. First, the subsystems nested within the systemic level being observed serve to define and constrain the systemic level of interest. Secondly, the suprasystem which environs the systemic level being observed provides the context in which the significance or meaning of the observed system can be assessed.

Organized Complexity

Complexity is a term often used to excuse one's inability to understand a system. To some, the term implies a haphazard conglomeration of unstructured phenomena. But complexity is a principal characteristic of systems which demands a more precise understanding. It is a truism that social systems, including information/communication systems, are complex systems. For Sorokin (1966, p. 642), complexity of such systems is related to the holistic characteristic of an open system which disallows deterministic or linearly causal explanations of systemic behavior. For Simon (1969, p. 118), the complexity of a system also emanates from holism so that the parts of a system "interact in a nonsimple way." For Simon this suggests pragmatically "that, given the properties of the parts and the laws of their interaction, it is not a trivial matter to infer properties of the whole." For van Gigch (1974, pp. 270-291), systemic complexity involves the hierarchical organization of a system as well as holism. To Schoderbek, Kefalas, & Schoderbek (1975, p. 13), the complexity of a system involves the specialization of functions performed by components.

Understanding systemic complexity requires explaining the structure-function complex of the system. The interaction among component parts of the system is complex when, according to Weiss (1971, p. 13), it cannot be explained through some deterministic explanation that the parts organize the whole or even that the whole determines how the parts are organized. Sorokin (1966, p. 642) terms this interaction among components of a complex system as "triple interdependence." He demands of empiricism that "the study has to proceed not only from parts to the whole and from each part to the other parts but still more so from the whole to the parts (along the lines of the triple interdependence)."

Simply speaking, complexity in a system means *differentiation*. Such differentiation can occur in the structural dimension so that the greater the number of different classes of component parts, the greater the complexity. For example, the complexity of a social system comprising two individuals and their interactions increases geometrically with the addition of a third individual to the system. In terms of a simple network in a message-exchange model, only one channel exists to connect the components of a dyad, while three channels exist in a three-person network.

Functional complexity implies differentiation among possible states (i.e., events) which may characterize the system at different points in time. For example, a decision model implies a finite number of possibilities in terms of alternative choices available as outcomes of the decision situation. The more complex the decision model, the larger the number of alternatives available to the decision-maker—that is, the greater the number of potential states the decisional system can enter.

To say that a system is complex is to say little about empirical approaches from system theory. Such systems approaches typically consider the systemic property of "organized complexity." Complexity by itself does not necessitate a systems approach. For example, Bales (1953) hypothesized an "equilibrium model" of group interaction which suggested that as a group increases in complexity (e.g., addition of new members, differentiation of roles, etc.) the group becomes less stable. This instability could be counteracted by, for example, a greater degree of centralized control to serve as a simplifying agent. But complexity is not a single property which characterizes all systems in the same way. It is far more valuable, then, to conceptualize the complexity characteristic of systems in terms of some degree of organized complexity.

Rapoport and Horvath (1968, p. 73) distinguish organized complexity from "organized simplicity" and "chaotic complexity." Organized complexity is thus a continuum bounded by the polar extremes of simplicity and chaos. According to Rapoport and Horvath:

> The organization of a system is simple if the system is a serial or an additive complex of components each of which is understood. . . . [for example,] a time-linear chain of events, each a determinate consequence of the preceding one. . . .
> At the other extreme is "chaotic complexity" where the number of entities involved is so vast that the interactions can be described in terms of continuously distributed quantities or gradients. (p. 73)

A system governed by physical quasi-causal laws exemplifies a simple system. Bales's equilibrium hypothesis probably visualized the complexity of a group as chaotic rather than organized. An axiom of open systems indicates that they tend to evolve to states of ever-increasing complexity across time. In terms of structural complexity, such an evolutionary process is observable, as Darwinian theory has demonstrated, in the growth and increasing differentiation of material forms (e.g., biological species), typically through the mode of natural selection.

Increased growth and differentiation are also characteristic of organized complexity in the time dimension. Differentiation and growth in time, however, refer not to material objects but to systemic states or events. Pringle (1968) discusses complexity in time:

> This space-time transposition is not easy to visualize, since . . . complexity implies verifiability of observation. Verifiability in this case cannot mean repeatability of successive observations, but must imply confirmation by simultaneous observations in different places. Behaviour is thus fully ordered when it consists of an indefinite repetition of the same event, and chaotic when the sequence of events does not contain any element of repetition whatever. The complexity of a description of the behaviour resides in the number of independent rhythms [i.e., patterns] into which it can be analysed, and it relies for its objectivity on the fact that several simultaneous observations yield the same result. (p. 264).

Organized complexity (either in space or time), then, implies some selection process. That is, among all the possible differentiations of material forms or event-states, only some are selected while others are not selected. Unlike a simple system, the resultant selections cannot be predicted from initial conditions or primal cause. And unlike a chaotic system, selections of event-states or forms are not totally accidental or random. An analysis of organized complexity in systems strongly implies longitudinal observation utilizing a model of probability. These evolutionary explanations which result from a probabilistic model involve some attempt to determine the degree of organized complexity, that is, a position on the continuum somewhere between simplicity and chaos, in order to maximize understanding of systemic functioning. Systemic complexity is thus not an empirical "problem" which needs to be overcome by simplifying the system conceptually. Rather, organized complexity is a property of the system which needs to be confronted empirically in any systems approach to scientific inquiry.

Self-regulation

The regulatory mechanisms of systems are rather common knowledge to members of division 1. Regulation implies feedback processes, both negative and positive, which serve to counteract or amplify deviations in the system. The significance of these feedback processes to empirical systems approaches is well known. Of more importance to our purpose in relating system theory to information/communication systems is the principle of self-regulation, which characterizes all open systems.

The property of self-regulation is inherent within open systems and is what Sorokin (1967, p. 113) calls, "immanent self-regulation and self-direction." According to Sorokin:

> Any functional or logical system as a unity has a certain degree of autonomy and inherent self-regulation in its functioning and change. . . . The autonomy of any system means further existence of some margin of choice or selection on its part with regard to the infinitely great number of varying external agents and objects which may influence it. . . . The functions, change, and destiny of the system are determined not only and not so much by the external circumstances (except in the case of catastrophic accidents), but by the nature of the system itself and by the relationship between its parts.

This systemic principle of self-regulation thus demands the consideration of regulatory processes *inherent* within a system, which largely determine the influence of forces external to the system rather than visualizing the system as determined by those forces.

Under any circumstances, open-systems approaches rarely search for antecedent conditions or causes as the basis for explanation of systemic functioning. The environment does not influence the system as much as the system influences itself. To a large extent, the environment is a *creation* of the self-regulating system, especially in the case of a social system. Weick (1977) terms this phenomenon of social organizing the "enacted environment." In any case, antecedent or causally-based explanations are ill-suited to the self-regulating open system. Jackson (1969, p. 390) suggests that this traditional model of scientific explanation "does not encompass those feedback processes of a system which *achieve outcomes*. . . . Thus the study of single elements or static 'before and after' situations will not be too enlightening. . . . Adopting the premise of . . . a system requires us to *attend only to present (observable) process*, that is, to ecology rather than genesis."

Systems approaches to empirical inquiry are undoubtedly unconventional, at least in the sense of traditional and time-tested modes of explanation and conceptualizations. The systemic principle of self-regulation, particularly, requires revision of many of our traditional modes of thought. And this is the phenomenon which we shall later call "thinking systems." Specific reconceptualizations obligated by "thinking systems" will be discussed later.

CHARACTERISTICS OF INFORMATION/COMMUNICATION SYSTEMS

Applying system theory to any empirical inquiry requires that the investigator consider those characteristics which are intrinsic to the empirical phenomena. Certainly the phenomena of communication/information systems are no exception. In no way do these characteristics imply a redefinition or even adaptation of the properties of systems in general. Those properties reflect axiom-like epistemological assumptions. On the other hand, the systemic principles, discussed earlier, are so abstract as to resist immediate application in the absence of some consideration of the phenomenal characteristics of communication.

Hierarchy of Social Systems

It seems clear that the study of communication is implicitly a study of *human* communication. Communication/information systems are, above all, social systems, and components of social systems are people. Although some may distinguish between human communication and mass communication, I must reject the viability of such a distinction. A similar dichotomy is present in separating "hardware" from "software" in computer systems. But like hardware and software in mass communication, their relationship is complementary, not dichotomous. A systems approach to communication, thus, inevitably concerns itself with a social system. It may or may not include technological components.

Certainly the components of any social system are people—human beings or collectivities of human beings. But this does not mean to imply necessarily that the unit of empirical analysis is a person or collection of persons. The holistic principle of systems suggests that the relationship or connectedness between people is of greater analytical import. Thus, systems approaches in social sciences have used such analytical units as roles, interactions, or relationships. The isolated individual is rarely the same as the individual component in a system.

In discussing systems approaches in psychiatry, Jackson (1969, p. 389) remarks, "It is likely that what we mean by the term "individual" when we take the family system into account may be quite different from what this term presently describes" (author's emphasis deleted). Jackson's point is not that the individual's self experiences some change when it enters a system. Rather, he suggests that our understanding of, in this instance, human behavior changes in considering the systemic context. He goes on to provide an example of that changed understanding. "The important point here is that the behavior which is usually seen as symptomatic [of a psychiatric pathology] in terms of the individual can be seen as adaptive, even appropriate, in terms of the vital system within which the individual operates" (p. 393).

The unit of analysis in a systems approach thus implies the relatedness feature which connects the components in a social system. The systems approach, then, subordinates explanations from the viewpoint of the individual in favor of holistic explanations from the view of the system. Jackson provides another example of this shift in explanatory level when he rejects the notion "that a sadist met a masochist and they lived happily ever after because they were 'made for each other.' On the contrary, we are constantly defining and *being defined* by the nature of our relationships."

We are well aware that social systems exist inherently in a hierarchy of systems—i.e., interpersonal, group, organizational, mass communication. Each level in the hierarchy includes those properties or characteristics of its subsystems. But each level in the hierarchy generates new emergent properties of that suprasystem which are not evident in any of the subsystems. Grobstein (1973) terms this phenomenon of emergent properties "neogenesis." He suggests that emergent properties at each succeeding level of the hierarchy can be observed only at that level and simply do not exist in the sublevel. He states:

> The new information generated by the relationships that are established as the new set [i.e., suprasystem] appears must be read in the context of the next higher order set . . . in both the developmental and in the functional sense, important new properties arise at the transition between a given set and its higher order set. Conversely, such properties tend to be lost if components of a set are dispersed or if a set is dissociated from its context of superset." (p. 45, author's emphasis deleted)

In terms of communication systems some properties emerge at an hierarchical level which simply do not exist at the lower level. For example, who is the deviant in a dyad? Can an individual be a leader in the absence of a follower. In this way, transitions upward in the hierarchy of social systems inherently involve increases in complexity. That is, group communication is more complex than dyadic communication; organizational communication is more complex than the group system; mass communication is still more complex, and so forth. The hierarchy of social systems, then, can be called levels of complexity of communication/information systems, in the sense that different phenomenal characteristics of a system are created at each higher-order level of the systemic hierarchy.

While transitions to a higher-order communication system involve increases in complexity, such complexity does not necessarily mandate empirical consideration of all the systemic properties of each subordinate level contained within the system. That is, as analysis moves upward in the hierarchy of social systems, those properties significant to the lower levels become less distinct. In this way, individual differences of personalities, attitudes, or perceptual sets of individuals in a dyad or group are less distinct and thereby less meaningful in mass communication. The increasing level of complexity implicit in the systemic hierarchy does not necessarily imply greater problems in empirical analysis at a more complex level.

Systems approaches, consistent with earlier discussions, do not emphasize causal or quasi-causal models of explanation. Phrased another way, the phenomena of communication/information systems are indeterminate. Pattee (1973, pp. 135-144) specifically attributes the indeterminancy inherent in systems approaches to the hierarchical organization of systems. He advocates a multilevel analysis of systems to solve what he calls "the central problem of hierarchy theory."

Pattee demands that systems approaches concern themselves with both the structural and the descriptive levels of systemic hierarchy, that is, "the epistemological relation between events and descriptions of events—between matter and symbol" (p. 136). He cites the paradox inherent in deterministic explanations relevant to communication/information systems. That paradox exists when the explanatory model assumes behavior governed by an irreversible and time-symmetric law while at the same time assuming the availability of choice among behavioral alternatives. He argues, "How can we be governed by inexorable natural laws and still choose to do whatever we wish? These questions appear paradoxical only in the context of single-level descriptions" (p. 142).

Applying the levels of structure and description to our earlier human-mass communication distinction, Pattee seems to be arguing that systems approaches to empiricism within hierarchy theory necessarily involve inquiry into both the "hardware" and "software" elements of communication/information systems. Looking solely at the structural (hardware) level of analysis allows for deterministic explanations which are quite inappropriate at the descriptive (software) level.

Without a doubt, systems approaches to communication necessarily involve empirical consideration of the hierarchy of social systems—hierarchy of subsystem-suprasystem relationships as well as structural-descriptive-epistemological relationships. To ignore the hierarchy of information systems is to unfairly delimit our understanding of the complexity of human communication.

Event Data

A year ago, Krippendorff (1977, pp. 154-155) noted what he called "institutional barriers" to systems approaches in communication. He suggested that the basis for these barriers lies in the fact that systems approaches to communication include "*no obvious materiality as referent*." In an earlier discussion (Fisher, 1978, pp. 103-104), I have referred to the material existence of components as a tenet of a mechanistic perspective of communication. The point is, as Krippendorff indicates, central to systems approaches to communication inquiry. Systems approaches endow the time dimension of communication with centrality and correspondingly reduce the significance of the spatial aspects of communication.

The most obvious implication of the centrality of the time dimension is reflected in the nature of the data to be employed. As Dore (1961) stipulates in discussing functionalism, a first cousin to system theory, events are paramount in the explanation. Data are typically events. They occur in time. They are fleeting and have no material existence as such. Hence, communication within a systems approach is clearly not "thing-like." The resultant view of communication process is perhaps best exemplified by Birdwhistell's rather eloquent statement cited by Watzlawick, Beavin, and Jackson (1967):

> An individual does not communicate; he engages in or becomes part of communication. He may move, or make noises. . . . but he does not communicate. In a parallel fashion, he may see, he may hear, smell, taste, or feel—but he does not communicate. In other words, he does not originate communication; he participates in it. Communication as a system, then, is not to be understood on a simple model of action and reaction, however complexly stated. As a system, it is to be comprehended on the transactional level. (p. 70)

As Birdwhistell implies, a systems approach to communication not only utilizes events as the principal data in the inquiry but proceeds to analyze those data by searching for patterns of connectedness or relatedness among those event-data. Perhaps the best summary of such analysis is provided by Cappella (1977, pp. 45-48), who provides three recommendations: "Communication phenomena must be conceived as time-dependent processes. . . . Communication must be studied as an ever-changing, unbounded, unsequenced, and totally interdependent process. . . . Communication processes must be studied as interaction sequences."

The greatest problem in utilizing events as data within systems approaches to communication theory and inquiry is conceptual rather than analytical. Conceiving of a communication/information system composed of events, one gets the uneasy feeling that the system becomes somehow less "real"—less tangible and less distinctive than one might imagine. In many respects, communication systems are less distinctive, but they are no less significant. To the contrary, the centrality of event-data implies further conceptual revisions of communication. The spatial or thing-like conceptualizations of communication from other approaches are not directly applicable to systems approaches. Again, the principal problem for the communication scientist employing a systems approach is to learn how to "think systems."

Rule-Conforming Explanations

Cappella's (1977, pp. 48-49) fourth recommendation for communication inquiry regards the formalization of explanation: "Communication must be studied as a system of constitutive and regulative rules." Unfortunately, Cushman and Pearce (1977, pp. 175-177) imply that systems approaches to communication provide a perspective which is somehow different from a rules perspective. I say "unfortunately" because there appears to be nothing which would prohibit an amalgamation of systems approaches within a theoretical formalization of rules. Of course, all systems approaches need not employ rule-conforming explanations, nor are all rule formalizations systems approaches. Nevertheless, systems approaches to communication/information systems, as defined, are more amenable to explanation within a rule formalization than from a covering-law model.

System theory provides an epistemological basis for communication theory and inquiry, but a rules perspective does not necessarily contain an epistemology. In fact, the various applications of rules to communication have not always been in agreement on the epistemological basis of communication rules. For example, Cushman (1977) utilizes the self-concept as the epistemological source for his rules-based explanation of communication. Pearce (1976, see also Cushman & Pearce, 1977) employs motivation of the social actors in the form of von Wright's (1971) "practical syllogism." Such an epistemology is in the same spirit as Schutz's (see, e.g., 1970, pp. 126-129) "in-order-to motives," as distinguished from "because motives," in which the social actor bestows meaning upon his ongoing action as an intention to bring about a projected goal.

Emshoff (1971) provides yet another potential epistemological basis for a rules-based explanation of communication. He seeks to identify the "causal factors which occur prior to the behavioral actions" and then develop "objective procedures for measuring how the subject perceives each of the factors" in order to construct "a model which shows how a subject will act under each possible combination of perceptions of the causal factors."

A fourth possible epistemology for communication rules lies within the constraint inherent within the regularity of the interaction sequences themselves (see Fisher, 1976). Such an epistemology emanates directly from what Watzlawick, Beavin, and Jackson (1967, pp. 131-132) call "the limiting effect of communication." Unlike the other epistemological bases, which require that the social actor be consciously aware of the rules operant in the situation, Watzlawick, Beavin, and Jackson suggest that such awareness may be superfluous. They state:

> *Context*, then, can be more or less restricting, but always determines the contingencies to some extent. But context does not consist only of institutional, external (to the communicants) factors. The manifest messages exchanged become part of the particular interpersonal context and place their restrictions on subsequent interaction. . . . Even to disagree, reject, or redefine the previous message is not only to respond but thereby to engender an involvement that need not have any other basis except the relationship definition and the commitment inherent in *any* communication. (p. 132)

The epistemological bases for rules explanations of human communication therefore include Cushman's self-concept, Pearce's goal-directed motivation, Emshoff's perceived antecedent factors, and Watzlawick, Beavin, and Jackson's limitation principle. Which is the appropriate epistemology for communication rules? Apparently all are appropriate. As Cappella (1977, p. 49) points out, "most rules theories offer a prominent place to the individual's subjective choice." All of these epistemologies include subjective choice on the part of the social actor. The epistemological difference lies in whether one chooses to seek a primal basis for that subjective choice (in terms of goals, self-concept, or antecedent conditions) or whether one views choice making as simply inevitable and inescapable. According to Watzlawick, Beavin, and Jackson, then, why seek the reason or cause for the initial choice when the choice, having been made, results in a limitation or constraint on subsequent interaction patterns? There appears no necessary rationale for choosing one epistemology over another. The rationale for one's epistemology inevitably comes down to a question of faith. Certainly there can be no direct proof that one is true and all others are false.

The important issue of rules-based explanations, therefore, is not so much whether a subjective choice is made, but the extent to which the actor must be aware of some basis for making the choice. All rules theorists will undoubtedly agree that rules serve to explain human behavior because the actors choose to conform to those rules. To the extent that they are aware of why they made the choice or even that they did make a choice may depend upon the communicative situation. Toulmin (1974) provides a "heptachotomy" of typical situations which range from a high-level awareness of rules operating in the situation to no such awareness. He suggests, then, that the actor's awareness of choice is a matter of degree rather than a prerequisite axiom.

It seems clear that systems approaches to communication theory and inquiry are more appropriately formalized within a rule-conforming model of explanation, rather than law-governed models. Systemic complexity argues against making inferences on the basis of antecedent conditions, a characteristic typical of a covering-law model of theory. Thus, systems analysts in communication will probably opt for rule-conforming models of explanation. In this sense, system theory provides the epistemology for communication theory and inquiry, while rules provide the explanatory form or model. Whether the epistemological basis is self-concept, in-order-to motivation, or the limitation principle, a systems approach is conceptually practicable. Naturally, all systems approaches are not identical. One person's systems approach may indeed be quite different from another person's.

SYSTEMS RESEARCH IN COMMUNICATION

A few years ago, my father-in-law suffered a heart attack, his first. Several years prior to that, my brother also survived a heart attack. With my medical naivete, I found it difficult to comprehend why one was required to curtail his diet and activity while the other had few such limitations. It soon became apparent to me that there are many varieties of heart attacks. Their causes are different; their symptoms are different; their treatments are different. I was naive enough not to be aware of these differences. The same is true of systems approaches to communication inquiry. In our naivete we often tend to lump them all together in the mistaken belief that system theory is system theory.

The abstractness of system theory allows for many disparate methodologies and conceptualizations within its parameters. As Rosen has already pointed out, system theory does not provide any empirical categories to load the system. Those categories, the most significant element of empiricism, are left to the investigator. Thus, systems approaches are quite disparate when one considers the disparity among investigators' intentions, purposes, empirical phenomena observed, and analytical techniques employed. The following paragraphs attempt to delineate a few of the major approaches to communication theory and inquiry which utilize system theory as a central rationale.

Networks

System research in communication networks provides a conceptual advantage unlike many other systems approaches. That is, it endows the communication/information system with a quasi-materiality. Unlike earlier network studies in social psychology (e.g., Bavelas, 1950; Leavitt, 1951), network research in communication has expanded the "connectedness" dimension from that of merely a message-exchange channel to a broader concept of relationship or kinship. While much of the network analysis in communication has been adapted to the analysis of formal organizations (see, e.g., Farace, Monge, & Russell, 1977), network analysis has also been applied to families (e.g., Edwards & Monge, 1977). Few network analyses in communication have been published. They include mostly unpublished research, principally from Michigan State University (see, e.g., Amend, 1971; Farace & Morris, 1969; Guimaraes, 1970; MacDonald, 1970; Jacob, 1972; Monge, 1972). On the other hand, analyses of structural aspects of information systems have been popular in such related fields as anthropology, sociology, and business management. It is likely that their popularity in communication research will increase in the future.

Modelling and Theorizing

Much of the earlier literature employing system theory in communication has included theoretical "thinkpieces." To a great extent, these articles (e.g., Fisher & Hawes, 1971; Monge 1973; Thayer, 1972; Krippendorff, 1975; Thayer, 1975; and Monge, 1977) reflect several purposes: to popularize system theory as a viable alternative approach in communication, to explicate the parameters of a general theoretical model, and to provide the prerequisite model preliminary to performing empirical research.

A general reading of these thinkpieces leads one to the realization that the authors espouse a number of different approaches to communication from essentially the same methatheoretical perspective of system theory. They are, above all, models for inquiry. In the sense that these models circumscribe and isolate processes, they reflect epistemologically different approaches to communication inquiry. That is, although the general properties of systems are common to all models, the suggested isomorphisms with empirical phenomena of communication vary widely, depending on the authors' emphases and interests.

Recently, system theorists in communication have taken a mathematical bent in their modelling of communication/information systems (see, e.g., Cappella, 1976; Hawes & Foley, 1976; Hewes, Brazil, & Evans, 1977; Capella, 1974). These mathematical models employ the formalistic assumptions of pathway analysis and cybernetics (e.g., Cappella, 1975) as well as the probabilistic modeling of stochastic and Markov processes (e.g., Hewes, 1975). It is probably from such a specific approach to communication that one infers the undue emphasis on mathematical formalization within all systems approaches. Certainly, attempts to employ modeling procedures as a systems approach to communication do rely heavily on mathematical formalization. Much more data-based research needs to be performed, as empirical tests of these models, before anyone is able to assess their significance and empirical worth.

Interaction Patterning

Unquestionably the most prolific (in terms of sheer number of published research reports) systems approach to communication inquiry is the study of interaction sequences. The most common approach to the discovery of interaction sequences has been to analyze ongoing interaction into specific action categories for the purpose of discovering recurrent patterns or sequences within the stream of communicational behavior. The typical research methodology, termed interaction analysis, probably had its greatest impetus in Bales's (1950) popular twelve-category system called "Interaction Process Analysis." In terms of system theory, however, Bales did not utilize the methodology as an attempt to discover interaction sequences but, rather, sought only gross variations in category use within his "equilibrium model."

Attempts to discover interaction sequences reflect a variety of research purposes. One common purpose deals with the longitudinal development or change over time of interaction patterns (e.g., Fisher, 1970; Valentine & Fisher, 1974; Mabry, 1975b; Ellis & Fisher, 1975; Fisher & Beach, 1977b). Other research purposes have included a variety of communicative settings, such as decision-making groups, encounter groups, consciousness-raising groups, families, medical teams, and so forth (e.g., Hawes & Foley; 1973; Glover, 1974; Mabry, 1975a; Thornton, 1976; Drecksel & Fisher, 1977). Specific interpersonal variables such as leadership (e.g., DeStephen, 1977; Geonetta & Gouran, 1977), have also served as the focus of research in interaction sequences. Recently, research in sequences has focused on relational aspects of communication, notably Bateson's (1958) use of control modes (see, e.g., Mark, 1971; Millar & Rogers, 1976; Parks, et al., 1976; Drecksel & Fisher, 1977; Ellis, 1977; Fisher & Beach, 1977b).

Perhaps the most significant innovations in the search for interaction sequences have included the techniques used to analyze data generated from interaction analyses. Much of the earlier research employed nonparametric statistics such as chi-square (e.g., Scheidel & Crowell, 1964, 1966; Fisher, 1970; Gouran & Baird, 1972; Baird, 1974). More recently, statistics from information theory adapted to stochastic probability models, specifically Markov processes, have achieved popularity in analyzing interaction data (see, e.g., Hewes, 1975; Hawes & Foley, 1976; Fisher, Glover, & Ellis, 1977; Fisher & Beach, 1977a, 1977b; Stech, 1970, 1975, 1977).

These three systems approaches to communication theory and inquiry certainly do not exhaust the potential uses of system theory in communication. They are included, not as a comprehensive survey of systems approaches in communication, but as examples of systems approaches. The intent is to provide some appreciation for various uses of system theory in communication, not to provide a comprehensive bibliography of systems research in communication. With these approaches in mind, then, it is now possible to turn to a discussion of prerequisites to performing systems research in communication, preliminary to providing a realistic assessment of its worth.

DIFFICULTIES IN PERFORMING SYSTEMS RESEARCH

Unlike other epistemological perspectives in communication inquiry, systems research requires more than the decision to do it. Inquiry from a systems perspective implies a frame of mind, a methodology, data analysis, and interpretations of results which are somewhat unique. Traditional training for performing empirical inquiry does not typically include these unique traits of systems research. On the other hand, neither are systems approaches to communication mystical, in the sense that rules for performing such research are not explicable. They are simply different from the traditional modes of inquiry. Some of these differences are discussed in the following pages in an attempt to achieve some appreciation for systems approaches to communication.

Thinking Systems

Huse and Bowditch (1977, p. 39) suggest that "the most important concept to keep in mind is the need to *think* in systems terms. This thought process overrides the importance of attempting to *measure* each variable." The first prerequisite to performing systems research, then, is to develop this mental framework, that is, to think in systems terms. Emory (1969), for example, summarizes his view of systems theory as "systems thinking." To think systems is difficult only because it is unconventional. For years we have taught and rewarded progress in analytical or critical thinking. The traditional thought processes involve dissecting or reducing a whole into its component parts or categories, for example, propositions into issues, arguments into premises and warrants, problems into causes and needs.

Systems thinking avoids such reductionistic processes. To think in systems terms is not to categorize but to search for connectedness principles, isomorphisms, interrelationships—in short, a holistic approach. To isolate many variables is equally problematic. In fact, multivariate (as distinguished from univariate) analysis is simply not an issue in system thinking. Some have even suggested that systems thinking is to reject thinking in terms of variables. Under any circumstances, the mind-set which avoids the tendency to analyze and categorize in favor of seeking transactions among phenomena is the goal. But, as Lindsey (1972) points out, "the shift to systems thinking will be by no means simple. . . . Categorical thinking is so firmly rooted a habit that the change to systems thinking will be as difficult as the transition from a three-dimensional to a four-dimensional geometry."

Time Analysis

A few years ago, it was popular to debate the "true" meaning of "process" in communication theory and inquiry (e.g., Smith, 1972). While that debate is now outdated and relatively trivial, it did spawn a greater interest in longitudinal analyses of communicative phenomena conceived as a series of events. It focused interest on what Vickers (1971, p. 202) terms a "sense of history, which is the awareness of time as a dimension." Not only is communication thus conceived as a series of events, but also as an ongoing phenomenon demanding longitudinal analysis. Considerably more research avoiding the pretest-posttest research model in favor of ongoing observation now appears in our journals.

Such time analyses of communication seek ultimately to discover patterns, in the form of interaction sequences, kinship relations, feedback loops, and so forth, which persist and serve to characterize and regulate communication/information systems. Orchard (1972) suggests that the systems approach searches for systemic behaviors, defined as "a particular time-invariant relation specified for a set of quantities . . . based on samples of a certain pattern." He distinguishes among "permanent behaviors," "relatively permanent behavior," and "temporary behavior" which are organized into "programs" within the system. Scheflen (1969) also discusses "behavioral programs" within an interpersonal system of communication. The observation of an ongoing system is thus time consuming and tedious. But if communication is to be characterized as a series of events, then collection, analysis, and interpretation of event-data must maintain the integrity of those data as events which occur in time.

Statistical Analysis

Communication students typically receive their statistical training in the "traditional" paradigm of the social sciences. Such training involves inferential statistics, emphasizing ANOVA, as well as principles of experimental design in an hypothesis-testing model. Those statistics often used in systems approaches to communication inquiry, however, are seldom included in the traditional statistical modes. The nontraditional modes include information theory ($\log_2$-based) statistics, Markov chains, stochastic probability, path analysis, and so forth. The search for new statistics continues (see, e.g., Spillman, Spillman, & Bezdek, 1977).

The "new" statistics are not more sophisticated thatn inferential statistics. They are simply different, that is, unconventional. The problem thus lies in the fact that they are seldom available in formal training received by past and present generations of communication scholars. Hence, those communication scientists wishing to employ systems approaches which demand unconventional statistical analyses have been forced to acquire an understanding of those statistics on their own. While not all systems approaches require nontraditional analyses, it is nonetheless mandatory that analytical treatments of data be appropriate to the data themselves. Acquiring a knowledge of other statistical forms, at the very least, increases the arsenal of analytical tools available to the communication researcher.

Confronting Empirical Complexity

Too often, systemic complexity has been conceptualized as the difference between multivariate and univariate analysis. Such a conceptualization is myopic. The problem is one of analyzing complexity itself and undoubtedly stems from the difficulty in thinking systems, or what Livesey (1972, p. 160) calls "our lack of 'complexity-consciousness' . . . our inability to see things whole because we do not know where to begin and have no teachers who can help us make a start." Complexity itself is a complex phenomenon. In a communication/information system, complexity exists in terms of the various hierarchical levels of analysis, the sheer number of different concepts to be accounted for, the exponential increase in possible interrelationships among concepts, as well as organized complexity in time. A few efforts to confront such empirical complexity (see, e.g., Stech, 1977; Fisher, Glover, & Ellis, 1977) have explored this problem methodologically. Much more remains to be done.

Validity of Action Categories

The validity of the categories used to define and interpret communication/information systems has long been a matter of concern among scholars engaged in researching interaction sequences. Cappella (1977, p. 48) discusses this issue of validating interaction categories specifically "in terms of the perceptions of the participants." He, along with Hawes (1972b), treats this validity issue as an empirical problem and assumes that any interpretation of action must be validated in terms of its consistency with the actor's perception of his or her own action. I have discussed this validity issue elsewhere (Fisher, 1977a, pp. 14-15) as more of a theoretical than an empirical issue—that the basis for validating action categories differs from one theoretical framework to another.

To insist that action categories be validated as similar to actors' perceptions, is probably an "argument from synonymy" and misses the issue somewhat. More important, perhaps, is the epistemological assumption inherent in the connection between cognitive and behavioral phenomena. A superior approach, perhaps, is not to mandate a specific method for validation but, rather, to investigate, empirically and theoretically, the nature of that cognitive-behavioral relationship (see Fisher & Beach, 1977b). In the absence of such definitive investigations, however, we are probably restricted to questioning the validity of action categories until they can be interpreted as being isomorphic with actors' perceptions. As Vickers (1971, pp. 201-202) indicates, "The variables we select are chosen from their relevance to our interests and to the time span of our concern; and we must often choose between the simplification which makes the problem manageable but gravely unrealistic and the more complex representation which makes it realistic but gravely unmanageable." At this point, we have no choice but to attempt to hold the balance even between manageability and realism.

Interpreting Results

The earlier discussions of complexity imply a truism in systems research—if complexity resides within the analysis, then complexity will also exist in the results generated from such analysis. Complexity of analysis, then, creates new problems in interpreting the complexity in the results. One example of such an interpretative problem is the question of how much redundancy (or information) within interaction sequences is optimal. We already know that too much redundancy, for example, the monotony of assembly-line work groups, renders the interactions humanly meaningless. Of course, too little redundancy is equally meaningless since it contains insufficient information to interpret the meaning of the patterns. The problem, then, resides in interpreting how much redundancy may be regarded as an optimal amount. Our own studies of interaction sequences during the past several years have yielded a range of stereotypy (a measure of interactional redundancy) from less than .10 to more than .60 (minimum = 0, maximum = 1.00). How much stereotypy is to be desired? Kolaja (1969, p. 76) has identified this as a problem which has not been resolved, even theoretically.

A second problem in interpreting results from systems analysis of communication is the phenomenon of reciprocity. Researchers typically characterize reciprocity as a response-in-kind. That is, *A* self-discloses to *B*, so *B* responds by self-disclosing to *A*. On the other hand, Bateson (1972, pp. 68-70) suggests that interpretations of reciprocity may be more complex than simply the obvious similarity of responses. For example, although a single instance of an interaction may be asymetrical, in the sense that the response is different from the preceding act, symmetry may characterize the interaction when the analysis considers a large number of instances. That is, *A* attempts to dominate *B*, and *B* submits to the dominating attempt. Given this single instance of interaction, the relationship exhibits no reciprocity and is complementary (dominant-submissive). But over a large number of instances, the analysis might reveal that *A* also responds to *B*'s dominating attempts with submissive acts. Thus, symmetry and reciprocity is regained when, over a large number of instances, the *A*-*B* relationship is characterized by both a dominant-submissive and a submissive-dominant relationship. The result is symmetry—that is, reciprocity.

These are simply two of the possible problems in interpreting the complexity of results generated from a systems approach to communication inquiry. Other possibilities exist in interpreting the stationarity of time parameters in ongoing interaction. For example, where does $Time_1$ end and $Time_2$ begin? Is $Time_1$ of Group *A* equivalent to $Time_1$, in Group *B*? Or is it possible that Group *A*'s $Time_1$ is Group *B*'s $Time_2$? Placing such time parameters "in phase" across different communicative situations and populations is a potentially significant empirical problem. In any case, interpretation of results is inevitably an intervention of the investigator into the "realism" of the phenomenon.

The complexity inherent in the phenomena suggests a multiplicity of possible interpretations of the same results gained from observing the same phenomena. Communication scientists engaged in employing systems approaches to communication research often long for the "good old days" when the null hypothesis was either rejected or it was not. But interpretation of results within the traditional hypothesis-testing paradigm was subject to prior constraints assumptively placed on the investigation. On such *a priori* criteria are available in most systems approaches to communication.

RECONCEPTUALIZATIONS PREREQUISITE TO SYSTEMS INQUIRY

When one engages in systems thinking, one soon discovers that old and familiar concepts assume new and added meaning. The benefit from systems thinking is not so much the application of specific how-to-go-about-it guidelines but, rather, the innovative and mind-expanding approaches to familiar phenomena. To the systems thinker, such innovations are intuitively obvious. But given the whole of inquiry into communication, such innovations are actually reconceptualizations. The ensuing paragraphs treat three of those common reconceptualizations.

Information

It is common in traditional communication research to conceive of information as thing-like—something to be transported from one place to another. Systems thinking revises the concept of information from a materialistic reality to a concept which is *created* within the process of communication. In this sense, information (a la information theory) is created by the connectedness or relatedness among components of a system, rather than transmitted from one component to another. In this way information tends to be less "real," in the sense that it possesses no material referent or physical existence. As Wilden (1972, p. 222) states, "Nor is the unit of survival 'in' entities—'in' the organism or 'in' the environment—the unit of survival is in their relationship, which is nowhere. It is nowhere because it is information." In other words, information has no material or quasi-material referent. Rather, it is created by the apparent connectedness between events which occur as normal systemic functioning.

Another way to visualize information in an analysis of social systems is to conceptualize it as the social system's counterpart of energy as it functions in a physicalistic system. Wilden (1972, p. 361) goes on to point out, "In the open system, therefore, homogeneity can only be sought in the relationships of the system. Since information itself is a relation, the study of open systems must involve the dialectics of their informational relationships, whereas the closed system is amenable to additive energy-entity analysis." Wilden suggests that physical systems imply the existence of material entities and thus are subject to physical laws involving the concept of energy which is necessary to conceptualize the force of entropy.

But the physicalistic concept of energy stipulates that it cannot be created; it can only be transformed from one form to another, given the Second Law of Thermodynamics (i.e., entropy). In the open system, such as a communication system, however, energy is less appropriate to the time-based nature of the data. Thus, information serves as the counterpart of energy. Unlike the physicalistic sense, information can not only be transformed but can be created within a social system. In this way, information (i.e., the connectedness between events), in what Wilden calls "the dialectics of their informational relationships," serves to "energize" the system. Information endows events with meaning, that is, significance. This characteristic is intrinsic to the self-organizing and self-regulating capacity of open systems and is similar to what Weick (1977) terms "enactment processes."

Reconceptualizing information as the energizing force of open systems emphasizes the equifinal nature of open systems. Communication outcomes within a systems approach are not deducible from antecedent states or conditions. Information may be generated in the interim between the antecedent state of initial arrangement of components and the outcome of systemic functioning. That information may serve to modify the trajectory of the system's activity. This antiphysicalistic depiction of systems is a corollary to the substitution of information for energy in open-systems approaches to communication inquiry.

Message

A decade ago, Becker (1968) intimated that our traditional view of message as central to communication, or even as a viable concept within communication, was questionable. His view of message "bits," acquired by information processors over an extended period of time, revised our conventional notion of message as a unified and thing-like entity transmitted on a channel between source and receiver. I have discussed elsewhere (Fisher 1978, pp. 165-283) the various conceptualizations of message (e.g., as transmitted signal, as structural form, as social influence, as interpretation, as reflection of self, as commonality) and have argued that the concept of message may have outlived its usefulness.

A systems approach to communication does not require message in any of its conventional conceptualizations. Rather, such approaches tend to utilize nonmessage concepts such as acts, relationships, or sequences. These nonmessage concepts are generally more explanatory than that of message. Rather than reiterating that argument here, I will merely state the conclusion that the usefulness of the message concept, particularly within a systems approach to communication, is highly limited and probably insignificant.

Control

Our traditional research methodologies have virtually sanctified the concept of control, often at the sacrifice of the complexity inherent within systems approaches. For example, we have tended to assume the existence of situation-dependent constraints on communication and sought to discover those constraints by empirically controlling our observations. That is, we have assumed differences across communicative situations and have attempted to control for those differences, or we have attempted to search for situational differences within a quasi-experimental research paradigm. A systems approach, however, searches, not for differences, but for similarities across contexts. Indeed, if one assumes and seeks differences across communicative situations, he will undoubtedly find them. Situational differences unquestionably exist. But this is not to deny that communicative situations also reflect significant similarities.

The empirical issue is not that communication does not differ from one situation to another. Of course it does. All situations are, to some extent, heterogeneous. On the other hand, many situations are homogeneous in numerous respects. Hence, different situations may be, communicatively speaking, homogeneous in terms of some aspects (i.e., categories) and, at the same time, heterogeneous in terms of others (see, e.g., Fisher, Glover, & Ellis, 1977). To ask, under the guise of empirical control, how a situation does affect or constrain communication is to beg the question. It assumes the inevitability and significance of situational constraints or communication which must be controlled for. More important to the systems thinker are the questions, "In what ways are communicative situations similar? In what ways are they different?'' (see, e.g., Pattee, 1973, pp. 138ff.).

How, then, does one conceptualize control within a systems approach. Pattee (1973) views control as a function of systemic hierarchy. He states clearly that systemic control must satisfy two conditions:

> First, an effective control event cannot be simply a passive, spatial constraint, but must actively change the *rate* of one particular event, reaction, or trajectory relative to the unconstrained rates. . . . Second, the operation of the constraint must be *repeatable* without leading to the freezing up of the system. Another way to say this is that control constraints must limit the trajectories of the system in a regular way without a corresponding freezing out of its configurational degrees of freedom. (pp. 83-84)

Control, then, in a systems approach affects not the outcome of the system so much as it affects the rate of progress toward that outcome or goal-state. Furthermore, systemic control affects the repeatability (or informational patterning) of systemic events while maintaining the system's capacity for choice (or degrees of freedom). In this way, systemic control in a communication/information system is unlike control in a physicalistic system. Unlike laws of physics (e.g., gravity or electrical fields) which constrain or control end-states by allowing no freedom at all, communicative events maintain many degrees of freedom while reflecting constraint or control evident in the degree of patterning (information) of events. This same phenomenon of systemic control was discussed earlier as organized complexity in time, phrased within a model of rule-conforming explanations.

The distinction between the traditional concept of control, and control within a systemic hierarchy should not be misinterpreted as similar to Heisenberg's uncertainty principle. Systems reflect complexity, equifinality and probabilistic connections between events. Outcomes and predictions are not certain, to be sure, but connectedness between events can be computed at a level of expected probability, unlike a random and thus unmeasurable degree of uncertainty. Constraints exist within the system in the form of information. They affect the rate of locomotion along a goal trajectory or the degree of repeatability or patterning of related events, but they also exhibit a typically high number of degrees of freedom. Simply speaking, systemic control is relative rather than absolute.

ON ASSESSING SYSTEMS APPROACHES TO COMMUNICATION

The field of communication is certainly not what Thomas Kuhn (1970) would call a "mature science." That is, communication cannot be characterized within a single unified "paradigm" or "disciplinary matrix" with a single list of "exemplars" shared by communication scholars. Communication is preparadigmatic or, more accurately, multiparadigmatic. Our research reflects many theoretical perspectives, of which system theory is but one. At this point in the development of our discipline, no one perspective can claim the allegiance of all or nearly all members of our scientific community. Choosing any perspective demands that one "buy into" both its strengths and weaknesses. The choice is inevitably a matter of "trade-offs." Choosing a systems approach to communication inquiry, then, should involve an awareness of those trade-offs.

Strengths of Systems Approaches

I shall not dwell long on the strengths of systems approaches to communication. My biases are well known. Clearly the most significant strength of system theory in communication is its potential for integration, and the need for integration is apparent. As Ruben and Kim (1975) point out:

> In areas ranging from anthropology, art, and biology to neurophysiology, psychology, and zoology, scholars have for years concerned themselves with communication, and yet extensive cross-disciplinary fertilization and integration has simply not yet occurred. Journalism, speech communication, mass communication, semiotics, and information sciences have all too frequently been victimized by a similar intellectual isolationsim. For this set of problems, general systems seems to provide a potential solution. (p. 2)

Integrating the domain of inquiry reflected in the study of communication across a broad range of disciplines is certainly a benefit, whose potential, while not yet achieved, is blatantly obvious. Certainly, attempts to integrate various domains of systems inquiry are rampant in the literature (e.g., Jantsch, 1975, pp. 196ff.). Of more immediate import, perhaps, is the need to integrate specific approaches within communication itself. One clear example seems to be that of the cognitive-behavioral underpinnings of communication. On an abstract level, Laszlo (1972, pp. 153-154) implies there are no barriers to their integration: "First, we allow that systems of mind-events of physical events can be internally viewed. We then note that the theories applying to natural and to cognitive systems are isomorphic, with the consequence that when switching from the one to the other system, we do not necessitate changes in theory. The *content* or *referent* of the theory changes; its *form* remains invariant." Laszlo, of course, is not discussing communication specifically, although at least one attempt (Beach & Fisher, 1977) to integrate theoretically cognitive and behavioral dimensions of communication does exist. In a similar vein, empirical integration of content and relationship dimensions (see Fisher & Beach, 1977a) are also necessary.

Of course, many other strengths of system theory have been espoused by systems advocates. Monge (1977, p. 29) has indicated three major advantages of systems approaches to communication: "First, the framework . . . consists of a set of concepts and relationships that are theoretically and logically interrelated. Second, it is a framework which should permit integration of knowledge from a variety of currently disparate academic areas. Third, it is parsimonious, in that it uses far fewer concepts and theories than those generated by alternative approaches. To the already discussed advantage of integration, Monge adds two additional advantages—theoretical consistency and parsimony. Certainly these advantages have not been fully realized empirically in communication research. Those extant examples of systems research, however, have demonstrated their potential and remain, at the very least, some of the principal innovations in communication research of the past decade.

Weaknesses

To a considerable extent, the weaknesses of systems approaches to communication are the same weaknesses which characterize virtually every perspective currently in vogue. The most seldom recognized problem of system approaches is its ontological weakness. Phrased another way, epistemological strength typically involves ontological weakness. System theory is no exception. This problem does not necessarily imply epistemological error in system theory, even though some critics have argued against certain epistemological assumptions of systems. For example, Bateson (1972, p. 405) criticizes the cybernetic method of negative explanation and suggests that there is a difference between "being right" and "not being wrong." The weakness of systems approaches is, rather, that insight into the ontological nature of observed phenomena is sacrificed for its epistemological strength in empirical observation. For example, Hawes (1977, p. 68) states, "before we search for . . . theories to answer 'why' questions, let's be certain we have sufficient descriptive and interpretive work for these explanations."

A comparison of phenomenology and empiricism (in a radical sense) may serve to explain this issue. Phenomenology is ontologically based. Its fundamental question asks, "What is the nature of being-ness in objects observed?" Empirical science is more epistemologically based. Its principle question is, "What is the nature of how we know what we know?" A phenomenological method, then, attempts to achieve ontological reduction of observed phenomena into their essential foundations. A scientific method applies rules for relating observational data to empirical claims. Given this overly general framework, then, the ontological-epistemological dichotomy is more apparent. If results from two phenomenological studies differ, the only way to determine which study is more accurate or adequate is to engage in argument, dialogue, and ultimately persuasion among phenomenological scholars. On the other hand, if results from two "scientific" studies differ, then *a priori* criteria of relating data to claims are applied in order to determine which set of results is more accurate or adequate.

In general philosophical terms, ontology should precede epistemology. It is in this sense that Hawes advocates greater attention to questions asked before we ask them. In practice, however, the greater tendency is to choose an observational approach which is *either* ontologically based or epistemologically based. The choice among methods or theoretical perspectives is, practically speaking, which trade-off the scholar wishes to make—ontological strength and epistemological weakness or epistemological strength and ontological weakness. Systems epistemologists rarely ask the question, "What is it we wish to know?" Conversely, phenomenologists rarely address the question, "How do we come to know what we know?"

The systems scholar, then, finds himself squarely between the horns of the epistemological-ontological dilemma. The way out is typically a rationalization. Beer (1966, p. 243) exemplifies this attitude when he characterizes applications of systems principles to phenomena as "acts of mental recognition rather than characteristics of physical things." He goes on to state: "We select, from an infinite number of relations between things, a set which, because of coherence and pattern and purpose, permits an interpretation of what might otherwise be a meaningless cavalcade of arbitrary events. It follows that the detection of system in the world outside ourselves is a subjective matter." This does not mean to imply that systems approaches cannot have an ontology. Indeed Laszlo (1972, pp. 143-163) has suggested a general ontology within a general systems framework. However, empirical approaches employing system theory in communication, at this point in their development, must accept an ontological weakness along with epistemological strength. Hopefully, such acceptance need be only a temporary condition.

Like many other theoretical perspectives in communication, as well as in other fields, system theory exhibits rather substantial disagreement among its exponents. Only one of those disagreements will be discussed here as representative of such lack of unanimity. Monge (1977, p. 22) specifies among his conceptualizations of communicative phenomena within an open system a prerequisite logical condition—"stipulation of the environment. In open systems this is crucial because the system's exchange with the environment, that is, its inputs and outputs, must be explained." Monge's notion is a prevalent one among systems theorists, in that they assume that the parameters or boundaries of a system (its interface with an environment) must be distinctly determined.

On the other hand, Weick (1977) argues that open social systems typically create, invent, or "enact" their environment in the sense that "the environment is located in the mind of the actor and is imposed by him on experience in order to make that experience more meaningful" (p. 274). Weick's notion of an enacted environment thus blurs the distinction between inputs and outputs of a system. In fact, the mere existence of an enacted environment becomes itself an output of the system so that the environment, in the form of what Weick calls "sensemaking episodes," is stored in the retention processes of the system as past wisdom (p. 279).

In the typical sense that an environment serves to constrain a system, an enacted environment becomes an event constrained by the system. Enacted environments of the past can serve to constrain contemporary enactments of the environment, as well as contemporary enactments' serving to constrain past enactments. At best, then, an environment and a system are only loosely coupled through the related interactions within the system itself.

While other epistemological disagreements exist among systems theorists, the environment-system boundaries disagreement is one of the most glaring. To some theorists, the stipulation of systemic parameters is an *a priori* and axiomatic assumption. To others, apparently, the issue is defined more ontologically. To the extent that an environment loses any semblance of physicalism, it becomes part of the information or organizing processes. In this way, systems are empowered to create their environments in the same sense that they can create information. A different situation, of course, exists in a closed-system analysis in which systems, isolated from their environments, exhibit clear and evident parameters, across which there is no transfer of energy or interaction.

A third weakness of systems approaches to communication is certainly not unique. Within the general and abstract methatheory of systems has been a proliferation of wide-ranging and disparate empirical approaches, techniques, and methodologies. In some cases, this proliferation has involved theoretical conceptualizations as well as differences in observational techniques. As Delia (1977, pp. 51-53) points out, this proliferation stems more from the metatheoretical stance of the systems theorist and less from substantive claims made. This weakness, of course, is the other side of the coin in the quest for theoretical integration. According to Delia, "The attainment of 'unity' among concepts simply through provision of a framework for organizing and relating existing theoretical perspectives is not to attain a genuinely general and integrated conceptual stance" (p. 52).

To be perfectly frank, systems theorists have been guilty of searching for appropriate analytical units in the form of substantive claims. And that problem is an understandable reflection of the early stage of substantive development of systems theory in communication. Systems theorists in communication simply have not solved this fundamental conceptual problem. Coleman (1971, p. 79) explains, "The fundamental question of what is the subject of action, i.e., what is the appropriate unit of analysis, is the same in both fields [biology and social science] as are many of the other conceptual problems." Coleman advocates shifting the conceptualization of social systems from the individual, that is, the "whole person," to the concept of "role."

Whether role, self-concept, in-order-to motivation, or pragmatic sequence is the appropriate unit of analysis remains an unanswerable question at this point. More importantly, as Delia indicates, any theoretical integration claimed for systems theory must await the unification of substantive theory development. And that integration will be organized principally around analytical units to reflect a stance identifiable as "the" system approach to communicative phenomena. While other more traditional approaches differ principally in modes of operationalizing those concepts, systems approaches to communication reflect proliferation of both concepts, (i.e., equivocation of same and similar concepts) and operationalizations.

What, then, is the conclusion of this attempt to assess strengths and weaknesses of system approaches to communication. Unfortunately, no such conclusion can be definitive. The choice of one's own theoretical perspective remains a function of the individual scholar's interests, purposes, desires, and goals. Moreover, each scholar *must* make such a choice—to be able to claim a perspective as one's own to stand up and be counted. Delia (1977) is emphatic on this point.

> While multiple perspectives ought to be encouraged at the community level, . . . at the individual level, multiple perspectivism ought to be discouraged. To work with a theory requires a degree of existential commitment to its categories as a way of organizing reality and as providing a way of studying a domain of phenomena. Shifts from perspective to perspective all too often result in conceptual ambiguities and confusions in the theoretical stances of individual researchers and in discontinuities in research programs. . . . While it may be highly desirable to have competing multiple perspectives at the community level, the task of the individual researcher is to develop, utilize, and defend a coherent theoretical system. (p. 61)

I could not agree more with Delia's assessment of requiring a choice among theoretical perspectives at the individual level. I have elsewhere (Fisher, 1978) termed the failure to do so (i.e., shifting from perspective to perspective) "intellectual dilletantism." Such multiple perspectivism by an individual is simply not defensible from any rational or scientific basis of inquiry. To choose a perspective, however, requires that a scholar-researcher "buy into" both the strengths and weaknesses of that perspective. Whichever perspective is chosen is inevitably the individual's answer to the question, "What does it do for me?"

CONCLUSION

To understand system theory and to think systems with any degree of sophistication is to understand the magnitude of the task at hand—understanding and explaining the complexities of human communication. Few systems theorists are so naive that they possess a blind faith in the abstract principles of systems in the belief that such concepts hold all the answers to desired knowledge. To the contrary, systems theorists tend to evaluate the potential of the goal and plod forward in the direction of its accomplishment, despite the difficulty in gathering, analyzing, and interpreting data generated from systems analyses.

Systems approaches to communication reflect a

variety of empirical and conceptual attempts to explain and understand the complex phenomena of human communication. At this point, systems approaches can claim only marginal significance in the whole of communication theory and inquiry. Sorokin (1966, p. 645) explains, "No significant theory can be purely abstract and devoid of relevant empirical content, nor can it consist of a mere collection of empirical facts devoid of an adequate explanatory theory" (author's emphasis deleted). Whereas, one systems approach may exhibit greater theoretical strength and another may reflect greater empirical support, the combination of both, essential to Sorokin's view of a "significant theory," has not yet been realized.

Drawing together empirical support and abstracted systemic properties within a unified theory of some significance is extraordinarily difficult. Borrowing Weick's (1977, p. 287) description of enactment processes, one could say that systems approaches to communication are: "About inductions rather than deductions, about likelihoods rather than certainties, about contingencies rather than necessities, about plausible explanations rather than proofs, about exceptions rather than uniformities, about invention rather than discovery, and about the pragmatically sensible rather than the strictly logical." It is simply impossible to be definitive about systems approaches to communication given this relativistic conception of system theory. We have been too often guilty of claiming theoretical integration of too much of the entire world and have neglected integration within systems approaches themselves. Nevertheless, systems theorists reflect unbridled optimism. My own optimism is totally consistent with that of Churchman's (1968, pp. 230-232):

> It's not as though we can expect that next year or a decade from now someone will find the correct systems approach and all deception will disappear. This, in my opinion, is not in the nature of systems. What is in the nature of systems is a continuing perception and deception, a continuing reviewing of the world, of the whole system, and of its components. The essence of the systems approach, therefore, is confusion as well as enlightenment. The two are inseparable aspects of human living.

And finally, my bias:
. . . *The systems approach is not a bad idea.*

REFERENCES

ACKOFF, R.L., & EMERY, R.E. *On purposeful systems.* Chicago: Aldine-Atherton, 1972.

AMEND, E. Liaison communication roles of professionals in a research dissemination organization. Unpublished doctoral dissertation, Michigan State University, 1971.

BAIRD, J.E., JR. A comparison of distributional and sequential structure in cooperative and comparative group discussions. *Speech Monographs*, 1974, 41, 226-232.

BALES, R.F. *Interaction process analysis.* Reading, Mass.: Addison-Wesley, 1950.

BALES, R.F. The equilibrium problem in small groups. In T. Parsons, R.F. Bales, & E. Shils (Eds.), *Working papers in the theory of action*. New York: Free Press, 1953, 111-161.

BATESON, G. *Naven* (2nd ed.). Stanford, Cal.: Stanford University Press, 1958.

BATESON, G. *Steps to an ecology of mind.* San Francisco: Chandler, 1972.

BAVELAS, A. Communication patterns in task-oriented groups. *Journal of the Acoustical Society of America*, 1950, 22, 725-730.

BEACH, W.A., & FISHER, B.A. Communication as social relationship: Implications of the cognitions-behaviors controversy for communication theory. Paper presented at the annual meeting of Western Speech Communication Association, Phoenix, 1977.

BECKER, S.L. What rhetoric (communication) theory is relevant for contemporary speech communication? Paper presented at University of Minnesota Symposium in Speech Communication, Minneapolis, 1968.

BEER, S. *Decision and control.* New York: Wiley, 1966.

BERLO, D.K. *The process of communication.* New York: Holt, Rinehart & Winston, 1960.

BERRIEN, F.K. *General and social systems.* New Brunswick, N.J.: Rutgers University Press, 1968.

BERTALANFFY, L.V. *General system theory.* New York: Braziller, 1968.

BOHM, D. Science as perception-communication. In F. Suppe (Ed.), *Structure of scientific theories*. Urbana: University of Illinois Press, 1974, 374-391.

BUCKLEY, W. Society as a complex adaptive system. In W. Buckley (Ed.), *Modern systems research for the behavioral scientist*. Chicago: Aldine, 1968, 490-513.

CAMPBELL, J.H., & MICKELSON, J.S. Organic communication systems: Speculations on the study, birth, life, and death of communication systems. In B.D. Ruben & J.Y. Kim (Eds.), *General systems theory and human communication*. Rochelle Park, N.J.: Hayden, 1975, 222-236.

CAPPELLA, J.N. A cybernetic-coorientation model of interpersonal communication. Paper presented at the annual meeting of the International Communication Association, New Orleans, 1974.

CAPPELLA, J.N. An introduction to the literature of causal modelling. *Human Communication Research*, 1975, 1, 362-377.

CAPPELLA, J.N. Modelling interpersonal systems as a pair of machines coupled through feedback. In G.R. Miller (Ed.), *Explorations in interpersonal communication*. Beverly Hills, Cal.: Sage, 1976, 59-85.

CAPPELLA, J.N. Research methodology in communication: Review and commentary. In B.D. Ruben (Ed.), *Communication yearbook I*. New Brunswick, N.J.: Transaction-International Communication Association, 1977, 37-53.

CHURCHMAN, C.W. *The systems approach*. New York: Delacorte, 1968.

COLEMAN, J.S. Social systems. In P.A. Weiss (Ed.), *Hierarchically organized systems in theory and practice*. New York: Hafner, 1971, 69-79.

CUSHMAN, D.P. The rules perspective as a theoretical basis for the study of human communication. *Communication Quarterly*, 1977, 25, 30-45.

CUSHMAN, D.P., & PEARCE, W.B. Generality and necessity in three types of human communication theory—special attention to rules theory. In B.D. Ruben (Ed.), *Communication yearbook I*. New Brunswick, N.J.: Transaction-International Communication Association, 1977, 173-182.

DELIA, J.G. Alternative perspectives for the study of human communication: Critique and response. *Communication Quarterly*, 1977, 25, 46-62.

DeSTEPHEN, R.S. Leadership and sex: Behavioral differences in the small group context. Paper presented at the annual meeting of the Western Speech Communication Association, Phoenix, 1977.

DIESING, P. *Patterns of discovery in the social sciences*. Chicago: Aldin, 1971.

DORE, R.P. Function and cause. *American Sociological Review*, 1961, 26, 843-853.

DRECKSEL, L., & FISHER, B.A. Relational interaction characteristics of women's consciousness-raising groups. Paper presented at the annual meeting of Western Speech Communication Association, Phoenix, 1977.

EDWARDS, J.A., & MONGE, P.R. The validation of mathematical indices of communication structure. In B.D. Ruben (Ed.), *Communication yearbook I*. New Brunswick, N.J.: Transaction-International Communication Association, 1977, 183-193.

ELLIS, D.G., & FISHER, B.A. Phases of conflict in small group development. *Human Communication Research*, 1975, 1, 195-212.

ELLIS, D.G. A social system model of relational control in two ongoing group systems. Paper presented at the annual meeting of the Speech Communication Association, Washington, D.C., 1977.

EMORY, E.E. (Ed.). *Systems Thinking*. London: Penguin, 1969.

EMSHOFF, J.R. *Analysis of behavioral systems*. New York: Macmillan, 1971.

FARACE, R.V., MONGE, P.R., & RUSSELL, H.M. *Communicating and organizing*. Reading, Mass.: Addison-Wesley, 1977.

FARACE, R.V., & MORRIS, C. The communication system of Justin Morrill College. Unpublished paper, Michigan State University, 1969.

FISHER, B.A. Decision emergence: Phases in group decision making. *Speech Monographs*, 1970, 37, 53-66.

FISHER, B.A. Communication study in system perspective. In B.D. Ruben & J.Y. Kim (Eds.), *General systems theory and human communication*. Rochelle Park, N.J.: Hayden, 1975, 191-206.

FISHER, B.A. Relationship rules. Paper presented at the annual meeting of the International Communication Association, Portland, 1976.

FISHER, B.A. Evidence varies with theoretical perspective. *Western Journal of Speech Communication*, 1977a, 41, 9-19.

FISHER, B.A. Interaction analysis: An underutilized methodology in communication research. Paper presented at the annual meeting of the Western Speech Communication Association, Phoenix, 1977b.

FISHER, B.A. *Perspectives on human communication*. New York: Macmillan, 1978.

FISHER, B.A., & BEACH, W.A. Empirical correlates of content and relationship communication: An exploratory study. Paper presented at the annual meeting of the Speech Communication Association, Washington, D.C., 1977a.

FISHER, B.A., & BEACH, W.A. The ongoing process of relational development in dyads: A preliminary report. Unpublished paper, Department of Communication, University of Utah, 1977b.

FISHER, B.A., GLOVER, T.W., & ELLIS, D.G. The nature of complex communication systems. *Communication Monographs*, 1977, 44, 231-240.

FISHER, B.A., & HAWES, L.C. An interact system model: Generating a grounded theory of small groups. *Quarterly Journal of Speech*, 1971, 57, 444-453.

GEONETTA, S.C., & GOURAN, D.S. Patterns of interaction as a function of the degree of leadership centralization in decision-making groups. *Central States Speech Journal*, 1977, 28, 47-53.

GLOVER, T.W. Interpersonal power in family groups: An analysis of complementary and symmetrical interaction. Unpublished thesis, University of Utah, 1974.

GOURAN, D.S., & BAIRD, J.E., JR. An analysis of distributional and sequential structure in problem-solving and informal group discussions. *Speech Monographs*, 1972, 39, 16-22.

GROBSTEIN, C. Hierarchical order and neogenesis. In H.H. Pattee (Ed.), *Hierarchy Theory: The challenge of complex systems*. New York: Braziller, 1973, 31-47.

GUIMARAES, L.L. Network analysis: An approach to the study of communication systems. Unpublished paper, Michigan State University, 1970.

HAWES, L.C. The effects of interviewer style on patterns of dyadic communication. *Speech Monographs*. 1972a, 39, 114-123.

HAWES, L.C. Development and application of an interview coding system. *Central States Speech Journal*, 1972b, 23, 92-99.

HAWES, L.C. Alternative theoretical bases: Toward a presuppositional critique. *Communication Quarterly*, 1977, 25, 63-68.

HAWES, L.C., & FOLEY, J.M. A Markov analysis of interview communication. *Speech Monographs*, 1973, 40, 208-219.

HAWES, L.C., & FOLEY, J.M. Group decisioning: Testing in a finite stochastic model. In G.R. Miller (Ed.), *Explorations in interpersonal communication*. Beverly Hills, Cal.: Sage, 1976, 237-254.

HEWES, D.E. Finite stochastic modelling of communication processes: An introduction and some basic readings. *Human Communication Research*, 1975, 1, 271-283.

HEWES, D.E., BRAZIL, A.J., & EVANS, D.E. A comparative test of two stochastic process models of messages, mediating variables, and behavioral expectations. In B.D. Ruben (Ed.), *Communication yearbook I*. New Brunswick, N.J.: Transaction-International Communication Association, 1977, 195-214.

HUSE, E.F., & BOWDITCH, J.L. *Behavior in organizations* (2nd ed.). Reading, Mass.: Addison-Wesley, 1977.

JACKSON, D.D. The individual and the larger contexts. In W. Gray, F.J. Duhl, & N. Rizzo (Eds.), *General systems theory and psychiatry*. Boston: Little, Brown, 1969, 387-396.

JACOB, M.A. The structure and functions of internal communication in three religious communities. Unpublished doctoral dissertation, Michigan State University, 1972.

JANTSCH, E. *Design for evolution*. New York: Braziller, 1975.

KAPLAN, A. *Conduct of inquiry*. San Francisco: Chandler, 1964.

KIM, J.Y. Feedback in social sciences: Toward a reconceptualization of morphogenesis. In B.D. Ruben & J.Y. Kim (Eds.), *General systems theory and human communication*. Rochelle Park, N.J.: Hayden, 1975, 207-221.

KOESTLER, A. Beyond atomism and holism—The concept of the holon. In A. Loestler & J.R. Smythies (Eds.), *Beyond reductionism*. London: Hutchinson, 1969, 192-216.

KOLAJA, J. *Social system and time and space*. Pittsburgh: Duquesne University Press, 1969.

KRIPPENDORF, K. The systems approach to communication. In B.D. Ruben & J.Y. Kim (Eds.), *General systems theory and human communication*. Rochelle Park, N.J.: Hayden, 1975, 138-163.

KRIPPENDORFF, K. Information systems theory and research: An overview. In B.D. Ruben (Ed.), *Communication yearbook I*. New Brunswick, N.J.: Transaction-International Communication Association, 1977, 149-171.

KUHN, A. *The logic of social systems*. San Francisco: Jossey-Bass, 1974.

KUHN, T. *The structure of scientific revolutions* (2nd ed.). Chicago: University of Chicago Press, 1970.

LASZLO, E. *Introduction to systems philosophy*. New York: Gordon & Breach, 1972.

LEAVITT, H.J. Some effects of certain communication patterns on group performance. *Journal of Abnormal and Social Psychology*, 1951, 46, 38-50.

LINDSEY, G.N. A future of communication theory: Systems theory. Paper presented at the annual meeting of the Western Speech Communication Association, Honolulu, 1972.

LIVESEY, L.J., JR. Noetic planning: The need to know, but what? In E. Laszlo (Ed.), *The relevance of general system theory*. New York: Braziller, 1972, 147-162.

MABRY, E.A. Sequential structure of interaction in encounter groups. *Human Communication Research*, 1975a, 1, 302-307.

MABRY, E.A. Exploratory analysis of a developmental model for task-oriented small groups. *Human Communication Research*, 1975b, 2, 66-73.

MacDONALD, D. Communication roles and communication content in a bureaucratic organization. Unpublished doctoral dissertation, Michigan State University, 1970.

MARK, R.A. Coding communication at the relationship level. *Journal of Communication*, 1971, 21, 221-232.

MARUYAMA, M. The second cybernetics: Deviation-amplifying mutual causal processes. *American Scientist*, 1963, 51, 164-179.

MEEHAN, E.J. *Explanation in social science: A systems paradigm*. Homewood, Ill.: Dorsey, 1968.

MILLAR, F.E., & ROGERS, L.E. A relational approach to interpersonal communication. In G.R. Miller (Ed.), *Explorations in interpersonal communication*. Beverly Hills, Cal.: Sage, 1976, 87-103.

MONGE, P.R. The conceptualization of human communication from three system paradigms. Unpublished doctoral dissertation, Michigan State University, 1972.

MONGE, P.R. Theory construction in the study of communication: The system paradigm. *Journal of Communication*, 1973, 23, 5-16.

MONGE, P.R. The systems perspective as a theoretical basis for the study of human communication. *Communication Quarterly*, 1977, 25, 19-29.

ORCHARD, R.A. On an approach to general system theory. In G.J. Klir (Ed.), *Trends in general systems theory*, New York: Wiley-Interscience, 1972, 205-250.

OZBEKHAN, H. Planning and human action. In P.A. Weiss (Ed.), *Hierarchically organized systems in theory and practice*. New York: Hafner, 1971, 123-230.

PARKS, M.R., FARACE, R.V., ROGERS, L.E., ALBRECHT, T., & ABBOTT, R. Markov process analysis of relational communication in marital dyads. Paper presented at the annual meeting of the International Communication Association, Portland, 1976.

PATTEE, H.H. The physical basis and origin of hierarchical control. In H.H. Pattee (Ed.), *Hierarchy theory: The challenge of complex systems*. New York: Braziller, 1973, 73-108.

PATTEE, H.H. Postscript: Unsolved problems and potential applications of hierarchy theories. In H.H. Pattee (Ed.), 1973, 131-156.

PEARCE, W.B. The coordinated management of meaning: A rules-based theory of interpersonal communication. In G.R. Miller (Ed.), *Explorations in interpersonal communication*. Beverly Hills, Cal.: Sage, 1976, 17-35.

POPPER, K.R. *Conjecture and refutation*. New York: Basic, 1962.

PRINGLE, J.W.S. On the parallel between learning and evolution. *Behaviour*, 1951, 3, 174-215. Reprinted in W. Buckley (Ed.), *Modern systems research for the behavioral scientist*. Chicago: Aldine, 1968, 259-280.

RAPOPORT, A. Foreword. In W. Buckley (Ed.), *Modern systems research for the behavioral scientist*. Chicago: Aldine, 1968, viii-xxii.

RAPOPORT, A., & HORVATH, W.J. Thoughts on organization theory. *General systems*, 1959, 4, 87-91. Reprinted in W. Buckley (Ed.), 1968, 71-75.

RUBEN, B.D. Intrapersonal, interpersonal, and mass communication processes in individual and multi-person systems. In B.D. Ruben & J.Y. Kim (Eds.), *General systems theory and human communication*. Rochelle Park, N.J.: Hayden, 1975, 164-190.

RUBEN, B.D. & KIM, J.Y. (Eds.). *General systems theory and human communication*. Rochelle Park, N.J.: Hayden, 1975.

SCHEFLEN, A.E. Behavioral programs in human communication. In W. Gray, F.J. Duhl, and N. Rizzo (Eds.), *General systems theory and psychiatry*. Boston: Little, Brown, 1969, 209-228.

SCHEIDEL, T.M., & CROWELL, L. Idea development in small discussion groups. *Quarterly Journal of Speech*, 1964, 50, 140-145.

SCHEIDEL, T.M., & CROWELL, L. Feedback in small group communication. *Quarterly Journal of Speech*, 1966, 52, 273-278.

SCHODERBEK, T.P., KEFALAS, A.G., & SCHODERBEK, C.G. *Management systems*. Dallas: Business Publications, 1975.

SCHUTZ, A. On phenomenology and social relations. Chicago: University of Chicago Press, 1970.

SIMON, H.A. *The sciences of the artificial*. Cambridge, Mass.: M.I.T. Press, 1969.

SMITH, D.H. Communication research and the idea of process. *Speech Monographs*, 1972, 39, 174-182.

SOROKIN, P. *Sociological theories of today*. New York: Harper & Row, 1966.

SOROKIN, P. Causal-functional and logico-meaningful integration. In J.J. Demerath, III, & R.A. Peterson (Eds.), *Systems, change, and conflict*. New York: Free Press, 1967, 99-113.

SPILLMAN, B., SPILLMAN, R., & BEZDEK, J. New methodologies for communication research: Applications of fuzzy mathematics. Paper presented at the annual meeting of the Western Speech Communication Association, Phoenix, 1977.

STECH, E.L. An analysis of interaction structure in the discussion of a ranking task. *Speech Monographs*, 1970, 37, 248-263.

STECH, E.L. Sequential structure in human social communication. *Human Communication Research*, 1975, 1, 168-179.

STECH, E.L. The effect of category system design on estimates of sequential and distributional structure. *Central States Speech Journal*, 1977, 28, 64-69.

SUPPE, F. (Ed.). *The structure of scientific theories*. Urbana: University of Illinois Press, 1974.

SUTHERLAND, J.W. *A general systems philosophy for the social and behavioral sciences*. New York: Braziller, 1973.

THAYER, L. Communication systems. In E. Laszlo (Ed.), *The relevance of general systems theory*. New York: Braziller, 1972, 95-121.

THAYER, L. Knowledge, order, and communication. In B.D. Ruben & J.Y. Kim (Eds.), *General systems theory and human communication*. Rochelle Park, N.J.: Hayden, 1975, 237-245.

THORNTON, B.C. Communication and health care teams: A multimethodological approach. Unpublished doctoral dissertation, University of Utah, 1976.

TOULMIN, S.E. Rules and their relevance for understanding human behavior. In T. Mischel (Ed.), *Understanding other persons*. Totowa, N.J.: Rowam & Littlefield, 1974, 185-215.

VALENTINE, K.B., & FISHER, B.A. An interaction analysis of verbal innovative deviance in small groups. *Speech Monographs*, 1974, 41, 413-420.

van GIGCH, J.P. *Applied general systems theory*. New York: Harper & Row, 1974.

VICKERS, G. *Freedom in a rocking boat*. New York: Basic, 1971.

von WRIGHT, G.H. *Explanation and understanding*. Ithaca, N.Y.: Cornell University Press, 1971.

WATZLAWICK, P., BEAVIN, J.H., & JACKSON, D.D. *Pragmatics of human communication*. New York: Norton, 1967.

WEICK, K.E. *The social psychology of organizing*. Reading, Mass.: Addison-Westley, 1969.

WEICK, K.E. Enactment processes in organizations. In B. Staw & G. Salancik (Eds.), *New directions in organizational behavior*. Chicago: St. Clair, 1977, 267-300.

WEISS, P.A. The living system: Determinism stratified. In A. Koestler and J.R. Smythies (Eds.), *Beyond reductionism*. London: Hutchison, 1969, 3-42.

WEISS, P.A. The basic concept of hierarchic systems. In P.A. Weiss (Ed.), *Hierarchically organized systems in theory and practice*. New York: Hafner, 1971, 1-43.

WILDEN, A. *System and structure*. London: Tavistock, 1972.

COMMUNICATION MODELS OF THE MESSAGE-BELIEF CHANGE PROCESS

JEFFREY E. DANES
University of Connecticut

This research developed and then tested three mathematical communication models of the message-belief change process: the proportional change, the belief certainty, and the information inertia model. For each model, the change (difference) equations are presented as well as the over-time recursive predictive equations. Focusing only upon the empirical evaluation of the change equations, strong support was obtained for the information inertia model. The information inertia model was then re-evaluated when accumulated information was given (1) as *subjective information*, and (2) as *ln information*: Logarithmic transformations of the remembered total number of messages received from the following media sources: electronic, print, books, and personal contacts. The ln information measure proved to be the superior measure of accumulated information. The regression curves for the *ln* information model suggested however slightly the possibility of yet another message-belief change model to be considered: One in which belief change resistance is proportional to the product of ln information and belief certainty. This model failed as did the original belief certainty model. Overall, the belief certainty model was the most inferior of all models tested, indicating that the degree to which one is certain in belief is unrelated to the change of "authority" or "informational" beliefs. The model which fit the data obtained in the two experiments gave belief change as a function of the discrepancy between the original belief and the belief value communicated in the message; as an inverse function of the natural logarithmic transformation of the remembered number of times receivers had decoded messages from previous communication sources.

THE THREE MODELS

A current view adopted by many communication scholars is that communication has its *primary* effect upon the ways in which the human structures, maps, or organizes the symbolic environment so that it becomes understandable (Roberts, 1971). The structuring and restructuring of one's symbolic environment goes by many different terms; however, the term currently in vogue for much of communication research is the construct of the "image." Boulding (1956) has conceptualized the image to be what one *believes to be true*—one's subjective knowledge of the various aspects of the physical, social, and symbolic world. By another name, the image construct has also been referred to as *belief*; Bem (1970) has offered the following treatment of belief:

> If a man perceives some relationship between two things or between something and a characteristic of it, he is said to hold a belief. For example, he might suppose asteroids to be round, the dean to be square, God to be dead, men to love freedom, himself to dislike spinach, and Republicans to promote congress. Collectively, a man's beliefs compose his understanding of himself and his environment. (pp. 4-5)

The focus of this study is upon the change of beliefs using messages; the belief of primary concern is what Rokeach (1968) has termed the "authority" belief and Fishbein and Azjen (1975) have called "informational" beliefs.

> Many of our beliefs are formed neither on the basis of direct experience with the object of belief nor by way of some inference process. Instead, we often accept information about some object provided by an outside source. Such sources include newspapers, books, magazines, radio and television, lectures, friends, relatives, coworkers, etc. Beliefs formed by accepting the information provided by an outside source may be termed *informational* beliefs (Fishbein & Ajzen, 1975, p. 133).

The relationship between communication and

belief change has been of central interest to communication scholars for decades. In an attempt to clarify the ways in which communication changes belief, this research tested three mathematical models of communication and belief change: the proportional change model, the belief certainty model, and an information inertia model. In each model, the change variable is the original belief (b_0) in some claim such as: "The nuclear production of electricity is potentially more dangerous than the conventional methods of producing electricity." Belief is assessed as a subjective probability where 0 = completely true, 50 = uncertain, and 100 = completely false; the change message (M) is a "factual" communication derived from a news source such as a popular news magazine. Thus, a message (M) which warrants the truth of a claim should cause the original belief to change in the direction of true, i.e., toward zero (0). Clarification of the cognitive-communication mechanisms responsible for the belief changes produced by communication was the central focus of this research.

The Proportional Change Model

The proportional change (or "message-belief" discrepancy) model was first suggested by French (1956) and has since been elaborated by a variety of authors (Anderson, 1959, 1965, 1971; Anderson & Hovland, 1957; Hovland & Pritzker, 1957; Hunter & Cohen, 1972, 1974; Whittaker, 1967; Woelfel & Danes, in press). The recursive structure of this model as specified by Anderson and Hovland (1957) took the following from:

$$(1) \quad b_1 = b_0 + \alpha (M - b_0)$$

This model states that after the reception of a message (M), the new belief (b_1) is given by the last belief (b_0) plus the degree to which the belief changed: $\alpha (M - b_0)$. Belief change (Δb_0) after the reception of one message (M) may therefore be written as:

$$(2) \quad \Delta b_0 = \alpha (M - b_0)$$

Where α is a constant of proportionality that depends upon the discrepancy of the belief value communicated in the message and the original belief held by the receiver: $(M - b_0)$. Therefore, this model gives the change in belief as the proportion (α) of the discrepancy $(M - b_0)$ between the receiver's original belief and the belief value communicated in the message, M. If α equals zero, the receiver is unaffected by the message; as α assumes larger values, the receiver's original belief changes more so in the direction of the message M. With a message that warrants the truth of a claim i.e., M = 0, the proportional change model as expressed above becomes:

$$(3) \quad \Delta b_0 = \alpha (0 - b_0)$$

$$(4) \quad \Delta b_0 = -\alpha b_0$$

The parametric curves illustrating the theoretical relationships between belief change as a function of the original belief when M = 0 are presented in Figure 1.

Nonlinear versions of this model have been proposed by Sherif, Sherif, and Nebergall (1965) in their social judgment theory; by Aronson, Turner, and Carlsmith (1963) in their version of dissonance theory; by Hunter and Cohen (1972); and by Fishbein and Ajzen (1975, p. 469) in a model which they derive from McGuire (1968).

Proportional change: Over time. If it were true that the amount of belief change obtained was proportional to the amount of change advocated, then once α was measured, the future states of b_0 (i.e., b_n) could be clearly and unambiguously predicted by the calculation of the predictive equation latent within this difference model. The change in b_0 (Δb) may also be written as:

$$(5) \quad \Delta b = b_1 - b_0$$

$$(6) \quad b_1 = b_0 + \Delta b$$

Equation (4), however, specifies that Δb is equal to $-\alpha b_0$; thus:

$$(7) \quad b_1 = b_0 - \alpha b_0$$

$$(8) \quad b_1 = (1 - \alpha) b_0$$

As such, the model predicts that after one exposure to a belief-change message, the next belief (b_1) will be $(1 - \alpha)$ times the last belief (b_0). Thus, the general predictive equation for n repeated exposures to a change message becomes:

(9) $b_n = (1 - \alpha)^n b_0$

The resulting predictive equation for *n* message repetitions of one change message results in an exponentially declining sequence, indicating that as *n* grows large, the acceptance of the truth claim increases; that is, as $n \rightarrow \infty$, $b_n \rightarrow 0$. As such, it is clear that even with relatively minute changes, the accumulative effects of message repetition may be quite dramatic.[1]

The Belief Certainty Model

For many years investigators have believed that people with extreme beliefs are more resistant to change than those with more neutral beliefs (Brim, 1955). This principle was dubbed the "polarity" principle by Osgood and Tannenbaum (1955) when they incorporated it into their congruity theory. The polarity principle was used in conjunction with discrepancy theory in a version of "information processing" theory by Hunter and Cohen (1972) and the model presented below is adapted from theirs. The belief-certainty hypothesis states that belief change is proportional to the message-belief discrepancy and inversely proportional to the certainty to which a receiver holds a particular belief. Thus, those who are uncertain in their convictions should be the most susceptible to change:

(10) $\Delta b_0 = \alpha (M - b_0)/(1c_0)$

And with M = true = 0, the model becomes:

(11) $\Delta b_0 = -\alpha\, b_0/(1+c_0)$

With belief certainty (c_0) explicitly defined as the deviation from an uncertain response (maximum uncertainty = b_0 = 50), a precise operationalization of belief certainty becomes:

(12) $c_0 = \beta \left| b_0 - 50 \right|$

Where β is a scale dependent parameter which governs the potential range of values; with $\beta = 1$, the belief certainty scale runs from 0 for minimum certainty (maximum uncertainty) to 50 for maximum certainty. With $\beta = 2$, the scale runs from 0 for minimum certainty to 100 for maximum certainty. Thus, in order to keep the belief and the belief certainty values equivalent, β was sent to 2

FIGURE 1
Parametric Curves for the Proportional Change Model with α Parameterized

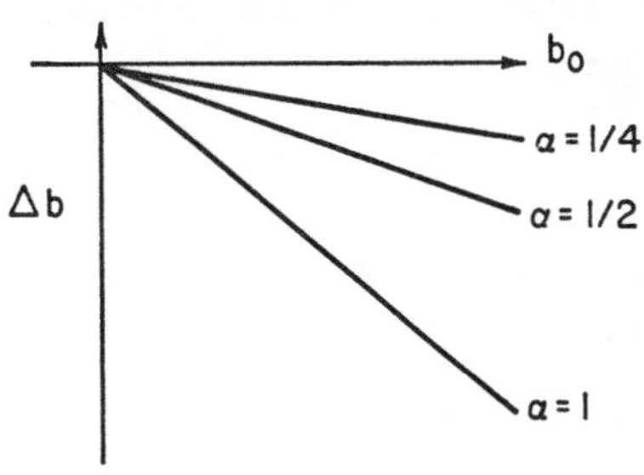

for the parametric curves derived from (11) above (see Figure 2). Most importantly, however, the setting of $\beta = 2$ enables the model to behave mathematically in a way that is consistent with the theoretical expectation: those with extreme beliefs, regardless of whether the beliefs are true or false, should be more resistant to discrepant messages. Smaller values for β would not reflect this theoretical expectation and this is evident when $\beta \rightarrow 0$; for in this instance, when β is very small (.1 or .001), the belief certainty model would then more closely reflect the underlying theoretical expectation extant in the proportional change model as presented in (4) above. Although larger values for β do produce the theoretical expectation, as $\beta \rightarrow \infty$, the resulting distributions become unrealistically leptokurtic.

FIGURE 2
Parametric Curves for the Belief Certainty Model With α Controlled

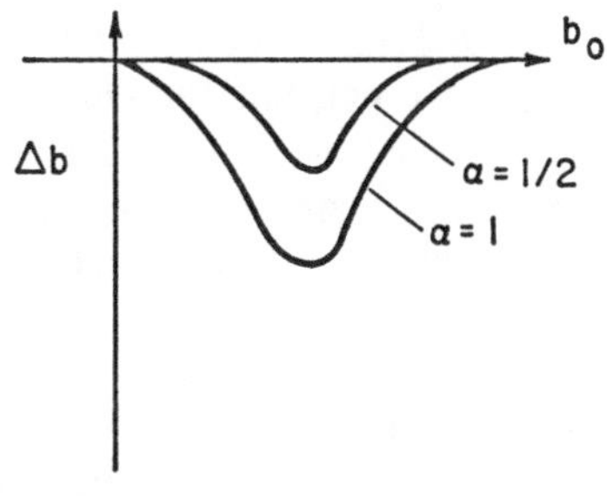

Belief certainty: Over time. Given that the next belief is determined by the original belief plus the change:

(13) $b_1 = b_0 + \Delta b_0,$

the over time recursive structure of the belief certainty model may be readily calculated. Substituting the belief certainty change equation in (11) above yields:

(14) $b_1 = b_0 - \alpha b_0/(c_0+1)$

(15) $b_1 = \left[1 - (\alpha/(c_0+1))\right] b_0$

As such, the model states that the next belief (b_1) is given by:

(16) $\left[1 - (\alpha/(c_0+1))\right]$

times the last belief (b_0). Therefore, b_2 may be determined by:

(17) $b_2 = \left[1 - (\alpha/c_1+1))\right] b_1$

where c_1 is defined as:

(18) $c_1 = \beta|50 - b_1|$

However, since b_1 has already been defined, b_2 may be determined from b_0 in the following way:

(19) $b_2 = \left[1 - (\alpha/(c_1+1))\right]\left[1 - (\alpha/c_0+ 1))\right] b_0$

(20) $b_2 = b_0 \prod_{k=0}^{1} \left[1 - (\alpha/(c_k+1))\right]$

Thus, the generalized over time equation for *n* message repetitions when M = true = 0 becomes the following:[2]

(21) $b_n = b_0 \prod_{k=0}^{n-1} \left[1 - (\alpha/(c_k+1))\right]$

The Accumulated Information Model

For some years communication researchers have known that "established" beliefs are more difficult to change than are "de novo" beliefs (Hovland, 1959; Roberts, 1971). Anderson (1959, 1965) and Rosenberg (1968) suggested that this effect could be accounted for within the context of the discrepancy model if the parameter α were to decrease as a function of accumulated information:

(22) $\Delta b_0 = \alpha(M - b_0)/(1 + i_0)$

And with M = true = 0, the model becomes:

(23) $\Delta b_0 = -\alpha b_0/(1 + i_0)$

where i_0 is the level of information at the time of the message.

Using the average number of times an individual has communicated with his or her significant others about a particular topic (a composite of American values) as a measure of accumulated information, Saltiel and Woelfel (1975) have provided path analytic support for this hypothesized relationship. Saltiel and Woelfel, however, failed to present a conceptual definition for "information" or for "accumulated information"; nonetheless, they do assert that messages carry information and that the reception of messages causes information to internally accumulate within the receiver. On the definition of information for human communication, Lin (1973) has argued that information exists only when a receiver is familiar with the symbols of a message: unfamiliar symbols convey little to no information. Further, Lin (1973) has argued that *information* may be ". . . defined as a set of symbols which both the source and receiver are familiar" (p. 23). As such, *accumulated information* may be defined as the mental aggregation (storage) of a set of familiar symbols sent from a source to a receiver. Accumulated information is seen to differ from "knowledge" in that knowledge implies "correctness"; whereas the notion of accumulated information makes no such implication.

The relationship of accumulated information to belief-change messages may be interpreted in the following way: when a receiver decodes a message advocating belief change, the receiver according to the proportional change model, makes a mental comparison between his or her initial belief and the proposed belief, and then yields proportionately. However, other mental comparisons are likely; the accumulated information hypothesis implies that a receiver not only makes belief comparisons but also assesses the degree to which he or she is "informed" about the belief topic. If one is *not* informed; that is, if one cannot retrieve prior message content (pro or con) then this new information compared to the old (none) takes precedent and consequently alters the original belief. Further, if one has accumulated much information, then during the comparison process this information might be retrieved and used in defense (compare with Roberts & Maccoby, 1973) of the initial belief, resulting in little to no belief change. The parametric curves which illustrate the theoretical relationships between belief change as a function of message-belief discrepancy and accumulated information are presented in Figure 3.

Accumulated information: Over time. Given that the next belief is determined by the last belief plus the change:

(24) $b_1 = b_0 + \Delta b_0$

the over time recursive structure of the accumulated information model may be readily calculated. Substituting the accumulated information change equation in (23) above yields:

(25) $b_1 = b_0 - \left[(\alpha b_0/(1+i_0))\right]$

(26) $b_1 = \left[1 - (\alpha/(1+i_0))\right] b_0$

As such, the model states that the next belief (b_1) is given by:

(27) $\left[1 - (\alpha/(1+i_0))\right]$

times the last belief (b_0). Thus, b_2 may be determined by:

(28) $b_2 = \left[1 - (\alpha/(1+i_1))\right] b_1$

(29) $b_2 = \left[1 - (\alpha/(1+i_1))\right] \left[1 - (\alpha/(1+i_0))\right] b_0$

(30) $b_2 = b_0 \prod_{k=0}^{1} \left[1 - (\alpha/(1+i_k))\right]$

Thus, the generalized over time equation for *n* message repetitions when M = true = 0 becomes the following.[3]

(31) $b_n = b_0 \prod_{k=0}^{n-1} \left[1-(\alpha/(1+i_k)\right]$

All of the recursive time models presented above make the following assumptions: (1) the *same* message value is repeated over time; and (2) that the parameter α remains *unchanged* as a function of message repetition. However, each of the models specify distinct ways in which belief changes as a function of one message. Thus, the first step in the evaluation of these models is the

FIGURE 3
Parametric Curves for the Accumulated Information Model with α Held Constant at One

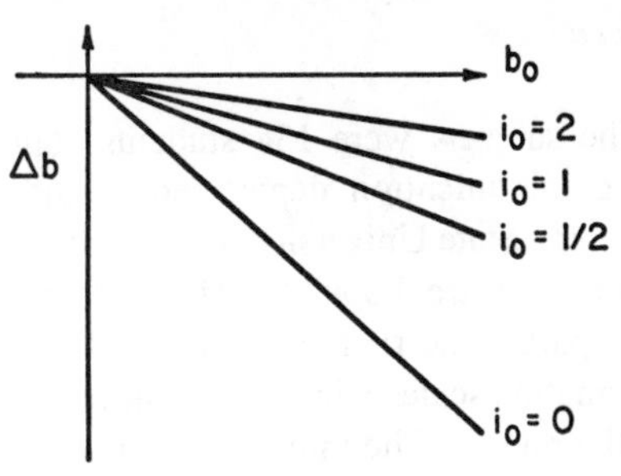

empirical evaluation of the *change equations*; the experiment presented below deals only with this problem.

METHOD

Message-belief Topics

The following belief statements were used for the experiment: (1) the nuclear production of electricity is potentially more dangerous than the conventional methods of producing electricity, and (2) the U.S.S.R. military forces are becoming superior to the military forces of the U.S.A. Hereafter the first belief topic is referred to as the *nuclear belief* and the second as the *military belief*. The belief-change messages dealt specifically with these two beliefs, both argued as "true," and both were abstracted from actual news stories presented in the March 8, 1976 issue of *Time*: "The struggle over nuclear power" and "That alarming Soviet build-up."

To insure that the "truth" argument came across clearly, each of the actual news stories were modified slightly. Included in the nuclear experimental message was: ". . . nuclear power is potentially more dangerous than conventional sources of power" and "to those in the antinuclear camp, the danger is clear, 'the nuclear production of electrical power poses a severe threat to the lives and health of millions of Americans' . . ." For the military message similar modifications were made. Included in the military experimental message was "Whether the Soviets actually plan to attack the Western world, one thing is clear according to NATO Commander in Chief . . ., 'The massive

Soviet build-up clearly indicates that the U.S.A. is becoming the weaker of the two military giants.' "

Procedure

The subjects were 134 students solicited from the communication department subject pool at Michigan State University. Each subject was given a questionnaire booklet which was made up of three parts. The first part contained the belief and information scales which the subject was to fill out for the pretest. The middle section was one of the two messages. The subject was asked to "carefully read and underline the main points of the article." The third section of the booklet consisted of the same belief and information scales which the subject was asked to fill out again as the post-test scores. For the purpose of double checking reliability, a third questionnaire was given one week later. In this design, those subjects who were randomly assigned the nuclear message acted as a control group to those subjects assigned the military message, and vice versa.

Instruments

The belief index was composed of six items. Three were bipolar scales from unlikely to likely, from improbable to probable, and from false to true. The other three items used a different format. First, the subject was asked to make a forced choice between two endpoints such as true or false, and then to rate his or her confidence in that rating on a 6-point Likert scale from "just guessing" to "certain." This pair of responses was then combined to provide a scale by starting from 50 for "just guessing" and counting either up or down in steps of 10 to either 0 for certain and true or 100 for certain and false. The three items of the compound type used the same endpoints as did the three bipolar scales. All six items proved correlationally equivalent when subjected to a cluster analysis.[4] All six measures were scored so that 0=true and 100=false.

For the measurement of information "non-objective" information scales rather than the "objective" knowledge scales were used to account for those receivers who may have been misinformed on the two experimental topics. Knowledge implies that the information accumulated is "correct"; whereas, the accumulated information construct makes no such implication. The information index consisted of eight items. Four of the tiems were global judgments on 7-point bipolar scales: "know a little—know a lot," "not aware—aware," "not informed—informed," "not knowledgeable—knowledgeable." Four of the items were counts (numerical judgments) of the *number of times* the belief topic had been decoded via the four media categories: television and radio, newspapers and magazines, books, and personal contacts. In a pilot study, these counts did not relate linearly to the global information judgments. The maximal linear correlation was found for the logarithmic transformation.[5] In the main study, each numerical count was transformed by the formula $x' = ln(x + 1)$ where ln is the natural log function.

RESULTS

Scale Construction

Since each variable is measured by several indicators, the reliability of each instrument can be measured in two ways: by Cronbach's (1951) coefficient alpha or by an over time reliability coefficient such as is given by Wiley and Wiley (1970). Coefficient alpha for the nuclear belief was .97 and for the military belief was .96, while the Wiley and Wiley (1970) reliability coefficients were .90 and .93 respectively. Coefficient alpha for the nuclear information index was .94 and for the military information index was .91, while the Wiley and Wiley reliability coefficients were .98 and .94. For each instrument, index scales were created by averaging the multiple indicators.

Message Effect

The means and the standard deviations for the pretest, post-test, and belief change are shown in Table 1. For those who read the nuclear message, there was a mean change of −12.6 units on a 100 point scale; for those who did not read this message, there was a mean change of .4 units. The

TABLE 1
Pretest and Posttest Belief-Change Means and Standard Deviations for the Experimental and Control Situations

Message Treatment	Belief Topic.	Pretest	Posttest	Belief Change
Nuclear	Nuclear	33.7(21.7)	21.1(26.4)	-12.6(18.7)
Control	Nuclear	35.4(27.0)	35.8(26.7)	0.4(15.3)
Military	Military	38.9(26.2)	34.3(26.4)	-4.6(16.3)
Control	Military	43.6(23.7)	46.0(26.4)	2.4(14.5)

TABLE 2
Correlations Between Δb, d, Accumulated Information, and Belief Certainty for the Nuclear and Military Topics in both the Experimental and Control Situations

Variable		Nuclear Message	Nuclear Control	Military Message	Military Control
Proportional Change	$d=b_0$	-.65*	-.30	-.30	-.27
Accumulated Information	$d=b_0/(1+i_0)$	-.76*	-.26	-.38*	-.12
Belief Certainty	$d=b_0/(1+c_0)$	-.16	-.13	-.08	.07
Accumulated Information	i_0	.51*	.04	.32	.16
Belief Certainty	c_0	.39	.26	.14	.06

*Indicates that the experimental correlation was significantly different from the control correlation (.05 level).

point biserial correlation for this message effect is .36 which is significant (F=19.62, df=1, 132; p<.001). For those who read the military message there was a mean change of −4.6 units while for those who did not read this message there was a mean change of 2.4 units. The point biserial correlation for this message effect is .21 which is significant (F=6.42; df=1, 132; p<.01) though only two-thirds as large as the effect for the nuclear message.

Screening the Models: A Quick Check

Each of the three models has the form:

$$\Delta b = -\alpha d$$

where *d* is either the message-belief discrepancy or a modification of that discrepancy. In each case, *d* can be calculated from the other variables. Thus, one quick check of the relative power of the three models is to compare the correlation $r_{d\Delta b}$ for each of the three models. These correlations are presented in Table 2.

The first column of Table 2 has the correlations for the nuclear message group. The correlation for the proportional change model in which $d = b_0$ is −.65 which is substantial. In part, this is the well-known regression artifact, but only in small part. The control group correlation for change on the nuclear belief is found in column two of Table 2 and is only −.30 with 95% confidence limits including the values: −.07 to −.50. The upper limit of this range represents the maximum value of this correlation that could be created by a regression artifact. The correlation for the accumulated information model in which $d = b_0/(1+i_0)$ is −.76 for the nuclear message group, which is not only substantial in size, but is larger than the −.65 for the proportional change model (t=1.93, df=63, p<.05). Thus, belief change is smaller for those whose belief is based upon more accumulated information. The correlation for the belief certainty model in which $d = b_0/(1+c_0)$ is .16 which is negligible in comparison to the fit for the other two models.

The correlations for the military message group are presented in column three of Table 2 and the corresponding control group correlations are found in column four. The correlation for the proportional change model is −.30, the correlation for the accumulated information model is −.38, and the correlation for the belief certainty model is −.08. These correlations are all lower than those obtained for the nuclear message group and reflect as indicated earlier a difference in the basic effectiveness of the two messages. However, the comparative size of the correlations is the same: the belief certainty model shows almost no fit at all, while the accumulated information model shows better fit than the proportional change model. However, the difference between these two correlations was not significant (t = −0.91; df = 65, p>.05).

Testing the Models

Thus far, the "fit" of each of the models was discussed in correlation terms; the problems associated with the correlational approach to the "testing" of mathematical models are well known (cf., Birnbaum, 1974). Therefore, to determine the functional form of communication to belief change more precisely, a graphic method was used to analyze the communication and belief change models: a nonlinear bivariate regression which results in an empirical "plot" of the functional relationship of belief change to communication (Hunter & Cohen, 1974).

The above correlational analyses suggested that the accumulated information model was the superior of the three; thus for the analysis presented below, initial belief (b_0) was divided into the following three levels: 0−35 = true, 35.001−65 = uncertain, and 65.001 − 100 = false. Initial accumulated information was divided into the following three levels: 0 − 1.75 = low, 1.75001−3.25 = moderate, and those values greater than 3.25001 were scored as high. Two criteria were used in producing the three-way splits for the belief (b_0) and the information (i_0) variables: (1) the split was made so that the proportions of scale values were equivalently distributed at the minimum and maximum regions, with the remainder assigned to the "uncertain" region for belief and the "moderately" informed region for information. And, (2) so that an approximately equal

TABLE 3
Belief-Change Means and Sample Size for the Three Levels of Accumulated Information and the Three Levels of Belief for the Nuclear Message

		Accumulated Information (i_0)			
		Low (1)	Moderate (2)	High (3)	
Belief (b_0)	False (3)	-53.9(2)	-26.3(2)	-11.7(1)	-34.4(5)
	Uncertain (2)	-27.1(18)	-11.7(5)	-2.7(1)	-22.9(24)
	True (1)	-7.0(11)	-1.0(21)	-2.1(5)	-2.9(37)
		-21.7(31)	-4.7(28)	-3.6(7)	-12.6(66)

number of receivers were present in each cell. However, it was discovered that belief and information were nonlinearily related; thus the production of cells with roughly equal numbers of receivers was not possible. For the nuclear message, the belief change means and number of subjects are presented in Table 3. Since the reliabilities average .95, no correction such as that recommended in Hunter and Cohen (1974) was made on the data before cell membership was determined.

From Tables 3 and 4, a nonlinear relationship between belief and information is graphically revealed by the distribution of the receivers in the cells. For those who are "informed," practically none are "uncertain." For those who are "uninformed," the majority are "uncertain"; however, a substantial number of the "uninformed" are "certain" in their convictions. The existence of this nonlinear relationship between information and belief precluded an unequal number of receivers in each cell.

If the proportional change model is more correct than the others, the resulting "plots" would reflect this if three *parallel* negatively sloped lines resulted from the analysis. If the accumulated information model is more correct than the others, the resulting "plots" would reflect this, if the three lines form a negatively sloped *bilinear fan* such that steeper slopes obtain with lesser amounts of accumulated information. If the belief certainty model is more correct than the others, the resulting "plot" should form three *collinear*, *v-shaped* curves, reflecting the theoretical expectation that those with extreme convictions are the most resistant to change.

The regression of belief change (Δb) onto the three levels of initial belief (b_0) and the three levels of initial accumulated information (i_0) produced the parametric curves for the nuclear message in Figure 4. The results of the regression analysis reported in Figure 4 clearly support the accumulated information model. The parametric curves almost exactly reproduce the accumulated information parametric curves reported in Figure 3: the empirical "plots" produce a *bilinear fan*.

Table 4 contains the mean change as a function of initial belief and information for the military message. These means are plotted in Figure 5.

FIGURE 4
Regression Curves of Nuclear Belief-Change on Initial Belief with Accumulated Information Parameterized

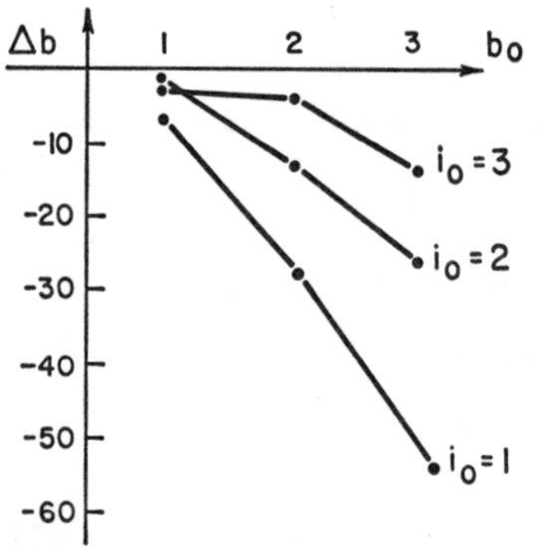

These parametric curves are also essentially of the same form as the information model in Figure 3, though the value of α is not so large as for the nuclear message. The one point which appears to be deviant is that for $b_0 = 2$, $i_0 = 2$. However, this mean is based on only 5 subjects, and has a standard deviation of 18.9, and does not differ significantly from the -6.35 value that would make the parametric curve a straight line ($t = 1.30$, df $= 4$, $p > .05$).

Accumulated Information: Further Explorations

The accumulated information variable thus far consisted of two very much different operational measures: seven-point Likert type scales designed to assess the degree to which receivers *felt* "informed," and logarithmic transformations of the number of times receivers have heard or read about a belief topic. The correlation (corrected for attenuation) between these two measures equaled .81 for the nuclear measures and .73 for the military measures—indicating that roughly one-half of the variance was unaccounted for. Thus, although there was extended overlap between these two different operational measures, they clearly were not tapping exactly the same construct. Therefore, the next set of analyses separated the two information measures and re-evaluated the accumulated information model. Summing the Likert global information scales yielded what hereafter will be called *subjective information* (si_0); summing the numerical counts and taking the natural logarithm of this sum yielded what hereafter will be called *ln information* (ln_0).

The correctional quick check. Each of the two information models has the form:

$$\Delta b = -\alpha d$$

where d is the ratio of belief (b_0) to either $ln_0 + 1$ for the ln information model of $si_0 + 1$ for the subjective information model. Hence, the relative power of these two models may be assessed though the comparison of the correlations $r_{d\Delta b}$, as was done above. Along with the correlations for the proportional change model in which $d = b_0$, these correlations are presented in Table 5.

The first column of Table 5 has the correlations for the nuclear message group. The correlation for the *ln* information model in which $d = b_0/(ln_0+1) = -.82$ which is substantial and significantly larger than the $-.65$ correlation for the proportional change model ($t = 3.27$, df $= 63$, $p < .05$). The control group correlation for change on the nuclear belief is found in column two of Table 5 and is only $-.28$. The second entry in column two of Table 5 has the correlation for the subject information model in which $d = b_0/(si_0+1)$ is $-.65$, a correlation that is identical to the $-.65$ correlation for the proportional change model. Thus, belief change is more accurately accounted for when information is given as the logarithm of the remembered total number of messages received from the four major media categories: television and radio, newspapers and magazines, books, and personal contacts. Belief change is unaffected by the degree to which receivers *feel* "informed" about the belief topic.

The correlations for the military group are presented in column three of Table 5 and the corresponding control group correlations are found in column four. The correlation for the ln information model is $-.44$, the correlation for the proportional change model is $-.30$. Only the *ln* information model correlation is significantly different from its corresponding control correlation. Further, the military *ln* information correlation is also significantly different from the $-.30$ correlation for the proportional change model ($t = -1.68$, df $= 65$,

TABLE 4
Belief-Change Means and Sample for the Three Levels of Accumulated Information and the Three Levels of Belief for the Military Message

		Accumulated Information (i_0)			
		Low(1)	Moderate(2)	High(3)	
Belief (b_0)	False(3)	-25.0(3)	-12.7(4)	0.3(6)	-9.5(13)
	Uncertain(2)	-10.8(17)	6.0(5)	--(0)	-6.9(22)
	True(1)	-6.9(6)	0.0(22)	0.2(5)	-1.3(33)
		-11.5(26)	-.07(31)	.007(11)	-4.6(68)

p<.05). Again, the correlations for the military group are all lower than those obtained for the nuclear message group and reflect as indicated earlier a difference in the basic effectiveness of the two messages. However, the comparative size of the correlations is the same: the subjective information and the proportional change models fit equally well and the *ln* information model provided a much superior fit.

Nonlinear bivariate regression. The above correlation analyses suggested that the *ln* information model was the superior of the two accumulated information models. But, might there be an even better functional form of communication to belief change? To find out just how well the *ln* information model fit the belief change data, a nonlinear bivariate regression (Hunter & Cohen, 1974) was used to create an empirical "plot" of communication to belief change. Since the reliability estimates (Spearman-Brown) equaled .83 and .80 for the nuclear and the military *ln* information measures, the correction procedures recommended in Hunter and Cohen (1974) were employed before cell membership was determined. Similar to the analyses presented earlier, initial belief was divided into the following three levels: 0 – 35 = true, 35.001 – 65 = uncertain, and 65.001 – 100 = false. And, for the *ln* information variable: 0 – 2.64 = low, 2.65 – 3.39 = moderate, and 3.40 – and above = high information. Again, as in the above analyses, equal cell membership was not found due to the basic nonlinear relationship between information and belief.

FIGURE 5
Regression Curves of Military Belief-Change on Initial Belief with Accumulated Information Parameterized

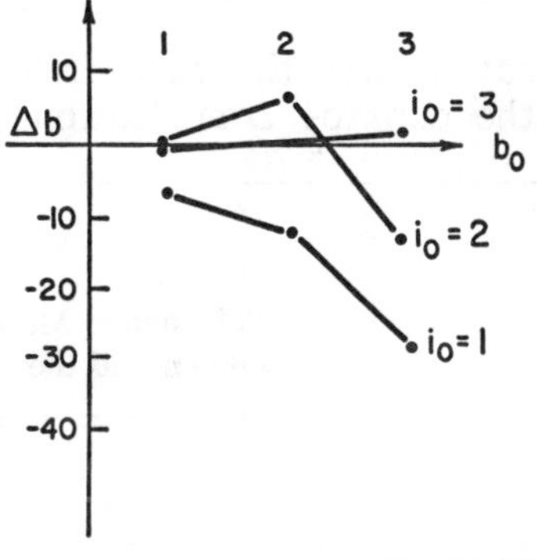

For the nuclear message group, the belief change means the the number of subjects are presented in Table 6; the regression of belief change (Δb) onto the three levels of belief (b_0) and

TABLE 5
Correlations Between Δb, d Ln Information, and Subjective Information for the Nuclear and Military Topics in both the Experimental and Control Situations

Variable	Nuclear Message	Nuclear Control	Military Message	Military Control
Ln Information $d = b_0/(ln_0+1)$	-.82*	-.28	-.44*	-.14
Subjective Information $d = b_0/(si_0+1)$	-.65*	-.20	-.31	-.09
Proportional Change $d = b_0$	-.65*	-.30	-.30	-.27
Ln Information (ln_0)	.48*	.03	.23	.09
Subjective Information (si_0)	.50*	.04	.30	.15

*Indicates that the experimental correlation was significantly different from the control correlation (.05 level).

TABLE 6
Belief-Change Means and Cell Size for the Three Levels of Ln Information and the Three Levels of Belief for the Nuclear Message

		Ln Information (ln_0)			
		Low(1)	Moderate(2)	High(3)	
Belief (b_0)	False(3)	-77.2(2)	-12.8(1)	-2.5(2)	-34.4(5)
	Uncertain(2)	-28.2(17)	-11.5(2)	-9.2(5)	-22.9(24)
	True(1)	-3.4(12)	-2.5(8)	-2.8(17)	-2.9(37)
		-21.8(31)	-5.1(11)	-4.1(24)	-12.6(66)

the three levels of *ln* information (ln_0) produced the parametric curves in Figure 6. For the military message group, the belief change means and the number of subjects are presented in Table 7; the regression of belief change (Δb) onto the three levels of belief (b_0) and the three levels of *ln* information (ln_0) produced the parametric curves in Figure 7.

The visual inspection of Figure 6 indicates that the data based parametric curves provided an excellent fit. The only deviant change score, −9.2, is the one in which $b_0 = 2$ $ln_0 = 3$ has a cell size of five, a standard deviation of 18.01, and is not significantly different from −2.65, the value which would occur if the curve were a straight line ($t = -1.32$, df = 4, $p > .05$). The data based parametric curves for the military message likewise provided an excellent fit. The only slightly deviant point is the mean −7.5 for the cell $b_0 = 2$; $ln_0 = 2$. This value has a standard deviation of 20.24, a cell size of 6, and is not significantly different from −2.85, the value expected if the curve were a straight line ($t = -0.51$, df = 5, $p > .05$).

The visual inspection of both Figures 6 and 7 nevertheless suggests however slightly that there might be some interaction between information and belief certainty. Could it be that the belief certainty function comes into operation at the higher levels of accumulated information? If this were the case, the following message-belief change model should be true:

(32) $\Delta b_0 = \alpha(M - b_0)/(ln_0 c_0 + 1)$

Verbally, this model states that belief certainty minimally inhibits belief change as accumulated information decreases; that belief certainty maximally inhibits belief change as information increases. The quick correlation check was employed and the results of this speculation were not confirmed. The correlation for the nuclear message group equaled −.58, and the correlation for the military message group equaled −.14, correlations trivial in magnitude when compared to those obtained from the *ln* information model.

DISCUSSION

The ability of the proportional change model to more accurately account for belief change was en-

FIGURE 6
Regression Curves of Nuclear Belief-Change on Initial Belief with Ln Information Parameterized

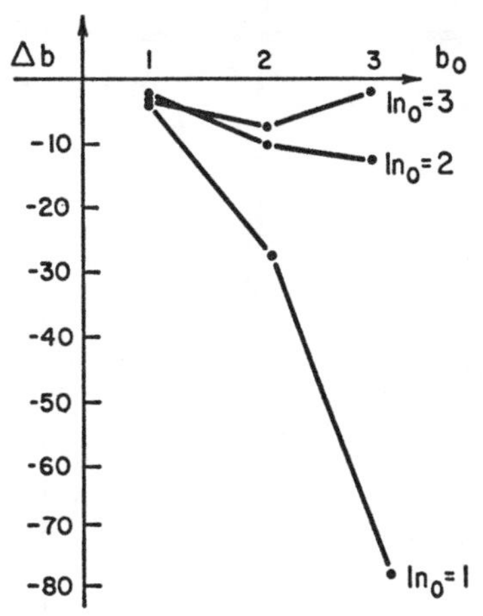

hanced when this model included the accumulated information operator, a finding which supports the theorizing by Anderson (1959, 1965), Rosenberg (1968), and Saltiel and Woelfel (1975). It was discovered, however, that of the two different operational procedures used to assess accumulated information, the logarithmic transformation of the number of times receivers had remembered decoding prior messages about the belief topic was a much superior measure of the accumulated information construct. The information inertia model did no better than did the proportional change model when accumulated information was given only by measures of subjective information. This finding strongly suggests that the degree to which receivers *feel* "informed" is unrelated to the message-belief change process. This research has, therefore, discovered a new form for the accumulated information change equation:

(33) $\Delta b_n = \alpha(M - b_n/(ln(X_n+)+1)$

Where X_n is the remembered total number of messages received at time *n*; ln is the natural log function.

The discovery of this newer *ln* informational interia model, now permits at least a partial specification of the ways in which information accumulates as a function of over-time message repetition. In the over-time equation for the accumulated in-

TABLE 7
Belief-Change Means and Cell Size for the Three Levels of Ln Information and the Three Levels of Belief for the Military Message

		Ln Information (ln_0)			
		Low(1)	Moderate(2)	High(3)	
	False(3)	-37.8(3)	-3.7(3)	0.1(7)	-9.5(13)
Belief (b_0)	Uncertain(2)	-9.4(10)	-7.5(6)	-2.1(6)	-6.9(22)
	True(1)	-1.7(2)	-2.0(12)	-0.8(19)	-1.3(33)
		-14.0(15)	-3.8(21)	-0.9(32)	-4.6(68)

formation model given above in (31), the subscripted information variable i_k was deliberately left undefined. The model only stated that information accumulates, but it did not specify the way in which it accumulates. With the simplifying assumption of *perfect* memory, one can now specify the behavior of i_k. Earlier ln_0 was defined as:

(34) $ln_0 = \ln(X_0+1)$

Where X_0 is the remembered total number of messages received at time 0; thus, with the assumption perfect memory, the next value for *ln* information after the reception of a new message is:

(35) $ln_1 = \ln(X_0+2)$

And, with the replacement of i_1 with ln_1 in equation (28) given above yields:

(36) $i_1 = \ln(X_0+2)$

which ultimately leads to the following definition of i_k:

(37) $i_k = ln_k = \ln(X_0+n+1)$.

Which is now the first best estimate for the way in which information accumulates. The perfect memory assumption, however, is likely to be a false assumption in "real" communication transactions; therefore, this deterministic model may be made probabilistic by relaxing the perfect memory simplifying assumption via the incorporation of a recall probability parameter (*p*).

Taking into account that fact that memory (R) may not be perfect and that it is subject to individual differences, i_k could be estimated in the following way:

(38) $i_k = \ln(X_0+E(R))$

Where E(R) is the expected value of R and the binominal R may be defined as:

(39) $R = \sum_{m=0}^{n+1} r_m$

FIGURE 7
Regression Curves of Military Belief-Change on Initial Belief with Ln Information Parameterized

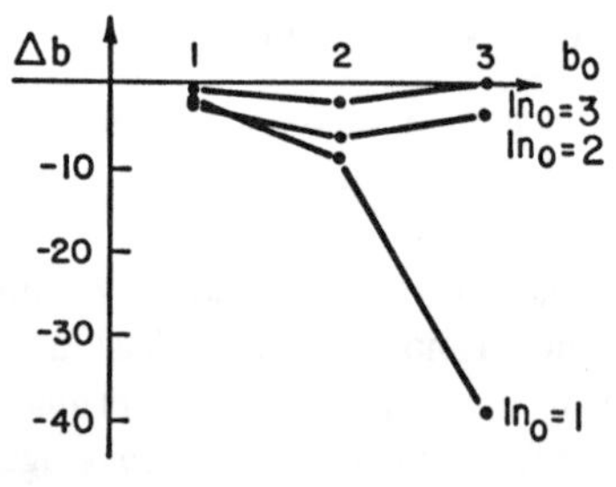

With the bernoulli r_m given as:

$$(40)\quad r_m = \begin{cases} 1 \text{ if the message is remembered} \\ 0 \text{ if the message is forgotten} \end{cases}$$

Thus, the expected value of R after n−1 additional message repetitions is given as:

$$(41)\quad E(R) = (n+1)p$$

Where p is the probability of whether the additional message counts will be remembered. The result is a probabalistic model which becomes increasingly accurate as n grows large; that is, as $(n+1) \rightarrow \infty$, the value of E(R) becomes an increasingly accurate estimate of the remembered total number of messages received from communication sources.

Of the three message-belief change models tested above, the belief certainty model was clearly the most inferior. It failed, and its failure suggests that the certainty which one ascribes to a belief is unrelated to belief change, a result which was also found by Saltiel and Woelfel (1975), who report no net effect of certainty on "attitude" change in a field setting across a six-month interval of time. Furthermore, even when the belief certainty operator was incorporated into the "interaction" model (equation 32), the resulting correlations with belief change were definitely inferior in comparison to those obtained from both the proportional change and the *ln* information models. Overall, the results of this research indicates that resistance to informational belief change is best viewed as being linked to accumulated information, rather than to the certainty associated with a particular belief.[6]

NOTES

1. A more general predictive equation for the proportional change model is one in which the message (M) takes on any value from 0 − 100; such an equation takes the following form:

$$b_n = \alpha M + \alpha M(1-\alpha) + \alpha M(1-\alpha)^2 + \ldots + \alpha M(1-\alpha)^{n-1} + (1-\alpha)^n b_0$$

2. A more general predictive equation for the belief certainty model is one in which the message (M) takes on any value from 0 − 100; such an equation takes the form:

$$b_n = \frac{\alpha M}{1+c_{n-1}} + \frac{\alpha M}{1+c_{n-2}}\left(1 - \frac{1}{1+c_{n-1}}\right) + \frac{\alpha M}{1+c_{n-3}} \prod_{k=n-2}^{n-1}\left(1 - \frac{1}{1+c_k}\right) + \ldots + \frac{\alpha M}{1+c_0} \prod_{k=1}^{n-1}\left(1 - \frac{1}{1+c_k}\right) + b_0 \prod_{k=0}^{n-1}\left(1 - \frac{\alpha}{1+c_k}\right)$$

3. A more general predictive equation for the accumulated information model is one in which the message (M) takes on any value from 0 − 100; such an equation takes the following form:

$$b_n = \frac{\alpha M}{1+I_{n-1}} + \frac{\alpha M}{1+i_{n-2}}\left(1 - \frac{1}{1+i_{n-1}}\right) + \frac{\alpha M}{1+i_{n-3}} \prod_{k=n-2}^{n-1}\left(1 - \frac{1}{1+i_k}\right) + \ldots + \frac{\alpha M}{1+i_0} \prod_{k=1}^{n-1}\left(1 - \frac{1}{1+i_k}\right) + b_0 \prod_{k=0}^{n-1}\left(1 - \frac{\alpha}{1+i_k}\right)$$

4. See Danes (1976) or Hunter (1977) for a detailed description of the cluster analysis used for the construction of the measures used in this research.
5. The correlation between the raw counts and the subjective information measures, averaged over 18 items equaled .45; the same correlation when the counts were logarithmically transformed equaled .70.
6. The author is grateful for the theoretical and mathematical assistance of Dr. John E. Hunter, Professor of Psychology and Mathematics, Michigan State University. Portions of this manuscript have been recently accepted for publication in *Human Communication Research*, see Danes, Hunter, and Woelfel, in press.

REFERENCES

ANDERSON, N. Test of a model of opinion change. *Journal of Abnormal and Social Psychology*, 1959, 59, 371-381.

ANDERSON, N. Primacy effects in personality impression formation. *Journal of Personality and Social Psychology*, 1965, 2, 1-9.

ANDERSON, N. Integration theory and attitude change. *Psychological Review*, 1971, 78, 171-206.

ANDERSON, N., & HOVLAND, C. The representation of order effects in communication research. In C. Hovland (Ed.), *The order of presentation in persuasion*. New Haven, Conn.: Yale University Press, 1957.

ARONSON, E., TURNER, J., & CARLSMITH, J. Communicator credibility and communication discrepancy as determinants of opinion change. *Journal of Abnormal and Social Psychology*, 1963, 67, 31-36.

BIRNBAUM, M. Reply to the devil's advocates: Don't confound model testing and measurement. *Psychological Bulletin*, 1974, 81, 854-859.

BOULDING, K. *The image*. Ann Arbor: University of Michigan Press, 1956.

BRIM, O. Attitude content-intensity. *American Sociological Review*, 1955, 20, 68-76.

CRONBACH, L. Coefficient alpha and the internal structure of tests. *Psychometrika*, 1951, 16, 297-334.

DANES, J. *Mathematical models of communication and belief change: Proportional change, accumulated information, and belief certainty*. Unpublished doctoral dissertation, Department of Communication, Michigan State University, 1976.

DANES, J., HUNTER, J., & WOELFEL, J. Mass communication and belief change. A test of three mathematical models. *Human Communication Research*, in press.

FISHBEIN, M., & AJZEN, I. *Belief, attitude, intention, and behavior*. Reading, Mass.: Addison-Wesley, 1975.

FRENCH, J. A formal theory of social power. *Psychological Review*, 1956, 63, 181-194.

HOVLAND, C., & PRITZKER, H. Extent of opinion change as a function of amount of change advocated. *Journal of Abnormal and Social Psychology*, 1957, 54, 257-261.

HOVLAND, C. Reconciling conflicting results derived from experimental and survey studies of attitude change. *American Psychologist*, 1959, 14, 8-17.

HUNTER, J. Cluster analysis: Reliability, construct validity, and the multiple indicators approach to measurement. Unpublished manuscript, Department of Psychology, Michigan State University, 1977.

HUNTER, J., & COHEN, S. Mathematical models of attitude change in the passive communication context. Unpublished manuscript, Department of Psychology, Michigan State University, 1972.

HUNTER, J. & COHEN, S. Correcting for unreliability in nonlinear models of attitude change. *Psychometrika*, 1974, 39, 445-468.

LIN, N. *The study of human communication*. New York: Bobbs-Merrill, 1973.

McGUIRE, W. Personality and susceptibility to social influence. In E.F. Borgotta and W.W. Mabert (Eds.), *Handbook of personality theory and research*. Chicago: Rand McNally, 1968, 1130-1187.

OSGOOD, C., & TANNENBAUM, P. The principle of congruity in the prediction of attitude change. *Psychological Review*, 1955, 62, 42-55.

ROBERTS, D. Nature of communication effects. In W. Schramm & D. Roberts (Eds.), *The process and effects of mass communication*. Urbana: University of Illinois Press, 1971.

ROBERTS, D. & MACCOBY, N. Information processing and persuasion: counterarguing behavior. In P. Clarke (Ed.), *New models for mass communication research*. Beverly Hills, Cal.: Sage, 1973, 269-307.

ROSENBERG, S. Mathematical models of social behavior. In G. Lindzey and E. Aronson (Eds.) *The handbook of social psychology*. Reading, Mass.: Addison-Wesley, 1968.

SALTIEL, J., & WOELFEL, J. Inertia in cognitive processes: The role of accumulated information in attitude change. *Human Communication Research*, 1975, 1, 333-344.

SHERIF, C., SHERIF, M., & NEBERGALL, R. *Attitude and attitude change*. Philadelphia: Saunders, 1965.

WHITTAKER, J. Resolution of the communication discrepancy issue in attitude change. In C.W. Sherif and M. Sherif (Eds.), *Attitude, ego-involvement, and change*. New York: Wiley, 1967, 159-177.

WILEY, D., & WILEY, J. The estimation of measurement error in panel data. *American Sociological Review*, 1970, 35, 112-117.

WOELFEL, J., & DANES, J. Models for the metric multidimensional analysis of communication, conception, and change. In P. Monge & J. Cappella (Eds.), *Multivariate analysis in communication research*. New York: Academic Press, in press.

CYCLES IN CHILDREN'S ATTENTION TO THE TELEVISION SCREEN

ROBERT KRULL *WILLIAM G. HUSSON*
ALBERT S. PAULSON
Rensselaer Polytechnic Institute

This study deals with the relationship between TV program variables and children's attention to the TV screen. Children were individually shown sample versions of either *Sesame Street* or the *Electric Company*. The attention levels of each child, the levels of four measures of program complexity, and two measures of visual/verbal interaction of program material were measured at 30-second intervals. The data were analyzed using frequency-domain time series techniques.

Young children's attention to *Sesame Street* was found to be moderately affected by the program variables measured. Older children's attention to the *Electric Company* was more strongly affected by the program variables, particularly visual variables. Older children also showed anticipatory attention changes prior in time to changes in program variables.

The communications literature has moved progressively to a position from which receivers of messages are regarded as actively involved in the process of communication. Researchers interested in the gratifications of mass media audiences have taken this stance, for example. In this paper we examine children's attention to the TV screen in a way which emphasizes the activeness of their role in viewing and which raises questions regarding both the theory and methods required to operate from a pro-active perspective.

Prior to a preceding study (Krull & Husson, 1977) we had expected children to be rather selective about the kinds of television material to which they pay attention. This expectation was based in part on the information available about adult viewers. A number of studies have shown that viewers engage in several activities while viewing and that different types of programs are watched with different degrees of attentiveness (Robinson, 1969; Bechtel, Achelpolk, & Akers, 1972; LoSciuto, 1972; Murray, 1972). A good deal of research has shown the same kind of selectivity to be found among young children.

Children's Attention to the TV Screen

In studies of television commercials, Ward and his coworkers found older children (ages 11 to 12) paid less attention to the TV set, and were more selective about what was paid attention to than were younger children (Ward, Levinson, & Wackman, 1972; Ward & Wackman, 1973). In a related study, Wartella and Ettema (1974) found that second graders and kindergartners paid more attention than nursery school children, and that the older children were more selective in attention, preferring more complex material.

The most elaborate set of studies of children's attention to the TV screen is that done on Children's Television Workshop (CTW) programs. In surveying formative research on *Sesame Street*, Reeves (1970) reported children's attention in general to be very fluid, and to be higher for segments containing animation, children, animals, and rapidly paced action. Anderson and Levin (Anderson & Levin, 1976; Levin & Anderson, 1976) found the number and duration of visual fixations on the TV screen by children to increase between the ages of 1 and 4 years. They also found that attention correlated negatively with the length of program segments (bits) and positively with the appearance on the screen of adult females, children, nonhuman characters, physical activity, lively music, and special effects. They also noted one dimension underlying many of their variables to be the amount of action present.

Lasker (1974) found similar results in a study of

Jamaican children who were introduced to *Sesame Street* after never having seen television of any kind. He found older children (ages 9 to 10) to be more selective in attention, to be more visually oriented than younger children and to prefer the more complex production techniques.

Taken together, these studies of children's attention seem to show both fluidity of attention and a change in the aspects of programs eliciting attention as children mature. We examined these two issues using an information processing perspective on program variables in a setting which allowed an assessment of the information processing speeds of children (Krull & Husson, 1977). We duplicated the results of other researchers in many respects, but we also found that older children seemed to be able to anticipate changes in program information rates before they occurred.

In this paper we use the same theoretical framework as we did in the preceding study. However, we employ more elegant techniques which allow us to examine children's behavior, particularly the anticipation effects, in greater detail.

Children's Informaiion Processing of Television Messages

In the aforementioned study we had taken two different tacks on the information processing children are likely to do. One of these involves the information theory concept of entropy and was used to develop program variables already applied in several studies; the other tack drew from research in cognitive psychology based on the writings of Piaget (1969).

Program form complexity and children's attention. Information theory was used to generate measures of program form complexity—that is, measures of the noncontent, structural aspects of programs. Of the several variables generated, four are used in this paper: *set time entropy, verbal time entropy, shot entropy* and *nonverbal dependence entropy*. Definitions of these variables are given in Appendix A; more detailed descriptions are available elsewhere (Watt & Krull, 1974).

The rationale for a relationship between program complexity and the behavior of television viewers is that viewers are likely to choose programs on the basis of the amount of information processing offered. Some viewers would be expected to prefer high rates of information processing and should, therefore, choose programs with high information rates. Other viewers might prefer lower information rates and should, therefore, choose programs with lower information rates. The same kind of rationale might hold for the information rates of program content rather than program form, but the content variables required to test such a rationale have not yet been developed.

Program form complexity has been found to be related to the behavior of adults in several studies. When ratings were used as a measure of viewer preference, the levels of complexity of commercial programs appeared to be near the optimum for most viewers. Public television programs were found to be lower overall in form complexity than commercial programs, as were their ratings; but increasing complexity correlated with increasing ratings for public television shows (Krull & Watt, 1975).

Viewers were found to cluster their program preferences around certain complexity values when viewing was measured by the average frequency of tuning in (Watt & Krull, 1974), but were not found to cluster their liking of programs (Krull, Watt & Lichty, 1974). However, young adults were found to prefer higher levels of program complexity for both viewing and liking, than were other age groups (Krull, Watt & Lichty, 1977).

In examining the effects of program complexity on viewers, Watt and Krull found that viewers of highly complex programs were more aggressive (Watt & Krull, 1976) and were more aroused physiologically (Watt & Krull, 1974). Both the aggression and arousal were argued to be outcomes of high rates of information processing.

These studies dealt with children only as small parts of some samples. In addition, the time frame of these studies was very long, given the likely rates of young children's responding to programs. The Krull and Husson (1977) study focused directly on children using a comparatively short time frame.

Krull and Husson examined the behavior of

children watching *Sesame Street* and the *Electric Company* shows. The four complexity measures used were set entropy, verbal entropy, shot entropy and nonverbal dependence entropy. Children's attention was assessed at 30-second intervals using time-domain time series analysis. Time series analysis was used to determine the delay between changes in program variables and the children's responses, to determine the sizes of effects at their strongest point, and to determine the duration of effects.

As expected, the duration of what could be called attention span was relatively short for all children. The interdependence (partial autocorrelation) between neighboring measurement intervals was found to last only about 30 seconds. That is, a child's attention to the TV screen at one point during a program depended on his or her attention in one preceding 30-second interval only. The partial correlations between attention levels at intervals 60 seconds or more apart were not statistically significant. Surprisingly, younger children showed interdependence at longer lags than did older children. This indicated that the attention spans of younger children are longer than those of older children, and this was rather puzzling.

When the correlations between program complexity variables and children's attention were examined, correlations were found, in general, to reach a maximum within 60 seconds. In other words, the correlations were at a maximum either during the interval in which the program variables changed or in the immediately following 30-second interval. This indicated children react fairly quickly to what happens in programs.

Older children were found to be more strongly affected by changes in program variables than were younger children. Older children were also found to be more affected by visual variables, while younger children were more affected by verbal variables. Much of this could have been anticipated from previous studies showing the higher selectivity and visual orientation of older children. One unanticipated result, however, was that the data indicated older children anticipated changes in programs.

Ordinarily, correlations at negative lags, correlations which showed changes in programs following changes in attention in our study, indicate that the causal order chosen by the researcher is the reverse of that holding in nature. That interpretation made little sense for our study. Children are not able, directly, to change what happens in programs by changing their attention. It is possible that older children could anticipate changes in programs after having learned how typical programs are constructed. Then they could pay attention to those parts they liked and could avoid those parts they did not like. Using such a technique of viewing, children could "change" the programs they were viewing (see Krull & Husson, 1977; Krull & Husson, in press; and Krull & Paulson, in press).

We constructed models without anticipation effects, but including two visual/verbal interaction variables to be described in the next section, which accounted for over 40% of the variance in attention for older children and over 50% of the variance in attention for younger viewers (Krull & Husson, 1977). These are fairly strong models, given the current state of communication research. But when the anticipation effects were added to a time-domain time series model, the amount of variance explained in attention of older viewers rose to nearly 80% (Krull & Husson, in press).

These very strong results argue that children chose program segments on the basis of the information processing offered, and that they become more selective about their information processing as they get older. However, the explanation of the anticipation effects is rather crude, and we plan to elaborate on it substantially in this paper. Before we do that, let us look at the Piaget-based cognitive processing variables we included in the models just described.

Visual/verbal interaction and children's attention. To the program complexity measures we added two more variables: visual/verbal congruence and visual/verbal independence. These variables measured the degree of interaction between verbalization and visual representation on the television screen.

The variables were measured in the following way. First, each show's spoken verbal content was categorized as a set of discrete meaningful utterances. These utterances could be of any length of syntactic form—from a single word (or letter) to a complete sentence. The sole criterion for counting any utterance as a discrete unit was whether that utterance conveyed a meaning which was separate and distinct from that of contiguous verbal sequences.

Congruent utterances were utterances that were paired with images in the visual frame of reference. For example, the spoken word "one" (paired with a graphic of the number) was counted as a congruent utterance. Similarly, letters of the alphabet which were recited with accompanying graphic representation were each treated as individual utterances. More complex forms of congruent utterances were sentences such as, "Look at all this old stuff I have lying around here," "There's a bird on me," and "And now we have a picture of Bert."

Conversely, visual/verbal independence was operationally defined by utterances which were not paired with images on the screen. Examples were statements like "How was your day," "Hey, I'm just kidding," and "I've got a little system that I use sometime."

It is clear that this verbal coding system dichotomizes verbalization on what is essentially an abstractness-concreteness dimension. This dimension has previously been found to be predictive of paired associate learning in children. (Reese, 1965; Rohwer, et al., 1976; Dilley & Paivio, 1968). The basic paradigm of these studies is to vary concreteness on both the stimulus and response side of a paired associate unit in order to determine which stimulus-response combination of concrete and abstract terms is easiest for children to learn. In general, these studies have found a strong facilitory effect due to concreteness (both for pictures and concrete words), particularly when a concrete term appears as a stimulus item in the paired associate unit. The interaction between stimulus and response items has also been found to be significant.

The theoretical interpretation of the facilitory effect of concreteness in paired associate learning differs among the researchers cited. However, these studies are cited not for their support of a particular theoretical viewpoint, but rather for their indirect validation of the relevance of the abstractness/concreteness dimension measured in the present study. Insofar as congruent versus independent verbalization reliably cuts across a dimension of abstractness/concreteness it might be fair to predict differences in children's attention as a function of the facilitory learning effect of concreteness—that is, children should attend more to congruent verbalization sequences because they facilitate learning, whereas attention should decline during the more abstract, independent verbalization sequences.

While the paired associate learning experiments provide some indirect empirical support for the attention hypothesis with respect to verbalization, they do not suggest a strong theoretical rationale for the hypothesis. A rationale is provided, however, by Piaget's theory of intellectual development. The crux of Piaget's theory is that the child organizes his or her experience in a manner that can be described by progressively more complex and systematic rules of logical organization (Ginsburg & Opper, 1969). Clearly, such structuring or organization occurs at a perceptual as well as at an overt physical level (Piaget, 1969) and hence is subject to the same rules of logical organization which have been used to describe the child's physical manipulation of objects in conservation tasks, class inclusion tasks, and the like.

Given this assumption, which follows from Piaget's theory, congruent verbalization can be construed as an instructional set to perceptually organize the visual field in a certain way, while independent verbalization can be construed as a set for assimilation of verbal, rather than perceptual, information. Considered in this way, differential attention patterns as a function of these variables can easily be predicted from Piaget's theory. Attention should be high during periods of visual/verbal congruence, since congruent verbalization implies a set of task instructions in which the child is required to concretely act on the visual field (albeit only at a perceptual level). Inasmuch as the children in our sample fall within the age range of children whose mental operations are characterized by "concrete" characteristics (both preoperational and concrete operational stages), this perceptual task would be well within their capabilities and hence attention should be high. Conversely, since visual/verbal independence carries no set for perceptual organization, attention should decline (because the child is required to assimilate information which is predominantly verbal rather than visual).

Krull and Husson (1977) found that independent verbalizations uniformly depressed attention levels of children, as predicted. Congruent verbalizations were found to increase levels of attention for only some of the sample TV shows used. Both measures were found to be more important in explaining the viewing behavior of the younger viewers of *Sesame Street*.

Analysis of Children's Attention in the Frequency Domain

Now that we have outlined the theoretical rationales and findings regarding the effects of program variables on children's attention, we are ready to describe what these links should look like in the frequency domain. The reason for using frequency domain analysis is that our findings point to this domain as the source for some answers about children's behavior.

If children are anticipating changes in programs, these changes must appear with some regularity. If they did not, children could not develop implicit mental models for how programs are constructed and they would not have a basis for deciding when to change their attention levels. This interplay between program changes and children's viewing implies that there are cycles in both program variables and attention. Time-domain time series analysis examines these cycles indirectly, frequency-domain time series analysis examines cycles directly.

Spectral methods are described at length elsewhere (Bloomfield, 1976; Blackman & Tukey, 1959; Granger & Hatanaka, 1964; Jenkins & Watts, 1968). Space limitations preclude our explaining them here, but a brief outline of what to look for in graphs of spectral statistics will be provided in conjunction with each set of hypotheses.

Cycles in children's attention. Prior to running the preceding study (Krull & Husson, 1977), we had expected older children to show more consistent levels of attention than younger children. Our data instead showed more consistent levels of attention among younger children, as indicated by higher autocorrelations. While autocorrelations are useful for estimating short-term changes, they are less useful for detecting long-term changes such as long cycles in attention. To detect long cycles, one is advised to examine the power spectrum.

The power spectrum indicates the contribution of cycles of different length to variance in data series. Series dominated by short-term changes are expected to have high power in the short cycle, or high frequency, part of the spectrum. Series dominated by long-term changes are expected to have high power in the long cycle, or low frequency, part of the spectrum.

If our prior theory is correct, younger children's attention should show higher power in the high frequency part of the spectrum. If the autocorrelations obtained by Krull and Husson are correct, older children should show higher power in the high frequency part of the spectrum. We stuck to the hypothesis based on our theory:

H_1: The power spectra of younger children's attention will show more power in the high frequencies than will the spectra of older children.

Spectral analysis of program variables. *Sesame Street* and the *Electric Company*, the sample programs we used in our study, are produced by the same organization using roughly the same kind of structure. We had expected, and found, very similar autocorrelations for the program variables for both series. This indicates that the program variables in the two series changed from one point to another with similar probability structures. If the effects of program variables on viewers are linear, as we found by testing for curvilinear effects, differences in the raw levels of program variables should not produce large differences in the responses of children. This set of conditions allowed a weak comparison between different viewers of the two series. For this paper, we examined the spectra as well to see if there were large differences invalidating the comparison in the frequency domain.

Program variables and children's attention. Assessing these causal links in the frequency domain involves balancing several factors: the natural response tendency of children (attention "cycle"), the dominance of cycles in programs, and the time delay between changes in program variables and the behavior of the children. Let us take each of these in turn, listing hypotheses as we go.

If children have natural attention cycles, they may avoid paying attention to program changes which occur at radically different cycle lengths. This would make it appear as if children were suddenly paying attention although nothing had happened in a program, or that they stopped paying attention though interesting material was still being presented. The children and programs would appear to be in synchrony only when changes in attention and program material occurred with the same frequency, and when children responded with little delay.

Correlations between cycles can be obtained from a number of spectral statistics, of which we have used the simplest to interpret. The *coherence* spectrum gives the correlation between two data series for a specified range of cycle lengths. The coherence values run between 0.0 and 1.0, and may be interpreted like ordinary correlations. However, their statistical significance must be looked up in special tables. Further information is available from the reference sources cited.

We used rationales described in preceding sections to produce the following rather crude hypotheses. These hypotheses were tested using coherences.

- H_2: Cycles in set entropy will produce cycles in children's attention.
- H_3: Cycles in verbal time entropy will produce cycles in children's attention.
- H_4: Cycles in shot entropy will produce cycles in children's attention.
- H_5: Cycles in nonverbal dependence entropy will produce cycles in children attention.
- H_6: Cycles in visual/verbal independence will produce cycles in children's attention.
- H_7: Cycles in visual/verbal congruence will produce cycles in children's attention.

We did not make these hypothesis age specific because there were no previous spectral studies from which to draw guidelines. However, studies in other settings led us to expect older children to be less perceptually bound, and hence to respond more strongly to program variables. Our own data from the time-domain time series analysis also supported this expectation.

Anticipation effects in children's attention. If children react just to changes in programs after they occur, there would be a delay in the correlations between the program and attention variables. On the other hand, if children anticipate changes in programs, there should be a lead in the correlations between the program and attention variables. As we have already mentioned, we found an apparent anticipation effect in our time-domain time series analysis. Our rationale for this effect is as follows.

If cycles in TV program variables are very strong, children may be able to perceive them after some viewing experience and to pick points in programs when something interesting is likely to occur. Older children would have more viewing experience and more integrated mental machinery, and would be more likely to show the anticipation effects, as we found.

The *phase* spectrum gives the relative degree of lead or lag between specified cycles of two or more variables. The phases are computed at the same cycle lengths as the coherences, and the two statistics must be used together to obtain a proper interpretation of the phases. The major reason for this is that small coherences give rise to very large, spurious phases.

Our previous findings and theoretical rationale led us to hypothesize anticipation-indicating phase leads for older children and certain program variables only. However, we did examine the phases for all cases.

- H_8: Older children should show phase lead for set entropy.
- H_9: Older children should show phase lead for shot entropy.
- H_{10}: Older children should show phase lead for nonverbal dependence entropy.

METHOD

Samples

Television program material. Children's Television Workshop (CTW) provided us with four videotapes, two *Electric Company* and two *Sesame Street* programs. These shows were taken to be representative of the two series, but no comparative figures for the program variables are available. The *Sesame Street* shows were 47 (SS#1) and 58 (SS#2) minutes in length; the *Electric Company* shows were 28 (EC#2) and 19 (EC#1) minutes in length. *Electric Company* show #1 was somewhat shorter than most programs in that series, but was similar in other respects.

Viewing samples. CTW also provided data on children watching the four sample programs. Ten children watched each tape. The *Sesame Street* viewers were 4 to 5 years old; the *Electric Company* viewers were 7½ to 8½ years of age.

Measurement

Program complexity measures. Scoring the videotapes proceeded in several stages. First, the videotapes were timed to determine the boundaries of program content segments (bits) and the program was divided into 30-second intervals. This was done to provide markers to check the accuracy of variable measurements with respect to time in the program. Then entire videotapes were coded in 30-second intervals, one complexity variable at a time.

One coder ran the videotape machine and stopped it every 30 seconds using the machine's pause control. The other coder scored program variables on a machine consisting of ten electric clocks and a keyboard, noting the results for each 30-second interval. Some program segments were of very high complexity, so the average of several coding passes was used to represent the interval.

Entropy values for each complexity variable were computed after coding was completed.

Visual/verbal interaction measures. The verbal parts of each videotape were transcribed. Then we determined whether each utterance fell into the congruent or independent category.

Since the length of utterances varied greatly, the number of words per utterance was used as a weight. For example, the word "one" or the letter *g* were counted as single utterances. So was the statement, "Look at all this old stuff I have lying around here." The latter utterance clearly occupies more "space" of the interval than either of the unit utterances. We felt that a weighted measure of verbal density would take this into account.

Each scale was completed by summing the number of weighted utterances in each category.

Children's attention measure. The attention data was collected by CTW as part of its research program. Children were individually shown a videotape. A colored-slide projector, changing slides every 7.5 seconds, was placed at the same height as the television set and about 45 degrees to one side.

With the exception of one *Sesame Street* tape, the attention of each child was noted every 7.5 seconds by a coder using a push-button connected to a recording device. Attention was weighted as follows: 3 — eyes on the screen throughout the interval, 2 — eyes on the screen more than half the time, 1 — eyes on the screen less than half the time, 0 — eyes off the screen throughout the interval. One of the *Sesame Street* tapes was scored for attention only every other 7.5 second interval.

These figures were then averaged over all of the ten children watching a particular show. This averaging procedure does not allow an assessment of individual differences in viewing behavior. However, the intent of the two series, and of this analysis, is to determine the reactions of large numbers of children in aggregate rather than to aim programs at individual children.

Entropy values were computed over 30-second intervals because we felt much shorter intervals might give erroneous results because of errors in stopping the videotape machine, and the like. The attention data were averaged over 30 seconds to make the measurement intervals comparable to that used for the program variables. This was pos-

FIGURE 1
Spectral Densities for Children's Attention

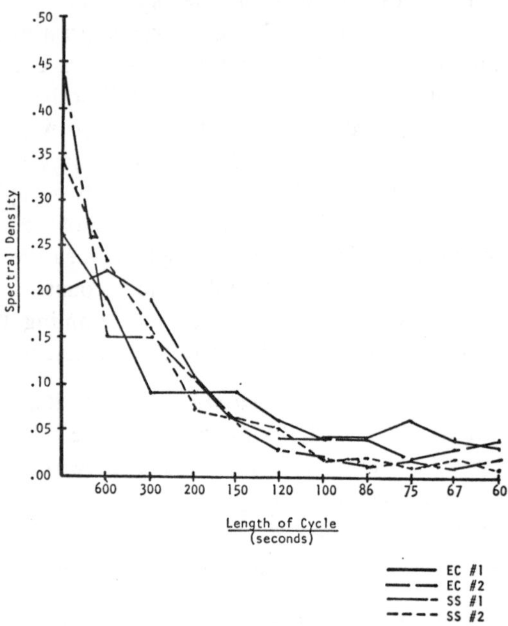

FIGURE 2
Spectral Densities for Set Entropy

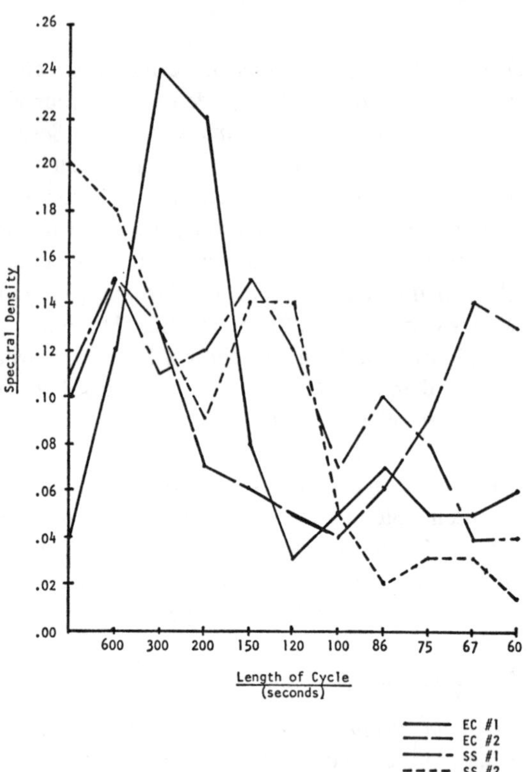

sible because four 7.5-second intervals corresponded to one 30-second interval and we took care to make sure that the boundaries matched.

Statistical Analysis

Estimates of the spectral statistics were obtained using a commercial package of routines. The package computed raw spectral estimates by using a cosine transform of the autocorrelation coefficients. It then smoothed the estimates by averaging three adjacent frequencies using the following scheme (the Tukey-Hanning window, see Granger & Hatanaka, 1964, ch. 4):

$$\text{Smoothed Spectral Power } (\omega) = .23\, p^{(\omega-1)} + .54\, p^{(\omega)} + .23\, p^{(\omega+1)}$$

where p is the raw power estimate at a given frequency and w is the frequency of interest. These estimates were then divided by the variance of the series to yield spectral densities. Spectral densities, rather than spectra, were graphed because the former can be read as correlations between cycles and data and are hence easier to interpret.

Coherences were obtained from the Fourier transforms of the cross-correlations between program variables and children's attention. The estimates were smoothed in the same way as the spectra. Phases were computed from the co- and quadrature spectra. Please see the spectral methods references for additional information on how these computations are performed.

RESULTS

Cycles in Single Series

Children's attention. Figure 1 shows the power spectra for children's attention for both the *Electric Company* and *Sesame Street* series. We had hypothesized that the younger children watching *Sesame Street* should show shorter attention spans than the older children watching the *Electric Company* (H_1).

The figure shows the attention levels of both

FIGURE 3
Spectral Densities for Verbal Entropy

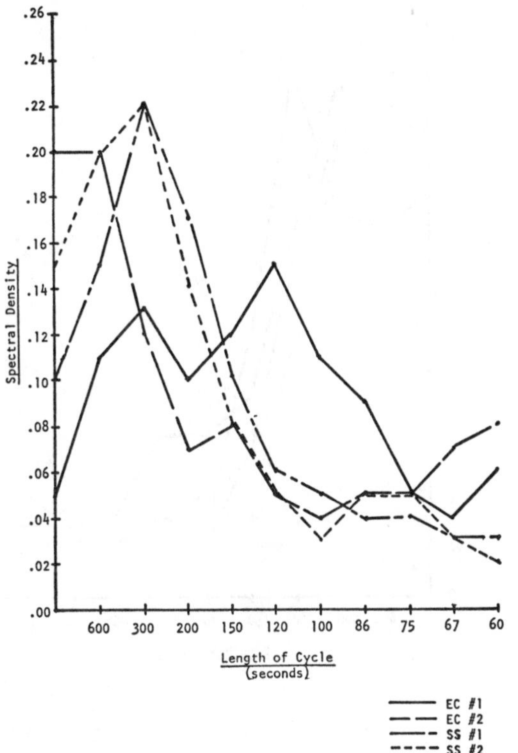

FIGURE 4
Spectral Densities for Shot Entropy

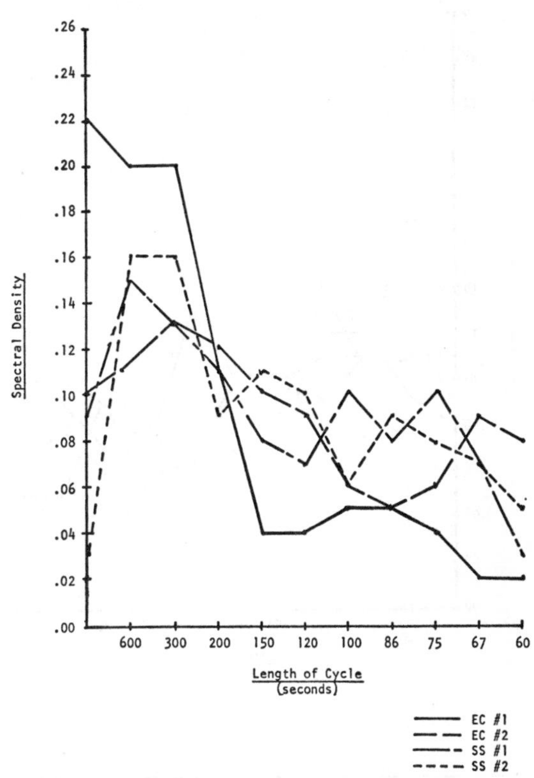

older and younger children to be dominated by cycles longer than 200 seconds. Younger children show much more power in the 600-plus-second region than do older children. Older children show consistently more power in cycles shorter than 100 seconds, but these cycles seem to contribute relatively little to the variability in the data. Hypothesis 1 does not seem to be supported by the data. *Entropy measures of program complexity*. Figure 2 shows the power spectra for set entropy. We had hoped that these spectra would be roughly similar to one another so that comparisons between viewers of the two programs could be more easily made.

Electric Company #1 has a very strong power peak in the 200 to 300-second range. *Electric Company* #2 has considerable power in the 70-second range. Both *Sesame Street* programs have considerable power near 150 seconds. These differences should be kept in mind in interpreting the coherences between set entropy and children's attention.

Figure 3 shows the power spectra for verbal entropy. Three shows have power at 300 to 600 seconds. *Electric Company* #1 is a bit of an oddball again, showing power at about 125 seconds.

Figure 4 shows the spectra for shot entropy. All of the shows have high power in the 300 to 600-second range and relatively less elsewhere. *Electric Company* #1 exhibits the same pattern, but more strongly than the rest of the series.

Figure 5 shows the power spectra for nonverbal dependence entropy. With the exception of *Electric Company* #1, all of the patterns indicate little dominance by cycles at any particular frequency. *Electric Company* #1 shows slightly more power in the 600-plus-second range.

Taken together, these figures seem to indicate that three of the show are roughly similar in their spectral properties for the complexity variables.

FIGURE 5
Spectral Densities for Nonverbal Dependence Entropy

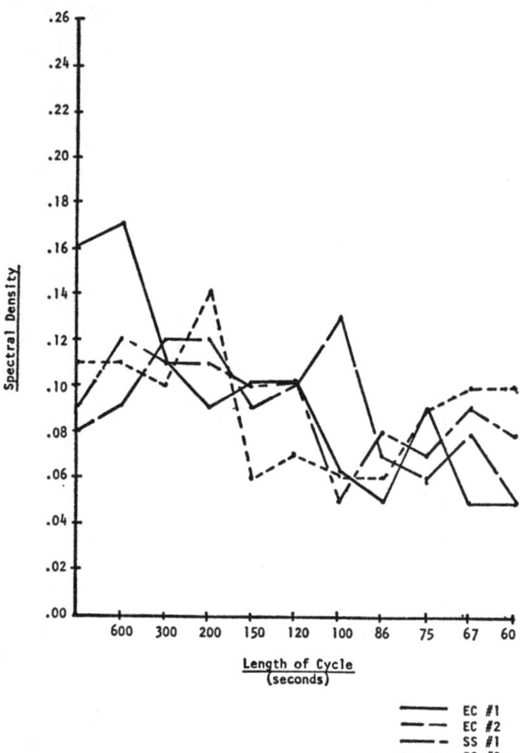

FIGURE 6
Spectral Densities for Visual/Verbal Congruence

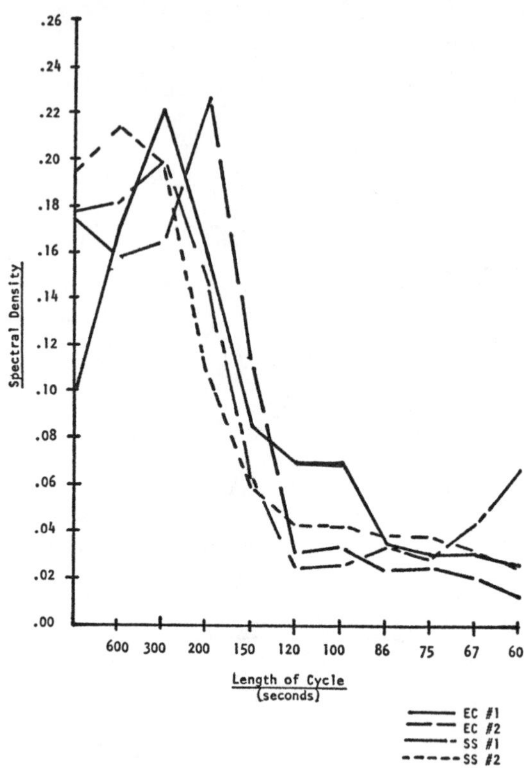

For three of the complexity variables, all but nonverbal dependence, there is considerable relative power at the longer cycles. Electric Company #1 appears to be a bit of an oddball and its cross-spectral coefficients should be interpreted with caution.

Visual/verbal interaction measures. Figure 6 shows the power spectra for visual/verbal congruence. The patterns for all of the programs seem to be rather similar, with the greatest concentration of power being at cycles 200 seconds and longer. Figure 7 shows the power spectra for visual/verbal independence. All of the series are again dominated by cycles longer than 200 seconds, but the amount of power in the region is not as large as for the congruence variable. The spectra for the two different series weave in and out of one another through most of the full range examined, but there is a small peak for *Electric Company* #1 near 86 seconds.

Considering all of the six TV program measures together, one sees a fairly good similarity between the spectra for *Sesame Street* and those for the *Electric Company*. There seems to be some justification for a weak comparison between the viewing behavior of the two different sets of children watching the two series.

Program Variables and Children's Attention

Given the sample sizes for our test programs, the coherences reaching significance at the .05 probability levels are: .80, EC #1; .67, EC #2; .55, SS #1; .50, SS #2. The coherences required for significance are rather high for the shorter *Electric Company* shows because of the small number of measurement intervals. The levels were estimated from Granger and Hatanaka (1964, p. 79). Phases were more complicated to assess (see Granger & Hatanaka, 1964, for tables).

FIGURE 7
Spectral Densities for Visual/Verbal Independence

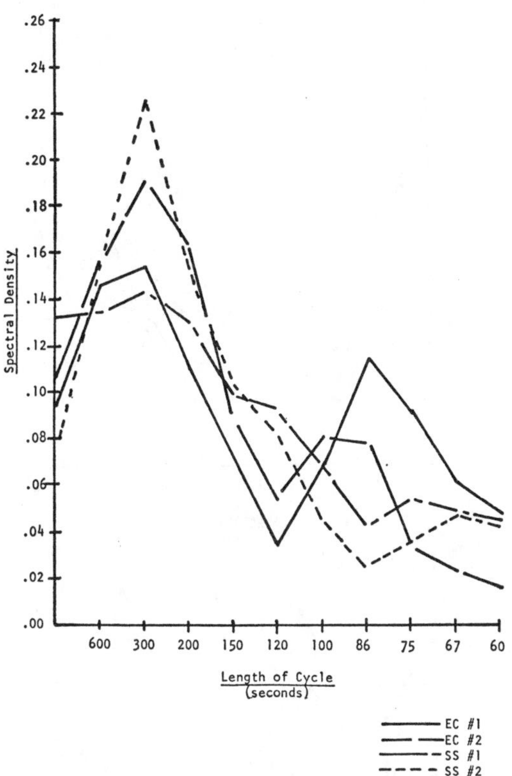

FIGURE 8
Spectral Correlations Between Set Entropy and Attention

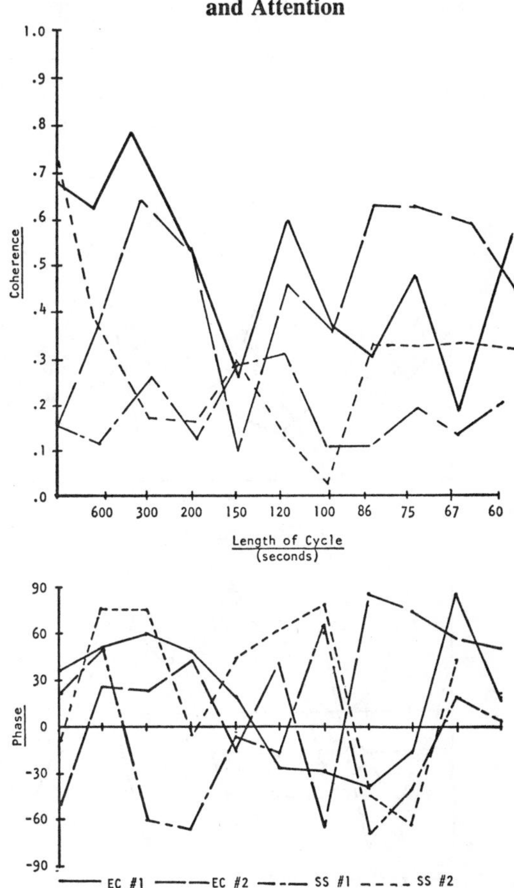

Program complexity and children's attention. Figure 8 shows the coherences and phases for the relationship between set entropy and children's attention. The coherences for *Sesame Street* are not particularly powerful, with the exception of very long and relatively short cycles for *Sesame Street* #2. Since *Sesame Street* #1 does not show power in the same area, these high coherences may be idiosyncratic to program #2.

Both *Electric Company* programs exhibit roughly the same pattern: high power in the 200 to 300-second range and the odd power peak at higher frequencies. Although *Electric Company* #1 has considerable power in its set entropy spectrum for the 200 to 300 range, *Electric Company* #2 does not. It is likely, therefore, that the high coherences here do reflect the reactions of the children. The peaks at 300 seconds barely reach significance for both shows.

Figure 8 also shows the phase spectra for this relationship. Since the coherences for the Sesame Street shows are small, their phases are likely to be uninterpretable. The *Electric Company* shows both had high coherences in the 300-second range. The corresponding phases both show phase leads (positive degrees) from 200 to 600 seconds, and are twice as large as required for significance at the .05 level. EC #2 had high coherences in the 67 to 86-second range and the phases for that range are also correspondingly high and show a lead. Since EC #2 shows relatively little coherence and not nearly the length of phase lead in this area, the correlations in the 67 to 86-second range appear to be idiosyncratic to EC #2. The data support H_2 with respect to the *Electric Company* shows and H8 with respect to phase lead for these shows.

Figure 9 shows the coherences and phases for

FIGURE 9
Spectral Correlations Between Verbal Entropy and Attention

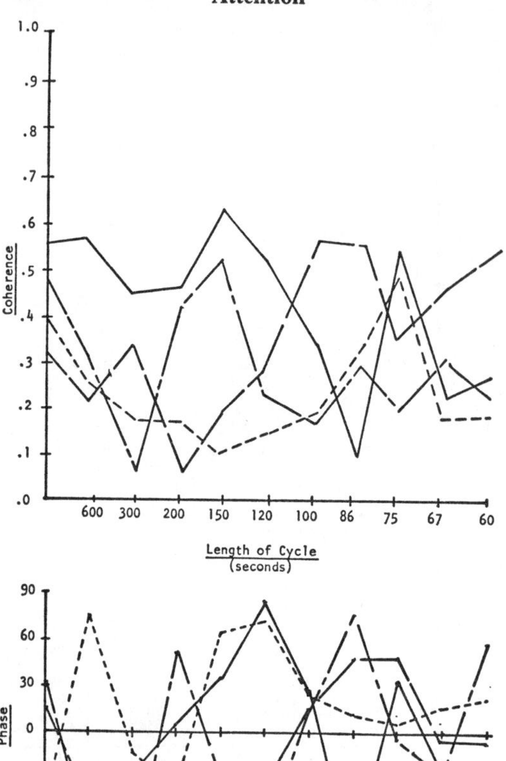

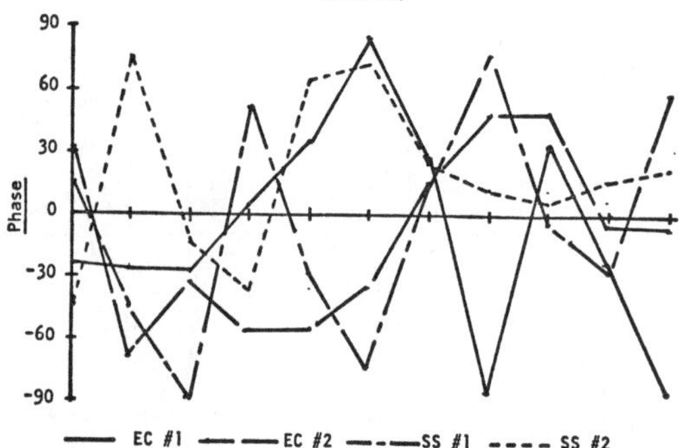

FIGURE 10
Spectral Correlations Between Shot Entropy and Attention

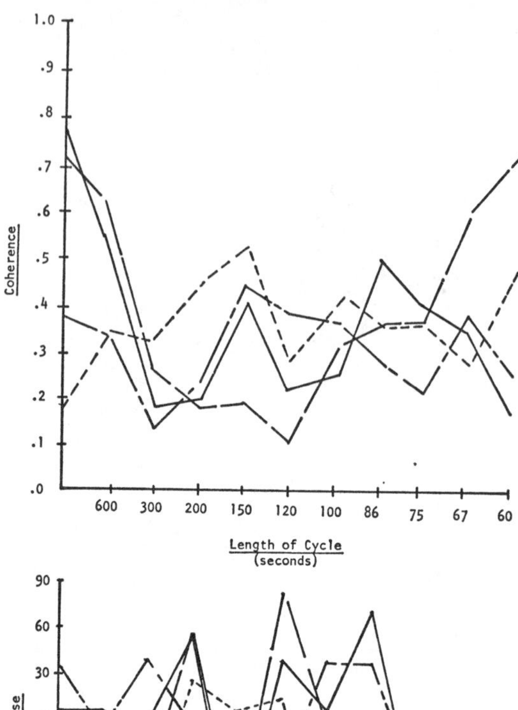

verbal entropy and attention. *Sesame Street* #1 shows highest coherence at about 150 seconds, *Sesame Street* #2 shows highest coherence at about 75 seconds. Although both coherences nudge significance, each occurs where the other series shows almost no coherence at all. *Electric Company* #1 shows coherence in the 120-plus-second range, *Electric Company* #2 shows coherence at about 80 to 100 seconds. Again the coherences are near significance, and again they occur at very different places for the two programs.

The phases given in the same figure show negligible leads or lags for the *Sesame Street* shows. There is a significant phase lead for *Electric Company* #2 at 86 seconds, but none at 100 seconds. *Electric Company* #1 shows significant phase lags at 300-plus seconds and significant phase lead at 120 seconds. Since these patterns show little consistency among programs it is difficult to conclude anything with respect to H_3.

Figure 10 shows the coherences and phases for set entropy and children's attention. *Sesame Street* #2 shows significant coherence at 600-plus seconds, and *Electric Company* #2 shows high coherence at 60 to 67 seconds.

Sesame Street #2 shows negligible lead or lag near its only high coherence. Both *Electric Company* shows have negligible lead or lag in the 600-plus-second range, *Electric Company* #2 shows some lag in the 60 to 67-second range. The 60 to 67-second statistics for EC #2 are probably idiosyncratic to that program. The coherences and

FIGURE 11
Spectral Correlations Between Nonverbal Dependence and Attention

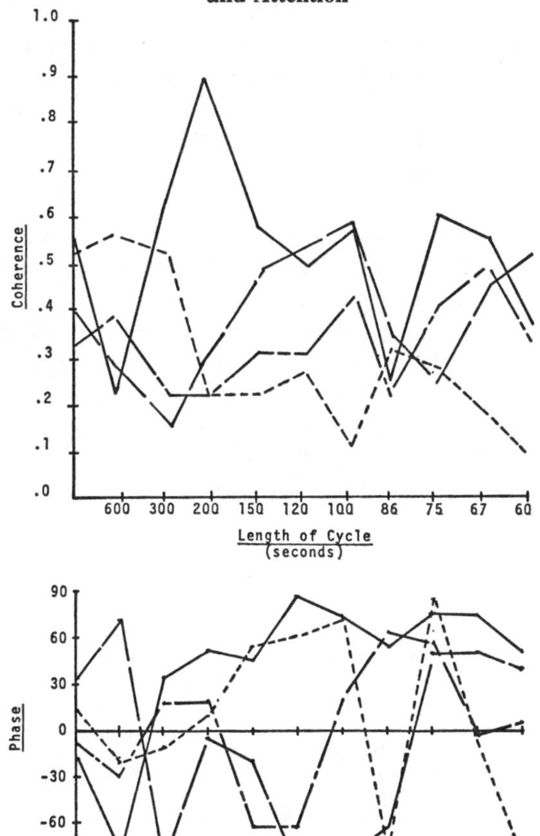

FIGURE 12
Spectral Correlations Between Visual/Verbal Congruence and Attention

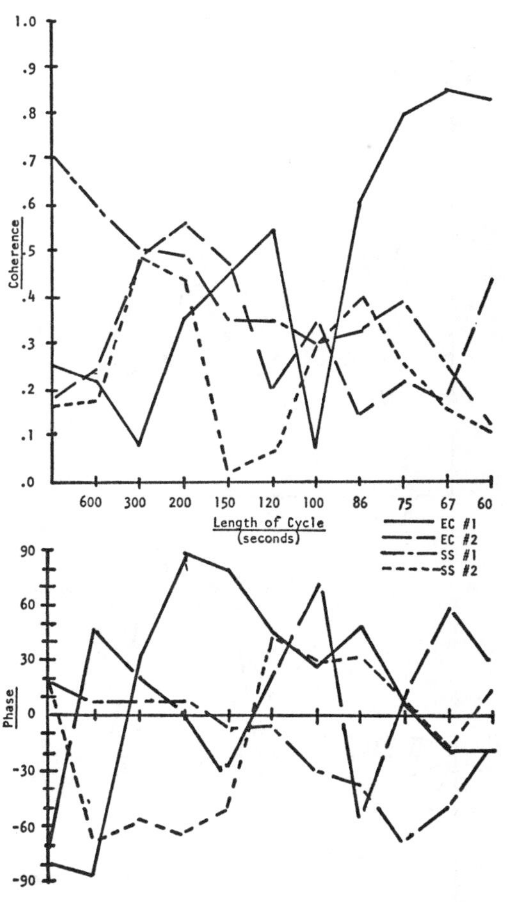

phases support H_4 and H_9 with respect to the *Electric Company* programs.

Figure 11 shows the correlations for nonverbal dependence entropy and attention. *Sesame Street #2* shows significant coherence in the 300-plus-second range, *Sesame Street #1* fails to show significant coherences anywhere. *Electric Company #1* shows very large coherence at 200 seconds and moderate, nonsignificant coherences at 100 seconds and 67 to 75 seconds. *Electric Company #2* shows little coherence at 200 seconds, but does have moderate, nonsignificant coherences at the other places where *Electric Company #1* does.

Sesame Street #2 shows no phase lead or lag in the range of its significant coherences. *Electric Company #1* shows significant phase leads for most of its range, but *Electric Company #2* shows significant lags through most of its range. The data showed mixed support for H_5 and H_{10}.

Visual/verbal interaction and children's attention. Figure 12 shows the correlations between visual/verbal congruence and children's attention. *Sesame Street #1* shows statistically significant coherence in the 300-plus-second range and progressively less throughout the rest of the spectrum. *Sesame Street #2* shows significant coherence only at 200 to 300-second cycles. So the data for these two shows seem to agree only in the 200 to 300-second interval. The *Electric Company* shows exhibit even less agreement. The only region of significant coherences is that from 60 to 75-second

FIGURE 13
Spectral Correlations Between Visual/Verbal Independence and Attention

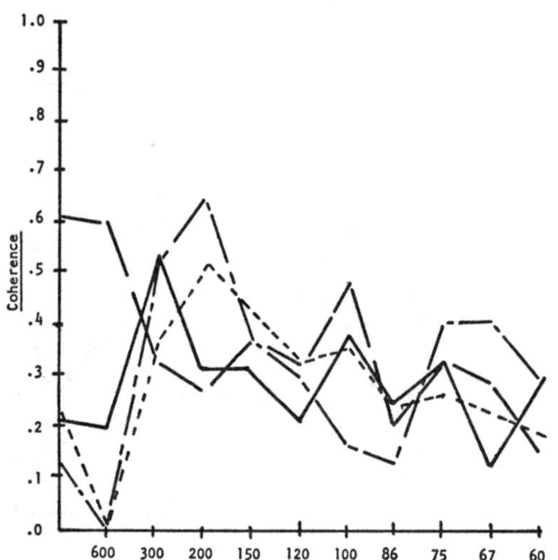

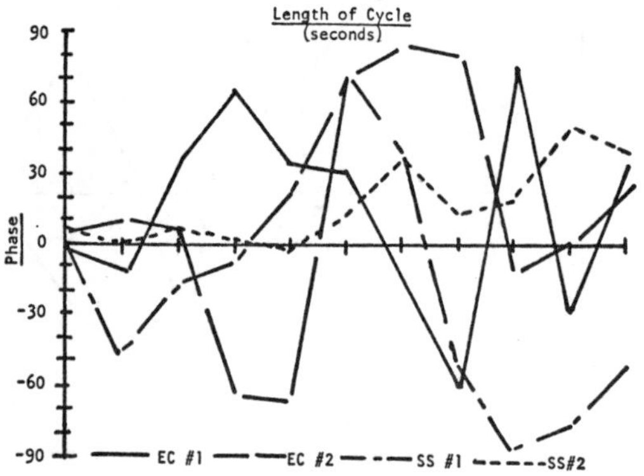

cycles for *Electric Company* #1.

The phases for *Sesame Street* show as little agreement as did the coherences. In the 200 to 300-second region where the coherences agreed, the phases are null in one case and 60-degree lag in the other. The phases for the *Electric Company* shows have even less agreement than those for *Sesame Street*. In the range of significant coherences for *Electric Company* #1, the phase gradually shifts from moderate lead to moderate lag. The support for H6 from these data is decidedly mixed.

Figure 13 shows the correlations between visual/verbal independence and attention. The patterns for the coherences are surprisingly similar, considering the patterns for the other variables. Unfortunately, few of the coherences are significant statistically. With one exception, both the *Electric Company* and *Sesame Street* shows have greatest coherence around 200-second cycles and less coherence at other cycles. *Electric Company* #2 is slightly different from the other programs in having high coherence in the 600-plus-second range.

The phases also given in the figure are as different as the coherences were similar. Both *Sesame Street* shows have negligible phase shifts in the 200-second range where the coherences were high. Their phases are very dissimilar in other regions. The *Electric Company* phases are almost mirror images of one another about the horizontal axis.

Taken together, the coherences and phases provide somewhat mixed support for H_7.

DISCUSSION

The purpose of this paper was to examine the relationship between TV program variables and children's attention, so as to determine how active the child is in television viewing. We did this by examining time series data in the frequency domain with particular emphasis on anticipation effects. The pattern of findings was more ambiguous than we would have liked, but the following summary and interpretation seem fair.

Our theory predicted that older children should have longer attention spans (cycles) than younger children. The data seem to indicate, however, that younger children have longer attention cycles, particularly in the 600-plus-second range. The autocorrelations from the preceding study had also shown higher attention spans for younger children, but that was for 30-second lags. These two sets of findings tap attention spans in different time frames, but there may be one unifying explanation for them.

The *Sesame Street* shows are twice as long as the *Electric Company* shows. It is possible that the children watching *Sesame Street* get tired of viewing during the second half of the show. This fatigue effect would produce a long-term trend in the data which would certainly appear in the 600-second region of the spectra and which might increase the size of the short-term autocorrelations. This explanation could be assessed by removing the trend from the data and recomputing the spectra.

Our theory also indicated that children should choose to pay attention to program segments on the basis of the amount and kind of stimulation provided. Roughly, we had expected children to pay more attention to perceptually complex, but cognitively concrete, material. We also expected older children to be more affected by program variables, to prefer visual variables and to anticipate program changes.

Some of our expectations were confirmed. Most program variables showed some correlation (coherence) with children's attention. However, there was often only moderate consistency among the findings for the four sample programs and many coherences did not reach statistical significance. The phases also showed relatively little stability, although many reached statistical significance even when the coherences did not.

On the favorable side we can say the following. Our coherences were actually fairly high in absolute value and only the shortness of our data series precluded their being of greater statistical significance. As expected, the older children were more affected by program variables, were more affected by the visual variables, and showed anticipation effects (phase leads) for many variables.

Taking our interpretation at face value, our data seem to indicate that older children are rather strongly affected by our program variables, while younger children are only weakly affected. This implies either that children in the 4 to 5 age range are so perceptually bound that they will watch anything, or that young children respond to program variables we have not yet measured. There is probably a little truth to each explanation. Young children may not be able to sort out programs sufficiently well to respond quickly when programs change, and *Sesame Street*'s popularity may be based on other factors we have not tapped.

The implications of our findings for older children are very interesting. Older children seem to respond to a larger range of program variables and to anticipate changes in programs. The latter implies that 8-year-old children have fairly sophisticated mental models of programs. The analysis of these mental models promises to be a fruitful avenue for understanding children's cognitive development in general.

One way of ferreting out the structure of these theoretical mental models would be to combine several program variables in a single statistical model. We did this for our time-domain models and found them to have very high predictive power. One interesting feature of multivariate spectral models is the opportunity they provide to assess which variables trigger the anticipation of children. Some verbal program variable might lead a visual program variable. Children then could be reacting to the verbal variable with a short delay, but statistically they would be seen as anticipating the visual variable.

We feel that the multivariate models are fairly easy to test, but that there is relatively little substantive theory to guide us in making detailed predictions about what their parameters should be, or metatheory to guide us in integrating an overall explanation. Small pieces of substantive theory could be developed by running a fairly large number of studies of the kind reported in this paper. The metatheoretical problem seems less easy to solve.

Implicitly, the anticipation effects discussed in this paper refer to complicated causal loops, probably feedforward loops. While complicated causalities often appear in articles in theoretical discussions (this is particularly true of feedback), there is rarely an attempt to study these causalities empirically. This may be true in part because loops require very complicated methodologies to evaluate, but it may also be true because the state of communications theory is so rudimentary.

For example, our hypotheses about coherences were very crude. Most communications theories are stated in "if, then" terms, or at best in "as *X* increases, *Y* increases" terms. This form of theory seems reasonable from the point of view of the people to be explained, but leaves us with the kind of hypotheses we used in this paper. The kind of theory necessary for future work seems to be one which allows specification of parameters, like the expected length of delay between program variables and viewers' responses, but which does so in a way which includes aspects of the machinations of the viewers themselves.

REFERENCES

ANDERSON, D.R., & LEVIN, S.R. Young children's attention to Sesame Street. *Child Development*, 1976, 47, 806-811.

BLACKMAN, R.B. & TUKEY, J.W. *The measurement of power spectra*. New York: Dover, 1959.

BECHTEL, R.B., ACHELPOLK, C., & AKERS, R. Correlates between observed behavior and questionnaire responses on television viewing. *Television and social behavior* Vol. 4. Washington: Government Printing Office, 1972, 274-344.

BLOOMFIELD, P. *Fourier analysis of time series: An introduction*. New York: Wiley, 1976.

DILLEY, M.G., & PAIVIO, A. Pictures and words as stimulus and response items in paired-associate learning of young children. *Journal of Experimental Child Psychology*, 1968, 6, 231-240.

GINSBURG, H., & OPPER, S. *Piaget's theory of intellectual development: An introduction*. Englewood Cliffs, N.J.: Prentice-Hall, 1969.

GRANGER, C.W.J., & HATANAKA, M. *Spectral analysis of economic time series*. Princeton, N.J.: Princeton University Press, 1964.

JENKINS, G.M., & WATTS, D.G. *Spectral analysis and its applications*. San Francisco: Holden-Day, 1968.

KRULL, R., & HUSSON, W.G. Children's attention to the television screen: A time series analysis. Paper presented at the annual meeting of the Association for Education in Journalism, Chicago, 1977.

KRULL, R., & HUSSON, W.G. Children's anticipatory attention to the TV screen. Article submitted for review, in press.

KRULL, R., & PAULSON, A.S. Time series analysis in communication research. In P.M. Hirsch, P.V. Miller and F.G. Kline (Eds.), *Methodological strategies for communication research*. Beverly Hills, Cal.: Sage, in press.

KRULL, R., & WATT, J.H. Television program complexity and ratings. Paper presented at the annual meeting of the American Association for Public Opinion Research, 1975.

KRULL, R., WATT, J.H., & LICHTY, L.W. Structure and complexity: Two factors in television viewership. Paper presented at the annual meeting of the International Communication Association, 1974.

KRULL, R., WATT, J.H., & LICHTY, L.W. Structure and complexity: Two measures of complexity in television programs. *Communication Research*, 1977, 4, 61-86.

LASKER, H.M. *The Jamaican project*. Cambridge, Mass.: Center for Research in Children's Television, 1974.

LEVIN, S.R., & ANDERSON, D.R. The development of attention. *Journal of Communication*, 1976, 26, 126-135.

LOSCIUTO, L.A. A national inventory of television viewing behavior. *Television and social behavior*, Vol. 4. Washington, D.C.: U.S. Government Printing Office, 1972, 33-86.

MURRAY, J.P. Television in inner-city homes: Viewing behavior of young boys. *Television and social behavior* Vol. 4. Washington, D. C.: U. S. Government Printing Office, 1972, 345-394.

PIAGET, J. *The mechanisms of perception*. New York: Basic, 1969.

REESE, H.W. Imagery in paired-associate learning in children. *Journal of Experimental Child Psychology*, 1965, 2, 290-296.

REEVES, B.F. *The first year of Sesame Street: The formative research*. New York: Children's Television Workshop, 1970.

ROHWER, W.D., JR., LYNCH, S., SUZUKI, N., & LEVIN, J. Verbal and pictorial facilitation of paired-associate learning. *Journal of Experimental Child Psychology*, 1967, 5, 294-302.

ROBINSON, J. Television and leisure time: yesterday, today and (maybe) tomorrow. *Public Opinion Quarterly*, 1969, 33, 210-222.

WARD, S., LEVINSON, D., & WACKMAN, D. Children's attention to television advertising. *Television and social behavior* Vol. 4. Washington, D. C.: U. S. Government Printing Office, 1972, 491-515.

WARD, S., & WACKMAN, D. Children's information processing of television advertising. In P. Clarke (Ed.), *New models for communication research*. Beverly Hills, Cal.: Sage, 1973, 119-146.

WARTELLA, E., & ETTEMA, J.S. A cognitive developmental study of children's attention to television commercials. *Communication Research*, 1974, 1, 69-88.

WATT, J.H., & KRULL, R. An information theory measure for television programming. *Communication Research*, 1974, 1, 44-68.

WATT, J.H., & KRULL, R. An examination of three models of television viewing and aggression. *Human Communication Research*, 1976, 3, 99-112.

Appendix A

DEFINITIONS OF PROGRAM COMPLEXITY VARIABLES

Set time entropy is defined as the degree of randomness of the time of visual duration of discrete physical locations in a program.

Verbal time entropy is defined as the degree of randomness of the time of audible behavior on the part of characters in a program.

Nonverbal dependence entropy is defined as the degree of randomness of the use of visuals only to carry the narrative in a program.

Shot entropy is defined as the degree of randomness of the duration of different apparent distances between the camera and the object in view.

This new variable was added to tap visual aspects of television programs not handled by the set entropy measure. It was coded by scoring the amount of time spent on close-up, medium, and long shots. These three categories were used as a compromise between having sufficient categories to make discriminations and not so many that categorization became unreliable.

Both one and two person close-ups (showing upper chest and head) were coded into the close-up category. Shots which showed more than the upper chest and head, but less than the entire figure, were coded as long shots. These distinctions were rather difficult to make with puppets and some animated figures.

LABORATORY VERIFICATION OF "FREUDIAN" SLIPS OF THE TONGUE AS EVIDENCE OF PREARTICULATORY SEMANTIC EDITING[1]

MICHAEL T. MOTLEY
Ohio State University

BERNARD J. BAARS
State University of New York, Stony Brook

Earlier research has shown that spoonerisms (e.g., *wage rate* → *rage wait*) can be elicited by a laboratory technique in which subjects attempt to articulate a target (*wage rate*) preceded by biasing word items containing certain phonological characteristics of the designed error (*rage wait*). The frequency of errors on various targets depends more upon the linguistic characteristics of their potential spoonerism than upon the characteristics of the targets themselves, suggesting that subjects "edit" phoneme strings prior to articulation. Phonological and lexical criteria have been established within the prearticulatory editing operations. The present report describes two experiments designed to determine whether these prearticulatory edits involve semantic criteria. In Experiment 1, the base-rate of errors produced by the phonetic bias technique was dramatically increased by adding (to the phonological bias) items which were semantically synonymous to the designed target errors. In Experiment 2, the base-rate of errors was increased by manipulating subjects into a situational cognitive set consonant with the semantic implications of the designed target errors. Results imply a semantic criterion in the prearticulatory editing operations of natural speech encoding—a semantic criterion very much like that which has been assumed for "Freudian slips." Implications are discussed.

INTRODUCTION

Ever since Freud first popularized the suggestion that verbal slips may provide insights to cognitive processing, linguists and psycholinguists have examined slips of the tongue in pursuit of such insight. The verbal slip research since Freud has discounted Freud's original notions, however. Freud claimed that verbal slips are instigated by the global cognitive (and affective) state of the speaker, and that linguistic factors do not influence the outcome of the errors. Subsequent research, on the other hand, has ignored the Freudian notion of influence by global cognitive states, while focusing on the linguistic factors which influence verbal slips. The present study, though based upon the recognition that linguistic factors *do* instigate or mediate verbal slip outcomes, also pursues the explanation outlined by Freud (1965).

Freud's view of verbal slips was, in effect, a prediction that semantic influences which are independent of a speaker's intended utterance can create a distorted utterance such that the mutilated outcome more closely resembles the meaning of the semantic interference than the meaning of the originally intended verbal output. Freud proposed that a source of this semantic interference is the cognitive set which accompanies the speaker's utterance. Although the notion of the "Freudian slip" has enjoyed intuitive popularity, there has been no replicable empirical evidence of the phenomenon, and there has been very little evidence of specific speech encoding processes which could account for this type of verbal slip. More specifically, there has been no experimental evidence that the kinds of semantic considerations present in "higher" and presumably more remote stages of encoding (e.g., semantic and presemantic stages) can distort the more immediate phonological or articulatory stages. Since evidence for Freudian slips has always been anecdotal, corresponding theories have always been post hoc.

In recent years, researchers have succeeded in artificially eliciting various types of slips of the tongue (Motley & Baars, 1975a, 1976a; for a review of methods, see Baars, 1977). Laboratory-

FIGURE 1
Sample Word List, Basic SLIP Technique (With explanation)

WORD PAIRS	CUED FOR VOCALIZATION	EXPECTED ORAL RESPONSE	FUNCTION
⋮			
big sun	no	none	neutral filler
lucky man	no	none	neutral filler
pencil shove	yes	pencil shove	neutral filler
make pool	no	none	interference
tame mule	no	none	interference
taste food	no	none	interference
fake tool	yes	TAKE FOOL	spoonerism target
⋮			

generated verbal slips now allow a precisely replicable investigation of the potential of semantic factors (and/or cognitive set) to influence verbal slips. The present study investigates this question via a laboratory technique which elicits *spoonerisms*—the type of verbal slip in which phonemes are switched with one another (e.g., the intended utterance *blue chip stocks* accidentally spoken as *blue chop sticks*). The spoonerism has been an especially popular type of verbal slip for psycholinguistic research, partially because of the clarity of its mutilation (see MacKay, 1970; Motley, 1973).

This study employed the spoonerism elicitation technique developed by Motley and Baars (1976a). The basic procedure (to be detailed below) consists of a tachistoscopic presentation of a word-pair list. The word pairs are read silently by the subject, with the exception of certain word pairs which are cued to be spoken aloud; these being *target* word pairs designed by the experimenter to elicit spoonerisms. The target word pairs are preceded by *interference* word pairs (read silently) which are designed to more closely resemble the phonology of the desired spoonerism error than the phonology of the subject's intended target. (See Figure 1.) This SLIP technique (Spoonerisms of Laboratory-Induced Predisposition) elicits spoonerisms on approximately 30% of the target word pairs attempted by the subject. (For details and variations of the technique, see Motley & Baars, 1976a. For an introduction to other laboratory techniques for eliciting various kinds of verbal slips, see Baars, 1977.)

While on the one hand pursuing Freud's explanation of verbal slips, the present study was conceived primarily as an extension of earlier studies using the SLIP technique. Previous research with the SLIP procedure has demonstrated that spoonerism frequencies are affected by certain linguistic characteristics of the spoonerism error itself, independent of the characteristics of the target. Motley and Baars (1975a) demonstrated, for example, that spoonerism frequencies increase according to the transitional probability of the initial phoneme sequence of the error: word-initial spoonerism frequencies increase for errors with higher word-initial phonotactic probabilities. Baars, Motley, and MacKay (1975) demonstrated that spoonerism frequencies increase according to the lexical legitimacy of the error, independent of the lexical characteristics of their targets: spoonerism frequencies are greater for lexically legitimate errors than for lexically anomalous errors, regardless of their targets.

These earlier studies allowed conclusions regarding the probable linguistic characteristics of spoonerism outcomes. More importantly, however, these studies also allowed conclusions regarding the subjects' cognitive encoding operations during the SLIP task. Specifically, the cognitive processing which precedes the subject's eventual articulation involves not only a consideration of the target, but also an evaluative consideration of its recoded (spoonerized) phoneme sequence. Notice, for example, that subjects provided with an equal number of targets such as *long root* (/lɔŋ rut/—rɔŋ lut/) versus matched targets such as *lawn roof* (/lɔn ruf/→/rɔn luf/) will produce a significantly greater number of slips on those targets which allow lexically legitimate spoonerisms (e.g., *long root* → *wrong loot* versus *lawn roof* → **rawn loof*, see Baars, et al., 1975). Since the targets themselves are similar in all respects, subjects' spoonerism behavior (e.g., favoring /rɔŋ lut/ over /rɔn luf/) cannot be dependent in any direct way upon subjects' evaluations of the targets. Rather, the spoonerism behavior can be explained only by allowing that subjects considered the spoonerized version of the targets prior to articulation, and *evaluated* the corresponding phoneme sequences by applying the criterion of lexical legitimacy. Thus, Motley and Baars (1975b) explain the subjects' SLIP encoding experience as follows:

1. Subjects attempt to articulate the phoneme string associated with the target.
2. The task's interference words, however, created confusion and uncertainty within the phoneme sequence.
3. The confusion multiplies the available choices of phoneme sequences to be articulated (e.g., at least the target sequence and spoonerized sequence are available in choices).
4. The eventual articulatory decision is determined by "editing" (i.e., evaluating) the available choices, with the phoneme sequence fitting the criteria of the editing decision being identified for articulatory output.

The encoding of naturally occurring spoonerisms may be explained as analogous to the encoding of SLIP errors (Motley & Baars, 1975b): Speakers prepare to articulate a phoneme sequence, discover that confusion or uncertainty accompanies the phoneme sequence information, edit the potential phoneme sequences by applying certain evaluative criteria, and select for articulation the phoneme sequence which first (or best?) passes their edit. On occasion, a spoonerized phoneme sequence is approved by the editing mechanism.

This brief description of a 'prearticulatory editing' component of natural encoding raises a variety of questions, some of which have been addressed as follows. (For a more detailed discussion of these issues, see Motley & Baars, 1975b.)

A. What is the role of prearticulatory editing in normal (error-free) encoding? The edit probably performs a passive role during most speech encoding, becoming activated for those situations in which noise (interference, confusion, competition, etc.) exists in the phoneme sequence being prepared for articulation.

B. What is the source (or cause) of noise in the phoneme sequence information? It is possible that a variety of causes instigate the noise which accompanies some prearticulatory phoneme sequences. Empirical research suggests that an especially profound source of prearticulatory noise is the competition of encoding plans (see especially Baars, 1976; also Baars, 1977). That is, once a speaker has decided to encode a given thought for speech output, a variety of choices and options (semantic, lexical, and syntactic) are available. Baars's competing plans hypothesis postulates that encoding progresses not simply by initially eliminating all but one option and linearly encoding that final choice, but rather by allowing decisions on options during the encoding of the initial (not necessarily final) choice(s). If two (or more) output plans are in competition as late as the phonological phase of encoding, noise may be present in the phoneme sequence information.

C. If phoneme sequences are edited, how is it that phoneme sequence errors (e.g., verbal slips) can occur in natural speech? One explanation for the existence of errors in edited phoneme sequences is simply that the editing mechanism occasionally fails. One likely reason for failure is associated with the timing schedule which appears to accompany encoding operations (see Motley, 1974). That is, the editing operations may begin to evaluate the options of a confused phoneme sequence, fail to complete its evaluation in the 'allotted' time, and be 'ordered' to output a phoneme sequence before all editing operations upon that sequence are complete (Motley & Baars, 1975b). A second explanation of naturally occurring edited phoneme sequence errors is more germane to our present concern. The editing mechanism is presumed to compare phoneme sequences against linguistic criteria independent of the "target" phoneme sequence. That is, a phoneme sequence may be "incorrect" based upon the intended utterance, yet be quite "correct" according to the linguistic criteria of the editing mechanism. For example, the spoonerism, *right leading* (from intended *light reading*), might be approved by an editing mechanism evaluating only phonotactic integrity and lexical integrity.

D. What are the criteria of the prearticulatory editing decisions? The research discussed above suggests two criteria upon which the editing mechanism evaluates phoneme strings destined for articulation—phonotactic integrity (Motley & Baars, 1975a), and lexical integrity (Baars, et al., 1975). The present study investigates the presence of additional editing criteria.

Within the context of a prearticulatory editing model, Freud's prediction of semantic influences upon verbal slips may be approached as a prediction of editing based upon semantic criteria (in addition to the phonotactic and lexical criteria already established). This paper reports investigations of two levels of semantic editing criteria. Experiment 1 investigates the influence of *verbal* semantic interference upon spoonerism outcomes. Experiment 2 investigates the influence of *cognitive* semantic interference.

EXPERIMENT 1[2]

Hypothesis

Frequencies of spoonerisms will be significantly greater for word-pair targets preceded by both semantic and phonological interference than for targets preceded by phonological interference only.

Subjects

Subjects were 44 experimentally naive students of an introductory communication course at California State University, Los Angeles. All were native speakers of American English.

Apparatus

The SLIP word pairs were tachistoscopically presented by a memory drum (Lafayette, Model 303BB), each word pair being exposed for one second, with less than 0.10 second between exposures. The cue for subjects to speak aloud the target word pairs (and certain neutral control word pairs) was a buzzer. This cue followed the conclusion of each target word-pair exposure by approximately 0.5 second.

Stimuli

Two matched lists of 264 word pairs were constructed: one for the Semantic Interference treatment, and one for the Semantically Neutral treatment; identical except for their semantic bias items. Each word pair list contained 20 target word pairs as potential spoonerisms, each target preceded by 8 interference word pairs (actually, 4 interference pairs, each presented twice). Target word pairs were designed to elicit lexically legitimate spoonerism switches of the words' initial consonants. For example, the target *bad mug* would be expected to spoonerize to *mad bug*. (See Figure 2.) The interference preceding each target consisted of 2 word pairs (each presented twice) containing phonological interference, and 2 word pairs (each presented twice) containing semantic interference. The phonological interference word pairs were constructed such that the initial consonants and subsequent vowels of both words were identical to the corresponding phonemes of the expected spoonerism (e.g., phonological interference pairs *mashed buns* and *massive bus* for target *bad mug* → *mad bug*, see Figure 2.) The semantic

FIGURE 2
Sample for Experiment 1 Word Pair Lists (With explanations)

SEMANTIC INTERFERENCE TREATMENT				SEMANTICALLY NEUTRAL TREATMENT			
	Word pair list (in order of presentation)	Cued	Expected Oral Response		Word pair list (in order of presentation)	Cued	Expected Oral Response
A	Golf ball	no	none	a	Golf ball	no	none
	Golf ball	yes	Golf ball		Golf ball	yes	Golf ball
	Tan siphon	no	none		Tan siphon	no	none
	Flour tray	yes	Flour tray		Flour tray	yes	Flour tray
	Chisel tip	no	none		Chisel tip	no	none
B	Irate wasp	no	none	b	Irene's watch	no	none
	Irate wasp	yes	Irate wasp		Irene's watch	yes	Irene's watch
C	Mashed buns	no	none	c	Mashed buns	no	none
	Mashed buns	no	none		Mashed buns	no	none
D	Angry insect	yes	Angry insect	d	Angle insert	yes	Angle insert
	Angry insect	no	none		Angle insert	no	none
E	Massive bus	no	none	e	Massive bus	no	none
	Massive bus	no	none		Massive bus	no	none
F	Bad mug	yes	MAD BUG	f	Bad mug	yes	Mad bug (?)

Designed function of word pairs:

A & a: neutral control words to minimize predictability of cues and patterns (cued randomly)
B : semantic interference toward spoonerism of F
b : phonological relative of B, semantically neutral to spoonerism of f
C & c: phonological interference toward spoonerism of F and f
D & d: same as B & b, respectively
E & e: same as C & c
F & f: spoonerism target pair (hypothesis predicts greater frequency of spoonerisms for F than for f.

interference word pairs (for the Semantic Interference treatment list only) were constructed such that their meaning would be similar to that of the expected spoonerisms, while independent of the meaning of their target word pairs (e.g., semantic interference pairs *irate wasp* and *angry insect* for target *bad mug* → *mad bug*, see Figure 2.) These semantic interference word pairs (of the Semantic Interference treatment list) were matched on the Semantically Neutral treatment list by word pairs which were similar in phonology (to their semantic interference "mates") but which were semantically independent of their corresponding target or expected spoonerism. (For example, the semantic interference words *irate wasp* and *angry insect* were matched by the semantically neutral *Irene's watch* and *angle insert*, for target *bad mug* → *mad bug*, see Figure 2.)

The interference words for each of the 20 targets were ordered and cued to be spoken aloud as shown in Figure 2. Each set of interference and target items was separated by 4 to 7 neutral control words, some of which were randomly assigned to be repeated and/or cued to be spoken aloud.[3]

A counterbalanced within-subjects design was employed. Each subject's trial consisted of a performance on the first half of one treatment's word list, followed immediately by the second half of the other treatment's word list.

Instructions

Subjects were instructed to read the word pair list silently. Upon hearing the buzzer cue, subjects were to speak aloud the word pair which had immediately preceded the buzzer.[4]

Results

As predicted, the 44 subjects committed a significantly greater number of spoonerism errors for the Semantic Interference treatment than for the Semantically Neutral treatment. Specifically, 75 spoonerisms occurred under the Semantic Interference treatment, versus 27 spoonerisms for the Semantically Neutral treatment, with 31 subjects performing in the predicted direction ($T(34) = 30$, 10 ties, $p < 0.001$; Wilcoxon Signed Ranks test). We may thus accept the hypothesis.

DISCUSSION

Experiment 1 demonstrates that the subjects' speech encoding systems were sensitive to semantic influence from the 'semantic interference' word pairs. Notice that since subjects in both treatments were considering the *same* targets, the differences in spoonerism frequencies cannot be due to an encoding evaluation of the target itself. Rather, the increased frequency of semantically biased spoonerisms must be due to some evaluation of the spoonerized phoneme sequence. That is, the subjects' encoding process must have involved an evaluation of recoded (i.e., spoonerized and perhaps alternative) phoneme strings since the semantic bias relates only to the error *outcome*, independent of the target.[5] These semantic evaluations of recoded phoneme sequences served either to inhibit the eventual articulation of semantically anomalous phoneme sequences, or to facilitate the articulation of semantically appropriate phoneme sequences, or both.

As in the earlier SLIP studies, prearticulatory editing of recoded phoneme strings is evident in Experiment 1. In this case, however, the editing criterion is a semantic criterion. Moreover, the edit seems to base its semantic evaluation not so much upon what is semantically congruous with the target, but rather upon what is semantically congruous with the verbal context which accompanies the target. In effect, the semantic criterion overrides the target criterion.

Experiment 1, by demonstrating the ability of semantic criteria to override target criteria during prearticulatory encoding, comes close to demonstrating the effects proposed by Freud. As in Freud's theory, the SLIP task demonstrates that semantic interference may contribute to a distortion of the articulated phonology of a speaker's intended utterance, and that the distortion may result in an utterance whose meaning is closer to that of the semantic interference than to that of the intended utterance. There is, however, a primary difference between the type of verbal slip discussed by Freud and the verbal slips generated in Experiment 1. In Freud's verbal slip examples, the semantic interference is supposed to originate from "outside" of the total semantic context of the intended utterance. The condition was only partially present in Experiment 1, since our interference was verbal interference within the context of the task, and was in close proximity to the targets (although semantically independent of the targets). That is, the semantic editing criteria were established by the verbal context of the SLIP lists.

Experiment 2 seeks evidence of semantic editing criteria based not upon verbal context, but rather upon a more global "cognitive set." The procedure was similar to that of Experiment 1, except that the source of semantic interference was designed to be found not on the word lists, but rather within the treatments' situational environments. While being virtually a direct test of Freud's theory, Experiment 2 seeks an extension of the semantic editing criteria established by Experiment 1.

EXPERIMENT 2

Hypothesis

Frequencies of spoonerisms will be significantly greater for targets yielding errors semantically congruous with subjects' situational cognitive set than for targets yielding errors semantically incongruous with subjects' situational cognitive set.

Subjects

Subjects were 90 experimentally naive male students of an introductory communication course at California State University, Los Angeles. All were native speakers of American English.

Apparatus

The apparatus was the same as that of Experiment 1.

Treatments

Subjects were randomly assigned to one of three treatment conditions designed to manipulate cognitive set (30 subjects per condition):

1. One condition was designed to create a situational cognitive set toward electric shocks. For this "Electricity Set" treatment, subjects were attached to false electrodes ostensibly connected to an electric timer. Subjects were told that the timer was capable of emitting random, moderately painful, electric shocks; and that during the course of their task they may or may not receive such a shock. (No shocks were administered.) The Electricity Set treatment was administered by a male experimenter.
2. A second treatment condition was created to establish a situational cognitive set toward sex. For this "Sex Set" treatment, the task was administered by a female confederate experimenter who was, by design, attractive, personable, provocatively attired, and seductive in behavior. The Sex Set treatment was administered in the absence of electrical apparatus.
3. A "Neutral Set" control treatment was administered by a male experimenter in the absence of electrical apparatus.

Stimuli

Subjects in all treatments performed the SLIP task on the same word-pair list. Spoonerism targets were nonsense words for which a switch of initial consonants would create real words related either to electricity or sex. The word-pair list contained 7 targets designed to elicit spoonerism errors related to the Electricity Set (e.g., *shad bock* → *bad shock*, *vani molts* → *many volts*, etc.) alternated with 7 targets designed to elicit spoonerism errors related to the Sex Set (e.g., *goxi furl* → *foxi girl*, *lood gegs* → *good legs*, etc.).

Each target was preceded by three "interference" word pairs designed to create phonological bias toward the expected spoonerism error. For example, the target *bine foddy*—expected to spoonerize to *fine body*—was preceded by the interference word pairs, *fire Bobby*, *five toddies*, and *line shoddy*.[6] Each set of interference and target items was separated by 4 to 6 neutral control word pairs, some of which received randomly assigned cues to be spoken aloud. Interference words were semantically independent of expected spoonerisms. Interference and control items consisted of both nonsense-word pairs and real-word pairs. (See Figure 3.)

Instructions

Instructions were as for Experiment 1.

FIGURE 3
Sample from Experiment 2 Word Pair List (With explanation)

	WORD PAIR LIST	CUED	EXPECTED ORAL RESPONSE Electric Set	Sex Set
A	leet rud	no	Ø	Ø
	tire chain	no	Ø	Ø
	big table	yes	big table	big table
	ruf gam	no	Ø	Ø
B	dad lock	no	Ø	Ø
	bagged rocks	no	Ø	Ø
	back shot	no	Ø	Ø
C	shad bock	yes	BAD SHOCK	bad shock?
D	paper match	no	Ø	Ø
	slof puz	yes	slof puz	slof puz
	dog tail	no	Ø	Ø
	fal keeb	no	Ø	Ø
	noot wib	yes	noot wib	noot wib
E	rocky world	no	Ø	Ø
	folly curl	no	Ø	Ø
	father girth	no	Ø	Ø
F	goxi furl	yes	foxi girl?	FOXI GIRL

Designed function of word pairs:
A: neutral control words to minimize predictability of cues and patterns (cued randomly)
B: phonological interference toward spoonerism of C
C: spoonerism target -- Electricity Error
D: same as A
E: phonological interference toward spoonerism of F
F: spoonerism target -- Sex Error

Results

As predicted, spoonerism frequencies were significantly higher for the targets whose errors matched the treatment's cognitive set than for targets whose errors were unrelated to the treatment. Figure 4 shows the frequency of spoonerism errors in all three treatment conditions. A signifi-

FIGURE 4
Frequencies of Electricity Error and Sex Error Spoonerisms in Electricity Set, Neutral Set, and Sex Set Treatments

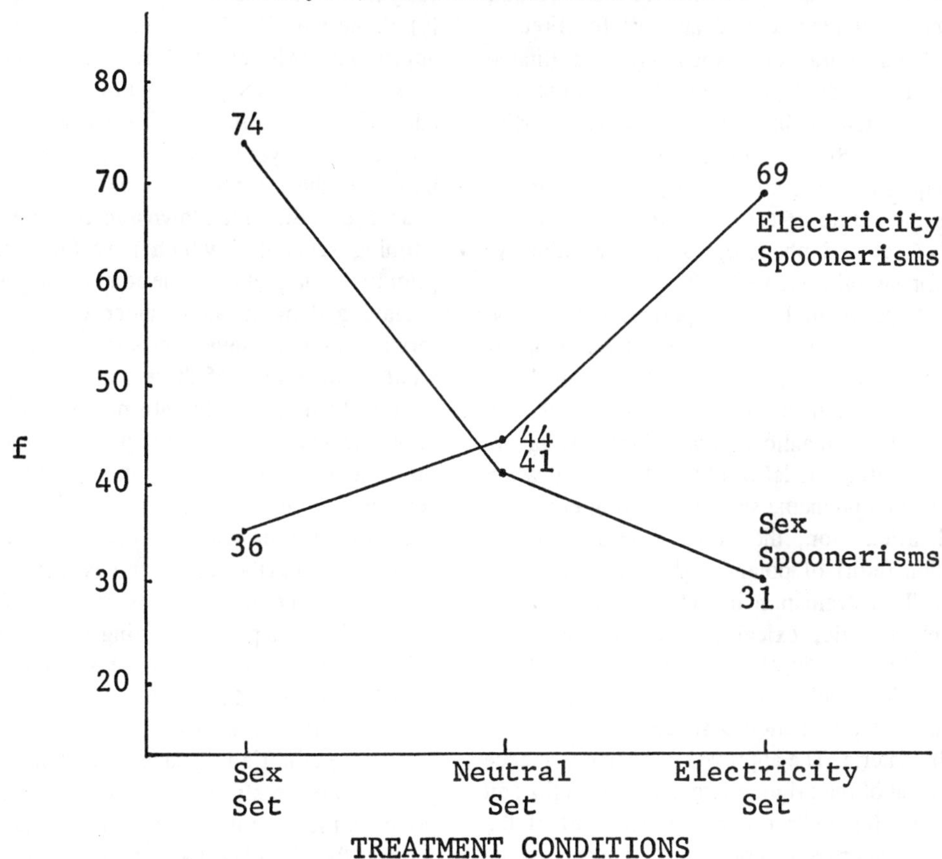

cant interaction occurred between the Cognitive Set factor (Electricity, Sex, and Neutral Sets) and the Error Outcome (Electricity and Sex Errors) factor ($F(2, 87) = 24.91$, $p < .001$; Two Factor ANOVA, Repeated Measures on One Factor). A test for simple main effects demonstrated a significant difference in the effect of the Error Outcome factor for the Sex Set ($p < .001$) and for the Electricity Set ($p < .001$), though not for the Neutral Set ($p > .25$); as well as a significant difference in the effect of the Cognitive Set factor for the Sex Errors ($p < .01$), and for the Electricity Errors ($p < .01$). That is, for the Sex Set, sex errors were significantly more frequent than were electricity errors, while the reverse was true for the Electricity Set, and no difference was found for the Neutral Set. These results support the hypothesis.

DISCUSSION

Experiment 2 demonstrates that subjects' speech encoding systems were sensitive to semantic influence from their situational cognitive set. Notice again that since subjects in all treatments were considering the same targets. Since the situational bias related only to the spoonerism outcome, the differences in spoonerism frequencies cannot be due to an encoding evaluation of the target itself, but rather must be due to an evaluation of the target's recoded phoneme sequence. Again, the evaluation was based upon criteria independent of the target itself; again, these evaluations of recoded phoneme sequences served to inhibit incongruous sequences and/or to facilitate congruous sequences.

As in Experiment 1, Experiment 2 presents evidence of prearticulatory editing of recoded phoneme strings on the basis of semantic criteria. In Experiment 2, however, the semantic editing criterion is oriented toward support for Freud's proposal that natural verbal slips may be facilitated by a cognitive set independent of the semantic context of an intended utterance. Moreover, earlier work with the SLIP technique allows us to consider a question not addressed by Freud; namely, what is the nature of the encoding interaction of cognitive set and phonological (or articulatory) output for natural speech errors?

Both Experiment 1 and Experiment 2 may be viewed as evidence of additional criteria of prearticulatory editing. That is, to the phonological and lexical criteria evidenced in earlier studies, we may now add semantic criteria. Thus, the prearticulatory editing model would postulate that when noise enters a phoneme sequence during encoding toward articulation, the noise is treated by an evaluation (edit) of potential phoneme sequence options. This evaluation includes a consideration of the phonotactic, lexical, and semantic integrity of the phoneme sequences; rejecting those sequences which fail to meet the criteria, and "approving" for articulation a sequence which does meet the criteria. The approved phoneme sequence may be that of the original target; but since the edit criteria are linguistic criteria independent of the target, the approved phoneme sequence may be one other than that of the original target (i.e., may be a verbal slip).

To postulate the presence of such semantic editing is not necessarily inconsistent with the fact that some natural spoonerisms (and other verbal slips) violate lexical and semantic restrictions. We may assume that the function of phonological, lexical, and semantic prearticulatory edits in natural speech encoding is to insure that the speech output is (as intended) phonologically, lexically, and semantically appropriate. Likewise, it would appear that the prearticulatory edits of the subjects engaged in the SLIP task also function to facilitate output which is phonologically, lexically, and semantically appropriate—appropriate for the language, albeit at variance with the target. Spontaneous spoonerisms may be phonologically, lexically, and semantically appropriate; or phonologically and lexically appropriate, while semantically inappropriate; or phonologically appropriate, while lexically and semantically inappropriate; or (very rarely) phonologically, lexically, and semantically inappropriate (Motley, 1973). Inappropriate output presumably results from a failure in the performance of one or more edits. The causes of these edit failures are as yet unknown. As suggested above, however, there are indications that one potential source of edit breakdowns is a prearticulatory "timing schedule" which may force an output prior to its completion of the edit operations.

Having demonstrated evidence of prearticulatory editing upon several criteria, we must wonder what is the source of these edit criteria. That is, what is the nature of the information against which phoneme sequences are compared during an editing evaluation? The issue is more complex for the semantic editing demonstrated in Experiments 1 and 2 than for the phonological and lexical editing demonstrated in the earlier studies. Given the question, "Is phoneme string *X phonotactically* appropriate?," or "Is phoneme string *X lexically* appropriate?", an editor could make a simple "yes" or "no" decision. Moreover, this decision may be made simply on the basis of the linguistic parameters of the editor's language as a whole. That is, a given phoneme string simply either does or does not meet the phonotactic criteria of the language; if it does, then it either does or does not represent an existing lexical entity within the language. Thus, since we have evidence that phonotactic and lexical prearticulatory editing decisions are not based upon comparisons with the target, we might conclude that the decisions are based upon comparisons with phonotactic and lexical information for the language as a whole.

However, given the question, "Is phoneme string *X semantically* appropriate?", an editor could *not* make a simple yes/no decision without further information. That is, phoneme sequences are not semantically appropriate or inappropriate on the basis of linguistic criteria alone, but rather are appropriate or inappropriate on the basis of contextual considerations. Whereas each phonotactic or lexical editing decision may be determined by reference to the *same* information, each semantic editing decision must be determined by reference to *new* information.

Experiment 1 suggests that one source of reference information for semantic edits may be the global verbal context of the utterance. That is, the semantic properties of the recoded phoneme sequences are compared to the semantic properties of the target's verbal context. Since these semantic properties vary from utterance to utterance, the representation of the semantic reference information is presumably dynamic and transient. Thus, two sources of semantic reference information seem plausible: (1) The edit may check semantic associates of the portions of the utterance which have already been encoded and articulated, and/or (2) the edit may check semantic associates of the portions currently being encoded. Notice that if phoneme sequence interference is typically a result of competition between two or more encoding plans (see Baars, 1976, 1977), then all competing plans (i.e., all considered versions of the utterance) may serve as reference information for the semantic edit. That is, perhaps the semantic edit checks the meaning of an edited phoneme sequence against (all) meanings related to all encoding plans considered as options for the utterance. Notice also, that although we are discussing semantic reference to verbal context, the reference information itself need not be verbal, but rather is probably pre-verbal (pre-lexical) semantic representation.

Experiment 2 suggests that a source of reference information for semantic edits may be nonlinguistic stimuli to which the speaker is, on some cognitive level, attending. Thus, we may speculate that a variety of internal and external stimuli, though unrelated to a speaker's message, may be represented within the speaker's "semantic space," and may thus serve as reference information for semantic phases of prearticulatory editing. Notice that this representation is not necessarily separate from the verbal reference information discussed above. Pre-verbal associates of verbal stimuli would presumably occupy the same semantic space as the pre-verbal associates of the nonverbal stimuli.

Although we cannot be certain of the information to which the prearticulatory edit feeds back, we can be reasonably certain that some sort of prearticulatory feedback loops do exist. As discussed elsewhere by Baars (1977), our earlier demonstrations of prearticulatory editing evidence "bottom-up" encoding in addition to the commonly accepted "top-down" (semantic-lexical-syntactic-phonological-articulatory) encoding processes. With phonotactic and lexical editing, however, we could not be certain that the reference was one which goes back up to higher (earlier) encoding levels. Since the reference information for phonotactic and lexical decisions is static, it is at least possible (though intuitively unattractive) that this reference information enters the flow of control at stages lower than phonological encoding. In the case of semantic editing, however, we can be certain of a bottom-up feedback process. Since the reference information is dynamic and situation-specific, and since part of the same reference information initiated the intended utterance, the semantic edit (and now, we can infer the phonological and lexical edits as well) must flow upward to a very high level of encoding.

In summary, this paper has supported Freud's notion of verbal slips, although differing in certain particulars. We would not support Freud's claim that linguistic factors do not influence verbal slips, for phonotactic and lexical information appear to be important factors in the outcome of verbal slips. We would not support Freud's view that cognitive set is a direct cause of verbal slips, but would claim instead that noise in the phonological sequencing operations is the more direct cause, and that one source (cause) of this noise is the competition of more than one encoding plan. This paper, however, does provide the first empirical support for Freud's more general notion that semantic influences which are independent of a speaker's intended utterance can influence verbal slips to be closer in meaning to the semantic interference than to the originally intended utterance.

NOTES

1. The authors wish to acknowledge Sandra Gary for her assistance with Experiment 2.
2. Experiment 1 has been reported in more detail elsewhere. (See Motley & Baars, 1976b.)
3. These neutral control word pairs served as "fillers" to prevent the subjects from noticing a pattern by which to predict the cue for target word pairs.

4. That is, the target's exposure was concluded immediately before the buzzer cue. This procedure forces subjects to attend to all word pairs, including interference items. (See Motley & Baars, 1976a.)
5. Motley and Baars (1976b) have demonstrated that these laboratory-generated spoonerisms are not the result of reading errors or other errors of the target's input into the encoding process, but rather are clearly the result of errors in attempting the target's articulatory output.
6. The phonological pattern for these interference word pairs was constant for all targets. The pattern used was that of Motley and Baars (1976a).

REFERENCES

BAARS, B.J. The competing plans hypothesis: An heuristic approach to the problem of speech errors. Unpublished paper, Department of Psychology, UCLA, 1976.

BAARS, B.J. On eliciting predictable speech errors in the laboratory; Some methods and results. Paper presented at the Twelfth International Congress of Linguists, Vienna, Austria, 1977.

BAARS, B.J., & MOTLEY, M.T. Spoonerisms as sequencer conflicts: Evidence from artificially elicited errors. *American Journal of Psychology*, 1976, 83, 467-484.

BAARS, B.J., MOTLEY, M.T., & MACKAY, D.G. Output editing for lexical status in artificially elicited slips of the tongue. *Journal of Verbal Learning and Verbal Behavior*, 1975, 14, 382-391.

FREUD, S. In A. Tyson (Trans.), *Psychopathology of everyday life*. New York: Norton, 1965.

MACKAY, D.G. Spoonerisms: The structure of errors in the serial order of speech. *Neuropsychologia*, 1970, 8, 323-350.

MOTLEY, M.T. An analysis of spoonerisms as psycholinguistic phenomena. *Speech Monographs*, 1973, 40, 66-71.

MOTLEY, M.T. Acoustic correlates of lies. *Western Speech*, 1974, 38, 81-87.

MOTLEY, M.T., & BAARS, B.J. Encoding sensitivities to phonological markedness and transitional probability: Evidence from spoonerisms. *Human Communication Research*, 1975a, 2, 351-361.

MOTLEY, M.T., & BAARS, B.J. Toward a model of integrated editing processes in prearticulatory encoding: Evidence from laboratory generated verbal slips. Paper presented at the annual meeting of the Speech Communication Association. Houston, Texas, 1975b.

MOTLEY, M.T., & BAARS, B.J. Laboratory induction of verbal slips: A new method for psycholinguistic research. *Communication Quarterly*, 1976a, 24, 28-34.

MOTLEY, M.T., & BAARS, B.J. Semantic bias effects on the outcome of verbal slips. *Cognition*, 1976b, 4, 177-187.

INTERPERSONAL COMMUNICATION

Theory and Research: An Overview
Selected Studies

INTERPERSONAL COMMUNICATION THEORY AND RESEARCH: A METAMETHODOLOGICAL OVERVIEW

DEAN E. HEWES
University of Wisconsin

In *Communication Yearbook I*, Berger (1977a) presented an extensive compilation of literature on interpersonal communication produced within our field. While research in interpersonal communication has certainly advanced since Berger's review, the importance of further review at this time has been subborned by the emergence of another issue in that same volume of *Communication Yearbook*. In particular, numerous contributors, including Budd (1977), Berger (1977a), Berlo (1977), and Cappella (1977), echoed a growing concern over the influence of methodologies on the construction of theories of communication.

Over thirty years ago, Kurt Lewin coined the phrase "law of the hammer" to describe the problem these authors perceived in contemporary communication research. In Lewin's terms, the "law of the hammer" was the tendency of social scientists to inflict an available methodology on phenomena regardless of the appropriateness of that methodology. The consequences of this "law" were distorted descriptions of social life and ambiguous links between theorizing and data.

Thirty years ago, the social sciences were in their methodological infancy, and the empirical component of communication a less than fond gleam in some rhetoricians' eyes. Despite our 30 years of maturation, the "law of the hammer" remained a salient part of our research endeavors. The problem has reached such proportions that philosopher Rom Harré (1977) has argued that "experimental social psychology [and, therefore, most of interpersonal communication research], as practiced in the positivist, behaviorist tradition, is not a genuine science, developing out of real problems of a given and growing subject matter, but an artificial construction based on an unsound philosophical theory of science, that is not an attempt to study human social behavior as such, but an effort to fulfill an *a priori methodology. And the assumptions behind this methodology are demonstrably at variance with the character of the problems to be investigated and the nature of the individuals and structures involved*" (p. 155, my italics).

While one might question the solutions to this problem proposed by Harré and his colleagues (cf., Douglas, 1976; Harré & Secord, 1972; Harré, 1973), the existence of the problem is self-evident. Sociologists such as Blumer (1972), Coser (1975), and Phillipson (1972) have recognized the problem in their own field; Delia (1977), Cappella (1977), and Budd (1977) have raised the issue forcefully within the field of communication.

Identifying the general problem of methodological interference in theory testing is only part of the solution. Greater precision in phrasing the problem, clear identification of consequences and potential solutions are necessary as well. Recent critical reviews of the state of our field have made moves in these directions. For instance, Budd (1977) provided a broad overview of the problem across the areas of communication research, although he advance no explicit solutions. Similarly, Delia (1977) provided a comprehensive analysis of the problem, augmented by a well-developed, though controversial philosophical framework, suggestive of methodological reforms. Unfortunately, the nature of those reforms remains somewhat opaque, pending further clarification. Finally, Cappella (1977) has documented the methodological implications of certain "god" and "devil" terms in our discipline. In many ways, Cappella's treatment is the most suggestive of the three, in that it is both more specific and unwed to a particular philosophical framework; however, it does not focus on interpersonal communication, nor does it delve deeply into the causes and consequences of the "law of the hammer."

In order to build on the foundations laid by these

scholars, I have focused my concern in the following ways. First, the domain of the problem has been narrowed from social science in general to interpersonal communication. Second, following Miller's (in press) theoretical overview, my examples are drawn from "situationist" and "rules" approaches to the interpersonal area.[1] Third, I have attempted to document *particular types* of methodological interference with research and theorizing in those content areas. Finally, I have suggested some general guidelines for blunting the impact of the "law of the hammer" which are quite different from those proposed by many of those critics who share my concern over methodological determinism (e.g., Blumer, 1972; Budd, 1977; Douglas, 1976; Harré & Secord, 1972; Phillipson, 1972). No claims are made that this paper has uniquely identified these problems nor proposed the solutions, but my remarks can contribute to a more general call-to-arms against a major problem in our field.

THESIS

Briefly, the thesis of this paper is that methodological conventionality has been allowed to dictate theoretical moves and observational strategies in ways which are detrimental to the study of interpersonal communication. The mechanism which produces this sad state of affairs can be described as follows. Social scientists hold differing, broad perspectives which dictate the way in which they approach research. For example, one may *impose* a theoretical structure on the world to gain explanatory power (cf., Meehan, 1968, and numerous indictments of empirical sociology by "phenomological" sociologists such as Mehan & Wood, 1975), one could *induce* an explanation from actors in everyday life (Delia, 1977; Douglas, 1976; Shutz, 1970; Tudor, 1976), or one could *combine* these strategies in some way (cf., Bem & Allen, 1974; Hawes, 1972, 1975).[2] These broad perspectives then dictate conventional applications of available methodologies—and here is the crux of the problem. Conventional applications may introduce into the perspective additional requirements and constraints which influence observation and theory in ways not clearly or even consciously chosen by the researcher (Magnusson, 1976, and Nowakowska, 1973, illustrate a similar process in personality research.) This point is documented below.

THE INFLUENCE OF THE "LAW OF THE HAMMER" ON INTERPERSONAL COMMUNICATION: SOME EXAMPLES AND SPECIFIC SOLUTIONS

In this section, I examine the impact of "law of the hammer" conventionality on situationist and rules approaches to interpersonal communication. Two perspectives under each of these approaches are used to illustrate the consequences of methodological conventionalism; ways of circumventing these consequences are suggested.

Situationist Approaches to Interpersonal Communication

Situationist approaches to interpersonal communication begin with the assumption that some aspect of the social "field" in which the individual is located determines subsequent communication behaviors. Situational variables can (1) produce changes in output variables, (2) delimit the range of applicability of causal explanations, or (3) moderate the effects of other input variables in producing changes in output. For example, situational ambiguity *produces* certain types of interchanges directed toward clarifying the definition of the situation (Craig, Johnson, & Shaw, 1976; McHugh, 1968); the acquaintanceship context has been hypothesized to *delimit* a set of relationships among self-esteem, attitude similarity, liking, and communication-bound anxiety distinctively different from those found in other contexts (e.g., Snavely, Merker, Becker, & Book, 1976); instrumental approaches to interpersonal message strategies dictate different causal sequences between message implications and effect contingent upon the context (Miller & Steinberg, 1975; Miller, Boster, Roloff, & Seibold, 1977).

These distinct approaches to situational variables share at least one common methodological problem. In order to be viable, each must provide some method of defining relevant situational variables. It is precisely at this step that the "law of the hammer" functions. Depending upon the global perspective of the researcher, certain methodological choices are made which unduly influence subsequent observation and theorizing. Let us consider two global perspectives, their methodological implications, and the subsequent effects on situationalist approaches to interpersonal communication.

Theoretically imposed perspectives. Communication researchers such as Miller and Steinberg (1975) and social psychologists such as Sells (1963) and the Sherifs' (Sherif & Sherif, 1963) have advanced theoretically imposed definitions of situations as explanatory variables of interpersonal interaction. Typically such approaches are based on the assumptions that objective, theorist-imposed situational variables are either more precise, more easily controlled, or more explanatory than definitions derived from other sources (Arnoult, 1963; Proshansky, Ittelson, & Rivlin, 1970; Sells, 1963).

This point of view seems to have two obvious implications for research methodology. First, self-report measures of theorist-defined variables become second-class data since these data are neither objective nor unambiguously related to the theorist's definition of the underlying construct being measured (for instance, see Cozby, 1973, for an illustration in the self-disclosure literature and Jacob, 1975, for a similar example in the analysis of family interaction).[3] Second, since theorist-defined situations can be objectively manipulated, ANOVA becomes the convenient and, therefore, the conventional methodology for this kind of research (e.g., Miller et al., 1977; Roloff, 1978).

These two methodological implications create innumerable theoretical problems. For example, *the variance accounted for by main effects or interactions may be seriously biased*. Coleman (1964) suggested that while obtaining significant differences is important in the early stages of a science, estimates of the magnitudes of those effects is crucial for later development. Recent advances in ANOVA have emphasized the value of estimating the magnitude of experimental effects in that methodology (Cohen, 1966; Dodd & Schutz, 1973; Dwyer, 1974; Vaughan & Corballis, 1969). Yet, the theoretically inappropriate choice of nominal-level independent variables can seriously bias magnitude estimates (cf., Falzer, 1974). This occurs when information is lost through "nominalization" of continuous variables (Bryson & Phillips, 1975). For instance, Hewes and Wotring (1974) reported an example where the magnitude of the bias created by moving from interval to nominal independent variables ranged between 10 and 60%. Further, if the relationship between independent and dependent variables is in fact nonlinear, an inappropriate choice of the number of treatment levels could destroy the ability to detect any relationship (Acock & Martin, 1974; see also Adams & Freedman, 1976, pp. 54-55, for a discussion of this issue in relation to equity theory).[4]

These problems have serious ramifications for interpersonal communication. Nonlinear relationships have been either hypothesized or explained in a number of recent studies addressing such wide-ranging topics as personal space (Burgoon & Jones, 1976), communication effectiveness (Alpert & Anderson, 1973), and relationship development (Berger, Weber, Munley, & Dixon, 1977). While comparison of effect sizes has been less frequently made, recent work in relational communication (Folger & Sillars, 1977), interactionist psychology (Endler & Magnusson, 1976), personality/behavior relationships (Cartwright, 1975) and task effects in small group research (Bochner, 1974; Hackman, 1968) provides some evidence of its importance. The deleterious effects of "law of the hammer" applications of ANOVA can impede progress in interpersonal communication research.

Consider a second consequence of "law of the hammer" applications of ANOVA to situational analysis: *resulting causal sequences may be "ecologically invalid."* Brunswick (1947) stressed the importance of ecological validity, or generalizability of findings to the "real world." ANOVA approaches to situations carry with them ontological assumptions which may weaken ecological validity. Foremost among them is the conventional assumption that treatments must be "unconfounded" in n-way designs. This implies that the number of observations in each cell in the design should be proportional, so as to ensure that the treatments are all orthogonal (uncorrelated, unconfounded) to one another. This convention is so strong that extensive journal space has been dedicated to finding ways to compensate for the "unfortunate" side-effects of accidently nonorthogonal designs (cf., Gocka, 1973; Overall & Spiegel, 1973; Rawlings, 1972, 1973; Wolf & Cartwright, 1974). Certainly no competent researcher would intentionally violate this convention and "confound" an otherwise clean design, although, in contradiction, no one seriously believes that situational causes of interpersonal behavior generally operate orthogonally to other variables. In fact, recent theorizing in "rules," social learning theory, and psychodynamic approaches to social behavior would suggest that nonorthogonality of situational and individual difference variables is the rule, rather than the exception (Argyle, 1977; Mischel, 1977; Wachtel, 1973).

The potential consequences of these apparently contradictory beliefs concerning design requirements and social reality are easily demonstrated in the following example. Suppose that one wished to study the independent and conjoint effects of "fed" versus "open" questions (Scheff, 1973) and floor time (cf., Rogers & Jones, 1975) in determining perceived dominance. A conventional approach to this study would be to cross these two variables in a two-way ANOVA design. Stimulus tapes could be created which typify high versus low floor times and fed versus open questions in a 2 x 2 design.

The problem arises when one or more cells in this design are atypical of everyday interaction. For example, when employing open questions, that is, questions whose answers require elaboration, the questioner is unlikely to hold a great deal of floor time; consequently, the "high-floortime/open-question" cell of our design is unusual. This cell in our design is potentially confounded since it may force the subject to make a judgment concerning an unfamiliar situation, requiring attention to other details of the interaction not considered in the three other cells. As a consequence, this cell of the design may contain implicitly confounding treatment variables whose presence is introduced by an explicit attempt to *prevent* confounding (see Hewes & Wotring, 1974, for other examples of this problem). Further, the results of such a design also may not be generalizable to the "real world," since the two independent variables do not function orthogonally outside the laboratory. Unless evidence can be mustered to refute the claim that this cell presents an atypical interaction, the requirement of orthogonality in ANOVA designs may well result in ungeneralizable main effects and interactions. Forced orthogonalization of correlated causes can produce ecologically invalid causal sequences. When the process of orthogonalization results in cells that do not correspond to real-world conditions, results of such an experiment have low interpretability and weak external validity, a problem which Falzer (1974) notes is "rampant" in the communication literature.

Problems of both level of measurement and orthogonality of causes in ANOVA research are consequences of "law of the hammer" methodological conventionality. Neither problem is insuperable, but remedies require unconventional solutions. For instance, combinations of methodologies can help alleviate the problem of measuring the magnitude of effects of theoretically continuous-level independent variables in ANOVA. The first step is to perform a manipulation check on each of the treatment variables in the design. This can be accomplished by having the subjects respond to an appropriately blinded continuous-level measure of the independent variable. Typically, responses to this self-report measure at each level of the treatment are tested to determine if they are significantly different, thus providing a manipulation check. If they are, the manipulation is generally assumed successful; however, instead of stopping there, an extra step can be taken. The continuous-level measure can be used as a covariate in the design. The intraclass correlation between this covariate and the dependent variable is an estimate of the population correlation between the theoretically continuous independent variable and the dependent variable.[5] Further, if an analysis of covariance employing the manipulation check as the covariate does *not* remove all of the statistically significant main effects and interactions, then one can question (1) whether the experimental treatment is a "pure" operationalization of the theoretical variable, (2) whether the covariate is a "pure" operationalization of the theoretical variable, or (3) whether both the treatment and the covariate suffer from operational inadequacy. While the proposed methodology does not answer these questions, it does raise them—and knowing the answers is important. Further, if all statistically significant variation *is* removed by the covariate, strong evidence has been garnered for the validity of both covariate and treatment. Clearly, a slight twist on conventional methodology can result in many benefits.

This same kind of slight twist can be applied to the problems created by forced orthogonalization in ANOVA designs as well. The answer to this problem was suggested by this author in an earlier paper (Hewes & Wotring, 1974; see also Falzer, 1974). Simply put, one solves the problem of forced orthogonalization by intentionally "unorthogonalizing" the design. This requires prior information concerning the degree of overlap between independent variables. Once such information is available, one can create a design where the distribution of observations across cells approximates the population distribution. Alternatively, Keren and Lewis (1976) have developed an elegant method of weighting observations in correspondence to population distributions so that an orthogonal design can be analyzed in a nonorthogonal manner ex post facto. Either of these two techniques provides that slight methodological twist necessary to blunt some of the worst potential effects of "law of the hammer" conventionalism.

Induced perspectives. Attempts to base situationist explanations of interpersonal behavior on imposed, theorist-based variables are flawed by "law of the hammer" conventionalism. These flaws are not inherent in the theorist-based perspective. Rather, if my thesis is correct, any broad approach to theorizing is open to difficulties if linked to methodological conventionalism. Support for the thesis depends upon cross-perspective evidence. Such evidence is forthcoming from an alternative approach to theorist-based situationism.

The "induced perspective" is represented by a loose confederation of approaches which emphasize the subject, rather than the theorist, as the primary source of situational variables. Schutz's (1970) phenomenological sociology, Delia's (1977) "constructivism," various ethnomethodological perspectives (for instance, Cicourel, 1974; Garfinkel, 1967; Phillipson, 1972), and the work of Endler, Ekehammar, and Magnusson (see Endler & Magnusson, 1976, for a summary) illustrate various versions of the induced perspective relevant to interpersonal communication. Of these various approaches, the work of Endler, Ekehammar, and Magnusson, as well as the various schools of ethnomethodology, provide the clearest methodological implications. Since ethnomethodological approaches are discussed under rules methodologies, the induced perspective is exemplified here by the work of Endler, Ekehammar, and Magnusson.

These investigators have been vitally interested in discovering a set of underlying dimensions for describing the perception of situational influences on behavior. The motivation behind their research resides in their justifiable belief that perceived situational variables represent either significant causes of interpersonal behavior, important moderators between individual predispositions and behavior (Bowers, 1973; Ekehammar, 1974; Mischel, 1973), or both. Thus, for example, the development of measures of perceived situational dimensions becomes a crucial enterprise as communication apprehension is reconceptualized as a "state" (context-controlled), rather than a "trait" (predispositional), variable (cf., Lamb, 1972; Snavely et al., 1976). Similarly, a set of stable perceptual dimensions of relational contexts would prove highly useful to studies of relationship development (e.g., Berger et al., 1977) or social style (e.g., Garrison & Powell, 1977; Garrison, Sullivan, & Pate, 1976; Snavely et al., 1976). In short, Endler, Ekehammar, and Magnusson have addressed a question fundamental to interpersonal communication research; that is, what are the defining characteristics of "situations" (cf., Bateson, 1972; Bochner, 1976).

Endler, Ekehammar, and Magnusson have engaged in a large research program designed to identify a stable set of dimensions for characterizing situational influences. This program is characterized by three assumptions: (1) the subject's interpretation of the environment, rather than the "true," "objective," or "geographic" environment (Koffka, 1935), is the primary source of situational influence on behavior (cf., Magnusson, 1971); (2) the subject's naive judgments of perceived similarity of situations provide a viable basis for inducing dimensions of situations (cf., Ekehammar & Magnusson, 1973; Magnusson & Ekehammar, 1973); (3) dimensions derived from perceived stimulus similarity of situations should correspond to dimensions derived from similarity of perceived responses to situations (cf., Ekehammar, Schalling, & Magnusson, 1975).

Assumption 1, and to some extent assumption 3, follow logically from the induced perspective. Assumption 2, that similarity judgments provide the basis for determining situational dimensions, appears to be an outgrowth of methodological convenience (see arguments by Magnusson, 1971; Magnusson & Ekehammar, 1973; Ekehammar & Magnusson, 1973), in particular the accessibility of multidimensional scaling (MDS) algorithms. As a result, typical studies of situational dimensions employ either global stimulus similarity measures or response probability metrics derived from a set of written descriptions of situations. These data are converted into a similarity matrix which is then subjected to some form of MDS. The factors derived from the MDS are labeled in traditional factor analytic fashion. These labels "explain" why the situations are similar and, presumably, why similar situations would cause subsequent behavioral similarity.

The problem with these conventional approaches to the induced perspective on situationalism resides in their failure to provide what they claim—an explanation. The conventional induced perspective methodologies are simply inadequate for this task. Global stimulus similarity judgments, and the factor structures which summarize them, do not tell us what part or parts of the situations trigger subsequent behavior; they do not allow us to generalize our explanations to other situations not part of the original sample, since we have no rational basis for sampling situations (Arnoult, 1963; see also Magnusson, 1971, for a more reserved version of this argument).

Comparable problems in explanation arise from attempts to derive situational dimensions from response similarity. While there have been intriguing attempts to base situational similarity on similarities in affective reactions (Ekehammar, Schalling, & Magnusson, 1975), in "situated identities" (Alexander & Knight, 1971), in motives (Mills, 1940) and in response probabilities (Frederickson, 1972, p. 120), all of these approaches share the same common flaw. *If the situation is defined solely in terms of the response it elicits or facilitates, no explanation of the relationship between situation and response is possible*; their relationship is merely tautological (cf., Arnoult, 1963). Further, this problem is not necessarily solved by appealing to the comparability of dimensions obtained through stimulus and response similarity methods (assumption 3) since we have no basis for determining the independence of the two methods. If global stimulus similarity judgments are based on response similarity, the two approaches are redundant, rather than mutually supportive. Together they may take us no further toward explaining the relationship between situation and behavior than they do separately.

The problems in explanation found in induced perspective research are not inherent in that perspective. The problem, it seems, rests with "law of the hammer" conventionalism. The difficulty in circumventing the conventionalism is that induced perspective theorists have done little to bridge the gap between their statements of epistemic prescriptions and methodology. For instance, Schutz's (1970, p. 279) Postulate of Adequacy stipulates that a phenomenological explanation of a social act would be comprehensible to the individual actor "in terms of a common-sense interpretation of everyday life." While this postulate is suggestive, it is far from adequate to tell a researcher how to *do* science (Tudor, 1976). In the same vein, Delia's (1977) subject-based paradigm for communication research supplies an intuitively satisfying world view, but is ambiguous when it comes to implementation. Fortunately, the same kind of unconventional methodological twists discussed earlier hold promise for extricating us from this methodological hiatus.

The crux of the problem with the induced approaches to situationism outlined here is that they do not provide sufficient explanatory power. The cause of this problem is that the conventional methodologies, by themselves, do not provide us with sufficient information on which to base an explanation. If additional information were made available from other methodological approaches, the deficiencies in existing methodologies could be exorcised.

Our major task is to determine the nature of the perceptual dimensions of situations. Why are certain situations seen as being more similar than others? To provide an answer to this question, we need to impose explanatory factors on raw similarity judgments.[6] Imposed factors might be chosen on the basis of existing theory, open-ended explanations provided by subjects, the researcher's intuitions, or some combination of the three.[7] However the imposed factors are chosen and related to one another, the researcher now possesses an *a priori* factor structure against which similarity judgments can be compared. Techniques such as confirmatory factor analysis (Burt, 1973; Jöreskog, 1966, 1969, 1973; Mulaik, 1972, 1975) and Woelfel's Galileo system (cf., Gillham & Woelfel, 1977; Woelfel & Danes, in press) provide much of the necessary software.

If the number of factors derived from similarity judgments, the relationships among factors (orthogonal or oblique) and the internal structure of each factor (i.e., how each situation loads on each factor) can be replicated by factor analysis of a set of meaningful variables, then we are one step closer to explaining situational influences. Further, if the relationships among variables within each situation remain relatively constant across situations, those variables provide a strong basis for a theory of situational influence on interpersonal behavior.[8] Various forms of confirmatory factor analysis, when added to conventional techniques, yield a methodological twist sufficient to overcome many of the present barriers to induced situational explanations.

Rules Approaches to Interpersonal Communication

As we have seen above, situationist approaches to interpersonal communication have suffered from excessive dependence on orthodox methodologies. Commitment to a general perspective (theorist-based or induced) seems to have dictated conventional methodological choices which, in turn, unnecessarily constrained explanation. In many ways this problem is not necessarily as severe in the rules approach to interpersonal communication. Rules approaches are in their theoretical and methodological infancy (Cushman & Pearce, 1977; Miller, in press); consequently, many of the problems discussed in relation to situationist approaches have not had an opportunity to arise. Nevertheless, some emerging problems are apparent. Pointing them out at this early stage of theory formation could have a salutory effect on subsequent research.

In order to highlight these methodological problems, I have adopted the same organization as employed in the discussion of situationist approaches. Thus, rules approaches are divided into "theorist-based" and "induced" categories, the effects of the "law of the hammer" are documented in each, and unconventional methodologies are suggested to remedy extant problems.

Theoretically imposed perspectives. There are a variety of ways to impose structure on interpersonal interaction so that one can detect "rules," or normative regularities, of interaction. For instance, sociolinguists, working in the tradition of Noam Chomsky, proceed (1) by choosing a set of formally defined nominal-level "variables" (this fragment of the interaction is or is not of type X), and (2) by imposing a logical calculus on the relationships between variables. Variables and calculus are then invoked to explain examples of the domain of discourse to be analyzed (for instance, Labov, 1972; Mohan, 1974; Nofsinger, 1976). The domain of discourse to be analyzed is usually limited to those statements or interactions which are intuitively deemed to be the part of a corpus that would have to be generated by a "competent" member of the social community being sampled. Rules are invoked as explanations only for those statements or interactional sequences which can be classified as "competent." The remaining statements or interactions are considered to be the result of some unexplained failure to follow the hypothesized rules.

As in Chomsky's approach to syntax, the precision of the formal machinery vastly outweighs the precision of criteria for determining what is or is not a legitimate part of a "competent" corpus. For instance, Pearce's (1976) rules-based theory of interpersonal communication contains a category of action labeled as "creative," that is, action of an individual which involves "following the rules [described in the theory] in a novel way or acting independently of the rules" (p. 19). No criteria are specified for determining when an action is "creative" or when it is merely governed by rules as yet unknown. Thus, any action observed to be in violation of a theoretically specified rule may be merely classified as "creative." As a result, the theory remains essentially unfalsifiable since contradictory data can be explained away. Similar problems arise in all rules theories since, at their heart, they all permit the actor to choose not to follow the rule (for instance, Cushman & Pearce, 1977; Goffman, 1969; Toulmin, 1969). Thus all rules theories face the problem of "domain imprecision," that is, imprecision in specifying a set of criteria independent of the rules themselves which distinguish those behaviors, acts, or interaction sequences representative of underlying rules from those which are due to accident or choice (Kaufer, 1976). Without a precise set of criteria for specifying the domain of observations amenable to rules explanation, all rules theories are inherently unfalsifiable; that is, any counter-examples can be dismissed as having been the result, either of choice not to follow the rule, or accident (see Berger, 1977a, p. 221, for a more specific statement of this problem in other areas of interpersonal communication research). The difficulties created by this "domain imprecision" have been widely and rigorously discussed in the literature on linguistics (Cohen, 1974; Cohen & Wirth, 1975; Wirth, 1976; see particularly Wirth, 1975). Frankly, I can see no obvious *methodological* solution to this problem. The solution to the problem requires increased *theoretical* precision instead.

Fortunately, the field of communication is not solely dependent on this particular theorist-based perspective on interpersonal rules. A more likely candidate for both methodological critique and improvement is the finite state Markov chain (cf., Hewes, 1975, in press). Markov chain models have been linked to rules theorizing by a number of authors (for instance, Hewes, 1976; Lenk, 1976; Riskin, 1963), and rightly so. Several of the properties of rules theories are compatible with Markov technology. Markov models can represent the contingent sequential structure of spoken acts, a property of rules theories (Cushman & Pearce, 1977).[9] These models are useful for summarizing statistical, as opposed to deterministic, regularities in interaction, another suggested property of rule-based phenomena (Pearce, 1976).

Markov chains are rapidly becoming the accepted methodology for analyzing sequential interaction data (cf., Ellis & Fisher, 1975; Hawes & Foley, 1973, 1976; Hewes, in press). The problem with Markov chain models is that they have been widely applied without apparent thought to the nature of the phenomena being modeled (see Hewes, in press, for an extensive discussion of this issue). As a result, the methodological conventionalism associated with Markov chain models, if applied to rules theories, is likely to have the same crippling effects as extreme methodological orthodoxy in situational approaches to interpersonal communication.

Elsewhere (Hewes, 1976) I have documented the disjunctions between finite state Markov chain models as methodological tools and rules theories of the type advocated by Toulmin (1969, 1974) and others (Cushman & Whiting, 1972; Cushman, 1977; Cushman & Pearce, 1977). These disjunctions center around the formal requirements of the model. As an illustration, the *interpretation* of "states," or items in the "behavioral repertoire" of the rule-user, must not change across the time. This requirement is not necessarily consistent with rules approaches based on symbolic interactionist assumptions (cf., Cushman & Whiting, 1972; Pearce, 1976). Other requirements of Markov chain models such as "stationarity"[10] place undue restrictions on the form of sequential rules. While methods for circumventing these restrictions are available (for instance, G.A. Miller, 1952, pp. 445-447; Hewes, in press), they all involve departures from conventionality.

The formal restrictions on rules theorizing imposed by finite state Markov chain assumptions are not nearly as serious as the explanatory blind spots engendered by that methodology. The various Markov models are extremely useful for summarizing interact sequences which happen "as a rule" (Toulmin, 1974); however, the truly distinctive feature of rules theories is that the explanatory mechanism, the rule, has normative force only (Cushman & Pearce, 1977; Toulmin, 1969, 1974). Actors consciously choose to follow rules or choose not to violate them. Unlike natural laws, rules can be violated.

Markov chain models are not composed of the components necessary for explaining choice-governed regularities. At the very most, they can summarize observed regularities of the following form:

> If action A performs some behavior s_i at any time $t+k$, then actor B will perform some behavior s_j at $t+k+1$ with probability p_{ij}
>
> A does s_i at a particular time $t+k$
>
> B does s_j at $t+k+1$ with probability p_{ij}.

Clearly, the explanatory syllogism above contains no reference to choice. Markov models are extremely good at summarizing what happens "as a rule" but not at explaining why something happens "because of a rule." Additional information must be added before Markov chain explanations of the type described above can fully represent choice-governed behavior. If Markov chain models are imposed on rules theorizing without appropriate modifications, the worst kind of "law of the hammer" distortion is a likely result.

What can we do about this problem? The answer is to meld the descriptive power of Markov-type models with exogenous variables which represent the decision-making process. The Markov chain captures the regular sequential structure of the units specified as states or categories in the theory; the exogenous variables contained in the decision procedures describing the conditions under which an individual is likely to choose to either violate a rule or pick one rule over another. Combined, these two methodologies can be used to capture both the stable, probabilistic, sequential structure generated by rules and the choice mechanisms which make such actions distinct from law-governed behavior.

Spilerman (1972; Singer & Spilerman, 1974; see also Hewes, 1977, in press) has introduced the general technology. Specific decision models based on regression analysis, sequential elimination methods, mathematical programming, spatial proximity (MacCrimmon, 1973), and exchange theories (e.g., Thibaut & Kelley, 1959) can provide the structure and some of the content for the requisite exogenous variables. The tactic of adding unorthodox twists to orthodox methodologies aids in circumventing problems created by the "law of the hammer."

Induced perspectives. Probably the largest body of rules research has been undertaken from an induced perspective. Most of this work is grounded on Schutz's (1970) requirement that "each term in a scientific model of human action must be constructed in such a way that a human act performed within the life world by an individual actor in the way indicated by the typical construct would be understandable for the actor himself as well as his fellowmen in terms of common-sense interpretations of everyday life" (p. 279).

In application, however, induced perspective theorists usually go a bit further. In creating their "accounts" or "interpretations" of everyday life, these theorists hope to infer underlying rules which describe how an actor can create and/or apply surface rules of social interaction (cf., Eglin, 1975; Garfinkel, 1967; Mehan & Wood, 1975). The problem in this enterprise, and even many of those concerned with inducing surface rules (e.g., Goffman, 1955, 1969; Pearce, 1976) is the conventionalism which dictates that both the theoretical constructs and the relationships among constructs must be cast in terms understandable to actors in the "life world" (for example, Pfohl, 1975, pp. 252-254; Wieder, 1974). As a consequence, such rules gain comprehensibility at the cost of precision. The predictive power of a theory is a direct function of its constructs *and* the precision of the relationships among its constructs. The language of everyday life is not notoriously precise.

This loss of precision may well be acceptable, if intuitive understanding or ex post facto explanation are the goals of the theorist. If, on the other hand, prediction is also desired, the rules theorists may need to compromise their adherence to the induced perspective. This can be accomplished by imposing formal relationships on constructs derived from actors in the "life world." To the extent that one can choose the formal representational system so that it does minimal violence to subject-based intuitions, to that extent one may be able to attain the twin goals of understanding and prediction. The problem, of course, is how one makes the "correct" choice of a methodology which leaves subjects' intuitions unbloodied, or at least unbowed. The greatest weakness of arguments for an induced view of communication (Delia, 1977) seems to be the lack of guidance provided in this area. Similar moves in other fields have apparently fared no better (e.g., Tudor, 1976).

I am afraid that I, too, have no methodological rabbits up my sleeve. The problem of determining the "correct" induced perspective methodology is likely to go unanswered for some time, simply because criteria for a solution are not at hand. In every other methodological problem discussed in this paper, criteria for solution were easily accessible. If theoretically interesting information are lost in ANOVA designs because the independent variables are nominal, then one figures a way to incorporate continuous independent variables in an experimental design; if choice behavior must be added to finite state Markov chain models to capture the essential character of a "rule," then one merely fuses the two. But if one must base the choice of methodology on subjects' intuitions, then neither I, nor any other theorist, can propose methodological solutions in the absence of information from subjects. We certainly do not have sufficient subject-based descriptions of relationships at this time to prescribe solutions. In fact, if literature on human judgment (Goldberg, 1970; Slovic & Lichtenstein, 1971), creativity (Ghiselin, 1952), attributional processes (Nisbett & Wilson, 1977), cognitive psychology (Mandler, 1975), and recent work in selective perception (Dixon, 1971; Erdelyi, 1974), is any indication, subjects may be unable to give clear insights into the ways in which they perform cognitive operations (see Nisbett & Wilson, 1977, for a review). I am afraid that much groundwork has yet to be laid before induced perspective rules theories can be usefully employed in interpersonal communication. The evidence cited above casts doubt on the reliance that can be placed on subject-based descriptions of their cognitive processes as a source of methodologies.[11]

SUMMARY AND SUGGESTIONS FOR FUTURE RESEARCH

In the previous section, I tried to document the inner workings of a methodological "law of the hammer." Both situationist and rules approaches to interpersonal communication were shown to be subject to this "law," and the consequences of its operation were outlined. It should be clear that such difficulties are not limited to these particular approaches to interpersonal communication, or even to the interpersonal area itself. The problem of "law of the "hammer" conventionalism appears to be widespread.

The tack I have taken in describing this problem is markedly different from those taken by many of the critics cited in my introductory warrant (e.g., Blumer, 1972; Budd, 1977; Douglas, 1976; Harré & Secord, 1972; Phillipson, 1972). Nevertheless, when one examines the worst instances of distortion noted by these critics, those distortions appear to be more a result of carelessness and unimaginative uses of extant methodologies than of inherent flaws in the techniques of modern social science. We may ultimately have to reconceptualize the nature of human beings (e.g. Harré & Secord, 1972) or allow subjects to become active participants in the process of discovery (e.g., Delia, 1977; Mixon, 1971) as these critics suggest. However, we must also cope with the methodological blind spots created by unthinking methodological conventionalism, and we must cope with these blind spots whether we need new assumptions about the nature of human beings or not, whether we need a new ethos of communication research or not.

The problem of "law of the hammer" conventionalism in interpersonal communication is clearly much broader than the few instances I have highlighted in this brief article; nevertheless, I have attempted to sketch specific solutions to specific methodological problems as models of the kind of flexibility that is needed in our methodological thinking. Let me also propose two recommendations which may be of assistance in combating the general problem. *First, researchers must remember that any test of a theory is really a test of the assumptions of that theory and the assumptions of the methodology used in the study.* All too often these two sets of assumptions are treated as disjunct when, in fact, they are not (cf., Magnusson, 1976). Researchers should compose a list of all the assumptions of the methodologies that they plan to use and ask themselves whether or not those assumptions conform to the assumptions of the theory. (Many of the chapters in Monge and Cappella's (in press) new multivariate text address these issues from the standpoint of communication theorists.) If the assumptions of theory and methodology are found to be compatible, then the potential interference with substantive conclusions caused by invalidation of methodological assumptions must be assessed. This kind of two-stage assessment procedure may suggest alternative methodologies which produce less theoretical distortion or inspire methodological innovations to improve theory/observation fit.

Second, researchers should have at their disposal the widest possible range of methodological tools. As Cappella (1977) implies, "to adore one methodology is the only sin." If the "law of the hammer" is a methodological fact of life, and I believe it is, then the best way to circumvent it is to have many "hammers." As the number of methodologies increases, so does the chance of finding one which fits the problem at hand. Though there are practical limits to implementing this suggestion, intuitive understanding of a wide range of methodologies is a reasonable goal for any researcher. Once a researcher knows that a particular methodology is available and applicable, expert advice can be sought on the methodological details.

Neither of these two suggestions is sufficient, alone or together, to solve the problem noted by Kurt Lewin so many years ago. Interpersonal communication, as well as the social sciences in general, will always find its methodologies lagging behind its theoretic structures. If this were not the case, then we should let statisticians take over the job of theory construction. Since we must cope with methodologies which constrain the testing of our theories, our best solutions would appear to be broad methodological training coupled with a low animal cunning in contriving methodological twists. The "law of the hammer" will likely remain with us, but its effects can be moderated through constant vigilance.

NOTES

1. Miller (in press) discussed two other approaches to interpersonal communication, "laws" and "developmental," which will not be explored here. The laws approach is sufficiently close to the situationist approach discussed here to make a separate presentation unnecessary. Detailed analyses of the philosophical and pragmatic problems with the laws approach have been discussed elsewhere (e.g., Achinstein, 1971; Berger, 1977b; Cushman, 1977; Monge, 1977). The developmental and rules approaches share many of the same methodological problems, though they are conceptually distinct; thus, the methodological problems discussed under rules approaches has implications for the study of relationship development. The unique methodological aspects of developmental approaches have been treated extensively elsewhere (e.g., Nesselroade & Reese, 1973), in the time-series analysis literature (Box & Jenkins, 1976; Glass, Willson, & Gottman, 1975) and in catastrophe theory (e.g., Isnard & Zeeman, 1976; Sussman, 1975). Discussion of this extensive literature is beyond even the potential scope of a paper such as this.
2. These alternatives may well originate with some methodological commitment; however, no attempt will be made to resolve this "chicken and egg" argument.
3. This is evidenced by the use of self-report measure as manipulation checks in experimental studies. The continuous-level self-report data are only employed to validate nominal-level treatment levels. The continuous-level information is then thrown away in preference to nominal information.
4. The most obvious example of this is when a quadratic relationship exists but only two treatment levels are taken, one on each side of the "turning point" of the curve.
5. Note that the term intraclass correlation as used here does not refer to the correlation between the nominal-level, independent variables and the dependent variable in the design, which is the normal usage of the term found in most design texts. It refers here to the correlation between continuous independent and dependent measures controlling for cell mean differences, assuming a fully balanced design.
6. I am presuming that to "explain" means to subsume under a more general set of principles (Rescher, 1970). While I am not limiting myself to the case where those more gen-

eral principles are laws, subsumption under *some kind* of more general principle appears to be necessary for a satisfying explanation. Thus, to say that a pattern of similarity judgments, stable across a large sample of individuals, exists *because that is the way those situations are related* is less satisfactory than saying that the pattern exists *because those situations are being judged on a stable set of perceptual dimensions used to evaluate all situations*.

7. Clearly, to remain completely true to the induced perspective, factors and relationships among factors would be drawn from actors in everyday life. Thus, for example, listening to a class lecture, going out on a first date, and having a candle-light dinner at an apartment might fall along a single dimension based on intimacy. If one could determine that judgments about the relative intimacy of those three situations were sufficient to reconstruct the similarity-base dimension, one could "explain" that dimension in a more meaningful way.
8. If the relationships among variables is situation specific, then the causal relationship between perceived situation and behavior may itself be subject to higher-order situational influence. Obviously, explanation becomes much more complicated in this instance.
9. As noted in 1, developmental approaches to interpersonal communication share properties with rules approaches. Contingent, sequential structure is one such property. Thus, much of the following discussion is relevant to developmental approaches.
10. Stationarity implies that the conditional probability of moving from one "state" to the next, for all possible pairs of states, is independent of time.
11. By this I am not implying that subject reports are invalid for purposes *other* than the description of cognitive *processes*. Subject-based insights into the important variables in a given social milieu or their own cognitive states at a given point in time may still be highly useful.

REFERENCES

ACHINSTEIN, P. *Law and explanation*. Oxford: Oxford University Press, 1971.

ACOCK, A.C., & MARTIN, J.D. The undermeasurement controversy: Should ordinal data be treated as interval? *Sociology and Social Research*, 1974, 58, 427-433.

ADAMS, J.S., & FREEDMAN, S. Equity theory revisited: Comments and annotated bibliography. In L. Berkowitz & E. Walster (Eds.), *Advances in experimental social psychology*. Vol. 9. New York: Academic, 1976, 43-91.

ALEXANDER, C.N., & KNIGHT, G.W. Situated identities and social psychological experimentation. *Sociometry*, 1971, 34, 65-82.

ALPERT, M.E., & ANDERSON, W.T., JR. Optimal heterophily and communication effectiveness: Some empirical findings. *Journal of Communication*, 1973, 23, 328-343.

ARGYLE, M. Predictive and generative rules models of P x S interaction. In D. Magnusson & N.S. Endler (Eds.), *Personality at the crossroads*. New York: Wiley, 1977, 353-370.

ARNOULT, M.D. The specification of "social" stimulus. In S.B. Sells (Ed.), *Stimulus determinants of behavior*. New York: Ronald Press, 1963, 16-30.

BATESON, G. *Steps to an ecology of mind*. San Francisco: Chandler, 1972.

BEM, D.M., & ALLEN, A. On predicting some of the people some of the time: The search for cross-situational consistencies in behavior. *Psychological Review*, 1974, 81, 506-520.

BERGER, C.R. Interpersonal communication theory and research: An overview. In B. Ruben (Ed.), *Communication yearbook I*. New Brunswick, N.J.: Transaction-International Communication Association, 1977a, 217-228.

BERGER, C.R. The covering law perspective as a theoretical basis for the study of human communication. *Communication Quarterly*, 1977b, 25, 7-18.

BERGER, C.R., WEBER, M.D., MUNLEY, M.E., & DIXON, J.T. Interpersonal relationship levels and interpersonal attraction. In B. Ruben (Ed.), *Communication yearbook I*. New Brunswick, N.J.: Transaction-International Communication Association, 1977, 245-266.

BERLO, D.K. Communication as process: Review and commentary. In B. Ruben (Ed.), *Communication yearbook I*. New Brunswick, N.J.: Transaction-International Communication Association, 1977, 11-28.

BLUMER, H. Sociological analysis and the "variable." In J.G. Manis & B.N. Meltzer (Eds.), *Symbolic interaction* (2nd ed.). Boston: Allyn & Bacon, 1972, 92-101.

BOCHNER, A.P. Task and instrumentation variables as factors jeopardizing the validity of published group communication research, 1970-1971. *Speech Monographs*, 1974, 41, 169-178.

BOCHNER, A.P. Conceptual frontiers in the study of communication in families: An introduction to the literature. *Human Communication Research*, 1976, 2, 381-397.

BOWERS, K.S. Situationalism in psychology: An analysis and a critique. *Psychological Review*, 1973, 80, 307-336.

BOX, G.E.P., & JENKINS, G.M. *Time series analysis: Forecasting and control* (2nd ed.). San Francisco: Holden-Day, 1976.

BRUNSWICK, E. *Systematic and representative design of psychological experiments with results in physical and social perception*. Berkeley: University of California Press, 1947.

BRYSON, K.R., & PHILLIPS, D.P. Method for classifying interval-scale and ordinal scale data. In D.R. Heise (Ed.), *Sociological methodology 1975*. San Francisco: Jossey-Bass, 1975, 171-190.

BUDD, R.W. Perspectives on a discipline: Review and commentary. In B. Ruben (Ed.), *Communication yearbook I*. New Brunswick, N.J.: Transaction-International Communication Association, 1977, 29-36.

BURGOON, J.K., & JONES, S.B. Toward a theory of personal space expectations and their violations. *Human Communication Research*, 1976, 2, 131-146.

BURT, R.S. Confirmatory factor-analytic structures and the theory construction process. *Sociological Methods and Research*, 1973, 2, 131-190.

CAPPELLA, J.N. Research methodology in communication research: Overview and commentary. In B. Ruben (Ed.), *Communication yearbook I*. New Brunswick, N.J.: Transaction-International Communication Association, 1977, 37-54.

CARTWRIGHT, D.S. Trait and other sources of variance in the S-R inventory of anxiousness. *Journal of Personality and Social Psychology*, 1975, 32, 408-414.

CICOUREL, A.V. *Cognitive sociology*. New York: Free Press, 1974.

COHEN, D. (Ed.). *Explaining linguistic phenomena*. New York: Wiley, 1974.

COHEN, D., & WIRTH, J.R. (Eds.). *Testing linguistic hypotheses*. New York: Wiley, 1975.

COHEN, J. Some statistical issues in psychological research. In B.B. Wolman (Ed.), *Handbook of clinical psychology*. New York: McGraw-Hill, 1966, 95-121.

COLEMAN, J.S. *Introduction to mathematical sociology*. New York: Free Press, 1964.

COSER, L.A. Presidential address: Two methods in search of a substance. *American Sociological Review*, 1975, 40, 691-700.

COZBY, P.C. Self-disclosure: A literature review. *Psychological Bulletin*, 1973, 79, 73-91.

CRAIG, R., JOHNSON, B., & SHAW, M. The process of coorientation toward a definition of the situation. Paper presented at the annual meeting of the Speech Communication Association, San Francisco, 1976.

CUSHMAN, D.P. The rules perspective as a theoretical basis for the study of human communication. *Communication Quarterly*, 1977, 25, 30-45.

CUSHMAN, D.P., & PEARCE, W.B. Generality and necessity in three types of theory about human communication. In B. Ruben (Ed.), *Communication yearbook I*. New Brunswick, N.J.: Transaction-International Communication Association, 1977, 173-182.

CUSHMAN, D.P., & WHITING, G.C. An approach to communication theory: Toward consensus on rules. *Journal of Communication*, 1972, 22, 217-238.

DELIA, J. Constructivism and the study of human communication. *Quarterly Journal of Speech*, 1977, 63, 66-83.

DIXON, N.F. *Subliminal perception: The nature of a controversy*. London: McGraw-Hill, 1971.

DODD, D.H., & SCHULTZ, R.F., JR. Computational procedures for estimating magnitude of effect for some analysis of variance designs. *Psychological Bulletin*, 1973, 79, 391-395.

DOUGLAS, J. *Investigative social research*. Beverly Hills, Cal.: Sage, 1976.

DWYER, J.H. Analysis of variance and the magnitude of effects: A general approach. *Psychological Bulletin*, 1974, 81, 731-737.

EGLIN, P. What should sociology explain—regularities, rules or interpretations? *Philosophy of Social Science*, 1975, 5, 377-391.

EKEHAMMAR, B. Interactionism in psychology from a historical perspective. *Psychological Bulletin*, 1974, 81, 1026-1048.

EKEHAMMAR, B., & MAGNUSSON, D. A method to study stressful situations. *Journal of Personality and Social Psychology*, 1973, 27, 176-179.

EKEHAMMAR, B., SCHALLING, D., & MAGNUSSON, D. Dimensions of stressful situations: A comparison between a response analytic and a stimulus analytic approach. *Multivariate Behavioral Research*, 1975, 10, 155-164.

ELLIS, D.G., & FISHER, B.A. Phases in conflict in small group development: A Markov analysis. *Human Communication Research*, 1975, 1, 195-212.

ENDLER, N.S., & MAGNUSSON, D. *Interactional psychology and personality*. New York: Wiley, 1976.

ERDELYI, M.H. A new look at the new look: Perceptual defense and vigilance. *Psychological Review*, 1974, 81, 1-25.

FALZER, P.R. Representative design and general linear model. *Speech Monographs*, 1974, 41, 127-168.

FOLGER, J., & SILLARS, A.L. Relational coding and perceptions of dominance. Paper presented at the annual meeting of the Speech Communication Association, Washington, D.C., 1977.

FREDERIKSEN, N. Toward a taxonomy of situations. *American Psychologist*, 1972, 27, 114-123.

GARFINKEL, H. What is ethnomethodology? In H. Garfinkel (Ed.), *Studies in ethnomethodology*. Englewood Cliffs, N.J.: Prentice-Hall, 1967, 1-7.

GARRISON, J.P., & POWELL, R.G. Interpersonal solidarity and communication contexts: The study of relational communication in a mutual-causal paradigm. Paper presented at the annual meeting of the International Communication Association, Chicago, 1978.

GARRISON, J.P., SULLIVAN, D.L., & PATE, L.E. Interpersonal valence dimensions as discriminators of communication contexts. Paper presented at the annual meeting of the Speech Communication Association, Houston, 1976.

GHISELIN, B. *The creative process*. New York: Mentor, 1952.

GILLHAM, J., & WOELFEL, J. The Galileo system of measurement: Preliminary evidence for precision, stability, and equivalence to traditional measures. *Human Communication Research*, 1977, 3, 222-234.

GLASS, G.V., WILLSON, V.L., & GOTTMAN, J.M. *Design and analysis of time-series experiments*. Boulder: Colorado Associated University Press, 1975.

GOCKA, E.F. Regression analysis of proportional cell data. *Psychological Bulletin*, 1973, 80, 25-27.

GOFFMAN, E. On face work. *Psychiatry*, 1955, 18, 213-231.

GOFFMAN, E. *Strategic interaction*. Philadelphia: University of Pennsylvania Press, 1969.

GOLDBERG, L.R. Man versus model of Man: A rationale, plus some evidence for a method of improving clinical inferences. *Psychological Bulletin*, 1970, 73, 422-432.

HACKMAN, J.R. The effects of task characteristics on group products. *Journal of Experimental Social Psychology*, 1968, 4, 162-187.

HARRÉ, R. Some remarks on "rule" as scientific concept. In T. Mischel (Ed.), *On understanding other persons*. Oxford: Blackwell, 1973.

HARRÉ, R. Science as representation: A reply to Mr. MacKinnon. *Philosophy of Science*, 1977, 44, 146-158.

HARRÉ, R., & SECORD, P.F. *The explanation of social behavior*. Oxford: Blackwell, 1972.

HAWES, L.C. Development and application of an interview coding scheme. *Central State Speech Journal*, 1972, 33, 92-99.

HAWES, L.C. Response to Grossberg and O'Keefe: Building a human science of communication. *Quarterly Journal of Speech*, 1975, 61, 209-219.

HAWES, L.C., & FOLEY, J.M. A Markov analysis of interview communication. *Speech Monographs*, 1973, 40, 208-219.

HAWES, L.C., & FOLEY, J.M. Group decisioning: Testing a finite stochastic model. In G.R. Miller (Ed.), *Explorations in interpersonal communication*. Beverly Hills, Cal.: Sage, 1976, 237-254.

HEWES, D.E. Finite stochastic modeling of communication processes: An introduction and some basic readings. *Human Communication Research*, 1975, 1, 271-283.

HEWES, D.E. Rules theories and Markov chains: An attempted integration. Presented to the Seminar on Rules, Department of Communication, Michigan State University, Summer 1976.

HEWES, D.E. The analysis of social interaction: What do we know and when should we stop knowing it? Paper presented at the annual meeting of the Speech Communication Association, Washington, D.C., 1977.

HEWES, D.E. Stochastic modeling of communication systems. In P. Monge & J.N. Cappella (Eds.), *Multivariate techniques in communication research*. New York: Academic, in press.

HEWES, D.E., & WOTRING, C.E. Methodology in socialization research: A causal analysis. Presented at the annual meeting of the International Communication Association, New Orleans, 1974.

ISNARD, C.A., & ZEEMAN, E.C. Some models from catastrophe theory in the social sciences. In L. Collins (Ed.), *The uses of models in the social sciences*. London: Tavistock, 1976, 44-100.

JACOB, T. Family interaction in disturbed and normal families: A methodological and substantive review. *Psychological Bulletin*, 1975, 82, 33-65.

JÖRESKOG, K.G. Testing a simple structure hypothesis in factor analysis. *Psychometrika*, 1966, 31, 243-260.

JÖRESKOG, K.G. A general approach to confirmatory maximum-likelihood factor analysis. *Psychometrika*, 1969, 32, 443-482.

JÖRESKOG, K.G. A general method for estimating a linear structural equation system. In A.S. Goldberger & O.D. Duncan (Eds.), *Structural equation models in the social sciences*. New York: Seminar, 1973, 85-112.

KAUFER, D. Developing a rule theoretic approach to communication as opposed to a dictionary of rules: Some considerations and criteria. Paper presented to the Doctoral Honors Seminar on Rules, Amherst, Mass., 1976.

KEREN, G., & LEWIS, C. Nonorthogonal designs: Sample versus population. *Psychological Bulletin*, 1976, 83, 817-826.

KOFFKA, K. *Principles of Gestalt psychology*. New York: Harcourt, 1935.

LABOV, W. Rules for ritual insult. In D. Sudnow (Ed.), *Studies in social interaction*. New York: Free Press, 1972, 120-169.

LAMB, D.H. Speech anxiety: Towards a theoretical conceptualization and preliminary scale development. *Speech Monographs*, 1972, 39, 62-67.

LENK, D. The use of stochastic model for discerning rule guided communication behavior. Paper presented to the Doctoral Honors Seminar on Rules, Amherst, Mass., 1976.

MAGNUSSON, D. An analysis of situational dimensions. *Perceptual and Motor Skills*, 1971, 32, 851-867.

MAGNUSSON, D. The person and the situation in an interactional model of behavior. *Scandinavian Journal of Psychology*, 1976, 17, 253-271.

MAGNUSSON, D., & EKEHAMMAR, B. An analysis of situational dimensions: A replication. *Multivariate Behavioral Research*, 1973, 8, 333-339.

MacCRIMMON, K.R. An overview of multiple objective decision making. In J.L. Cochrane & M. Zeleny (Eds.), *Multiple criteria decision making*. Columbia: University of South Carolina Press, 1973, 18-44.

MANDER, G. *Mind and emotion*. New York: Wiley, 1975.

McHUGH, P. *Defining the situation*. Indianapolis: Bobbs-Merrill, 1968.

MEEHAN, E.J. *Explanation in social science: A systems paradigm*. Homewood, Ill.: Dorsey, 1968.

MEHAN, H., & WOOD, H. *The reality of ethnomethodology*. New York: Wiley, 1975.

MILLER, G.A. Finite Markov processes in psychology. *Psychometrika*, 1952, 17, 149-167.

MILLER, G.R. Current perspectives in interpersonal communication theory and research. *Human Communication Research*, in press.

MILLER, G.R., BOSTER, F., ROLOFF, M., & SEIBOLD, D. Compliance-gaining message strategies: A typology and some findings concerning effects of situational differences. *Communication Monographs*, 1977, 44, 37-51.

MILLER, G.R., & STEINBERG, M. *Between people*. Chicago: Science Research Associates, 1975.

MILLS, C.W. Situated actions and vocabularies of motive. *American Sociological Review*, 1940, 5, 904-913.

MISCHEL, W. Toward a cognitive social learning reconceptualization of personality. *Psychological Review*, 1973, 80, 252-283.

MISCHEL, W. The interaction of person and situation. In D. Magnusson and N.S. Endler (Eds.), *Personality at the Crossroads*. New York: Wiley, 1977, 333-352.

MIXON, D. Instead of deception. *Journal of the Theory of Social Behavior*, 1971, 2, 145-177.

MOHAN, B.A. Do sequencing rules exist? *Semiotica*, 1974, 12, 75-96.

MONGE, P. The systems perspective as a theoretical basis for the study of human communication. *Communication Quarterly*, 1977, 25, 19-20.

MONGE, P., & CAPPELLA, J.N. *Multivariate techniques in communication research*. New York: Academic, in press.

MULAIK, S.A. *The foundations of factor analysis*. New York: McGraw-Hill, 1972.

MULAIK, S.A. Confirmatory factor analysis. In D.J. Amick & H.J. Walberg (Eds.), *Introductory multivariate analysis*. Berkeley, Cal.: McCutchan, 1975.

NESSELROADE, J.R., & REESE, H.W. *Life-span developmental psychology: Methodological issues*. New York: Academic, 1973.

NISBETT, R.E., & WILSON, T.D. Telling more than we can know: Verbal reports on mental processes. *Psychological Review*, 1977, 84, 231-259.

NOFSINGER, R.E., JR. On answering questions indirectly: Some rules in the grammar of doing conversation. *Human Communication Research*, 1976, 2, 172-181.

NOWAKOWSKA, M. The limitations of the factor analytical approach to psychology with special application to Cattell's research strategy. *Theory and Decision*, 1973, 4, 109-139.

OVERALL, J.E., & SPIEGEL, D.K. Comment on Rawlings' nonorthogonal analysis of variance. *Psychological Bulletin*, 1973, 164-167.

PEARCE, W.B. The coordinated management of meaning: A rules-based theory of interpersonal communication. In G.R. Miller (Ed.), *Explorations in interpersonal communication*. Beverly Hills, Cal.: Sage, 1976, 13-35.

PFOHL, S.J. Social role analysis: The ethnomethodological critique. *Sociology and Social Research* 1975, 59, 243-265.

PHILLIPSON, M. Phenomenological philosophy and sociology. In P. Filmer, et al. (Eds.), *New directions in sociological theory*. Cambridge, Mass.: MIT Press, 1972, 119-164.

PROSHANSKY, H.M., ITTELSON, W.H., & RIVLIN, L.G. The influence of the physical environment on behavior:

Some basic assumptions. In H.M. Proshansky, W.H. Ittelson, & L.G. Rivlin (Eds.), *Environmental psychology: Man and his physical environment*. New York: Holt, Rinehart & Winston, 1970, 27-37.

RAWLINGS, R.R. Note on nonorthogonal analysis of variance. *Psychological Bulletin*, 1972, 79, 373-374.

RAWLINGS, R.R. Comments on the Overall and Spiegel paper. *Psychological Bulletin*, 1973, 79, 168-169.

RESCHER, N. *Scientific explanation*. New York: Free Press, 1970.

RISKIN, J. Methodology for studying family interaction. *Archives of General Psychiatry*, 1963, 8, 343-348.

ROGERS, W.T., & JONES, S.E. Effects of dominance tendencies on floor holding and interruption behavior in dyadic interaction. *Human Communication Research*, 1975, 1, 113-122.

ROLOFF, M. The situational use of pro- and antisocial compliance-gaining strategies for high and low Machiavellians. Paper presented at the annual meeting of the International Communication Association, Chicago, 1978.

SCHEFF, T. Negotiating reality: Notes on power in assessment of responsibility. In B. Franklin & F. Kohout (Eds.), *Social psychology and everyday life*. New York: McKay, 1973.

SCHUTZ, A. *On phenomenology and social relations*. H.R. Wagner (Ed.). Chicago: University of Chicago Press, 1970.

SELLS, S.B. Dimensions of stimulus situations which account for behavior variance. In S.B. Sells (Ed.), *Stimulus determinants of behavior*. New York: Ronald Press, 1963, 3-15.

SHERIF, M., & SHERIF, C.W. Varieties of social stimulus situations. In S.B. Sells (Ed.), *Stimulus determinants of behavior*. New York: Ronald Press, 1963.

SINGER, B., & SPILERMAN, S. Social mobility models for heterogeneous populations. In H.L. Costner (Ed.), *Sociological methodology 1973-74*. San Francisco: Jossey-Bass, 1974, 356-402.

SLOVIC, P., & LICHTENSTEIN, S. Comparison of Bayesian and regression approaches to the study of information processing in judgment. *Organizational behavior and human performance*, 1971, 6, 651-730.

SNAVELY, W.B., MERKER, G.E., BECKER, L.L., & BOOK, V.A. Predictors of interpersonal communication apprehension in the acquaintance context. Paper presented at the annual meeting of the Speech Communication Association, San Francisco, 1976.

SPILERMAN, S. The analysis of mobility processes by the introduction of independent variables into a Markov chain. *American Sociological Review*, 1972, 37, 277-294.

SUSSMAN, H.J. Catastrophe theory. *Synthese*, 1975, 31, 229-270.

THIBAUT, J.W., & KELLEY, H.H. *The social psychology of groups*. New York: Wiley, 1959.

TOULMIN, S. Concepts and the explanation of human behavior. In T. Mischel (Ed.), *Human action*. New York: Academic, 1969, 71-104.

TOULMIN, S. Rules and their relevance for understanding human behavior. In T. Mischel (Ed.), *Understanding other persons*. Oxford: Blackwell, 1974, 185-215.

TUDOR, A. Misunderstanding everyday life. *Sociological Review*, 1976, 24, 479-503.

VAUGHN, G.M., & CORBALLIS, M.C. Beyond tests of significance: Estimating strengths of effects in selected ANOVA designs. *Psychological Bulletin*, 1969, 72, 204-213.

WACHTEL, P.L. Psychodynamics, behavior therapy, and the implacable experimenter: An inquiry into the consistency of personality. *Journal of Abnormal Psychology*, 1973, 82, 324-334.

WIEDER, D.L. Telling the code. In R. Turner (Ed.), *Ethnomethodology*. Baltimore: Penguin, 1974, 144-172.

WIRTH, J.R. Logical considerations in the testing of linguistic hypotheses. In D. Cohen & J.R. Wirth (Eds.), *Testing linguistic hypotheses*. New York: Wiley, 1975, 211-220.

WIRTH, J.R. (Ed.). *Assessing linguistic arguments*, New York: Wiley, 1976.

WOELFEL, J., & DANES, J. Metric multidimensional scaling in communication research. In P. Monge & J. Cappella (Eds.), *Multivariate techniques in communication research*. New York: Academic, in press.

WOLF, G., & CARTWRIGHT, B. Rules for coding dummy variables in multiple regression. *Psychological Bulletin*, 1974, 81, 173-179.

STUDIES IN INTERPERSONAL EPISTEMOLOGY I: SITUATIONAL ATTRIBUTES IN OBSERVATIONAL CONTEXT SELECTION[1]

CHARLES R. BERGER *JOSEPH W. PERKINS*
Northwestern University

The present studies investigated the bases upon which persons choose social contexts in order to maximize information acquisition about a stranger. In Experiment 1, persons expressed information acquisition preferences for pictures in which a target person was in either solitary or social situations. Judges strongly preferred social contexts for information acquisition. In Experiment 2, persons made preference judgments on the informational value of pictures in which a target person was with either similar or dissimilar others and was either involved or uninvolved with the others. Multidimensional scaling analyses revealed that the similarity and involvement dimensions were used as bases for information preference choices. Persons showed strong preferences for situations in which the target person was highly involved. Similarity preferences were more variable. Findings were discussed in terms of social comparison theory. The implications of the findings for the utility of rule-governed approaches to interpersonal communication were considered.

Recent theory and research in interpersonal communication and related areas has emphasized the *active role* that man plays in perceiving and constructing his social environment. Several lines of inquiry from several different disciplines assume that man is not always at the mercy of environmental events and that persons frequently plan and choose courses of action in accordance with rules or some other set of criteria. Within the discipline of communication, several researchers (Cushman & Whiting, 1972; Delia, Clark & Switzer, 1974; Hale & Delia, 1976; Pearce, 1976; Cushman, 1977) have articulated theoretical positions which emphasize the active role that persons play in perceiving and acting, and the critical role that volition plays in human communication.

The above contributions to theory and research in interpersonal communication have been spawned by theory and research from other disciplines. The notion that man is an active construer of social reality is a central assumption of several attribution theories (Kelly, 1955; Heider, 1958; Hones & Davis, 1965; Kelley, 1967; Jones, Kanouse, Kelley, Nesbitt, Valins & Winer, 1972; Kelley, 1973). In addition, those identified with the rules perspective (Harré & Secord, 1972; Harré, 1974; Toulmin, 1974) have stressed both the active nature of man's attempts to understand and "negotiate" his social relationships and the various rules by which human conduct is guided. In addition, some researchers in the area of perception and human information processing (e.g. Weimer, 1977) have raised questions concerning the traditional distinctions between sensory and motor components of the nervous system. Weimer has argued that the mental or cognitive realm is motoric and suggests a return to the active epistemologist's conception of mind as both a generator of its output *and* its input.

While an impressive array of theorists and researchers emphasize the active nature of perception, it should be kept in mind that persons do respond to stimuli which are out of their awareness. Nisbett and Wilson (1977) have cogently advanced and extensively documented the generalization that persons may have little awareness of the higher order mental processes underlying judgment, evaluation, and the initiation of complex behavior. Specifically, these researchers cite several studies which show that a particular stimulus has affected a particular response, but that sometimes subjects are (1) unaware of the existence of the stimulus, (2) unaware of the existence of the responses, or (3) unaware that the stimulus has affected the response. These findings indicate definite limitations on the awareness persons have of their higher mental processes. Moreover, Nisbett and Wilson's conclusions raise serious questions about the usefulness of self-report measures which ask subjects why they have behaved in a certain way. Nisbett and Wilson suggest that cognitive structures which mediate the verbal understanding of phenomenal experience may be different from those which underly complex judgments and behavior.

The above discussion of the awareness issue provides a counterweight to the notion that persons are all knowing and all understanding of their own as well as others' behavior. Persons are influenced by stimuli about which they are unaware and about which they cannot speak or write. Thus, self-reports which attempt to ascertain the reasons or explanations for certain actions may be misleading for the reasons that Nisbett and Wilson have outlined. Moreover, some attribution theorists (Shaver, 1975) have noted that persons do not *always* attempt to predict and explain the behavior of others. It is only under certain conditions that persons behave as "naive scientists" or active attribution generators.

The above discussion provides a critical context for the present work. Specifically, we assume that *under certain conditions* persons attempt to reduce their uncertainty about themselves and others in order that they be able to select optimal messages from their available repertoire to accomplish their goals in an interaction. In previous work on this issue (Berger, 1976; Berger, Gardner, Parks, Schulman, & Miller, 1976; Berger, 1977), we have attempted to specify some of the variables responsible for increased awareness about another person's behavior and increased interest in gathering information about the person. Specifically, Berger (1976, 1977) has suggested that such factors as the incentive value of the other person, the extent to which the other person deviates from rules and norms, and the probability of future interaction with the other person will be related to the desire to find out more about a particular target individual.

In addition, we further assume that once a person begins to focus his or her attention on the task of gathering information about another, there are several different strategies that a person uses to glean such information. Berger, et al. (1976) and Berger (1976, 1977) have suggested numerous strategies for gathering information about others. Conceptually, these strategies have been viewed as occurring at one of three levels. First, an individual can gather information as an unobtrusive observer. That is, he can observe the target person and attempt to find out things about him without actually interacting with him. These strategies have been called *passive strategies*. It should be kept in mind that we do not mean to imply that information gathering is a "passive" activity. This term is used to contrast with more active strategies which require the manipulation of the environment by the information gatherer.

A second set of information gathering strategies we have called *active strategies*. These strategies involve the active manipulation of the environment by the information seeker, but do not involve direct interaction between the seeker and the target person. Arranging chairs at a meeting so that the target person can be observed interacting with others would be one active strategy. Finally, *interactive strategies* are those which involve the direct interaction of the information seeker with the target person. Question asking and self-disclosure might be strategies used to gather information in this face-to-face interaction mode (Berger, et al, 1976). The present paper focuses upon the *passive strategies*. No claim is made that the strategies examined in this paper are exhaustive of the set of passive strategies that might be used to gather information about an unknown other.

When a person assumes the role of unobtrusive observer of a particular target person, are certain observational contexts perceived to be more informative than others when an unobtrusive observer wishes to gather information about a target person? Gibbs-Smith (1973) has recommended that in order to be an effective observer, a person should compare new items to similar items which have been noticed before. According to Gibbs-Smith, the act of comparison with similar things aids memory. This advice is given within the context of police training, but does give us at least one lead in answering the above question.

Aside from the recommendations of practitioners of the art of observation, various social-psychological theories and research studies suggest that there may be crucial personal and situational attributes which observers might use to glean information about target persons. For example, Festinger's (1954) social comparison theory and research designed to test the theory (Schachter, 1959; Gerard, 1963; Rabbie, 1963; Zimbardo & Formica, 1963) indicated that when persons are unsure of their abilities and opinions, they will seek out others in order to reduce their uncertainties about their abilities or opinions. Furthermore, Schachter's (1959) work demonstrated that persons prefer *similar others* to dissimilar others when they seek the comparison information which will help to reduce their uncertainties about themselves. Thus, the criterion of *perceived similarity* of the other serves as a basis for information search. Of course, perceived similarity of others, especially in the area of attitudes and opinions, has been shown to be consistently related to interpersonal attraction (Byrne, 1971; Huston, 1974). If we extend the line of reasoning of social comparison theory and research to the situation in which an individual is attempting to reduce his uncertainty about *another person* rather than himself, we might argue that a person would prefer to observe an unknown target person (1) in the presence of others rather than alone, and (2) with *similar others* rather than dissimilar others.

The reasoning for the first of the above two predictions is simply that viewing a target person alone makes social comparison more difficult and thus makes information gathering more difficult. When a person is engaged in solitary activity, the range of responses the person is likely to give is restricted. When a person is in the presence of others, he or she may display a wider range of responses because of the behavior of others in the situation. Thus, the unobtrusive observer is more likely to gain more unique information about the person when the person is with others. This is not to say that observing a person engaged in a solitary activity is not informative or that *some* solitary situations cannot be relatively informative. The hypothesis stipulated here is predicated on the notion that both social comparison and information generation in general will be facilitated by observing the target individual embedded in a social context rather than a solitary context.

Assuming observers' preferences for social situations over solitary situations as observational contexts, we can ask what attributes of *social situations* might subserve observers' selections of observational contexts. That is, if the observer had a choice of contexts in which to observe the target person, how would he or she employ attributes of the situation in making a choice of observational contexts? Social comparison theory suggests that observers might choose to see the target with similar others rather than dissimilar others, as was suggested above. This expectation could be reasoned from the theory in the following way. Observing a target person with similar others provides a more stable baseline from which to evaluate his or her behavior. One's behavior in the presence of similar others might more confidently be attributed to factors which reside within the individual; that is, the person's behavior is due to his or her "personality." By contrast, observing a target embedded in a situation with dissimilar others might lead to less attributional confidence about the target's "personality" because any behavioral uniqueness displayed by the target person might be attributed to the fact that dissimilar others are present in the situation rather than to individual idiosyncrasies of the target person.

It should be noted that both extentions of social comparison theory discussed above do *not* necessarily assume that the target person is actually interacting with those present in the situation. Schachter (1959) argues that social comparison can occur in the absence of verbal communication. Thus, the hypothesis that observers prefer social to solitary contexts and observational contexts with similar others rather than dissimilar others present does not assume that the target person is actually interacting with the others in the social modes.

One difficulty with the preference for similarity hypothesis derived from social comparison theory is that it could be plausibly argued that an observer might wish to observe the target in the presence of *dissimilar others* rather than similar others. The line of reasoning for this hypothesis would be an extension of the argument presented for the alone versus social situation hypothesis. That is, a given target person might display a *greater variety of responses* with dissimilar others than with similar others. The presentation of such variety might be potentially more informative for the observer than the responses shown in the presence of similar others. Moreover, the observer might be able to more confidently ascertain how the target deals with possible stress and anxiety associated with being in the presence of dissimilar others. Thus, the derivation from social comparison theory may not be directly applicable in the present case. Of course, it is possible that observers might prefer to observe both types of interaction situations in order to glean different kinds of information about the target person. Given the potential ambiguity of a direct prediction from social comparison theory regarding the similarity variable, we feel that it is best to state that there is some kind of systematic relationship between target-other similarity and preference for observational context.

It is possible to consider types of similarity other than the similarity between the target person and the other persons present in the social situation being observed. The degree of similarity between the observer and the other persons in the situation might be investigated. Or, the extent to which the observer feels similar to the target person might be significant. We feel, however, that the degree of similarity between the observer and the target might be more of a determinant of selection of target to be observed rather than a criterion for choosing some kind of observational context. Observer-target and observer-other similarities were not examined in the present study but may have more impact upon observational context selection.

In addition to the solitary-social and the similar-dissimilar hypotheses, the present study also examined the role that *target involvement* plays in observational context selection. Specifically, it was reasoned that since the two hypotheses presented above only stipulate that observers prefer to observe the target person *with others* and *with similar/dissimilar others*, a critical attribute of the social context might be the extent to which the target person is actually interacting with the others present in the situation. Under the notion that the mere presence of others in a situation will produce more response variety in the target than solitary situations, it could be argued that the more the target person is *actively involved* with the others in the situation, the more likely it is that response variety will increase and the observational context will have more potential information value to the observer. Viewing a target person reading a book with others present in the situation would be of low potential information value because the opportunity for the target to display a wide variety of verbal and nonverbal behaviors is limited. Thus, the straightforward prediction in this case would be that observers will prefer to observe the target person in social contexts where the target is actively involved in the social situation rather than in social contexts where the target person is relatively passive.

In summary, the present investigation examined the following three hypotheses:

H_1: Observers attempting to gain information about a target person will prefer to observe the target person in social rather than solitary situations.

H_2: The degree of similarity between the target person and the others present in the social situation will affect the preferential choices of observational contexts by observers.

H_3: Observers will prefer to gain information from observational contexts in which the target person is actively interacting with others rather than social situations in which the target is passive relative to the others present.

We would like to reemphasize that we do not believe that persons necessarily *consciously make* the kinds of calculations we have suggested when trying to gather information about a stranger. Moreover, we also do not believe that persons spend large amounts of time in their daily lives trying to reduce their uncertainties about other persons. We do believe that when persons have decided, for whatever reason, that they want to "get to know" someone, they may employ the kinds of information gathering criteria we have outlined above. Persons *may not be able* to report these criteria verbally, even when they are preoccupied with information gathering activities. However, we feel that by studying the *preferences* that persons manifest for observational contexts, we can determine whether the criteria suggested above are used for context selection. In order to accomplish this task, participants in the present study made paired comparison judgments of slide pictures of various situations involving a target person. These paried comparison judgments were analyzed in a number of different ways, including multidimensional scaling procedures, in order to test the hypotheses advanced above.

METHODS AND PROCEDURES

Two separate investigations were conducted in order to test the three hypotheses of the study. The first experiment tested Hypothesis 1, while the second experiment tested the latter two hypotheses.

Stimulus Materials

One male and one female theater student at Northwestern University each served as a target person. Two male and two female theater students were used as "others" in the social situations. In addition, two male and two female residents of retirement homes were used as "others" in some of the pictures. Approximately 200 35mm color slides were taken of the target persons engaging in both solitary activities and activities with other persons. The male and female target persons never appeared in the same picture. In taking the pictures, an effort was made to vary two attributes of the situation: (1) the degree of similarity between the target and the others present, and (2) the extent to which the target was involved in interacting with the others present in the situation. Similarity was varied by having the college student target person in the presence of, or interacting with either the college age "others" or the elderly persons. In addition, different sex combinations were used within each of the two age groups. Involvement was manipulated by having the target person vary his or her body orientation, eye contact, and direct verbal interaction with the others present. The similarity and involvement attributes were not relevant to the pictures in which the target person appeared alone. However, each target person was photographed in the following three solitary situations: reading alone, typing, and playing solitaire.

From the original pool of approximately 200 slides, 67 slides were selected which were judged by the investigators to be the best representatives of the similarity and involvement dimensions. The best slides of the three solitary situations for each target person were among the 67 slides. In order to further reduce the size of the picture pool, 21 Northwestern University undergraduate students rated each of the 67 pictures on the following four dimensions: (1) Preference for information acquisition about the target person; (2) similarity of target to others pictured; (3) involvement of target with others; and (4) the happiness of the target. The happiness dimension was included because it was not possible to control totally the facial expressions of the target in each of the situations. The results of this pretest were used to select the best eight social slides for each target person. Those slides which received the most extreme ratings along the similarity and involvement dimensions were used to fill a 2 X 2 stimulus matrix consisting of two levels of similarity and two levels of involvement. The best two slides for each cell were chosen for each target. In addition, three solitary slides were chosen for each target. In the present studies, only the slides for the female target person were used, since those slides achieved the largest extremes on the two attribute dimensions. The results of the pretest indicated that the target was judged to be most similar to the others pictured when the others were of the same age as the target. Slides in the low similarity cells all involved the target interacting with the elderly persons. Also, very large differences in involvement were produced by manipulating the dimensions discussed above.

Experiment 1

Stimulus selection. Of the eight stimuli used to fill the 2 X 2 matrix of social situations, the four best representatives of the design (on the basis of the pretest) were chosen to test Hypothesis 1. In addition, three slides depicting the target in the three different solitary situations (reading, typing, and playing solitaire) were used.

Participants. Judges for Experiment 1 were 72 students enrolled in summer courses in the Department of Communication Studies and the Department of Communicative Disorders at Northwestern University. These students ranged in age from 18 to 56 years old with a mean age of 26.38 years. The sample was predominantly female (74%).

Procedures. Participants received written instructions which asked them to assume that they wanted to get to know the target person whose picture they would see at the beginning of the series of slides. The instructions then indicated that the participant would be presented with pairs of slides involving the target person. The participant was requested to choose the situation (slide) which would give him or her the *most information* about the target person; assuming that he or she could *not* interact with the target person and could only act as an unobtrusive observer in the situation. This latter point was emphasized at different points in the instructions. This limitation clearly placed the participant in the *passive strategy* information acquisition mode. Participants were asked whether they had any questions about the instructions. In no case did any participant give any indication that he or she did not understand the judgment task.

Not all possible paired comparisons were made among the seven stimuli (four social and three solitary) since Hypothesis 1 dealt only with the contrast between social and solitary observational contexts. Instead, each solitary stimulus was paired with each of the four social stimuli for a total of 12 paired comparisons. The 12 comparisons were arranged in such a way that position effects (left versus right) were controlled and no stimulus followed or preceded itself in the series (see Guilford, 1954). In the actual presentation of the stimuli, the participants first viewed a single slide of the target person in a full-face, head-on pose. This slide was shown for 15 seconds. Then, each stimulus pair was shown for a period of 15 seconds during which the participants made their judgments.

Experiment 2

Stimulus selection. Since the aim of Experiment 2 was to test the latter two hypotheses concerning social situations, only social stimuli were used. A total of eight stimuli, two from each cell of the 2 X 2 design, were employed. Two stimuli from each cell were employed to increase ecological validity.

Participants

Ninety-one students enrolled in summer courses at Northwestern University participated in Experiment 2. The mean age of the students was 25.90. The sample was predominantly female (76%).

Procedures

Participants were randomly assigned to one of the following four judging conditions: (1) context preference; (2) target similarity; (3) target involvement; and (4) target happiness. The instructions for the context preference condition were exactly the same as those used in Experiment 1. Participants in the *target similarity* condition were asked to choose the slide in each pair in which the target was most similar to the others pictured in the slide. Persons in the *target involvement* condition were asked to indicate in which of the two slides the target was most involved with the other persons. The final judgment group was asked to decide in which of the pairs the target appeared to be most happy. The judgments of the *target similarity* and the *target involvement* groups served to check the manipulations represented in the pictures and to double check the pretest results. The happiness judgments were included for exploratory reasons.

All possible pairs of the eight slides were judged for a total of 28 comparisons. The stimuli were arranged to avoid position biases. Participants were shown the same single picture of the target person as was used in Experiment 1. This stimulus again was shown for 15 seconds. Then, each of the 28 pairs was shown for a period of 15 seconds. None of the participants indicated confusion about the task and many were interested in the purpose of the project. Of course, before and during the judging, persons were not aware of the instructions that others were following. Only after the experiment

TABLE 1
Preference Distribution for Experiment 1 Comparisons

	Comparisons*											
Situation	1	2	3	4	5	6	7	8	9	10	11	12
Social	89%	73%	86%	84%	84%	70%	89%	76%	89%	73%	92%	89%
Solitary	11	27	14	16	16	30	11	24	11	27	8	11

*Each comparison based upon an n of 72 judges.

did the participants learn of the four different judgment groups.

RESULTS

Experiment 1

The results for Experiment 1 are quite straightforward. As Table 1 indicates, in all of the 12 comparisons, the stimulus in which the target person was with others (social context) was much more frequently chosen than the situation in which the target was alone (solitary context.) Of the total of 864 comparisons made by the 72 judges, 83%were made in favor of the social context alternative. Individual binominal tests were run for each of the 12 comparisons. In order to adjust for the possibility of spurious significance by repeated use of the same test, we divided the traditional .05 alpha level by a factor of 12 (.004). Even with this extremely conservative alpha level, the probability value for each comparison far exceeded the critical value of .004. The smallest difference between the two situations was comparison six in which 70% chose the social situation. The difference observed in this comparison was significant at the .0002 level. Even though the binominal test does *not* take into account the correlation between comparison groups introduced by using the same judges in each comparison, we feel that if such a correlation could be taken into account, it would serve to lower the obtained probability values even more.

Although it is amply clear that the judges in Experiment 1 overwhelmingly preferred social contexts for information acquisition, it is also the case that not all comparisons produced the same magnitude of difference. A *Cochran Q* test of Table 1 indicated that some of the social slides drew significantly more selections that others, or alternatively, that some of the alone slides drew significantly more selections than other alone slides ($Q = 39.23$, $df = 11, p < .001$). Examination of the comparisons revealed that no particular picture within the social and solitary sets consistently drew a high or low level of preference. Certain combinations of slides produced the variations shown in Table 1. Perhaps certain combinations of attributes in each picture produced the fluctuations; however, the data of Experiment 1 could not be used to explore this particular issue. In general, we can confidently assert that for this set of pictures, social situations were preferred to solitary situations as information acquisition contexts by unobtrusive observers.

It is of further interest to note that when the eight and nine-year-old sons of the senior author were presented with some of the comparisons used in Experiment 1, they both *always* chose the social situations over the solitary situations. Thus, the

TABLE 2
Obtained Scale Values and Scale Value Intercorrelations

Picture Type**		Context Preference (n = 23)	Involvement (n = 24)	Similarity (n = 22)	Happiness (n = 22)
High Involvement-High Similarity	(1)	1.24	2.28	1.37	2.02
High Involvement-High Similarity	(2)	1.06	2.14	1.77	1.82
High Involvement-Low Similarity	(3)	1.16	1.49	1.05	1.29
High Involvement-Low Similarity	(4)	1.14	1.60	.92	1.64
Low Involvement-High Similarity	(5)	.47	.91	.85	.58
Low Involvement High Similarity	(6)	.51	.91	.54	.69
Low Involvement-Low Similarity	(7)	.15	.19	.22	.07
Low Involvement-Low Similarity	(8)	.00	.00	.00	.00

*Scale values were obtained by the composite standard method (Guilford, 1954)
**Classification of picture type based upon *a priori* selection by investigators and pretest

Intercorrelations Among Dimensions*

	Context Preference	Involvement	Similarity	Happiness
Context Preference	--	.95	.86	.96
Involvement		--	.95	.98
Similarity			--	.90
Happiness				--

* All correlations based upon N=8

selection criterion so strongly manifested in the present sample may develop at a relatively early age.

Experiment 2

Manipulation checks. In order to ascertain whether

or not the involvement and the similarity dimensions were clearly represented in the eight slides, two different sets of judges did paired comparison judgments of the eight slides in terms of the degree of involvement of the target person with the other persons in the picture and the extent to which the target person was similar to the others in the slide. In addition, a third group judged the extent to which the target person appeared to be happy. Table 2 contains the scale values for each of the eight stimuli for each of the three sets of judges. In addition, the scale values for the judging group which evaluated the information of each pair of stimuli are displayed and the correlations among all four sets of judges scale values are shown. Table 2 reveals that the involvement manipulation was highly successful. The four stimuli designed to represent high involvement obtained considerably higher scale values than the four stimuli designed to represent low involvement. These results are consistent with both the investigator's selection of the stimuli and the pretest data cited earlier. It should be noted that the happiness scale values and the involvement scale values are similar and that the correlation between them is almost perfect (.98). Thus, when we refer to involvement in the present study we are talking more in terms of *intense positive affiliation* rather than intensity per se.

The scale values for the similarity dimension are a bit less consistent than those for the involvement dimension. The top two and the bottom two stimuli in terms of similarity scale values are in line with our expectations. However, it is evident that the two low similarity stimuli of the high involvement condition were judged to have greater target-other similarity than the two high similarity stimuli in the low involvement condition. Another way of looking at the similarity scale values is that high involvement tended to increase perceived similarity between the target and the others present, while low involvement tended to lead to judgments of dissimilarity between the target and the others present. In the present study, this meant that when the young female target was present with peers but not interacting with them, she was seen as *more dissimilar* to her peers than to elderly persons with whom she was actively involved. Thus, it appears that high levels of involvement can overcome other visible differences, such as age, and induce perceptions of greater similarity. While there does seem to be some reciprocal effect of similarity on judgments of involvement, such that judgments of involvement are increased by more similarity (see involvement scale values of Table 2), the effects of involvement upon judgments of similarity seem to be more pronounced.

The above results indicate that, although the involvement manipulation was very successful, it to some extent swamped the similarity manipulation as well. Of course, it should be kept in mind that when persons made judgments of involvement, similarity, and happiness, they were *not judging* the information utility of the pictures for getting to know the target person. It is possible that when persons make information utility judgments, their weighting of the similarity and involvement dimensions change in such a way that both dimensions are employed equally and in a non-interactive way to produce an information preference judgment. The only way to answer that particular question is by an internal analysis of the information preference judgments themselves. This analysis is taken up in the next section.

Context preference analyses. The data presented in this section are relevant to Hypotheses 2 and 3. For purposes of this discussion we will ignore the happiness data and observe the limitation on interpretation of the involvement dimension in view of its high correlation with the happiness dimension.

Reference to Table 2 shows that context preference seems to have been dominated by the involvement dimension. The four most preferred situations for information acquisition about the target were high involvement situations. The large impact of involvement on preference is further substantiated by the high magnitude of correlation between information preference and involvement (.95). Among the four most preferred slides, differences in similarity seem to exert less of an effect; however, among the four lowest slides in terms of context preference, the rank order of similarity scale values is identical with the rank order of context preference values. The lesser impact of similarity on preference is indicated by the correlation of .86 between similarity and preference.

While the above analyses of the context preference data are instructive, they do not directly answer the question of how or if involvement and similarity dimensions were used to arrive at context preferences. In order to ascertain whether these two dimensions were actually employed by the 23 persons who judged the information utility of the eight slides, the data for these persons were submitted to the multidimensional scaling program MDPREF (Green & Rao, 1972; Green & Wind, 1973). Usually, when one wishes to recover perceptual dimensions used by judges, one has the judges do similarity/dissimilarity judgments and then employs one of several multidimensional scaling programs such as INDSCAL, TORSCA 8, or KYST to determine what perceptual dimensions judges used to arrive at their similarity/dissimilarity decisions. In the present case, judgments were not of the similarity/dissimilarity type but were *dominance* or *preference* data. However, it is possible to recover perceptual dimensions from such dominance or preference data using MDPREF.

Since we hypothesized that two dimensions would underlie the context preference judgments, a two-dimensional solution was computed first. The plots of the eight stimuli in the two-dimensional solution are presented in Figure 1. The two-dimensional solution on the average accounted for 56% of the variance in the 23 judges' judgments. The solution accounted for 50% or more of the variance in the judgments of 14 judges and for 10 of the 23 judges, the two dimensions accounted for over 70% of the variance in each of their sets of judgments.

Moreover, Figure 1 reveals that the two dimensional solution comes fairly close to recovering the original 2 X 2 stimulus matrix. First, all of the high involvement stimuli (1,2,3, and 4) are found on the high involvement side of the coordinate system, while the low involvement contexts are found on the other side. And, all of the high similarity contexts (1,2,5, and 6) are found above the abscissa, while all of the low similarity stimuli (3,4,7, and 8) are found below the abscissa. In a rough way, the four quadrants of Figure 1 correspond to the four cells of the 2 X 2 stimulus matrix.

Figure 1 also reveals, however, that low similarity stimulus 7 of the low involvement condition was not as extremely dissimilar as one would have liked. Ideally, stimuli 7 and 8 should have been as extreme as stimuli 3 and 4 in terms of their locations in their quadrant. Also, stimulus 2 should have been closer to stimulus 1, stimulus 6 should have been closer to stimulus 5. The general picture revealed by Figure 1 suggests that the involvement dimension produced more consistent and dramatic differences than did the similarity dimension. This conclusion is consistent with the one drawn from an examination of the rank order data and the correlations between the ranks for involvement, similarity, and context preference.

The MDPREF analysis also indicated the preference of each individual judge with reference to the perceptual space generated in Figure 1. These judge vectors show the direction of preference for each judge. Figure 2 shows the placement of each judge in the two dimensional space according to the pattern of the judge's preference ratings. Figure 2 vividly indicates the extent to which the high involvement contexts were preferred to the low involvement contexts. Of the 23 judges, only two consistently preferred low involvement situations. Moreover, it is also apparent from Figure 2 that there is a slight tendency for judges to fall on the positive side of the ordinate, indicating a slight preference for similar over dissimilar contexts. These findings provide further support for the conclusion that the involvement dimension was a more consistent determinant of context preference than was the similarity dimension. It also should be noted that a three-dimensional solution for the present set of data resulted in very little change in the placement of judge vectors.

DISCUSSION

Lest the reader conclude that the present studies were merely an exercise to see whether persons could perceive the same dimensions in visual stimuli that researchers tried to build into those stimuli, let us reemphasize that the critical focus of the study was on the dimensions of *context preference*. When persons were asked to make judgments of the potential information value of the situation in Experiments 1 and 2, they were initially

FIGURE 1
Two-Dimensional Plot of Context Stimuli

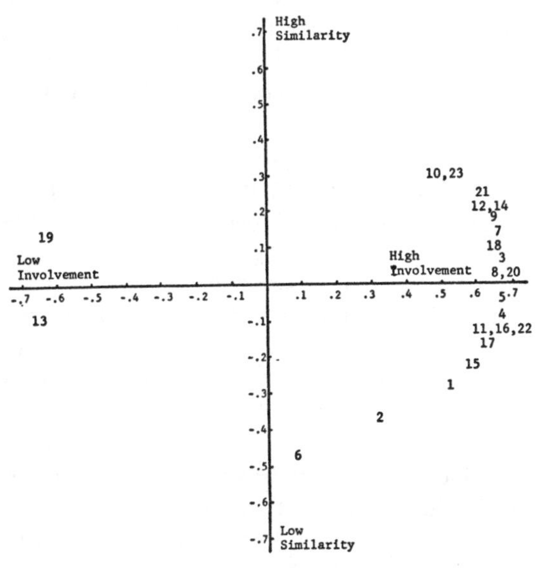

FIGURE 2
Two-Dimensional Plot of Judges' Preferences

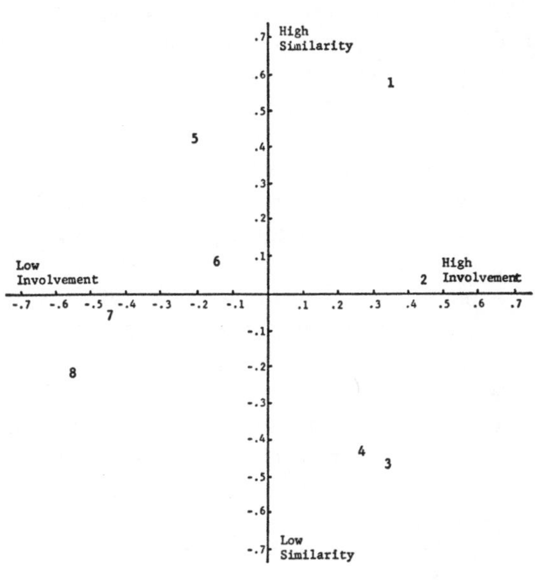

unaware that the various dimensions were systematically manipulated in the stimuli. No instructions compelled the judges to base their preference decisions on any particular attributes other than information utility. In theory, the judges could have chosen attributes other than those manipulated in the slides as bases for making their preference judgments.

In fact, however, both studies provided relatively strong support for the hypotheses. First, Experiment 1 clearly demonstrated that when persons wish to gain information about a target person whom they have never met, and they are given the choice of observing the target in solitary or in social situations, there is an overwhelming preference for social situations. Experiment 2 demonstrated that when observers wish to gain information about an unknown target, they will prefer to gather their information by observing the target actively engaged in positive interaction with the others, as opposed to observing the target person with others present but uninvolved with them. The role of similarity in context preference choice is less clear. However, the results of the MDPREF analyses suggest that judges did use the criterion of similarity between the target and the others present in the situation for determining observation context choice.

Part of the difficulty with the similarity results may be traced to the way in which similarity was manipulated in the slides. Similarity was based upon *age*. Although there is no question that in the dissimilar slides the 19-year-old target female was significantly younger than the other persons in the slide (all of whom were over 65) and that in the similar slides the 19-year-old target female was similar in age to her college student peers, it may be that age itself was not the best way in which to induce visual perceptions of similarity or dissimilarity. Perhaps racial differences or differences in socio-economic class as revealed by dress might be more powerful ways in which to operationally manipulate similarity. A second problem with the entire concept of visual similarity is simply that such attributes as perceived involvement may be at least partially confounded with similarity perceptions. This possibility has a basis in Heider's (1958) attribution analysis, since *unit relations* such as proximity and similarity are assumed to be related to *sentiment relations* such as liking. Whether similarity and involvement can ever be disentangled totally is a problem for future research.

While the involvement manipulation was seemingly more successful than the similarity manipulation, there was at least one difficulty with it. The happiness judgments clearly confirmed that the target appeared happier in high involvement situations. This means that our conclusions must be amended to indicate that contexts with *positive involvement* on the part of the target will be preferred to contexts in which the target is uninvolved. The question remains whether highly involving situations which are *negatively toned* would be as preferred as positive involvement situations. We are in the process of developing a new set of slides in which the target person will be highly involved in what appears to be an argument with the others present in the situation. Comparisons with these situations should provide an answer to the question posed above.

Besides the limitations present in the manipulations cited above, there are a few other methodological issues which might be problematic. First, it is obvious that the samples of persons used in the present studies were somewhat limited. However, since the students were from summer school classes, there was considerably more heterogeneity in age than in the usual sample of college students. A sampling problem of potentially greater import is that associated with stimulus selection. Although we attempted to include a number of different social and solitary situations in the experiments to increase ecological validity, there is little doubt that a wider sample of situations would strengthen our confidence in the findings of the present study. In Experiment 1, some persons did indicate that there might be some solitary situations that they would choose over social situations in order to find out things about the target person. One person suggested that if the target person were looking in a mirror, he would most probably choose that solitary situation to observe over a social context. Thus, a wider sampling of situations is necessary in order to further buttress the conclusions of Experiment 1. The same recommendation holds for Experiment 2.

At a theoretical level, the findings of the present study raise some interesting questions. First, it will be recalled that our derivation from social comparison theory suggested that observers would tend to prefer to observe the target person interacting with similar others rather than dissimilar others. While there was a tendency for this to occur for some judges, the effect was far from robust. These findings raise a question concerning the uncertainty-reducing value of similar others. Perhaps under certain conditions, similar others will be used as a kind of stable baseline from which to judge the target's behavior. One condition where this might occur is at the very beginning of a relationship. However, as the observer learns more about the target, he might want to observe the target with dissimilar others in order to determine the kind of response variety the target is capable of displaying. This speculation should be tested in subsequent research; since it is clear that there is considerable variation in the use of the similarity dimension as a determinant of context preference.

A second theoretical issue raised by the present study concerns the extent to which the context preference judges were actually conscious of their use of the stimulus dimensions in their decision-making. While no systematic attempt was made to collect data on this issue, persons who participated in Experiment 1 generally reported that their choices were "easy," while those in Experiment 2 reported that their decisions were "hard." It is not clear whether this means that persons in Experiment 1 were more aware of the solitary versus social attribute in their stimulus series, while those in Experiment 2 were less aware of the criterial attributes present in their stimulus series. Data germane to the awareness issue would bear directly upon some of the basic assumptions of the "rules" perspective discussed earlier. For if persons cannot accurately report why they made a particular set of preference judgments, but the perceptual dimensions that were explicitly placed in the stimuli can be recovered, as we did in the present study, then how can it be argued that man consciously makes actional choices on the basis of rules? (Unless of course any kind of regularity is defined as a rule.) When one uses the term "rule" to explain why someone has conformed consciously to a set of norms, that situation is quite different from the present one. *If* persons were generally not aware of the critical attributes subserving their choices in Experiment 2, yet we find that they made their preferences judgments on the basis of certain attribute dimensions, do we call that "rule-governed" behavior?

We noted at the beginning of the present paper that there are those who have argued for an active, choice-making conception of man as opposed to a conception of man as acted upon. It seems that the methodology of the present study meets these suggestions on both grounds. First, persons were placed in the role of actively making judgments rather than "acted upon" by the stimulus manipulations. Secondly, persons were placed in the position of explicitly making choices. But, it should also be noted that stimulus conditions were manipulated in the present study. Thus, in the study of knowledge-gaining strategies there is room for a wide variety of methodological approaches.

One final issue should be dealt with at this point. This concerns the question of whether research of the type reported here properly belongs within the domain of communication research. The answer to this question is simple and straightforward. Before persons utter words to others, they do obtain information which helps them to determine what they will say and how they will say it. In other words, persons communicate with others on the basis of what they think they know about them. Thus, the questions of how persons generate knowledge about others and how that knowledge influences their communication choices are central to any kind of interpersonal communication inquiry. The primacy of the former question seems obvious.

NOTE

1. The authors would like to express their deep appreciation to Doris Kistler, Department of Communicative Disorders, Northwestern University, and to Glen W. Clatterbuck, Department of Communication and Theatre, Miami University for their help in various phases of this research. The authors also would like to thank Daniel and Matthew Berger for taking time from their games to help us play ours.

REFERENCES

BERGER, C.R. Beyond initial interaction: Uncertainty, understanding, and the development and disintegration of interpersonal relationships. Paper presented at the annual meeting of the Speech Communication Association, San Francisco, December 1976.

BERGER, C.R. Beyond initial interaction: Uncertainty, understanding, and the development of interpersonal relationships. Unpublished paper, Department of Communication Studies, School of Speech, Northwestern University, 1977.

BERGER, C.R., GARDNER, R.R., PARKS, M.R., SCHULMAN, L., & MILLER, G.R. Interpersonal epistemology and interpersonal communication. In G. Miller (Ed.), *Explorations in interpersonal communication*. Beverly Hills, Cal.: Sage, 1976, 149-171.

BYRNE, D. *The attraction paradigm*. New York: Academic Press, 1971.

CUSHMAN, D.P. The rules perspective as a theoretical basis for the study of human communication. *Communication Quarterly*, 1977, 25, 30-45.

CUSHMAN, D.P., & WHITING, G.C. An approach to communication theory: Toward consensus on rules. *Journal of Communication*, 1972, 22, 217-238.

DELIA, J.G., CLARK, R.A., & SWITZER, D.E. Cognitive complexity and impression formation in social interaction. *Speech Monographs*, 1974, 41, 299-308.

FESTINGER, L. A theory of social comparison processes. *Human Relations*, 1954, 7, 117-140.

GERARD, H.B. Emotional uncertainty and social comparison. *Journal of Abnormal and Social Psychology*, 1963, 66, 568-573.

GIBBS-SMITH, C.H. *The art of observation*. London: Bedford Square Press, 1973.

GREEN, P.E., & RAO, V.R. *Applied multidimensional scaling*. Hinsdale, Ill.: Dryden, 1972.

GREEN, P.E., & WIND, Y. *Multiattribute decisions in marketing*. Hinsdale, Ill.: Dryden, 1973.

GUILFORD, J.P. *Psychometric methods*. New York: McGraw-Hill, 1954.

HALE, C., & DELIA, J.G. Cognitive complexity and social perspective-taking. *Communication Monographs*, 1976, 43, 195-203.

HARRÉ, R., & SECORD, P.F. *The explanation of social behavior*. Oxford: Blackwell, 1972.

HARRÉ, R. Some remarks on 'rule' as scientific concept. In T. Mischel (Ed.), *Understanding other persons*. Oxford: Blackwell, 1974, 143-184.

HEIDER, F. *The psychology of interpersonal relations*. New York: Wiley, 1958.

HUSTON, T.L. A perspective on interpersonal attraction. In T. Huston (Ed.), *Foundations of interpersonal attraction*. New York: Academic Press, 1974, 3-28.

JONES, E.E., & DAVIS, K.E. From acts to dispositions: The attribution process in person perception. In L. Berkowitz (Ed.), *Advances in experimental social psychology*, Vol. 2. New York: Academic Press, 1965, 219-266.

JONES, E.E., KANOUSE, D.E., KELLEY, H.H., NISBETT, R.E., VALINS, S., & WEINER, B. (Eds.), *Attribution: Perceiving the causes of behavior*. New Jersey: General Learning Press, 1972.

KELLEY, H.H. Attribution theory in social psychology. In D. Levine (Ed.), *Nebraska symposium on motivation*. Lincoln: University of Nebraska Press, 1967.

KELLEY, H.H. The processes of causal attribution. *American Psychologist*, 1973, 28, 107-128.

KELLY, G. *The psychology of personal constructs*. New York: Norton, 1955.

NISBETT, R.E., & WILSON, T.D. Telling more than we can know: Verbal reports on mental processes. *Psychological Review*, 1977, 84, 231-259.

PEARCE, W.B. The coordinated management of meaning: A rules-based theory of interpersonal communication. In G. Miller (Ed.), *Explorations in interpersonal communication*. Beverly Hills, Cal.: Sage, 1976, 17-35.

RABBIE, J.M. Differential preference for companionship under threat. *Journal of Abnormal and Social Psychology*, 1963, 67, 643-648.

SCHACHTER, S. *The psychology of affiliation: Experimental studies of the sources of gregariousness*. Stanford, Cal.: Stanford University Press, 1959.

SHAVER, K.G. *An introduction to attribution processes*. Cambridge: Winthrop, 1975.

TOULMIN, S.E. Rules and their relevance for understanding human behavior. In T. Mischel (Ed.), *Understanding other persons*. Oxford: Blackwell, 1974, 185-215.

WEIMER, W.B. A conceptual framework for cognitive psychology: Motor theories of the mind. In R. Shaw & J. Bransford (Eds.), *Perceiving, acting, and knowing*. Hillsdale, N.J.: Lawrence Erlbaum Associates, 1977, 267-311.

ZIMBARDO, P., & FORMICA, R. Emotional comparison and self-esteem as determinants of affiliation. *Journal of Personality*, 1963, 31, 141-162.

TRAIT PREDICTORS OF RELATIONAL CONTROL[1]

DONALD G. ELLIS
Purdue University

This study attempted to identify clusters of traits which best predicted the use of relational control style. After 125 subjects interacted in different settings, their interaction was coded using two interaction analysis systems designed to code relational control. Subjects were then assigned to control style groups. Each subject completed a battery of trait measures. Results of a discriminant analysis indicated that people who consistently use submissive control modes were apprehensive about communication but still desired social relationships. Members of the one-up group needed to express control and to structure their environment, but were very concerned about how other people perceived them.

Any activity as varied in scope as human communication has many dimensions. In our efforts to make the science of human communication a coherent system of ideas with some legitimate claim to reality, we must recognize and pay empirical attention to the multifaceted levels of human communication. Possibly the most important dimension of human communication is the definition of the relationship between interactants. Issues concerning the acquisition of self-concept through interaction, the delineation of role dependencies, and metacommunicational messages about control all bear upon relational communication. Relational communication shifts the emphasis from individuals to the relationships between individuals. As Parks (1977) cogently argues, the relational dimension of human interaction dictates how a receiver should assign meaning to a message.

The concept of "relational" communication emerged from the collective efforts of Bateson (1935, 1958) and Watzlawick, Beavin, and Jackson (1967). Their studies provided the initial impetus for what has become a persistent line of research: how communicators exchange messages and thereby define their relationships. The theoretical nature of relational communication is important to reemphasize. Relational communication is *not* a "type" of communication which is usually characteristic of a particular setting. Family interaction, for example, is not the only interaction which is relational. Members of intimate dyads are not the only people who produce relational communication. And relational communication is not simply communication which is about a relationship. Rather, relational communication is that aspect of all communication which signals how a message should be understood or interpreted with respect to the definition of the relationship. The relational level is a logical dimension of communication and complements the content level. All messages convey information (content), but in the process the communicator instructs the receiver on how he is defining their relationship. Again, this is true of all communication. Even two strangers who communicate momentarily about the weather are sending messages which have relational implications.

The control dimension of a relationship has received the brunt of theoretical and empirical attention. Very simply, when two people interact their talk suggests who will control the definition of the relationship. Messages have been classified according to when an interactant asserts relational control (one-up) and seeks to dominate the definition of the relationship, or when a message accepts control from another (one-down) and relegates the individual to a submissive position in the relationship. Recently Ericson and Rogers (1973) added the one-across mode which signals an unwillingness to accept either relational definition. Although research remains sparse, most empirical efforts concentrate on either category systems designed to classify instances of relational control (see Sluzki & Beavin, 1965; Mark, 1971; Ericson

& Rogers, 1973; Folger & Puck, 1976; Ellis, 1976), clinical settings (Bateson, Jackson, Haley, & Weakland, 1956; Watzlawick, Beavin, & Jackson, 1967), or family interaction (Lederer & Jackson, 1968; Mark, 1970; Ericson, 1972; Millar, 1973). Moreover, Ellis (1976) and Folger and Puck (1976) have observed the process of relational control in decision-making groups and physician-patient interviews, respectively.

To date, most research considers the research setting as a communicative system and then begins the process of coding relationship definitions offered by each interactant. These procedures are useful and yield important results but they overlook any input attributable to the individual. That is, it may be possible that certain individuals have a "relational style" which characterizes their communicative encounters. Some people, regardless of the setting, probably use one type of control mode to the near exclusion of the other. If the coding schemes which purport to measure relational control are adequate, then instances of relational control should correlate with certain trait measures which attempt to predict similar behavior. The purpose of this investigation was to examine the relationship between two styles of relational control (one-up and one-down, or controlling and submissive) and trait variables which best discriminate between these two styles. An understanding of this relationship should extend the conceptual boundries of relational control and provide some insights into the interaction analysis schemes used to code relational control.

This approach rests on the assumption that interpersonal behavior is the consequence of both trait and social influences. While communication scholars have often over-emphasized personality traits (see Hewes et al., 1976), the search for clusters of traits which best predict communicative behavior has produced interesting results. Correlations between any single trait and a behavior will be low, but predictability is increased when clusters of traits are examined. Moreover, Campus (1974) argues that data generated from the *a priori* classification of behaviorally consistent individuals are especially useful. The specific purpose of this study, then, was to *identify trait correlates of relational control by determining whether use of each control mode could be distinguished from the other by a unique trait profile*.

METHOD

Subjects

The original subject pool consisted of 125 undergraduates. From these subjects 56 were used in the final analysis. Following the procedures described below these 56 subjects were divided into one of two groups. Group 1 (one-up style) contained 30 subjects and Group 2 (one-down style) had 26 subjects.

Procedures

All 125 subjects interacted in two settings. First, subjects were randomly assigned to dyads and asked to talk for 15 minutes. The dyads were given no instructions regarding what to talk about or how to proceed. This allowed the interaction to develop naturally. Second, all subjects were assigned to one of 25 groups. Each group had five people and completed a task which required interaction among the members. All dyadic and group interaction was audio-recorded.

The recorded interaction was then coded using two interaction analysis systems designed to code relational control. The first category scheme, developed by Rogers and Farace (1975), refines the formulations outlined by Sluzki and Beavin (1965) and Mark (1971). The second coding scheme was developed by Ellis (1976). For a verbal statement to be considered a one-up or a one-down, it had to be reliably classified by both systems. This allowed for an extra check on the validity of the coding. Any statement which was inconsistently measured by the two coding schemes was eliminated from further analysis. Each subject, then, produced interaction from two different settings which was coded into either a one-up, one-down, or one-across category. Although the one-across function was not used in the final analysis, it was retained for the determination of style groups.

Over a period of one week, subjects responded to 16 trait measures. Although precise predictions based on sound theory was difficult, if not impossible, it is important to avoid unjustifiable data dredging. Therefore, the final list of measures were either commonly used in communication studies or could be conceptually related to one of the control modes. The following instruments were used. PRCA (CMAP) measures anxiety related to oral communication and includes items related to dyadic and group interaction (McCroskey, 1970). Communication apprehension is a determinant of numerous interaction behaviors and should characterize those subjects who rely on one-down response modes. Machiavellianism (MACH) measures the degree to which someone feels others are manipulable (Christie & Geis, 1970). The Machiavellian individual should be aware of the appropriate or desired response for a particular situation and vary his interaction accordingly. Therefore, Machiavellianism should not distinguish one group from the other. Least Preferred Coworker (LPC) taps interpersonal versus task orientation toward others (Fiedler, 1964). The low LPC or task-oriented individual will probably use dominant control messages. Unwillingness to Communicate (UWC) is a two-factor construct measuring avoidance of communication (Burgoon, 1976). The UWC scale was separated into its two factors. The first factor is approach-avoidance (UWCAA), which measures general anxiety and the likelihood of approaching and participating in communication. The second factor is labelled reward (UWCR) and estimates an individual's tendency to find communication rewarding. Similar to CMAP, this measure should predict the one-down style. The need to express Affection, Inclusion, and Control (NEA, NEI, NEC). These measure a need to express love and affection, association, and power, respectively (Shutz, 1966). NEC should be most predictive of the one-up group. An individual who always needs to express inclusion (NEI) is probably easily controlled and therefore a one-down type. The same may be true of those with needs to express love and affection. Rhetorical Sensitivity (RHETSEN) is a measure of attitude toward encoding spoken messages (Hart & Burks, 1972). The rhetorically sensitive person is very conscious of the interaction around him and usually offers socially acceptable messages. Therefore, RHETSEN should not discriminate between the groups. Dogmatism (DOG) taps openness or closedness of belief system (Troldahl & Powell, 1965) and might be typical of someone who always seeks relational control. Feelings of Inadequacy (FINAD) is concerned with self-esteem in terms of assertiveness (Skolnick & Shaw, 1970) and should represent the one-down group. Anomia (ANOMIA) taps a sense of disintegration or self-to-other alienation (Srole, 1956). Since it is correlated with UWC (Burgoon, 1976, p. 69), ANOMIA should characterize those who consistently employ submissive control styles. Intolerance For Ambiguity (MAT-50) uncovers a tendency for certain types of information to generate discomfort or threat (Norton, 1975). Someone who is highly intolerant of ambiguity should need to structure his interaction and therefore use one-up control modes. Concern for Status (COFORST) measures the value placed on symbols of status (Kaufman, 1957) and might be a stereotypical trait of one who wishes to dominate the definition of his relationships with others. Interpersonal Communication Inventory (ICI) is a general measure of interpersonal communication skills (Bienvenu, 1971) and could characterize either group. Finally, Internal-External Locus of Control (INEX) is a measure of the extent to which a person feels that rewards result from his own behavior or outside forces (Rotter, 1966). Anyone who believes that he alone is responsible for his own rewards should be in the one-up group.

Data Analysis

To determine group membership (control style) a chi-square analysis was performed on the frequencies generated by each subject. For a subject to be classified as a member of the one-up or one-down group he needed a significant chi square. Moreover, the significance must have been attributable to frequencies which significantly exceeded chance expectations.

After subjects were classified and the dependent groups were formed, a multiple discriminant analysis was computed to test the degree of separation between style groups and to calculate the contributions of each trait variable. The SPSS subprogram DISCRIMINANT was used to test for differences between group centroids. The obtained discriminant function defined the weighted combination of traits which maximized group separation.

RESULTS

A test for reliability (Guetzkow, 1950) was performed on a sample of 150 units of interaction. Reliability for the Ellis (1976) system was .80 ($p. < .05$), while coders obtained a reliability figure of .77 ($p. < .05$) for the Rogers and Farace (1975) coding system. There were 56 of the original 125 subjects that had significant chi-square analyses. The formation of the nominal groups for the dependent measure resulted in 30 subjects for the one-up group and 26 subjects for the one-down group.

The reliabilities for the independent variables were as follows: CMAP (.90); MACH (.54); LPC (.82); UWCAA (.86); UWCR (.70); NEA (.90); NEI (.92); NEC (.91); RHTSEN (.48); DOG (.55); FINAD (.48); ANOMIA (.79); MAT-50 (.83); COFORST (.75); ICI (.77); and INEX (.89). Four measures (MACH, RHTSEN, DOG, and FINAD) were considered unreliable and dropped from further analysis.

From the remaining 12 variables, 10 entered the final equation in the following manner: CMAP ($F=64.09$; $df=1,54$); LPC ($F=38.67$; $df=2,53$); NEI ($F=28.33$; $df=3,52$); UWCAA ($F=19.79$; $df=4,51$); ANOMIA ($F=17.0$; $df=5,50$); MAT-50 ($F=15.13$; $df=6,49$); COFORST ($F=13.92$; $df=7,48$); ICI ($F=11.97$; $df=8,47$); NEA ($F=10.48$; $df=9,46$); and NEC ($F=9.23$; $df=10,45$). The final variables were internal-external locus of control and the reward factor of the Unwillingness-to-Communicate scale. These variables did not significantly contribute to the separation of the two groups.

The linear combination of variables produced significant between-group differences (Wilks' Lambda=.32; $X^2=55.79$; $p. < .001$). The eigenvalue was 2.05 with a canonical correlation of .82. A set of discriminant coefficients was computed to assign subjects to either the one-up or one-down groups. Since group membership was known beforehand, it was possible to check the accuracy of the classification. This procedure produced Table 1 which reports the percentage of correct classifications. Subjects were assigned to the correct group 92.9 percent of the time $X^2=41.14$; $df=1$; $p. < .001$. These data provide evidence for the degree of dissimilarity between the two groups. The low number of misclassifications indicates considerable dissimilarity between the two groups.

However, statistical significance does not ensure a strong separation between the two groups. To test the extent of *discriminatory power*, Tatsuoka's (1970, p. 48-53) multivariate extension of omega square was computed. These data indicate strong discriminatory power ($\hat{w}^2_{multi}=.662$). That is, 66 percent of the total variability in discriminant space is attributable to group differences.

Table 2 reports the resultant discriminant coefficients. The function mean for the one-up group was -1.309 and $+1.511$ for the one-down group. Therefore, to score high and be classified as a member of the one-down group a subject was ideally high on CMAP, NEI, UWCAA, and ICI with low scores on MAT-50, ANOMIA, NEC, COFORST, LPC, and NEA. The reverse pattern is ideal for the one-up group.

DISCUSSION

The emergent trait profiles for the two groups are interesting. In many cases the initial reasoning was supported; however, in others the exact opposite resulted. The person who consistently uses one-down control functions scores high on CMAP, which means he tends to avoid interaction. Moreover, he also scores high on UWCAA. This is not surprising since the general unwillingness scale is correlated with PRCA (.53 in Burgoon, 1976; .48 in this study), and the approach-avoidance factor in particular is substantially correlated with PRCA (.69 in Burgoon, 1976; .61 in this study). The unwillingness scale, however, contains a reward factor which was fairly unreliable and did not enter the final equation. Apparently, the one-down control style avoids interaction and rarely communicates with others; however, he does not find communication unrewarding. That is, people using this control style do not necessarily see others as dishonest communicators who are inattentive or simply trying to use others (see Burgoon, 1976, p. 64).

Yet, as predicted, this individual scores high on

TABLE 1
Classification Matrix for Discriminant Predictors

Actual Group	N of Cases	Predicted Group 1	Predicted Group 2
Group 1	30	27 90.0%	3 10.0%
Group 2	26	1 3.8%	25 96.2%

92.9% Correct Classifications

TABLE 2
Standardized Discriminant Coefficients

Variable	Coefficient
CMAP	1.88
MAT-50	-.65
ANOMIA	-.45
NEI	.50
UWCAA	.39
NEC	-.38
ICI	.15
COFORST	-.46
LPC	-.64
NEA	-.12

NEI. This means that even though he characteristically avoids interaction, he desires association with others. McCroskey and Sheahan (1977) also found support for this occurrence. They reasoned that high and low apprehensives would not differ with regard to desire for social relationships. They found this to be true even though the two types had very different patterns of social relationships. The one-down style has a need to be included, but with an attendant and possibly frustrating fear of interaction.

These data also indicate that a person characterized by this control style would ideally score high on a general measure of interpersonal skills. However, Tatsuoka (1970, p. 53) suggests that when the smallest discriminant coefficient is half the size of the next highest, it is best to focus on the larger variables for a clearer interpretation. Also, to conclude that the one-down style is representative of good communication skills as measured by ICI would be misleading. The ICI contains a number of dimensions, such as patient-listening and controlled verbal behavior, which are predictable for the one-down style. And while these behaviors may be appropriate in some contexts, their consistent use should not be equated with exemplary communication.

The submissive control style scores low on intolerance for ambiguity, is not anomic, has little need for control or affection, and is not relationship-oriented or concerned with status symbols. The low score on NEA or LPC is contrary to expectations but consistent with the resultant profile. This individual simply does not tamper with his interpersonal experiences. He needs to associate with others but fears the process of communication. When a member of this group does interact with others he is quite willing to accept the submissive role in a relationship. In short, the best predictor of this control style is communication apprehension. This individual is a passive participant in communicative encounters with little concern for controlling relational definitions.

The one-up style is interpretable and interesting. This individual is composed of two clusters of traits. First, this person is intolerant of ambiguity with a considerable desire to structure his environment. He is uncomfortable and threatened when his interaction with others is unclear or unstructured. Moreover, the person tends to feel anomic and has feelings of aimlessness. However, his need to express control, which is manifest in his verbal behavior, is possibly an attempt to cope with the desire for structure in the environment. Yet members of the one-up group express a "relational orientation." They are concerned about how they appear to others; they score high on LPC which indicates a preference for quality interpersonal relations as opposed to task demands; and although the discriminant function is low, there is some need to express affection. We have, then, an individual who demands much from others but who is very concerned about the impressions others have of their relationship with him. This type of style is representative of the person who needs to control and influence others, but whose control attempts must be acceptable to others. Otherwise he will experience anxiety.

The high score of anomia is confusing. One might argue that a member of this relational style group seeks to overcome feelings of powerlessness or estrangement by constantly trying to control his relational definitions. On the other hand, Burgoon (1976) reports a significant correlation between anomia and unwillingness to communicate. Therefore, anomia should predict submissive rather than controlling behavior. In any case, the connection between anomia and relational control remains unclear. In brief, this control style is exemplified by the person who wants to be liked and respected but needs to structure his relationships with others on his own terms.

The trait profiles for each relational control style allowed subjects to be classified according to style and provided a description of characteristics unique to each style. These data also lend support for the coding systems used to code relational interaction. There is a growing collection of research centering around verbal utterances coded according to category systems measuring relational control. Future research should continue to combine actual communicative behavior with individual difference measures. Such an integration will produce accurate predictions and a clearer understanding of relational interaction.

NOTE

1. The author wishes to acknowledge Linda Skerchock and Steve Axley who assisted with the data collection.

REFERENCES

BATESON, G. Culture contact and schismogenesis. *Man*, 1935, 35, 178-183.

BATESON, G. *Naven*. Stanford, Cal.: Stanford University Press, 1958.

BATESON, G., JACKSON, D.D., HALEY, J., & WEAKLAND, J. Toward a theory of schizophrenia. *Behavioral Science*, 1956, 1, 251-264.

BIENVENU, M.J., SR. An interpersonal communication inventory. *Journal of Communication*, 1971, 21, 381-388.

BURGOON, J.K. The unwillingness-to-communicate scale: Development and validation. *Communication Monographs*, 1976, 43, 60-69.

CAMPUS, N. Transituational consistency as a dimension of personality. *Journal of Personality and Social Psychology*, 1974, 29, 593-600.

CHRISTIE, R., & GEIS, F. *Studies in Machiavellianism*. New York: Academic Press, 1970.

ELLIS, D.G. An analysis of relational communication in ongoing group systems. Unpublished doctoral dissertation, Department of Communication, University of Utah, 1976.

ELLIS, D.G. Relational interaction in decision-making groups. A paper presented at the annual meeting of the International Communication Association, Portland, Oregon, April 1976.

ERICSON, P.M., & ROGERS, L.E. New procedures for analyzing relational communication. *Family Process*, 1973, 12, 245-267.

ERICSON, P.M. Relational communication: Complementarity and symmetry and their relation to dominance-submission. Unpublished doctoral dissertation, Department of Communication, Michigan State University, 1972.

FIEDLER, F.E. A contingency model of leadership effectiveness. In L. Berkowitz (Ed.), *Advances in Experimental Social Psychology*, Vol. 1. New York: Academic Press, 1964, 149-190.

FOLGER, J., & PUCK, S. Coding relational communication: A question approach. A paper presented at the annual meeting of the International Communication Association. Portland, Oregon, April 1976.

GUETZKOW, H. Unitizing and categorizing problems in coding qualitative data. *Journal of Clinical Psychology*, 1950, 6, 47-50.

HART, R.P., & BURKS, D.M. Rhetorical sensitivity and social interaction. *Speech Monographs*, 1972, 39, 75-91.

HEWES, D.E., HAIGHT, L., & SZALAY, S.M. The utility and cross-situational consistency of measures of verbal output: An exploratory study. A paper presented at the annual meeting of the International Communication Association. Portland, Oregon, April 1976.

KAUFMAN, W.C. Status-concern scale in status, authoritarianism, and antisemitism. *American Journal of Sociology*, 1957, 62, 379-382.

LEDERER, W.J., & JACKSON, D.D. *The mirages of marriage*. New York: Norton, 1968.

MARK, R.A. Parameters of normal family communication in the dyad. Unpublished doctoral dissertation, Department of Communication, Michigan State University, 1970.

MARK, R.A. Coding communication at the relational level. *Journal of Communication*, 1971, 21, 221-232.

McCROSKEY, J.C. Measures of communication bound anxiety. *Speech Monographs*, 1970, 37, 269-277.

McCROSKEY, J.C., & SHEAHAN, M. Communication apprehension, social preference and social behavior in a college environment. A paper presented at the annual meeting of the International Communication Association, Berlin, Germany, June 1977.

MILLAR, F.E. A transactional analysis of marital communication patterns: An exploratory study. Unpublished doctoral dissertation, Department of Communication, Michigan State University, 1973.

NORTON, R.W. Measurement of ambiguity tolerance. *Journal of Personality Assessment*, 1975, 39, 607-619.

PARKS, M.R. Relational communication: Theory and research. *Human Communication Research*, 1977, 3, 372-381.

ROGERS, L.E., & FARACE, R.V. Analysis of relational

communication in dyads: New measurement procedures. *Human Communication Research*, 1975, 1, 222-239.

ROTTER, J.B. Generalized expectancies for internal versus external control of reinforcement. *Psychological Monographs*, 1966, 80 (1 whole no. 609).

SCHUTZ, W.C. *The interpersonal underworld*. Palo Alto, Cal.: Science and Behavior, 1966.

SKOLNICK, P., SHAW, J. Brief note on the reliability of the Janis and Field "Feelings of inadequacy" scale, *Psychological Reports*, 1970, 27, 732-734.

SLUZKI, C.C., & BEAVIN, J. Simetria y complementaridad: Una definicion operacional y una tipologia de parejas. *Acta Psiquicatricia Y Psiocologica de American Latina*, 1965, 2, 321-330.

SROLE, L. Social integration and certain corollaries: An exploratory study. *American Sociological Review*, 1956, 21, 709-716.

TATSUOKA, M.M. *Discriminant analysis: The study of group differences*. Champaign, Ill.: Institute for Personality and Ability Testing, 1970.

TROLDAHL, V., & POWELL, F. Short dogmatism scale. *Social Forces*, 1965, 44, 211-214.

WATZLAWICK, P., BEAVIN, J., & JACKSON, D.D. *Pragmatics of human communication*. New York: Norton, 1967.

THE SITUATIONAL USE OF PRO- AND ANTISOCIAL COMPLIANCE-GAINING STRATEGIES BY HIGH AND LOW MACHIAVELLIANS

MICHAEL E. ROLOFF
University of Kentucky

EDWIN F. BARNICOTT, JR.
University of Kentucky

This study examined the influence of Machiavellianism on a person's decision to employ compliance-gaining strategies. Subjects indicated the likelihood they would use 16 techniques in interpersonal and noninterpersonal relationships for long-term and short-term consequence rewards. The 16 techniques were placed into two categories: prosocial strategies and antisocial strategies (composed of psychological force techniques and punishing activity techniques). Machiavellianism was found to be significantly correlated with the general use of prosocial techniques and psychological force techniques. Machiavellianism had a greater influence on psychological force techniques than either prosocial or punishing activity techniques. When examining the compliance-gaining behavior in relationships, high Machiavellians were found to be more active than low Machiavellians. A significant interaction between relationships, compliance-gaining strategies and Machiavellianism was observed. When examining long-term and short-term consequences, high Machiavellians were found to be more active than low Machiavellians.

The desire to exert strong control over one's environment through communication has long been of interest to scholars and lay persons alike. The works of Machiavelli (1940) and Hitler (1943) exemplify how communication has been viewed as an instrument for political control. Yet not all control need be political; some individuals seek to dominate others in relationships. Both Berne (1964) and Shostrom (1967) analyzed the desire to manipulate others through game playing.

Christie and Geis (1970, pp. 3-4) argued for the existence of a control-oriented personality type labeled Machiavellianism. A high Machiavellian, they asserted, manifests: (1) relative lack of affect in interpersonal relationships, (2) lack of concern with conventional morality, (3) lack of gross psychopathology, and (4) low ideological commitment. Furthermore, Christie and Geis argued that the high Machiavellian would be cool (not distracted by irrelevant affect), and oriented toward self-defined goals, task success, and explicit cues and responses; the low Machiavellian, they noted, would be open (susceptible to affective involvement), and oriented toward the interaction process, getting carried away (distractibility), and implicit cues and responses.

Research has largely supported this description of the Machiavellian. High Machiavellians tend to be more suspicious in their interactions with others (Geis & Christie, 1970). Saling (1973) found that high Machiavellians tended to be inaccurate in their perceptions of others and that in interactions for rewards, high Machiavellians tended to view competitors as being more dissimilar to themselves than was really the case. Low Machiavellians, Saling found, were more accurate in their perceptions of similarity between themselves and others. Christie and Lehmann (1970) factor-analyzed the responses of college students to Machiavellianism scales and three factors emerged: affirmative negativism, disbelief in people, and duplicity. The duplicity factor provides insight into the principles that guide the high Machiavellian's communication. Christie and Geis (1970) observed that high Machiavellians were skillful bargainers, achieving success in every experimental situation, whereas low Machiavellians were less likely to attain success in their bargaining. Geis, Christie, and Nelson (1970) allowed subjects to play the role of experimenter and deceive other subjects into taking a personality test. High Machiavellians manipulated their subjects more often and in ways judged to be more creative. Exline, Thibaut, Rickey, and Gumpert (1970) observed the cheating behavior of Machiavellians, and found that high Machiavellians would deny their cheating longer and would do so when looking their accuser in the eye longer than low Machiavellians.

The high Machiavellians' desire to deceive and win should have profound impact on the communication strategies they employ to control their environment. Specifically, we would expect the degree of Machiavellianism to have a great effect on the likelihood that a person will attempt to control another through communication. Bochner, Di Salvio, and Jonas (1972) observed that high Machiavellians contributed more in significant phases of group discussion. The high Machiavellians tended to influence the group decision-making by saturating the group with task-relevant information. Bochner and Bochner (1972) found greater acceptance of others' views in low Machiavellian groups. Low Machiavellian groups tended to focus on socioemotional means, such as acknowledgment, agreement, and disagreement to fulfill the group task. By contrast, high Machiavellian groups tended to rely on task-oriented information as a means of completing the group task. Hacker and Gaitz (1970) found that high Machiavellians participated more in discussion, asked for more information, and more often provided their own orientation. Rim (1966) reported that high Machiavellians exerted more personal control over their environment than low Machiavellians; Braginsky (1966) reported the same behavior among children.

Solar and Bruehl (1971) observed that a great deal of the high Machiavellian's desire to actively control his or her environment stems from a paranoia that the external environment controls him or her. They found that subjects ranking high in external locus of control also rank high in Machiavellianism. Furthermore, Harris (1967) reported that high Machiavellians tended to perceive others with whom they interact as being more negative than did low Machiavellians. Solar and Bruehl (1971) summarized: "Finally, since they (high Machiavellians) do not see themselves as capable of obtaining by themselves those reinforcements required for survival, they may feel compelled to manipulate others to obtain those reinforcements. In coping with external expectancies, Machiavellian attitudes therefore appear an almost necessary defense" (p. 1081).

We would predict an increased likelihood of attempts to control another person by high Machiavellians. Furthermore, we would predict that certain types of strategies would be more likely to be employed by high Machiavellians to gain rewards. Several studies have focused on the types of compliance-gaining techniques a person may use to secure rewards from the environment. Marwell and Schmitt (1967) analyzed the responses of undergraduate students to questions concerning the likelihood they would use 16 compliance-gaining techniques in 4 situations. They were concerned with how specific compliance-gaining techniques would cluster into broader strategies. They viewed a strategy as a set of techniques which a person would consider him or herself likely to use. The responses were summed across the 4 situations and an oblique factor analysis done. Five factors emerged: rewarding activity, punishing activity, expertise, activation of personal comitment, and activation of impersonal comitment. These oblique factors were then correlated and produced 2 second-order factors: tendency to use socially acceptable techniques, and tendency to use socially unacceptable techniques.

Roloff (1976) argued that by examining the basic thrust of a communication strategy, one can predict the influence of the strategy on interpersonal relationships. He theorized that strategies can be categorized as prosocial if the strategy attempts to gain relational rewards by explaining one's position and attitudes, and as antisocial if the strategy attempts to gain relational rewards through force or deception.

Given the distinct nature of the high Machiavellian, we would predict that, as Machiavellianism increases, the general use of all compliance-gaining strategies will increase. However, Machiavellianism should have a greater influence on the use of antisocial strategies than prosocial strategies.

Moreover, it would be interesting to examine how Machiavellians behave in certain specific situations. Since the high Machiavellian is described as being emotionally uninvolved in relationships, we might expect that he or she would not view the type of relationship as a key determinant of the type of strategy to be employed. For example, Miller and Steinberg (1975) distinguished between interpersonal and noninterpersonal relationships based upon the type of information shared between the relational partners. Interpersonal relationships involve the sharing of psychological information and are therefore rare and highly valued. Noninterpersonal relationships involve the sharing of information based on groups and cultural membership; such information is more readily shared, making noninterpersonal relationships more common and less valued.

We would expect high Machiavellians to rely on prosocial strategies, more so than antisocial strategies, in both types of relationships, because prosocial strategies involve less risk—people normally do not want to comply with others who deceive or threaten them (Brehm, 1966; Deutsch, 1969). But we would also expect high Machiavellians not to show much variation in their use of prosocial and antisocial strategies across relationships. On the other hand, low Machiavellians are very involved in their relationships, and particularly with people with whom they have an interpersonal relationship. We would also expect low Machiavellians to be more likely to employ prosocial strategies than antisocial strategies. However, we would further expect low Machiavellians to be significantly more likely to employ prosocial strategies in interpersonal relationships and significantly more likely to employ antisocial strategies in noninterpersonal relationships than in interpersonal relationships.

Another situational cue that should interact with Machiavellianism deals with the nature of the reward that two people are communicating about. Miller, Boster, Roloff, and Seibold (1977) investigated the use of Marwell and Schmitt's (1967) compliance-gaining techniques in situations where the object of the interaction had long or short-term consequences. For example, rewards having short-term consequences could be interactions between two people about where they should go on a date; rewards with long-term consequences could be interactions between two people about whether to move to a distant part of the country. Given the importance of long-term decisions, we would predict high Machiavellians to attempt to persuade another to comply with their wishes to a greater extent in long-term consequence situations than in short-term consequence situations. However, we would also expect the high Machiavellian to show caution in what strategies he or she chooses to employ. Specifically, high Machiavellians would be significantly more likely to employ prosocial strategies in long-term situations than short-term situations, and significantly more likely to employ antisocial strategies in short-term consequence situations than in long-term consequence situations. Low Machiavellians should be less concerned about the nature of the reward. They should show less situational variation in their use of complaince-gaining strategies because of the nature of the reward.

PROCEDURES

Sample

Data were collected from 124 undergraduate students enrolled in introductory communication classes at a large southern university. Analysis of demographic data provided by respondents revealed a sex ratio of 43% female and 56% male (1% declined to answer). The model age for the sample was 18 years (median = 20 years; mean = 20 years). All respondents were fulltime students: 50% of the sample were freshmen, 27% sophomores, 15% juniors, and 8% seniors.

Questionnaire Construction

A questionnaire was constructed which consisted of 3 sets of self-administered items and appropriate instructions for completing each set. First, a set of items developed by Miller, Boster, Roloff, and Seibold (1977) were administered. These items elicited respondents' judgments on their likelihood of using 16 compliance-gaining techniques in 4 situations. Table 1 contains the list of the 16 compliance-gaining techniques. Each respondent indicated how likely he or she would use

TABLE 1
Sixteen Compliance-Gaining Techniques

	Technique	Description
1.	Promise	If you comply, I will reward you.
2.	Threat	If you do not comply, I will punish you.
3.	Expertise (Positive)	If you comply, you will be rewarded because of the "nature of things."
4.	Expertise (Negative)	If you do not comply, you will be punished because of the "nature of things."
5.	Liking	Actor is friendly and helpful to get target in "good frame of mind" so that he will comply with request.
6.	Pre-giving	Actor rewards target before requesting compliance.
7.	Aversive Stimulation	Actor continuously punishes target making cessation contingent on compliance.
8.	Debt	You owe me compliance because of past favors.
9.	Moral Appeal	You are immoral if you do not comply.
10.	Self-Feeling (Positive)	You will feel better about yourself if you comply.
11.	Self-Feeling (Negative)	You will feel worse about yourself if you do not comply.
12.	Altercasting (Positive)	A person with "good" qualities would comply.
13.	Altercasting (Negative)	You will feel worse about yourself if you do not comply.
14.	Altruism	I need your compliance very badly, so do it for me.
15.	Esteem (Positive)	People you value will think better of you if you comply.
16.	Esteem (Negative)	People you value will think worse of you if you do not comply.

each technique on an 8-point scale ranging from extremely likely (8) to extremely unlikely (1).

The 4 situations were based upon the Miller and Steinberg (1975) distinction between interpersonal and noninterpersonal relationships and the Miller, Boster, Roloff and Seibold (1977) distinction between rewards with long and short-term consequences. The 4 situations were: interpersonal relationship with long-term consequences, noninterpersonal relationship with long-term consequences, interpersonal relationship with short-term consequences, and noninterpersonal relationship with short-term consequences. A complete description of each situation may be found in Miller, Boster, Roloff, and Seibold (p. 43).

The second set of items were demographic ques-

TABLE 2
Factor Loadings: Principal Components Factor Analysis with Varimax Rotation, Sixteen General Compliance-Gaining Techniques

	Factor 1	Factor 2	Factor 3
Self-Feeling (Negative)	.784	.259	.269
Esteem (Negative)	.704	.301	.351
Moral Appeal	.678	.095	-.009
Altercasting (Negative)	.668	.087	.123
Esteem (Positive)	.571	.514	.225
Debt	.540	.449	.302
Liking	.160	.635	-.039
Promise	-.099	.604	.057
Self-Feeling (Positive)	.426	.597	.179
Expertise (Positive)	.380	.506	.135
Altruism	.311	.476	.047
Expertise (Negative)	.328	.449	.295
Altercasting (Positive)	.422	.425	.218
Pre-Giving	.057	.331	-.036
Threat	.144	.000	.861
Aversive Stimulation	.428	.028	.450
Eigenvalue	5.91	1.21	.70
% of Variance	75.7	15.4	8.9

tions which have already been reported.

The third set of items consisted of a personality battery. Responses were made to the Mach IV scale. The 20 items utilized a 6-point scale ranging from strongly agree (6) to strongly disagree (1). The sum of the 20 items represented the respondent's degree of Machiavellianism. Christie and Geis (1970) argued that a constant of +20 be added to every total score (p. 27). The potential range was from 40 to 140. Robinson and Shaver (1973, pp. 590-591) report an average item-total correlation of .38 and split-half reliability of .79.

Preliminary Analysis

To determine the prosocial and antisocial compliance-gaining strategies, the responses made to each technique were summed across the 4 situations. This provided a general measure of the likelihood that each technique would be used, regardless of the situation. These 16 general measures were then factor analyzed with a varimax rotation. Table 2 contains the results of the analysis.

Three factors emerged. Although, some heavy cross-loadings appeared, factor 1 is an antisocial cluster entitled psychological force. It consists of negative self-feeling, negative esteem, moral appeal, negative altercasting, positive esteem, and debt. With the exception of positive esteem, all the items implied some negative consequence that will occur to the target person's self-concept unless he or she complies with the request. Factor 2 is the prosocial factor consisting of liking, promise, positive self-feeling, positive expertise, altruism, negative expertise, positive altercasting, and pregiving. With the exception of negative expertise, all the items implied some positive outcome that will occur if the target person complies with the request. In order to maintain content purity in the factors, positive esteem was inserted into the prosocial factor and negative expertise became part of the psychological force factor. In both cases, heavy cross-loadings existed between the two factors. Factor 3 is also an antisocial cluster and is entitled punishing activity; it consists of threat and aversive stimulation.

After the factor analysis, the dependent measures were formed. Each measure was formed in 3 steps. First, the likelihood that a given technique would be used was summed across the appropriate situations. For the general use, the technique was summed across all 4 situations. For use in interpersonal relationships, each technique was summed across interpersonal relationship, long-term consequences and interpersonal relationship, short-term consequences. Likewise for use in noninterpersonal relationships, each technique was summed across the 2 noninterpersonal situations; for long-term consequences, each technique was summed across the 2 long-term situations, and for short-term consequences, each technique was summed across the 2 short-term situations.

Second, the scores (step #1) of each technique having the highest factor loading on a single factor were summed. This sum was then divided by the number of techniques used to form it. (Psychological force was divided by 8, prosocial was divided by 6, and punishing activity was divided by 2.) Thus, the dependent measures consisted of the average use of psychological force techniques, prosocial techniques, and punishing activity techniques. The average use for the 3 general strategies ranged from 8 to 32; the average use for the strategies in interpersonal and noninterpersonal relationships and long and short-term consequences ranged from 2 to 16. Third, the internal reliability of each dependent measure was computed using coefficient alpha (Nunnally, 1967). Table 3 contains the alphas for all the measures. Overall, the alphas are high (13 of the 15 are greater than .60). As expected the lowest reliabilities were obtained for the two item scales (punishing activity techniques).

An examination of the Machiavellianism scores indicates that the mean value was 81.1 and standard deviation was 9.5. The values ranged from 53 to 106. Since these values are somewhat biased toward low Machiavellians, quartile deviations were used in some analyses. Subjects having scores higher than 87 were categorized as high Machiavellians and subjects having scores lower than 75 were categorized as low Machiavellians.

TABLE 3
Coefficient Alphas for Three Compliance-Gaining Strategies in Relationships Situation, Consequent Situation, and General Use

	Pro-Social Techniques	Psychological Force Techniques	Punishing Activity Techniques
Interpersonal Relationship	.717	.784	.680
Noninterpersonal Relationship	.725	.847	.619
Long-Term Consequences	.750	.799	.411
Short-Term Consequences	.685	.827	.523
General Use	.789	.878	.633

RESULTS

Two sets of procedures were employed in testing the hypotheses. For the hypotheses dealing with the relationship between Machiavellianism and the general use of compliance-gaining strategies, Pearson correlation coefficients were computed followed by a test for the difference between dependent correlations (Bruning & Kintz, 1968). For the hypotheses dealing with the proposed interactions between Machiavellianism, situations and compliance-gaining strategies, a three factor analysis of variance with repeated measures on the last two factors was computed (Winer, 1971). Planned comparisons were made utilizing one-tailed tests since direction was hypothesized. The analysis of Machiavellianism in the ANOVA utilized quartile splits forming high and low Machiavellians. It was expected that the influence of Machiavellianism on general use could be observed using the entire distribution of Machiavellianism. However, the interactions would be best observed in the outer segments of the distribution.

The Pearson correlations were computed between Machiavellianism and each of the three general measures of compliance-gaining strategies. Two of the three correlations were significant although they varied in magnitude. The correlation between Machiavellianism and the general use of prosocial techniques was .2131 ($p < .013$). The correlation between Machiavellianism and the general use of psychological force techniques was .3443 ($p < .001$) and the general use of punishing activity techniques was .1015 ($p < .145$). The tests for the difference between dependent correlations indicated that, as predicted, the correlation between Machiavellianism and psychological force techniques was significantly greater than the correlation between Machiavellianism and prosocial techniques ($t = 1.66$, $p < .05$). However, two unpredicted results occurred. First, the correlation between Machiavellianism and prosocial techniques, and Machiavellianism and punishing activity techniques did not differ significantly. Since punishing activity techniques was categorized as antisocial, we expected that Machiavellianism would have a stronger influence on its use than on prosocial techniques. The opposite was found in the correlations although the correlations did not differ significantly. Second, we thought that the correlations between Machiavellianism and psychological force techniques, and Machiavellianism and punishing activity techniques should be similar since both are antisocial. However, we found that the correlation between Machiavellianism and psychological force was significantly greater than the correlation between Machiavellianism and punishing activity (t = 2.57, p < .01). Thus, Machiavellianism influenced only one dimension of antisocial activity.

The analysis of variance for the interpersonal and noninterpersonal relationships is presented in Table 4. Significant main effects are observed for compliance-gaining activity in the relationships (F = 16.98, p < .001) and the use of the three compliance-gaining strategies (F = 100.96, p < .001). However, the two variables did not interact significantly.

Of particular importance was a main effect for Machiavellianism. The planned comparisons indicate that in interpersonal relationships there is no significant difference in the likelihood that high and low Machiavellians will use prosocial techniques. However, the comparisons indicate that in interpersonal relationships, high Machiavellians are significantly more likely to employ psychological force techniques than low Machiavellians (t = −2.36, p < .025) and high Machiavellians are significantly more likely to employ punishing activity techniques than low Machiavellians (t = −1.66, p < .05). When examining noninterpersonal relationships, we observed that high Machiavellians are significantly more likely to employ prosocial techniques than low Machiavellians (t = −2.37, p < .025) and significantly more likely to employ psychological force techniques than low Machiavellians (t = −2.61, p < .025). However, we observed no difference between the likelihood that high or low Machiavellians would use punishing activity techniques.

The predicted interaction between Machiavellianism and compliance-gaining strategies only approached significance (F = 2.38, p < .10). However, the predicted interaction between Machiavellianism, relationships, and compliance-gaining strategies did reach significance (F = 4.81, p < .01).

The planned comparisons indicate that both high and low Machiavellians are significantly more likely to employ prosocial techniques than either psychological force techniques (high Machiavellians: t = 10.57, p < .01; low Machiavellians: t = 12.01, p < .01) or punishing activity techniques (high Machiavellians: t = 6.26, p < .001; low Machiavellians: t = 7.30, p < .01) in interpersonal relationships. Furthermore, there is no significant difference between the use of psychological force techniques or punishing activity techniques for either high or low Machiavellians in interpersonal relationships.

When examining noninterpersonal relationships, we observed that both high and low Machiavellians are significantly more likely to employ prosocial techniques than either psychological force techniques (high Machiavellians t = 7.14, p < .001; low Machiavellians: t = 9.01, p < .01) or punishing activity techniques (high Machiavellians: t = 5.74, p < .01; low Machiavellians: t = 2.87, p < .01). However, when examining the use of psychological force techniques and punishing activity techniques we find that while no difference exists in their use by high Machiavellians, low Machiavellians are significantly more likely to use punishing activity techniques than psychological force techniques (t = −2.87, p < .01).

When comparing the use of a given strategy by high and low Machiavellians in both relationships, we observe that for low Machiavellians, the use of prosocial and punishing activities do not differ significantly, regardless of the situation, while they are significantly more likely to employ punishing activity techniques in noninterpersonal rather than interpersonal relationships. High Machiavellians, on the other hand, differ in their use of two strategies: high Machiavellians are significantly more likely to employ prosocial techniques in noninterpersonal relationships than in interpersonal relationships (t = −3.08, p < .01) and they are significantly more likely to employ psychological force techniques in noninterpersonal relationships than in interpersonal relationships (t =

TABLE 4
Analysis of Variance: Machiavellianism x Relationship x Compliance-Gaining Strategies

Category Means

	Interpersonal Relationships			Noninterpersonal Relationships		
	Pro-Social	Psych. Force	Pun. Act	Pro-Social	Psych. Force	Pun. Act
Low Mach	9.59	6.19	6.37	9.59	6.82	8.19
High Mach	9.93	7.19	7.33	10.70	8.22	7.70

Source of Variation	SS	df	MS	F
Total	1789.59	323		
Between Subjects	544.43	53		
Machiavellianism (A)	42.25	1	42.25	4.37*
Error (a)	502.17	52		
Within Subjects	1245.17	270		
Relationships (B)	48.22	1	48.22	16.98**
A x B	.15	1	.15	<1
Error (b)	147.46	52	2.84	
Compliance-Gaining Strategies	531.06	2	265.53	100.96**
A x C	12.52	2	6.26	2.38 (p < .10)
Error (c)	273.09	104	2.63	
B x C	6.84	2	3.42	1.72
A x B x C	19.14	2	9.57	4.81**
Error (bc)	206.69	104	1.99	

*$p < .05$

**$p < .01$

−3.31, $p < .01$). High Machiavellians do not differ significantly in their use of punishing activity techniques across the relationships. It would appear that the interaction may be explained primarily by the tendency of low Machiavellians to be more likely to employ punishing activity techniques in noninterpersonal relationships (predicted) and the tendency of high Machiavellians to be more likely to employ prosocial and psychological force techniques in noninterpersonal relationships (not predicted).

The analysis of the long and short-term consequence situations is presented in Table 5. We observed a significant main effect for compliance-gaining strategies ($F = 89.19$, $p < .001$) but not for consequences. We also observed a significant interaction for compliance-gaining strategies by consequence situation ($F = 15.79$, $p < .001$) and the expected main effect for Machiavellianism ($F = 5.32$, $p < .05$). An examination of the category means indicates that the difference is in the predicted direction in all but one case. High Machiavellians are more active in their use of all strategies and in all situations, except for punishing activities, in long-term consequence situations. However, an analysis of the planned comparison reveals that only two comparisons are significantly different: high Machiavellians are significantly more likely to employ psychological force techniques in long-term consequence situations ($t = -3.25$, $p < .01$) and in short-term consequence situations ($t = -2.39$, $p < .025$). The use of prosocial techniques in both interpersonal ($t = -1.56$, $p < .10$) and noninterpersonal relationships ($t = -1.62$, $p < .10$) approach significance.

The predicted interaction between Machiavellianism and compliance-gaining strategies approaches significance ($F = 2.84$, $p < .07$). The interaction between Machiavellianism and compliance-gaining strategies and consequence situations was not significant.

DISCUSSION

Two important issues are raised in this research. First, the research provides some verification for Christie and Geis's (1970) description of Machiavellians, but also some surprising invalidations. As predicted, high Machiavellians are significantly more active in compliance-gaining situations than low Machiavellians. Most importantly, Machiavellianism has a stronger influence on the use of psychological force techniques than either prosocial or punishing activity techniques. We initially predicted that Machiavellians would influence both antisocial strategies equally, but this was not confirmed. While high Machiavellians are oriented toward psychological punishing activity, physical aggression (real or implied through threats) is not highly influenced by high Machiavellianism. It may well be the case that high Machiavellians find threats and aversive stimulation too obvious. Their deceptive nature may lead them to be more covert.

When examining the individual situations, the results are mixed. Again, we find that high Machiavellians are significantly more active in relationships and consequences than low Machiavellians. However, the predicted coolness in interpersonal relationships seemingly did not affect compliance-gaining activity. High Machiavellians varied their use of prosocial techniques and psychological force techniques sc that they used them more often in noninterpersonal relationships. This does indicate that high Machiavellians are not partial to those with whom they have interpersonal relationships. They were not more likely to employ prosocial techniques with people with whom they have a close relationship. However, high Machiavellians were not likely to use the psychological force techniques equally in both relationships. It is possible that high Machiavellians viewed noninterpersonal relationships as situations where they can manipulate someone who has little information about them. In other words, the risk would be less than deceiving someone who knows them well.

Another surprise was the low Machiavellians tendency to use both prosocial and psychological force techniques equally in all relationships. It may be the case that low Machiavellians feel compassion for all people, hence they treat all people equally in terms of their strategies. However, their differential use of punishing activity does not fit this description. If low Machiavellians show com-

TABLE 5
Analysis of Variance: Machiavellianism x Consequences x Compliance-Gaining Strategies

Category Means

	Short-term Consequences			Long-term Consequences		
	Pro-Social	Psych. Force	Pun. Act	Pro-Social	Psych. Force	Pun. Act
Low Mach	9.04	6.59	7.67	10.00	6.26	6.96
High Mach	9.74	7.70	8.33	10.74	7.85	6.85

Source of Variation	SS	df	MS	F
Total	1696.18	323		
Between Subjects	536.01	53		
Machiavellianism (A)	49.78	1	49.78	5.32*
Error (a)	486.23	52	9.35	
Within Subjects	1160.17	270		
Consequences (B)	.37	1	.37	1
A x B	.15	1	.15	1
Error (b)	106.97	52	2.06	
Compliance-Gaining Strategies	494.10	2	247.05	89.19**
A x C	15.73	2	7.87	2.84 ($p < .07$)
Error (c)	287.89	104	2.77	
B x C	58.10	2	29.05	15.79**
A x B x C	5.51	2	2.76	1.50
Error (bc)	191.40	104	1.84	

*$p < .05$
**$p < .01$

passion towards others, why do they exhibit increased use of punishing activity in noninterpersonal relationships where they do not know the person well? It may be that they view this strategy as a mode of influence never to be used in interpersonal relationships and used only in noninterpersonal relationships after prosocial activity has failed.

The lack of support in the long and short-term consequence situation is troublesome. While high Machiavellians were again more active in compliance-gaining activity (particularly psychological force techniques in both situations) they did not vary their activity significantly. The solution to this problem may stem from the stimulus situation. Since there was no significant main effect for the consequence situations, it is possible that people generally do not distinguish between the two descriptions.

The second important issue which is raised in this study is the general influence of Machiavellianism in compliance-gaining activity. By examining the amount of variance explained by the main effects and interaction in each of the analyses, we can make an estimate of their influence on the intention to use the strategies. While we admit that the compliance-gaining activity measured here deals with the intention to use each strategy in the situations, Fishbein and Ajzen (1975, pp. 368-381) argued that behavioral intention should normally predict actual behavior, barring situational and time constraints.

The squared Pearson correlations indicate that the amount of variance explained varied with the type of compliance-gaining technique. At best, Machiavellianism explains 12% of the variance in psychological force techniques. The amount of variance explained in the general use of prosocial techniques was 5% and 1% for punishing activity techniques.

When examining the eta squared statistic, we can determine the amount of variance explained in ANOVA (Nunnally, 1967, pp. 133-136). In relationships, the main effects and interactions have a total eta of .61 and eta squared of 37%. However, the influence of the main effect of Machiavellianism explained only 2.4% of the variance. None of the interactions explain as much variance. The main effect of compliance-gaining strategies explained 30% of the variance.

When examining eta squared for consequence situations, we find a similar pattern. The total amount of variance explained was 36%. The amount of variance explained by the Machiavellianism main effect was 3%. Again, the interactions explained little variance. The greatest amount of variance explained again resulted from the compliance-gaining strategies main effect (30%).

This would indicate that, while Machiavellianism can predict the general direction of a person's behavior, it is not the key factor in determining the person's specific behavior in these compliance-gaining situations. Other factors should be investigated along with Machiavellianism.

REFERENCES

BERNE, E. *Games people play*. New York: Grove Press, 1964.

BOCHNER, A.P., & BOCHNER, B. A multivariate investigation of Machiavellianism and task structure in four-man groups. *Speech Monographs*, 1972, 4, 277-285.

BOCHNER, A.P., DISALVIO, V., & JONAS, T. How they control groups structure: A WORDS computerized content analysis of Machiavellian message strategies. Paper presented to the annual meeting of the Speech Communication Association, Chicago, 1972.

BRAGINSKY, D.D. Machiavellianism and manipulative interpersonal behavior in children: Two explorative studies. Unpublished doctoral dissertation, Department of Psychology, University of Connecticut, 1966.

BREHM, J.W. *A theory of psychological reactance*. New York: Academic Press, 1966.

BRUNING, J.L., & KINTZ, B.L. *Computational handbook of statistics*. Glenview: Scott, Foresman, 1968.

CHRISTIE, R., & GEIS, F.L. *Studies in Machiavellianism*. New York: Academic Press, 1970.

CHRISTIE, R., & LEHMANN, S. The structure of Machiavellian orientations. In R. Christie and F.L. Geis (Eds.), *Studies in Machiavellianism*. New York: Academic Press, 1970, 359-387.

DEUTSCH, M. Conflicts: Productive and destructive. *Journal of Social Issues*, 1969, 25, 7-41.

EXLINE, R., THIBAUT, J., HICKEY, C., & GUMPERT, P. Visual interaction in relation to Machiavellianism and an unethical act. In R. Christie and F.L. Geis (Eds.), *Studies in Machiavellianism*. New York: Academic Press, 1970.

FISHBEIN, M., & AJZEN, I. *Belief, attitude, intention and behavior: An introduction to theory and research*. Reading: Addison-Wesley, 1975.

GEIS, F.L., & CHRISTIE, R. Overview of experimental research. In R. Christie and F.L. Geis (Eds.), *Studies in Machiavellianism*. New York: Academic Press, 1970, 285-313.

GEIS, F.L., CHRISTIE, R., & NELSON, C. In search of the Machiavel. In R. Christie and F.L. Geis (Eds.), *Studies in Machiavellianism.* New York: Academic Press, 1970, 77-95.

HACKER, S., & GAITZ, C.M., Interaction and performance correlates of Machiavellianism. *Sociological Quarterly*, 1970, 2, 94-102.

HARRIS, T. Machiavellianism, judgment, independence and attitudes toward teammate in a cooperative judgment task. Unpublished doctoral dissertation, Department of Psychology, Columbia University, 1966.

HITLER, A. *Mein kampf.* Boston: Houghton Mifflin, 1943.

MACHIAVELLI, N. *The prince. The discourses.* New York: Modern Library, 1940.

MARWELL, G., & SCHMITT, D.R., Dimensions of compliance-gaining behavior: An empirical analysis. *Sociometry*, 1967, 30, 350-364.

MILLER, G., BOSTER, F., ROLOFF, M., & SEIBOLD, D. Compliance-gaining message strategies: A typology and some findings concerning effects of situational differences. *Communication Monographs*, 1977, 44, 37-51.

MILLER, G., & STEINBERG, M. *Between people: A new analysis of interpersonal communication*, Palo Alto: Science Research Associates, 1975.

NUNNALLY, J., *Psychometric methods*, New York: McGraw-Hill, 1967.

RIM, Y. Machiavellianism and decisions involving risks. *British Journal of Social and Clinical Psychology*, 1966, 5, 36-50.

ROBINSON, J., & SHAVER, P. *Measures of social psychological attitudes.* Ann Arbor, Mich.: Institute for Social Research, 1973.

ROLOFF, M.E. Communication strategies, relationships and relational change. In G. Miller (Ed.), *Explorations in interpersonal communication.* Beverly Hills, Cal.: Sage, 1976, 173-196.

SALING, N. An investigation of the effects of competition and cooperation on the accuracy and congruency of communication in cooriented dyads. Unpublished masters thesis, Department of Speech, University of Kentucky, 1973.

SHOSTROM, E.L. *Man the manipulator: The inner journey from manipulation to actualization.* Nashville: Abingdon, 1967.

SOLAR, D., & BRUEHL, D. Machiavellianism and locus of control: Two conceptions of interpersonal power. *Psychological Reports*, 1971, 29, 1079-1082.

WINER, B.J. *Statistical principles in experimental design.* New York: McGraw-Hill, 1971.

MASS COMMUNICATION

Theory and Research: An Overview

Selected Studies

MASS COMMUNICATION THEORY AND RESEARCH: AN OVERVIEW

JOSEPH M. FOLEY
Ohio State University

The field of mass communication research and theory continues to grow at a rapid rate. A bibliography of all the books and articles in this field which have been published since the last edition of *Communication Yearbook* would have to include several thousand titles. There have been far too many important studies to begin to discuss all of them here. Rather than trying to summarize the many fine recent studies, this overview will present an analysis of the current status of this rapidly developing research field.

Each year, the research in mass media becomes more voluminous and more diverse. As more and more researchers conduct mass communication studies, the field of mass communication research grows in scope and complexity. The more we study, the more new questions we raise. The more new questions we raise, the more we are led to question whether the old questions were really important. Most of our studies show that the processes of mass communication are vastly more complex than we hypothesized initially. This complexity becomes a challenge to our ingenuity, for it appears that our present research methods are barely able to penetrate the surface of the processes underlying mass communication.

This makes mass communication research a dynamic and exciting area, and an area where there is a sense of urgency for many of our research investigations. It is clear that the mass media have had a major impact on individuals and social systems around the world. It is less clear exactly what the nature of this impact has been, but we are finding disturbing evidence that suggests some of the impacts of the media are harmful.

Mass communication research can also be a frustrating field. This frustration comes from two primary causes. First, the frustration arises because the processes of mass communication are so complex that it is not at all clear whether we are making any meaningful progress toward a better understanding of them. In fact, we continue to be far from agreement about which processes and variables need to be studied. Second, the frustration comes from the increasing use of mass communication research findings as "evidence" for various points of view in the continuing controversies over the setting of social policies for the mass media. The many scholarly qualifications we place on our studies often seem to get lost as our findings become rhetorical ammunition for individuals promoting particular mass communication policies. These frustrations have provided a healthy stimulus for much mass communication research.

MASS COMMUNICATION AS A RESEARCH FIELD

In examining the present status of mass communication as a research field, it is helpful to posit three characteristics which are associated with an established scientific research field: (1) self identification, a group of people who identify themselves as researchers in the field; (2) range of problems, a well defined set of problems which are generally agreed to be germaine for the field; (3) methodology, a set of methodologies which are generally agreed to be appropriate for studying these problems. These three characteristics focus on the sociological dimensions of a research field—in particular, on the characteristics of the field as they are perceived by those who identify with it.

A field could also be defined in terms of the logical and philosophic unity of its research investigations and theoretic formulations. This type of definition is not appropriate for the field of mass communication as its exists today. The field is marked by an excitement and optimism which grows from the diversity of views which are held by the many people who identify themselves as mass communication researchers. The field is still searching for a clearly defined conceptual unity.

Self Identification

The number of people identifying themselves as mass communication researchers has grown rapidly in the past several years. There is no precise way to measure this growth, but the following two measures provide an indication.

Dissertation Abstracts first used "Mass Communications" as a category for grouping abstracts in 1967. Each year, there has been substantial growth in the number of dissertations grouped under this heading. During the year from July 1969 to June 1970, there were 38 dissertations under this heading; during the year from July 1976 to June 1977, there were 101 dissertations under this heading. This increase represents a growth of about 15% per year throughout this 8-year period.

The *Comprehensive Dissertation Index 1861-1972* requires 72 pages to present its keywork listings for "Mass Communications" dissertations from that 113-year period. The three annual supplements for 1973, 1974, and 1975 require a total of 43 pages for the keywork listings for dissertations from just those 3 years. If this trend continues for the 1976 and 1977 volumes, the number of pages required for listings for the last 5 years (1973-1977) will be greater than the number of pages required for all the years prior to 1973. This suggests that there may have been as many mass communication dissertations from 1973 to 1977 as there were during all the years before 1973.

Since both these indexes classify dissertations based on the description given in the dissertation title and abstract, they provide a guide to the rapidly growing number of people who are identifying their work as mass communication research. This is a dramatic influx of new people into the field. As the authors of these recent dissertations continue their careers, they will play a decisive role in shaping the development of mass communication research. In sheer number these new people will have a massive impact; the immediate thrust of this impact will be further enhanced by the fact that many researchers are more productive during the early years of their careers than they are during their later years. Much of the research published in the next few years will be conducted by people who have recently begun their research careers; this may well result in some significant new research directions.

This rapidly growing number of mass communication dissertations is representative of the growth in mass communication research in general. The implications of working in a research field in which the amount of knowledge may be doubling in five years are staggering. Simply trying to keep up with the field places the researcher in an impossible dilemma. If one really takes the time to keep up to date, there is little time left for conducting research. If one ignores the mass of new material and concentrates on individual research projects, one quickly looses touch with the current state of the field.

One of the solutions to this dilemma has been for researchers to become increasingly specialized, focusing on a limited range of mass communication topics and not trying to be eclectic. This trend toward specialization will certainly continue. It is becoming increasingly difficult to develop the broad perspective needed to analyze the most important problems. At this time, it is not at all clear which specializations will prove to be the most fruitful. Looking at the diversity of some recent research articles illustrates the broad range of topics being studied.

Range of Problems

The range of problems included in recent mass communication is extremely wide. Perhaps the most studied area is the influences of media content on the audience. Recent examples include the Zanna, Darley, and Klosson (1976) study of television news viewers; the Payne (1976) study of the relationship between television drug advertising and drug abuse among the young; the Weigel (1976) study of audience conventionality and U.S. television; and the Tuchman (1976) analysis of media values. There have also been many studies of the ways the audience uses the media; one recent example is the Dotan and Cohen (1976) study of family use of media in Israel. There have been a number of studies of the processes within media organizations—for example, the Anderson (1977) study of social responsibility theory—and there have been increasingly sophisticated analyses of the economic structure of the media, for example, the Beebe (1977) study of program choice in U.S. television markets.

As the studies mentioned above suggest, much of the research has looked at the medium of television. But mass communication research certainly is not limited to television. Two recent studies suggest the diversity of topics being investigated. Sanches (1977) studied the stories in Japanese comic books. Pool (1977) provides an outstanding anthology of analyses of the impact of a precursor of the electronic mass media—the telephone.

One of the problems faced by mass communication researchers is the growing evidence that all these topics (and a host of others) are closely interrelated. They all need to be studied together—a task that is impossible for any single researcher or team of researchers. Most of the articles in mass communication are written as though the author expects that the work will contribute to some as yet unseen unified field. The authors hope that each finding will eventually become an important link. In time, we will know which types of study are most fruitful. Today we are very far from knowing which insights ultimately will be important; most of them appear to offer great (but unrealized) potential.

Since we are faced with a situation where everything appears to be interrelated with everything else, we need to strive to identify some broad simplifying assumptions which we can use as a basis for developing a sound theoretic framework for the study of mass communication. Because there is so much research to be done and so many variables to study, we often fail to go beyond our immediate research findings to analyze their importance in light of various theoretic frameworks.

Mass communication research appears to be in the luxurious position where almost any variable which is studied leads to the discovery of relationships which are interesting in themselves, and which appear to have important implications for the as yet to emerge general theory of mass communication. Since there is no shortage of variables which produce significant findings, we need to challenge ourselves to go beyond these findings to seek deeper relationships.

Faced with the diverse range of topics which comprise the field of mass communication research, it is tempting to specialize into narrow groups of researchers who all study the same narrow set of topics. To some extent this is necessary, but we should not lose sight of the insights a diversity of approaches can provide. At present, the field of mass communication is not characterized by having a well-defined set of problems which researchers generally agree are germaine. Rather, there are almost as many conceptions of the most important problems as there are researchers in the field.

Methodologies

Not surprisingly, mass communication research is using a rapidly increasing variety of research methods. In recent years the field has followed the general trend in the social sciences to become increasingly mathematical in its analyses. This has made much of the research increasingly obscure for most readers.

A few examples will suffice to illustrate this diversity of method. Krull, Watt, and Lichty (1977) used an information theory based analysis to develop entropy measures of television program complexity. Rossiter and Robertson (1976) used canonical analysis to study the relationship between a child's developmental level and understanding of television advertising. Spence (1977) used an econometric analysis to study the market structures of pay television and advertiser supported television.

It is clear that the field of mass communication research cannot be characterized by its use of a narrow set of research methods. Its researchers are as eclectic in their choice of research method as they are in their choice of problems for investigation. It is impossible for any individual to thoroughly grasp the many methodological approaches which are being used. We each must restrict our reading to the research which has used a method with which we are familiar.

Information Overload

This review of the characteristics of the field of mass communication research indicates that the researchers and theorists are faced with a classic information overload situation. The number of people working in the field is so large that it is impossible to keep track of the work being done by more than a very small percentage of them. The range of problems is so broad that it is impossible to keep up with them. The methodologies being used are so diverse that an individual can grasp only a relatively small set of them.

In addition to these problems, the sheer volume of work being published is gargantuan. For the year July 1976 to June 1977, McKerns and Delahave (1976, 1977) included nearly 800 articles in their mass communication bibliography. Just reading mass communication articles would be a full-time job. Mass communication researchers must develop strategies to cope with this information overload.

As we know from the research studies of people faced with information overload, the classic response is to selectively attend to only a small part of the information presented. In this way an individual is able to reduce the overload to manageable proportions. As we do this, we often assume that we are attending to the most part of the available information. In mass communication, we are faced with an impossible amount of information but we have no clear cut criteria for selecting the most important part. We often use a variety of relatively nonsystematic and counterproductive strategies.

To some extent, we cope with the information overload along the lines which have been discussed above. We focus our attention on a limited topic; we restrict ourselves to analyzing research which has used a familiar methodology; and we look at the research produced by a relatively small group of people.

We also tend to use a series of less well-articulated methods for coping with the information overload. Some of these methods can have undesirable consequences. In reviewing research, we often limit ourselves to a few "favorite" journals for our basic literature review. Because important mass communication articles are published in so many journals, a thorough literature search is very time consuming to conduct. Even after potentially important articles are located, we may find the journal is not available in any accessable library. With the rapidly rising costs of journal publication, it appears that this problem will become more serious in the future. Libraries, as well as individual researchers, are unable to keep up with the mass of important studies being published.

Researchers in the United States have a particular problem of failing to recognize the work which is being done in other parts of the world. Because there is so much work being published by people in U.S. universities and research institutions, it is easy to lose sight of the work being done in other countries by being swamped with an overload of domestic information.

If mass communication is to develop into a truly significant research field, we must find ways to increase the exchange of information and ideas among researchers throughout the world. We need to try to bridge the barriers of language and distance, even though we will thereby increase the problem of information overload. This process is beginning as individual researchers actively seek to relate their studies to similar work being done in other countries. Mass communication researchers and theorists need to work actively to develop a global awareness of the research being done in their areas.

Mass Communication as a Research Field

It seems paradoxical that so many people are choosing to identify their research with a field which is not clearly defined. It appears that as more and more people identify their research as focusing on mass communication, the field becomes more and more diverse. Both the range of problems studied and the range of methodologies used to study these problems are growing rapidly. There is little indication that the field of mass communication research is becoming more well-defined. Rather, its heterogeneity appears to be increasing almost at an exponential rate.

This makes the field of mass communication appear deficient when it is compared with research in fields which (at least from a distance) appear to be more well-defined. Fields such as physics, economics, biology, and astronomy appear to be better focused. Rather than dwelling on this type of comparison, it is more appropriate to recognize the field of mass communication as a field which is challenging the traditionally accepted ways of organizing knowledge. It is in the company of many other new fields which challenge the conventional disciplines. Examples of such fields include environmental studies and space science, which both cut across broad areas of the physical and social sciences. These fields are characterized by the attempt to study a broad set of phenomena by using a wide range of techniques. Mass communication is a field of this type. Its success will be based on its ability to integrate a variety of approaches which come from many different traditional disciplines. This breadth is a challenge and even a mandate for mass communication research and theory.

POLICY DIMENSIONS OF MASS COMMUNICATION RESEARCH

There are a variety of pressing social problems which add a sense of urgency to many mass communication studies. The field has developed an impressive body of evidence which shows that the mass media have an important impact on almost every aspect of daily life. This impact is felt throughout the world. Increasingly, policy makers and concerned citizens are asking for research information which will aid them in dealing with important problems of national and international mass media policy.

Often, the people asking for policy guidance have little understanding of the necessity for building well-organized research and theory. Policy makers around the world are faced with the need to make immediate decisions about the mass media. Because they must make the decisions *now*, they have little patience with the researcher's plea that the processes of mass communication are extremely complicated and that years of additional study are needed. Many researchers have been moved by this challenge and have directed their efforts in areas which have clear policy implications.

Media and Children

In the past year, the study of media and children has been an extremely important area of policy related research. The potential impact that mass media may have on the young is a concern in all societies. If aspects of this impact are harmful, researchers are obligated to suggest ways to reduce the harm. If aspects of this impact are beneficial, researchers are obligated to suggest ways of increasing the benefits. The studies mentioned below provide an indication of the range of studies being conducted in this area. Wackman and Wartella (1977) provide an excellent overview of the present status of research and theory on the ways children respond to television. One of the trends in this research area is increased interest in the ways children perceive the mass media. Hawkins (1977) and Reeves and Greenberg (1977) are good examples of different research analyses of this area.

In the U.S., there is continuing concern with the impact television advertising is having on children. The articles in the *Journal of Communication* symposium on "How TV Sells Children" (1977, 27, 100-157) provide a good review of much of this research. Rosengren, et al. (1976) discuss Swedish adolescents' responses to television and develop three scales for measuring this response. Himmelweit and Swift (1976) conducted a follow-up of the children from the Nuffield study. They found that adolescent media taste was a good predictor of adult media use 20 years later. Rosenblatt (1976) provides an interesting analysis of the models television presents for children growing up in the United States. Murray (1976) reviews the research on children and television from a number of cultures in his discussion of the Australian experience.

The need for guidance in dealing with policy issues, such as controlling, or not controlling the kind of television available to the young, adds an additional dimension of concern for media researchers. In addition to the need to conduct research which is theoretically sound and scientifically rigorous, media researchers are also asked to make their research extremely practical.

CONCLUSION

The field of mass communication research and theory is growing rapidly, both in quantity and in quality. Each of our studies provides new evidence for the complexity of the processes of mass communication. The rapidly emerging new mass communication technologies will add to this complexity.

Lefèvre (1977) provides a good summary of the current status of the research.

> Telecommunications, electronic techniques and audio-visual media will . . . have an increasing role to play in the economic and social activities of the societies of tomorrow, whether these are developed or developing. Their influence in every sector of activity is potentially very important.
>
> The current state of research nevertheless does not make it possible either to quantify this importance with any accuracy or to forecast how these forms of technology can be expected to make their influence particularly felt. The information we possess and the knowledge we have acquired concerning other systems nevertheless allow us to see how important and urgent it is to carry out thorough studies in this field. They further emphasize the need for accurate planning of communications and telecommunications as an integral part of national planning. (p. 237)

Research and theory in mass communication is making significant progress. The increased understanding of the complexities of mass communication processes is leading to an increased recognition of the importance of improving the conceptualization of the immense number of variables which are known to be important.

REFERENCES

ANDERSON, H. An empirical investigation of what social responsibility theory means. *Journalism Quarterly*, 1977, 34, 33-39.

BEEBE, J. Institutional structure and program choices in television markets. *Quarterly Journal of Economics*, 1977, 91, 15-37.

DOTAN, J., & COHEN, A. Mass media use in the family during war and peace: Israel 1973-1974. *Communication Research*, 1976, 3, 393-402.

HAWKINS, R. The dimensional structure of children's perceptions of television reality. *Communication Research*, 1977, 4, 299-320.

HIMMELWEIT, H., & SWIFT, B. Continuities and discontinuities in media usage and taste: A longitudinal study. *Journal of Social Issues*, 1976, 32, 133-156.

KRULL, R., WATT, J., & LICHTY, L. Entropy and structure: Two measures of complexity in television programs. *Communication Research*, 1977, 4, 61-68.

LEFÈVRE, B. The impact of electronic communications on town and regional planning. *Impact of Science on Society*, 1977, 27, 227-238.

Mc KERNS, J., & DELAHAYE, A. Articles on mass communication in U.S. and foreign journals. *Journalism Quarterly*, 1976, 53, 778-787; 1977, 54, 209-221, 428-440, 647-659.

MURRAY, J. Beyond entertainment: Television's effects on children and youth. *Australian Psychologist*, 1976, 11, 291-300.

PAYNE, D. Relationship between television advertising and drug abuse among youth: Fancy and fact, *Journal of Drug Education*, 1976, 6, 215-220.

POOL, I. de SOLA. *The social impact of the telephone*. Cambridge, Mass.: M.I.T. Press, 1977.

REEVES, B., & GREENBERG, B. Children's perceptions of television characters. *Human Communication Research*, 1977, 3, 113-127.

ROSENBLATT, R. Growing up on television. *Daedalus*, 1976, 105, 61-68.

ROSENGREN, K., WINDAHL, S., HAKANSSON, P., & JOHNSSON-SMARAGDI, U. Adolescents' TV relations: Three scales. *Communication Research*, 1976, 3, 347-366.

ROSSITER, J., & ROBERTSON, T. Canonical analysis of developmental, social, and experiential factors in children's comprehension of television advertising. *Journal of Genetic Psychology*, 1976, 129, 317-327.

SANCHES, M. Contemporary Japanese youth: Mass media communication. *Youth & Society*, 1977, 8, 389-416.

SPENCE, M. Television programming, monopolistic competition, and welfare. *Quarterly Journal of Economics*, 1977, 91, 103-126.

TUCHMAN, G. Mass media values. *Society*, 1976, 14, 51-54.

WACKMAN, D., & WARTELLA, E. A review of cognitive development theory and research and the implication for research on children's responses to television. *Communication Research*, 1977, 4, 203-224.

WEIGEL, R. American television and conventionality. *Journal of Psychology*, 1976, 94, 253-255.

ZANNA, M., DARLEY, J., & KLOSSON, E. How television news viewers deal with facts that contradict their beliefs: Consistency and attribution analysis. *Journal of Applied Social Psychology*, 1976, 6, 159-176.

TIME SERIES ANALYSIS OF ALTERNATIVE MEDIA EFFECTS THEORIES[1]

JAMES H. WATT, JR.
University of Connecticut

SJEF A. VAN DEN BERG
University of Connecticut

The necessary conditions for discriminating among direct and indirect theories of mass communication, null effects, agenda-setting, reverse effects, and reverse agenda-setting theories are outlined. The conditions are tested on a nine-month series data set. Media performance is represented by daily measurements of mass media assertions and story prominence about the Concorde supersonic aircraft trial in Washington, D.C. Behavioral response is represented by daily levels of Concorde noise complaints. Time series cross-correlation analysis indicates the minimal conditions for support are present only for direct and indirect effects, agenda-setting and reverse agenda-setting theories. Interpretation of the time lag information between presumed cause and effect further limits the plausible theories to one: direct effects.

INTRODUCTION

Theory in mass-communication effects can be grouped into several general categories. Each category implies a somewhat different process occurring in audiences.

The *direct effects* perspective assumes that mass media teach audiences behaviors and attitudes directly. This perspective includes three major theories: the hypodermic theory, the one-step flow theory, and observational learning theory.

The *hypodermic theory* of mass communication effects was prevalent among early researchers into the political effects of communication (see Katz, 1963, for a discussion of these early assumptions). This simple stimulus-response theory merely assumed that exposure to mass communication would affect audiences in a way consistent with media content.

The *one-step flow* model is an elaboration of the hypodermic theory. It introduces audience selectivity processes between the media stimulus and the audience response (Troldahl, 1966; Rogers, 1973). Thus the media are not assumed to have the same effect on all audience members. The effect is presumed modified by selective exposure or attention, selective perception, and selective retention of content on the part of the audience.

Observational learning (Bandura & Walters, 1963; Liebert, Neale & Davidson, 1973) has been used primarily in the context of children's response to televised violence, but it applies to the learning of any mass medium content. In essence, it adds a number of message content attributes to the one-step flow model. It postulates that learning from media involves stages of exposure to the message, retention of its content (usually expressed as recall of behaviors exhibited by a model), and some acceptance phase which consists of inhibition or disinhibition toward the class of actions represented in the message content. Each of these stages are affected by message attributes such as the status of the source, the closeness to the audience member in age and sex of the source, the vicarious rewards and punishments depicted in the message, and so forth.

The *indirect effects* perspective introduces the interpersonal communication process into the study of mass media effects. The major theories in this class are the two-step flow and the multi-step flow. The two-step flow (Lazarsfeld, et al., 1944; Rogers, 1962) states that information from the mass media flows first to opinion leaders, who then pass on the information or opinions via interpersonal channels to others. The mass media content may be modified by its relay through these opinion leaders, but it ultimately affects large numbers of persons.

The multi-step flow (Rogers, 1973) is an elaboration of this theory to accomodate many relays of information through interpersonal channels. It thus allows a more complex communication network, and removes the mass medium message even further from its ultimate effect on an audience member.

The commonality shared by all these theories is that of a cause-effect relationship between mass media content and the effect of this content. To be sure, the effect can be greatly reduced or modified by the intervening processes of selectivity and interpersonal communication, but *some* effect as a result of exposure to mass communication is predicted by all the theories.

Another class of theories disputes this cause-effect conceptualization. These can be called the *null-effects* theories, although this may be overstating the case. Klapper (1960) proposed that mass media be considered only one of many causes of change in audience behavior and/or attitudes, and further that it was generally subordinate to other, nonmediated communication causes of such changes. Klapper's view of media effects includes most of the processes contained in the one-step flow model and the multi-step flow model, but considers the nonmedia processes to be dominant over the mass communication processes. A similar theory of limited effects in political communication has found some support (Becker, McCombs, & McLeod, 1975; Blumler & McLeod, 1974). In oversimplified terms, this theory contends that, because of selectivity processes, only persons already holding similar views to those advocated in the message will be affected by the message.

A somewhat different approach to mass communication effects is provided by the *agenda-setting* theories (McCombs & Shaw, 1972; Cohen, 1963). This theory posits that the mass media set the public agenda for discussion, not by persuading the audience of the correctness of particular attitudes or behaviors, but by teaching them what is important and what is not.

Agenda-setting differs from the direct and indirect effects theories in predicting that the media will affect the saliency of issues perceived by the audience, rather than affecting audience behavior or attitude. Thus the amount of exposure of an audience member to messages about a topic should affect the perceived importance of the topic by the audience, and by implication, should result in behavioral action related to the topic.

There are two other classes of theory which are little considered. These can be considered mirror-image forms of the direct effects theories and the agenda-setting theories. The *reverse effects* class would state that the media content responds to public opinion or behavior, and thus the causal direction is opposite of that postulated by the direct effects theories. Reverse effects are most often mentioned in discussions of whether the mass media create audience taste, or merely reflect it (Bogart, 1969).

Reverse agenda setting would predict that the prominence of stories about a topic in the mass media is produced by the salience of the issue to the audience, that is, the public sets the agenda, and the mass media reflect this decision in their coverage. This proposition has received very little attention from mass media researchers.

Determining the Correct Theory

In general, it is difficult to distinguish between direct and indirect effects, while it is fairly easy to distinguish between these two classes of theory and null effects and agenda setting. Considering indirect and direct effects as a single class, the following findings should be observed in order to choose a particular paradigm.

Indirect and direct effects. Exposure to media content (advocated behavioral actions or attitudes) should predict subsequent audience behavior or attitudes. Note that the media content measure must include both an evaluation of advocated positions or behaviors, and either the amount of exposure reported by audience members or a measure of the message prominence, which should predict aggregate exposure.

Null effects. Media content should not predict subsequent behaviors or attitudes.

Agenda setting. The prominence of media content in a particular area should predict the salience of the issue observed in the audience, and by implication should predict the *amount* of, but not the *direction* of subsequent behaviors. The assumption here is that more salient issues are acted on more frequently, although the particular nature of the action cannot be predicted.

Reverse effects. Audience behavior or attitudes should predict later media coverage. Again, both advocated behaviors and attitudes and message prominence should be predicted.

Reverse agenda setting. The salience of a topic to the audience should predict message prominences, but not the behaviors or attitudes advocated in the messages.

Information for Theory Discrimination

The tests between theories just outlined imply that a researcher should obtain the following minimum information:

1. A measure of exposure to mass media messages by the audience. This exposure measure can be either direct, as by asking media-use recall questions on a questionnaire or by using a media-use diary, or it can be indirect, by measuring the prominence of mass media messages and making the reasonable assumption that more prominent messages reach more audience members.
2. A measure of mass media content which taps the content attribute central to the effect being tested. For example, if community attitudes on a topic were being studied, this might be a positive-negative evaluative dimension. For information-gain studies, it might be number of factual statements presented. This analysis will be called *assertions analysis* for the remainder of this paper.
3. A measure of audience attitude or behavior. Typical studies might use attitude shift on particular issues, knowledge gain, shifts in frequency of advocated behaviors, and so forth.
4. A measure of the salience or importance of a topic perceived by the audience. Again, this may be directly assessed by questioning audience members or inferred by observing audience behavior.
5. All the above measures must be taken over time, at as many time points as possible, as the time order of variables is necessary to discriminate between some theories, for example, direct effects and reverse effects.

METHOD

The research described in the remainder of this paper involves a test of mass media effects in a community controversy. The five requirements just outlined were operationalized and used in an attempt to discriminate which general class of media effects theory was the best description of reality, at least for the community and topic studied.

The Problem

In May 1976, the British and French national airlines were given permission to begin a 16-month test period of Concorde supersonic transport flights into Dulles International Airport in Washington, D.C. Concurrent with this test period, the Federal Aviation Administration conducted noise and pollution monitoring of Concorde operations. As part of this monitoring, a noise complaint telephone number was publicized. Calls to this number were coded into type of complaint categories, and the number of calls received each day were tabulated. Monitoring of mass media coverage of the controversy was also initiated at this time. The research reported here draws from these two data bases.

The Media Measures

In the Washington area, the *Washington Post* and evening news broadcasts on WTOP, a local television station, were monitored. WTOP had the highest rated local news programs in May 1976, when monitoring began. Concorde-related statements on NBC, CBS, and ABC national network newscasts were also tabulated. Data for the first 253 days of the trial period, from May 24, 1976 to January 31, 1977, are used in this analysis. All media, with the exception of WTOP, were recorded on a daily basis. WTOP newscasts were monitored in four separate three-week periods at approximately equal intervals, giving data for 91 of the 253 days.

Prominence coding. This measure was constructed to fulfill the need for a measure of probable exposure to the story being coded (for direct effects tests) and as a measure of the importance assigned the story by news organizations (for agenda setting tests).

Two operational formulae for prominence were developed, one for television news stories and one for print media stories. The formula for television prominence follows:

$$TVPROM = ((TPT-TNS)/TPT) + (DS/150) + (.5*TSG/DS) + (TFV/DS)$$

TPT is total news program time in seconds.
TNS is time from beginning of newscast to start of story in seconds.
DS is the duration of the Concorde story in seconds.
TSG is the time of appearance of stills and graphics during the story in seconds.
TFV is the time of appearance of film and videotape during the story in seconds.

Stories nearer the beginning or lead position of the newscast score higher in prominence, as do longer stories, stories which use still graphic aids, and stories which use film or videotape.

The 150 divider for the duration of story term represents an arbitrary estimate for the duration in seconds of an average news story. Actual average for Concorde stories was about 120 seconds. The .5 weight for stills and graphics is an arbitrary weight reflecting the lesser visual impact of still presentations, as compared to film or videotape.

The formula for print prominence follows.

$$PRPROM = .1\,(SW)\,[(CW \cdot CI) + (ZG)]\,[e^{-\{(PG-1) + (NS-1)\}/10}]$$

SW is a Section Weight (for newspapers, the front section is given a weight of 1.5, other sections 1.0).
CW is the column width used for the story in inches.
CI is the length of the story in column inches.
G is the area of graphics, cartoons, and headlines, in square inches.
PG is the page number.
NS is the number of sections in the particular issue of the newspaper from which the story was obtained.

This formula represents a number of common sense decisions about the nature of a prominent story in the print medium. That is:

1. A story in the front section of a newspaper is more prominent than a story in later sections.

2. The more text, as measured by the square area devoted to the text (column inches times column width), the more prominent is the story.

3. The more square area devoted to graphics, the more prominent the story. The graphics serve as an attention-getting device, and so serve to make the story more prominent to the reader. An arbitrary weight of 2 is assigned graphics, reflecting the assumption that they are more important, per square area, than is story text.

4. The further back in a section the story appears, the less prominent it is in a newspaper.

5. The more sections a newspaper has, the less prominent is any story appearing near the front of any single section. For example, a story appearing near the front of a section in a newspaper with three sections is more prominent to a reader than the same story appearing near the front of a section of a newspaper which has seven sections.

6. The prominence of any story decreases more rapidly as it goes from the front page of a section to the second page, slightly less rapidly as it goes from the second to the third, less yet from third to fourth, and so forth. This is the reason for the exponential (natural logarithm based) decay term in the prominence formula.

7. The front page of a section in a newspaper with a small number of sections is a more prominent position than is the front page of a section in a newspaper with a large number of sections, as there is less competition for attention by front page stories in a newspaper with fewer sections. The adjustment for the number of sections in a newspaper in the exponential decay term reflects this assumption.

The constants in the equation are scale factors to make the range of the print prominence scores comparable to those for television, so that the two can be summed in an overall prominence index.

Both prominence measures were tested for face validity by coding the first month's Concorde stories with the operational definitions, and comparing the ranking of story prominence to prior subjective rankings of story prominence made by two persons. When split into high, medium, and low prominence categories, the operational measures gave virtually the same results as the subjective rankings.

Assertions analysis. Assertions are defined as a simple declaration of fact or opinion. Any sentence spoken or printed may contain many assertions, if it is grammatically complex, or it might contain no assertions relevant to the topic being coded.

Assertions in each Concorde story were coded into one of 38 content categories. Full descriptions of these categories and their development can be found in Watt (1977). Intercoder reliability tests gave a 92% agreement between redundant coders of 20 stories on the number of assertions in each story, thus validating the ability of coders to recognize the basic unit of analysis.

Each assertion was also coded as being either positive, negative, or neutral toward the Concorde. These terms were not defined, but left to the interpretation of the coder. Mean agreement by coders of the same material on positive assertions was 92%, on neutral assertions was 88%, and on negative assertions was 89%. It was concluded that coders could agree reasonably well on positive, negative, and neutral assertions when they were classified into the content categories.

Only seven of the categories which were related to Concorde noise were used in this study, as the audience effect measurement of interest was noise complaints. The seven categories were:

1. Noise physiological effects
2. Noise measurement by FAA
3. Noise measurement by other groups
4. Noise measurement, general
5. Subjective reactions to noise
6. Concorde noise compared to other planes
7. Other mentions of Concorde noise

Strength-direction index. In order to test the direct/indirect effects model and the reverse effects model, it is necessary to combine the prominence of a story with its assertions score to create an index of potential effects. A highly negative, but nonprominent story might be expected to have less effect than a mildly negative, but highly prominent story. The formula for the index used follows:

STRDIR = (NPOS − NNEG)*PROM

NPOS is the number of positive assertions in the category for the story.

NNEG is the number of negative assertions in the category for the story.

PROM is the prominence score for the story.

The strength-direction index for a single story is computed by summing the strength-direction values for each of the seven assertions categories used.

Each story in the monitored media which mentioned the Concorde was coded by at least three different coders. The assertions value for each evaluation level of each content category was determined by computing the mean for all coders of the same story. Over the 253-day period, 76 Concorde stories were located and coded; 49 were print stories and 27 appeared on television.

The Audience Measure

The measure of audience behavior used in the tests of the models was the number of complaints received each day by the FAA noise complaint telephone service. This measure is the audience response in tests of direct/indirect theories, and the causal agent in reverse effects tests. The measure also is taken to represent perceived salience of the noise issue in the audience, by assuming that more complaints represent a higher salience condition. This implied salience can then be used in tests of agenda setting and reverse agenda setting models.

Time Series Analysis

As was outlined previously in the discussion of the requirements of theory discrimination, both the media measurements and the audience measurements were taken over a number of time periods (253 daily time points). A time series analysis utilizing autocorrelations and cross-correlations was carried out to provide significance tests for observed relationships. (See Krull & Husson, 1977, for a discussion of time series analysis.)

Autocorrelations. An autocorrelation is the correlation of a variable with itself at different time intervals. It is thus a measure of consistency over time of a particular variable. A variable which increased and decreased slowly over long periods (for example, seven days of increase, followed by seven days of decrease) would show high autocorrelations for adjacent days, as the level of the variable on any given day would be predictive of the level the next day.

Autocorrelations can be computed for differing time intervals, in order to determine how long this predictive ability persists. In the above example, the autocorrelations for a one-day lag (the ability of today's value to predict tomorrow's) would be high, the autocorrelation of a two-day lag somewhat lower, and so forth, until the autocorrelation reached non-significance, probably somewhere around seven days. This would indicate that one could predict future values of the variable for about six days, given the current value. This interval represents the consistency window of the variable.

Autocorrelations are not directly used to test the alternative models, but they are indicative of the reasonableness of postulated cause-effect relationships. It is reasonable to expect that a cause and its effect have similar consistency windows; that is, a cause which persists for two days should be linked to an effect which persists for a similar time. It is possible for a cause to produce a longer lasting effect (e.g., brief exposure to a poison may produce long-lasting effects), but it is not plausible for the reverse to occur (e.g., the effects of a poison to wear off before exposure to the poison is terminated).

The computational formula (Fuller, 1976) for autocorrelation follows:

$$\text{RAUTO} = \frac{\sum_{i=1}^{n-j+1} (A_i - \text{MEAN})(A_{i+j-1} - \text{MEAN})}{(N-L+1)(\text{VAR})}$$

N is the number of time points.
L is the time lag interval (from 1 to some maximum).
MEAN is the arithmetic mean of the variable taken over all time points.
VAR is the variance of the variable taken over all time points.
SIGMA is the standard summation function.

Cross-correlations. Cross-correlation of two-time series variables is similar to simple Pearsonian correlation. The major difference is that the values for one variable are correlated with the values for the other variable a fixed number of time intervals away. For example, the values of an *X* variable will be paired with values of a *Y* variable one time interval away, to produce one cross-correlation, then recomputed with *X* and a value of *Y* two time intervals away to produce another cross-correlation, and so forth. The results can be interpreted as the ability of current values of *X* to predict subsequent values of *Y* at differing lengths of time in the future. Cross-correlations with a zero time interval difference are simple Pearson correlations, computed with values of the same two variables at a number of time points.

Cross-correlations can be used to infer causal direction. If *X* significantly predicts values of *Y* at later time intervals, and *Y* does not predict *X* at later times, one would infer that at least the temporal sequence implied in the statement "*X* causes *Y*" was satisfied, if not the other requirements of causality.

The time interval between the *X* and later values of *Y* for the highest cross-correlation provides information about the length of time required for the possible cause to produce the effect. If one observed increasingly larger cross-correlations as one computed time intervals of 1, 2, and 3, then observed decreasing cross-correlations with larger time intervals, one would conclude that three time intervals was the point at which the effect was strongest.

This ability to test causal sequence and to estimate effect time makes cross-correlations ideal for contrasting models in which the causal direction is in question, such as between direct effects and reverse effects theories. The computational formula for the cross-correlation at each time interval (x at time t) correlated with Y at $t+L$ follows:

$$\text{X CORR} = \frac{\sum_{i=1}^{N-L+1} (Y_i - \text{MEAN}_y)(X_{i+l-1} - \text{MEAN}_x)}{(N-L+1)(SD_x)(SD_y)}$$

N is the number of observations in the X and Y time series.
L is the time interval between X and the Y value being correlated.
X and Y are the time series being correlated.
MEAN_X and MEAN_Y are the means of all the values of *X* and *Y* respectively for the entire series.

TABLE 1
Autocorrelations of Story Prominence, Story Strength, Direction Index, and Noise Complaints

TIME LAG	PROMINENCE	STR-DIR INDEX	COMPLAINTS
0	1.00	1.00	1.00
1	.39***	.27***	.22***
2	.09	-.09	.23***
3	.06	.03	-.07
4	.02	-.03	-.08

*** indicates $p < .01$
** indicates $p < .02$
* indicates $p < .05$

SD_X and SD_Y are the standard deviations of the same values.
SIGMAO is the standard summation function.

RESULTS AND CONCLUSIONS

Table 1 contains the results of the autocorrelations analysis for the three variables of interest. As it shows, story prominence is reasonably stable over a two-day period; about 16% of the variance in tomorrow's prominence can be predicted by today's prominence. After a one-day period, however, current prominence of Concorde stories could predict subsequent story prominence at no better than chance levels.

The strength-direction index which included story prominence as well as an evaluative direction assigned to noise assertions was also fairly stable over a single day period only, but only 8% of the variance of the next day's index was explained by current values.

Noise complaints were somewhat more stable, with current numbers of complaints predicting the number of complaints for two days at better than chance levels. A little more than 4% of the variance in both day's complaints was explained.

All variables are seen to have similar consistency windows from the autocorrelation analysis. No causal information is provided by this analysis, as the similar autocorrelations indicate that any variable could reasonably be the cause of any other. The cross-correlation analysis must be used to determine temporal sequences.

The tests between an agenda setting effect and a reverse agenda setting effect are found in the cross-correlations summarized in Table 2. As that table indicates, only the zero-lag, or normal Pearsonian correlation between prominence and noise complaints is significant. This would indicate that agenda setting, if it is taking place at all, takes place in the same day as the media stories which produce it. Since the time lag of zero cannot establish temporal sequence, reverse agenda setting cannot be ruled out, if it also takes place very rapidly.

Both these suppositions are not very plausible. If prominent stories changed the salience of issues and this increase in salience led to the behavioral action of complaining, then one would expect the effect to persist longer than 24 hours. It is here that the value of a time-series technique such as cross-correlation becomes evident. If one simply corre-

TABLE 2
Cross-Correlations Between Story Prominence and Noise Complaints

TIME LAG (DAYS)	COMPLAINTS PREDICT PROMINENCE	PROMINENCE PREDICTS COMPLAINTS
0	.15***	.15***
1	.01	.07
2	.01	.00
3	-.03	-.02
4	.06	-.01
5	.00	.01

*** indicates $p < .01$
** indicates $p < .02$
* indicates $p < .05$

lated story prominence with complaints, with no time lagging, one would conclude that story prominence and complaints were related, and thus an agenda-setting effect was likely. The addition of a cause-effect time estimate makes this conclusion much less acceptable.

Table 3 summarizes the cross-correlations which contrast the reverse effects and the direct/indirect effects models. As this table clearly indicates, there is no support for the reverse effects or mirror model. None of the correlations are above chance levels when complaints predict the strength-direction (prominence combined with evaluation) index.

On the other hand, the strength-direction index predicts the number of complaints one day later at better than chance levels. The amount of variance explained (about 2%) is small, but it is unlikely that the relationship is due to chance. Further, the negative sign for the cross-correlation indicates that the more negative the index, the higher the number of complaints. Thus we have evidence that prominent stories having a preponderance of noise related assertions negative to the Concorde are followed a day later by an increase in complaints about Concorde noise. Interestingly, there is no significant relationship between the strength-direction index and complaints in the same day.

DISCUSSION

Within the limitations of this study (and these will be discussed below), we have received empirical support for three general theories: direct/indirect effects, agenda setting and reverse agenda setting. All other media effects theories were rejected, as they gave predictions counter to observed data.

We can expand from the statistical tests somewhat and argue that agenda setting and reverse agenda setting, while not ruled out by the data, are not convincing models of the data. The results indicate that these processes occur immediately and their effects disappear before 24 hours have

TABLE 3
Cross-Correlations Between Story Strength-Direction Index and Noise Complaints

TIME LAG (DAYS)	COMPLAINTS PREDICT STR-DIR INDEX	STR-DIR INDEX PREDICTS COMPLAINTS
0	-.04	-.04
1	.04	-.14**
2	.05	-.08
3	-.07	-.02
4	-.01	-.01

*** indicates $p < .01$
** indicates $p < .02$
* indicates $p < .05$

elapsed. Thus the only agenda setting effect consistent with the data would have to be translated into behavior immediately, or changes in audience salience level reflected in behavior would have to be reported upon by the media in the same day in which they take place. Neither explanation is convincing.

Direct/indirect effects seems the better model to impose on this set of data. The effect is seen to follow the cause by a day, consistent with the fact that most of the media exposure to Concorde stories by the audience probably took place in the afternoon or early evening, and that reaction to this exposure would thus quite likely occur the next day. It might be further argued that direct effects is a better explanation than indirect effects, simply because the effect is observed so soon after exposure. The interpersonal communication necessary in indirect effects would have little time to take place. But indirect effects cannot be ruled out.

However, this study has limitations which certainly rule out its presentation as the definitive word on mass media effects theories. For example, agenda setting may have received little support because of unmeasured media coverage before the beginning of the project. If the salience of the Concorde trial period has already been set in the minds of the audience, further stories might have little effect. In other words, perhaps audience salience with respect to the Concorde had already reached a ceiling.

It can be further argued that noise complaints are not the best operationalization of audience salience possible. But from a public policy making viewpoint, it can also be argued that salience which does not lead to behavior is not terribly critical.

There is also a possibility of a "third-variable" problem in the conclusions presented. For example, media coverage was highest in the spring of 1976 and tapered off in the fall and winter. It could be that more complaints were telephoned in during the spring and summer because people were outside during these seasons and were responding to actual outside noise levels. When the weather cooled, and, coincidently, so did the news coverage, the complaints may have decreased as people went inside. This would give the same pattern of results as was observed, but the necessary connection between the presumed cause (media coverage) and the effect (noise complaints) would be missing.

A last limitation of the study is in the small

amount of variance in noise complaints explained by the media indices. This is not totally unexpected, as there are many nonmedia variables ignored in this study which might account for differences in the number of telephoned complaints. The actual noise level of the Concorde comes immediately to mind as a relevant variable ignored in this analysis, as does the outside temperature, for the reasons explained above.

Another factor contributing to the small amount of variance explained might be the sampling of WTOP stories. Unlike the other media outlets which were continuously monitored, the local television station output was sampled. Thus stories which might have produced change in the audience could have been missed.

Clearly variables such as these should be included in analyses attempting to explain as much of the variance as possible in noise complaints. But ignoring them does not remove the non-chance findings attributable to media observed in these analyses.

NOTES

1. This research was partially supported by U.S. Department of Transportation, Federal Aviation Administration Award No. DOT-FA76WA-3820.

REFERENCES

BANDURA, A. & WALTERS, R. *Social learning and personality development*. New York: Holt, Rinehart & Winston, 1963.

BECKER, L., McCOMBS, M., & McLEOD, J. The development of political cognitions. In S.H. Chaffee (Ed.), *Political communication*. Beverly Hills, Cal.: Sage, 1975.

BLUMLER, J. & McLEOD, J. Communication and voter turn out in Britain. In T. Leggart (Ed.), *Sociological theory and survey research*. Beverly Hills, Cal.: Sage, 1974.

BOGART, L. How the mass media work in America. In R. Baker and S. Ball (Eds.), *Mass media and violence*. Washington, D.C.: U.S. Government Printing Office, 1969.

COHEN, B. *The press, the public and foreign policy*. Princeton, N.J.: Princeton University Press, 1963.

FULLER, W.A., *Introduction to statistical time series*. New York: Wiley, 1976.

KATZ, E. The diffusion of new ideas and practices. In W. Schramm (Ed.), *The science of human communication*. New York: Basic, 1963.

KLAPPER, J., *The effects of mass communication*. New York: Free Press, 1960.

KRULL, R. & HUSSON, W. Children's attention to the television screen. Paper presented to the Association for Education in Journalism, 1977.

LAZARSFELD, P., BERELSON, B. & GAUDET, H., *The people's choice*. New York: Duell, Sloan & Pearce, 1944.

LIEBERT, R., NEALE, J., & DAVIDSON, E. *The early window: Effects of television on children and youth*. New York: Pergamon Press, 1973.

McCOMBS, M. & SHAW, D. The agenda setting function of the mass media. *Public Opinion Quarterly*, 1972, 36, 176-187.

ROGERS, E. *Diffusion of innovations*. New York: Free Press, 1962.

ROGERS, E. Mass media and interpersonal communication. In I. de Sola Pool & W. Schramm (Eds.), *Handbook of communication*. Chicago: Rand McNally, 1973.

TROLDAHL, V. A field test of a modified 'two-step flow of communication' model. *Public Opinion Quarterly*, 1966, 30, 609-623.

WATT, J. Content analysis of Concorde mass media depictions: Interim report. Washington, D.C., Federal Aviation Administration, Department of Transportation, 1977.

THE VARIABLE NATURE OF NEWS MEDIA INFLUENCE

HAROLD GENE ZUCKER
University of California-Irvine

It is widely held in the social science community that the news media have little influence on public opinion. In this paper, it is argued that this counterintuitive belief is based on weak theories derived from studies with faulty methodologies. A theory of variable news media influence is presented, which states that the less obtrusive an issue is, and the less time the issue has been prominent in the media, the greater is the news media's influence on opinion about that issue. Data is presented which demonstrate that network television news has influenced national public opinion about certain issues in a pattern consistent with the theory.

Many social scientists still believe that the mass media do not have any important effect on public opinion. This belief was, and is, counterintuitive to most people, but it appears to be based on the bulk of the empirical data. Prominent among the data, a few large scale voting studies (e.g., Lazarsfeld, Berelson, & Gaudet, 1948; Berelson, Lazarsfeld, & McPhee, 1954) seem to indicate that this lack of influence is, in fact the case. The main results of these studies and their authors' interpretations of these results have never been seriously challenged. These studies, together with a few other studies of mass communications and society (e.g., Star & Hughes, 1950) had the effect of convincing most of the social science community that the news media have little or no effect on society. These studies and several major summary works, which furthered the no-media-influence theory (e.g., Klapper, 1960; Berelson & Steiner, 1964) had the effect of stifling research in this area until the latter part of the 1960s.

When research into the effects of the news media resumed, even the authors of the most prominent new studies (Funkhauser, 1973; McCombs & Shaw, 1972) did not question the findings of the earlier studies. Instead, they said that the classic studies had not looked at the whole picture. They had only examined one of the two possible types of influence the media could have. The new researchers said that while the old studies had shown that the media could not tell people what to think, the new studies show that the media can tell people what to think *about*. These new studies convinced many people, but failed to convince many others, mainly due to weaknesses in the methodologies employed.

Despite the long-term general acceptance of the no-media-influence conclusion of the voting studies, those studies have a fatal design flaw. The claim that the media have no influence is based on the observation that self-reported high exposure groups and low exposure groups did not exhibit any significant difference in knowledge or opinion attributable to media exposure. However, this claim is not a valid inference from this observation.

There are actually three possible basic relationships between news media exposure and news media influence on society. The first is that the media can never influence anybody, regardless of exposure. The second is that the media can only influence heavy media users. The third is that the media can influence society as a whole, heavy and light users alike. The methodology employed by the voting studies is incapable of distinguishing between the first and third possibilities. Both would predict that there would be no difference found between the high and low exposure groups. But the third possibility was never even considered. It was just assumed that since the second possible relationship was not supported, the first one must be true. This assumption was not justified by the data. Studies are still being made using the same faulty methodology and making the same unwarranted claims (e.g., Patterson & McClure, 1976).

The theoretical case for the third possible relationship, that the media influence everybody, is at least as good as the case for the first possible relationship, that the media influence nobody. Those who declared the importance of personal influence in the form of peer group pressure, opinion leaders, and so forth (e.g., Katz, 1957) may have missed the most significant part of the "two-step flow of information" from the media. Personal influence is, indeed, an important part of the mechanism of public opinion formation. But this fact does not mean that the media have little influence. On the contrary, it means that the media's influence can reach and affect even those that do not watch, read, or listen.

Katz and Lazarsfeld (1955) and others claim that opinion leaders use the mass media more than nonleaders. It is quite possible, even likely, that high media use is one of the main reasons some people are opinion leaders. The nonleaders may speak to the leaders about an issue in order to find out what the media have been saying. If high media users are more influential than nonusers, then this fact indicates the media have much influence, not little influence. When Katz and Lazarsfeld investigated the news media-opinion leader-low media user link, they were (mistakingly) looking for an explanation as to why the media had little or no effect on public opinion, so they concentrated on the idea that the opinion leaders could filter and distort messages in the media as the most important part of the relationship. The most consequential part of the relationship, however, is actually that the link exists at all, that information in the media reaches the nonusers.

The theoretical case that the news media have no effect on public opinion has two main components. The first is the existence of opinion leaders as middlemen between the media and a large part of the public. This idea has been reexamined above. The other main component is selective perception. This phenomenon has been adequately dealt with elsewhere. Sears and Freedman (1967) have reviewed the main studies in that area and found that selective perception is the exception rather than the rule. McCombs and Shaw (1972) have produced further good data that selective perception is not the rule in the knowledge of issues in political campaigns. Thus, both the data and theory behind the no-media-influence idea resulting from the first generation of news media effects studies are seen to be weak.

While the authors of the most prominent second generation studies (Funkhauser, 1973; McCombs & Shaw, 1972) claim that these studies demonstrate that the media play a major role in setting the political agenda, many social scientists remain unconvinced. The reason these studies are not more convincing is that they, too, suffer from a critical design flaw. This flaw is that the methodologies employed produced only synchronous correlations between the media and opinion.

The problem with synchronous correlations is that they can only say that *A* is related to *B*. They cannot, by their nature, provide any indication as to whether this finding is due to *A* causing *B*, *B* causing *A*, or *C* causing both. In this case, *A* is news content, *B* is public opinion, and *C* is "reality" (i.e., factors external to both *A* and *B*).

Funkhauser makes a credible case that, at least for some issues, the newsmagazine coverage and public opinion seemed to vary together and to vary independently of the real world importance of the issue area (thus tending to rule out the third rival explanation of the correlation), but he did not (could not with his data) address the possibility that opinion was causing coverage (i.e., the news magazines were giving the public what it wanted—the second rival explanation). McCombs and Shaw (1972) addressed that second explanation by saying that the news media they studied did not originate in the city in which they conducted their study and, therefore, the news producers were not giving the people in that city what they wanted. They did not (could not) address the possibility that both the media and public opinion were reflecting reality. Thus, in both these important studies, after the correlation between news content and opinion was produced, evidence was presented against only one of the three rival explanations of that correlation.

It is unfortunate that these studies changed the best part of the methodology of the election studies as well as the worst part. The best way to make claims about the media and public opinion is to look at changes in both over time, and to use small enough intervals so that it is possible to determine if changes in one preceded changes in the other.

Some more recent agenda-setting studies have utilized cross-lagged (two points in time) comparisons and produced some interesting results. Tipton, Haney, and Basehart (1975) found little evidence for agenda setting by any medium in a pair of state and local campaigns. McLeod, Becker, and Byrnes (1974) also found only very weak support for agenda-setting by newspapers, while McCombs and Weaver (1977) found some evidence for newspaper use predicting the personal agendas of users (nonusers were not examined), but no similar evidence for television use, though they found that television use might sometimes stimulate political interest.

Perhaps these crosslagged studies did not support the agenda-setting hypothesis more strongly than they did because they were based on what might be an incorrect assumption; that is, that the influence of the news media is the same toward opinion about all the different sorts of issues. This assumption is implicit in the design of these studies, for only if it were true, could we expect that the entire list of issues in the media's agenda would transfer to the public's agenda and retain the same relative positions. This transfer is the test for agenda setting used by virtually all the studies in this area.

VARIABLE NEWS MEDIA INFLUENCE: A THEORY

Despite its wide use, it is not clear that the assumption, that the news media's influence is the same for all sorts of issues, should be accepted without an adequate test. It actually seems more likely that the assumption is not true, and that the news media can influence public opinion about some issues more than other issues. Therefore, it would seem that a useful question to ask is under what conditions is the news media's influence on public opinion maximal or minimal.

Accordingly, a theory of variable news media influence was devised. The theory consists of two principles. The first is *obtrusiveness*. The rationale behind this principle is straightforward. The less direct experience the people have with a given issue area, the more they will rely on the news media for information and interpretation in that area. The public does not need the mass media to see, or be upset with, rising prices or a line at the gas pump. When they exist, these conditions are obtrusive in the daily life of the public. However, there are other sorts of conditions which can be just as serious, without being obtrusive. Pollution can be one of these conditions. Increasing dependence on foreign oil can be another. In these cases, direct experience is not a clear guide, and the public derives many of its ideas about the importance and implications of these types of issues from the news media. When the news media emphasize a concern with a problem of this sort, it becomes a major national issue. When they give little or no coverage to a problem of this sort, it does not become, or ceases to be, a major issue.

The second principle is *duration*. The rationale for the duration principle is twofold. First, after a few years of an issue's being prominent in the media, most people have already made up their minds about the issue and are, thus, less subject to being influenced by the media than when the issue first gained prominence. It is generally accepted that attitudes only change in response to new information. After an issue has been prominent in the news for a few years, the information currently being given by the news media may be new in detail, but only rarely is it new in kind. Relatively few people are receiving new information, so relatively few attitudes will be changed. Repetition of similar stories is an effective technique for a while, and is, in fact, the most effective method by which the evening newscasts establish the importance of an area;[1] but eventually it wears thin. Of course, it is always possible that some really new information will be presented, in which case the news media may regain their influence in that area for a time.

The second basis for the duration principle is that the public seems to have a limited attention span toward nonobtrusive issues. After a few years, people get bored with an issue (unless that issue *is* obtrusive). It appears from the data below that problems such as pollution and the energy crisis exist as major issues for about three or four years, even though the problems themselves may exist for many more years, both before and after their time of national prominence.

METHOD

From all the above it would appear that a more useful way to examine the influence of the news media on public opinion might be to employ running measures of both news coverage and opinion for each of a set of issues and compare the changes in each over time. The key question would be whether coverage led opinion, or the two varied concurrently, or opinion led coverage.

If changes in coverage are seen to lead corresponding changes in opinion, a case for high media influence could be made. The case would be strengthened if a prima facie case could be made that the changes in both opinion and news coverage do not correspond to changes in the real-world seriousness of the issue area. Useful measures of both coverage and opinion on a national level are available.

There have been numerous studies indicating that television is the most used and trusted news media (e.g., Carter & Greenberg, 1965; Jacobson, 1969). It is also the most centralized medium, so, despite some evidence from some community studies (e.g., McCombs, 1976; Tipton, Haney, & Basehart, 1975; Patterson & McClure, 1976) that newspapers correlate better than television with voter agendas, this researcher believes that, at the national level at least, the public is more influenced by the three television networks' newscasts than any other medium.

It was hypothesized that the news decision of greatest consequence is whether or not to cover a given issue, and that the pro or con slants to the coverage and the length of the individual news items were secondary. Practical considerations unfortunately prevented the inclusion of these secondary areas in the study. The time periods of analysis are calendar months, primarily because the data source for network news coverage, the *Television News Index*, is published on a monthly basis. The measurement of news content used was, thus, the monthly number of items about a given issue on the networks' evening news. The study period coincides with the availability of this data.

The sources used for public opinion were the Gallup polls. The answers to the question, "What is the most important problem facing the country today?" were used as a measure of public concern for national problem areas, and the answers to the question, "Who would you like to see get the 1976 presidential nomination of your party?" were used to assess the public perception of the importance of national politicians.

Predictions were made and tested for each usable national problem area. An area was considered usable if it appeared in at least ten polls, thereby providing at least a minimum number of data points for analysis, and if it was an area that was directly or indirectly included in the *Television News Index*. Areas such as "moral problems" and "corruption in government" are examples of problems that appeared in the polls, but were not indexed. When these criteria were applied, six useable problems were found: pollution, drug abuse, the energy crisis, the cost of living, unemployment, and crime.

Judgments on the obtrusiveness of each issue area are included in the discussion of each area below. It should be noted here, though, that only obtrusiveness on the national level is considered, as the indicator of opinion used applies only to the national level.

Using the theory, it was predicted that the first three areas should demonstrate a pronounced lead effect, since reality was relatively unobtrusive in these cases. The energy crisis is a partial exception in the area of obtrusiveness which will be dealt with later. The prediction was borne out in each case. Simultaneous plots of opinion and coverage are presented in Figures 1-6.[2]

When the plots of the nonobtrusive issues of pollution and drug abuse are examined, it is seen that their initial rises in both coverage and opinion fall early in the study period. Hence, for simplicity and consistency (in the statistical comparisons) it was decided to divide the study period in half for examination vis-a-vis the duration principle. The study periods for the issues of the cost of living and crime were divided in the same manner so that the statistical comparisons could be based on the same number of data points.

FIGURE 1
Pollution

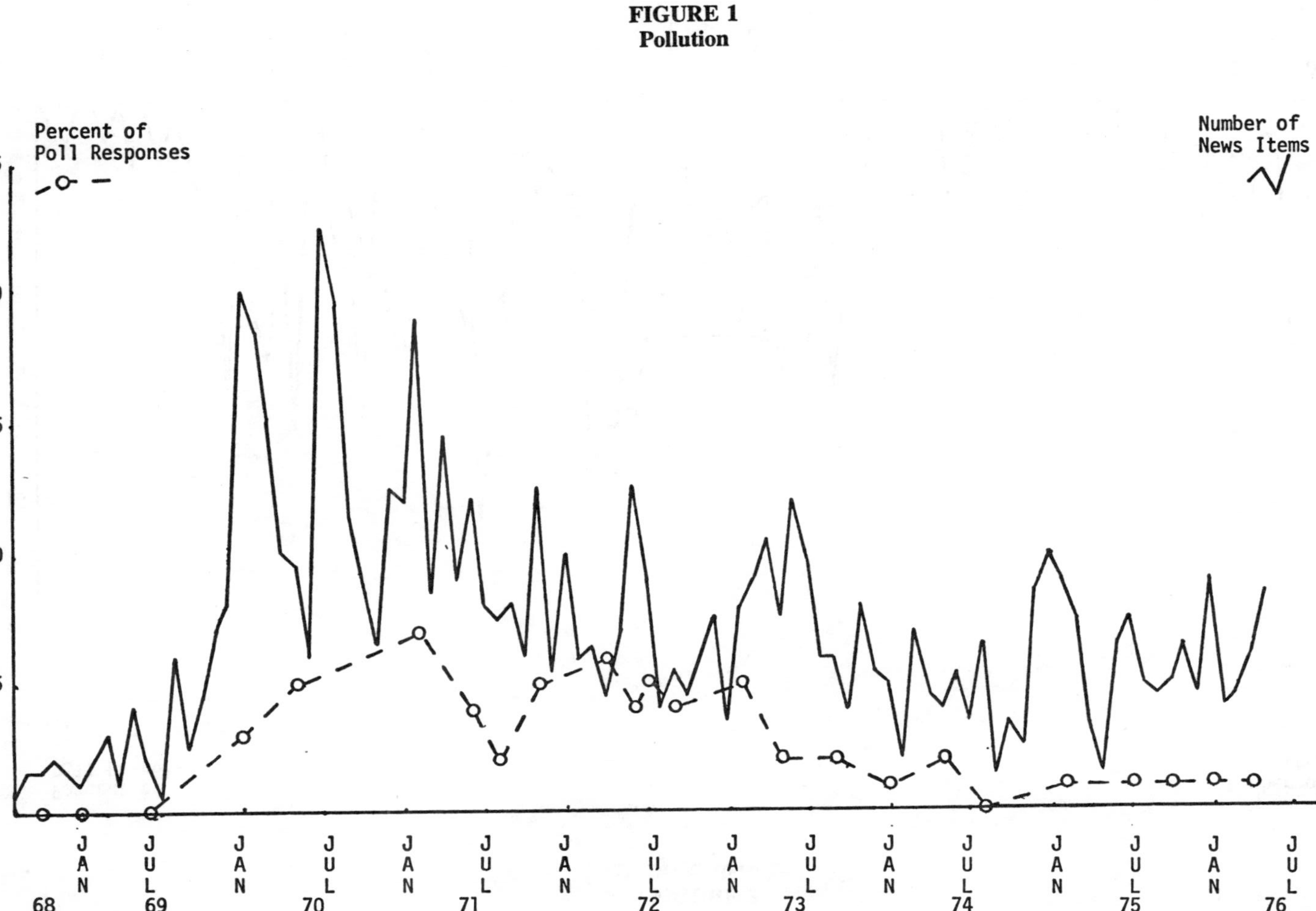

FIGURE 2
Drug Abuse

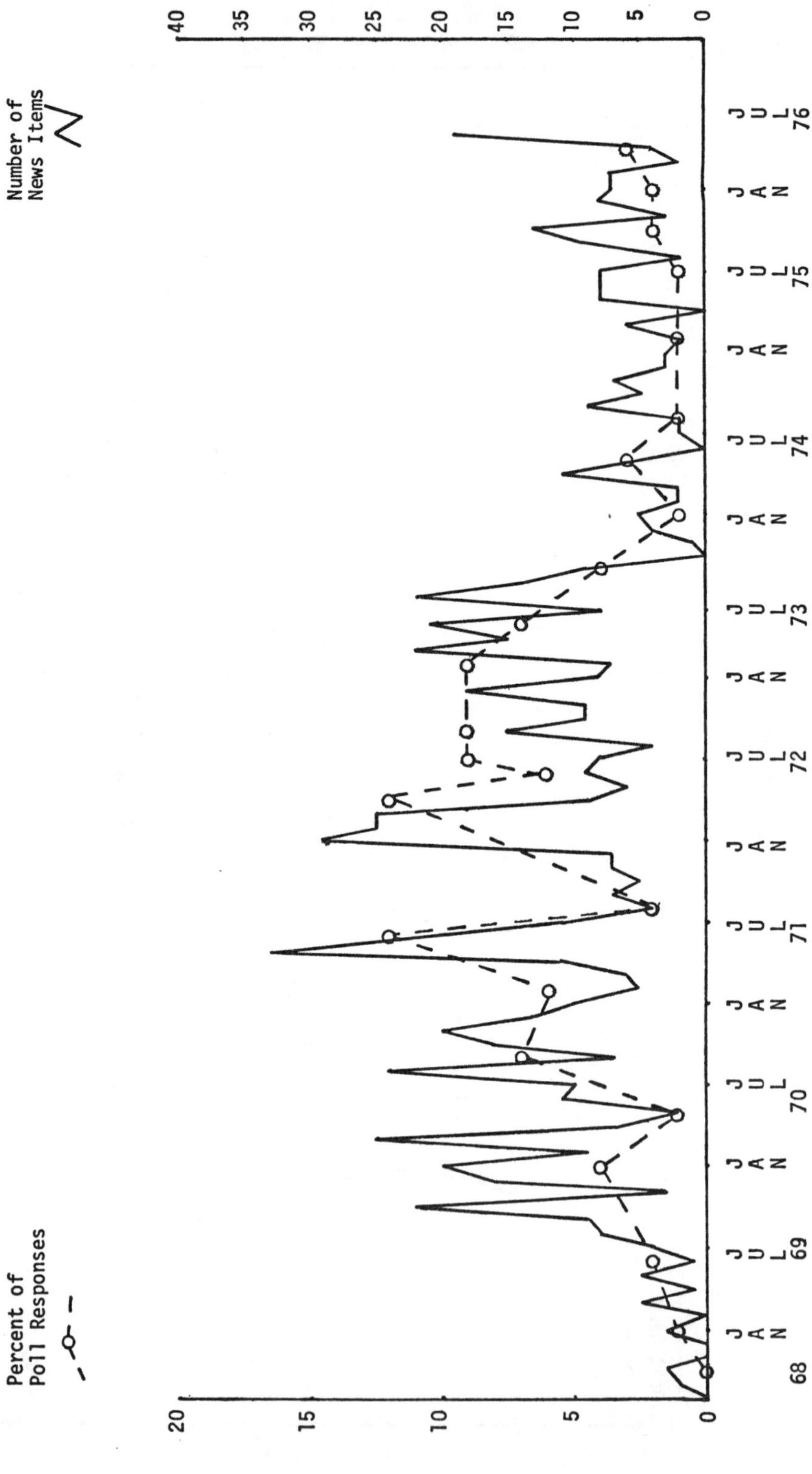

FIGURE 3
Energy

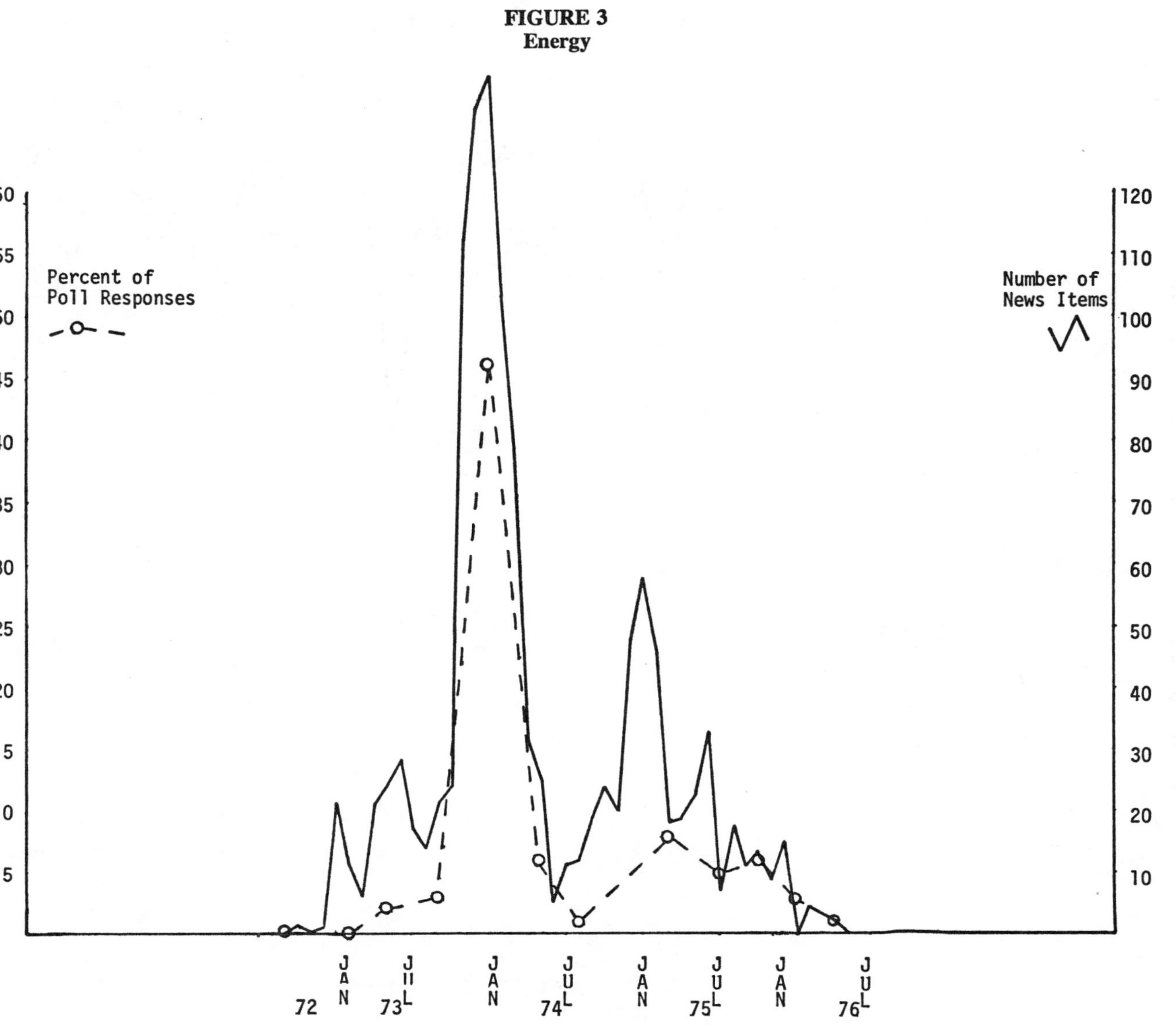

FIGURE 4
Cost of Living

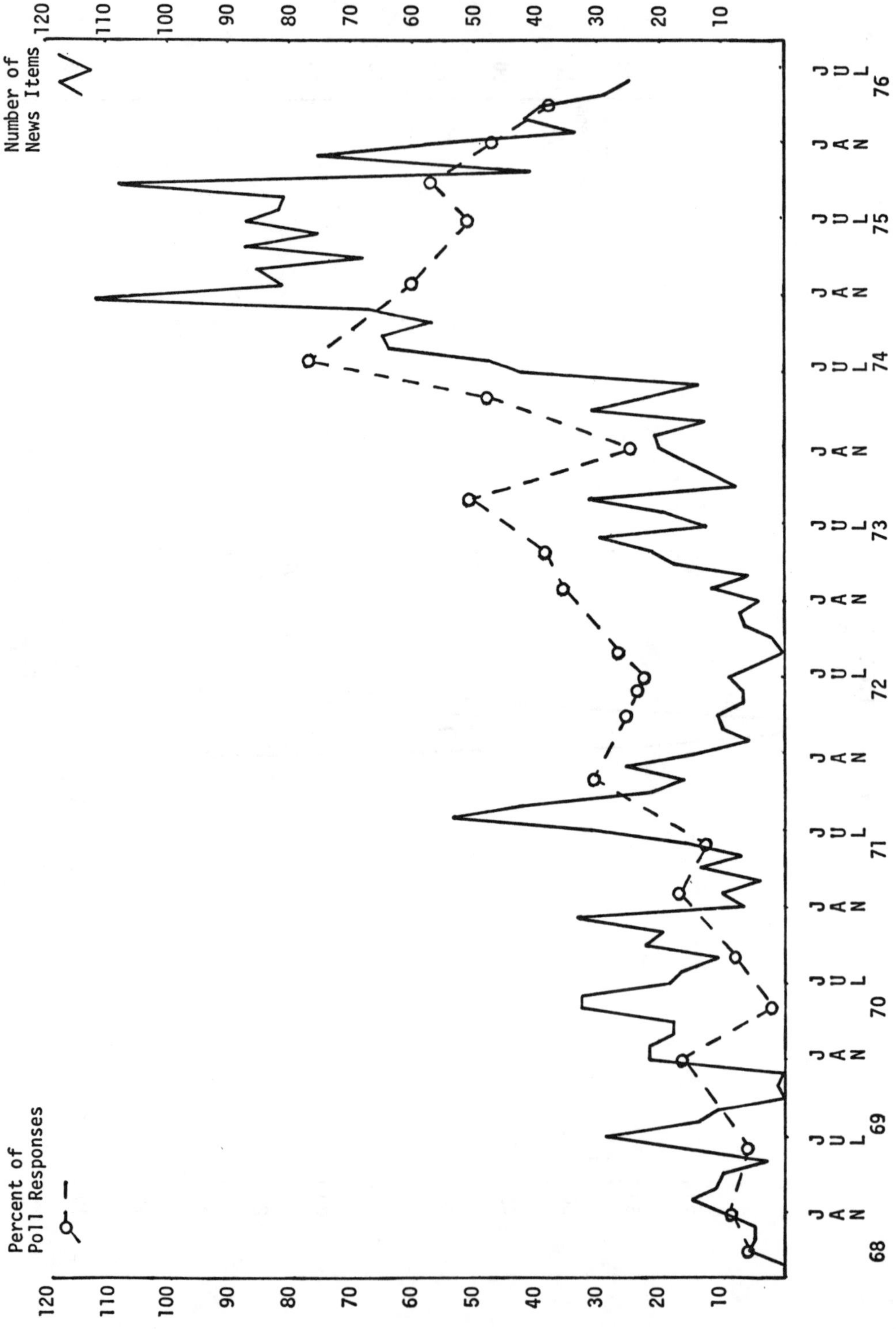

FIGURE 5
Unemployment

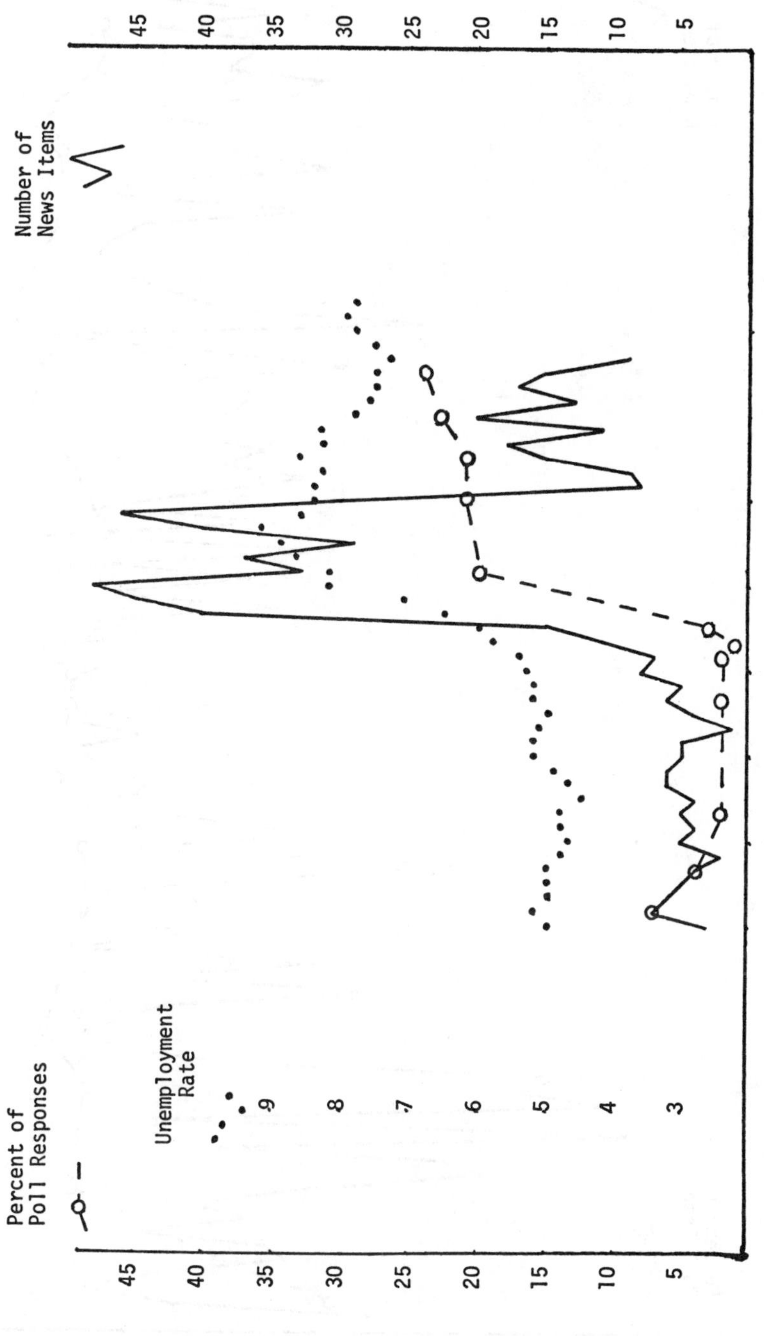

FIGURE 6
Crime

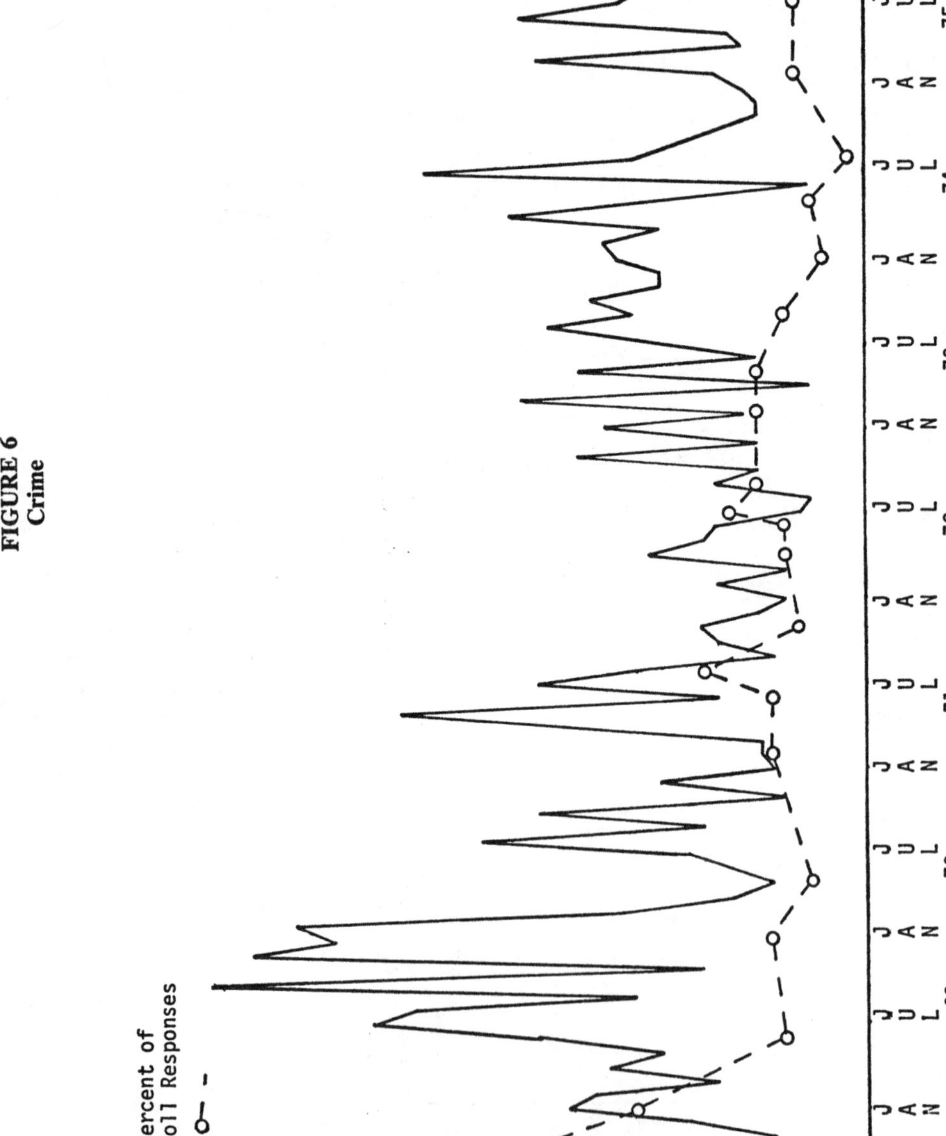

TABLE 1
Pearson Correlation Coefficients (Zero order)

	Period	Preceding Months		Current Months		Following Months		N	Predict
		r	s	r	s	r	s		
Pollution	68-72	.79	.001	.64	.013	.39	.107	12	high
	72-76	-.19	ns	.01	ns	.36	ns	12	low
Drug Abuse	68-72	.80	.001	.61	.018	.38	ns	12	high
	72-76	.29	ns	.60	.020	.50	.047	12	low
Energy	72-76	.71	.011	.33	ns	.31	ns	10	high
Cost of Living	68-72	.20	ns	-.29	ns	-.37	ns	12	low
	72-76	.59	.021	.62	.016	.65	.010	12	low
Unemployment	72-76	.60	.014	.74	.002	.18	ns	13	low
Crime	68-72	.19	ns	.04	ns	-.08	ns	12	low
	72-68	-.47	ns	-.16	ns	.05	ns	12	low

In order to have statistical, as well as visual, comparisons of the data, Pearson correlation coefficients were calculated for each issue and time period. Three correlations are reported for each period; the poll results with the coverage of the months preceding the months of each poll, with the months of the polls, and with the months following the months of the polls. The results of these correlations are presented in Table 1.

RESULTS

Pollution and Drugs

The pollution and drug abuse issues are nonobtrusive (see explanation below). Because of the duration principle, the prediction was that the lead effect of the news would be large in the first half of the sample and much reduced or absent in the second half. The data were found to be as expected. The preceding months' correlations are both high and account for nearly twice as much of the variance as the current months' correlations, in the first half of the data. The lead effect is absent in the second half of the data.

After demonstrating that changes in public opinion in a given area correspond to preceding changes in news coverage, it is necessary to answer those critics who would attempt to explain the correlations and lead effect as either the result of an ability of the networks to anticipate changes in public opinion and give the people what they want before they want it, or as a result of an ability of the networks to pick up on real-world changes in the problem areas in advance of the public. In both the pollution and drug abuse cases the data provide evidence against both of these interpretations. If the networks had an ability to either predict trends in public opinion or to pick up on real-world changes faster than the general public, why does the lead effect appear only in the first half of the data? It seems much easier to posit that network influence diminishes over time, than to posit that a network ability to either anticipate opinion or discern reality in advance of the public diminishes over time.

To further discredit the notion that the correlation between opinion and preceding news content can be explained as the result of a network ability to discern reality faster than the public, it is necessary to compare the fluctuations in both opinion and news to any fluctuations of the real-world importance of the problem areas. In the case of pollution, no figures are available, but it seems manifestly untrue that the severity of actual pollution varied in the same manner as the risings and fallings of both coverage and opinion as seen in Figure 1.

This lack of correspondence between the real world and the opinion and coverage curves is also the best defense for the judgment that pollution is nonobtrusive. If the issue area were obtrusive, one would expect a closer correspondence between opinion and the real-world seriousness of the problem. Pollution has built up gradually in most areas, so most people either do not realize it is there, or do not consider it other than natural, unless it is talked about as a problem in the media.

In the case of drug abuse, estimates of the real-world seriousness of the problem are available. According to the Department of Health, Education, and Welfare (O'Donnell, 1976), drug use rose sharply until about 1970 and then gradually leveled off. This pattern does not explain the risings and fallings seen in coverage and opinion. In this case too, the lack of correspondence between reality and coverage and opinion supports the contention that this area is nonobtrusive. Most people either have no contact with drug users or do not consider drug use a problem, unless the news media bring it to their attention as a problem.

Energy

The case of the energy crisis is more complex. There was a relatively short period—the oil embargo—during which the problem was extremely obtrusive, and a much longer period during which it was not obtrusive. Based on the obtrusiveness principle, we would expect that there would be a high media influence effect, except during the coming and going of the gas lines. This prediction, too, was borne out. Without the obtrusive period, the preceding months' correlation is both relatively high and much above the current months' correlation.

If the obtrusive period is included, the correlations become a clear case of both the media and opinion reflecting an unavoidable reality. With this period included, the correlations for both the preceding and current months rise to about .96. The correlations of this magnitude are also an artifact of adding an extreme point to a Pearson correlation coefficient calculation.

The energy problem ceased to be obtrusive when the gas lines ended and the domestic prices stabilized. The average American simply came to accept higher gas prices as normal. If the problem had continued to be obtrusive, not only would energy have consistently remained as a major national problem in the polls, but per capita energy use would not still be increasing and sales of gas-guzzling automobiles would have decreased much more than they have.

For a comparison of the public perception of the importance of the energy problem to reality, there are some measures available. Excluding the embargo period, the best measure of the energy problem is probably the percentage of our fuel use supplied by foreign sources. This is a direct measure of our vulnerability to another embargo. This percentage has risen dramatically since 1973. It was 29% before the embargo and was over 41% in 1976 (Finlay, 1976). Total fuel use, another measure of the problem, has also risen rapidly since 1972.

Cost of Living, Unemployment, and Crime

The cost of living is certainly an obtrusive problem. People can see rising prices without any help from the media. Unfortunately, the *Television News Index* does not index the "cost of living"

TABLE 2
First Order Partial Correlations

	Preceding Months, controlling for current months		Current months, controlling for preceding months	
	r	s	r	s
Pollution	.63	.019	.22	.260
Drug Abuse	.67	.012	.10	.390
Energy	.66	.026	.01	.494

[a]partial correlations were only calculated for the high influence cases.

or "inflation" per se. The overall heading "Economy-U.S." was used as a proxy measure of network coverage of this area. No lead effect was expected in either half of the data. None was found.

Unemployment is obtrusive—people know people who are out of work. Therefore, little network influence was predicted. No lead effect was evidenced. The correlations were substantial, but they can be easily interpreted as the result of correlations between both news content and public opinion with reality. A comparison of the news content and poll results with the monthly unemployment statistics supports this view. The correlation of opinion and the statistics is over .9, and that of the news and the statistics is within .04 of the opinion-news correlation. The correlation of over .9 supports the obtrusiveness of the problem. The public perception of the importance of the unemployment problem is directly related to the number of people who are unemployed.

While crime appears as a concern in the national polls, the public perception of crime as a problem probably reflects the amount of crime news in the local news more than the amount in the national news. Local news certainly devotes a much higher percentage of its time to crime news. People know they are much more likely to be personally affected by pollution or oil consumption a hundred miles away than by a murder a hundred miles away. However, they may still cite crime as a national problem if they feel that the federal government should be doing more to reduce crime in their area.

As was expected, there is no correlation between the public perception of crime as a national problem and network news coverage. However, it must be noted that this lack of correlation can be explained by the considerations above, without reference to the two principles, and is, therefore, not really a test of the theory.

Partial Correlations

In two of the three cases in which high media influence was predicted, while the correlations of opinion with the preceding months' coverage was well above the correlations of opinion with the current months' coverage, these later correlations were still substantial. Since it was observed that there is some continuity of coverage from month to month, it was hypothesized that part of the correlation between the current months' coverage and opinion may be based on correlations of both of these with the preceding months' coverage. In order to test this hypothesis, first order partial correlations of the current months' coverage with opinion, controlling for the preceding months' coverage, and of the preceding months' coverage with opinion, controlling for the current months' coverage, were calculated for each of the high influence cases.

The results supported the hypothesis (see Table 2). In each case, the current months' correlation with opinion dropped to the negligible level, while the preceding months' correlation with opinion remained relatively high. It seems that for each of these cases, virtually all of the correlation of opinion with what *is* (or has very recently been) on the news is the result of a correlation of both of these with what *has been* (a little while ago) on the news.

Politicians

It was also desired to test the predictions based on the theory of variable news media influence on the risings and fallings of national politicians. The period studied was 1973-1975. Election years could not be included in the study. The monthly numbers of news items in those years is not comparable to the numbers in other years, since all potential candidates receive much more coverage in the election years.

Unfortunately, there were found to be two serious problems with an attempt to demonstrate network influence on the choice of candidates. The first is that in the poll results of each party there is a major noise factor preventing the results of some of the polls from being strictly comparable to the results of the other polls. On the Republican side, Agnew led each of the polls until his resignation, after which he did not appear at all. On the Democratic side, Kennedy, who led each of the polls he was in by a wide margin, was allowed as a choice by the interviewers in some of the polls, but not in others. The inclusion or exclusion of Kennedy or Agnew unavoidably had an effect on the percentages received by the other candidates.

The second problem is that nearly all of the politicians to receive noticeable shares of the choices have been prominent for many years. Thus, the duration principle would indicate that there should be little media influence on opinion about them. The only politician who was not too prominent for too many years before the study period, and who received enough of the choices to make his rise and fall worth analyzing was Howard Baker. In his case the lead effect was crystal clear. The preceding months correlation was .81, while the current and following months correlations were approximately zero. The networks seem to have first established, then eliminated, Baker as a credible candidate.

As a parting word on presidential candidates, it should be noted that Jimmy Carter continuously received more network news coverage than any other Democratic candidate from January 1976 on, even though he only received 4% of the responses in both January polls. This priceless publicity may well have been the major factor in the success of his bid for the nomination.

The Lag Period

It should be reported that, although it was not anticipated, there appears to be some natural significance to the two to six-week before-a-poll time period, which is the lag represented by the use of the preceding calendar months. In addition to the zero order correlations already reported, two other sorts were calculated for the high influence cases. One was opinion with an average of the preceding months' numbers of items and the current months' numbers. The other was the preceding months' numbers and the months preceding those months' numbers (weighted toward the former). In all but one case, the correlation of opinion with the preceding months alone was higher than the other two correlations. The exception was found when the months preceding the months preceding the polls were included in the energy correlations. As a group, these correlations would seem to indicate that the news of approximately two to six weeks ago is much more influential on current opinion than is the news of more than six or less than two weeks ago. Perhaps the news of more than six weeks ago is considered old or is already forgotten, while the news of only one week ago may not yet have had enough time to spread from the high media users to the rest of society.

It must be stressed, however, that further work in this area, using actual two to six-week periods before a poll (and variations thereof), rather than calendar months, is needed before any claims about the maximum influence of the two to six-week ago period can be made.

DISCUSSION AND CONCLUSIONS

In the first part of this paper, the highly influential classic voting studies were reexamined, and it was seen that they (and other studies using a high exposure-low exposure comparison) suffered from a fatal design flaw, which rendered the no-media-influence conclusion of their authors invalid, despite its long-term general acceptance. The main theories that support the no-media-influence theory are shaky.

A rival theory of variable news media influence was proposed. This theory states that the less direct experience people have with an issue area, and the less time that that area has been prominent in the news, the greater is the news media's influence on public opinion on that issue. A test of the theory was presented. All of the test cases supported the theory. The correlations between news coverage and public opinion in the high influence cases cannot be readily explained as either the result of opinion causing coverage, due to a network desire to give the people what they want,[3] or as the result of "reality" causing both coverage and opinion. The correlations *can* be explained as coverage changes causing opinion changes. Further research is needed to confirm and refine the two principles and, perhaps, add other principles as well to the theory, until a fuller understanding of news media influence is achieved.

People today live in two worlds: a real world and a media world. The first is bounded by the limits of the direct experience of an individual and his acquaintances. The second spans the world, bounded only by the decisions of news reporters and editors. The individuals in our society have no real-world experience with many national and virtually all international problems. When they have to deal with (or have to choose whether or not to deal with) these problems, media-world experience must suffice.

An individual who pays little attention to the media world is nonetheless affected by it, because the only information he has about the world beyond his small, direct experience, real world is through people who *do* pay attention to the media world. The direct influence of the mass media on public opinion is not the properly discredited "injecting" of ideas into each individual mind, but is instead the creation of the media world. The inclusion or exclusion, prominence or inconspicuousness, and favorable or unfavorable slants of items of information in that world form a large part of the information environment on which the public bases its opinions and attitudes.

Evidence now exists that the media world affects national public opinion about the importance of issues. The main evidence that the media cannot affect opinion about the different sides of an issue has been shown to be invalid. New research in this vital area is clearly needed.

NOTES

1. Patterson and McClure (1976) maintain that network news is not capable of distinguishing the important from the trivial, because the typical network half-hour newscast is, essentially, all headlines. They may be right as far as a single broadcast goes, but they are wrong about network news in general. The networks do not establish the importance of a subject so much by its position in an individual broadcast, or by having the anchorman calling it a "top story," as by including a series of related stories in many different broadcasts. This latter technique *is* an effective way of imbuing the subject with importance in the public's mind.
2. It is important to note that on these plots there are monthly points for the coverage data, while there is only an average of three points a year for the opinion data. The lines connecting the opinion points have only been drawn in order to make the points easier to find. It cannot be assumed that public opinion follows those lines in the months between two polls.
3. It is not maintained that the networks do not tailor their coverage somewhat to give the people what they want. They do (see e.g., Patrick, 1975). The high current months' coverage correlation with opinion in the second half of the study period for the drug abuse issue may well be evidence of such tailoring. What is maintained is that, for the high influence issues, any such tailoring has a much smaller effect on the relationship between coverage and opinion than the effect of preceding changes in coverage causing subsequent changes in opinion.

REFERENCES

BERELSON, B., LAZARSFELD, P., & McPHEE, W. *Voting*. Chicago: University of Chicago Press, 1954.

BERELSON, B., & STEINER, G. *Human behavior*. New York: Harcourt Brace, 1964.

CARTER, R., & GREENBERG, B. Newspapers or television: Which do you believe. *Journalism Quarterly*, 1965, 42, 29-34.

FINLAY, D. How OPEC Meeting could affect prices. America's oil outlook. *Miami Herald*, December 15, 1976, p. 19A.

FUNKHAUSER, G.R. Public opinion in the sixties. *Public Opinion Quarterly*, 1973, 37, 62-75.

JACOBSEN, H. Mass media believability: A study of receiver judgments. *Journalism Quarterly*, 1969, 46, 20-28.

KATZ, E. The two-step flow of communication. *Public Opinion Quarterly*, 1957, 21, 61-78.

KATZ, E., & LAZARSFELD, P. *Personal influence: The part played by people in the flow of mass communications*. Glencoe, Ill.: Free Press, 1955.

KLAPPER, J. *The effects of mass communication*. New York: Free Press, 1960.

LAZARSFELD, P., BERELSON, B., & GAUDET, H. *The people's choice* (2nd ed.). New York: Columbia University Press, 1948.

McCOMBS, M. Press and public agendas of community issues. Paper presented at the annual meeting of the American Association for Public Opinion Research, Ashville, N.C., 1976.

McCOMBS, M., & SHAW, D. The agenda-setting function of the mass media. *Public Opinion Quarterly*, 1972, 36, 176-187.

McCOMBS, M., & WEAVER, D. Voters and the mass-media: Information-seeking, political interest, and issue agendas. Paper presented at the annual meeting of the American Association for Public Opinion Research, Buck Hill, Pa., 1977.

McLEOD, J., BECKER, L., & BYRNES, J. Another look at the agenda-setting function of the press. *Communication Research*, 1974, 1, 131-166.

O'DONNELL, J., et al. *Young men and drugs - a nationwide survey*. Washington, D.C.: U.S. Government Printing Office, 1976.

PATRICK, W. Network television news and public opinion polls. Unpublished doctoral dissertation, Ohio University, 1975.

PATTERSON, T., & McCLURE, R. *The unseeing eye: The myth of television power in national politics*. New York: Putnam, 1976.

SEARS, D., & FREEDMAN, J. Selective exposure to information: A critical review. *Public Opinion Quarterly*, 1967, 31, 194-213.

STAR, S., & HUGHES, H. Report of an educational campaign: The Cincinnati plan for the United Nations. *American Journal of Sociology*, 1950, 55, 389-400.

TIPTON, L., HANEY, R., & BASEHART, J. Media agenda-setting in city and state campaigns. *Journalism Quarterly*, 1975, 52, 15-22.

ORGANIZATIONAL COMMUNICATION

Theory and Research: An Overview
Selected Studies

ORGANIZATIONAL COMMUNICATION THEORY AND RESEARCH: AN OVERVIEW OF RESEARCH METHODS

HARRY S. DENNIS III
The Executive Committee
Milwaukee, Wisconsin

GERALD M. GOLDHABER
State University of
New York-Buffalo

MICHAEL P. YATES
State University of
New York-Buffalo

In *Communication Yearbook I,* it was reported that the field of organizational communication remains composed of a *collection* of disciplines *in search of a domain* (Richetto, 1977); apparently, no discipline has obtained preeminence in the quest for a single, unifying, theoretical perspective for attacking problems that are indigenous to the study of organizational communication.

Perhaps nowhere is this more evident than in the seeming multitude of diverse research methodologies and analytical procedures which proliferate in the field. Threads of distinguishable continuity in these undertakings are fleeting at best, not because research designs have necessarily been poorly conceptualized or ineffectually executed, and not because resulting instrumentation has produced findings of questionable validity and/or generalizability.

The problem, in short, which each discipline encounters is no different than the problem experienced, more or less, by the seven other ICA divisions; a problem echoed by many, but most recently by Scott (1977), "If we are to study communication, then something must *not* be communication" (p. 258). In the field of organizational communication, this question continues to be deliberated, and there does not appear to be any evidence of consensus in sight. For this reason, we cannot be assured that the field, as it is known today, will continue to attract, generate, and sustain the degree of research interest and enthusiasm that it has in the past.

Given that a search for *some* domain will continue for the short term, it seems fitting to us in this second annual overview to conduct an examination of representative research methods and procedures that have been used to study communication phenomena within complex organizations. Our proposed task, however, presents an interesting design problem within its own right. The most expedient solution would be to select a chronological design, but to do so would undermine any logical integrity which, from a research methods viewpoint, would necessarily be absent in the chronology. A second alternative would involve selecting an appropriate symbolic, empirical, or heuristic model against which "tests of apparent fitness" could be made; the drawback, of course, is that retrospective modeling seldom produces an accurate representation with very much present-day usefulness. A third option would entail a hypothetical but relatively complete representation of a research system from a methodological viewpoint against which organizational communication research methods could be both described and evaluated. Our attraction to this third option will become evident later.

REPRESENTATION OF THE RESEARCH SYSTEM

Figure 1 illustrates the representation of the research system, which we developed to accomplish our proposed task.[1] Organizational communication research has been accomplished in laboratory and field locales, incorporating either descriptive or predictive research designs. A time dimension, ranging from "one-shot" to longitudinal, with samples composed of individuals, defined organizational subunits, or entire organizations, has been subjected to scrutiny. Both behavioral and nonbehavioral data have been collected using survey, interview, observation, and content analytic data collection procedures. Analysis of results has been quantitative and qualitative, accounting for various

FIGURE 1
Representation of Research System

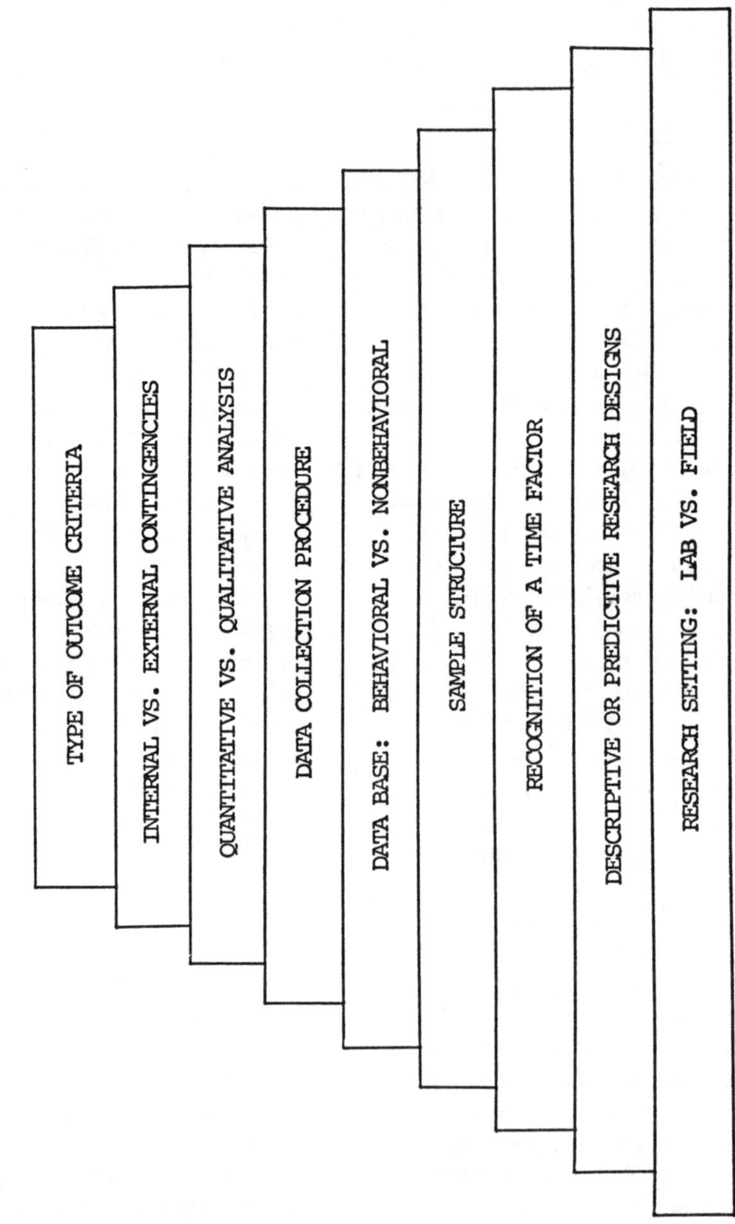

internal organizational and external (environmental) contingencies. To varying degrees, either internal or external criteria have been used to evaluate the performance of the communication variables manipulated in the research.

In the sections that follow, we intend to direct this representation toward an evaluation of a cross-section of organizational communication research. In so doing, a research methodological profile will be presented. This profile will identify areas of underemphasis and overemphasis, and methodological and procedural strengths and weaknesses, which seem to prevail in the study of organizational communication.

Unfortunately, due to limitations of time, space, and perhaps, hindsight, we cannot promise that all methodological innovations and contributions in the field will be incorporated in this overview. However, we did endeavor to include research examples that met the following criteria:[2]

1. The studies surveyed contain some historical value to the field of organizational communication.
2. In addition to historical value, the research has some seminal quality about it, in that it continues to serve as a foundation for inquiry and research output.
3. The research describes a current developmental trend or interest in the contemporary study of organizational communication.
4. The research describes a reasonable representative slice of methodological alternatives available for use in the study of organizational communication.

We hasten to add that no attempt was made to construct either a scientific or prescientific conception of the generic term "organizational communication." For the interested reader, definitions of such are as abundant as are the disciplinary searches for the domain described earlier (see Redding, 1972, for example). We did narrow our specific search, however, to research produced under the obvious rubric of "organizational communication," that maintained a recognizable, message-centered conceptual perspective, and that examined some characteristics of formal or emergent organizational relationships.

The remainder of this overview treats each one of the components of the research system presented in Figure 1 by describing the component's historical development, followed by an evaluation of its status, and concluding with recommendations to enhance its pursuit by the field.

RESEARCH SETTING: LAB VERSUS FIELD

Miller (1970) noted that "it appears that the setting of any research undertaking must be placed at some point on a continuum ranging from relatively 'pure' field research, on the one hand, to relatively 'pure' laboratory research on the other" (p. 77). Stressing that differences between the lab and the field are in degree rather than in kind, he suggested that (1) the structuring of the research environment by the investigator, (2) the rigor maintained over variables capable of affecting research outcomes, and (3) the use of restricted parent populations, are the dominant characteristics of laboratory research.

In the same volume, Redding (1970) maintained that "probably the least ambiguous, although not necessarily the most valuable, way of defining field research is in terms of *locale*" (p. 105). Like Miller, Redding reported that the "lab-field" dichotomy is probably a false one and that many of the "pure" characteristics of the laboratory can be found in the field, and vice versa. In place of the dichotomy, he recommended that we consider the presence (or absence) of researcher controls *in connection with* subject perceptions; that is, (1) do subjects perceive variances arising from the experimental investigation—different from the everyday routine—as research induced; (2) do subjects perceive deviations from their experienced routine, but do not link these deviations to the investigator; or (3) do subjects—in spite of the experimental investigation—perceive no departures from their regular routine?

Historical Development

Using the Miller and Redding perspectives described above, we found that approximately 30% of our organizational communication research sample, representing research accomplished since 1948, has been conducted in laboratory locales. Prior to 1961, 25 separate laboratory studies were reported (including, among others, Bavelas, 1950; Heise & Miller, 1951; Leavitt, 1951; Macy, Christie, & Luce, 1953; Guetzkow & Simon, 1955; Guetzkow & Dill, 1957; Roby & Lanzetta, 1957; Cohen, 1958; Shaw, 1959). Using artificially created networks, such variables as net size and type, channel restrictiveness, information overload, semantic ambiguity, and message distortion, among others, were pitted against speed, accuracy, organization, leader emergence, morale, task completion effectiveness and efficiency, and personal satisfaction criteria.

The prevalence of experimental research in laboratory locales has diminished considerably since 1961. Whereas the pioneers wrestled with seemingly compatible theoretical constructs, operationalized in congruent laboratory environments, the past 15 years have witnessed divergence in construct emphasis and experimental elegance. Examined variables include: organizational structure (Carzo, 1963; Cain, 1964; Carzo & Yanouzas, 1969); information filtration (O'Reilly & Roberts, 1974); group cohesiveness (D'Augelli, 1973); media effectiveness (Smith, 1962); listening competence (Kelly, 1962); communication conflict strategies (Ellis, 1965); social exchange strategies (Organ, 1974); participation in decision making (Ponder, 1973); orientation and consensus (Knutson, 1972; interpersonal expectations (Thomas, 1973); interaction quality (Leathers, 1972); upward communication distortion (Athanassiades, 1974); and communication openness (Jablin, 1977).

By far, the greatest preponderance of organizational communication research has been accomplished in field locales, where the stringent application of research controls has varied considerably from one study to the next. Settings have included governmental, industrial, and educational environments, for the most part, in both the public and private sector. The majority of this research can be categorized as quasi-experimental at best,[3] and, with the exception of ECCO analysis (Davis, 1953) and network analysis research (Danowski & Farace, 1974; Richards, 1976), there has been little concerted effort to translate and apply findings generated from controlled laboratory environments to field settings. Finally, most organizational communication research conducted in field locales has been characterized, using Scott's (1965) terminology, by *transitory* investigator participation in the situation under study.

In spite of these limitations, much progress has been made. Historically, for example, the well-known Hawthorne studies (Roethlisberger & Dickson, 1943) produced the first concentrated and systematic use of the *interview* in an industrial setting. The interview was also a popular research tool in early rumor research (see Back et al., 1950).

After the introduction of the interview as a data collection device, the trend in field research witnessed the development of survey, observation, and content analytic tools for exploring communication phenomena in organizations. Examples would include "Living-In," "Duty Study," "Indirect Analysis," "Cross-Section Analysis," "ECCO Analysis," and Odiorne's (1954) often cited "Communication Audit." (For a detailed review of these techniques, see Ayres, 1976.) This trend continued throughout the 1950s, tapered off in the 1960s, and has regained some momentum in the 1970s with the refinement of various network analysis methodologies and comprehensive communication audit procedures. (Network studies use both Duty Study and Cross-Section Analysis techniques, among other variations of sociometic methodologies—see Burns, 1954; Schwartz, 1968; Farace & Morris, 1969; Conrath, 1973; MacDonald, 1976.) The LTT Communication Audit (Wiio, 1976) and the ICA Communication Audit (Goldhaber, Porter, & Yates, 1977) represent two comprehensive communication auditing procedures that have, perhaps, the longest on-going administrative history in field locales, next to the well-known "Survey of Organizations," a product with over 20 years of field testing (from a theoretical model supplied by Likert, 1961), including repeated *time-series* applications, by the Institute for Social Research at the University of Michigan (Taylor & Bowers, 1972).

Numerous researchers over the years have used, to varying degrees of success, the field locale for the testing of hypotheses and the development of specific instrumentation relating to perceptions and attitudes toward communication acts or other human behavioral events occurring in the organization. Representative research includes Katz, Maccoby, and Morse (1950), on the relationship of supervisory communication behaviors to employee morale and productivity; Browne and Nietzel (1952), on the disparity between superior-subordinate perceptions of authority, responsibility, and delegation; Odiorne (1954), on the effectiveness of management communication; Perry and Mahoney (1955), on the relationship between employee knowledge of their company and employee morale; Likert (1961), on managerial perceptions of communication accuracy and effectiveness; Read (1962), on proclivities to distort upward communication; Maier, Hoffman, and Read (1963), on superior-subordinate communication; Lawler, Porter, and Tannenbaum (1968), on how superior-subordinate dyads view their interactions with one another; Roberts and O'Reilly (1974), on the development of an instrument purporting to measure a number of perceptual communication variables; Dennis (1975) on the construction of a managerial communication climate instrument; Falcione (1975) and Daly, McCroskey, & Falcione (1976), on the development of measures of perceived supervisory credibility and homophily; Goldhaber, Porter, and Yates (1977), on the development of an instrument purporting to measure perceptions of downward and upward communication effectiveness, channel adequacy, quality of human relationships, and evaluation of several perceived organizational effectiveness dimensions; and Schiemann and Graen (1977), on the construction of a questionnaire that purports to integrate previously isolated communication constructs. Similar descriptions of this type of field research can be found in Redding's (1972) comprehensive review. (For other integrations, see Baird, 1977; Downs, Linkugel, & Berg, 1977; Farace, Monge, & Russell, 1977; Johnson, 1977; Wofford, Gerloff, & Cumins, 1977.)

Turning, however, to the issue of experimental manipulation and rigorous control in field locales, a somewhat scant history emerges. Coch and French (1948) experimentally manipulated the extent to which employees of an industrial organization could participate in planning in an organizational change process and evaluated the effects of these manipulations on several criterion variables. Sherif, et al. (1954), in an undisputed classical contribution to conflict theory, experimentally induced conflict production and then introduced superordinate goals to achieve conflict resolution. These investigators did not, however, direct their research problem toward organizational communication phenomena per se; nonetheless, the indirect impact of their work on the field has been great (see Redding, 1972).

Examples of experimental field manipulations specifically concerned with the behavior of communication phenomena include Dahle's (1954) comparison of the effectiveness of five different methods for transmitting employee benefit information, using three separate industrial and business samples, and Miraglia's (1973) pre- and post-measurement of a communication training program.

Evaluation

Research in laboratory locales. That the laboratory has largely disappeared as a popular research location for organizational communication research is perplexing. Guetzkow (1965) noted, "It may not be accidental that research in communication has lagged behind studies concerning other features of organizational life, such as authority, division of work, and status" (p. 569).

He went on to remark that the *contingent nature* of typical organizational communication research results may account for this observation; and most of the results to which Guetzkow was referring did obtain in laboratory settings. Nevertheless, since 1965, we have witnessed a further decline of research interest in the laboratory locale.

Aside from the decline, there are a number of needs which organizational communication laboratory research typically fails to adequately meet. Weick (1965), speaking for lab research in general lists several, which we believe are crucially important for organizational communication researchers: (1) the need to achieve greater experimental *realism*; (2) the need to provide for realistic subgroupings, mediated interactions, and hierarchical relations; (3) the need to create a sense of "real-life" duration through effective *time-compression* techniques; (4) the need to incorporate membership and career progression problems common to organizational experience; (5) the need to use deliberately induced feedback processes to enhance the experimental group's knowledge of its performance results; and (6) the need to make laboratory tasks *interdependent*, as tasks are in real organizations.

The early communication net studies represented ingenious attempts in contrived settings to obtain control of the complexity of "contingent" variables that affect and/or interact with communication performance in real organizations. However, laboratory network research is subject to at least two major criticisms. First, the inclusion and hypothesized effects of multiple net structures and "nets" within nets to provide for more meaningful mediated interactions has been largely ignored. Second, net tasks have not been structured effectively to translate real organizational concerns into laboratory analogues. As a result, knowledge of how the task interacts with given variations of communication structures is incomplete. Current network research in the field setting partially sidesteps these criticisms, but for different reasons which, to date, no investigator has adequately linked to the formidable laboratory net research accomplished over 15 years ago.

Whereas the net research of the 1950s and the early 1960s was generally derived from a relatively contiguous, theoretical perspective, subsequent laboratory research in organizational communication resembles a theoretical dart board. The use of games in interpersonal conflict research is one bright exception where a discernible research trend and fairly uniform research methodology is evident (for examples, see Steinfatt's, 1974, review).

Finally, the obvious paucity of empirical communication research in laboratories either reflects researcher disappointment with the productive potential of this setting, or indicates that organizational communication investigators have been somewhat remiss in recent years. An inspection of the laboratory procedures used by 12 of the investigators cited in this overview indicated that not more than three of Weick's (1965) needs are met in any single research undertaking. If this is indeed characteristic of the field of organizational communication as a whole, then researchers must review their commitment to execute and report laboratory research that endeavors to satisfy higher standards of external validity.

Research in field locales. Field settings have grown exponentially over the years, and their diversity has been very pronounced.[4] The enthusiastic graduate student who exclaims, "I have hypotheses, where can I test them?" captures the essence of the problem we see in the arbitrary selection of field research locales. Little attention has been given to the relative influence of the locale itself on the behavior of communication phenomena occurring within the locale. Furthermore, field settings, especially industrial and business organizations, possess a potentially dangerous research trap—not new by any means—but one that organizational communication researchers should acknowledge as a serious contaminating threat to unbiased study results; that is, the question of how the research is sponsored and financed. Depending upon the arrangement, the obligation of the investigator to produce usable results for his client organization first and the scientific community second can promote the acceptance of research procedures and the interpretation of research findings that are thinly extrapolated well beyond what is reasonably acceptable to the scientific community.

Methodological rigor in field locales, especially from the Miller (1970) and Redding (1970) viewpoints expressed earlier, remain subject to strong criticism. Other than the very few (true) experimental studies that have been executed in natural setting, few investigators (notwithstanding the usual economical problems associated with field research) have taken the time to build research designs that meet minimally acceptable external validity requirements (a la Campbell & Stanley, 1966). This is especially true for the vast quantities of research instruments that have been developed to measure communication phenomena. With the exception of network analysis instruments, few of these research aids have ever been successfully validated against one another or against other external criteria. In fact, many of these instruments obscure the underlying concepts under study to such a point that reliable replication is all but impossible.

Aside from the question of methodological rigor in the field, the whole issue of the investigator's role—whether active or passive participation is more appropriate for the research problem—is seldom expressed as a design decision. Yet the issue speaks directly to the degree of control maintained over unwanted sources of extraneous influence. Beyond the question of active versus passive participation, there is the related issue of transitory versus sustained researcher involvement as a way of describing alternative field approaches (Scott, 1965). This survey of organizational communication research produced examples meeting both the sustained and transitory criteria; in few cases, however, could we discern that the approach taken was *as a consequence* of deliberating the merits of transitory or sustained involvement. Obviously, study design parameters, characteristics of the research problem, types of data needed, data collection procedures, and the time available to conduct the research are factors that will influence this decision. We are simply pointing out that each approach taken by the investigator has its own set of corollary research conditions, which should be anticipated when the field setting is contemplated.

Finally, it appears that most organizational communication scholars (following the Miller, 1970, and Redding, 1970, distinctions made earlier) have expended considerable effort in the structuring of the immediate data collection environment in particular, but not the overall research environment in general. Contaminating error sources, such as social desirability, nonanonymous response profiles, and voluntary versus involuntary subject participation, are seldom adequately accounted for in the description of the research design. This is primarily true, of course, for the mainstream of organizational communication data that are collected through self-report, paper-and-pencil means.

Recommendations

The distinctions made by Miller (1970), and Redding (1970), and others, should be weighed carefully before an arbitrary decision is made to conduct research in a field or laboratory locale. Sometimes, useful "mutations" are in order. For example, Jablin (1977) tested the effects of various conditions of perceived communication openness by employing a germane subject population drawn from a cross-section of organizations, and by exposing his sample to stimulus materials administered in a carefully controlled laboratory setting.

Not only is a return to the relatively neglected laboratory locale suggested by this review, but the greater use of *true experimental designs* in field studies is strongly urged. We sense that the study of organizational communication has been overharvested with the production of too many overlapping instruments and questionnaires purporting to measure the same communication phenomena (e.g., "communication satisfaction," "communication climate," "communication openness," and "communication style" questionnaires). There is an urgent need to assess the real empirical and theoretic merit of these paper-and-pencil concepts in deliberately manipulated and experimentally controlled laboratory and field settings. Conservatism, not compromise, should govern decisions affecting the research locale.

Lastly, for the past ten years, many scholars have accepted a "contingent" or "situational" view of organizational communication concepts (Derry, 1972; Redding, 1972). This view implies that the direction and strength of perceptions and behaviors will vary from one context to the next. We urge that the research *setting* be hypothesized as a contingency, both in the research design phase of a study and in the measurement of the dependent variables. Until comparisons can be made on the basis of research locale, the external validity of organizational communication findings will remain subject to uncertainty.

DESCRIPTIVE OR PREDICTIVE RESEARCH DESIGNS

Of the studies reviewed here, 73% used descriptive research designs. The remainder either deliberately employed a predictive research design or attempted to use predictive statistics on a design with suspicious parametric features.[5]

Historical Development

In the early years of organizational communication research (circa late 1940s and early 1950s), a good proportion of the research accomplished was rightfully termed "exploratory," and, as such, descriptive designs were in order. Outside the realm of dissertation research, hypothesis testing per se was subordinated to the development of procedures and techniques for operationalizing organizational communication concepts. The few experimental manipulations that were conducted in both the laboratory (principally, the communication network studies) and the field were not supported by very powerful inferential statistics.

Typical of research designs executed during this early period included the one-shot case study, such as the excellent Katz, Maccoby, and Morse (1950) work cited before and a classic piece by Lawrence (1958). However, by 1959, there was such a proliferation of organizational studies of single cases (or multiple cases subjected to single interpretive analyses), including a rash of hastily developed surveys, that one review of 178 descriptive studies concluded that the study of organizational communication was characterized by a nearly total absence of sound research procedures (Sexton & Staudt, 1959).

Also influencing the descriptive emphasis of researchers were the rather crude tools available for quantifying data obtained through qualitative means. Interview and observation strategies are cases in point. Only recently have techniques been developed to incorporate qualitative data within an overall predictive research design. Some of these techniques are discussed in the data analysis section of this review.

Historically and currently, it is also true that researchers have devoted considerable attention to the establishment of satisfactory internal validity requirements. Tests for external validity require predictive designs, which are useless if internal validity objectives have not been met. Research in the 1970s, however, is being accompanied with the gradual employment of improved multivariate techniques, which, *if used in conjunction with true experimental designs*, should lead to a shift of emphasis from descriptive to prescriptive research in organizational communication (see, for example, Daly & McCroskey, 1975; Dennis, 1975; Falcione, 1975; Daly, McCroskey, & Falcione, 1976; Scott, McCroskey, & Sheanon, 1976; Goldhaber, Porter, & Yates, 1977).

Evaluation

Laboratory research excluded, most organizational communication investigators over the years (whether "communication" represented their disciplinary allegiance or not) have been confronted with the dilemma of meeting a scientific obligation as well as a pragmatic one to the organizational client. Hence, it is not surprising that we have seen heavy reliance on descriptive designs and corresponding descriptive statistics for the evaluation of communication concepts and hypotheses. Experimental manipulations, with tight controls, in organizational environments are not only costly, if executed effectively, but can be somewhat threatening to naive organizational subjects. Experimental deception in one form or another, while practical in the laboratory, is unsettling to the organizational client who is providing time—and, therefore, money—to the research project. Thus the historical absence of predictive research designs in organizational communication research outside the "pure" laboratory is somewhat understandable.

Our review suggests that organizational communication scholars need to reassess what constitutes a "predictive research design." It should not be interpreted to mean collecting self-report data, which is scored and analyzed statistically, and then related, coincidentally, to some separate measurement representing past history; it does suggest that the rigor of experimental manipulation, with adequate controls, is used to predict the behavior of organizational communication phenomena while accounting for "other" sources of variation influencing the phenomena under study.

We are by no means condemning further use of descriptive research. Communication is, after all, a process variable, the multiple peculiarities of which are more subject to extensive observation using descriptive techniques rather than exotic experimental methodologies. But descriptive designs have one obvious failing which predictive designs do not: their theoretical power is limited, by definition, to the sample under study.

Recommendations

Organizational communication researchers should screen the descriptive techniques that have accumulated over the years and concentrate upon refining those empirical tools which have consistently yielded the most substantive research output. New tools with predictive value should be incorporated in *true* experimental designs; old tools with questionable predictive value, if not discarded altogether, should be reexamined for their current worth. (For an example of a new descriptive strategy for studying "contact systems" which seems especially encouraging—see Thorngren, 1970.)

To solve the problem of simultaneously meeting client expectations and researcher needs, we urge that greater attention be given to clients who recognize the value of and need for empirical research—*and who are willing* to sacrifice immediate organizational "returns" for an important scientific contribution. It has been our collective experience that such organizations, if correctly approached, are responsive to the enhancement of scientific knowledge, realizing that, in the long run, *enhancement* is the precursor to improved organizational functioning.

RECOGNITION OF A TIME FACTOR

Organizational life is ongoing and continuous: certain properties remain fixed over the organization's life span and others change or disappear. In a profit-making organization, the annual or quarterly balance sheet is a statement to the stockholders of the firm's asset and liability condition. To management, however, the balance sheet only represents one day in the life of the company. Perhaps, more importantly, the whole concept of organizational planning and budgeting is weighted by a time factor, which represents the constraints imposed on the organization as it attempts to develop, maintain, and allocate human, material, and financial resources. Finally, the context and process of planned organizational change (involving tasks, structures, technologies, and people—Leavitt, 1965) is subject to a time dimension ranging from "immediate" on the one hand, to "long-term" on the other.

Historical Development

The issue of time has at least two important research dimensions. First, it can refer to the extent to which the investigator *sustains* in the research environment to collect the data under study; second, it can refer to the *total research period*, during which time the investigator intervenes in the research environment (Scott, 1965). Furthermore, while the amount of time devoted to the data collection activity in a descriptive study may strongly influence the quality of data collected through observation, self-report, or interview methods, time, if not controlled carefully, can seriously threaten the internal validity of an experiment due to subject maturation (Campbell & Stanley, 1966).

Most organizational communication research continues to produce "snapshots" of the phenomena under study. For example, Muchinsky (1977) reports a questionnaire study where he attempted to assess relationships between his measures of "organizational communication," "organizational climate," and "job satisfaction." His questionnaires were administered concurrently in a single wave to his respondent population. The assumption, of course, was that these concepts could be accurately measured with a one-shot administration. Historically, however, there are examples of studies that used extended research interventions to obtain some indication of measurement stability.

Coch and French (1948), for example, devoted several months to their pre- and post-experimental change program at the Harwood Manufacturing Corporation. Burns (1954), also employing a *sustained* approach, worked with four departmental executives in a British firm, having them self-report their interactions over a five-week period. Also in 1954, Roy (1969) used a participant-observer technique in a manufacturing company for a one-year period to collect data about communication and emergent group processes. Piersol

(1955) conducted a case study in which he used unobtrusive observer techniques to record the communication behavior of industrial foremen for a one-month period. Then, using an experimental design, Miraglia (1963) spent six weeks administering his experimental treatment (a communication training program), followed by an immediate and delayed posttest (given four months after the treatment).

Until recently, the mainstream of organizational communication research simply has not given serious attention to time as a potential, independent research influence. As early as 1961, Likert (1967) was admonishing industrial clients that behavioral change programs require a minimum of five years to accomplish successfully, with a corresponding set of repeated measurement and observation required to determine the overall effectiveness of the change effort. Taylor and Bowers (1972) refer to their extended effort to refine the "Survey of Organizations" as an "inter-company" longitudinal program of data collection and instrument refinement. In the specific area of communication research, Thorngren (1977) reports ten years of systematic, longitudinal study in connection with his recently published theory of organizational contact systems. Finally, Schiemann and Graen (1977) describe their research, wherein they attempted to predict the behavior of several communication variables based upon interpersonal and structural antecedents, as longitudinal in design (hypothesized antecedents were collected at time 1 and dependent measures were assessed four months later).

Evaluation

The consideration of time as a factor in organizational communication research appears, historically, to have been dictated more by the conveniences of research method requirements rather than by the structure of the research problem under study. Clearly, some communication variables are "time-bound" and others are "time-free." For example, the directionality of messages occurring within the organization's formal structure represents a time-free variable cluster; the directionality of messages associated with emergent structures seems time-bound, especially in diffusion networks (Pool, 1973).

Also, the time structure within which humans must perform varies from one organization to the next (e.g., an organization that produces output for consumption on a daily basis, contrasted with one that produces output for consumption on an annual basis). These organizationally-related contingencies involving time suggest that research interventions must be planned accordingly. We have observed little systematic effort on the part of organizational communication researchers to construct and coordinate their interventions in this manner.

A second problem encountered is obtaining an empirically-derived measure of a significant time unit for research (i.e., seconds, minutes, hours, days, etc.). This is both a researcher intervention concern (how long should one sustain?) and a data collection problem (what are the smallest time units by which data are meaningfully collected?).

A third problem with time in organizational communication inquiry is even more perplexing: are time-bound variables—cast in a time-series research design—significantly influenced by one unit of time, but not significantly influenced by another unit of longer or shorter duration? We can cite no research which has addressed this problem.

In summary, we suspect that investigators in the field of organizational communication have perceived the time variable to be more indicative of a research design limitation than to be conceptualized as a separate research dimension affecting the degree to which new research opportunities can be explored.

Recommendations

The methodological problem with time. Communication scholars are encouraged to accelerate the use of multiple, repeated-measure and time-series types of designs. But multiple or repeated measures alone are obviously insufficient if administered concurrently: they must be truly extended over time (for one example, see Warner, Falcione, & Temkiewicz, 1978). We believe, too, that greater use of a "research team" approach in longitudinal studies will enhance the likelihood that objective data collection and analysis procedures will obtain. We also urge greater use of unobtrusive data collection in those designs requiring sustained investigator participation in the research locale.

The "variable" problem with time. Few studies introduce time (defined in controlled and measured units) as an independent or dependent variable in the research design. We encourage this. Few investigators follow up a research project with successive interventions to determine if, over time, the results of the research project are affected by organizational contingencies that were ignored or not present in the original research undertaking (for an exception, see Wiio, 1976). When these recommendations cannot be followed, we suggest that every investigator, regardless of the research design employed, sufficiently document any time-bound organizational contingencies existing at the moment of the research which could change, and, therefore, affect the success of any subsequent replication.

SAMPLE STRUCTURE

Historical Development

Sample sizes and sampling plans have varied considerably over the past thirty years. Excluding case histories, in the 1950s, most organizational communication research designs used sample sizes under 100; in the 1960s, this increased to approximately 200 persons per study. More recent samples in the 1970s have averaged slightly over 300 per study. Sampling plans have called for measurements taken from individuals, entire work groups, or total organizations. A majority of the research, however, seems to be based upon samples of individuals drawn randomly, purposively, or accidentally, from their organizations.

The sampling of individuals can be illustrated by Read's (1962) classic study in which 52 pairs of supervisors and subordinates were randomly sampled to determine their perceptions of each other's mobility aspirations, trust, and influence. Davis (1953) also sampled individuals, but did so purposively, when he asked 67 managers to report on the content of a message he planted in the company. Sometimes, individuals are selected from a cross-section of organizations in an attempt to produce external validity. Such was the case in the recent study by Bacharach & Aiken (1977), who distributed 1,005 questionnaires to 44 local administrative bureaucracies in Belgian cities.

Samples can also be constructed with members of different work groups, as was the case with Browne & Nietzel (1952), who administered a disparity measure to 100 persons in several different work groups, and with Coch & French (1948), whose 28 subjects were obtained similarly from several existing work groups. More recently, Mintzberg (1975) illustrated that these sampling units can be very small, especially in a longitudinal study: he observed 5 managers and the amount of time they spent in various forms of interaction and decision making.

Although Sanborn (1961), perhaps, was one of the earliest organizational communication investigators to sample an entire organization of substantial size, this trend is seeing renewed interest in the 1970s. Primarily associated with studies and attempts to develop standard survey instruments and network analysis methodologies, many researchers are now reporting large samples, or samples of entire organizations (Taylor & Bowers, 1972; Wiio, 1974; Richards, 1976; Goldhaber et al., 1977).

In summary, although the bulk of the methodologies in organizational communication were developed by sampling small numbers of individuals (particularly in diary-type studies), the trend seems to be towards larger sample sizes—over 300 per study, including studies of entire organizations.

Evaluation

In addition to the obvious criticism that, in general, sample sizes have been far too small over the years to allow for meaningful conclusions and external generalizability, a far more pervasive criticism seems in order. Although samples and sampling are critical to the conduct of any research design, there has been no *systematic* reporting of sample characteristics and sampling procedures. Organizational communication researchers, including most of those investigators responsible for the development of the various research methods reported in this overview, have been unwilling or unable to address sampling efficiency as an issue. Researchers have not, for example, consistently reported their method for establishing the sample size. (In surprisingly several studies, the sample size was not even mentioned.)

Besides sample size requirements, the related subject of sampling errors is almost never discussed. References to other studies and their sampling characteristics and methods, no matter how seminal, have been missing. Reports of sampling power have been absent, too, and, in many cases, statistical errors have been committed by not accounting for demographic or organizational factors in sampling variations. Dennis (1975), for example, adjusted his sample higher in a manufacturing company because he discovered a significantly higher turnover rate in that organization than in an insurance company he was also studying. In short, most organizational communication research over the past 30 years has, for a number of reasons (e.g., entry opportunities, time, economics, geography, availability, etc.), ignored serious sampling considerations.

Recommendations

When possible, organizational communication researchers (especially researchers who employ multivariate analytical techniques) should consider studying entire organizations or, minimally, intact suborganizational units. This will allow for examinations of the systematic properties of the organization and will also facilitate the proper use of more advanced multivariate analytical techniques.[6] More importantly, however, all researchers should mention: (1) sample size; (2) sampling plan and method (e.g., "randomly selected 6 organizations from 32 available by using a table of random numbers"); (3) sampling error and confidence level (e.g., 3% error at the 95% confidence level); (4) reasons for selecting the particular sample (e.g., prior research, cross validation, organizational restrictions, economics, etc.); (5) clear descriptions of the demographic nature of the sample; (6) how the sample under study compares and contrasts with samples used in related research.

DATA BASE: BEHAVIORAL VERSUS NONBEHAVIORAL

Let us state at the outset that it is not our intention to undertake the challenge posed by the very mass of existing literature relating to the study of "behavioral" versus "nonbehavioral" variables in organizational communication research, or to renew the debate concerning the "attitude-versus-behavior" controversy which prevails in the general study of communication and psychology.

For the purposes of this section, "behavioral" will refer to observable, verifiable acts; "nonbehavioral" will denote any description of a human communication experience which is not observable and verifiable through some methodologically sound practice.[7] Thus, a paper-and-pencil self-report of communication behaviors occurring in the past, which has not been independently verified, constitutes nonbehavioral data. (Nebergall, 1965, specifically distinguishes paper-and-pencil responses from "other" kinds of behavior.)

Historical Development

Over 70% of the studies surveyed here made use of a nonbehavioral data base. Some early examples would include Davis (1953), who introduced the ECCO analysis procedure wherein respondents must "recall" their knowledge, if any, of a planted message; Burns (1954), who found that although diaries of supervisors (supposedly accurately maintained) indicated that they had given 165 *clear* instructions to subordinates during the experimental observation period, the subordinates themselves recorded receiving instructions on only 84 of these occasions; Perry and Mahoney (1955), who correlated scores from an employee information test with scores from a morale survey; Simpson (1959), who asked supervisors in a textile mill how many work-related communication contacts they had typically with every other supervisor; and Walton (1959), who evaluated the effectiveness of several management information channels by asking employees to hypothetically rate the channels.

More recent examples would include the measures of upward, downward, and lateral organizational communication in the Taylor and Bowers (1972) work described earlier; the use of Fault Tree Analysis (Witkins & Stephans, 1972); the development of paper-and-pencil measures of perceived communication satisfaction (Downs, Hazen, & Quiggins, 1973); perceived managerial communication climate (Dennis, 1974); perceived communication freedom (Dennis, Richetto, & Wiemann, 1974); perceived supervisory credibility (Falcione, 1975); perceived communication apprehension (Scott, McCroskey, & Sheahan, 1976); the use of self-report measures in those network analysis methodologies that require subjects to recall their behaviors (Richards, 1976); and a battery of dyadic interpersonal questionnaire instruments reported by Schiemann and Graen (1977).

Early examples of behavioral research include the laboratory net research reported by Bavelas (1950) and others; the classic in small group research, of course, was Bales's (1950) Group Interaction Analysis behavior recording technique; the classic in rumor research was the "participant-observation" method—developed when self-report measures proved inaccurate, by Back, et al. (1950); and, using the *shadow* observation technique, Piersol (1955) followed his subjects for one month recording their on-the-spot communication behaviors.

Later, a cross-section of behavioral communication research can be seen in the work of Hinrichs (1964), who had subjects record their communication behavior at random periods at the sound of a buzzer; Sadler (1974), who used several behavioral and nonbehavioral techniques to examine a number of communication variables; and Mintzberg (1975), who used direct observation and content analysis to record the individual communication behavior of five executives.

Evaluation

Organizational communication researchers have not, historically, emphasized a strict operational definition pertaining to the collection of behaviorally-based communication data (for some exceptions, see Redding, 1972). Intuitively, it seems reasonable to have one. Small group research, for example, has generated abundant observation techniques over the years, many of which were specifically designed to capture small group properties and processes (Golembiewski, 1965). Further, the careful use of terminology by organizational communication investigators, describing the precise nature of the data base, is often times overlooked, especially in discussing the implications of research findings.

A case in point. One study reviewed here concluded from the administration of a questionnaire-survey that employees were unable to send grievance messages through formal union channels. However, no evidence to support the actual incidence of channel blockage was supplied by the investigator. Other examples could be cited where researchers have taken the liberty of reporting perceptual data as if they were, in fact, a true representation of actual communication experiences.

Attempts to determine the extent to which data obtained from nonbehavioral measures correlate with behaviorally-based data are markedly absent in the study of organizational communication. Network analysis methodologies are apparently equipped to collect communication experience information at the moment of occurrence, and, therefore, offer an excellent opportunity, if used in conjunction with other acceptable self-report, perceptual tools, to overcome this criticism.

Recommendations

Behaviors in complex organizational environments are often difficult to precisely measure on the individual level, and much more so with aggregates. The laboratory continues to present a fruitful environment (using audio-video support) for this purpose. Hence, we suggest the increased use of the laboratory locale—if possible, in field settings—for the collection and analysis of enriched, behaviorally-based data. For example, the subject of organizational and communication climates has been extremely difficult to conceptualize theoretically and then operationalize for use in the field (see Hellriegel & Slocum, 1974). Almost all of the data collected pertaining to these concepts are nonbehavioral, with real-world references seriously lacking. And yet we have reason to suspect, rather strongly, that perceived "climate" is associated with specific organizational communication behaviors (Redding, 1972; Dennis, 1974).

Perhaps a more concentrated reliance on nonreactive measurement procedures (i.e., physical traces, archives, and contrived observation) in organizational environments would also help remedy what we believe to be a fallible reliance on perceptually-based interview and questionnaire research methods (see Webb, Campbell, Schwartz, & Sechrest, 1971). Finally, to the extent that it is feasible and practical, organizational communication researchers should collect both behavioral and nonbehavioral data—if possible, concurrently—within the same overall research design.

DATA COLLECTION PROCEDURE

Historical Development

Almost all organizational communication researchers have gathered their data with survey questionnaires, interviews, observation techniques, or content analyses. About 75% of the studies examined here used survey questionnaires to measure respondents' feelings, perceptual evaluations, or reports about their communication experiences. In the 1950s, the most popular data gathering technique was the questionnaire, which was used to have respondents report the information they possessed about their organization's policies and practices, or information about their perceived role in the organization.

In the 1960s, researchers collected much data by either employing self-reports of behavior-estimates or actual logs of current communication behaviors. In the 1970s, there has been a shift toward the collection of either self-reports (through large surveys) of feelings and perceptions or the use of trained observers to log participants' communicative behaviors.

Due to its obvious economy of usage and ability to reach large numbers of people in short periods of time, the questionnaire survey has been the most popular data collection tool in organizational communication research. Surveys allow organizations to assess the effectiveness of their downward communication systems by asking such knowledge-related questions as: "How many sick leave days per month are you allowed?" or "How much money does the company contribute to your pension fund?" (for an example, see Funk & Becker, 1952). Inferences about communication problems existing in the organization were drawn from "disparity scores" of some survey instruments: "Describe your specific job duties and responsibilities." The answer would then be compared with what the respondent's superior or subordinate had indicated, as a measure of potential disparity (Browne & Neitzel, 1952). One other type of survey, mentioned earlier, asked respondents to indicate the amount of a particular message that they had received, the source of the message, the time they first heard it, their location, and the channel used for its transmission (Davis, 1953).

More recent surveys developed in the 1970s measure respondents' perceptions of communication topics, channels, sources, interpersonal relationships, feedback, and outcomes (Wiio, 1974; Roberts & O'Reilly, 1974). The ICA Communication Audit Survey Questionnaire (Goldhaber et al., 1977) measures communication needs by comparing discrepancies between the amount of information received versus the amount of information desired. The Network Analysis Survey Instrument (Richards, 1976) asks respondents to indicate from recall the frequency and importance of interaction with others over a given period of time (usually five working days).

The interview has been typically administered either concurrently or subsequent to the employment of a survey instrument. Although some interview guides (Foltz, 1973) have been developed as primary data-gathering techniques for organizational studies, most have been used in conjunction with another research instrument. The ICA Communication Audit system has developed an interview procedure based upon the use of two interviewers for every interviewee. This allows the lead interviewer the freedom to concentrate upon the questions and interaction dynamics, rather than upon precision in note taking. Further, after each interview episode, the two interviewers meet to discuss their observations and notes, as well as any implications of their particular interview experience for future interviews.

Observation techniques involve perceiving and recording the communication experiences of either self ("Duty Studies") or others ("trained" or "participant" observers). The Duty Study, for example, provides the respondent with a means of recording his or her own communication experiences either continuously or periodically. Burns (1954), discussed elsewhere in this overview, was one of the first to use this technique; he obtained information about communication activities of subjects who recorded the length of time an interaction lasted, who was involved, what the subject of the discussion was, and who initiated the encounter. This information resulted in findings about the direction of communication and the amount of time spent in various types of communication activities.

Other terms by which the Duty Study or variations thereof are known are: "self-recording technique," "communication log," "communication flow sheet," and "communication diary." Typically, the categories for observing communicative behavior have evolved out of discussions between the researcher(s) and the respondents. Much of the work in organizational communication being done in Canada (Conrath, 1973) and in Sweden (Thorngren, 1977), coincidentally, is of the duty study variety.

Trained observers perceive and describe the behavior of people other than themselves; participant observers perform similarly, but actually assume membership status in the group they are observing. Piersol (1955) introduced his version of this approach to observation in a study of the communication behavior of industrial foremen. He pointed out that a trusting relationship is necessary if "natural" data are to obtain. Sanborn (1961) used the same technique to follow executives of a large retail organization for four hours each, recording all detectable oral communication behavior.

Finally, content analysis techniques have been used by organizational communication researchers for analyzing message content and handling. This technique entails (1) selecting the message for study; (2) deciding upon a representative sample; (3) developing mutually exclusive and/or sign categories for measurement; (4) measuring the frequency of appearance of the categories in accordance with appropriate, verifiable coding rules; (5) applying proper statistical tests to the data; and (6) drawing final conclusions about the universe from which the data were drawn. For example, Dee (1960) analyzed common themes appearing in a union newspaper. Purdom (1963) content-analyzed messages sent through formal channels of a health organization. Goldhaber (1971) used content analysis to study two companies' employment manuals. His categories were two types of words—negative words (e.g., cannot, never, no, do not, etc.) and command words (e.g., always, must, essential, required, etc.).

Evaluation

Each of the above four data-gathering methods has both advantages and disadvantages. For example, questionnaires are fast, reliable, and economical; but are also prone to sampling error (especially with mail surveys), semantic problems, and interpretation problems (e.g., what is the real significance between a "fair" and "good" rating on an evaluative scale—from the *respondent's* viewpoint?). Interviews allow a maximum of researcher/respondent interaction, but at the expense of time, money, and coding problems. Observation studies provide detailed information about the amount of communication, the network used and the direction followed with a minimum of bias; but take a lot of time, require the processing of large amounts of data for typically small samples (some of which are unusable), and depend greatly upon respondent willingness to cooperate (no small task, as most researchers who have used observation techniques will testify). Content analysis allows careful scrutiny of written messages, but is sometimes subject to the valid criticism that post hoc hindsight is used to develop content categories.

Another recurring difficulty with the utilization of these research methods in organizational communication research is the lack of an agreed upon set of standards and rules for method application. Other than Taylor and Bowers (1972) and Goldhaber et al. (1977), no published set of norms exists for any communication behaviors or perceptions of behaviors. Norms cannot be developed without first agreeing upon a standardized procedure and instrumentation for gathering the data. With normative data, organizations can begin to compare themselves with other organizations against a common yardstick, whether it be perceptually or behaviorally based (e.g., job satisfaction, career commitment, productivity, profitability, etc.). With norms, in short, we believe that research in organizational communication will truly establish some much needed external validity.

Recommendations

Researchers should take whatever steps are necessary to guarantee the internal validity and reliability of their instrumentation (e.g., compute, as a matter of routine practice, appropriate reliability coefficients; correlate scores on surveys with "hard" measurements of organizational performance, such as turnover, absenteeism, productivity, and so on; use two interviewers and an immediate debriefing period; and develop objective, independently verifiable, content analytic categories). Further, the results of all validity and reliability computations should be reported with the description of the methodology.

Researchers should use at least two data-gathering techniques in every study in order to facilitate cross-validation of the results. Where discrepancies occur, a third methodology may be called for or a reported refinement of the instruments and a recollection of the data. In the case of new instrumentation, testing on a reported pilot population should be mandatory for all research projects. While the use of unobtrusive measurement techniques has not been discussed in this section on data collection procedures, mainly because nonreactive measurement has simply not been used in organizational communication research, our recommendations with respect to behavioral versus nonbehavioral data bases apply here.

Finally, when instrumentation has been developed satisfactorily, and the procedures for their administration standardized, collection of normative data should begin, hopefully, to permit comparisons and external validation of selected theoretical arguments.

QUANTITATIVE VERSUS QUALITATIVE ANALYSIS

We are reminded that the subject of what constitutes quantitative versus qualitative data analytical techniques is becoming blurred with sophistications brought through computer technology. Avoiding that argument, we wish to stress what we perceive to be a more important theme: the relative value to the study of organizational communication of *both* analytical techniques. In this regard, our position is clear: they are mutually valuable and needed.

Historical Development

The development of the use of quantitative measurement analysis in organizational communication research has paralleled the growing use of mathematical models in all of the social sciences. The general direction of this progression has been from the early use of aggregated scores of ratings, through the use of comparative statistical procedures and tests of significance, to the increasing use of correlative and regressive techniques and the development of complex multivariate models and clustering procedures.

Early survey work, such as the Funk and Becker (1952) research cited earlier, used means and percentages to describe the distribution of scores or ratings, as did the observational studies (Piersol, 1955; Sanborn, 1961) in describing frequencies within behavioral categories. While many of these studies did not employ conventional tests of significance, a number used relatively sophisticated tests of difference and correlation. For example, Browne and Nietzel (1952) submitted their survey scores to simple Pearson Product Moment correlation analysis, and Funk (1956) utilized analysis of variance and discriminant analysis.

With the advent of computerized storage and manipulation of data in the late 1950s, researchers began to employ increasingly complex statistical models to represent their data and provide tests of significant difference or association. As standardized statistical packages became available which provided multivariate statistical procedures, researchers began to employ these models to analyze their data.

Increasingly complex analysis of variance models was also used by investigators such as Taylor and Bowers (1972), Wiio (1974), and Goldhaber et al. (1977). Multiple regression has become widely used in tests of the predictive ability of multivariate measures (Dennis, 1974; Sadler, 1974; Daly, McCroskey & Falcione, 1976). Factor analysis and smallest space analysis have been employed to identify clusters of variables which share strong association with a common vector, thus allowing the identification and validation of multiple dimensions within the domain of measurement (Taylor & Bowers, 1972; Dennis, 1974; Roberts & O'Reilly, 1974; Falcione, 1975; Yates, Goldhaber, Porter, Dennis, & Richetto, 1976).

Recently, canonical correlation models have been utilized to test relationships between multiple sets of independent and dependent variables (Dennis, 1975; Muchinsky, 1977). Concomitantly, pattern recognition and matrix manipulation techniques are beginning to be employed in the identification and description of the structural typology of the interactive network operating in an information system (Richards, 1976). Finally, the internal consistency and stability of quantitative measures have been assessed throughout the use of inter-item, split-half, and test-retest correlation analysis as a means of instrument development and refinement (Taylor & Bowers, 1972; Scott, McCroskey, & Sheahan, 1976; Yates *et al.*, 1976; Goldhaber *et al.*, 1977).

Qualitative analyses, while not as widely employed as quantitative methods, have increased in sophistication and reliability, and have become more closely integrated with quantitative approaches. At present, the majority of researchers use qualitative analysis as an adjunct to, rather than as a substitute for, quantitative techniques.

The early participant-observation techniques and content-analytic methods discussed in the preceding section were primarily qualitative, reporting subjective judgments of events and thematic trends in messages. The earlier organizational communication studies employing interviews were also qualitative (e.g., Sanborn, 1961; Pace & Simons, 1963), yet the quantification of responses in categories inductively derived from the data has increased (Foltz, 1973; Yates *et al.*, 1976). The use of computer programs to count key words and phrases and compute frequencies is bringing quantitative procedures to previously qualitative methods of content analysis (Goldhaber, 1971).

Evaluation

While the advent of computerized analysis has allowed increasing sophistication in the models and designs utilized in testing hypothesized relationships and developing measures of communication variables, it has also made it possible for researchers to use, or abuse, statistical procedures without knowledge of the assumptions upon which these procedures are based. This has led to a proliferation of studies in which the most basic assumptions of sample size and characteristics, level of data and distribution of variance have been consistently violated or ignored. Early researchers such as Funk & Becker (1952) or Burns (1954) may be faulted primarily for small sample sizes and/or for using parametric procedures on nominal or ordinal level data. Yet the level of analysis in these investigations was such that findings were presented in close to raw data form, so that misleading distortion due to data reduction and manipulation was minimal. As data manipulation sophistication and the complexity of the statistical procedures used increased, however, so did the magnitude of errors in the use of these procedures.

Also, historically, researchers who employed analysis of variance designs gave no indication that they tested for the validity of the assumptions made in the particular designs chosen. In Funk's (1956) study, for example, no test for homogeneity of variance was reported. This failure to make, or report, appropriate tests continues to the present (Scott et al., 1976; Goldhaber et al., 1977).

Perhaps the most consistent violation occurs in the use of survey scores which constitute ordinal level data in parametric procedures, which assume at least interval level data. Researchers make the argument that because Likert, Guttman, or semantic differential scaling techniques were used which are *capable* of producing interval level data, they are justified in assuming that the requirements of known intervality between data points and additivity of responses have, in fact, been met. Yet few researchers have replicated the extensive psychometric and perceptual judgment tests, which were made originally with these scaling techniques.

If pressed, however, investigators may point to

the "power" and "robustness" of the statistics used, asserting that, even if several underlying assumptions are violated, the statistic is powerful enough to avoid rejecting a null hypothesis which is, in fact, true. Yet this argument, if not spurious, is an apology for violating the underlying assumptions of a statistic, not a reason to consistently do so.

In the rush to quantification, many researchers assumed that statistical modeling could replace conceptual modeling, and have attempted to use the results of multiple correlation, regression, or factor analysis, to discover the relationships in their data, rather than use them to test relationships which have been derived from cohesive theory and which have been hypothesized with precision. McCroskey and Young (1975) have described the pitfalls of factor analysis in communication research with sufficient thoroughness such that there is no reason to repeat them here. Let it suffice to say that the pitfalls are as prevalent in the area of organizational communication in particular, as they are in the field of communication in general.

Additionally, there is a limit to the utility of "brute force" pooling and partialing of variance in identifying important, as distinguished from significant, relationships and differences in a universe of data-points. Procedures which are powerful from the viewpoint of data reduction and manipulation may be weak in their ability to identify slight, but important, anomalies in the structure of that universe. Time series analysis and pattern recognition procedures may be more appropriate means of representing and analyzing that structure, but these techniques are only now beginning to be understood and used to analyze organizational communication systems as structural entities (Richards, 1976).

Finally, the need to establish the predictive ability of a measurement system has led some researchers to employ predictive statistical models, such as multiple regression, in research designs which are, in fact, associative (Daly, McCroskey, & Falcione, 1976). Researchers should temper their interpretation of such results with the realization that, lacking a direct manipulation, or a design incorporating a pre/post or longitudinal time dimension, their findings are not truly predictive. The central consideration is that designs test hypotheses, statistics do not. Indeed, researchers may wish to reconsider the use of multiple regression in light of the theoretical nature of the communication process as a complex system. Models which employ multiple predictors of a single criterion may be inappropriate in the investigation of multiple predictors and multiple criteria which characterize the most common descriptions of communicative causal factors and end results. Canonical models, if the underlying assumptions are carefully met, may be a more appropriate means of representing such relationships (see Dennis, 1974).

Qualitative analysis, while not as subject to strict criteria and procedures as quantitative analysis, has suffered from a lack of systematization. As a result, findings are not directly comparable or replicable, and this potentially useful and conceptually-rich form of analysis has been used principally as an anecdotal source of Gestalt impressions (e.g., Roy's 1954 research, 1969; Sanborn, 1961).

Recommendations

The primary remedy for errors in the use of statistics in the study of organizational communication is in education, updating, and control. Students, educators, and practitioners should be trained and kept informed in at least the basics of multivariate analysis, and the goal of all researchers should be to maintain a "state of the art" awareness of mathematical modeling procedures. Quality control of published research should be upgraded so that mistakes and omissions in statistical procedures will not be circulated as acceptable research procedures. A commitment as investigators to improving the quality and accuracy of research is the only ultimate solution to this problem.

Greater systematization can be brought to the analysis of interview and message content. If no *a priori* categories of response are available or desired, this may be inductively derived from the data by comparing the independent judgments of a number of investigators in a Delphi method (Rogers, 1973), or a variation of the method employed by IÇA Communication Audit researchers in analyzing "Critical Incident" data (see Yates *et al.*, 1976).

On the other hand, where categories of responses are available, such as in the results of a structured interview, a series of data reduction steps may be taken which aggregate responses while maintaining the quality of the data. Raw transcripts or notes from the interview are structured according to the interview guide. Responses to questions and follow-up probes are listed for each respondent and pooled across respondents by question categories. The common categories of responses are then identified within each question category by repeated passes through the aggregated responses. The response frequencies within each subcategory are then tabulated, identifying general trends in the data. From these frequencies, percentages are calculated. Summary conclusions are generated and listed for each question, along with examples of responses for each category—which have been edited to remove any references—which could be used to identify the source. This summary may then be reported without violating the confidentiality of the interview.

INTERNAL VERSUS EXTERNAL CONTINGENCIES

The recognition that "contingencies" affecting the organization may also impact upon certain organizational communication variables has gained only recent operational emphasis in the study of organizational communication, while the general concept of "organizational contingencies" has been researched in the study of organizational behavior for over a decade (see, for example, Woodward, 1965; Lawrence & Lorsch, 1967; Hellriegel & Slocum, 1973; Hofer, 1975; Luthans & Stewart, 1977). As used here, the term "contingencies" will denote events that are liable to occur in a given organizational situation, but which are most likely not intended.

Historical Development

Contingencies affecting communication behaviors and perceptions may be grouped as *internal*—derived from the organization (i.e., organization structure, outputs, space/time, demographics, and traditions), or *external*—derived from outside the organization (i.e., economy, technology, laws, and the external socio/political/cultural environment). Approximately 50% of the organizational communication research surveyed here has collected data relating, largely, to internal contingencies; interestingly, very few investigators have actually used or acknowledged these contingencies in their data analyses.

In the 1950s, for example, job classification and organizational role were of primary concern. In the 1960s, type of structure (e.g., "tall versus flat") and organizational size were studied. In the 1970s, attention has been given to personal demographics, particularly job tenure, mobility, education, and status.

In an extensive study of several small to middle-sized organizations, Sadler (1974) collected data on such internal contingencies as job classification and tenure, technical complexity and task variability, size, structure, and unionization—as well as economic and consumer external contingencies. Bacharach and Aiken (1977) correlated frequency of communication contacts with such internal contingencies as organizational size, shape, decentralization, routinization, and boundary spanning. They found that these organizational contingencies accounted for about 50% of the variance in the frequency of subordinate communication, but little or none of the variance in the frequency of department head communication.

Goldhaber et al. (1977) have shown differences in communicative behaviors and perceptions among different types of organizations (as a function of differences in organizational outputs—a hospital contrasted with an educational institution, for example). They reported that governmental organizations have a greater need to both send and receive information than do private enterprise, health care, and educational organizations. Further, they reported that workers in governmental organizations tend to be less satisfied with organizational outcomes (such as perceived organizational effectiveness) than those in other organizations.

In a series of European studies, Wiio (1976) has

also reported significant relationships between selected organizational demographics and communication behaviors and perceptions. Age and job tenure were the most potent predictors, for example, of communication information needs and communication satisfaction. Older employees and those with the greatest job tenure tended to want less, but indicated that they received more information than their younger, less experienced counterparts; not surprisingly, the latter were more dissatisfied with their perceived communication environment.

With implications for most multinational corporations, Throngren (1977) has concluded that after relocation (space viewed as an internal contingency), Swedish workers retained 30% of their old communication contacts. Similarly, Pye (1977) maintained that the increased economic benefits a company may obtain from relocations can be offset by the increased costs of communication (to maintain old contacts). Finally, in a test of the relationship between communication satisfaction and the *external* contingency of cultural language differences, Jain, Kanungo, and Goldhaber (1978) found that French-speaking employees were more satisfied than English-speaking employees in a landing hospital, with information sent and received while on the job, with the organization's communication channels, and with their overall jobs.

Evaluation

Very little empirical research has been reported which deals with the effects of internal and external contingencies upon communication perceptions, attitudes, and behavior in the general area of organizational communication. As a consequence, it is difficult to evaluate the prospective methodologies which may be employed to study contingencies. Suffice to say that the very absence of hypothesized contingency relationships in organizational communication research indicates neglect, in so far as our survey of the literature is concerned (for one exception, see Derry, 1972; for other comments on the issue, see Redding, 1972).

Recommendations

Organizational communication researchers can no longer avoid the systematic collection and reporting of communication data. Recent findings by Wiio and Goldhaber, cited above, have demonstrated the viability of contingency theory for communication researchers.

To repeat, internal contingencies should be measured, such as *structure* (including the degree of formality and type of structure chosen to organize the functions and relationships in the organization, as well as the size and shape of the system); *outputs* (the amount of diversity and degree of market uniqueness affecting the organization's products and services); *demographics* (the degree of variation among people working for the organization in such characteristics as age, education, job tenure, and supervisory status); *spatiotemporal characteristics* (the degree of variation in both spatial characteristics—design, amount, location, distance, including barriers, and temporal characteristics—timing of events and activities, including duration and permanence); and *traditions* (the degree of conformity with organizational norms and expectations—such as willingness to accept job relocations—history, value orientations, and so on).

Additionally, external contingencies should all be considered, such as the *economy* (amount of stability in current markets, the activities of competition, the effects of inflation, and the general impact of economical events upon capital resources needed by the organization); *technology* (the degree of industry innovation with equipment, science, research and development, and its impact on the organization); *laws* (the degree of impact of local, state, and federal regulations and guidelines which directly affect organizational operations); *socio/political/cultural* (the degree of impact of social, political, and cultural changes occurring within a given society); and *environment* (the degree of impact on the organization of the climate, geography, population/density, and energy availability).

TYPE OF OUTCOME CRITERIA

In this concluding section, we examine the use of criterion measurement in organizational communication research. A distinction is made between internal and external criteria for the purposes of illustration only. Generally speaking, dependent measures which are generated by the researcher, and which only operate within the realism of the research itself, tend to be classified as internal criteria; objective measures, which sustain in organizations to evaluate other organizational and/or communication performance phenomena, are termed external criteria.

Historical Development

Our tabulations indicate that approximately 65% of organizational communication research has employed at least one internal criterion measure, 5% of the literature surveyed cited the use of at least one external criterion, and 30% of the studies reviewed used no internal or external criterion measure at all.

In the 1950s and 1960s, typical internal criteria included knowledge of organizational information (Funk & Becker, 1952); morale (Browne & Neitzel, 1952); communication satisfaction (Level, 1959; Sanborn, 1961); communication sophistication (Sanborn, 1961); semantic information distance (Tompkins, 1962); perceived trust and perceived upward influence (Read, 1962); ratings of supervisory communication ability (Pace & Simons, 1963); perceived superior-subordinate agreement (Maier, Hoffman, & Read, 1963); and evaluations of managerial interaction episodes (Lawler, Porter, & Tannenbaum, 1968).

During this same period, typical external dependent variables and criterion measures studied were: production per unit of time (Coch & French, 1948); problem-solving speed and accuracy (Bavelas, 1950); decision-making efficiency (Carzo, 1963); and profitability and rate of return on sales (Carzo & Yanouzas, 1969).

In the 1970s, additions to both lists described above would include, representing internal criteria, perceived environmental uncertainty (Huber, O'Connell, & Cummings, 1975; perceived job satisfaction (Roberts & O'Reilly, 1974; Dennis, 1975; Falcione, 1975, Daly, McCroskey, & Falcione, 1976; Richards, 1976); perceived coordination (Sadler, 1974); managerial performance ratings (Dennis, 1975); and perceived organizational effectiveness (Goldhaber et al., 1977; and, representing external criteria, productivity (Burhans, 1971; Taylor & Bowers, 1972); sales performance (Sadler, 1974); accidents, grievances, turnover, value added, cost of information (Taylor & Bowers, 1972; Thorngren, 1977); absenteeism (Dennis, '1975); and return on investment (Thorngren, 1977).

Evaluation

There seems to be an under-utilization of organizationally-relevant external criteria, or "end-result" variables, to use Likert's (1967) terminology, in organizational communication research. We recognize, however, that the ability of a hypothesis or research instrument to account for external criterion variance is an aim that, perhaps, some organizational communication scholars do not view as a priority at this stage of the field's development. Nevertheless, we wish to mention three criticisms for researchers who endorse our view, that if we claim to be organizational communication specialists, and if we hold the notion that *effective* communication in organizations is important, then we must be able to show how improvements in communication functioning will affect the end results that organizations seek.

Our first criticism relates to the widespread use of internal criterion measures that have no acceptable measure of validity beyond the immediate research project for which the measures were designed. When criterion measures are designed for general usage in the field, few researchers make a deliberate attempt to incorporate the measures in their own research, or take the time to subject the measures to a series of cross-validation efforts. Communication satisfaction, for example, has been tossed about as a criterion for years. To date, however, there has been little systematic effort to determine the extent to which this internal criterion shares any significant variance with other, organizationally germane, external criteria. As one colleague put it, "What does it mean if you do not possess high communication satisfaction in your organization?" In short, we have multiple internal criteria, none of which to our knowledge share any meaningfully verified, significant variance with any of several important external criteria. Part of this problem relates to our earlier discussion on individual research designs; until the field of organizational communication finds a way to use more "true" research designs, it is doubtful that this criterion problem will be solved.

Second, human communication performance is

a multidimensional variable, as is human work performance. People scoring high on one dimension may score low on another, and their scores may change over time or literally over organizations. Thus, we run into the difficulty of asking ourselves, "Should we be measuring performance on these dimensions separately or should they be combined to reach an overall judgment?" Organizational communication researchers have yet to come to grips with this question, and until this is done, we will risk wandering aimlessly in the development of satisfactory internal and external criteria.

Third, few researchers report convergent and discriminant validity tests in connection with their internal criterion, nor do they report any other rigorous assessments of these measures. For example, has the investigator insured that the criterion is not contaminated by the predictor itself? Is the criterion comprehensible and relevant to the sample to which it has been applied?

Recommendations

Put simply, more external, organizationally relevant criteria should be incorporated in the design of organizational communication research. Internal criteria need to be correlated with external criteria, whenever possible, to establish a form of concurrent validity; criterion measures generated internally should be carefully inspected to insure that basic principles of sound, psychometric measurement have not been violated. Perhaps, when these steps are taken, we will be able to abandon many of the circular and self-serving descriptions which, unfortunately, characterize our current efforts to define "effective organizational communication."

CONCLUSION

Richetto (1977) opened his overview of the organizational communication field by asserting that "organizational communication, like the teary-eyed little girl in party dress, appears to be 'all dressed up with no place to go' " (p. 331). From a research methods perspective, we would add that she is overdressed in some places and underdressed in others.

To summarize, most organizational communication research has been accomplished in field locales, using predominantly descriptive research designs and a relatively short research intervention period, with only incidental recognition of a time factor. It has employed samples consisting principally of individuals, composed of data bases that are mainly nonbehavioral, with data collection methods dominated by self-report instruments, and with analyses of data primarily quantitative. It has described internal contingencies, when included, as either an intervening variance source, or as a post hoc supplementary explanation to major research findings; it has engaged the use of mainly internal criteria, again, when included, to establish the validity of research results.

We reiterate areas we believe are in need of strengthening.

1. There is a need to accomplish more research in laboratory locales and then translate and apply this research in field settings in order to establish theoretically and empirically contiguous research results.
2. More true experimental designs should be used, regardless of the research locale, to enhance the predictive power of the concepts and constructs tested.
3. Longitudinal and time series research, employing multiple research methodologies, with *time* treated as a significant—if not independent or moderating—variable should replace the historical emphasis on the one-shot case study and/or the single measurement of variables undifferentiated in terms of their time-bound or time-free properties.
4. Avoidance of incidental sampling, the prevention of self-selection in sample compositions, the use of *meaningful* organizational sampling units, and the use of power calculations to establish sample strength should increase the generality of organizational communication research.
5. Making the assumption that unverified self-report data constitute true behavioral statements, attaching unqualified significance to perceptual observations, and failing, in general, to make a uniform distinction between behavioral and nonbehavioral data are errors that can be easily rectified by adhering to strict criteria for operationalizing variables and specifying how the

sample population supplied their behavioral experiences and/or perceptual reports. The need for more relevant, behaviorally-based data is also suggested.

6. The use of multiple data gathering procedures, including unobtrusive measurement techniques, the careful reporting of reliability and validity data, and the use of *already existing* data collection instruments should be substituted for the current trend of developing a new measuring technique for each conventional data collection procedure that is used.

7. Data analysis—both quantitative and qualitative—should be elevated from an all too frequent prescientific misuse of descriptive and inferential statistics, especially in connection with the use of multivariate models, to a scientific application of rigid rules, based upon similarly strictly-maintained assumptions, that are appropriately applied to the research problem and its corresponding research design. (The reporting of simple percentages and uncorrected means is far more valuable in the long run than is the reporting of a multiple regression that is based upon truly ordinal data points established from a non-random, non-representative, sample population.)

8. The collection and/or reporting of contingent organizational data should be accompanied with a description of how these data interacted with other data obtained during the research intervention. How these data produced significant criterion variance, if any, should especially be mentioned.

9. In the final analysis, the capability of organizational concepts, constructs, and theories to explain and predict variations in human and organizational performance is implicit to the sine qua non of the emerging field. Never has the need been greater than now to show that such relationships do exist, that communication performance and communication perceptions do predict and explain significant variance in human and organizational performance. Never will the challenge be greater than it is now to produce results that practitioners can accept, understand, and use to improve the functioning of their organizations.

Lastly, Grunig (1973) maintained that:

> . . . most 'theories' of organizational communication are of little use for the professional because they are generally descriptive (e.g., they tell how information flows through an organization) or predictive (e.g., some say that upward communication will be biased in favor of the superior's expectations). Seldom is such theory explanatory. Most organizational communication theory falls into the category . . . empirical generalizations rather than theory because it leaves unanswered the question of *why* the empirical generalization occurs. (pp. 8-9)

We would argue that the explanatory ability of a theory, which is subject to empirical verification, is not unrelated to the ability of a research design to minimize unwanted sources of error variance. Yes, the study of organizational communication appears abundant with empirical generalizations, as Grunig claimed, some more fruitful and beneficial than others to professional researchers and practitioners alike. But the theory to which these generalizations have been applied will continue to prevail without sufficient explanatory power, until such time that adequate research methods are utilized and true research designs are consistently employed to satisfy the skepticism of many who claim that the study of organizational communication has not yet found a position in the social science hierarchy.

The challenge, as we see it, is to make a methodological "mid-course" correction. We have the skills and knowledge to do it. Only time will tell if we have made the correction wisely.

NOTES

1. The first draft of this review contained a section entitled, "Communication Variable Classification," which was inserted after the fifth tier in Figure 1 (i.e., "Data Base: Behavioral vs. Nonbehavioral"). An editorial decision was made to eliminate this section because most of the content in it duplicated Richetto's historical overview reported in *Communication Yearbook I*. (See Richetto, 1977.)
2. We originally consulted well over 200 primary and secondary sources representing research accomplished during the period 1948 to 1977. A problem quickly emerged: how do you distinguish between research which has had direct bearing on the embryonic development of the field, from research accomplished in allied disciplinary areas that tangentially has influenced theoretical contributions made to date? The reader will judge if our final sample of 100 plus studies seems to maintain an internal consistency which properly represents the study of organizational communication. No doubt other important contributions from the disciplines of psychology, sociology, anthropology, and the management sciences have been inadvertently omitted. But we feel, given the eclectic emphasis of many researchers for the past 30 years, our sample is reasonably representative.
3. By quasi-experimental, we mean research that lacks sufficient experimental control to establish acceptable claims for

external validity. In organizational communication research, we see this illustrated in semiscientific sampling procedures and in the relative absence of counter-balanced control group designs that include pre- and post-measurement on the dependent variable(s). Aside from these restrictions, we accept the customary distinction between the presence or absence of experimental treatment manipulation.

4. Settings have included manufacturing companies, wholesale and retail businesses, insurance companies, financial institutions, health care institutions, military organizations, public utilities, governmental bureaucracies, high schools, colleges, universities, penal institutions, law enforcement agencies, volunteer associations, and religious institutions.
5. A predictive design is a true experimental design (Campbell & Stanley, 1966) which permits the investigator to select and utilize statistics appropriate for a parametric model; the design is "true" because certain requirements for internal and external validity have been met. A descriptive design should not call for the use of inferential statistics and cannot make any claims beyond the sample under study.
6. For a typical canonical correlation analysis, for example, a sample of from 500 to 1,000 is customary to maintain a ratio of about 20 subjects for each dependent variable analyzed.
7. Certainly, the use of audio/visual techniques, as well as the unobtrusive use of available evidential "traces" (e.g., memos, letters, appointment records, meeting minutes, and other organizational artifacts) to "freeze" behavioral acts constitute two variations of a methodologically sound practice.

REFERENCES

ATHANASSIADES, J.C. Investigation of some communication patterns of female subordinates in hierarchical organizations. *Human Relations*, 1974, 27, 195-209.

AYRES, J. Techniques for the study of communication in organizations. In J.L. Owen, P.A. Page, & G.I. Zimmerman (Eds.), *Communication in organizations*. New York: West, 1976, 290-295.

BACHARACH, S.B., & AIKEN, M. Communication in administrative bureaucracies. *Academy of Management Journal*, 1977, 20, 365-377.

BACK, K., FESTINGER, L., HYMOVITCH, B., KELLY, H., SCHACTER, S., & THIBAUT, J. The methodology of studying rumor transmission. *Human Relations*, 1950, 3, 307-312.

BAIRD, J.E., JR. *The dynamics of organizational communication*. New York: Harper & Row, 1977.

BALES, R.F. *Interaction process analysis: A method for the study of small groups*. Cambridge, Mass.: Addison-Wesley, 1950.

BAVELAS, A. Communication patterns in task oriented groups. *Journal of the Acoustical Society of America*, 1950, 22, 307-312.

BROWNE, C.G., & NIETZEL, B.J. Communication, supervision, and morale. *Journal of Applied Psychology*, 1952, 36, 86-91.

BURHANS, D.T. The development and measuring of two internal communication measuring instruments. Paper presented at the annual meeting of the International Communication Association, Atlanta, 1972.

BURNS, T. The direction of activity and communication in a departmental executive group. *Human Relations*, 1954, 7, 73-97.

CAIN, G.S. Some effects of organizational structure on problem solving. Unpublished doctoral dissertation, Pennsylvania State University, 1964.

CAMPBELL, D.T., & STANLEY, J.C. *Experimental and quasi-experimental designs for research*. Chicago: Rand McNally, 1966.

CARZO, R. Some effects of organizational structure on group effectiveness. *Administrative Science Quarterly*, 1963, 7, 393-424.

CARZO, R., & YANOUZAS, J.N. Effects of flat and tall organization structure. *Administrative Science Quarterly*, 1969, 14, 178-191.

COCH, L., & FRENCH, R.J. Overcoming resistance to change. *Human Relations*, 1948, 1, 512-532.

COHEN, A.R. Upward communication in experimentally created hierarchies. *Human Relations*, 1958, 11, 41-53.

CONRATH, D.W. Communication environment and its relationship to organizational structure. *Management Science*, 1973, 20, 586-603.

DAHLE, T.L. An objective and comparative study of five methods of transmitting information to business and industrial employees. *Speech Monographs*, 1954, 21, 21-28.

DALY, J., & McCROSKEY, J. Occupational choice and desirability as a function of communication apprehension. *Journal of Counseling Psychology*, 1975, 22, 309-313.

DALY, J., McCROSKEY, J., & FALCIONE, R. Homophily-heterophily and the prediction of supervisor satisfaction. Paper presented at the annual meeting of the International Communication Association, Portland, 1976.

DANOWSKI, J.A., & FARACE, R.V. Communication network integration and group uniformity in a complex organization. Paper presented at the annual meeting of the International Communication Association, New Orleans, 1974.

D'AUGELLI, A.R. Group composition using interpersonal skills: An analogue study on the effects of members' interpersonal skills on peer ratings and group cohesiveness. *Journal of Counseling Psychology*, 1973, 20, 531-534.

DAVIS, K. Methods of studying communication patterns in organizations. *Personnel Psychology*, 1953, 6, 301-312.

DEE, J. Oral communication in a trade union local. *Journal of Communication*, 1960, 10, 77-86.

DENNIS, H.S., III. A theoretical and empirical study of managerial communication climate in complex organizations. Unpublished doctoral dissertation, Purdue University, 1974.

DENNIS, H.S., III, RICHETTO, G.M., & WIEMANN, J.M. Articulating the need for an effective internal communication system: New empirical evidence for the communication specialist. Paper presented at the annual meeting of the International Communication Association, New Orleans, 1974.

DENNIS, H.S., III. The construction of a managerial "communication climate" inventory for use in complex organizations. Paper presented at the annual meeting of the International Communication Association, Chicago, 1975.

DERRY, J.O. A correlational and factor-analytic study of attitudes and communication networks in industry. Unpublished doctoral dissertation, Purdue University, 1972.

DOWNS, C.W., HAZEN, M.D., & QUIGGINS, J. An empirical and theoretical investigation of communication satisfaction. Paper presented at the annual meeting of the Speech Communication Association, New York, 1973.

DOWNS, C.W., LINKUGEL, W., & BERG, D. *The organizational communicator*. New York: Harper & Row, 1977.

ELLIS, D.S. An analysis of the differential effects of various types and degrees of communication opportunity on conflict between groups. Unpublished doctoral dissertation, Purdue University, 1965.

FALCIONE, R.L. Subordinate satisfaction as a function of perceived supervisor credibility. Paper presented at the annual meeting of the International Communication Association, Chicago, 1975.

FARACE, R.V., & MORRIS, C. The communication system at Justin Marrill College. Unpublished paper, Department of Communication, Michigan State University, 1969.

FARACE, R.V., MONGE, P.R., & RUSSELL, H.M. *Communicating and organizing*. Reading, Mass.: Addison-Wesley, 1977.

FOLTZ, R. *Management by communication*. New York: Chilton, 1973.

FUNK, H.B., & BECKER, R.C. Measuring the effectiveness of industrial communications. *Personnel Journal*, 1952, 29, 237-240.

FUNK, F.E. Communication attitudes of industrial foremen as related to their productivity. Unpublished doctoral dissertation, Purdue University, 1956.

GOLDHABER, G.M. A content analysis of two employment manuals with implications for theory X-Y assumptions. *EPS*, 1971, 11, 1-8.

GOLDHABER, G.M., PORTER, D.T., & YATES, M.P. The ICA communication audit survey instrument: 1977 organizational norms. Paper presented at the annual meeting of the International Communication Association, Berlin, 1977.

GOLEMBIEWSKI, R.T. Small groups and large organizations. In J.G. March (Ed.), *Handbook of organizations*. Chicago: Rand McNally, 1965, 87-141.

GRUNIG, J.E. Information seeking in organizational communication: A case study of applied theory. Paper presented at the annual meeting of the International Communication Association, Montreal, 1973.

GUETZKOW, H., & SIMON, H.A. The impact of certain communication nets upon organization and performance in task-oriented groups. *Management Science*, 1955, 1, 233-250.

GUETZKOW, H., & DILL, W.R. Factors in the organizational development of task-oriented groups. *Sociometry*, 1957, 20, 175-204.

GUETZKOW, H. Communication in organizations. In J.G. March (Ed.), *Handbook of organizations*. Chicago: Rand McNally, 1965, 534-573.

HEISE, G.A., & MILLER, G.A. Problem-solving by small groups using various communication nets. *Journal of Abnormal and Social Psychology*, 1951, 46, 327-335.

HELLRIEGEL, D., & SLOCUM, J.W. Organization design: A contingency approach. *Business Horizons*, 1973, April, 59-68.

HELLRIEGEL, D., & SLOCUM, J.W. Organizational climates: measures, research, and contingencies. *Academy of Management Journal*, 1974, 17, 255-280.

HINRICHS, J. Communications activity of industrial research personnel. *Personnel Psychology*, 1964, 17, 193-204.

HOFER, C.W. Toward a contingency theory of business strategy. *Academy of Management Journal*, 1975, 18, 784-810.

HUBER, G.P., O'CONNELL, M.J., & CUMMINGS, L.L. Perceived environmental uncertainty-effects of information and structure. *Academy of Management Journal*, 1975, 18, 725-740.

JABLIN, F.M. An experimental study of message-response in superior-subordinate communication. Unpublished doctoral dissertation, Purdue University, 1977.

JAIN, H., KANUNGO, R., & GOLDHABER, G. Communication differences between Anglophones and Francophones in a Canadian hospital. Unpublished manuscript, McMaster University, Hamilton, Ontario, 1978.

JOHNSON, B. *Communication: the process of organizing*. Boston: Allyn & Bacon, 1977.

KATZ, D., MACCOBY, N., & MORSE, N. *Productivity, supervision, and morale in an office situation: Part I*. Ann Arbor: University of Michigan, Institute for Social Research, 1950.

KELLY, C.M. Actual listening behavior of industrial supervisors as related to listening ability, general mental ability, selected personality factors, and supervisory effectiveness. Unpublished doctoral dissertation, Purdue University, 1962.

KNUTSON, T.J. An experimental study of the effects of orientation behavior on small group consensus. *Speech Monographs*, 1972, 39, 159-165.

LAWLER, E.E., PORTER, L.W., & TANNENBAUM, R. Manager's attitudes toward interaction episodes. *Journal of Applied Psychology*, 1968, 52, 432-439.

LAWRENCE, P.R. *The changing of organizational behavior patterns*. Boston: Harvard University Press, 1958.

LAWRENCE, P.R., & LORSCH, J.W. Organization and environment: Managing differentiation and integration. Boston: Harvard University Press, 1967.

LEATHERS, D.G. Quality of group communication as a determinant of group product. *Speech Monographs*, 1972, 39, 166-173.

LEAVITT, H.J. Some effects of certain communication patterns on group performance. *Journal of Abnormal and Social Psychology*, 1951, 46, 38-50.

LEAVITT, H.J. Applied organizational change in industry: Structural, technological, and humanistic approaches. In J.G. March (Ed.), *Handbook of organizations*. Chicago: Rand McNally, 1965, 1144-1170.

LEVEL, D.A. A case study of human communication in an urban bank. Unpublished doctoral dissertation, Purdue University, 1959.

LIKERT, R. *New patterns of management*. New York: McGraw-Hill, 1961.

LIKERT, R. *The human organization: Its management and value*. New York: McGraw-Hill, 1967.

LUTHANS, F., & STEWART, T. A general contingency theory of management. *The Academy of Management Review*, 1977, 2, 181-195.

MacDONALD, D. Communication roles and communication networks in a formal organization. *Human Communication Research*, 1976, 365-375.

MACY, J., CHRISTIE, L.S., & LUCE, R.D. Coding noise in a task-oriented group. *Journal of Abnormal and Social Psychology*, 1953, 48, 401-409.

MAIER, N.R., HOFFMAN, L.R., & READ, W.H. Superior-subordinate communication: The relative effectiveness of those who held their subordinates' position. *Personnel Psychology*, 1963, 26, 1-11.

McCROSKEY, J., & YOUNG, T. Uses and abuses of factor analysis in communication research. Paper presented at the annual meeting of the International Communication Association, Chicago, 1975.

MILLER, G.R. Research settings: Laboratory studies. In P. Emmert & W.D. Brooks (Eds.), *Methods of research in communication*. Boston: Houghton-Mifflin, 1970.

MINTZBERG, H. The manager's job: Folklore and fact. *Harvard Business Review*, 1975, 53, 49-61.

MIRAGLIA, J.F. An experimental study of the effects of communication training upon perceived job performance of nursing supervisors in two urban hospitals. Unpublished doctoral dissertation, Purdue University, 1963.

MUCHINSKY, P.M. Organizational communication: Relationships to organizational climate and job satisfaction. *Academy of Management Journal*, 1977, 20, 592-607.

ODIORNE, G.S. An application of the communications audit. *Personnel Psychology*, 1954, 7, 235-243.

O'REILLY, C.A., & ROBERTS, K.H. Information filtration in organizations: Three experiments. *Organizational Behavior and Human Performance*, 1974, 11, 253-265.

ORGAN, D.W. Social exchange and psychological reactance in a simulated superior-subordinate relationship. *Organizational Behavior and Human Performance*, 1974, 11, 132-142.

PACE, W.R., & SIMONS, H.R. Preliminary validation report on the Purdue basic oral communication evaluation form. *Personnel Journal*, 1963, 42, 191-193.

PERRY, D., & MAHONEY, T.A. In-plant communications and employee morale. *Personnel Psychology*, 1955, 8, 339-346.

PIERSOL, D. A case study of oral communication practices of foremen in a Midwestern corporation. Unpublished doctoral dissertation, Purdue University, 1955.

PONDER, A.A. The effects of involvement in decision-making on the productivity of three-man laboratory groups. Unpublished doctoral dissertation, University of British Columbia, 1973.

POOL, I. de SOLA. Communication systems. In I. de Sola Pool, W. Schramm, N. Maccoby, & E.B. Parker (Eds.), *Handbook of communication*. Chicago: Rand McNally, 1973.

PURDOM, P. Organization decentralization in a government executive agency as measured by communications: A study of the community health services of the Philadelphia Department of Public Health. Unpublished doctoral dissertation, University of Pennsylvania, 1963.

PYE, R. Office location and the cost of maintaining contact. *Environment and Planning*, 1977, 9, 150-154.

READ, W. Upward communication in industrial hierarchies. *Human Relations*, 1962, 15, 3-15.

REDDING, W.C. Research setting: Field studies. In P. Emmert and W.D. Brooks (Eds.), *Methods of research in communication*. Boston: Houghton Mifflin, 1970.

REDDING, W.C. *Communication within the organization: An interpretive review of theory and research*. New York: Industrial Communication Council, 1972.

RICHARDS, W.D. Using g-network analysis in research. Paper presented at the annual meeting of the International Communication Association, Portland, Oregon, 1976.

RICHETTO, G.M. Organizational communication theory and research: An overview. In B.D. Ruben, (Ed.), *Communication yearbook I*. New Brunswick, N.J.: Transaction-International Communication Association, 1977.

ROBERTS, K.H., & O'REILLY, C.A. Measuring organizational communication. *Journal of Applied Psychology*, 1974, 59, 321-326.

ROBY, T.B., & LANZETTA, J.T. Conflicting principles in man-machine system design. *Journal of Applied Psychology*, 1957, 41, 170-178.

ROETHLISBERGER, F.J., & DICKSON, W.J. *Management and the worker*. Cambridge, Mass.: Harvard University Press, 1943.

ROGERS, D.P. A systems analysis of correlates of network openness in organizational communication. Unpublished doctoral dissertation, Ohio University, 1973.

ROY, D. Efficiency and "the fix": Informal intergroup relations in a piecework machine shop. In J.A. Litterer (Ed.), *Organizations: Structure and behavior*. Vol. 1 (2nd Ed.). New York: Wiley, 1969.

SADLER, W.J. Communications in organizations: An exploratory study. Unpublished doctoral dissertation, University of Wisconsin, 1974.

SANBORN, G.A. An analytical study of oral communication practices in a national retail sales organization. Unpublished doctoral dissertation, Purdue University, 1961.

SCHIEMANN, W.A., & GRAEN, G. The predictability of communication in organizations: An empirical investigation and integration. Management working paper, Georgia Institute of Technology, College of Industrial Management, Atlanta, 1977.

SCHWARTZ, D.F. Liaison-communication roles in a formal organization. *Communimetrics reports, no. 1*. Fargo: North Dakota State University, 1968.

SCOTT, M.D., McCROSKEY, J.C., & SHEAHAN, M.E. The development of a self-report measure of communication apprehension in organization settings. Paper presented at the annual meeting of the International Communication Association, Portland, Oregon, 1976.

SCOTT, R.L. Communication as an intentional social system. *Human Communication Research*, 1977, 3, 258-268.

SCOTT, R.W. Fields methods in the study of organizations. In J.G. March (Ed.), *Handbook of organizations*. Chicago: Rand McNally, 1965, 261-304.

SEXTON, R., & STAUDT, V. Business communication: A survey of the literature. *Journal of Social Psychology*, 1959, 50, 101-118.

SHAW, M.E. Acceptance of authority, group structure, and the effectiveness of small groups. *Journal of Personnel*, 1959, 27, 196-210.

SHERIF, M., HARVEY, O.J., WHILE, B.J., HOOD, W.R., & SHERIF, C.W. *Experimental study of positive and negative intergroup attitudes between experimentally produced groups: Robbers cave study*. Norman: University of Oklahoma, 1954.

SIMPSON, R.L. Vertical and horizontal communication in formal organizations. *Administrative Science Quarterly*, 1959, 4, 188-196.

SMITH, R.L. An experimental comparison of oral and written media for communicating information in industry. Unpublished thesis, Purdue University, 1962.

STEINFATT, T.M. Communication and conflict: A review of new material. *Human Communication Research*, 1974, 1, 81-89.

TAYLOR, J.C., & BOWERS, D.C. *Survey of organizations*. Ann Arbor, Mich.: Malloy Lithographing, 1972.

THOMAS, D.R. Managerial bias: The effects of interpersonal expectations in a work group situation. Unpublished doctoral dissertation, University of Washington, 1973.

THORNGREN, B. How do contact systems effect regional involvement. *Environment and Planning*, 1970, 2, 409-427.

THORNGREN, B. Silent actors: Communication networks for development. In I. de Sola Pool (Ed.), *Social impact of the telephone*. Boston: M.I.T. Press, 1977.

TOMPKINS, P.H. An analysis of communication between headquarters and selected units of a national labor union.

Unpublished doctoral dissertation, Purdue University, 1962.

WALTON, E. Communicating down the line: How they really get the word. *Personnel*, 1959, 36, 78-82.

WARNER, E., FALCIONE, R., & TEMKIEWICZ, J. A communication audit of a federal agency at two points in time. Paper presented at the annual meeting of the International Communication Association, Chicago, 1978.

WEBB, E.J., CAMPBELL, D.T., SCHWARTZ, R.D., & SECHREST, L. *Unobtrusive measures: Nonreactive research in the social sciences*. Chicago: Rand McNally, 1971.

WEICK, K.E. Laboratory experimentation with organizations. In J.G. March (Ed.), *Handbook of organizations*. Chicago: Rand McNally, 1965, 194-260.

WIIO, O.A. Auditing communication in organizations. A standard survey. Paper presented at the annual meeting of the International Communication Association, New Orleans, 1974.

WIIO, O.A. Organizational communication: Interfacing systems in different contingencies. Paper presented at the annual meeting of the International Communication Association, Portland, Oregon, 1976.

WITKIN, B.R., & STEPHANS, K.G. A fault tree analysis approach to analysis of organizational communication systems. Paper presented at the annual meeting of the Western Communication Association, 1972.

WOFFORD, J., GERLOFF, E., & CUMINS, R. *Organizational communication: The keystone to managerial effectiveness*. New York: McGraw-Hill, 1977.

WOODWARD, J. *Industrial organization: Theory and practice*. London: Oxford University Press, 1965.

YATES, M.P., GOLDHABER, G.M., PORTER, D.T., DENNIS, H.S., III, & RICHETTO, G.M. The ICA organizational communication audit: The results of six studies. Paper presented at the annual meeting of the International Communication Association, Portland, Oregon, 1976.

CRITERIA FOR EVALUATION OF ORGANIZATIONAL COMMUNICATION EFFECTIVENESS: REVIEW AND SYNTHESIS

RICHARD V. FARACE
Michigan State University

JAMES A. TAYLOR
Temple University

JOHN P. STEWART
Michigan State University

This paper contains a discussion of 21 potential criteria for assessing the effectiveness of communication in organizations. The criteria are derived from a systematic, computer-based search of the literature in communication, management, organizational behavior, and allied fields. The criteria are grouped under the general heading of *communication rules*, since the formal and informal rule structure of the organization provides the framework within which individual criteria operate. Five categories of criteria are described: structure, messages, media, communicator, and potpourri. The media category is omitted for brevity purposes from the present paper.

For each criterion, the major literature identified by the authors is summarized, and a discussion is given of the conditions under which the criterion can exemplify more or less effective communication. The set of criteria, while not exhaustive, offers a focus for a continuing attempt to transform the multifaceted notion of "communication effectiveness" into more operational terms that have both theoretic and practical utility. The paper concludes with a brief outline of the next steps involved in developing this initial effort—the derivation of propositions or assertions, operationalization and measurement, and research that will yield empirical evidence about the criteria (their reliability, validity, and value).

Scholars of organizational communication have long had to grapple with the problem of explicating, measuring and applying the concept of "communication effectiveness." Since the concept has, by its treatment and its typical conceptualization, been very broad in nature, little progress seems to have been made in making it useful in either a scholarly or pragmatic sense—even though the need to do so is widely felt. The present paper is an initial explication of some of the elements of organizational communication effectiveness as described and summarized on the basis of a comprehensive literature review. Subsequent papers will deal with the development of propositions concerning the criteria, measurement techniques, and potential research investigations. Initially, some comments will be made about the authors' conceptualization of communication.

Some communication scientists define the principal function of communication as the reduction of uncertainty (Farace, Monge, & Russell, 1977). Many scholars argue that this is the sole motivation for communication. The reduction of uncertainty is directed toward the specific goals of the message source, so as to achieve as much control over the receiver during the process of uncertainty reduction as possible. Thus, uncertainty reduction through communication—whether this is labelled education, information, public relations, specification, explanations, and so forth—is fundamentally designed to limit the range of alternatives a receiver may engage in after receipt of the message. This means that communication is directed at, in some fashion, controlling the behavior of the receiver.

Similarly, the function of the process of organization is the reduction of variability in human behavior. Organizations render the collective behavior and the outcomes of many individuals predictable. This occurs through communication; hence, there can be no separation between "organizing" functions and communicating functions in organizations (Weick, 1969).

Communication scholars argue that three categories of change through communication are knowledge, attitudes, and behavior. In general, knowledge is designed to re-direct the focus of a receiver's available choices. Attitude change communication is designed to increase the tendency that a receiver will act in a particular way at subsequent points in time. Communication aimed at behavioral change, the most difficult of the three to achieve, is designed to produce immediate compliance or to instill a long-term behavioral pattern in a receiver. It should be obvious that most communication events contain elements of all three of these factors, particularly communication in organizations.

Communication increases the probability that the receiver will come into greater compliance with the source, and hence, communication acts to render the world more predictable. This same comment can be applied to the processes involved in the formation of organizations. Organizations allow predictions to be made about the conversion of the resources into some product. Organizations exist because it is easier for a large group of people, acting interdependently, to transform resources, than the same set of individuals could accomplish if their entire efforts were spent working alone. Organizational processes focus centrally on the control and coordination of people and resources. The mechanism through which control and coordination is accomplished is communication.

The objective of this review is to present in outline form some major concepts used in viewing communication and organizations. Our interest is in establishing criteria by which the effectiveness of communication in organizations may be judged and evaluated. At a macro-level, the criteria are: (1) does the communication event increase the ability of the organization's managers to control production processes; and (2) does the communication event enhance the ability to coordinate these same processes. These two categories are, in themselves, too broad to be useful, and they give organizations a stigma of possessing a lack of sensitivity to the human needs of its members. Scholars have long noted that managers are responsible for the adjudication of the balance between organizational productivity norms and the needs of the individual members of the organization (Simon, 1947). Thus, an extensive list of criteria which incorporates both the control and coordination notion, and the human dimension of organizational functioning, is proposed.

Communication effectiveness can be defined in general as the degree to which the response to a message transmission event is consonant with the overall objectives of the initiator of the event. Thus, from an individual's point of view, communication is effective when the receiver complies with the intent of the source's message. From a managerial viewpoint, communication is effective when subordinates as a group respond behaviorally in congruence with the manager's message; in such a case, the manager is thus able to accurately predict the outcome of the message that he or she disseminates, and can encourage that outcome through the message itself, the choice of medium, and the code system employed.

Further analysis of this definition reveals that communication is effective when: (1) the objectives of the sender, with respect to particular messages, will have a high probability of being fulfilled; and (2) the uncertainty of fulfillment is due to failures other than the communication process itself. While one can concur that communication is effective when there is a high probability of understanding, or responsive behavior, exception should be taken to the implicit notion that effectiveness is dichotomous. Communication effectiveness is not "caused" in the classical sense of Event *A* being a necessary and sufficient antecedent of Event *B*. Rather it "emerges" when the sum of scores for an organization on a set of factors produces a value within a specified range. Communication can be ineffective, and it can be *too* effective. When it is ineffective, an organization suffers from excessive error. When it is too effective, the organization suffers from various dysfunctions (e.g., boredom, apathy) resulting from an excessive concentration of resources on communication acts.

In summary, communication is effective when the outcome of a message event can be accurately

FIGURE 1
Determinants of Communication Effectiveness

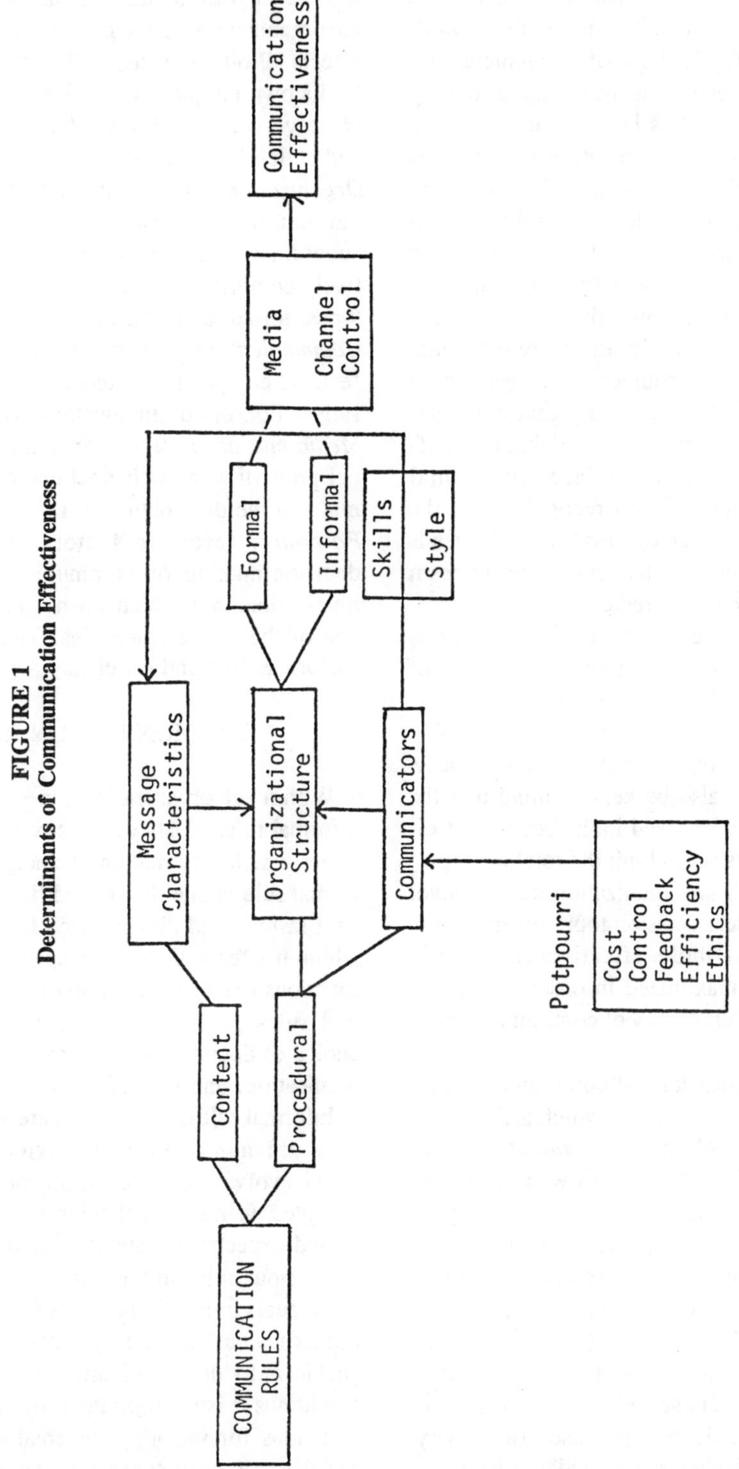

predicted. To the extent prediction is incorrect, then the communication involved is ineffective.

This definition of communication effectiveness should be contrasted with a definition of *communication efficiency*. While the goal of predictability in communication events is generally a worthy one, that goal must always be conditioned by the cost of achieving it. Communication efficiency is the outcome of the relationship between the amount of resources expended in transmitting information or messages, and the utility of the transmission event. The more important the expected outcome, the greater the utility of the transmission event. Similarly, the more important the outcome, the more resources a manager should be willing to expend in achieving that outcome. Since efficiency is a conditional variable (i.e., efficiency and effectiveness are functional covariants), it is important to recognize that the degree of effectiveness an organization achieves is ultimately dependent upon the level of resources it brings to bear to achieve predictability.

Consequently, the concept of effectiveness is clearly a macro-level entity; one composed of numerous elements. Each of these elements, in itself and in conjunction with others, contributes to the organization's overall level of effectiveness. However, it should also be kept in mind that the resource constraints involved in the concept of efficiency will always act to limit the total aggregate effectiveness which an organization can achieve. Therefore, the critical decision topic for managers is the selection of those effectiveness criteria which need to be maximized in order to achieve the greatest overall efficiency of communication in the organization.

Five primary dimensions of communication effectiveness are proposed, all of which are subordinate to the nature of the *communication rules* which govern and control the flow of messages throughout the organization. The five primary dimensions are: (1) the *structure* or patterning of message movement; (2) the *messages* that move through the structure; (3) the *communicators* that send and receive the messages; (4) *media* characteristics, and (5) a potpourri of additional effectiveness criteria. These relationships are diagramed in Figure 1. For purposes of brevity, media characteristics are not considered here.

Communication rules refer to the norms or rules which govern and control the content and protocol associated with the transmission of information in an organization. This is a macrocategory which affects all others, since each category is governed by its own unique set of rules.

Message characteristics refer to content, format, and style of messages.

Organizational structure refers to the pattern of communication relationships and supervisor-subordinate communication relations which collectively comprise the organization. They are of two types: formal and informal.

Communicators possess characteristics which affect the composition, frequency, competence and satisfaction of communication events.

Media characteristics refer to the channels, channel properties, and channel choices which can be made in the distribution of information.

Potpourri refers to factors which affect the decision-making of communicators about communication, but which do not primarily fit in to one of the above categories. These refer to such factors as cost and efficiency.

COMMUNICATION RULES

Within all organizations, a set of formal and informal rules exists which governs the conditions under which information exchange takes place. A formal rule is one that is codified in some permanent fashion and disseminated to those individuals whom it affects. Generally, specific organizational sanctions exist for violation of a formal rule. Formal rules govern access to superordinates, the choice of documents to be used for types of communication, and so forth.

Informal rules, in contrast, are similar to norms; they are non-codified behavioral expectations which evolve over time as non-specified, generally accepted forms of behavior which are mutually shared expectations about the individuals occupying various roles in the organization. They enable individuals to have guidelines for behavior regarding topics not covered by formal rules. They also enable individuals to learn when and under what conditions it is appropriate to bypass formal rules. Sanctions for violating informal rules also exist, and they can be as severe as sanctions for violating formal rules. Sanctions include criticism, ostracism, and ridicule. In addition, consistent violation of informal rules can seriously hamper upward organizational mobility. The majority of communication events in an organization will tend to be governed by informal communication rules (Downs, 1967). Informal communication rules are likely to be relatively uniform within hierarchical levels within the organization.

Another important distinction which can be applied to communication rules is the difference between *content* and *procedural* rules (Cushman & Whiting, 1972). Content rules govern the standard usage or consensus among communicators on how to describe a concept or issue, the attributes of concepts or issues, and the functions of the concepts or issues for the organizations. Content rules describe the conditions under which given topics may be addressed, the appropriate terminology to use in discussing them, and the types of "meaning" invoked by a communication. Conventional language allows a communicator considerable flexibility in the application of these rules. However, effective mangement of communication requires, at a minimum, a baseline level of agreement among the members of the organization as to how these content rules are to be observed. Note that this issue of agreement pertains to both formal and informal rules.

Procedural rules, in contrast, guide the choices individuals make about method of transmission of messages, appropriate sources, routing protocol, and the myriad of other scheduling events involved in bringing about and concluding communication events. Procedural rules specify relevant media, timing of information flow, distribution policies, the conditions under which and the persons to whom information may be addressed, and other aspects of the circulation of information in the organization. Procedural rules specify who is to be included in various distribution lists, the specific format of the document, and individuals who must review a document prior to dissemination. Consequently, procedural rules have the capability of exercising as much, if not more, influence on the character and nature of communication as do content rules. Again, effective management of communication requires, at a minimum, a baseline agreement among the members of the organization as to how these procedural rules are to be observed. Given this brief review of the concept of communication rules in organizational settings, we will next describe the procedures by which the potential effectiveness criteria were developed for each of the four areas grouped under the "rules" heading.

SEARCH PROCEDURES

The authors used two basic strategies in obtaining the literature used for this report. They drew upon their own materials from the fields of organizational and management theory, communication theory, and related fields. Second, access was obtained to broad-based sources of potential literature with which the authors might not be familiar. The initial literature set was augmented by a computer search of the following automated data bases: Social Science Search; Sociological Abstracts; Psychological Abstracts; Inform—a collection of materials devoted to organizational processes; Educational Resources Information Center (ERIC); National Technical Information Service (NTIS); and Dissertation Abstracts. Summed, these data bases contain more than two million separate citations of articles, books, bibliographies, monographs, and other materials.

To search these data bases, the following procedure was used. First, a set of key terms related to communication (with emphasis on print messages) was identified on the basis of a preliminary review of recent literature on organizational communication. The search procedure required that at least one of the key terms appear in the title of the cited item. Separately, a list of 49 key words, each reflecting a possible criterion or subcriterion element, was linked to the initial set of terms. The set of 49 terms was allowed to range freely, that is, to appear anywhere in the citation—title, abstract, index term, and so forth. This procedure was implemented on each data base and yielded a total of 3,555 separate citations. The search terms are shown in Table 1.

Next, the citations and their abstracts (if present) were screened by the authors for relevance. All citations considered germane by one or more persons were then sought out for photocopying and retrieval. An attempt was made to locate the mate-

TABLE 1
Search Terms for Communication Effectiveness Criteria

Title Terms	Criterion Terms		
communication	clarity	rate	guidelines
information	accuracy	flow	procedures
messages	timeliness	movement	regulations
text	believability	value	policy(ies)
print	utility	content rules	efficiency
technology transfer	completeness	procedural rules	persuasiveness
documents	complexity	appeal(s)	acceptance
	conciseness	organization	goals
	readability	competence	change
	attractiveness	regulation	aims
	comprehensiveness	specification	objectives
	comprehension	networks	results
	understanding	consensus	outcomes
	agreement	relevance	effectiveness
	volume	dissemination	impact
	intensity	distribution	effects
		format	

rials in three sites: the State of Michigan Library, Lansing; the Michigan State University Library, East Lansing; and the University of Michigan Library, Ann Arbor. Further screening of the relevance of citations took place as each item was located. The result of this activity produced a new sub-list and a library of some 450 items.

These items were read and reviewed, and incorporated into the present paper.

COMMUNICATION EFFECTIVENESS

In the sections that follow, four categories of communication effectiveness will be presented. Within each dimension, specific communication effectiveness criteria will be described, and relevant literature will be cited and discussed. The first of these dimensions is "communication structure."

Communication Structure

Organizations are composed of two principle kinds of relationships. The first relations exist because of the provisions for hierarchical authority found in organizations. Hierarchical relations are typically described as a pyramid, where control is manifested at the top, and different levels within the pyramid indicate different amounts of power and authority. Hierarchical relations can also be identified as a network; the network indicates the direction of information flow, and the hierarchical levels provide rules for the direction of flow. Depending on the context of a communication event, organization members are more or less likely to use this formal, hierarchical network.

In conjunction with a formal network, a network of informal or subformal relationships coexists in organizations (Etzioni, 1966). Informal networks are central to the overall functioning of the organization. They can be conceptualized as patterns of communication links governed by the organization's informal rules. Downs (1967) argues that most communication in an organization travels along a subformal or informal network. Such networks, regardless of whether they operate on a face-to-face, print, or other media basis, are composed of two main elements: nodes and links. A node in such a network can be an individual, and organizational subunit, or the organization itself. Links are demonstrated by the flow of information between nodes. This flow may proceed in varying directions and degrees; that is, formal procedures may specify that one unit must initiate contact with another before moving ahead on a project. This has important implications for the way information may be handled, and the way that decisions based on that information can be made. For example, in an analysis of a network problem, we may find that the directionality of flow between two key nodes is contrary to the needs and desires of the two nodes. Such a situation might constitute a serious impediment or threat to effective communication. Thus, by comparing the "actual" network with the "desired" network, it becomes possible to develop specific strategies to organize the system's communication capabilities more adequately. The following criteria are relevant to the concept of communication structure.

Accessibility. This can be defined as the degree to which any node in the network can be reached in one-step (or more) communication from all other possible nodes in the network. Accessibility is independent of hierarchical position. Downs (1967, p. 125) notes that in organizations in which all individuals are accessible to one another, without reference to normal supervisor-subordinate relationships, middle level managers are likely to be discontented. In those organizations in which a high rate of "bypassing" is encouraged by higher management, there will usually be an informal norm which mitigates against the practice. Downs discusses several reasons for encouraging high accessibility. These include the ability: (1) to eliminate or reduce distortion; (2) to validate information before placing it into formal communication channels; (3) to circumvent certain subordinates who refuse to communicate certain ideas upward; (4) to increase the speed of information flow, particularly information that arises in stressful situations; and (5) to involve subordinates more fully in the process of decision-making.

Rothwell and Robertson (1975) state that organizations often do not develop specific policies that promote the effective flow of information. One systematic technique for encouraging reasonable accessibility is the formation of an "information department," which in effect reroutes intelligence around hierarchical levels in the organization. However, these departments are frequently among the first to suffer the consequences of an economic downturn; they are eliminated in times of economic stringency. This tendency contradicts the purpose of such a department, since it is in precisely such times that it should be of greatest value. In addition, the authors indicate that with knowledge of communication processes, an information department can generate and facilitate innovation in the organization.

Schneider (1971) urges that communication accessibility be made important when an organization has highly complex and variable tasks. Specifically, he recommends that organizations develop a system for routinely distributing information to those individuals with unique competencies. To support his view, he cites research suggesting that 30% of scientific manpower is wasted because needed information is not available to the correct person at the correct time. In our view, this is an accessibility (as well as a timeliness) problem.

Chakrabarti (1972) emphasizes the importance of communication channel access. If channels of communication are not well understood, communication will be less effective. He also indicates that communication will be more effective when: (1) channels exist linking every member; (2) the lines of such channels are kept as short as possible; (3) complete lines are employed; (4) the individual nodes have sufficient communication competence; (5) the lines of communication cannot be easily broken; and (6) procedures exist to authenticate communication acts.

One important aspect of accessibility (as well as of a number of other criteria presented in this paper), is the degree to which *perceptual* processes determine how organizational members respond to the specific criterion. In the case of accessibility, it is important to examine whether system members perceive that other key actors, with whom they may or may not be in direct contact, are accessible. While the formal hierarchy may prescribe a routing plan for the movement of information, individuals may not perceive that they can, in fact, use that pathway. In addition, organizational members may not know where the best targets for the information are (i.e., the roles of others are not clearly defined). They may not know how to develop an appropriate "game plan" to transmit the information. Problems of accessibility often cause people not to have the information they need to perform their work properly.

Flow control. Flow control refers to the ability of managers to regulate the dissemination of a message. High flow control exists when a manager can make clear-cut decisions about whether, and in what form or timing, a message will pass through his or her office—to either higher levels or lower levels in the organization (Rothwell, 1975).

Implicit in the concept of flow control is the possibility that a manager may not specifically know the intended recipient of a given communication. Communication becomes effective to the degree that the manager knows the appropriate "gatekeepers," "opinion leaders," or "key communicators" who serve as information managers. By virtue of their position in the communication structure, key information managers (whether formal or not) can initiate message routing sequences (Oniki, 1974). Effective communication thus presumes a wide knowledge of which organizational members comprise this key group, and how they themselves may be reached. In time of conflict, flow control becomes critical because competing organizational subunits will only communicate formally (Downs, 1967). In popular terms, "information (flow control) is power."

O'Reilly and Roberts (1974) provide evidence that considerable distortion of information occurs as it travels through an organization. This problem is more severe when a large proportion of the information flow is up the organizational hierarchy. Communication will be more effective when communicators know the shortest feasible paths for transmitting information. Communication will also be more effective when the information sent up the hierarchy (or received from lower levels) passes through the fewest possible intermediate steps. The problem of upward communication in particular is that *intentional* distortion through flow control is likely to aggravate other more naturally occurring distortion processes involved in transmission of information.

Allen and Cohen (1969) and Downs (1967) supplement the comments above by reporting that more information is transmitted within status levels than across levels. Furthermore, lower status individuals attempt to send information upward more often than high status individuals initiate downward flow. Therefore, high status individuals contribute to blockage which restricts upward flows of information to them; unfavorable but important information is often denied the higher level decision-makers, who are nevertheless dependent on traditional hierarchical communication flows. Allen and Cohen further indicate that low status individuals tend to have large numbers of contacts with individuals outside the organization, since they are less likely to have been in the organization as long as high status members. This further indicates the restriction on information incurred by high status individuals as a consequence of flow control decisions made at lower levels.

One consequence of limited upward communication is due to the failure of managers to act on undesireable conditions that have previously been brought to their attention. This often results in a loss of faith by subordinates, both in the sincerity of management, and, more importantly, in the value of communicating with management in general (Planty & Machaver, 1952).

Flow control is an equally important problem, if not more so, for downward communication, where the opportunity for information restriction, modification, enhancement, and so forth is very common. A companion loss in communication effectiveness is also a byproduct of downward flow control.

Hierarchiality. As modern organizations incorporate wider spans of supervision, the "pyramid of control" has become substantially wider at the base, and shorter in height. Hierarchiality refers to communication which occurs between levels of authority, or across a specific level of authority. It is complicated by the differences between staff and line functions, and, within levels, the differences between competitive and cooperative subunits of equal hierarchical authority (Carzo & Yanouzas, 1969).

Further analysis reveals that as organizations seek to reduce hierarchical conflict by decreasing the number of supervisory levels (and thus increase the ratio of subordinates to supervisors), communicative complexity is radically increased. Also, as subordinates are added to a supervisor's work group, the amount of time that the supervisor can spend with the individual is proportionally decreased. Consequently, decreases in the amount of hierarchiality in an organization's structure has a marked impact on the amount of time a supervisor can spend communicating with subordinates, and this in turn affects the probability that high agreement and accuracy will be able to exist in supervisory-subordinate relationships. Changes in hierarchiality will therefore have a definite impact on the level of communication effectiveness. The trade-off here appears to be the communication problems involved in requiring information to pass through a number of hierarchical levels versus the individual problems associated with many subordinates reporting to fewer supervisory levels.

A similar problem exists between staff and line distinctions in organizations. Etzioni (1966) points out that higher and lower ranking line personnel often form coalitions against staff personnel, which obfuscate existing hierarchical distinctions, and hence, the very function the hierarchy is intended to perform. To the extent this problem exists, it mitigates against effective communication.

Network role distribution. In addition to hierarchical positions, which are more formal assignments of communication roles, individuals may be classified into informal communication roles (Monge & Lindsey, 1973). An organization can be analyzed, and communication problems diagnosed, by examining the pattern of distribution in the informal communication roles. The roles are:

1. communication members of cliques (Festinger, Schachter & Back, 1950; Porter & Lawler, 1965);
2. bridges, individuals who are themselves members of groups, and who link other groups, and thus provide an avenue for information to flow between large bodies of people;
3. liaisons, individuals who link groups, but who

are not themselves members of groups, and perform key gatekeeping roles (Guetzkow, 1965; Farace & Danowski, 1973; & Taylor, 1976) and as a result influence the behavior of the system far in excess of their formal role assignment;
4. isolates, persons who have minimal or no contacts with other members of the organization (Richards, 1974) and who are usually poorly informed, poorly integrated, and least participative.

If there are a large number of group members, there will be a higher level of tolerated organizational conflict, and more organized formal and informal politicking (Taylor, 1976). If there are relatively few bridges and liaisons in the organizations, the organization will be highly differentiated, and information flow will be seriously impeded (Farace & Danowski, 1973), particularly when the organization lacks liaisons between subunits (Wigand, 1975). In any organization, it is imperative that management make a careful assessment of the placement of bridges and liaisons to ensure that appropriate linkages between subunits are in fact in place and operating.

If more than a small percentage (perhaps 5-10%) of the members of an organization are only minimally connected to the other members—that is, are classed as isolates—and if the organization's members perform complex tasks requiring considerable interdependence, there will be a considerable problem in overall communication effectiveness.

An issue closely related to the precise distribution of organizational members into communication roles—and one which dramatically affects the performance of a communication network—is the degree to which members of the network are transient. While little or no research has touched upon the issue, it seems clear that transferring personnel may create havoc with networks, particularly if the individual occupies a key communicative role in the informal network. Taylor, Farace, & Monge (1976) indicate that "key communicators" can be used effectively to disseminate important information to the larger network of which they are a part. Conversely, if these same key communicators are not given adequate information about a particular topic, they can act to block attempts to introduce information made through other means. One of the consequences of routine transfer of personnel, for example, is that they are less likely to emerge as important members of an informal network. This suggests that whenever transients are a "fact of life" in an organization, its communication will be less effective; in addition, more emphasis must necessarily be placed on the formalization of communication roles to ensure that the movement of information throughout the organization occurs as needed.

Integrativeness. This refers to the degree an individual is linked within a communication network to others who are also linked together. Thus, the criterion of integrativeness is related to the degree to which an organization and its sub-units are composed of dense linkage patterns (Jacobson and Seashore, 1951). Danowski (1974) indicates that integrativeness is a good predictor of the overall level of redundancy of information in a communication network. Highly integrated individuals are likely to encounter the same information more than once (through more than one network pathway), and hence have more opportunity to comprehend or verify it. Therefore, organizations composed of highly integrated individuals have higher levels of redundancy and lower levels of distortion and error, and hence have more effective communication.

Connectedness. This is ordinarily a measure of the interaction density of organizational subgroups. It differs from integrativeness in that it is an aggregate variable which describes varying density values for organizational sub-units formed according to certain criteria, such as work groups, friendship, kinship, and so forth. Taylor (1976) reported that groups higher in connectedness show lower variance in member attitudes. Danowski (1974) found that connectedness was a good predictor of the level of homogeneity (or similarity) with respect to key norms and goals within a network. Mitchell (1969) argued that connectedness can be taken to be critical to the development of morale and satisfaction, inasmuch as it is related to the development of affective rewards in the work place.

Overload and Underload. Overload may in general be defined as the inability of a member of an organization to adequately process information received. Quite simply, it occurs when a person receives more information per time period than he or she can cope with (Wofford, Gerloff & Cummins, 1977). A second condition under which overload often occurs is when large quantities of information are systematically routed through the same point in a network. Miller (1964) notes that there are seven typical responses to communication overload:

1. omission—failure to adequately process information;
2. incorrectly processing all information;
3. queueing—arbitrary sequencing information with no regard to importance;
4. filtering—separating out according to some category scheme using some set of rules, usually idiosyncratic;
5. approximation—categorizing information and using blanket responses;
6. employing multiple channels—altering flow by manipulating channels and directing information away;
7. escaping—avoiding information.

It should be clear that certain of these techniques are more rational for the individual in some circumstances than others.

Any organization experiencing widespread overload among its members is quite probably exhibiting a very high level of error. Gross and Springer (1967) argue that overload creates an organizational "intelligence gap" by causing the accumulation of large quantities of unused information. Since the techniques members may use to reduce overload are often random in the aggregate, policy makers will be misled and lack critical information for decision making. A related problem first touched upon by Emery and Trist (1965) occurs when the rate of change for an organization constantly induces increased information processing demands at the same time that environmental pressure causes considerable internal turbulence and the perception of crisis. Over time, expanding demands create increased irrational responses, causing increased uncertainty and expanded perception of crisis, eventually leading to significant organizational breakdown.

Huber, O'Connell, and Cummings (1975) note that high information overload increases perceived organizational uncertainty. As a result, organizational structure may vary substantially with perceived environmental uncertainty. Thus, in part, the structure of an organization is influenced by those positions within its network at which overload occurs. By learning where overload is a constant factor, organizational managers can predict structural change, and, hence, plan those changes. Another possible phenomenon which is associated with variable distribution of information load (some people overloaded, some people not) is the misperception of slack resources, and the consequent misallocation of resources (Galbraith, 1974; Summers, 1974).

Underload has been defined as the absence of sufficient information to achieve peak productivity. It is the obverse of overload. Implicitly, underload means that an individual is not receiving enough information to keep busy. Danowski (1975), Farace, Monge and Russell (1977), and Johnson (1977) argue that underload causes extreme dissatisfaction with the work environment. Some of the typical consequences of underload are employee boredom, the tendency of personnel to fabricate time-consuming activities that are usually of a nonconstructive nature, the use of free time in which grievances lead to dissatisfaction, and finally, an increase in accident rates resulting from carelessness or neglect of duty.

Purposive information acquisition. One technique organizations develop to cope with uncertainty is to "routinize" common topics of uncertainty. This means that organizations identify those areas in their operations about which they are consistently uncertain. To resolve the uncertainty, they store information, and develop techniques for scanning the relevant environment so that when the uncertain topic re-emerges, the necessary information is available.

Among the devices now in use by organizations are the computer-based information systems. Lucas (1975) reports that, unfortunately, there is little research at the present time which adequately evaluates the impact of information systems or suggests ways to better utilize these systems. Evaluations of information systems should consider the relationship between the use of the system and performance. In any kind of a management system, there are various classifications of decision-making with which the manager is confronted. These decisions can range from extremely perfunctory kinds of decisions to highly complex ones. Typically, decisions can be classified into three general categories: strategical, tactical, and technical. The key interest in using an information system is to produce timely information that is pertinent and applicable to any of these three categories. The specific needs of the organization will determine what type of information system must be gathered and restructured to meet the decision-making needs of the organization on a productive and efficient basis.

Burch and Strater (1973) found that formal information systems are severely limited as to how much relevant information they can provide any given level of decision-making. Therefore, information systems are substantially more effective and serve better tactical and technical decision-making even though there is still a great potential for analysts to serve the strategical level. Informational needs at all levels can be met more effectively if the individual analyst and the information system work together in tailoring the information output to fit the users' needs.

Turpin (1972) found that a company can reduce 10 to 20% of its paper work by taking a critical look at internal information control procedures. Hidden in these procedures are any of several check and cross-check requirements, which if found to be extremely time-consuming and costly, can be discontinued without great risk to the overall efficiency of the organization. (In fact, this particular study emphasizes the fact that general efficiency in the use of an information system greatly enhances general communication efficiency.) As noted earlier in this paper, efficiency and effectiveness are highly interdependent concepts (cf., Allen & Cohen, 1969).

Kneitel (1975) points out that one of the primary goals of communication is to ensure that data are transmitted within a given network without loss. Fulfilling this goal is a major criterion for incorporating an information system into the everyday workings of an organization, thus realizing to a greater degree communication effectiveness. Ways of viewing this criterion might include the degree to which storage and retrieval methods are systematic, are understood, the accessibility of data, and human factors problems. (See: Gallagher, 1974; Bentley, 1974; Kneitel, 1975; Murdick & Ross, 1972; Ensign, 1974; Turpin, 1972; Schneyman, 1976; Miller, 1977; David & Pruett, 1975; Burch & Strater, 1973; Floyd & Zimud, 1976; Lucas, 1975; Adelberg, 1975).

Uncertainty. Uncertainty is perhaps the central concept in organizational communication research. Previously, it was noted that a major purpose of communication is to bring about the reduction of variability in response, that is, to achieve control. This implies that communication serves to reduce the number of alternatives in a situation, and/or cause the probability that a certain one of the alternatives will be selected (i.e., have a probability of choice of 1.0). These two factors—namely, the number of alternatives in a situation, and their probabilities—are the core elements in the standard definition of uncertainty. Shannon and Weaver (1949) defined uncertainty on the basis of the logarithmic value of the division of two probabilities. The dividend is the *a postiori* probability that the message received is the message actually transmitted. The divisor is the *a priori* probability that a particular message is transmitted. Many scholars have focused on these two relationships.

Lawrence and Lorsch (1967) indicate that organizational structure is a function of environmental uncertainty. For them, an organization's environment is more uncertain if the information describing the environment is unclear, if causal relationships have not been defined, and if the time span between production of messages and feedback is relatively slow. A strong correlation was found between a general measure of environmental uncertainty and an organization's willingness to expend resources on more efficient means of information transfer. Similarly, Galbraith (1974) found that the greater the net task uncertainty, the greater the amount of information that must be processed among decision makers during task execution to achieve a given level of performance. Huber, O'Connell, and Cummings (1975) argue that perceived environmental uncertainty is a critical intervening variable in the linkage connecting organizational environment with organizational process, structure, and performance. When administrators perceive their organizational environment to be uncertain, they will expand the organization's information processing capacity, and hence, its task performance. Continuing, Huber, et al., argue that environmental uncertainty is a function of: (1) information load; (2) organizational structure; (3) the background of organizational respondents; (4) the duration of participation in organizational tasks; and (5) the stability of the perceived environment. They argue that administrators can control and manipulate, to a degree, organizational structure and information load to minimize perceived environmental uncertainty. Therefore, when managers perceive environmental uncertainty, and act upon it informationally, net organizational communication effectiveness will be enhanced.

Duncan, Featherman & Duncan (1972) clearly support management's responsibility for the reduction of environmental uncertainty. They state that the organization's internal environment is a function of its perceived external uncertainty. They conceptualize environmental uncertainty as: (1) lack of information about relevant factors that impact a decision; (2) lack of knowledge about organizational decisions; and (3) lack of ability to assign probabilities to the distribution of environmental impacts upon the success of an organizational decision. Their views are quite similar to what March and Simon (1958) term "uncertainty absorption":

> Uncertainty absorption takes place when inferences are drawn from a body of evidence, and the inferences, instead of the evidence itself, are then communicated. . . . in all of these cases, the person who summarizes and assesses his own direct perceptions and transmits them to the rest of the organization becomes an important source of information premises for organizational action. The 'facts' he communicates can be disbelieved, but they can only rarely be checked. Hence, by the very nature and limits of the communication system, a great deal of discretion and influence is exercised by those persons who are in direct contact with some part of the 'reality' that is of concern to the organization. Both the amount and the locus of uncertainty absorption affect the influence structure of the organization.

Thus, it should be clear that positions of informational leadership (for example, liaisons and bridges) intervene powerfully, and, in concert with technological gatekeepers (cf. Allen & Cohen, 1969) radically affect an organization's perception of its own level of uncertainty. To the degree that general levels of organizational uncertainty can be measured, and to the extent that key communicators' levels of uncertainty can be measured, powerful predictors of both organizational priorities (particularly informational priorities) and organizational information processing performance can be generated (Holland & Stead, 1976). As these authors crucially point out, the greater the overall organizational uncertainty about needed information, regardless of information concerning task processes, the greater the amount of organizational tension and stress.

It is important to note that a continuing theme underlying this discussion of uncertainty is that some optimal level of uncertainty provides for the most efficient level of processing for an organization. The point that low levels of uncertainty have the capability of being as dysfunctional as extremely high levels has already been noted. Therefore, uncertainty in an organization should be considered in terms of some optimal level, based upon the preferred tolerance for uncertainty (Danowski, 1975; Barnard, 1938) existing among individual members.

The point concerning optimal levels of uncertainty can also be applied to specific units within an organization. Alpert and Anderson (1973) state that while it is fundamental to human communication research that source-receiver similarity promotes communication effectiveness, it is the case that near-complete similarity produces lack of sustained interest in interpersonal relationships. Thus, particularly in organizations, it is important to optimize the dissimilarity, or the uncertainty, between members of work groups—between pairs of members, their relationships, and the data which they process.

Message Criteria

Absolute vs. distributed information. Messages, and the information they contain, may be more or less distributed throughout an organization. Absolute information refers to the total quantity or amount of information possessed by all the members of an organization (or in its "memory" units). Distributed information refers to the degree of dispersal or homogeneity of knowledge of a given piece of information by the members of the organization. The distinction affects communication effectiveness in at least two ways: (1) it influences the degree to which critical organizational data circulate .throughout its networks, and (2) it influences the degree to which individuals with access to organizational data are evaluated.

Organizations which have a high degree of information distribution are perceived as "open" (Bennis, 1969). Schneider (1971) indicates that total distribution of information in a scientific organization (or other types as well) is impossible, due to the technicality of most scientific specialties. Thus, the concept of distribution is also an optimizing one, rather than a maximizing one. Glazer (1973) indicates that distribution capability in the attempt to disseminate cross-discipline data. by the attempt to disseminate cross-discipline data. It was also reported that distribution problems, particularly problems related to a difficulty in cross-discipline linguistics, have presented adequate dissemination of research knowledge.

Distribution is therefore both an organizational and a technological problem. The absolute information criterion refers to the total amount of information available somewhere in the organization, as noted above. Muller (1974) has shown that by measuring the amount of knowledge within an organization, one is more capable of predicting the degree to which an organization approaches its "optimality frontier." By this he meant that those organizations which enjoy a high degree of absolute information operate at the edge of their productive capacity. Absolute information is also a criterion of communication effectiveness because it predicts the degree to which an organization will have to expend resources to inform systems members about crucial organizational responsibilities.

Frequency and volume. Frequency is defined as the rate of transmission of messages per unit time period, and volume represents the total aggregate of messages within that time period. To many communication scholars, measures of message frequency and volume are fundamentally related to the development of cognitive processes in individuals (Newcomb, 1953; McPhee, 1972; Saltiel & Woelfel, 1975).

In general, these authors argue that the effect of a large volume of information advocating an attitude or behavior of a particular valence and magnitude is to *shift* the attitude or behavior of a receiver in the advocated direction (Barnett, Serota & Taylor, 1976). By identifying important attitudinal or behavioral issues in the organizational context, and maintaining a record of the number, degree and direction of the messages being transmitted concerning these cognitive elements, relatively crude counting procedures can yield quite accurate estimates of the shifts that will take place in the organization's cognitive makeup. Nystedt and Magnusson (1972) argue that the greater the frequency of a specific message, the greater the reliability of judgment on phenomena associated with the message (i.e., the more frequently a goal is stated, the greater the reliability of the judgment that the goal will be used).

Simon (1947) states that planning reduces the amount of information processing required by subordinate elements within a hierarchy by reducing the amount of discretion exercised at lower levels. In effect, he, like Taylor, Farace and Monge (1976), argues that frequency becomes important when a message inherently lacks contents which creates a psychological bridge between the symbols employed in the message and the symbols employed in the individual's cognitive definition of self.

Galbraith (1974) indicates that as the number of formal subdivisions involved in a response to a problem increases (N greater than 7-8), the amount or volume of information increases; as the amount increases, the decision-making capability of the departments taken as individual units exceeded. On this point, Katzman (1974) states that new information-processing technologies have been adopted as a response to the perceived total volume of data connected with individual phenomena, and that the output of the increased processing capability only tends to increase the information responsibilities of individuals. Hence, while one may obtain an exponential decrease in de facto levels of information, the individual still receives a multiplicative increase in the level of *in situ* data.

The developers of management information systems have established several *caveats* affecting the tolerable volume of human information processes (Katzman, 1974). From a variety of sources, these are: (1) All individuals receive more information after the adoption of a new communication technology. (2) With the adoption of a new communication technology, individuals who already have high levels of information and ability will gain more than will individuals at lower initial levels. (3) Human beings have a limited capacity to process and store information. (4) Compared to human beings, machines now have unlimited capacity to store and process information. (5) New communication technologies and techniques create new information gaps before old information gaps are closed.

In the conceptualization of a message used here, it is considered as a discrete piece of data, reflecting meaning for some individual phenomenon. Data are, by definition, an aggregate of many symbolic stimuli. As the volume of messages increases, the individuals within organizations demand more processing technology. As the caveats above indicate, new technology carries with it its own demands. As we will discuss in a subsequent report on communication media, the imposition of new processing technology and new transceiving technology may satisfy the constraint of demand, but at the cost of human capacity.

Message organization. This refers to the degree to which messages, or a particular message, are consonant with the syntactic expectations of a receiver. When messages consistently deviate from established grammatical protocols, the message will be ineffective. This is a particular problem in government bureaucracies, which are compelled by regulations and specifications requirements to construct elaborate, often redundant, and usually grammatically difficult descriptions of organizationally relevant phenomena. To the individual receiving such a communication, the message can become so complex as to be uninterpretable.

Most of the variables that have traditionally been examined under the heading of message organization deal with such factors as the placement of the conclusion, degree of internal redundancy, arrangement of main and supporting points, logical structures, and so forth (Bettinghaus, 1973; Miller & Burgoon, 1973). Relatively little of this research has been done in organizational settings, taking into account the constraints noted above.

Uncertainty of the message. Uncertainty also manifests itself at the message level. Messages are a response to a perceived uncertainty, and they vary in their ability to reduce uncertainty. As uncertainty is increased, the frequency of messages about a specific phenomenon will also increase (Huber, O'Connell, & Cummings, 1975). Whittmore & Yovits (1973) note that the greater the uncertainty associated with a specific observation, the greater the level of information to be derived—and the greater the volume of message production about the observed event.

Secondly, as Korzenny (in press) notes, the lower the channel bandwidth through which a message is disseminated, the higher the uncertainty of the receiver. In that vein, Holland & Stead (1976) argue the following points:

1. Managers should maximize the richness of content form during periods of uncertainty.
2. The greater the degree of economic unease, the greater the uncertainty—no matter what the content of the message.
3. Employee training should include the processing of highly uncertain messages.
4. Where formal channels are encouraged, and informal channels are discouraged, organizational members will experience higher uncertainty, no matter what the message.

Communication function/purpose. Communication function refers to the organizational purposes to which various kinds of communication are dedicated. Recognizing the differences discussed below in the potential types of communication functions enables managers to discriminate and differentiate communication content. Simply put, this prevents confusion. If these criteria can be optimized in an organization, that organization will be both more effective, and composed of personnel who give more careful attention to the production and distribution of messages that lead to desired, intended effects.

Three general categories of communication functions that are frequently applicable to bureaucracies are production, innovation, and maintenance (Farace, Monge and Russell, 1977). Production communication refers to messages that deal with the work flow—issuing directives, receiving reports, specifying regulation and procedures, and so forth. Innovation communication is primarily directed towards messages from higher level managers that substantially encourage and reward lower-level subordinates for generating new ideas, suggestions, and comments for organizational improvements. Finally, maintenance communication deals with messages that seek to bolster the self-concept of the organizational member as a worthy human being, and that address the issue of building organizational affiliation and identification in members.

Schuler and Blank (1976) argue that there are four types of communication in organizations. Unlike the list of Farace, et al., Schuler and Blank's characteristics represent dimensionalities of intent, rather than message content. They are: informative, regulatory, status-quo, and integrative. Schuler and Blank found that integrative communication, or communication aimed at increasing perceived member cohesiveness, is the most satisfying form of the four, and that it inspires high productivity. We suspect, however, that consistently high levels of integrative communication reduce its value in general; that is, it has an optimum level beyond which further investment of communication resources is counterproductive.

March and Simon (1958) describe five types of communication in organizations: (1) communication for nonprogrammed activities; (2) communication to initiate and establish programs; (3) communication to provide data for the application of strategies for the execution of programs; (4) communication to evoke programs; and (5) communication to provide information on the results of activities. March and Simon suggest that there is a need to balance planning, innovation, production, and evaluation activities in the organization's overall message dissemination. Failure to consciously proceed induces information gaps which significantly affect decision-making abilities.

The issue underlying this criterion is not so much which of the category systems should be selected; instead, for the purposes of effective communication, it is imperative to select some system and to develop procedures for monitoring its use. Our research indicates that communication networks in organizations vary quite radically depending on the content category on which they are defined. Consequently, management of communication networks becomes inextricably tied to the conscious use and measurement of selected category systems that reflect the range of important content issues in the organization. The specific set of content categories is typically chosen uniquely for a given organization.

Communicators. The next set of criteria deal with selected individual characteristics of organizational members. Organizations, by virtue of their particular specialty, tend to adopt personnel procedures which retain individuals with homogeneous characteristics. The processes of socializing in an organization also work to make the communication styles of individuals more similar over time. Organizations differ, however, in the amount of individual variation in communicator characteristics they will tolerate. Large organizations, and in particular bureaucracies with extensive histories, are generally willing to tolerate far less deviation in communicator characteristics. The environment of some organizations often places strenuous demands on it to accomplish greater rates of innovation. Thus, its dilemma becomes one of balancing its own flexibility and creativity with the necessary level of rigidity to function efficiently. (It should be emphasized that "rigidity" is a necessary, not a derogatory, characteristic of an organization.) Thompson (1967, p. 17) describes the problem in the following way:

> The modern bureaucratic organization is dominated by the monocratic stereotype. The stereotype is institutionalized in a system of bossman roles. Modifications of the stereotype, therefore, come through variations in individual role-playing. The monocratic organization stresses hierarchical authority and

> communication (going through channels). It is highly oriented toward control, predictability, and reliability. Control is facilitated by defining jobs narrowly, programming activities into routines to the greatest extent possible, and fixing responsibilities by avoiding all overlapping and duplication.

Thompson points out that this concept of an organization mitigates against innovation and change. Communicator characteristics must therefore be seen as a reflection of allowed individual differences in key personal attributes which facilitate communication, given the constraint of a particular organizational environment.

Cognitive style. Cognitive style refers to the stereotypical affective perceptual set of organizational members. Research has shown that cognitive style will vary both in the aggregate case (i.e., across all employees) and in the individual case, depending upon whether the organization is highly bureaucratic (Thompson, 1967), task oriented (Woodward, 1965), subject to environmental stress (Drucker, 1974), or subject to fluctuations in level of uncertainty (Lawrence & Lorsch, 1967). Miller, Galanter, & Pribram (1960) point out that cognitive style is an outcome of environmental factors. Since organizational environments are systematic collectivities of stimuli, there is a tendency for similar cognitive styles to emerge within an organization. Communication is the vehicle through which cognitive style is developed and manifested. Miller and Steinberg (1975) state that the self-concept of an individual is a direct function of his/her communication behavior; that is, individuals define themselves as human beings and as workers by observing their own communication behavior, and the behavior of others in their immediate environment. Note that this is the inverse of the classical psychological assumption that communication behavior is solely an *outgrowth* of unconscious motivations

An organization which, at the management level, understands the principle noted above, and takes advantage of it in communication—particularly communication aimed at socializing new employees—will be more effective than one which does not (see also Pines & Julian, 1972).

Competence—communication skills. Communicator competence is a collection of specific skills dealing with an individual's ability to encode and decode, seek information, and otherwise engage in communication activities within the organization. These skills can be both related to the formal or the informal communication system. Competence skills relate to the employee's understanding of the communication rules of the organization, and his or her ability to work with (and around) the rules. Competent individuals know how to "cut the red tape." Berlo, Lemert, and Mertz (1969) provide research that indicates that perceived communicator competence is a key dimension of communicator credibility. At an operational level, competence involves writing skills, speaking skills, listening skills, information acquisition skills, the ability to organize information, and so forth.

Argyris (1962) states that interpersonal competence is the best communication predictor of organizational success, as defined by the organization's balance sheet. Similarly, interpersonal competence is frequently cited as a key attribute in the rise in managerial levels of organizational members. Argyris indicates that competence and its importance as an organizational criterion are widely seen to stem from three basic values held by all formal organizations (p. 39): (1) the important human relationships are those that are related to achieving the organization's objectives; (2) effectiveness in human relationships increases as behavior is rational, logical and clearly communicated, while effectiveness decreases as emotionality increases; and (3) human relationships are most effectively influenced through directions, coercion, and control, as well as a set of rewards and penalties that serve to emphasize rational behavior and "getting the job done." Argyris criticizes this notion by stating that while such values may be consonant with minimal standards of productivity and performance, encouraging *higher* levels of interpersonal competence increases productivity and promotes a healthier organizational environment. Therefore, communication competence relates to effectiveness in two senses: it encourages high production values, and it fosters a greater personal commitment in the organization (McGregor, 1960).

Agreement and accuracy. Agreement refers to the degree to which two individuals (often, a supervisor-subordinate dyad) have the same perception of some social object in their environment. Accuracy reflects whether one or the other can predict the position or view held by the other member of the pair (Farace, Monge, and Russell, 1977).

When an organization is characterized by high levels of agreement and accuracy, it exhibits consensus. Newcomb (1953) developed a theory of co-orientation which predicts different behavioral outcomes for different combinations of agreement and accuracy. He argued that imbalances in accuracy and/or agreement can cause communication to occur. For instance, when two individuals are inaccurate about their perception of each other, their relationship is imbalanced and, in most cases, they will communicate to restore accuracy to the situation. Highly unbalanced relationships cause organizational conflict; high levels of conflict can be extremely dysfunctional to the organization.

The concepts of accuracy and agreement can be applied to any objects of importance in an organizational setting. In the context of communication effectiveness, however, the concepts are most commonly applied to the communication rules and other specific communication behaviors that take place in the organization. Thus, while the logic is the same as for other types of co-orientation objects, the application for communication effectiveness is much more specific.

Homogeneity or similarity. Individuals in organizations vary in the amount to which they are like one another along a variety of dimensions; furthermore, perceptual differences come into play in the decision process that individuals undergo in estimating the degree of similarity between themselves and others. Alpert and Anderson (1973) suggest that communication effectiveness is related to the level of influence a source exercises over the actions of message recipients. That is, communication is effective when it causes a receiver to change his or her behavior in some desired way. They state, "Communication, and hence the potential for influence, occurs most frequently among individuals who are similar, alike, that is, homophilous" (p. 328).

For an organization, some level of homophily is crucially important with respect to goals, perception of mission, and productivity. When an organization encourages similarity through its message policies, it can take advantage of: (1) higher levels of interpersonal attraction and frequency of interaction (Guetzkow, 1965; Rokeach, 1968); (2) higher potential for communication effectiveness (Lazarsfeld & Merton, 1964); (3) higher perceived communication instrumentality, that is, communication will be perceived as more valuable (Rogers and Shoemaker, 1971); and (4) greater employee satisfaction through more effective interpersonal relationships (Alpert & Anderson, 1973).

Alpert and Anderson caution that too much similarity can be dysfunctional. Following from the research of Simon (1969), Alpert and Anderson note that certain dissimilarities augment the persuasive effect of communication. Therefore, they introduce the concept of "optimal total heterophily," or "optimal dissimilarity." Thus the effective organization is one which both encourages similarity yet tolerates certain levels of dissimilarity. Communication "stasis" is the equilibrium point which results from the balance of these two forces. This is a conceptualization familiar to conflict theorists, who argue that in the absence of dissensus, an organization will tend to be non-creative, unresponsive to environmental changes and relatively inflexible (Huse, 1975).

Uncertainty. Uncertainty has already been discussed as a structural and a message criterion. It is also important to note the important effects of perceived uncertainty on communicating individuals. Huber, O'Connell and Cummings (1975) point out that administrative and management behavior is largely predicated upon the perception of environmental uncertainty. For the individual, environmental uncertainty is of two types—internal and external. Internal uncertainty refers to uncertainties associated with status quo operations of an organization. This would include uncertainties about information load, employee behavior, the security of one's position, and about the organization itself.

External uncertainty refers to an individual's perceptions of the relative rate of change in the environment and the quality of information being received about the environment. Huseman, Logue, & Freshly (1977) suggest that message ambiguity, or the amount of uncertainty in a specific communication, promotes message distortion and increases the level of organizational conflict. Weick (1969) states that absolute certainty is never required; instead, individuals "enact" task roles in order to reduce apparent uncertainty (or, in his terms, "equivocality"). In fact, Weick states that it is uncertainty which provides the motivation for the members of an organization to engage in organizing behaviors.

Lawrence and Lorsch (1967) identify four measurable features of organizations which vary with uncertainty levels. These are: (1) the degree of reliance on formalized rules and formal communication channels; (2) the time horizons of managers and professionals; (3) the orientation of managers and professionals towards goals, either diffuse or concentrated; and (4) the interpersonal style of managers and professionals, either relational or task-oriented. They found that high-performing companies had a close degree of fit between the attributes of organizational subunits and the demands and perturbations of the environment to which the subunits responded. They noted that where a high degree of environmental uncertainty existed, high-performing companies engaged in a large amount of information flow across the organization's boundaries.

Along a similar line, Duncan, Featherman & Duncan (1972) conceptualized uncertainty as (1) a lack of information about relevant factors that impact on decisions; (2) a lack of knowledge about organizational decisions; and (3) a lack of ability to assign probabilities to the distribution of environmental impacts on the success of an organization. A strong correlation was found between general uncertainty in an organization and its use of more efficient means of information transfer. Holland and Stead (1976) argue that employees who spend a great deal of time working with highly uncertain problems should probably be geographically isolated. However, isolation decreases access to and among employees; this in turn increases information transfer costs and penalizes those personnel who are likely to be the most creative and innovative. They further argue that environments which discourage informal contact and stress formality induce organizational members to experience far higher levels of uncertainty than would otherwise be the case.

A final point to be made deals with communicators' intentional manipulation of levels of uncertainty. Carzo and Yanouzas (1969) state that, "one of the reasons why people are able to gain power that is greater than the administrative authority allocated to their position is that they are strategically located in the flows of information and/or the relationships between or among organizational components" (p. 199). Such individuals gain power through the discretionary release or withdrawal of important information. In effect, they manipulate the uncertainties of those with whom they interact. We have noted that individuals tend to be liaisons and bridges, and their influence is often discussed in organizational literature (Schwartz & Jacobson, 1977); however, the effect of that influence on either overall organizational performance or communication effectiveness is unknown.

Uncertainty is related to organizational communication effectiveness in two ways. First, high levels of perceived uncertainty increase the flow of information from the environment (Lawrence & Lorsch, 1967), and hence, increase the demand upon the communication system. If adjustments are not made during periods of organizational stress, overall communication effectiveness will be inhibited. Second, uncertainty should be considered in terms of optimal levels that exist within the acceptable boundaries established by organizational members or units. Danowski (1975) states that people have "preferred" levels or tolerances for uncertainty. They seek to maximize this uncertainty, and willfully induce error when their uncertainty drops below a preferred level to some significant degree. The organization that seeks to routinize all uncertainty, and hence, to minimize its impact, should find new and imaginative sources of error occurring as a result.

Potpourri

We use the term potpourri as a label for those criteria which either cut across all other categories above, or which do not fit into one of the other criterion dimensions. The criteria to be considered in this section are: cost of information and efficiency.

Cost of information. Interestingly, most communication scholars have paid relatively little attention to the cost of communication or information, except in the context of costs involved in technology/hardware. However, it is commonly recognized that all communication events in an organization consume a certain amount of time and resources, and hence should be attributed a certain level of cost. Golightly (1973) found that, by accounting for information expense in a multiple regression model of productivity, he was able to markedly improve the ability of the Pareto economic model of the firm to account for variability in the productivity of a firm. In effect, then, he was able to give some empirical support for the contention that all communication in an organization has cost and, furthermore, that efficiencies in information processing costs are an important component of overall productivity.

In the case of bureaucracies, a large percentage of all activities taking place is in the form of communication events. This suggests that efficiencies in the conduct of these events bear a strong relationship to the organization's ability to transform the resources it acquires into the outcomes it desires. While little research has been done on cost per se, some literature does incorporate it. Glazer (1973) argues that success in knowledge transfer in achieving institutional change is a function of the organization's willingness to expend resources. Unfortunately, Huber, O'Connell, and Cummings (1975) indicate that, while economic constraints increase uncertainty and hence the demand for information, information-processing technology is usually the first area to suffer resource cutbacks.

Efficiency. Efficiency simply refers to the relative rate of return on energy (time and resources) invested in communicating. In the sense of Simon (1947), returns on investment take the form of any number of inducements or perquisites. It can range from a "pat on the back," a responsive behavior, or monetary compensation. In general, communication is efficient when the returns achieved exceed the amount of energy invested in the communication event.

A more useful concept is perhaps that of relative efficiency, in which alternative communication media and/or strategies are employed to achieve the same end results. By careful accounting of the investments required to bring about desired goals through each communication means, measures of relative efficiency can be obtained. Relatively little research has been performed that examines large-scale communication systems (particularly those composed chiefly of human components) and that defines and operationalizes their relative efficiency.

CONCLUDING REMARKS

This paper provides a description of 21 potential criteria for assessing the effectiveness of organizational communication processes. For each criterion, a computer-based literature search was used to supplement materials available to the authors. Important works related to each criterion are summarized, and the discussion centers on the conditions under which the criterion might be taken to reflect a component of the macro-concept of "organizational communication effectiveness."

The paper clearly represents only the first step in the process of more fully coming to grips with the concept. Criteria involving organizational media are in the process of being outlined in the same fashion that the structure, message, communicator, and potpourri criteria categories are treated in the present paper. The next step in the process is the development of testable propositions and the identification of measurement procedures and research contexts that will enable the propositions to be evaluated. As this work is completed by organizational communication scholars, it will then become considerably easier to respond competently to the query: "What do you mean by effective communication in organizations?"

REFERENCES

ADELBERG, A.H. Management information systems and their implications. *Management Accounting*, 1975, 53, 328-330.

ALLEN, T.J., & COHEN, S.I. Information flow in research and development laboratories. *Administrative Science Quarterly*, 1969, 14, 12-20.

ALPERT, M.I., & ANDERSON, W.T. Optimal heterophily and communication effectiveness—Some empirical findings. *Journal of Communication*, 1973, 23, 328-343.

ARGYRIS, C. *Interpersonal competence and organizational effectiveness*. Homewood, Ill.: Irwin-Dorsey, 1962.

BARNARD, C.I. *The functions of the executive*. Cambridge, Mass.: Harvard University Press, 1938.

BARNETT, G., SEROTA, K., & TAYLOR, J. Campaign communication and attitude change: A multidimensional analysis, *Human Communication Research*, 1976, 2, 227-244.

BENNIS, W.G. *Organization development: Its nature, origins, and prospects*. Reading, Mass.: Addison-Wesley, 1969.

BENTLEY, T.J. Designing an information system that meets the needs of management. *Management Accounting*, 1974, 52, 299-303.

BERLO, D.K., LEMERT, J.B., & MERTZ, R.J. Dimensions for evaluating the acceptability of message sources. *Public Opinion Quarterly*, 1969, 33, 119-128.

BETTINGHAUS, E.P. *Persuasive communication* (2nd ed.). New York: Holt, Rinehart & Winston, 1973.

BURCH, J.G. & STRATER, F.R. Tailoring the information system. *Journal of Systems Management*, 1973, 24, 34-38.

CARZO, R. & YANOUZAS, J. Effects of flat and tall organizational structure. *Administrative Science Quarterly*, 1969, 14, 178-191.

CHAKRABARTI, A.K. A dissonance theory approach to communication channel usage. *Indian Journal of Social Research*, 1972, 13, 98-110.

CUSHMAN, D.P., & WHITING, G.C. An approach to communication theory: Toward consensus on rules. *Journal of Communication*, 1972, 22, 217-238.

DANOWSKI, J.A. An uncertainty model: Friendship communication networks and media-related behavior. Unpublished paper, Department of Communication, Michigan State University, 1974.

DANOWSKI, J.A. An information theory of communication function: A focus on information aging. Unpublished doctoral dissertation, Michigan State University, 1975.

DAVID, C.J., & PRUETT, J.M. Information systems—Information life span considerations. *Information & Records Management*, 1975, 9, 24, 27-28.

DOWNS, A. *Inside bureaucracy*. Boston: Little, Brown, 1967.

DRUCKER, P.F. *Management: Tasks, responsibilities, practices*. New York: Harper & Row, 1974.

DUNCAN, D.O., FEATHERMAN, D.L., & DUNCAN, B. *Socio-economic background and achievement*. New York: Seminar Press, 1972.

EMERY, F.E., & TRIST, E.L. The causal texture of organizational environments. *Human Relations*, 1965, 18, 21-32.

ENSIGN, R.B. Measuring the flow of management information. *Journal of Systems Management*, 1974, 25, 40-43.

ETZIONI, A. *Modern organizations*. Englewood Cliffs, N.J.: Prentice-Hall, 1966.

FARACE, R.V., & DANOWSKI, J.A. Analyzing human communication networks in organizations: Applications to management problems. Unpublished paper, Department of Communication, Michigan State University, 1973.

FARACE, R.V., MONGE, P.R., & RUSSELL, H.M. *Communicating and organizing*. Reading, Mass.: Addison-Wesley, 1977.

FESTINGER, L., SCHACHTER, S., & BACK, K. *Social pressures in informal groups: A study of human factors in housing*. New York: Harper & Row, 1950.

FLOYD, H.F., & ZIMUD, R.W. Daily information reporting. *Business Horizons*, 1976, 19, 39-44.

GALBRAITH, J.R. Organization design—Information processing view. *Interfaces*, 1974, 4, 28-36.

GALLAGHER, C.A. Perceptions of value of a management information system. *Academy of Management Journal*, 1974, 17, 46-55.

GLAZER, E.M. Knowledge transfer and institutional change. *Professional Psychology*, 1973, 4, 434-444.

GOLIGHTLY, H.O. The what, what not, and how of internal communication. *Business Horizons*, 1973, 16, 47-50.

GROSS, B.M., & SPRINGER, M. New goals for social information. *Annals of the American Academy of Political & Social Science*, 1967, 373, 208-218.

GUETZKOW, H. Communication in organizations. In J.G. Marsh (Ed.), *Handbook of organizations*. Chicago: Rand McNally, 1965.

HOLLAND, E. & STEAD, B.A., et al. Information channel/source selection as a correlate of technical uncertainty in a research and development organization. *IEEE Trans. on Eng. Mgmt.*, 1976, 23, 163-167.

HUBER, G.P., O'CONNELL, M.J. & CUMMINGS, L.L. Perceived environmental uncertainty—Effects of information and structure. *Academy of Management Journal*, 1975, 18, 725-740.

HUSE, E. *Organizational development*. New York: Wiley, 1975.

HUSEMAN, R.C., LOGUE, C.M. & FRESHLY, D.L. *Readings in interpersonal and organizational communication*. 3rd ed. Boston: Holbrook Press, 1977.

JACOBSON, E., & SEASHORE, S. Communication practices in complex organizations. *Journal of Social Issues*, 1951, 7, 28-40.

JOHNSON, B.M. *Communication: The process of organizing*. Boston: Allyn & Bacon, 1977.

KATZMAN, N. Impact of communication technology—Some theoretical premises and their implications. *Ekistics*, 1974, 38, 125-130.

KNEITEL, A.M. Management-information-systems-EDP management—Where the action is. *Infosystems*, 1975, 22, 61-62.

KORZENNY, F. A theory of electronic propinquity: mediated communication in organizations. *Communication Research*, 1978, 5, 3-24.

LAWRENCE, P.R., & LORSCH, J.W. *Developing organizations: Diagnosis and action*. Reading, Mass.: Addison-Wesley, 1967.

LAZARSFELD, P.F., & MERTON, R.K. Friendship as social process: A substantive and methodological analysis. In M. Berger et. al. (eds.). *Freedom and control in modern society*. New York: Octagon, 1964.

LUCAS, H.C., JR. Performance and the use of an information system. *Management Science*, 1975, 21, 908-919.

MARCH, J.G., & SIMON, H. *Organizations*. New York: Wiley, 1958.

McGREGOR, D. *The human side of enterprise*. New York: McGraw-Hill, 1960.

McPHEE, W. Studies in theories of large groups. Final report submitted to Department of Health, Education, and Welfare, 1972 (ERIC).

MILLER, G.E., GALANTER, E., & PRIBRAM, K. *Plans and the structure of behavior*. New York: Holt, Rinehart & Winston, 1960.

MILLER, G.R., & BURGOON, M. *New techniques of persua-*

sion. New York: Harper & Row, 1973.
MILLER, G.R., & STEINBERG, M. *Between people: A new analysis of interpersonal communication*. Chicago: Science Research Associates, 1975.
MILLER, J.G. Psychological aspects of communication overloads. In R.W. Waggoner and D.J. Clark (Eds.), *International psychiatry clinics: Communication in a clinical practice*, Boston: Little, Brown, 1964.
MILLER, L.R. Law and information systems. *Journal of Systems Management*, 1977, 28, 21-29.
MITCHELL, J.C. (Ed.). *Social networks and urban situations*. Manchester, England: Manchester University Press, 1969.
MONGE, P.R., & LINDSEY, G. Communication patterns in large organizations. Unpublished manuscript, San Jose State University, 1973.
MULLER, J. Sources of Measured Technical Efficiency—Impact of Information. *American Journal of Agricultural Economics*, 1974, 56, 730-738.
MURDICK, R.G., & ROSS, J.C. Future management—Information-systems. *Journal Systems-Management*, 1972, 23, 32-35.
NEWCOMB, T.M. An approach to the study of communicative acts. *Sociological Review,* 1953, 60, 393-404.
NYSTEDT, L., & MAGNUSSON, D. Predictive efficiency as a function of amount of information. *Multivariate Behavioral Research*, 1972, 7, 441-450.
ONIKI, H. Cost of communication in economic organization. *Quarterly Journal of Economics*, 1974, 88, 529-550.
O'REILLY, C.A.I., & ROBERTS, K.H. Information filtration in organizations—Three Experiments. *Organization Behavior and Human Performance*, 1974, 11, 253-265.
PINES, H.A., & JULIAN, J.W. Effects of task and social demands on locus of control differences in information processing. *Journal of Personality*, 1972, 40, 407.
PLANTY, E., & MACHAVER, W. Upward communication: A project in executive development using the syndicate method. *Personnel,* 1952, 28, 66-70.
PORTER, L., & LAWLER, E. Properties of organizational structure in relation to job attitudes and job behaviors. *Psychological Bulletin,* 1965, 64, 23-51.
RICHARDS, W.D. Network analysis in large complex systems: Metrics. Unpublished paper, Institute for Communication Research, Stanford University, 1974.
ROKEACH, M. *Beliefs, attitudes and values*. San Francisco: Jossey-Bass, 1968.
ROGERS, E., & SHOEMAKER, F. *Communication of innovations: A cross-cultural approach*. New York: Free Press, 1971.
ROTHWELL, R. Patterns of information-flow during innovation process. *ASLIB Proceedings*, 1975, 27, 217-226.
ROTHWELL, R., & ROBERTSON, A.B. Contribution of poor communication to innovative failure. *ASLIB Proceedings*, 1975, 27, 393-400.
SALTIEL, J., & WOELFEL, J. Accumulated information and attitude change. *Human Communication Research*, 1975, 1, 333-344.
SCHNEIDER, J.H. Selective dissemination and indexing of scientific information. *Science*, 1971, 173, 300-308.
SCHNEYMAN, A.H. Management information systems for management sciences. *Interfaces*, 1976, 6, 52-59.
SCHULER, R., & BLANK, L.F. Relations among types of communication, organizational level, and employee-satisfaction and performance. *IEEE Transactions of Eng. Mgt.*, 1976, 23, 124-129.
SCHWARTZ, D.F., & JACOBSON, E. Organizational communication network analysis—The liaison communication role. *Organizational Behavior and Human Performance*, 1977, 18, 158-174.
SHANNON, C., & WEAVER, W. *The mathematical theory of communication*, Urbana: University of Illinois Press, 1949.
SIMON, H.A. *Administrative behavior: A study of decision-making processes in administrative organizations* (2nd ed.). New York: Macmillan, 1947.
SIMON, H.A. *The sciences of the artificial*. Cambridge, Mass.: MIT Press, 1969.
SUMMERS, J.O. Less information is better? *Journal of Marketing Research*, 1974, 11, 467-468.
TAYLOR, J.A. An empirical examination of the referential function of informal communication groups. (Unpublished master's thesis, Michigan State University, 1976).
TAYLOR, J.A., FARACE, R.V., & MONGE, P.R. Communication and the development of change among educational practitioners. Unpublished paper, Department of Communication, Michigan State University, July 1976.
THOMPSON, J.D. *Bureaucracy and innovation*. University: University of Alabama Press, 1967.
TURPIN, J.B. Communication needs of MIS. *Journal of Systems Management*, 1972, 23, 28-30.
WEICK, K.E. *The social psychology of organizing*. Reading, Mass.: Addison-Wesley, 1969.
WHITTMORE, B.J., & YOVITS, M.C. Generalized conceptual development for analysis and flow of information. *Journal of the American Society for Information Science*, 1973, 24, 221-231.
WIGAND, R.T. Communication network analysis in urban development. Paper presented at the annual meeting of the International Communication Association, Chicago, April 1975.
WOFFORD, J.C., GERLOFF, E.A., & CUMMINS, R.C. *Organizational communication: The keystone to managerial effectiveness*. New York: McGraw-Hill, 1977.
WOODWARD, J. *Industrial organization: Theory and practice*. London: Oxford University Press, 1965.

MESSAGE-RESPONSE AND "OPENNESS" IN SUPERIOR-SUBORDINATE COMMUNICATION[1]

FREDRIC M. JABLIN
University of Wisconsin-Milwaukee

This study summarizes a field experiment analyzing relationships among "openness" of superior-subordinate communication, and attitudes toward five basic types of message-responses occurring in a dyad: confirmation, disagreement, accedence, repudiation and disconfirmation. Results indicated that regardless of perceived climate of "openness" of communication, subordinates (subjects) predicted (and preferred) that a superior respond to an unfavorable message from a subordinate more often with a confirming or disagreeing response, than with an acceding, or repudiating, or disconfirming response. However, dependent upon the degree of perceived "openness" or "closedness" of the communication relationship with the superior, subordinates evaluated the appropriateness of these responses differently. Moreover, the object (superior or subordinate) of the subordinate's initial message was found to play an important role in determining the superior's and subordinate's later responses. Subjects also predicted that a subordinate would respond to a superior's message with either a confirming or disagreeing response, more often than with an acceding, or repudiating, or disconfirming response.

Perhaps one of the most common complaints aired by managers and supervisors is that employees are not "open" and honest when communicating with their superiors (e.g., Gemmill, 1970). For example, researchers have discovered that subordinates are afraid to tell their superiors how they feel (e.g., Vogel, 1967), distort information they pass on to their bosses (e.g., Read, 1962; Downs, 1967; Athanassiades, 1973; O'Reilly and Roberts, 1974; Roberts and O'Reilly, 1974a, 1974b), and generally feel that if they disclose negative or unfavorable information to their superiors they will be punished in some way (e.g., Blau & Scott, 1962; Argyris, 1966). At the same time, however, we find that many management theorists and researchers argue that openness of communication between subordinates and superiors is a vital element of a successful organizational climate (e.g., Haney, 1967; Likert, 1967). Along these lines, investigations by Burke and Wilcox (1969), Baird (1973) and Jablin (1977) have revealed that employees are more satisfied with their jobs when openness of communication exists between subordinate and superior, than when the relationship is "closed." Of even greater significance are several studies which report that openness of communication is directly correlated with organizational performance (e.g., Indik, Georgopoulos, & Seashore, 1961; Willits, 1967).

A dilemma would then appear to exist: on the one hand, subordinates are reluctant to be open when communicating with their superiors; however, on the other hand, communication openness is ostensibly essential to organizational success. Given this apparent contradiction, the major predicament for superiors is to develop relationships with subordinates such that the subordinate does *not* feel he or she will be penalized for being open in communication. In essence, subordinates need to feel that their openness will not be discouraged, but rather, rewarded by their superior (Gemmill, 1970; Stull, 1974).

At this point, the question arises concerning which superior and subordinate interpersonal behaviors are conducive to the development and maintenance of open communication relationships. Few empirical studies have attempted to specifically examine the effects of perceived message-responses upon openness of communication between superiors and subordinates. The present investigation attempts, in part, to fill this hiatus by addressing itself to the following question: *What types of communicative responses characterize open and closed communication relationships between superiors and subordinates*?

REVIEW OF LITERATURE

Open Communication in the Organization

Reviews examining the nature and definitional properties of openness of communication are available in the research literature (e.g., Baird, 1973). Hence, the following discussion will address itself solely to investigations related to open communication in the organization. A review of this literature reveals only two major investigations directly examining openness of communication between superiors and subordinates; both inquiries are doctoral dissertations, the first by Baird (1973), and the second by Stull (1974).

The design of Baird's (1973) study provided for an examination of subordinates' "upward communication freedom" with superiors, as well as perceptions of openness with peers. Results of the research revealed that both supervisor-subordinate and peer-peer dyads were more willing to (and actually did) talk more about task than nontask topics. Further, these same dyads were more willing to *listen* on task-related and positive topics, than on nontask-related and negative topics. Perhaps the most general conclusion that can be drawn from Baird's research is that, regardless of dyad-type, both willingness to talk and actual talk about a topic is a function of the individual's perception of the other's willingness to listen.

Building upon Baird's study, Stull (1974) attempted to ascertain subordinate and supervisor attitudes toward three types of supervisory responses (*accepting*, *reciprocating* and *neutral-negative*) to task-relevant and nontask-relevant open messages sent by subordinates. Analyses disclosed that all response types were viewed as important and that, for task and nontask topics, subordinates and supervisors preferred supervisory responses that were accepting (encouraging) or reciprocating ("owning-up" to one's feelings, ideas, etc.), rather than neutral-negative (unfeeling, cold or "nonaccepting").

In summary, the above studies provide support to the notion that openness of communication involves both message-sending and message-receiving behaviors (Redding, 1972), and more specifically that in an open communication relationship between superior and subordinate both parties: (1) perceive the other interactant as a willing and receptive listener, and (2) refrain from responses which might be perceived as neutral-negative or "nonaccepting."

Interpersonal Message-Response

Generally, interpersonal response is associated with investigations of feedback (e.g., Weiner, 1950). However, as Leth (1976) notes, most research on feedback has operationalized the concept as a relatively general response type. In contrast to such conceptualizations of interpersonal response, other researchers (e.g., Ruesch, 1953; Rokeach, 1960; Watzlawick, Beavin, & Jackson, 1967; Hawes, 1973) have suggested that interpersonal responses are made at two basic levels, one a content level (the report aspect of the message), and the other a relational level (the command dimension of the message).

Probably the most widely accepted schemata of message-response categories are those advanced by Watzlawick, et al. (1967): confirmation, rejection, and disconfirmation. *Confirmation* is a response which provides a speaker with positive content and positive relational feedback; *rejection* is a response which provides a speaker with negative content feedback, but positive relational feedback; *disconfirmation* is a response which provides a speaker with irrelevant (or inappropriate) content and equally irrelevant relational feedback. Sieburg and Larson (1971) characterize a disconfirming response as inappropriate-unclear-impersonal.

On the surface, it would appear that two of the responses that Stull (1974) studied, acceptance and neutrality, are synonymous with the Watzlawick, et al. concepts of confirmation and disconfirmation. There are similarities, yet there are substantial differences in the meanings assigned to the terms. Acceptance, for Stull, is a response which reflects "unconditional positive regard" (Rogers, 1961) to the discloser of the message. However, Stull's definition of acceptance as a positive rela-

FIGURE 1
Proposed Categories of Interpersonal Message Responses

		Relational Level		
		Positive	Negative	Irrelevant
Content Level	Positive	Confirmation	Accedence	
	Negative	Disagreement	Repudiation	
	Irrelevant			Disconfirmation

tional feeling between interactants does *not* consider the role of message *content* in response behavior. On the other hand, the concepts of confirmation and rejection are more specific, defining both relational and content dimensions of interpersonal response. The meaning of Stull's concept of neutral-negative responses appears congruous with the idea of disconfirmation, but again we find there are differences. A neutral-negative response infers a lack of recognition of the relational component of the communication interaction; however, it also includes a negative reaction to the content of the message. On the other hand, the Watzlawick, et al. concept of disconfirmation implies a recognition of neither relational or content dimensions of communication.

As is evident from the preceding discussion, researchers have used a variety of similar, yet subtly distinct, message-response categories to analyze communicative behavior. Moreover, we find that no single response-category schema really adequately covers relevant "response space" (i.e., both content and relational dimensions of messages). For example, the Watzlawick, et al. taxonomy does not provide for responses which could be classified as both negative-content *and* negative-relational messages. Stull's response categories present problems, in that they confuse content and relational levels of communication. Given this situation, proposed here is a new category system which is intended to combine the strengths of previous taxonomies. This categorization is outlined in Figure 1.

The above taxonomy provides for five different types of message-response. *Confirmation* and *disconfirmation* correspond in meaning to the Watzlawick, et al. definitions. *Disagreement* is similar in meaning to the Watzlawick, et al. concept of "rejection"; however, it was felt that the term "rejection" was inappropriate for describing a response which includes a positive relational component. *Accedence* refers to a response in which one agrees on the content level, but expresses negative affect on the relational level. *Repudiation* is a response where one sends the listener both negative content and negative relational feedback.

At this juncture, the reader should be cautioned that, despite the apparent exclusiveness of each of the categories, message-responses are typically not entirely positive or negative on any one dimension. Rather, responses must be perceived as possessing degrees of valence on both content and relational levels. Furthermore, it should be noted that four cells in the 3x3 matrix are empty. The rationale for this decision is simple: a response cannot be irrelevant on a content level and at the same time command positive or negative qualities on the relational level. Conversely, a response cannot be irrelevant on the relational level and retain positive or negative content attributes.

THE PRESENT RESEARCH

The goal of the present research is to determine which kinds of interpersonal response behaviors (i.e., confirmation, disagreement, accedence, repudiation, and disconfirmation) correspond to openness in superior-subordinate communication. Based upon the above literature review, some basic conceptualizations and predictions of this relationship can be tentatively proposed. Succinctly stated, one requisite of an open communication climate between a superior and subordinate is *reciprocal acceptance* of the other by both interactants. In other words, for open communication to exist each party needs to believe (to some degree) that his or her communication will be accepted by the other individual (Stull, 1974; Gilbert & Horenstein, 1975; Gilbert & Whiteneck, 1976; Gilbert, 1976). Once reciprocal acceptance develops in relationships between supervisors and subordinates, a tolerance for a variety of response behaviors emerges. For example, Fleishman and Harris (1962, p. 53) have found that "workers under foremen who establish a climate of mutual trust, rapport and tolerance for two-way communication with their work groups are more likely to accept higher levels of structure." In a very real sense, we may postulate that the supervisor has accumulated "idiosyncratic credit" (Hollander, 1958) via his or her "consideration" behavior, allowing him or her to violate some communication norms of the work group.

In summary, it would appear that in a truly open communication relationship between superior and subordinate, both individuals possess a freedom to respond to the other's messages in any of the five response styles outlined earlier. Each interactant believes the other party will accept messages that are sent. Further, each individual has a certain degree of leeway in the number of negative relational and content messages he or she sends because of reciprocal acceptance, and from the "idiosyncratic communication credit" he or she has accumulated. However, it is unlikely that responses will be acceding, repudiating, or disconfirming, since inherently these behaviors will normally lead to a deterioration of reciprocal acceptance.

Hypotheses and Research Question

With an understanding of the issues related to openness of communication and interpersonal message-response discussed earlier, the following hypotheses are advanced:

H_1: Regardless of perceived climate of openness of communication, subordinates will *prefer* to receive from superiors communicative responses which are, in descending rank order, confirming, disagreeing, acceding, repudiating, and disconfirming.

H_{2A}: Subordinates who perceive an *open* climate of communication between themselves and their superior will feel it is *appropriate* for a superior to respond to messages from a subordinate in any of five response styles (i.e., confirming, disagreeing, acceding, repudiating, and disconfirming).

H_{2B}: Subordinates who perceive a *closed* climate of communication between themselves and their superior will feel it is *not appropriate* for a superior to respond to messages from a subordinate with an acceding, repudiating, or disconfirming response.

H_{3A}: Subordinates who perceive an *open* climate of communication between themselves and their superior will *predict* that a superior will respond to a message sent by a subordinate with either a confirming or disagreeing response, more often than with an acceding, repudiating, or disconfirming response.

H_{3B}: Subordinates who perceive a *closed* climate of communication between themselves and their superior will *predict* that a superior will respond to a message sent by a subordinate with any one of these responses: acceding, repudiating, or disconfirming.

H_{4A}: Subordinates who perceive an *open* climate of communication between themselves and their superior will *predict* that a subordinate will respond to a superior's message with either a confirming or disagreeing response, more often than with an acceding, repudiating, or disconfirming response.

H_{4B}: Subordinates who perceive a *closed* climate of communication between themselves and their superior will *predict* that a subordinate will respond to a superior's message with any of three responses: acceding, repudiating, or disconfirming.

Despite the rationale presented earlier to support

the above hypotheses, there is another important variable which may affect these predictions. Specifically, a potential interaction may exist between the object of the superior's or subordinate's message and the other person's response. For example, will a superior be as accepting of a subordinate if the subordinate discloses a negative statement *about the superior*, as when the subordinate discloses a negative statement about himself? No organizational communication study has examined this issue, and a search of relevant literature reveals only one empirical study by Levinger and Seen (1967) approaching this problem. Their study examined how marital satisfaction is related to the *object* of valence statements. Preliminary results indicated that the more satisfied spouses were less likely to discuss negative feelings pertaining to their mates, but more likely to discuss negative feelings about external events. Hence, the present research poses the following research question:

> Question 1: Is there an interaction between the object (superior or subordinate) of a message and the receiver's response to that message?

METHODOLOGY

Research Design

The research design was comprised of two basic conditions, one depicting an *act* and the other an *interact* (Weick, 1969; Fisher & Hawes, 1971; Hawes, 1973). In the act condition, subjects (all experimental subjects used in the study were real-life subordinates) saw one of two videotapes. Regardless of the videotape, the subject always saw a subordinate initiate a message directed to his superior. (However, at the very beginning, the subject was unaware of which party was the superior and which the subordinate.) In one of the tapes, the subordinate always began the conversation by sending a message to the superior, the content which was *unfavorable to the superior*. In the other tape, the subordinate initiated the conversation with a message, the content of which was *unfavorable to the subordinate* (himself). (It will be noted that all initial messages were unfavorable in content; for pragmatic reasons no favorable initiating messages were included in the design.) The subjects were then informed that the person who initiated the interaction on the designated topic was the subordinate, and that the listener was his boss. Following this disclosure, subjects were asked to (1) predict what they thought the superior would say in response to the subordinate's comment (i.e., predict the second element in the interact), and (2) what they would *prefer* this response to be. Subjects responded in each instance by actually writing out the words of the response.

At this point, the videotape was again started and subjects saw one of ten interact condition tapes; that is, they now saw the superior make his actual response (on the videotape) to the subordinate's initial message. This response of the superior was experimentally manipulated to be one of five types: (1) confirming, (2) disagreeing, (3) acceding, (4) repudiating, and (5) disconfirming. Subjects were then requested to indicate the *appropriateness* of the superior's actual response. Finally, the experimenter asked subjects to predict how they thought the *subordinate* would respond to the superior's response; that is, they wrote out the words of a message representing the final (third) element of a complete *double-interact*.

Research Setting

The companies. Seven different business/industrial organizations participated in the research study. All organizations were located in the midwest United States, ranging in size from around one hundred employees to several thousand. These organizations included a manufacturer of specialized office equipment (n=45), a grain refining plant (n=86), a hospital (n=48), an investor-owned utility (n=91), two separate units of a public utility type of company (n=48, n=59), and an insurance company (n=8).

The subjects. In total, usable data were collected from 385 subjects. Each subject who participated in the study was a member of the organization who had a superior to whom he or she reported, that is, all subjects were subordinates. The subject population can be characterized as follows:

1. Approximately 60% were male and 40%

female, with over 50% between the ages of 26 and 45.

2. The great majority of subjects completed high school, but fewer than 14% held college degrees.
3. Over 90% of the subjects had been employed with their organization for at least one year, suggesting that interaction patterns between subordinates and superiors were probably quite stable.
4. Approximately 64% of the sample perceived themselves to be in lower levels of the organization's hierarchy, 31% in the middle of the hierarchy, and only 5% in the upper echelons of the organization.

Data-Gathering Instruments

Two paper-and-pencil questionnaires, and ten videotape superior-subordinate communication enactments (stimulus materials) were prepared by the investigator. The first questionnaire, arbitrarily labeled Questionnaire-A, contained the independent-variable scale, and seven demographic questions. The second questionnaire, arbitrarily labeled Questionnaire-B was used in conjunction with the videotape stimulus materials and provided subjects with the opportunity to evaluate supervisor message-responses, as well as to predict both superior and subordinate message behaviors.

Questionnaire-A. This questionnaire contained the Superior-Subordinate Communicative Openness Scale (SSCO). The SSCO was constructed after a review of relevant empirical and theoretical literatures, and is concerned soley with *task-related* issues surrounding its fundamental construct. The scale contains 18 items, utilizing a five-point Likert-type response format. Data collected from a pilot study using student subjects (n=194), and data secured from organizational field subjects (n=385) indicate that the scale is quite stable and reliable. Factor analyses (Principal Components-Varimax Rotation) on the SSCO for both populations revealed identical and unidimensional factor structures, and comparable factor loadings (range: .60–.87). Moreover, reliability analyses suggest that the SSCO is extremely reliable (Cronbach's alpha=.96).

In addition to the SSCO, Questionnaire-A contained seven demographic questions, concerning information about the respondent's age, education, length of service with the organization, superior's span of control, size of the organization, perceived position in the organization's hierarchy, as well as the individual's general job title.

Videotaped stimulus materials. Several issues regarding the general content of the videotapes require explanation. As has been noted, the subordinate always initiated the interaction (on the chosen topic) with the superior. The rationale for this decision is quite simple: in order to investigate openness in message sending it was necessary to begin the conversation with an open message. Research on self-disclosure indicates that a "genuine disclosure" (Miller & Steinberg, 1975) involves some kind of risk on the part of the speaker. Hence, in the present study the subordinate initiated the interaction with a message which was *unfavorable* either to himself or to the superior. The assumption was that when the subordinate initiated the interaction with an unfavorable, risky message he was engaging in open communication. This assumption was validated by four judges who viewed each of the ten videotapes and responded to the following question on a 7-point semantic differential-type scale (1=strongly agree, 7=strongly disagree): "Do you feel the subordinate was being 'open' in communication when offering his initial comments?" The mean rating for the videotapes was 2.25, indicating that the subordinate's unfavorable message was considered to be significantly open.

It was further determined to limit the topic of conversation between the subordinate and superior to a task-related matter. This decision is founded upon results of recent research which suggest that the majority of superior-subordinate interaction concerns task issues (Richetto, 1969; Baird, 1973). Additionally, in all videotaped episodes the topic of conversation was impersonal (focus on something external to self) rather than personal (topic directly related to self). This judgment was based upon results of Baird's (1973) study in which he found superiors and subordinates talk more about impersonal than about personal topics. Finally, in an attempt to control for sex and age interaction within the videotape sequences, the same two male actors of approximately the same age (30-35) were employed in all ten videotapes.

With the above considerations in mind, a topic for the superior-subordinate interaction was chosen: one concerned with alleged breakdowns in a newly acquired piece of equipment in a manufacturing firm—specifically, breakdowns with a "press in the Stamping Department." It was felt that the topic met the requirements outlined above, and was easily related to by all subjects, that is, regardless of the type of organization in which one works, equipment invariably is breaking down.[2]

Each tape began in the same manner, with the same initial two-shot profile edited into the beginning of each sequence. The subordinate's message concerning the press in the Stamping Department was identical for all tapes except for changes in the pronouns "I" and "you." The superior's response was manipulated dependent upon the interact condition (i.e., confirming, disagreeing, acceding, repudiating, or disconfirming). However, all superior responses were approximately the same number of words in length (range: 37-42 words). Camera positions and shots were standardized for all tapes.[3]

The validity of the content (experimental manipulation) of each of the five types of messages enacted in the videotapes was established by having four judges view each tape, classifying each of the superior's responses into one of five categories: confirmation, disagreement, accedence, repudiation, and disconfirmation. All four judges were correctly in agreement in categorizing the message-response of the superior 100% of the time.

Questionnaire-B. This questionnaire provided subjects with the opportunity to predict (in a written message): (1) what the superior would probably say in response to the subordinate's initial message, and (2) the words they would *prefer* the superior should say. After subjects viewed the superior's actual response (on the videotape), they responded to the following semantic differential-type question: "How *appropriate* was the superior's response to what the subordinate said?" (1=not appropriate, 7=very appropriate). Subsequent to completing this item, subjects were asked to write the actual words he or she thought the subordinate would say in response to the superior's response (on the videotape). Also included within Questionnaire-B were several manipulation-check questions.[4]

Data Analysis

Rater reliability. In order to examine the "predicted" and "preferred" message-responses collected from subjects, three judges coded the written messages into one of five response styles: confirming, disagreeing, acceding, repudiating, or disconfirming. Judges were instructed in the taxonomy of message-responses described earlier, and employed this classification schema as their criteria for assigning each message to a category. Each judge was aware of the context in which the responses were made, and was instructed to consider both the scenario and the preceding message(s) in coding any single response. In total, each judge coded 1,155 messages.

Both inter-rater and intra-rater reliability estimates were computed for the three judges. The kappa statistic (Cohen, 1960; Cohen, 1968) was employed to measure the degree of agreement between raters. For the present data $k=.80$, with a standard error of .015.[5] Intra-rater reliability was assessed by randomly selecting one subject from each of the ten videotape conditions, and asking each judge to again code this subject's three message-responses. Thus, each judge made a total of 30 ratings. These 30 ratings collected at the end of the coding session were compared to the same ratings made during the session. Judge 1 was in self-agreement 26 out of 30 times (86.6%); Judge 2, 26 out of 30 times (86.6%); and Judge 3, 27 out of 30 times (90%). Based on these results it was concluded that there was a satisfactory degree of inter-rater and intra-rater reliability.

Statistical analyses. Prior to testing hypotheses and examining the research question, a median-split (Median=64.14, Mean=60.03, SD=16.5) was computed for the data obtained from the SSCO. This dichotomization of scores into two groups enabled the researcher to assign subjects into one of two groups: (1) high openness between superior and subordinate ("open" group), and (2) low openness between superior and subordinate ("closed" group).

TABLE 1
Contingency Table for Preferred Superior's Response

Object of Subordinate's Message	Preferred Superior's Response					
	Confirm	Disagree	Accede	Repudiate	Disconfirm	
Superior	116	58	7	9	2	192
Subordinate	142	25	20	5	1	193
	258	83	27	14	3	385

After coding the subject generated message-responses, 2x5 contingency tables (2 levels of the object of the subordinate's initial message and 5 levels of message-response) were prepared for the predicted and preferred superior's response, and the predicted subordinate's response, for both the open and closed groups. Hypotheses 1, 3a, 3b, 4a, and 4b were tested by chi-square tests of goodness-of-fit across the response marginals of their respective contingency tables. Following this test, a series of 1x2 chi-square tests between pairs of response marginals were conducted, in accordance with the relationships predicted by the hypotheses. Each hypothesis was tested and then immediately followed by findings related to the research question. This approach was utilized since the research question inquired into the possibility that there was an interaction between the object (either superior or subordinate) of the subordinate's initial unfavorable message, and the superior's subsequent response (as well as the subordinate's later messages). The research question was explored by chi-square tests of independence for 2x5 contingency tables, followed by orthogonal partitions (Castellan, 1965; Bresnahan & Shapiro, 1966) of these tables. (It should be noted that these partitions were in accordance with the relationships predicted by the hypotheses.)[6]

Hypotheses 2a and 2b were tested by 2x5 analyses of variance (ANOVA) for unequal cells. Where appropriate, probing techniques were employed. The alpha level for all statistical tests was set at the .05 level of significance. All hypotheses were tested by one-tailed tests, and the research question by a two-tailed test.

RESULTS

In order to insure that the open and closed groups were significantly different from each other, a *t*-test was computed on SSCO scores between the two groups. The resulting *t*-ratio ($t=26.56$, $df=383$, $p<.001$) was significant, indicating that statistically the open group ($\overline{X}=75.33$, $SD=7.55$) was different from the closed group ($\overline{X}=48.81$, $SD=11.61$) in superior-subordinate communicative openness. Further evidence that the open and closed groups formed within the SSCO scale were really different is supplied by the fact that scores for the scale ranged from the lowest to highest possible value (range: 18-90), and were approximately normally distributed.

Hypothesis 1

Hypothesis 1 predicted that, regardless of perceived climate of openness of communication, subordinates would *prefer* to receive from superiors responses which were, in descending rank-order, confirming, disagreeing, acceding, repudiating, and disconfirming. Table 1 reports the contingency table for data pertaining to the preferred superior's response. The chi-square tests on the response marginals of Table 1 supported Hypothesis 1. Since the chi-square test for the contingency table was significant ($\chi^2=23.13$, $df=3$,

$p<.0001$, Cramer's $V=.25$), the interaction between the object of the subordinate's unfavorable message, and the preferred superior's response was explored by orthogonally partitioning the table. These partitions revealed three significant sources of variation within the contingency table: confirm *x* disagree ($\chi^2=15.60$, df=1, $p<.001$), disagree *x* accede ($\chi^2=15.74$, df=1, $p<.001$) and accede *x* repudiate ($\chi^2=5.43$, df=1, $p<.01$).

Hypotheses 2a and 2b

Hypostheses 2a and 2b pertain to perceptions of the appropriateness of the superior's actual response (on the videotape), for the open and closed groups, respectively. These hypotheses were tested by 2x5 ANOVA for unequal cells. For Hypothesis 2a to be supported, a main effect for the superior's message-response should *not* obtain (essentially a *null* hypothesis); that is, all messages should be perceived as equally appropriate. For Hypothesis 2b to be supported, a main effect for the superior's message-response *should* obtain. Moreover, multiple comparison tests should reveal that acceding, repudiating, and disconfirming responses were rated as significantly less appropriate than confirming or disagreeing responses.

Contrary to expectations, a main effect was found for the superior's message-response ($F=14.38$; df=4, 182; $p<.001$), for the open group. Hence, Hypothesis 2a was not supported. Apparently, subordinates who perceived an "open" communication relationship with their superiors did not feel that all types of superior responses were appropriate. In order to determine which responses were perceived as appropriate, a Newman-Keuls multiple comparison test was computed between the main effect means. Results of this test indicated that *disconfirming* responses ($X=1.78$) were considered inappropriate when compared to all other kinds of responses; a *repudiating* response ($\overline{X}=3.34$) was perceived as inappropriate when compared to confirming ($\overline{X}=4.50$) or disagreeing ($\overline{X}=4.64$).

As expected, a main effect for the superior's message-response did emerge ($F=13.86$; df=4,183; $p<.001$), for the closed group. However, a main effect for the object of the subordinate's message also became evident ($F=6.13$; df=1,183; $p<.05$), along with a significant interaction ($F=4.09$; df=4, 183; $p<.005$). Since the interaction was significant, an ANOVA for simple main effects was computed.[7] This analysis indicated three significant simple main effects. First, a significant effect for a superior's repudiating response according to the object of the subordinate's message was found ($F=15.34$; df=1, 183, $p<.001$). An examination of these means disclosed that it was highly appropriate ($\overline{X}=5.21$) for a superior to respond to a subordinate with a repudiating message, if the subordinate (in a closed climate) had already sent to the superior an unfavorable message about the *superior*. On the other hand, if such a subordinate had sent to the superior an unfavorable message about *himself* it was inappropriate ($\overline{X}=3.00$) for the superior to respond in a repudiating manner.

The two other significant main effects related to the object of the subordinate's message for the various superior responses. In order to determine which responses were perceived as appropriate within each of these two effects, Newman-Keuls multiple comparison tests were computed for the respective means.

The multiple comparison tests revealed several interesting findings. First, when the superior was the object of the subordinate's unfavorable message, a disconfirming response ($\overline{X}=1.81$) from the superior was considered inappropriate when compared to the other responses. It was also evident that when the superior was the object of the subordinate's unfavorable message, a *repudiating* response ($\overline{X}=5.21$) by the superior was perceived to be more appropriate than a disagreeing response ($\overline{X}=3.68$). On the other hand, when the subordinate was the object of his own unfavorable message, a disconfirming response ($\overline{X}=2.00$) from the superior was considered inappropriate when compared to acceding ($\overline{X}=3.35$), disagreeing ($\overline{X}=4.37$), and confirming messages ($\overline{X}=4.15$). It is of interest to note that there was no significant difference between a repudiating ($\overline{X}=3.00$) and disconfirming response—both were considered to be inappropriate. In summary, the data did not fully support Hypothesis 2b.

TABLE 2
Contingency Table for Predicted Superior's Response for the "Open" Group

Object of Subordinate's Message	Predicted Superior's Response					
	Confirm	Disagree	Accede	Repudiate	Disconfirm	
Superior	26	51	7	18	1	103
Subordinate	53	17	12	5	2	89
	79	68	19	23	3	192

TABLE 3
Contingency Table for Predicted Superior's Response for the "Closed" Group

Object of Subordinate's Message	Predicted Superior's Response					
	Confirm	Disagree	Accede	Repudiate	Disconfirm	
Superior	29	38	4	17	1	89
Subordinate	64	15	22	3	0	104
	93	53	26	20	1	193

Hypotheses 3a and 3b

Hypotheses 3a and 3b relate to the superior's response to the subordinate's initial unfavorable message, as *predicted* by the open and closed groups, respectively. Table 2 reports the contingency table for the predicted superior's response for the open group; and Table 3 reports these predictions for the closed group. The chi-square tests on the response marginals of these contingency tables supported Hypothesis 3a, but did not support Hypothesis 3b. However, it should be emphasized that the chi-square tests on the response marginals of Table 3 were significant, but the findings were all in the direction *opposite* to that predicted. Thus, the data indicate that subordinates who perceived either an open or closed climate of communication between themselves and their superior, predicted that a superior would respond to an unfavorable message from a subordinate more often with a confirming or disagreeing response, than with an acceding, or repudiating, or disconfirming response. But, unlike subjects within the open group, the closed group predicted significantly more confirming responses than disagreeing responses from the superior ($\chi^2=10.96$, $p<.001$).

Since the chi-square test on the contingency tables for the open group ($\chi^2=33.91$, df=3, $p<.0001$, Cramer's V=.42), and the closed group ($\chi^2=44.39$, df=3, $p<.0001$, Cramer's V=.48)

TABLE 4
Contingency Table for Predicted Subordinate's Response for the "Open" Group

Object of Subordinate's Initial Message	Predicted Subordinate's Response to the Superior					
	Confirm	Disagree	Accede	Repudiate	Disconfirm	
Superior	39	35	11	16	2	103
Subordinate	53	25	6	2	2	88
	92	60	17	18	4	191*

*One missing observation

TABLE 5
Contingency Table for Predicted Subordinate's Response for the "Closed" Group

Object of Subordinate's Initial Message	Predicted Subordinate's Response to the Superior					
	Confirm	Disagree	Accede	Repudiate	Disconfirm	
Superior	31	27	9	20	1	88
Subordinate	59	22	6	14	1	102
	90	49	15	34	2	190*

*Three missing observations

were significant, the interaction between the object of the subordinate's initial unfavorable message and the predicted superior's response were examined by orthogonally partitioning the tables. The orthogonal partitions for the open group indicated two significant sources of variation within the contingency table: confirm x disagree ($\chi^2=26.06$, df=1, $p<.001$), and confirm x repudiate ($\chi^2=14.75$, df=1, $p<.001$). The partitions of the contingency table for the closed group revealed four significant sources of variation: confirm x disagree ($\chi^2=22.32$, df=1, $p<.001$), confirm x repudiate ($\chi^2=19.20$, df=1, $p<.001$), disagree x accede ($\chi^2=22.28$, df=1, $p<.001$), and disagree x repudiate ($\chi^2=6.82$, df=1, $p<.01$).

Hypotheses 4a and 4b

Hypotheses 4a and 4b are concerned with the subordinate's response to the superior's response (to the subordinate's initial message), as *predicted* by the open and closed groups, respectively. Table 4 presents the contingency table for the predicted subordinate's response for the open group; and Table 5 reports these predictions for the closed group. The chi-square tests on the response marginals of these contingency tables supported Hypothesis 4a, but did *not* support Hypothesis 4b. As was the case earlier, the chi-square tests on the response marginals in Table 5 were all significant, but in the direction *opposite* to that predicted. In summary, both subordinates perceiving an open or closed climate of communication between themselves and their superior predicted that a subordinate would respond to a superior's message with either a confirming or disagreeing response, more often than with acceding, or repudiating, or disconfirming. Moreover, they predicted that the subordinate would respond with significantly more confirming responses than with disagreeing responses.

Since the chi-square test for the contingency tables for the open group ($\chi^2=15.07$, df=4, $p<.005$, Cramer's V=.28), and the closed group ($\chi^2=9.89$, df=3, $p<.02$, Cramer's V=.23) were significant, the interaction between the object of the subordinate's initial unfavorable message, and the predicted subordinate's response to the superior's response (to the unfavorable message) were explored by orthogonally partitioning the contingency tables. The orthogonal partitions for the open group indicated two significant sources of variation within the contingency table: confirm x repudiate ($\chi^2=13.10$, df=1, $p<.001$) and disagree x repudiate ($\chi^2=5.20$, df=1, $p<.05$). The partitions for the closed group revealed only one significant source of variation: repudiate x confirm ($\chi^2=5.90$, df=1, $p<.02$).

The reader will note that the preceding analyses have not taken into account the effect of the superior's response (to the subordinate's initial unfavorable message), upon the subordinate's predicted response to the superior. Hence, one additional level of analysis is required to accurately interpret the interaction between the object of the subordinate's initial unfavorable message, and the subordinate's predicted response to the superior's response (to the unfavorable message). An examination of the contingency tables for the five superior responses (i.e., confirmation, disagreement, accedence, repudiation, and disconfirmation) to the subordinate's initial unfavorable message, should reveal the effects of each of the superior responses upon the subordinate's subsequent response.

These analyses are not statistically reported here due to their length and complexity. However Tables 6 and 7 summarize the "emergent" patterns of communication suggested by such analyses. These tables are graphically structured in terms of the three components of a dyadic *double-interact* (i.e., initial message, response, response to response). Table 6 relates to those subjects who perceived an open communication relationship with their superiors; Table 7, to those who perceived a closed communication relationship.

DISCUSSION

The present investigation was designed to experimentally analyze the relationships among openness of superior-subordinate communication and attitudes toward five basic types of message-responses occurring in a dyad: confirmation, disagreement, accedence, repudiation, and disconfirmation. Despite the fact that not all hypotheses were entirely supported, the results of the study suggest certain patterns of communication characteristic of open and closed superior-subordinate relationships.

Data collected for preferred and predicted superior message-responses to a subordinate (delivering an unfavorable message) unequivocally indicate that *disconfirming* responses are not acceptable in superior-subordinate communication. Results from the present investigation parallel the conclusions of earlier research (e.g., Sieburg and Larson, 1971) which have suggested that a disconfirming response is a "destructive" response, and one that should be avoided in "healthy" communication relationships. Moreover, the present study found, to some extent, one's preference for a certain type of message-response is dependent upon the object (target) of the preceding message.

Perhaps of even greater significance is the fact that the overwhelming majority of subjects (subordinates) indicated that they preferred to receive from superiors the combination of confirming and disagreeing responses (86.6%), rather than the combination of acceding, repudiating, and disconfirming responses (11.4%). These results suggest that, in general, the relational valence of a message *may* play a more salient role in an individual's overall evaluation of a message, than the content of that message. In other words, findings in the present study indicate that subordinates prefer messages from superiors which provide positive relational feedback, or something resembling Carl Roger's (1961) "unconditional positive regard." This conclusion supports Stull's (1974) research, in which he found that an "accepting" response was the most desirable superior reaction to a message. Findings from the present investigation suggest the additional conclusion that, regardless of the object of a message (i.e., superior or subordinate) an accepting message is preferred to a nonaccepting message.

Whether or not a subordinate perceived an open climate of communication between himself or herself and his or her superior did affect evaluations of the appropriateness of a superior's response, as well as predictions of superior and subordinate message-responses. In general, subordinates who perceived an open climate of communication between themselves and their superior felt that it was inappropriate, regardless of the object of the message (superior or subordinate), for a superior to react to a subordinate's message with a repudiating or disconfirming response. In contrast, subordinates who perceived a closed communication relationship with their superior judged the appropriateness of a superior's response by not only the type of response expressed, but by *whom the message was about* (i.e., superior or subordinate). These results suggest that in open relationships, superiors and subordinates possess a greater freedom in their response repertory than do subordinates and superiors in closed communication relationships. The rules for determining an appropriate message-response appear simpler in an open relationship than in a closed one. A subordinate who perceives a closed relationship with his or her superior not only considers the actual response-type of the superior's message, in evaluating the superior's communication, but also the object of the subordinate's own preceding message to the superior. Seemingly, these processes would lead to less spontaneity, greater evaluativeness and greater strategy in the subordinate's communicative behavior—all of which, Gibb (1961) claims, create a "defensive communication climate."

In general, both subordinates who perceived a closed and those who perceived an open climate of communication between themselves and their superior predicted that a superior will respond to an unfavorable message from a subordinate more often with a confirming or disagreeing response, than with an acceding, or repudiating, or disconfirming response. However, subordinates who perceived an open relationship with their superior predicted an equal number of confirming and disagreeing responses, while subordinates who perceived a closed relationship expected the superior to respond with significantly more confirming than disagreeing responses. These findings may imply that a subordinate experiences more discordant communication from a superior in an open than in a closed relationship; in other words, there is more room for disagreement in an open than in a closed relationship.

The above conclusion would appear justified, except that it must be kept in mind that both subjects perceiving a closed and those perceiving an open communication climate between themselves and their superior, also indicated that the object (superior or subordinate) of the subordinate's preceding message would affect their prediction of the superior's response. Specifically, when the *superior* is the object of the subordinate's initial unfavorable message, subjects expect the superior to respond to the subordinate with fewer confirming, and more disagreeing and repudiating responses than if the *subordinate* were the object of his own initial unfavorable message. Yet, subjects who perceived an open communication relationship with their superior also felt that confirming and disagreeing responses were significantly more appropriate than a repudiating response, while sub-

TABLE 6
Emergent Communication Pattern for Subjects Who Perceived an "Open" Communication Relationship with their Superior

Object of Subordinate's Initial Message (On Videotape) ("ACT")	Actual Superior's Response (On Videotape) ("INTERACT")	S Prediction of Subordinate's Response to Superior* ("DOUBLE-INTERACT")
Superior <u>or</u> Subordinate	Confirmation	Confirmation
Superior <u>or</u> Subordinate	Disagreement	Confirmation/ Disagreement
Superior <u>or</u> Subordinate	Accedence	Confirmation, Disagreement
Superior only	Repudiation	Repudiation, Disagreement, Confirmation
Subordinate only	Repudiation	Disagreement, Confirmation
Superior <u>or</u> Subordinate	Disconfirmation	Disagreement, Confirmation, Repudiation

*Responses are listed in rank-order of their frequency of prediction; a slash (/) indicates approximately the same rank ordering.

jects with closed relationships perceived a repudiating response from the superior to be significantly more appropriate than a disagreeing response. Hence, we find that, regardless of perceived openness or closedness of the communication relationship with their superior, subordinates *expect* the same type of responses from a superior, but *evaluate* the appropriateness of these responses differently.

Results of the study have also indicated that both subordinates who perceived an open and those who perceived a closed climate of communication between themselves and their superior, predicted that a subordinate would respond to a superior's message with either a confirming or disagreeing response, more often than with an acceding, or repudiating or disconfirming response. However, again we discover that the object of the subordinate's initial message plays an important role in determining the subordinate's later response to the superior's response (to the subordinate's initial unfavorable message); that is, if the superior is the object of the subordinate's initial unfavorable message then the subordinate will respond to the superior's response, with more repudiating and fewer confirming statements, than if the subordinate were the object of his own initial message.

Tables 6 and 7, presented earlier, have traced the emerging communication pattern (act/interact/double-interact) between superior and

TABLE 7
Emergent Communication Pattern for Subjects Who Perceived a "Closed" Communication Relationship with their Superior

Object of Subordinate's Initial Message (On Videotape) ("ACT")	Actual Superior's Response (On Videotape) ("INTERACT")	S Prediction of Subordinate's Response to Superior* ("DOUBLE-INTERACT")
Superior <u>or</u> Subordinate	Confirmation	Confirmation
Superior only	Disagreement	Disagreement, Confirmation
Subordinate only	Disagreement	Confirmation, Disagreement
Superior <u>or</u> Subordinate	Accedence	Confirmation, Disagreement, Repudiation
Superior <u>or</u> Subordinate	Repudiation	Confirmation, Disagreement/ Repudiation
Superior <u>or</u> Subordinate	Disconfirmation	Confirmation, Disagreement/ Repudiation

*Responses are listed in rank-order of their frequency of prediction; a slash (/) indicates approximately the same rank ordering.

subordinate as perceived by subjects in this study. An analysis of these patterns leads to the following interesting conclusions:

1. For both open and closed groups, a substantial degree of reciprocity exists for confirming messages.
2. As soon as a superior's message contains negative relational valence toward the subordinate, subjects who perceive a closed relationship with their superior are prepared to retort with a response that also transmits negative relational valence toward the superior—but this is not true for subjects who perceive an open relationship with their superior.
3. The great majority of all subordinates do not respond to a superior's message (regardless of the type of message) with either an acceding or disconfirming response.
4. Both subjects in the open and closed groups tend to respond to a *disconfirming* message from a superior with a positive relational remark, and to a lesser extent with negative relational feedback.

In conclusion, the overall results of this research support the basic thrust of the earlier studies of Baird (1973) and Stull (1974) concerning openness of communication between superiors and subordinates. Further, the investigation corroborates, in an organizational field setting, the clinical and empirical observations of many researchers who have explored interpersonal response behavior. Moreover, the research supports the notion that openness of communication between superiors and subordinates is a multidimensional construct, one which is contingent upon numerous message-response alternatives, upon perceptions of organizational and communication climate, as well as upon individual differences between organizational members.

NOTES

1. This research, supported through a General Electric Foundation Grant, at Purdue University, is part of the author's doctoral dissertation completed under the direction of Professor W. Charles Redding. Acknowledgment is given to Professor Redding for his valuable assistance throughout this project.
2. To further insure that subjects could relate to the topic, the experimenter instructed the subjects, prior to viewing the videotape, to keep in mind any piece of equipment with which they were familiar on the job, while they were listening to a boss and his subordinate discuss (on the videotape) a "press in the Stamping Department."
3. Superior-subordinate interaction scripts, and specific video and audio production instructions are available from the researcher, upon request.
4. Manipulation-checks included tests examining the effects of:
   (1) demographic variables upon perceived openness of communication between superior and subordinate;
   (2) similarity/dissimilarity of subject prediction of the superior's response to the superior's *actual* response;
   (3) differential levels of subject perception of the difficulty of the assigned task;
   (4) differential levels of subject self-perceived ability to assume the roles of the superior and subordinate viewed on the videotape; and
   (5) initial attributions of the role/status identities of the interactants viewed on the videotape. These tests indicated that the above potentially confounding variables did not distort obtained results.
5. "Under the hypothesis of no agreement beyond chance, k/SE_k will, by the central limit theorem, be approximately distributed as a standard normal variate" (Fleiss, 1971, pp. 380-381). In the present data $k/SE_k = 54.12$, which is significant beyond the $p<.0001$ level; hence, we can infer that the obtained overall agreement with this group of coders reflected an exceptionally high level of reliability.
6. When the degrees of freedom (df) within a contingency table were larger than 1, the chi-square test was used if no cell contained an *expected* frequency less than 2. According to McNemar (1969), when df is 2 or more, "expected frequencies as low as 2 will not produce misleading values" (p. 254). If a cell contained an *expected* frequency of less than 2, the cell was dropped from analysis.
7. Winer (1971) suggests that, "should the interaction term in the analysis of variance prove to be statistically significant, it is generally desirable to analyze the simple main effects rather than the overall main effects" (p. 435).

REFERENCES

ATHANASSIADES, J.C. The distortion of upward communication in hierarchical organizations. *Academy of Management Journal*, 1973, 16, 207-226.

ARGYRIS, C. Interpersonal barriers to decision making. *Harvard Business Review*, 1966 (March-April), 44, 84-97.

BAIRD, J. An analytical field study of "open communication" as perceived by superiors, subordinates and peers. Unpublished doctoral dissertation, Department of Communication, Purdue University, 1973.

BLAU, P.M. & SCOTT, W. *Formal organizations*. San Francisco: Chandler, 1962.

BRESNAHAN, J.L., & SHAPIRO, M.M. A general equation and technique for the exact partitioning of chi-square contingency tables. *Psychological Bulletin*, 1966, 66, 252-262.

BURKE, R.J., & WILCOX, D.S. Effects of different patterns and degrees of openness in superior-subordinate communication on subordinate job satisfaction. *Academy of Management Journal*, 1969, 12, 319-326.

CASTELLAN, N.J., JR. On the partitioning of contingency tables. *Psychological Bulletin*, 1965, 64, 330-338.

COHEN, J. A coefficient of agreement for nominal scales. *Educational and Psychological Measurement*, 1960, 20, 37-46.

COHEN, J. Weighted kappa: Nominal scale agreement with provision for scaled disagreement or partial credit. *Psychological Bulletin*, 1968, 70, 213-220.

DOWNS, A. *Inside bureaucracy*. Boston: Little, Brown, 1967.

FISHER, B.A., & HAWES, L.C. An interact system model: Generating a grounded theory of small groups. *Quarterly Journal of Speech*, 1971, 57, 444-453.

FLEISHMAN, E.A., & HARRIS, E.F. Patterns of leadership behavior related to employee grievances and turnover. *Personal Psychology*, 1962, 15, 43-56.

FLEISS, J.L. Measuring nominal scale agreement among raters. *Psychological Bulletin*, 1971, 76, 378-382.

GEMMILL, G. Managing upward communication. *Personnel Journal*, 1970, 49, 107-110.

GIBB, J.R. Defensive communication. *Journal of Communication*, 1961, 11, 141-148.

GILBERT, S.J. Empirical and theoretical extensions of self-disclosure. In G.R. Miller (Ed.), *Explorations in interpersonal communication*, Beverly Hills, Cal.: Sage, 1976, 197-215.

GILBERT, S.J. & HORENSTEIN, D. The dyadic effects of self-disclosure: Level versus valence. *Human Communication Research*, 1975, 1, 316-322.

GILBERT, S.J., & WHITENECK, G.G. Toward a multidimensional approach to the study of self-disclosure. *Human Communication Research*, 1976, 2, 347-355.

HANEY, W.V. *Communication and organizational behavior—Text and cases* (2nd ed.). Homewood, Ill.: Irwin, 1967.

HAWES, L.C. Elements of a model for communication processes. *The Quarterly Journal of Speech*, 1973, 59, 11-21.

HOLLANDER, E.P. Conformity, status and idiosyncracy credit. *Psychological Review*, 1958, 65, 117-127.

INDIK, B.P., GEORGOPOULOS, B.S., & SEASHORE, S.E. Superior-subordinate relationships and performance. *Personnel Psychology*, 1961, 14, 357-374.

JABLIN, F.M. An experimental study of message-response in superior-subordinate communication. Unpublished doctoral dissertation, Department of Communication, Purdue University, 1977.

LETH, S.A. Interpersonal response: Confirmation, rejection and disconfirmation in established friendships. Unpublished doctoral dissertation, Department of Communication, Purdue University, 1976.

LEVINGER, G., & SENN, D.J. Disclosure of feelings in marriage. *Merill-Palmer Quarterly*, 1967, 13, 237-249.

LIKERT, R. *The human organization*. New York: McGraw-Hill, 1967.

McNEMAR, Q. *Psychological statistics* (4th ed.). New York: Wiley, 1969.

MILLER, G.R., & STEINBERG, M. *Between people*. Palo Alto, Cal.: Science Research Associates, 1975.

O'REILLY, C., & ROBERTS, K. Information filtration in organizations: Three experiments. *Organizational Behavior and Human Performance*, 1974, 11, 253-265.

READ, W.H. Upward communication in industrial hierarchies. *Human Relations*, 1962, 15, 3-15.

REDDING, W.C. *Communication within the organization: An interpretive review of theory and research*. New York: Industrial Communication Council, 1972.

RICHETTO, G.M. Source credibility and personal influence in three contexts: A study of dyadic communication in a complex aerospace organization. Unpublished doctoral dissertation, Department of Communication, Purdue University, 1969.

ROBERTS, K., & O'REILLY, C. Failures in upward communication: Three possible culprits. *Academy of Management Journal*, 1974a, 17, 205-215.

ROBERTS, K., & O'REILLY, C. Measuring organizational communication. *Journal of Applied Psychology*, 1974b, 59, 321-326.

ROGERS, C. *On becoming a person*. Boston: Houghton Mifflin, 1961.

ROKEACH, M. *The open and closed mind: Investigations into the nature of belief systems and personality systems*. New York: Basic, 1960.

RUESCH, J. Synopsis of the theory of human communication. *Psychiatry*, 1953, 16, 215-243.

RUESCH, J. The tangential response. In P.H. Hock and J. Zubin (Eds.), *Psychotherapy of communication*. New York: Grune & Stratton, 1958, 37-48.

SIEBURG, E., & LARSON, C. Dimensions of interpersonal response. Paper presented at the annual meeting of the International Communication Association, Phoenix, 1971.

STULL, J.B. "Openness" in superior-subordinate communication: A quasi-experimental field study. Unpublished doctoral dissertation, Department of Communication, Purdue University, 1974.

VOGEL, A. Why don't employees speak up? *Personnel Administration*, 1967, 30, 18-24.

WATZLAWICK, P., BEAVIN, J., & JACKSON, D. *Pragmatics of human communication: A study of interactional patterns, pathologies, and paradoxes*. New York: Norton, 1967.

WEICK, K.E. *The social psychology of organizing*. Reading, Mass.: Addison-Wesley, 1969.

WEINER, N. *The human use of human beings: Cybernetics and society*. Garden City, N.Y.: Doubleday, 1950.

WILLITS, R.D. Company performance and interpersonal relations. *Industrial Management Review*, 1967, 7, 91-107.

WINER, B.J. *Statistical principles in experimental design* (2nd ed.). New York: McGraw-Hill, 1971.

THE DETERMINANTS OF COMMUNICATION AND COMMUNICATION STRUCTURE IN LARGE ORGANIZATIONS: A REVIEW OF RESEARCH[1]

PETER R. MONGE
San Jose State University

JANE A. EDWARDS
University of California-Berkeley

KENNETH K. KIRSTE
Systems Development Corporation
Sunnyvale, California

Research findings from the literatures of administrative science, communication network analysis, industrial and personnel psychology, sociometry, social psychology, and sociology were combined in an attempt at generating principles regarding determinants of organizational communication structure which might have generality across organization types and methodologies. Studies were classified into two groups: those which considered only emergent structure, and those which compared an organization's emergent structure with its formally specified structure. Within each of these two groupings, studies were further subdivided into quantitative and qualitative sections according to the nature of the communication variables for which determinants were proposed. In the final section, 17 general statements were offered which summarize the best substantiated findings of the literature. Finally, several current shortcomings of the literature were noted and suggestions were made for future research.

Communication and communication structure in large organizations have been examined from so many disciplinary perspectives that the task of summarizing this literature is like assembling a puzzle composed of cubes with pictures on all facets. Several good but very different pictures are possible depending upon which facets are exposed and how they are arranged together.

Past reviews have been of basically two types: (1) those which emphasized general organizational behavior but mentioned communication behavior incidentally (e.g., James & Jones, 1974c; Porter & Lawler, 1965); and (2) those which focused primarily on communication (e.g., Guetzkow, 1965; Porter & Roberts, 1973). Considerable variety is found within each of these types.

This diversity of perspectives seems invaluable to the eventual formulation of a theory of organizational communication having validity at multiple levels of analysis (e.g., intrapersonal, dyadic, intragroup, etc.). Progress toward a multidisciplinary synthesis has begun. The present review attempts another step in that direction. It surveys empirical studies[2] from business, communication, industrial and social psychology, and sociology dealing with determinants[3] of communication structure in large, long-term, profit-making organizations. The focus on large corporate organizations excludes most small group studies,[4] and studies of service organizations and foreign societies,[5] where they suggest relationships which should be tested in corporate settings. Within these constraints, the review attempts a representative sampling of major trends and offers synthesizing hypotheses based on this sampling.

Before beginning, a few definitions are in order. A *network* may be defined as the set of stable person-to-person relationships through which information flows in an organization. For any organization of more than three individuals, several different configurations of relationships are theoretically possible. The configuration which actually exists is called that network's *structure*. Organizational structures may be represented as schematic diagrams, in which dots represent network members and lines represent relationships among them. Alternatively, structures can be represented as numerical values on mathematical indices (Edwards, 1976; Glanzer & Glaser, 1959; Guimaraes, 1970; Proctor & Loomis, 1951). With either method, the structures of different networks can be compared and predictor variables may then be sought to explain their differences.

Past comparisons of structures have led to two tenets which appear to be universally accepted in current literature: (1) organization members may be linked together through any of several possible types of relationships (e.g., communication, friendship, authority, work dependencies); and (2) different relational networks (e.g., friendship, power, kin) may differ radically in structure even when they share some of the same dyadic links (the shared links are called "multi-plexes" by Gluckman, 1967).

While commonplace today, the importance of relationship type has not always been appreciated. In fact, a preoccupation with formally specified (chain-of-command) relationships to the exclusion of all others was a major shortcoming of the classical theoretical approach to organizational behavior (Roberts, O'Reilly, Bretton, & Porter, 1963).

It is now generally believed that the formally specified relationships represent a bare minimum of interconnections needed for an organization to function, and that organization members must often forge many additional links in order to meet the exigencies of everyday situations (e.g., Wickesberg, 1968). In fact, these two types of structure (formal and emergent) probably never completely coincide. Not only may the emergent structure contain a greater density of relationships (Danowski, 1974), but it may also contain a larger number of status distinctions (Jacobson & Seashore, 1951) than is specified by the formal chart. Further evidence for the importance of unexpected situational demands in shaping organizational structure is the fact that two organizations with identical formal charts may develop grossly different emergent structures (Thompson, 1956).

This important distinction between formal and emergent structure has been handled in basically two ways in the literature. In the first, emergent structure has been examined with explicit reference to formal structural characteristics. Researchers in this tradition have examined such variables as direction of communication flow (i.e., vertical, horizontal, or diagonal), and the effects of status differences on communication initiation, content, and quantity. Researchers in the second tradition have focused strictly on emergent structure without explicit reference to formal characteristics. These people have described various communication roles found in emergent structures, distinguished among people enacting different roles, and noted various characteristics (fluid or static) of emergent networks. The present review is divided into two sections in accordance with these traditions. Variables within each division are further distinguished, mainly in terms of their quantitative or qualitative emphases.

EMERGENT CHARACTERISTICS RELATED TO FORMAL STRUCTURE

Quantitative Aspects

Quantitative variables discussed in this section include: overall amount of communication; the relative quantities of horizontal, vertical, and diagonal communication; and the rates of initiation of communication by individuals at various levels of organizational status.

Total amount of communication. The single best predictor of a person's total communication amount appears to be his organizational status. In general, higher status individuals spend more time communicating than lower status people (Farace & Pacanowsky, 1974), and devote more time to communication than they do to their other activities (Dubin, 1962; Hinrichs, 1964; Klemmer & Snyder, 1972; Thomason, 1966). Along with this, they tend to be better informed of the rumors circulating through the organization (K. Davis, 1953a; Sutton & Porter, 1968), even when rumors are planted at lower levels in the hierarchy (K. Davis, 1953a).

Technology and task variables may also influence communication amount. Though global effects of technology are difficult to assess (James &

Jones, 1974c; Mohr, 1971), several regularities have been found involving component aspects of the technology variable.

Communication among top executives may increase with the amount of novelty or innovation in a company (Thomason, 1966). Other important factors include the differentiation of jobs, the density of people in work area, and interpersonal proximity. Form (1972) reported that these technological variables exercised far more influence over interaction quantity and quality than either seniority or age (i.e., two measures of nonformal status).

Finally, communication amount appears related to the amount of discretion a person is allowed to exercise in performing the job (Blau, 1954; Wade, 1968). This correlation, however, may be merely an indirect result of the close relationships between discretion and status (Blau, 1960), and between status and communication.

Amount of vertical, horizontal, and diagonal communication. In addition to their total amount, communication behaviors of network members may differ in terms of their "direction" of flow within the organization. Horizontal or lateral communications are those which flow between people having the same hierarchical status. Vertical communications are those which flow between subordinates and their superiors in the same chain of command. Vertical communications may be either upward (subordinate to superior) or downward (superior to subordinate). Diagonal communications involve people of differing status in different chains of command.

The first question which arises is the relative importance of these various types of communication. Classical organizational theory (reviewed by Roberts, O'Reilly, Bretton, & Porter, 1973) emphasized the importance of only the formal control structure, which includes mainly vertical communications. In that view, superiors sent directions downward and subordinates sent performance feedback upward. Other types of communication (which were not so clearly specified on the formal chart) seemed somewhat incidental. However, more recent writers (e.g., Dubin, 1962; Dubin & Spray, 1964; Guetzkow, 1965; Simpson, 1959) agree with Burns (1954) that "the 'vertical' system would be virtually unworkable without the considerable flow of information laterally" (p. 92).

Estimates of the amount of horizontal communication generally hover around 30-40% (Porter & Roberts, 1973, p. 61). Estimates of vertical communication run as high as 67% (Porter & Roberts, 1973). However, studies suggest that the proportion of communication distributed among the various directions may vary greatly as a function of organizational size, members' organizational status, task requirements, and anticipated satisfaction.

While the importance of network size in other aspects of organizational functioning has been noted by several authors (Ingham, 1970; Meyer, 1972; Porter & Roberts, 1973), only one study was encountered which related it specifically to communication behavior. In this study of the League of Women Voters (an unpublished study by Donald, cited by Guetzkow, 1965), the rate of upward vertical communication was found to decrease with increases in network size, while the rate of horizontal communication remained roughly the same. While this result is intriguing, considerably more research is needed before firm conclusions may be drawn regarding the size variable.

Dubin (1962) investigated the influence of hierarchical status on directionality. After examining prior empirical studies, he postulated that people of lower organizational status (down to the level of the general foreman) would devote progressively less time to downward communication, and progressively more time to both upward and horizontal communication than would people of higher status. More recent empirical research, however, (including Dubin & Spray, 1974) has not supported this hypothesis.

Believing Dubin's hypothesis to be an oversimplification, Thomason (1966) emphasized the importance of work dependencies. In his view, the need for greater coordination between some pairs of individuals than others (e.g., between "director" and "assistant to the director") may cause the communication structure to look more like "a patch-work quilt of centres and lacunae" than like the simple gradient Dubin proposed.

This coordination, or work dependency, has received considerable research attention. Rosengren (1967) observed a positive correlation between task autonomy and the amount of restricted and formalized communications in a hospital. .Weiss and Jacobson (1960) found a similar relationship within a corporate setting. Vertical communications were preferred by workers having autonomous jobs (i.e., jobs for which they were solely responsible); horizontal or diagonal communications predominated when members specialized in subportions of the job and needed coordinated effort for its completion.

While Thomason (1966) denied the possibility of a simple gradient across individual positions in the hierarchy, he implied that a gradiant might be found at the level of coordinated pairs. Consistent with this, Marting (1969) reported that managers engaged in more communication with other departments (i.e., horizontally or diagonally) than did nonmanagers. Wickesberg (1968), however, found virtually no differences between the two groups in their amounts of horizontal and diagonal communication. This inconsistency may reflect instability in the relationship between hierarchical status and total amount of nonvertical communication. Further research is needed to properly evaluate this possibility.

One final factor influencing direction of communication flows might be satisfaction one anticipates obtaining from the communication. While horizontal and upward vertical communications seemed highly similar in perceived satisfaction and importance, they were perceived as much more satisfying and important than downward vertical communication (Berkowitz & Bennis, 1961). Similarly, perceptions of organizational functioning were found to be more favorable among employees whose organizations tended more toward upward than toward downward or multidimensional communication flows (Zaenglein & Smith, 1971).

Amount initiated versus amount received. One final quantitative variable is the proportion of an individual's communications with others which he himself initiates. Two general findings include a systematic overestimation of one's own initiation rate (Webber, 1970), and a generally high correlation between the number of communications a person initiates with others and the number of communications initiated by others with that person (Wade, 1968). More interesting findings pertain to patterns of initiation as they are nested within the hierarchical system.

Though upward vertical communication may be perceived as more satisfying and more important than downward vertical communication (Berkowitz & Bennis, 1961), it is much less frequent than downward initiation (Berkowitz & Bennis, 1961; Burns, 1954; Dubin, 1962; Dubin & Spray, 1964; Webber, 1970). This could be because high status persons are sought after by so many more people (because of their power and information) (Davis & Leinhardt, 1972; Homans, 1950), that it is impossible for them to communicate with all who wish to communicate with them. Alternatively, it may be due to a tacit organizational etiquette that prohibits excessive fraternizing with high status persons (Berkowitz & Bennis, 1961). Support for the second view is found in the greater equality of initiation seen in unusual situations (like conferences) in which organizational constraints were somewhat relaxed (Blau, 1955; Hurwitz, Zander, & Hymovitch, 1953). These constraints on upward communication suggest yet another way in which horizontal communications may be vital to the organization: they provide a valuable compromise between the less satisfying but easily initiated communication to subordinates and the very satisfying but difficult to initiate communication to superiors (Berkowitz & Bennis, 1961).

From this section several promising determinants of quantitative status-related communication behaviors have emerged: hierarchical rank, organizational size, novelty, and discretion. The best substantiated or most promising hypotheses involving these variables are listed separately at the conclusion of this review.

Qualitative Aspects

In addition to the quantitative aspects just discussed, several qualitative characteristics of communication have been related to formal structural variables. Of particular concern are determinants of message content, channel or modality, and message fidelity.

Content. Though essential to the study of content distributions, the use of content typologies is problematic for two reasons. First, subjects may have difficulty discriminating accurately or reliably among highly similar content categories (Sadler & Barry, 1967). Second, terminological and operational differences between typologies may complicate the comparison of results from different studies (see Dubin, 1962; Jacob, 1972). These factors may explain why results concerning content have not been as consistent as results in other areas of organizational communication. Even so, several interesting findings have emerged.

Content flows in an organization may be influenced by the patterned communications of certain individuals, called "magnetic centers," who systematically attract particular types of communications (e.g., authority, power, expertise, or sociability) (Walton, 1963).

Content flows may also be influenced by task dependencies and role expectations. Superiors and subordinates may differ in the communication contents they seek (e.g., problem feedback versus task supportiveness and understanding) (Berkowitz & Bennis, 1961; Slote, 1971). Wager (1972) suggests they may also differ in the communication contents expressed in their own communications, but this difference was observed in only half of Wager's subjects, and was not replicated by Wickesberg (1968). The inconsistency between studies could reflect unreliability in content judgments (Sadler & Barry, 1967) or an independence of some content categories from status or task variables (see, for example, Marting, 1969). More research is clearly needed.

Channel. Though face-to-face communication may be generally preferred to other types of communication (Conrath, 1973), great individual differences in channel preference have also been observed (Dubin & Spray, 1964). Channel preference may also be modified by role expectations (Thomason, 1966), novelty of the organization's operations (Burns, 1954), and the perceived information-sharing norms of one's work group (Dewhirst, 1971).

The relationship between message content and channel choice has received several speculative treatments (Guetzkow, 1965; Melcher & Beller, 1967; Porter & Roberts, 1973), but this review uncovered only one empirical treatment. That study found that the formal and work flow structure resembled the face-to-face communication structure much more closely than did the structures of either written or telephone communications (Conrath, 1973).

Channel choice has also been related to the physical distance separating interactants (known conversely as "proximity"). A strong negative relationship has been found between distance and face-to-face communication (Barnlund & Harland, 1963; Conrath, 1973; Kirste & Monge, 1974), but no complementary compensation for distance was observed in the other two channels (Conrath, 1973). This may be due to the insensitivity of the traditional fixed space measures of proximity. It might be fruitful to retest the latter hypothesis using the more dynamic joint probability measure proposed by Kirste and Monge (1974).

Message distortion. Information is essential at virtually every stage of organizational functioning. Due to limited resources of time and personpower, however, not all available information can be fully processed at every stage. Instead, the organization must rely on "gatekeeping"[6] *at* its boundaries and "filtering" *within* its boundaries to reduce the available information to usable proportions. While the resulting information is usually sufficiently accurate for its purposes, important distortions occasionally occur. The present section focuses on determinants of these two processes, both when they are functional and when they are not.

1. *Gatekeeping*. Potential determinants of gatekeeping behavior include: the manner in which authority is exercised in the organization (Whitley & Frost, 1972), message importance, message acceptability, and the influence of one's reference group (Porter & Roberts, 1973). Rather than the result of any one of these variables, however, Whitley and Frost (1972) suggest that gatekeeping is a product of a number of them in combination. A thorough discussion of gatekeeping variables is available in these two sources.

2. *Filtering*. The two types of variables most strongly linked to filtering are: (1) message content, and (2) particular aspects of the relationship between the interactants.

a. *Content*. Rumor content may partly dictate who receives a rumor as well as who transmits it.

Rumors with general appeal might be expected to spread broadly and somewhat indiscriminately through the organization. In two studies (Berkowitz & Bennis, 1961; K. Davis, 1968), work-oriented or production-oriented rumors were found to spread further than any other type. These results are weakened, however, by methodological flaws. First, questionnaires were completed in the place of work during regular hours, a situation which might spuriously inflate the number of task-related responses. Second, Davis's so-called "production-oriented" message concerned the possible layoff of 50 employees, a topic with considerable personal salience independent of its task relevance.

Results are contradictory concerning the spread of "general interest" information. Davis (1953a) reported a greater spread between departments than within them; Sutton and Porter (1968) reported the reverse. The discrepancy may reflect differences in the operational definition of "general interest," or differences in the internal cohesiveness of the two subject populations.

Rumors concerning more specialized topics may tend to spread chiefly toward "those who are seen as being most affected by the information" (Festinger, Schachter, & Back, 1950). Albaum (1964), however, reported great inefficiencies in this channeling process. Only two of his six planted messages reached their appropriate destinations and one of those arrived distorted. This conflicts with Marting's (1969) finding of 80% accuracy in rumor flows. The discrepancy may reflect different criteria for judging accuracy, or differences in the content of planted rumors used in the two studies. An especially important content variable may be a message's congruity with respondents' past experience or present beliefs (Pool, 1973). If Albaum's messages were relatively less congruent than Marting's, the discrepancy might be easily explained. This variable should be more carefully examined in future research concerning rumor content.

Results are mixed regarding the influence of content in determining who will transmit a rumor. Davis (1953a) found no set of individuals who served as transmitters regardless of task relevance. In contrast, Sutton and Porter (1968) found 71% who did. These studies may have differed in the precision of rumor tracking or in the validity of their content typologies relative to their subject populations. More research is needed for all ideas in this section.

b. *Relational variables*. Vertical filtering has been studied mainly within superior-subordinate dyads. Laboratory studies of this type are reviewed by Roberts and O'Reilly (1973). The present section considers only field studies.

There are two types of vertical filtering: downward filtering, which involves withholding information from one's subordinates; and upward filtering, which involves withholding information from one's superiors. K. Davis (1968) invoked downward filtering to explain why the employees below the general foreman knew only the work-related rumors which had been planted. A foreman's avoidance of non-essential downward communication would be understandable, given Berkowitz and Bennis's (1961) finding that downward links are associated with lower satisfaction and lower perceived importance, but at present this is mere speculation.

Upward filtering has received more research attention. It may be measured directly, by asking respondents to estimate their degree of openness with their superiors, or else indirectly, by calculating the degree to which superiors and subordinates agree about the subordinates' work problems and responsibilities. Upward filtering may be affected by the subordinate's satisfaction (Burke & Wilcox, 1969) or vice versa (Gemmill, 1969); by his trust in his superior (Roberts & O'Reilly, 1973); and by his own mobility aspirations (Maier, Hoffman, & Read, 1963; Read, 1962). The superior's perceived influence, however, appears to be relatively unimportant (Roberts & O'Reilly, 1973; Read, 1962).

EMERGENT CHARACTERISTICS EXAMINED WITHOUT REFERENCE TO FORMAL STRUCTURE

Studies in the last section explicitly related formal and emergent structures. The use of formal structure as a reference point for emergent phenomena has methodological and theoretical advantages. The relatively static and overt formal structure is imposed intact upon the individual all at once. This greatly eases boundary identification and clarifies the direction of causation among important variables.

The present section examines emergent structure largely independently of formal hierarchical variables. Boundary identification in these studies may be determined from differential flows of communication and energy at the organization's periphery (Danowski, 1974; Phillips & Conviser, 1972), but formal organizational boundaries are also commonly used.

The specification of causality is more difficult. In fact, many emergent structure relationships may be mutually causal. For example, a person's total number of communication partners may be both the result and the cause of his status in the group (Blau, 1954). For this reason, we will usually speak of "correlates" rather than "determinants" of communication structure. As before, studies are divided into quantitative and qualitative sections. Variables in the quantitative section include total amount of communication, and initiation rate; variables in the qualitative section include communication roles and network characteristics.

Quantitative Aspects

Amount. Several correlates of amount of communicative involvement have been mentioned in the literature. They include sociometric status, task competence, and proximity, to be discussed in that order.

Analogous to the positive correlation between hierarchical status and amount of communication (noted in the first section of this review) Larsen (1971) reported a positive correlation between *sociometric* status and amount of communication. This relationship is obviously tied to Homan's (1950) generalization that people tend to interact with those they are attracted to, a generalization which Collins and Raven (1969) termed one of the best supported in all of social psychology.

A second important correlate of communication amount is task competence. Graham (1971) found people rated high by others on either social or task criteria tended to be considered more desirable partners, regardless of the social or task status of the person doing the rating. Similarly, Blau (1954) found that highly competent law enforcement agents and those with extensive informal relations received a disproportionately large number of contacts. Interestingly, even though task competence and extent of informal relations were each directly related to integration, they were inversely related to one another. This finding seems to parallel the finding in the small group literature of two distinctly different types of group leaders: task leaders and socioemotional leaders. While the precise meaning of this parallel is presently unclear, it seems an especially promising area for cross-situational verification in future research.

One final influence on degree of communicative involvement is proximity. In line with the sizable social-psychological research on proximity, Gullahorn (1952) found the distance among the desks of clerical workers to be inversely related to the amount of communication among the workers, modified by the constraints of row arrangement and barriers such as filing cabinets. Similarly, Form (1972) appreciated the strong constraining influence of spatial arrangement and the density of people in the work spaces on interaction in factories. Barnlund and Harland (1963) asserted that, while physical proximity may be important initially in constraining and promoting communication along certain gradients, once the social structure stabilizes, prestige may be a more important determining variable, with communication tending to be polarized around high status members. Earlier work (Larsen & Hill, 1958) supports the same conclusion and also indicates that the influence of social structure upon interpersonal communication increases with the stability of the social structure.

Initiation. In general, the number of communications an individual initiates is positively correlated with the number of communications to that person which are initiated by others (Wade, 1968). Yet, the person's absolute rate of initiation appears to be a function of his or her sociometric status.

Although initiation rate may eventually be found to correlate with sociometric status in much the same way that it correlates with hierarchical status, the present sampling of research provides no support for this conclusion. Borgatta (1954) reported a (nonsignificant) correlation of only .20 between these variables. No other studies were found which pertained to this relationship.

Qualitative Aspects

This section is divided into two parts. First, traits and behaviors of people assuming particular communication roles are identified. Second, correlates of various network characteristics are noted.

Communication roles. In the past, researchers have distinguished among numerous communication roles. Monge and Lindsey (1974) list several such roles: participant, isolate, bridge, liaison, tree node, and dyad. Yet most research pertains to only two of those roles, isolate and liaison, which are discussed below. In general, the use of multiple operational definitions for the same communication roles, and insufficient research devoted to any one of them, complicates the interpretation of conflicting findings, making it difficult to determine whether the inconsistencies are due to differences in the constructs being measured, differences in the organizations under study, or simply instability of the communication role relationship being studied. Yet despite these difficulties, available research reflects several exciting regularities concerning these two communication roles.

1. *Isolate*. The most fundamental distinction among communication roles is that between individuals who do participate in a communication network, called "participants," and those who do not, called "isolates." The measurement problems associated with distinguishing between these two groups have prompted some controversy in the literature.

Killworth and Bernard (1973) suggested that isolates may be merely artifacts of insufficiently sensitive measurement techniques. They believed that network isolates might disappear altogether if respondents listed all of their associates, instead of only their closest three associates (as is customary in the sociometric approach described in Moreno, 1960). Empirical data from Moreno and Jennings (1938), however, do not support this view. Although the number of isolates initially declined with increases in the number of sociometric choices, the number of isolates soon stabilized, and additional sociometric choices only caused greater inequality in the choice distribution as these choices went disproportionately to individuals at the upper end of the distribution.

Additional evidence of the actual existence of isolates comes from K. Davis (1953a) who was unable to identify a group of individuals who were consistently active in rumor flows, yet observed that there were some individuals who were reliably isolated from them.

Thus, it appears that isolates may be more than a mere artifact of measurement procedures. However, the necessity for task interdependence within work organizations seems to preclude the possibility of *absolute* isolation. Instead, it seems that isolation should be viewed as a matter of degree, and thus that isolates and participants should be seen as two points on the same continuum. Hurewitz (1962) suggests that the continuum should be subdivided even more finely. Specifically, he advocates discriminating between neutral isolates (those who receive no more than one positive or negative choice in a sociogram), and isolates who are actively disliked (that is, receive many negative nominations).

The idea of making successively finer distinctions between communication roles has obvious merits for precision, but remains rare in the literature. Fortunately, the present isolate/participant distinction is refined enough for use in identifying difference between individuals occupying these two communication roles.

Network participants may differ from so-called isolates in terms of their (1) status and tenure with the organization; (2) job satisfaction; (3) work performance; and (4) perceptions of the accuracy of communications within the organization.

Network participants in a naval training sample were found to have significantly higher mean rank and tenure, and to be significantly older on the average than isolates (Roberts & O'Reilly, 1974).

While the two groups did not differ in terms of satisfaction with pay, promotion opportunities or work demands, isolates were significantly less satisfied with their supervisors and co-workers than were network participants (Roberts & O'Reilly, 1974). As might be expected from their relative dissatisfaction with supervisors and co-workers, isolates tended to perceive their work groups as performing at a significantly lower level, and tended to be, themselves, poorer performers than were network participants (Roberts & O'Reilly, 1974).

In addition to being less productive themselves, isolates may actually hinder the performance of others. According to Jennings (1960), isolates tend to "conduct themselves in ways which imply a marked lack of orientation . . . to elements of the total group situation," and their " 'externalizing' of private feelings of irritability" may harm morale in their immediate social environment (p. 91).

These two groups may also differ in their perceptions of communication accuracy within their organization. "Participants indicate higher interpersonal trust and feel information transmitted in their organization is more accurate, more often summarized, less gatekept, less changed, and more frequently expanded than do isolates" (Roberts & O'Reilly, 1974, p. 43). It is less clear whether people "become untrusting when they find themselves isolates" or whether people "who generally have low interpersonal trust seek out isolate communication roles" (Roberts & O'Reilly, 1974).

2. *Liaison*. As with the role of communication isolate, "liaison" has been defined differently by different authors. Schwartz (1969) identified two different but complementary functions performed by liaisons: network cohesion and information dissemination. Both of these functions have served as the basis for operationally defining liaisons.

Weiss and Jacobson (1960), and other researchers who emphasize the cohesion function, have defined a liaison as "an individual who [works] with at least two individuals who [are] members of work groups other than his own." A person's most frequent communications, however, need not be with those in his own work group. A variety of algorithms have been devised to identify emergent communication "cliques" without respect to work-group structure (see Abelson, 1967; Guimaraes, 1970; Richards, 1976). Researchers in this tradition (e.g., Farace & Pacanowsky, 1974; Monge & Lindsey, 1974; Richards, 1976) define liaisons as group linkers who are *not* group members. (In this terminology, Weiss and Jacobson's liaisons are called "bridges.")

Despite differences in definition and methodology, all researchers in this tradition emphasize the critical cohesive function served by liaisons over the long term. A liaison may sometimes be the only link connecting two otherwise isolated parts of a network (Bernard & Killworth, 1975, p. 2).

For K. Davis (1953a) and others who emphasize the information function, a liaison is a person who both receives and transmits a rumor or other piece of information to other members of the organization. These researchers emphasize the importance of liaisons in the short-term dynamics of message flows. When group members are highly homophilous (i.e., similar in knowledge, beliefs, information sources, etc.), new information may be less common. A link to a heterophilous person may greatly increase the likelihood of encountering a new item of information (Liu & Duff, 1972).

Their heterophilous nature may cause these links to be "weaker" in frequency or affective strength, but this does not diminish their importance. Rapoport and Horvath (1961) suggested that information transmitted through weak ties may actually "reach a larger number of people than if sent through strong ties." Granovetter (1973) reemphasized the importance of weak ties.

The extreme importance of these links has led several authors to examine characteristics which might distinguish liaisons from nonliaisons. Demographics have seldom been helpful in this regard. For example, in a university setting, Schwartz (1969) found liaisons (defined in terms of network cohesion) to be quite similar to nonliaisons in terms of age, sex, academic rank, degrees held, administrative positions, years employed by the university, percentage of time allotted to teaching, research, consulting, and administration, number of committee memberships at various levels and number of articles published recently.

However, liaisons and nonliaisons may differ in terms of general personality characteristics. As Porter and Roberts (1973) expressed it: "Certain individuals probably have a much greater propensity for wanting to serve as key communication links than do other individuals, thus indicating that personality factors may play an important role in the quality and quantity of such communication" (p. 55). Sutton and Porter (1968) administered personality inventories to both liaisons (defined as rumor transmitters) and nonliaisons. While the differences were not statistically significant, liaisons appeared to be relatively more interaction-oriented; dead-enders (those who received but did not transmit the rumor) appeared to be more task-oriented; and isolates (those who neither received nor transmitted the rumor) appeared to be more self-oriented. Using the cohesion definition of liaison, Schwartz (1969) further substantiated the interaction orientation of liaisons. In his study, liaisons reported roughly twice as many committee meetings per month, listed nearly twice as many communication contacts, and had nearly three times as many of these contacts reciprocated as did nonliaisons. These differences in communicative involvement were so great as to have been perceived even by the nonliaisons. In addition to their greater involvement in communication networks (a cohesion function), liaisons tended more often than nonliaisons to be the *initial sources*, or gatekeepers, of information relating to changes, new ideas, or new developments in the organization (informational function). Thus, results from these two research traditions may be closely complimentary.

Liaisons may be more productive at their work (Allen & Cohen, 1960), and may have higher organizational status than their colleagues (Frost & Whitley, 1971). Even when they do not have higher formal status than nonliaisons, they appear to be perceived as more influential within the power structure of the organization, by virtue of their communication links to more important secondary contacts (Schwartz, 1969).

Despite differences in operational definition, these studies present a remarkably consistent profile of the liaison member as an energetic, dynamic, committed organization member, fulfilling a vital communication service for his organization. This is in stark contrast to the profile of the communication isolate provided in the preceding section. While this contrast in personalities makes intuitive sense, more research is needed to determine its generality.

3. *Distribution of communication roles*. Having noted several systematic differences between isolates and liaisons, discussion now turns to the relative distribution of these communication roles within the organizational context. (Please see Table 1.)

From these data several interesting regularities emerge. First, the percentages of liaisons generally seem very similar for rumor studies and static structure studies, the only exception being the Farace and Johnson (1974) study. Farace and Johnson, themselves, remark on their very small percentage, attributing it to "the greater stringency of criteria we impose before an individual is considered a liaison, plus the uniformity of application of the criteria that the computerized routine gives over the prior 'by hand' analysis" (p. 13). This seems a plausible explanation of the observed discrepancy.

The relative distribution of liaisons and isolates in a communication network may vary as a function of the type of communication content carried by the network. Farace and Johnson (1974) reported finding more isolates in innovation and maintenance networks than in production networks. Since it is much more difficult to keep one's membership in a work organization while isolated from the production network than it is when isolated from the innovation or maintenance networks, this finding may once again reflect the importance of job requirements.

The relative number of liaisons versus isolates may also vary with the stage of organizational development and the stage in the diffusion of a message. No results were found bearing on this first factor. Regarding the stage of diffusion, however, Pool (1973) suggested that the number of liaisons in a diffusion network may increase as an S-shaped function of the time since the rumor began its spread. When the rumor is first planted, the number of people transmitting it is very few and this number increases only gradually. At a certain point of expansion, the number of people who have both received and transmitted the rumor increases very rapidly while the number of people who have neither received nor transmitted the

TABLE 1
Average Percentages of Isolates and Liaisons in Communication Networks

TYPE OF STUDY	REFERENCE	PERCENT ISOLATES	PERCENT LIAISONS
RUMOR FLOWS	Festinger, Cartwright, et.al. (1948)	41.0	27.0
	Marting (1969)	48.0	18.0
	Sutton & Porter (1968)	33.0	10.0
STATIC PATTERNS	Farace & Johnson (1974)	23.0[a]	1.1[b]
	Schwartz (1969)	13.0	16.0
	Weiss & Jacobson (1960)	0.5	18.0

[a]The authors distinguish between "Type 1" and "Type 2" isolates. This figure represents the average of both groups combined.
[b]The authors report an average of 5.9 "bridges" (cf. text, p. 33).

rumor declines correspondingly. Eventually, the percentage of each should stabilize as the number of people still unfamiliar with the rumor reaches a lower limit. Since the three rumor studies mentioned here employed different time periods for assessing the messages' progress through the organization, it is surprising that the percentages of liaisons and isolates were as similar as they were. However, more research is needed to determine for certain the importance of the time-period variable in explaining their differences.

Network characteristics. One property common to all organizations (and indeed to all systems) is what might be called "stability in flux." Organizations change and evolve over time, but may remain relatively stable for long periods in between. Communication relationships between particular individuals may persist despite great changes in their work group membership and organizational status (Whitley & Frost, 1972). Emergent communication relationships between different organizational positions may persist despite changes in personnel (Jennings, 1960, p. 89). It is this type of stability which explains why sociometric data gathered at one point in time may be highly successful in predicting rumor flows at a subsequent point in time (Katz, 1960). In general, it is the property which enables researchers to generate meaningful and testable hypotheses.

While networks themselves remain relatively stable, however, time may be an important consideration in other ways when reviewing this literature. With respect to the role of time, Coleman (1964) distinguishes two basic types of studies in network structure: (1) those studying forces responsible for a network's structure at one particular point in time ("source-oriented" studies of static structural characteristics); and (2) those examining the flow of messages through particular networks over time ("consequence-oriented" studies of dynamic message flows). The results of these two types of studies are summarized separately and in this order.

1. *Static structural characteristics*. Writers have long noted the nonrandom nature of social networks. Different yet complimentary aspects of this nonrandomness have been elucidated through the use of many diverse methods. Starting with a random network (i.e., one in which links between

TABLE 2
Percentages of Reciprocated Links in Social Networks

SUBJECT POPULATION	REFERENCE	PERCENT
High School Senior Males	Alexander (1966)	60
Medical Doctors	Coleman, Katz, & Menzel (1966)	37
Groups of Oceanographers on a Scientific Cruise	Bernard & Killworth (1975)	57 67 75 100 100
Native-Born Urban White Males	Laumann (1971)	43
College Professional Staff	Schwartz (1969)	50

pairs of individuals are assigned on a random basis), Rapoport (1963; also, Rapoport & Horvath, 1961, summarized in Abelson, 1967) imposed successive constraints (called "biases") upon linkage assignment as needed to bring the simulated network into closer correspondence with actual social networks. The constraints which appeared to be most successful in this regard were: (1) popularity, the tendency for there to be more individuals involved in very many as well as in very few relationships than would be expected in a random network; (2) reciprocity or symmetry, the tendency for a partner in a reported relationship to reciprocally acknowledge the relationship; and (3) transitivity, the tendency in social triads for the relationships among the component dyads to all be the same (e.g., the tendency for people to be friends with the friends of their own friends). Empirical research by other authors has further affirmed the existence of these properties.

The popularity constraint is seen in Moreno and Jennings's (1938) "sociodynamic effect," a "distortion of choice distribution in favor of the more chosen as against the less chosen." They report that this tendency is "characteristic of all groupings which have been sociometrically tested" (p. 359).

Jennings (1960) stressed the importance of reciprocity, stating that it may be "a more critical factor than the quantity of interaction, for the individual's choice-status and the choice-structure of the community as a whole" (p. 97). Estimates of percent of reciprocated relations vary among studies from different research traditions (see Table 2), yet they are consistently above chance level. Reciprocation rate appears unrelated to occupational status, education, religious preference, or political party preference (Laumann, 1971). It does correlate, however, with respondent age (Moreno, 1960); the frequency of contact of the two friends, their proximity, and the subjective closeness of their friendship (Laumann, 1971); the size of the network (Moreno, 1960); social distance among group members (Foster & Horvath, 1971); and the degree of interlock of the network (Laumann, 1971).

The study of transitivity necessarily involves also the study of the more restrictive yet closely related properties of balance and clusterability. Balance (Heider, 1946) in affective networks is the tendency for friends to like each other's friends and to dislike each other's enemies. The initial concept of balance was applied only to three-member networks composed of signed (i.e., positive or negative) affective relationships. More recently, it has been extended to larger networks (Cartwright & Harary, 1956; Flament, 1963) and to those composed of unsigned (i.e., merely present or absent) relationships (by J.A. Davis, 1967, cited in Abelson, 1967).

The basic definition of balance has several mathematical implications, the most important being the "structural principle," which allows, at most, two mutually isolated cliques within the network. Considering this restriction unrealistic for describing naturally occurring networks, J.A. Davis (1967) proposed "clusterability" as an alternative. A clusterable network may have any number of cliques within its boundaries so long as none of its 3-cycles has a negative line.

The degree to which a total network is balanced can be determined from an evaluation of the balance of its component triads (Flament, 1963). The same is true of clusterable networks. This fact sparked an interest in the triads themselves. Davis and Leinhardt (1972) hoped in this way to lend empirical support to Homans's (1950) idea that social networks are composed of two structures: differentiation into cliques (clusterability), and elaboration into ranks.

Davis and Leinhardt identified three types of dyadic relationships: mutually positive, mutually nonpositive, and asymmetrical. They expected asymmetrical relationships (i.e., those in which one individual feels a positive relationship while the other individual feels a nonpositive relationship) to occur chiefly among individuals at different levels of status (formal or informal), and mutual relationships (either positive or nonpositive) to occur chiefly among status equals. They also expected that only mutually positive relationships would occur *within* cliques, and that only mutually nonpositive relationships would occur *between* them, at the same level of status. The logistical constraints these hypotheses imposed (with respect to the status level at which each interactant is placed) lead to the expectation that 7 out of 13 possible triad types should rarely occur in natural networks. These authors examined sociomatrices from 427 groups and found only 2 of these 7 triads to occur more often than chance expectation. Thus, they reported obtaining general support for the two hypotheses, and, indirectly, for Homans's theory.

Continuing to be troubled by the remaining two triads, however, Davis (1970) subsequently proposed a refinement of the model which involved the idea of pair sums (the sum of the degree of liking of each member of a pair for the other, used as an index of the degree of clusterability of the pair as a whole). This modification not only resolved the problem of the final two triads but also made the model itself more parsimonious.

Hallinan (1972) questioned the adequacy of the data pool with which Davis and Leinhardt had tested their hypotheses. Specifically, she noted that those data reflected a conglomeration of sociometric questions (e.g., "Who would you vote for for president?", "Who would you prefer to have as a roommate?", etc.), and the frequent use of a fixed number of sociometric choices (e.g., "List your *three* best friends") which effectively precluded the occurrence of at least half a dozen of the triad types under examination. Hallinan (1974) tested those hypotheses through the use of her own data collection and analysis procedures (based on the six "triplets" contained in each triad) and obtained similar results.

As the result of these and similar systematic research efforts in this area, considerable information has arisen regarding transitivity, balance, and clusterability. Available data suggest tendencies in affective networks toward all three of these properties: transitivity (Hallinan & Felmlee, 1975, p. 195), positive balance, and clusterability (Killworth & Bernard, 1973). Several potential determinants of transitivity have also emerged from the literature.

The most important determinant of transitivity may be relationship type. Affective (i.e., sentiment) relationships in natural groups tend clearly toward transitivity (Hallinan & Felmlee, 1975, p. 195), but this trend may be considerably weaker for effective (i.e., actual behavior) networks (Bernard & Killworth, 1975)[7]—even though these two types of networks may overlap by as much as 60% (Bernard & Killworth, 1975).

A second factor influencing the degree of transitivity may be the number of liaisons in the network. Bernard and Killworth (1975) suggest an attenuation in transitivity as the number of liaisons increases.

Laumann (1971) mentions social background and personality variables as additional factors mediating degree of transitivity in affective networks. He compared basically two types of networks: (1) "interlocking" networks, in which the best friends of the respondent all knew each other; and (2) "radial" networks, in which they did not. Respondents in these two groups did not differ significantly with respect to age, intergenerational mobility, ethnic affiliation, relative educational attainment, relative socioeconomic status, or time in present neighborhood. However, they did differ in terms of religious preference, Catholics and Jews having more interlocked (or "transitive") networks than Protestants or others. They also differed in preferred job type. People with radial networks preferred individualistic, autonomous jobs, supposedly because of their greater tolerance for diversity and ambiguity than people with interlocked networks. Laumann (1971) also observed that the degree of *homogeneity* of the respondent's friends with respect to ethno-religious group membership, occupational activity, and political party preference might be a good predictor of transitivity. One final predictor he mentioned was friendship intensity (reported also in Hallinan & Felmlee, 1975), measured in terms of frequency of interaction, reported feelings of intimacy, and length of association.

Several other network-level properties have received research attention. Foremost among them is the degree of internal complexity of the network, measured most frequently in terms of either the raw total of relationships existing within the network or the percentage of existing within-network relationships out of the total number of such relationships which would have been theoretically possible (termed network "density," or "connectedness").

Danowski (1974), and Roberts and O'Reilly (1974) found a network's internal density to be inversely related to its size. However, Edwards and Monge (1975) provided evidence that a large spurious correlation between size and the density measure could be expected simply due to the use of network size when calculating density. Clearly this relationship warrants further study.

Several authors have examined possible influences of the organization's environment on its internal communication structure.

Wade (1968) reported a significant positive relationship between the raw frequency of incoming telephone calls and the number of calls either initiated or received internal to the network (a government agency). In contrast, Roberts and O'Reilly (1974) found a negative correlation between the number of communication links going externally from a network and the number of communication links within the network. The apparent discrepancy between these studies could arise from differences in the relationships these authors studied (symmetric only, or symmetric plus asymmetric), or the criteria used to define organizational boundaries (formal specifications versus actual interaction patterns).

Other researchers expected a network to adjust its internal complexity to the level of complexity in its environment (Danowski, 1974; Roberts & O'Reilly, 1974; Weick, 1969; Wigand, 1974), but empirical results have been mixed. This may be due to insufficient precision in measuring internal and external complexity.

2. *Dynamic flows*. Some researchers (Back, Festinger, Hymovitch, Kelley, Schachter, & Thibaut, 1950; Caplow, 1947; K. Davis, 1953a, 1953b, 1968; Festinger, Cartwright, Barber, Fleischl, Gottsdanker, Keyser, & Leavitt, 1948; Marting, 1969; Sutton & Porter, 1968) have used rumor flows as a source of structural information. From this research it appears that rumors:

1. may follow a small number of well-defined paths (Caplow, 1947; Moreno, 1960);
2. may travel more quickly through these channels than through formally specified channels (Guetzkow, 1965; K. Davis, 1953a);
3. may spread toward (and maybe not spread beyond) groups for which their content is of high interest (K. Davis, 1953a; Festinger, Schachter, & Back, 1950);
4. may spread through these channels only on the company premises and during company time (K. Davis, 1953a);
5. may reach the greatest percent of people close to the site of rumor initiation (K. Davis, 1953a; Guetzkow, 1965).

Data for each of these characteristics, however, remain scarce.

One final concern has been the relationship between rumor networks and formal communication structure. Though it would be pragmatically desirable if a weak formal structure were supplemented by a strong rumor network, this need not occur (K. Davis, 1953a), due perhaps to the primarily social forces which shape the rumor network (Marting, 1969). But here again, more research is needed.

SUMMARY AND CONCLUSIONS

A number of intriguing regularities have emerged in the course of this review of interdisciplinary findings. While the thinness of the data base precludes definitive conclusions, this section presents a number of "assertions" intended to summarize the material. The label "assertion" rather than the more traditional term "proposition" is intended to alert the reader to the variability in the form and quality of the knowledge claims that are offered. Many "propositional inventories" exist in social science which include statements that are clearly not in propositional form and cannot be used as hypotheses or as components in axiomatic theories, at least not without considerable transformation. Some of the "assertions" listed in this section are in propositional form and can be used as propositions, axioms, or postulates as they are phrased. Other assertions are simply existence statements; others might best be considered boundary conditions. The difference rests largely upon the *nature* of the research which generated the assertion and the *strength* of the support for the statement.

Following the assertions, several shortcomings of the literature are noted and several suggestions are made for future research in the area.

Four variables were mentioned as possible determinants of quantitative formal communication: organizational status, task responsibility, task requirements, anticipated satisfaction from communication, and network size. Assertions suggested by this section are:

1. High-ranking individuals communicate more while performing their jobs than do lower status persons.
2. Though the functions served by horizontal and vertical communication may differ, both types are essential to continued organizational functioning.
3. Job responsibilities and job requirements may significantly influence the quantity and direction of communication flows.
4. Communications between organizational members who differ in hierarchical status are usually initiated by the person with the higher status.

The second section of the review examined potential determinants of three kinds of qualitative status-related behaviors: content choice, channel selection, and message distortion. Potential determinants of message content included differential status of the interactants, contento-tropic behaviors, task variables, and role expectations. While several intriguing relationships are proposed in that section, only one seems sufficiently supported to warrant restatement here:

5. Organizational equals are more likely to discuss problems or proposed changes in the organization than are individuals who differ in status.

Choice of channel may be the result of: a general popularity of one channel over another, individual differences in channel preference, message content, distance, work demands, or organizational climate. However, the data base is too thin in this area to justify offering even tentative assertions.

Message distortion and filtering appear to be affected by both message content (e.g., social versus task communication) and relational variables (e.g., trust, mobility aspirations, superior's perceived influence, superior's own prior job experience, and subordinate's job satisfaction). Tentative assertions suggested by these data are:

6. The content of a message determines which people will transmit it, which people will receive it, and how accurately it will arrive.
7. The subordinate's satisfaction with his work situation, his trust in the superior, and his own mobility aspirations may be the most important variables affecting upward filtering.

The second half of this review examined correlates of emergent structure without regard for its relationship to formal structure. The correlates of its quantitative aspects include sociometric status, task competence, and proximity. Regarding these variables, it can be asserted that:

8. Informal status within a work group or organization correlates with amount of communicative involvement.
9. Proximity to others in the work group or organization correlates with amount of communicative involvement.
10. The number of communications a person initiates is generally related to the number of communications that person receives.
11. Communications between organizational members who differ in informal status may more often be initiated by the higher status person (compare with 4).

The qualitative aspects of emergent structure fall into two categories: communication roles and their distribution, and characteristics of the network as a whole. Assertions concerning communication roles are:

12. Communication isolates and communication liaisons have markedly different personalities and behavioral tendencies.
13. Liaisons serve both cohesion and gatekeeping functions for the organization, which may explain why their presence in a network is of such vital importance.

Assertions concerning network characteristics follow:

14. Two recurring characteristics of organizational structure are the distortion of social nominations toward the more chosen persons and away from the less chosen persons (popularity bias), and a tendency for a partner in a reported relationship to reciprocally acknowledge the relationship (reciprocity bias).
15. The structure of an organization's external environment may affect its internal structure.
16. There may be a natural tendency toward transitivity, balance, and clusterability in large networks.
17. Dynamic flows may tend toward content dependence and linkage gradients.

These 17 assertions all need further research before they achieve more definitive status, but their interdisciplinary origins may make them ultimately more fruitful than more parochial postulates. The basic reason for this is their efficient treatment of the "levels problem."

Organizational behavior may be studied from several different levels of analysis (individual's general response tendencies; group interactions; etc.), each with somewhat unique characteristics from all the others (see Hannan, 1971, regarding the aggregation issue). When the same phenomena are studied by several disciplines, an interdisciplinary approach could provide converging operations for disentangling reliable relationships from methodological artifacts. When particular levels of analysis are studied by only one discipline, an interdisciplinary synthesis would be essential to achieve comprehensive coverage of levels.

To date, this synthesis has been hindered by two important factors. First, differences in terminology and methodology require a translation of labels and findings. Guidelines for such translation might be helpful (see Edwards & Monge, 1976). In their absence, the enterprise requires a virtual immersion in both relevant literatures, a luxury for which few researchers have adequate time and resources. A more serious problem is the methodological inadequacy of many studies—inadequacy which limits the generality of their findings, even within the confines of their home disciplines.

Methodological flaws mentioned by previous researchers (especially Evan, 1971; James & Jones, 1974a; and Porter & Roberts, 1973) include problems in sampling methods, measurement, statistical analysis, and design.

Sampling problems include the examination of too few types of individuals, organizations, and technologies; the tendency toward incidental sampling rather than random or representative sampling; and the great possibility (as a result of low questionnaire return rates) of self-selection bias within the populations which are observed (see, for example, Dunteman, 1966.)

Measurement problems arise from a general absence of validity and reliability information for the numerous structural indices (Edwards, 1976; Edwards & Monge, 1975, 1977) as well as for the measures of nonstructural variables. Smith, Kendall, and Hulin's (1969) measure of job satisfaction is a welcome exception to this.

Many of the studies are flawed statistically by either an avoidance of significance tests (resorting instead to direct comparisons of raw frequencies and proportions) or a misuse of significance tests. Concerning their misuse, many authors appear to use the *p* value as an index of the "degree of significance" (see Bakan, 1966), an error which is reflected in the sometimes lengthy theoretical interpretations made of nonsignificant "trends." Another frequent error is the computation of a multitude of post hoc analyses without readjustment of the alpha level. (The misuse of multivariate statistics in this literature is discussed at length in James & Jones, 1974a).

Major flaws in the designs used in organizational literature include: (1) an over-reliance on cross-sectional rather than longitudinal data; (2) the typical use of only one measurement technique and subject population in each study; (3) the failure to specify hypotheses in advance of data collection; and (4) inadequate control over relevant variables.

This array of methodological and analytic problems greatly hinders theoretical development. In future research, samples, both larger in size and drawn more scientifically, are needed; the validity and reliability of structural and nonstructural measures should be systematically determined; greater care should be taken in statistical treatment of the data; *a priori* hypotheses should become expected procedure; and greater use should be made of multimethod and longitudinal designs.

Though the future of research in this area is presently uncertain, an improved data base might encourage future, more comprehensive interdisciplinary syntheses which might in turn direct research toward more fruitful and more cumulative directions. Through these complimentary pursuits—theoretical synthesis and theory-guided research—we may ultimately approach the comprehensive, data-based theory of organizational communication toward which so many have labored for so long.

NOTES

1. This manuscript was prepared in connection with research under the Office of Naval Research, Organizational Effectiveness Research Programs, Contract No. N00014-73-A-001; Peter R. Monge, Principal Investigator.
2. Theoretical approaches are avoided since no theory currently exists which unifies these findings (Porter & Roberts, 1973). However, comprehensive coverage of past theoretical positions concerning the role of communication in organizational functioning is found in Roberts, O'Reilly, Bretton, and Porter (1973), and Porter and Roberts (1973).
3. The focus on *determinants* rather than *consequences* of communication structure excludes most studies of job satisfaction and organizational climate. Research on organization climate is reviewed by James and Jones (1974b), and Redding (1972).
4. Many authors (e.g., Cohen, Robinson, & Edwards, 1969; Danowski & Farace, 1974; Evan, 1971; Monge, Kirste, & Edwards, 1974; Porter & Roberts, 1973; Rome & Rome, 1961; Wager, 1972; Weick, 1969) have questioned the applicability of small group network findings to operations in large organizations. In addition to relying heavily on the use of college students as subjects, small group studies generally involve the performance of highly artificial tasks within an arbitrary (randomly assigned) status hierarchy in a short-term environment, which lacks the history, tradition, and long-range goals typical of actual large ongoing organizations. Finally, as Guetzkow (1965, p. 565) noted, where differences are observed between different network types, they "may be temporary, due to initial problems involved in organizing the group for task performance," and hence be inconsequential to the long-range concerns of organizational researchers, even if applicable. This suspicion was substantiated by Burgess (1969), who found that differences in performance between wheel and circle networks virtually disappeared by the time the groups had finished 500 trials on the experimental task. Because of these problems, which limit the generality of small group studies, this literature is seldom cited in this review. However, several excellent summaries of this research may be found elsewhere (Collins & Raven, 1969; Glanzer & Glasser, 1961; Guetzkow, 1965; Haythorn, 1968; Shaw, 1964).
5. Cross-cultural research relevant to organizational behavior is reviewed by Roberts (1972).
6. While this definition is consistent with Allen and Cohen's (1969) use of the terms and fits the purpose of the present discussion, it should be noted that Roberts, O'Reilly, Bretton, and Porter (1973) prefer a different definition. In their words: "A number of authors have differently interpreted gatekeeping (Allen & Cohen, 1969; Bass, 1969; Breed 1955; Lewin, 1966). . . . We believe that gatekeeping is the conscious or unconscious withholding of information but that the information allowed through the gate may still be accurate, or it may be distorted. Gatekeeping, then, in our terms, is independent of distortion or accuracy" (p. 10).
7. Bernard and Killworth (1975) claim that rather than transitivity, intransitivity is the organizing principle. They attribute prior findings favoring transitivity to a counting error which is easily made when analyzing affective data.

REFERENCES

ABELSON, R.P. Mathematical models in social psychology. In L. Berkowitz (Ed.), *Advances in experimental social psychology*. New York: Academic Press, 1967.

ALBAUM, G. Horizontal information flow: An exploratory study. *Academy of Management Journal*, 1964, 7, 21-33.

ALEXANDER, C.N., JR. Ordinal position and sociometric status. *Sociometry*, 1966, 29, 41-51.

ALLEN, T.J., & COHEN, S.I. Information flow in research and development laboratories. *Administrative Science Quarterly*, 1969, 14, 12-20.

BACK, K., FESTINGER, L., HYMOVITCH, B., KELLEY, H., SCHACHTER, S., & THIBAUT, J. The methodology of studying rumor transmission. *Human Relations*, 1950, 3, 307-312.

BAKAN, D. The test of significance in psychological research. *Psychological Bulletin*, 1966, 66, 423-437.

BARNLUND, D.C. & HARLAND, C. Propinquity and prestige as determinants of communication networks. *Sociometry*, 1963, 26, 467-479.

BASS, A.F. Refining the "gatekeeper" concept: A U.N. radio case study. *Journalism Quarterly*, 1969, 46, 352-355.

BERKOWITZ, N.H., & BENNIS, W.G. Interaction patterns in formal service-oriented organizations. *Administrative Science Quarterly*, 1961, 6, 25-50.

BERNARD, H.H., & KILLWORTH, P.D. *Some formal properties of networks*. Tech. Rep. Arlington, Va.: Office of Naval Research, January 1975 (Contract No. N00014-73-A-0417-0001-117-949).

BLAU, P.M. Patterns of interaction among a group of officials in a government agency. *Human Relations*, 1954, 7, 337-348.

BLAU, P.M. *Dynamics of bureaucracy*. Chicago: University of Chicago Press, 1955.

BLAU, P.M. Patterns of deviation in work groups. *Sociometry*, 1960, 23, 245-261.

BORGATTA, E.F. Analysis of social interaction and sociometric perception. *Sociometry*, 1954, 17, 7-31.

BRAGER, G. Commitment and conflict in normative organizations. *American Sociological Review*, 1969, 34, 482-491.

BREED, W. Social control in the newsroom. *Social Forces*, 1955, 33, 326-335.

BURGESS, R.L. Communication networks and behavioral consequences. *Human Relations*, 1969, 22, 137-159.

BURKE, R.J., & WILCOX, D.S. Effects of different patterns and degrees of openness in superior-subordinate communication on subordinate job satisfaction. *Academy of Management Journal*, 1969, 12, 319-326.

BURNS, T. The direction of activity and communication in a departmental executive group: A quantitative study in a British engineering factory with a self-recording technique. *Human Relations*, 1954, 7, 73-97.

CAPLOW, T. Rumors in wars. *Social Forces*, 1947, 25, 298-302.

CARLSON, E.R. Clique structure and member satisfaction in groups. *Sociometry*, 1960, 23, 327-337.

CARTWRIGHT, D., & HARARY, F. Structural balance: A generalization of Heider's theory. *Psychological Review*, 1956, 63, 277-293.

COHEN, A.R. Upward communication in experimentally created hierarchies. *Human Relations*, 1958, 11, 41-53.

COHEN, A.M., ROBINSON, E.L., & EDWARDS, J.L. Experiments in organizational embeddedness. *Administrative Science Quarterly*, 1969, 14, 208-221.

COLEMAN, J.S. *Introduction to mathematical sociology*. New York: Free Press, 1964.

COLEMAN, J.S., KATZ, E., & MENZEL, H. *Medical innovation: A diffusion study*. Indianapolis: Bobbs-Merrill, 1966.

COLLINS, B.E., & RAVEN, B.H. Group structure: Attraction, coalitions, communication, and power. In G. Lindsey & E. Aronson (Eds.), *Handbook of social psychology*. Vol. 4. (2nd ed.). Reading, Mass.: Addison-Wesley, 1969.

CONRATH, D.W. Communications environment and its relationship to organizational structure. *Management Science*, 1973, 20, 586-603.

DANOWSKI, J.A. An information processing model of organizations: A focus on environmental uncertainty and communication network structuring. Paper presented at the annual meeting of the International Communication Association, New Orleans, 1974.

DANOWSKI, J.A., & FARACE, R.V. Communication network integration and group uniformity in a complex organization. Paper presented at the annual meeting of the International Communication Association, New Orleans, 1974.

DAVIS, J.A. Clustering and structural balance in graphs. *Human Relations*, 1967, 20, 181-187.

DAVIS, J.A. Clustering and hierarchy in interpersonal relations: Testing two theoretical models of 742 sociograms. *American Sociological Review*, 1970, 35, 843-852.

DAVIS, J.A., & LEINHARDT, S. The structure of positive interpersonal relations in small groups. In J. Berger, M.J. Zelditch, & B. Anderson (Eds.), *Sociological theories in progress*. Vol. 2. New York: Houghlin-Mifflin, 1972.

DAVIS, K. Management communication and the grapevine. *Harvard Business Review*, 1953a, 31, 43-49.

DAVIS, K. A method of studying communication patterns in organizations. *Personnel Psychology*, 1953b, 6, 301-312.

DAVIS, K. Success of chain-of-command oral communication in a manufacturing group. *Academy of Management Journal*, 1968, 11, 379-387.

DEWHIRST, H.D. Influence of perceived information-sharing norms on communication channel utilization. *Academy of Management Journal*, 1971, 14, 305-315.

DUBIN, R. Business behavior *behaviorally* viewed. In G.B. Strother (Ed.), *Social science approaches to business behavior*. Homewood, Ill.: Dorsey Press, 1962.

DUBIN, R., & SPRAY, S. Executive behavior and interaction. *Industrial Relations*, 1964, 3, 99-108.

DUNTEMAN, G.H. Organizational conditions and behavior in 234 industrial manufacturing organizations. *Journal of Applied Psychology*, 1966, 50, 300-305.

EDWARDS, J.A. The validation of mathematical indices of communication structure. Unpublished thesis, Department of Speech-Communication, San Jose State University, 1976.

EDWARDS, J.A., & MONGE, P.R. Descriptive communication structure metrics: A preliminary logical and empirical analysis. A paper presented at the annual meeting of the International Communication Association, Chicago, 1975.

EDWARDS, J.A., & MONGE, P.R. *A comparison of data collection procedures for the study of communication networks and structure*. Tech. Rep. Arlington, Va.: Office of Naval Research, 1976 (Contract No. N00014-75-C-0445).

EDWARDS, J.A., & MONGE, P.R. The validation of mathematical indices of communication structure. In B.D. Ruben (Ed.), *Communication yearbook I*. New Brunswick-Transaction-International Communication Association, 1977.

EVAN, W.M. (Ed.) *Organizational experiments: Laboratory and field research*. New York: Harper & Row, 1971.

FARACE, R.V., & JOHNSON, J.D. Comparative analysis of human communication networks in selected formal organizations. Paper presented at the annual meeting of the International Communication Association, New Orleans, 1974.

FARACE, R.V., & PACANOWSKY, M. Organizational communication role, hierarchical level and relative status. Paper presented to the Academy of Management Association, Seattle, 1974.

FESTINGER, L., CARTWRIGHT, D., BARBER, K., FLEISCHL, J., GOTTSDANKER, J., KEYSEN, A., & LEAVITT, G. The study of a rumor: Its origin and spread. *Human Relations*, 1948, 1, 464-486.

FESTINGER, L., SCHACHTER, S., & BACK, K. *Social pressures in informal groups*. New York: Harper, 1950.

FLAMENT, C. *Applications of graph theory to group structure*. Englewood Cliffs, N.J.: Prentice-Hall, 1963.

FORM, W.H. Technology and social behavior of workers in four countries: A sociotechnical perspective. *American Sociological Review*, 1972, 37, 727-738.

FOSTER, C.C., & HORVATH, W.J. A study of a large sociogram, III: Reciprocal choice probabilities as a measure of social distance. *Behavioral Science*, 1971, 16, 429-435.

FROST, P.A., & WHITLEY, R.D. Communication patterns in a research laboratory. *Journal of R & D Management*, 1971, 1, 71-79.

GEMMILL, G. Comments on "Effects of different patterns and degrees of openness in superior-subordinate communication on subordinate job satisfaction" by R. Burke and D. Wilcox—September, 1969. *Academy of Management Journal*, 1969, 12, 506-507.

GESCHWENDER, J.A. Status inconsistency, social isolation, and individual unrest. *Social Forces*, 1968, 46, 477-483.

GLANZER, M., & GLASER, R. Techniques for the study of group structure and behavior: I. Analysis of structure. *Psychological Bulletin*, 1959, 56, 317-332.

GLANZER, M., & GLASER, R. Techniques for the study of group structure and behavior: II. Empirical studies of the effects of structure in small groups. *Psychological Bulletin*, 1961, 58, 1-27.

GLUCKMAN, M. *The judicial process among the Barotse of Northern Rhodesia* (2nd ed.). Atlantic Highlands: Humanities Press, 1967.

GRAHAM, G.H. Correlates of perceived importance of organizational objectives. *Academy of Management Journal*, 1968, 11, 291-300.

GRAHAM, G.H. Interpersonal attraction as a basis of informal organization. *Academy of Management Journal*, 1971, 14, 483-495.

GRANOVETTER, M.S. The strength of weak ties. *American Journal of Sociology*, 1973, 78, 1360-1380.

GREENBERGER, E., & SORENSON, A. Interpersonal choices among a junior high school faculty. *Sociology of Education*, 1970, 44, 198-216.

GUETZKOW, H. Communication in organizations. In J.G. March (Ed.), *Handbook of organizations*. Chicago: Rand McNally, 1965.

GULLAHORN, J.T. Distance and friendship as factors in the gross interaction matrix. *Sociometry*, 1952, 15, 123-134.

GUIMARAES, L.L. Network analysis: An approach to the study of communication systems. Unpublished manuscript, Department of Communication, Michigan State University, 1970.

HALLINAN, M. Comment on Holland and Leinhardt. *American Journal of Sociology*, 1972, 77, 1201-1205.

HALLINAN, M. *The structure of positive sentiment*. New York: Elsevier, 1974.

HALLINAN, M., & FELMLEE, D. An analysis of intransitivity in sociometric data. *Sociometry*, 1975, 38, 195-212.

HANNAN, M.T. *Aggregation and disaggregation in sociology*. Lexington, Mass.: Lexington Press, 1971.

HAYTHORN, W.W. The composition of groups: A review of the literature. *Acta Psychologica*, 1968, 28, 97-128.

HEIDER, F. Attitudes and cognitive organization. *Journal of Psychology*, 1946, 21, 107-112.

HINRICHS, J.R. Communications activity of industrial research personnel. *Personnel Psychology*, 1964, 17, 193-204.

HOLLAND, P.W., & LEINHARDT, S. Some evidence on the transitivity of positive interpersonal sentiment. *American Journal of Sociology*, 1972, 77, 1205-1209.

HOMANS, G.C. *The human group*. New York: Harcourt, Brace, 1950.

HUREWITZ, P. The neutral isolate—An operational definition: A criticism of the use of the normal curve of distribution. *International Journal of Sociometry and Sociatry*, 1962, 2, 151-157.

HURWITZ, J.L., ZANDER, A.F., & HYMOVITCH, B. Some effects of power on the relations among group members. In D. Cartwright & A.F. Zander (Eds.), *Group dynamics: Research and theory*. Evanston, Ill.: Row, Peterson, 1953.

INDIK, B.P. The scope of the problem and some suggestions toward a solution. In B.P. Indik & F.K. Berrien (Eds.), *People, groups and organizations*. New York: Teachers College Press, Columbia University, 1968.

INGHAM, G. *Size of industrial organizations and work behavior*. Cambridge: Cambridge University Press, 1970.

JACOB, M.A. The structure and functions of internal communication in three religious communities. Unpublished doctoral dissertation, Department of Communication, Michigan State University, 1972.

JACOBSON, E., & SEASHORE, S.E. Communication practices in complex organizations. *Journal of Social Issues*, 1951, 7, 28-40.

JAMES, L.R., & JONES, A.P. *A note on problems related to rationale, models, and methodology in organizational analysis*. Tech. Rep. Arlington, Va.: Office of Naval Research, 1974a (Contract No. N00014-72-A-0179-0001).

JAMES, L.R., & JONES, A.P. Organizational climate: A review of theory and research. *Psychological Bulletin*, 1974b, 81, 1096-1112.

JAMES, L.R., & JONES, A.P. *Organizational structure: A review of structural dimensions and their conceptual relations with individual attitudes and behavior*. Tech. Rep. No. 74-19. Arlington, Va.: Office of Naval Research, 1974c (Contract No. N00014-72-A-0179-0001).

JENNINGS, H.H. Sociometric choice process in personality and group formation. In J.L. Moreno (Ed.), *The sociometry reader*. Glencoe, Ill.: Free Press, 1960.

KATZ, L.B. Statistical methods and models: Introduction. In

J.L. Moreno (Ed.), *The sociometry reader*. Glencoe, Ill.: Free Press, 1960.

KELLEY, H.H. Communication in experimentally created hierarchies. *Human Relations*, 1951, 4, 39-56.

KELLEY, J. The study of executive behavior by activity sampling. *Human Relations*, 1951, 4, 39-56.

KILLWORTH, P.D., & BERNARD, H.R. *CATIJ: A new sociometric and its application to a prison living unit*. Tech. Rep. No. 102-73. Arlington, Va.: Office of Naval Research, 1973 (Contract No. N00014-73-A-0417-0001).

KIRSTE, K.K., & MONGE, P.R. *Proximity: Location, time and opportunity to communicate*. Tech. Rep. No. 3. Arlington, Va.: Office of Naval Research, 1974 (Contract No. N00014-73-A-0476-0001).

KLEMMER, E., & SNYDER, F. Measurement of time spent communicating. *Journal of Communication*, 1972, 22, 142-158.

LARSEN, K.S. Dogmatism and sociometric status as determinants of interaction in a small group. *Psychological Reports*, 1971, 29, 449-450.

LARSEN, O.N., & HILL, R.J. Social structure and interpersonal communication. *American Journal of Sociology*, 1958, 63, 497-505.

LAUMANN, E.O. *Bonds of pluralism*. New York: Wiley Interscience, 1971.

LAWLER, E., PORTER, L., & TENENBAUM, A. Manager's attitudes toward interaction episodes. *Journal of Applied Psychology*, 1968, 52, 432-439.

LEWIN, K. Group decision and social change. In H. Proshansky & B. Seidenberg (Eds.), *Basic studies in social psychology*. New York: Holt, 1966.

LIU, W.T., & DUFF, R.W. The strength in weak ties. *Public Opinion Quarterly*, 1972, 36, 361-366.

LYKKEN, D.T. Statistical significance in psychological research. *Psychological Bulletin*, 1968, 70, 151-159.

MAIER, N.R.F., HOFFMAN, L.R., & READ, W.H. Superior-subordinate communication: The relative effectiveness of managers who held their subordinates' positions. *Personnel Psychology*, 1963, 16, 1-11.

MARTING, B.J. A study of grapevine communication patterns in a manufacturing organization. *Academy of Management Journal*, 1969, 12, 385-386. (Abstract)

MELCHER, A.J., & BELLER, H. Toward a theory of organization communication: Consideration in channel selection. *Academy of Management Journal*, 1967, 10, 39-52.

MEYER, M.W. Size and the structure of organizations: A causal analysis. *American Sociological Review*, 1972, 37, 434-441.

MOHR, L.B. Organizational technology and organizational structure. *Administrative Science Quarterly*, 1971, 16, 444-459.

MONGE, P.R., KIRSTE, K.K., & EDWARDS, J.A. A preliminary causal model of the formation of communication structure in large organizations. Paper presented at the annual meeting of the International Communication Association, New Orleans, 1974.

MONGE, P.R., & LINDSEY, G.N. The study of communication networks and communication structure in large organizations. Paper presented at the annual meeting of the International Communication Association, New Orleans, 1974.

MORENO, J.L. (Ed.). *The sociometry reader*. Glencoe, Ill.: Free Press, 1960.

MORENO, J.L., & JENNINGS, H.H. Sociometric measurement of social configuration. *Sociometry*, 1938, 1, 342-374.

PELZ, D.C. Some social factors related to performance in a research organization. *Administrative Science Quarterly*, 1956, 1, 310-325.

PETTIGREW, A. Intergroup conflict and role strain. *Journal of Management Studies*, 1968, 5, 205-218.

PHILLIPS, D.P., & CONVISER, R.H. Measuring the structure and boundary properties of groups: Some uses of information theory. *Sociometry*, 1972, 35, 235-254.

POOL, I. de SOLA Communication systems. In I. de Sola Pool, W. Schramm, N. Maccoby, & E.B. Parker (Eds.), *Handbook of communication*. Chicago: Rand McNally, 1973.

PORTER, L.W., & LAWLER, E.E. Properties of organization structure in relation to job attitudes and job behavior. *Psychological Bulletin*, 1965, 64, 23-51.

PORTER, L.W., & ROBERTS, K.H. *Communication in organizations*. Tech. Rep. No. 12. Arlington, Va.: Office of Naval Research, ERIC (microfiche) ED-066-773, 1973. Revised version published in M. Dunnette (Ed.), *Handbook of industrial and organizational psychology*. Chicago: Rand McNally, in press.

PROCTOR, C.H., & LOOMIS, C.P. Analysis of sociometric data. In M. Jahoda, M. Deutsch, & S.W. Cook (Eds.), *Research methods in social relations*. New York: Dryden, 1951.

RAPOPORT, A. Mathematical models of social interaction. In R.D. Luce, R.R. Bush, & E. Galanter (Eds.), *Handbook of mathematical psychology*. Vol. 2. New York: Wiley, 1963.

RAPOPORT, A., & HORVATH, W.J. A study of a large sociogram. *Behavioral Science*, 1961, 6, 279-291.

READ, W.H. Upward communication in industrial hierarchies. *Human Relations*, 1962, 15, 3-15.

REDDING, W.C. *Communication within the organization: An interpretive review of theory and research*. New York: Industrial Communication Council, 1972.

RICHARDS, W.R., JR. A coherent systems methodology for the analysis of communication systems. Unpublished doctoral dissertation, Department of Communication, Stanford University, 1976.

ROBERTS, K.H. On looking at an elephant: An evaluation of cross-cultural research related to organizations. *Psychological Bulletin*, 1972, 74, 327-350.

ROBERTS, K.H., & O'REILLY, C.A., III. *Failures in upward communication: Three possible culprits*. Tech. Rep. No. 1. Arlington, Va.: Office of Naval Research, April 1973 (Contract No. N000314-69-A-0200-1054). Revised version published in *Academy of Management Journal*, 1974, 17, 205.

ROBERTS, K.H., & O'REILLY, C.A., III. *Empirical findings and suggestions for future research on organizational communication*. Tech. Rep. No. 6. Arlington, Va.: Office of Naval Research, 1974 (Contract No. N000314-69-A-0200-1054).

ROBERTS, K.H., O'REILLY, C.A., III, BRETTON, G., & PORTER, L.W. *Organizational theory and organizational communication: A communication failure*? Tech. Rep. No. 3. Arlington, Va.: Office of Naval Research, May 1973 (Contract No. N000314-69-A-0200-1054). Revised version published in *Human Relations*, 1974, 27, 501-524.

ROME, S.C., & ROME, B.K. A Leviathan technique for large-group analysis. *Behavioral Science*, 1961, 6, 148-152.

ROSENGREN, W.R. Structure, policy, and style: Strategies of organizational control. *Administrative Science Quarterly*, 1967, 12, 140-164.

SADLER, R.J., & BARRY, B.A. Organizational characteristics of growing companies. *Journal of Management Studies*, 1967, 4, 204-219.

SCHWARTZ, D.F. Liaison roles in the communication structure of a formal organization: A pilot study. A paper presented at the annual meeting of the National Society for the Study of Communication, Cleveland, 1969.

SHAW, M.E. Communication networks. In L. Berkowitz (Ed.), *Advances in experimental social psychology*. Vol. 1. New York: Academic Press, 1964.

SIMPSON, R.L. Vertical and horizontal communication in formal organizations. *Administrative Science Quarterly*, 1959, 4, 188-196.

SLOTE, L.M. Superior-subordinate role conflict. *Dissertation Abstracts International*, 1971, 32(A), 538. (Abstract)

SMITH, P.C., KENDALL, L.M., & HULIN, C.L. *The measurement of satisfaction in work and retirement: A strategy for the study of attitudes*. Chicago: Rand McNally, 1969.

SUTTON, H., & PORTER, L.W. A study of the grapevine in a governmental organization. *Personnel Psychology*, 1968, 21, 223-230.

THOMASON, G.F. Managerial work roles and relationships—Part I. *Journal of Management Studies*, 1966, 3, 270-284.

THOMPSON, J.D. Authority and power in "identical" organizations. *American Journal of Sociology*, 1956, 62, 290-301.

WADE, L.L. Communications in a public bureaucracy: Involvement and performance. *Journal of Communication*, 1968, 18, 18-25.

WAGER, L.W. Organizational "linking pins": Hierarchical status and communication roles in interlevel conferences. *Human Relations*, 1972, 25, 307-326.

WALTON, E. A study of organizational communication systems. *Personnel Administration*, 1963, 26, 46-49.

WEBBER, R.A. Perceptions of interactions between superiors and subordinates. *Human Relations*, 1970, 23, 235-248.

WEICK, K. *The social psychology of organizing*. Reading, Mass.: Addison-Wesley, 1969.

WEISS, R.S., & JACOBSON, E. The structure of complex organizations. In J.L. Moreno (Ed.), *The sociometry reader*. Glencoe, Ill.: Free Press, 1960.

WHITLEY, R.D., & FROST, P.A. Authority, problem solving approaches, communication and change in a British research laboratory. *Journal of Management Studies*, 1972, 9, 337-361.

WICKESBERG, A.K. Communications networks in the business organization structure. *Academy of Management Journal*, 1968, 11, 253-262.

WIGAND, R.T. Communication, integration, and satisfaction in a complex organization. Paper presented at the annual meeting of the International Communication Association, New Orleans, 1974.

ZAENGLEIN, M.M., & SMITH, C. An analysis of individual communication patterns and perceptions in hospital organizations. *Human Relations*, 1972, 25, 493-504.

INTERCULTURAL COMMUNICATION

Theory and Research: An Overview
Selected Studies

INTERCULTURAL COMMUNICATION THEORY AND RESEARCH: AN OVERVIEW OF MAJOR CONSTRUCTS[1]

MICHAEL H. PROSSER
University of Virginia

In *Communication Yearbook I* (1977), Tulsi B. Saral's overview of intercultural communication stresses primarily the definitional aspects which have been provided by a growing number of authors in collections, authored books, and essays on the subject. In this overview, I shall provide my developing orientation toward major constructs in the field of intercultural communication, stressing significant issues which ought to be considered, and the interrelational components between these terms: communication and culture.

It is important to note that, as Saral indicates, the study of intercultural communication is still in its early stages. Except for Robert T. Oliver's *Culture and Communication* (1962) and Alfred Smith's *Communication and Culture* (1966), virtually no full-length texts on the theoretical aspects of intercultural communication existed until the early 1970s. Within the last half-dozen years, this deficiency has been lessened by the appearance of various new texts: Samovar and Porter, *Intercultural Communication: A Reader* (1972, revised edition, 1976); Prosser, *Intercommunication among Nations and Peoples* (1973); Harms, *Intercultural Communication* (1973); Condon and Yousef, *An Introduction to Intercultural Communication* (1974); Ruhly, *Orientations to Intercultural Communication* (1976); Sitaram and Cogdell, *Foundations of Intercultural Communication* (1976); Dodd, *Perspectives on Cross-Cultural Communication* (1977); Fischer and Merrill, *International and Intercultural Communication* (1977); Prosser, *Cultural Dialogue* (1978); Weaver, *Crossing Cultural Barriers* (1978); and others still to come out shortly. Various specialized texts on interracial and interethnic communication have been published: Smith, *Transracial Communication* (1973); Rich, *Interracial Communication* (1974); and Blubaugh and Pennington, *Crossing Differences: Interracial Communication* (1976).

Simultaneously, as a result of various intercultural conferences, other specialized publications have been made available, such as: Prosser, *Syllabi in Intercultural Communication* (1974, 1975); Jain, Prosser, and Miller, *Intercultural Communication: Proceedings of the SCA Summer Conference X* (1974); Condon and Saito, *Intercultural Encounters with Japan: Communication—Contact and Conflict* (1974); and Jain and Cummings, *Proceedings of the Conference on Intercultural Communication and Teacher Education* (1975). Various selected bibliographies have been published, the most up-to-date being Seelye and Tyler's *Intercultural Communicator Resources* (1977). Two sets of volumes which now regularly report on developing constructs in intercultural communication, as well as describing and including ongoing research are the *International and Intercultural Communication Annual* (Casmir 1974, 1975, 1976; Jain, 1977); and *Readings in Intercultural Communication* (Hoopes 1971, 1972, 1973, 1974). A new quarterly journal, which began publishing in 1977 and is expected to report studies of particular interest to those interested in intercultural communication, is *The International Journal of Intercultural Relations* (Landis, 1977).

It is encouraging to recognize that, while cultural anthropologists such as Dell Hymes, Ethel Albert, Clifford Geertz, Roy Wagner, and Edward T. Hall have long considered the study of communication as an essential ingredient of the study of culture, intercultural communication specialists have begun to take more seriously the works of cultural anthropologists in relation to their own study of the relationships between communication and culture. While our graduate programs still are not producing intercultural communication specialists in as systematic a fashion as they should, it is also encouraging to recognize that cultural anthropology is more and more likely to serve an important role in the training of such specialists. Thus with the increasing published texts, essays, journals, and specialized collections; improving graduate programs; frequent specialized conferences on intercultural communication; a growing recognition of the importance of intercultural communication in such organizations and associations as the International Communication Association, the Speech Communication Association, the Society for Intercultural Education, Training, and Research, and the International Division of the Association for Education in Journalism; many new colleges and university level courses; and the increasing sophistication of field studies in various aspects of intercultural communication; it is likely that we can predict a wholesome continuation of progress and diversity in the study of intercultural communication. However, it is also likely, just as when the areas of communication theory and interpersonal communication were in their initial stages of development, we will begin to agree slowly about what are the major constructs which help to define and give structure to the study of intercultural communication. Such reasons lead me to suggest cautiously that the following suggested major constructs in intercultural communication are personalized speculations, many of which require much more substantial testing than has so far been offered. It is in this spirit that I undertake such an overview, assuming that others will seek to correct and clarify any over-generalized assumptions, and also noting that, since an overview is at best a synthesis, their more substantative support may be found in many of the various published materials noted above.

BASIC PREMISES

Communication and culture are both processes. Communication, like culture, is a human necessity. Communication always occurs at the human level both intrapersonally and interpersonally when human interaction is involved. Certain communicative acts are involuntary causing the communicator never to exercise total control of the communication environment. At the same time, culture itself makes it possible for every human being to exert partial control both over his or her culture and his or her communication. Often we seek voluntarily to control or influence the attitudes or behavior of others in a positive or negative way. Communication and culture are inseparably linked. Both are of central importance, either to the student of communication or of culture. They become linked through communication within our cultural setting and context, and whenever we engage in either the intercultural communication of an interpersonal nature or the cross-cultural communication of a collective nature. Thereby, intercultural communication becomes a subset of both communication and culture. Most of the writers cited above would tend to agree with this minimum set of premises in considering the study of intercultural communication.

CRITICAL ISSUES IN THE STUDY OF INTERCULTURAL COMMUNICATION

Similarities and Differences

Central to the study of communication between members of different cultures is the importance of similarities and differences as they affect all intercultural and cross-cultural communication. All cultural groups share certain traits, but differ enough so that we can describe the world as being made up of many distinct cultures, rather than just a single world culture as some authors propose, for example McLuhan in his global village concept. A key thinker in the study of intercultural communication, Edward Stewart (1974), argues that the value of similarities rather than differences becomes a major assumption in American thinking and value systems, but that in many cultures, including those adhering to various Eastern philosophies of life, the value of differences is considered paramount. Stewart proposes that, "It is on this issue of difference, either naturally or by acquisition, that intercultural communication rests its claim for identity." By stressing either actual or perceived cultural contrasts and on the communicative contrasts between members of different cultures, Stewart contends that intercultural communication, thereby, becomes a most urgent extension of all human communication. Even the terms "communication'' and ''culture'' are viewed entirely differently in Western and Eastern cultures. In Western cultures, these terms are considered explicit, but in Eastern cultures they are considered implicit. This contrasting view plays an important role in the consideration of such terms.

Conflict

A second critical issue in the study of intercultural communication stems from the endemic nature of conflict both in human communication and culture. Almost every theory of the development of the human situation reflects the notion that we seem constantly to be in conflict. There is an important logic in Herbert Simons's assumption that communication is the means by which conflict gets socially defined; the instrument through which influence in conflict is exercised; and the vehicle by which partisans or third parties may prevent, manage, or resolve conflict (1974). Opposing schools of thought among social scientists argue, on the one hand, that conflict in communication and culture is a deviation from the norm, or communication breakdowns and culture shock, and must be corrected, and on the other hand, that conflict is at least necessary and inevitable as a part of the general social and cultural structure. Simons defines conflict as that state of a social relationship in which incompatible interests between two or more parties give rise to a struggle between them. In the intercultural setting, such conflict often arises when the parties cannot agree on similarities in language codes; nonverbal patterns; and attitudinal, perceptional, value-oriented, and thought-patterning cultural components.

Control

A third critical issue in the study of intercultural communication relates to the control of communication and culture. Although a basic premise has been suggested that individuals always exercise only partial control over communication and culture, it would seem likely that, the higher the status of the communicator and the more complex the communication setting or context, the more likely will control pervasively affect communication and culture. Norbert Wiener calls ''cybernetics'' the science of communication and control with an emphasis on automatic control. He proposes that the seventeenth and early eighteenth centuries were the age of clocks and the twentieth century is the age of communication and control (1966, pp. 25-35). The very notion of *homo faber*, or man the maker, implies that, especially in the Western tradition, ''man is the measure of all things.'' Clifford Geertz (1973) proposes two specific ways of viewing culture. The first proposal challenges our normal definition that culture consists of the complexes of concrete behavior patterns—customs, usages, traditions, and habit clusters. Instead, he suggests that culture may be seen as a set of control mechanisms—plans, recipes, rules, instructions, or what engineers and computer experts call programs, for the governing of behavior. The second concept is that humans are precisely the animals most desperately dependent upon such extragenetic, outside-the-skin control mechanisms, such cultural programs, for ordering their behavior (1973). Edward Hall (1976) indicates that the world is currently caught in a double crisis, the population/environment crisis, and the crisis of contemporary man himself, who is caught in the controls that his cultural communication have placed upon him. The solution which he recommends is to look beyond culture, ''because the greatest separation feat of all is when one manages to gradually free oneself from the grip of unconscious culture'' (p. 210).

Technology

A fourth interrelated issue of critical importance in the study of intercultural communication is the impact exerted by technology. Such authors as Jules Henry (1963), Jacques Ellul (1964), and B.F. Skinner (1971) appear to be cultural determinists who express less hope in the release of technology's hold on communication and culture than other authors, such as Hall (1976). As quoted by Ellul (1964), Ernst Junger's reminder in the early 1900s that ''technology is the real metaphysics of the twentieth century'' has been borne out if one accepts the views of Henry, Ellul, and Skinner. Ellul expands Junger's notion with the assumption that twentieth-century technique has overcome culture as civilization, culture as institution, culture as a specific society, and culture in the most personalized sense, what Triandis calls subjective culture (1972). Ellul argues that technique is civilization; it has absorbed the basic cultural institutions; it is the universal language; it has absorbed the sacred and its messages, mysteries, and myths; in effect, it is the new god. Essentially, technology and technique, in Ellul's view, have become synonymous with both communication and culture. These cultural determinists agree that, as technology becomes the master and therefore becomes the ultimate channel and medium of communication, the members of the culture so affected will have everything that their hearts desire except their freedom and dignity (see especially Skinner, 1971). If the cultural determinist's view is accepted, or even if one attempts to disprove its premises, the role in communication and culture of technology becomes of prime importance in the study of intercultural communication.

Stability and Change

A fifth interrelated issue of concern to the student of intercultural communication are the contrasting positions about the importance of cultural stability versus cultural change. If survival is the chief value of any culture which wishes to perpetuate itself, we need to ask how that survival is to be obtained, whether by cultural stability or cultural change. In contrast to the views of the cultural determinists, Daniel Bell (1970) argues that culture is the most dynamic component of a civilization, outreaching the dynamism of technology itself, and that it is committed to a ceaseless impulse toward change, "searching for a new sensibility" (p. 17). Harold L. Nieburg (1973) notes, however, that culture represents contradictory functions: as a means of containing chaos and background noise, it maintains arbitrary order. This very order causes it to lose its adaptability, and it becomes vulnerable because of dissidents in the culture or through environmental changes. The very success of a culture helps to initiate fundamental change in the culture itself. And yet, Nieburg argues, the principle of cultural reality lies in the continued legitimacy of any culture in a given population over a period of time. Jules Henry (1963) contends that "inherent in the human condition is the fact that we must conserve culture while changing it; that we must always be more sure of surviving than of adapting—as we see it. Whenever a new idea appears our first concern as animals must be that it does not kill us; then, and only then, can we look at it from other points of view . . ." (p. 261).

Imperialism and Dependency

The concept of cultural stability versus cultural change leads to a final critical issue in the study of intercultural communication. This is the question of cultural imperialism versus cultural dependency, a subject given extensive treatment in the *Journal of Communication* in 1975. Most cultures, given the opportunity, probably would wish to extend their culture both geographically and temporally by forcing others to accept their cultural controls. All of the great cultural thrusts of history have sought cultural control over others. Whether it is a matter of forcing cultural customs, traditions, norms, and values on others with entirely different inclinations directly or indirectly, cultural imperialism and its counterpart, cultural dependency, both appear to be inherent factors in culture. Cultural activity over space and time can be expressed communicatively through architecture, sculpture, city planning, armed forces, weapon systems, and modern conveniences. Such activity becomes an index of power. Surprisingly, we could argue that the transistor radio is perhaps the foremost symbol of cultural imperialism and dependency, as perhaps more people in the world are potentially influenced by this medium than through any other communications media. Through the radio, with its ability to transmit messages across cultures, members of one culture find things in one culture which they wish to emulate. The irreversability of technology suggests as well that the transistor radio is likely to be followed in every developing culture with further communicative and cultural symbols that directly or indirectly extend the control of one culture over another.

THE CHIEF COMPONENTS OF COMMUNICATION

The components of communication refer to those essential factors which must be present for an effective minimal study of communication in a community or culture. An understanding of the chief components of communication which interact with components of culture leads to an understanding of social discourse in the cultural context, especially when it occurs between or across cultures. A cultural anthropologist who views communication as essential to the study of culture, Dell Hymes (1973), suggests that "the starting point is the ethnographic analysis of the communicative habits of a community in their totality, determining what count as communicative events, and as their components, and conceiving no communicative behavior as independent of the set framed by some setting or implicit question. The communicative event is thus central" (p. 46). Hymes considers the study of communication and its components one of the greatest challenges in the broader study of culture. He stresses that the interactional nature of the components is important, although we can isolate one or more of them for specific analysis. This frame of reference leads Hymes to such questions as follow. What are the communication events, and their components, in a community? What are the relationships between them? What capabilities and stages do they have in general, and in specific cases? How do they work? Among the various components which Hymes delineates, the communication message, the communication participants, the codes which they utilize, and the channels or media which they apply as they interact would seem to be among the most important of the communication components in the communication events which take place within and between cultures.

John Weakland (1967) suggests that communication always involves a multiciplicity of channels, of context, and of messages. While Edward T. Hall (1976) would stress the contextual nature of any communication event, Dell Hymes (1973) believes that the message includes all other components in a balanced ratio, and therefore, we could presume that from his perspective, the message carries with it its own context. The source with no message to send is not in need of channels in which to send it, linguistic or nonverbal patterns in which to code it, or of a receiver to decode it. Typically, every message carries its own situational context, according to Hymes, and has its own range of topics in and between cultures which may be addressed in the message itself. All messages require focused interaction between senders and receivers in order for any sort of basic functions as messages. The status of communicators plays a role in the sending and receiving of messages. The higher-status communicator generally sends and receives more messages than the lower-status communicator. The latter is likely to receive a large number of messages, but only to send back more routinized and formalized messages to the high status communicator. The selection and control of messages provide important roles for both senders and receivers. Within and between cultures, propaganda is often utilized to attempt to control members of a culture, or imperialistically to expand the boundaries of one culture over the parameters of another.

Among the various ways of considering communication participants, senders and receivers, one can classify them according to the number of participants engaged in sending or receiving a message, the given characteristics of the communicators, and the directionality of the message flow. An overlapping continuum of communication participants can be developed, ranging from intrapersonal, to interpersonal, to cultural, to collective, to what may be described ambiguously as global communication. Within these hierarchical sets, each system can be subsumed by the others, especially in terms of numbers of participants, their characteristics, and the directionality of the message flow among them. As we move along the continuum, more and more participants are involved. Characteristics such as the utilization of the individual senses in the communication event change from a highly personal involvement of sense relationships to a highly impersonal, formalized, and less involved relationship by the bulk of the participants. The directional flow of the communication is one-way at the intrapersonal level; it becomes two-way in interpersonal and cultural communication; and again changes essentially back to one-way in collective and global communication. The more participants, the more interactional feedback is minimized, delayed, and routinized. As I have indicated, intercultural communication is an extension of interpersonal communication, but it adds a heightened emphasis on cultural characteristics such as linguistic and nonlinguistic codes, perception, attitudes, values, and thought patternings as they are similar or different from culture to culture. Since collective communication subsumes earlier sets of participants, it emphasizes larger numbers of participants, and much less two-way communication except through formalized, delayed, or ritualized responses. As I define cross-cultural communication, it is a subset of collective communication, in that it tends to have the characteristics of collective communication and crosses cultural and national boundaries, often in the form of propaganda of one sort or another. Global communication participants are often those described by Colin Cherry (1971) when he writes of such supranational systems as the post, telephone, airways, monetary regulations, time zones, and satellites, all of which are essential for building a global communication system and which, according to Cherry, are more an ideal than an actuality.

While linguistic and nonverbal codes could equally well be placed among cultural components as well as among communicative components, I have included them in the latter, partially because both language and nonverbal codes provide a chief means of communication quite apart from what makes a culture's essential ingredients. In fact, I would argue that verbal linguistic codes provide one of the key links for cultural communication. As symbol-builders and manipulators, we can encode and decode a nearly limitless variety of verbal and nonverbal messages, depending upon our own capacities for coding and decoding. Colin Cherry proposes: "It is their [humans] powers of language which set them apart from the creatures by a gulf, a gulf which Susanne Langer has seen as 'one whole day of Creation'—a whole chapter of evolution. All races of man, all nations, all tribes everywhere have language" (1971, p. 2). By its very nature, language is the key link between our ability to communicate and to pass down our cultural traditions to our children and to those who come after us either across space or time. Speech itself is the basic coding procedure, followed by language, followed by nonverbal cues. Language symbolizes and catalogs our perceived reality. The linguistic universals which cut across cultures serve as a primary linkage between communication and culture, and as a base for intercultural communication. In fact, a key communication participant who links one culture to another through intercultural communication is the bilingual or polylingual individual when the cultures in contact are actually separated by different language systems. Nonverbal codes complement the linguistic codes and often actually cause more difficulties interculturally, because it is easier to decipher verbal codes than the more subtle, and often unconscious, nonverbal codes. The whole sense ratio is tied up with nonverbal communication within and between cultures, allowing one almost to be able to define a culture by the particular ratio that the senses play in that culture, with some cultures being more tactually-oriented than others; or more visually-oriented; or more orally-oriented. Each separate orientation plays a role that helps to direct both the linguistic and nonverbal codes which develop in and between cultures.

Intracultural, intercultural, and cross-cultural communication almost literally cannot take place without the availability of channels and media, whether of a traditional form such as the drum or the technological form such as the transistor radio or satellite communication. Some writers have assumed that such communication takes place almost entirely in the interpersonal setting. This view misses the point that technology and the technological communication systems have the most profound effect on all human interaction. Since modern society is developed and supported by transport, power, and communication networks, they are tied in directly to the concept of man the symbol-builder and user and man the tool-builder and user as he relates within his own culture and with members of other cultures. Channels and media serve as the transmitters and mediators for our own culture and for other cultures as well. Control over such channels and media provide a singular monopolistic advantage toward those who collectively control them within a culture or between cultures.

THE CHIEF CULTURAL COMPONENTS AND LINKAGES

Four major theoretical orientations have led to many of the current theories of culture: cultural evolutionism, cultural functionalism, cultural history, and cultural ecology. Cultural evolutionism refers to the cumulative, collective experience of mankind. Sometimes it is called "Culture Writ Large." Among men, symbol-building and using and tool-building and using are key cultural characteristics which are progressive in their development, and thereby can be seen to be evolutionary in nature.

Cultural functionalism is currently the major recent emphasis in cultural anthropology, especially in relation to ethnographic research as suggested by Hymes in developing an ethnography of communication for a specific community or culture. The functionalist seeks for ways that institutions and structures of a society interconnect to form a system which is a working unit. The functionalist seeks to explain why these elements relate as they do, why certain cultural patterns exist, and why they continue to persist.

Cultural history ethnographically studies the contemporary history of a culture as seen through time and space. All study of culture is a study of history and a study of contemporary history, at least for the informants, documents, artifacts, and other historical evidence available from the period of history of a culture or interacting cultures being studied.

Cultural ecology stresses man's interaction with his cultural environment. Cultural ecology is characterized by a concern with adaptation on two levels, first with regard to the way that cultural systems adapt to their total enviornment, and second, with regard to the way that institutions of a given culture adapt or adjust to one another. Each of these four cultural orientations, considered both separately and jointly, provides useful insights to the study of intercultural and cross-cultural communication (Kaplan & Manners, 1972).

Various cultural components and communicative components can be isolated to see how they interact within and between cultures. The most cultural of cultural characteristics are values and value orientations which are translated communicatively through beliefs, attitudes, stereotypes, myths, perception, thought patterning, and behavior. When one considers language, nonverbal codes, perceptions, attitudes, thought patterning, and values, similarities and differences in each element make intercultural and cross-cultural communication increasingly more complex as one moves from component to component. Communication acts to spread the simple and most diffusable ideas so easily from culture to culture that objective notions like skills and precise artificial coding systems are easily transferred. Values and subjective ideas, such as religious or political philosophies and ideologies, spread very slowly and often painfully from one culture to the next. It is with value differences that the most intense aspects of culture clash. As a number of cultural anthropologists have done in the past, it is possible to identify specific value orientations as universal to all peoples, others as specific to certain types of culture, and others to particular cultures. Every culture can be seen as having a dominant value-oriented profile, but there are always varient or substitute profiles possible. Kluckhohn and Strodtbeck's (1961) identification of six basic problems as common to all human groups and cultures—human nature orientation, man-nature orientation, time-orientation, activity orientation, relational orientation, and space orientation—has provided researchers of intercultural communication with many important and interesting variables to consider in their research. An understanding of such orientations and their variables is critical also to those who expect to engage in intercultural communication.

In conjunction with an understanding of values as a critical element in intercultural communication for cultures in interaction, it is also important to study subjective culture, which can be described as the study of human cognitive processes. These processes may be nonlinguistic, such as perceptual styles, motivational patterns, and skills, or linguistic, such as meanings, beliefs, and the linguistic structures which express them (Osgood, May, & Myron, 1975). The memory of past structured, stable, and meaningful experiences form our present perceptions and constitute an important component of culture. Perceptually significant experiences are always culturally derived in part, and their responses are culturally affected. Beliefs and perception link tangible objects of culture and intangible subjective elements of culture, such as values. As an expression of culture, thought patterning determines much of the way that perception operates individually within the culture. When members of contrasting cultures are interacting, culturally-derived individual perceptions increase the difficulties in communication. For the individual, there exists only subjective reality, that is, the universe as he perceives it. More important than genetic factors sometimes, an individual's perceptions of the external world are the experiential elements which help him to see the world as stable, structured, and meaningful. Both because of genetic and cultural environmental reasons, no two persons can completely share perceptions of themselves, the objects and things of their world, or other persons in their world in precisely the same way. Thus subjective culture includes the most personal of cultural components. Marshall Singer (1971) suggests that it is precisely such patterns—when shared beyond individuals, even in an unarticulated way, of perceptions, communication, and behavior—which can be referred to as a culture. Singer notes that group-based perceptions often do not recognize national or cultural boundaries. Such perceptions may be shared internationally or interculturally by members of similar groups, but not necessarily by other individuals within a nation or culture. He suggests that, the fewer group identities that a person shares and the less intensely held the identities which exist with individuals with whom he must communicate, the more cross-culturally he is operating on the basis of a perceptual continuum.

SUMMARY

In this overview of what I consider to be major constructs in the study of intercultural communication, I have first noted the main published books which have stressed contributions to the growing literature of intercultural communication. I then provided a statement of basic premises in intercultural communication which I believe that most authors in the area would find acceptable. My discussion of six critical issues agrees generally with issues raised by some other authors, but may also highlight some issues not considered as important by other authors. The issues which I stressed include: the importance of similarities and differences, the nature of conflict in human communication and culture, the control of communication and culture, the impact of technology on communication and culture, the importance of cultural stability versus change, and cultural imperialism versus dependency. Following this discussion, I suggested as an important viewpoint for those considering intercultural communication as the components of communication. Among the communicative components which I find especially important for the ethnographic study of a community or culture are communication messages, communication participants, linguistic and nonverbal codes, and channels or media. Finally, I considered briefly cultural orientations and specific cultural components and linkages with communication. I noted the existence of four major theoretical orientations: cultural evolutionism, cultural functionalism, cultural history, and cultural ecology. Among various possible cultural components, I emphasized two: values as the most cultural of cultural characteristics, and perception as an example of subjective culture or the most personal attributes of culture.

The overview itself does not emphasize all the possible variables which bear upon the intercultural or cross-cultural communication setting or context. Rather, it is suggestive of the range of linkages which might be successfully considered when an effort is made to tie together the basic premises, the critical issues, the components of communication, and the cultural orientations and components of culture into a coherent mapping of what I consider to be major constructs which ought to be understood by the seriously-interested student of intercultural and cross-cultural communication. As I have suggested, a more substantative development of the overview can be found in my *Cultural Dialogue* (1978), as well as in other published books cited initially. Additionally, Edward Stewart's "An Overview of the Field of Intercultural Communication" (1974) provides a still more fully developed notion of the field. Stewart's work is one to which all of us actively interested in developing a theoretical base for the study of intercultural and cross-cultural communication are indebted. The accumulating evidence is strong that the study of intercultural and cross-cultural communication is steadily becoming more sophisticated. As this occurs, such study will also help to demonstrate the important relationship between intercultural and cross-cultural communication and all other forms of communication, and also its study as central to the study of culture itself.

NOTE

1. A substantial portion of this overview serves as a synthesis of ideas which are more fully developed in my full-length text on intercultural communication, *Cultural Dialogue* (Houghton Mifflin, 1978). Naturally, it is to be expected that some of the major constructs which I have emphasized will agree with other authors' views, while others will be at variance with the views of other authors.

REFERENCES

BELL, D. The cultural contradictions of capitalism. *The Public Interest*, 1970.

BLUBAUGH, J.A., & FENNINGTON, D.L. *Crossing differences: Interracial communication*. Columbus, Ohio: Bobbs-Merrill, 1976.

CASMIR, F.L. (Ed.). *International and intercultural communication annual*. Vols. 1-3. Falls Church, Va.: Speech Communication Association, 1974, 1975, 1976.

CHERRY, C. *World communication: Threat or promise*. New York: Wiley Interscience, 1971.

CONDON, J.C., & SAITO, M. (Eds.). *Intercultural encounters with Japan: Communication—contact and conflict*. Tokyo: 1974.

CONDON, J.C., & YOUSEF, F. *An introduction to intercultural communication*. Indianapolis, Ind.: Bobbs-Merrill, 1975.

DODD, C.H. *Perspectives on cross-cultural communication*. Dubuque, Iowa: Brown, 1977.

ELLUL, J. *The technological society*. New York: Random House, 1964.

FISCHER, H., & MERRILL, J.C. (Eds.). *International and intercultural communication*. New York: Hastings House, 1976.

GEERTZ, C. *The interpretation of cultures*. New York: Harper & Row, 1973.

HALL, E.T. *Beyond culture*. New York: Doubleday, 1976.

HARMS, L.S. *Intercultural communication*. New York: Harper & Row, 1973.

HENRY, J. *Culture against man*. New York: Random House, 1963.

HOOPES, D.W. (Ed.). *Readings in intercultural communication*. Vols. 1-4. Pittsburgh: University of Pittsburgh Press, 1971, 1972, 1973, 1974.

HYMES, D. Toward ethnographics of communication. In M.N. Prosser (Ed.), *Intercommunication among nations and peoples*. New York: Harper & Row, 1973.

JAIN, N.C. (Ed.). *International and intercultural communication annual*. Vol. 4. Falls Church, Va.: Speech Communication Association, 1977.

JAIN, N.C., & CUMMINGS, R.L. (Eds.). *Proceedings of the Conference on Intercultural Communication and Teacher Education*. Milwaukee: Milwaukee Urban Observatory, University of Wisconsin-Milwaukee, 1975.

JAIN, N.C., PROSSER, M.H., & MILLER, M.H. (Eds.). *Intercultural communication: Proceedings of the Speech Communication Association Summer Conference X*. Falls Church, Va.: Speech Communication Association, 1974.

KAPLAN, D., & MANNERS, R.A. *Culture theory*. Englewood Cliffs, N.J.: Prentice-Hall, 1972.

KLUCKHOHN, F.R., & STRODTBECK, F.L. *Variations in value orientations*. Evanston, Ill.: Greenwood, 1961.

LANDIS, D. (Ed.). *International journal of intercultural relations*, New Brunswick: Transaction, 1977.

NIEBURG, H.L. *Culture storm*. New York: St. Martin Press, 1973.

OLIVER, R.T. *Culture and communication*. Springfield, Ill.: Thomas, 1962.

OSGOOD, C.E., MAY, W.H., & MIRON, M.S. *Cross-cultural universals of effective meaning*. Urbana: University of Illinois Press, 1975.

PROSSER, M.H. *Cultural dialogue* Boston: Houghton Mifflin, 1978.

PROSSER, M.H. (Ed.). *Intercommunication among nations and peoples*. New York: Harper & Row, 1973.

PROSSER, M.H., (Comp.) *Syllabi in intercultural communication*. Charlottesville: University of Virginia, 1974, 1975.

RICH, A. *Interracial communication*. New York: Harper & Row, 1974.

RUHLY, S. *Orientations to intercultural communication*. Chicago: 1976.

SAMOVAR, L., & PORTER, R.E. (Eds.). *Intercultural communication: A reader*. Belmont, Cal.: Wadsworth, 1972; revised edition, 1976.

SARAL, T.B. Intercultural communication theory and research: An overview. In B.D. Ruben (Ed.), *Communication yearbook I*. New Brunswick, N.J.: Transaction-International Communication Association, 1977.

SEELYE, N., & TYLER, V.L. (Eds.). *Intercultural communicator resources*. Provo, Utah: Brigham Young University, 1977.

SIMONS, H. The carrot and stick as handmaidens of persuasion in conflict situations. In G.R. Miller & H.W. Simons (Eds.), *Perspectives on communication in social conflict*. Englewood Cliffs, N.J.: Prentice-Hall, 1974.

SINGER, M. Culture: A perceptual approach. In *Readings in intercultural communication*. Vol. 1. Pittsburgh: University of Pittsburgh Press, 1971.

SITARAM, K.S., & COGDELL, R.T. *Foundations of intercultural communication*. Columbus, Ohio: Bobbs-Merrill, 1976.

SKINNER, B.F. *Beyond freedom and dignity*. New York: Knopf, 1971.

SMITH, A. (Ed.). *Communication and culture: Readings in the codes of human interaction*. New York: Holt, Rinehart & Winston, 1966.

SMITH, A.L. *Transracial communication*. Englewood Cliffs, N.J.: Prentice-Hall, 1973.

STEWART, E.C. An overview of the field of intercultural communication. Mimeograph released by Intercultural Communications Network, University of Pittsburgh, 1974.

TRIANDIS, H.C. *The analysis of subjective culture*. New York: Wiley, 1972.

WEAKLAND, J. Communication and behavior—An introduction. *The American Behavioral Scientist*, 1967.

WEAVER, G. *Crossing culturai barriers*. Dubuque, Iowa: Brown, 1978.

WIENER, N. Cybernetics. In A. Smith (Ed.), *Communication and culture: Readings in the codes of human interaction*. New York: Holt, Rinehart & Winston, 1966.

THE ROLE OF PERSONALITY IN INTERCULTURAL COMMUNICATION

PERRY M. NICASSIO and TULSI SARAL
Governors State University

This paper discusses the value of integrating the construct of personality into the study of intercultural communication. Heretofore, intercultural communication researchers have analyzed the communication process almost exclusively from the perspectives of the cultures represented by the communicators and have not given sufficient theoretical or empirical attention to the unique characteristics of the communicators as influencing the communication behavior. The authors point out the potential problems that may arise when intercultural communication researchers steadfastly rely on cultural stereotypes based on normative data to interpret the communication which takes place between individuals who share in various degrees the "typical" behavior patterns of the cultures that they represent. The authors propose that intercultural communication researchers adopt a new perspective which views the communication process as resulting from the dynamic interplay between the cultures of the communicators, their unique response dispositions, and the situational context in which the communication takes place.

In his overview of intercultural communication theory and research, Saral (1977) points out the need for isolating numerous variables that affect the nature and process of communication interaction that takes place among individuals with varying cultural orientations. He specifies that, in the process of intercultural communication, a communicant does not lose his or her individual uniqueness and that, like culture, each member of a culture is also subject to the continuous process of growth, evolution, and change, experienced by different individuals at different speeds and in different directions. One way to look at such differences is to examine the role of personality in the process of intercultural communication. A review of literature in the field reveals no study specifically designed to examine this critical variable of individual differences in intercultural communication. The present paper is an attempt to lay forth a theoretical and conceptual framework for the study of personality variables in the process of communication among members from different cultural groups.

In the most general sense, theorists agree that the purpose of studying personality is to strive for a comprehensive, detailed understanding of the uniqueness of individual behavior patterns, thoughts, and emotions. While considerable disagreement exists over the precise role that heredity, the external environment, and conscious and unconscious forces play in the development of the human being, the major thrust of personality research has been to focus the attention of behavioral scientists on the various behavioral, cognitive, and affective dimensions that can reliably distinguish one individual from another. Thus, the field of personality has often been equated with the scientific study of individual differences.

An important assumption often made by personality researchers is that the construct of personality itself refers to the more enduring or stable characteristics of individuals. Irvin Child (1968), for example, asserts that "personality consists of all those more or less stable internal factors that make one person's behavior consistent from one time to another, and different from the behavior other people would manifest in comparable situations" (pp. 82-83). Social learning theorists like Mischel (1974), however, point out that the temptation to describe the stable characteristics of individuals has caused researchers to exaggerate the degree of consistency in human behavior across situational settings. Indeed, one of the common biases in the personality approach to the study of human behavior has been the tendency to focus on individual variation and response stability to the extent that the impact of environmental factors is often minimized. Mainly for this reason, the construct of personality has little meaning for radical behaviorists like Skinner who instead emphasize the plasticity of human behavior in the face of often subtle environmental variations. Stated simply, the radical behaviorist attributes whatever stability exists in the behavior of humans to constancies in environmental contingencies and not to dispositional, enduring characteristics of the individuals themselves.

While both positions have led to significant advances in understanding human behavior, an integrated perspective which recognizes the import of both individual uniqueness and environmental setting deserves special merit. An interactionist perspective allows the behavioral scientist to take into account variability in the behavior within individuals across situations and variability between individuals to identical environmental events. Robert Levine (1973) acknowledges the logic of this dualistic perspective by stating that "personality is the organization in the individual of those processes that intervene between environmental conditions and behavioral response" (p. 5). In this sense, personality is a construct which is best used to account for the multitude of factors which cause individuals to respond differently to the same stimulus situations.

Common, everyday experiences serve to illustrate the tenability of this perspective. Consider, for example, the divergent reactions of two college students whose term papers are harshly criticized by their psychology professor. Student *A*, after receiving his paper, immediately becomes depressed, angry at himself for not doing a better job of writing, and self-effacing to the extent that he openly apologizes to the professor for not having put forth more effort. In contrast, Student *B* openly displays his anger to the professor for what he thought was an unfair evaluation of his work, demands that the paper be reconsidered on different criteria, and upon being informed that his work would not be reevaluated, storms to the dean's office to file a formal complaint against the professor. Clearly, in the foregoing illustration, knowledge of the external stimulus situation above would not have been sufficient to predict the behavior of either student. However, prior knowledge of Student *A*'s lack of self-confidence and self-critical tendencies, and Student *B*'s arrogance and assertiveness, in combination with an understanding of the external situation, would have been quite illuminating and allowed for a much more accurate prediction.

Numerous other examples could have been used just as easily to illustrate the salience of the interactionist perspective. Without belaboring the issue any further, suffice it to say that the construct of personality permits us to acknowledge the contribution of individual differences in human behavior to stimulus situations, without which our understanding of the complexity of human behavior would be inadequate, and often erroneous.

INTERCULTURAL COMMUNICATION: CULTURES, CONTEXTS, INDIVIDUALS

The thesis that the recognition and study of individual differences is important to the behavioral sciences in general may also be extended specifically to the field of intercultural communication. Although the precise delineation of this area of study is difficult, principally because of the inherent ambiguity of the terms "culture" and "communication," we will refer to intercultural communication as the processes of interaction, both verbal and nonverbal, that take place between members of different cultural groups in various situational contexts. In analyzing communication from an intercultural perspective, then, we must acknowledge and study the interaction of three major forces: the cultures under consideration with their attendant norms and value systems which guide human behavior, the situational context or specific environment in which the interaction takes place, and the unique characteristics of the individuals themselves as participants in the communication process.

Heretofore, the primary emphasis in the study of intercultural communication has been to analyze the process of communication almost exclusively from the perspective of the cultures that the individuals represent. A common assumption, of course, is that the cultures are definitely influencing the communication, and therefore, an appropriate understanding of their impact is of the utmost importance. Although there is considerable face validity to the proposition that culture indeed has an effect on human behavior in general, and on the manner in which individuals of disparate cultural groups relate to each other in particular, the precise manner in which culture exerts its influence has been the subject of considerable controversy in the behavioral sciences.

At the core of this issue is a larger dilemma which all cross-cultural researchers must acknowledge, and which, unfortunately, is never totally soluble. An inherent difficulty in the concept of culture is its very abstractness, a quality which complicates the task of parceling out its effect on human behavior from other variables. If, for example, research demonstrates a significant difference between two cultures on some dimension of behavior, the overriding concern may be reduced to the question of the degree of confidence that we may have, as investigators, that the observed difference is a function of the variable, culture, and not other extraneous variables which are not under experimental control. It is always problematic to ascribe causal significance to culture for differences in individual behavior patterns because culture is a subject variable, and as such, does not lend itself to being studied independently of the individuals themselves who are emitting the behavior. The same, of course, applies to other subject variables, such as age, sex, race, and social class, which often appear to be potent sources of variability in behavior, but upon closer analysis, may "mask" the effect of other uncontrolled sources of variation. In a general sense, then, those of us who purport to study the effect of culture on behavior, communication, and other human processes, operate under the influence of a bias which may cause us to confuse and exaggerate the contribution of culture with other variables that are not immediately identifiable. Although we may approximate the solution to this dilemma through refinements in research methodology such as, (1) employing sampling procedures which select subjects within cultures for comparison on the basis of their similarity on other attributes that may exert effects on the dependent variable under scrutiny, and (2) measuring subjects to insure equivalence on other dimensions that may pose rival explanations for cultural differences (Brislin, Lonner, & Thorndike, 1973), we can never be fully certain in a scientific sense that we have indeed isolated a cultural effect.

These notes of caution notwithstanding, the new and controversial field of intercultural communication has attracted scholars from many different disciplines into its ranks to embark on the challenging, if problematic task of studying the ways in which that elusive variable, culture, affects human interaction. A prevailing view among researchers and theoreticians in this area of study is that culture principally affects communication through the development of norms and role expectations which establish boundaries of acceptable behavior in different situations. Underlying the development of behavioral norms and role definitions are values which are transmitted via cultural institutions such as religion, art, folklore, various other expressive media, and child-rearing practices. From a theoretical perspective, communicators in an intercultural context may not only be affected by their own culture's norms but also by what they have learned about the norms of the culture represented by the other communicator.

The subjective culture model developed by Triandis (1972) takes into account the norms of the communicators based on a "map" of culturally-molded cognitions and perceptions derived from elaborate statistical analyses. In essence, the "map" reflects the attitudes and norms of different cultural groups and is then used to predict interactive behaviors between members of the cultures concerned. To train a member of one culture to interact with members of another culture, therefore, has been viewed as a process whereby the individual must learn the norms governing the behavior of the members of the other culture in a number of situations. This learning process actually involves an act of assimilation, in which a member of the out-culture acclimates himself or herself to the in-culture through an acquired understanding of the prevailing attitudes, values, and behaviors of the in-culture, which he or she should presume to be operating in a variety of contexts.

The culture assimilator, which is based on the subjective culture model, has been used to provide such cultural "education" by giving members of a given culture feedback concerning the appropriateness of specific behaviors, based on an analysis of normative data of the culture into which they are "assimilating." The purpose of this training is to provide a match between the response of the member of the out-culture and the normative response of the in-culture. With this knowledge, it is assumed that the member of the out-culture will know how to behave appropriately when interacting with members of the in-culture.

The culture assimilator approach acknowledges the import of the context in intercultural interactions, to the extent that the training is geared to specific situations. However, as Saral (1977) points out, human interaction never occurs in a vacuum but in varying environments which occasion different behaviors. An important point in the study of the setting in which the communication takes place is that the context of the interaction may vary markedly in complexity depending on the particular situational cues that are present. Because of the potency of specific cues in certain situations, some responses have a much higher likelihood of being emitted than others, because individuals can readily perceive the cues and adjust their behavior accordingly. Clearly, in such situations, we may anticipate considerable uniformity in human behavior because of the environmental "pull" for certain responses, and thus, the normative response of a cultural group would fairly accurately represent how members of the culture typically behave. From the standpoint of the individual who is learning about the culture in question, adherence to the norm would be recommended, since doing so would have rather high probability of being "accurate" or appropriate. Some human behavior in different cultural settings has a stereotypic flavor. In American culture, standing to salute the flag and giving applause after a well-received concert performance are examples of stereotypic responses in settings which simply do not allow for a great range of behaviors to be emitted. Members of other cultures may exhibit other behaviors under basically the same situations, but the variability in responsiveness within the various cultural groups may be minimal.

However, the issue of the degree of intracultural variability in behavior patterns in different contexts is an extremely vital one for understanding, in a general sense, the magnitude of influence that culture may have on behavior, and for educating individuals about the nature of the behavior patterns of other cultural groups. Most contexts are not nearly as delimiting as those cited in the preceding examples, in that members of the same cultural group may exhibit significant variability in their behavior. The normative response, taken here to mean the modal responses of members of the culture in such contexts, may present a very oversimplified, misleading representation of the behavior of the culture, especially when such behavior is couched in terms such as "appropriate" or "correct" for intercultural training. When there is widespread variability in behavior in a particular context between members of the same culture, the entire philosophy of studying the behavior of the individuals from a cultural perspective may be questioned. It is definitely a truism that individuals reflect in their behavior patterns, to various degrees, what are considered to be the predominant cultural norms. While the behavior of some individuals may approximate quite closely the cultural stereotype in a particular context, the behavior of others may be very atypical of the culture and highly idiosyncratic.

An important implication of intracultural variability in responsiveness in different contexts is that the cultural assimilator approach to intercultural training may be most appropriate when little variability exists, and the normative response of the cultural group in question has a very high likelihood of being expressed in the *individual behavior patterns* of its members. In contexts in which substantial variability exists, the training should include a description of the cultural norms, but it also must go beyond such norms to account for the behavior of the members of the culture as individuals who, while possessing some common characteristics considered to be representative of the culture as a whole, also are significantly different from each other on a number of cognitive, affective, and behavioral dimensions.

The study of personality would appear to have much to contribute to the field of intercultural communication because it focuses attention on individual differences in responsiveness which account for variability in behavior within cultures in various contexts. The construct of personality also emphasizes the importance of examining the process of human communication as an interaction which occurs between individuals, a fact which is often easily ignored when the concept of culture is introduced into this interaction and cultural stereotypes are invoked to explain individual behavior patterns. Thomas Maretzki (1974) has also drawn attention to the position that culture may or may not tell us much about individual behavior patterns, and that such a realization is crucial, in general, for people living in a multicultural society, and in particular, for the clinician who not only must learn to be aware of cultural differences in the behavior patterns of his or her clients, but must also be able to construe and interpret psychological problems on an individual basis. In short, he is asserting that the principle of culture has analytic value to groups, but not to individuals, a position that we feel has substantial merit.

THE CONSTRUCT OF PERSONALITY IN INTERCULTURAL COMMUNICATION

A question may now justifiably be raised concerning how scholars of intercultural communication should take into account the construct of personality in the study of the communication process. The acknowledgment of individual differences in cultural behavior patterns in specific contexts logically leads to the even more important issue of how, in fact, they influence communication which takes place between members of different cultural groups. As complex as this problem is, both theoretically and methodologically, we may advance significantly towards its solution if we are able to focus our analytic energies on the communicators themselves, and not exclusively on the cultural groups that they represent. Specifically, it would be extremely helpful to understand how the individuals have learned to behave in the various contexts prior to interacting in them. Particular attention should be given to the learning histories of the individuals, in order to obtain information about the development and range of behaviors that they have emitted over an extended period of time in the designated contexts.

Such individualized attention may possibly lead to the identification of "styles" of communication that may be more valuable in predicting the nature of the intercultural interaction than the mere knowledge of the cultures represented by the communicators, particularly in cases where the behavior of the communicators deviates significantly from the normative behavior pattern of their respective cultures. Consider, for example, a situation in which two students of different cultures find themselves collaborating on a class project. Without knowing each other personally, the students look forward to working together because of the cultural stereotypes that they have of one another. Student *X*, while from a culture which stresses a diligent work ethic with a premium on intellectual and scholastic achievement, nevertheless is a rather unserious student and is somewhat lazy and inefficient in his study habits. On the other hand, Student *Z*, who hails from a culture which places a higher value on personal enjoyment than on success and scholastic achievement, fashions himself as an extremely ambitious, hard-working individual who aspires to being the best student in his class. Aware of the other's cultural heritage and its associated values and norms, the students anticipate that they will get along quite well together in their collaborative effort, but for different reasons. Student *X*, thinking that his counterpart, like himself, will not take the work seriously, considers their collaboration as a diversion and possibly, an opportunity to develop a friendship. Student *Z*, in contrast, looks forward to working together with his counterpart because he assumes that he will be collaborating with someone like himself who is intellectually-oriented and motivated to produce the best possible project. Needless to say, after getting to know one another, they realize the unfortunate consequences of being misled by the cultural stereotype which they held. This dilemma could have been largely avoided, however, if they had learned more about each other's unique dispositions and behavior patterns prior to interacting.

Although the foregoing illustration represents an extreme case in which the cultural stereotype, though accurate in a normative sense, was a totally inappropriate standard by which to interpret the behavior of the students as individuals, other situations in which intercultural communication takes place are also subject to varying degrees of the same type of error that befell our two bemused students. Other individuals in the same context, for example, may have had other response dispositions which may have more closely approximated their respective cultural norms, thus allowing such norms to be a more accurate guide for the interaction. Very seldom does it occur, though, when the individual behavior patterns of the communicators perfectly match the stereotypes of the cultures that they represent in a particular context.

In instances in which there is interaction between members of two cultural groups, the relative weights of the cultures of the individuals, the context, and the unique response dispositions of the individuals on the process of communication are likely to vary. The relative impact of culture, for example, may depend on the nature of the communication context and the unique characteristics of the communicators as individuals. In a model which takes into account these three sources of variation, it is possible for one variable to be prepotent over the other two. For example, even though all communication occurs in a particular setting, the context may be such a powerful determinant of behavior that neither culture nor individual response dispositions may have any significant bearing on the nature of the interaction. This would occur in situations in which there is uniformity in the response norms of the two cultures and no significant variability in individual behavior. An exchange of a greeting, carried out in the same manner in two different cultures may illustrate this type of communication. Although there may be subtleties in the manner in which the greeting is exchanged that may reflect cultural or individual differences, basically the interchange is highly stereotypic and dominated by each individual's recognition of the other. In this type of context, we may even question if intercultural communication is taking place since the cultures represented by the two communicators are not influencing the interaction to any appreciable degree.

In reality, most situations typically involve a dynamic interplay among these three factors. Analyzing intercultural communication from this three-dimensional perspective permits a more comprehensive analysis of the communication process, in that we may study the independent contribution of these sources of variation as well as their interaction. Such a perspective also possesses heuristic value since experimental research may be generated which addresses the impact of these factors on various aspects of the interaction, such as congruity in the meaning of various messages; interpersonal attraction, which may be measured both behaviorally and attitudinally; the quality of the end product of the communication; and others. Actually, studies which examined specific variables related to the three dimensions pending the development of more refined measurement strategies would be most appropriate. For example, we may first study the degree to which various cultures differ from one another on various dimensions and then examine the effect of the composite variable cultural similarity-dissimilarity of the communicators in different contexts which vary in some important qualitative aspects; for example, social, occupational, and so forth, among communicators who differ cognitively, affectively, and behaviorally as individuals.

With more theoretical development and the generation of specific hypotheses based on research in several areas of the social and behavioral sciences, we may begin to understand more thoroughly the nature of the intercultural communication process. And in our scientific efforts, above all, let us not forget the fact, humbling as it may be, that our task must involve the complex analysis of interaction occurring between individuals and not cultural stereotypes.

REFERENCES

BRISLIN, R., LONNER, W., & THORNDIKE, R. *Cross-cultural research methods*. New York: Wiley, 1973.

CHILD, I. Personality in culture. In E.F. Borgatta & W.W. Lambert (Eds.), *Handbook of personality theory and research*. Chicago: Rand McNally, 1968.

LeVINE, R. *Culture, behavior and personality*. Chicago: Aldine, 1973.

MARETZKI, T. Culture and the individual. In Wen-Shing Tseng, J.F. McDermott, & T.W. Maretzki (Eds.), *People and cultures in Hawaii*. Honolulu: University of Hawaii, School of Medicine, Department of Psychiatry, 1974.

MISCHEL, W. *Introduction to personality*. New York: Holt, Rinehart & Winston, 1974.

SARAL, T.B. Intercultural communication theory and research: An overview. In B.D. Ruben (Ed.), *Communication yearbook 1*. New Brunswick, N.J.: Transaction-International Communication Association, 1977.

TRIANDIS, H. *The analysis of subjective culture*. New York: Wiley, 1972.

THE INEFFABLE: AN EXAMINATION OF THE LIMITS OF EXPRESSIBILITY AND THE MEANS OF COMMUNICATION

W. BARNETT PEARCE
University of Massachusetts

ROBERT J. BRANHAM
Bates College

Recurrent claims of ineffable experience and their importance for communication theory are analyzed. Four positions are identified: (1) the "complete effability/complete communicability" position is historically identified with Western culture but repudiated by modern thought; (2) the "complete ineffability/complete communicability" position has some adherents but is self-defeating; (3) the "complete effability/limited communicability" position provides the conceptual base for most of the work in twentieth century communication theory; and (4) the "complete ineffability/limited communicability" position has consistent support but requires a new form of theory which differentiates "coordination" and "consubstantiation" as genres. Explication of the features of situations which prompt recognition of ineffability and the characteristics of individual and cultural attempts to express the ineffable necessitates a reanalysis of the function of several social institutions. This analysis suggests new directions for the development of communication theory.

Wittgenstein (1961, p. 151) concluded the *Tractatus* by saying "whereof one cannot speak, thereof one must be silent." We disagree. Granted that the inexpressible—by definition—may not be spoken, yet it may —with difficulty—be spoken about, perhaps profitably.

Throughout history, persons have claimed to have experiences which are uniquely significant or valid, but which they cannot convey to others. As Stapledon (1939, . 418) said, "the ecstatic experience, which is the mystic's supreme reward, is said to give profound insight into the essential nature of reality, along with a stammering inability to describe *what* has been revealed, save in the most metaphorical and paradoxical terms." Among these "stammerers" is Lao Tzu (1972), who claimed that "the Tao which can be expressed is not the real Tao." Otto (1957) alluded to the "tremendous mystery" of religious experience, then cordially advised all those without this experience to read no further since they would be unable to comprehend the argument. Buddhist koans (such as: "What is the sound of one hand clapping?") are answered in such a way as to demonstrate the futility of logic or language as a means to discover or express reality. The formula, "I just can't tell you . . ." (e.g., "how excited I am") has become a commonplace expression of intensity. Depending on one's perspective, such claims for inexpressible knowledge and experience may be seen as arrogant and obscurantist attempts to withhold propositional knowledge from public scrutiny; as evidence of deficiency in communication ability or interest; or as profound comments on the nature of the human condition.

Communication theorists have seldom dealt with experiences claimed to be ineffable: scientific analysis has focused on descriptions of regularly recurring communication processes, and critical works have selected unusual examples of common forms of communication. An unintended consequence of these selective processes has been the virtual exclusion from scholarly purview of those experiences which persons claim to be their most significant, such as moments of mystical insight, rapturous "peak experiences," artistic perception, or religious ecstasy. There are at least three reasons why such phenomena should receive systematic analysis. First, excluding them beggars communication theory by limiting it to the province of the commonplace. Precisely those events which illumine and infuse our lives with energy are defined outside its competence. Second, a cool-eyed study of the ineffable permits a reasoned assessment of the claims for mystic experiences. To the extent that "seers" introduce their art or ideology into human society, it will be through communication, and a complete theory of communication should account for the processes by which new visions become social cliches. Finally, there is reason to believe that there are different genres of communication, each of which requires a different explanatory structure and each of which must be included in a theory of communication. Specifically, communication utilizing socially-constructed meanings may be coordinated by rules, but communication between cultures or about non-socially-sanctioned meanings must rely on symbolic artistry in evoking archetypes. The former genre is exemplified by greeting rituals, the latter by great literature.

The following section contextualizes the inquiry by describing four claims about the existence of the ineffable and the possibility of communication. The contrast between these positions forces the articulation and organization of the basic assumptions from which any theory must proceed. Each position implies the development of a communication theory considerably different from the others; the assumption that experience is ineffable leads to a novel claim about the form of communication theory.

FOUR CLAIMS ABOUT EXPRESSIBILITY AND COMMUNICATION

Historically and analytically, four positions about the ineffable may be identified based on contrasting assumptions about the expressibility of experience and the possibility of communication.

Complete Effability; (Potentially) Complete Communication

The existence of the ineffable is denied by the claim that there exist modes of expression adequate (at least in principle) to represent any human experience. From this perspective, it is assumed that experience is isomorphic with reality. Further, problems in communication are attributable to situational factors (e.g., noise) or deficiencies in individuals' communication skills. Western culture has until recently endorsed this position, and has considered claims of ineffable experience as obscurantism or confessions of personal inadequacy. With characteristic industry, the rhetoricians, social scientists, and engineers of Western societies have worked toward complete communication by removing semantic, syntactic, and technical barriers. This activity has produced what Matson and Montagu (1967) described as a series of three revolutions: a technological revolution in which the problem of distributing messages over time and distance was reduced; a cybernetic revolution in which the techniques of feedback and control were applied to machinery and society; and an "unfinished" revolution in which concern for human values was introduced.

The "complete effability" position is consistent with the programs of both the classical Greeks and the logical positivists. The Greeks celebrated speech as the means for employing reason and discovering knowledge. Plato portrayed Socrates as debating about truth by using speech to critique the use of speech: noncontradictory usages were accepted as correct. Aristotle's three "laws of thought" (identity, exclusion, and noncontradiction) provided the basis for logic, which was considered a compendium of rules for the correct use of language which would produce certain (as opposed to merely probable) knowledge. In this century, the logical positivists selected Wittgenstein's picture theory of meaning as the ideal form of scientific language. According to the picture theory, the logic of language is representative of the structure of reality (Morrison, 1968). The positivists argued that synthetic statements, the terms of which could be fully defined operationally and the prediction of which could be empirically verified, met this criterion. By organizing these carefully selected statements into valid syllogistic patterns, certain knowledge could be achieved (see, for example, Rapoport, 1969).

The communication theory which derives from this position stresses the fidelity and efficiency of messages, and is most clearly exemplified by Shannon and Weaver's (1949) *The Mathematical Theory of Communication*.

Complete Ineffability; Complete Incommunicability

This position is the polar opposite of the preceding one and represents the solipsist claim that persons are the prisoners of their own experience, unable to know whether it corresponds to any non-subjective reality, and unable to communicate it with anyone else (assuming that others exist). If this position were true, we could neither know it nor do anything about it, and no communication theory follows from it. We include it here because it is part of the analysis of positions and because, along with the position of complete effability/complete communicability, it conceptually bounds the next two positions.

Complete Effability; Limited Communicability

This position denies the existence of ineffable experience but affirms real problems in communication which arise because persons' experiences are not isomorphic. A person's experience is not mysterious to himself and adequate modes of representation exist for him to express that experience, but others may be unable to recognize those expressions if they have no comparable experience. This position assumes that experience is separated from reality by a perceptual process which is not neutral, and that different persons may well experience the "same" event very differently.

This concept underlies much of the work in social science during this century. William James's (1947) concept of a "pluralistic universe" describes reality as a "big, booming, buzzing confusion" out of which persons carve their own perceived environment, which may differ significantly from that of their fellows. Studies of perceptual processes (e.g., Gibson, 1966) have stressed the translation processes which occur from event (e.g., light waves), to percept (neural electrical impulses), to concept (experience). Kelly's (1955) "personal construct theory" assumes that encounters with reality are meaningless until interpreted by being filtered through a system of constructs. Since constructs are an individual's own, different persons may construe particular events very differently, or an individual may change his experiences by reconstruing events. Although concepts may be preverbal, they are potentially articulatable, given the ministrations of a therapist or researcher. Communication is possible to the extent that individuals have similar constructs or can construe the construct system of the other.

The "linguistic relativity" argument is consistent with this position. Rejecting the notion of language as a passive instrument of thought, Sapir, Whorf, and others argued that experience is shaped by, and to some extent limited to, the categories and logical structures of language (see Slobin, 1971). In addition to creating a discontinuity between reality and experience, this process assures that the person will have a language adequate for representing his experience, although he may have difficulty communicating with persons who do not belong to his speech community.

Finally, the *Weltanschauugen* school in the philosophy of science forcefully argues a comparable position. Criticizing the positivists' search for a set of observations which would scientifically prove the validity of statements which could be used as the propositions of a theory, Hanson, Kuhn, and Feyerabend claimed that all observation is theory-dependent. Although *seeing that* (e.g., something is there) is a physical response to the environment, *seeing it as* (e.g., a sunrise) requires the use of meanings in the "theory" of the observer. Persons with different theories do not see the same thing even when the physical stimulus is similar for both, leading to problems in the testing of theories and in communication (see Suppe, 1974).

The communication problems identified by this approach are typified by the physicist asked to explain his craft to a 3-year-old boy ("run along, sonny") or to a benighted humanist colleague ("I'm sorry, but you simply haven't the math"), and by the suppression of experience or preclusion of means of expression by taboo, censorship, or social disapproval. The communication theory deriving from this position deals with the difficulty in moving between two fields of experience, each of which is (in principle) known and expressible by its inhabitant but which may be quite foreign to the other. Exemplars of this approach include Wiseman and Barker's (1974) *Speech/Interpersonal Communication*, ethnographies of the meanings constructed by various societies (Philipsen, 1975), and analyses of social rules which facilitate coordination (Jackson, 1966).

Complete Ineffability; Limited Communicability

This position claims that experience per se is

inexpressible: each of the various modes of representation has a particular logic which imposes its own distortion when used to describe experience, and the distortion constitutes a loss. To paraphrase Huxley: the problem that we all face is to have Shakespearean feelings and, unless by chance we happen to be Shakespeare, to talk like accountants or college professors; to touch the pure lyrics of experience and reduce them to verbal equivalents of tripe and hogwash.

The general semanticist's critique of Aristotelian modes of thought is consistent with this claim. The fundamental tenet of the Korzybskian program is the dissimilarity between reality and language (Korzybski, 1933; Condon, 1975). Several academic traditions which have attempted to describe human awareness have reported an inarticulable substratum of experience. Freud and Jung described the unconscious, which is symbolic rather than rational and is at most only dimly perceived. The Wurzburg school described the *aufgabe* of thought, which are primitive experiences which cannot be verbally depicted. Arieti's (1976) analysis of creativity postulated the existence of the "endocept" as a description of these phenomena. Endocepts are "primitive" organizations of experience which are expressed only by being translated at some price into words, music, art, and so forth.

The Buddhist world view is based on an assumption that truth and experience are ineffable because the nature of reality is unlike the nature of language or propositional knowledge. Knowledge claims are general while reality is absolutely particular, unique and unrelated; propositions are abstract while reality is pure existence, a point-instance in the stream of existence, unextended and unenduring.

The theory which derives from this position differentiates two genres of communication. When enacting socially patterned episodes, such as greeting rituals upon entering an office, conventions (Lewis, 1969) or language games (Wittgenstein, 1968) may enable persons to coordinate adequately despite the ineffability of experience: the salt gets passed even though true "saltiness" or the explosion of taste-on-tongue is not experienced or described by any of the messages. Other situations, however, such as an encounter with a significant work of art, prompt recognition of ineffability and, in the absence of social rules, require communication by means of symbolic artistry which evokes (rather than describes) meaning. The former genre consists of coordination; the latter of consubstantiation.

Summary

Of these four positions, the latter two deserve considerable attention. The first seems refuted by the discoveries of a score of disciplines and the second is futile regardless of its veracity. The third, the "complete effability/limited communicability" position, is well-represented in the literature; the fourth, the "complete ineffability/limited communicability" position, is not. Because it has received relatively little attention and because it has the potential of accounting for those significant events which people report as inexpressible, this paper will develop the fourth position.

An analysis of this position appropriately focuses on two phenomena: the expressibility of human experience and the means by which persons achieve communication.

EXPERIENCE AND EXPRESSION

The assumption that experience is ineffable seems to require that a discussion of it be idiosyncratic, exotic, and mystical. However, the fact that the *content* of experience is ineffable does not preclude a rigorous and general inquiry into the *phenomenon* of ineffability. The implications of a provisional acceptance of the claim that experience is inexpressable may be explored through the answers to three questions: (1) What prompts recognition of ineffability? (2) When and in what manner is the communication of ineffable experience attempted? (3) What is the cultural importance of the recognition of and attempts to communicate the ineffable?

The Recognition of the Ineffable

Based on relevant testimony, we can conclude that the recognition of the ineffable is not limited to particular types of phenomena (e.g., spiritual) and does not necessarily result in traumatic revolutions of one's perceptual sets. Static and relatively familiar phenomena such as Huxley's (mescaline-induced) vision of a vase of flowers, Keats' Grecian urn, and Warhol's soup can may become evocative, significant, and ineffable through a process of what the Russian Formalists would call "radical defamiliarization" or the phenomenologists "making uncanny" (Duff, 1970; Huxley, 1954). By the same token, even truly exceptional events can be trivialized, as some have claimed about the ritualized degeneration of Taoism, and as the sixth century B. C. prophets, and later Jesus, claimed about Judaic religious rituals. Recognition of ineffability thus is an aspect of the "I" of the beholder: it is more an epistemic attribute of experience than an ontologic claim for the existence of a special category of reality. Further, recognition of the ineffable may be a temporally isolated experience, such as a drug-induced vision or a lifelong, cognitively integrated enlightenment or conversion. Such experiences may be the result of diligent searching, as in classical Zen training, or accidentally encountered, as in the case of the conversion to Christianity of the agnostic C.S. Lewis (1955), who described himself as "surprised by joy."

Regardless of the type of phenomenon or persistence of the experience, persons seem to recognize the ineffable when they confront their experience with language (or some other representation system) in a social context. The history of rhetorical theory is filled with more or less organized opposition to language as a sufficient means of describing experience. The Cynics of Diogenes, early scientific societies (Wenzel, 1974), general semanticists, contemporary protest movements, and Zen monks all concur in a desire to move "beyond the veil of words" whether by diatribe, number, subscripts, conventions, mass demonstrations, or the koan (Hoffman, 1975; Miura & Sasaki, 1966). In Swift's satire of the Academy, the problem of the relation between language and reality is solved by the simple expedient of carrying sacks of useful referent objects: one converses with one's colleagues by pointing rather than speaking. (It is interesting to note that a truly learned professor, according to Swift, is easily discernable by his pronounced stoop.)

According to the theory proposed in this paper, individuals coordinate their own and others' behavior relevant to particular experiences by learning language games which, although the statements made may have absolutely no *descriptive* relation to the experience, serve to *create* the conditions necessary for the experience to occur. For example, the utterance "please pass the salt" (or better, the cryptic "after you're finished . . .") may resist philosophic analysis as propositions but may make possible an inexpressible tangy explosion of taste on tongue. With repetition, these language games tend to obscure the ineffability of experience, so much so that a rather conventional member of a homogeneous culture may never have occasion to communicate about an experience for which there is no available language game. Such a person may well have, as Chesterton (1927) warned, forgotten that these means of coordination were manmade, artificial implements, and not the thing itself. Those who do remember become the critics decrying the meaninglessness and decadence of their cultural institutions.

Two types of social contexts impel recognition of the ineffable: those in which the language games are unavailable or unsuccessful, as when a person has a culturally unique experience or is communicating cross-culturally; and those in which the society has deliberately circumvented normal means of coordination.

Most societies have in some sense provided contexts in which normal means of coordination do not work, thus forcing a confrontation between experience and mode of representation. The process in each resembles the three stages of brainwashing: unfreezing (dislocation); change; and refreezing (Schein, Schnieier, & Barker, 1961). The dislocation is produced by a conscious punctuation of quotidian reality in law, logic, language, or convention: monastic communities seek physical isolation and take vows of sanctioned deviancy; artists assume an elitist creativity in concept or execution; drug experience is contextualized as ritualized discovery (as in Yaqui peyote rites) or conscious violation of social mores (as in a furtive high school drinking spree), and rites of passage are marked by awesome ceremony and physical danger. Change is produced by ascribing particular significances or expectations to events. Zen initiates follow a strictly imposed discipline leading toward the socially identified goal of enlightenment. Drug users expect alterations in their experience of reality and are often directed toward its recognition and appreciation by other people. Refreezing consists of social labeling or typing processes, sometimes aided by the individual who marks the reality of his experience by adopting new manners of speech, dress, action, or association, for example, as a "born again Christian" reinforces and is reinforced by the spiritual community in the belief that he has experienced a uniquely significant event.

From this perspective, formal and informal social institutions which circumvent normal processes of coordination are interpretable as manifestations of a (perhaps latent) cultural recognition of the ineffability of experience, and the necessity to acknowledge it, at least periodically. This interpretation suggests a reassessment of the role of monastic orders, of art which strains to annihilate itself by denying its own expression, and of scholarly reminders of the gap between the mode of representation and that which is represented (Sontag, 1969): they are seen as cultural anchors which function to slow and inhibit too easy dependence on a limited repertoire of language games. Representing the systemic wisdom of a viable culture, they comprise sanctioned alarms which disrupt the social order by reminding it that it is artificial and limited. This line of reasoning suggests that formal social contexts which prompt recognition of the ineffable would occur most frequently in homogeneous, isolated cultures, since frequent cross-cultural contact would serve much the same function.

While certainly not all private experience is prompted by social institutions, the recognition of ineffability requires social reference. For those instances of visionary experience which occur independent of social direction or whose breadth or intensity transcend the disectional institution, social reality—whether linguistic or conventional—still serves as a basis for comparison. For example, the question and answer pattern of the Zen koan offers an intriguing but ultimately futile exercise in logic and language. There is no verbally significant or "logical" answer; what is achieved is a sense of necessary transcendence of the "frame" in which the question is asked. The koan does not attempt to express the ineffable, but to cue and confirm its existence. In this sense the koan has been compared to a brick used to knock upon the gate of enlightenment; once the gate is opened, the brick is discarded because it bears no intrinsic meaning. "What is the nature of enlightenment?", the novice inquires in one classic interchange. "A bowl full of snow," the master responds.

Attempts to Express the Ineffable

Paradoxically, the most intense experiences are those which persons would most like to communicate, but are least likely to be able to communicate. Intense emotions, vivid sensation, aesthetic appreciation, religious ecstasy all function as "irreducible metaphors" beyond the normal limits of intersubjectivity (Alston, 1964, pp. 103-106).

Like the man who discovered the existence of the sun in Plato's myth of the cave, those who would carry the message that appearential reality consists of shadows are thwarted by the limitations of the "language of the tribe," and must purify it (Huxley, 1963). These attempts sometimes produce bizarre consequents: ecstatic Christians engage in glossalalia, the "barks" or the "shakes"; and enlightened monks may be inflicted with "Zen sickness," a malady whose primary symptom, an incessant composition and recitation of poetry, can be cured only by extended isolation. More systematic attempts to express the ineffable are art and science. Science refines the language of the tribe by increasing the precision of its use and by verifying truth-claims. Artists refine the language of the tribe, according to Huxley, for "the express purpose of creating a language capable of conveying, not the single meaning of some particular science, but the multiple significance of human experience, on its most private as well as its more public levels." (Huxley, 1963, p. 118).

The artistic enterprise is based on the assumption that there are strong commonalities in human experience—we will later designate these as archetypes—which can be evoked if not necessarily described. The achievement of consubstantiality in communication involves the elicitation of appropriate meanings, not their bald or precise description (Burke, 1969a, 1969b). The characteristics of literature which is "great"—that is, perceived as meaningful by persons in diverse cultures and epochs—seem to focus on a particular type of ambiguity.

Three paradoxical attributes appear to be universal in manifestations of artistic greatness: the forcing of attention beyond the representational icon itself—poesis rather than mimesis; the evocation of multiple ranges of meaning—the appeal to universals with an infinite scope of individual applications; and the vivacity of evoked experience—the stark chill of profound recognition as opposed to the "warm fuzzy feeling" of simple identification (Branham, 1977). Mona Lisa's smile is ambiguous yet universally evocative, representing an artistically valid use of symbolism. The famed "flower sermon" of Gautama operated in a similar fashion. The Buddha is said to have slowly twirled a flower in his fingers, never speaking, but watching his gathered disciples for a sign of understanding. Upon observing a monk named Kashyapa who had apparently been enlightened by the wordless and ambiguous "sermon," the Buddha smiled and presented him with his begging bowl and robe as a sign of the transmission. Kashyapa in turn is said to have conveyed that smile to several succeeding generations of monks.

The literary genre most consistently devoted to the explicit interplay of private experience and public expression is that of fantastic fiction. Proceeding from the accepted premise of impossibility, fantasy attempts to convey an internal consistency and reality of the supernatural, the imaginary world, or cosmic vision. As Dante ascends through Paradise, he pronounces that "what I must now delineate no voice / Ever communicated nor ink wrote; nor was it ever grasped by the imagination" (III, 19). The task facing the author of fantasy is an awesome one. While all fiction in some sense seeks to portray and elaborate an imaginary world peopled with imaginary beings, fantasy goes one step farther: it depicts characters and settings beyond our repertoire of perceptual bases which operate upon physical and social orders in direct violation of our knowledge of reality. The objective fantasy is an intensely private vision driven toward communicability. The danger of incomprehensibility is ever present, as Lord Dunsany (1969) cautions in *The King of Elfland's Daughter*: "If through fault of mine my reader should fail to picture the peaks of Elfland, my fancy should never have strayed from the fields we know."

The fantasists have provided an impressive array of techniques designed to blend the ineffable with communicable fiction. Olaf Stapledon (1937), who in *Star Maker* undertakes the modest objectives of determining the place of community in the universe and portraying the true nature of the supreme being, employs an intellectual quasi-history of intelligence in this cosmos and others. Stapledon's evolutionary narrator rises with the breadth of historical scope to a level finally capable of at least glimpsing, if not fully understanding, the nature of the *Star Maker*. David Linsay (1968), in *A Voyage to Arcturus*, portrays a Nietzchean world illuminated by two suns which bear unearthly spectra. The difficulty of describing a color, particularly a color never seen such as Lindsay's "ulfire" or "jale," is enormous; as Lindsay notes, "As regards the Alppaine colors, blue stands in the middle and is therefore not existence, but relation, Ulfire is existence, so it must be a different sort of existence." Through musical and emotional referents, Lindsay conveys at least a functional understanding of unseen physical phenomena. H.P. Lovecraft, acknowledged master of supernatural horror, takes an entirely different route of expressing a profoundly private vision. Instead of attempting to expand the narrative perspective to accommodate the vision or establishing philosophical frames of reference, Lovecraft (1971) appeals to the "gibbering nameless horrors of chaos" lurking in some form in the reader's mind. The intense, if private, fears of the individual reader are seen as infinitely more powerful than the fear instilled through direct physical description in textual display.

In whatever communicative form chosen, fantastic fiction at its best provides a compelling transmission, if not translation, of ineffability. The vision produced remains vivid, if undefinable. As philologist Elwin Ransom in C.S. Lewis's (1968) *Perelandra* returns to earth from a visionary experience on Venus and is asked to describe his adventures, he responds: "It is words that are vague. The reason why the thing can't be expressed is that it's too *definite* for language."

In any of its expressive formats, the social context of ineffability provides a relational bridge between the realms of private and public experience. Effective translation need not involve literal expression; indeed, private vision can be shared at the level of social direction and value (as in sanctioned religious enlightenments), commonality of inducement (as in drug subcultures), or appreciation of the ambiguous expression itself (as in art and literature). Thus, while glossalalia communicates no direct connotative meaning in its use of language foreign to the speaker (and almost always to the listener), it serves as a "supernatural sign that God was in the midst of these believers" and evokes recognition and understanding from worshippers who have had similar visions (Christenson, 1968). The diverse sensory experiences of drug use may be unique for every participant, yet a relational bond exists among users based upon the drug inducement and its attendant rituals. Even in the description of experience unrelated to drug use, the accepted terminological referents of the drug experience bear meaning for members of the subculture. In fantasy fiction, the limits of imagination are ever-stretched; yet where description fails, communication still often succeeds.

The dual continua of experience and expressive competence thus intersect. While the most gifted poet may never be able to deal directly with the most private of human experience, our contextually shared private experiences may often be conveyed to some degree by common cultural tools or perhaps without words at all.

The Significance of Attempts to Express the Ineffable

Those who tamper with the language of the tribe in an attempt to express the ineffable have met a variety of social responses. Visionaries have been burned as witches, revered as prophets, feted as artists, canonized as saints, and incarcerated as lunatics. Depending in part of the expressor's artistry and the culture's receptivity, responses have ranged from outrage to gratitude, from bewilderment to comprehension, from rejection to incorporation.

For the most part, society seems to operate on the "automatic pilot" of coordinated activities produced by reenacting sanctioned episodes, scripts, and games. If the ineffable is successfully evoked, the expressor is likely to be honored (perhaps posthumously) and society is the richer for its contact with the mystery of existence. If the society rejects the attempted expression, the expressor may be alienated or driven insane by a persistent reminder of his lack of symbolic and experiential commonality, and the society becomes more rigid and artificial. Reactions to Stapledon's (1937) *Star Maker* illustrate these societal effects. Some readers found the description of the *Star Maker* exhilarating because it expanded the scope of their consciousness; others found it depressing because the role of the human species was depicted as short and futile.

Reflecting Rogers and Shoemaker's (1971) analysis of the adoption of innovations, however, most of those who attempt to express the ineffable are confronted with a mixed response, including a small number of enthusiastic endorsees and more or less formal rejection by the majority. If opposing forces are repressive, as in the case of Christians in the USSR or the drug culture in the U.S., the persecution creates strong community ties within the group which may facilitate the development of elaborate means of symbolizing the commonly-acknowledged experience. If the opposing forces are tolerant, bi-experiential actors capable of communicating within multiple private and social realms may be produced. Swift's (1933) Laputans, for example, spent most of their time in private contemplation of the abstract, but could be called upon to attend the interactive necessities of social life and trivial conversation when reminded by a servant, who would strike the appropriate speaker's mouth and listener's ear with a pebble-filled bladder. Or perhaps, as a consequence of the ascent of man in progressive civilization, we have learned largely to avoid the realm of private experience, or repress its contemplation and expression as we concentrate upon the daily business of society.

No matter how private and incommunicable the experience and its interpretation, human action operates within a social context. This context, in varying degrees, directs attention toward, and prompts recognition of, the experience, generates the means or limits for its attempted expression, and most certainly issues an interactive response to attempted expression with concomitant effects upon future experiential and communicative patterns of the individual or social group. Even if the premise of ineffability is accepted for all human experience, particular modes and contexts of ineffable experience have traditionally appeared as culturally constant: religious enlightenment, artistic vision, and drug-induced consciousness being the most obvious. In each instance, the operation of the social context has assumed an important role in the shaping, expression, and social response of private experience.

THE MEANS OF COMMUNICATION

The assumption that all experience is ineffable makes the phenomena of communication problematic. Two questions are suggested: (1) How is it that persons are able to communicate at all?; (2) How do persons communicate well? The answers to these questions reinforce the utility of some lines of communication theorizing and suggest some novel integrations and extrapolations.

The position developed in this paper pictures persons in direct experiential contact with their fellows and their environment. This experience is characterized as broad, vivid, common, and ineffable. The broadness and vividness of primary experience has frequently been attested to by psychoanalysts, whose portrayals of subconscious dreams, images, and urges indicate that these are unrestricted and undiluted; and by mystics and artists, whose behavior and descriptions frequently scandalize the refined elements of society (see Bettelheim, 1976). A key assumption is that experience is common. Because all members of the human species have comparable perceptual equipment and live in an environment which operates according to the same physical laws, they develop ''archetypes'' which function as the irreducible templates for the perception or generation of patterns. Koch's (1955) analysis of signs indicated that a vertical stroke means something different than a horizontal one in all cultures (presumably because all humans have lived in an environment in which gravity is a factor). Similarly, Jung (1964) noted that round symbols in all cultures mean something different than long, narrow or pointed ones (presumably because of the permeability of skin to things with points). Only the most heavily enculturated Occidental would describe Yang and Ying as a dichotomy—or even as a bipolar continuum. Finally, it is assumed that any mode of representation of this experience is a map rather than the territory: the experience itself is ineffable.

A society is, by definition, a group which has achieved a means of replacing anarchic chaos with some form or order. This order consists in part of the constitutive definitions of the acts, agents, scenes, purposes, and agencies which comprise reality (Searle, 1969; Burke, 1969b), and in part of the norms and rules which govern and guide behavior (Jackson, 1966). When an individual is socially constructed, he superimposes the social constructed reality on his own direct experience and learns to communicate within this confined, pale surrogate for experience.

We can now answer the first question. Communication occurs in two forms. The first consists of coordination, and reinforces the social order. Based on a knowledge of social reality and the rules which govern behavior, persons may coenact episodes such as church, classroom, or barroom brawl. There is no way for individuals to be certain that their experiences of the event are comparable to others, but this is irrelevant as long as each produces actions which the others can interpret as those which constitute the events in which they think they are participating. Usually, a gadfly who questions the ''real'' meaning of an event is perceived as a threat to the social order and is ostracized as ''philosopher,'' ''egghead,'' or more parsimoniously, ''wet blanket.'' The practical value of coordination is that it facilitates the maintenance of order—most persons can pick the way through the bulk of their day's requirements on "automatic pilot," without having to spend considerable amounts of energy struggling to express or understand. The price of coordination is that it limits communication to the range of experiences sanctioned and symbolized by the society, and these may well become sterile and repetitious.

The second form of communication is consubstantiation, in which a person evokes in others but does not describe experiences. By the artistic use of symbols, a skilled rhetor may allude to needs or attitude clusters associated with an archetypal experience and refresh awareness of it without describing it (Burke, 1969a, pp. 20ff.). Consubstantiation is always a threat to the existing social order because it reminds persons of the narrowness and tepidness of social reality. However, as we argued above, such reminders may be necessary for the long-run viability of a system.

The second question, that of how persons manage to communicate well, presupposes different criteria for each kind of communication. Coordination is successful when two or more persons are able to generate a series of actions which mesh. An exemplary performance is one in which the communicators have conformed carefully to the center of the permissible latitudes of meanings and messages, and thus best approximated a stereotypic interaction; for example, a "hi, how are you" exchange. Consubstantiation is successful when a person is able to transcend or penetrate cultural meanings and evoke the vivid primal experience. An exemplary performance is one in which the participants may be stammeringly unable to account for what happened, but they know beyond doubt that it was significant.

The two forms of communication are not mutually exclusive, however, and an integration of them is perhaps the maximally effective communicative experience. Primitive societies institutionalized combinations of coordination and consubstantiation in rituals and myths. To the extent that these served as substitutes for technology, science, and entertainment and were not pale repetitions of form, they provided scripts; thus assuring coordination, which fused the common activities of the tribe (relocating, the agrarian cycle, life-stages) with primal fears (spirits, monsters) and cultural myths (creation, continuation, heroic deeds) (Becker, 1975; Eliade, 1963). Modern societies are more individualistic. While the social order retains some formal intercourse between coordination and consubstantiation (as in literary genres, temples, sports, and drug use) by the demythologizing and de-ritualizing social reality, many episodes have become bareboned scripts permitting considerable flexibility in enactment. Those individuals who enact these episodes with flawless coordination are considered safe, conventional, and a bit dull. Those who mix consubstantiation-play into their enactment—who achieve both coordination and the energy and vivacity of evoked primal experience—are prized and praised as conversationalists, orators, and artists. Obviously, consubstantiation-play risks disrupting coordination: "We must not assume that the sole purpose of communication is to insure full understanding by every hearer. Such an ideal would entail the banishment of with and vivacity from human discourse and the anaesthetization of keener intellects by laborious explanation. In these matters, the speaker must at times take calculated risks: sometimes his remarks will fall on stony ground and he will have lost the gamble" (Parry, 1967, p. 95).

CONCLUSION

This inquiry has shown that the assumption that all experience is ineffable does not preclude the possibility of accounting for communication. On the contrary, it permits the inclusion of a category of events which otherwise must be ignored. The personal and social significance of communication situations which provoke recognition of ineffability were assessed, and the implications of ineffable experience for communication theory were discussed. Two forms of communication, coordination and consubstantiation, were contrasted, each of which requires a theory with different primitive terms and a different logic of explanation.

The theories presented here proffer a powerful and sensitive way to account for human communication. However, they are far from fully worked out. In fact, the confrontation between the formal apparatus of theory, and the diversity and vivacity of ineffable experience may create a situation comparable to that in modern physics where theoretical elegance is unobtainable. Stapledon (1939, p. 418) warned that "all intellectual descriptions and interpretations of the mystical experience must be regarded with great suspicion. It is after all very unlikely that human thought and language, which are adapted to much more simple, more commonplace experience, should be able to cope with experience of a very different order." To paraphrase a common assessment, more thinking needs to be done, and that, resourcefully and innovatively. The importance of ineffability for the further development of communication theory lies in its ability to provoke, to challenge, to lay bare metatheoretical assumptions and to coalesce vast ranges of significant human action heretofore ignored in disciplinary construction.

REFERENCES

ALSTON, W.P. *Philosophy of language*. Englewood Cliffs, N.J.: Prentice-Hall, 1964.

ARIETI, S. *Creativity: The magic synthesis*. New York: Basic, 1976.

BECKER, R. *Escape from evil*. New York: Free Press, 1975.

BETTELHEIM, B. *The uses of enchantment*. New York: Knopf, 1976.

BRANHAM, R.J. Translating the ineffable: Olaf Stapledon's cosmic 'stammering.' Unpublished paper, Bates College, 1977.

BURKE, K. *A rhetoric of motives*. Berkeley: University of California Press, 1969a. Originally published in 1950.

BURKE, K. *A grammar of motives*. Berkeley: University of California, 1969b. Originally published in 1945.

CHESTERTON, G.K. *Orthodoxy*. New York: Dodd, Mead, 1927.

CHRISTENSON, L. *Speaking in tongues*. Minneapolis: Dimension, 1968.

CONDON, J., JR. *Semantics and communication* (2nd Ed.). New York: Macmillan, 1975.

DUFF, R.A. *Poetic vision and the psychodelic experience*. New York: Delta, 1970.

DUNSANY, L. *The king of Elfland's daughter*. New York: Ballantine, 1969. Originally published in 1923.

ELIADE, M. *Myth and reality*. New York: Harper, 1963.

GIBSON, J.J. *The senses considered as perceptual systems*. Boston: Houghton Mifflin, 1966.

HOFFMAN. Y. *The sound of one hand*. New York: Basic, 1975.

HUXLEY, A. *The doors of perception*. New York: Harper & Row, 1954.

HUXLEY, A. *Literature and science*. New York: Harper & Row, 1963.

JACKSON, J. A conceptual and measurement model for norms and roles. *Pacific Sociological Review*, 1966, 9, 35-47.

JAMES, W. *Essays in radical empiricism and a pluralistic universe*. New York: Longmans Green, 1947.

JUNG, C. *Man and his symbols*. Garden City, N.Y.: Doubleday, 1964.

KELLY, G. *The psychology of personal constructs*. Vols. 1-2. New York: Norton, 1955.

KOCH, R. *The book of signs*. New York: Dover, 1955. Originally published in 1930.

KORZYBSKI, A. *Science and sanity*. Lancaster, Pa.: Science Press, 1933.

LEWIS, C.S. *Perelandra*. New York: Macmillan, 1968. Originally published in 1944.

LEWIS, C.S. *Surprised by joy*. New York: Harcourt, Brace & World, 1955.

LEWIS, D.K. *Convention: A philosophical study*. Cambridge, Mass.: Harvard University Press, 1969.

LINDSAY, D. *A voyage to Arcturus*. New York: Ballantine, 1968. Originally published in 1927.

LOVECRAFT, H.P. *At the mountains of madness*. New York: Ballantine, 1971. Originally published in 1934.

MATSON, F., & MONTAGU, A. *The human dialogue*. New York: Free Press, 1967.

MIURA, I., & SASAKI, R.F. *Zen dust: The history of the koan and koan study in rinzai Zen*. New York: Harcourt, Brace & World, 1966.

MORRISON, J.C. *Meaning and truth in Wittgenstein's 'Tractatus.'* The Hague: Mouton, 1968.

OTTO, R. *The idea of the holy*. London: Oxford University Press, 1957. Originally published in 1936.

PARRY, J. *The psychology of communication*. London: University of London Press, 1967.

PHILIPSEN, G. Speaking 'like a man' in Teamsterville: Culture patterns of role enactment in an urban neighborhood. *Quarterly Journal of Speech*, 1975, 61, 13-22.

RAPOPORT, A. *Operational philosophy: Integrating knowledge and action*. San Francisco: International Society for General Semantics, 1969. Originally published in 1953.

ROGERS, E., & SHOEMAKER, F. *Communication of innovations: A cross-cultural approach*. New York: Free Press, 1971.

SCHEIN, E., SCHNEIER, I., & BARKER, C. *Coercive persuasion: A socio-psychological analysis of the 'brainwashing' of American civilian prisoners by the Chinese communists*. New York: Norton, 1961.

SEARLE, J. *Speech acts: An essay in the philosophy of language*. Oxford: Oxford University Press, 1969.

SHANNON, C., & WEAVER, W. *The mathematical theory of communication*. Urbana: University of Illinois Press, 1949.

SHERIF, M. *The psychology of social norms*. New York: Harper, 1966. Originally published in 1936.

SLOBIN, D. *Psycholinguistics*. Glenview, Ill.: Scott, Foresman, 1971.

SONTAG, S. *Styles of radical will*. New York: Delta, 1969.

STAPLEDON, W.O. *Star maker*. London: Methuen, 1937.

STAPLEDON, W.O. *Philosophy and living*. Vol. 2. London: Hazell, Watson & Viney, 1939.

SUPPE, F. The search for philosophic understanding of scientific theories. In F. Suppe (Ed.), *The structure of scientific theories*. Urbana: University of Illinois Press, 1974, 125-220.

SWIFT, J. *Gulliver's travels*. New York: Oxford Press, 1933, Book II, Ch. 2.

TZU, L. *Tao te ching*. Gia-Fu Feng & Jane English (Trans.). New York: Vintage, 1972.

WENZEL, J.W. Rhetoric and anti-rhetoric in early American scientific societies. *Quarterly Journal of Speech*, 1974, 60, 328-336.

WISEMAN, G., & BARKER, L. *Speech/interpersonal communication* (2nd Ed.). New York: Chandler, 1974.

WITTGENSTEIN, L. *Tractatus logico-philosophicus*. London: Routledge & Kegan Paul, 1961. Originally published in 1921.

WITTGENSTEIN, L. *Philosophical investigations*. New York: Macmillan, 1968. Originally published in 1953.

INTERCULTURAL COMMUNICATION INDICATORS (A "LANGUETICS" MODEL)

V. LYNN TYLER
Brigham Young University

"Languetics" as a science deals with essential elements, considered according to pertinent cultural differences and similarities, which inhibit or enhance the desired results of intercultural communicative events. This paper reviews salient "intercultural communicative indicators" of meaning in messages which must cross cultural boundaries. It reviews the need to mark and take advantage of contexts, suggests a patterning of participant factors, and makes note of other aids which are necessary for perceiving or expressing that which might otherwise be a miscue or missed cue. "Intercultural grammars" are proposed as helps in bridging misunderstanding which could result from: (1) data which may be required for a message receiver but which are not apparently present in a source situation or expressed message; (2) data which are absent or ambiguous for either the message originator or receptor; (3) data which are implied but which must be made explicit for message perception; and/or (4) data which may need distinct treatment in new cultural frames of reference. This new science provides for a system to deal with all "differences which make a difference" in intercultural encounters with a purpose.

The following incidents have been repeated, sometimes with disastrous results, all over the world day after day, and in as many variations as there are people who are "different."

While visiting in the Middle East, an American was invited to dinner at the home of an Arabic friend. As he was leaving, he made a special effort to thank the host and hostess for their hospitality and generosity. But, as he spoke with them, he realized that his sincere compliments had somehow been misunderstood.

An American supervising a building project in the Orient was responsible for some of the errors that had been made on the job. He called a meeting to review some of the real problems. He also wanted to try to justify some of his actions. He sought to explain how anyone in his position could make similar mistakes and asked for understanding and forgiveness. He passed around written materials and asked for a written list of suggestions for follow up. He became uneasy when he sensed that something he was trying to communicate "just didn't fit."

The visiting professor felt that his international audience in a South Pacific colloquium was ably following his presentation. He had been cautioned about humor being difficult to transfer across cultural boundaries, but felt his gestures could be exaggerated to make up for differences—especially if he spoke slowly and distinctly. He later learned that almost everyone else was embarrassed by his remarks.

What happened? What false illusions of communication took place?

When language and cultures are somehow different, many people have learned to anticipate such experiences—to expect challenges to human understanding. Unfortunately, many people mistakenly assume that problems stem from language differences alone, and that they can easily be resolved through interpreters or with appropriate language training.

Actually, verbal communication comprises only a portion of a total message that is conveyed, fed back, and reacted to. In the cases reviewed above, English language could have been used, but not to deter misunderstanding. The situations described all give a broad spectrum of communicative indicators. Signals that are nonverbal (such as gestures, assumptions, and entire situations) often surround and greatly influence normal language expressions and perceptions.

To communicate effectively in or with varied cultural constraints, one must take into consideration many factors which have often been overlooked by people whose life experiences widely differ.

The intercultural communicator should consistently try to discover pertinent differences and similarities regarding expectations, assumptions, values, and behavior unique to different peoples. He should become familiar with factors and conditions which may either inhibit or enhance culturally loaded messages. He is most effective when using any cue to communicate which is affected by contextual and environmental factors influencing participants.

In every intercultural communication context, certain "gaps" must be bridged if communication is to reach its highest potential. Understanding and using *c*ulturally *h*idden *u*nits of *m*eaning (CHUMs) in effect bridge otherwise entrapping chasms of concern for those sending and receiving messages, as these are processed interculturally.

These hidden meanings may inhibit messages if they are in the form of *miscues* (which may be defined as communicative elements that are in some real way, even if assumed to be, offensive, provocative or intolerable), or *missed cues* (which are unclear, have varied meanings, are meaningless in certain contexts, or are simply "too different"). Miscues lead to miscommunication, while missed cues result in noncommunication.

CHUMs may also be manipulated to enhance communication if they are in the form of *cues* (perceivable CHUMs which can be learned and then appropriately used), or *clues* (less noticeable hints that can lead to increased understanding).

The term "languetics" has been coined recently to mark the study of verbal, nonverbal, paraverbal, and other indicators of language-based communication. Languetics refers to more than linguistics (the scientific study of verbal language, written or spoken), or communication (studies of modes and media—for focused purposes), or behavioral sciences (which study mental and physical behavior based on cultural or other influences), as these deal with communication systems and results. Languetics encompasses all *language markers* (or their notable absence) and their *cultural indicators*, or other influences on or from language—as these are significant in an intercultural setting.

"Intercultural grammars" are presently being developed to bridge "culture grammars" as these are identified in distinct populations. Each culture has the yet unwritten grammar which is composed of values, assumptions, perceptions of the world, sets of communicative expressions, and so forth. Intercultural grammars can provide the means of developing individual and holistic evaluative competence in communicating interculturally. It is then feasible to provide systems for teaching people to increase communication proficiency and performance. Until such a system is available to the intercultural communicator(s), undesired miscommunication or noncommunication is all the more likely to occur.

In order to develop intercultural grammars, a readily retrievable and practical system of data availability is essential for detecting and then effectively utilizing the pertinent required information. This must include:

1. Data required for the receptor (receiver) of the message, but which are not present in a source situation or message per se.
2. Data that are absent or ambiguous or otherwise unavailable for either the originator or receptor of the message.
3. Data that are implied but which must be made explicit in a new cultural context.
4. Data which are explicit but which may need distinct treatment because they may be offensive or otherwise potentially not acceptable in a new cultural perspective.

Already available are tools for the intercultural communicator, such as those developed (and developing) at the Brigham Young University Language and Intercultural Research Center: (1) InterCultureGrams, with references; (2) bridges of understanding: experiential learning aids. (people-specific); (3) intercultural guidelines (how-to's); (4) resource references to others doing similar work in a variety of methods. At the LIRC/BYU, other developments include: connotative lexicons, data bank systems, resource materials, and one-to-one counseling.

The Intercultural Communicative Indicators model (of languetics) now to be considered, is aimed at identifying and defining the basic and essential components and factors involved in intercultural communicative encounters. It is designed to provide working relationships involving all elements of understanding. The requirements for such a model have been well spelled out in Smith's report ''Research and Theory in Intercultural Communication''—prepared for the State of the Art Study of the Society of Intercultural Education, Training, and Research (1977).

THE MODEL

The need to expedite the improvement of communication between peoples of differing cultures is increasing faster than the actual improvement. This is particularly so among professionals: translators and interpreters, international businessmen, government employees, and others whose skills and knowledge place them in touch with people throughout the world.

Psychologists, anthropologists, sociologists, communication researchers, and linguists have suggested a wide variety of systems and models—attempting to explain and in some ways use the selected factors which must be considered when interacting with different peoples. (Most, if not all, recognize that the complexity between cultural differences is often greater within cultures. Both require consideration, and may equally fit in the ''languetics'' model design.)

As Hall points out in *Beyond Culture* (1977), models have been used for centuries to deal with the ''enormous complexity'' of life and its manifestations. Many models dealing with culture and communication are theoretically too abstract or incomplete, often leaving out factors which are as important as, if not more important than others considered. Hall maintains that what is often left out gives the very needed structure and form to the system! (Others included in the reference list which follows also make these points—some very culturally specific. See Fuglesang, 1973, for example.)

Also emphasized by Hall (1977) is the importance of ''looking at the way things are actually put together, [rather] than at theories.'' He cautions against overstated emphasis of ''the process of classification, and the decisions it involves, at the expense of the information about'' that being studied or used. Since classification actually makes it much more difficult to integrate the different components into a ''usable, intelligible pattern,'' what is needed is a new type of paradigm which shows significant relationships.

Each of the major factors of the Intercultural Communicative Indicators model of languetics, which follows, has been horizontally segmented into its several categorical components (each of which are potentially ad infinitum, though are finitely focused). However, on the model itself, the *interrelationships* should be emphasized and used in concert, as applicable. While the model illustrates some of the complexity of intercultural communication, it is also designed to demonstrate how a message changes as it goes from one cultural context into another, and returns—showing that these elements of change are not always related directly to language alone, but can usually be stated in language descriptions.

In languetics analysis, each factor and component can be demonstrated as influencing or being influenced by messages as these confront cultural barriers.

The *explicit* (surface or ''plain'') meaning of a message may be acceptably translated in many cases, but the cultural communicative mode, or context and environment of the message situation affect the *implicit* (deeper, usually hidden, except to culture-participants) meaning(s) of that message.

Intercultural communication includes much more than explicit definitions of ''culture,'' which may have already been delineated acceptably for many anthropologists, sociologists, linguists, and others. However, a thorough investigation is now required of those aspects of communication which affect how a person perceives ''the world,'' and which influences messages he or she expresses or perceives.

The Intercultural Communicative Indicators model of languetics serves as a framework into which relevant data can be organized and analyzed. In such a complex system, data will undoubtedly fit into several of the model categories.

It is intended that the model account for such overlap and interrelationships, and to make these manageable. It would be unrealistic to isolate all of the factors, components, and their configurations

FIGURE 1
Intercultural Communicative Indicators

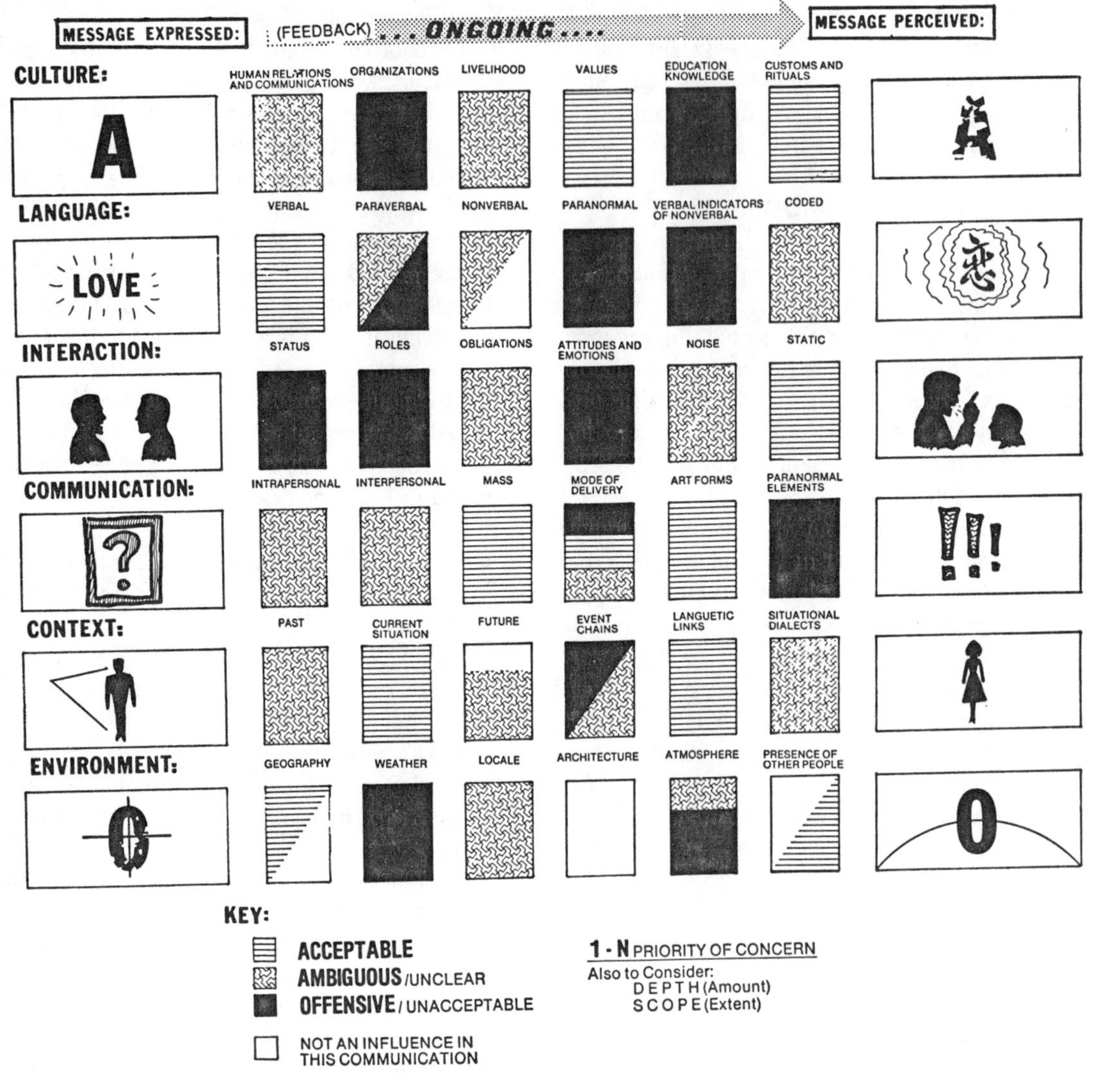

and permutations—as these would constitute the "whole" of any given set of intercultural communications (or, as currently denominated: "languemes").

The emphasis will be on reducing uncertainties, after a determination of the risk that is acceptable in terms of the expected benefits from componential intercultural communication analyses. Critical areas where differences in meaning and misunderstandings regularly occur, or where such have high impact somehow, will be surveyed and validated—so that in any intercultural communication that is replicatable, these areas might be taken into consideration for adjustments to be made. Error and miscommunication can then be avoided. Likewise, "what works best for whom" can be defined and replicated.

HOW THE MODEL CAN WORK

The attached demonstration model of Intercultural Communicative Indicators (or languetics) can be illustrated with an example from Fuglesang's (1973) text, *Applied Communication in Developing Countries*. Though somewhat exotic, its overstatement can serve to highlight at least several significant considerations.

Some sanitation experts went to a Zambian village to lecture on the harmful effects of the tsetse fly. The lecturers, from an English-speaking country, could not speak the native language of the villagers. Interpreters were used. Intending to make the presentation more visual and impressive, the lecturers brought a large model of the tsetse fly. They were using an instructional technique which their own culture allowed to be quite appropriate.

For the Zambian villagers, however, the use of a large-scale model was completely foreign to their culture, and the meaning of the message was unacceptable, or lost. The villagers' reaction was, "It may be true what you say about this . . . but it cannot concern us, because the flies are not so big in our place."

As Stewart suggests, "The Zambian villagers' mode of instruction and learning focuses on the perception of the physical world. They do not (so readily) respond to the abstract conceptualizations of the world suggested by this type of model, charts, and symbolization. One might say that they do not subscribe to the convention of pictorial representation found among Westerners. Because of this cultural difference, the message was very ambiguous, at best." Indeed, it was offensive to many!

Interpretation of the message from English into another language may have caused some real problems, since many scientific or technical terms used by the sanitation experts do not exist in that particular use of the Zambian language. The interpreters themselves may have been unfamiliar with the terms and approach used by the specialists, with the result that much of the message was either misinterpreted to their audience, or not interpreted at all. Again: offense possible.

Interactions seen in this situation are also influenced by status, roles, obligations, and attitudes—as perceived by both parties. The specialists, for example, may have considered themselves as "helpers, guiding lights" to this group of people. The villagers, on the other hand, may have seen the specialists as intruders. Misunderstanding should and could have been avoided if, for example, real effort had been made by the specialists to establish leading clues to effective communication with the respected people of the village.

The communication mode—a lecture with a sizeable model of the tsetse fly—was obviously ineffective in communicating the desired message. The specialists should have first learned what modes of communication could be most effective in this particular culture: dance, story-telling, and so forth.

The context of the messages refers to those significant elements of the past, current, and anticipated situations. The future results the experts anticipated did not coincide with the opinion the villagers held of other "specialists" who always seemed to come to patronizingly disrupt their calm atmosphere. Had the specialists made a meaningful attempt to understand this "past" context of the villagers, they could have more easily established communicative relations enabling their expectations.

The environment of this particular situation also created problems. The lecture was held in a tiny, stuffy village hut (at the insistence of the specialists), on a very warm day. Everyone was hot and extremely uncomfortable. That, among other considerations, was important to the message getting through.

Other components of the unsuccessful communication could be considered. But there is a point to be made. Fuglesang's (1973) plea is: "Beware of your own reaction to this story. If you find it intriguing, there is hope. But if you find it just [amusing] you had better get out of the communication business."

In many cases, the separate components (horizontally listed on the model) of the six major factors (vertically categorized) indicate by special marking when there was an acceptable cultural equivalent established. In each factorial category, at least one communicative component registered "ambiguous," or "offensive"—distorting the entire message. On the attached model, very general

TABLE 1
Representative and Sample Coding

I. CULTURE (SOME EXAMPLES)
- A. HUMAN RELATIONS AND COMMUNICATIONS
  - 1. AFFECTION
  - 2. BURIAL RITES/CONSTRAINTS
  - 3. DATING
  - 4. ELDERLY, CARE OF
  - 5. ENTRANCE RITES/CONSTRAINTS
  - 6. ETIQUETTE, NONVERBAL
  - 7. ETIQUETTE, VERBAL
  - 8. FRIENDLINESS
  - 9. GIFT EXCHANGE, SHARING
  - 10. GREETINGS
  - 11. MALE/FEMALE ROLES
  - 12. MARRIAGE RITES/CONSTRAINTS
  - 13. POLITICS
  - 14. SOCIAL GATHERINGS
- B. ORGANIZATIONS
  - 1. COMMUNITY SERVICE
  - 2. EDUCATIONAL SYSTEMS
  - 3. FAMILY UNIT
  - 4. GOVERNMENT, POLITICAL
  - 5. RELIGIOUS DENOMINATIONS
  - 6. SOCIAL CLASSES/INSTITUTIONS
- C. LIVELIHOOD
  - 1. MEALS AND DIET
  - 2. WORKING CONDITIONS/CONSTRAINTS
- D. VALUES
  - 1. COSMIC ORDER
  - 2. ECONOMIC CONSTRAINTS
  - 3. HUMAN NATURE (GOOD/EVIL)
  - 4. RELATIONSHIPS (SELF/OTHERS/AUTHORITY/NATURE)
  - 5. RELIGION
  - 6. STATE OF HAPPINESS/DISTRESS
  - 7. STATUS/SUCCESS
  - 8. VALUES AND IDEALS
- E. EDUCATION/KNOWLEDGE
  - 1. CHANGE/GROWTH
  - 2. CHILD-REARING
  - 3. GROUP VS. INDIVIDUAL IDENTITY
  - 4. SCHOOLING
- F. CUSTOMS AND RITUALS (Acceptable/Unacceptable ways of doing things)
  - 1. UNWRITTEN CODES
  - 2. WRITTEN CODES
- G. TIME
  - 1. CALENDAR, CLOCKS
  - 2. HABITS
  - 3. PUNCTUALITY
  - 4. SENSE
- H. SPACE AND MOVEMENT
  - 1. INTIMACY DIMENSIONS
  - 2. INTRUSION FACTORS
  - 3. MOBILITY
  - 4. SOCIAL DISTANCE
  - 5. TERRITORIAL MARKERS
- I. LEISURE/RECREATION
  - 1. GAMES, SPORTS
  - 2. HOLIDAYS AND CELEBRATIONS
  - 3. RELAXATION
  - 4. VALUES OF TIMES AND SPACE
- J. MATERIALITY
  - 1. COMMUNITY LIVING
  - 2. FASHION
  - 3. HOMES
  - 4. MODESTY
  - 5. PROPERTY:COMMUNITY
  - 6. PROPERTY:PRIVATE
  - 7. PROPERTY:UTILITARIAN
- K. SYMBOLS
  - 1. MOURNING
  - 2. RESPECT
  - 3. WEALTH
- L. HUMOR
  - 1. NEGATIVE
  - 2. NEUTRAL
  - 3. POSITIVE
- M. TYPES (HIGH VS. LOW CONTEXTS)
  - 1. IDEOLOGICAL
  - 2. "PRIMITIVE"
  - 3. TECHNOLOGICAL
  - 4. TRADITIONAL

II. LANGUAGE (REPRESENTATIVE)
- A. VERBAL
  - 1. SEMANTICS (DENOTATION, CONNOTATION)
  - 2. SOUNDS (PHONOLOGICAL)
    - a. Change
      - assimilation
      - consonantal sandhi
      - metathesis
    - b. Contraction
    - c. Exchange of Meaning--Puns
    - d. Repetition
      - alliteration
      - assonance
      - consonance
      - rhyme
      - rhythm
  - 3. SYNTAX AND DISCOURSE
    - a. Change in Meaning
      - allegory
      - antipersonification
      - colloquialism
      - comparison by implication
      - digression
      - double-meaning
      - enigma
      - fable
      - idiom
      - irony
      - metaphor
      - parable
      - personification
      - proverb
      - simile
      - slang
      - symbol
      - wise-folly
    - b. Change in Word Order
      - anastrophe
      - transposition
    - c. Expansion
      - description
      - enumeration
      - exaggeration
      - parenthetic remark
    - d. Omission
      - assumption
      - asyndeton
      - gapping
      - honorifics
      - insinuation
      - reasoning and logic
      - sudden silence
      - syllepsis
    - e. Repetition
      - chiasmus
      - correspondence
      - parallelism
      - redundancy
      - refrain
      - restatement
      - summarization
  - 4. WORDS
    - a. Combinations
    - b. Ellipsis
    - c. Exchange
      - antonomasia
      - euphemy
      - metonymy
      - permutation
      - synecdoche
    - d. Repetition
      - anaphora
      - cliches
      - double negative
      - duplication
      - word-folding
  - 5. OTHER COMPOSITE PATTERNS
    - a. Logic
    - b. Rhetoric
    - c. Stylistics
    - d. Other thought patterns
- B. PARAVERBAL
  - 1. ALLOPHONIC VARIATIONS
  - 2. ARTICULATION
  - 3. INTONATION PATTERNS
  - 4. JUNCTURE
  - 5. NONFLUENCES/GRUNTS
  - 6. PITCH
  - 7. RATE OF SPEECH
  - 8. SILENCE
  - 9. STRESS
  - 10. STYLE MARKERS
  - 11. VOICE QUALITY
    - a. Harsh
    - b. Nasal
    - c. Soft
    - d. Stuttering
    - e. Throaty
  - 12. VOLUME
- C. NONVERBAL
  - 1. VISUAL
    - a. BODY POSTURE
      - 1. Body Stiff and Straight
      - 2. Leaning Back
      - 3. Leaning Forward
      - 4. Legs Crossed
      - 5. Slouching
      - 6. Turning Away
    - b. COLORS
    - c. DANCE
    - d. FACIAL EXPRESSIONS
      - 1. Eyebrows
        - one raised
        - raised, arched in the middle
        - raised at the ends toward nose
      - 2. Eyes
        - looking down
        - looking straight ahead
        - looking to one side
        - winking
      - 3. Mouth and Lips
        - frown
        - lips tightly pressed
        - mouth wide open
        - pout
        - smile
        - sticking tongue out
        - yawning
    - e. GESTURES
      - 1. Arm(s)
        - drawing toward body
        - folding in front of chest
        - hands on hips
        - pushing away from body
        - raising right arm to square
        - rocking, folded
        - shrugging shoulders
        - waving, high in air
      - 2. Feet, Legs, Toes, etc.
      - 3. Finger(s)
        - crossing
        - fist clenched--thumb up
        - index finger circling ear
        - index, up
        - middle finger pointed out
        - pinching nose
        - scratching top of head
        - snapping
        - tapping side of head
        - thumb and index forming "O"
        - thumb pointing in one direction
      - 4. Hand(s)
        - clapping
        - clenching one or both fists
        - covering heart
        - crossed across chest
        - drawing across throat
        - hands covering ears or face
        - hitting throat or forehead
        - holding up--palm out
        - rapping knuckles on head
        - rubbing
      - 5. Head
        - chin
        - nodding up and down
        - shaking from side to side
        - tilting head back, down
      - 6. Shoulders and Torso
      - 7. Signing (Deaf, et al.)--"Total Communication"
    - f. OBJECTS
    - g. PICTURES
    - h. SIGN LANGUAGE
    - i. SIGNS
    - j. SYMBOLS

TABLE 1 (Cont.)

- 2. AUDITORY
  - a. BELCHING
  - b. BLOWING THROUGH FLAPPING LIPS
  - c. CLEARING ONE'S THROAT
  - d. CLICKING
  - e. COUGHING
  - f. DRUMS
  - g. DUCK CALL
  - h. GASPING
  - i. GRUNTS
  - j. HISSING
  - k. HUSHING
  - l. INTONATION PATTERNS NOT ACCOMPANIED WITH VERBAL
  - m. KISSING
  - n. MUSIC
  - o. NOISES
    - 1. Non-Human
    - 2. Vocalic
  - p. RHYTHM
  - q. SCREAMING
  - r. SHRILL WHISTLE
  - s. SIGHING
  - t. SIRENS
  - u. VOLUME
  - v. WHINING
  - w. WHISTLE
  - x. YAWNING
- 3. OLFACTORY
  - a. BABY SMELLS
  - b. BODY ODOR
  - c. BREATH ODOR
  - d. BURNT ODORS
  - e. CHEMICAL ODORS
  - f. DISINFECTANT
  - g. FLOWER SCENTS
  - h. FOOD ODORS
  - i. FRESH SMELLS
  - j. PERFUMES
  - k. ROOM ODORS
- 4. TACTILE
  - a. CARESSING
  - b. CLUTCHING TIGHTLY
  - c. EMBRACING
  - d. HITTING
  - e. KINESTHETIC
  - f. KISSING
  - g. PAIN
  - h. PINCHING
  - i. PLEASURE
  - j. PRESSURE
  - k. RUBBING
  - l. SLAPPING
  - m. SPANKING
  - n. TEMPERATURE
  - o. TICKLING
  - p. TOUCHING
- 5. GUSTATORY
  - a. AGREEABLE
  - b. BITTER
  - c. BLAND
  - d. DISAGREEABLE
  - e. FAMILIAR
  - f. HOT
  - g. SALTY
  - h. SOUR
  - i. STRANGE
  - j. SWEET
- 6. VESTIBULAR
  - a. BALANCE
- 7. SPACIAL
  - a. CLOSENESS
  - b. SEATING ARRANGEMENTS
- 8. TEMPORAL
  - a. FUTURE ORIENTED
  - b. LENGTH OF TARDINESS
  - c. MAKING MOST OF PRESENT
  - d. PAST ORIENTED
  - e. PUNCTUALITY
  - f. TARDINESS
- 9. CLOTHES TEXTURE
  - a. COURSE BURLAP
  - b. FURRY
  - c. HEAVY DENIM
  - d. LIGHT CHIFFON
  - e. SCRATCHY WOOL
  - f. SILKY
  - g. SOFT KNIT
  - h. THIN NYLON
- 10. CLOTHES, HAIR
  - a. CASUAL
  - b. CONSERVATIVE
  - c. EXTRAVAGANT
  - d. FEMININE
  - e. FESTIVE
  - f. FORMAL
  - g. INFORMAL
  - h. IMMODEST
  - i. MASCULINE
  - j. MOURNING
  - k. TAILORED
- 11. EVENTS, SITUATIONS, ETC.
- 12. EMOTION AND CHARACTER COMPOSITES
- 13. OTHER PATTERNS AND STYLES (E.G. MICRO-MOMENTARY)

D. PARANORMAL (see communication modes)
E. VERBAL INDICATORS OF NONVERBAL
F. CODED (filtered, spliced)

III. INTERACTION

- A. STATUS
  - 1. EQUAL
  - 2. PERCEIVED TRAITS
  - 3. UNEQUAL
- B. ROLES/RELATIONSHIPS
  - 1. CANDIDATE/VOTER
  - 2. CHAIRMAN/MEMBER
  - 3. CLERGYMAN/LAYMAN
  - 4. DOCTOR/PATIENT
  - 5. EMPLOYER/EMPLOYEE
  - 6. HUSBAND/WIFE
  - 7. INTERMEDIARIES
  - 8. MALE/FEMALE
  - 9. MEMBER/OUTSIDER
  - 10. OFFICER/ENLISTEE
  - 11. PARENT/CHILD
  - 12. PERFORMER/AUDIENCE
  - 13. RULER/SUBJECT
  - 14. SELLER/BUYER
  - 15. TEACHER/PARENT
  - 16. TEACHER/STUDENT
- C. OBLIGATIONS
  - 1. GREAT
  - 2. INDEPENDENCE
  - 3. NON-EXISTENT
  - 4. SLIGHT
- D. ATTITUDES AND EMOTIONS (EGS ONLY)
  - 1. ANNOYED
  - 2. COMPROMISING
  - 3. CONFUSING
  - 4. CONTROLLED
  - 5. COOPERATIVE
  - 6. DISGUSTED
  - 7. EMPATHY
  - 8. EXCITED
  - 9. FATALIST
  - 10. HOSTILE
  - 11. INSULTED
  - 12. LOVING
  - 13. SHOCK
  - 14. SYMPATHETIC
  - 15. THREATENED
- E. NOISE (NON-DISTRACTIVE)
- F. STATIC (INTERFERENCE)

IV. COMMUNICATION

- A. INTRAPERSONAL
  - 1. DREAMS
  - 2. FEELINGS
  - 3. PRAYER
  - 4. VISIONS
- B. INTERPERSONAL
  - 1. INTIMATE
  - 2. CONSULTATIVE
  - 3. SMALL GROUP
- C. MASS
  - 1. CEREMONY--RITUAL
  - 2. CONCERT
  - 3. CRUSADE
  - 4. DEMONSTRATION
  - 5. RALLY
  - 6. REVIVAL MEETING
  - 7. SPEECH
- D. MODE OF DELIVERY
  - 1. COMPUTER
  - 2. CORRESPONDENCE
  - 3. DISCUSSION GROUP
  - 4. DRUMS
  - 5. FILM, STILLS
  - 6. FLAGS
  - 7. LECTURE
  - 8. LIGHTS
  - 9. MOTIONS PICTURES
  - 10. PRINT
  - 11. RADIO
  - 12. RECORD
  - 13. SATELLITE
  - 14. SMOKE SIGNALS
  - 15. TAPE
  - 16. TELEGRAPH
  - 17. TELEPHONE
  - 18. TELETYPE
  - 19. TELEVISION
  - 20. VIDEOTAPE
- E. ART FORMS (AND COMBINATIONS)
  - 1. ARCHITECTURE
  - 2. DANCE
  - 3. DRAMA
  - 4. INTERIOR DESIGN
  - 5. LANDSCAPE
  - 6. LITERATURE
  - 7. MUSIC--INSTRUMENTAL
  - 8. MUSIC--VOCAL
  - 9. PAINTING
  - 10. PHOTOGRAPHS
  - 11. PICTURES
  - 12. SCULPTURE
- F. PARANORMAL ELEMENTS
  - 1. EXTRA-SENSORY PERCEPTION
    - a. Clairvoyance
    - b. Precognition
    - c. Postcognition
    - d. Telepathy
  - 2. ILLUSION
  - 3. INSPIRATION
  - 4. INTUITION
  - 5. MEDITATION
  - 6. PSI-KAPPA (MIND OVER MATTER)
  - 7. REVELATION

V. CONTEXT "SETTING" (REAL OR ASSUMED)

- A. PAST
  - 1. BACKGROUND
  - 2. EDUCATION
  - 3. EXPERIENCE
  - 4. MEMORIES
  - 5. TRAINING
- B. CURRENT SITUATION
  - 1. FEELINGS
  - 2. INSIGHT
  - 3. INTUITION
  - 4. PREDISPOSITIONS
  - 5. TALENTS
- C. FUTURE
  - 1. ANTICIPATIONS
  - 2. ANXIETIES
  - 3. ASSUMPTIONS
  - 4. EXPECTATIONS
  - 5. INTENTIONS
- D. EVENT CHAINS: (Composite of behavioral units of communicative situations.)
- E. LANGUETIC LINKS: (All verbal/non-verbal composites of meaningful interrelated expressions/perceptions essential to a message being understood.)
- F. SITUATIONAL DIALECTS: (Manner of speech used for specific circumstances.)

VI. ENVIRONMENT

- A. GEOGRAPHY
- B. WEATHER-CLIMATE
- C. LOCALE
- D. ARCHITECTURE
- E. ATMOSPHERE
- F. PRESENCE OF OTHER PEOPLE

representative illustrations are used to indicate varied types of application. (Numbers may be used to mark priorities to be rectified, and so forth. The depth and scope determinants would vary, of course, in each situation.)

Each of the components could be broken down into significant elements to be considered—as illustrated in the attached representative and sample coding lists. This makes possible the pinpointing of problems so that specific solutions can be dealt with. A simple formulation might be:

W W C	(*W* is *W*anted to be *C*ommunicated)
− w w c	(*w*hat *w*as (actually) *c*ommunicated)
Y C	[Equals=] (That *Y*et to be *C*ommunicated) (or apologized for, or somehow rectified!)

Obviously, every message includes some potential miscommunication in its own language and culture. The model is applicable intraculturally as well as interculturally, though it has been devised specifically for use with intercultural encounters of any type.

FUTURE IMPLICATIONS AND APPLICATIONS

The model can serve as a type of blueprint for interpersonal, mediated, and other forms of communication. It could also be developed (as indeed it is projected to be) for computer retrieval uses or other analytic paradigms with special applications. For any given intended, perceived, or analyzed message, the factors and components involved can be marked for expressing that message in a given cultural situation. This can be compared realistically with intentions, perceptions, and misperceptions noted in intercultural encounters, expressly marking feedback or other follow up considerations.

Where elements of the message are expressed and perceived equivalently, that part of the message can be shown to be "acceptable." (This can be very helpful in seeking replications of what works well.) Where communications are ambiguous or offensive, they can be appropriately noted. The significant differences between these can be marked and dealt with appropriately.

A point needs to be made that individual and group communications (such as in the media: film, illustrations, and so forth) can be analyzed componentially using the same format. Detail is not given here because this is an early look at uses of the model. Sufficient testing has been done, however, on a variety of communicative situations and modes, and others will be tested as the model is developed into a much broader model featuring significant components—with factors being refined as found to be expedient. The development of intercultural grammars with guidelines for their use also will focus on the solution of dilemmas that today are known but yet unsolved.

It is intended that all cultural data which are analyzed with interrelationships demonstrable through the use of the model eventually will be placed into computer formats so that anyone desiring to express to a person or group in a particular culture a specific message can retrieve pertinent data. What communication and interaction modes, environments, culture-language, and so forth, would be most effective in given situations can be marked. Precautionary measures can be noted for avoiding miscommunications and misinterpretations.

Currently, information is being gathered, correlated and validated in each of the areas noted on the model. That a computer-assisted data bank is needed is evident to anyone directly involved in any form of intercultural communication.

Although much, much work is still needed, many current projects and insights will open the doors to further research in the componentialized analysis of intercultural communication. Now that specific elements for data acquisition and sharing are better outlined and a system formulated for their use, there is a much better chance for understanding and more adequately using the interrelationships between peoples who want greater success in communication.

REFERENCES

ALLEN, V.F. Understanding the cultural context. *Modern Language Journal*, May 1969, 324-326.

BASS, B.M. The American advisor abroad. *The Journal of Applied Behavioral Science*, 1971, 7, 285-308.

BRISLIN, R.W. Comparative research methodology: Cross-cultural studies. *International Journal of Psychology*, 1976, 11, 215-229.

BRISLIN, R.W. *Translation: Applications and research*. New York: Gardner Press, 1976.

COLBY, B.N. Culture grammars. *Science*, 1975, 187, 913-919.

CONDON, J.C., & YOUSEF, F.S. *An introduction to intercultural communication*. Indianapolis: Bobbs-Merrill, 1975.

FARB, P. *Word play: What happens when people talk*. New York: Bantam, 1973.

FUGLESANG, A. *Applied communication in developing countries*. Sweden: Dag Hammarskjold Foundation, 1973.

GERBNER, G. The need for cultural indicators. *Audio-Visual Communication Review*, 1969, 17, 137-148.

HALL, E.T. *Beyond culture*. Garden City, N.Y.: Anchor, 1977.

HAVILAND, J.B. Folk systematics. *Science*, April 4, 1975.

HOLTON, G. On the role of themata in scientific thought. *Science*, 1975, 188, 328-334.

KAPLAN, R.B. *The anatomy of rhetoric: Prolegomena to a functional theory of rhetoric*. Philadelphia: The Center for Curriculum Development, 1972.

KOHLS, R.H. Communicating across cultures. Unpublished USIA presentation, 1976.

KOLERS, P.A. It loses something in the translation. *Psychology Today*, May 1969, 32-35.

LANGUAGE RESEARCH CENTER. *Guidelines and thesaurus for solving cross-cultural mis-cues and missed-cues*. Provo, Utah: Brigham Young University, 1976.

LANGUAGE RESEARCH CENTER. *Intercultural communicating*. Provo, Utah: Brigham Young University, 1976.

LONNER, W.J. The search for psychological universals. In H.C. Triandis (Ed.), *Handbook of Cross-Cultural Psychology*. In preparation for 1977 press date.

NEWMARK, P. Further propositions on translation: Part I. *The Incorporated Linguist*, 1974, 13.

NEWMARK, P. Further propositions on translation: Part II. *The Incorporated Linguist*, 1974, 13.

NIDA, E.A. *Componential analysis of meaning: An introduction to semantic structures*. The Hague: Moulton, 1975.

NIDA, E.A. *Exploring semantic structures*. Munich: Fink, 1975.

NIDA, E.A. Dynamic equivalence. Address to F.I.T. Congress, Montreal, May 1977.

NIDA, E.A., & TABER, C.R. *The theory and practice of translation*. Netherlands: Brill, 1974.

OLIVER, R.T. *Culture and communication: The problem of penetrating national and cultural boundaries*. Springfield, Ill.: Thomas, 1962.

OSGOOD, C.E., MAY, W.H., & MIRON, M.S. *Cross-cultural universals of affective meaning*. Champaign: University of Illinois Press, 1974.

POYATOS, F. Analysis of a culture through its culturemes: Theory and method. Unpublished manuscript. Brigham Young University, 1976.

POYATOS, F. *Man beyond words*. Oswego: New York SEC Monograph, 1976.

RICKS, D.A., FU, M.Y.C., & ARPAN, J.S. *International business blunders*. Columbus, Ohio: Grid, 1974.

SMITH, A.G. Research and theory in intercultural communication. Prepared for State of the Art Study of Intercultural Education, Training, and Research, March 15, 1977.

SMITH, A.G. The taxonomy of communication. In B. Ruben (Ed.), *Communication yearbook I*. New Brunswick, N.J.: Transaction-International Communication Association, 1977.

SZALAY, L.B. Adapting communication research to the needs of international and intercultural communication. *International and Intercultural Communication Annual*. Vol. 1, December 1974, 1-16.

TAYLOR, C.V. A schema for the contextual study of language. In *Linguistics*, Brigham Young University, n.d.

TRIANDIS, H.C. Subjective culture and interpersonal communication and action. *International and Intercultural Communication Annual*, 1974, 1, 17-23.

TYLER, V.L. Dimensions, perspectives, and resources of intercultural communication. *International and Intercultural Communication Annual*. 1974, 1, 65-74.

UNESCO. *DARE information management system*. Paris: UNESCO Press, 1975.

UNESCO. *Spines thesaurus: . . . policy-making, management and development*. Vols. 1-3. Paris: UNESCO Press, 1976.

POLITICAL COMMUNICATION

Theory and Research: An Overview
Selected Studies

POLITICAL COMMUNICATION THEORY AND RESEARCH: AN OVERVIEW 1976 - 1977[1]

KEITH R. SANDERS
Southern Illinois University-Carbondale

LYNDA LEE KAID
University of Oklahoma

The burden of this essay is to present the work of political communication scholars published, or otherwise made available, from spring, 1976 to early fall, 1977. It is written with the first overview in this series (Nimmo, 1977) as a point of departure and with the hope that it, and those to follow, will provide a brief intellectual history of the major theoretical and methodological themes and controversies which have preoccupied those who study the role of communication in the acquisition and distribution of power.

The studies reviewed here have been drawn principally from the fields of mass communication, speech communication, and political science. Also included are studies from psychology, and from the abundant popular literature on the topic. Responding to severe space limitations, we have chosen to emphasize the voluminous periodical literature rather than the scores of books published in 1976. These volumes will have been widely read and reviewed elsewhere by the time this essay is published. Books published in 1977, articles, and convention papers of quality, therefore, receive primary emphasis.

In order to make this essay as congruent as possible with its predecessor, we will examine literature relevant to: (1) political communicators, (2) political messages, (3) the media of political communication, (4) the political audience, and (5) methods in the study of political communication. Our intent is to provide description and synthesis, eschewing evaluation. Temptation, however, sometimes overcomes even the best of intentions.

POLITICAL COMMUNICATORS

The study of persons in positions of political power has, since the days of the Greeks, been a source of fascination to communication scholars. So much so, in fact, that Cronkhite (1975) has contended that far too much contemporary scholarship views human communication narrowly as a sequence of linear events set in motion by an establishment source for the sole purpose of achieving audience compliance. While this criticism may be more applicable to speech communication scholarship than to scholarship in mass communication and political science, it is, nevertheless, true that leaders—politicians (Barber, 1977; Chandler, 1976; Hess, 1976), institutional advocates (Bogart, 1976; Tunstall, 1977), managers (Agranoff, 1976), journalists (Filler, 1976), lobbyists (Bachrack, 1976), and opinion leaders—continue to attract much scholarly attention.

The objective and perceived attributes of sources and the manifest content of messages are seen by many as being critical variables in the explanation of changes in audience attitudes, values, and behavior. A study by Stimson (1976), however, examined levels of presidential approval, as measured by the classic Gallup question, from Truman's first term through Nixon's first term, and concluded that it was all a matter of *time*. Approval levels, he decided, reflect regular parabolic cycles among the "less well-informed" members of the public, leading to the conclusion that "presidential approval may be almost wholly independent of the President's behavior in office, a function largely of inevitable forces associated with time" (p. 1).

Upon first reading this report, we were inclined to wonder why Eisenhower's curve was so much less parabolic than others; why no data were presented to support the claim that the ill-informed were primarily responsible for cyclical indulations in presidential approval, a point later challengea by Prosser and Converse (1976-1977); and what contributes to high expectations and later cynicism, if it is not, in part, the behavior of presidential candidates during campaigns and their subsequent performance in office as reported by the mass media?

It is difficult for us to conceive a variable as apparently complicated as presidential popularity fluctuating, sometimes dramatically, in an informational vacuum. Cornwell (1976), arguing from empirical but nonquantitative data, also saw presidential popularity as a cyclical, largely parabolic, phenomenon exhibiting much the same behavior as Stimson observed. Cornwell, however, offered an explanation having little to do with time. The rate at which presidential popularity declines is, he said, a function of whether the president was elected or succeeded from the vice-presidency; the skill with which he deals with the press; and the extent to which he is willing to trade on his popularity for "partisan" causes.

Other challenges to the Stimson analysis can be found in the literature on the relationship between the press and the presidency. Considerable attention has been focused on the access which the president has to the media and to the potential power of this access in rallying favorable public opinion (Balutis, 1976; Grossman & Rourke, 1976; Herbers, 1976; Minow & Mitchell, 1976; Rutkus, 1976). Quantitative studies have tended to confirm the importance of press coverage. Haight and Brody (1977) developed a regression analysis in which they included as predictor variables previous levels of presidential popularity, a news discrepancy variable reflecting the ratio of good-to-bad news about the president, and the number of appearances of the president (Nixon) on the electronic media. The three variables accounted for 64% of the variance in presidential approval, with each variable contributing a significant amount of unique variance. Moreover, Singleton (1976) reported that positive coverage of the president on the network evening television news correlates significantly with presidential popularity levels. Taken together, these studies suggest that " 'time' is no more likely to *cause* presidential approval than to move the tides and the seasons" (Stimson, 1976, p. 7; italics are Stimson's), but that the content of time, as interpreted by the media, may hold part of the explanation for its fluctuations.

A second important controversy has to do with the question of whether the adversary model or the exchange model can best explain the relationship between public officials and the press (Miller, 1976). In a tightly argued essay, Grossman and Rourke (1976) faulted the adversary model, contending that it "provides no mechanism for understanding the enormous amount of cooperation and even collaboration that takes place in the interaction between the press . . . and the government" (p. 455). They proposed an exchange model which embodies "the notion that reporters and officials have reason and resources to trade with each other, and that this interdependence is the key to understanding their interaction" (p. 456).

The adversary model receives more popular attention and is often used to describe the government-press relationships from both sides. Diamond (1976) and Rosenbloom (1976) characterized the relationship as the constant struggle of candidate/official with the press. Reedy (1976) described President Johnson's attitude as being closer to that of an adversary than a partner. Johnson had poor relations with the press, said Reedy, because, contrary to the advice of his aides, he took a partisan view of the press, attempted to make reporters look bad, and tried to buy their souls with promises to "make great men" of them.

That Nixon adopted an adversarial stance toward the press is well known. Porter (1976) maintained that the Nixon administration actively sought to "intimidate, harass, regulate and in other ways damage the news media" (p. vii). But data presented by Blankenburg (1977) on network revenues, stock market levels, and other indicators disputed the view that the Nixon campaign against the media had a serious *economic* impact on the media. In any event, it is clear that although the exchange model may hold greater explanatory value, the adversary model remains predominant in the minds of academics and practitioners.

A long-standing argument over the determinants of political imagery has centered on whether images are "stimulus-determined," (Atkin & Heald, 1976; Baskin, 1976; Sanders & Pace, 1977) or "perceiver-determined" (Blumler, 1977). Nimmo and Savage (1976) found neither model to be sufficient, seeing images as "reciprocal relationships reflecting continuing exchanges between leaders and followers'' (p. 89). After considerable thought (Nimmo, 1974) and a series of empirical studies (Nimmo & Savage, 1976), Nimmo (1976) proposed a model of political image formation which involves an interaction between and among politicians, professional communicators, and political audiences. In a campaign context, the model asserts that political candidates possess certain objective characteristics which are, in turn, mediated by professional ''image-makers,'' such as campaign managers, reporters, and editors. The electorate develops an image of the candidates through an interaction between the information available to it and its projected needs. This model is a significant contribution in that it integrates under a single conceptual umbrella several competing explanations and suggests new relationships which the models it replaces could not investigate. (See Davis, Dyson, & Scioli, 1976, for another interactive approach to image formation and change.)

The ''opinion leader'' has also been traditionally viewed as a source of political messages, especially in the context of the ''two-step flow'' model, wherein elites are viewed as a distinctive part of the electorate with influence flowing from them to less active citizens (Garrison & Anderson, 1977; Mansfield & Borman, 1977; McCain & Wall, 1976; Wall & McCain, 1977). But Robinson (1976), while confirming that opinion leaders receive information from a variety of sources, questioned the validity of the two-step hypothesis in light of his findings that over one-half of a national sample neither gave nor received opinions. He also found that opinion-giving and opinion-receiving took place, to a large extent, among the same persons, and that the traditional hypothesis was accurate only in the context of the nuclear family. This study raised new questions about the adequacy of one of the most important notions to come out of *The People's Choice* (Lazarsfeld, Berelson, & Gaudet, 1944).

POLITICAL MESSAGES

The dispute over the validity of studies attempting to establish the ''direct effects'' of political messages remains a recurrent theme in the most recent literature. Despite the fact that it has been fashionable for some time to decry the usefulness of ''effects'' research, the majority of political communication research is, implicitly or explicitly, of this genre. While the assumptions, methods, and findings of the voting studies upon which the ''limited effects'' model was based have been questioned (Chisman, 1976), the death knell for direct effects research was sounded prematurely. Kraus and Davis (1976), while acknowledging many faults in the classic voting studies, reviewed evidence which supports the view that the mass media have important direct effects on political socialization and electoral behavior. Within the broad confines of the continuing controversy over the theoretical efficacy of direct effects research, we have chosen to review several studies which analyzed the content of political reportage, searched for political bias, and dealt with other topics of contemporary concern.

Any treatment of a political message appropriately begins with an examination of its content. Analyses of the content of nonpurposive messages, particularly in television news and newspapers, have shown that the media devote relatively little attention to the coverage of substantive policy issues in political campaigns. Graber (1976a, 1976b) has demonstrated that coverage of the 1968 and 1972 presidential campaigns by both newspapers and television was dominated by information about the candidate's personal qualities. Patterson and McClure (1976) have been particularly critical of television's coverage of the 1972 campaign. They found, as did Hofstetter (1976), that television news devotes an excessive amount of time to coverage of campaign ''hoopla,'' at the expense of issues. Similar findings have surfaced in more restricted studies of coverage of the 1976 presidential election in magazines and newspapers (Cigler & Bliss, 1977; Kay, 1977), in analysis of the content of the 1972 presidential convention coverage (Paletz & Elson, 1976), in a study of television coverage of the early 1976 presidential primaries (Robinson & McPherson, 1977), and in reports on the coverage of lower-level races in the press and on television (Carey, 1976; Kaid, 1976a; Leary, 1977; Windhauser, 1977). Buss and Hofstetter (1977) analyzed transcripts of television network news during the 1972 presidential campaign according to the logical styles used by the newscasters in presenting stories. They found similarity among the three networks and demonstrated that "cognitive maneuvers" were far more frequent that actual logical fallacies. (See Buss & Hofstetter, 1976, for an application of this approach to political advertising.)

An issue of paramount social concern in recent years has been the question of the existence, extent, and effect of political bias in media reporting (Rubin, 1977), but most studies have not shown the presence of substantial bias. For example, little unexplainable political imbalance has been found in newspaper coverage (Parsons, 1976; Windhauser, 1976; Windhauser, 1977). The most ambitious efforts to date to investigate political bias in electronic media in coverage are those of Hofstetter and his colleagues (Hofstetter, 1976; Hofstetter & Buss, 1976). They advocated moving from a language view of bias which may be value-based to a "selectivity" view, recognizing that the decision to select some news stories or details may be a result of structural constraints of a given medium as well as of any political bias. Applying content analysis methods to coverage of the 1972 campaign, Hofstetter (1976) uncovered no overwhelming evidence of political bias in newspapers or television but identified some indications of structural bias. Structural bias in television has been discussed in depth by Altheide (1976) in his participant/observer study of local and national news operations. He concluded that the "news perspective," derived from commercialism, ratings competition, and commitment to entertainment inevitably results in distortion of the news. Studies of content and potential bias of media coverage remain basically in the descriptive mode. Researchers have yet to link bias characteristics directly with audience effects.

Within the continuing controversy over direct effects research in general, some of the most interesting disputes revolve around the agenda-setting hypothesis. Unlike the general descriptive studies of bias, the agenda-setting model commendably attempts to link content with effects. It posits that the agenda reflected in the mass media become the agenda held by the public. Since the initial empirical test of this concept by McCombs and Shaw (1972) with undecided voters in Chapel Hill, North Carolina, a number of studies have investigated the concept, producing generally supportive results (McCombs, 1976).

Shaw and McCombs (1977) compiled a book which included much previously published and unpublished work on agenda setting. One of its several contributions was the discussion of some of the conditions which mediate the agenda-setting effect. Three of these conditions are: the need for orientation (Weaver, 1977), frequency of media exposure (D.L. Shaw & Clemmer, 1977), and amount of interpersonal communication (E.F. Shaw, 1977). There are undoubtedly other such conditions (Williams & Semlak, 1976), and as they are discovered, it is likely that the focus of agenda-setting research will shift from an excessive concern with message variables to a greater concern for source, channel, and, especially, receiver variables.

Recent studies have emphasized the need for a cautious interpretation of the power of the agenda-setting function. Meadow (1976b) found little support for the hypothesis in his attempt to correlate coverage of network television news and newspapers reporting with Gallup poll data. Neither Williams and Larsen (1976) in their study of agenda setting in a non-election context, nor Kaid, Hale, and Williams (1977) in their test of the agenda-setting influence of a specific political event, found supportive evidence.

In addition, several conceptual and methodological problems remain to be solved. Among them are: concern over the direction of causality (surely the agenda of the viewer/reader have some influence over media agenda); questions as to what constitutes a "significant" or "meaningful" correlation and as to which correlational statistic should be used (Murdock, 1975); and issue categories which are so broad that they are difficult to interpret. However, researchers seem to be aware of these and other difficulties, and are, for example, beginning to expand their conception of their dependent variable (Becker & McCombs, 1977; Benton & Frazer, 1976; McCombs & Weaver, 1977). The agenda-setting hypothesis remains one of the most heuristic ideas in the contemporary study of political communication, and is primarily responsible for the rediscovery of cognition as a dependent variable in political communication research.

Purposive Messages

During peak political campaign periods, a great many mass communication messages aimed at voters are purposive—intentionally persuasive. The analysis of these messages raises issues which go to the heart of the direct effects controversy and are basic to the study of political communication, for it is here that fears of demagoguery and propaganda wax strongest. Despite the potential importance of this area, relatively few efforts fall into it in the most current research, although some scholars continue to describe and analyze the practical techniques of preparing messages designed for image making (Nimmo, 1976), and practitioners reiterate their confidence in the direct effects of television advertising (Napolitan, 1976). Agranoff (1976) has written a text blending the empirical data on political behavior and communication with practical recommendations for running political campaigns.

Although a few scholars have analyzed the content characteristics of political advertising (Buss & Hofstetter, 1976; Kaid, 1976a; Patterson & McClure, 1976) or the impact of varying media (Cohen, 1976), most empirical research in this area has concentrated on measuring the effects of the advertising message on voter attitudes, cognitions, and behavior. Survey research on political advertising effects generally relies on voter recall of exposure and/or effects. For instance, Mendelsohn and O'Keefe (1976) found that one-fourth of the voters in the 1976 presidential campaign claimed that television ads influenced their vote selections. On the other hand, Patterson and McClure (1976) could isolate only a small percentage of voters who claimed political advertising as a reason for changing voting intentions or attitudes. In a study of multiple forms of political advertising in a 1972 state senate campaign, Kaid (1976a) found that political advertising variables did not make a strong unique contribution to voting behavior.

Survey researchers have been more successful in attributing increased voter knowledge of issues to political advertising exposure (Atkin & Heald, 1976; Patterson & McClure, 1976; Surlin & Gordon, 1977), but not in attributing increased positive evaluations of candidate image traits (Hale, Kaid, & Fahey, 1977; Patterson & McClure, 1976).

Advances have been made in another area which might be classified as purposive, although the message is generated by a presumably objective source. The first empirical tests of the impact of "instant analysis" commentaries by newscasters have recently been conducted. Commentaries shown after "The Selling of the Pentagon" documentary mitigated the effectiveness of the program's ability to change beliefs about the military (M.J. Robinson, 1976; M.J. Robinson, 1977). Kaid, Singleton, and Davis (1977) also found that affective evaluations of a political speaker were not significantly altered by the presence of a neutral, positive, or negative commentary by a newscaster, but the presence of a commentary tended to result in more recall of the content of the speech than did the speech alone.

Regens and Matthews (1977) found that subjects exposed to a presidential debate plus commentary did not rate the candidates differently from those exposed to the debate alone. So far, then, research seems to indicate little affective change as a result of instant analysis, but considerable possibility of cognitive effects. Davis, Kaid, and Singleton (in press) have provided further confirmation for cognitive effects with their exploration of commentary effects from an information-processing viewpoint, concluding that the type of commentary can affect the number and kinds of attributes and issues ascribed to a speaker.

Message Characteristics and Strategies

The traditional study of public speaking by political actors is concerned with analysis of rhetorical message characteristics and strategies (Black, 1976; Brock, 1977; Hayes, 1977; McKerrow, 1977; Whalen, 1976). Innovative variations on this theme produced analyses of political messages from a "costs" perspective (Alexander, 1976;

Maisel, 1976); a detailed yet imaginative content analysis of the debates between Giscard d'Estaing and Mitterrand (Cotteret, Emeri, Gerstle, and Moreau, 1976); an enlightening study of the rhetoric of "civil piety" in America (Hart, 1977), and the most comprehensive, and hopefully, the most heuristic single volume yet written on the importance, functions, effects, and situational implications of political linguistics (Graber, 1976c).

THE MEDIA OF POLITICAL COMMUNICATION

Harold Innis's (1950) contention that the nature of a society's communication systems determines its social and political structure is one of the strongest assertions ever made about the power of the mass media. This contention, and McLuhan's (1964) "probes," generated much scholarly and popular discussion, but they did not generate much systematic theorizing or basic research. Recent literature suggests that this is beginning to change. The deterministic, single variable model suggested by Innis and McLuhan is being rejected in favor of a multivariate, interactive perspective. Recent theorizing and research leads to the tentative conclusion that channel variables do not singularly account for much variance in audience responses, but that they do interact powerfully with source, message, situational, and receiver variables to help produce important changes.

Manheim's (1976) eloquent article contending that democracy may not be able to survive television is the most systematic reformulation of the arguments of Innis and McLuhan that we have read recently. At the crux of Manheim's case is the proposition that "not only is the political content of television generally uninvolving, but the medium itself, *in the structure of its interaction with the user*, requires a relatively low level of participation in the reception of information" (p. 87, italics added).

Most recently published studies do not support Manheim's position, but one study does adopt a similar attitude. Robinson and Zukin (1976) reported that heavy reliance on television during the 1968 campaigns correlated highly with political conservatism. But, do political conservatives watch more television or does television induce political conservatism? The authors suggested that either television coverage of politics or television programming in general "made viewers more anxious and more frustrated about the present state of politics. And those anxieties and frustrations played themselves out as an affinity for Wallace in 1968" (p. 82).

Most studies reported in the recent past support a more interactive perspective (Fulero & Fischoff, 1976; Worchel, Andreoli, & Eason, 1975). For example, Cohen (1976) found that, for Hebrew University students, whether candidates were presented on radio or television accounted for no significant variance in image. However, there was an interaction between channels and candidates.

An interesting channel question permeates the agenda-setting literature. Are newspapers or television the more influential agenda setter? Several studies have found television to be a less effective medium for issue transmission than newspapers (McCombs, 1977; Patterson & McClure, 1976; Tipton, Haney, & Baseheart, 1975; Williams & Larsen, 1976). Without the benefit of actual media content data, McCombs and Weaver (1977) and Weaver, Becker, and McCombs (1976) made similar claims for their study of the 1976 presidential election on the basis of the stability of issue correlations over time.

McCombs (1976, 1977) has given this question thoughtful attention. He argued that, on the basis of data from the 1972 presidential study in Charlotte, North Carolina, newspapers play the dominant role early in the campaign, but that television catches up and becomes predominant later in the campaign. Patterson and McClure (1976) argued, on the other hand, that television may be more effective than newspapers when it makes exciting and highly relevant visual presentations. This newspaper-versus-television dispute is not solely a channel question, since findings on the contingent conditions of agenda setting mentioned in the previous section indicate that receiver and message variables must be taken into account.

In a different context, Zukin (1977) found that partisan stability was apparently not affected by channel variables. In the 1976 election, however, Lucas and Adams (1977) found that media use patterns constituted the only important distinctions between decided and undecided voters. Sanders and Atwood (1977) reported that the channel through which self-confrontational information about the values of "freedom" and "equality" were presented made no difference in the amount of value change which occurred. Live, print, and televised presentation of self-confrontational stimuli all produced changes in the two values, which persisted over a period of six weeks. The much researched self-confrontational technique (Grube, Rankin, Greenstein, & Kearney, 1977; Rokeach, 1973) is apparently not "channel bound."

Influenced by the earlier work of Lang and Lang (1968), Kaid, Corgan, and Clampitt (1976) conducted a study of audience responses to a campaign speech by Gerald Ford. Those who attended the event recalled more issues, were better able to recall accurately the specific points made in the speech, and were more inclined to vote for the candidates endorsed by Ford than were those who were not present but received information about the event from the media. This study, although in some ways supportive of the view that the channel through which a message is received *can* make a difference, leads us to wonder whether the issue should be viewed solely in terms of channel variables or whether it should be viewed in terms of channel and "environmental" variables. Viewing the televised report of a political speech in the comfort of one's living room with one's immediate family is certainly different from attending a partisan political rally with its hoopla and frenzy. In addition, the type and level of the election campaign may interact with channel variables. Although the environmental and situational aspects of media attendance have, in the past, been much neglected, two studies reported in the past year are relevant.

Atwood and Sanders (1976) found that subjects reported different patterns of media use and credibility in primary, as opposed to general election environments. However, neither perceived media use, nor perceived media credibility correlated significantly in the primary or in the general election with voting preferences. This later finding and a previous study by Atwood and Sanders (1975) increase our skepticism about the relationship which DeVries and Tarrance (1972) assert between media use patterns and ticket-splitting. We found no statistically analyzed, quantitative evidence which supports the widely held belief that ticket splitting is, somehow, a function of perceived media use or perceived media credibility.

Situational influences seem also to have been at work in studies reported by O'Keefe, Mendelsohn, and Liu (1976), and Mendelsohn and O'Keefe (1976). Voters in Summit County, Ohio, reported differences in the sources of information they counted on in the presidential elections of 1972 and in the off-year elections of 1974. Evidence is mounting that voters change their informational preferences as circumstances change, and that those changes may be due to the amount and type of coverage. At any rate, it is risky to generalize about the influence and use of media from general presidential elections, where they have been most often investigated, to primary elections and elections at lower levels.

THE AUDIENCES OF POLITICAL COMMUNICATION

There is no theme in the wide range of topics drawing on the talents of political communication researchers that involves more productive controversy than does the ubiquitous dispute over the essential nature of the political audience. Traditionally (Doob, 1935), it was thought that influence passed from sources, through messages and channels to gullible, captive, atomistic publics willing to comply with even the most outrageous persuasive design. This viewpoint was submerged by the weight of empirical evidence generated by the "limited effects" position which saw audiences as exceedingly difficult to persuade, largely because of the operation of selective exposure, perception, and recall (Klapper, 1960). Recently, the uses and gratifications position (Blumler, 1977) asserted that individuals with compelling social and psychological needs dominate the communication process in their search for gratifications. Essentially the argument is waged between those who contend that sources, media, and messages *do things* to people and those who argue that *people do things with* sources, media, and messages. We have organized the following discussion around this controversy, as we examine research involving the Watergate scandal, the role of mass communication in political socialization, and other related topics.

Studies which examined the effects of Watergate on the political process are now beginning to appear regularly in published form (Becker, 1976; Becker & Towers, 1976; Besen & Mitchell, 1976; McLeod, Brown, & Becker, 1977; Soule & Marx, 1976; Stevenson & Laing, 1976; Tillinghast, 1976; Wilson & Williams, 1977). A thorough review of this interesting literature is well beyond the scope of this essay; however, one exchange does deserve special attention.

McLeod, Brown, Becker, and Ziemke (1977a) designed a study which could investigate the effects of the scandal and the uses made of the reportage of Watergate events. The study is unique in that it controls for pre-Watergate levels of several variables through the use of panel data and regression analysis. Although they found marked increases in anti-Nixon attitudes, the authors could find little evidence of change in more general orientations such as political efficacy and trust. Reading about the Watergate hearings and talking with others about them did, however, produce a number of significant relationships. The authors gathered and analyzed their data in a manner which allowed either the active or passive view of the Watergate audience to be confirmed.

Davis (1977) objected to the McLeod, et al. (1977a) study, characterizing it as "a sophisticated lineal descendant of *The People's Choice*" (p. 24). He proposed an alternative to such studies, which would involve the study of mass communication in situations wherein normal social processes had been disrupted. Only during periods when the normal functioning of social-structural variables are disrupted are we likely, he thinks, to find significant changes in behavior which can be attributed to the mass media. We agree with McLeod, et al. (1977b) that Davis's proposal for radical changes in the direction of political communication research is exciting, in spite of our concern that such an approach would preclude the proper investigation of the long term socializing influences of the mass media.

As Kraus and Davis (1976) observed, studies of the role of mass media in political socialization are recent. Most early studies in this rapidly evolving area omitted communication variables, especially mass communication variables, from consideration, and this is not surprising. If one assumes that the political audience is moved largely by a compelling desire to achieve psychological consonance, and that it is largely under the socializing influence of peers, family, and school, there is little room for a concern for mass communication variables. It is also true, incidentally, that most of the early studies also failed to shed much light on the role of interpersonal communication in socialization even though all of the forces they posited as being influential were presumably at work in informal, face-to-face settings. (See Atkin, 1976, for a review of socialization studies which include communication variables.)

Recent literature supports the notion that mass communication does play a role in political socialization. Rubin's (1976) study of seventh graders produced evidence of a significant relationship between television exposure levels and attitudes toward political objects and institutions. Atkin and Gantz (1977) reported a positive relationship between television viewing and levels of political information among children. Adoni (1977) reported a positive relationship between exposure to a daily newspaper, and information preference and importance attached to political and civic activities among high school students in Israel; and Woelfel (1977) found high path coefficients between political information and frequency of interpersonal discussion about politics, and the number of sources children and adolescents consult on political topics. (See also Meadow, 1976a; Tan & Vaughn, 1976; and White, 1976, for other perspectives on the role of communication in political socialization.)

The development of political attitudes and cognitions in adults also appears to be related to communication behavior. That there is a positive relationship between reported public affairs exposure and levels of political knowledge has been documented in diverse settings in the United States and abroad (Atkin, Galloway, & Nayman, 1976; Barbic, 1976; Feigert, 1976; Hofstetter, Zukin, & Buss, 1976; M.J. Robinson, 1976; Wimmer, 1976).

Conventional wisdom was under attack on several fronts in the literature of the past year, but nowhere did it suffer a more lethal blow than in two studies reassessing levels of political knowledge and sophistication in underdeveloped countries. It is widely assumed that the electorate in these countries possesses little political knowledge and is largely ignorant of political processes, national leadership, and political organizations. This notion was strongly contradicted by data generated by Hayward (1976) in Ghana. His survey data revealed that his respondents' knowledge of political parties, political leaders, national boundaries, and so forth, was high, and in some cases higher than in the United States. Hayward speculated that Ghanaians find politics more salient than do most Westerners, that they have not yet been saturated with information, and that any absence of variety may enhance the effectiveness of the information that is available.

A study reported by Barkan (1976) supported the findings of Hayward and added that peasants in Kenya in a 1974 election had a well-defined conception of the roles their political leaders should play, that these conceptions were the basis for evaluations of the candidates, and for their voting decisions. It is apparently necessary to revise conventional wisdom regarding the sophistication and information-seeking activities of the electorate in underdeveloped countries, and to rethink the notion that there is an immutable, positive relationship between the amount of political information available and levels of political knowledge.

The period under review here also witnessed the publication of several historical and conceptual analyses of much merit, all reflecting a different view of the body politic. They include Roelof's (1976) pessimistic "critique of a national political mind" in which he examines the role of ideology and myth in the political system; Combs's and Mansfield's (1976) collection of essays reflecting, comprehensively, a dramaturgical approach to political communication studies; Goodwyn's (1976) history of the populist "moment" in America; Witcover's (1977) detailed recounting of the presidential campaign in America; Chesebro's (1976) persuasive argument that all communication is political; Farrell's (1976) invitation to apply a system's perspective to the investigation and "praxis" of political communication, and Martin's (1976) thoughtful review and critique of mass communication theory as it applies to political campaigns. Thus, we conclude this discussion of the political audience with one of the most interesting conceptual disagreements we have recently encountered.

Swanson (1977a, 1977b) is one of the most persistent American critics of the highly heuristic uses and gratifications approach. (For recent confirmation of his model, see O'Keefe, Mendelsohn, & Liu, 1976; Mendelsohn & O'Keefe, 1976; and Lometti, Reeves, & Bybee, 1977.) He has argued that there are four conceptual problems which must be solved before the approach can achieve the ends which its advocates envision. They are: (1) a vague conceptual framework in confusion over whether the rationale is or is not functionalism revisited; (2) a lack of precision in the definitions of major concepts and terms; (3) a confused explanatory apparatus; (4) an ironic failure to view perception as an active process. The latter problem seems especially serious since the active audience construct is the most exciting aspect of the uses and gratifications rationale.

The cause of these difficulties, said Swanson (1977a), is that uses and gratifications research has utilized the variable analytic approach—a model which can document new relationships but which cannot be much concerned with systematic theory building. He also argued that the variable analytic approach is inherently incapable of investigating the receiver as an active agent.

Blumler (1977) responded to these and other criticisms of the uses and gratifications rationale by insisting that researchers in the effects tradition were not forced into a single set of theoretical commitments, and that uses and gratifications research is and ought to be multitheoretical. There is not a single theory, but many theories, all sharing a common field of concern, and a basic set of concepts. Blumler reviewed the range of meanings which have been attached to the active audience concept and suggested that these meanings need to be sorted out and operationalized in an effort to determine under what circumstances, if any, each applies.

Blumler's recent research suggests that audience orientations to the mass media fall into three categories: (1) a cognitive or information seeking orientation; (2) a search for diversion; and (3) a separate personal identity orientation in which messages are used to give salience to aspects of an audience member's life. He offered a series of hypotheses which assert a relationship between these orientations and media effects.

We would not attempt here to mediate this provocative exchange, except to say that it has reminded us of a truism often ignored. Conceptual analysis and criticism of the sort reflected in this controversy is an enterprise in which all of us must engage.

METHODS IN THE STUDY OF POLITICAL COMMUNICATION

The methods used by political communication researchers during the year past reflect the diversity of their backgrounds and the richness of their subject matter. Some new initiatives were made, some old techniques were improved upon, and survey research received critical attention.

Gouran (1977) wrote a convincing rationale for an application of the theory and method of group dynamics to the study of political decision making, and demonstrated their explanatory efficacy in a study (Gouran, 1976) of the dynamics of the Watergate cover-up. Kirkpatrick, Davis, and Robertson (1976) also profitably studied political decision making in small groups.

More researchers used panel designs instead of "one shot" surveys, which were the staple of the field for some time. The use by McLeod, et al. (1977a) of regression analysis and a panel design was innovative, in that it increased the strength of causal inferences which could be drawn from their data. Path analysis is growing in popularity and although it has been profitably applied (Kimsey, 1977), it is the best example of "law of the instrument" in the field. The technique's potential is, at the moment, ahead of the field's ability to use it. Multidimensional scaling continues to hold much promise (Barnett, Serota, & Taylor, 1976; Serota, Cody, Barnett, & Taylor, 1977), and may, if it can be applied across diverse populations, become a popular and productive tool. The usefulness of respondent participation in the creation of measuring instruments and the value of open-ended questions was again demonstrated by Stevenson and Laing (1976).

Hofstetter (1976) applied content analytic techniques and made a contribution, especially in his operationalization of the notion of "structural bias" in the media. Again, however, the visual aspects of television and film have escaped careful notice. Hart (1976) constructed, via computer assisted content analysis, an interesting "linguistic map" of the public discourse of Richard Nixon.

There were few examples over the past year of studies which utilized intensive analytic procedures, although they have clearly advanced our knowledge of how individuals form and maintain political images (Nimmo & Savage, 1976; Brown, 1976; Brown, 1977). The success which has accompanied the use of such procedures is a reminder of the limitations of aggregate data analysis. Surely, there is as much to learn from observing individuals, per se, as there is to learn from observing groups. With renewed theoretical interest in the "active" audience, and the increasing influence of humanistic psychology, we anticipate an increase in the utilization of intensive techniques.

Finally, large sample survey research was subjected to several critical reviews this past year. Vatz (1976) wondered whether public opinion is actually there to be measured, and Weiner (1976-1977) contended that "the highly competitive environment for British political polls created strong pressures for them and their consumers to derive certainty and significance from ambiguous information" (p. 673). However, the most ambitious critique came from Wheeler (1976), who reported that he once saw an interviewer walk past a house because a German shepherd was sitting on the porch. Wheeler went on to make more penetrating observations about the uses and abuses of polling as referenda.

CONCLUSION

The literature under review here exhibits several deficiencies. Rhetorical and media critics are far ahead of their empirically-oriented counterparts in recognizing the political importance of film and "prime-time" television. Relatively few theorists and researchers have taken up the challenge implicit in the assertion that *all* communication is political, and, that instead of investigating the role of communication in politics, researchers should be investigating the role of politics in communication. The law of the instrument remains unrepealed, with some researchers thinking in terms of numbers instead of ideas. There also remains a considerable lack of knowledge on the part of some researchers of related research in other disciplines.

There are, however, a number of encouraging trends. The source-message dominated view of communication is rapidly giving way to a multivariate, interactive perspective in movement toward a process orientation. Univariate and bivariate models are under great conceptual pressure as is the conventional wisdom underlying the two-step flow model, the assumed relationship between mass media exposure and ticket splitting, and the imperialistic view of levels of political intelligence and sophistication in the third world. New independent, dependent, and intervening variables are being conceptualized, and channel variables are beginning to acquire theoretically interesting dimensions. Although still present, disciplinary chauvinism is on the decline. Most researchers are more interested in explaining the phenomena they study than they are in conforming to the conventions of their disciplinary habitat. Thus, the one inescapable conclusion which can be drawn from this review is that political communication is clearly emerging as a distinguishable, provocative field of inquiry.

NOTE

1. The authors wish to express their appreciation to John J. Chalfa, Jr., and Jim Fahey for their bibliographic contributions to this essay.

REFERENCES

ADONI, H. The functions of the mass media in the political socialization of adolescents. Paper presented at the annual meeting of the International Communication Association, Berlin, 1977.

AGRANOFF, R. *The management of election campaigns*. Boston: Holbrook, 1976.

ALEXANDER, H.E. *Campaign money: Reform and reality in the states*. New York: Free Press, 1976.

ALTHEIDE, D.L. *Creating reality: How TV news distorts events*. Beverly Hills, Cal.: Sage, 1976.

ATKIN, C. Communication and political socialization. *Political Communication Review*, 1976, 1, 2-6.

ATKIN, C., GALLOWAY, J., & NAYMAN, O.B. News media exposure, political knowledge and campaign interest. *Journalism Quarterly*, 1976, 53, 231-237.

ATKIN, C., & GANTZ, W. Political socialization effect of television. Paper presented at the annual meeting of the American Association for Public Opinion Research, Buck Hill Falls, Pennsylvania, 1977.

ATKIN, C., & HEALD, G. Effects of political advertising. *Public Opinion Quarterly*, 1976, 40, 216-228.

ATWOOD, L.E., & SANDERS, K.R. Perception of information sources and likelihood of split ticket voting. *Journalism Quarterly*, 1975, 52, 421-428.

ATWOOD, L.E., & SANDERS, K.R. Information sources and voting in a primary and general election. *Journal of Broadcasting*, 1976, 20, 291-302.

BACHRACK, S.D. *The committee of one million: "China lobby" politics, 1953-1971*. New York: Columbia University Press, 1976.

BALUTIS, A. Congress, the president and the press. *Journalism Quarterly*, 1976, 53, 509-515.

BARBER, J.D. *The presidential character: Predicting performance in the White House*. Englewood Cliffs, N.J.: Prentice-Hall, 1977.

BARBIC, A. Participation or escape? *Journal of Communication*, 1976, 26, 36-42.

BARKAN, J.D. Comment: Further reassessment of "conventional wisdom": Political knowledge and voting behavior in Kenya. *American Political Science Review*, 1976, 70, 452-455.

BARNETT, G.A., SEROTA, K.B., & TAYLOR, J.A. Campaign communication and attitude change: A multidimensional analysis. *Human Communication Research*, 1976, 2, 227-244.

BASKIN, O. Effects of televised political advertisements on candidate image. Paper presented at the annual meeting of the International Communication Association, Portland, Ore., 1976.

BECKER, L.B. Two tests of media gratifications: Watergate and the 1974 election. *Journalism Quarterly*, 1976, 53, 28-33.

BECKER, L.B., & McCOMBS, M. U.S. primary politics and public opinion: The role of the press in determining voter reactions. Paper presented at the annual meeting of the International Communication Association, Berlin, 1977.

BECKER, L.B., & TOWERS, W.M. Attitudes vs. cognitions: Explaining long-term Watergate effects. Paper presented at the annual meeting of the International Communication Association, Portland, Ore., 1976.

BENTON, M., & FRAZER, J.P. The agenda-setting function of the mass media at three levels of "information holding." *Communication Research*, 1976, 3, 261-274.

BESEN, S.M., & MITCHELL, B.M. Watergate and television: An economic analysis. *Communication Research*, 1976, 3, 243-260.

BLACK, E. *Southern governors and civil rights: Racial segregation as a campaign issue in the second reconstruction.* Cambridge, Mass.: Harvard University Press, 1976.

BLANKENBURG, W.B. Nixon vs. the networks: Madison Avenue and Wall Street. *Journal of Broadcasting*, 1977, 21, 163-175.

BLUMLER, J.G. The role of theory in uses and gratifications research. Paper presented at the annual meeting of the International Communication Association, Berlin, 1977.

BOGART, L. *Premises for propaganda: The United States Information Agency's operating assumptions in the Cold War*. New York: Free Press, 1976.

BROCK, B.L. A dramatistic film strip model for the study of political campaigns and social movements. Paper presented at the annual meeting of the Central States Speech Association, Detroit, 1977.

BROWN, S.R. Observational standpoints in the study of political communication. Paper presented at the annual meeting of the International Communication Association, Portland, Ore., 1976.

BROWN, S.R. Political literature and the response of the reader: Experimental studies of interpretation, imagery and criticism. *American Political Science Review*, 1977, 71, 567-584.

BUSS, T.F., & HOFSTETTER, C.R. An analysis of the logic of televised campaign advertisements: The 1972 presidential campaign. *Communication Research*, 1976, 3, 367-392.

BUSS, T., & HOFSTETTER, C.R. The logic of televised news coverage of political campaign information. *Journalism Quarterly*, 1977, 54, 341-349.

CAREY, J. How media shape campaigns. *Journal of Communication*, 1976, 26, 50-57.

CHANDLER, D.L. *The natural superiority of southern politicians: A revisionist history*. Garden City, N.Y.: Doubleday, 1977.

CHESEBRO, J.W. Political communication. *Quarterly Journal of Speech*, 1976, 62, 289-300.

CHISMAN, F.P. *Attitude psychology and the study of public opinion*. University Park: Pennsylvania State University Press, 1976.

CIGLER, A.J., & BLISS, W. Setting the agenda of the campaign: Periodical coverage of the 1976 Democratic nomination process. Paper presented at the annual meeting of the Southwest Political Science Association, Dallas, 1977.

COHEN, A.A. Radio vs. TV: The effect of the medium. *Journal of Communication*, 1976, 26, 29-35.

COMBS, J.E., & MANSFIELD, M.W. *Drama in life: The uses of communication in society*. New York: Hastings House, 1976.

CORNWELL, E.E., JR. The president and the press: Phases in the relationship. *Annals of the American Academy of Political and Social Science*, 1976, 427, 53-64.

COTTERET, J.M., EMERI, C., GERSTLE, J., & MOREAU, R. *Giscard d'Estaing and Mitterrand: 54774 mots pour convanincre*. Paris: Presses Universitares de France, 1976.

CRAGAN, J.F., & SHIELDS, D.C. Foreign policy communication dramas: How mediated rhetoric played in Peoria in campaign '76. Paper presented at the annual meeting of the Central States Speech Association, Detroit, 1977.

CRONKHITE, G. Persuasion: Parochialism or process. *Quarterly Journal of Speech*, 1975, 6, 101-104.

DAVIS, D.K. Assessing the role of mass communication in the social processes: A comment on "Decline and Fall at the White House." *Communication Research*, 1977, 4, 23-24.

DAVIS, D.K., KRAUS, S., & LEE, J. Opinion formation process during the resignation and pardon of Richard Nixon: A pilot study of critical events analysis. Paper presented at the annual meeting of the World Association for Public Opinion Research, Montreux, Switzerland, 1975.

DAVIS, D., DYSON, J.W., & SCIOLI, F.P. Messages, conceptual rules and information search in candidate image formation. Paper presented at the annual meeting of the Southwest Political Science Association, Dallas, 1976.

DAVIS, D., KAID, L.L., & SINGLETON, D.L. Information effects of political commentary. *Experimental Study of Politics*, in press.

DeVRIES, W., & TARRANCE, L. *The ticket splitter: A new force in American politics*. Grand Rapids, Mich.: Eerdmans, 1972.

DIAMOND, E. The new campaign journalism. *Columbia Journalism Review*, March-April 1976, 14, 11-14.

DOOB, L.W. *Propaganda, its psychology and technique*. New York: Holt, Rinehart & Winston, 1935.

FARRELL, T.B. Political communication: Its investigation and praxis. *Western Speech Communication*, 1976, 40, 91-103.

FEIGERT, F.B. Political competence and mass media use. *Public Opinion Quarterly*, 1976, 40, 234-238.

FILLER, L. *The muckrakers*. University Park: Pennsylvania State University Press, 1976.

FULERO, S.M., & FISCHOFF, B. Differential media evaluation and satisfaction with election results. *Communication Research*, 1976, 3, 22-36.

GARRISON, J.P., & ANDERSON, P. Media consumption and population characteristics of political opinion leaders. Paper presented at the annual meeting of the International Communication Association, Berlin, 1977.

GOODWYN, L. *Democratic promise: The populist moment in America*. New York: Oxford University Press, 1976.

GOURAN, D.S. Small group research and the demystification of the political process. *Political Communication Review*, 1977, 2, 1-5.

GOURAN, D.S. The Watergate cover-up: Its dynamics and its implications. *Communication Monographs*, 1976, 43, 176-186.

GRABER, D. Effect of incumbency on coverage patterns in the 1972 presidential campaign. *Journalism Quarterly*, 1976a, 53, 499-508.

GRABER, D. Press and TV as opinion resources in presidential campaigns. *Public Opinion Quarterly*, 1976b, 40, 285-303.

GRABER, D. *Verbal behavior and politics*. Urbana: University of Illinois Press, 1976c.

GROSSMAN, M.B., & ROURKE, F.E. The media and the

presidency: An exchange analysis. *Political Science Quarterly*, 1976, 91, 455-470.

GRUBE, J.W., RANKIN, W.L., GREENSTEIN, T.N., & KEARNEY, K.A. Behavior change following self-confrontation: A test of the value mediation hypothesis. *Journal of Personality and Social Psychology*, 1977, 35, 212-216.

HAIGHT, T.R., & BRODY, R.A. The mass media and presidential popularity: Presidential broadcasting and news in the Nixon administration. *Communication Research*, 1977, 4, 41-60.

HALE, K.D., KAID, L.L., & FAHEY, J. Measuring the impact of a televised political program: Combining three research perspectives. Paper presented at the annual meeting of the Speech Communication Association, Washington, D.C., 1977.

HART, R.P. Absolutism and situation: Prolegomena to a rhetorical biography of Richard M. Nixon. *Communication Monographs*, 1976, 43, 204-228.

HART, R.P. *The political pulpit*. West Lafayette, Ind.: Purdue University Press, 1977.

HAYES, J.T. Ronald Reagan's address to the 1976 Republican national convention: A case study in generic and biographic rhetorical criticism. Paper presented at the annual meeting of the Central States Speech Association, Detroit, 1977.

HAYWARD, F.M. A reassessment of conventional wisdom about the informed public: National political information in Ghana. *American Political Science Review*, 1976, 70, 433-451.

HERBERS, J. *No thank you, Mr. President*. New York: Norton, 1976.

HESS, S. *Organizing the presidency*. Washington, D.C.: The Brookings Institution, 1976.

HOFSTETTER, C.R. *Bias in the News*. Columbus: Ohio State University Press, 1976.

HOFSTETTER, C.R., & BUSS, T. Some concerns in evaluating news coverage: The case of biased reporting of political events. Paper presented at the annual meeting of the International Communication Association, Portland, Ore., 1976.

HOFSTETTER, C.R., ZUKIN, C., & BUSS, T.F. Political imagery in an age of television: The 1972 campaign. Paper presented at the annual meeting of the American Political Science Association, Chicago, 1976.

INNIS, H.A. *Empire and Communication*. London: Claredon Press, 1950.

KAID, L.L. Measures of political advertising. *Journal of Advertising Research*, October 1976a, 16, 49-53.

KAID, L.L. Newspaper treatment of a candidate's news releases. *Journalism Quarterly*, 1976b, 53, 135-37.

KAID, L.L., CORGAN, C., & CLAMPITT, P. Perceptions of a political campaign event: Media vs. personal viewing. *Journal of Broadcasting*, 1976, 20, 303-312.

KAID, L.L., HALE, K., & WILLIAMS, J.A. Media agenda setting of a specific political event. *Journalism Quarterly*, 1977, 54, 584-587.

KAID, L.L., SINGLETON, D., & DAVIS, D. Instant analysis of televised political addresses: The speaker vs. the commentator. In B. Ruben (Ed.), *Communication yearbook I*, New Brunswick, N.J.: Transaction-International Communication Association, 1977, 453-464.

KAY, J. Agenda setting applied to Detroit news coverage of the 1976 Ford-Carter campaign. *Michigan Speech Association Journal*, 1977, 12, 47-56.

KIMSEY, W. A path analysis of attitudes and cognitions in the 1976 presidential campaign. Unpublished doctoral dissertation, Southern Illinois University, 1977.

KIRKPATRICK, S.A., DAVIS, D.F., & ROBERTSON, R.D. The process of political decision-making in groups: Search behavior and choice shifts. *American Behavioral Scientist*, 1976, 20, 33-64.

KLAPPER, J.T. *The effects of mass communication*. Glencoe: Free Press, 1960.

KRAUS, S., & DAVIS, D.K. *The effects of mass communication on political behavior*. University Park: Pennsylvania State University Press, 1976.

LANG, K., & LANG, G.E. *Politics and television*. Chicago: Quadrangle, 1968.

LAZARSFELD, P.F., BERELSON, G., & GAUDET, H. *The people's choice*. New York: Duell, Sloan & Pearce, 1944.

LEARY, M.E. *Phantom politics: Campaigning in California*. Washington, D.C.: Public Affairs Press, 1977.

LOMETTI, G.E., REEVES, G., & BYBEE, C.R. Investigating the assumptions of uses and gratifications research. *Communication Research*, 1977, 4, 321-338.

LUCAS, W.A., & ADAMS, W.C. The undecided voter and political communication in the 1976 presidential election. Paper presented at the annual meeting of the Southwest Political Science Association, Dallas, 1977.

MACALUSO, T.F. Political information, party identification and voting defection. *Public Opinion Quarterly*, 1977, 41, 255-60.

MAISEL, L. (Ed.). *Changing campaign techniques: Elections and values in contemporary democracies*. Beverly Hills, Cal.: Sage, 1976.

MANHEIM, J.B. Can democracy survive television? *Journal of Communication*, 1976, 26, 84-90.

MANSFIELD, M.W., & BORMAN, J.C. Identifying belief structures of leaders and the public: An application of Q methodology. Paper presented at the annual meeting of the International Communication Association, Berlin, 1977.

MARTIN, L.J. Recent theory on mass media potential in political campaigns. *Annals of the American Academy of Political and Social Science*, 1976, 427, 125-133.

McCAIN, T.A., & WALL, V.D., JR. River Ridge III: The campaign that failed. *Human Communication Research*, 1976, 2, 245-254.

McCLURE, R.D., & PATTERSON, T.E. Print vs. network news. *Journal of Communication*, 1976, 26, 23-28.

McCOMBS, M.E. Agenda setting research: A bibliographic essay. *Political Communication Review*, 1976, 1, 1-7.

McCOMBS, M.E. Newspapers versus television: Mass communication effects across time. In D.L. Shaw and M.E. McCombs (Eds.), *The emergence of American political issues*. St. Paul, Minn.: West, 1977, 89-105.

McCOMBS, M.E., & SHAW, D.L. The agenda-setting function of the mass media. *Public Opinion Quarterly*, 1972, 36, 176-187.

McCOMBS, M.E., & WEAVER, D. Voters and the mass media: Information-seeking, political interest, and issue agendas. Paper presented at the annual meeting of the American Association for Public Opinion Research, Buck Hill Falls, Pa., 1977.

McKERROW, R.E. Truman and Korea: Rhetoric in the pursuit of victory. *Central States Speech Journal*, 1977, 28, 1-12.

McLEOD, J.M., BROWN, J.D., & BECKER, L.B. Watergate and the 1974 congressional elections. *Public Opinion Quarterly*, 1977, 41, 181-195.

McLEOD, J.M., BROWN, J.D., BECKER, L.B., &

ZIEMKE, D.A. Decline and fall at the White House: A longitudinal analysis of communication effects. *Communication Research*, 1977a, 4, 3-22.

McLEOD, J.M., BROWN, J.D., BECKER, L.B., & ZIEMKE, D.A. Decline and fall at the White House: A rejoinder to Professor Davis. *Communication Research*, 1977b, 4, 35-39.

McLUHAN, M. *Understanding media*. New York: McGraw-Hill, 1964.

MEADOW, R.G. Information and maturation in the political socialization process. Unpublished doctoral dissertation, University of Pennsylvania, 1976a.

MEADOW, R.G. Issue emphasis and public opinion: The media during the 1972 presidential campaign. *American Politics Quarterly*, 1976b, 4, 177-192.

MENDELSOHN, H., & O'KEEFE, G. *The people choose a president: Influences on voter decision making*. New York: Praeger, 1976.

MILLER, S.H. Congress and the news media: Coverage, collaboration and agenda setting. Unpublished doctoral dissertation, Stanford University, 1976.

MINOW, N.N., & MITCHELL, L.M. Incumbent television: A case of indecent exposure. *Annals of the American Academy of Political and Social Science*, 1976, 425, 74-87.

MURDOCK, J. The agenda-setting function: A critical review. Paper presented at the annual meeting of the Speech Communication Association, Houston, 1975.

NAPOLITAN, J. Media costs and effects in political campaigns. *Annals of the American Academy of Political and Social Science*, 1976, 427, 114-124.

NIMMO, D. *Popular images of politics*. Englewood Cliffs, N.J.: Prentice-Hall, 1974.

NIMMO, D. Political image makers and the mass media. *Annals of the American Academy of Political and Social Science*, 1976, 427, 33-44.

NIMMO, D. Political communication theory and research: An overview. In B. Ruben (Ed.), *Communication yearbook I*, New Brunswick, N.J.: Transaction-International Communication Association, 1977, 441-452.

NIMMO, D., & SAVAGE, R. *Candidates and their images*. Pacific Palisades, Cal.: Goodyear, 1976.

O'KEEFE, G.J., MENDELSOHN, H., & LIU, J. Voter Decision making 1972 and 1974. *Public Opinion Quarterly*, 1976, 40, 320-330.

PALETZ, D.L., AND ELSON, M. Television coverage of presidential conventions. *Political Science Quarterly*, 1976, 91, 109-131.

PARSONS, M.B. A political profile of newspaper editors. *Journalism Quarterly*, 1976, 53, 700-705.

PATTERSON, T.E., & McCLURE, R.D. *The unseeing eye*. New York: Putnam, 1976.

PORTER, W.E. *Assault on the media: The Nixon years*. Ann Arbor: University of Michigan Press, 1976.

PROSSER, S., & CONVERSE, J.M. On Stimson's interpretation of declines in presidential popularity. *Public Opinion Quarterly*, 1976-1977, 40, 538-541.

REEDY, G.E. The president and the press: Struggle for dominance. *Annals of the American Academy of Political and Social Science*, 1976, 427, 65-72.

REGENS, J.L., & MATTHEWS, H.G. Political information and candidate evaluation: An experimental analysis of vote choice. Paper presented at the annual meeting of the Southwest Political Science Association, Dallas, 1977.

ROBINSON, J.P. Interpersonal influence in election campaigns: Two-step flow hypotheses. *Public Opinion Quarterly*, 1976, 40, 304-319.

ROBINSON, M.J. Public affairs television and the growth of political malaise: The case of "The Selling of the Pentagon." *American Political Science Review*, 1976, 70, 409-432.

ROBINSON, M.J. The impact of "instant analysis." *Journal of Communication*, 1977, 27, 17-23.

ROBINSON, M.J., & McPHERSON, K.N. Television news coverage before the 1976 New Hampshire primary: The focus of network journalism. *Journal of Broadcasting*, 1977, 21, 177-186.

ROBINSON, M.J., & ZUKIN, C. Television and the Wallace vote. *Journal of Communication*, 1976, 26, 79-83.

ROELOF, H.M. *Ideology and myth in American politics: A critique of a national political mind*. Boston: Little, Brown, 1976.

ROKEACH, M. *The nature of human values*. New York: Free Press, 1973.

ROPER ORGANIZATION. *Changing public attitudes toward television and other mass media, 1959-1976*. Washington, D.C.: Television Information Office, 1977.

ROSENBLOOM, D.L. The press and the local candidate. *Annals of the American Academy of Political and Social Science*, 1976, 427, 12-22.

RUBIN, A.M. Television in children's political socialization. *Journal of Broadcasting*, 1976, 20, 51-60.

RUBIN, B. *Media, politics, & democracy*. New York: Oxford University Press, 1977.

RUTKUS, D.S. Presidential television. *Journal of Communication*, 1976, 26, 73-78.

SANDERS, K.R., & ATWOOD, L.E. Influence of channel variables on values and behavior. Paper presented at the annual meeting of the International Communication Association, Berlin, 1977.

SANDERS, K.R., & PACE, T.J. The influence of speech communication on the image of a political candidate: "Limited effects" revisited. In B. Ruben (Ed.), *Communication yearbook I*, New Brunswick, N.J.: Transaction-International Communication Association, 1977, 465-474.

SEROTA, K.B., CODY, M.J., BARNETT, G.A., & TAYLOR, J.A. Precise procedures for optimizing campaign communication. In B. Ruben (Ed.), *Communication yearbook I*, New Brunswick, N.J.: Transaction-International Communication Association, 1977, 475-491.

SHAW, D.L., & CLEMMER, C.L. News and the public response. In D.L. Shaw and M.E. McCombs (Eds.), *The emergence of American political issues*. St. Paul, Minn.: West, 1977, 33-51.

SHAW, D.L., & McCOMBS, M.E. (Eds.). *The emergence of American political issues*. St. Paul, Minn.: West, 1977.

SHAW, E.F. The interpersonal agenda. In D.L. Shaw and M.E. McCombs (Eds.), *The emergence of American political issues*. St. Paul, Minn.: West, 1977, 69-87.

SINGLETON, D.L. The role of broadcasting in presidential popularity: An exploration in presidential power. Paper presented at the annual meeting of the International Communication Association, Portland, Ore., 1976.

SOULE, J.W., & MARX, P. Cognitive dissonance and public reactions to Watergate. *Experimental Study of Politics*, 1976, 5, 1-19.

STEVENSON, R.L., & LAING, R.B. The audience for the impeachment hearings. *Journal of Broadcasting*, 1976, 20, 159-168.

STIMSON, J.A. Public support for American presidents: A cyclical model. *Public Opinion Quarterly*, 1976, 40, 1-21.

STONE, P., & BRODY, R.A. Modeling opinion responsiveness to daily news: The public and Lyndon Johnson 1965-1968. *Social Science Information*, 1970, 9, 95-122.

SURLIN, S., & GORDON, T.F. How values affect attitudes toward direct reference political advertising. *Journalism Quarterly*, 1977, 54, 89-98.

SWANSON, D.L. Information utility: An alternative perspective in political communication. *Central States Speech Journal*, 1976, 27, 95-101.

SWANSON, D.L. Political communication research and the uses and gratifications model: A critique. Paper presented at the annual meeting of the International Communication Association, Berlin, 1977a.

SWANSON, D.L. The uses and misuses of uses and gratifications. *Human Communication Research*, 1977b, 3, 214-221.

TAN, A., & VAUGHN, P. Mass media exposure, public affairs knowledge and black militancy. *Journalism Quarterly*, 1976, 53, 271-279.

TILLINGHAST, D.S. Information seeking on Watergate and President Nixon's resignation and attitudes toward Nixon in the mass media. Unpublished doctoral dissertation, Michigan State University, 1976.

TIPTON, L.P., HANEY, R.D., & BASEHEART, J.R. Media agenda setting in city and state election campaigns. *Journalism Quarterly*, 1975, 52, 15-22.

TUNSTALL, J. *The media are American*. New York: Columbia University Press, 1977.

VATZ, R.E. Public opinion and presidential ethos. *Western Journal of Speech Communication*, 1976, 40, 196-206.

WALL, V.D., JR., & McCAIN, T.A. River Ridge II: The effects of social system modernity on perceptions of a school bond proposal. *Western Journal of Speech Communication*, 1977, 41, 160-174.

WEAVER, D. Political issues and voter need for orientation. In D.L. Shaw and M.E. McCombs (Eds.), *The emergence of American political issues*. St. Paul, Minn.: West, 1977, 107-119.

WEAVER, D., BECKER, L.B., & McCOMBS, M.E. Influence of mass media on issues, images and political interest. Paper presented at the annual meeting of the Midwest Association for Public Opinion Research, Chicago, 1976.

WEINER, S.L. The competition for certainty: The polls and the press in Britain. *Political Science Quarterly, 1976-1977*, 91, 673-696.

WHALEN, A.C. The presentation of image in Ella T. Grasso's campaign. *Central States Speech Journal*, 1976, 27, 207-211.

WHEELER, M. *Lies, damn lies, and statistics*. New York: Norton, 1976.

WHITE, T.B. Civil rights and socialization: Political beliefs among a black elite. Unpublished doctoral dissertation, Princeton University, 1976.

WILLIAMS, W., & LARSEN, D. The agenda-setting function of the mass media in a signal starved market. Paper presented at the annual meeting of the International Communication Association, Portland, Ore., 1976.

WILLIAMS, W., & SEMLAK, W.D. Campaign '76: The agenda setting effects of television network news and a local daily newspaper on interpersonal and intrapersonal agendas during the New Hampshire primary. Paper presented at the annual meeting of the Speech Communication Association, San Francisco, 1976.

WILSON, C., & WILLIAMS, E. Watergate words: A naturalistic study of media and communication. *Communication Research*, 1977, 4, 169-178.

WIMMER, R.D. Mass media and the older voter. *Journal of Broadcasting*, 1976, 20, 313-322.

WINDHAUSER, J.W. How the metropolitan press covered the 1970 general election campaigns in Ohio. *Journalism Quarterly*, 1976, 53, 264-270.

WINDHAUSER, J.W. Reporting of campaign issues in Ohio municipal election races. *Journalism Quarterly*, 1977, 54, 332-340.

WOELFEL, J.C. Changes in interpersonal communication patterns as a consequence of need for information. *Communication Research*, 1977, 4, 235-256.

WORCHEL, S., ANDREOLI, V., & EASON, J. Is the medium the message? A study of the effects of media, communicator, and message characteristics on attitude change. *Journal of Applied Social Psychology*, 1975, 5, 157-172.

YALCH, R.F. Pre-election interview effects on voter turnout. *Public Opinion Quarterly*, 1976, 40, 331-336.

ZUKIN, C. A reconsideration of the effects of information on partisan stability. *Public Opinion Quarterly*, 1977, 41, 244-254.

CANDIDATE IMAGES: STEREOTYPING AND THE 1976 DEBATES[1]

JOHN E. BOWES
University of Washington

HERBERT STRENTZ
Drake University

The process of formation and change in images of political candidates is described in terms of stereotyping of candidate attributes and issues. Four stereotyping components are described and examined: homogenization, polarization, fixedness, and reification. A fifth variable, issue congruity, is also examined. The rotating panel of approximately 200 students was questioned on four occasions (August through October, 1976) in order to bracket each of the three televised debates. Polarization and reification explain the most variance in candidate images. Their strongest stereotyping effects are upon candidate attributes rather than issues. The debates themselves showed little impact on attributes, though the effects of direct exposure were difficult to separate from commentary and conversation about the debates as "events." Sources most influential in altering attributes were largely personal or organizational. The influence of direct contact with politicians was quite pronounced.

CONCEPTUALIZATION

A candidate's image—his or her publicly perceived attributes—has become an essential consideration in political campaigns.[2] While ties to traditional party and class loyalties have waned, the persona of the candidate has waxed in explanations of what sways voter preferences. As Gans (1977) states in a recent issue of the *Columbia Journalism Review*, the candidates used television to reach an audience of:

> . . . general voters: people who were deciding whether to vote and for which man, and who judged the candidates on the basis of such criteria as capability and trust. The candidates were less concerned with issue oriented voters who also wanted to know how the candidates stood on specific issues. (p. 25)

Much earlier, Katz and Feldman (1971), in their review of research of the 1960 Kennedy-Nixon debates, arrived at about the same conclusion. They found that the debates changed few opinions on issues and focused more on personalities and presentation style.

The literature suggests that what the voter derives as candidate images from televised debates depends on what criteria they use to evaluate candidates. For social scientists who hold the debates to be powerful influences, the image could be considered "stimulus-determined." Another view is that images are a product of partisan affiliation and standing vote intentions. Thus, input from the debates will be conditioned by a need to keep images harmonious with partisan beliefs and candidate choice, for example, prior experience. Images in these circumstances are clearly more predetermined. Balance theorists would call this "perceiver-determined" (McGrath & McGrath, 1962).

The origins of the image may be further complicated, as Sigel (1964) suggests, by components of the image that are being considered. She proposed that perception of candidates is stimulus-determined when one considers a candidate's personality or appearance, and is perceiver-determined (especially by partisan inclinations) when the candidate's stand on political issues is examined. Gans (1977) acknowledges this distinction in describing campaign strategy, criticizing President Carter and former president Ford for a lack of responsiveness to issue-based questions. Candidates instead seemed to emphasize personalities.

Thus, both editorial comment and research suggest the importance of images as a focus of attention. But as Nimmo and Savage (1976) comment, "There has been insufficient research into. . . . how [voters] organize perceived traits into overall images of what a candidate stands for." (p. 102). It seemed especially useful, therefore, to examine image formation under the purposive conditions of the presidential debates within a structure sensitive to how images are constructed.

Walter Lippmann (1922) suggested that the world is too complex and fleeting for direct acquaintance; rather, people reconstruct their environment using more simple and manageable categories for experience: stereotypes. In stereotyping, the individual achieves a condition of "belief or attitude . . . oversimplified in content in which the unique attributes of the subject are not observed, and which is resistant to change" (Krech & Crutchfield, 1958, p. 668). As suggested by Lippmann and others (see Bauer, Pool, & Dexter, 1963), stereotypes in their formative stages may be necessary to the voter, allowing him to categorize new experiences in familiar, helpful frameworks. Allowed to progress, however, the stereotype becomes a rigid and extreme image, insensitive to change or moderation. The stereotyping process, thus, may be seen as the means by which formation of candidate images is achieved.

R.F. Carter (1962), in an analysis of the 1960 Presidential debates, described three dimensions of stereotyping:

1. Stereotyping suggests a *process* of categorical responding, where the characteristics of a situation are increasingly interrelated and predictable from each other, i.e. the image components are *homogenized*. Seen in moderation, the process of stereotyping may be beneficial—a reflection of one's progress toward a "stable, focussed evaluation of the stimulus" (p. 78). In excess, however, homogenizing levels the distinctive attributes of an individual.
2. The more negative aspects of stereotyping are suggested when characteristics are not only homogenized, but become polarized as well. The application of characteristics in the extreme, applying them to the full degree, is *polarization*.
3. When a polarized and homogenized image persists over time, resistant to changing conditions and events, it is an instance of *fixedness*. What is implied in this structuring is that a process of stereotyping, starting with homogenizing of characteristics, may be a normal, often useful consequence of categorizing events. The process becomes malignant when the individual cannot recognize unique or changing qualities.

In this conceptualization of stereotyping, images were composed of attributes describing single events or individuals. The voter might, for example, depict a candidate in polar extremes (e.g., *very* honest) or homogenously across attributes (e.g., *somewhat* honest, *somewhat* hard working, etc.). Yet stereotyping can be conceptualized as other than an individual phenomenon. Voters, for example, could believe that "all politicians are alike," failing to distinguish among them in terms of attributes and salient issues.

Stamm, Bowes, and Bowes (1973) developed this concept as a special case of stereotyping: *reification*; e.g., assigning members of a group equally to an attribute so that *each candidate is highly predictable from the others*. By contrast, homogenization in stereotyping considers the array of attributes for a given candidate—*each attribute is highly predictable from the others*.

But if voters converge candidates to a common description, could they be similarly converging candidates toward their own views? Thus *congruency*, or the discrepancy between the respondent's own views on the importance of issues and those he or she ascribes to the candidates, was incorporated into the analysis as a control and covariable. If stereotyping and congruency are closely linked and this association increases with the course of the campaign, congruency becomes an important adjunct of stereotyping. For not only is the respondent erasing distinctions among attributes describing each candidate (homogenization) and differences among candidates (reification), but he or she is removing the distinction between the candidate and his own vision of what is politically important. We should see this by an increase in congruency with the respondents' own views as the campaign progresses. The following questions were suggested:

1. Were images more closely tied to candidates' personality attributes or, rather, to the importance candidates assigned to issues? Did respondents stereotype equally with respect to issues and attributes, or were there differences?

2. What were the effects of the televised debates as contrasted to other information sources on stereotyping of candidates? What was the impact of the debates as a source compared with exposure to general news sources, personal sources, or politicians directly?
3. What influence did intended vote—Carter or Ford—have? Do some candidates elicit more stereotyping; e.g., project more stable images than do others? What was the strength of this influence relative to use of media, personal sources, and exposure to the debates?

In attending to these major questions, we may learn more about stereotyping itself and the interrelationships among its several dimensions.

METHODOLOGY

Subjects were drawn from undergraduate journalism courses at Drake University, Des Moines, Iowa. A rotating panel design was used, meaning that a given subject was interviewed at least several times during the campaign. In all, there were four waves of interviewing. The waves took place approximately one week before each of the three debates and after the final debate, immediately prior to election day. After the second survey, 35 students in the group were replaced with new subjects. Following the four waves, a core of 150 subjects were interviewed all four times, while two smaller groups were measured only twice. About 70 additional subjects comprised the rotating segment of the panel. Rotation allowed a check on sensitization resulting from repeated measures. No significant sensitization effects were apparent.

The first step in the measurement process was the administration of nine attributes based on Carter (1962), but modified to describe candidate characteristics commonly cited during the 1976 debates (e.g., fair, hard working). Next, scales based on nine major issues (developed from opinion poll and editorial accounts of current issues) asked the respondent to estimate the importance candidates assigned to each.[3]

Nine Candidate Attributes

Homogenization. For each different scale position for the nine attributes or issues possible, the respondent was assigned a 1. Marking nonredundant positions across the scales would result in a highly heterogeneous score of 9. Contrarily, indicating on all scales, say, a 3 would result in a highly homogeneous score of 1. With few exceptions, respondents completed all scales. Those with incomplete scales were excluded from analysis.

Polarization. This was indexed by assigning a value of 1 to scales where the extreme categories of 9 or 10 (attributes: "strongly applies"; issues: "very important") were marked. Use of other scale positions were scored 0. Thus an individual marking the 9 or 10 category for all of the nine issues or attribute scales would have a maximum score of 9. In the relatively few instances where the scale was blank or marked "IDK," the scale was scored 0. (Highly polarized scales also tend to be homogenous inasmuch as respondents were clustered at extreme scalar positions. Prior use of these scales, however, has shown the considerable independence of these two stereotyping components outside of the instance of extreme polarization.)

Fixedness. Since we were able to track the same population over a four-month interval prior to the 1976 election, we could gauge the rate of change in issue and attribute scales over time. A pattern of *decreasing* change would suggest fixedness.

Reification. This variable was derived separately for candidate attributes and major campaign issues. In each of these two sets of scales, the scalar difference between challenger Carter's rating and President Ford's were summed for each respondent. The closer the two candidates were rated on personal attributes or the importance they assigned to issues, the lower the reification index. Other potential candidates (Reagan, Maddox, etc.) were measured on attribute scales, but owing to the comparatively few respondents who regarded these individuals as salient, analysis was limited to Ford and Carter. Listwise deletion was used to control for blank or missing scales.

Congruency. The measurement was made by com-

FIGURE 1
Mean Attribute and Issue Polarization for Ford and Carter Across Four Surveys

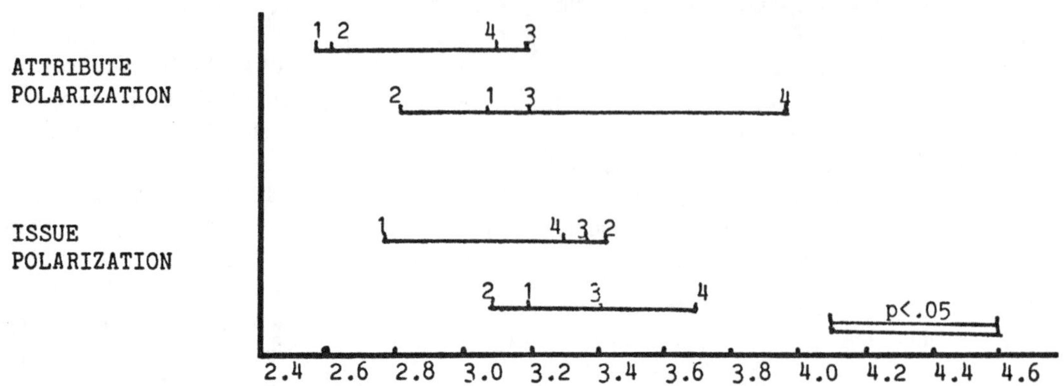

MEAN POLARIZATION
(higher values indicate greater polarization)

*In this and similar tables to follow, numbers on trend lines indicate the survey plotted. Survey 1, 2 and 3 were administered prior to the three debates respectively. Survey 4 followed the last debate. Letters indicate: F=Ford, C= Carter. The significance of difference is determined by comparing distances on trend lines against the ruler provided. This ruler represents a "worst case" estimate of sample n and standard error for this table. Sample size varied somewhat by survey, but was approximately: Carter, n=55; Ford, n=75.

---

paring for each subject the absolute difference between his rating of Ford or Carter on the issues scales with the importance he himself assigned to the issue. These differences were summed separately for Ford and Carter across the nine issues scales.[4]

RESULTS

Stereotyping: Issues versus Attributes

With respect to stereotyping, our respondents showed major differences between issue orientation and attributes of candidates. The two major candidates differed noticeably in the manner and degree to which they were stereotyped.

As Figure 1 shows, *polarization* increased as the election drew close, though the effect was by no means uniform and linear over time. The greatest polarization of Ford's attributes occurred after the second debate (Survey 3) while that of Carter occurred after the first debate (Survey 2). Polarization of issues did not vary nearly as much, indicating, as suggested by Sigel (1964), their more stable anchoring in the respondents' political preferences and philosophies. Given the generally Republican leanings of the sample, there were understandable tendencies to rate the Republican candidate higher on issues interest, as well as more favorably on personal attributes.

Ford's personal attributes were far less *homogenized* than were Carter's (see Figure 2), indicating greater differentiation of Ford's strengths and weaknesses. Issues were not strongly differentiated; there was somewhat greater homogenization of Carter. Few changes in homogenization were evident over the campaign period. Though a slight increase in homogenization occurred as the campaign progressed, this was likely an artifact. Since polarization increased greatly during the same time, homogenization of a given candidate may have been forced by increasingly polar responses. (As more scales are marked

FIGURE 2
Mean Attribute and Issue Homogenization for Ford and Carter Across Four Surveys

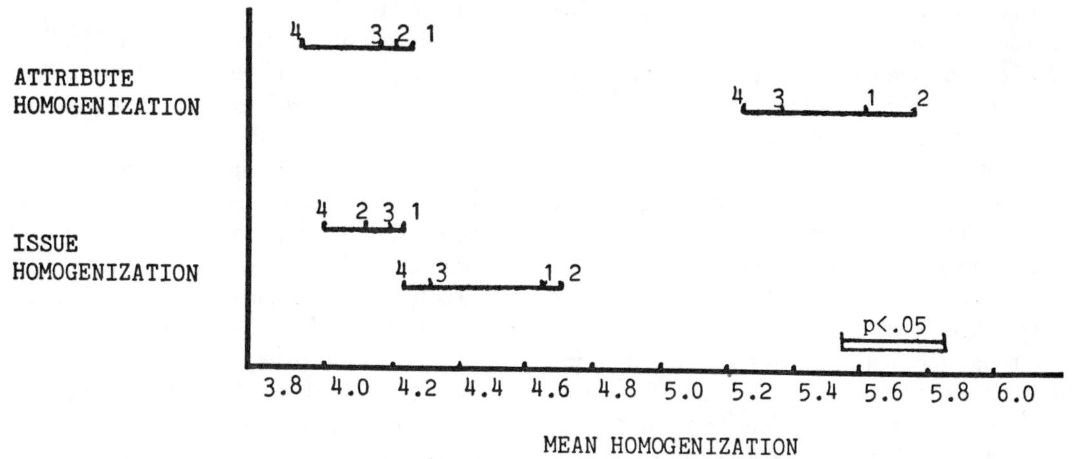

FIGURE 3
Reification of Ford and Carter for Issues and Attributes Across Four Surveys

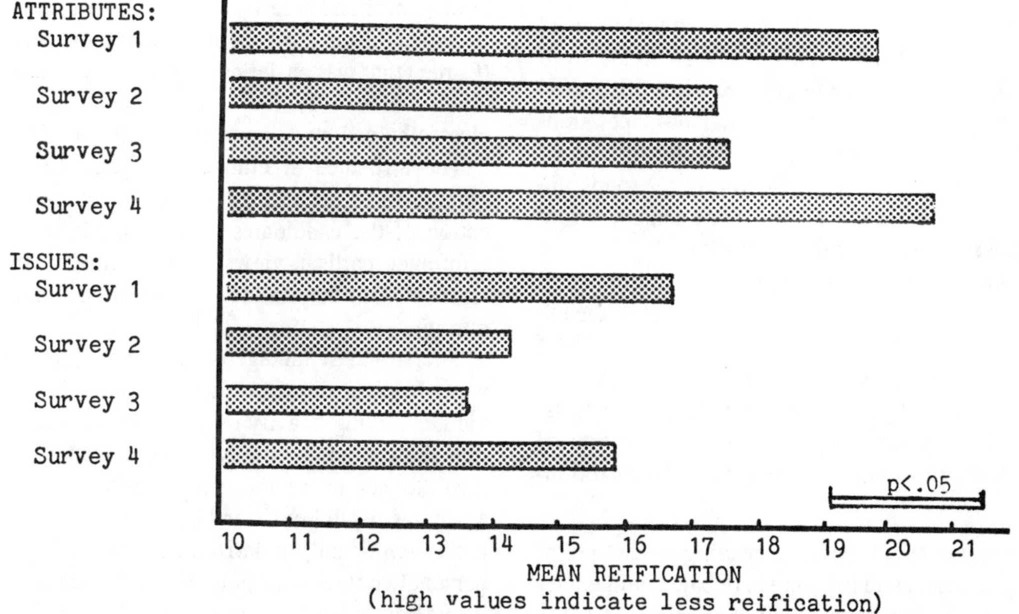

at their extreme, there is less variability of marking and consequently more homogenization.)

Fixedness was not apparent in these analyses. Very possibly the time span for observing this effect was inadequate.

Reification parallelled in part the findings for homogeneity and polarization (Figure 3), but was much greater for attributes than for issues. Thus, what contrasted the candidates was based more on personality than on the importance they accorded to issues. This outcome underscores the folk wisdom of campaign managers who view campaigns more as an exhibition of personality than a sharpening of the issues.

Although the first three surveys showed an increase in reification, the third debate (Survey 4) produced a different effect. Here respondents contrasted the candidates to the level obtained prior to the *first* debate. These findings suggest that the din of campaign oratory and advertisements may dwell so much on issues that candidates become less distinct over time. But confronted with the immediacy of an election (shortly following Survey 4) and a choice to be made, voters may have felt required to contrast the candidates.

Influence of Debates and Other Information Sources

What effect on candidate images could be traced to the televised debates themselves? Apart from viewing the debates on television, the probable exposure of respondents to radio, newspaper transcripts, news commentaries, and so forth, left few opportunities for escape. Comparison groups unexposed to the debates and commentary about them were very difficult to constitute.

Acknowledging this media "contamination," several observations can be made about each source of debate exposure (see Table 1). There were no consequences of exposure to the debates reflected in polarization of both attributes and issues, homogenization of issues or reification of attributes. However, two consistent effects did result:

1. Exposure to TV debates, reading transcripts of the debates, and listening to debate commentary decreased homogenization of candidates following the first debate only. Measures taken after the third debate no longer showed a strong difference, suggesting a waning influence of debate information.
2. Debate exposure increased the reification of Ford and Carter on *issues*, but reduced their reification on *attributes*. But exposure to news commentary about the debates *decreased* the reification of issues. In short, the TV debates helped respondents distinguish candidates on personality attributes but made candidates appear more alike on issues. The results show that exposure to news commentators mitigated this effect. These outcomes were only significant after the third debate, suggesting that the nearness of the election magnified the importance of commentators as sources.

Exposure to political information from local and network TV news (other than the televised debates) also showed little influence on candidate image (see Table 2). By contrast, group and interpersonal sources were highly influential. Contact with friends strengthened the polarization of Ford's attributes, suggesting the reinforcement by peers of candidate characteristics. The effects of class discussion were even more pervasive, especially following the third debate. Those using classes as political information sources tended more to homogenize and polarize Carter. Classes may have provided information about the underdog candidate (Carter) that was easier and more likely ignored by other sources. By the time of the third debate, classes helped students to reify both candidates.

The influence of clubs and organizations was quite different, showing a strong reduction in reification of the candidates on issues. These groups reinforced partisan views, accentuating issues differences. But they failed to contrast candidates on attributes.

The strongest linkage of source to stereotyping was a result of direct contact with politicians. Individuals relying heavily on politicians for information showed an especially strong tendency to contrast (to not reify) the candidates on issues and attributes. Both Ford's and Carter's attributes were more significantly polarized by those having high personal contact with politicians. But homogenizing of Ford's attributes was lowered, while Carter's

TABLE 1
Mean Homogenization, Polarization, and Reification by Type of Exposure to the Presidential Debates for Second and Fourth Questionnaires

	Attribute Polarization		Issue Polarization		Attribute Homogenization		Issue Homogenization		Attribute Reification		Issue Reification	
Survey:	S 2	S 4	S 2	S 4	S 2	S 4	S 2	S 4	S 2	S 4	S 2	S 4
Exposure: TV												
Yes:	4.21	5.80	5.34	5.75	7.53*	7.03	6.98	6.48	17.26	25.57*	14.25	10.40
No:	5.81	4.73	6.37	5.25	6.79	6.74	6.12	6.35	17.83	21.11	14.29	16.40*
TRANSCRIPT												
Yes:	4.50	6.03	5.35	5.75	7.68**	7.09	7.01	6.59	17.48	20.39	14.31	16.56
No:	4.58	4.86	5.43	5.39	6.96	6.73	6.57	6.37	15.51	22.80	14.40	15.36
COMMENTARY												
Yes:	4.58	5.60	5.48	5.60	7.53	6.82	6.81	6.57	17.82	22.07	14.08	17.23**
No:	4.00	5.21	5.41	5.38	6.76	7.51	6.82	6.20	16.22	18.47	15.16	12.18

Significance is noted by the highest mean of the pair.
* .05
** .01
*** .001

TABLE 2
Partial Correlations Between Political Information Sources and Stereotyping of Issues and Attributes

	ATTRIBUTES				ISSUES				REIFICATION	
SOURCE:	Carter Polariz.	Carter Homog.	Ford Polariz.	Ford Homog.	Carter Polariz.	Carter Homog.	Ford Polariz.	Ford Homog.	Attrib.	Issues
FRIENDS:										
Survey 1	-.194	-.105	-.122	-.122	-.112	.020	-.077	-.093	.104	.042
Survey 3	.027	-.149	.251**	-.012	.004	-.054	-.0017	.062	.185*	.087
CLASSES:										
Survey 1	-.164	.050	-.017	-.112	.017	-.206*	.201*	.116	-.182	.035
Survey 3	-.115	.023	-.063	.134*	.205*	.232**	-.021	.135	.220*	.253**
ORGANIZA.:										
Survey 1	-.076	-.091	-.048	-.133	-.224*	-.168	-.053	-.033	-.072	-.191
Survey 3	.124	.034	.115	.029	.176	-.201	-.004	-.014	-.173	-.356**
NTWK TV NEWS:										
Survey 1	.183	-.014	-.045	.013	.077	.049	.044	-.059	-.108	.001
Survey 3	.022	.072	-.007	.038	-.004	.103	.163	.005	-.092	.187*
POLITICIAN:										
Survey 1	.082	.087	.063	.053	.056	-.273*	.234*	-.006	-.147	-.173
Survey 3	.286**	-.062	.228	-.199**	.216*	.066	-.012	-.144	-.281**	-.417***

remained unaffected, by contact with politicians.

The irregularities in these findings raise many questions. Why, for example, did classes, clubs, and organizations polarize Carter and not Ford on issues? Why did local and network television news have so little effect in promoting stereotypes, given popular criticism that this is a prominent effect? It should be recalled that, with the exception of reification, effects of information sources on stereotyping were generally weak. Our timing may have been partly at fault. Many media effects were examined in the first and third surveys only, meaning that the impact of the first debate (Survey 2) and the immediacy of election day (Survey 4) may have been lost.

Another possible reason that so little influence on candidate images was attributed to media may be traced to our limitation to *political* information sources. Media news contains much "nonpolitical" information that has, nevertheless, political consequences which may not be readily recognized. We were, however, forced to reject this possibility. Frequency of use of TV news, radio news, magazines, and newspapers was correlated with stereotyping indices. As before, few strong correlations resulted (see Table 3). The one consistent result was a link of TV news to issue stereotyping, the effect being to increase homogeneity for Carter and polarization for both candidates. This effect only showed prior to the televised debates (Survey 1). Exposure to newspapers had no discernable effects either prior to or during the debates. News magazines, together with radio, showed weak correlations with stereotyping indices only late in the campaign after the second debate (Survey 3).

Influence of Candidate Preference

Preferences for candidates demonstrated influences on images that were more subtle and enduring than the short-term impact of televised debates. Thus, stereotyping should be more intense for one's preferred candidate. Popular conceptions might suggest otherwise; that is, one stereotypes the opposition (presumably less well-known) as an easy way of dealing with the object.

The collective preference for Ford is clear when congruity is examined (Figure 4). Respondents continually decreased the distance between themselves and Ford as the campaign progressed. Congruency also increased with Carter until the last debate (Survey 4) when he was contrasted. The trend to congruity with both candidates suggested the influence of similar issues being stressed by both candidates.

This process did not predict respondent judgments of debate winners.[5] Voters seemed, instead, to put distance between themselves and the disfavored candidate; an action based on standing intentions rather than the short-term influence of the debates.

Figures 5 through 9 show the strong effects of treating the samples by intended vote. Clearest is candidate attribute polarization shown in Figure 5. Respondents strongly polarized their favored candidate and increasingly did so as election day approached.

Outcomes for disfavored candidates were less consistent. Ford voters did not significantly polarize their evaluation of Carter's attributes. Contrarily, Carter voters significantly polarized Ford as the election progressed. This may signal a greater ambivalence towards Carter by his adherents. Carter voters began to polarize their candidate earlier in the campaign (following the first debate) more than did Ford voters, who showed significant movement only after the third and final debate.

Issue polarization (Figure 6) followed the pattern just described. Respondents tended more to polarize the importance their candidate gave to major campaign issues. However, the differences were less distinct and the pattern more irregular as election day moved closer. As with attributes, Ford was more polarized by Carter voters.

Effects of intended vote upon homogenization (Figures 7, 8) were less apparent. For both attributes and issues, the greatest homogenization occurred for Carter voters, the least for Ford by both Carter and Ford voters. The suggestion in these findings is that Ford was seen by supporter and nonsupporter alike as having more definitive strengths and weaknesses, yielding a less homogenous portrait across the attribute-rating scales. However, this conclusion for issues was marginal at best and was apparent only in the beginning stages of the campaign.

As has been shown, Carter voters tended to rate

TABLE 3
Partial Correlations Between Frequency of Media Use and Stereotyping of Issues and Attributes

	ATTRIBUTES				ISSUES				REIFICATION	
SOURCE:	Carter Polariz.	Carter Homog.	Ford Polariz.	Ford Homog.	Carter Polariz.	Carter Homog.	Ford Polariz.	Ford Homog.	Attrib.	Issues
TV NEWS:										
Survey 1	.095	-.004	-.073	.056	.313**	.216	.280**	.014	-.101	.077
Survey 3	-.111	.126	-.073	.169	-.056	.139	.077	-.079	.016	.106
NEWS MAGS:										
Survey 1	-.078	-.123	.143	-.200	-.184	-.073	.125	-.053	-.107	-.065
Survey 3	.157	.013	.201*	-.036	.176*	.002	-.012	-.089	-.098	-.117
RADIO:										
Survey 1	-.041	.034	-.088	-.065	.039	.040	.157	.029	-.036	-.136
Survey 3	.139	.232**	-.0003	.161*	-.006	-.065	-.092	.044	-.015	-.119

* .05
** .01
*** .001

FIGURE 4
Congruency with Ford and Carter on Issue Importance Across Four Surveys

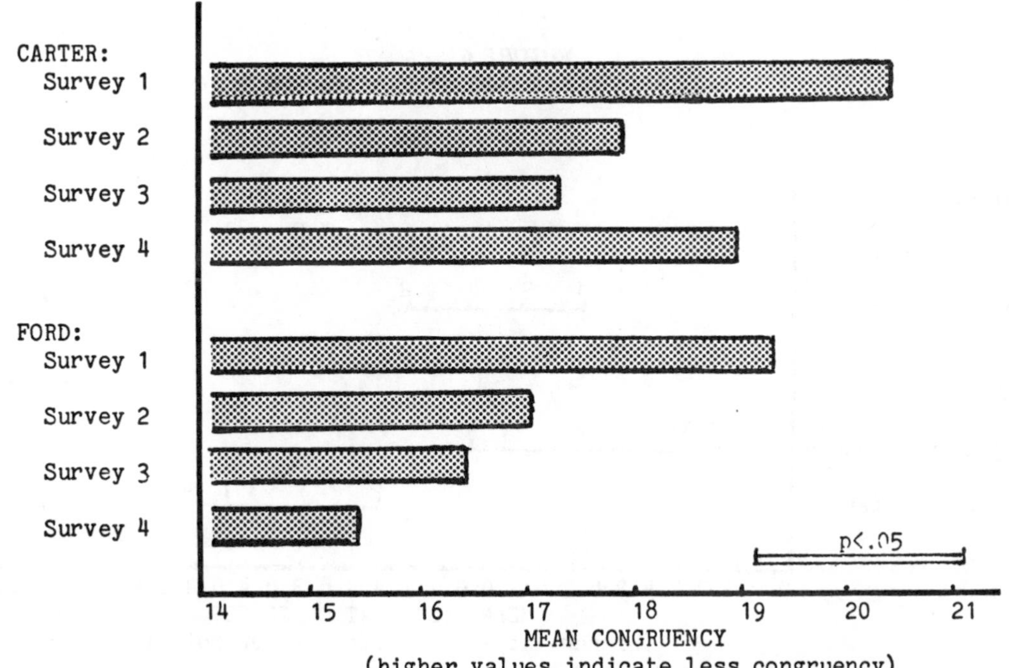

FIGURE 5
Effect of Intended Vote on Attribute Polarization Across Four Surveys

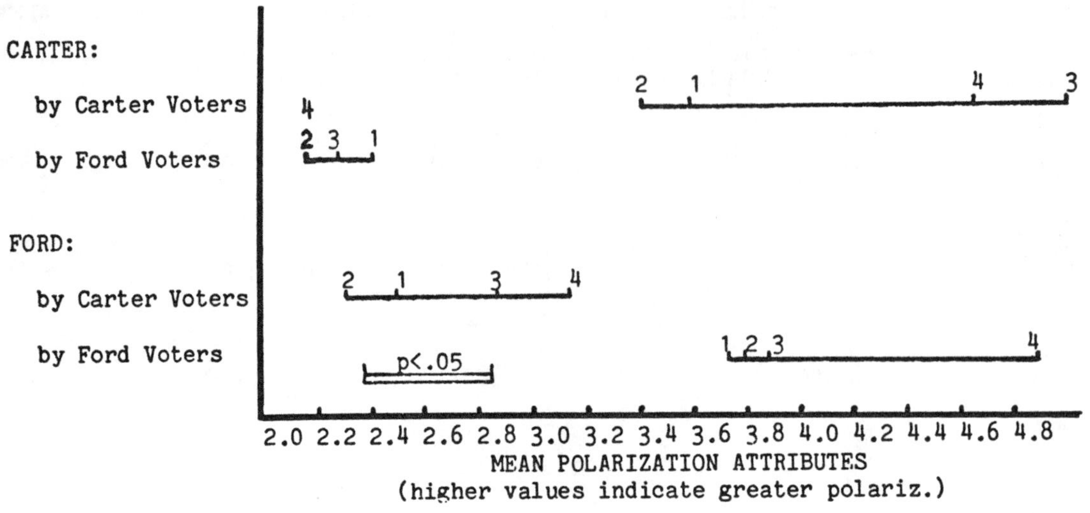

FIGURE 6
Effect of Intended Vote on Issue Polarization Across Four Surveys

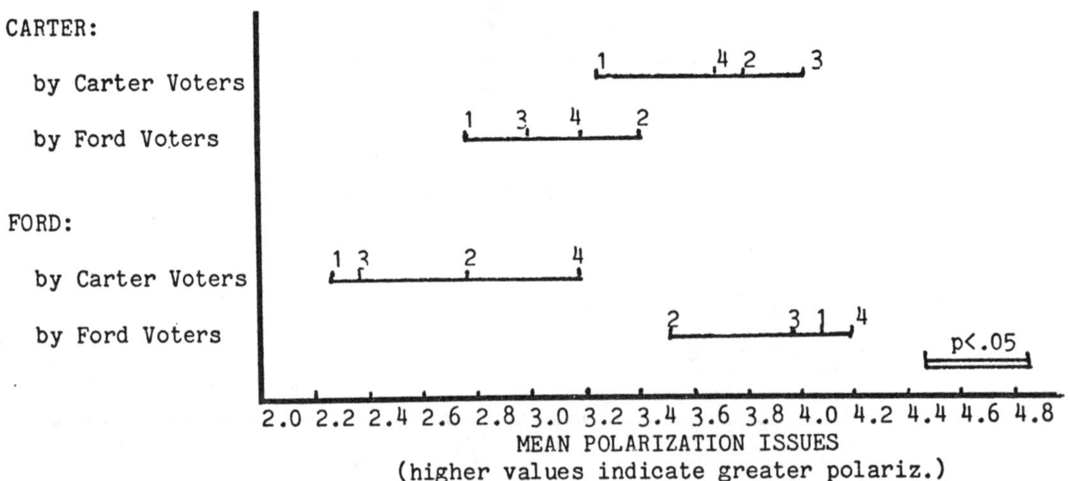

FIGURE 7
Effect of Intended Vote on Attribute Homogenization Across Four Surveys

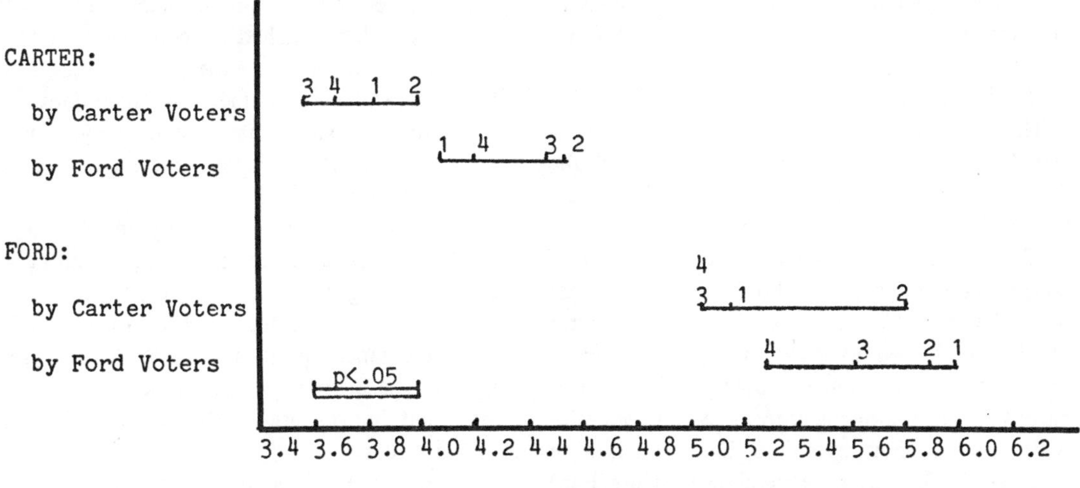

FIGURE 8
Effect of Intended Vote on Issue Homogenization Across Four Surveys

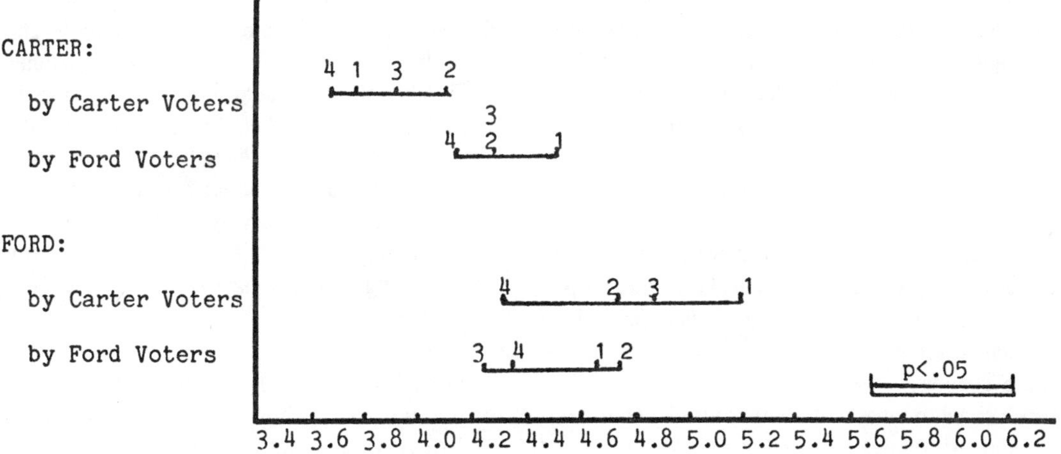

Ford higher than in the analogous situation for Ford voters. This ambivalence by Carter supporters was also suggested by the reification findings in Figure 9. These showed Carter voters perceiving much less distance between the two candidates on personality attributes than was perceived by Ford supporters. The two candidates were only marginally contrasted on the issues.

The trend over the campaign period was for respondents to move to greater congruency with the candidate of their choice (Figure 10). However, they did not move farther away from the opposing candidate. Carter voters moved to a position of congruity on the issues with Ford fully equal to that of Ford voters. Contrarily, congruity with Carter was heavily biased toward the Carter voters. Ford voters kept their distance, showing only a marginally significant movement to increased congruity with Carter. In short, over time, Carter voters were as close to Ford as to their choice, while Ford supporters contrasted themselves with Carter.

Though no separate scaling of fixedness was attempted, visual inspection of homogeneity, polarization, and reification showed little of this effect as the campaign progressed. The active communication environment of campaign oratory, heavy news coverage, the debates, and the impending election date may have defeated fixedness. More likely, our span of measurement was too short for fixedness to become apparent, especially outside of the charged atmosphere of the campaign period. Perhaps, too, our sample of college students—many first-time voters—were less willing than established, older voters to become set early in the campaign.

CONCLUSIONS

These findings suggest the utility of stereotyping measures and provide insight into how college-age voters come to picture and distinguish contenders in a major national election. Since data were gathered over time, some idea of process and flux was introduced into what would otherwise be static impressions of political image formation.

Personal attributes were stronger indicants of image than issues. The pronounced effects of personal contact with politicians on reducing reification was especially notable. The overall influence of information sources was, as Sigel suggests, more on attributes than issues.

The impact of the debates appeared slight with the important exception of reification. Direct TV exposure seemed to support debate critics: candidates were distinguished on personality attributes but blended together on the issues. What is difficult to resolve is whether this outcome resulted from any purposive strategy by candidates or was simply the result of people's interest more in personality than election issues.

Intended vote, a presumably more complex product of social experience and partisan beliefs, exerted stronger influence on respondents' political images than did the short-term impact of debates and general political information through the media. These findings run counter to the impression that images are easily swayed, short-term media forces.

Polarization, homogenization, and reification varied in their ability to explain and track image formation. Reification and polarization provided more distinct findings when compared to homogenization, which proved weak and possibly confounded with polarization. Later analysis will control this confounding, better isolating homogenization effects. Fixedness was not apparent. Congruency was remarkable for its interplay with stereotyping over the four sample points. Together with polarization, it clearly showed the movement of respondents towards their chosen candidate in a way unrelated to debate winners.[6]

Finally, since stereotyping measures bracketed each debate, changes could be closely isolated in time to the debate. Changes, for example, signalled strong gain by Carter following the first debate and a later recovery by Ford in the last two. In short, enough sensitivity was shown in several stereotyping dimensions to "track" debate performance.

Several problems with stereotyping as a measure need emphasis, both as a caution to interpretation of findings and to show the needs of future study.

1. Isolating the effects of exposure to debates was troublesome, given that exposure was nearly universal, if not to the debates themselves, at least to commentary and news reports about them. Only 6 (of some 200 or so respondents) indicated no expo-

FIGURE 9
Effect of Intended Vote on Issue and Attribute Reification Across Four Surveys

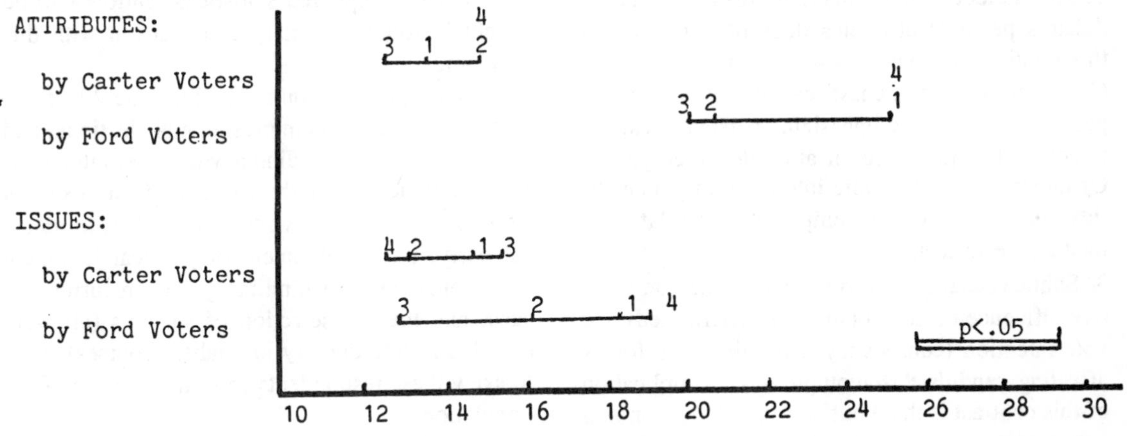

FIGURE 10
Congruency with Ford and Carter on Issue by Intended Vote Across Four Surveys

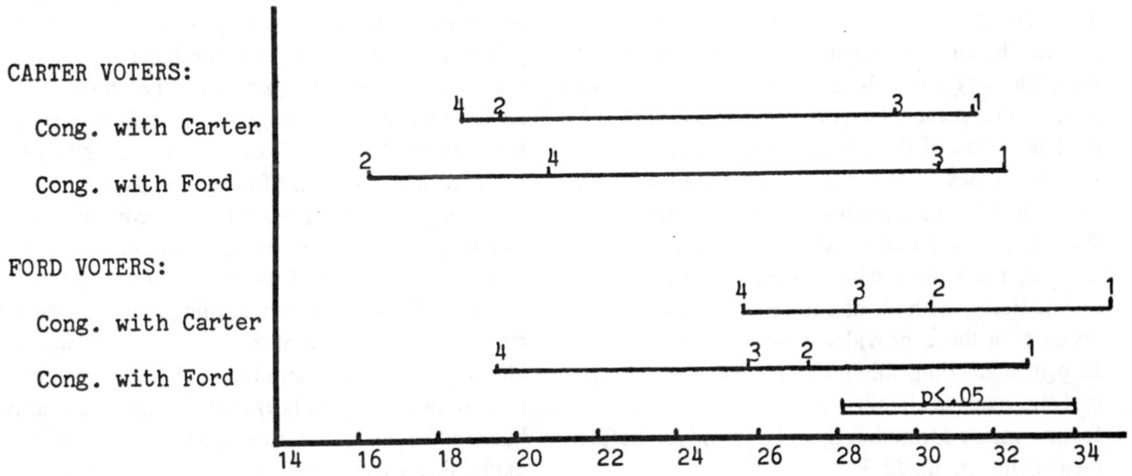

sure to any information about the debates—far too few for adequate comparison to those who did. Instead, only kinds of exposure could be contrasted without much attention to their redundancy.
2. That stereotyping occurs more readily on a candidate's personal attributes does little to explain this relationship. The answer is important. Gans (1977), for example, chastises the media and campaign strategists for emphasizing personalities, not issues. Is this the origin of attribute stereotyping? Or rather, are voters more interested in personalities, regardless of the emphasis candidates or media give to them?[7]
3. Subtle causal questions intrude on the comparative influence of media (stimulus determined) and vote intention (consistency determined) as forces affecting candidate stereotyping. The implication of this contrast is that consistency is long standing and based on personal values and experience. Stimuli such as media, on the contrary, are invasive, short-term forces affecting image. The strong influences of intended vote in this study and the strong movements of respondents toward congruity suggest the latter. But definite media relationships to stereotyping were also apparent. Some of these occurred early in the campaign. Attribute homogenization, for example, was increased by exposure to the first debate. Increased exposure to television news was linked to the polarization of both candidates on issues *before* the debates had begun. The unanswered question is: to what extent are such early media-based influences later incorporated into personal experience and political values? Is a span of three months sufficient time for such processes to take place? With this in mind, the distinction of stimulus versus consistency influence becomes one fixed in time, vulnerable to campaign processes which antedate the measures taken. Better methods of coping with causal influences than those provided here may be of some help in untangling this problem. But the conceptual structures available suggestive of processes affecting image formation must be improved before clear gains are made.
4. The intrinsic correlation between homogeneity and polarization hampered isolation of homogenization change over the campaign. How much of this was due to polarized responses? Correlations between homogenization and polarization yielded an average coefficient of concordance of 38%, indicating enough overlap to cause serious distortion, but not enough to suggest the two are redundant indices. Improved statistical controls will be sought in follow-up analyses to reckon with this problem.
5. This sample was young (average age 20), most were first-time voters in presidential elections, and all were students attending a Midwestern university. The typicality of the sample and its external validity must be taken with caution. Ties to political party, the development of political judgment based on long-term familiarity with recurrent issues, and the self-selection of students (all were enrolled in introductory journalism courses) serve to skew these respondents from the balance of the population.
6. It was difficult to detect in these data any stable rate-of-change patterns. Our failure to note any progressive "fixedness" of image with time is indicative. That is, did most movement in polarization, homogenization, and reification take place early in the campaign or later on? A related question concerns changes with time in the joint effects of stereotyping components. Is stereotyping, for example, a process of successive rather than simultaneous influences? It could be hypothesized that homogenization shows an initial, stable formation of image. Later in the campaign, reification and polarization might become dominant in terms of movement as one struggles with the choice to be made. Both questions suggest the limitation of our three-month "window" on process as well as the stability and precision of measures used.
7. Finally, the conceptual link of congruency to stereotyping processes needs additional explication. Congruency does not align well with Lippmann's original stereotyping implications of rigid, categorical thinking, but it does suggest identification with a candidate. Viewed in a context of increasing polarization of candidate attributes and issues, congruency is perhaps useful in explaining why images become stereotyped.

It should come as no surprise that stereotyping and evolution of candidate images should pose difficult questions, especially interpreted in the context of fast-moving political events surrounding a presidential election. Yet despite many unresolved points, stereotyping provided a conceptually and operationally sensitive indication of candidate image. It suggests—beyond knowing their content—that images can be viewed cognitively as a process developing along major, measurable dimensions.

NOTES

1. The authors wish to thank Professor Alex Edelstein of the School of Communications, University of Washington, for his suggestions and editorial advice on this manuscript, and Barbara Bowes for her assistance with data processing.
2. See Nimmo and Savage (1976) for a detailed discussion of candidate images, definitions, and origins. Their working definition of image is "a human construct imposed on an array of perceived attributes projected by an object, event or person." This is essentially the usage of "candidate image" here. We have taken "attribute" to include the usual array of personality traits, but as well, the importance the candidate is perceived as assigning to various major issues. See note 3 for a listing of issues used. Kraus and Davis (1976) provide a summary and annotated bibliography of current communication research relevant to candidate images and media impacts on them.
3. Methods used to assess stereotyping bear resemblance to those used by Carter (1962) and close similarity to those used by Stamm, Bowes, and Bowes (1973) and Bowes (1977). Questions forming the basis of stereotype formation were based on common personal attributes and key campaign issues. They were as follows:

   > Question 1: "We'd like you to look over a list of characteristics frequently used to describe political candidates. If you feel there are important descriptors left out, add them in the blank spaces at the bottom of the list. Now there are two things we would like you to do with the list:"
   > "#1: Rank the three most important characteristics to you. Mark a '1' by the most important, a '2' by your second choice, and a '3' by the third choice."
   > "#2: Describe the candidates you're aware of on all scales. You may use an "F" for Ford and a "C" for Carter. . . ."

   Respondents could also rate Reagan, McCarthy, and Maddox. Few chose to do so. Attributes rated, in addition to what the respondent might add to the list, were: "trustworthy," "sincere," "works hard," "experienced," "fair," "intelligent," "imaginative," "safe," and "tough." Scales were divided into equal intervals numbered 1 to 10, indicating (1) "not at all" to (10) "very."

   > Question 2: "We'd like to know what major issues *you feel* are central to the Presidential campaign and the debates between Ford and Carter. Look over the list below. Are there any issues left out? If so, add them in the blanks at the bottom of the list. Then: Indicate on the scales the importance you personally place on each issue. Mark the scale position closest to your feelings with an 'X'."

   After the respondent finished this task, he or she was asked:

   > "Now: Go back through the list, indicating how you think Ford would honestly rate the importance of issues on the list. Mark your estimate with an 'F' on each scale. Do the same for Carter, marking your estimate of his ratings with a 'C' on each scale."

   Issues rated, in addition to what the respondent added to the list, were: Jobs, Full Employment; Control of Inflation; Equal Rights for Women; Environmental Protection; Busing and Integration; Honesty in Government; Abortion and Right to Life; U.S. Foreign Policy (Kissinger); and Government Spending (Taxes). Each was rated on a 1 to 10 scale, from "not at all important" (1) to "extremely important" (10).
4. Several minor methodological points need clarification:

   a. The influence of candidate preference on stereotyping was determined by dividing and comparing the sample on intended vote.
   b. Because there were so many possible information sources to be examined, they were divided roughly in half; each half being measured in Surveys 1 and 3, or 2 and 4. Consequently, information sources were measured only twice during the course of the debates. In Surveys 1 and 3, frequency of information source use was determined for both political and general news. These were continuous measures covering media and personal sources. Surveys 2 and 4 measured exposure to the debates with simple dichotomous items.

   c. The polarization and homogenization of attributes or issues could be seriously contaminated by the interest respondents placed in certain attributes or issues. Low interest scales could, for example, be suspect of vulnerability to response set. Response set by this analysis is not separable as a bias from the homogenization measure. Too, high interest scales might be more likely to be polarized. To test the effects of salience in a limited way, attributes were ranked by respondents according to their importance. Respondents could add attributes to the set, should the prepared set be unsatisfactory. Comparing responses on an individual basis for top ranked (I to III) scales versus those ranked lower showed no significant differences in either polarization or homogenization. Only five respondents added attributes to the scale set provided.
5. Respondents were asked to rate overall performance of Ford and Carter before and following each debate. The difference between these two measures provided a rough indication of relative "winning" or "losing." Carter improved while Ford declined as a result of the first debate, a situation reversed by the second debate, though Carter's loss here was not equal to Ford's gain. The third debate showed no significant movement at all.
6. While most movement was toward the respondents' favored candidate, respondents also moved appreciably, though to a lesser degree, closer to opposition candidates.
7. These causal problems resemble closely those of media agenda-setting research. See McLeod, Becker, and Byrnes (1974) and Bowes (1973).

REFERENCES

BAUER, R.A., POOL, I. de S., & DEXTER, L.A. *Amer-*

ican business and public opinion. New York: Atherton, 1963.

BOWES, J. Stereotyping and communication accuracy: Problems in effective citizen-government communication. *Journalism Quarterly*, 1977, 77, 70-76.

BOWES, J. A discussion of four papers: Political communication. Paper presented at the annual meeting of the Association for Education in Journalism, Fort Collins, Col., August, 1973.

CARTER, R.F. Stereotyping as a process. *Public Opinion Quarterly*, 1962, 26, 77-91.

GANS, H.J. Lessons 1976 can offer 1980. *Columbia Journalism Review*, 1977, 15, 25-27.

KATZ, E., & FELDMAN, J.J. The debates in light of research: A survey of surveys. In W. Schramm and D.F. Roberts (Eds.), *The process and effects of mass communications*. Urbana: University of Illinois, 1971, 701-793.

KRAUS, S., & DAVIS, D. Construction of political reality in society. In S. Kraus & D. Davis, *The effects of mass communication on political behavior*. University Park: Pennsylvania State University Press, 1976, 209-227.

KRECH, D., & CRUTCHFIELD, R.S. *Elements of psychology*. New York: Knopf, 1958.

LIPPMANN, W. *Public opinion*. New York: Macmillan, 1922.

McGRATH, J., & McGRATH, M. Effects of partisanship on perception of political figures. *Public Opinion Quarterly*, 1962, 26, 236-248.

McLEOD, J., BECKER, L., & BYRNES, J. Another look at the agenda-setting function of the press. *Communication Research*, 1974, 2, 131-166.

NIMMO, D., & SAVAGE, R.L. *Candidates and their images*. Pacific Palisades: Goodyear, 1976.

SIGEL, R.S. Effect of partisanship on perception of political candidates. *Public Opinion Quarterly*, 1964, 28, 484-485.

STAMM, K.R., BOWES, J.E., & BOWES, B.J. Generation gap a communication problem? A coorientational analysis. *Journalism Quarterly*, 1973, 50, 629-637.

WHY JOHN Q. VOTER DID NOT LEARN MUCH FROM THE 1976 PRESIDENTIAL DEBATES

DORIS A. GRABER
University of Illinois-Chicago Circle

YOUNG YUN KIM
Governors State University

The results reported in this paper about political learning from the 1976 presidential debates are based on a year-long study of all aspects of political learning of a small panel of voters. Debate learning is put into general learning perspectives and distinguishes various levels of learning. Judged in the context of learning throughout the campaign year, new learning from the debates was quite modest, even when the standards for scoring learning are low and inadequate to support the goal of intelligent voting. The knowledge-deficient learned at lower rates, quantitatively and qualitatively, than the better informed. Several factors which are known to inhibit learning were present in the debate scenarios. These include redundancy of information with predebate news supply, excessive complexity of issues with inadequate time for analysis, sketchy postdebate commentary, and general dullness. The audience watched the spectacle only partially and with mixed attention and discounted much of it as mere "campaign rhetoric."

On September 23, 1976, 94 million Americans watched the first of three 90-minute debates between Gerald Ford, the Republican incumbent, and Jimmy Carter, the Democratic challenger, in the 1976 presidential race. On October 6, and again on October 22, an audience of 85 million in the United States, along with people in 113 other countries of the world, watched the second and third debates between Ford and Carter. Seventy million Americans also watched the 60-minute debate on October 15 between Senators Robert Dole and Walter Mondale, the respective vice-presidential running mates of Ford and Carter. Many other persons read or heard commentary about the debates in addition to, or in place of, watching them.

The mass media covered the event in a style reserved for major political occurrences. There were repeated predebate announcements, extensive and prominent live coverage of the debates, and a moderate amount of postdebate summaries, analyses, and editorials. Numerous polls elicited audience reactions to the event and these reactions were widely publicized.[1]

The Education Fund of the League of Women Voters sponsored the debates to help "voters become better informed on the issues" and "in the hope of promoting a wider and better-informed participation by the American people in the election."[2] Translated into specific learning goals, this means that the league, and other proponents of presidential debates, hoped that voters would gain information about the issues beyond that held prior to the debates. This information about the nature of the issues, the stands of the candidates, and their capabilities to cope with the issues would be specific and detailed enough to enable voters to better determine which candidate deserved their vote, in light of the voter's own political preferences and concerns. Did the debates fulfill this important task?

To find out whether they had been the intended major learning event about campaign issues and candidate personalities and qualifications, we looked at three types of data. First, we examined the substance of the debate to discover the amount and comprehensibility of information made available to debate listeners. We also scrutinized press and television news coverage of the debates, which had been available to a small panel of voters, to determine how much the media helped these voters in digesting the information presented to them during the debates. Finally, we investigated how much and what kinds of knowledge about issues, candidate stands, and candidate qualifications, members of this panel had gained from the debates.

Since "learning" involves various levels of complexity, which are blurred by most studies, we carefully distinguished various learning levels. We tested for *awareness* (remembering an information item after it had been mentioned by the interviewer), and *spontaneous recall* (information initiated without any assistance from the interviewer). We also distinguished among bare recall without facts, recall with facts which might be correct or incorrect, and reconstruction of facts based on correct or incorrect inferences. Additionally, when measuring for knowledge about issues, we distinguished between knowledge about the nature of the issue, and knowledge about the position of one or both candidates on this issue.

THE SAMPLE

The respondents, whose knowledge gains from the debates are discussed here, were part of a panel study of voters whose political learning we had closely observed during an entire year. From January 1976 to January 1977 we kept in close touch with four small panels of voters through a series of 9 to 10 intensive interviews spaced throughout the year. An average of 165 individuals were contacted for each interview.[3]

Members of the panels were selected from a randomly drawn sample of registered voters in Evanston, Illinois, a suburban community near Chicago, as well as from metropolitan Indianapolis, Indiana, and Lebanon, New Hampshire, a small New England town. The final sample was drawn to assure a balance of such demographic characteristics as age, sex, and occupational status. It was also designed to represent various levels of interest in politics, availability of time for following political news, and various patterns of media use, such as major reliance on print media, major reliance on television, or major reliance on both print and television for political news. For each panel, content analyses of the major print and electronic media used by the respondents permitted an analysis of the relationship between information supply and information use.

The findings of debate learning presented here are based on the experiences of 21 members of our Evanston panels who were selected for especially intensive analysis. The findings from the larger group support the intensive-panel data when we compare data on political learning recorded throughout the election year (Becker, Weaver, Graber, & McCombs, 1977). Furthermore, a comparison of responses by our panel members with election-related responses by Gallup and Roper poll interviewees throughout 1976 shows no significant discrepancies.[4] This gives us confidence that our respondents do not differ significantly in their political learning behavior from that of general population samples. Intensive study of their political learning behaviors should reveal patterns found commonly among voters with similar learning propensities (Lane, 1962, pp. 1-11; Keniston, 1968; Brown, 1974; Lamb, 1975, pp. vii-xiii, 3-23).

The reason for using a small panel, of course, is the desire to investigate the political learning process intensively, over an extended period of time. The intensive nature of the investigation, which demanded close and prolonged monitoring of the information supply of specific respondents, collecting daily diaries, and researching lifestyle details of panel members, made it mandatory to limit the number of respondents under study. The reward of this intensive effort is a far more intimate knowledge of respondents than is ordinarily possible. This knowledge is essential in putting their verbal responses and their learning behaviors into appropriate contexts.

The interviews with members of the intensive panel were tape recorded and averaged two hours in length. Most questions were open-ended and designed to permit the respondent to formulate the major outlines of the problem as she or he perceived them. These broad questions were then followed by more focused questions designed to insure that all respondents covered the same major knowledge areas related to political learning. To elicit as broad a response as possible, probes and follow-up questions were unlimited. Probes routinely asked for reasons which had prompted particular answers.[5]

The initial interview with each of the respondents elicited detailed life histories, with special emphasis on the context and the substance of political learning during childhood, adolescence, and during various phases of the respondent's adult life. General attitudes towards the mass media, the scope and nature of information sources aside from the mass media, the felt needs for political information, and the uses of political information in the respondent's current life situation were also ascertained.

Table 1 groups the panel of 21 into four cells, depending on their interest in politics and on the time available for direct and indirect exposure to the mass media. Group assignments are based on replies to nine questions about interest and participation in politics, media use patterns, and general lifestyle characteristics. The replies were used to construct indexes of interest in politics and availability of time for news exposure. In the course of the election year, the lifestyle of a number of the respondents changed, increasing or decreasing the time available for media use. In each case, media use patterns changed. When a change of patterns was noted for two successive interviews, respondents were reassigned to newly appropriate cells. All of the reassignments took place during the first four months of the study. Table 1 reflects these reassignments.

The members of the intensive panel also completed daily diaries throughout the year in which they recorded news stories which had come to their attention from the mass media or through personal contacts. They were instructed to enter in a diary—at a designated time—any news story which they remembered, noting briefly the main theme, the source, the length of the story, the reasons for their interest in the story, and their reaction to it. A minimum of 30 minutes was to elapse between story exposure and diary entry to allow normal forgetting processes to operate. In most instances, the actual interval was four hours or more. In addition, members of the intensive panel were questioned during each interview about an array of 20 to 30 news stories which had been covered by the newspapers or television news programs to which they normally paid attention.

To detect possible sensitization effects which might appear in interviews and in the diaries because of the frequent repetitions, several checks were run using respondents who had not been included in the regular panels. Test results indicate that sensitization was not a major problem. For instance, the mean news awareness scores of panel members and nonmembers, based on responses about knowledge of randomly selected specific recent news stories, showed no significant differences.[6]

Information sources which were content-analyzed on a daily basis were the *Chicago Tribune*; the national evening news broadcasts by ABC, CBS, and NBC; and the CBS and NBC local news. These were the major sources of political news used by the Evanston panels.

THE FINDINGS ABOUT LEARNING

To test learning increments beyond debate knowledge, we asked each of our respondents whether she or he had learned anything new from the debates about Ford, Carter, Dole, or Mondale We also asked whether anything new had been learned about the issues. If the answer was positive, we then asked what the new information was and probed for as much detail as the respondent could recall. Since our respondents knew from previous interviews that their self-appraisals would be followed up by specific questions about new knowledge, the replies recorded here tend to be more conservative than responses when no follow-up is expected. Likewise, learning ratings based on unaided recall of "new" information are likely to be lower than ratings based on factual statements which respondents identify as true or false to varying degrees. However, since the voting decision involves choices made on the basis of freely recalled information—if, indeed, it is made on the voter's independent appraisals of the issues and the candidates' characteristics—we feel that the more rigorous learning tests applied here are necessary to measure whether the stated goals of the debates were achieved.

Table 2 shows the results when the respondents

TABLE 1
Background Characteristics of the Intensive Study Panel

1. High Interest -- High Availability Group

Age	Sex	Education**	Occupation	Marital Status***
25	M	College	Research Engineer	Single
38	M	College	Administrator	Married
45	M	College	Academic	Married
74	M	College	Lawyer	Married
75	M	Grade School	Blue Collar	Married

2. High Interest -- Low Availability Group

Age	Sex	Education**	Occupation	Marital Status***
28	F	College	Home/Child Care	Married
28	F	College	Corporation Executive	Single
30	F	College	Job/Home/Child Care	Married
33	F	College	Government Admin.	Married
36	M	College	Editor	Married

3. Low Interest -- High Availability Group

Age	Sex	Education**	Occupation	Marital Status***
25	M	College	Grocery Clerk	Single
46	F	High School	Dress Shop Owner	Married
50	F	College	Homemaker	Widowed
65	F	High School	Bookkeeper	Widowed
78	F	High School	Homemaker	Widowed

4. Low Interest -- Low Availability Group

Age	Sex	Education**	Occupation	Marital Status***
23	M	High School	Hospital Clerk	Single
27	M	College	Retail Sales	Single
28	F	High School	Insurance Clerk	Single
36	F	High School	Nurse	Married
56	F	3rd Grade	Maid	Widowed
62	M	College	Plant Manager	Married

*Group assignments are based on replies to nine questions which ascertained interest and participation in politics, media use patterns, and life style characteristics. The latter two gave clues to the availability of mass media information for particular respondents. Scores were based on a combination of self-assessment and objective measures.

**The designations indicate completion of degree requirements.

***Age and sex are not significantly related to interest in the election, learning from the debates, or to political learning in general. Education was significantly related to learning from the debates and to political learning in general. The data presented from this panel are therefore biased in the direction of exaggerating general learning and knowledge levels. Occupational needs, and social needs related to marital status had a strong impact on frequencies of political discussion.

TABLE 2
Number of Respondents Who Reported Various Degrees of Debate-Learning About Candidates and Issues (N equals 21 respondents)

Subject	None	Some	Lot	Debate
Ford	11	10	0	1st
Ford	9	11	1	2nd
Ford	12	9	0	3rd
Dole	11	7	3	V.P.
Carter	12	9	0	1st
Carter	7	14	0	2nd
Carter	9	11	1	3rd
Mondale	12	7	2	V.P.
Issues	21	0	0	1st
Issues	9	12	0	2nd
Issues	15	4	2	3rd
Issues	14	6	1	V.P.

gave their own assessment of learning about candidates and issues which had taken place as a consequence of the debates.[7] Learning a lot about presidential and vice-presidential candidates and about issues was rare. It was mentioned only once for Ford (for the second debate) and once for Carter (for the third debate). The report of learning about the vice-presidential candidates was somewhat more optimistic. Three respondents out of 21 thought that they had learned a lot about Senator Dole and two respondents felt that they had learned a lot about Senator Mondale. With some variations, apparent from Table 2, approximately half of the panel members claimed to have learned nothing new at all about the candidates in the course of the four debates.

Claims about issue learning were even more modest. The entire panel concluded that no new issue information was conveyed in the first debate; two-thirds made equally negative assessments for the third presidential debate and for the vice-presidential debate. The second debate was the only one for which more than half of the respondents claimed to learn a moderate amount about the issues. Only two respondents claimed to learn a lot about the issues from any one of the debates, in this case the third one. Only one respondent learned a lot about the issues from the vice-presidential debate. In each case, those who claimed a lot of learning about candidates or issues were primarily respondents from the high-interest, low-availability group identified in Table 1. For these respondents, the debates presented a chance to "catch up" on desired information to which they had been unable to expose themselves earlier.

The record of learning about candidates and issues looked even more meager when respondents were asked to spontaneously and specifically recall what they had learned about each candidate and about the issues. Table 3 gives the figures for both candidate and issue learning. It indicates how many specific items of information panel members could recall from each debate. The bulk of respondents learned nothing, or just one single item of information, about either candidate or issues during the individual debates and the debate aftermath, when the ability to spontaneously recall specific information is used as the test. Table 3 also shows that panel members could recall more information about the candidates than about the issues. This confirms the findings of other studies which have shown that the public more readily learns informa-

TABLE 3
Number of Respondents Who Recalled Zero to Three or More Items of Information About Candidates and Issues (N equals 21 respondents)

Subject	0	1	2	3 or more	Debate
Ford	11	8	2	0	1st
Ford	8	12	1	0	2nd
Ford	11	6	4	0	3rd
Dole	10	8	3	0	V.P.
Carter	12	9	0	0	1st
Carter	6	14	1	0	2nd
Carter	9	8	4	0	3rd
Mondale	11	8	2	0	V.P.
Issues	21	0	0	0	1st
Issues	8	9	3	1	2nd
Issues	13	3	1	3	3rd
Issues	14	4	3	0	V.P.

TABLE 4
Average Number of Information Items Learned by Groups of Respondents About Candidates and Issues (N equals 107 candidate qualities, 44 issue mention)

Group	Candidates qualities	Issues
High Interest, High Availability	5.0	2.8
High Interest, Low Availability	5.0	4.6
Low Interest, High Availability	4.2	0.6
Low Interest, Low Availability	2.7	0.7

tion about candidates than information about issues (Graber, 1972; Graber, 1974; Pomper, 1975; Asher, 1976).

A look at learning patterns of individual respondents shows that the two groups who had been rated as high in political interest (see Table 1) and whose record of learning about the election had been comparatively high prior to the debates, learned far more from the debates than did the two low-interest groups. The group with high interest and low availability learned the most, probably because it had the highest unsatisfied need for information. The groups with low interest, irrespective of available time, gained little from the debate presentations.[8] Table 4 presents the average number of information items learned by members of the groups listed in Table 1.

To test the recall of specific issue information which was extensively discussed during the first and second debates, we asked panel members early in October to report what each of the candidates had said about designated aspects of policy concerning—jobs, taxes, draft evaders, U.S. policy in Africa, U.S. relations with the Soviet Union, and

TABLE 5
Number of Respondents Who Recalled Various Amounts of Precise Information About Candidate Positions on Selected Issues (N equals 21 respondents)

Issue	Ford Position			Carter Position		
	None	Some	Lot	None	Some	Lot
Jobs	20	0	1	20	0	1
Taxes	21	0	0	10	7	4
Draft	11	6	4	12	6	3
Africa	8	7	6	3	11	7
Soviet	14	4	3	6	10	5
Defense	15	5	1	11	8	2

the adequacy of national defense. The question was: "Do you recall anything that Governor Carter/President Ford said during the first/second debate about what should be done to (increase jobs, reform the tax system, etc.)." Respondents were scored as learning "a lot" if they could spontaneously recall four or more facts that had actually been mentioned in the debates. They were scored as having gained "some" knowledge if they recalled from one to three facts. The score was "none" if nothing was recalled spontaneously. Table 5 presents the results.

Table 5 indicates that nearly 75% of the respondents could not accurately state President Ford's positions on the issues in question. An average of half of the respondents failed similarly for Carter. Very few respondents knew "a lot" about most of the issues. Here, again, knowledge about Carter was slightly greater than knowledge about Ford. In view of the many complaints that Carter was fuzzy on the issues, it is ironic that our panel members found it easier to recall parameters of Carter's policies than of Ford's.

When laxer learning standards were applied—whereby respondents were credited with learning if they were able to cite *any* facts about the policy areas under investigation, even if they referred to information which had not been included in the debates, and even if the statements contained major errors or were based on inferences—knowledge levels remained unimpressive. Using the standard of simultaneous knowledge of the positions of both candidates—a sine qua non for rational decision-making—only 3 respondents could recall the specifics about both Carter's and Ford's stands on Africa. Seven respondents could cite the stands of both candidates on jobs and on foreign policy towards the Soviet Union. Ten could cite the stands of both candidates for taxes, 16 for national defense, and 17 for amnesty. Table 6 presents the information and also indicates the various learning levels, from bare issue recall to knowledge of the stands of both candidates.

An answer-by-answer analysis of the first and second debates shows that job creation policies and defense policies were discussed extensively on four occasions by each of the candidates; tax reform and relations with the Soviet Union were the main subject of three Ford and four Carter replies; U.S. policy towards Africa was discussed in three Ford and two Carter replies; and the fate of draft evaders was the subject of one lengthy exposition by each of the candidates. All of the issues, except for the treatment of draft evaders, had been

TABLE 6
Number of Respondents Who Recalled Various Amounts of Imprecise Information About Both Candidates' Positions on Selected Issues (N equals 21 respondents)

Issue	No Awareness	Awareness	Know Issue Only	Know Issue & 1 Cand. Stand	Know Issue & 2 Cand. Stands
Jobs	4	3	4	3	7
Taxes	3	3	0	5	10
Draft	1	0	1	2	17
Africa	6	2	4	6	3
Soviet	5	0	5	4	7
Defense	3	0	2	0	16

mentioned repeatedly by most of our respondents as personally important to them in answers to the open-ended question: "Of the various problems and issues now facing the United States, which is the most important to you personally? Why?"

Given the fact, then, that these were important issues to our panel members, and that the candidates' positions on these issues had been frequently reported in the press and on television, as is apparent from our content analyses, our expectation had been that most respondents would be able to state two or three elements in the position of at least one of the candidates following the debates. That this expectation was not fulfilled is taken as evidence that learning from the campaign in general, and the debates in particular, was minimal when measured by the ability of panel members to cite candidate characteristics, campaign issues, and candidate positions on these issues. While the debates may have reinforced existing knowledge, the data presented here reveal unimpressive knowledge gains about candidates and issues linked to the debates.

Our expectations about likely learning rates are based on the assumption that an attentive citizen, in a presentation geared to his or her interest and level of understanding, should be able to recall at least 1 out of every 100 issues mentioned, especially when many issues were covered repeatedly. A total of 166 questions was asked in the three presidential debates, each of which was watched in whole or in part by two-thirds of the panel members. Coding up to 3 issue mentions for each response, 297 issue mentions occurred, covering diverse aspects of 26 issues. Nearly half of the issues were mentioned more than 10 times.[9] Yet the 1% learning rate, which would have meant an average of 3.0 statements reflecting issue learning, was not achieved. The average issue learning rate for the three presidential debates was 1.6 issues.

If one assumes that the answer to each of the 166 questions in the presidential debates provided an opportunity to evaluate the personal and professional qualifications of the candidates, then our respondents had 332 opportunities to judge the candidates along the dimensions which they had used in previous judgments. A total of 81 qualities were learned for the three presidential debates; this puts the average learning rate at 3.9 qualities. This is slightly higher than the bottom rate of 1% for learning, yet certainly no proud achievement.

REASONS FOR MODERATE LEARNING

Having established that learning was modest—a condition which appears to be quite common for most aspects of political learning—we attempted to ascertain why the information dispensed in the 4-stage, 5½-hour television spectacular, which was widely announced and described by press and television commentators and watched by an average of 85 million Americans, produced so little political learning. To answer this question, we looked at a variety of factors which communications researchers have identified as important in the political message transmission process (Kraus & Davis, 1976).

Debate effects might be small, we reasoned, because of learning deterrents which came into play in the interaction of audience characteristics with message or message-sender characteristics. More specifically, voters may have been unreceptive to the message because of a lack of interest in politics, a saturation with political information which made debate information redundant, or a lack of time or conflicting engagements which made it undesirable or impossible to pay attention to media events such as the debates. Forgetting the date or malfunctioning equipment might be other environmental causes which prevented attention to the debates.

Another group of deterrents relate to disinterest or distrust between the sender and the receiver of the message. If voters are cynical about the credibility of politicians in general, or about the credibility of one or both of the candidates, or if they consider their own views as clashing with those of one or both of these candidates, this cynicism might lead to minimal attention to and learning from the debates. In addition, voters who had already made a choice might lose interest in hearing the candidates further expound on their positions, since the incentive of gathering decision-making information had passed.

Finally, voters might have been repelled by the substance or format of the message. If the voters found the debates dull or carried on at the "gutter" level, if they found them overly complex and confusing, or if they deemed them manipulative and staged, they might decide to skip them or pay minimal attention. For the second and third presidential debates and for the vice-presidential debate, the perceived quality of previous debates became an additional factor in determining attention to and learning from the subsequent performances.

A look at the data which we have concerning these various explanatory factors shows that some, but not all, of these possible deterrents appeared during the 1976 presidential debates. Looking first at audience characteristics, we find that a lack of interest in politics in general, or in the debates in particular, was not a factor. During the debate period, two-thirds of the panel members stated that they were very interested in the presidential campaign, and the remainder had expressed moderate interest. When we looked at behavioral indexes of election interest, such as the frequency with which the respondents mentioned election stories, including debate stories in their diaries, the ease with which they recalled specific election stories, and the frequencies with which they listed the election as a matter of personal importance and concern in open-ended questions, the impression of substantial interest in the election was sustained. Likewise, 16 of our respondents claimed that issues were important to their presidential vote decision, and 17 claimed that personal and professional qualities of the candidates were significant in their choice.

However, these high interest levels did not produce regular and faithful watching of the debates, as might have been assumed. As Table 7 indicates, a third of the respondents were dropouts in each presidential debate and one-half of the respondents missed the vice-presidential debates entirely. Two individuals missed all four debates and two others saw only one. All of these absentees were from the low-interest, low-availability group (see Table 1). Of those who watched the debates, only half managed to pay attention to the entire broadcast. Only two individuals watched an hour or more of all four debates. Only six individuals saw portions of all four debates.

The bulk of the excuses offered for not watching the debates were that the respondent had other things to do, rather than that interest was lacking.[10] Examination of the interview transcripts shows that high interest was readily counteracted by other demands on the respondent's time. Politics was salient, but compared to other concerns, it readily yielded in competition for the limited time resources of the respondents. An invitation to dinner, a chance to make some money baby-sitting,

TABLE 7
Number of Respondents Who Watched Each Debate on Television for Varying Periods of Time (N equals 21 respondents)

	None	1-29 min.	30-59 min.	60-90 min.
1st debate	6	6	2	7
2nd debate	7	3	4	7
3rd debate	7	3	3	8
V.P. debate	11	1	2	7

an ordinary shopping trip, or a trip to the movies, provided ready excuses for ignoring the debates. The respondents were generally not motivated to catch up on debate learning through other sources. Less than one-third of the respondents reported learning from the debates through secondary channels. The fact that the print and electronic media used by our panel made little effort to summarize the substance of each debate on the days following the event may partly explain the low level of learning from secondary sources.

The conclusion which emerges from a comparison of data about political interest with data about debate attention is that inferences about the likely effects of high interest must be made in light of competing interest patterns within an individual. In such a competing interest scheme, the priorities assigned to political concerns, such as information about a pending political election, tend to be low.[11]

When we asked whether debate information was redundant with information previously presented to voters, the answer was a resounding "yes." Analysis of the print and television news stories which had been available to our respondents indicates that nearly all of the topics discussed in the debates had been amply covered from the early primary season on. Both presidential candidates had received a great deal of media exposure and questioning for many months prior to the debates, so that it was unlikely that any important questions remained untouched by the time the last campaign weeks rolled around. The vice-presidential candidates, being tied to their mentors' political positions, were not likely to strike out in new directions during the debates.

We know from responses in seven predebate interviews that our respondents were aware of the issues discussed in the debates and that most of them, by the time of the debate, had fairly firm conceptions about the personalities and qualifications of the candidates. We had specifically asked about awareness of five of the six specific issues on which we had tested respondents' debate learning. Nearly all respondents indicated awareness of these issues. More generally, a check of recall of election stories during prior interviews indicated familiarity with the type of information conveyed by the debates.[12]

A number of respondents commented explicitly that the debates contained nothing new. In addition, by the time of the debates, most of the respondents whose political interests were high, informed us that they already had sufficient information about candidates and issues to make a choice, confident that the choice was based on sufficient knowledge of the total situation. The information needs which were unfulfilled, as yet, related to matters of personal rather than general public interest, or to questions of future performance which could not possibly be answered prior to the candidate taking office. Half of the low interest group expressed the need for additional information, but it was an unfocused need. Most of them said they wanted to know more, or felt they ought to know more, but found it difficult to specify what information they wanted. Besides, most of them conceded that their own lack of motivation to pay attention to election information would probably bar additional learning, even if information was available in a format and at a time suited to their tastes.

The conclusion suggested by these data, then, is

that the information presented during the debates was familiar to most respondents. Those who were already knowledgeable about the election found little new to add to their knowledge. Those who had not yet learned much, for a variety of reasons, were generally prevented by these same reasons from learning more (Tichenor, Donohue, & Olien, 1970; Donohue, Tichenor, & Olien, 1975).

Turning to learning deterrents which might arise from cynicism about politicians or lack of incentives for paying attention to their campaign efforts, we again find a mixed picture. Throughout our interviews, there were a number of off-hand comments by our respondents about the unreliability and even deceitfulness of politicians. But the answers to specific questions concerning trust in public officials do not reveal high levels of distrust. For instance, in expressing agreement or disagreement with a statement that Ford or Carter as president could be trusted, only two respondents disagreed for Ford and only three disagreed for Carter.[13] On a series of statements about trusting public officials in general, from one-half to two-thirds of the respondents generally expressed some degree of trust. However, a number of respondents voiced doubts about the credibility of what they termed "campaign rhetoric" or "political jargon" with the implication that politicians should not be blamed for their vacuous rhetoric since the nature of the politics requires it. Audiences, for their part, should routinely discount what politicians say in the heat of a campaign.

We gather from these data that even voters who trust political figures may discount their campaign pronouncements. As a consequence, they may not be inclined to learn the information which is submitted to them. In addition, when there is a feeling, as happened during the debates, that the voter is viewing a carefully rehearsed performance designed to manipulate his judgment of the comparative merits of the candidates, learning resistance factors come into play. The evaluation that the debates were a "show" put on to deceive the voters, runs through the transcripts of our interviews.

If completion or near-completion of a voting decision was a depressant to debate learning, then the bulk of our respondents should have been affected. Half of the respondents had definitely decided for whom they would vote and one-quarter had made a tentative voting decision. However, it is not at all clear that the completion or near-completion of the voting decision did deter learning. With one exception, the totally undecided voters all came from the low-interest groups. As indicated earlier, the learning levels of these groups were low compared to the levels of members in the high-interest panels. We therefore have no conclusive evidence that undecided voters learned more than those who had already decided. However, it is possible that those who had already made a voting decision would have learned more than they actually did, if they had possessed the additional incentive of having to make a voting decision. Table 8 shows that decisional status bore no relation to the respondents' debate watching.[14]

The validity of linking voting decision to learning propensities is further called into question because the precise effect of the debates on the voting decision-making process is unclear. Of the four respondents in our sample who decided after the debates, three votes went to Ford, the presumptive loser of the debates, and one went to McCarthy. All of these voters had earlier leaned to Carter. None of the voters who had made a predebate decision, tentative or firm, changed their decision as a result of the debates. To confuse the situation even further, in response to a direct question, one-third of the panel claimed that the debates influenced their voting decision. The remainder saw no influence. It seems that "influence" in this case, meant reinforcement of prior decisions, rather than influence to make or change a decision. Since a number of respondents indicated that even their "firm" decision might be upset by some major event, the influence of the debates may have been appraised in terms of this unfulfilled potential.

Turning to the substance and format of the debates as possible deterrents to learning, a number of factors indicate that much was wrong with the highly-touted spectacular. It was, among other things, partly boring, overly complex, and inadequately analyzed. Whether a change in some or all of these facets would be able to overcome the deterrent power of the other factors mentioned earlier in this paper remains a matter for conjecture.

The question of the dullness of the debates, like

TABLE 8
Number of Decided and Undecided Voters Who Watched the Televised Debates for Varying Periods of Time (N equals 21 respondents)

	None	1-45 min.	45-90 min.
Decided Voters	1	6	4
Undecided Voters	1	5	4

other debate-related questions, yields a mixed answer. A direct question about whether the first debate was interesting elicited 6 comments that it was highly interesting, 14 comments that it was somewhat interesting, and 1 comment that it was boring.[15] The second debate was considered highly interesting by 2 respondents, 10 called it somewhat interesting, and 6 found it boring, while 3 did not know. These overall judgments of fairly high audience appeal are partly contradicted in many instances by some of the reasons given for watching less than the full debate.

Here people called portions of the debates dull, repetitive of previous campaign information, hard to follow, and the like. The most frequent reason cited for watching only the early portions of the debates was, "I fell asleep." Hence it seems that an overall judgment that the debates were interesting may mask strong impressions that debate quality was uneven throughout the communication event. Apparently, press personnel gathered similar impressions. While an early *Tribune* editorial (September 25), for instance, claimed that the first debate "struck sparks and shed light," a headline, prior to the second debate, queried "Can 'Sominex Twins' Wake the Nation?" Such a headline (October 5) certainly was not conducive to conditioning readers to expect an interesting presentation.

A number of people were disappointed that they were treated to parallel press conferences, rather than true debates in which the candidates would interact directly with each other. Their expectations for a true debate were unrealistic since most campaign issues are unsuitable for the debate format. They do not involve relatively narrow, clearcut situations on which debaters can take opposing stands. They deal with comparatively small differences in emphasis and approach, rather than differences in outcomes. Yet regardless of the validity of the expectation, the disappointment was real.

To many panel members, the debates seemed rehearsed and phoney. This impression was enhanced by the fact that the day before the first debate, the *Tribune* carried a long story about the briefing which the candidates had received which had "programmed" them with set answers. The story told of Ford sparring with a mock panel over a three-day period and described the careful tests of cameras, clothing, and make-up. This air of watching an unreal situation, a "show" that had little to do with the actors' abilities to be president, probably reduced the impact of the debate.

The complexity of the issues chosen for debating made dullness almost inevitable. Are wage and price controls necessary to stop inflation? Can taxes be cut without budget cuts? Is zero-based budgeting sound? Were the numerous Ford vetoes of legislation evidence of a lack of leadership by Ford, or evidence that Congress was obstructionist and spendthrift? Are U.S. defenses sufficiently strong and is the U.S. respected and trusted abroad? How good is the Helsinki agreement? Can human rights be protected without endangering the relations with other countries? These were some of the highly complex and controversial questions which listeners were asked to judge amid cleverly phrased claims and counterclaims, several of them partly inaccurate. As Tom Wicker put it in a *New York Times* story on October 26, the debates "afforded the two candidates opportunity to make more misrepresentations, false claims, calculated appeals and empty promises than probably ever were offered so directly to a long-suffering electorate."

While the issues were complex, the time allotted for discussion was totally inadequate. Judging from listener comments, confusion, rather than enlightenment, was prevalent. The format called for a three-minute reply to the initial question (2½ minutes in the third debate) and two minutes for a follow-up. Then there were two minutes for rebuttal. Closing statements were limited to three minutes each. Had the candidates really tried to explain the issues, state their positions, and delineate the consequences of various alternatives, they would have found the time constraints intolerable. As it happened, they made no such attempts and, in most instances, did not even use the full time allotted to them.

What the candidates attempted to do instead was to use the answers as a springboard to convey impressions about their personal competence, erudition, poise, and credibility. Both cited a wide array of confusing facts and statistics. Ford tried to show his mastery of complex issues and governmental functions and tried to depict Carter as confused, inexperienced, and lacking in leadership qualities. Carter attempted to appear sure and knowledgeable, sound in political judgment, sensitive to human needs, and generally sound in his priorities. He made skillful use of emotion-laden abstractions, claiming that America, under a Ford administration, was short on morality, openness, leadership, compassion for human rights, and lacked the respect of its own people and of the world. The listener, caught in this cross fire of the image battle, had an understandably difficult time in attempting to formulate distinct impressions about each candidate.

Media commentary did little to help listeners to make sense out of the confusion. The texts of the debates were not reprinted in the *Tribune* and there was no outline of the candidates' stands, or a pointing out of the errors in the statements made by Ford and Carter. A review of television and radio commentary and of postdebate coverage in the *Tribune* revealed very little interpretation and analysis of the information covered by the debates. Instead, the bulk of the commentary related to the performance of the candidates as winners or losers in the debate battle. Three out of four postdebate stories stressed this aspect, as did a series of public opinion polls taken in the wake of each debate. A *Tribune* headline and story on October 7 capture the flavor. The front-page, banner headline announced that "Ford, Carter Take Off the Gloves in Round 2," while the story described how the candidates, "wearing shiny new mean streaks" had stood before the television cameras "growling, glaring, gouging, and generally taking each other apart as they should have done and didn't do two weeks ago in Philadelphia."

SUMMARY AND CONCLUSIONS

This study has distinguished various levels of political learning and has found that learning from the debates was quite modest, even when the standards for scoring learning are low and inadequate to support the goal of intelligent voting. Those voters who were most deficient in knowledge prior to the debates learned at lower rates, both quantitatively and qualitatively, than those who were already better informed. Several factors which are known to inhibit learning, or are suspected of doing so, were present in the debate scenarios. Much of the information transmitted during the encounters was redundant with what respondents already knew prior to the debates. The debates could thus reinforce prior knowledge, but could contribute little to new knowledge acquisition. When the first debate turned out to be barren of new information, some respondents reported that their motivation to search for new information in subsequent debates was depressed.

While most of our panel members had no particular antipathies toward politicians in general and trusted both Ford and Carter to varying degrees, they nonetheless distrusted the debates and labelled them derisively as "rhetoric." Research on the effects of credibility on message impact suggests that such attitudes of scepticism about the credibility of debate messages may have served as a strong deterrent to learning (Anderson & Clevenger, 1953; Hovland, Janis, & Kelly, 1953). Similarly, an excessive complexity of messages, so evident in the debates, has been shown to be a deterrent to message comprehension and learning (Maccoby & Markle, 1973).

The fact that postdebate commentary was

sketchy and concentrated more on the impact of the debates on voting decisions, than on assessing the substance of the information which had been conveyed, posed further barriers to learning. Finally, the respondents, as such, did not treat the debates as a matter of high importance. While they were interested, few of them took the time to watch all the debates; when they did watch, it was generally an abbreviated exercise. This scattered attendance pattern sharply reduced the opportunities for learning since our data show that the bulk of debate learning was associated with actual watching of the televised event.[16]

It would take a separate paper to discuss the policy implications of our findings in terms of staging future debates. One could speculate about learning improvements which might have taken place if the debates had been scheduled earlier, if they had taken a different format, or if they had covered different subject matter. But prior to asking and answering such questions, serious thought should be given to the wisdom of assigning a major burden of voter enlightenment to comparatively brief and pressured encounters among presidential contenders. If the debates continue to be billed as spectaculars which facilitate instant, informed decision making and if large numbers of voters decide to use them in this fashion, the net result may be less, rather than more, voter learning. Our data show strong voter inclination to postpone political learning and wait for the single event which will settle the dust of election confusion. The debates may become this single, crucial event.

NOTES

1. The following sources were monitored for predebate and postdebate coverage: early evening network news on ABC, CBS, and NBC; local news on CBS and NBC; press coverage in the *New York Times*, *Philadelphia Inquirer*, *Boston Globe*, *Bangor Daily News*, *Chicago Tribune*, *Cleveland Plain Dealer*, *Detroit Free Press*, *Topeka Daily Capital*, *Houston Chronicle*, *Miami Herald*, *Raleigh News & Observer*, *Atlanta Constitution*, *Los Angeles Times*, *Seattle Daily Times*, *Denver Post*, *Salt Lake City Tribune*, *Chicago Daily Defender*, *National Observer*, *Wall Street Journal*, and *Washington Post*.
2. The first part of the quotation is from the debate text reprinted in the *New York Times* of October 8, 1976, quoting Pauline Frederick. The second part is from the debate text reprinted in the *New York Times* of September 23, 1976, quoting Edwin Newman.
3. Other collaborators in this research effort were Maxwell McCombs and Lee Becker and associates of Syracuse University, and David Weaver and associates of Indiana University.
4. See, for example, the candidate preference polls and "Most Important Problem" polls in the *Gallup Opinion Index* starting with No. 126 in January 1976 and extending throughout the calendar year. See also the Roper polls on election knowledge published in the *New York Times*, as well as the CBS-*Times* polls. Examples are polls published on June 3 and 4 under the heading "Poll Finds Voters Unsure about Candidates' Positions" and "Poll Finds Public Hazy on Candidates." For most polls, there was no significant difference between the distribution of responses of our panel members and those of the poll respondents.
5. These probes resulted in some very interesting insights into the broad range of quite different interpretations given by various respondents to many of the standard questions in national surveys, such as the election surveys of the University of Michigan Center for Political Studies. These different interpretations of questions cast serious doubts on the validity of a number of the answers and on the inferences drawn from them.
6. Panel members: $\bar{x} = 2.3$; control group: $\bar{x} = 2.4$ ($p < .05$). Recall of stories was scored on a 4-point scale, ranging from 1 for "none" to 4 for "a lot." The latter rating was awarded whenever respondents could spontaneously relate 3 or more aspects of a news story.
7. The self-assessment measure and the objective test of learning which measured ability to spontaneously recall facts were correlated significantly. The scores were $r = .68$ ($p < .001$) for issue learning, and $r = .62$ ($p < .001$) for candidate learning.
8. The correlation between prior interest and learning about issues is $r = .21$; for learning about candidates it is $r = .37$ ($p < .01$). The correlation between prior knowledge and learning about issues is $r = .56$ ($p < .05$); for learning about candidates it is $r = .67$ ($p < .001$).
9. The data are based on a content analysis performed by David Weaver in connection with the Becker, Weaver, Graber, & McCombs study.
10. Only in the vice-presidential debates did half of the nonwatchers indicate lack of interest.
11. High interest is, however, correlated with higher learning, as indicated in note 8, above.
12. When the knowledge scores from previous interviews, based on examination of recall of election stories, were compared with the respondents' specific knowledge of candidate qualifications and campaign issues, measured after the primaries, these two measures were significantly correlated ($r = .65$, $p < .001$). We also found that learning about issues and candidates was highly correlated. Those who learned the most about issues from the debates, learned the most about candidates as well. The correlation coefficient between the two aspects of debate learning was .75 ($p < .001$), when both variables were measured by specific information learned. In a similar manner, the learning about the two candidates from the debates was closely related. Those who learned more about Ford as a person also learned more about Carter ($r = .75$, $p < .001$).
13. On a 7-point scale, ranging from "strongly agree" (1) to "strongly disagree" (7), with 4 as the neutral point, Carter and Ford were ranked trustworthy as follows:

Strongly Agree	*1*	*2*	*3*	*4*	*5*	*6*	*7*	*Strongly Disagree*
Ford	5	6	7	1	1	1	0	
Carter	2	4	4	6	1	1	1	

14. For purposes of this table, respondents who had made a tentative decision only were listed as "undecided voters." The no-difference finding is significant at the .01 level.
15. Those who had not actually watched the debates reported the impression which they had received from other sources.
16. The correlation coefficient between television watching and issue learning was .41 ($p < .05$). For learning about the candidates it was .45 ($p < .05$).

REFERENCES

ANDERSON, K.E., & CLEVENGER, T., JR. A summary of experimental research in ethos. *Speech Monographs*, 1963, 30, 59-78.

ASHER, H. *Presidential elections and American politics: voters, candidates and campaigns since 1952*. Homewood, Ill.: Dorsey Press, 1976.

BECKER, L., WEAVER, D., GRABER, D.A., & McCOMBS, M. Influence of the debates on public agendas. In S. Kraus (Ed.), *Great debates, 1976, Ford vs. Carter*. Indianapolis: University of Indiana Press, 1978.

BROWN, S.R. Intensive analysis in political research. *Political Methodology*, 1974, 1, 1-25.

DONOHUE, G.A., TICHENOR, P.J., & OLIEN, C.N. Mass media and the knowledge gap: A hypothesis reconsidered. *Communication Research*, 1975, 2, 3-23.

GRABER, D. Personal qualities in presidential images: The contribution of the press. *Midwest Journal of Political Science*, 1972, 16, 46-76.

GRABER, D. Press coverage and voter reaction. *Political Science Quarterly*, 1974, 89, 68-100.

HOVLAND, C., JANIS, I., & KELLY, H. *Communication and persuasion*. New Haven, Conn.: Yale University Press, 1953.

KENISTON, K. *Young radicals*. New York: Harcourt, Brace & World, 1968.

KRAUS, S. & DAVIS, D. *The effects of mass communication on political behavior*. University Park: Pennsylvania State University Press, 1976.

LAMB, K. *As Orange goes: Twelve California families and the future of American politics*. New York: Norton, 1975.

LANE, R. *Political ideology: Why the American common man believes what he does*. New York: Free Press, 1962.

MACCOBY, N., & MARKLE, D.G. Communication and learning. In I. de Sola Pool and W. Schramm (Eds.), *Handbook of communication*. Chicago: Rand McNally, 1973.

POMPER, G. *Voters' choice: Varieties of American electoral behavior*. New York: Dodd, Mead, 1975.

TICHENOR, P.J., DONOHUE, G.A., & OLIEN, C.N. Mass media and differential growth in knowledge. *Public Opinion Quarterly*, 1970, 34, 151-170.

PHYSIOLOGICALLY-BASED CONTENT ANALYSIS: AN APPLICATION IN POLITICAL COMMUNICATION[1]

THOMAS C. WIEGELE
Northern Illinois University

This study examined the verbal behavior of former president Richard M. Nixon under conditions of severe psychological stress. After noting Nixon's written comments on stress in his book *Six Crises*, two of his extemporaneous speeches which dealt with failure—the 1962 California gubernatorial concession speech and the 1974 farewell to his staff address—were subjected to voice stress analysis. This technique utilizes an electronic instrument to obtain graphic representations of physiological disturbances in the voice. The analysis presented in this article demonstrates that underlying substantive themes in a speaker's voice can be physiologically detected by remote analysis.

The famous sign on President Harry S. Truman's desk which stated that "The Buck Stops Here" tells us something not only about the nature of bureaucracy but also about the decisional milieu in which central decision makers perform their responsibilities. That critically important decisions inevitably find their way to the president's desk indicates, in all likelihood, that a president performs his role in a stress-laden political environment. Indeed, Roger Hilsman (1971, p. 14) has implied that the words "turmoil" and "confusion" aptly portray the process that others have described as "rational decision making."

Elsewhere (Wiegele, 1977) stress has been defined as the anxiety, fear, and/or biophysiological change which develops as the internal response of an individual to an external load placed on it by a pathogenic agent, stressor, or life crisis which is perceived as posing a severe threat to one or more values of a political decision maker.[2] Decisional situations and political events can be conceptualized as external loads or stressors which pose severe threats to certain values of a decision maker and induce in an individual leader anxiety, fear, and/or biophysiological change. Such a decision maker could be described as being in a state of stress.

PROBLEMS OF STRESS MEASUREMENT

Until recently, it was virtually impossible even to conceive of measuring the stress states of individual decision makers, removed and well insulated as they are from the immediate concerns of the practicing political scientist. Within the past two or three years, however, an electronic voice analysis technique has been developed which makes possible the remote measurement of the stress states of leaders, using a device known as a Psychological Stress Evaluator, or PSE.[3]

The PSE processes an audio-tape recording of a speech or statement to produce on a heat sensitive strip a chart of the patterns of physiologically detected psychological stress. An example of these charts can be seen in Figure 1.

The physiological principles on which the process rests can be described quite simply. When an individual experiences psychological stress, the muscles associated with the vocal cords are subject to a degree of involuntary tensing. This tensing, though normally undetectable by the human ear, affects the electronic quality of the tape recording of the voice. Differing degrees of stress produce differing electronic configurations. For example, the unstressed charts in the top row of Figure 1 are patterns produced by completely relaxed vocal cords, as indicated by the undulating wave form. The tight "squarish" configurations in the bottom row result from tensed vocal cords. The almost rectangular pattern on the far right of the bottom row indicates extreme stress. Thus, the PSE records electronically the physiological evidences of psychological stress.

The PSE has been used in a variety of research

FIGURE 1
Visual Display of Stress Patterns

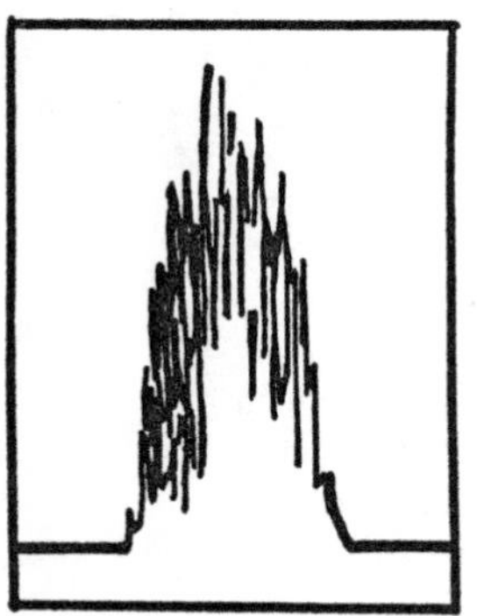
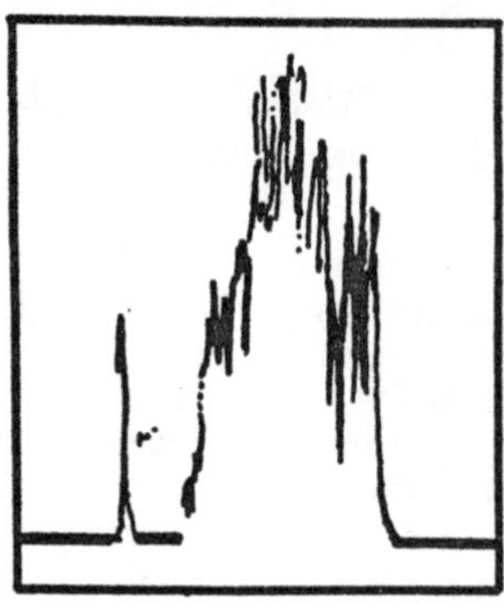
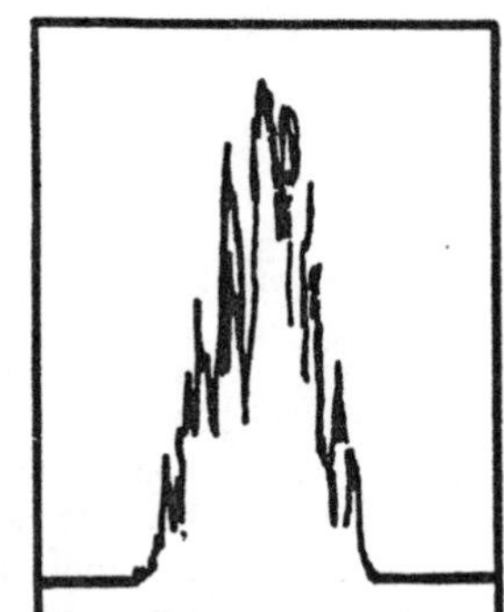

Unstressed Words

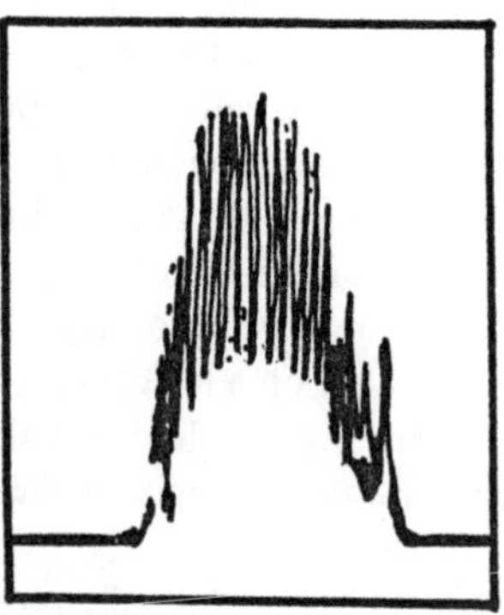

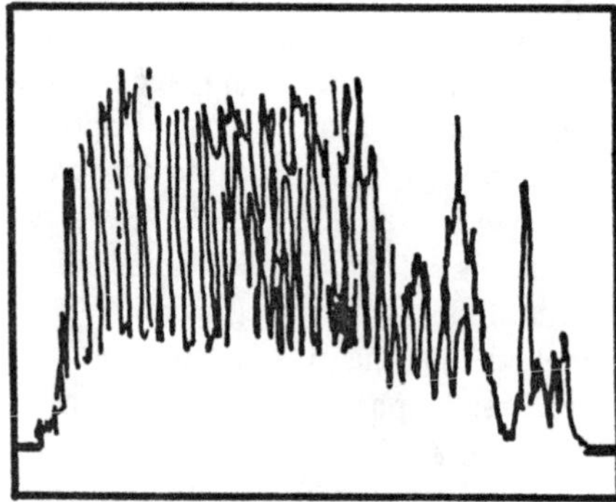

Stressed Words

and test environments. A representative sample of these studies can be cited. Lewis and Worth (n.d.) explored the emotional impact upon individuals (stress) of certain types of emotion-laden and neutral words. Brenner (1974) used the PSE to examine the evidences of stress in subjects experiencing stage fright. Psychiatric patients were probed by Wiggins, McCranie, and Bailey (1975). Reeves (1976) correlated PSE measures of stress with paper and pencil psychological tests designed to measure similar stress states. Borgen and Goodman (1976) tested the experiential effects of anti-anxiety drugs on patients by utilizing the PSE. Wiegele (1976a and 1976b) examined the international crisis speeches of U.S. presidents to search for evidences of stress. Normal and pathological anxiety states were analyzed by Smith (in press). In all of these very recent efforts, the PSE has been found to be a powerful instrument for the detection of stress.

The present paper examines the behavior of former president Richard M. Nixon under conditions of extreme psychological stress. Two of Nixon's public speeches, which were presented in the context of events which we will term political failures, will be examined through PSE analysis.

Comparisons will be made between these analyses and Nixon's written reflections on stress. Thus, before proceeding to a physiological analysis of Nixon's speeches, let us briefly review his written comments on the nature of stress in political decision-making situations.

NIXON'S REFLECTIONS ON STRESS

One of the behavioral characteristics of the experienced administrator is that he has learned to recognize the fact that he is confronted by a crisis situation which is inducing in him a good deal of psychological stress. Most, if not all, political decision makers have been through numerous stress-inducing situations. Few, however, have been able to commit to paper their reflections on stress.[4] Still fewer have been able to conceive of stress as an analytic category worth exploring. Richard M. Nixon, however, is an exception. In the Introduction to his *Six Crises*[5] Nixon spells out, with a sensitivity and an attention to detail unequaled among political decision makers, his views on the nature of stress as it affects political behavior among elites. His reflections deserve attention.

"There is one lesson, from my own experience," says Nixon, "that seems especially clear: reaction and response to crisis is uniquely personal in the sense that it depends on what the individual brings to bear on the situation—his own traits of personality and character, his training, his moral and religious background, his strengths and weaknesses." This "sense of the personal" is, of course, spelled out in great detail in *Six Crises*, but it should be emphasized that the intensity with which Nixon holds this position is not shared by many leaders. Indeed, Nixon writes that his book is an account "of great events—and how *one man* responded to them" (emphasis supplied).

Coolness and courage assume a good deal of importance for Nixon as qualities which an individual should possess in handling the stress of a political crisis:

> Coolness—or perhaps the better word is "serenity"—in battle is a product of faith. And faith apart from that which stems from religious heritage and moral training, comes to an *individual* after he has gone through a necessary period of indecision, of doubt and soul searching, and resolves that his cause is right and determines that he must fight the battle to the finish.
>
> Courage—or, putting it more accurately, lack of fear—is a result of *discipline*. Any man who claims never to have known fear is either lying or else he is stupid. By an *act of will*, he refuses to think of the reasons for fear and so concentrates entirely on winning the battle. (p. xv, emphasis supplied)

On the other hand, again emphasizing the individual perspective, the former president writes:

> I do not believe, for example, that some men are just "naturally" cool, courageous, and decisive in handling crisis situations, while others are not. . . . Of course some men may be stronger, less emotional, quicker, smarter, bolder than others. But I think these qualities are for the most part acquired and not inherited, and many times acquired suddenly under stress. . . . I have found that leaders are subject to all the human frailties; they lose their tempers, become depressed, experience the other symptoms of tension. Sometimes even strong men will cry. (p. xiv)

Moreover, observes Nixon "no one really knows what he is capable of until he is tested to the full by events over which he may have no control." It is this "testing process" which prepares the leader through experience to have confidence in his own behavior. Such behavior involves individual creativity, particularly in crises, by engaging all of an individual's personal resources and talents.

Various models of stress focus on the physiological distortions which take place in the human body that interact with psychological processes which have often been referred to as comprising "fight or flight syndrome." Nixon writes:

> Experience [in stress-inducing situations] is a vitally important factor. When a man has been through even a minor crisis, he learns not to worry when his muscles tense up, his breathing comes faster, his nerves tingle, his stomach churns, his temper becomes short, his nights are sleepless. He recognizes such symptoms as the natural and healthy signs that his system is keyed up for battle. Far from worrying when this happens, he should worry when it does not. Because he knows from experience that once the battle is joined, all these symptoms will disappear. (p. xv)

Note the clarity with which Nixon views a political situation as having powerful physiological effects upon an *individual* decision maker. Moreover, the imposition of stress can be highly ennervating:

> A man will look forward to the end of the battle. He thinks, "Just as soon as this is over I'll feel great." But except for a brief period of exhilaration if the fight ended in victory, he will then begin to feel the full effects of what he has been through. He may even be physically sore and mentally depressed. What has happened, of course, is that he is just too spent emotionally, physically, and mentally to enjoy the fruits of victory he so eagerly anticipated. (p. xv)

Over the course of a crisis, the stress which must be borne by an individual decision maker reaches a peak in the period of indecision which precedes the decision of "whether to fight or run away." Moreover, "the most dangerous period," Nixon asserts, "is the aftermath" because it is during this phase that "with all his resources spent and his guard down, . . . an individual must watch out for dulled reactions and faulty judgement."

Nixon understands that crises can be more broadly encompassing in a political sense and more historically significant than the individuals involved in them. Nevertheless, losing oneself in a larger political situation leads to the development of keener individual talents. For example, Nixon writes: "A man who has never lost himself in a cause bigger than himself has missed one of life's mountaintop experiences. Only in losing himself does he find himself. Only then does he discover all the latent strengths he never knew he had and which otherwise would have remained dormant" (p. xvi). Thus, "the natural symptoms of stress in a period of crisis," Nixon comments, "do not become self-destructive as a result of his worrying about himself but, on the other hand, become positive forces for creative action."

In summary, then, Nixon believes that crisis exerts its stresses on the personal capabilities of the individual decision maker. During the course of the crisis, it is the decision maker as an individual who is being tested. His personality, character, moral and religious background, coolness, courage, and experience come into play. The condition of stress can be looked upon as a battle with oneself to be won by recognizing the qualities of stress. Decision makers are cautioned to realize that the physiological effects of stress are temporary and can be overcome. Crises have a psychological ebb and flow which the experienced political decision maker recognizes and anticipates.

THE NIXON SPEECHES

Two of Nixon's public speeches were selected for PSE analysis: the California gubernatorial concession speech of November 7, 1962 and the farewell to his staff upon leaving the office of president on August 9, 1974. Both of these speeches deal with events which can only be described as political failures: the loss of the governor's race in California and the forced resignation from the presidency as a result of the Watergate affair. Each was for Nixon a real crisis in the sense that he described crisis in the previous section. Each was for Nixon an extemporaneous speech. That is, Nixon did not speak from a prepared written text that might have embodied phraseology that was the result of a staff or aide's proposal. Instead, it was the individual subject himself who made the rhetorical and substantive choices in his presentation. As a result of the crisis character of the events which immediately preceded the speeches, each is assumed to have created in Nixon a good deal of psychological stress. With the PSE analysis of these stress-laden failure speeches, we can determine the extent to which his general comments on the stressful nature of political decision making accurately describe his behavior in these two situations.

The procedures used to accomplish this were quite straightforward. A PSE wave-form chart (or spectral analysis) was produced for each word in the two oral documents. All the recordings were charted in Mode III on the PSE, with the tape speed at 1⅞ inches per second, and the chart drive at 20 millimeters per second.[6] The strip output of the PSE was then visually analyzed to determine which words exhibited the characteristic square blocking configuration of high stress, and these words were marked accordingly on the printed text of the speech.[7]

The general substantive theme of each paragraph was then determined, and a count made of the total number of words in each paragraph. Dividing this figure into the number of high-stress words in the paragraph (multiplied by 100) produced a standardized *score of high-stress words per paragraph*, and therefore a standardized measure of stress for each theme in any given oral document. To state it somewhat differently, this method can be looked upon as a physiologically-based content analysis procedure with aggregation at the paragraph level.

Two methodological problems immediately present themselves: the problem of controls and/or base levels of stress in individuals, and the problem of directionality.

Let us deal with the control issue first. As we have seen, the voice stress procedure detects physiological evidences of psychological stress, which is a form of psychological arousal. The general level of arousal in an individual at any given moment is a product of many factors. For a political decision maker these factors might include: his perceptions of a specific crisis event requiring immediate resolution, a future campaign for reelection, a recent family quarrel, a bitter personal dispute with a colleague, past political experiences, and an idiosyncratic constellation of psychological predispositions. Given the present state of social-psychophysiological research, it is, of course, not possible even to guess the relative weight of such factors. Thus, we cannot establish a control or baseline measure for an individual decision maker by measuring his arousal state (stress) in a variety of situations because not only is each situation idiosyncratic, but also equally idiosyncratic is the arousal level at any given point in time. In the research reported here I have assumed that, because of its immediacy, a known stress-producing political event will be the *single* most important factor determining the arousal level in an individual decision maker. This assumption is not unwarranted, given what is known about attention structures.

For these reasons, instead of attempting to identify possible multiple causes of stress which might be brought to bear on an individual, or to identify permanent baseline measures, we have simply taken the *overall* percentage of high stress words[8] in an oral document under consideration as a summary measure of the general state of physiological arousal in the subject at that point in time. This overall mean stress level can be viewed as a self-anchoring control because it is against this value that paragraph-aggregated stress percentages are compared. Deviations from the mean (the general arousal state) then form the focus of inquiry. That is, the researcher asks himself which substantive themes are producing the highest stress in the individual under examination.

The question of directionality presents us with a somewhat different type of problem. What do we know when we learn that speaking about a particular theme was accompanied by notable signs of stress? Based on solid experimental work,[9] we can state that evidences of high stress in a speaker indicate that the theme about which he is speaking is of great concern and importance to him, and that very likely such a theme is causing him a good deal of discomfort. This concern and discomfort produces physiological manifestations in the vocal cords, the sounds emanating from which can be electronically detected and analyzed by a PSE.

Clearly, the challenges confronting Nixon after his defeat in California and his resignation from the presidency required him to engage in problem-solving appraisals brought about by noxious or threatening stimuli. It is not unreasonable to assume that increased levels of stress resulted from his perception of discomforting or disliked stimuli, and that evidence of the stress can be found in the speeches to which we now turn.

THE 1962 CALIFORNIA GUBERNATORIAL CONCESSION SPEECH

The political future of Richard Nixon seemed very uncertain as the year 1960 came to a close. John Kennedy had narrowly defeated him in the 1960 presidential election. With the intention of returning to private life, Nixon and his family journeyed to California on February 28, 1961. There was much speculation in the press over whether Nixon would make a political comeback. The former vice-president attempted to quiet such speculation by declaring in a speech on March 11 in Sacramento that he did not intend to run for the California governorship in 1962 (*New York Times*, March 11, 1961, p. 1).

However, California Republicans perceived the situation quite differently. They saw Nixon as their means for winning the governorship (Mazo and

Hess, 1968, p. 260). The pressures of state Republican leaders coupled with those of prominent national Republican leaders forced Nixon to relent, and on September 27 he announced his intention to seek the Republican nomination for the governorship (*New York Times*, September 28, 1961, p. 1). At the same time, Nixon also stated that he would not be a candidate for president in 1964. He undoubtedly felt, on the basis of arguments pressed on him by such national leaders as Senators Hugh Scott and Barry Goldwater that he had to remain in the public view if he wished to maintain any influence in national Republican affairs (Mazo and Hess, 1968, p. 261). Such arguments made the gubernatorial campaign critical for Nixon's political future.

Nixon won the California Republican nomination for governor in the June 5th primary, but he suffered a chilling defeat in the final election. Thus, instead of demonstrating his ability to make a political comeback, the gubernatorial election resulted in weakening his position in the political arena.

On the day following the election, Nixon made his concession speech, an emotional presentation which reflected the frustration and bitterness which he felt at the time. The speech might more properly be called an extemporaneous statement to an excited audience. His words often rambled into incomplete sentences—a mark of heavy psychological stress—and he stumbled on words and exhibited numerous points of hesitation in the statement.[10]

In his talk, Nixon touched upon many topics, including reflections on the just-completed campaign and election, national politics, the press, defeat, and so forth. Despite the fact that he said early in the speech that, "I have no complaints about the press coverage," he devoted a good deal of commentary to a stinging critique of press attitudes toward his candidacy. Indeed, it was at this time that Nixon uttered one of the most quoted statements in American political history:

> You won't have Nixon to kick around any more, because, gentlemen, this is my last press conference; and it will be one in which I have welcomed the opportunity to test wits with you.
>
> But, unlike some people [President Kennedy], I've never cancelled a subscription to a paper and also I never will.

Reflecting on his defeat, Nixon stated that in spite of his loss, "I'm proud to have run for Governor. Now I would have liked to have won. But, not having won, the main thing was that I have battled—battled for the things I believed in." This comment, of course, is quite consistent with Nixon's reflections in his *Six Crises* on the necessity of "battling" under stress.

The gubernatorial concession speech contained 42 paragraphs with the *overall* percentage of high-stress words across all paragraphs at 3.27. On the basis of our earlier discussion, we can take this average score of 3.27 as a summary measure of Nixon's general level of psychological arousal at the time he delivered this speech. Of the 42 paragraphs, 16 had *paragraph* stress percentages that exceeded the *overall* percentage of high stress words for the speech. Table 1 arrays the themes on which Mr. Nixon exhibited stress which *exceeded* the overall or average percentage of stress for the speech.

The column on the left of Table 1 gives the percentage of high stress words out of the total number of words in each individual paragraph whose theme is identified in the column on the right. The original paragraph position is indicated in the center column for reference purposes. It should be noted that only paragraphs whose percentage of high-stress words exceeded the overall percentage of high-stress words for the entire speech are presented. As stated earlier, this decision is based on the assumption that the high-stress paragraphs indicate the themes of most concern to a speaker.

The themes arrayed in Table 1 can be grouped into four broad composite themes, as shown in Figure 2.

As Figure 2 indicates, the high-stress composite themes comprise four categories: the press, Nixon the man, the campaign, and the economy. The averaged stress levels for each theme are, respectively: 8.98, 7.22, 5.44, and 3.77. Not only was the problem of the press of greatest concern to Nixon, as evidenced by the fact that nine paragraphs cluster around this theme, but also the

TABLE 1
Gubernatorial Concession Speech of Richard M. Nixon, November 8, 1962: Paragraphs Which Exceeded the Average Percentage of High Stress Words Across the Entire Speech

Percentage of High Stress Words	Original Paragraph Position	Paragraph Theme
17.77	41	Last press meeting; Nixon no longer a target.
14.28	33	Sixteen years of press attack.
10.00	10	Reporters requested my comments on press.
10.00	34	Nixon verbal "flub" reported in press.
7.33	37	Newspapers have professional responsibilities.
7.31	40	Goodbye to press.
7.22	28	Defeated, but fought the battle.
7.14	1	Congratulations to Gov. Brown.
7.14	11	Gratitude to campaign workers.
5.88	9	Reporter Greenberg wrote facts.
5.35	18	Republicans need new leadership in California.
4.16	31	Nixon views on press unknown.
4.04	5	No _ad hominem_ attacks on Brown.
3.77	26	Economy must move forward.
3.57	4	Gov. Brown a decent man.
3.44	42	Admonition about press responsibility.
3.27		Percentage of high stress words across all paragraphs.

problem was the most stressful, as indicated by the fact that the average of the stress levels of the individual paragraphs comprising this theme, 8.98, are the highest of the composite themes.

Nixon did not dwell on the fact of his defeat in this speech—he devoted only one paragraph to it, but voice stress analysis with a score of 7.22 shows it is a clearly disturbing element, as indeed one would suspect.

Five paragraphs dealing with the campaign make up the third composite high-stress theme and it is to be expected that the campaign, so recently concluded, would produce a good deal of stress in Nixon. But it is not clear why the fourth theme, the

FIGURE 2
Composite High Stress Themes in Richard M. Nixon's Gubernatorial Concession Speech of November 8, 1962

Composite Theme 1:	Composite Stress Level	Paragraph Themes
The Press	8.98	(a) Last press meeting; Nixon no longer a target. (b) Sixteen years of press attacks. (c) Reporters requested my comments on press. (d) Nixon verbal "flub" reported in press. (e) Newspapers have professional responsibilities. (f) Goodbye to press. (g) Reporter Greenberg wrote facts. (h) Nixon views on press unknown. (i) Admonition about press responsibility.
Composite Theme 2:		
Nixon the Man	7.22	(a) Defeated, but fought the battle.
Composite Theme 3:		
The Campaign	5.44	(a) Congratulations to Brown. (b) Gratitude to campaign workers. (c) Republicans need new leadership in California. (d) No ad hominem attacks on Brown. (e) Gov. Brown a decent man.
Composite Theme 4:		
The Economy	3.77	(a) Economy must move forward.

question of the economy, should appear on the high-stress list.

While 16 paragraphs exceeded the percentage for stress for the speech, 26 paragraphs were lower than that average in their percentages of high-stress words. Themes for these latter paragraphs dealt with the importance of the governorship, voter turnout, the congressional elections, Republican successes in the other states, President Kennedy's popularity and character, international problems, general domestic affairs, future plans of Mr. Nixon, and expectations about future leadership. There were many topics that were discussed by Nixon that might have produced a good deal of stress in him. But it was those themes dealing with the press and his own defeat that created the very highest levels of stress as evidenced by PSE analysis.

Nixon's words regarding the press make it clear that he is expressing a deep-felt, *personal anger* at what he considered unfair treatment toward himself. His comment that he fought the good fight even though he went down to defeat likewise reflects a concern with himself as an individual. The sense of personal test and battle expressed by Nixon in his book is displayed with equal clarity by the psychophysiological analysis of this speech.

THE FAREWELL SPEECH

The events leading up to Richard Nixon's resignation from the office of the presidency on August 9, 1974 are so familiar to observers of contemporary American politics that they need no repeating. Suffice it to say that the chain of events began on June 17, 1972 when the now well-known "plumbers unit" broke into the national headquarters of the Democratic party located in the Watergate apartment complex in Washington, D.C. The 26 months that followed the break-in must have been for Nixon one of the most extended, intense, and stress-laden periods ever confronted by an American political leader. This lengthy period concluded with his farewell speech on August 9 to his White House staff, cabinet members, and close friends.[11] As stated previously, this speech was selected for PSE analysis because it was, like the gubernatorial concession speech, extemporaneous (the carefully prepared resignation speech was delivered the evening before the farewell speech, i.e., on August 8).

Nixon's farewell remarks covered a variety of topics which were presented in an atmosphere of strong emotion, sadness, and dejection. He thanked his staff for 5½ years of faithful service and encouraged them to dedicate themselves to assisting the new president. He regretted that he had not had more personal contact with his aides, but he reminded himself and them that service is its own reward.

Nixon told his audience that he had made honest mistakes, but that they had not been made for personal gain. He went on, in an almost stream-of-consciousness manner, offering reflections on his father, his mother, and President Theodore Roosevelt's autobiographical account of the death of his wife. At the conclusion of his remarks, Mr. and Mrs. Nixon left the White House for Andrews Air Force Base, where they boarded an aircraft for the journey to San Clemente, California.

The farewell speech was subjected to PSE analysis in the same manner that has been described above. It contained 24 paragraphs with an overall percentage of high stress words of 14.76, considerably more than the 3.27 of the gubernatorial concession speech. As before, we take this figure as Nixon's general level of arousal at the time he uttered these words.

Of the 24 paragraphs, 12 had a percentage of high-stress words exceeding the overall percentage for the speech. Table 2 arrays the themes for these high-stress paragraphs. Following the same procedure as for the earlier speech, the themes arrayed in Table 2 have been grouped into three broad composite themes, as shown in Figure 3.

The 9 paragraphs that comprise the personal, human tragedy theme produced the highest levels of stress: 22.28% of the words in these paragraphs were high-stress words. The composite theme relating to the staff reached 18.64% high-stress words; and the press theme, represented by only one paragraph, was just barely over the average of the entire speech with 15.62%.

Taking a closer look at these composite themes, we can see that again the "sense of the personal" comes through very strongly as supported by the physiological evidences of stress in Nixon's voice. The loss of the presidency is viewed by Nixon not as a political but as a personal tragedy. Nixon's historical reflections are not about a political leader (Theodore Roosevelt) who experienced a political crisis, but rather about a political leader who experienced a personal crisis: the death of his wife. Here is a portion of the quotation from President Roosevelt's diary read by Nixon in his farewell:

> When she [Mr. Roosevelt's wife] had just become a mother, when her life seemed to be just begun, and when the years seemed so bright before her, then by a strange and terrible fate death came to her. And when my heart's desire died, the light went out in my life forever. (p. 632)

However, Nixon continued,

> That was T.R. in his twenties. He thought the light had gone from his life forever—but he went on. And he not only became president but, as an ex-president, he served his country, always in the arena, tempestuous, strong, sometimes wrong, sometimes right, but he was a man. (p. 632)

TABLE 2
"Farewell to His Staff Speech" of Richard M. Nixon, August 9, 1974: Paragraphs Which Exceeded the Average Percentage of High Stress Words Across the Entire Speech

Percentage of High Stress Words	Original Paragraph Position	Paragraph Theme
33.33	13	Careers outside of govt. are rewarding.
31.14	17	President T. Roosevelt reports death of his wife.
24.61	18	Reading of quote from Roosevelt about death of wife.
21.53	9	Honest mistakes/no personal wealth.
20.00	11	Exhortation to strength and sacrifice.
19.19	24	Staff will be remembered.
18.58	20	We all experience low points in life.
18.09	3	Staff should serve next president well.
17.64	19	Admiration for Roosevelt's ability to carry on.
17.04	15	Reflections about his mother.
16.66	21	Disappointment can be a beginning.
16.62	1	Press will charge a staged conference.
14.79	Percentage of high stress words across all paragraphs.	

The mark of a great man, said Mr. Nixon, is that he can view disappointment as a beginning.

> Greatness comes not when things go always good for you, but the greatness comes and you are really tested, when you take some knocks, some disappointments, when sadness comes, because only if you have been in the deepest valley can you ever know how magnificent it is to be on the highest mountain [sic]. (p. 632)

That this theme produced extreme stress in Mr. Nixon suggests that he is viewing his resignation as a test of his own strength, a test which, if he survives it, will guarantee favorable recognition by later observers. An analyst might very well argue that Nixon viewed his life after the resignation as another crisis in precisely the same sense of personal test that he spelled out in his book. It should be noted that the single paragraph in which Nixon exhibited the highest stress in this speech is the one

FIGURE 3
Composite High Stress Themes in Richard M. Nixon's "Farewell to His Staff Speech" of August 9, 1974

Composite Theme 1:	Composite Stress Level	Paragraph Themes
Personal, Human Tragedy	22.28	(a) Careers outside of govt. are rewarding. (b) President T. Roosevelt reports death of his wife. (c) Reading of quote from Roosevelt about death of wife. (d) Honest mistakes/no personal wealth. (e) Exhortation to strength and sacrifice. (f) We all experience low points in life. (g) Admiration for Roosevelt's ability to carry on. (h) Reflections about his mother. (i) Disappointment can be a beginning.
Composite Theme 2:		
The Staff	18.64	(a) Staff will be remembered. (b) Staff should serve next president well.
Composite Theme 3:		
The Press	15.62	(a) Press will charge a staged conference.

in which he states that "there are many fine careers" outside of government. Conceivably, he viewed his return to private life as a new career (or crisis) which would test his ability and determination to survive the challenges ahead.

The second high-stress composite theme dealt with the farewell to his staff which, of course, was the occasion for the speech. Seven paragraphs were devoted to commentary regarding the loyalty, responsibility, and quality of the staff. Only two paragraphs, however, exceeded the overall percentage of high-stress words for the speech. But those two paragraphs were distinctive: rather than being reflective about past services, they constituted, literally, the farewell itself. The people to whom Nixon was talking were those whom he saw in the White House, including his personal quarters, on a daily basis. They were staying; he was leaving. Nixon was undoubtedly aware that he had disappointed them: the leader who should have been above reproach had been reproached. Consequently, his farewell in all likelihood had a deep, personal meaning for him.

The third composite theme, the press, occupied only one paragraph. Nixon began this speech with the observation that, "I think the record should show that this [gathering] is one of those spontaneous things that we always arrange whenever the President comes in to speak, and it will be so reported in the press, and we don't mind, because they have to call it as they see it [sic]." This can be viewed as simply another element in Nixon's continuing public quarrel with the press that began when he was a junior congressman from California. That this theme should have been one of high stress is not surprising in view of Nixon's traditional reactions to the press in very personal terms.

Thus, the physiological analysis of the tape recording of this speech reveals Nixon showing high stress on themes relating to his own personal tragedy, his staff, and the press. Low-stress themes, that is, themes which fell below the overall percentage of high-stress words for the speech, dealt with reflections on the White House as a home, pride in staff work, congeniality and helpfulness of the staff, Nixon's regret of not having had more personal contact with the staff, and the lack of personal dishonesty in his administration. One other theme dealing with reflections about his father fell immediately below the overall percentage cut-off point. That is, it was almost a high-stress theme which would have put it in the personal, human tragedy category.

That Nixon did not exhibit high stress when he commented that "not one single man or woman" in his administration is in government service for the purpose of personal gain, suggests that, contrary to the Watergate revelations, he did indeed view his administration's record as perfectly honorable.

SUMMARY AND CONCLUSIONS

We have examined Richard Nixon's views on the behavior of leaders acting under conditions of severe stress. His comments, based essentially on his experiences as vice-president of the United States, are insightful. We summarized them by saying that Nixon viewed the impact of crisis as exerting stress on the personal capabilities of the individual political decision maker.

The second section of the paper reported PSE analysis, a method of physiologically-based content analysis, of two extemporaneous speeches delivered by Nixon after experiencing two situations which can only be described as political failures, and therefore stress producing.

Several conclusions can be drawn from the evidence presented. From Nixon's written reflections on crisis, one would hypothesize that, in moments of stress, he would tend to fall back on his well-developed "sense of the personal." Our physiological analysis of the two speeches clearly supports such a hypothesis. The highest of the high-stress composite themes in each speech dealt with intensely personal themes: the alleged injury done Nixon by the press in his campaign for governor of California, and the human tragedy that had befallen him in his forced resignation from the presidency. Judging from the percentage of high-stress words that clustered around these themes, it seems highly likely that they were exceedingly disturbing to him.

Events that are traditionally viewed by the electorate as political failures, that is, those which were discussed in this paper, were perceived by Nixon as serious personal failures. Indeed, in the two speeches that were analyzed, Nixon never addressed the broader political consequences of the occurences. Further research with the PSE might be able to demonstrate that other leaders in similar situations also might view their political misfortunes in highly personal terms. Additional work regarding elite behaviors under these conditions might provide policy-oriented insights regarding the psychological disposition of such leaders. Decisional choices designed to restore personal worth or prestige might be fundamentally different from those directed at the precise resolution of a political problem. This knowledge might be particularly useful in assessing the stress states of foreign leaders in crisis confrontations.

Another finding is that PSE analysis appears to have differentiated between themes that are important to a speaker and those that are not. In our analysis, themes that relate to Nixon's sense of the personal, and other themes that one might intuitively judge to be most salient for the circumstances, produced the highest amount of stress in the subject. Other topics which were essentially reflective, or which dealt with less salient themes, produced considerably less stress in the speaker.

Traditional methods of analyzing political documents lean heavily on inference and on idiosyncratic, nonrigorous, and subjective searching for substantive patterns. Elaborate methods of content analysis do introduce a greater rigor and eliminate some of the subjectivity. But unfortunately, because of their complexity, high cost, and the difficulty in developing the routines, solid content analyses are seldom performed. Research relating to written and oral political behavior continues to depend upon inferences based upon presumptions of well functioning rationality on the part of both the observer and the subject of the observation. Combining PSE analyses with more traditional methods of inference should enable us to reach far sounder conclusions. Moreover, the PSE is a tool by which the researcher can probe the inner arousal state of his subjects in a purely unobtrusive way. The PSE thus promises to open the door to a range of studies never before contemplated and limited only by the imagination of the researcher himself.

NOTES

1. I wish to express my sincere thanks to three dedicated research assistants: Kim Carter, Terry Mullen, and Deborah Wathen. The Graduate School Fund of Northern Illinois University provided financial assistance for this project. Dektor, CIS., Inc. contributed generous help in the use of the Psychological Stress Evaluator. Richard Cady, Richard Johannesen, John Wahlke, and Manfred Wenner very kindly offered comments on a first draft of this paper.
2. See Wiegele (1977). This definition combines definitions which were offered by Holsti and George (1976, p. 6) and Scott and Howard (1970, pp. 259-278).
3. The scientific basis upon which the PSE operates and a variety of research issues associated with the PSE methodology are spelled out in detail in Wiegele (1976b).
4. For a review of the memoirs of statesmen regarding their perceptions on stress see Wiegele (1977).
5. All the quotations from Nixon on stress are from his *Six Crises* (1962, pp. xiii-iv).
6. The PSE can be set to produce charts in any of four modes. Each results in different pattern characteristics. The clearest patterns are produced by Mode III. Audio tape speed for PSE input is routinely run slower than recording speed. A chart drive of 20 millimeters per second is normal for the instrument.
7. This procedure, of course, ignores low and moderate stress data. As work with the PSE becomes more refined, such data will have to be incorporated into PSE analyses. However, at this stage in the emergence of this technology as a method of political research, it was felt that the analyst would have more confidence in the validity of his judgments if he confined his observations to those based on the high-stress words alone.
8. This is calculated by summing the paragraph stress percentages and dividing by the total number of paragraphs in the speech.
9. Wundt found that unpleasant or disliked stimuli produced high arousal levels as measured by cardiac acceleration. In this regard, see J.I. Lacey (1967, pp. 33-34). Lacey and Lacey (1970, p. 211) found that "tasks requiring internal cognitive elaboration . . . produced massive cardiac acceleration." Watts and Sumi (1976) have replicated these findings in a political context. See also Watts (1976).
10. It should be noted that in the tape recording of this speech, the first three paragraphs are virtually inaudible. The printed text of the document indicates, however, a more than routine beginning. For the record, these paragraphs deserve to be quoted:

    "Good morning, gentlemen. Now that Mr. Klein has made his statement, and now that all the members of the press are so delighted that I have lost, I'd like to make a statement of my own.

    "I appreciate the press coverage in this campaign. I think each of you covered it the way you saw it. You had to write it in the way according to your belief on how it would go [sic]. I don't believe publishers should tell reporters to write one way or another. I want them all to be free. I don't believe the FCC or anybody else should silence (words lost in transmission).

    "I have no complaints about the press coverage. I think each of you was writing it as you believed it."

    Unfortunately, these paragraphs, because they are almost inaudible, could not be included in the PSE analysis. My numbering of the paragraphs of this speech begins with the fourth paragraph which I call number 1.

    All quotations from this speech are from the text published in the *Los Angeles Times*, November 8, 1962. Audio recordings for this and the farewell speech were obtained from the U. S. National Archives and Records Service.
11. The text of this speech can be found in *The Public Papers of the Presidents: Richard Nixon, 1974* (Washington, D. C., U. S. Government Printing Office, pp. 630-632). All quotations in the present paper are from this text.

REFERENCES

BORGEN, L.A., & GOODMAN, L.I. Audio stress analysis, anxiety, and anti-anxiety drugs. Park Davis Research Laboratories, 1976.

BRENNER, M. Stagefright and Stevens law, paper presented at the annual meeting of the Eastern Psychological Association, 1974.

HILSMAN, R. *The politics of policy making in defense and foreign affairs*. Garden City, N.Y.: Doubleday, 1971.

HOLSTI, O., & GEORGE, A. The Effects of Stress on the Performance of Foreign Policy Makers. In C.P. Cotter (Ed.), *Political science annual*. Indianapolis, Ind.: Bobbs-Merrill, 1976.

LACEY, J.J. Somatic response patterning and stress: Some revisions of activation theory. In M.H. Appley and R. Trumball (Eds.), *Psychological stress: Issues in research*. New York: Appleton-Century-Crofts, 1967.

LACEY, J.J., & LACEY, B.C. Some autonomic-central nervous system interrelationships. In P. Black (Ed.), *Physiological correlates of emotion*. New York: Academic Press, 1970.

LEWIS, B.J., & WORTH, J.W. Transfer of stress through written and verbal communication, n.d.

MAZO, E., & HESS, S. *Nixon: A political portrait*. New York: Harper & Row, 1968.

NIXON, R.M. *Six crises*. Garden City, N.Y.: Doubleday, 1962.

REEVES, T.E. The measurement and treatment of stress through electronic analysis of subaudible voice stress patterns and rational-emotive therapy. Unpublished doctoral dissertation, Indiana State University, 1976.

SCOTT, R., & HOWARD, A. Models of stress. In S. Levine and N. Scotch (Eds.), *Social stress*. Chicago: Aldine, 1970.

SMITH, G.A. Voice analysis for the measurement of anxiety. *British Journal of Medical Psychology*, in press.

WATTS, M. Stress and physiological aspects of political behavior: The psychophysiological component of political attitudes. Paper presented at the Tenth Congress of the International Political Science Association, Edinburgh, 1976.

WATTS, M. & SUMI, D. Attitudes and physiological response to audiovisual display of aggressive social behavior. Paper prepared for delivery at the annual meeting of the Midwest Political Science Association, Chicago, 1976.

WIEGELE, T.C. Voice stress analysis: The application of a physiological measurement technique to the study of the Cuban missile crisis. Paper presented at the annual meeting of the International Studies Association, Toronto, 1976a.

WIEGELE, T.C. The psychophysiology of elite stress in five international crises: A comparative test of a voice measurement technique. Paper presented at the Tenth Congress of the International Political Science Association, Edinburgh, 1976b.

WIEGELE, T.C. Models of stress and disturbances in elite political behaviors: psychological variables and political decision making. In R.S. Robins (Ed.), *Psychopathology and Political Leadership*. New Orleans: Tulane Studies in Political Science, 1977.

WIGGINS, S.L., McCRANIE, M., & BAILEY, P. Assessment of voice stress in children. *Journal of Nervous and Mental Disease*, 1975, 160.

INSTRUCTIONAL COMMUNICATION

Theory and Research: An Overview
Selected Studies

INSTRUCTIONAL COMMUNICATION THEORY AND RESEARCH: AN OVERVIEW OF THE RELATIONSHIP BETWEEN LEARNING THEORY AND INSTRUCTIONAL COMMUNICATION

VELMA J. LASHBROOK
Wilson Learning Corporation

LAWRENCE R. WHEELESS
West Virginia University

Instructional communication can be conceptualized as the study of communication variables, strategies, processes, technologies, and/or systems as they relate to formal instruction and the acquisition and modification of learning outcomes. From this perspective, instructional communication is applicable to many disciplines, educational levels, and environments. In the first *Communication Yearbook*, Scott and Wheeless (1977) presented an overview of instructional communication, with a focus on current *research* findings and recommendations for future research. A recent volume (Hurt, Scott, & McCroskey, 1978) has presented direct *applications* of communication theory and research to classroom instruction and learning. Another useful approach is an examination of relevant learning theories and taxonomies as they relate to instructional communication. Such exploration can help refine and provide sound conceptual bases for communication theory, research, and application.

The purpose of this overview is to derive conceptual relationships from major learning taxonomies and theories. Due to the plethora of approaches to learning, this discussion is limited to those which appear to have the most application to instructional communication. Numerous cognitive and behavioral theories were rejected because little effort has been made to apply them to classroom situations (e.g., Pavlovian classical conditioning, Hullian hypothetico-deductive behavior theory). The theories or conceptualizations included have the following characteristics: (1) prescriptive instructional principles and/or techniques have either been derived from the theoretical position or are consistent with it; (2) a substantial amount of research has focused on classroom applications of the theory. Bloom's taxonomy of educational objectives and Gagnè's types of learning are considered in terms of their implications for diagnostic and measurement purposes, and for constructing instructional communication strategies to maximize learning. Instructional applications and research implications are drawn from Piaget's theory of cognitive development, Skinner's approach to operant learning, Bandura's psychological modeling, and Bruner's approach to discovery learning. In terms of instructional applications, these positions are viewed as complementary and integratable, not as approaches from which to choose. For research purposes, they provide conceptual frameworks to be used, extended, and/or integrated for the development of instructional communication theory and research.

LEARNING TYPOLOGIES

Several methods have been developed for classifying types of learning. Some educators have classified learning types according to educational objectives (Bloom, 1956; Krathwohl, Bloom, & Masia, 1964), while others have categorized learning based on the conditions necessary for each to occur (e.g., Gagnè, 1965). This section examines two of these typologies as they relate to applications and research in communication instruction.

Taxonomy of Objectives

Bloom and numerous educators and psychologists contributed to the development of a taxonomy of educational objectives. Three domains were considered: cognitive, affective, and psychomotor. Although there are several affective and psychomotor skills which are relevant to communication instruction (e.g., positive attitudes toward the course, its content, and the instructor; ability to communicate without verbal or nonverbal distractions), the cognitive domain appears to be the dominant concern for those involved in instructional communication. Since both the objectives and evaluation procedures for most instruction focuses on cognitive goals, this section emphasizes that domain.

Thorough discussions of the three domains and related taxonomies are readily available from original and secondary sources (Bloom, 1956; Brooks & Friedrich, 1973; Kibler, Barker, & Miles, 1970; Krathwohl, Bloom, & Masia, 1964). For each domain, the objectives are ordered in a hierarchy from simple to complex types of learning. The six cognitive objectives involve: knowledge, comprehension, application, analysis, synthesis, and evaluation. The affective goals include: attending, responding with interest and compliance, valuing, and organizing a value system. The psychomotor domain includes the following objectives or levels: gross bodily movements, finely coordinated movements, nonverbal behavior, and speech behavior.

Although the objectives were originally written in general terms, several writers (e.g., Mager, 1962; Vargas, 1972) have explained how to make them behavioral. This taxonomy of objectives, when used in conjunction with behavioral objectives, has several useful applications for the classroom. First, it provides a useful method for organizing the content of the course. Second, it prescribes the level and type of learning required of the student. Third, the behavioral objectives suggest ways to measure whether learning occurs. For both students and teachers, it provides a clear statement of the behavioral expectations.

Objectives can be useful to instructional communication researchers concerned with measurement. They suggest methods of test construction consistent with a given level of learning and allow researchers to target learning assessment at specific levels. For example, a researcher may be interested in examining the comparative effectiveness of passive reception and active participation. The researcher may have reason to believe that there are no learning differences for lower levels of learning (e.g., knowledge and comprehension), but that active participation is more effective than passive reception for higher levels of learning (e.g., application, analysis, synthesis, and evaluation). The use of cognitive/behavioral objectives could aid the instructional communication researcher in test construction and in selecting items appropriate to the behaviors of interest.

Probably the most significant research implication involves the treatment of behavioral objectives as a specific message/communication strategy designed to cue the learner to attend to relevant information. Some previous researchers (e.g., Kaplan, 1974; Kaplan & Rothkopf, 1974; Kaplan & Simmons, 1974; Rothkopf & Kaplan, 1972) have found that the use of objectives facilitates learning. While recent analyses of research (e.g., Duchastel & Merrill, 1973; Faw & Waller, 1976; Hartley & Davies, 1976; Kibler, Bassett, & Byers, 1977) highlight inconsistent and, perhaps, inconclusive findings, there is no evidence to suggest that the use of objectives detrimentally affects relevant learning. When considered as a cueing strategy, objectives generally appear to enhance learning.

Related research concerning the use of *directions* (e.g., Frase & Kreitzberg, 1975), *questions* (e.g., Bull, 1973; Felker & Dapra, 1975; Frase, 1967, 1968a, 1968b, 1970; Frase & Schwartz, 1975; Ladas, 1973; LaPorte & Voss, 1975; Rothkopf & Bisbicos, 1967), *pretests* (Frase, 1970; Hartley, 1973; Hartley & Davies, 1976; Lumsdaine, 1963; Rothkopf, 1970; Warr, Bird, & Rackman, 1970; Welch & Walberg, 1970), *underlining* (e.g., Cashen & Leicht, 1970; Crouse & Idstein, 1972; Idstein & Jenkins, 1972; Rickards & August, 1975) and *advance organizers* (e.g., Ausubel, 1963a, 1963b, 1968; Barnes & Clawson, 1975; Hartley & Davies, 1976; Lawton & Wanska, 1977; Snelbecker, 1974) suggests that such cueing strategies can help the learner select information and, thus, enhance intended learning. The primary proposition to be derived from this literature is:

P1: Cueing facilitates learning.

Additionally, the research provides general support for the following subpropositions:

P1a: Specific cues are more effective than general cues. (In other words; directions, objectives, questions, underlining, etc., that focus on specific aspects of the content to be learned [e.g., "List the three types of conflict"] will be more effective than ones which are general in nature [e.g., ''Understand conflict''].)

P1b: Cues enhance relevant learning, but may inhibit incidental learning. (This statement refers to the general finding that individuals tend to learn more about the content which is cued, but may learn less about the content that is not cued.)

P1c: The degree of similarity between the cues and the evaluation procedures to be used is positively related to the amount of intended learning. (Questions which are similar to those used for testing, objectives which specify the behavior to be tested, etc., generally result in greater relevant learning than cues which are dissimilar in focus.)

P1d: Cues given subsequent to an instructional message produce greater incidental learning than cues given prior to a message. (Although cue placement has little affect on relevant learning, placement after the message tends to improve incidental learning.)

P1e. The number of cues is nonlinearly related to the amount of learning. (The frequency of cue usage seems to be positively related to the amount of learning up to a point, after which, learning is decreased. For example, when underlining, it is important to cue all main ideas, but, if nearly everything is underlined, the cue loses its effectiveness.)

P1f: Reviewable cues are more effective than nonreviewable cues. (The degree to which the cues can be used for subsequent review is related to their effectiveness. In general, written cues are more reviewable than oral cues unless the latter have been stored in some way, such as notes, audiotape, or videotape.)

P1g: The relative effectiveness of specific cueing strategies is a function of the learner's motivation and abilities. (If a learner is not motivated or lacks the ability to use a specific cue, the strategies are unlikely to have a significant impact. Additionally, if the learner is highly motivated and has high ability relevant to the task, the effects of specific techniques may be minimized.)

Although the research related to these propositions has generally not been theoretically based, the concern for cueing learners seems to be founded, in large part, on Ausubel's approach to meaningful receptive learning (Ausubel, 1963a, 1963b, 1968). Ausubel posits a model of cognitive organization based on the *subsumption process*. The model assumes the existence of a hierarchically organized cognitive structure which consists of highly inclusive conceptual traces plus specific information. New information is processed by subsumption under existing categories or reorganization of the individual's cognitive structure (these processes are similar to Piaget's assimilation and accommodation concepts). Ausubel argues that the use of extrinsic organizing devices can be used to alter a learner's cognitive structure and, thus, facilitate positive transfer and reduce proactive inhibition. Although he advocated the use of general overviews as advance organizers, the research trend appears to be toward the use of more specific cues.

In general, the effectiveness of a variety of cueing strategies has received sound empirical support. Although the propositions outlined here provide a summary of the cueing literature, it should be noted that the actual effect of specific cues may not be easy to predict, due to potential interactions with learner characteristics and alternative techniques. However, the integration of cueing literature into instructional communication theory and research seems viable.

Types of Learning

Gagnè's (Gagnè, 1965, 1970; Gagnè & Briggs, 1974) typology concentrates on the conditions that must be met before learning occurs, rather than on goal behaviors. He has described eight types of learning, which have been labeled: signal learning, stimulus-response learning, chaining, verbal-association learning, multiple discrimination, concept learning, principle learning and problem solving.

The first type, *signal learning* (S-R), involves involuntary, diffuse, emotional responses which have been acquired through establishment of a conditioned response. Although signal learning is rarely intentionally used in instruction, there are several facilitating or interfering behaviors which may have been learned in this way. Two of the most notable interfering behaviors are test anxiety (e.g., Mandler & Sarason, 1952) and communication apprehension (e.g., McCroskey, 1970; McCroskey & Wheeless, 1976).

Stimulus response learning (Ss → R) "involves making very precise movements of the skeletal muscles in response to very specific stimuli or combinations of stimuli" (Gagnè, 1965, p. 35). The response is voluntary, precise, and includes a skeletal muscular act. Such learning generally includes shaping and the process of discrimination. This type of learning is not common in communication instruction. Nevertheless, this type is useful in overcoming interfering behaviors such as communication apprehension. Systematic desensitization (McCroskey, 1972; Wolpe, 1958), a method commonly used to minimize anxieties, requires the learner to relax muscles in response to specific stimuli situations (imagined or real). This technique can be used to help modify interfering behaviors of learners.

Chaining (Ss → R Ss → R) refers to the connection of two or more stimulus-response links. This type of learning requires that each link has been previously developed and that there is contiguity between links. When the conditions specified in the previous statement have been met, the chain usually occurs on a single occasion. A more specific type of chaining is called *verbal association learning* (Ss → r s → r s → R). Because it involves coding connections which are dependent on the learner's prior history, it is treated as a separate type of learning. This type involves the association of words with visual images, other words, and so forth. For example, children are taught to associate the word "media" with pictures, objects, and/or words such as "television," "radio," "film," and so forth.

Multiple discrimination involves differentiation among chains. First, a learner must acquire individual chains or verbal associations which connect a specific stimulus to a specific response. Second, stimuli must be made as distinctive as possible so that interference is reduced. Memorization is an important factor in multiple discrimination, but most important is the need to reduce interference to assure retention. This type of learning is prevalent in communication instruction. Students are required to discriminate among communication settings, theories of communication, types of message strategies, and so forth.

Concept learning essentially involves the processes of generalization and discrimination. The learner must be able to generalize across a variety of stimulus situations which incorporate the conceptual property, and discriminate among a variety of different stimulus situations. This, too, is a common type of learning. For example, to learn the concept "small group," students must learn to generalize across a variety of stimulus situations which incorporate properties such as size, interdependence, face-to-face contact, interaction, and goal orientation. Students must also discriminate small groups from collections of individuals, organizations, and so forth, on the basis of different stimulus properties.

Principle learning refers to the understanding of the relationship between concepts, or the acquisition of a chain of two or more concepts. To learn a principle, the student must learn the relevant concepts and develop the chain connecting them. An example relevant to communication is learning the principle that: "Information seeking is selective." The student must learn the concepts "information seeking" and "selective" and then link the two together.

Problem solving, the highest level of learning, involves the application of previously learned principles to solve new problems. The learner must be able to identify the goal, recall relevant principles, combine principles into new ones, and solve the problem. One of the primary objectives in graduate education, for example, is to teach the student to develop and test research hypotheses. Such a process involves problem solving.

Gagnè has suggested that these types of learning can be viewed as a hierarchy of learning, with each type serving as a prerequisite for those which follow it. For example, multiple discrimination learning requires that verbal associations or other chains and stimulus-response learning occur. Gagnè, however, does not include signal learning as a prerequisite, due to the lack of evidence supporting its necessity.

Gagnè's explication of the eight types of learning suggests differences in terms of prerequisites, requirements, and goals. These differences have several implications for instructional communication. Ultimately, they suggest refined adaptation of instructional messages for individual receivers. A readiness factor may be identified and operationalized in terms of the person's mastery of prerequisites. Readiness could be diagnosed and, if necessary prior learning has not occurred, instruction could be directed at establishing prerequisites before advancing to the desired learning type. Because it is quite likely that individuals differ on the basis of prerequisites, learners could have the opportunity to have remedial work or individualized instruction. Such approaches would allow the instructional communication system to be adapted to individual differences. When prerequisites are mastered, the learning process is simplified.

Various instructional methods can be employed as long as they enhance the development of the necessary links among variables. Gagnè does not prescribe the techniques to use, but communication researchers can provide a valuable service by investigating the effectiveness of various methods on achieving clearly specified learning goals. One way to judge the efficacy of a given strategy is to test its effectiveness in producing the desired behavior. For each learning type, there are different goals which can be specified in terms of behavioral objectives. For example, problem-solving requires the use and combination of old principles to solve a problem. Using cognitive objectives, an instructor might relate problem-solving learning to application, analysis, synthesis, and/or evaluation objectives. However, knowledge and comprehension objectives could not be used to test problem-solving ability, since they do not require that the principle be used.

Gagnè's typology also has several implications for instructional communication research. First, it suggests measurement and diagnosis of readiness to learn based on mastery of appropriate prerequisites. Based upon such assessment, facilitation of subsequent learning may be accomplished through adaptation of instructional communication to the receiver-learner. Second, the typology suggests a way to target measurement of learning to the appropriate learning type and to select communication strategies to maximize learning. In regard to the former implication, the following proposition is offered:

P2: Adaptation of instructional communication to individual differences facilitates learning.

P2a: Adaptation of instructional communication to differences in levels of prerequisite mastery facilitates learning.

The individual differences of concern are the varying levels of prerequisite mastery. To the degree that the differences are large, adaptation of messages and communication strategies through more individualized instruction becomes important. To the degree that the differences are small, mass communication strategies may become more practical for efficiency reasons.

A second implication concerns the selection of techniques and the type of learning. Gagnè's typology identifies eight types of learning and, due to the different processes involved, implies that the laws and strategies associated with each may be different. Moreover, specific measurements of each type may be targeted. Thus, it is posited that:

P3: The effectiveness of an instructional communication strategy is a function of the type of learning desired.

Although relatively little is known about which methods are most effective for given types of learning, it seems obvious that some are more effective for certain types than for others. Researchers in instructional communication can make worthwhile contributions by helping to develop communication strategies referencing different types of learning, and by identifying the conditions under which selected methods are effective or ineffective. Further, it seems apparent that some of the conflicting findings of previous research may be explained when differences in learning types are identified.

It also seems clear that Gagnè's typology does imply an external or internal order for preparing instructional messages/activities. Assuming that entry levels are known, the learning sequence should begin with the last acquired level and progress, step by step, to higher levels. Therefore, the following proposition is offered:

P4: The effectiveness of an instructional communication strategy is a function of the order by which stimuli are presented.

P4a: Ordering communication stimuli from lower to higher levels of learning is more effective than ordering from higher to lower levels.

It is important to note that the acquisition of each type of learning should be considered a prerequisite to the next type, and that no step should be skipped as one moves up the hierarchy.

LEARNING THEORIES AND STRATEGIES

The task of selecting a limited number of theoretical perspectives for inclusion in this overview was a difficult one. We selected the works of Piaget, Skinner, Bandura, and Bruner because these writers appear to have had the greatest impact on our contemporary educational system. The heuristic value of these approaches is evidenced by the large number of classroom applications which have been derived from them. Although the theories are philosophically different, the instructional principles generated from these perspectives do not seriously conflict with one another.

Cognitive Development

Piaget, a developmental psychologist, has outlined a theory of cognitive development which is particularly appropriate for examining how children learn (e.g., Elkind & Flavell, 1969; Flavell, 1963, 1970; Hilgard & Bower, 1975; Phillips, 1969; Piaget, 1950, 1952, 1954, 1957, 1969, 1970a, 1970b; Piaget & Inhelder, 1969). Piaget's approach focuses on both the psychomotor and cognitive domains and involves all of the types of learning discussed by Gagnè. Three major concepts are central to understanding Piaget's developmental approach: schema, assimilation, and accommodation. *Schemata* are the cognitive structures which individuals use to adapt to and organize the environment. They are concepts or categories which are used to process, generalize, and differentiate stimuli. *Assimilation* refers to the process by which an individual integrates stimuli into existing schemata. It is a method of adapting experiences to fit an existing cognitive structure. *Accommodation* is the process of creating or modifying schemata to provide a structure for new stimuli. It is a method of adapting the cognitive structure to fit experiences.

Piaget postulates that individuals progress through four stages of development, which are posited to be invariant with respect to order. The central explanatory factors for development are: biological maturation, experience with the physical environment, experience with the social environment, and equilibration (a progressive, self-regulating process that leads, step by step, to a final state of reversibility which is a characteristic of higher cognitive structures). Developmental changes affect the individual's ability to process new information and, thus, their ability to learn.

The first stage, the *sensorimotor period*, usually occurs between birth and 2 years of age. This stage is characterized by the development of reflex and motor skills. The sensorimotor period consists of six substages: exercising reflex schemata (0-1 month), primary circular reactions (1-4.5 months), secondary circular reactions (4.5-8 months), coordination of secondary schemata (8-12 months), tertiary circular movements (12-18 months), and mental combinations (18-24 months). During this period, an individual progresses from simple repetition of a behavior to active experimentation.

The *preoperational period*, the second stage, occurs between 2 and 7 years of age and consists of two major phases. Between 2 and 4 years of age, the individual experiences the fastest language growth of life. In addition to language acquisition, the person experiences the beginnings of logic. Basically, the child assumes causality when two things occur simultaneously. The second phase occurs between 4 and 7 years and is characterized by object and quantity permanence, awareness of contradictions between concepts and the environment, reversibility, and some conservation of quantities.

The *concrete operations period* occurs between 7 and 11 years of age. The individual develops decentration of thought, quantity conservation, social cooperation, and an understanding of time and three-dimensional space. Major developments in unidimensional logic and reasoning also occur.

The *formal operations period* begins at 11 years

of age. Thinking becomes multidimensional. The individual develops the ability to construct an argument, solve complex problems, abstract hypotheses, design experiments, and so forth.

Piaget's theory has several implications for the instructional practitioner. Sigel (1969) notes that teachers should adapt to the developmental changes of learners, construct curricula based on developmental sequences, and provide the child with multiple experiences to facilitate learning. Since a child structures the environment differently from an adult, it is important for a child to engage in learning experiences adapted to his or her verbal and nonverbal development. Further, because reasoning and multidimensional thinking occur late in development, it is important for children to experience the environment through physical manipulation. Concrete, participative activities are much more effective than verbal, receptive learning for young children.

Probably the best representation of an applied version of Piaget's theory is the Montessori school. Although not totally isomorphic with the theory, Montessori schools (Montessori, 1955, 1964, 1973) do employ a prepared and enriched environment to give the learner a variety of sensory experiences.

There are also numerous research implications associated with Piaget's theory of cognitive development. Like Gagnè's hierarchical typology, Piaget is concerned with adapting strategies to individual differences (Proposition 2) and ordering learning according to some sequence (Proposition 4). Specifically, the following subpropositions may be added:

P2b: Adaptation of instructional communication to individual developmental differences facilitates learning.

P4b: Primary instructional communication which is ordered according to developmental stages is more effective than instruction which follows a nondevelopmental sequence.

As with Gagnè's hierarchy, the acquisition of one of Piaget's stages should be considered a prerequisite to the next and no stage should be skipped. Whereas Gagnè's typology focuses on ordering within a given content area, Piaget's emphasis is on sequencing within curricula or disciplines. Additionally, Piaget's theory applies to instruction prior to adolescence. Gagnè's includes adolescent and adult learning as well.

Piaget's approach also suggests several additional propositions. The importance of sensory and social experiences is central to his explanation of development. He argues that favorable environments may advance development and unfavorable environments may retard it. The following proposition may be offered:

P5: Rate of development is a function of the social and sensory environment of the individual.

Research (e.g., Berlyne, 1960; Kagan & Kogan, 1970; Munsinger & Kessen, 1964) suggests several message or stimulus properties that may positively affect learning: novelty, complexity, surprisingness, repetition, size, and contrast. Physiological work by Hebb (1960) also points to three major characteristics of environmental stimuli that facilitate learning: the number of external stimuli, the repetition of external stimuli, and the variance among stimuli. Integrating this work with Piaget's theory, the following subpropositions may be suggested:

P5a: Rate of development is positively related to the number of message and environmental stimuli to which the individual is exposed.

P5b: Rate of development is increased by repetition of message and environmental stimuli.

P5c: Rate of development is positively related to variability (novelty, surprisingness, size, contrast, complexity, etc.) of message and environmental stimuli.

The role of practice and active versus passive learning are also addressed by Piaget. He argues that for early childhood, active discovery is essential and practice is useful for acquiring basic information, but has limited utility for learning operative skills. This view would suggest that practice has little effect on the development of communication behaviors once the basic skills are acquired. Thus, the following propositions are posited:

P6: The effectiveness of practice varies with

the developmental stage.

P6a: Repetitive practice facilitates the development of sensorimotor skills and the acquisition of basic figurative information, but has little effect on the development of operative skills.

P7: Active participation, through discovery, is more effective than passive reception learning.

Finally, the stages of development suggest different strategies and/or goal behaviors for research in instructional communication for children. For example, Ward and Wackman (1973) have examined the information processing of television advertising for preoperational and concrete operational stages of development. Children in the advanced stage of development demonstrated higher levels of generalization, differentiation, dimensionality, complexity, reasoning, attention, retention, and so forth, than those in the preoperational stage. Thus, it may be argued that:

P8: Complexity of information processing increases with each stage of development.

In examining the information processing of children, developmental stages cannot be ignored. Understanding these important differences can assist the process of designing instructional communication systems and selecting goals. Likewise, Piaget's theory is extremely useful for instructional communication researchers and practitioners concerned with children. However, it has limited utility for explaining adolescent and adult learning differences.

Operant Conditioning and Behavior Modification

Skinner's operant conditioning approach is an elaboration and extension of Thorndike's law of effect: "When a modifiable connection between a situation and response is made and is accompanied or followed by a satisfying state of affairs, that connection's strength is increased. When made and accompanied or followed by an annoying state of affairs, its strength is decreased" (Thorndike, 1913, p. 4). In other words, individuals do what is pleasant and avoid situations which are unpleasant. As one of the first theorists and researchers to focus on instructional problems, Thorndike (like Gagnè) argued that, in order to learn complex behaviors, the learner must first develop the simpler behaviors which are prerequisites.

Skinner's (Ferster & Skinner, 1957; Skinner, 1938, 1953, 1957, 1968, 1969, 1972, 1974) extension differs in several fundamental ways from Thorndike's. Rather than limiting the explanation to satisfying or annoying states of affairs, Skinner discusses positive and negative reinforcers, extinction, and punishment. He does not use an internal condition, such as satisfaction, to explain reinforcement. He simply states that, if a consequence increases the probability of a response, it is reinforcing. *Positive reinforcers* are rewarding stimuli which follow a response and *negative reinforcers* are aversive stimuli from which the organism is able to escape or which the organism may avoid. *Extinction* is the process of eliminating a response and usually results from providing no consequence for the behavior or from reinforcing an incompatible response. *Punishment* refers to the application of aversive stimuli following a response. Skinner contends that punishment is ineffective unless used continuously with constant monitoring and may produce undesirable side effects. He advocates positive, rather than aversive, forms of control.

Several other characteristics of the operant approach should be noted. First, Skinner proposes a three-term contingency model (discriminative stimuli, behavior, consequences) which suggests that, in learning, an individual should be exposed to discriminative stimuli which maximize the probability that a behavior will be emitted and that, when the behavior occurs, it should be reinforced in order to increase the probability of its occurrence. Second, Skinner advocates the use of functional analysis of situations for the identification of appropriate behaviors and reinforcers. Third, Skinner recommends the use of successive approximations and shaping. *Successive approximation* involves breaking down a goal behavior into small steps which are to be mastered one at a time. For example, the learner may identify before producing, work from easy to fine discriminations, learn parts before wholes, master the simple before the complex, and so forth. *Shaping* refers to the process of reinforcing mastery of each step. An essential feature of this procedure is that the reinforcer should be positive and immediate. This technique is similar to Thorndike's suggestion of breaking down complex acts and systematically rewarding practice. Moreover, successive approximation and shaping may be viewed as instructional communication procedures for blocking and organizing materials, as well as strategies for providing verbal and nonverbal reinforcement. Fourth, Skinner argues that generalization and discrimination are both essential for concept formation. *Generalization* refers to making similar responses to similar stimuli and *discrimination* involves making dissimilar responses to different stimuli. For example, to learn the concept "nonverbal communication" the learner must generalize from obvious forms (e.g., body language, physical appearance) to less obvious forms (e.g., vocalics, personal space) and discriminate between nonverbal and verbal communication.

Bijou (1970) reports an educational programming sequence based on the operant approach. This outline provides a useful guide for organizing educational objectives in a manner consistent with operant theory and has been applied in numerous individualized or self-paced courses. It should be noted that Piaget's developmental stages, Gagnè's hierarchy of learning, and Bloom's taxonomy of cognitive objectives can also be used to help break down the learning steps and assist in the ordering of communication stimuli for instruction.

In order to minimize aversive control and make learning intrinsically reinforcing, Skinner has also advocated the use of programmed instruction and teaching machines. Programmed instruction and teaching machines present instructional materials in small steps (using successive approximation principles), require students to actively respond to the material, and provide feedback concerning the correctness of the responses. *Programmed instruction* refers to the general instructional communication system and *teaching machines* are technological devices which can be used in applying this technique. The steps must be small enough that the learner masters each step before progressing to the next. Correct responses must be immediately and positively reinforced. The learner must play an active role and be allowed to move at his or her own pace. Many programmed, instructional materials use branching procedures which allow the student to enter different tracks based on his or her initial performance on a step. This communication strategy would, of course, be useful for teaching content (concepts, principles, theories, etc.) in communication courses, but would have limited utility in shaping behaviors (e.g., leadership, role adaptation).

A more recent system derived from the operant approach is the *Personalized System of Instruction* (Keller & Sherman, 1974; Ruskin, 1974; Scott & Young, 1976; Sherman, 1974). This method is characterized by the following features: self-pacing, mastery of content, emphasis on written materials, the use of peer-proctors, and the use of lectures as motivational devices. This strategy has proven to be very effective when applied to a wide variety of content areas.

Techniques designed for shaping behaviors include contingency management, token economies, contingency contracting, precision teaching, desensitization, and a variety of other behavior modification techniques (e.g., Bandura, 1969; Homme & Tosti, 1971a, 1971b; MacMillan, 1973; Mikulas, 1972; Snelbecker, 1974; Vargas, 1977). Most of these strategies were originally developed for special education students or psychiatric patients, but have proven useful in a wide variety of learning contexts. In general, these strategies involve the following steps: (1) specify the behavior in observable terms; (2) record the rate at which the behavior occurs; and (3) give small, frequent, immediate reinforcers following the occurrence of the desired behavior. Specific approaches involve some variations, but the basic procedure includes these steps. These procedures can be applied in communication to increase certain behaviors in groups or dyads, or to shape particular behaviors in a variety of communication-learning situations.

In a recent book for classroom teachers, Vargas (1977) has provided a thorough explanation of how to apply operant principles to instruction. Among the topics included are: behavioral measurement, precision teaching, stimulus control, contingency change, maintaining transfer, alternatives to punishment, shaping complex behavior, teaching attitudes and values, motivation, and individualizing mass instruction.

In summary, the operant approach emphasizes the use of positive control in the classroom and specifies procedures for achieving objectives. Operant theorists and researchers have produced numerous instructional strategies which can be applied to almost every aspect of instruction. Bijou's educational programming outline and the Personalized System of Instruction can serve as guides for designing courses and curricula. Vargas's explanation of how to apply operant principles can guide instruction in all design phases. Programmed instruction techniques can be used to teach content, and behavior modification strategies can be applied to the development of specific behaviors. We would argue that the operant approach provides the best philosophical, scientific, systematic, and practical approach for the design and execution of instructional communication strategies. The most useful applications of other theories may also be used within an operant framework with only minor modifications.

The multitude of research implications associated with the operant approach makes it difficult to select only a few for inclusion here. In terms of previously stated propositions, the operant approach has implications for both the adaptation to individual differences and the ordering of instructional communication stimuli. Thus, the following subpropositions may be added:

P2c: Adaptation of instructional stimuli to individual behavioral repertoires and/or mastery levels facilitates learning.

P2d: Adaptation of behavioral consequences based on a functional analysis of the individual is more effective than the use of consequences designed for a group.

P4c: Instructional communication stimuli which are ordered in small steps from simple to complex are more effective than ones which are ordered from complex to simple.

Since both reinforcement and punishment commonly take the form of verbal or nonverbal messages, the following propositional examples highlight the relevance of this theory to researchers in instructional communication. Probably the most central notion is that behaviors are a function of their consequences. Related to this basic operant learning principle are the following representative propositions:

P9: Reinforcement strengthens a response.

P9a: Immediate reinforcement is more effective than delayed reinforcement.

P9b: Small reinforcers are more effective than large ones.

P9c: Frequent reinforcement is more effective than infrequent reinforcement.

P9d: Intermittent schedules of reinforcement are more effective than continuous schedules.

P9e: Unpredictable schedules (variable) of reinforcement are more effective than predictable schedules.

P10: Effective punishment weakens a response.

P10a: Immediate punishment is more effective than delayed punishment.

P10b: Certainty of punishment is more effective than uncertainty.

P10c: Providing alternatives to the punished behavior is more effective than not providing alternatives.

P10d: Reinforcing incompatible behaviors is more effective than punishing the behavior.

P10e: Under conditions where an individual controls the consequences of a behavior, extinction is more effective than punishment.

P10f: Punishment increases hostility, aggression, fear, avoidance, and escape.

P10g: The effectiveness of punishment is negatively related to its frequency of use.

A final research implication provided by operant theory and research is in the area of measurement. Operant communication researchers require that the behavior be active, observable, and countable. Further, the basic unit of measurement is usually rate, or the ratio of the number of behaviors to the time observed. Although measurement need not be restricted in this manner, the use of rate may be useful in many instructional communication studies. When efficiency is of concern, rate of learning is probably more important than how much is learned.

Psychological Modeling

Although Bandura (1965, 1969, 1971) generally supports the operant approach, he argues that the Skinnerian group has operated from a restrictive paradigm. First, he contends that learning and performance can be distinguished and that no-trial learning can occur. He argues that the acquisition or *learning* of a matching response occurs through contiguous association of sensory events and that *performance* may depend on reinforcements administered to the model or anticipated by the learner.

Second, Bandura notes that operant conditioning is effective for shaping and maintaining behaviors when the essential responses are part of the behavioral repertoire of the organism. However, for developing new behavioral repertoires or unique complex combinations of responses, or for cases in which there are no reliable discriminative stimuli, operant conditioning is likely to be extremely time consuming and inefficient. Modeling is recommended as a strategy for learning new behavioral repertoires. *Modeling* requires a skilled model demonstrating the behavior, a pictorial representation of the behavior, or a verbal description of the behavior. The learner is a passive participant, but must perceive the stimuli in order to learn. Clearly, nonverbal and verbal communication messages are involved.

Modeling serves three primary functions. First, learners may acquire new behaviors by observing others. Second, modeling may strengthen or weaken inhibition. Increased inhibition is often produced via observation of a model who receives punishing consequences, and disinhibition generally occurs as a result of observing a model perform a threatening behavior without receiving aversive consequences. A third function is response facilitation. The response is commonly one which is socially accepted and part of the learner's repertoire, but is prompted by the behavior of others.

Essentially, there are four subprocesses involved in modeling: attention, retention, motor reproduction, and motivation. Bandura (1971) argues that when a learner is confronted with a modeling stimulus, he or she must first attend. Characteristics of the model and the observer affect *attention*. Modeling stimuli which are effective in getting attention are characterized by: distinctiveness, affective valence, complexity, prevalence, and functional value. The observer characteristics which affect attention are: sensory capacities, arousal level, motivation, perceptual set, and past reinforcement. Second, the *retention* process requires the observer to symbolically code, cognitively organize, symbolically rehearse, and engage in motor rehearsal of the behavior observed. Third, the *motor* reproduction process is dependent on the observer's physical capabilities, the availability of component responses, self-observations of the modeled behavior, and the accuracy of feedback. Finally, *motivation* is affected by external, vicarious, and self-reinforcement. Information acquisition and processing play key roles in this instructional approach. The modeling process might be diagrammed as follows:

MOTIVATION → ATTENTION → STIMULUS → RETENTION → RESPONSE

This approach to learning differs from an operant perspective by the inclusion of such cognitive constructs as motivation, attention, and retention and by the exclusion of reinforcement following the response. Reinforcement, however, is included in the motivational and attention processes and, thus, by implication, is an important part of the modeling process, although it is not considered to be the primary determinant of learning.

Vicarious reinforcement has been extensively researched by social learning theorists. Bandura (1971) concludes that vicarious reinforcement may produce the following effects: (1) it informs the learner about behaviors that are likely to meet with approval or disapproval; (2) it may enable the learner to discriminate between situations in which a behavior is acceptable or unacceptable; (3) it may provide an incentive for the observer to behave in the prescribed manner due to the anticipation of reinforcement; (4) it may extinguish or elicit emotional arousal in the learner; (5) it may modify the observer's perception of the model's status; (6) it may modify the learner's perception of the reinforcing agents. The consequences received by the model may affect the observer in any of these ways. Therefore, vicarious reinforcement is an extremely important aspect of the modeling process.

Another variable which should be considered is the model's status. Model characteristics seem to be most important when the behavioral consequences are unknown. If the model's status is high, the observer may engage in the prescribed behavior. However, if the consequences are undesirable, the behavior will be extinguished and the model's future influence will be diminished. Within this context, the model serves as the communication source in a similar manner to that described in the communication literature.

The modeling process is almost unavoidable in instruction. For example, learners may be required to operate computer simulations of various human interactions. They must learn to code, keypunch, and interpret data. In order to learn these skills, they may be given written instructions, examples, videotape demonstrations, and so forth. By modeling such examples, they should be able to acquire the necessary skills. Modeling procedures can also be used to teach students the behaviors associated with effective communication.

Modeling, as a theoretical perspective, has several implications for instructional communication research, since a verbal and/or nonverbal message is the primary stimulus employed. Specifically, the following propositions are particularly relevant:

P11: For acquiring new behavioral repertoires, modeling is more effective and efficient than shaping.

P12: Attention is a function of model and observer properties.

P12a: The model's distinctiveness, affective valence, complexity, prevalence, and functional value are positively related to attention.

P12b: The observer's sensory capacities, arousal level, motivation, perceptual set, and past reinforcement impact attention.

P13: Retention is a function of symbolic coding, cognitive organization, symbolic rehearsal, and motor rehearsal.

P14: Motor reproduction is a function of physical capabilities, mastery of component responses, self-observations of the modeled behavior, and accuracy of feedback.

P15: Motivation is a function of external, vicarious, and self reinforcement.

P16: The effect of a model's status is a function of the predicted consequences.

P16a: When consequences are unknown, the model's status is positively related to the learner's response.

P16b: If the consequences are undesirable, the model's future influence will decrease.

Essentially, these propositions deal with different phases of information processing and the model and learner characteristics that influence performance. The strength of this approach is in its application for the development of complex behavioral patterns. For simpler behaviors, the operant approach is probably more useful.

Discovery Learning

Bruner (Anglin, 1973; Bruner, 1966; Bruner, Goodnow, & Austin, 1956; Shulman, 1968; Snelbecker, 1974) takes a more cognitive approach to instruction. This perspective is based on several assumptions about the educational process. First, he characterizes institutional learning as intellectual growth (Bruner, 1966). He describes growth in the following ways:

1. Growth is characterized by increasing independence of response from the immediate nature of the stimulus.
2. Growth depends upon internalizing events into a "storage" system that corresponds to the environment.
3. Intellectual growth involves an increasing capacity to say to oneself and others, by means of words or symbols, what one has done or what one will do.
4. Intellectual development depends upon a systematic and contingent interaction between a tutor and a learner.
5. Teaching is vastly facilitated by the medium of language, which ends by being not only the medium for exchange but the instrument that the learner can then use himself in bringing order into the environment.
6. Intellectual development is marked by increasing capacity to deal with several alternatives simultaneously, to tend to several sequences during the same period of time, and to allocate time and at-

> tention in a manner appropriate to these multiple demands. (pp. 5-6)

The emphasis is placed on frequent symbolic interaction, increased verbalization, improving information processing capabilities, decreasing the importance of specific stimuli and extrinsic reinforcers, and increasing internalization and intrinsic reinforcement. Probably more than any of the other approaches, Bruner's appears to be most directly related to instructional communication theory and research as it is presently practiced.

A second assumption is that in learning, it is important to consider how knowledge is structured. Shulman (1968) interprets Bruner's spiral curriculum as beginning with the complex and learning the fundamentals or simple components in order to solve the complex. Although this may be perceived as contradicting the positions of Gagnè, Piaget, and Skinner, we believe that Bruner is arguing that exposure to the complex or terminal goal behavior can serve to motivate an individual to learn the small steps that lead to that objective. He does not argue that one masters the complex before the fundamentals.

Third, Bruner argues that the concept of readiness has been misused. It is his contention that readiness is taught, and that learning consists of mastering simple skills in order to achieve complex skills. Bruner suggests that learning involves three almost simultaneous processes: (1) acquiring new information, (2) transforming or manipulating information, (3) and evaluating or determining the adequacy of the transformation for a given task (Anglin, 1973).

A fourth assumption is that intuition plays a valuable role in education. He argues that instruction should be designed to develop intuitive thinking. Essentially, he is referring to the context of discovery as philosophers of science conceptualize it. Learners should be encouraged to develop tentative formulations or "educated guesses" which can later be put to the test. He also suggests that educators should avoid the notion that every question has one right answer. In essence, he argues that learners need to know the scientific method.

Finally, Bruner assumes that motivation is essential for learning to occur. He acknowledges that extrinsic reinforcers are sometimes useful in initiating or sustaining learning, but argues that the ideal motivation exists when reinforcement comes from learning per se. Bruner suggests that intrinsic motivation comes from a natural curiosity, a drive to achieve competence, and reciprocity, or the drive to respond and work with other human beings. Activities which allow a learner to actively participate and experience competence in dealing with the world are ones which will motivate the student to learn. It should be noted that this interpretation of motivation is not really very different from Skinner's and Bandura's positions. Each of these theorists argues that motivation or reinforcement should move from extrinsic to intrinsic factors. The main distinction among the approaches is that Bruner attributes motivation to drive states, and Skinner and Bandura attribute it to reinforcers or behavioral elements.

Based on these assumptions, Bruner has identified four basic features for a prescriptive theory of instruction (Bruner, 1966). The first feature is that such a theory must specify strategies for developing predispositions favorable toward learning or, more specifically, toward exploring alternatives. Bruner prescribes three conditions for developing predispositions: activation, maintenance, and direction. *Activation* involves curiosity, which he contends is a response to optimal uncertainty. Learning tasks must provoke exploration. *Maintenance* occurs when the benefits exceed the risk of exploration. Bruner contends that the consequences of error behaviors should not be too aversive. *Direction* depends on understanding the task goal and the relevance of alternatives for achieving that goal. Students must be made aware of the results of their explorations.

A second feature of a prescriptive theory is that it must specify how knowledge is to be structured. Bruner identifies three characteristics of such structure: the *mode of representation*, its *economy*, and its *power*. Knowledge can be represented in terms of actions required for achieving a goal (concrete or enactive), images or graphics that broadly stand for a concept (visual or auditory or iconic), and symbolic or logical propositions (words or numbers or symbolic). Developmentally, people learn to deal with a concept or problem first on a concrete level, than graphically, and finally symbolically. Therefore, instructional communicators must consider the entry level of the learner. Economy refers to a learner's information-processing ability and varies with the mode of representation (e.g., it is easier to handle symbols than concrete operations). Economy also depends on the sequence by which material is presented in a problem-solution format. Finally, power depends on the learner's ability to generate new propositions and solve problems based upon the information acquired. Educators should continuously examine the effects of various learning tasks in terms of power.

The third element of an instructional theory is that it should specify the *sequence* by which materials should be presented. Such sequences depend on the educational objectives, but should be adapted to the learner's entry level and enhance his or her ability to transform and transfer what is being learned. Additionally, the instructor should consider the developmental progression from concrete to symbolic operations and motivational factors, when designing the sequential presentation of material.

The final feature involves the form and pacing of *reinforcement*. Bruner recommends that reinforcement be used for informative functions; that is, educators should provide feedback which lets the student know when he or she is making progress, or which provides the learner with economical information that will encourage self-correction. Again, reinforcement should be primarily intrinsic.

The most significant application of Bruner's approach is the strategy which he has labeled *discovery learning*. It involves minimal teacher guidance, maximal student exploration, and trial-and-error learning. The emphasis is on the learning process rather than outcomes. He contends that such a strategy can produce maximal transfer from one learning situation to another because the emphasis is on broad principles rather than the specifics of the task. If properly designed, discovery tasks should also produce a shift from extrinsic to intrinsic reinforcement. He also argues that discovery learning improves the information retrieval process by allowing the learner to organize material in terms of his or her own cognitive structure. The learner is an active participant in communicating, information processing, selecting, transforming, and in constructing and testing hypotheses. Discovery learning can be conceived of as either a method or goal of instruction.

As an instructional communication method, discovery can be used in courses to help students understand the relationships among concepts (e.g., communication variables). Students can engage in mini-studies to investigate such relationships and discover for themselves how variables operate. General areas for study and possible alternatives for approaching a problem can be suggested by the instructor and/or generated by the students. The educator should avoid providing too much structure to such tasks. Evaluation procedures should be designed to reinforce the process rather than the outcome. For example, mini-studies could be evaluated in terms of the justification and criticism of the selected alternatives rather than the result.

As an objective or goal of instruction, discovery can be used to help students understand the scientific method or the problem-solving process. For example, one of the most common activities in a small group course requires students to complete a problem-solving task. If students are required to analyze and employ the attitudes, strategies, and skills of problem solving, and are evaluated in terms of their ability to generate alternatives and evaluate their effectiveness via discovery, such a task should help achieve the goal of learning how to explore and solve problems.

We would suggest that discovery learning can be incorporated in a course which is designed primarily from an operant perspective. Behavioral objectives and mastery of the discovery process can be used in conjunction with each other. Discovery methods can also help bring behaviors under the control of intrinsic reinforcers.

Many of the research implications of Bruner's theory for instructional communication are similar to those of other theorists presented here. For example, Propositions 2a, 7, and 8 could also be derived from this position. Several additional subpropositions may be added:

P4d: Instructional communication activities which progress from concrete to symbolic operations are more effective than ones which work from symbolic to concrete operations.

P9f: Intrinsic reinforcers are more effective than extrinsic reinforcers.

P15a: Intrinsic motivation is more effective than extrinsic motivation.

The discovery approach is also suggestive of several additional propositions:

P17: An individual's attitude toward learning is a function of activation (optimal uncertainty), maintenance (benefits exceed risks), and direction (clear and relevant goal).

P18: The effectiveness of an instructional communication stimulus is a function of its mode of representation, its economy, and its power.

Again, these propositions are representative rather than exhaustive of the types of relationships that can be drawn from Bruner's instructional theory.

Discovery learning also suggests another learning measure that is not typically employed in instructional communication literature. A learner's ability to generate new propositions and solve problems based on information acquired, when used as a measure of learning, seems useful for those researchers concerned with higher levels of learning.

SUMMARY

The learning typologies, theories, and strategies discussed in this overview are certainly not presented as being exhaustive of all approaches to learning. They are, however, representative of approaches that have implications for instructional communication theory and research. Further, we contend that most of the approaches cited here can be used in conjunction with one another.

The distinctions among these perspectives do not necessitate the selection of one approach. The operant view of learning has produced the most comprehensive applications to instruction and provides the underlying principles to guide the design of curricula, courses, instructional materials, activities, evaluation, and so forth. Bijou's educational programming outline, Vargas' guide for teachers, and Keller's Personalized System of Instruction provide basic assistance in instructional design. Programmed instruction can be an effective method for teaching content, and behavior modification techniques may be employed to develop or alter behaviors. An educational system designed from an operant perspective is characterized by positive rather than aversive forms of control, clearly stated behavioral objectives, steps to achieve the desired behaviors, individualized rather than mass instruction, active rather than passive learners, and criterion-referenced rather than norm-referenced evaluation.

Within an operant framework, Bloom's taxonomy of objectives, Gagnè's hierarchy of learning, and Piaget's stages of development can be used to aid in the diagnosis of entry level skills, identification of the appropriate steps and sequences for presenting instructional material or modifying behaviors, construction of behavioral objectives and evaluation procedures, and so forth. The cueing literature suggests discriminative stimuli which may aid in course design and preparation of instructional materials and activities. Bandura's modeling techniques can be used to help develop new behaviors or complex combinations of responses, and Bruner's discovery learning can be used as a method for teaching people how to learn or as an evaluation method to test transfer of principles learned in other ways.

Although the applications based on these varied perspectives can be used in conjunction with one another, it is important to note the major theoretical differences that do exist. The major distinctions among the approaches are based on differing conceptualizations of learning and its locus of control. Piaget is concerned with the development of sensorimotor and cognitive operations and how development affects the cognitive structure of the individual. Piaget believes that the explanation for learning rests with biological maturation, experience with the physical environment, experience with the social environment, and equilibration. Skinner views learning as synonymous with behavior change and argues that the consequences are the primary determinant of behavior. Bandura distinguishes between learning and performance, arguing that learning occurs through contiguous association of events, and that performance or behavior occurs when reinforcement is anticipated. Learning is dependent on attention, retention, motor reproduction, and motivation processes. For Bruner, learning is an internal unobservable state which may or may not be evident by behavior. Further, he believes that the determinants of learning are basically internal drive states and cognitive structuring.

Instructional communication research needs to be more conceptually based. Although the approaches discussed in this overview may not meet the rigid criteria necessary to be called a "theory," we would argue that each has demonstrated its heuristic value in terms of explanation/prediction and the numerous instructional systems and strategies which have been generated. These approaches also allow for explanation of why certain instructional communication strategies are effective or ineffective and clarify the conditions under which they should be used. One reason that these approaches have been particularly useful is that each has clearly defined the type of learning to be examined and the reasons for its occurrence. The differences in research designs and methodologies and instructional applications may be attributed to the differing conceptualizations and explanations of learning.

In spite of the variance among the approaches, several principles consistently emerge in the learning literature: (1) learners benefit from having clearly defined goals or objectives; (2) instructional methods should be adapted to the individual; (3) instructional stimuli should be ordered from lower to higher levels of learning; (4) learners benefit when instructional stimuli are numerous, varied, and repetitious; (5) active participation is more effective than passive reception; (6) reinforcement improves performance. Ideally, reinforcement should move from the extrinsic to the intrinsic. Although methods for implementing these principles may vary with the approach, the basic ideas remain the same.

A major task before instructional communication researchers is to clearly conceptualize what we mean by "learning," why it occurs, and what role communication plays in the learning process. One approach is to identify the communication variables, strategies, and systems which effectively operationalize the contingencies of learning theories. Since instruction for higher levels of learning relies heavily on communication, the integration of instructional communication research and learning theories may provide greater prediction and explanation. What is needed is a careful evaluation of alternative instructional systems which specifies the conceptual basis of the strategy and identifies the communication components which may maximize effectiveness.

REFERENCES

ANGLIN, J.M. (Ed.). *Jerome S. Bruner: Beyond the information given*. New York: Norton, 1973.

AUSUBEL, D.P. Cognitive structure and the facilitation of meaningful verbal learning. *Journal of Teacher Education*, 1963a, 14, 217-230.

AUSUBEL, D.P. *The psychology of meaningful verbal learning*. New York: Green & Stratton, 1963b.

AUSUBEL, D.P. *Educational psychology: A cognitive view*. New York: Holt, Rinehart & Winston, 1968.

BANDURA, A. Behavioral modifications through modeling procedures. In L. Krasner & L.P. Ullman (Eds.), *Research in behavior modification*. New York: Holt, Rinehart & Winston, 1965.

BANDURA, A. *Principles of behavior modification*. New York: Holt, Rinehart & Winston, 1969.

BANDURA, A. *Psychological modeling: Conflicting theories*. Chicago: Aldine-Atherton, 1971.

BARNES, R.B., & CLAWSON, E.U. Do advance organizers facilitate learning? Recommendations for further research based on an analysis of 32 studies. *Review of Educational Research*, 1975, 45, 637-659.

BERLYNE, D.E. *Conflict, arousal and curiousity*. New York: McGraw-Hill, 1960.

BIJOU, S.W. What psychology has to offer education now. In P.B. Dews (Ed.), *Festschrift for B.F. Skinner*. New York: Appleton-Century-Crofts, 1970, pp. 401-407.

BLOOM, B.S. (Ed.). *Taxonomy of educational objectives* (Handbook I: Cognitive domain). New York: McKay, 1956.

BROOKS, W.D. & FRIEDRICH, G.W. *Teaching speech communication in the secondary school*. Boston: Houghton-Mifflin, 1973.

BRUNER, J.S. *Toward a theory of instruction*. New York: Norton, 1966.

BRUNER, J.S., GOODNOW, J.J., & AUSTIN, G.A. *A study of thinking*. New York: Wiley, 1956.

BULL, S. The role of questions in maintaining attention to textual material. *Review of Educational Research*, 1973, 43, 83-87.

CASHEN, V.M., & LEICHT, K.L. Role of the isolation effect

in a formal educational setting. *Journal of Educational Psychology*. 1970, 61, 484-486.

CROUSE, J.H., & IDSTEIN, P. Effects of encoding cues on prose learning. *Journal of Educational Psychology*, 1972, 63, 309-313.

DUCHASTEL, P.C., & MERRILL, P.F. The effects of behavioral objectives on learning: A review of empirical studies. *Review of Educational Research*, 1973, 43, 53-69.

ELKIND, D., & FLAVELL, J.H. (Eds.). *Studies in cognitive development: Essays in honor of Jean Piaget*. New York: Oxford University Press, 1969.

FAW, H.W., & WALLER, T.G. Mathemagenic behaviours and efficiency in learning from prose materials: Review, critique, and recommendations. *Review of Educational Research*, 1976, 46, 691-720.

FELKER, D.B., & DAPRA, R.A. Effects of question type and question placement on problem-solving ability from prose material. *Journal of Educational Psychology*, 1975, 67, 380-384.

FERSTER, C.G., & SKINNER, B.F. *Schedules of reinforcement*. New York: Appleton-Century-Crofts, 1957.

FLAVELL, J.H. *The developmental psychology of Jean Piaget*. Princeton, N.J.: Van Nostrand, 1963.

FLAVELL, J.H. Concept development. In P.H. Mussen (Ed.), *Carmichael's manual of child psychology*. Vol. 1. New York: Wiley, 1970.

FRASE, L.T. Learning from prose material: Length of passage, knowledge of results, and position of questions. *Journal of Educational Psychology*, 1967, 58, 266-272.

FRASE, L.T. Effect of question location, pacing, and mode upon retention of prose material. *Journal of Educational Psychology*, 1968a, 59, 244-249.

FRASE, L.T. Some data concerning the mathemagenic hypothesis. *American Educational Research Journal*, 1968b, 5, 181-189.

FRASE, L.T. Boundary conditions for mathemagenic behaviors. *Review of Educational Research*, 1970, 40, 337-348.

FRASE, L.T., & KREITZBERG, V.S. Effect of topical and indirect learning directions on prose recall. *Journal of Educational Psychology*, 1975, 67, 320-324.

FRASE, L.T., & SCHWARTZ, B.J. Effect of question production and answering on prose recall. *Journal of Educational Psychology*, 1975, 67, 628-635.

GAGNÈ, R.M. *The conditions of learning*. New York: Holt, Rinehart & Winston, 1965.

GAGNÈ, R.M. *The conditions of learning* (Rev. ed.). New York: Holt, Rinehart & Winston, 1970.

GAGNÈ, R.M., & BRIGGS, L.J. *Principles of instructional design*. New York: Holt, Rinehart & Winston, 1974.

HARTLEY, J. The effect of pre-testing on post-test performance. *Instructional Science*, 1973, 2, 193-214.

HARTLEY, J., & DAVIES, I.K. Preinstructional strategies: The role of pretests, behavioral objectives, overviews, and advance organizers. *Review of Educational Research*, 1976, 46, 239-265.

HEBB, D.O. *Organization of behavior*. New York: Wiley, 1960.

HILGARD, E.R., & BOWEN, G.H. *Theories of learning*. Englewood Cliffs, N.J.: Prentice-Hall, 1975.

HOMME, L., & TOSTI, D. *Behavior technology: Motivation and contingency management* (Units I & II). San Rafael, Cal.: Individual Learning Systems, 1971a.

HOMME, L., & TOSTI, D. *Behavior technology: Motivation and contingency management* (Units III & IV). San Rafael, Cal.: Individual Learning Systems, 1971b.

HURT, T., SCOTT, M.D., & McCROSKEY, J.C. *Communication in the classroom*. Reading, Mass.: Addison-Wesley, 1978.

IDSTEIN, P., & JENKINS, J.R. Underlining versus repetitive reading. *Journal of Educational Research*, 1972, 65, 321-323.

KAGAN, J., & KOGAN, N. Individual variation in cognitive processes. In P.H. Mussen (Ed.), *Carmichael's manual of child psychology*. Vol. 1. New York: Wiley, 1970.

KAPLAN, R. Effects of learning with part v. whole presentations of instructional objectives. *Journal of Educational Psychology*, 1974, 66, 787-792.

KAPLAN, R., & ROTHKOPF, E.Z. Instructional objectives as directions to learners: Effect of passage length and amount of objective relevant content. *Journal of Educational Psychology*, 1974, 66, 448-456.

KAPLAN, R., & SIMMONS, F.G. Effects of instructional objectives used as orienting stimuli or as summary/review upon prose learning. *Journal of Educational Psychology*, 1974, 66, 614-622.

KELLER, F.S., & SHERMAN, J.G. (Ed.), *The Keller plan handbook*. Menlo Park, N.J.: Benjamin, 1974.

KIBLER, R.J., BARKER, L.L., & MILES, D.T. *Behavioral objectives and instruction*. Boston: Allyn & Bacon, 1970.

KIBLER, R.J., BASSETT, R.E., & BYERS, J.P. Behavioral objectives and communication instruction: State of research. *Human Communication Research*, 1977, 3, 278-288.

KRATHWOHL, D.R., BLOOM, B.S., & MASIA, B.B. *Taxonomy of educational objectives* (Handbook II: Affective domain). New York: McKay, 1964.

LADAS, H. The mathemagenic effects of factual review questions on the learning of incidental information: A critical review. *Review of Educational Research*, 1973, 43, 71-82.

LaPORTE, R.E., & VOSS, J.F. Retention of prose materials as a function of post acquisition testing. *Journal of Educational Psychology*, 1975, 67, 259-266.

LAWTON, J.T., & WANSKA, S.K. Advance organizers as a teaching strategy: A reply to Barnes and Clawson. *Review of Educational Research*, 1977, 47, 233-244.

LUMSDAINE, A.A. Instruments and media of instruction. In N.L. Gage (Ed.), *Handbook of research on teaching*. Chicago: Rand McNally, 1963.

MacMILLAN, D. *Behavior modification in education*. New York: Macmillan, 1973.

MAGER, R.F. *Preparing instructional objectives*. Belmont, Cal.: Lear Siegler, 1962.

MANDLER, G., & SARASON, S.B. A study of anxiety and learning. *Journal of Abnormal and Social Psychology*, 1952, 47, 166-173.

McCROSKEY, J.C. Measures of communication-bound anxiety. *Speech Monographs*, 1970, 37, 269-277.

McCROSKEY, J.C. The implementation of a large scale program of systematic desensitization for communication apprehension. *Speech Teacher*, 1972, 21, 255-264.

McCROSKEY, J.C., & WHEELESS, L.R. *Introduction to human communication*. Boston: Allyn & Bacon, 1976.

MIKULAS, W.L. *Behavior modification: An overview*. New York: Harper & Row, 1972.

MONTESSORI, M. *Childhood education.* New York: New American Library, 1955.
MONTESSORI, M. *Spontaneous activity in education.* Cambridge: Bentley, 1964.
MONTESSORI, M. *The Montessori elementary material.* New York: Schocken, 1973.
MUNSINGER, H., & KESSEN, K.W. Uncertainty, structure, and preference. *Psychological Monographs*, 1964, 78, 586.
PHILLIPS, J.L., JR. *The origins of intellect: Piaget's theory.* San Francisco: Freeman, 1969.
PIAGET, J. *The psychology of intelligence.* New York: Harcourt, Brace & Jonavich, 1950.
PIAGET, J. Autobiography. In C. Murchison & E.G. Boring (Eds.), *A history of psychology in autobiography.* Vol. 4. Worchester, Mass.: Clark University Press, 1952, 237-256.
PIAGET, J. *The construction of reality in the child.* New York: Basic, 1954.
PIAGET, J. *Logic and psychology.* New York: Basic, 1957.
PIAGET, J. *The mechanisms of perception.* New York: Basic, 1969.
PIAGET, J. *Science of education and the psychology of the child.* New York: Viking, 1970a.
PIAGET, J. Piaget's theory. In P.H. Mussen (Ed.), *Carmichael's manual of child psychology.* Vol. 1. New York: Wiley, 1970b.
PIAGET, J., & INHELDER, B. *The psychology of the child.* New York: Basic, 1969.
RICKARDS, J.P., & AUGUST, G.J. Generative underlining strategies in prose recall. *Journal of Educational Psychology*, 1975, 67, 860-865.
ROTHKOPF, E.Z. The concept of mathemagenic behaviours. *Review of Educational Research*, 1970, 40, 325-336.
ROTHKOPF, E.Z., & BISBICOS, E.E. Selective facilitative effects of interspersed questions on learning from written materials. *Journal of Educational Psychology*, 1967, 58, 56-61.
ROTHKOPF, E.Z., & KAPLAN, R. Exploration of the effect of density and specificity of instructional objectives on learning from text. *Journal of Educational Psychology*, 1972, 63, 295-302.
RUSKIN, R.S. *The personalized system of instruction: An educational alternative.* Washington, D.C.: ERIC/Higher Educational Research Report No. 5, 1974.
SCOTT, M.D., & WHEELESS, L.R. Instructional communication theory and research: An overview. In B.D. Ruben (Ed.), *Communication yearbook I.* New Brunswick, N.J.: Transaction-International Communication Association, 1977.
SCOTT, M.D., & YOUNG, T.J. Personalizing communication instruction. *Communication Education*, 1976, 25, 211-221.
SHERMAN, J.G. (Ed.). *Personalized system of instruction.* Menlo Park, N.J.: Benjamin, 1974.
SHULMAN, L.S. Psychological controversies in the teaching of science and mathematics. *Science Teacher*, 1968, 35, 34-38, 89-90.
SIGEL, E.G. The Piagetian system and the world of education. In D. Elkind & J.H. Flavell (Eds.), *Studies in cognitive development: Essays in honor of Jean Piaget.* New York: Oxford University Press, 1969.
SIGEL, I.E., & HOOPER, F.H. (Eds.). *Logical thinking in children: Research based on Piaget's theory.* New York: Holt, Rinehart & Winston, 1968.
SKINNER, B.F. *The behavior of organisms.* New York: Appleton-Century-Crofts, 1938.
SKINNER, B.F. *Science and human behavior.* New York: Free Press, 1953.
SKINNER, B.F. *Verbal behavior.* Englewood Cliffs, N.J.: Prentice-Hall, 1957.
SKINNER, B.F. *The technology of teaching.* New York: Appleton-Century-Crofts, 1968.
SKINNER, B.F. *Contingencies of reinforcement: A theoretical analysis.* New York: Appleton-Century-Crofts, 1969.
SKINNER, B.F. *Cumulative reçord: A selection of papers.* New York: Appleton-Century-Crofts, 1972.
SKINNER, B.F. *About behaviorism.* New York: Knopf, 1974.
SNELBECKER, G.E. *Learning theory, instructional theory, and psycho-educational design.* New York: McGraw-Hill, 1974.
THORNDIKE, E.L. *Educational psychology: The psychology of learning.* Vol. 2. New York: Columbia University Press, 1913.
VARGAS, J.S. *Writing worthwhile behavioral objectives.* New York: Harper & Row, 1972.
VARGAS, J.S. *Behavioral psychology for teachers.* New York: Harper & Row, 1977.
WARD, S., & WACKMAN, D.B. Children's information processing of television advertising. In P. Clarke (Ed.), *New models for mass communication research.* Beverly Hills, Cal.: Sage, 1973.
WARR, P.B., BIRD, W.W., & RACKMAN, N. *Evaluation of management training.* London: Gower Press, 1970.
WELCH, W.W., & WALBERG, H.S. Pre-test and sensitization effects in curriculum evaluation. *American Educational Research Journal*, 1970, 7, 605-614.
WOLPE, J. *Psychotherapy by reciprocal inhibition.* Stanford, Cal.: Stanford University Press, 1958.

COMMUNICATION APPREHENSION, INTELLIGENCE, AND ACHIEVEMENT AMONG SECONDARY SCHOOL STUDENTS[1]

GARY F. DAVIS
Purdue University

MICHAEL D. SCOTT
West Virginia University

This study investigated the impact of communication apprehension and intelligence on achievement, as well as the relationships among these variables. Two hypotheses were tested and one research question was explored. Hypothesis 1, which predicted that levels of communication apprehension and intelligence were linearly related, was confirmed. Hypothesis 2, which predicted that low communication apprehensives would exhibit significantly higher IQ scores than moderate and high communication apprehensives, was also confirmed. Exploration of the research question netted findings contrary to much of the previous research concerning communication apprehension and achievement.

Questions about differential levels of classroom achievement are not new. Likewise, scientific research concerning variables thought to be associated with the answers to these questions also is not new. For almost a century, social scientists (Crandall, 1963; Crandall & Rabson, 1960; Guilford, 1967; Hull, 1928; Jensen, 1969; Krechevsky, 1938; Moss & Kagan, 1961; Mowrer, 1947; Piaget, 1950, 1952; Seligman & Hager, 1972; Spearman, 1904, 1923; Thorndike, 1911; Thurstone, 1935) have repeatedly sought to ferret out the anthropological, psychological, and sociological roots of a student's success or failure in achieving at an acceptable level. Although much important information has been compiled during this span of time, many questions about why students succeed or fail remain.

For example, theorists, researchers, and educators alike have long agreed that academic achievement and verbal ability are strongly associated with one another (e.g., Carroll, 1960; Merrifield, 1971; Wechsler, 1971). Furthermore, this agreement is rather evident in the fact that standardized measures of verbal ability are the most common means of determining success in achieving (e.g., Bond, 1940; Terman, 1917, 1937, 1960; Wechsler, 1949). Yet, academic achievement is often associated with more than the analytical skills commonly tapped by standardized measures of achievement. Very recent research suggests it is also associated with a different kind of skill—oral communication (Bashore, 1971; McCroskey & Andersen, 1976). While much is known about the relationship between traditional analytic skills and achievement, less is known about how this other type of skill is related to academic achievement. Still less is known about the relationships among these different indicants of verbal ability and academic achievement.

Two variables that are presumably associated with one's verbal abilities—communication apprehension and intelligence quotient—also appear to be associated with differential classroom achievement (Anastasi, 1961; Thorndike, & Hagan, 1969; Bashore, 1971; Binder, Jones, & Strowig, 1970; McCroskey & Andersen, 1976). Whereas communication apprehension is a generalized anxiety or fear about oral communication, intelligence quotient is a measure of one's verbal as well as mathematical abilities and is significantly influenced by verbal skills (e.g., Carroll, 1960; Merrifield, 1971; Mussen, Conger, & Kagan, 1969).

A substantial body of literature suggests that intelligence quotient is a superior predictor of classroom achievement (e.g., Binder, Jones, & Strowig, 1970; Thorndike & Hagan, 1969). While considerably more modest, the body of literature concerning communication apprehension also indicates this construct may be a heuristic tool in predicting academic achievement (e.g., Bashore, 1971; McCroskey & Andersen, 1976; Scott & Wheeless, 1977a).

Although communication apprehension and intelligence quotient have been studied in isolation from one another, only one study to date has examined the relationship between the two constructs (Bashore, 1971) as they relate to student achievement. Furthermore, the inconclusive nature of the results of this single study, coupled with another study reporting that communication apprehension failed to significantly correlate with the *intelligence dimension of a personality measure* (McCroskey, Daly, & Sorensen, 1976), appears to have given weight to the conclusion that communication and intelligence have little in common in the prediction and explanation of differential levels of academic achievement (e.g., McCroskey, 1977a).

The paucity of research focusing on communication apprehension and intelligence suggests that the preceding conclusion is premature. And while this alone provides at least some rationale for further study of the two variables, a more compelling one can be found in the relevant literature. In brief, most of the researchers who have investigated the relationship between communication apprehension and achievement not only have advanced conclusions that appear to exceed the generalizability of their findings, but have also failed to concern themselves with the mediational impact of variables that appear to be conceptually linked to communication apprehension, for example, intelligence. This study, therefore, investigated the relationships among communication apprehension, intelligence, and academic achievement.

REVIEW OF RELEVANT RESEARCH

At least four areas of theory and research are important to questions concerning the relationships among the variables examined in this study: (1) theory and research concerning the relationship between communication apprehension and academic achievement; (2) studies where the findings provide some explanation of the relationship between communication apprehension and achievement; (3) theory and research focusing on the conceptualization and measurement of intelligence; and (4) theory and research based on the relationship between specific measures of intelligence and achievement.

Communication Apprehension and Achievement

Communication apprehension refers to a general anxiety or fear about real or anticipated communication with other people. High levels of apprehension have been found in approximately 15 to 20% of American college students (McCroskey, 1977a). Communication apprehension is a personality trait. That is to say, an individual who is apprehensive has a tendency of predisposition to be anxious about orally communicating across all situations (McCroskey, 1970). As used here, this trait should not be confused with state anxiety toward orally communicating. Whereas state anxiety refers to an apprehension or fear towards communicating in specific situations and is often referred to as "stage fright," the trait of communication apprehension is not contextually bound. Likewise, communication apprehension should also not be confused with general anxiety, which is an apprehension or fear of many situations which may or may not include oral communication.

While communication apprehension can be measured reliably and appears to be a viable construct in light of the general findings concerning its impact (McCroskey, 1977b), research focusing on the relationship between communication apprehension and achievement is relatively new. In what is probably the earliest study focusing on communication apprehension and achievement, Bashore (1971) found negative correlations of differing magnitudes between communication apprehension and the American College Test, the Illinois State High School Test, the verbal portion of the College Entrance Examination Board Test, and the Preliminary Scholastic Aptitude Test. Notably, Bashore also found a slight, negative correlation between IQ scores and communication apprehension among females. However, the small sample size of this study severely restricted its generalizability.

Even so, in a similar and more comprehensive study, comparable results were found by McCroskey and Andersen (1976). In this study, high communication apprehensives were reported to score significantly lower on the social science, natural science, math, and English portions of the American College Test, as well as the overall composite score of this test. Students with high communication apprehension were also reported to have lower grade point averages than students with low communication apprehension.

Scott and Wheeless (1977a) conducted a related study, the exception being that they were interested in the impact of oral communication on measures of achievement in a conventional classroom—tests and assigned projects. Scott and Wheeless's results suggested that the achievement differences reported by McCroskey and Andersen appeared to generalize to conventional classrooms employing less sophisticated measures of achievement than the ACT.

While the preceding two investigations found differential achievement among high and low communication apprehensives, it is interesting to note that moderately apprehensive subjects were never statistically compared to their verbal and reticent counterparts in either study. It is also interesting to note that in the absence of such a comparison, the only legitimate claim that could be made by either pair of researchers is that high and low communication apprehensives achieve differently. Yet, both pairs of researchers suggested that high communication apprehension appeared to be linked to less than normal levels of achievement.

The preceding conclusion was recently challenged by Scott, Wheeless, Yates, and Randolph (1977). These researchers examined the effects of communication apprehension and test anxiety on achievement in a nonconventional educational setting. Scott et al. hypothesized that a linear combination of communication apprehension and test anxiety would be significantly correlated with achievement, and explored the relationship among these variables. These researchers also included moderate apprehensives in the analysis. Results indicated that high apprehensives achieved no differently than moderate apprehensives and, contrary to previous research, low apprehensives achieved less efficiently than did highs or moderates. The results of this study also indicated that test anxiety was superior to communication apprehension as a predictor of achievement. These findings prompted Scott et al. (1977) to reexamine the results of an earlier study (Scott & Wheeless, 1977a) where moderate apprehensives were not included in the primary analysis. An examination of the means indicated that in the earlier study, moderates and highs in a conventional classroom also achieved at the same level, whereas low apprehensives excelled. As a result, Scott et al. argued that the achievement findings of prior research failed to warrant the conclusion that high communication apprehensives learn at substandard levels.

Studies with Explanatory Power

Although many explanations as to how communication apprehension mediates achievement have been offered, those which appear most credible have concerned the relationships between communication apprehension and teacher expectancies, communication apprehension and student attitudes, and communication apprehension and verbal abilities.

McCroskey and Daly (1976), for instance, examined the relationship between communication apprehension and teacher expectancies by constructing descriptions of two hypothetical school children. The descriptions were identical except that one student was described as highly verbal, whereas the other student was described as reticent. McCroskey and Daly hypothesized that teacher expectations of academic success among low apprehensive students would be more positive than those of academic success among high apprehensives. According to McCroskey and Daly, their results indicated that teachers formed negative perceptions of high apprehensives, expecting them to achieve less than low apprehensives. One possible explanation of the research findings on achievement, then, might be that teachers develop negative predispositions about reticent students. These predispositions, moreover, may lead to subjective and negative teacher evaluations of the highly apprehensive student.

In addition to differential teacher expectancies, the research also suggests that student attitudes may lead to different levels of achievement among students with varying levels of apprehension. In this regard, Hurt, Preiss, and Davis (1976) investigated student attitudes and communication apprehension in a middle school. They found communication apprehension to be significantly correlated with affective learning or attitudes toward school, and cognitive learning or grades. More specifically, they found that, as the level of communication apprehension increased, student attitudes toward school became more negative and grades lower.

In another study, Scott and Wheeless (1977b) investigated the relationships of three types of communication apprehension to student attitudes and levels of satisfaction. Scott and Wheeless also found that high communication apprehensives exhibited less favorable attitudes and expressed less satisfaction with classroom activities requiring them to orally communicate. They speculated that these two findings might assist in explaining research where highly apprehensive students did not achieve as well as low apprehensive students.

In a more indirect fashion, McCroskey and Andersen (1976) also found evidence in support of the notion that the attitudes of high communication apprehensives may undermine their academic performance. Using classroom preference instead of attitudes, McCroskey and Andersen found that, whereas low apprehensives prefer small classrooms characterized by high interaction, the reverse is true for high apprehensives.

Thus, like negative teacher expectancies, differential achievement among individuals with varying degrees of communication apprehension also may be partially a result of negative attitudes. These negative attitudes toward oral communication may also result in communication avoidance which, in turn, would lessen the highly apprehensive students exposure to needed classroom information.

Finally, evidence gleaned from the Scott, Wheeless, Yates, and Randolph (1977) study offers yet another explanation for the research findings. After examining earlier research, Scott et al. suggested a potential link between communication apprehension, achievement, and verbal ability. They argued that differential achievement effects observed in previous research may have been the result of differential verbal abilities among students with varying degrees of communication apprehension. Such a linkage appears plausible. If, for example, low communication apprehensives are more verbally skilled than their moderately to highly reticent counterparts, this might help explain why they tend to excel on both objective (e.g., ACT) and subjective (e.g., teacher evaluations) measures of achievement.

This reasoning is based on two factors. First, verbal ability and intelligence are interdependent and this might account for the low communication apprehensives tendency to excel on standardized measures of achievement which, in part, are based on one's verbal ability. Second, teachers may assume that verbally active students are more intelligent, and this may account for the low apprehensive's tendency to excel in conventional classrooms.

In summary, research concerning the relationship between communication apprehension and academic achievement is not as conclusive as some have suggested (e.g., McCroskey, 1977a). While there is some evidence in support of the notion that high communication apprehension negatively affects achievement, this evidence stems from research where only the extremes of the communication apprehension contribution were investigated. By way of contrast, where the full range of the distribution was investigated, high communication apprehensives appeared to achieve normally.

Also, the research has yet to yield an unequivocal explanation for differential levels of achievement among individuals with varying degrees of communication apprehension. While teacher expectancies and student attitudes may be at the root of the problem, the intelligence literature appears to lend support to the notion that achievement differences may be most associated with differential verbal abilities among students with varying degrees of communication apprehension.

The Nature of Intelligence Quotient

Intelligence has been defined as abstract reasoning, learning or profiting from experience, a capacity to adapt, and the ability to solve problems. Wechsler (1971) maintained that these definitions are insufficient but not entirely incorrect. Intelligent behavior may call on all of the cognitive attributes listed above or any of them separately. Humphreys (1971) defined intelligence as the entire repertoire of acquired skills, knowledge, learning sets, and generalization tendencies considered intellectual in nature that are available at any period of time. Intelligence tests consist of items that sample the totality of such acquisitions (Humphreys, 1971). Humphreys's definition, although circular in nature because of the use of the term "intellectual," is redeemed by the consensus among psychologists as to the kinds of behavior labelled "intellectual." This is exemplified by the use of highly similar tests of intelligence; for example, the Stanford-Binet (Terman, 1960) and the Wechsler tests (Wechsler, 1949).

Intelligence tests put a heavy reliance on the individual's language skills (Merrifield, 1971). Merrifield contended that those who are less verbal are virtually certain to fail on such tests. Humphreys (1971) maintained that exposure is needed for a student to acquire the knowledge and skills necessary to succeed on intelligence tests.

In summary, then, IQ can be generally defined as acquired skills and knowledge, as well as the ability to manifest those behaviors on a verbal skills test. Moreover, the literature suggests that students more proficient in verbal skills do better on IQ tests than those with less exposure and, consequently, less skills.

IQ and Achievement Studies

One thoroughly researched way of predicting academic achievement is the use of intelligence measures. Anastasi (1961) investigated the relationships among IQ, school grades, teacher ratings, and achievement test scores. The correlations among the variables were typically between .40 and .75. Sartain (1946), in a comparison of intelligence tests, found IQ and achievement to have a correlation of .58. Lorge, Thorndike, and Hagan (1964) conducted a study in which the verbal and nonverbal sections were correlated separately with achievement test scores. Typically, the verbal battery was more highly correlated (.77 to .80) than the nonverbal battery (.66 to .77). Clelland and Toussaint (1962) investigated the interrelationships of reading ability with reading comprehension and .73 resulted. Significant correlations between IQ and achievement have also been found by a number of other researchers (e.g., Bond, 1940; Deb & Ghosh, 1971; Sinha, 1972). Thorndike and Hagan (1969) and Binder, Jones, and Strowig (1970), in reviews of the research, found that IQ and academic achievement were consistently correlated at .50 and .60, thus establishing a fairly predictive paradigm.

Based on the research, then, it is apparent that IQ is clearly related to an individual's academic achievement. Also, verbal abilities seem to be highly related to intelligence quotient (Clelland & Toussaint, 1962; Lorge, Thorndike, & Hagan, 1964), and are thus at least indirectly related to achievement.

RATIONALE

Given the preceding review of the literature, it appears that communication apprehension and IQ may both be tied to verbal skills. Typically, communication apprehension gives rise to a consistent pattern of communication avoidance or withdrawal from situations where communication is likely to occur. Assuming this pattern of behavior manifests itself relatively early in the life of the individual, it could severely limit the individual's exposure to environmental information. Moreover, this limited exposure could conceivably affect the individual's verbal abilities in general which, in the long run, could affect the individual's level of achievement.

As proposed by Merrifield (1971) and Wechsler (1971), individuals who do not receive as much exposure to their environment are not as proficient in their verbal behaviors as others. As a result, they are virtually certain to do poorly on the IQ tests. The research inside and outside the classroom environment suggests that high communication apprehension may reduce the probability of this exposure and thereby lessen proficiency in verbal behaviors. This, of course, is related to a potentially low IQ level. Conversely, as communication apprehension decreases, students should have increased exposure to their environment, which could conceivably lead to increased verbal ability and higher IQ scores. Thus, hypothesis one predicts:

> H_1: Levels of communication apprehension and IQ are linearly related.

Although a linear relationship between communication apprehension and IQ is predicted in Hypothesis 1, there is reason to believe that high communication apprehensives achieve at a level that is comparable to their moderate counterparts (Scott, Wheeless, Yates, & Randolph, 1977). Further, it does not seem unreasonable to speculate that this comparable level of achievement might be partially attributable to similar levels of intelligence between high and moderate apprehensives. While high and moderate apprehensives would be expected to exhibit lower intelligence scores than low apprehensives, high and moderates themselves would not be expected to statistically differ. Hypothesis 2, therefore, predicts:

> H_2: Students with low levels of communication apprehension will have significantly higher IQ scores than those with moderate or high levels of communication apprehension.

Finally, the research of Scott et al. (1977) suggests: (1) that high levels of communication apprehension may not be as debilitating to achievement as some have concluded, and (2) high levels of communication apprehension may be of secondary importance to other variables associated with achievement. In the effort to assess the generalizability of the findings that prompted these conclusions, therefore, the following research question is advanced:

> Q_1: What are the relationships among IQ, communication apprehension, and achievement?

METHOD

Procedures and Sampling

The subjects employed in this study were 429 secondary school students (grades 9-12) at a major high school in a southeastern state. The subjects were given a 30-item measure of communication apprehension during the first week of the second semester, under the auspices of the student counselor. Also obtained from the student counselor during the same period of time were indices of intelligence and prior achievement.

Measurement

Communication apprehension was assessed with a self-report measure recently developed by McCroskey (1977c). This measure was comprised of 10 items from the Personal Report of Communication Apprehension (McCroskey & Wheeless, 1976), 10 items from the Personal Report of Communication Fear, (McCroskey, 1977c), and 10 items from a measure of Verbal Activity (McCroskey, 1977c).

High, moderate, and low levels of communication apprehension were determined upon the standard deviation criterion. The subjects scoring beyond a standard deviation above the mean were classified as high, those within a standard deviation above or below the mean were classified as moderate, and those below a standard deviation of the mean were classified as low.

IQ scores were obtained from the student counselor. These scores, moreover, were derived from measures which were developed independently, but presumed to be equivalent. Senior and junior subjects' IQ scores were derived from a standardized measure of achievement developed by Science Research Associates. Sophomore subjects' IQ scores were derived from the Iowa Test of Basic Skills, and freshmen subjects' IQ scores were derived from a test developed by the State Board of Education. Where necessary, high, moderate, and low levels of IQ were determined on the standard deviation criterion previously described.

Finally, achievement was determined on the basis of two measures: (1) subjects' composite scores on the Standardized Reading Achievement Test developed by Science Research Associates, and (2) grade point average.

STATISTICAL ANALYSES AND RESULTS

For all tests, statistical significance was established at the .05 level. It should be noted, moreover, that the N varied in most statistical analyses because scores on all relevant dependent measures were not available for all subjects.

Communication Apprehension

Since communication apprehension was assessed with an instrument comprised of items from three different measures thought to be associated with the general construct, the 30-item instrument was factor analyzed using oblique rotational solutions (N = 429, MSA = .82). In order to determine the number of valid factors present, an eigenvalue of 1.0 was established as the initial cut-off point. Each factor extracted was required to have two items loaded at .60 with no secondary loading of .40 or greater. Additional items were accepted as loaded on a factor if its primary loading was on the factor and had no secondary loading above .30. These additional items were selected on this basis until reliability was not increased. The magnitude of the relationships among extracted factors was assessed via Pearson product-moment correlations. Reliabilities were subsequently computed using the split-half method and Nunnally's recommended procedure (1967).

The oblique solution yielded two factors accounting for 40% of the total variance with 18 items meeting the minimum criterion established (see Table 1). The number of items were equally divided between the two factors. The first independent dimension was comprised of 9 items which, on face validity, appeared to be most associated with communication apprehension and communication fear. The second independent dimension was comprised solely of 9 items formerly associated with the verbal activity scale. The first factor, therefore, was labeled as communication apprehension and the second factor was labeled as verbal activity.[2]

The measure of communication apprehension displayed the following descriptive statistics: $\overline{x}$ = 29.9, SD = 6.9, split-half reliability = .84, and Nunnally's reliability r = .81. The second measure of verbal activity displayed: x = 25.1, SD = 7.0, split-half reliability = .91, and Nunnally's reliability r = .81. The correlation between the two factors was −.27, accounting for only 7% shared variance. While the two factor structures were correlated, the amount of shared variance was not highly meaningful.

Measure of Intelligence

Due to inconsistent testing procedures at the high school under investigation, three different tests of IQ were used. The use of three different intelligence tests required an analysis to determine if the three distributions were equivalent. The distributions of each specific IQ test were statistically compared via chi-square, goodness-of-fit procedures. A 3 x 3 matrix (3 levels of IQ x 3 tests) was obtained and the resulting total chi-square was not significant (x^2 = 8.66, df = 4). Thus, these measures were assumed to be equivalent and treated as such in relevant statistical analyses.

While most of the descriptive information concerning the three IQ measures is reported in Table 2, it should be noted that raw scores for each of the three measures were impossible to obtain. This, of course, precluded any statistical estimate of their reliability.

Measurement of Achievement

Achievement was measured by two methods, standardized achievement test scores and grade point average (GPA). The standardized achievement test (SRA) scores were only obtainable for the seniors and juniors (N = 160). As such, the subjects' test scores had a mean of 58.4 out of a possible 100, and a standard deviation of 26.4.

Grade point average was the second measure of achievement. The mean grade point average for the subjects was 2.26 with a standard deviation of .80. Grade point averages were not available for the freshmen and thus the total sample used in the analyses concerning GPA had an N of 304 and included only sophomores, juniors, and seniors.

Tests of Hypotheses

Analysis of variance was employed in the test of Hypothesis 1, along with a F-ratio comparison

TABLE 1
Factor Loadings of Extracted Apprehension—Verbal Activity Items

Items	Communication Apprehension	Verbal Activity
1	0.597	0.047
3	0.645	0.017
5	-0.479	-0.117
7	0.497	0.262
10	0.646	-0.070
14	0.754	-0.023
15	0.698	-0.029
16	-0.509	0.004
19	0.715	-0.019
21	0.174	0.542
22	-0.073	-0.560
23	0.061	-0.555
24	0.033	0.678
26	0.007	0.679
27	0.044	-0.629
28	0.148	0.731
29	-0.100	-0.514
30	0.042	0.750

TABLE 2
Intelligence Quotient Data

	N	Mean	SD	Range
IQ SRA	169	103.18	16.85	40-140
IQ-State testing	120	99.24	18.60	70-140
IQ-Iowa basic skills	100	98.12	16.26	70-140
Combined IQ tests	389	100.00	17.37	40-140

TABLE 3
Levels of Apprehension—Verbal Activity and IQ Means

	N	IQ
Communication Apprehension		
Low	63	107.35_{ab}
Moderate	255	99.72_{a}
High	71	98.13_{b}
Verbal Activity		
Low	52	96.15_{c}
Moderate	270	99.84_{d}
High	67	107.49_{cd}

Means with common subscript significantly different, $p < .05$.

TABLE 4
Correlation Coefficients

	COMAPP	VB	SRA	GPA
COMAPP				
VB	-0.3456*			
SRA	-0.2743*	0.2072*		
GPA	-0.2115*	0.1670*	0.6522*	
IQ	-0.1596*	0.2076*	0.8787*	0.6832*

*Significant at the .05 level.

test. Specifically, the correlation coefficient between communication apprehension and IQ was compared to the eta-square value as a test of linearity. The difference between eta and *r*, representing the correlation between the independent variable (communication apprehension) and the dependent variable (IQ) was tested using an F-ratio. Results of the hypothesis testing failed to reveal significance with either the 9 items tapping communication apprehension (F = 2.17, df = 2/386, c.v. = 3.00), or the 9 items tapping verbal activity (F = 1.10, df = 2/386, c.v. = 3.00). In the absence of a significant nonlinear trend, consequently, levels of communication apprehension and IQ were judged to be linearly related, as were levels of verbal activity and IQ (see Table 3 for display). Hypothesis 1, therefore, was confirmed.

Two separate analyses of variance were employed in the test of Hypothesis 2, along with *t*-tests for planned comparisons. The first analysis (3 levels of communication apprehension x IQ) was significant (F = 5.95, df = 2/386, $p < .05$). Low apprehensive IQ scores significantly differed in the predicted direction from the IQ scores of moderate (t_{LSD} = 3.16, df = 3.86, cv. = 1.645) and high (t_{LSD} = 3.02, df = 3.86, c.v. = 1.645) apprehensive (see Table 3).

The second analysis (3 levels of verbal activity x IQ) was also significant (F = 7.48, df = 2/386, $p < .01$). The IQ scores of high verbally actives significantly differed in the predicted direction from the IQ scores of moderate (t_{LSD} = 3.28, df = 386, c.v. = 1.645) and low (t_{LSD} = 3.59, df = 386, c.v. = 1.645) verbally actives (see Table 3).

Finally, post hoc analyses further revealed no significant difference in IQ between high and moderate communication apprehensives (t_{LSD} = 69, df = 386, c.v. = 1.645) or moderate and low verbally actives (t_{LSD} = 1.42, df = 386, c.v. = 1.645). Thus, Hypothesis 2 was also confirmed.

Exploration of the Research Question

The research question, which concerned the relationships among communication apprehension, IQ, and achievement, was explored first by use of Pearson product-moment correlations (see Table 4), since the direction and magnitude of these correlations should give some indication of the variables' relationships with one another. While the communication apprehension and verbal activity factors in the oblique solution were minimally correlated in the previous analyses (r = .27), the actual correlation based on the total of the items measuring each construct was somewhat higher (r = .35).

Low order, significant correlations were observed between IQ and the verbal activity items (r = .21). These correlations suggested a low level of shared variance between the two constructs, as would be suggested by the confirmation of Hypothesis 1.

The correlations between the two measures of communication apprehension and the two measures of achievement accounted for between 3.5% and 7% of the accountable variance. Communication apprehension and SRA (the measure of standardized achievement) were found to have a correlation of −.27, while verbal activity and SRA were found to correlate at .21. Communication apprehension and GPA correlated at −.21 and verbal activity and GPA were found to correlate at .17.

The correlations between IQ and the achievement measures, however, were substantially higher. IQ and SRA were highly associated (r = .88). IQ and GPA were more moderately associated (r = .68). Thus, when compared to the correlations between communication apprehension as well as verbal activity and achievement, IQ clearly shared more variance with achievement.

Since the correlations between IQ and achievement indices were so high, and since there was at least a low level of shared variance between IQ and the measures of communication apprehension and verbal activity, multivariate analysis of covariance subsequently was employed in the exploration of the research question. The question was, if the variance in achievement attributable to IQ was removed, would there be any residual variance attributable to communication apprehension and verbal activity alone?

With SRA and GPA as the dependent variable, IQ as the covariate, and three levels of communication apprehension as the independent variable, multivariate analysis of covariance was computed. The results of this procedure indicated that the IQ

TABLE 5
Means Adjusted for IQ

Level	N	SRA	GPA
Communication Apprehension			
Low	30	64.47	2.35
Moderate	94	56.80	2.28
High	35	57.21	2.21
Verbal Activity			
Low	28	56.94	2.28
Moderate	109	58.57	2.23
High	22	59.00	2.51

TABLE 6
Canonical Means for Variate Representing Achievement

Level	N	Canonical Mean
Communication Apprehension		
Low	30	0.2165
Moderate	95	0.1686
High	35	0.1575
Verbal Activity		
Low	28	0.2351
Moderate	110	0.2427
High	22	0.2912

covariate was significant ($F = 271.27$, $df = 2/155$, $p < .0001$), and according to Wilks's criterion, accounted for 88% of the variance. The communication apprehension effect on achievement, with IQ covaried out, failed to reach significance ($F = 2.25$) and would have accounted for only 6% of the variance. The correlations of the dependent variables (SRA and GPA) with the canonical variable did not adequately reflect *both* SRA ($r = .99$) and GPA ($r = .23$).

Since the canonical variable did not adequately reflect both dependent variables, the univariate statistics were also examined. With SRA as the dependent variable, the IQ covariate was significant ($F = 555.63$, $df = 2/155$, $p < .0001$) and accounted for 78% of the variance. The independent variable (communication apprehension) was also significant ($F = 4.44$, $df = 2/155$, $p < .01$), but the residual variance was only 1%. With GPA as the dependent variable, the IQ covariate was again significant ($F = 111.71$, $df = 2/155$, $p < .0001$) accounting for 42% of the variance. The independent variable (communication apprehension) was not, however, significant ($F = .39$) and the residual variance would have been only 5%. The SRA and GPA means adjusted for IQ appear in Table 5. For the significant effect of SRA, the largest difference in means was clearly between low communication apprehensives and the other two conditions.

With SRA and GPA as the dependent variables, IQ as the covariate, and three levels of verbal activity as the independent variable, multivariate analysis of covariance again indicated that the IQ covariate was significant ($F = 265.40$, $df = 2/155$, $p < .001$) and, according to Wilks's criterion, accounted for 88% of the variance. The verbal activity effect on achievement with IQ covaried out, however, failed to reach significance ($F = 1.22$) and would have accounted for only 3.2% of the variance. The correlations of the dependent variables with the canonical variate did not adequately reflect both SRA ($r = .04$) and GPA ($r = .98$). As a result, the univariate statistics were again examined.

With SRA as the dependent variable, the IQ covariate was significant ($F = 526.99$, $df = 2/155$, $p < .0001$) and accounted for 77% of the variance. The independent variable (verbal activity) was not significant ($F = .21$) and the residual variance would have been only .2%. With GPA as the dependent variable, the IQ covariate was again significant ($F = 114.29$, $df = 2/155$, $p < .001$) accounting for 43% of the variance. The independent variable (verbal activity) was not significant ($F = 2.19$) and the residual variance again would have been small, accounting for only .9 percent. The SRA and GPA means adjusted for IQ appear in Table 5.

Because of the unknown causal relationship between IQ, the measure of communication apprehension, and the measure of verbal activity, it was deemed useful to examine the direct relationship between achievement and the latter two measures by way of multivariate analysis of variance.

With SRA and GPA as the dependent variables and three levels of communication apprehension as the independent variable, Pillai's trace test indicated a significant effect ($F = 2.65$, $df = 4/314$, $p < .03$), and Wilks's criterion indicated that only 7% of the variance was accounted for by this effect. Moreover, the canonical variate was more highly correlated with SRA ($r = .99$) than with GPA ($r = .61$). The canonical means for the first characteristic root representing achievement (see Table 6), reflected the pattern of differences in achievement for low communication apprehension (.2165), moderate apprehension (.1686), and high apprehension (.1575). Clearly, the major difference was between the low apprehensives and the other two classifications.

With SRA and GPA as the dependent variables and three levels of verbal activity as the independent variable, Pillai's trace test indicated a significant effect ($F = 2.38$, $df = 4/314$, $p < .05$), and Wilks's criterion indicated that only 6% of the variance was accounted for by this effect. In this case, the canonical variate was more highly correlated with GPA ($r = .99$) than SRA ($r = .67$). The canonical means again reflected the pattern of differences in achievement: high VA (.2912), moderate VA (.2427) and low VA (.2351). The major difference once again was between the high verbally active (low apprehensive) and the other two conditions.

INTERPRETATION OF RESULTS AND DISCUSSION

This study was concerned with the impact of communication apprehension and intelligence on achievement, as well as the relationships among these variables. It was argued that most of the researchers who have investigated the relationship between communication apprehension and intelligence not only have advanced conclusions that appear to exceed the generalizability of their findings, but have also failed to concern themselves with the mediational impact of variables conceptually linked to communication apprehension. In light of previous research suggesting that both communication apprehension and intelligence are associated with verbal skills, and previous research indicating that high communication apprehensives are average achievers, two research hypotheses and one research question were explored.

Hypothesis 1 predicted that levels of communication apprehension and intelligence were linearly related. It was found that the specific relationship between levels of the two constructs was an inverse linear one.

Hypothesis 2 predicted low communication apprehensives would exhibit significantly higher IQ scores than either moderate or high communication apprehensives. This hypothesis was also confirmed. It was found that low communication apprehensives not only exhibited higher IQ scores than either moderate or high apprehensives, but also found that individuals high in verbal activity exhibited higher IQ scores than individuals either moderate or low in verbal activity. Finally, post hoc analyses demonstrated that moderate and high communication apprehensives exhibited similar IQ scores, as did individuals moderate and low in verbal activity.

Exploration of the research question, which inquired about the relationships among the variables investigated in this study, also netted several findings of note. Briefly, the findings generated from this exploration suggested the following.

1. Communication apprehension and intelligence are significantly correlated but share little variance.
2. Intelligence is more substantially correlated with the indices of achievement examined in this study than either communication apprehension or verbal activity.
3. When intelligence is removed as a source of variance, achievement variance attributable to either communication apprehension or verbal ability is not particularly meaningful.
4. When intelligence is not a covariate, communication apprehension is most associated with standardized achievement and verbal activity is most associated with GPA.
5. When intelligence is not a covariate, moderate and high communication apprehensives achieve at a comparable level, but low apprehensives do better than either group, and moderate and low verbally actives achieve at a comparable level, but high verbally actives achieve better than either group.

The preceding findings deserve some comment. To begin with, the fact that intelligence was far more substantially associated with achievement than communication apprehension and verbal activity is anything but surprising. Put simply, this finding does little more than confirm what some might perceive to be intuitively obvious. However, the fact that communication apprehension and verbal activity failed to account for appreciable variance when intelligence served as a covariate, is surprising in light of what has been said about the relationships among communication apprehension, intelligence, and achievement.

For example, in his summary of the "Classroom Consequences of Communication Apprehension," McCroskey (1977a) asserted that the reported differences in achievement between low and high communication apprehensives cannot be attributed to differential levels of intelligence. The findings of this study offer little in the way of support to this assertion. While it is true that communication apprehension and intelligence are not substantially correlated with one another, the findings of this study suggest that intelligence mediates achievement effects which heretofore had been attributed to differential levels of communication apprehension. Moreover, the analyses performed in the exploration of this study's research question, clearly indicate that the mediating effects of intelligence are of major consequence.

The above conclusion indirectly raises yet another issue concerning previous research focusing on the relationship between communication apprehension and achievement. As is often the case with research that is exploratory in nature, most investigators have isolated communication apprehension from other variables in their studies of its impact on achievement. Aside from this study, only one other study has systematically examined the achievement effects of communication apprehension in conjunction with another learning related variable. Specifically, Scott et al. (1977) included test anxiety in their examination of the achievement effects of communication apprehension. And while that investigation focused on an unconventional learning environment, Scott et al. reported a finding similar to that found in this study. Put simply, they reported that test anxiety, like intelligence, was superior to communication apprehension in predicting achievement.

Beyond the preceding, the findings of this study are also at issue with the notion that high communication apprehension is functionally related to less than normal achievement. First, high communication apprehensives exhibited comparable intelligence scores to moderate communication apprehensives. Second, high and moderate communication apprehensives also achieved at a comparable level. Given the fact that this latter finding has now been replicated not only with the two different populations of subjects (ie., high school and college), but also in three different types of instructional settings (i.e., mass lecture classes, small recitation sections, and individualized classes), its generalizability and acceptability is enhanced significantly.

Finally, while the results of this study clearly speak to previous claims about the relationship between communication apprehension and achievement, they do not provide a clear picture of the relationship between communication apprehension and intelligence. Earlier, the case was made that both constructs are tied to verbal skills. Although the findings of this study do suggest such a linkage between intelligence and verbal skills as measured by verbal activity, post hoc analyses yielded findings indicating the linkage between communication apprehension and verbal skills (as measured by verbal activity) is not as substantial as the rationale for this study may have suggested. Specifically, these analyses indicated that while low communication apprehensives score higher in verbal activity than their counterparts, a majority of them fall within the category of moderate verbal activity.

In summary, the findings of this study are conclusive in one sense, and inconclusive in another. First, it is clear that cognitive learning is affected by variables other than communication apprehension, and some of these variables may be more important than communication apprehension. Second, it is not clear how the verbal skills tapped by analytical measures such as intelligence tests are tied to another type of verbal skill—oral communication.

NOTES

1. The authors would like to extend their sincere thanks to Dr. Lawrence R. Wheeless for his invaluable input to this study.
2. Please note high verbal activity would be comparable to low communication apprehension, whereas low verbal activity would be comparable to high communication apprehension.

REFERENCES

ANASTASI, A. *Psychological testing*. New York: Macmillan, 1961.

BASHORE, D.N. Relationship among speech anxiety, IQ, and high school achievement. Unpublished thesis, Illinois State University, 1971.

BINDER, D.M., JONES, J.G., & STROWIG, R.W. Non-intellective self-report variables are predictors of scholastic achievement. *Journal of Education Research*, 1970, 63, 364-366.

BOND, E.A. Tenth grade abilities and achievements. *Teachers College Contributions to Education*, 1940.

CARROLL, J.B. Language development. In C.W. Harris (Ed.), *Encyclopedia of Education Research*. New York: Macmillan, 1960, 744-752.

CLELLAND, D.L., & TOUSSAINT, I. The interrelationships of reading, listening, arithmetic computation and intelligence. *Reading Teacher*, 1962, 15, 228-231.

CRANDAL, V.J. Achievement. In H.W. Stevenson (Ed.), *Child Psychology*. Chicago: University of Chicago Press, 1963, 416-459.

CRANDAL, V.J., & RABSON, A. Children's repetition choices in an intellectual achievement situation following success and failure. *Journal of Genetic Psychology*, 1960, 92, 161-168.

DALY, J.A., & McCROSKEY, J.C. Occupational choice and desirability as a function of communication apprehension.

Journal of Counseling Psychology, 1975, 22, 309-313.
DALY, J.A., McCROSKEY, J.C., & RICHMOND, V.P. The relationships between vocal activity and perception of communicators in small group interaction. *Western Speech Communication*, in press.
DEB, M., & GHOSH, M. Relation between scholastic achievement and intelligence. *Behavioromatric*, 1971, 1, 136-137.
FINE, B. *The stranglehold of the IQ*. Garden City, N.Y.: Doubleday, 1975.
GUILFORD, J.P. *The nature of human intelligence*. New York: McGraw-Hill, 1967.
HULL, C.L. *Aptitude testing*. Chicago: World, 1928.
HUMPHREYS, L.G. Theory of intelligence. In R. Cancro (Ed.), *Intelligence: Genetic and environmental influences*. New York: Grune & Stratton, 1971.
HURT, H.T., PREISS, R., & DAVIS, B. The effects of communication apprehension of middle-school children on sociometric choice, affective and cognitive learning. Paper presented at the annual meeting of the International Communication Association, Portland, Oregon, 1976.
JENSEN, A.R. How much can we boost IQ and scholastic achievement? *Harvard Educational Review*, 1969, 39, 1-123.
KRECHEVSKY, I. A study of the continuity of the problem solving process. *Psychological Review*, 1938, 45, 107-134.
LORGE, I., THORNDIKE, R.L., & HAGAN, E. *The Lorge-Thorndike intelligence tests multi-level edition*. Boston: Houghton Mifflin, 1964.
McCROSKEY, J.C. Measures of communication bound anxiety. *Speech Monographs*, 1970, 37, 269-277.
McCROSKEY, J.C. Validity of the PRCA as an index of oral communication apprehension. Paper presented at the annual meeting of the Speech Communication Association, Houston, 1975.
McCROSKEY, J.C. Classroom consequences of communication apprehension. *Communication Education*, 1977a, 26, 27-33.
McCROSKEY, J.C. Oral communication apprehension: A summary of recent theory and research. Paper presented at the annual meeting of the International Communication Association, Berlin, 1977b.
McCROSKEY, J.C. Alternative measures of communication apprehension. Unpublished monograph. West Virginia University, 1977c.
McCROSKEY, J.C., & ANDERSEN, J.F. The relationship between communication apprehension and academic achievement among college students. *Human Communication Research*, 1976, 3, 73-81.
McCROSKEY, J.C., & DALY, J.A. Teachers expectations of the communication apprehensive child. *Human Communication Research*, 1976, 3, 67-72.
McCROSKEY, J.C., DALY, J.A., RICHMOND, V.P., & COX, B.G. The effects of communication apprehension on interpersonal attraction. *Human Communication Research*, 1975, 2, 51-65.
McCROSKEY, J.C., DALY, J.A., RICHMOND, V.P., & FALCIONE, R.L. Studies of the relationship between communication apprehension and self-esteem. *Human Communication Research*, in press.
McCROSKEY, J.C., DALY, J.A., & SORENSEN, G.A. Personality correlates of communication apprehension. *Human Communication Research*, 1976, 2, 376-380.
McCROSKEY, J.C., HAMILTON, P.R., & WEINER, A.N. The effect of interaction behavior on source credibility, homophily, and interpersonal attraction. *Human Communication Research*, 1974, 1, 42-52.
McCROSKEY, J.C., & LEPPARD, T. The effects of communication apprehension on nonverbal behavior. Paper presented at the annual meeting of the Eastern Communication Association, New York, 1975.
McCROSKEY, J.C., & RICHMOND, V.P. The effects of communication apprehension on perceptions of peers. *Western Speech Communication*, 1976, 40, 14-21.
McCROSKEY, J.C., & RICHMOND, V.P. Communication apprehension as a predictor of self-disclosure. *Communication Quarterly*, in press.
McCROSKEY, J.C., & SHEAHAN, M.E. Seating position and participation: An alternative theoretical explanation. Paper presented at the annual meeting of the International Communication Association, Portland, Oregon, 1976a.
McCROSKEY, J.C., & SHEAHAN, M.E. Communication apprehension, preference, and social behavior in a college environment. Unpublished monograph, Department of Speech Communication, West Virginia University, 1976b.
McCROSKEY, J.C., & WHEELESS, L.B. *An introduction to human communication*. Boston: Allyn & Bacon, 1976.
MERRIFIELD, P.R. Using measured intelligence intelligently. In R. Cancro (Ed.). *Intelligence: Genetic and environmental influences*. New York: Grune & Stratton, 1971.
MOSS, H.A., & KAGAN, J. The stability of achievement and recognition seeking behaviors. *Journal of Abnormal Social Psychology*, 1961, 62, 504-513.
MOWRER, O.H. On the dual nature of learning: A reinterpretation of "conditioning" and "problem solving." *Harvard Educational Review*, 1947, 17, 102-148.
MUSSEN, P.H., CONGER, J.J., & KAGAN, J. *Child development and personality*. New York: Harper & Row, 1969, 571.
NUNNALLY, J. *Psychometric theory*. New York: McGraw-Hill, 1967.
PHILLIPS, G.M. Reticence: Pathology of the normal speaker. *Speech Monographs*, 1968, 35, 39-49.
PIAGET, J. *The psychology of intelligence*. London: Routledge & Kagan Paul, 1950.
PIAGET, J. *The origins of intelligence in children*. New York: International University Press, 1952.
ROSENTHAL, R., & JACOBSON, L. *Pygmalion in the classroom: Teacher expectations in intellectual development*. New York: Holt, Rinehart & Winston, 1968.
SARTAIN, A.Q. A comparison of the new revised Stanford-Binet, the Bellevue Scale and Certain group tests of intelligence. *Journal of Social Psychology*, 1946, 23, 237-239.
SCOTT, M.D., McCROSKEY, J.C., & SHEAHAN, M.E. The development of a self-report measure of communication apprehension in organizational settings. *Journal of Communication*, in press.
SCOTT, M.D., & WHEELESS, L.R. The relationship of three types of communication apprehension to classroom achievement. *Southern Speech Communication Journal*, 1977a, 3, 246-255.
SCOTT, M.D., & WHEELESS, L.R. Communication apprehension, student attitudes, and levels of satisfaction. *Western Journal of Speech Communication*, 1977b, 41, 188-198.
SCOTT, M.D., WHEELESS, L.R., YATES, M.P., & RANDOLPH, F.L. The effects of communication apprehension and test anxiety on three indicants of achievement in an

alternative system of instruction: A follow up study. In B.D. Ruben (Ed.), *Communication yearbook I*. New Brunswick, New Jersey: Transaction—International Communication Association, 1977.

SELIGMAN, M.E.P., & HAGER, J.L. (Eds.). *The biological boundaries of learning*. New York: Appleton, 1972.

SHEAHAN, M.E. Communication apprehension and electoral participation. Unpublished thesis, West Virginia University, 1976.

SINHA, N.C. Intelligence and scholastic achievement. *MANAS*, 1972, 19, 59-63.

SPEARMAN, C. "General intelligence," objectively determined and measured. *American Journal of Psychology*, 1904, 15, 201-293.

SPEARMAN, C. *The nature of intelligence and the principle of cognition*. London: Macmillan, 1923.

TERMAN, L.M. *The Stanford revision and extension of Binet-Simon scale for measuring intelligence*. Baltimore: Warwick & York, 1917.

TERMAN, L.M. *Measuring intelligence. A guide to the administration of the new revised Stanford-Binet tests of intelligence*. Boston: Houghton Mifflin, 1937.

TERMAN, L.M., & MERRILL, M.A. *Stanford-Binet intelligence scale. Manual for the third revision for L-M*. Boston: Houghton Mifflin, 1960.

THORNDIKE, E.L. *Animal intelligence*. New York: Macmillan, 1911.

THORNDIKE, E.L., & HAGAN, E. *Measurement and evaluation in psychology and education*. New York: Wiley, 1969.

THURSTONE, L.L. *The vectors of the mind*. Chicago: University of Chicago Press, 1935.

WECHSLER, D. *The Wechsler intelligence scale for children*. New York: Psychological Corporation, 1949.

WECHSLER, D. Intelligence: Definition theory, and the IA. In R. Cancro (Ed.), *Intelligence: Genetic and environmental influences*. New York: Grune & Stratton, 1971.

WHEELESS, L.R., NESSER, K., & McCROSKEY, J.C. Relationships among self-disclosure, disclosiveness, and communication apprehension. Paper presented at the annual meeting of the Western Speech Communication Association, San Francisco, 1976.

WITTEMAN, H.R. The relationship of communication apprehension to opinion leadership and innovativeness. Unpublished thesis, West Virginia University, 1976.

A NONVERBAL COMMUNICATION CLASSIFICATION SYSTEM FOR TEACHING BEHAVIORS

BARRY F. MORGANSTERN
West Virginia University

This study examined three independently developed nonverbal communication classification systems for teaching behavior. Nonverbal teaching behaviors were defined, coded, and analyzed through the use of the Love and Roderick (1971), Grant and Hennings (1971), and Civikly (1973) category procedures.

Through the use of three trained coders and 18 categories of nonverbal behavior, nonverbal teaching behaviors were examined, identified, and subjected to analysis. The purpose of the analysis was to answer three research questions. The questions follow.

1. Is there a degree of agreement between the three independent nonverbal classification systems?
2. Are there characteristic clusters of nonverbal behaviors that occur with specific behaviors?
3. Are certain nonverbal behaviors contingent upon other behaviors?

The results of this investigation indicated that the combined use of these three category systems provided a more comprehensive description of teaching behaviors than any of the systems would provide on an independent basis. This finding suggested that the three observation schemes employed were compatible and that the development of a combined system for use in examining the nonverbal behaviors of teachers would be a reasonable possibility.

INTRODUCTION

One of the greatest stumbling blocks in the study of communication has been the fact that "there are so many behaviors that one can observe and study that it becomes difficult to know where to start, what to exclude or how to order the priorities" (Mehrabian, 1972, p. 179). Illustrative of this problem are the modern research efforts that intend to study the nonverbal communication behaviors of teachers within the classroom context.

The dynamics of nonverbal behavior as studied in the classroom have led to the recent development of many nonverbal analysis systems and several combined verbal-nonverbal analysis systems. Though far from the extent or sophistication of verbal research, the number of investigations directed at identifying, classifying, and coding nonverbal teacher behaviors has increased (Grant & Hennings, 1971; Ekman, Friesen, & Wallace, 1969; Love & Roderick, 1971; Galloway, 1962; Civikly, 1973). Unlike verbal behavior, there is an obvious lack of explicit coding rules for nonverbal behaviors, due to the fact that no generally accepted "dictionary of meanings across cultures," or within specific cultures, has been realized. Without the advantage of concise meaning, coding or syntactical rules, definitions and category systems, to date, are essentially informal concepts. These informal concepts are only capable of describing the significance of these behaviors in specified contexts.

The restriction confronting this increased interest in the identification of nonverbal behaviors of teachers in the instructional setting is one of specificity. Inherent in each available nonverbal category system, to date, is a lack of generalizability across systems, due to the individualized structure of each. Essentially, the problem is that specific definitions of teacher nonverbal behaviors, as observed, do not currently exist. This agreement regarding what to observe and what behaviors should be excluded is lacking, due to the ever-increasing number of independently created nonverbal category systems. That is, there is a lack of comparison between systems.

It is the premise of this study that, before progress in the study of classroom teacher behavior can continue, a nonverbal category system must be developed that is clearly based on existing research information and existing nonverbal systems. Moreover, the determination of such a system will increase consistency in the definition and analysis of nonverbal teaching behaviors.

To this end, the present study was designed to identify a nonverbal category system derived from, and based upon, existing research data that will allow for consistency in observation, identification, definition, and analysis of nonverbal behaviors of teachers. Specifically, existing category systems and the respective behaviors of each were empirically employed, compared, and analyzed in the effort to derive a single, more precise instrument for the identification, coding, and tabulation of teachers' nonverbal behaviors.

A Definition of Nonverbal Behaviors

Before specifying the goals of this paper, it is necessary to determine a definitional focus for this study that will provide a structure for the subsequent rationale and design. Due to the variety of nonverbal teacher motions currently identified by the various category systems, this definition must be sufficiently broad enough to incorporate this entire range of behaviors.

Several authors (Galloway, 1962; Birdwhistell, 1970; Grant & Hennings, 1971) have emphasized this need for a more global approach to the concept of nonverbal communication. Birdwhistell (1970) suggested that the role of nonverbal behavior in the total communication process is an interactive one, in that "participants in an interaction constantly contribute by messages of various, overlapping lengths along one or more channels; such as language, movement, and smell" (Birdwhistell, 1970, p. v). Perhaps even more global in scope, Ekman and Friesen (1969) argued that "any movement or position of the face and/or the body" should be identified as nonverbal behavior (Ekman & Friesen, 1969, p. 49).

By incorporating these less restrictive definitions of nonverbal behaviors into this study, it becomes possible to include both intentional/instructional and unintentional or personal motions of teachers. Grant and Hennings (1971) supported the need to incorporate all possible nonverbal behaviors when they identified 22.1% of the total number of motions of case study teachers as being personal or noninstructional behaviors.

Because of the necessity for providing a broad and interactive foundation for this study, the following definitions will be employed.

Nonverbal Communication—"Transmitting a thought or feeling from one person to another through gesture, posture, facial expression, tone and quality of voice, or physical contact, as an auxiliary function to speech or without speech" (Galloway, 1962, p. 8).

Teacher-Student Relationship—"An interdependent relationship that has been established by the teacher and the pupil through socio-emotional, physical, and intellectual contacts" (Galloway, 1962, p. 8).

A survey of literature reveals an increased research interest in the nonverbal interaction between teacher and student (Barr, 1929; Lail, 1968; Grant & Hennings, 1971; Strother, 1971; Love & Roderick, 1971; Woolfolk & Woolfolk, 1974). These exploratory probes consist of independent attempts to identify, tabulate, and analyze nonverbal moves of teachers in the educational setting (Love & Roderick, 1971; Grant & Hennings, 1971; Galloway, 1962; Civikly, 1973).

These researchers have developed and tested nonverbal category systems for the purpose of isolating and defining the necessary research variables within the context of nonverbal behavior in the classroom. However, the very independence of each of these systems has prevented researchers from being able to achieve consistency in (1) identifying a generally acceptable cluster of behaviors specific to the teaching environment, (2) defining or describing these behaviors, and (3) identifying the characteristic behavior sequences or clusters that may occur in time with other behaviors.

While several attempts at integrating existing verbal category systems with nonverbal coding systems are evident, no studies devoted to a comparison across nonverbal schemes have been located in an extensive review of research literature.

In the attempt to clarify the "state" and importance of research regarding nonverbal behavior within the classroom environment, two positions have been examined. They include (1) the research specific to nonverbal behavior, and (2) the pedagogical implications of nonverbal behavior underlying learning. In each case, investigations discussed pertain to the communicative behavior of the teacher within the educational setting.

Research Specific to Nonverbal Codes

The emphasis on the nonverbal communication that occurs in the classroom is essential in constructing forms of interaction analysis that will help in the understanding of human behavior. A survey of literature reveals an increased interest in the nonverbal interaction that occurs between teacher and student (Barr, 1929; Grant & Hennings, 1971; Love & Roderick, 1971; Galloway, 1972; Woolfolk & Woolfolk, 1974).

Most representative of these investigations involving the identification, registration and analysis of communicator influence in terms of nonverbal motions are Galloway (1962), Love and Roderick (1971), Grant and Hennings (1971), and Civikly (1973). Galloway's pioneering study established systematic techniques of investigating nonverbal motions during the interaction between teacher and students.

Grant and Hennings's (1971) study was a useful extension of Galloway's work. Though more comprehensive than Galloway's work, the nature of both study designs were limited in their interpretation of teachers' moves. Both approaches were descriptive examinations of teachers' moves, and each attempted only to compare each instructor along predetermined dimensions, such as a comparison between verbal and nonverbal motions. No attempt was made to compare teachers' nonverbal moves across the two systems.

In a similar fashion, the Love and Roderick nonverbal category system was designed specifically for comparison with Flanders's Verbal Classification system. Functioning from such a preconceived structure is restrictive, in the sense that acquired research data from external studies is ignored, thereby minimizing any consistency across nonverbal observation systems.

Civikly's (1973) proposed nonverbal category system was based on the need for a classification system that would fulfill the requirements of a specific research orientation. Civikly stated that: "the study of nonverbal observational techniques is still in an early developmental stage, and most researchers are devising their own descriptive category systems specific to their research orientation and goals (Knapp and Harrison, SCA National Convention, 1972). The system I have developed typifies this trend, and focuses on the area of nonverbal behavior in the . . . classroom" (p. 109).

Obviously, these researchers are committed to designing category systems sufficiently inclusive and precise so as to provide reliable coding of observable behaviors by trained coders. However, by continuing to develop systems for specific research enterprises, researchers will only increase the gap between theory and practice.

Pedagogical Implications

Perhaps the primary implications of this interest in nonverbal behaviors within the classroom are the attempts to identify and categorize effective nonverbal behaviors by teachers and to develop more meaningful programs/models for teacher improvement and training (Galloway, 1962; Young, 1968; Harrison & Knapp, 1972; Woolfolk & Woolfolk, 1974). The inherent, yet still somewhat tentative, assumption underlying these implications is that certain nonverbal behaviors are supportive of, or indicative of, effective and ineffective learning conditions in the classroom (Galloway, 1962; Rosenthal & Jacobson, 1968; Grant & Hennings, 1971). To extend and strengthen such conclusions, a single structure of coded behaviors must be established that will allow for the consistent identification and comparison of teachers' nonverbal moves.

Teaching Models

Assuming this need for comparison, in order to develop newer, more beneficial models, researchers must consider certain concepts underlying learning and the impact of nonverbal communication in the classroom.

A critical assumption is that through this comparative analysis of teachers' moves, models can be generated. Specifically, researchers design models by isolating elements of the total communication process for purposes of observing particular components of the total process, in order that they may use the observable elements in training situations. If Gibson's (1968) rationale for the use of teaching models is acceptable—that such models are among the most effective teaching instruments—it can be implied that the generation of more complete, real-to-life, teaching models based on a comparative analysis of teachers' nonverbal behaviors is justified. Gibson (1968) states:

> It is widely agreed that performance models are among our most effective teaching instruments. As teachers of speech, we instruct our students to read speeches acclaimed as classics. The preparation of teachers can follow the same general route. When a student micro-teaches a unit in an unusually effective and creative manner, his performance should be extracted from the videotape and preserved for replay to methods classes in succeeding terms. (pp. 107-108)

Allen and Ryan (1972) reaffirmed this conviction that "perhaps the most effective way to instruct teachers in the use of these nonverbal cues is to show them a model using these cues in a teaching context" (p. 78).

Restating the importance of studying teachers' nonverbal behaviors, the findings of Galloway (1962), Grant and Hennings (1971), and Adams and Biddle (1970) are illustrative of the impact of extralinguistic moves in the classroom. Indeed, if learning is defined as a "relatively permanent change in a behavioral tendency and is the result of reinforced practice . . . where the reinforced practice is the cause of the learning" (DeCecco, 1968, p. 243), it becomes apparent that the nonverbal and verbal behaviors of a teacher do act as reinforcers of behaviors (Thorndyke, 1913; Verplanck, 1955; Rosenthal & Jacobson, 1968).

The implications of this concept are that nonverbal behaviors can be either intentional or unintentional. The teacher can intentionally communicate (nonverbally) such things as: that students should be quiet, be seated, or that the class is not yet over (DeCecco, 1968). Additionally, the teacher may unintentionally exhibit personal moves such as posture changes, scratching his ear, or twisting a ring on his finger (Grant & Hennings, 1971). Regardless of the nonverbal cue, it serves to convey meanings to the students. Indeed, as Knapp (1972) states, "the subtle nonverbal influences in the classroom can sometimes have dramatic results" (p. 9). This conclusion can also be extended to other teacher roles, such as the student's concept of the teacher as human, as interested or disinterested, as excited or bored, and so forth (Biddle & Ellena, 1964, p. 196).

Investigating teacher influence in the classroom is a difficult task. Though most researchers would accept generally defined classifications of nonverbal motions (Ekman & Friesen, 1967; Knapp, 1972), identifying the meaning of these moves in a specific context requires more than an understanding of general labels.

Research Questions

Four observations are derived from an extensive review of the literature. First, existing capabilities for the identification, tabulation, and analysis of teachers' nonverbal behaviors are not as precise or sophisticated as the current verbal interaction analysis systems being employed. Second, to date, existing nonverbal analysis methodologies have been designed independently of each other and are therefore severely restrictive in their application. Third, as a result of such individualistic biases toward research, generalization across nonverbal coding systems and research settings cannot be achieved to any significant degree. Fourth, there is a lack of empirical research designed to draw together existing evidence to provide a consistent and complete method for identifying, coding, and analyzing nonverbal behaviors. Because of the nature of these observed research needs, the following research questions are in order:

1. Is there a degree of agreement between the three independent nonverbal classification systems?
2. Are there characteristic clusters of nonverbal behaviors that occur with specific behaviors?
3. Are certain nonverbal behaviors contingent upon other behaviors?

METHODS AND PROCEDURES

As previously stated, a variety of nonverbal teaching behaviors have been identified by several independent research attempts. Therefore, to obtain the required specificity of definition within this study, nonverbal communication behaviors of teachers were operationalized by three nonverbal systems: (1) Love and Roderick's (1971) nonverbal categories, (2) Grant and Hennings (1971) classification system of teacher behavior, and (3) Civikly's (1973) category system. The selection of each system was based on three criterion: (1) that the category system was developed for use in identifying, coding, and analyzing the nonverbal classroom behaviors of teachers; (2) that the use of the category system be subject to similar requirements for coder-training, tabulation of behaviors, and implementation procedures; (3) that each system must have demonstrated acceptable levels of reliability. The minimum level of reliability acceptable for this criteria was set at .70 (Fox, 1969).

The design of these systems (Love & Roderick, 1971; Grant & Hennings, 1971; Civikly, 1973) was intended for application within the classroom context. Teachers' nonverbal behavior during the classroom interaction is the focus of these category structures.

The coding technique designed for this study, for the implementation of various category systems is appropriate to each of the selected systems (Morganstern, 1976). Specifically, methods of coder-training, tabulation of observed behaviors, and analysis of data is applicable to the selected categories, allowing for consistency and maximum control in their application.

Finally, these three procedures have demonstrated acceptable levels of coder reliability. Stated reliability levels for intercoder agreement for the Love and Roderick system is approximately .88; for Grant and Hennings, levels range from .80-1.00 for various categories within the system; and for Civikly, coder reliability levels range from .551 - .732.

Selection of Subjects

Due to the scope of this study and the method of data analysis to be performed, the size of the subject pool was not the primary concern. Specifically, the purpose of this investigation was to examine and analyze a large number of nonverbal teaching behaviors through the use of three nonverbal classification schemes discussed herein (Love & Roderick, 1971; Grant & Hennings, 1971; Civikly, 1973). Three professors from the Department of Speech and Dramatic Art were randomly selected from the available pool of professors within the department. The three randomly selected subjects were videotaped for two one-hour actual teaching situations. Portions of these three videotapes were then subjected to analysis by a team of three independent coders using each of the three selected category systems. This coding procedure insured a total pool of nonverbal teacher behaviors of five minutes per teacher, randomly selected in ten-second sequences (30 ten-second sequences per professor).

Of importance to this study is the data derived from the total number of coded sequences per teacher for each of the category systems. The methodological position underlying this investigation is that the value of such a research design is based on the ability to study, in depth, a collection of nonverbal teaching behaviors. As previously stated, one goal of this analysis is to establish a stronger methodological and theoretical approach to the identification and study of teachers' nonverbal behaviors in the classroom.

Like much of the research in the field of nonverbal communication—such as current attempts to provide a neurophysiological explanation of nonverbal information processing (Andersen, Garrison, & Andersen, 1975)—the analysis of nonverbal teaching behaviors must, for the present, be restricted to a limited number of cases if in-depth study and definition of these behaviors is to be achieved (Grant & Hennings, 1971). Specifically, a foundation from which to proceed must first be established.

As previously stated, each of the teachers selected for videotaping represented a single academic department, for the purpose of maintaining sufficient control over such variables as content, experience, and environment.

Videotaping and Coding Procedures

The selected instructors were videotaped within the speech laboratory facilities of the University of Missouri-Columbia. Variables such as teaching format and represented discipline were controlled. Teaching format was controlled, in that each professor was requested to maintain a teaching approach that excluded the use of films, slides, or student-oriented activities that would preclude the instructor being seen by the camera's eye. For example, the use of slides or film would preclude the use of the camera due to the necessity of turning out the lights. Likewise, a small group assignment might result in the professor sitting at the desk or leaving the classroom for the entire period. For these reasons, instructors were asked to present lessons that required teacher activity and/or teacher-student interaction. Other intrusive variables such as time of videotaping, equipment, and location remained constant or were minimized. Specifically, each classroom hour was videotaped at approximately the same hour of the day. Classroom meeting times ranged from 9:30 A.M. to 11:30 A.M., thereby decreasing affects that might have accrued from early morning to late evening classes. Moreover, videotaping procedures and the classroom environment remained constant. The coding procedure was employed utilizing the Love and Roderick categories (Willett, 1976), and was expanded to include the Civikly category system and the Grant and Hennings categories. A panel of three trained coders conducted the analysis procedure.

The three coders were all undergraduate students in the areas of speech or nursing. Each coder had been a student in the basic speech course, Introduction to Speech Communication.

Coder Training

In order to build confidence and reliability for the team of coders as they applied the three category systems to real-life video presentations of teacher classroom behavior, a coder training program was prepared (Morganstern, 1976). The design featured the use of instructional technology for the recording of nonverbal moves, specified definitions based upon positive and negative exemplars of each category of moves, plus rules and training procedures based on concepts of applied learning theory. As stated, this training procedure was employed by Willett (1976) for the purpose of achieving a consistent, acceptable degree of coder agreement.

Obtained Coder Reliability Levels

Subjects were trained for each system employed and were tested for accuracy on both of the prepared practice tapes. Coders analyzed the final subject tapes after they had exhibited consistency in obtaining the specified reliability level of .700 or higher.

Results were obtained from this extensive coder training procedure that provided intercoder and intracoder reliability levels derived from both the practice tapes and the final teaching tapes for each of the three category systems employed. Fox's (1969) formula was selected to measure the amount of consistency of responses for two or more coders. Procedurally, intracoder and intercoder reliability was determined by computing the percentage of time independent coders agreed in analysis of the same material. This procedure for determining agreement levels has appropriately been used in previous research of this nature (Willett, 1976) and provides a concise evaluation of coder credibility.

Intercoder and intracoder reliability levels achieved for the Love and Roderick classification system ranged from .933 to .955 and from .930 to .955, respectively. Intercoder and intracoder levels of agreement for the Grant and Hennings classification system ranged from .933 to .981 and from .933 to 1.00, respectively. Likewise, reliability levels of .826 to .988 and .880 to 1.00 were achieved for the Civikly classification systems.

These results clearly indicate that the training procedure previously outlined is capable of providing sufficient levels of intercoder and intracoder reliability levels of agreement to warrant the continuation of this study.

As outlined earlier, each of the selected teachers were videotaped, and a five-minute segment of each tape was randomly selected for analysis. The three trained coders then analyzed and tabulated the nonverbal motions of the three teachers utilizing each of the three category systems. Specifically, each taped sequence was analyzed nine different times by the team of three observers.

Available from this data was information that pertained to two subsequent statistical treatments: (1) an hierarchical cluster analysis (o-analysis) of the combined tallies for each teacher on each category; (2) a hierarchical cluster analysis of the combined tallies for each of 30 ten-second intervals per teacher.

Analysis of Data

A cluster analytic technique was selected for this investigation. As previously noted, a large array of data was collected. The attempt to discover natural clusters or structures of nonverbal teaching behaviors demanded such a data reduction technique.

Use of this hierarchical clustering technique provided the capability for comparing each category of nonverbal behavior with every other category of behavior. Thus, category number 1 was compared to categories, 2, 3, 4, . . . 18, and so on. This procedure also allowed for the mathematical identification of those categories most similar to each other—the formation of "like" clusters of behaviors.

The nonverbal teacher behaviors identified, coded, and tabulated by the three coders, using each of the three category systems, were subjected to independent cluster analyses. The first hierarchical cluster analysis was performed on the total body of data collected. That is, the nonverbal teacher behaviors for each teacher, as identified by each coder, for each category, were combined and subjected to the cluster analysis (BMDPIM—cluster analysis on variables, 1975, pp. 307-339). This overall analysis provided a definite clustering of nonverbal teacher behaviors for examination and interpretation.

The occurrence of clusters resulting from the overall analysis warranted the individual analysis of the nonverbal behaviors of each teacher. Therefore, data matrices were formed for each teacher based on the total number of coded behaviors by the three coders for each category employed. These data were then subjected to the same clustering procedure that was applied to the overall data (BMDPIM—Cluster Analysis on Variables, 1975, pp. 307-339).

This analysis of individual teacher behaviors was intended to provide information on specific clustering effects that would provide a greater degree of precision in the interpretation of clusters.

Additionally, the data were submitted to an individual Pearson correlation analysis (SPSS, Pearson Correlation, pp. 276-86). The use of the Pearson correlation analysis yielded precision in the interpretation of the obtained clusters. While the initial analysis also specified an average distance table that indicates the average similarity between variables, a more precise indicator of relationship was needed to support the results of this study.

To insure an adequate measure of similarity, a .40 level of correlation was required. Kerlinger (1973, p. 201) suggested a minimum correlation of .30; whereas, Nunnally (1967, p. 129) recommended a .40 or higher, based on the fact that .40 is the averaged correlation reported in the literature. Based on these recommendations, a .40 was accepted.

RESULTS

The results are organized according to the following research questions:

1. Is there a degree of agreement between the three independent nonverbal classification systems?
2. Are there characteristic clusters of nonverbal behaviors that occur with specific behaviors?
3. Are certain nonverbal behaviors contingent upon other behaviors?

Agreement Between the Three Independent Nonverbal Classification Systems

The results of the cluster analysis on the combined data indicated a clear association between the three independent nonverbal category systems employed. Four distinct clusters emerged from this analysis.

An explanation of the variable clustering process showed that the process began with the clustering of the variables: accepts or praises student behavior, facilitates student-to-student interaction, body motion, personal acts, and personal motions.

This first major cluster was labeled as "teach-

TABLE 1
Major Clusters Derived from Combined Data Analysis

Number	Cluster Variable Name and Number	Variables Included in Cluster	Number of Items in Cluster	Distance or Similarity when Cluster Formed
1	(1) accepts or praises student's behavior (13) body motion (4) Facilitates student-to-student interaction (12) personal motions (18) personal acts	1, 13, 4 12, 18	5	56.22
2	(2) displays student's ideas (7) focuses student's attention on important points (10) acting (15) hand gestures (3) shows interest in student behavior (11) wielding (8) demonstrates or illustrates	2, 7, 10, 15, 3, 11, 8	7	63.15
3	(16) facial expression (17) vocal expression (6) shows authority	16, 17, 6	3	73.16
	(5) gives directions (9) conducting (14) posture position	5, 9, 14	3	60.00

Total number of variables accounted for = 18

er-to-student interaction,'' because the behaviors that combined to form this cluster were indicative of teacher behaviors that serve to reinforce and facilitate interaction between the students and the teacher (Travers, 1972; Gagne & Briggs, 1974). The emergence of this cluster was not surprising. That is, by definition, each of the variables included in this first cluster share common nonverbal behaviors that lend themselves to an interactive classroom environment (DeCecco, 1968).

The exhibited relationship between ''personal motions or acts'' and ''facilitates student-to-student interaction,'' ''accepts or praises student behavior,'' and ''body motion'' supported the assumption that certain nonverbal behaviors are supportive of, or indicative of, effective and ineffective learning conditions in the classroom (Galloway, 1962; Rosenthal & Jacobson, 1968; Grant & Hennings, 1971). Specifically, different teachers have different, individualized teaching styles that are grounded in personal motions that tend to affect the facilitation and reinforcement of desired student behaviors (Grant & Hennings, 1971; Civikly, 1973; Willett, 1976).

Since little research has been conducted into the effects of personal motions on learning conditions, an empirical basis for interpreting the results is lacking. It would seem plausible that this group of teachers exhibited various personal styles in their teaching that do affect the learning conditions in the classroom. One possible interpretation, however, suggests that consistency between nonverbal communications may establish a particular classroom atmosphere conducive to teacher-student interactions. For example, facilitating and reinforcing behaviors combined with personal motions and body motions that indicate openness and security on the role of the teacher might enhance the classroom interaction (Rogers, 1970; Hyman, 1970; Laing, 1971).

The second major cluster that occurred, ''teaching strategies,'' included the following behaviors: displays student ideas, focuses students' attention on important points, shows interest in student behavior, demonstrates and/or illustrates, acting, wielding, and hand gestures. The results indicated a clear relationship between each of these seven categories of behavior. Each of these behavior patterns becomes involved in the procedure of clarifying or amplifying meanings the teachers were trying to communicate to the students.

Indeed, these nonverbal teaching behaviors fit well with the notion that teaching strategies designed to explicate meanings and provide direction for the students' learning efforts are necessary prerequisites for achieving desired learning outcomes (Travers, 1972; Gagne & Briggs, 1974).

The third major cluster derived from the data analysis, ''management and control,'' was comprised of three categories of behavior: shows authority, facial expression, and vocal expression. This natural cluster of behaviors suggests that teacher authority is indicated and sustained by the combined effects of vocal and facial expression. Specifically, previous research indicates that there is a direct link between the vocal and nonvocal expressions of teachers (Galloway, 1962; Amidon & Flanders, 1967; Strother, 1971; Cambra, 1976). Indeed, the significance of facial expression in the conveyance of nonverbal communications has been well documented by Birdwhistell (1970), Knapp (1972), Mehrabian (1972). It would appear that the exercising of authority is directly based on various combinations of vocal and facial expressions.

The results indicated a fourth major cluster, ''involvement and participation.'' This cluster was formed by the behavioral categories: gives directions, conducting, and posture-position. As with the three major clusters previously discussed, a distinct relationship existed between these behaviors and was anticipated. Both categories are intended to channel, elicit, or direct student behavior in terms of what is to be done, focused upon, or attended to. Common to both categories are predetermined signals for behavior, such as being seated, raising one's hand for recognition, or responding to the teacher's request or question.

The physical act of conducting or directing the amount of participation in a classroom is inherently bound to the presence of the teacher. A teacher's posture or position, in relation to the students, will support the role distinction between teacher and student (spatially) and help indicate for the student what to do, what is expected, or what to attend to.

TABLE 2
Pairwise Clusters and Correlations

	Variables Included in Cluster	Pearson Correlation
Major Cluster No. One: Subclusters	(12) personal motions (18) personal acts	.624
Major Cluster No. Two: Subclusters	(2) displays student ideas (3) shows interest in student behavior	.542
	(2) displays student ideas (7) focuses student attention	.645
	(2) displays student ideas (10) acting	.614
	(2) displays student ideas (5) hand gestures	.481
	(3) shows interest (7) focuses student attention	.421
	(3) shows interest (10) acting	.471
	(3) shows interest (15) hand gestures	.543
	(7) focuses student attention (10) acting	.959
	(7) focuses student attention (15) hand gestures	.806
	(10) acting (15) hand gestures	.849
	(11) wielding (3) shows interest	.540
	(15) hand gestures (8) demonstrates/illustrates	.479
Major Cluster No. Three: Subclusters	(16) facial expression (17) vocal expression	.463
Major Cluster No. Four: Subclusters	(5) gives directions (9) conducting	.612

Pairwise Clusters

Characteristic clusters of nonverbal behaviors. Characteristic clusters of nonverbal behaviors did occur with specific behavior being identified. The overall analysis identified four major clusters that accounted for all 18 of the behavior categories. Moreover, significant pairwise clusters within each major cluster were obtained from the Pearson correlation measure. The emergence of strong pairwise clusters or subclusters within the overall structure indicated the strength of each major combination, and thereby attested to the existence of common, or characteristic clustering affects. The correlation levels or amount of association between related variables ranged from 42.15 to 95.92.

A final comparison between the overall structure obtained and the results of the cluster analysis for each of the individual teachers provided additional support for the logic of the natural clusters observed. Specifically, each of the significantly related pairwise clusters matched up with significant associations derived from the individual cluster analyses performed. This result clearly indicated that the clustering affects observed were not based on the contribution of a single teacher/subject. Indeed, each subject contributed to the overall structure; however, not all pairwise clusters were fully accounted for by the individual data analyses. Apparently, the behaviors observed were not typical of male or female teachers within the randomly chosen sample for this investigation. This result lends support to the previously stated fact that these behaviors were not atypical of generally observed nonverbal teaching behaviors. Moreover, a variety of personality variables, as they relate to teaching style, did contribute to the overall structure, but inconsistently due to individualized or idiosyncratic behavior patterns.

Contingency Structure

Nonverbal behaviors contingent upon other behaviors. The results did not support the third research question. Are certain nonverbal behaviors contingent upon other behaviors? The category, "shows interest in student behavior," was the only category that correlated highly with each of the variables within its own cluster (teaching strategies) as well as with a variety of variables outside its cluster boundaries. For example, this category, "shows interest in student behavior," correlated highly with six variables within its own cluster and with several other behavior categories such as, "accepts or praises student's behavior and vocal expression," both of which fell outside the original cluster.

Though the behavior, "showing interest," did correlate highly with multiple variables, it did not indicate a sufficient contingency structure. This behavior is defined as the teacher establishing and maintaining eye contact with the students. This single condition, eye contact, accounted for 11.5% of all behaviors identified and tabulated by the team of three coders. Such a high percentage of behaviors accounted for by a single nonverbal act indicated that these teachers did establish and maintain eye contact quite frequently and that this behavior would occur even in the absence of other behaviors. Since no other variables correlated across the three category systems to a sufficient degree, indication of a contingency structure was not evident.

The lack of a strong contingency structure strongly suggests a robustness or independence for each major cluster identified. Apparently, the four clusters that emerged reflect real differences in behaviors across this sample.

CONCLUSION

As previously stated, three independent nonverbal observation instruments were employed in this study: the Love and Roderick (1971), Grant and Hennings (1971), and Civikly (1973), category systems. The nonverbal teaching behaviors of three professors were analyzed separately by three coders using each of the indicated classification schemes. Obtained data were submitted to four cluster analyses plus a Pearson correlation measure designed to determine the existence of naturally occurring clusters of behavior. Subsequent interpretations and comparisons of the results were based on the reported average distance scores, correlation measures, and the definitive guidelines es-

TABLE 3
Common Cluster Affects

Subclusters	Overall	Teacher 1	Teacher 2	Teacher 3
(12) personal motions (18) personal acts	.626	.558	.332*	.484
(2) displays student ideas (7) focuses student attention	.645	99.000*	.664	99.000*
(2) displays student ideas (10) acting	.614	99.000*	.677	99.000*
(2) displays student ideas (15) hand gestures	.481	99.000*	.575	99.000*
(7) focuses student attention (10) acting	.959	.937	.957	.953
(7) focuses student attention (15) hand gestures	.806	.855	.429	.019*
(10) acting (15) hand gestures	.849	.884	.875	.027*
(11) wielding (3) shows interest	.540	.526	.577	.577
(15) hand gestures (8) demonstrates/illustrates	.479	.722	.146*	.371*

* Indicates correlations of less than .40 that are not acceptable based on the criteria stated previously. They are included here to indicate the extent of these pairwise clusters.

tablished for each category by the authors of those systems.

The results indicated that four logically formed clusters of behavior existed within the data. An examination of the association between variables within each cluster signified that the nonverbal activity observed in this investigation paralleled the combined behaviors of the three systems employed. Indeed, what appeared to be the most frequently occurring teaching behaviors, as dictated by the three systems, was what was actually going on in this sample of professors studied.

Based on the results of this investigation, it is reasonable to assume that in the instructional setting, the dimensions of teacher-to-student interaction, teaching strategies, classroom control and management, and involvement and participation, as viewed through teacher's nonverbal behavior, are basic functions of the communication pattern of teachers. Finally, the use of a more concise observation system, such as the structure indicated by the results of this study, could provide necessary information for programs of teacher training and self-analysis.

REFERENCES

ADAMS, R.S., & BIDDLE, B.J. *Realities of teaching: Explorations with video tape*. New York: Holt, Rinehart & Winston, 1970.

ALLEN, D., & RYAN, D. The component-skills approach. In D.M. Brooks (Ed.), *Speech communication instruction*. New York: McKay, 1972.

AMIDON, E. Interaction analysis applied to teaching. *The Bul-*

letin of the NASSD, 1966, 50, 93-97.

AMIDON, E.J. & FLANDERS, N.A. *The role of the teacher in the classroom.* Minneapolis: Association for Productive Thinking, Inc., 1967.

ANDERSON, P.A., GARRISON, J.P., & ANDERSEN, J.F. Defining nonverbal communication: A neurophysiological explanation of nonverbal information processing. Paper presented to the Behavioral Science Interest Group at the annual meeting of the Western Speech Communication Association, Seattle, Washington, November, 1975.

ASCHNER, M.J. & GALLAGHER, J.M. A preliminary report on analysis of classroom interaction. *Merrill-Palmer Quarterly*, 1963, 9, 183-195.

ATKINSON, R.C. Ingredients for a theory of instruction. *American Psychologist*, 1972, 921-931.

BALL, G.H., & HALL, D.J. A clustering technique for summarizing multivariate data. *Behavioral Science*, 1967, 12, 153-155.

BARR, A.S. *Characteristic differences in the good and poor teachers of the social sciences*. Bloomington, Ill.: Public Schools, 1929.

BIDDLE, D.J. & ELLENA, W.J. Contemporary research on teacher effectiveness. New York: Holt, Rinehart & Winston, 1964.

BIOMEDICAL COMPUTER PROGRAM. Berkeley: University of California Press, 1975.

BIRDWHISTELL, R.L. *Kinesics and context: Essays on body motion*. Philadelphia: University of Pennsylvania Press, 1970.

BOSMAJIAN, H.A. *The rhetoric of nonverbal communication: Readings*. Glenview, Ill.: Scott Foresman, 1971.

BOURNE, L.E., JR. *Human conceptual behavior*. Boston: Allyn & Bacon, 1966.

BREED, G. Nonverbal behavior and teaching effectiveness, final report. Special project sponsored by Office of Education; Department of Health, Education and Welfare; South Dakota State University; November, 1971; ERIC NO. ED 059 182.

CAMBRA, R.E. The development of a verbal and nonverbal interaction category system for use in learning situations. Paper presented to the Instructional Division at the annual meeting of the Speech Communication Association Convention, San Francisco, 1976.

CIVIKLY, J.M. A description and experimental analysis of teacher nonverbal communication in the college classroom. Unpublished doctoral dissertation, Florida State University, 1973.

COGAN, M. The behavior of teachers and the productive behavior of their pupils. *Journal of Experimental Education*, 1958, 27, 89-124.

DeCECCO, J.P. *The psychology of learning and instruction: Educational psychology*. Englewood Cliffs, N.J.: Prentice-Hall, 1968.

EKMAN, P. & FRIESEN, W. Repertoire of nonverbal behavior: Categories, origins, usage and coding. Semiotica, 1, 1969; 49-98.

FOX, D.J. *The research process in education*. New York: Holt, Rinehart & Winston, 1969.

GALLOWAY, C.M. Nonverbal communication in teaching. In R.T. Hyman (Ed.), *Teaching: Vantage points for study*. New York: Lippincott, 1968.

GALLOWAY, C.M. An exploratory study of observational procedures for determining teacher nonverbal communication. Unpublished doctoral dissertation, University of Florida, 1962.

GIBSON, J.W. Using video tape in the training of teachers. *The Speech Teacher,* March 1968, 17, 107-109.

GAGNÉ, R.M. & BRIGGS, L.J. *Principles of instructional design*. New York: Holt, Rinehart & Winston, 1974.

GRANT, B., & HENNINGS, D.G. *The teacher moves: An analysis of nonverbal activities*. New York: Teachers College Press, Columbia University, 1971.

HARRISON, R.P. & KNAPP, M.L. Toward an understanding of nonverbal communication systems. *Journal of Communication,* 1972, 22, 339-52.

HYMAN, R.T. *Teaching*. New York: J.D. Lippincott, 1968.

KERLINGER, F.N. *Foundations of behavioral research*, (2nd Ed.). New York: Holt, Rinehart & Winston, 1973.

KNAPP, M.L. *Nonverbal communication in human interaction*. New York: Holt, Rinehart & Winston, 1972.

LAING, R.D. *Self and others*. New York: Vintage Press, 1971.

LAIL, S.S. The model in use, *Theory into practice*, 1968, pp. 176-179.

LOVE, A.M., & RODERICK, J.A. Nonverbal communication: The development and field testing of an awareness unit. *Theory into practice,* 1971, 10, 295-299.

MEHRABIAN, A. *Nonverbal communication*. New York: Aldine Athtron, 1972.

MORGANSTERN, B.F. Rationale and training guides for a nonverbal classification system. Paper presented at the annual meeting of the Speech Communication Association, San Francisco, 1976.

NUNNALLY, J.C. *Psychometric theory*. New York: McGraw-Hill, 1967.

ROGERS, C. *The interpersonal facilitation of learning*. Dimensions of Oral Communication: An introduction, ed. K. Ericson. Dubuque, Iowa: William C. Brown, 1970.

ROSENTHAL, R. & JACOBSEN, L. *Pygmalion in the classroom*. New York: Holt, Rinehart & Winston, 1968.

SCHUM, W.C. The effects of training student teachers in self-analysis of nonverbal response patterns. Paper presented at the annual meeting of the American Educational Research Association, Chicago: April 1974, ERIC Number ED 088 829.

STROTHER, D.B. The effects of instruction in nonverbal communication on elementary school teacher competency and student achievement. Project sponsored by the National Center for Educational Communication, Department of HEW: Oct. 1971, ERIC No. ED 056 005.

THORNDIKE, E.L. *Psychology of learning*. New York: Teachers College Press, Columbia University, 1913.

TRAVERS, R.M.W. *Essentials of learning,* 3rd Edition. New York: Macmillan, 1972.

VERPLANCK, W.S. The control of the content of communication: Reinforcement of statements of opinion. *Journal of Abnormal and Social Psychology,* 1955, 51, 668-76.

WILLETT, T.H. A descriptive analysis of nonverbal behaviors of college teachers. Unpublished doctoral dissertation, University of Missouri-Columbia, 1976.

WOOLFOLK, K.L., & WOOLFOLK, A.E. Effects of teacher verbal and nonverbal behaviors on student perceptions and attitudes. *American Educational Research Journal*, 1974, 11, 297-303.

YOUNG, D.B. The analysis and modification of teaching behavior using interaction analysis, micro-teaching and video-tape feedback. Paper presented at the National Association of Secondary School Principles, 1968.

WHEN GALATEA IS APPREHENSIVE: THE EFFECT OF COMMUNICATION APPREHENSION ON TEACHER EXPECTATIONS

MARY-JEANETTE SMYTHE
University of Missouri

WILLIAM G. POWERS
University of Missouri

The effect of communication apprehension on teacher expectations was investigated in an ongoing educational environment composed of a multisection basic speech course. Students were classified as high or low communication apprehensives. The teacher expectations were assessed. Results strongly indicate high communication apprehensive students are perceived as having less success potential than their low communication apprehensive peers in the actual student-teacher encounter.

The role of a teacher's expectations in shaping students' academic achievement has become an issue of increasing importance in the decade following the publication of Rosenthal and Jacobson's (1968) *Pygmalion in the Classroom*. Although the relationship between student characteristics and teacher expectations remains somewhat unclear, there is general agreement that expectation or "pygmalion" effects do occur at all levels of education, often with profound consequences for student learning (Brophy & Good, 1974). Previous research on teacher expectations has identified a number of variables of potential significance in determining a teacher's expectations for students' performance. Such variables, however, do not appear to consistently affect teacher-student relationships (Brophy & Good, 1974). The lack of consistency precludes understanding, much less intervention and/or remediation, of the role of expectations in learning environments.

Current gaps in our understanding of the teacher expectations question may be attributed to two factors concerning the focus and execution of research on the topic. First, researchers have primarily examined static, personal variables (e.g., sex, race, etc.) as determinants of expectations. While these variables unquestionably affect a teacher's perception of students, most of the research ignores a single, critical characteristic of expectations. That is, expectations are an outgrowth of the dynamic communication exchanges between people. Teachers may develop performance expectations based on the color of a student's skin, but these initial expectations may be (and often are) changed through the routine processes of classroom communication. For this reason, it seems reasonable to argue that research should focus on communication behaviors which might influence teacher-student interchanges, if any coherent account of the "pygmalion effect" is to be achieved.

Closely related to matter of focus in teacher expectation research is the manner in which most studies have been conducted. Brophy and Good (1974) have aptly noted that much of the confusion concerning expectancy effects in the classroom results from the predilection of researchers toward investigations of experimentally-induced expectations. Such studies usually involve providing teachers with contrived information concerning their students, designed to influence performance expectations, prior to the initial teacher-student encounter, with a subsequent measure of learning gains. For obvious reasons, these studies have produced contradictory findings. Those studies which measure teachers' responses to hypothetical descriptions of student behavior are somewhat more productive. While these findings are often revealing, they remain of questionable relevance to the *actual* educational environment. Naturalistic studies, investigating students and teacher in ongoing classroom encounters, have contributed the most consistent and useful information to date on the operation of expectation effects. Therefore, it seems apparent that research should be directed toward examining the communication behaviors of students as they affect teacher expectations in actual classroom settings. The current study was designed to accomplish these goals.

COMMUNICATION APPREHENSION AND TEACHER EXPECTATIONS

Given the argument that expectations develop as a consequence of teacher-student interaction, the communication apprehension (CA) variable emerges as an immediate concern. Current research relating this variable to academic achievement (McCroskey & Andersen, 1976), and communication effectiveness (Freimuth, 1976) have indicated the dramatic effects of communication apprehension in the classroom quite clearly. Individuals who experience high levels of this anxiety or fear concerning the act of communication appear to share a number of communication behaviors which distinguish them from individuals whose anxieties concerning communication are low. Most notably, McCroskey and Leppard (1975) report that high communication apprehensives characteristically avoid communication encounters, prefer working alone, and remain withdrawn in most communication situations. The implications of this profile of behavior in a classroom setting for the formation of teacher expectations seem obvious, but remain to be documented.

Interest in the potential effects of CA on teacher expectations has generated one particularly noteworthy study. McCroskey and Daly (1976) investigated teacher expectancies toward elementary school children as a function of student communication apprehension levels. Teachers' expectations for high apprehensive and low apprehensive students were found to differ markedly. Specifically, teachers expected the high apprehensive student to have significantly less success in the academic areas of reading, arithmetic, social studies, science, and art. Moreover, teachers predicted that the high communication apprehensive student was less effective in relationships with other students and projected lower current and future academic success for the high apprehensive student. Combined with related research revealing that the high apprehensive students score significantly lower on composite and subscores of the ACT, and generally maintain lower GPAs than low communication apprehensive students, McCroskey and Daly's (1976) findings invite the inference that the "pygmalion effect" found to be prevalent with other variables (Brophy & Good, 1974; Beez, 1968; and Rubovits & Maehr, 1971, 1973) is equally operative with communication apprehension.

Such an inference can be drawn only with certain reservations. In the McCroskey and Daly (1976) study, teachers responded to written descriptions of two hypothetical elementary school children, with one description representing characteristic behaviors of a high apprehensive student and the other representing the characteristic behaviors of a low apprehensive student (McCroskey & Daly, 1976, p. 68). Although manipulation checks in both a pilot study and a full research project confirmed the validity of the written description strategy relative to the researchers' intent, the operation of communication apprehensive and teacher expectancies in ongoing educational environments needs further substantiation. These results provoke the question of whether such differences would emerge in actual educational instances, where teacher evaluations and ultimate expectancies were a function of classroom exposure to high and low CA students over the course of an entire semester. Indeed, McCroskey and Daly note that "of even more concern is the impact of expectancies generated in the natural teaching-learning environment and the causal agents which lead to these expectancies" (McCroskey & Daly, 1976, p. 67). To this end, the current study investigated the expectations teachers form for high and low CA students actually enrolled in their classes. Based on previous CA research, it was generally hypothesized that teachers would form less favorable expectations of success for high communication apprehensive students than they would for low communication apprehensive students.

METHOD

Data for hypothesis testing was collected from

the enrollment in a multisection basic speech communication course during the spring semester, 1977. All students enrolled in the class were asked to complete the Personal Report of Communication Apprehension (PRCA) approximately two weeks before the conclusion of classes. The PRCA was one among several descriptive instruments concerning the course content, teachers, and materials, which students completed during this period. Students and their teachers were told that the data was being gathered by the department for the purpose of determining future curricular and instructional procedures. A total of 723 usable PRCA forms were obtained. Student scores on the PRCA were used to operationally define high CA and low CA students for the purposes of this study.

The PRCA has consistently produced internal reliability indices above .90 and test-retest reliability indices above .80 (McCroskey, 1970). Predictive validity has been established in numerous studies (McCroskey, 1975). These findings suggested that the PRCA was a sufficiently rigorous instrument for assigning students to high and low CA categories. From the 723 PRCAs, a mean was computed (X=58.92) and students divided into groups on the basis of their scores. The criterion for inclusion in the high CA or low CA group was to have scores falling in the array at a point either less than or more than one standard deviation above or below the mean (SD=12.76). This resulted in 81 students being designated as low CA students and 83 students being classified as high communication apprehensive students.

Four weeks later, 12 members of the instructional staff for the basic course were asked to complete a questionnaire regarding each of the designated high or low apprehensive students they had taught during the just completed semester. Members of the teaching staff were graduate teaching assistants who all had at least one year's teaching experience. Their participation was determined by the distribution of the 164 high and low apprehensive students within all the sections of the course offered during the spring semester. The teachers had conducted classes with the students selected for evaluation two hours per week over a 16-week semester. They were relatively naive concerning the CA variable (i.e., no teachers were aware of any students' scores on the PRCA), and were not aware of the true purpose of the evaluations they were asked to complete. Rather, each teacher was simply given a list of students enrolled in the sections he had taught and asked to evaluate them on the basis of the questionnaire provided. The purpose of their evaluations was presented as an integral part of the larger departmental survey of the basic course and its enrollment, designed to "increase faculty knowledge regarding the students comprising the basic course."

The evaluation the teachers completed was based on the scales used in the McCroskey and Daly (1976) study, with appropriate linguistic modifications (e.g., "reading" as an area was changed to "English") to accommodate a college-level population. The questionnaire asked teachers to estimate the success of each student in nine areas by responding to ten-point scales (ranging from 0-9) bound at the extremes by "very poorly" and "very well." The nine areas included: English, mathematics, physical sciences, social sciences, art, deportment, relationships with other students, overall achievement, and success in future education. In addition to these categories included by McCroskey and Daly (1976), teachers were requested to estimate "success in future occupation" for each of the students. Items concerning class participation and students' level of anxiety about communication were included as manipulation checks.

Of the 164 students composing the high and low apprehensive groups, a total of 157 usable questionnaires were returned. Of these, 80 were classified as representing high apprehensive students and 77 were classified as representing low apprehensive students.

RESULTS

Data on each of the 12 scales were analyzed through analysis of variance. Results are summarized in Table 1. Manipulation check items on class participation and anxiety about communication indicated that the PRCA-based designations of students as high or low apprehensives were accurate. High communication apprehensive students were described by their teachers as substantially

TABLE 1
Mean Teacher Expectations for High CA and Low CA College Students

Area	High CA	Low CA	F	Probability
Manipulation Checks				
Anxiety About Communication	5.51	3.48	33.97	<.05
Class Participation	4.29	6.52	34.52	<.05
Success Variables				
English	5.38	6.49	13.78	<.05
Mathematics	5.20	6.01	8.11	<.05
Social Sciences	5.14	6.49	23.07	<.05
Physical Sciences	5.31	6.18	8.23	<.05
Art	5.09	5.95	9.50	<.05
Deportment	5.89	6.73	7.64	<.05
Relationship with other Students	5.56	6.77	18.08	<.05
Overall Achievement	5.64	6.92	19.30	<.05
Future Education	5.63	7.03	24.63	<.05
Future Occupation	5.98	7.08	16.10	<.05

more anxious about communication than their low apprehensive peers (F=33.97) and considerably less likely to participate in classroom interactions (F=34.52).

The general hypothesis of the current study was supported. As depicted in Table 1, significant differences were obtained on every one of the scales included on the questionnaire. Teacher expectations described by these data reflected the belief that low apprehensive students would perform better than the high CA students in all areas. Moreover, the high apprehensive students were viewed by their teachers as less capable of establishing good relationships with other students, and as far less likely to enjoy success in their future educational or occupational careers. These results demonstrate quite clearly that high levels of student communication apprehension are perceived by teachers and translated into negative expectations for future performance.

DISCUSSION

The results of this study are remarkable in several respects. Certainly the strength and direction of the effects observed illustrate that communication apprehension is a potentially powerful determinant of a teacher's perceptions and expectations for a student's performance. Our data seems irrefutable on the point that teachers can detect and respond differentially to students as a function of the students' communication behavior. What is perhaps surprising about these findings is that in each of the 12 categories, without exception, the high apprehensive student was negatively perceived by his teachers. The discrepancy on the deportment variable between this study and the McCroskey and Daly (1976) study is probably attributable to differing performance expectations operating in imaginary elementary and current college classrooms. The silence that characterizes the highly apprehensive student may be construed as positive in the elementary learning setting. However, in a college classroom, particularly a speech communication classroom, this silence is less likely to be considered desirable.

The evidence from this study strongly indicates that teachers discriminate among their students on the basis of communication behavior which reflects apprehension levels. The fact that these data were collected at the conclusion of a course, rather than in the early or midsemester period only serves to strengthen the suspicion that the negative expectations generated by high communication apprehensives become self-fulfilling prophecies. The negative expectations these teachers expressed regarding their high apprehensive students were an outgrowth of their sustained interactions over an entire semester. Although these data do not speak to the issue, it seems highly improbable that these expectations were not communicated to the high apprehensive students, and probably reflected in the teachers' evaluations of their achievement.

Without question, however, the most important implications of the current findings lie in the demonstration that, *in naturalistic classroom settings*, communication apprehension affects the expectations teachers form for their students. This consideration outweighs any limitations attributable to sample size, and so forth. Similarly, we doubt that the findings can be realistically discounted on the basis of academic level or subject matter biases. Investigations are currently underway to empirically support the conviction that where communication apprehension is concerned, teachers in a basic college speech communication course are not unique in their responses to the high and low apprehensive students. Rather, we suspect that these findings reveal, for the first time, empirical evidence on *why* students high in communication apprehension have lower GPAs and achievement test scores than their low apprehensive peers. The hypothetical question posed by the McCroskey and Daly (1976) study concerning the possibility of negative teacher expectations as a function of high communication apprehension has been affirmed by the current findings. The evidence seems quite clear. Teachers form negative expectations for the highly apprehensive student. The clearer understanding of the "pygmalion effect" afforded by these findings only heightens the urgency of the need for change in our programs for teacher preparation. Future studies of the naturalistic type should be aimed toward identifying the dynamics of expectancies in the classroom. As these become clearer, intervention and remediation strategies designed to reduce the pygmalion effect should be applied to both the teacher and the high apprehensive student. Student communication apprehension and teacher expectations constitute a genuine classroom problem of indeterminate dimensions. Available data indicate that immediate and sustained attention to its resolution is warranted.

REFERENCES

BEEZ, W.V. Influence of biased psychological reports on teacher behavior and pupil performance. *Proceedings of the 76th Annual Convention of the American Psychological Association*, 1968, 3, 605-606.

BROPHY, J., & GOOD, T. *Teacher-student relationships: Causes and consequences*. New York: Harper & Row, 1974.

FREIMUTH, V.S. The effects of communication apprehension on communication effectiveness. *Human Communication Research*, 1976, 2, 289-298.

McCROSKEY, J.C. Measures of communication-bound anxiety. *Speech Monographs*, 1970, 37, 269-277.

McCROSKEY, J.C. Validity of the PRCA as an index of oral communication apprehension. Paper presented at the annual meeting of the Speech Communication Association, Houston, December 1975.

McCROSKEY, J.C., & ANDERSEN, J.F. The relationship between communication apprehension and academic achievement among college students. *Human Communication Research*, 1976, 3, 73-81.

McCROSKEY, J.C., & DALY, J.A. Teachers' expectations of the communication apprehensive child in the elementary school. *Human Communication Research*, 1976, 3, 67-72.

McCROSKEY, J.C., & LEPPARD, T. The effects of communication apprehension on nonverbal behavior. Paper presented at the annual meeting of the Eastern Communication Association, New York, March 1975.

ROSENTHAL, R., & JACOBSON, L. *Pygmalion in the classroom: Teacher expectation and pupils' intellectual development*. New York: Holt, Rinehart & Winston, 1968.

RUBOVITS, P.C., & MAEHR, M.L. Pygmalion analyzed: Toward an explanation of the Rosenthal-Jacobson findings. *Journal of Personality and Social Psychology*, 1971, 19, 197-203.

RUBOVITS, P.C., & MAEHR, M.L. Pygmalion black and white. *Journal of Personality and Social Psychology*, 1973, 25, 210-218.

HEALTH COMMUNICATION

Theory and Research: An Overview
Selected Studies

HEALTH COMMUNICATION THEORY AND RESEARCH: AN OVERVIEW OF THE COMMUNICATION SPECIALIST INTERFACE

DONALD M. CASSATA
University of North Carolina School of Medicine

During the past decade, many authors have focused on the importance of communications within health and medicine. Psychiatrists and other physicians have addressed the topic (Bennett, 1976; Berger, 1977; Fletcher, 1973; Harlem, 1977). Allied health professionals have also contributed several books (Collins, 1977; Hein, 1973; Lewis, 1969; Purtillo, 1973; Travelbee, 1971). Social scientists have covered the subject as well (Anthony & Carkhuff, 1976; Ley & Spelman, 1967; Skipper & Leonard, 1965). Surprisingly, these authors are not within the discipline of communication. The primary purpose of this paper is to emphasize the importance of the study of communication in health settings and to describe the functions of communication specialists in health areas.

In recent reviews, Adler (1977) and Costello (1977) have assembled a body of literature and identified various parameters in the study of health communication. These reviews attest to the unique abilities of communication scholars to bring not only a broad understanding of communication processes but also a strong methodological approach to solving problems.

In health and medicine especially, the contribution which communication scholars can make is in implementing a communication methodology as part of a behavioral science perspective of medicine. Goldberg (1968, p. 45) states that such a scholar "goes beyond the formal speech setting and focuses on the implications of relevant theory and research in the behavioral sciences for resolving conflict and improving communication in a great variety of interpersonal situations." He further states (1968, p. 42) that communication can be referred to as a methodology "when it is systematic, deliberate, and based on a set of principles." Communication specialists perform one of their most important functions by applying this perspective to health provider-patient interaction and management processes.

Some of the specific methodologies which apply to medical situations are the use of audio or video equipment for feedback purposes, general semantics, rhetorical strategies, role playing, brainstorming, debate, parliamentary procedure, laboratory training, and so forth. These methods are just one part of the armamentarium of a communication specialist.

Besides having knowledge of and skills of various methodologies, communication specialists must be grounded in communication theory, be students of interpersonal processes within a variety of situations, and be able to conduct research and/or evaluation studies. These three contributions within health care contexts can aid the health field significantly.

Involvement of communication specialists in the health field is greatly needed. Walker (1973) identifies this need as a persistent health care problem. There is a lack of emphasis on communication as a significant variable, as well as a lack of overall knowledge and research in the patient-health provider arena. Lynn (1976) reports that the climate for communication input is right because of the demand for more personalized care and the rapid and extensive changes in health services delivery methods, manpower, and organizational structure.

Barnlund (1976, p. 722) discusses the need for including communication specialists in medical education because of the importance of human relationships in the practice of medicine: ". . . no profession has daily contact with so wide a spectrum of sub-cultures and none exerts influence over such sensitive matters." Emphasizing this understanding of the physician setting and the importance of communication skills in practicing medicine, Barnlund asks, "How many medical school courses are concerned with exploring the ways illness threatens the symbolic as well as physical self? How many class periods focus upon the communicative strategies patients use to cope with imminent threats to their survival? How much time is spent exploring the physician's own communicative style, the assumptions on which it rests, the impulses it reflects, and the consequences for those he or she treats?"

At the graduate level of medical education, there is increasing demand that primary care specialists develop their communication skills. Martin (1975) specifies some of the needs:

> The family practice trainee must acquire and develop identifiable communications skills using verbal and non-verbal (body language) techniques and physiological responses to emotion to evaluate properly the patient's state of 'disease'. He should be competent in communicating with patients, families, peers, society and himself. Is it any wonder that communication is probably the most important skill that a training program must impart to the family practice trainee? (p. 290)

He goes on to describe some of the functions communication serves for the practitioner:

> Appropriate communication provides the physician with an accurate data base from which he can extrapolate certain probabilities relating to the patient's condition. This process of extracting information never ceases in the family physician's clinical practice. The physician imparts information either to reinforce the patient's behavioral attitudes or to change such attitudes. His major role is to assess the patient to understand and gain the patient's acceptance of either behavioral change or reinforcement. Compliance with such counsel requires explanation, patient understanding, and motivation. Patient motivation relates directly to the physician's communicative skills, commitment, and the level of congruity in the encounter. (p. 290)

According to Costello (1977), diagnoses, cooperation, counsel, and education are the four basic functions served by communication between health professionals and patients. He stressed two reasons for the importance of the physician's interpersonal communication as part of the diagnostic function: (1) interpersonal communication contributes, along with technical skills, to diagnosing disease problems; and (2) interpersonal communication is critical in the treatment of nondisease problems. Inherent within these four functions is also the crucial ingredient of relationship building and contracting. Ideas gleaned from communication theory and negotiation theory can enhance both these inherent functions.

The importance of the study of communication and the value of communication specialists in meeting several identified needs within the health field have been discussed. The remainder of this paper will examine the skills of communication specialists—interpersonal, counseling and group—as they relate to needs in health contexts. Although some examples specify doctor-patient interaction, it is understood that the ideas can be applied to exchanges between clients and other health care providers as well.

DOCTOR-PATIENT INTERACTION

Doctor-Patient Interaction: The Medical Interview

There is solid agreement that good doctor-patient communication is essential to effective health care. Indeed, Tumulty (1970) posits that it is the essence of the clinical process. The medical interview forms the core of the doctor-patient interaction, clinical diagnosis, and therapeutic relationship. Several recently published books describe the parts and process of the medical interview (Bernstein, Bernstein, & Dana, 1974; Bird, 1973; Enelow & Swisher, 1972; Engel & Morgan, 1973; Froelich & Bishop, 1972; Stevenson, 1971).

Even though the dynamics of communication and relationships between health providers and patients during the medical interview are complex, they are essential to teach. In their review of the literature related to the training of medical students in interviewing techniques, Maguire and Rutter (1976) identify medical students' deficiencies in interviewing skills, show the inadequacies of traditional methods of interview training, and propose development of an interview model and training procedure. This model is unique since it incorporates the data (content) to be obtained and the interviewing techniques (process) that should be used.

FIGURE 1.
Medical Interview Skills Checklist

BIOLOGICAL INQUIRY

- ______ Patient Diagnosis
  - ______ Identification of patient's problem(s), pursuing presenting symptoms
  - ______ Past medical history
  - ______ Family medical history
  - ______ Review of systems
  - ______ Physical examination (talks patient through examination)
  - ______ Diagnostic decision-making process (differential)
  - ______ Problem list
  - ______ Tests, X-Rays, and laboratory studies

- ______ Patient Treatment and Education
  - ______ Formulation of treatment plan
  - ______ Explanation of treatment and prescription of medication
  - ______ Patient education
  - ______ Identification of positive aspects of health

PSYCHOLOGICAL INQUIRY

- ______ Patient Profile
  - ______ Demographics (age of patient, education, family size, religion, where from)
  - ______ Life situations (identify stresses, satisfactions, feelings)
    - ______ Occupational functioning
    - ______ Family functioning
    - ______ Marital functioning
    - ______ Sexual functioning
    - ______ Social relationships
    - ______ Leisure-time activities (What do you do for fun? Relaxation?)
    - ______ Alcohol, tobacco, and drug use
    - ______ "What is a typical day/evening/weekend like for you?"
    - ______ Support systems (identify and find out to whom person turns during times of need or crisis)
    - ______ Religious or spiritual support
  - ______ Impact of illness on the patient and on patient's family
  - ______ Identification of life-style
  - ______ Identification of psychosocial problems
  - ______ Identification of psychosocial strengths
  - ______ Problem list
- ______ Patient Treatment and Education
  - ______ Formulation of a treatment plan
  - ______ Discussion of a treatment plan
  - ______ Patient education

INTERVIEW ORGANIZATION

- ______ Organizational Plan
- ______ Organizational Process

Cassata, Conroe, and Clements (1977) report a method using videotape feedback for teaching the medical interview. A Medical Interview Skills Checklist (MISC), consisting of more than 75 items, was developed (see Figure 1). The MISC provides a structure for assessing biological and psychosocial data gathered, the organization of the interview, and the depth and breadth of the physician-patient relationship. It is a tool for measuring specific data-gathering and problem-solving skills. The ratings used for the MISC are "strong," "weak," or a check mark, meaning that there is not enough data to assess the skill as either strong or weak. However, for research purposes, there are three levels of competency which may be assigned to each skill: a student-physician will score 3 for a particular behavior if he or she demonstrates most skills, 2 for behavior if the student demonstrates some skills, and 1 for behavior if the student demonstrates little or no skills.

During the past several years, the teaching of medical interviewing and relationship skills as part of the medical school curriculum has increased. Even though this is occurring, few of the 116 medical schools have a systematic approach for the teaching of these skills. Communication specialists can bring both a theory and methodology for the achievement of this need.

Doctor-Patient Interaction: Patient Satisfaction

While much useful information has been written about ways to establish effective doctor-patient communication via the medical interview, several studies empirically document the problems inherent in such communication. The most notable work has been done by Korsch at the University of Southern California, and Ley at the University of Liverpool.

Korsch and her associates (Francis, Korsch, & Morris, 1969; Freemon, Negrete, Davis, & Korsch, 1971; Gozzi, Morris, & Korsch, 1969; Korsch & Aley, 1973; Korsch & Negrete, 1972; Korsch, Gozzi, & Francis, 1968; Korsch, Negrete, Mercer, & Freemon, 1971) used a modified Bales's Interaction Analysis to categorize in various ways statements made by physicians and patients, including a classification according to the affect expressed. In general, they found the expression of positive affect from the physician is associated with greater patient satisfaction and compliance. For instance, parents demonstrated an intense need for explanation of their child's disease and what caused it. Sixty-five percent of the parents stated that these expectations were not met. The investigators also noted a direct correlation between patients' expectations being met, patients' feelings of satisfaction, and patient compliance.

Ley and others investigated the problem of hospitalized patients' dissatisfaction with communication (Ley, 1972a, 1972b, 1972c, 1973, 1976; Ley & Spelman, 1967; Ley, Bradshaw, Eaves, & Walker, 1973; Ley, Bradshaw, Kincey, & Atherton, 1976). Using data from a number of studies, they showed that 11-65% of patients come out of the hospital feeling dissatisfied with the communication aspect of their hospital stay. Furthermore, attempts to improve communication by increasing the information given to the patient did not eliminate complaints about poor communication. They emphasize not only that understanding patients' information needs is necessary but knowledge of the best methods of imparting technical information is needed as well.

The following nine conclusions of their research may be viewed as specific applications to medical settings of principles of interpersonal communication:

1. Patients forget much of what the doctor tells them.
2. Instruction and advice are more likely to be forgotten than other information.
3. The more a patient is told, the greater the portion he or she will forget.
4. Patients will remember:
   a) what they are told first,
   b) what they consider most important.
5. Intelligent patients do not remember more than less intelligent patients.
6. Older patients remember just as much as younger ones.
7. Moderately anxious patients recall more of what they are told than highly anxious patients or patients who are not anxious.
8. The more medical knowledge a patient has, the more he or she will recall.
9. If the patient writes down what the doctor says, he or she will remember it just as well as if he or she merely hears it.

Another experimental study of patient satisfaction of medical communication yielded related conclusions. Kupst, Dresser, Schulman, & Paul (1975) investigated four communication methods: (1) single communication of medical information by the physician, (2) communication by the physician plus a written summary, (3) information presented twice by the physician through repetition, (4) single presentation by the physician with patient restatement and clarification by the physician. They found that recall is better in cases where information has been repeated orally than in cases where information was presented only once, or where a single presentation was followed by a written summary. For immediate recall, physician repetition and patient restatement with feedback are similar in effectiveness. However, patient restatement with feedback was preferable, increasing patient satisfaction.

As the above examples demonstrate, communication specialists not only have much to offer in developing better doctor-patient relationships, but also will find this topic an important and fruitful area for further research.

Doctor-Patient Interaction: Counseling

Given the emphasis in medical education on diagnosis and management of physical and organic conditions, teaching how to manage other problems, such as chronic disability, emotional illness, death, and bereavement, is often a deficient area of the educational experience. That medical education does not prepare physicians to identify and deal effectively with patients' and family members' feelings about the impact of illness or psychosocial problems is also a major weakness in the medical curriculum.

Communication specialists can have important input into teaching affective communication skills. These skills include contracting, self-disclosure, empathy, ventilation, active listening, support, reflection, confrontation, and others. These affective skills have great applicability in therapeutic settings as Carkhuff and Berenson (1976) demonstrate in their "teaching as treatment" counseling model.

Beyond uses in teaching and counseling, communication theory is essential for crisis intervention (Aguilera & Messick, 1974), conflict resolution (Johnson, 1974), patient counseling (Ireton & Cassata, 1976), death and dying situations (Kubler-Ross, 1969), chronic disability (Kiely, 1972; Strauss, 1975), and for communication in serious illnesses such as cancer (McIntosh, 1974).

GROUP INTERACTION

Group Interaction: Health Teams

Group process viewed from a communication perspective has important applications to the health field. Health care teams, physicians in group practice, allied health workers, patient support groups—the growth of such groups points to the need for education and research about their functions in medical settings. Thornton (1977) proposed that the team approach to health care is a viable alternative to the traditional doctor-patient model of health care. Leadership, team size and composition, role negotiation, communication patterns and conflict resolution, and decision making were identified as important characteristics of the health team. She posits that, through the study of communication patterns, researchers will discover how the team negotiates roles, makes decisions and delivers effective patient care.

Comparing team versus individual nursing care, Cassata (1973) examined the effect of these two systems of nursing care on the perceptions of patients and nursing staff. Patients in the individualized nursing system rated staff more positively than did patients receiving team nursing care. However, patient satisfaction was rated equally high under both systems. Individualized nursing staff viewed their care more positively than did team nursing staff, rated the personal attention given to patients significantly higher, and perceived their patients as more "demanding." On the other hand, team nursing staff had a higher level of job satisfaction and higher station effectiveness ratings. It was concluded that the development and adaptation to individualized nursing created dissatisfaction and frustration for the nursing staff. Judging from patient and nurse comments, dissatisfaction was apparently not directed toward patients, but was manifested by poor staff communication, rapport, trust, morale, and plans of leaving their jobs. As this research implies, communication specialists are needed within health care settings to participate in staff and organizational development (Bormann, Howell, Nichols, & Shapiro, 1969; Schein, 1969).

Group Interaction: Families

The effects of illness on the family and the family's importance in patient compliance and rehabilitation have been demonstrated (Arbogast & Scratton, 1977; Litman, 1974). Physicians charged with treating and caring for families especially need training in family dynamics and small group process. By regarding the family as a small group system, health providers can use knowledge of group dynamics to facilitate information gathering and provide counseling.

Interaction with more than one person at a time is essential also for effective assessment and management of health problems. For instance, interacting with a sick child and his or her mother, with a husband and wife in marital conflict, and with a family whose father has just died, are common situations in which health professionals are involved. Communication theory can assist health professionals in understanding marital and family communication as well (Miller, Nunnally, & Wackman, 1975; Satir, 1967, 1972; Wahlroos, 1974; Watzlawick, Beavin, & Jackson, 1967).

Other aspects of small group training that will not be discussed in this paper are the need for communication specialists to assist in practice management and hospital administration (Zola & McKinlay, 1974). For example, admission procedures, telephone usage, patient scheduling, personnel management, and record keeping systems are just a few of the administrative matters that health professionals must manage and communication specialists might address.

OTHER NEEDS

Much work needs to be done in the application of communication theory and research to patient and health education (Richards, 1975). Theories on the dissemination of health information and strategies for patient education still need to be explored by communication specialists. Recently, Brenner and Quesada (1977) reviewed the role of the mass media within this context.

Patient compliance is another major area in which communication specialists are needed in health communication (Davis, 1968; Marston, 1970; Vincent, 1971; Mitchell, 1974). Daly and Hulka (1975) show that interpersonal communication and patient satisfaction affect patients' compliance with medical advice and instructions. As discussed above, Ley (1976) and Korsch (1970) and Korsch et al. (1968) report similar results.

Communication scholars should become involved as well in such problematic areas as pediatric communication/interviewing (Helfer & Ealy, 1972; Helfer & Hess, 1970; Korsch et al., 1971), adolescent communication/interviewing (Stephenson, 1970; Rigg, 1970), middle years communication/interviewing (Sheehy, 1974), aged communication/interviewing (Cassata, 1976). Cross-cultural and ethnic communication is an area where many communication scholars can contribute also (Shuy, 1976; Zola, 1963).

Outcome and cost effectiveness studies are vital to the development of health communication theory. Three studies in particular demonstrate the therapeutic outcomes of communication in the health provider-patient dialogue. Egbert et al. (1963, 1964) report the value of encouragement, instructions and interpersonal contact on reducing postoperative pain, use of medication, and length of stay in the hospital. Dumas, Anderson, & Leonard (1965) show that psychological preparation (communication of anxieties and feelings) of surgical patients by a nurse reduces the incidence of postoperative vomiting.

CONCLUSION

Communication specialists may not be aware of the efficacy of their knowledge and skills, nor how broadly they might be applied in health fields. A communication perspective humanizes doctor-patient relationships. It emphasizes being person-oriented and family system-oriented, making contact, developing two-way communication, feedback, empathy, openness, trust, semantics, sociolinguistics, nonverbal behaviors, and so forth.

In order to have a significant impact on the health field, especially with medical doctors, communication specialists or methodologists must establish their skills and confidence in the clinical setting. This clinical skills interface promotes credibility and mutual understanding between the communication specialists and health providers. Clinical competency can be demonstrated through skillful interpersonal-interviewing, affective skills, knowledge and understanding of life stresses and the value of support systems, the philosophical conviction that an individual is able to help himself or herself, and an emphasis on wellness as a counterpoint to illness.

In certain circumstances, the attainment of professional certification may be necessary for credibility. However, communication specialists do not have to demonstrate that they can provide service to patients. What they do need to show is that they serve an integral educational function in the teaching and research related to the process and outcome of patient care.

To aid in the development of one's confidence, a working knowledge and understanding of anatomy, physiology, organic systems, and the rudiments of the medical history would be advantageous. Furthermore, internships and study within health care settings would instill a level of comfort and familiarity, through promoting an understanding of the particular health care delivery system, the impact of illness on patients and families, and the life and work of health providers.

Several associations and organizations may also provide peer support and professional growth, such as the Health Communication Division of the International Communication Association (ICA), the American Association of Medical Colleges (AAMC), the Association for the Behavioral Sciences and Medical Education (ABSAME), the Society of Teachers of Family Medicine (STFM), and the Health Divisions of the American Sociological Association (ASA) and of the American Psychological Association (APA).

The state of the art of health communication is embryonic, to say the least. Potential areas have been identified for the involvement of communication specialists in health fields. By applying communication theory and research, as well as interpersonal and group skills, communication specialists can enhance interactions in medicine, the health care delivery system, and health care in general.

REFERENCES

ADLER, K. Doctor-patient communication: A shift to problem-solving research. *Human Communication Research*, 1977, 3, 179-190.

AGUILERA, D.C., & MESSICK, J.M. *Crisis intervention: Theory and methodology*. St. Louis: Mosby, 1974.

ANDERSON, J.A., DAY, J.L., DOWLING, M.A.C., & PETTINGALE, K.W. The definition and evaluation of the skills required to obtain a patient's history of illness: The use of videotape recordings. *Postgraduate Medical Journal*, 1970, 46, 606-612.

ANTHONY, W.A., & CARKHUFF, R.R. *The art of health care*. Amherst, Mass.: Human Resource Development Press, 1976.

ARBOGAST, R.C., & SCRATTON, J.M. The family as patient: An assessment schema. Paper presented at the annual meeting of the Society of Teachers of Family Medicine, Atlanta, 1977.

BARNLUND, D.C. The mystification of meaning: Doctor-patient encounters. *Journal of Medical Education*, 1976, 51, 716-725.

BENNETT, A.E. (Ed.). *Communication between doctors and patients*. New York: Oxford University Press, 1976.

BERGER, M.M. *Working with people called patients*. New York: Brunner/Mazel, 1977.

BERNSTEIN, L., BERNSTEIN, R.S., & DANA, R.H. *Interviewing: A guide for health professionals* (2nd ed.). New York: Appleton-Century-Crofts, 1974.

BIRD, B. *Talking with patients* (2nd ed.). Philadelphia: Lippincott, 1973.

BORMANN, E.G., HOWELL, W.S., NICHOLS, R.G., & SHAPIRO, G.L. *Interpersonal communications in the modern organization*. Englewood Cliffs, N.J.: Prentice-Hall, 1969.

BRENNER, D.J., & QUESADA, G.M. The role of mass media in health communication. Paper presented at the annual meeting of the International Communication Association, Berlin, 1977.

CARKHUFF, R.R., & BERENSON, B.G. *Teaching as treatment*. Amherst, Mass.: Human Resource Development Press, 1976.

CASSATA, D.M. Communication and the aged. In J.T. Kelly & J. Weir (Eds.), *Perspectives on human aging*. Minneapolis: Craftsman Press, 1976.

CASSATA, D.M. *The effect of two patterns of nursing care on the perceptions of patients and staff in two urban hospitals*. Unpublished doctoral dissertation, University of Minnesota, 1973.

CASSATA, D.M. & CLEMENTS, P.W. Teaching communication skills through videotape feedback: A rural health program. *Bioscience Communication*, in press.

CASSATA, D.M., CONROE, R.M., & CLEMENTS, P.W. A program for enhancing medical interviewing using videotape feedback in the family practice residency. *Journal of Family Practice*, 1977, 4, 673-677.

CHARNEY, E. Patient-doctor communication: Implications for the clinician. *Pediatric Clinics of North America*, 1972, 19, 263-279.

COLLINS, M. *Communication in health care*. St. Louis: C.V. Mosby, 1977.

COSTELLO, D. Health communication theory and research: An overview. In B. Ruben (Ed.), *Communication yearbook I*. New Brunswick, N.J.: Transaction - International Communication Association, 1977.

DALY, M.B., & HULKA, B.S. Talking with the doctor, 2. *Journal of Communication*, 1975, 25, 148-152.

DAVIS, M.S. Variations in patients' compliance with doctors' advice: An empirical analysis of patterns of communication. *American Journal of Public Health*, 1968, 58, 275-288.

DUMAS, R.G., ANDERSON, B.J., & LEONARD, R.C. The

importance of the expressive function in preoperative preparation. In J.K. Skipper, Jr., & R.C. Leonard (Eds.), *Social interaction and patient care*. Philadelphia: Lippincott, 1965, 16-29.

EGBERT, L.D., BATTET, G.E., TURNDORF, H., & BEECHER, H.K. The value of the preoperative visit by an anesthetist. *Journal of the American Medical Association*. 1963, 185, 553-555.

EGBERT, L.D., BATTET, G.E., WELCH, C.E., & BARTLETT, M.K. Reduction of postoperative pain by encouragement and instruction of patients. *New England Journal of Medicine*, 1964, 270, 825-827.

ENELOW, A.J., & SWISHER, S.N. *Interviewing and patient care*. New York: Oxford University Press, 1972.

ENGEL, G.L. The need for a new medical model: A challenge for biomedicine. *Science*, 1977, 196, 129-136.

ENGEL, G.L., & MORGAN, W.L. *Interviewing the patient*. Philadelphia: Saunders, 1973.

FLETCHER, C.M. *Communication in medicine*. London: Nuffield Provincial Hospitals Trust, 1973.

FRANCIS, V., KORSCH, B.M., & MORRIS, M.J. Gaps in doctor-patient communication: Patients' response to medical advice. *New England Journal of Medicine*, 1969, 280, 535-540.

FREEMON, B., NEGRETE, B.F., DAVIS, M., & KORSCH, B.M. Gaps in doctor-patient communication: Doctor-patient interaction analysis. *Pediatric Research*, 1971, 5, 298-311.

FROELICH, R.E., & BISHOP, F.M. *Medical interviewing* (2nd ed.). St. Louis: Mosby, 1972.

GOLDBERG, A.A. Communication methodology. In C.E. Larson & F.E.X. Dance (Eds.), *Perspectives on communication*. Milwaukee: University of Wisconsin, 1968.

GOLDEN, J.S., & JOHNSON, G.D. Problems of distortion in doctor-patient communication. *Psychiatry in Medicine*, 1970, 1, 127-149.

GOZZI, E.K., MORRIS, M., & KORSCH, B.M. Gaps in doctor-patient communication: Implications for nursing practice. *American Journal of Nursing*, 1969, 69, 529-533.

HARLEM, O.K. *Communication in medicine*. Basel: Karger, 1977.

HEIN, E.C. *Communication in nursing practice*. Boston: Little, Brown, 1973.

HELFER, R.E., & EALY, K.F. Observations of pediatric interviewing skills. *American Journal of Diseases of Children*, 1972, 123, 556-560.

HELFER, R.E., & HESS, J. An experimental model for making objective measurements of interviewing skills. *Journal of Clinical Psychology*, 1970, 26, 327-331.

HELFER, R.E., WELL, W.B., & RYAN, M. Interviewing children. In A.J. Enelow & S.N. Swisher (Eds.), *Interviewing and patient care*. New York: Oxford University Press, 1972, 125-139.

IRETON, H.R., & CASSATA, D.M. A psychological systems review. *The Journal of Family Practice*, 1976, 3, 155-159.

JOHNSON, D.W. Communication and the inducement of cooperative behavior. In Conflicts: A critical review. *Speech Monographs*, 1974, 71, 64-78.

KIELY, W.F. Coping with severe illness. *Advances in Psychosomatic Medicine*, 1972, 8, 105-118.

KIMBALL, C.P. Medicine and dialects. *Annals of Internal Medicine*, 1971, 74, 137-139.

KORSCH, B.M., & ALEY, E.F. Pediatric interviewing technics. In *Current problems in pediatrics*. Chicago: Yearbook Medical Publishers, 1973, 1-42.

KORSCH, B.M., FREEMON, B., & NEGRETE, V.F. Practical implications of doctor-patient interaction analysis for pediatrics practice. *American Journal of Diseases of Children*, 1971, 121, 110-114.

KORSCH, B.M., GOZZI, E.K., & FRANCIS, V. Gaps in doctor-patient communication: Doctor-patient interaction and patient satisfaction. *Pediatrics*, 1968, 42, 855-871.

KORSCH, B.M., & NEGRETE, V.F. Doctor-patient communication. *Scientific American*, 1972, 227, 66-74.

KORSCH, B.M., NEGRETE, V.F., MERCER, A., & FREEMON, B. How comprehensive are well-child visits? *American Journal of Diseases of Children*, 1971, 122, 483-488.

KUBLER-ROSS, R.E. *On death and dying*. New York: Macmillan, 1969.

KUPST, M., DRESSER, K., SCHULMAN, J.L., & PAUL, M.H. Evaluation of methods to improve communication in the physician-patient relationship. *American Journal of Orthopsychiatry*, 1975, 45, 420-429.

LEWIS, G.K. *Nurse-patient communication*. Dubuque, Iowa: Brown, 1969.

LEY, P. Complaints made by hospital staff and patients: A review of the literature. *Bulletin of the British Psychological Society*, 1972a, 25, 115-150.

LEY, P. Comprehension, memory and the success of communications with the patient. *Journal for Institutional Health Education*, 1972b, 10, 23-29.

LEY, P. Primacy, rated importance and the recall of medical information. *Journal of Health and Social Behavior*, 1972c, 13, 311-317.

LEY, P. The measurement of comprehensibility. *Journal for Institutional Health Education*, 1973, 11, 17-20.

LEY, P. Towards better doctor-patient communication. In A.E. Bennett (Ed.), *Communication between doctors and patients*. New York: Oxford University Press, 1976, 77-98.

LEY, P., BRADSHAW, P.W., EAVES, D.E., & WALKER, C.M. A method for increasing patients' recall of information presented to them. *Psychological Medicine*, 1973, 3, 217-220.

LEY, P., BRADSHAW, P.W., KINCEY, J.A., & ATHERTON, S.T. Increasing patients' satisfaction with communication. *British Journal of the Society of Clinical Psychology*, 1976, 15, 403-413.

LEY, P., & SPELMAN, M.S. *Communicating with the patient*. London: Staples Press, 1967.

LITMAN, T.J. The family as a basic unit in health and medical care: A social-behavioral overview. *Social Science and Medicine*, 1974, 8, 495-519.

LYNN, E.M. Rapid change in the health care system and the increasing need for speech communication input. Paper presented at the annual meeting of the Speech Communication Association, San Francisco, 1976.

MAGUIRE, P., & RUTTER, D. Training medical students to communicate. In A.E. Bennett (Ed.), *Communication between doctors and patients*. New York: Oxford University Press, 1976, 46-74.

MARSTON, M.V. Compliance with medical regimens: A review of the literature. *Nursing Research*, 1970, 19, 312-323.

MARTIN, L.R. Liaison psychiatry and the education of the family practitioner. In R.O. Pasnau (Ed.), *Consultation-liaison psychiatry*. New York: Grune & Stratton, 1975, 285-294.

McINTOSH, J. Processes of communication, information seeking and control associated with cancer: A selective review of the literature. *Social Science and Medicine*, 1974, 8, 167-187.

MEDIA AND MEDICINE (special section). *Journal of Communication*, 1975, 25, 113-184.

MILLER, S., NUNNALLY, E.W., & WACKMAN, D.B. *Alive and awake: Improving communication in relationships*. Minneapolis: Interpersonal Communication Programs, 1975.

MITCHELL, J.H. Compliance with medical regimens: An annotated bibliography. *Health Education Monographs*, 1974, 75, (Serial No. 2 in new series).

PURTILLO, R. *The allied health professional and the patient: Techniques of effective interaction*. Philadelphia: Saunders, 1973.

RECORDON, J.P. Communication in the doctor-patient relationship. *Journal of the Royal College of General Practitioners*, 1972, 22, 818-827.

RICHARDS, N.D. Methods and effectiveness of health education: The past, present and future of social scientific involvement. *Social Science and Medicine*, 1975, 9, 141-156.

RIGG, C.A. On communicating with teenagers. *Australian Paediatrics Journal*, 1970, 6, 17-19.

SATIR, V. *Conjoint family therapy*. Palo Alto, Cal.: Science and Behavior Books, 1967.

SATIR, V. *Peoplemaking*. Palo Alto, Cal.: Science and Behavior Books, 1972.

SCHEIN, E.H. *Process consultation: Its role in organization development*. Reading, Mass.: Addison-Wesley, 1969.

SHEEHY, G. *Passages*. New York: Dutton, 1974.

SHUY, R.W. The medical interview: Problems in communication. *Primary Care*, 1976, 3, 365-386.

SKIPPER, J.D., JR., & LEONARD, R.C. (Eds.). *Social interaction and patient care*. Philadelphia: Lippincott, 1965.

SPELMAN, M.S., LEY, P., & JONES, C. How do we improve doctor-patient communications in our hospitals? *World Hospitals*, 1966, 2, 126-129.

STEPHENSON, J.R. Communication and adolescent medicine. *Clinical Pediatrics*, 1970, 9, 558-564.

STEVENSON, I. *The diagnostic interview* (2nd ed.). New York: Harper & Row, 1971.

STRAUSS, A.L. (Ed.). *Chronic illness and the quality of life*. St. Louis: Mosby, 1975.

THORNTON, B.C. Communication and health care teams. Paper presented at the annual meeting of the International Communication Association, Berlin, 1977.

TRAVELBEE, J. *Interpersonal aspects of nursing* (2nd ed.). Philadelphia: Davis, 1971.

TUMULTY, P.A. What is a clinician and what does he do? *New England Journal of Medicine*, 1970, 283, 20-24.

VINCENT, P. Factors influencing patient noncompliance: A theoretical approach. *Nursing Research*, 1971, 20, 509-516.

WAHLROOS, S. *Family communication: A guide to emotional health*. New York: Macmillan, 1974.

WAITZKIN, H., & STOECKLE, J.D. Information control and the micropolitics of health care: Summary of an ongoing research project. *Social Science and Medicine*, 1976, 10, 263-276.

WALKER, H.L. Communication and the American health care problem. *Journal of Communication*, 1973, 23, 349-360.

WATZLAWICK, P., BEAVIN, J., & JACKSON, D.D. *Pragmatics of human communication*. New York: Norton, 1967.

ZOLA, I.K. Problems of communication, diagnosis, and patient care: The interplay of patient, physician and clinic organization. *Journal of Medical Education*, 1963, 38, 829-838.

ZOLA, I.K., & McKINLAY, J.B. *Organizational issues in the delivery of health services*. New York: Prodist, 1974.

PEDIATRICIAN-PARENT COMMUNICATION: FINAL REPORT

PAUL ARNTSON *DAVID DROGE*

HARRY E. FASSL
Northwestern University

The research reported here is concerned with accurately describing doctor-parent communication in a pediatric setting, and analyzing how parental characteristics affect the nature of the interaction. Three sets of variables were used: parents' sociodemographic characteristics, categories of medical communication coded from the examinations, and the concomitant perceptions of the interactants. Five patterns of results emerged that help explain the effectiveness of medical communication.

1. A strong reciprocity norm exists for the communication of affect.
2. Parents tend to "medicalize" health problems more than doctors.
3. There is an active-passive role relationship. Doctors proportionally ask twice as many questions and make twice as many commands, while parents do not ask for explanations.
4. The higher the parents income and education, the more likely the examinations will be shorter, less symptoms discussed, and more "medical goods" delivered.
5. The more the family has a history of past illnesses, the more affective comments made by the doctors during the examinations.

INTRODUCTION

In 1975, we began studying communication between medical consumers and health care personnel in a pediatric setting. Based on the assumption that "the quality of medical care depends in the last analysis on the interaction of the patient and the doctor" (Korsch & Negrete, 1972, p. 66), our overall goal was to generate data useful in developing communication courses in premedical programs and medical schools. Of all health care delivery systems, oral communication has been the least systematically studied (Raimbault, Cachin, Limal, Eliacheff, & Rappaport, 1975). Yet it is primarily through oral communication that essential information is transferred, interpersonal trust established, and health care attitudes developed (Korsch, 1975).

The focus of our investigation was influenced strongly by the research of Davis (1968a, 1968b) and Korsch (Korsch, Gozzi, & Francis, 1968; Korsch, Freemon, & Negrete, 1971; Korsch & Negrete, 1972). These researchers examined the interrelationships between three sets of variables: the patients' sociodemographic variables, Bales' Interaction Process Analysis of the doctor-patient interactions, and the concomitant perceptions of the interactants.

We collected three sets of variables from 197 pediatrician-parent interactions. The parents' sociodemographic variables were taken from hospital records. Categories of medical communication were coded from transcriptions of the examinations. The perceptual variables came from four questionnaires. The parents responded to before-examination questionnaires, after-examination questionnaires, and phone questionnaires. The doctors filled out a short questionnaire after each examination. Our original research objectives were (1) to develop a content analysis system that would accurately describe pediatrician-parent communication; (2) to discover the interrelationships between the sociodemographic, communication, and perceptual variables; and (3) to relate the three sets of variables to the parents' satisfaction and comprehension.

Unlike previous research (Davis, 1968b; Korsch et al., 1971), we did not use compliance as an outcome variable for three reasons. First, we could not physically measure whether the parent and child had complied fully. Follow-up testing is the only reliable way to measure compliance (Davis, 1968b; Korsch et al., 1968; Harper, 1971). Second, because perceived satisfaction has been related positively to parental compliance (Francis, Korsch, & Morris, 1969), we were content to let satisfaction be an indirect measure of compliance. Third, compliance would have been an inappropriate variable for the large number of well-child examinations we analyzed.

In 1976, we reported on the project's progress. In this interim paper, we discussed the development, reliability, and utility of a system to content analyze pediatrician-parent communication, and we analyzed the interrelationships between the parents' sociodemographic variables and the parents' and doctors' perceptual variables. The present paper represents the final report for the project. We will discuss the results of the content analysis system and analyze the interrelationships between the communication variables and the sociodemographic and perceptual variables.

Because the 1976 paper provides the background for the present report, we must briefly summarize its results. The content analysis system proved to be reliable and more applicable to medical settings than Bales's system. Our category system was developed because Bales's IPA was designed primarily to assess personality characteristics through verbal behavior, was relatively content free, and was unable to show how doctors "deliver the medical goods" during examinations. Sixteen content categories emerged from listening to the examinations. The categories were organized into socioemotional, task, and procedural units. Besides coding the content of each thought unit, we also coded the form of the thought unit. Coders labelled each unit as a question, statement, command, or if explicitly answering a why question, an explanation. Interjudge reliability fluctuated around .80.

While the development and reliability of the coding system was encouraging, the frequency analysis of the sociodemographic and perceptual variables was decidedly discouraging. Only 71 out of 197 cases contained all of the medical history forms and the four questionnaires. Out of the 14 sociodemographic variables, only 9 varied enough to warrant further use. The perceptual variables for the parents and the doctors generated even worse descriptive statistics. Out of 23 patients' variables only 3 could be used. Three of the 9 doctors' variables could be used. For most of the perceptual variables, between 50% and 70% of the respondents chose the highest alternative. The most skewed variables in the study were parents' satisfaction, understanding, and confidence in the doctors—the variables of most interest. While none of the parents in the study indicated any dissatisfaction, a survey of parents who no longer use the center showed that over 20% of them were willing to indicate their dissatisfaction. Clearly, part of our sample was missing.

It is small consolation that our frequency distributions have ample precedent. Deisher, Engel, Spielholz, and Standfast (1965, p. 85) found that 98% of the 136 mothers in their survey "were very satisfied with the medical care that their children were receiving." In a recent study of mother-physician interaction by Liptak, Hulka, and Cassel (1977), only 8 out of 479 mothers indicated negative attitudes about the professional competence or personal qualities of the physician, or the cost and convenience of care. Only Korsch and her associates found any significant amount of parental dissatisfaction. Twenty-four percent of the 800 mothers were either moderately or highly dissatisfied. However, given the research setting, it is surprising that 76% of the mothers were satisfied. The study was conducted in an emergency clinic of a children's hospital. The children usually had acute illnesses or accidental injuries and were seen for a short period of time by residents unknown to the mothers. Whatever the setting, it is evident that patients respond "in a stereotyped, socially acceptable manner and only rarely express negative attitudes" about medical care (Hulka, Zyzanski, Cassel, and Thompson, 1970, p. 429).

The interrelationships of those sociodemographic and perceptual variables, whose distributions warranted further use, provided two interesting patterns of results. First, the higher the income and the more educated the parents were, the more likely they would carefully fill out the medical history forms. The number of illnesses for father, mother, child, and sibling were all significantly related to each other and to income and education levels. The higher the income and education, the more the number of illnesses reported. Researchers are getting more than a family's medical history when using medical data filled out by parents.

The second pattern of results indicated that the clinicians' communication preferences were positively correlated with the educational and income levels of the parents. Three measures of the doctors' perceptions—how well they think the parent is doing, how much they like talking to the parents, and how well they communicated with the parents—were correlated significantly with the income and educational levels of the parents. Two interesting findings that fit into this pattern are that the parents' perception of how much useful material they received was negatively correlated with education level of the father and with how much the doctor liked talking with the parent.

The results from the interim report make it necessary to alter the original research objectives. It is no longer possible to relate the sociodemographic, perceptual, and communication variables to the parents' levels of satisfaction and understanding. Given that the parents' satisfaction, understanding, and liking for the pediatricians were all positively skewed, it becomes increasingly important to accurately describe the parent-pediatrician interaction. Rarely do we find a naturalistic communication transaction that is perceived as being so successful. What is it about the actual communication that makes it so effective? We already know that the expectations of the parents and the credibility of the medical profession are important factors. Outside of a few analyses based on Bales's IPA, we know very little about the nature of the communication.

The findings from the interim report, which associated pediatricians' communication preferences to the income and education of the parents, suggest that we attempt to relate what actually happens in the examination to the parents' sociodemographic variables and the pediatricians' social perceptions.

METHOD

Subjects

The parents and children visiting the Child and Adolescent Center represent a bimodal section of the North Shore of Chicago. On an economic scale, families pay either all of their medical expenses or are subsidized by public welfare agencies. We audiotaped 197 examinations. Of that number, only 71 cases had complete sociodemographic and questionnaire data. Our sample size was reduced further by the nature of the examinations. Out of 71 examinations, 38 had sufficient audio quality to warrant transcription and analysis. Subject attrition due to incomplete data and inaudible or noisy examinations made this an expensive study. The demographic and medical data for these 38 cases compared favorably with the census tract data for the center's clients.

Design

Data were collected at several points during the parents' encounter with the center. Appropriate control groups were used to check for instrumentation and testing effects. The majority of parents were presented with a standardized questionnaire before the examination, immediately after the examination, and by phone two days later. One set of parents was questioned only after the examination and two days later. Five female and five male interviewers were used in administering the questionnaires. Each clinician was given a standardized questionnaire to fill out after every examination.

Instrumentation

Three sets of variables were collected for the project. The demographic and medical variables were taken from the Pediatric History and Pediatric Family forms given to each parent when they first started using the center. Surprisingly, very few parents filled these forms out. It took two mailings and several phone calls to get parents to send the forms back. Fourteen sociodemographic variables were taken from the forms. The 9 variables found to warrant further use were: (1) children's age in months, (2) illnesses first week, (3) illnesses first six months, (4) family income, (5) number of siblings, (6) education of mother, (7) education of father, (8) illnesses of father, and (9) illnesses of mother.

Members of the hospital's staff and researchers at the Center for Urban Affairs generated open and closed questions to be used in measuring the parents' expectations and perceptions of the examination and the clinician. Two pilot studies were conducted to improve the form and content of the questions. Many of the questions we wanted to ask did not register with the parents. Scales had to be easy to understand and weighted in the same direction. Our major difficulty was inducing variability in the parents' responses. The before, after, and phone questionnaires were constructed in order to compare the parents' expectations and perceptions to the communication behavior exhibited during the examination. Twenty-three variables were drawn from the three questionnaires. Only the two questions that asked the parents to make judgments about the doctors' perceptions had enough variability to be used. They were: "How good a job does the doctor think the parent is doing?" and "How much did the doctor like talking with the parent?"

After each examination, the clinicians filled out a brief questionnaire. The questions were designed to measure the doctors' perceptions of the children's health and the participants' communication. None of the questions from the 38 cases exhibited enough variability to be of further use.

The communication set of variables were taken from a content analysis system devised to measure the form, content, and social-emotional dimensions of the examinations. The examinations were taped, transcribed, and analyzed by one of five trained coders. Sixteen categories were organized into three subunits: social, task, and procedural. A description of each category follows.

Social

Social procedural.

1. Repetition, reaffirmation, clarification of given information—for example, "He's 2 years old."; "Two years old?"; "Really?"; "Is he?"; "Two years old."
2. Conversational regulators—statement used to extend or encourage conversation or to show understanding or lack thereof; for example, "I see"; "Right"; "Okay"; "Fine"; "Hogwash"; etc. when interspersed in another person's thought unit. They are *not* interruptions and must be complete words, which excludes sounds such as "Um Hum" "On Hunh" "Hmm" etc.

Rapport building.

3. Friendly or calming gestures—greeting and other forms of polite interchange, requests of the doctor to the child for permission to do something during the exam, promises to elicit cooperation, nonsense, non-exam related "chit chat," and anything else intended to relax or show friendship with the other person; for example, "Hello, how are you?"; "Can I look in your mouth?"; "You can have a lollipop."
4. Self-expression of concern—opportunity for or recognition of questions, worries, emotions, and so forth and the statement of worries and emotions. *Not* questions as they fall into other categories; for example, "Do you have any questions?" "Does not doing well in school bother you?"; "I'm worried about his fever."
5. Reassurance or approval—explicit seeking or giving of approval of one's own or others' actions or development; for example, "Is it normal for him to gain this much weight?"; "It was right to give him only fluids."

Tasks

6. Symptoms of health problem—actual behavioral indicators and/or physiological manifestations of health problems and also the effects that the symptoms will have and references to the problem in general; for example, eating and sleeping patterns and irritability as they indicate the nature of the problem in question, and pain, fever, vomiting, etc. "How do you feel today?"; "Where does it hurt?"; "He started vomiting last night."; "He hasn't been sleeping well since he got sick."
7. Diagnosis and inferences—based on symptoms or other nonexamination findings; for example,

"He looks like he has the flu."; "I think he has a virus."

8. Environmental factors—concerning the social and physical living environment, such as school, home, and social environments; hobbies and activities; for example, "Does he do well in school?"; "Is there peeling paint at home?"; "I ice skate everyday."; "He comes into contact with six or seven people a day."

9. Medication—pharmaceutical remedy to alleviate present health problem given for postexam use. Both prescription and nonprescription drugs are included; for example, aspirin, ear drops, and prescription medicines. "Give him 2 aspirin for fever."; "Should he have ear drops?"

10. Professional treatment—concerns treatment for health problem given by someone trained in a health care profession (shots are included in this category); for example, shots, physical therapy, etc.

11. Nonprofessional treatment—concerns treatment given at home by mother or other unskilled care; for example, restricted activity, home remedies, etc.

12. Testing—concerns tests run to gain information about health problem; for example, urine, blood, X-rays, etc.

13. Exam findings—concerns information derived from the present exam and inferences drawn from this information; for example, "I believe he has a viral infection," if said as a result of the exam. "What is wrong with him?"

Procedure

14. Physical direction—concerning movement of body or body part or sound production; for example, when the doctor asks the child to open his mouth or the parent to hold the child's hand, or when the parent tells the child to be quiet or be good.

15. Clinic or exam procedure—concerns the mechanical running of the clinic or exam; for example, "Call the clinic in 24 hours to find out the test result."; "What are the doctor's calling hours?"; "Cathy will be in in a minute to do the blood test."

16. Orientation—nonmedical background such as phone number, address, name, etc.; for example, "Who's John?"; "My address is 123 N.U. Road."

The speaker was identified for each thought unit. Thus each examination contained 16 categories for both the pediatrician and the parent. The form of the thought unit was identified by labelling the parents' and doctors' remarks as a question, statement, command, or explanation. The number of doctors' and parents' comments was counted for each examination. Finally, the total length of each interaction was computed.

Statistical Analysis

All of the analyses were descriptive in nature. Correlation coefficients were computed to examine linear relationships between variables. In all the analyses, significance levels were not as important as the magnitudes of effect. For the communication variables, zero-order correlational analysis was not appropriate. The total length of each examination confounded the correlations between the communication variables. Two methods could be used for controlling total length; neither is without its problems.

A ratio measure could be computed for each variable with total length in the denominator. While these ratio measures are intuitively understandable, they can lead to spuriously high correlations. According to McNemar (1969) and Fuguitt and Lieberson (1974), ratio variables that have a common denominator for each case may generate artificially high correlations, even when there is absolutely no relationship between the variables. Fuguitt and Lieberson suggest that partial correlational techniques are preferable to ratio measures for minimizing confounding variables.

Yet partial correlational analysis is not as intuitively understandable, nor is the technique immune from spurious findings. Blalock (1964) indicated that: "the numerical value of a correlation coefficient may be reduced not only because a confounding influence has been controlled, but it may also be altered because we have decreased the total variation in the independent variable relative to that in other causes of the dependent variable" (p. 87). Partial correlational analysis may artificially diminish measures of association based on zero-order coefficients. As the more conservative measure, partial correlational analysis was used to control for total length.

TABLE 1
Summary Proposition

Category	Parent	Doctor
1. Repetition, reaffirmation, clarification	.04	.04
2. Conversational regulators	.07	.09
3. Friendly or calming gestures	.25	.24
4. Self-expressions of concern	.03	.01
5. Reassurance or approval	.01	.03
6. Symptoms	.32	.23
7. Diagnosis and inference	.02	.02
8. Environmental factors	.10	.03
9. Medication	.04	.04
10. Professional treatment	.02	.03
11. Non-professional treatment	.03	.06
12. Testing	.02	.04
13. Exam findings	.003	.04
14. Physical direction	.02	.09
15. Clinic or exam procedure	.02	.04
16. Orientation	.01	.01
Statements	.86	.72
Questions	.12	.22
Commands	.02	.05
Explanations	.003	.01

RESULTS

The results will be reported in two sections. First, the correlations between the communication variables will be analyzed in order to describe the nature of the pediatrician-parent communication. Second, the correlations between the communication variables and sociodemographic variables will be examined in order to understand how the parents' characteristics affect the interaction. We report only those correlations that are statistically significant at alpha equals .05 one-tailed.

Communication Variables

The coding of the 38 transcripts yielded over 7,800 units of analysis, with the doctors accounting for 61.1% of the units, and the parents accounting for 38.9% of the total. The frequency distributions for the 16 categories were excellent.

The first seven tables are used in analyzing the communication variables. Table 1 contains the summary proportions for each category, Tables 2-4 show the zero-order correlation matrices of the communication variables. Because total length of the examination was significantly correlated with most of the categories, Tables 5-7 contain the first-order correlation matrices of the communication variables. Notice the differences between the zero-order and first-order correlations. While the zero-order correlations are all positive and fairly high, the significant first-order correlations are fewer, lower, and about half negative.

Three patterns of relationships emerge from these tables that are interesting and worth reporting.

1.Part of the effectiveness of the pediatrician-parent communication can be attributed to a strong reciprocity norm. Table 1 shows that the doctors and parents use the social-emotional categories in approximately the same proportions. Stronger evidence for the reciprocity norm comes from the diagonal in Table 7. The more the parents use any category, the more the doctors use the same category. The diagonal correlations are all positive, ranging from .31 to .81.

Another type of reciprocity that emerges from the data suggests that examinations may have either a social-emotional or task emphasis. Tables 5 and 6 show that an inverse relationship exists between the amount of symptoms and calming gestures for both parents and doctors. These are by far the two most frequently used categories; therefore, one might think that a negative relationship exists because of time. Yet Table 7 shows that the more one participant mentions a social-emotional category, the less the other participant mentions a task category. Consider the negative relationships between doctor and parent categories shown in Table 8.

It seems that the examinations have either a social-emotional or task tone to them that is respected by the participants. This is not to say that task and social-emotional functions are not present in every examination.

2. The parents may want to "medicalize" health problems more than the doctors. Tables 5 and 6 show that the more the doctors talk about symptoms, the more they also talk about environmental factors. The more the parents talk about

TABLE 2
Correlation Matrix—Parents' Communication Categories

	1	2	3	4	5	6	7	8	9	10	11	12	13	14	15	16
1. Repetition		.407	.471	.438		.495	.494	.359			.608		.372		.291	.301
2. Regulators					.417											
3. Calming gestures					.437	.323		.552					.349	.578		
4. Expressions of concern						.648	.456	.451			.293	.497	.282		.497	
5. Reassurance												.272				
6. Symptoms							.323	.533	.314		.301	.591	.411	.431	.582	
7. Diagnosis											.610	.455	.423	.314	.275	.390
8. Environment											.336	.534		.654	.269	
9. Medication											.361	.268	.398			
10. Professional treatment																
11. Non-professional													.441			.502
12. Testing													.270	.591	.370	
13. Exam findings														.422		.310
14. Physical direction																.268
15. Exam procedure																.383
16. Orientation																

TABLE 3
Correlation Matrix—Doctors' Communication Categories

	1	2	3	4	5	6	7	8	9	10	11	12	13	14	15	16
1. Repetition		.340	.382	.407	.325	.344	.289								.501	.449
2. Regulators				.267			.305							.429		
3. Calming gestures					.377	.357		.513				.340		.379		.309
4. Expressions of concern						.596		.567				.407		.319	.290	
5. Reassurance						.388		.307	.274			.318	.532		.323	.314
6. Symptoms								.697	.321			.447			.660	.385
7. Diagnosis											.348					
8. Environment									.343		.525				.500	.413
9. Medication													.300			
10. Professional treatment																
11. Non-professional															.294	.415
12. Testing														.271	.381	.267
13. Exam findings																.324
14. Physical direction																
15. Exam procedure																.740
16. Orientation																

TABLE 4
Correlation Matrix—Doctors' Communication with Parents' Communication

Parent	Doctor 1	2	3	4	5	6	7	8	9	10	11	12	13	14	15	16
1. Repetition	.712	.332	.465		.326	.366							.328		.481	.403
2. Regulators	.491	.696					.413									
3. Calming gestures			.754													
4. Expressions of concern	.437			.688	.468	.682		.533				.424			.427	
5. Reassurance		.307														
6. Symptoms	.316		.345	.440	.461	.905		.574	.356			.389			.613	.385
7. Diagnosis	.312				.297	.302			.356			.365	.576		.511	.472
8. Environment			.712	.502	.411	.594		.726			.283	.506		.276	.304	.307
9. Medication		-.296							.809							
10. Professional treatment										.739						
11. Non-professional	.351				.378						.516				.498	.505
12. Testing			.302	.451	.291	.630		.620	.545			.686			.416	
13. Exam findings						.278							.477			
14. Physical direction			.610			.398		.350	.456			.419				
15. Procedure	.392			.317	.282	.578		.421			.276				.631	.450
16. Orientation	.298										.500		.330		.421	.804

TABLE 5
Correlation Matrix—Parents' Communication Categories with Length Partialled Out

	1	2	3	4	5	6	7	8	9	10	11	12	13	14	15	16
1. Repetition		.352					.325	-.425			.484	-.303				
2. Regulators					.370	-.381		-.321								
3. Calming gestures				-.514	.435	-.298	-.290					-.335		.323	-.343	
4. Expressions of concern						.354	.286							-.273		
5. Reassurance						-.272										
6. Symptoms								-.344	.311	.344					.354	
7. Diagnosis								-.302			.527	.268	.319			.302
8. Environment										-.282				.300	-.291	
9. Medication												.344		.388		
10. Professional treatment																
11. Non-professional												-.301	.337			.431
12. Testing														.301		
13. Exam findings														.258		
14. Physical direction																
15. Exam procedure																.276
16. Orientation																

TABLE 6
Correlation Matrix—Doctors' Communication Categories with Length Partialled Out

	1	2	3	4	5	6	7	8	9	10	11	12	13	14	15	16
1. Repetition		.287					.264	-.359				-.263			.310	.277
2. Regulators						-.262	.289							.397		
3. Calming gestures				-.300		-.528									-.364	
4. Expressions of concern						.347		.318					-.382			
5. Reassurance													.522			
6. Symptoms								.306							.412	
7. Diagnosis											.331					
8. Environment																
9. Medication																
10. Professional treatment																
11. Non-professional																.358
12. Testing																
13. Exam findings																.275
14. Physical direction																
15. Exam procedure																.642
16. Orientation																

TABLE 7
Correlation Matrix—Doctors' Communication with Parents' Communication with Length Partialled Out

Parent	Doctor 1	2	3	4	5	6	7	8	9	10	11	12	13	14	15	16
1. Repetition	.597	.277				-.315		-.482					.282			
2. Regulators	.477	.692				-.313	.399									
3. Calming gestures			.580	-.530		-.579		-.415	-.294			-.310			-.578	-.330
4. Expressions of concern				.547		.426										
5. Reassurance		.286				-.250									-.355	-.330
6. Symptoms		-.414	-.537			.749	-.290							-.462	.317	
7. Diagnosis			-.455										.560		.367	.340
8. Environment	-.378		.271					.344							-.369	
9. Medication		-.338							.810							
10. Professional treatment										.739						
11. Non-professional			-.277								.476		.533		.343	.376
12. Testing	-.406		-.355					.282	.475	.314	-.309	.520				
13. Exam findings													.448			
14. Physical	-.298		.274						.352		-.277				-.310	
15. Exam			-.314			.347						-.282		-.392	.485	.271
16. Orientation						-.301					.464		.291		.311	.787

symptoms, the more they talk about medication and professional treatment, and the less they mention environmental factors.

3. The doctors proportionally ask twice as many questions and give twice as many commands as the parents. The doctors are clearly in control, as they are expected to be. It is unusual that the doctors give so few explanations. We believe this is because of the way the category was defined. What the extremely low amount of explanations means is that the parents did not explicitly ask for very many explanations. This finding further documents the dominant-passive role relationships between doctors and patients.

TABLE 8
Relationship Between Doctor—Parent Categories

Parent	Doctor	r
Calming gestures	Symptoms	-.579
Symptoms	Calming gestures	-.537
Calming gestures	Environment	-.415
Calming gestures	Exam procedures	-.578
Exam procedures	Calming gestures	-.314
Reassurance	Symptoms	-.250
Diagnosis	Calming gestures	-.455
Non-pro treatment	Calming gestures	-.277
Testing	Calming gestures	-.355
Calming gestures	Testing	-.310
Calming gestures	Medication	-.294

Communication and Sociodemographic Variables

Tables 9 and 10 contain the first-order correlations between the communication and sociodemographic variables. Total length was partialled out of these matrices because age, income, father's education, and the communication variables are significantly related to total length.

Two patterns of relationships emerge from Tables 9 and 10 that are worth reporting.

1. There is an experience factor among the parents that affects the communication variables. The parents with higher incomes, more education, older children, larger families, and more past family illnesses will have more experience with pediatric examinations. They will be more familiar with the medical aspects of the examination. Most of the correlations in Tables 9 and 10 document the effect of parental experience on the nature of the examination. Consider a few of the more obvious relationships:

Notice that the more experienced the parents, the less the doctors and the parents talk about symptoms or are repetitious, and the more they discuss medication and professional treatment. Since the symptoms category comprises over one-fourth of all the comments, this means that the examinations with experienced parents are shorter. The doctors can more quickly deliver the medical goods (medication and professional treatment). Our interpretations of these findings are supported by the negative correlations between the length of the examination and age (−.41), income (−.28), and fathers' education (−.40). No wonder the pediatricians enjoy talking more with parents who have higher incomes and more education.

2. Several correlations in Table 7 show that the pediatricians are sensitive to the needs of certain parents. The more past illnesses in the first week and the first six months, the more reassurance and expressions of concern given by the doctors to the parents. Table 5 also shows that there is a positive relationship between the amount of exam findings discussed by the doctor and the number of the doctor's reassurances.

Besides these findings, two correlations with the parents' perceptions of how well the doctor likes talking with them are worth noting. The more questions the doctors asked and the more symptoms the parents mentioned, the more the parents thought the doctors liked talking with them.

DISCUSSION

The results of the project have modestly increased our understanding of the doctor-parent communication process. To date, the research by Korsch and her associates remains the most thorough analysis of doctor-parent interaction. We replicated many of their findings. They found that doctors usually talked more than their patients (Freemon, Negrete, Davis, & Korsch, 1971). We found that our pediatricians talked twice as long,

TABLE 9
Correlation Matrix—Doctors' Communication Categories with Sociodemographic Variables with Length Partialled Out

	Age in Months	Illinesses First Week	Illinesses First 6 Monts	Income	Number of Siblings	Mother's Education	Father's Education	Mother's number of illinesses	Father's number of illinesses
1. Repetition	-.287								
2. Regulators									
3. Calming gestures							-.360		
4. Expressions of concern		.374							
5. Reassurance			.335						
6. Symptoms		-.275		-.272					
7. Diagnosis		.560	.331						.456
8. Environment	.600								
9. Medication			.292			.308			.312
10. Professional treatment						.337			
11. Non-professional		.589							
12. Testing									
13. Exam findings					-.341				
14. Physical direction	.446								
15. Exam procedure			.288	-.283					
16. Orientation									
Statements	.292								
Questions							-.314		
Commands	.286						-.284		.306
Explanations									

TABLE 10
Correlation Matrix—Parents' Communication Categories with Sociodemographic Variables with Length Out

	Age in Months Months	Illnesses First week	Illnesses First 6 months	Income	Number of Siblings	Mother's Education	Father's Education	Mother's number of illinesses	Father's number of illinesses
1. Repetition				-.295					
2. Regulators									
3. Calming gestures									
4. Expressions of concern									
5. Reassurance									
6. Symptoms	-.381			-.395					
7. Diagnosis									
8. Environment	.310							.336	
9. Medication									
10. Professional treatment				-.314		.306			
11. Non-professional		.294				-.429			
12. Testing						.335			
13. Exam findings									
14. Physical direction									
15. Exam procedure									
16. Orientation									
Statements	-.423						.406		
Questions									
Commands								.401	
Explanations									

TABLE 11
Doctor—Parent Relationships

The higher the	the less the
children's age	doctor's repetitions
parents' income	parents' repetitions
parents' income	doctor mentions exam procedures
children's past illness	doctor mentions symptoms
parents' income	doctor and parent mentions symptoms
mothers' education	parent mentions nonprofessional
children's age	parent mentions symptoms
number of siblings	doctor mentions exam findings

The higher the	the more the
children's age	doctor and parent mention environment
mothers' past illnesses	parent mentions environmental factors
mothers' education	doctor discusses medication
children's past illnesses	doctor discusses medication
fathers' past illnesses	doctor discusses medication
mothers' education	doctor and parent discuss professional treatment

and proportionally asked twice as many questions and gave twice as many commands as did the parents. As Davis (1968a) found, there is a predominant doctor-active/patient-passive role relationship. Using Bales's categories, Korsch reported that "gives information" was most commonly used by both physicians and mothers (Korsch & Negrete, 1972). They also found that medical history and treatment were most commonly discussed (Freemon et al., 1971). In our study, the statement form was used the most and symptoms was the largest category.

However, we also contradict several of Korsch's findings. They found that mothers expressed nearly twice as many affective statements as doctors. Proportionally, our pediatricians and parents expressed the same amount of social-emotional comments. There was a strong reciprocal affective relationship. If either participant expressed more affect, the other would respond by expressing more affect and less symptoms. The discrepancy between these findings may be explained by the settings. Pediatricians in a private practice are much more likely to interact affectively with parents than are unknown residents in an emergency clinic. We found that the pediatricians were quite aware of the affective needs of certain parents whose families had past health problems.

Korsch et al. (1968) reported that, although many mothers wish to know the cause of their children's illnesses, cause is only rarely discussed. Our results indicate that, while the pediatricians associated symptoms with environmental factors, the parents associated their children's symptoms with medication and professional treatment, rather than with environmental factors. Perhaps the residents in the clinic did not think it was their responsibility to discuss causation because they believed the parents' regular physicians would do that.

Korsch and her associates also reported that no relationship was demonstrated to exist between demographic characteristics of the parents and the communication styles of the physicians (Freemon et al., 1971). The sociodemographic variables in our study were strongly related to both length of the examination and the content. The more experienced the parents, the more likely the examination would be shorter, less symptoms would be discussed, and more "medical goods" delivered. The family's past illnesses also increased the likelihood that the physicians would use more social-emotional categories.

Even though the project has increased our understanding of pediatrician-parent communication, the research fell far short of its original goal. It is our conclusion that the kind of data needed to help develop medical communication courses must come from dysfunctional communication situations. Most medical communication is on "automatic pilot." There is no reason to think about the communication if it is functional. Many of the questions we asked the parents either did not register with them (large number of blanks), or their responses were, "of course," and they checked the highest alternative.

Another type of invariance was evident in the actual communication. There was almost an invarient process to the examinations: opening greeting, reasons for visit, symptoms/physical examination, diagnosis, treatment/medication/testing, next visit. Even in an emergency clinic, Korsch and Negrete (1972) found a highly stylized form of communication.

The problem of invariance can be avoided by selecting medical communication settings that do not solve the patients' health problems. Rimbault et al. (1975) interviewed chronically ill children and their parents. The parents were not at all reticent in showing their disatisfaction during the examination. The clinical approach used in this French research with 17 cases has been more informative than Korsch's research with over 800 cases. As a recent cancer patient, one author found that people at "Make Every Day Count" meetings were very interested in discussing the positive and negative aspects of medical communication. Before their cancers, they had taken medical communication for granted. By researching dysfunctional situational situations, data could be gathered that would be useful in improving medical communication.

Since the time of Empedocles, rhetoricians, and now communication researchers, have been trying to improve doctor-patient communication. The need for improvement has been based primarily on an intervention model of care. Given a mental or physical problem, a theraputic or medical intervention takes place that solves the problem. Improving the interventional process is clearly worthwhile. However, this process can socialize people into becoming clients of medical elites, making them feel incompetent to take care of themselves (Illich, 1976; McKnight, 1976). Improving doctor-patient communication can be disabling if the assumptions underlying the interaction are that the patient does not know what the problem is, cannot understand the problem or the solution, and cannot even decide whether the solution has dealt with the problem, while the doctor knows the problem and its solution, both of which must be dealt with in the doctor's terms (McKnight, 1976, p. 18).

These assumptions are not present in another health care model, prevention. In this model each individual and the community would have to be competent to take care of themselves. Health care would no longer be defined as a medical intervention, but as an individual and corporate physical, educational, and political activity. Our research focus has shifted to improving health communication within a preventative model of care.

REFERENCES

BLALOCK, H.M., JR. *Casual inferences in nonexperimental research*. Chapel Hill: University of North Carolina Press, 1964.

DAVIS, M. Variations in patients' compliance with doctors' advice: An empirical analysis of patterns of communication. *American Journal of Public Health*, 1968a, 58, 274-288.

DAVIS, M. Physiological, psychological, and demographic factors in patient compliance with doctors' orders. *Medical Care*, 1968b, 6, 115-122.

DEISHER, R., ENGEL, W., SPIELHOLZ, R., & STANDFAST, S. Mothers' opinions of their pediatric care. *Pediatrics*, 1965, 35, 82-90.

FRANCIS, V., KORSCH, B., & MORRIS, M. Gaps in doctor-patient communication: Patients' responses to medical advice. *New England Journal of Medicine*, 1969, 280, 535-540.

FREEMON, B., NEGRETE, V., DAVIS, M., & KORSCH, B. Gaps in doctor-patient communication: Doctor-patient interaction analysis. *Pediatric Research*, 1971, 5, 298-311.

FUGUITT, G.V., & LIEBERSON, S. Correlation of ratios or difference scores having common terms. In H.L. Cosmir (Ed.), *Sociological methodology 1973-1974*. San Francisco: Jossey-Bass, 1974.

HARPER, D. Patient follow-up of medical advice: A literature review. *Journal of Kansas Medical Society*, 1971, 72, 265-271.

HULKA, B., ZYZANSKI, S., CASSEL, J., & THOMPSON, S. Scale for the measurement of attitudes toward physicians and primary medical care. *Medical Care*, 1970, 8, 429-436.

ILLICH, I. *Medical nemesis*. New York: Random House, 1976.

KORSCH, B.M. Teaching interviewing. *Pediatrics*, 1975, 5, 305-306.

KORSCH, B., & NEGRETE, V. Doctor-patient communication. *Scientific American*, 1972, 227, 66-74.

KORSCH, B., GOZZI, E., & FRANCIS, V. Gaps in doctor-patient communication: Doctor-patient interaction and patient satisfaction. *Pediatrics*, 1968, 42, 855-871.

KORSCH, B., FREEMON, B., & NEGRETE, V. Practical implications of doctor-patient interaction analysis for pediatric practice. *American Journal of Diseases of Children*, 1971, 121, 110-114.

LIPTAK, G.S., HULKA, B.S., & CASSELL, J.C. Effectiveness of physician-mother interactions during infancy. *Pediatrics*, 1977, 60, 186-192.

McKNIGHT, J. Professionalized service and disabling help. Paper presented at the annual symposium on bioethics of the Clinical Research Institute of Montreal, Canada, 1976.

McNEMAR, Q. *Psychological statistics* (4th ed.). New York: Wiley, 1969.

RAIMBAULT, G., CACHIN, O., LIMAL, J.M., ELIACHEFF, C., & RAPPAPORT, R. Aspects of communication between patients and doctors: An analysis of the discourse in medical interviews. *Pediatrics*, 1975, 55, 401-405.

COMMUNICATOR STYLE DIFFERENCES IN FORMAL VS. INFORMAL THERAPEUTIC RELATIONSHIPS

LOYD S. PETTEGREW
Vanderbilt University

RICHARD C. THOMAS
Vanderbilt University

This paper presents the results of the second in a series of empirical investigations on communicator style in therapeutic relationships. This study focuses upon perceived therapist communicator style from the perspective of their helpees. A rationale is provided for studying potential stylistic differences between therapists in formal and informal therapeutic relationships. The nature of these two types of relationships are detailed and several research expectations are advanced. A global assessment of the interrelationships between the variables in the Therapeutic Communicator Style Measure is made. A configural comparison is performed on the TCSM variables for the formal and informal samples, and the structural reliability is confirmed by the results. Central tendency differences are assessed for each TCSM variable between test groups on both a univariate and multivariate basis. Finally, predictive relationships between the style variables and a collapsed dependent measure of positive therapeutic climate are investigated. A discussion of the results is made in light of previous research on formal and informal therapeutic relationships, and future directions for research are offered.

Interpersonal communication which has therapeutic value has existed since humans began to verbally and paraverbally relate to one another. We have evidence that therapeutic communication was a topic which held the interest of scholars during the classical rhetorical period (Zilboorg, 1941). Although therapeutic communication as a field of study and a vocational practice has undergone substantive change and refinement during the twentieth century, there remain large gaps in our knowledge and understanding of the therapeutic communication process.

One area which remains largely uncharted concerns the *structure* and *domain* of style-related variables which are operable in therapeutic relationships. Since it is the therapist whose communication with the client is the locus of social-psychological influence (Goldstein, Heller, & Secherest, 1966), it is reasonable to focus our attention on the way he or she communicates in helping relationships—the therapist's *communicator style*.

While there exists a body of research which has delved into style-related variables regarding the therapist's communication, the majority of the findings concern discrete variables studied in isolation. Even the copious findings on the style-related "essential therapeutic ingredients" have failed to incorporate a broader style perspective. To date, there has been no investigation which has taken a more *holistic* approach to the study of therapist communicator style in helping relationships. This study is the second in a series of empirical investigations designed to investigate therapist communicator style from a more holistic perspective.

Several steps are taken in the presentation of this research study. First, a rationale is presented which highlights both the theoretical perspective and the various research questions addressed in this research. Second, a detailed report of the empirical procedures used in this study is provided. Third, the results of this investigation are presented and discussed in light of characteristic differences between formal and informal therapeutic relationships detailed in the rationale. Finally, the limitations of this present study and directions for subsequent research endeavors are discussed.

RATIONALE

Previous research by the author (Pettegrew, 1977) has presented the notion that therapeutic communication is not necessarily restricted to a professional helper and client. Therapeutic communication can and does take place "whether a person seeks, in times of emotional uncomfortableness and stress, a quack, a clergy-man, a counselor, a therapist, a psychiatrist, a medical doctor, a teacher, an analyst, his buddy at the bar, or his neighbor over the back fence" (Shave, 1975, p. 108).

While Shave's characterization indicates that there are potentially a large variety of therapeutic relationships, they can all be conceptually classified as either "formal" or "informal." Formal therapeutic relationships consist of a helper who is professionally trained and monetarily compensated for his or her efforts with an identified client. Conversely, an informal therapeutic relationship consists of two individuals who assume the roles of helper and helpee in a relationship based on natural interpersonal selection out of mutual interest for each other's well being (and not professional compensation).

A second criterion by which formal and informal therapeutic relationships can be distinguished involves the degree of emotional uncomfortableness of the helpee. The formal therapist is usually confronted with a client who is more emotionally uncomfortable than helpees involved in informal relationships. This is due to the fact that the informal helping relationship represents an ongoing and successful social bond where the problems of human existence (and the resulting emotional uncomfortableness) can be resolved as they arise. As a result, the helpee is not caught up in a spiral of "communication breakdown" where the more he or she is in need of therapeutic communication the less able he or she is to establish and/or maintain it on an informal basis. The helpee in the informal therapeutic relationship, therefore, does not suffer from a buildup of emotional uncomfortableness and is not motivated to seek professional help through a formal therapeutic relationship. Shave (1975) hypothesizes that informal therapeutic relationships are consequently "less one-sided, less sustained, and less emotionally intense than a professional relationship" (p. 108).

Expectations for Helper Differences on the TCSM Variables

All interpersonal communication contains two characteristic components: report (content) and command (relationship) (Bateson, 1951, pp. 179-180; Watzlawick, Beavin, & Jackson, 1967, pp. 51-54). The command aspects of interpersonal communication act to supplement and further define how the message content should be understood. They are the multiplicity of personal behavioral actions—communication cues—which operate across specific contexts and represent the pragmatic features of all interpersonal interactions. The Communicator Style Construct (Norton, 1978) represents these command aspects in a specific, valid, and more holistic way. Thus, it serves as an adequate framework from which to investigate *how* people communicate within particular contexts like that of therapeutic communication.

The present research has utilized this construct, with certain modifications to more adequately reflect helper communicator style within the therapeutic context. Specifically, the communicator style construct has been expanded to include the Rogerian variables of *warmth, accurate empathy*, and *genuineness* (Truax & Carkhuff, 1967). While these variables are not style characteristics in and of themselves (they more closely represent emotional climates within the therapeutic transaction), they constitute elements in the therapist's communication which have proven vital to positive outcome across a broad range of therapeutic interactions (Ivey, 1971; Truax & Carkhuff, 1967). They will serve as important dependent measures in the present research.

The revised communicator style construct and measuring instrument—Therapeutic Communicator Style Measure (TCSM)—is composed of 12 independent variables (dominant, open, relaxed, attentive, dramatic, friendly, animated, contentious, impression-leaving, voice, precise, and communicator image) and 4 dependent variables (therapeutic satisfaction, accurate empathy, warmth, and genuineness). The general content of each of these TCSM variables is summarized in Appendix A.

While previous research has specified stylistic differences between a general interpersonal and therapeutic context (Pettegrew, 1977, pp. 600-602), it is reasonable to expect that there will also be stylistic differences *within* the therapeutic context itself. The criteria for distinguishing between formal and informal therapeutic relationships discussed earlier, in spite of their rather general nature, provide several substantive research expectancies regarding formal and informal helper differences. These expectations will now be detailed.

Accurate empathy and attentive. It is reasonable to expect that the therapist in formal helping relationships will be viewed by his or her client as more attentive and accurately empathic than the informal helper. Both attentiveness and accurate empathy involve receiver skills and conceptually overlap in this regard (Norton & Pettegrew, 1978). Training in these skills represents an important part of the professional therapist's vocational preparation (Ivey, 1971), and it is, therefore, reasonable to hypothesize that he or she will be able to make these skills more demonstrable during the helping encounter. Research by Martin, Carkhuff, and Berenson (1965) and Reismann and Yamokoski (1974) has revealed that professional therapists display more accurate empathy than do lay therapists in informal helping relationships.

Relaxed. It is also reasonable to expect that the helper in the formal relationship will be seen as more relaxed than his or her informal counterpart. Again, due to his or her professional training and experience with helpees who are emotionally uncomfortable, it is likely that the formal therapist will be more relaxed in his or her style—not display as much nervousness in linguistic and paralinguistic cues. Conversely, the informal helper is less frequently confronted with the helpee's problems; therapeutic interactions are less commonplace and, therefore, more likely to produce uncertainty and nervousness in the helper's communication.

Open. Although the informal therapeutic relationship represents a socially constituted bond where a broader range of interpersonal dynamics are operable, it is not clear that the helper in this relationship will be seen as more open. Especially in therapeutic relationships, openness—the helper's tendency to reveal personal feelings and information to the client—serves an important reciprocal function. Self-disclosing statements by the therapist serve to increase the amount and level of client self-disclosure (Bundza & Simonson, 1973; Jourard, 1971). In spite of the deeper, mutual friendship, both of these schools of thought advocate minimal communicative activity, and nonjudgmental responses by the therapist. Although it would be unfair to conclude that all professional helpers are equally influenced by this tradition, especially in light of newly popular confrontive techniques like "E.S.T.," it is reasonable to expect them to display less dominant and contentious behavior than helpers in informal relationships.

Impression-leaving and communicator image. These two style subconstructs concern the image the therapeutic communicator leaves on the helpee as a result of his or her helping intervention. Since helpers in both formal and informal relationships become emotionally significant transference figures to the helpee (Shave, 1974, 1975), it is doubtful that their communication will elicit significantly different impressions or images in the helpee. By virtue of the fact that therapists in both relationships assume a helping role with the client, they should also be equally evaluated as good communicators. This is perhaps a demand characteristic of the helper role; after all, one would not continue to seek therapeutic communication from a person one did not consider to be a good communicator.

Voice and precise. There is no reason to expect formal and informal helpers to differ on either the voice or precise subconstructs. The distinctiveness and loudness of one's voice is more attributable to developmental and biological differences than to professional training or the mutuality of the informal relationship. The same holds true for precise. Preciseness—requiring clear definitions and precise meanings—is an essential function in all therapeutic communication. Without it, any therapeutic communicator is burdened with ambiguity and doubt as to the helpee's problems.

Therapeutic satisfaction. In spite of the plethora of research questioning the efficacy of formal therapeutic communication (Bergin, 1971; Eysenck, 1952; Frank, 1961; Truax & Carkhuff, 1967), there is no reason to believe that helpers in formal therapeutic relationships will be seen by their clients as providing significantly less therapeutic satisfaction than their counterparts in informal relationships. The differing characteristics of each helping relationship would seem to balance out any inequities in therapeutic satisfaction. For example, although the helper in the formal relationship has the advantage of professional training and experience in providing a satisfying helping relationship for his or her client, the client is also more emotionally uncomfortable; this makes a satisfactory helping intervention more difficult to achieve. Conversely, the helper in the informal relationship has a less difficult task (with a more emotionally comfortable helpee) but lacks professional training and experience.

Friendly, warm, and genuine. There is good reason to expect that helpers in formal and informal therapeutic relationships will differ on friendliness, warmth, and genuineness. Because the informal helping relationship is mutually established and naturally constituted, it is reasonable to hypothesize that the informal helper will be seen as more friendly than the "professional friend" (Schofield, 1964). Because of this mutual friendship, the informal helper is liable to be more encouraging and willing to express admiration to the helpee than the formal therapist who does not have such a relationship with his or her client.

The Rogerian variable of warmth is closely related to the friendly subconstruct. Both concern therapist communication which serves to support and encourage the helpee. We should expect the therapist in the informal relationship to engage in more of this supportive activity because of the mutuality of the social bond. After all, the informal helper may be in need of such support from the helpee at some future date. This expectation that the helper-helpee roles will be reversed in the informal therapeutic relationship motivates the helper to provide the degree of supportive communication that he or she would desire as a helpee.

Because the helper in the formal therapeutic relationship has both a professional status and professional interest in the client, it is likely that he or she will be seen as less genuine than the informal helper. When a helper is being paid to engage in therapeutic conversations with a client, it is easier to question his or her genuineness than when the helper is a naturally selected friend and the relationship is premised on mutual concern for each other's well being. Several authors (Barnes & Berke, 1971; Cooper, 1967; Laing, 1962) suggest the pervasiveness of this relationship dynamic.

Previous Research on Types of Therapeutic Relationships

Much of the previous research purporting to analyze differences in therapist behaviors across "types" of therapeutic relationships has distinguished two major relationship types—"professional" and "paraprofessional" or "lay." Typically, therapists representing these relationship types are assessed in regard to differences on the Rogerian essential therapeutic ingredients (Gurney, 1969; Ivey, 1971; Shapiro, Kraus, & Truax, 1969; Shapiro & Voog, 1969; Truax & Silber, 1966); self-disclosure (Simonson & Bahr, 1974); and therapeutic ability (Poser, 1966).

Unfortunately, this research is not directly relevant to the concerns of the present study and is of questionable applicability to the therapeutic phenomenon itself. The professional therapeutic relationship operationalized in this body of research is comprised of a client and a professionally-trained helper. As such, it is equivalent to the formal therapeutic relationship operationalized in the present study. Problems arise, however, with the second type of therapeutic relationship. The paraprofessional or lay relationship is comprised of nonprofessionals (frequently college students) who are instructed to assume the role of a helper and helpees (strangers to these helpers who vary in their need for therapeutic intervention). This type of relationship is formed for research purposes and bears little resemblance to therapeutic relationships which occur outside of the experimental laboratory. Findings from this research body which address therapist differences between professional and paraprofessional relationships must, therefore, be treated with caution, for they do not necessarily reflect the bulk of real-life therapeutic interactions.

The present research avoids the artificially constituted paraprofessional relationship by substituting it with the informal therapeutic relationship. This operationalization is supported both theoretically and empirically, yet few studies have embraced this distinction (Martin, Carkhuff, & Berenson, 1965; Reisman & Yamokoski, 1974). While the term "lay" is used in this research to represent a nonprofessional therapeutic relationship, it is operationalized as "one friend helping another to deal with personal problems" (Reisman & Yamokoski, 1974, p. 270). It is a true life relationship instead of a therapy analogue.

Additional Research Concerns

Besides the assessment of stylistic differences between helpers in formal and informal therapeutic relationships, there are several other research questions which this study will address.

The TCSM data structure. This study will investigate the general structure of the TCSM data set, focusing on the style subconstructs which are most closely related to the Rogerian variables and therapeutic satisfaction. Currently, there is no information in the therapeutic communication literature which shows what specific therapist communicative behaviors are most strongly related to warmth, accurate empathy, and genuineness. It is reasonable to expect that both the friendly and attentive subconstructs will bare a strong relationship to these variables. The Rogerian variables should also be closely related to therapeutic satisfaction. Apart from these expectations, however, it is not clear which of the other style subconstructs will cluster with these aforementioned variables.

Structural reliability. Another important research question concerns the structural reliability of the TCSM. If the TCSM is to prove a useful measure of the command aspects of therapist communication, it is essential to assess its reliability on an ongoing basis. In order to address this question, a configural comparison will be made of the data structures representing formal and informal therapeutic relationships to see if they differ significantly.

Predictive relationships. The final research question involves the predictive relationship between the communicator style subconstructs and a combined dependent measure involving the Rogerian variables and therapeutic satisfaction. Information regarding which specific stylistic behaviors best predict "positive therapeutic climate" (the combined dependent measure) is presently lacking in the therapeutic communication literature. This information, combined with the assessment of the TCSM data structure, will provide an index of which stylistic variables are most important to the helping relationship.

EMPIRICAL PROCEDURES

Method

In order to investigate these questions, two sample populations were used. One sample represented therapists involved in formal helping relationships and the other represented therapists in informal helping relationships.

Subjects. The formal therapeutic sample consisted of 59 adults currently engaged in some type of formal helping relationship with a professional therapeutic communicator. These persons voluntarily completed the TCSM questionnaire in regard to their helper's general style of communication with them during therapeutic transactions. This sample was obtained from various outpatient psychological and counseling agencies in the San Diego and Ann Arbor areas. Psychiatrists, clinical psychologists, social workers, family counselors, and clinical psychology interns were represented in this sample. Such a diverse collection of therapeutic communicators insured a representative sample of formal therapeutic communicators.

The informal therapeutic sample consisted of 251 persons—University of Michigan and San Diego State University students enrolled in speech communication classes, and adults who were waiting at the Detroit Metro Airport. These subjects voluntarily completed the TCSM in regard to a self-designated helper. This helper was operationalized by the following instructions at the beginning of the TCSM: "Please answer the following questions in regard to that person whom

TABLE 1
Analysis of Variance for TCSM Variables in Formal vs. Informal Therapeutic Relationships

VARIABLE	F-STATISTIC	SIGNIFICANCE
Dominant	31.13	.0001*
Open	9.91	.002*
Relaxed	15.67	.0001*
Attentive	5.65	.02
Dramatic	25.59	.0001*
Friendly	16.18	.0001*
Animated	28.64	.0001*
Contentious	40.32	.0001*
Impression-leaving	7.47	.01
Voice	11.60	.0007*
Precise	1.58	.21
Communicator Image	.01	.90
Therapeutic satisfaction	5.22	.02
Accurate empathy	.37	.54
Warmth	22.21	.0001*
Genuineness	11.18	.0009*

Note: df = 1,308

*Variables meeting Dunn's multiple comparison criterion for significance.

TABLE 2
Group Means for TCSM Variables

VARIABLE	FORMAL	INFORMAL
Dominant	.47	-.11
Open	.26	-.06
Relaxed	-.34	.08
Attentive	-.19	.05
Dramatic	.42	-.10
Friendly	.32	-.07
Animated	.42	-.10
Contentious	.52	-.12
Impression-leaving	.26	-.06
Voice	.26	-.06
Precise	-.10	.02
Communicator image	.01	.00
Therapeutic satisfaction	.20	-.05
Accurate empathy	.06	-.01
Warmth	.39	-.09
Genuineness	.31	-.07

Note: All mean scores are standardized with a mean of 0 and a standard deviation of 1.0.

There is an inverse relationship between the magnitude of the score and the valence of the variable. For example, a score of -.34 on Relaxed indicates very relaxed and a score of .47 on Dominant indicates not very dominant.

you most desire to communicate with when you are feeling down, emotionally distressed, or have personal problems which need airing." None of the respondents expressed difficulty with identifying such a person.

Results

Several different statistical techniques were used to assess the research questions. A one-way analysis of variance and discriminant analysis were employed to assess central tendency differences between the formal and informal test groups on a univariate and multivariate basis, respectively.

To assess the interrelationships between the TCSM variables, two data reduction techniques were used in conjunction with each other—factor analysis and smallest space analysis.

To determine the structural reliability of the TCSM, smallest space analysis solutions were generated for the formal and informal samples. Both solutions were then submitted to PINDIS—a configural comparison routine—to determine whether the two configurations differed significantly.

Finally, a series of multiple regression analyses were performed to determine the predictive relationships between the communicator style subconstructs and the combined dependent variable for both sample populations, individually and collapsed.

Central tendency differences. In order to test for central tendency differences on the TCSM variables between the two sample populations, two different statistical analyses were performed. Univariate differences were assessed by a one-way analysis of variance.[1] Table 1 presents the results of the analysis of variance.

These results reveal differences for ten TCSM variables. Using Dunn's multiple comparison procedure to guard against trivial significance (Kirk,

1968, p. 84) an alpha level of .003 was required to insure significance at the $p<.05$ level. Dominant, open, relaxed, dramatic, friendly, animated, contentious, voice, warmth, and genuineness differed significantly between the formal and informal sample populations. Attentive, impression-leaving, communicator image, accurate empathy, and therapeutic satisfaction did not differ significantly between the sample populations on this univariate test.

The direction of these differences can be seen by examining the means for both test groups. Table 2 presents these means in standard score form. The following *tenative* characterization can be made from an inspection of Tables 1 and 2. Helpers in formal therapeutic relationships are seen as more relaxed than helpers in informal relationships. This finding is consistent with one of the aforementioned research expectations. Formal helpers, however, failed to differ from informal helpers on attentiveness or accurate empathy; these two research expectations were not confirmed by the univariate test.

Helpers in informal therapeutic relationships differed from those in formal relationships with respect to the following TCSM variables: dominant, open, dramatic, friendly, animated, contentious, voice, warmth, and genuineness. Two research expectations were confirmed by these results. Helpers in informal therapeutic relationships are seen as significantly more friendly and genuine than their professional counterparts. This is probably due to distinctive differences in the nature of a naturally occurring versus professionally motivated helping relationship.

These results must be treated with caution. Assessing central tendency differences via a simple univariate technique like analysis of variance is prone to problems of interpretability. As a general rule, the danger of getting a distorted picture of group differences tends to increase as the number of variables and the correlations between them increases (Tatsuoka, 1970, pp. 2-4). Judging from the large number of variables analyzed for central tendency differences and the relatively large correlations among many of these variables ($r>.45$), meaningful differences may not be so clear-cut as assumed in the one-way ANOVA. To gain a more representative view of group differences, a multivariate discriminant analysis was performed.

Discriminant analysis assigns weighting coefficients to all variables tested for each group. The means for these groups can then be transformed to a single (linear combination) score for each variable which has a maximum potential for discriminating between groups (Overall & Klett, 1972, p. 243). Thus, by examining the pattern of weights, one can gain a more accurate picture of the nature of group differences than when treating each variable discretely, regardless of their intercorrelations and overlapping information. Table 3 presents the variable weights for the canonical variate (discriminant function).

From the results of the discriminant analysis presented in Table 3, we are able to more accurately specify how therapists in formal helping relationships differ from those in informal relationships regarding their perceived style of communication. They differ maximally in their attentiveness and relaxedness; to a lesser (though significant) degree, they also differ in their dominance, friendliness, contentiousness, and genuineness. Returning to the means for both test groups, we discover that therapists in formal relationships are more attentive and relaxed, while their counterparts in informal helping relationships are more dominant, friendly, contentious, and genuine.

These findings more clearly support the initial research expectations, with the exception of accurate empathy, while more closely representing the complex (multivariate) nature of the TCSM construct. Since therapists in formal relationships represent professional helpers, it is reasonable to expect them to be more attuned to their clients (attentive) and more relaxed in their therapeutic efforts due to experience. Since the informal helpers are, by definition, naturally occurring significant others—friends of the helpee by mutual choice—it is likely that they will be viewed by the helpee as more friendly, genuine (not encumbered by professional status), and warm; these helpers can probably get away with being more contentious and dominant without risking a professional relationship. In other words, helpers in informal therapeutic relationships have at their disposal a wider range of communication behaviors which include

TABLE 3
Weighting Coefficients for Discriminant Analysis

VARIABLE	WEIGHTING COEFFICIENT
Dominant	.46*
Open	.34
Relaxed	-.50*
Attentive	-.87**
Dramatic	-.03
Friendly	.46*
Animated	.26
Contentious	.55*
Impression-leaving	.12
Voice	-.10
Precise	-.23
Communicator image	-.30
Therapeutic satisfaction	-.03
Accurate empathy	.29
Warmth	.69**
Genuineness	.48*

Note: The canonical correlation coefficient was .60 accounting for 36% of the canonical variate. The Mahalanobis D^2 statistic was 3.38 indicating the discriminant function was significant ($F=22.6$, $p < .00$).

** Variables providing maximum discrimination.

* Variables providing good discrimination.

TABLE 4
Principle Components and Varimax Rotation of TCSM Variables on Collapsed Therapeutic Relationships

VARIABLE	FACTOR I	FACTOR II	FACTOR III
Dominant	-.33 *-.24*	.72 *.79*	.26 *-.09*
Open	.25 *.29*	.62 *.52*	-.25 *.40*
Relaxed	.67 *.65*	-.03 *-.14*	-.18 *.20*
Attentive	.83 *.84*	-.14 *-.15*	.31 *-.30*
Dramatic	-.09 *-.03*	.71 *.68*	-.08 *.24*
Friendly	.79 *.82*	.21 *.15*	.11 *-.02*
Animated	.41 *.46*	.52 *.49*	.13 *.01*
Contentious	-.29 *-.22*	.39 *.51*	.43 *-.34*
Impression-leaving	.59 *.59*	-.02 *-.09*	-.02 *.04*
Voice	.28 *.34*	.47 *.48*	.26 *-.13*
Precise	.17 *.22*	-.01 *.14*	.73 *-.70*
Communicator image	.86 *.87*	.13 *.07*	.14 *-.06*
Therapeutic satisfaction	.84 *.83*	.00 *-.09*	.02 *.02*
Accurate empathy	.89 *.89*	-.06 *-.11*	.16 *-.13*
Warmth	.84 *.84*	.19 *.07*	-.13 *.21*
Genuineness	.79 *.79*	.05 *-.05*	-.05 *.09*
Sum of squares/ *Eigenvalue*	6.22 *6.28*	2.19 *2.22*	1.15 *1.10*
% Variance	38.9 *39.3*	52.6 *53.1*	59.8 *59.8*

*Note: Values for principal components factor analysis are represented in italics.

more aggressive dimensions. If the professional therapist becomes too aggressive or assertive, he or she risks alienating or losing the client and perhaps gaining an unfavorable reputation as a result.

TCSM data structure. Two different, complementary statistical analyses were employed to investigate the interrelationships between the TCSM variables *across* formal and informal therapeutic relationships—factor analysis and smallest space analysis. Both types of therapeutic relationships were collapsed for these structural analyses in order to gain a more global index of the variable interrelationships. Such an index, especially of the relationship between the Rogerian variables and specific stylistic behaviors, is currently lacking in the therapeutic communication literature.

Principle components factor analysis was used on the collapsed data set and the results were submitted to a varimax rotation in order to more closely obtain simple structure (Rummel, 1970). Table 4 presents the results of both the principle components factor analysis and the varimax rotation. Factor analysis revealed three major factors whose eigenvalues met the Kaiser criteria (Nunnally, 1967, p. 332).

Factor I was comprised of the following nine variables: relaxed, attentive, friendly, impression-leaving, communicator image, warmth, accurate empathy, genuineness, and therapeutic satisfaction. The composition of this factor suggests that it concerns elements which comprise *facilitative therapeutic conditions*. As indicated in the rationale, the stylistic subconstructs of attentive and friendly bear strong conceptual similarity to the Rogerian variables of accurate empathy and warmth. It is, therefore, not surprising to find that all of these variables loaded on this first factor. It is of particular interest to note that the variable of therapeutic satisfaction is also found in this first factor. Again, this is not surprising since there is both a strong empirical and conceptual tie between the essential therapeutic ingredients and positive therapeutic climate (under which therapeutic satisfaction is subsumed). Finally, impression-leaving and communicator image are also included in the first factor. We can conclude from this finding that being seen as a good communicator and leaving a strong impression on the helpee are both intergal parts of creating a facilitative therapeutic climate. This finding is supported by previous empirical research which has established a strong tie between personal impression and interpersonal attraction (Norton & Pettegrew, 1977), effectiveness and persuasability (Levitt, 1957; Truax & Carkhuff, 1967; Bergin, 1971).

Factor II is comprised of the following style subconstructs: animated, dominant, open, dramatic, and voice. These variables entail activity components in communication where the therapist assumes an expressive role in the helping interaction. This factor thus represents *communicative activity* by the therapist and appears to have little in common with those variables which constitute a facilitative therapeutic condition. Perhaps communicative activity, by itself, does not exert either a definitely positive or negative valence on the helping process and, therefore, must be mediated by the ambiance of the variables in Factor I. This finding is important because it adds a new perspective to previous research on therapist expressive behaviors (Gladstein, 1974; LaCrosse, 1975; Rice, 1965; Strong, Taylor, Bratton, & Loper, 1971). While expressive behaviors do seem to supplement or orchestrate the therapist's communication, such cues do not themselves influence the valence of the therapeutic climate. Rather, they must be seen as compliments to more therapeutically related behaviors such as attentiveness and friendliness.

Factor III is problematic and, therefore, of questionable utility in understanding how communicator style variables function in helping relationships. While the principle components solution reveals only the precise subconstruct as loading on Factor III, the varimax rotation process forces the contentious subconstruct out of the second factor and into the third. Considering the fact that this subconstruct still loads highly on both Factors II and III, it is not clear that contentious belongs with precise in the third factor. Considering the small amount of variance accounted for by this factor, its conceptual utility must be seriously questioned. Perhaps Factor III could be seen with more conceptual clarity as a demand dimension of communicative activity (Factor II) despite its orthogonal status in factor analysis. In other words, the precise and contentious subconstructs might be reasonably considered as a particular aspect of more general communicative activity—demanding or imparing.

Smallest space analysis. An equally valid way of analyzing the interrelationships between the TCSM variables is through smallest space analysis. Like factor analysis, smallest space analysis (SSA) is a data reduction technique. SSA, however, is a *nonmetric* multidimensional scaling technique whose object is to map a set of variables or objects into a set of points in metric space (Lingoes, 1973). In so doing, it accurately reflects the underlying organic relationship within a variable set. The closer the variables are mapped together, the stronger is their relationship. Figure 1 represents the SSA-I solution for the collapsed TCSM data set.

SSA-I outputs a *goodness-of-fit* measure which allows one to determine the adequate number of dimensions in which a data set can be accurately described. As a general rule, a Guttman-Lingoes Coefficient of Alienation of .15 or smaller indicates that the dimensionality used in the solution is sufficient to accurately represent the data structure.

The TCSM data set was accurately represented in two dimensions (G-L coefficient of alienation = .09). Looking at Figure 1, the variables represented by Factor I form a reasonably tight cluster—indicating a close interrelationship. The variables in Factor II form a somewhat looser cluster in the SSA-I solution but still show an interrelationship which is distinctly different from those in Factor I. It is informative to note that the contentious subcontract falls into the second cluster (Factor II) and appears to have little in common with the precise subconstruct.

Precise falls midway between the first two clusters in the SSA-I solution. Although this provides supplemental support for its presence in Factor III, it also indicates that this factor is of limited conceptual utility as a one-variable factor and that the

FIGURE 1
Smallest Space Analysis of Collapsed Communicator Style and Therapeutic Variables

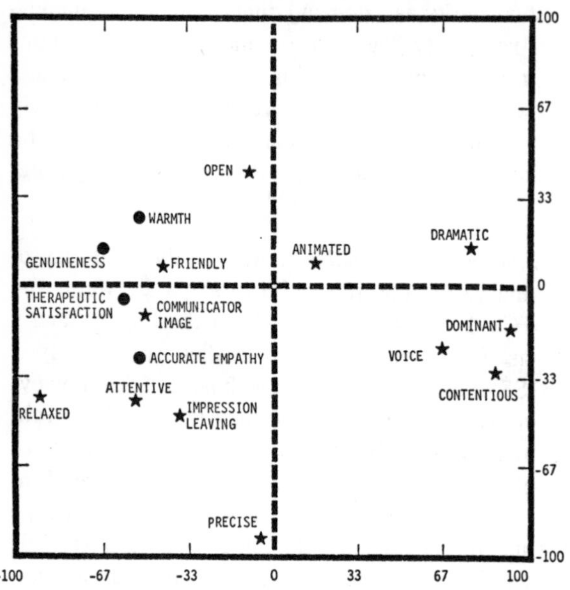

loading of the contentious subconstruct on the third factor was an artifact of the varimax forced rotation. It is probably most informative to consider the TCSM data set as represented by two distinct, yet substantive clusters or factors—facilitative therapeutic conditions and communicative activity—with the precise subconstruct bearing an equally distinct relationship to both factors.

Configural comparisons. A second research question involves possible differences in the TCSM data structure between formal and informal therapeutic relationships. More precisely put, regardless of any central tendency differences between the sample populations for the TCSM variables, do the interrelationships among the variables for the two sample populations differ in any meaningful way? This question is one way of assessing the structural reliability of the TCSM.

To answer this question, two separate SSA-I solutions were generated for the respective sample populations. These solutions were then submitted to a subroutine of smallest space analysis—PINDIS. PINDIS (Lingoes, 1973) compares data configurations by expanding and rotating both solutions to obtain the best possible fit. Once an optimal fit has been achieved, the program outputs a correlation coefficient for each dimension of the two solutions, as well as a measure of goodness of fit.

TABLE 5
Multiple Regression Analysis for TCSM Variables on Positive Therapeutic Climate by Relationship Type

Relationship Type	Best Predictors	β	T-Stat.	Significance
FORMAL	Communicator Image	.44	5.34	.0001
	Attentive	.33	3.33	.002
	Animated	.21	2.66	.01
	Impression-leaving	.12	2.27	.03
INFORMAL	Communicator Image	.24	5.30	.0001
	Impression-leaving	.18	5.00	.0001
	Attentive	.17	4.01	.0001
	Friendly	.19	3.74	.0002
	Dominant	-.14	-3.60	.0004
COMBINED	Impression-Leaving	.27	5.65	.0001
	Communicator Image	.31	4.83	.0001
	Friendly	.20	2.88	.004
	Dominant	-.15	-2.75	.01
	Attentive	.12	2.00	.05

The results of PINDIS showed the TCSM data sets representing formal and informal therapeutic relationships to be correlated r = .98 along the first dimension and r = .92 along the second dimension. The goodness-of-fit measure (G-L coefficient of alienation = .10) indicates that the PINDIS joint solution caused very little stress on the two original configurations. We can conclude from these results that the interrelationships between the TCSM variables are very similar for therapists representing both formal and informal therapeutic relationships. This also provides a good indication that the TCSM possesses good structural reliability—the data structure is stable across different sample populations.

Predictive relationships. The final research question concerns the predictive relationship between the communicator style subconstructs and the dependent measure. For this answer to possess optimal utility and reliability, the dependent measure was transformed. It was assumed that since the Rogerian variables are generally regarded as essential therapeutic ingredients which have been empirically demonstrated to be strongly related to positive therapeutic outcome (Truax & Carkhuff, 1967), a more stable dependent measure would entail a combination of these three variables with the therapeutic satisfaction variable. This transformation also has the advantage of avoiding multicollinearity in regression analysis.[2] Because the mean correlation of the Rogerian variables and therapeutic satisfaction is high ($r = .59$), the presence of the Rogerian variables as independent measures in the regression equation would inflate the standard errors of the regression coefficients and cause the coefficients to become unstable (Gordon, 1968, p. 596).

The resultant dependent measure for the regression analysis is termed "positive therapeutic climate"—the extent to which the helpee views the helper as warm, empathic, genuine, and providing a satisfying therapeutic relationship.

To test the predictive relationship between the communicator style subconstructs and the dependent measure of positive therapeutic climate, three separate multiple regression analyses were performed. The first analysis involved the combined test groups. This provides a global index of the predictive relationship between the style subconstructs. Table 5 presents the regression weights in this analysis. Five style subconstructs: dominant, attentive, friendly, impression-leaving, and communicator image, entered the regression equation to a statistically significant degree.

Two additional multiple regression analyses were performed on the formal and informal populations. Table 5 also presents the regression weights for these analyses. For the formal therapeutic communicator sample, communicator image, attentive, animated, and impression-leaving emerge as the best predictors of positive therapeutic conditions.[3] Communicator image, impression-leaving, attentive, friendly, and dominant are the best predictors for the informal therapeutic communicators.

It is important to note the consistent emergence of several style subconstructs as the best predictors of positive therapeutic climate across the three regression analyses. These subconstructs are communicator image, impression-leaving, and attentive. This finding is consistent with the information gained from SSA-I; these three subconstructs were most closely related to the individual components of the dependent measure. We can tenatively conclude from this analysis that the highly regarded therapeutic communicator is the one who projects a positive, impressionable image of himself or herself and, at the same time, is attentive to the communication and feelings of the helpee. While this finding does not bear directly on the prediction of successful therapeutic outcome, it is reasonable to speculate that communicative styles which best predict and are highly correlated with the helpee's positive evaluation of the therapeutic conditions will ultimately help foster positive change in the helpee as well.

DISCUSSION AND CONCLUSIONS

Several conclusions emerge from this study. First, there are several communicator style subconstructs which bear a strong relationship to the Rogerian essential therapeutic ingredients and therapeutic satisfaction. These subconstructs are friendly, attentive, relaxed, impression-leaving, and communicator image. Together they form a homogeneous cluster or factor which can be characterized as facilitative therapeutic conditions. This conclusion is supported by both the close intercorrelations between the variables and independent research concerning each individual variable. For example, the three Rogerian variables have been referred to as essential therapeutic ingredients (Truax & Carkhuff, 1967) and the style subconstructs of friendly and attentive bear a close conceptual and empirical tie to them. Additionally, work by Ivey (1971) and Shave (1974, 1975) suggests that attentive therapist behavior is vital to successful therapeutic communication. Research by Linden, Stone, and Shertzer (1965) indicates that a "comfortable therapeutic climate" is important to therapeutic success. Therapist behavior which is relaxed can be thought to contribute greatly to this climate. Finally, the therapist who leaves a strong impression on his or her client and projects a good image as a communicator will also contribute to facilitative therapeutic conditions. This is probably due to the fact that such behavior signals the competence of the helper and promotes the client's confidence in the therapist's ability to provide help.

One other major cluster of style subconstructs emerged which seems unrelated to the first. All of the subconstructs in this cluster concern specific types of activity in the therapist's communication. It is reasonable to characterize this cluster as communicative activity. It is important to note that these activities are not directly related to those communicative ingredients which directly facilitate therapeutic work. This finding mediates some of the research which has suggested a direct link between therapist behavioral cues and therapeutic climate (LaCrosse, 1975; Rice, 1965; Strong, Taylor, Bratton, & Loper, 1971).

The second conclusion which emerges from this study concerns the structural reliability of TCSM. The configural comparison analysis indicated that the interrelationships between the TCSM variables are stable across independent samples of therapeutic communicators. Subsequent research can now proceed with confidence in the reliability of the measuring instrument.

The third conclusion involves a partial confirmation of *a priori* research expectations. Specifically, helpers in informal therapeutic relationships were seen by their helpees as significantly more friendly and genuine than formal helpers. This is probably a function of their friendship bond, which is the result of natural social selection and is mutually formed. Informal helpers were also seen as significantly more dominant and contentious. This may be due to the fact that the helpee holds a greater latitude of acceptable behavior for the informal helper, while assertive or argumentative behavior from formal helpers might jeopardize their professional relationship with the client.

Therapists in formal helping relationships were viewed by their clients as significantly more attentive and relaxed. While the attentive subconstruct did not prove significant in the univariate analysis of variance, the discriminant analysis clearly showed it to be the best discriminator between the two test populations. Both of these findings support the research expectation. The variable of accurate empathy, however, did not differ significantly. While this finding is inconsistent with the initial research expectation, it probably indicates that attentiveness is only one of several parts of accurate empathy, and that the other parts are equally evoked by helpers in both formal and informal therapeutic relationships. In other words, while the formal therapist may be significantly more attentive, neither formal nor informal therapists differ in their sensitivities to the helpee's feelings and emotions. As Shapiro and Voog (1969, p. 509) indicated, accurate empathy is a fundamental characteristic of the inherently helpful person (informal therapeutic communicator); he or she shares this trait with the professional therapist.

Finally, several communicator style subconstructs emerge (across therapists in formal and informal relationships) as the best predictors of positive therapeutic climate. They are attentive, communicator image, and impression-leaving. This finding suggests that the helper who is able to provide a positive therapeutic climate for his or her clients (one in which the helpee will stand the greatest chance of positive change) communicates in such a way that he or she leaves a strong impression as a good communicator on the client and is capable of providing sufficient feedback to the client so that he or she knows the therapist is constantly with him or her.

It is also interesting to note that the friendly subconstruct failed to enter the regression equation for the formal therapeutic relationship sample. Perhaps the client implicitly knows that the therapist's interest in him or her is of a professional nature and is, therefore, less concerned with the therapist providing friendly cues during the helping interaction. The presence of the friendly subconstruct in the informal and combined regression equations, however, indicates that supportive and reinforcing cues are of considerable importance in many therapeutic transactions.

Finally, the relaxed subconstruct failed to enter any of the regression equations in spite of its close structural relationship with the dependent measures. We can speculate that being relaxed (absence of nervous mannerisms) acts only in a supplemental way to reinforce the positive therapeutic climate created by the positive image the helper projects and the attentive cues which he or she provides.

Limitations

There are several limitations to this study which must be articulated. First, the results of this research are only representative of therapists in general. The fact that individual therapists probably differ from this characterization does not diminish the value of the present findings; correlational research, like that presently under consideration, seeks to identify group similarities and test for differences between these broad sample groups. After general patterns have been identified and relative weights assigned to the importance of each style subconstruct, individual differences can be investigated with more confidence through experimental design.

Second, the fact that clients involved in formal therapeutic relationships are probably more emotionally uncomfortable and are experiencing a greater degree of transference with their helper than the informal helpee might serve to bias their evaluation of him or her. Although the researchers feel that such a biasing effect will be lessened by the fairly large sample size from a variety of therapeutic agencies and the expectation that extreme positive and negative conditions of client ambivalence will balance each other out, it is important to recognize the possibility of this bias. Further study, experimentally controlling the degree of client dysfunction or uncomfortableness, is certainly warranted.

The third limitation concerns the source of data. The present study used the perspective of the client or helpee to evaluate the therapist's style of communication. While this perspective is vital to complete understanding of how therapists communicate during helping interactions, it is also important to consider the therapist's own perspective. In so doing, the researchers will be better able to address the degree of congruence between these two perspectives, as well as gain a more stable index of therapist communicator style. The present study represents an important step toward this end.

NOTES

1. Although the researchers had no expectations regarding sex differences for the TCSM variables, a one-way ANOVA was performed to determine if such differences did exist. The results of this analysis indicated that there were, in fact, no sex differences for any of the TCSM variables. This is not surprising since communicator style is more likely to vary as a function of the individual, rather than sex differences for therapeutic communicators.
2. The research move of combining the Rogerian variables with therapeutic satisfaction is open to criticism. One might argue that this move tends to "contaminate" a relatively pure dependent measure of therapeutic satisfaction with other variables which may be only tangentially related. To assess this possibility, an MCA analysis was performed. The MCA analysis is a form of regression analysis using dummy variables; it has the capacity to show the effect of each predictor on the dependent variable both before and after taking into account the effects of all other variables (Andrews, Morgan, Sonquist, & Klem, 1973). An MCA on just therapeutic satisfaction indicated that the Rogerian variables accounted for 37% of the variance in therapeutic satisfaction in an additive regression model and 28% (genuineness), 19% (warmth), and 16% (accurate empathy) individually. There appears to be considerable justification in combining these variables into a collapsed dependent measure which capitalizes on their conceptual closeness and avoids problems with multicollinearity.
3. The issue of multicollinearity also arose in regard to the independent measures of friendly and attentive in the regression analyses. Friendly failed to enter the equation with statistical significance while attentive did. Since these variables are highly correlated, there was a possibility of multicollinearity affecting the results. An independent regression analysis was performed partialing out attentiveness. Friendly still did not enter the equation.

REFERENCES

ANDREWS, F.M., MORGAN, J.N., SONQUIST, J.A., & KLEM, L. *Multiple classification analysis: A report on a computer program for multiple regression using categorial predictors*. Ann Arbor, Mich.: Institute for Social Research, 1973.

BARNES, M., & BERKE, J. *Two accounts of a journey through madness*. New York: Ballantine, 1971.

BATESON, G. Information and codification: A philosophical approach. In J. Ruesch & G. Bateson, *Communication: The social matrix of psychiatry*. New York: Norton, 1951.

BERGIN, A.E. The evaluation of therapeutic outcomes. In A.E. Bergin & S.L. Garfield (Eds.), *Handbook of psychotherapy and behavior change: An empirical analysis*. New York: Wiley, 1971.

BUNDZA, K., & SIMONSON, N. Therapist self-disclosure: Its effects on impressions of therapist and willingness to disclose. *Psychotherapy: Theory, Research, and Practice*. 1973, 10, 215-217.

COOPER, D. *Psychiatry and anti-psychiatry*. New York: Ballantine, 1967.
EYSENCK, H.J. The effects of psychotherapy: An evaluation. *Journal of Consulting Psychology*, 1952, 16, 319-324.
FRANK, J. *Persuasion and healing*. New York: Schocken, 1961.
GLADSTEIN, G.A. Nonverbal communication and counseling/psychotherapy. *The Counseling Psychologist*, 1974, 4, 34-57.
GOLDSTEIN, A.P., HELLER, K., & SECHEREST, L. *Psychotherapy and the psychology of behavior change*. New York: Wiley, 1966.
GORDEN, R.A. Issues in multiple regression. *American Journal of Sociology*, 1968, 73, 592-616.
GURNEY, B.G. *Psychotherapeutic agents: New roles for nonprofessionals, parents, and teachers*. New York: Holt, Rinehart & Winston, 1969.
IVEY, A.E. *Microcounseling: Innovations in interviewing training*. Springfield, Ill.: Thomas, 1971.
JOURARD, S. *Self-disclosure: An experimental analysis of the transparent self*. New York: Wiley, 1971.
KIRK, R.E. *Experimental design: Procedures for the behavioral sciences*. Belmont, Cal.: Brooks-Cole, 1968.
LaCROSSE, M.B. Nonverbal behavior and perceived counselor attractiveness and persuasiveness. *Journal of Counseling Psychology*, 1975, 22, 563-566.
LAING, R.D. *The divided self*. Baltimore: Pantheon, 1962.
LEVITT, E.E. The results of psychotherapy with children: An evaluation. *Journal of Consulting Psychology*, 1957, 21, 189-196.
LINDEN, J., STONE, S., & SHERTZER, B. Development and evaluation of an inventory for rating counseling. *Personnel and Guidance Journal*, 1965, 44, 267-276.
LINGOES, J. *The Guttman-Lingoes nonmetric program series*. Ann Arbor, Mich.: Mathesis Press, 1973.
MARTIN, J.C., CARKHUFF, R.R., & BERENSON, B.G. A study of counseling and friendship. Unpublished manuscript, University of Massachusetts, 1965.
NORTON, R.W. Foundations of a communicator style construct. *Human Communication Research*, 1978, 4, 99-112.
NORTON, R.W., & PETTEGREW, L.S. Attentiveness as a style of communication. *Communication Monographs*, 1978, in press.
NORTON, R.W., & PETTEGREW, L.S. Communicator style as an effect determinant of attraction. *Communication Research: An International Quarterly,* 1977, 4, 257-282.
NUNNALLY, J. *Psychometric theory*. New York: McGraw-Hill, 1967.
OVERALL, J.E. & KLETT, C.J. Applied multivariate analysis. New York: McGraw-Hill, 1972.
PETTEGREW, L.S. An investigation of therapeutic communicator style. In B. Ruben (Ed.), *Communication yearbook*, I. New Brunswick, N.J.: Transaction-International Communication Association, 1977, 593-604.
POSER, E.G. The effect of therapists' training on group therapeutic outcome. *Journal of Counseling Psychology*, 1966, 30, 283-289.
REISMAN, J.M., & YAMOKOSKI, T. Psychotherapy and friendship: An analysis of the communication of friends. *Journal of Counseling Psychology*, 1974, 21, 269-273.
RICE, L.N. Therapist's style of participation and case outcome. *Journal of Consulting Psychology*, 1965, 29, 155-160.
RUMMEL, R.J. *Applied factor analysis*. Evanston, Ill.: Northwestern University Press, 1970.
SCHOFIELD, W. *Psychotherapy: The purchase of friendship*. Englewood Cliffs, N.J.: Prentice-Hall, 1964.
SHAPIRO, J.G., KRAUSS, H.H., & TRUAX, C.B. Therapeutic conditions and disclosure beyond the therapeutic encounter. *Journal of Consulting Psychology*, 1969, 16, 290-294.
SHAPIRO, J.G., & VOOG, T. Effects of the inherently helpful person on student academic achievement. *Journal of Consulting Psychology*, 1969, 16, 505-509.
SHAVE, D.W. *Communication breakdown: Cause and cure*. St. Louis, Mo.: Green, 1975.
SHAVE, D.W. *The therapeutic listener*. Huntington, N.Y.: Krieger, 1974.
SIMONSON, N.R., & BAHR, S. Self-disclosure by the professional and paraprofessional therapist. *Journal of Consulting and Clinical Psychology*, 1974, 42, 359-363.
STRONG, S.R., TAYLOR, R.G., BRATTON, J.C., & LOPER, R.G. Nonverbal behavior and perceived counselor characteristics. *Journal of Counseling Psychology*, 1971, 18, 554-561.
TATSUOKA, M.M. Discriminant analysis. In *Selected topics in advanced statistics* No. 6. Champaign, Ill.: The Institute for Personality and Ability Testing, 1970.
TRUAX, C.B. & CARKHUFF, R.R. *Toward effective counseling and psychotherapy*. Chicago: Aldine, 1967.
TRUAX, C.B., & SILBER, L.D. Personality and psychotherapeutic skills. Unpublished manuscript, University of Arkansas, 1966.
WATZLAWICK, P., BEAVIN, J.H., & JACKSON, D.D. *Pragmatics of human communication*. New York: Norton, 1967.
ZILBOORG, G. *A history of medical psychology*. New York: Norton, 1941.

APPENDIX A

TCSM VARIABLE DESCRIPTIONS

DOMINANT - This refers to the tendency to dominate therapeutic conversations—coming on strong and taking complete charge of things, speaking *very* frequently.

OPEN - This refers to how open you are as a communicator—whether you readily reveal personal things about yourself or openly express feelings and emotions.

RELAXED - This refers to how relaxed you are in therapy—whether you reveal any nervous mannerisms or are very calm and collected in your communication.

ATTENTIVE - This refers to how attentive you are to your client by encouraging him/her, listening carefully and deliberately reacting in such a way that they know they are being listened to.

DRAMATIC - This refers to how verbally alive you are—whether you exaggerate to stress a point, have picturesque speech or vocally act out what you are meaning.

FRIENDLY - This refers to whether you demonstrate kindly interest and goodwill toward your client without being hostile.

ANIMATED - This refers to how nonverbally active you are in your communication—whether you actively use facial expressions, gestures, and eye-contact.

CONTENTIOUS - This refers to how argumentative you are with your client—the extent to which you take issue with your client's opinions.

IMPRESSION-LEAVING - This refers to the impression you leave on your client as a communicator—whether what you say and do in therapy leaves a lasting impression.

VOICE - This refers to how loud and distinctive your voice is in therapy.

PRECISE - This refers to how precise your content of communication is in therapy and how accurate you insist on both you and your client's conversation to be.

COMMUNICATOR IMAGE - This refers to how good a communicator you are—whether you find it easy to talk on a one-to-one basis, maintain the conversation in nearly every encounter with your client.

THERAPEUTIC SATISFACTION - This refers to how helpful your client deems your therapeutic conversation—how much better he/she feels after talking with you and how lost he/she would feel without your help.

ACCURATE EMPATHY - This refers to how able you are to clarify and expand on your client's feelings—how accurately aware you are of his/her emotions and feelings.

WARMTH - This refers to how well you communicate deep interest, a warm attitude, and nonthreatening environment to your client.

GENUINENESS - This refers to your ability to come across as nonphony and nondefensive—always being yourself in your conversations with your client.

HEALTH CARE TEAMS AND MULTIMETHODOLOGICAL RESEARCH

B. C. THORNTON
University of Nevada

This study of health care teams used a multimethodological approach. Participant observation and interaction analysis results described the faculty and student health care teams at a university where health care was delivered to clients. The composite data base consisted of six student and three faculty health teams and 12,540 acts.

Conclusions were that a multimethodological approach provides rich data but that time and financial restraints must be considered in designing such studies. The methodologies proved to be useful descriptive tools, in that the participant observation provided a general perspective of the team program as well as information on incidents considered critical by the observer and participants. The interaction analysis supplied more objective data on the communication patterns that developed around the general systems variables of source of information, time orientation, information assembly rules, and equivocality reduction. Implications were suggested for small group research and more specifically for applications to health care teams.

THE PRESENT RESEARCH

One of the new models of health is the health or patient care team, a type of small group. Research on such health teams is minimal and it will be the purpose of this study to utilize multimethodological approaches to describe health care team communication in general systems and communication terminology. This study took place in a field setting (a university) rather than in a laboratory, and it is processually oriented.

A review of the literature on health teams has been presented elsewhere (Thornton, 1976). That review indicated that much health team research stressed the importance of communication in the health team. Research regarding communication and health teams however was sparse.

This present study did not attempt to predict the success of health care teams and it was limited to descriptions of team communication in the Family Health Maintenance Program at a university which utilizes the team concept for clinical training and family primary health care.

A general assumption of this study is that health care teams are no longer an experimental concept. They are a reality. The question became how to empirically describe this reality so that hypotheses could eventually be generated for research on the health care model. In order to discuss the research, a few definitions need to be given.

A *team* is a group with a purpose, the accomplishment of which requires interdependent and collaborative efforts of its members. A group of physicians sharing an office, each with his own patients, sharing only costs and staff, does not fit the team definition; whereas, a team working in the operating room would. "Teamness" is synergy; that is, the result of the team is more than a mere addition of the sum of its parts.

A *health care team* is defined by Boufford and Kindig (Wise, Beckhard, Rubin, & Kyte, 1974) as "a group of health workers who must work interdependently to accomplish a task" (p. 150). Although there are many compositions of health care teams, the teams for this research project consisted of a physician, a nurse, a medical technologist, and a social worker. The clinical assistants were also limited participants in the teams. The phrase "health care team" will be used synonymously with patient care team in the sense that both terms define a group of professionals, semiprofessionals and nonprofessionals who interact interdependently to provide needed services that bring them into direct personal and physical contact with the patient.

DESCRIPTION OF THE RESEARCH SETTING AND APPLICATION OF THE METHODOLOGIES

The university studied has a two-year medical school with a health science division. Awarded money by the Robert Wood Johnson Foundation to implement and study health care teams, the division began the team program in 1974. Teaching faculty were recruited to become voluntary role-modeling members of a team, and students were enlisted from the second year of medical school and the senior year of the social work, nursing, and medical technology programs to be on the student teams. The students were given university credit for the experience and were able to use the clinical health team setting to further their technical skills. In the semester in which this research was conducted, there were three faculty teams and six student teams. Each faculty team supervised two student teams.

The clients or the families were recruited by friends, faculty, and sometimes by the students themselves. The research project occurred over a five-month period and involved all participants in comprehensive health care known as the Family Health Maintenance Program.

The purpose of the program was to attempt to integrate students in the health-related disciplines in an effort to provide more efficient care for the client (patient), as well as to increase the job-related satisfactions of the professional health care deliverer. The rationale for the use of the health team model as a real alternative to traditional health care is provided in another paper (Thornton, 1976).

As stated previously, the intent of this research was to study the communication behavior of health care teams through a multimethodological approach. The constraints of the approach were evident: using more than one method is time consuming, costly and often takes more research personnel than are available. A combination of the methods of interaction analysis and participant observation, however, has several advantages. The interaction analysis provided an objective method of looking at the communication behavior of groups, i.e., the health care teams. These behaviors can be analyzed and described in various ways according to the interaction analysis scheme used. Interaction analysis allows the diversity of analyzing groups separately or, as in the case of this study, it provides a means to pool the team matrices into a composite in order to provide a large data sample. Additionally, participant observation allows a macro view of the research universe while interaction analysis provides the micro view.

AN OVERVIEW OF PARTICIPANT OBSERVATION

Participant observation, used initially in the field of anthropology, has in recent years become a major way to study interaction. Goffman (1974) uses this method as a way to organize experience. By joining a group, sharing in the life activities of the membership, and observing the group from that framework, the observer has a way (even though imperfect) of getting some conception of group synergy—a more overall perspective than can be reached from more limited experience. McCall and Simmons (1969) provide a major overview of important participant observation research studies. Advocates of the participant observation method also indicate the advantages of observing a group throughout its history to get some conception of the group's synergy. Further importance comes in allowing the researcher to develop theory while observing, and to use more than one theory in the same project.

Lofland (1971, p. vii) stresses the importance of this kind of qualitative research, noting that it ranks among the major research strategies of sociologists and other social sciences. Some examples of participant observation research on health care teams include Lashoff (1968), Brunetto and Burke (1972), Eichhorn (1973), and Wise et al. (1974).

The Application of Participation Observation in this Study

The participant observers in this study consisted of two researchers who worked in the team clinical setting. These persons attended all of the meetings of the student and faculty health care teams and any other relevant meetings or functions. The observers had a functional role with the team. Their responsibilities consisted of supplying the equipment and of helping both the teams and their clients keep track of appointments. This role was necessary and independent of the research. The observers looked for process and patterns in terms of acts, activity, meanings, participation, relationships, and settings (Lofland, 1971). Initially, all clients and team members were told about the participant observation and the interaction analysis.

Results of the participant observation and interaction analysis resulted in a composite description of the health care teams. The teams were described under the headings of leadership, roles, norms, and environmental and physical restraints. Results of the communication patterns as established under these variables were discussed. Selected participant observation results are presented in the composite description of health team interaction presented later in this paper.

OVERVIEW OF INTERACTION ANALYSIS AND THE SIPA SYSTEM

The essential characteristics of interaction analysis are mutually exclusive categories which (1) are content free, (2) act as units of measurement, and (3) provide the interstructuring of sequential events during group interaction (Fisher, 1974). The unit of analysis can be the act, interact, double interact or triple interact (see Table 1 for examples).

Methods of interaction analysis vary primarily in terms of the categories and the unit of measurement. Bales's (1950a, 1950b) pioneering system was based on task and social problems of the group and a single thought was the unit of analysis. The Amidon and Flanders system (Amidon & Hough, 1967) used primarily for classroom categorization, used time units of from three to five seconds. Crowell and Scheidel (1961) were interested in the acts related to the development of ideas, and their unit was a single thought. In recent years, interaction analysis has changed conceptually. Communication scholars and researchers have often looked at interacts and higher orders of communication in a general systems theory perspective. Some examples are Weick (1969), Mark (1971), Hawes (1972), Hawes and Foley (1973), Ellis and Fisher (1975), Mabry (1975), Rogers and Farace (1975), and Fisher, Glover, and Ellis (1977). The distinction between the content and relationship aspects of communication was clarified by Watzlawick, Beavin, & Jackson (1967). For this research project on health teams, an analytical system which processes content information at the level of the system rather than the individual was used. The SIPA (Social Information Processing Analysis) uses an utterance as the unit of analysis and contains the following four mutually exclusive and exhaustive dimensions $SIPA_1$, Source of Information; $SIPA_2$, Time Orientation; $SIPA_3$ Information Assembly Rules; and $SIPA_4$, Equivocality Reduction. The SIPA system was developed by Fisher, Drecksel, and Werbel (in press).

Reliability among coders was established according to the formula devised by Guetzkow (1950) for coding qualitative data. There were three pairs of raters. Results exceeded the .80 criterion ($p < .01$) on the first two dimensions and between .70 and .80 ($p < .01$) on dimensions 3 and 4.

The data was placed on computer matrices. A composite of both student and faculty teams was then analyzed for interaction patterns.

Results of Interaction Analysis

The final results of the interaction analysis application were based on a large data base. The student composite data base consisted of 11,174 acts from the six student teams. The faculty data base consisted of 1,366 acts from two faculty teams. The total data base was 12,540 acts. Each of these acts was coded four times on each of the four dimensions of SIPA, thus requiring 50,160 coding decisions. That is, they were coded for source of information ($SIPA_1$), time orientation ($SIPA_2$), information assembly rules ($SIPA_3$), and equivocality reduction ($SIPA_4$). In the initial stages of data analysis, the decision was made to study the composite teams at the interact level.

The double interact was found to be impractical for this research project, as the size of the matrix increases geometrically as complexity increases.

TABLE 1
Description of Interaction Sequences

Interaction Sequence	Description	Numerical Examples
Act	Each sentence is an act. All interacts, double interacts and triple interacts are a combination of acts. A speaks	-1-
Interact	An interact is a pair of contiguous acts: A speaks B speaks	1-2
Double Interact	A double interact is three contiguous acts: A speaks B speaks A speaks	1-2-1
Triple Interact	A triple interact contains four contiguous acts: A speaks B speaks A speaks B speaks	1-2-1-2

Dimension 4 of SIPA at the triple interact level requires a 7×7×7×7 matrix, or a total of 2401 cells. Therefore, the triple interact matrices were not analyzed, for even with the extremely large student data sample there were too many zero cells, and interaction was distributed too widely throughout the matrix.

The stereotypy statistic was utilized. It is an information statistic which employs an analysis of removal of uncertainty based on transitional probabilities from one state to another, in terms of redundancy or sequential patterning which is stereotypy. It is useful for the present study because it allows comparison of data of varying amounts (Miller & Frick, 1949, pp. 311-324). Stereotypy ranges from 0 to 1.0. It is cumulative, so that at one level of complexity the measured structure inherently contains within it all the structure contributed at each lower level; that is, stereotypy for double interacts will always be larger than for the interacts.

Stereotypy is described by Quastler (1955), Attneave (1959), and Garner (1962) and is summarized by Fisher, et al. (1977, p. 234). Derived from information theory, stereotypy is a measure of structure, sometimes called the C-function in information theory (Quastler, 1955, p. 90). It ranges from a minimum of 0 (randomness) to 1.0 (absolute predictability and absence of complexity).

Table 2 compares the health teams with decision-making and family groups (Fisher, et al. 1977). It indicates variations of stereotypy within the SIPA dimensions when these groups are compared to the health teams. The decision-making and family groups show higher structure on dimensions 1 and 2 of SIPA, and lower structure on dimensions 3 and 4 than the health teams. Details of the three group comparison appear on Table 2.

While stereotypy appears to be a very useful statistical device to describe the patterning that exists in a communication system, it is impossible

TABLE 2
Stereotypy Comparisons for Health Teams and Other Small Groups

Dimensions of SIPA	Families		Decision Making Groups		Student Health Teams		Faculty Health Teams	
	Interact	Double Interact	Interact	Double Interact	Interact	Double Interact	Interact	Double Interact
$SPIA_1$	.412	.425	.457	.487	.227	.276	.228	.256
$SIPA_2$	.456	.472	.442	.470	.213	.242	.147	.176
$SIPA_3$	.064	.080	.074	.091	.165	.175	.111	.119
$SIPA_4$	.181	.215	.154	.186	.256	.272	.313	.348

The information on family and decision making groups is adapted with permission from an article, 'The Nature of Complex Communication Systems" by B. Aubrey Fisher, Thomas W. Glover and Donald G. Ellis, Communication Monographs, 1977, 44, p. 237.

to indicate what is the "ideal" range of stereotypy in a team or small group. Only after a larger data base of studies is generated will a researcher be able to make hypotheses regarding structure for different kinds of groups. Furthermore, absolute structure (1.0) would indicate absolute predictability. Again, system principles indicate such a group would be uninteresting and repetitive, as well as bordering on being a closed system subject to entropy (Kuhn, 1975, p. 117).

$SIPA_1$—Source of Information

As indicated previously, SIPA is an attempt to indicate where information patterns originate in the group. This dimension of SIPA describes the communication patterns among the individual, the group, the immediate environing system, and the larger external environment.

An assumption of systems theory is that a group can only be observed in relation to its next highest level of environing system (Weick, 1969, pp. 27-29). Therefore, to understand the health team it is important to determine the group's source of information.

Table 3 represents the stereotypy calculated for each matrix for both composite teams on each dimension of SIPA. It duplicates part of the information in Table 2. Structure for $SIPA_1$ is .227 at the interact level and .276 at the double interact level for the student teams. The faculty interact stereotypy was .228 and .256 for the double interact.

Table 4 is a compilation of all the structured cells from the $SIPA_1$ (source of information) faculty and student composite matrices. The structured cell tables show cells which indicate structure, i.e., frequencies exceeding equiprobability (chance). The cells which are starred also indicate that while exceeding equiprobable frequency the cell does not have significant transitional probability to be analyzed for structure. The transitional probability indicates the probability of a cell's subsequent act following an antecedent act. To show structure, the transitional probability is computed for each cell of the matrix and then the transitional probability is computed for each individual matrix and each dimension. In $SIPA_1$, cells are considered significant which have a transitional probability of .25 or beyond (which is the equiprobable transition probability for the four categories of acts as contained in this dimension). The asterisk indicates the cells which do not have this transitional probability. The transitional probability is calculated for each matrix, so the asterisk should be rechecked by the reader for each structure table.

An analysis of Table 4 in the source of informa-

TABLE 3
Stereotypy for Health Care Teams

Dimensions of SIPA	Students Interact	Students Double Interact	Faculty Interact	Faculty Double Interact
$SIPA_1$	.227	.276	.228	.256
$SIPA_2$	.213	.242	.147	.176
$SIPA_3$	.165	.175	.111	.119
$SIPA_4$	.256	.272	.313	.348

tion dimension ($SIPA_1$) shows that group interactions center around "2" which is the group category of the $SIPA_1$ dimension. These group comments intermingle with individual or introspective, and immediate environment comments. This is apparent for both the student and the faculty teams. Both groups energized themselves by focusing information processing inward and the information exchanged with the environment was generally restricted to the groups, although there is some indication that the faculty when not interacting in group cycles did move to the immediate environing system. This is shown in Table 4 by the way that "2" and "3" comments pattern together. No cells which exceed equiprobability and transitional probability, however, indicate any faculty communication patterns with the larger environment. Analysis of the student teams shows that they did reach into the larger environment for information by the patterns involving "4's" in the double interact matrix of Table 4.

To summarize the results of the source of information dimension ($SIPA_1$), the matrices indicated that the faculty team obtained its information individually or from the group with some interaction occurring from immediate environment information. Groups that do not interact with the environment to a large extent are considered closed systems, and the faculty patterning on this dimension would indicate that they were certainly more "closed" than the students.

The students obtained their information from all four states: individual, group, immediate and larger environments.

$SIPA_2$—Time Orientation

Time orientation is considered to be crucial to the understanding of small groups (McGrath & Altman, 1966, p. 73). The assumption of this dimension of the SIPA system is that time helps the group to orient its current experience in terms of the multiplicity of past and future experiences. All time is seen in terms of the present. The work of Kolaja (1969, p. 9) on one-layer present and two-layer present provides the basis for the category. The states of the time dimension are (1) past to present, (2) present to present, (3) future to present, and (4) timeless present. The latter category refers to universal principles.

The stereotypy for $SIPA_2$ (Table 3) indicates some variation on structure. The student interact for the dimension has a composite stereotypy of .213, while the faculty interact has a low

TABLE 4
Structured Cell Table Indicating Cells Beyond Equiprobable Occurrence for SIPA₁ (Source of information dimension) +

	Composite Faculty	Composite Students
Interact	1-2 2-1* 2-2 2-3 3-2 2-3	1-2 2-1* 2-2 2-3* 3-2
Double Interact	1-2-1* 1-2-2 1-3-2 1-3-3 2-1-1* 2-1-2 2-2-1* 2-2-2 2-2-3 2-3-1* 2-3-2 2-3-3 3-1-2 3-1-3 3-2-2 3-2-3 3-3-1* 3-3-2 3-3-3	1-1-2 1-2-1 1-2-2 2-1-1 2-1-2 2-2-1 2-2-2 2-2-3* 2-2-4* 2-3-2 2-3-3 2-4-2 3-2-2 3-2-3 3-3-2 3-3-3 4-2-2 4-2-4

+Numbers in this table represent following states of the Source of Information Dimension:

1. Individual
2. Group System
3. Immediate Environing System
4. Environment

*A cell with a frequency exceeding equiprobability but which has a transitional proability of less than .25 on $SIPA_1$.

stereotypy of .147. The double interact of $SIPA_2$ for students is .242 while the double interact for the faculty is .176. This would indicate that there was very little patterning or structure of communication patterns for the faculty team on this dimension, particularly at the interact level.

Table 5 summarizes the structured cells for the students and the faculty. What is particularly interesting is the way that the faculty uses the third or future-to-present state of the time orientation dimension, which is the goal-oriented or predictive category. Faculty communication frequently consisted of sequences which involved the future-to-present interacting with the present-to-present or timeless present (universal category). The student patterns did not indicate this. Student sequences consisted of present-to-present comments cycling with past-to-present information or timeless present information.

In summary, the time orientation interactions of the faculty showed future-to-present or goal-oriented interaction, whereas the students did not. The students emphasized interaction which cycled with the present and sometimes the past.

TABLE 5
Structured Cell Table Indicating Cells Beyond Equiprobable Occurrence for $SIPA_2$ (Time orientation dimension) +

	Composite Faculty	Composite Students
Interact	1-2 2-2 2-3* 3-2 3-3	1-2 2-1* 2-2 2-4 4-2 4-4
Double Interact	1-1-1 1-1-2 1-2-1 1-2-2 2-1-1* 2-1-2 2-2-1* 2-2-2 2-2-3* 2-2-4* 2-3-2 2-3-3* 2-4-2 3-2-2 3-2-3 3-3-2 4-2-2 4-2-4 4-4-2	1-1-2 1-2-1 1-2-2 2-1-1* 2-1-2 2-2-1* 2-2-2 2-2-3* 2-2-4* 2-3-2 2-4-2 2-4-4 4-2-2 4-2-4 4-4-2 4-4-4

+ Numbers in this table represent the following states of the Time Dimension:

1. Past-to-Present
2. Present-to-Present
3. Future-to-Present
4. Timeless Present

*A cell with a frequency exceeding equiprobility but which has a transitional probability of less than .25 on $SIPA_2$.

$SIPA_3$—Information Assembly Rules

This category was adapted from the work of Weick (1969) who argued that assembly rules were the means by which the degree of equivocality was registered accurately in any process. The purpose of this dimension is to discover how and in what manner information is assembled with other information. This dimension categorizes as follows: (1) generation of additional information, (2) comparison with other information, and (3) reaction without additional information.

The stereotypy for $SIPA_3$ (Table 3) indicates much less structure than the other categories. As stated previously, while higher stereotypy does not indicate significance, it is expected that it will be similar within the dimensions of an interaction analysis schema. Fisher, Glover, and Ellis (1977)

TABLE 6
Structured Cell Table Indicating Cells Beyond Equiprobable Occurrence for SIPA₃ (Information assembly rule dimension)

	Composite Faculty Team	Composite Student Team
Interact	1-1 1-2* 2-1 3-1	1-1 1-3* 3-1
Double Interact	1-1-1 1-1-2* 1-1-3* 1-2-1 1-2-2* 1-3-1 2-1-1 1-1-2* 2-2-1 3-1-1	1-1-1 1-1-2* 1-1-3* 1-2-1 1-3-1 2-1-1 3-1-1

+ Numbers in this table represent the following states of the Information Assembly Rule Dimension:

1. Generation of Additional Information
2. Comparison with other information
3. Reaction without additional information

* A cell which is beyond equiprobability but which has a transitional probability of less than .33.

have already indicated that such low structure on this dimension might indicate it generates little information about communication structure and should possibly be discarded.

In this dimension, the structured patterns of student and faculty health care teams were similar as shown in Table 6. Wherever information was generated, the faculty team and students processed this information by generating additional information, as can be seen by the cells ending in "1's."

In summary, $SIPA_3$, information assembly rules analysis, exhibits low structure; however, the faculty and students show similar patterns of generating additional information with additional information. Comparison or reaction patterns are usually followed with more generation of information.

$SIPA_4$–Equivocality Reduction

The equivocality reduction dimension was also devised from the work of Weick (1969, p. 40). It seeks to give information on the organizational function of removing equivocality from the information environment. This dimension seeks to reveal the process of equivocality reduction, not to measure the equivocality reduced (Fisher, 1975). It is a scalar system ranging from the most to the least equivocality reduction. The scales are as follows: (1) clear-cut statement with support, (2) clear-cut statement, (3) reducing number of interpretations, (4) maintenance of equivocality, (5) adding another interpretation (move uncertain), (6) provides several interpretations, and (7) open-ended.

Analysis of the data for this dimension of equivocality reduction at the interact and the double interact level is complex. The interact matrix has 49 cells and the double interact has 343 (7×7×7 matrix) cells.

From the 11,352 acts analyzed in the seven categories of this dimension, it is interesting that only 170 acts were in category 3 (reducing the number of interpretations) and only 75 were in category 7 (the open-ended category of $SIPA_4$ where such comments as, "Where do we go from here?" are coded).

A return to Table 3 and a review of stereotypy indicates that student stereotypy on the composite interact matrix was .256 and the faculty was .313. Double interact stereotypy is .272 for the students and .348 for the faculty. This indicates that faculty structure on this dimension was not only higher than the students but higher than any other faculty or student stereotypy for any of the dimensions of SIPA, which indicates a highly structured pattern of attempts to reduce equivocality on the faculty teams. A summary of this dimension indicates that for both the faculty and student teams, patterns to reduce equivocality were prominent.

Table 7, the structured cell table for $SIPA_4$, displays the patterns of equivocality reduction which were similar for the student and faculty teams. Antecedent comments which indicated equivocality ("4's" or "5's") interacted with comments to reduce equivocality (with the lower numbers such as "1" or "2"). For example, cell "4-5-1" indicates that an antecedent comment maintaining equivocality when followed by a subsequent comment adding another interpretation was followed by a clear cut statement with support; an attempt to reduce the equivocality.

MULTIMETHODOLOGICAL RESULTS AND IMPLICATIONS

In this section the findings of interaction analysis and participant observation will be discussed in terms of leadership, roles, and norm setting, as well as environmental constraints.

Much of the health team literature overemphasizes the issue of leadership on the team. While leadership in any group is important, this strong focus in terms of the health team seems to arise from the interest in finding out what happens when you put a high-status professional (the doctor) in a more egalitarian setting. As Kane (1975, p. 5) indicates, one of the reasons health care teams are advocated by allied health professions is because it is in this setting that other disciplines can share leadership and decision making with the doctor. However, previous research does not indicate a preference for either the integrative leadership model where the doctor is always the leader or the coordinate pattern where decision-making and leadership are shared (Kane, 1975, p. 58).

In the present health team research project, the participant observation results indicated that both the integrative and the coordinate leadership models were successful. In fact, the two student teams that typified the extremes of these models met the faculty criteria of task accomplishment and team member satisfaction. In the successfully functioning teams, the combination pattern which both types of leadership had was their ability to reduce equivocality (Weick, 1969, pp. 99-101). The interaction analysis results confirmed the general pattern of equivocality reduction for the composite teams (see Table 7). This suggests that research in the future should look at the leader's potential for reducing equivocality as one indication of effectiveness.

Hage (1974) correlates roles, status, and communication in an organization by analyzing the interaction in a hospital setting and reviewing network theory. Hage's main thesis is that cybernetic (or controlled) organizations use sanctions and high feedback with socialization in order to maintain control. His contention is that the more complex an organization, the greater the need for high communication to achieve feedback because of the status differences that are generated. The problem for an organization becomes one of providing for functional roles that provide the system with high feedback. Weick (1969, p. 98) contends that it is

TABLE 7
Structured Cell Table Indicating Cells Beyond Equiprobable Occurrence for SIPA$_4$ (Equivocality reduction dimension) +

	Composite Faculty	Composite Students
Interact	1-2 1-4 2-1* 2-2 2-4 2-5* 2-6* 4-1* 4-2 4-4 4-2 5-4 6-2	1-2 2-1* 2-2 2-4 2-5* 2-6 4-2 4-4 4-5* 5-2 5-4 6-2
Double Interact	1-2-2 1-4-1 1-4-2 1-4-4 1-5-2 1-6-1 1-6-2 2-1-1* 2-1-2 2-1-4 2-1-5* 2-1-6* 2-2-1* 2-2-2 2-2-4 2-2-5* 2-2-6 2-2-7 2-4-1* 2-4-2 2-4-4* 2-4-5* 2-4-6* 2-5-1* 2-5-2 2-5-4 2-6-1 2-6-2 2-6-4 2-7-2 4-1-1* 4-1-2 4-1-4 4-1-5 4-2-1* 4-2-2 4-2-4 4-2-5 4-2-6* 4-4-2 4-4-4 4-5-1 4-5-2 4-5-4 4-6-1 4-6-2 5-1-2 5-2-1* 5-2-2 5-2-4 5-2-5* 5-2-6* 5-4-1* 5-4-2 5-4-5 5-6-2 6-1-1 6-1-2 6-2-1* 6-2-2 6-2-4 6-2-5* 6-2-6* 7-2-2	1-1-2 1-2-1 1-2-2 1-2-4 1-2-5* 1-2-6* 1-4-2 1-4-4 1-5-2 1-5-4 1-6-1 1-6-2 2-1-1* 2-1-2 2-1-4 2-1-5* 2-1-6* 2-2-1* 2-2-2 2-2-4 2-2-5* 2-2-6* 2-4-1* 2-4-2 2-4-4 2-4-5* 2-4-6* 2-5-1* 2-5-2 2-5-3* 2-5-4 2-5-5* 2-5-6* 2-6-1* 2-6-2 2-6-4* 2-6-6* 4-1-2 4-1-4 4-2-1* 4-2-2 4-2-4 4-2-5* 4-4-6* 4-5-2 4-5-4 4-6-2 4-6-4 5-1-2 5-1-5 5-2-1* 5-2-2 5-2-4 5-2-5 5-2-6* 5-3-5 5-4-2 5-4-4 5-4-5 5-4-6 5-5-2 5-6-2 6-1-2 6-2-1* 6-2-2 6-2-4 6-2-5 6-2-6 6-4-2 6-4-6

+ Numbers in this table represent the following states of the Equivocality Reduction Dimension:

1. Clear-cut statement with support
2. Clear-cut statement
3. Reducing number of interpretations
4. Maintenance of equivocality
5. Adding another interpretation (more uncertain)
6. Provides several interpretations
7. Open-ended

* A cell which is beyond equiprobability but which has a transitional probability of less than .14.

important to study network and role relationships in order to understand the interlocked behavior patterns that are the key to the understanding of an organization. Further, it is through the reduction of equivocality that roles are established, understood, and enacted. The conclusion implied from these general systems analyses, as well as from this current research project, is that rigid role definition is not as important for group functioning as the establishment of patterns of communication which stress high feedback that is generated within the organization (equivocality reduction). In terms of the health care teams, the participant observation reports indicated that there was role confusion which did influence the communication process. Participant observation findings indicated that role anxiety and rigidity began to occur when the director of the health team research program insisted that faculty teams who supervised students should be individual closed systems. In order to function, a system must have contact with the immediate and larger environment, meaning that on a team there must be communication patterns that diffuse beyond the group. The interaction analysis, as well as the participant observation findings, indicated that the original dictates of keeping parts of the program separate particularly influenced the communication of the faculty health care teams, so that role clarity was not easily obtained. In the $SIPA_1$ dimension, source of information, the faculty had no significant communication patterns which involved the outside environment, making it difficult to obtain feedback on their roles. A functional role is also enhanced in a group that has procedures for reducing the equivocality about roles as well as other issues (Weick, 1969, pp. 98-99). In this regard, both the faculty and student teams did attempt equivocality reduction as mentioned previously in regard to the interaction analysis.

Whereas leadership and roles are interrelated through such systems devices as environmental constraints and equivocality reduction, so is norm setting. On one of the teams for example, an incident was related regarding the manner in which the faculty social worker established the norm of self-disclosure and communication about sensitive issues such as sexuality. The initial insistence of the faculty social worker that the teams confront intimate and sensitive issues was an example of Weick's (1969, pp. 43-53) interlocked behavior process, wherein essential cycles are established by groups which set norms and then utilize these norms in their communication patterns. The observers also noted that tension seemed to reduce in the groups after these norms had been set, probably a consequence of reduced equivocality. The norm of the faculty was to deal with the group and within the group on communication patterns. The norm for the students was to deal with the immediate and outer environment, as well as with the group itself. The findings of the participant observation indicated that neither faculty teams, with the exception of a collective of faculty members that never became a team, were particularly closed systems in terms of norm settings. However, individuals in the faculty groups did, by their behavior, set norms which in turn affected student behavior.

HUERISTIC IMPLICATIONS FOR COMMUNICATION AND HEALTH TEAM RESEARCH

Perusal of the communication literature does not indicate many studies using a multimethodological base. The intention of this research project was to provide an empirical way of looking at communication on health care teams using the more subjective (though empirically designed) participant observation and the objective and qualitatively detailed interaction analysis. Since data are always lost in using a methodology, using more than one method compensates for this loss. It is hoped that this approach will be used more frequently in communication research. While using two methods is time consuming and expensive, it is particularly useful when there is no empirical data base on which to build a research project. Although there have been many studies on health care teams, few have been empirical, as indicated by Kane (1975).

Communication research which is processually oriented should not be generalized to the larger universe. Findings for the health care teams in this study do not apply to all small groups. Nevertheless, some provocative studies are suggested by the conclusions. For example, it would be enlightening for small group research to find out if task-oriented groups, other than health care teams, develop patterns (as did the student teams in this study) of going from the individual to the group system and then to the larger environment on the source of information dimension. It was only during the last phases of the group that patterning indicated the group was dealing with its more immediate (and more threatening?) environment. More studies on this dimension would have implications, as does this study in a limited manner, for systems research.

The time orientation results described interesting patterns of time orientation for the health care teams. The finding for the student teams was that structure or patterning revolved around the present-to-present time state, which is one of the characteristics of an intensive group or a more encounter-like group (Werbel et al., 1974). Weick (1969) indicates that a decision-making group should understand planning in the future perfect tense. "It isn't the plan that gives coherence to actions. Coherence comes from the fact that when the act to be accomplished is projected in the future perfect tense, the means for accomplishing the act become explicit, and the actions run off with greater coherence" (p. 102). Are these two findings diametrically opposed? Can an effective health team focus on the here-and-now and yet be an effective decision-making group? At this point, participant observation provides useful data. Groups that were observed with present-to-present patterns were the most "team oriented," however, groups that were future-to-present oriented (the faculty groups) were able to make decisions more readily. Therefore, it would be interesting to attempt health care or task group training which would enable groups to establish an early phasic pattern that is present-to-present oriented but which can change as the group develops to the future-to-present dimension of goal orientation.

As noted previously, the information assembly rule category gave little useful description. A study by Ellis and Fisher (1975) suggests the importance of understanding information assembly rules for the study of small group conflict, in order to understand how a group assembles information. However if this information is to be obtained from $SIPA_3$, the category should be redesigned to provide this information.

The dimension on equivocality reduction has intriguing implications for future research. Fisher et al. (1977) have suggested that this dimension would be interesting to study at the triple interact level if a functional way could be found to deal with the unusually large matrices. In the meantime, it does indicate interesting scalar information on equivocality reduction.

DISCUSSION OF THE RESEARCH PROCESS

As indicated, this was a long and costly study expected to be the data basis for longitudinal studies on health care teams. Because there were many people involved in all stages of the research, care was taken to preserve the accuracy of the data. One of the interesting findings in this area, however, was that even skilled typists have difficulty transcribing the tapes of group interaction. A review of a tape and of a transcript indicated that the typist was inadvertently ignoring the comments of children when they were interacting with a team. In the future, health teams should be isolated from other interaction for transcription purposes while participant observers are utilized to observe how the team interacts with the faculty, the clients, and others.

One of the major findings of this study was that the depth or focus of significant events is not indicated in the interaction analysis transcripts. It was only through the perceptions of the observer that critical incidents could be judged. Future research should consider use of participant observation and of the critical incident technique (Herzberg, Mausner, & Snyderman, 1959) on members of health teams so the ex post facto analysis of the data could analyze whether participants' views as to what was important to the interaction process correlated with the more objective interaction analysis.

For those who read this research report in terms of training health care teams, there are many implications. The first of these is that "time" should be given consideration, that is, time in the sense of duration as well as in the sense of the time dimension used in $SIPA_2$. If teams are to work effectively, they must be given time to do so. If they are going to interact with clients in a productive way for themselves and for the clients, they must have time to achieve "teamness," whatever that means for a particular team. Not only should time be used wisely, but students and faculty should learn to understand time in a general systems perspective (Brodey, 1969).

The results indicate that students want and need more training in group processes, but again time becomes a main consideration for students and faculty. Teams need time to reflect, and so they should be given only minimally necessary material for their effectual functioning.

In order to train and study health teams in terms of providing an "ideal" model, systems and communication theory principles should be utilized and goals for the teams should be manageable (Kane, 1975, pp. 64-71). It is possible that several alternative health team models will be seen as ideal.

The conclusion of this paper is that health teams are a potentially rich source for small group research. The results of well designed and carried out research on these teams could provide useful information to the communication and health care fields.

REFERENCES

AMIDON, E.J., & HOUGH, J.B. (Eds.). *Interaction analysis: Theory, research and application*. Reading, Mass.: Addison-Wesley, 1967.

ATTNEAVE, F. *Applications of information theory to psychology*. New York: Holt, Rinehart & Winston, 1959.

BALES, R.F. *Interaction process analysis*. Cambridge, Mass.: Addison-Wesley, 1950a.

BALES, R.F. A set of categories for the analyses of small group interaction. *American Sociological Review*, 1950b, 15, 181-187.

BRODEY, W.M. Information exchange in the time domain. In W. Gray, F.J. Duhl, & N.D. Rizzo (Eds.), *General systems theory and psychiatry*. Boston: Little, Brown, 1969.

BRUNETTO, E., & BIRK, P. The primary care nurse—the generalist in a structured health care team. *American Journal of Public Health*, 1972, 62, 785-794.

CROWELL, L., & SCHEIDEL, T.M. Categories for analyses of development in discussion groups. *Journal of Social Psychology*, 1961, 54, 155-168.

EICHHORN, S. *Becoming: The evaluation of five student health teams*. Institute for Health Team Development, 1973.

ELLIS, D.G., & FISHER, B.A. Phases of conflict in small group development: A Markov analysis. *Human Communication Research*, 1975, 1, 195-212.

FISHER, B.A. *Small group decision-making: Communication and the group process*. New York: McGraw-Hill, 1974.

FISHER, B.A. Communication study in system perspective. In B.D. Ruben & J.Y. Kim (Eds.), *General systems theory and human communication*. Rochelle Park, N.J.: Hayden, 1975.

FISHER, B.A., GLOVER, T.W., & ELLIS, D.G. The nature of complex communication systems. *Communication Monographs*, 1977, 44, 231-240.

FISHER, B.A., DRECKSEL, L., & WERBEL, W. Social information processing analyses (SIPA): Coding ongoing human communication. In *Small group behavior*, in press.

GARNER, W.R. *Uncertainty and structure as psychological concepts*. New York: Wiley, 1962.

GOFFMAN, I. *Frame analysis*. New York: Doubleday, 1974.

GUETZKOW, H. Unitizing and categorizing problems in coding qualitative data. *Journal of Clinical Psychology*, 1950, 6, 47-58.

HAGE, J. *Communication organization and control: Cybernetics in health and welfare settings*. New York: Wiley, 1974.

HAWES, L.C. The effects of interview style on patterns of dyadic communication. *Speech Monographs*, 1972, 39, 4-23.

HAWES, L.C., & FOLEY, J.M. A Markov analysis of interview communication. *Speech Monographs*, 1973, 40, 208-219.

HERZBERG, F., MAUSNER, B., & SNYDERMAN, B.B. *The motivation to work* (2nd ed.). New York: Wiley, 1959.

KANE, R.A. *Interprofessional teamwork*. Manpower monograph No. 8, Syracuse, N.Y.: Division of Continuing Education and Manpower Development, Syracuse University, 1975.

KOLAJA, J. *Social system and time and space*, Pittsburgh, Pa.: Duquesne University Press, 1969.

KUHN, A. Social organization. In B.D. Ruben & J.Y. Kim (Eds.), *General systems theory and human communication*. Rochelle Park, N.J.: Hayden, 1975.

LASHOFF, J.C. The health care team in the mile square area, Chicago. *Bulletin New York Academy of Medicine*, 1968, 44, 1363-1369.

LOFLAND, J. *Analyzing social settings*. Belmont, Cal.: Wadsworth, 1971.

MABRY, E.A. Sequential structure of interaction in encounter groups. *Human Communication Research*, 1975, 1, 302-307.

MARK, R.A. Coding communication at the relationship level. *Journal of Communication*, 1971, 21, 221-232.

McCALL, G.J., & SIMMONS, J.L. *Issues in participant observation: A text and reader*. Reading, Mass.: Addison-Wesley, 1969.

McGRATH, J., & ALTMAN, I. *Small group research: Synthesis and critique of the field*. New York: Holt, Rinehart & Winston, 1966.

MILLER, G.H., & FRICK, F.C. Statistical behavioristics and sequences of responses. *Psychological Review*, 1949, 56, 311-324.

QUASTLER, H. (Ed.). *Information theory in psychology*. Glencoe, Ill.: Free Press, 1955.

ROGERS, L.E., & FARACE, R.V. Analysis of relational communication in dyads: New measurement procedure.

Human Communication Research, 1975, 1, 222-239.
SCHEIDEL, T.M., & CROWELL, L. Idea development in small discussion groups. *Quarterly Journal of Speech*, 1964, 50, 140-145.
STECH, E.L. Sequential structure in human social communication. *Human Communication Research*, 1975, 1, 168-179.
THORNTON, B.C. Communication and health care teams: A multimethodological approach. Unpublished doctoral dissertation, Department of Communication, University of Utah, 1976.
WATZLAWICK, P., BEAVIN, J.H., & JACKSON, D.D. *Pragmatics of human communication: A study of interactional patterns, pathologies and paradoxes*. New York: Norton, 1967.
WEICK, K.E. *The social psychology of organizing*. Reading, Mass.: Addison-Wesley, 1969.
WERBEL, W., ELLIS, D., & FISHER, B. A comparative morphology of groups: A systems perspective. Paper presented at the annual meeting of the International Communication Association, New Orleans, 1974.
WISE, H., BECKHARD, R., RUBIN, I., & KYTE, A. *Making health teams work*. Cambridge, Mass.: Ballinger, 1974.

ABOUT THE AUTHORS

Paul Arntson received his Ph.D. from the University of Wisconsin. He has a joint appointment in the Department of Communication Studies and the Center for Urban Affairs at Northwestern University. His primary research interests include small group interaction, communication development, and health care in inner-city environments.

Bernard J. Baars, assistant professor of Psychology at SUNY-Stony Brook, studied at California State University-Los Angeles (M.A., 1973) under David Perrott, and at UCLA (B.A., 1970; Ph.D., 1977) under Donald MacKay. His primary areas of interest are psycholinguistics and cognitive psychology.

Edwin Barnicott, Jr. is a master's candidate in the Department of Human Communication at the University of Kentucky. His research interests include interpersonal relationships, family communication patterns, and family influences on the development of communication skills.

Sjef A. van den Berg is assistant professor in the Communication Research Program at the University of Connecticut. He received his B.B.A. (Personnel Management) and M.A. (Journalism) from the University of Oregon, and his Ph.D. (Mass Communication) from the University of Wisconsin-Madison. His current teaching and research interests include audience perceptions of television content, and organizational and cross-cultural communication.

Charles R. Berger is associate professor in the Department of Communication Studies, Northwestern University. His principal areas of research interest are development and disintegration of interpersonal relationships, knowledge processes in interpersonal communication, and social influence processes.

John E. Bowes (Ph.D., Michigan State, 1971) is an assistant professor of Communications at the University of Washington, where he has been active in research concerning political images and stereotyping, communication of technological information to non-experts and computer-based information systems. Before coming to Washington, he directed the communication program at the University of North Dakota. He is now an associate of the Communication Research Center, a director of the Center for Quantitative Studies in the Social Sciences and manager of the Gannett Computer Facility in the School of Communications.

Robert J. Branham is instructor of Speech at Bates College. He is an alumnus of Dartmouth College (B.A.) and the University of North Carolina (M.A.) and is a doctoral candidate at the University of Massachusetts. His research interests focused primarily on rhetorical aspects of literature.

Michael Burgoon received his Ph.D. in communication from Michigan State University in 1970. He is the author or coauthor of six books on communication. Dr. Burgoon has published numerous chapters in books and is widely published in professional journals in communication, speech, psychology and management. His main areas of research interest are persuasion, propaganda and compliance-gaining communication strategies.

Donald M. Cassata (B.A., M.A., University of Denver; Ph.D., University of Minnesota) is director of Medical Communications and associate professor, Department of Family Medicine, University of North Carolina School of Medicine. For the past six years, his responsibilities have included teaching medical students and family physicians in courses such as physician-patient relationship, medical interviewing and counseling skills, and psychological medicine. His research focuses on medical interview assessment, effects of videotape feedback, nursing care systems, and psychosocial evaluation. Currently, he chairs the Division of Health Communication, International Communication Association.

Frank E.X. Dance (B.S., Fordham University; M.S., Ph.D., Northwestern University) is currently professor of Speech Communication at the University of Denver. He is a past editor of *The Journal of Communication* and *Communication Education*. He served as president of ICA in 1967. Dance has authored or coauthored numerous articles and seven books dealing in whole or in part with the study of human communication theory.

Jeffrey E. Danes completed his graduate training at Michigan State University. He is currently affiliated with the Communication Research Program at the University of Connecticut. His primary areas of research include persuasion within the mass communication context, communication and change, quantitative communication models, and data analysis. He is coauthor (with Joseph Woelfel) of "Metric Multidimensional Models of Communication Conception and Change," in *Multivariate Techniques in Communication*, edited by Peter Monge and Joseph Cappella.

Gary F. Davis received his B.A. in psychology and M.A. in speech communication at West Virginia University. He is currently a doctoral candidate in the Department of Communication at Purdue University.

Harry S. Dennis III received his Ph.D. in organizational communication at Purdue, following six years of duty as an Air Force instructor pilot. Presently, he is chairman of the board and CEO of Nourse, Handy & Dennis, Inc., a Wisconsin firm which directs continuing education programs for presidents of small to medium-sized companies. He is also coauthoring a book with Gerry Goldhaber, Gary Richetto, and Osmo Wiio titled *Information Power and the Management Function: Developing Organizational Intelligence*, which is scheduled for release in 1978. He is the deputy director of the International Communication Association Communication Audit.

David Droge is a doctoral student and university fellow in the Department of Communication Studies at Northwestern University. He received his B.A. and M.A. in speech communication at San Francisco State University. He has been a member of the faculty at Oregon State University. He is currently interested in the study of small-group communication.

Jane A. Edwards obtained B.A. and M.A. degrees in Speech-Communication and an M.A. degree in psychology from San Jose State University. She is coauthor of several articles and technical reports dealing with organizational communication and communication networks. Currently, she is at the University of California-Berkeley, working toward a doctorate degree in cognitive psychology, with an emphasis in language behavior.

Donald G. Ellis (Ph.D., University of Utah) is assistant professor in the Department of Communication at Purdue University. His research interests include interpersonal and group behavior with special emphasis on relational communication. He has published in *Human Communication Research, Communication Monographs, Small Group Behavior*, and others. He is a member of the editorial board of *Human Communication Research* and a 1976 recipient of the Speech Communication Association Golden Anniversary dissertation award.

Richard V. Farace is professor and Director of Graduate Studies of the Communication Department at Michigan State University. The focus of his research efforts evolves around organizational communication, with primary emphasis on network analysis and multivariate methodologies and structure. He is coauthor of *Communicating and Organizing* (Farace, Monge, and Russell, Addison-Wesley, 1977) along with numerous related papers and articles.

Harry E. Fassl received his B.A. in psychology from Elmhurst College and his M.A. in educational psychology from Northwestern University. He is currently a student in the doctoral program in educational psychology at Northwestern. His primary interests are data analysis and measurement, along with group communication processes.

B. Aubrey Fisher (Ph.D., Minnesota, 1968) is professor of communication at the University of Utah. His research interests and publications include the areas of group decision making, interaction analysis, relational communication, and general system theory. He is the author of *Small Group Decision Making: Communication and the Group Process* and *Perspectives on Human Communication.*

Joseph M. Foley is an associate professor in the Department of Communication at Ohio State University. He received the Ph.D. and M.A. degrees from the University of Iowa, and a B.S. degree from Antioch College. His current research projects are in the areas of media policy formation and the assessment of the impact of changing media technologies.

Gerald Goldhaber is associate professor of Communication at State University of New York, Buffalo and Director of the ICA Communication Audit. He has authored, coauthored and coedited six books and over 100 chapters, articles, monographs, and papers. His books include *Organizational Communication*, *Communication Probes*, *Stand Up and Speak Out*, and *Information Power and the Management Function*. His articles appear in such journals as *Speech Monographs, Speech Teacher, Journal of Communication, Human Communication Research*, and the *Canadian Journal of Personnel*. He received his Ph.D. in 1970 from Purdue University.

Doris A. Graber is professor of Political Science at the University of Illinois-Chicago Circle. She is the author of *Public Opinion, The President and Foreign Policy* (1968) and *Verbal Behavior and Politics* (1976), as well as numerous articles dealing with mass media information supply and its effects on the mass public.

Edward T. Hall is author of *The Silent Language, The Hidden Dimension,* and *Beyond Culture*. He serves as a consultant to architects, business, government, and private foundations, and is a director of the Ansul Company, a Fellow of the American Anthropological Association, the Society of Applied Anthropology, and the Advisory Council of the National Anthropological Film Center. His previous teaching affiliations include Northwestern University, the Illinois Institute of Technology, the Harvard Business School, Columbia University, Bennington College, and the University of Denver.

Dean E. Hewes is assistant professor of Communication Arts, University of Wisconsin-Madison. At present, he is vice-chairperson of the Interpersonal Communication Division. His research interests include the analysis of social interaction, personality antecedents of communicative behavior, developmental approaches to communicator competence, the message-mediating variable-behavior relationship, and research methodology.

William G. Husson is a doctoral student in Communication at Rensselaer Polytechnic Institute.

Fredric M. Jablin (Ph.D., 1977, Purdue University) is assistant professor in the Department of Communication at the University of Wisconsin-Milwaukee. His research interests include the study of patterns of interpersonal and small group interaction in organizational settings, the impact of technology upon communicative behavior within organizations, and analysis of creative inhibition in problem-solving groups. He has also served as a consultant to several large private industrial/business organizations.

Lynda Lee Kaid, Ph.D., Southern Illinois University, is assistant professor in the School of Journalism and Mass Communication at the University of Oklahoma. She is coauthor of *Political Campaign Communication: A Bibliography and Guide to the Literature* and associate editor of *Political Communication Review*. Her articles have appeared in *Journalism Quarterly, Journal of Broadcasting, Journal of Advertising Research, Central States Speech Journal, Communication Research, Communication Yearbook 1*, and others. Her primary research is political communication.

Young Yun Kim is a professor in the Department of Human Communication at Governors State University. She earned a master's degree in speech-communication at the University of Hawaii and a Ph.D. in Communication Studies at Northwestern University. Her major research interests are in the field of intercultural communication.

Kenneth K. Kirste received his B.A. degree in Speech-Communication from San Jose State University. He is currently a senior system analyst at System Development Corporation in Sunnyvale, California. His research interests are in the areas of organizational communication, proxemics, and development of computer software for implementing research activities.

Robert Krull is assistant professor of Communication and director of the Communication Research Laboratory at Rensselaer Polytechnic Institute.

Velma J. Lashbrook (B.S., Iowa State University, 1970; M.S., Illinois State University, 1971; D.Ed., West Virginia University, 1976) is currently a private research consultant working for the Wilson Learning Corporation of Eden Prairie, Minnesota. Her current research interests include organizational climate, performance feedback systems, person perception, leadership, and learning systems. She has coauthored *PROANA5: A Computerized Technique for the Analysis of Small Group Interaction* (with William B. Lashbrook, 1974) and presented numerous scholarly papers in the interpersonal and small group, organizational, information systems, and instructional divisions of international, national, and regional communication associations. She has had top three papers in the Behavioral Science Interest Group of the Western Speech Communication Association and the Interpersonal and Small Group Interaction Division of the Speech Communication Association, and received an outstanding student award for a paper presented for the Instructional Communication Association of the International Communication Association.

Gerald R. Miller received his B.A. and M.A. in political science and his Ph.D. in psychology and speech from the University of Iowa. Currently, he is professor of Communication at Michigan State University. He was previously a member of the faculties at the University of Iowa and the University of Washington. He has authored or edited seven books and has written numerous articles for journals of communication, psychology, speech, and law. He is former editor of the journal, *Human Communication Research*, and is the president-elect of the International Communication Association. Professor Miller's honors include the Speech Communication Association's Golden Anniversary Award for outstanding scholarly publication in 1967, 1974, and 1976; the Distinguished Faculty Award and the *Centennial Review* Lectureship from Michigan State University; and a Joint Resolution of Tribute from the Michigan legislature for his research dealing with the courtroom uses of videotape.

Peter R. Monge (Ph.D., communication, Michigan State University) is associate professor in the Department of Speech-Communication at San Jose State University and currently visiting associate professor in the Department of Communication, Michigan State University. He has published several papers in the areas of systems theory, communication networks, and organizational communication. He is coauthor of the recently published book, *Communicating and Organizing*, and coeditor of the forthcoming book, *Multivariate Techniques in Communication Research*.

Barry F. Morganstern (Ph.D., Department of Speech and Dramatic Art at the University of Missouri-Columbia, 1977) is assistant professor of Speech Communication at West Virginia University.

Michael T. Motley, assistant professor of Communication at Ohio State University, studied at the University of Texas (B.A., 1965; M.A., 1967) under Theodore Clevenger, Jr., and at Pennsylvania State University (Ph.D., 1970) under George Borden. His primary areas of interest are psycholinguistics and communication theory.

Perry M. Nicassio, Ph.D., received his bachelor's degree in psychology from the University of Southern California and his masters and doctorate degrees in clinical psychology from Northwestern University. As a predoctoral research fellow of the Council of Intersocietal Studies at Northwestern, Dr. Nicassio spent more than a year in Colombia conducting cross-cultural research on the relationship between parental sex role identity and fertility. Dr. Nicassio has published articles that have appeared in scholarly journals that are based on his cross-cultural and clinical research activities. He is currently a university professor, and former Program Coordinator of Behavioral Studies at Governors State University, Park Forest South, Illinois.

Albert S. Paulson is associate professor of Operations Research and Statistics and an affiliated faculty member of the Communication Research Laboratory at Rensselaer Polytechnic Institute.

W. Barnett Pearce (M.A., Ph.D., Ohio University) is associate professor in the Department of Communication Studies, University of Massachusetts. He has taught at the University of North Dakota and the University of Kentucky. His research has been primarily in the area of interpersonal communication associated with coorientation and the theory of the coordinated management of meaning.

Joseph W. Perkins received his M.A. in speech from the University of Alabama. He is currently a second year doctoral student at Northwestern University with research interests in interpersonal, organizational, and mass communication.

Loyd S. Pettegrew (Ph.D., University of Michigan) is presently a research associate in the Office of Communication Research at Vanderbilt University Medical Center. His dissertation involved a three-stage investigation of communicator style in therapeutic relationships. He specializes in the areas of interpersonal, health, and organizational communication, and in philosophy of science and contemporary rhetorical theory. He has been involved during the last several years in helping develop and test the communicator style construct and is currently working on a program of planned change for the Vanderbilt Medical Center.

William G. Powers received his degree in Communication from the University of Oklahoma (1973) and is presently an assistant professor at the University of Missouri-Columbia. He is the co-author of *Interpersonal Communication: A Question of Needs*, and has been a contributor to *Human Communication Research*, *Communication Monographs*, *Communication Quarterly*, and *Psychological Reports*. His research interests include interpersonal and instructional communication.

Michael H. Prosser (Ph.D., University of Illinois) is professor of Speech Communication at the University of Virginia and was the department chairman from 1972 to 1977. He was the founding chairman of the Commission for International and Intercultural Communication of the Speech Communication Association from 1971 to 1973; chairman of the International Communication Development Council of the Midwest Universities Consortium for International Activities from 1971 to 1972; vice-president and chairman of the Intercultural Communication Division of ICA from 1974 to 1977; and member of the Governing Council of the Society for Intercultural Education,

Training and Research from 1974 to 1977. He has taught at the University of Virginia, Indiana University, SUNY at Buffalo, Queens College, Memorial University of Newfoundland, California State University at Hayward, St. Paul's University, and the University of Ottawa. Among his six edited or authored books are *Sow the Wind, Reap the Whirlwind: Heads of State Address the United Nations, 2 vols.; Intercommunication Among Nations and Peoples*; and *Cultural Dialogue*.

Michael Roloff (Ph.D., Michigan State University) is assistant professor of Human Communication at the University of Kentucky. His major research interests include interpersonal conflict resolution and compliance-gaining activity, interpersonal relationships, and relational change.

Keith R. Sanders, Ph.D., University of Pittsburgh, is professor of Speech Communication at Southern Illinois University-Carbondale. He is a former chairperson of the Political Communication Division of the International Communication Association. He is editor of *Political Communication Review*, coauthor of *Political Campaign Communication*, and has written for the *Journal of the American Forensic Association, The Quarterly Journal of Speech, The Central States Speech Journal, Journalism Quarterly, Journal of Broadcasting, Communication Research, Communication Yearbook 1*, and others. His research interests focus on the role of interpersonal and mass communication in political decision making.

Tulsi Saral is a professor of Communication Science at Governors State University, Park Forest South, Illinois, where he served as program coordinator of communication science program for four years, and as assistant dean of the College of Human Learning and Development for two years. He has authored several articles on intercultural communication and is currently the chairperson of the Intercultural Communication Division of the International Communication Association.

Michael D. Scott (Ph.D., University of Southern California, 1974) is associate professor of Speech Communication and Educational Psychology at West Virginia University, as well as director of the doctoral program in communication in instruction. He is vice-chairperson of the interpersonal and organizational communication division of the Eastern Communication Association. He is co-author of *Principles of Human Communication, Communication in the Classroom*, and *Interpersonal Communication: A Question of Needs*. Examples of his work appear in *Speech Monographs, The Journal of Communication, Communication Education, Western Speech Communication, The Southern Speech Communication Journal*, and *Communication Yearbook 1*.

Mary-Jeanette Smythe received her Ph.D. from Florida State University (1973) and is currently an assistant professor at the University of Missouri. Primary research interests include instructional communication and nonverbal communication.

John P. Stewart completed his M.A. at Brigham Young University and is presently a doctoral candidate in communication at Michigan State University. The focus of his research is in organizational communication and behavior. He is currently working with network analysis and systems research, along with methodological design and application.

Herbert Strentz (Ph.D., Northwestern, 1969) is dean of the School of Journalism and associate professor at Drake University. He has been active in research concerning media accounts of unidentified flying objects, the problems of group image differences on political issues and the relations between reporters and their news sources. He was chairman of the Department of Journalism at the University of North Dakota before coming to Drake. Prior to graduate study, he was a reporter for the Fresno (Cal.) *Bee* and the Associated Press. Dr. Strentz is author of *News Reporters and News Sources*, published by the Iowa State University Press.

James A. Taylor completed his Ph.D. at Michigan State University and is now an assistant professor of communication at Temple University. He has been extensively involved in evaluative research projects in organizational communication. Author of several papers on innovation technology and diffusion, his primary areas lie in health systems research and behavior.

Lee Thayer is distinguished professor of Communication at the University of Houston. Trained as a psychologist, Professor Thayer has for many years been active as an author and researcher in a wide range of communication-related subjects. His most recent book, *The Idea of Communication*, will appear in 1978.

Richard C. Thomas (M.A., San Diego State University) teaches interpersonal communication, nonverbal communication, sexism and communication, family communication, and intercultural communication at San Diego Junior Colleges. He is a communication consultant/counselor for Garrard Center for Psychology and is researching therapeutic transactions from a communication perspective.

B.C. Thornton (Ph.D., University of Utah) is an assistant professor at the School of Medical Sciences at the University of Nevada-Reno, and is the research director for a longitudinal study of communication on health care teams. Thornton's research interests include small groups, communication theory, and new approaches to the study of communication. She has written in the areas of health communication, interpersonal and small groups, and political communication.

V. Lynn Tyler is associate director of the Language and Intercultural Research Center at Brigham Young University and has worked on intercultural communication concerns for nearly 30 years as a missionary of the Church of Jesus Christ of Latter-day Saints (Mormon), as curriculum coordinator, and as a director of "transcultural services." He is a member of the Board of Directors of the American Translators Association and has served on several Intercultural Communication Association committees.

James H. Watt, Jr. received his Ph.D. in mass communication from the University of Wisconsin in 1973, and has been associated with the Communication Research Program in the Department of Speech at the University of Connecticut since that time. His research includes investigations of television form attributes and their effects on viewer attention, physiological arousal, and learning; television form and content attribute effects on adult viewers' pro- and antisocial behavior; and audience perceptions of network programming.

Walter Baker Weimer (Ph.D. University of Minnesota) has taught at the Pennsylvania State University since 1969. His research interests include cognitive psychology, history and philosophy of science and psychology, methodology of scientific research, and interdisciplinary relationships between psychology, speech-communication and economics.

Lawrence R. Wheeless received his Ph.D. from Wayne State University (1970) and is associate professor of Speech Communication at West Virginia University. He is chairperson of the Instructional Communication Division of the International Communication Association. He is the author of *Practical Experiences in Interpersonal Communication* and coauthor of *An Introduction to Human Communication*. He is the author or coauthor of numerous research reports and reviews which appear in *Speech Monographs, The Speech Teacher, The Journal of Communication, Language and Style, The Journal of Broadcasting, Journal of the American Forensic Association, Southern Speech Communication Journal, Communication Yearbook, Western Speech Communication,* and *Human Communication Research*. Also, he is president of the West Virginia Communication Association, vice-chairperson of the Organizational and Interpersonal Communication Division of the Eastern Communication Association, and chairperson of the Instructional Communication Division (VII), International Communication Association.

Thomas C. Wiegele (B.S., Marquette University; A.M., Ph.D., University of Pennsylvania) is director of the Center for Biopolitical Research and associate professor of Political Science at Northern Illinois University. His writings have focused on blending natural science orientations into the study of political decision making, particularly in international crisis situations. To this end he has examined the impact of stress from several perspectives.

Michael P. Yates received his M.A. in Speech Communication from West Virginia University (1975) and currently is completing his doctoral studies at The State University of New York, Buffalo.

Harold Gene Zucker is a Ph.D. candidate in Social Sciences at the University of California-Irvine. He received his M.A. from State University of New York, Buffalo and his A.B. from Cornell, both in anthropology. His major research interests center on the deliberate use of the mass media to direct social change, particularly through covert techniques. His other major interests are intercultural communication and the general impact of the mass media on society.

INDEX

SUBJECTS

NAMES